Encyclopedia of American Prisons

Encyclopedia
of American Prisons

Editors
Marilyn D. McShane
Frank P. Williams III

GARLAND PUBLISHING, INC.
New York & London
1996

Library of Congress Cataloging-in-Publication Data

Encyclopedia of American prisons / editors, Marilyn D. McShane, Frank
   P. Williams III.
       p.   cm. — (Garland reference library of the humanities ; vol.
1748)
      Includes index.
      ISBN 0-8153-1350-0 (alk. paper)
      1. Prisons—United States—History—Encyclopedias.   2. Prison
administration—United States—History—Encyclopedias.   I. McShane,
Marilyn D., 1956– . II. Williams, Franklin P. III. Series.
HV9471.E425 1996
365'.973—dc20   95-41593
                                                      CIP

Cover photographs: Inmate count (upper right) by James A. Bolzaretti.
Aerial view of Eastern State Penitentiary as it appeared in 1935 (lower left),
reprinted by permission of The Library Company of Philadelphia.

Cover design by Lawrence Wolfson Design, N.Y.

Printed on acid-free, 250-year-life paper
Manufactured in the United States of America

To Mary Rae Schmidt

On whom we have come to rely for so many things

Contents

Acknowledgments

Many people encouraged and guided us through this massive undertaking. Our special thanks go to our editor and the vice president at Garland, Gary Kuris, who not only posed the challenge but also provided enthusiastic support throughout the process, greasing all the right wheels in the bureaucratic labyrinth of the publishing world. Also at Garland, Phyllis Korper, Eileen Sutter, Brian Pilicer, and Adrienne Makowski were of great help to us. Our mentor for this project was Bill Bailey, who laid out all the ground rules and potential pitfalls from his experience with the *Encyclopedia of Police Science*. He patiently answered hundreds of questions and only once moved without leaving a forwarding address.

We are also indebted to Kathleen Maguire and Tim Flanagan with the Prison Research Group for helping us launch the search for contributing authors. Mary Rae Schmidt, our loyal and hardworking office manager, fielded hundreds of frantic phone calls and last-minute faxes. She is now on a first-name basis with all the overnight carrier representatives. We also thank our colleagues at CSUSB for their collegial support throughout this project, including Penny Robbinette for her assistance with indexing and our chair, Chuck Fields.

Finally, we express our heartfelt appreciation to all of our contributing authors, those who volunteered and those who answered the call. We are convinced that this collection of articles represents everything the general reader needs to know about prisons in America. The cooperation and team spirit the many authors brought to this project was inspiring, and we look forward to working with all of them again in the future.

Introduction

Although prisons were used in Europe as early as the twelfth and thirteenth centuries, they were not considered necessary by the founders of this country. A careful look at the development and use of prisons in the United States tells us much about ourselves, our view of humanity, our hopes and our fears. The literary and cinematic image of the prison has gripped the imagination of everyone who has ever contemplated punishment. Prisons, and those who live and work in them, have generated many stories, films, and legends.

The history of prisons is both colorful and full of controversy. Debates have raged over everything from philosophy to architecture. There have been miracles and setbacks, heroes and villains, in each state and in every institution. Most systems have a great deal in common; trends are easily discerned, and problems seem to transcend the decades.

There is something unmistakably American about the prison system we have created. Just as the solitary fortresses of the early 1900s attracted visitors from all over the world, American institutions are still drawing international attention. Today, over one million people are incarcerated—and we are not through yet. The money spent on building and running prison systems now exceeds that allocated to higher education in many states. The federal government and most states are presently engaged in a building program that will add over one hundred new prisons in the next ten years, and the budgetary allocations for incarceration will only increase. If statistics can be believed, the United States already incarcerates its citizens at a higher rate than any other country. Whether they be houses of darkness, warehouses for the socially unfit, "country clubs," or models of reform, prisons continue to haunt our American dream.

This work was compiled in the belief that everyone should be familiar with the history and current operations of American prison systems. Many of the entries in this encyclopedia begin with a historical discussion to help frame the issues. Any understanding of contemporary problems must begin with an appreciation for where we have been. The more we know about prisons, the better we can plan for their design and future use.

The entries included here are by no means exhaustive. That would have taken a great many more entries than we had room for, and far more than one volume. These entries, however, are critical to an understanding of prisons in America. Each is written by an author who knows the subject matter well and, in many cases, is preeminent in the field. We believe that these entries compose a comprehensive collection that tells the story of the people, places, and ideas behind the American prison system.

Contributors

Patrick R. Anderson
Florida Southern College

B. Jaye Anno
Consultants in Correctional Care, Santa Fe

Sarah Barbo
Whitman College

Clemens Bartollas
University of Northern Iowa

Barbara Belbot
University of Houston

Robert L. Bing III
University of Texas, Arlington

Robert Blair
College of Wooster

Michael Blankenship
East Tennessee State University

Barbara Bloom
Barbara Bloom and Associates,
Petaluma, California

Mark Blumberg
Central Missouri State University

Robert M. Bohm
University of Central Florida

Michael Braswell
East Tennessee State University

Velmer Burton Jr.
Washington State University, Pullman

Tory Caeti
Huntsville, Texas

Jack E. Call
Radford University

Lisa Callahan
Russell Sage College

Bonnie Carlson
University at Albany,
State University of New York

Leo Carroll
University of Rhode Island

Robert Carter
University of Southern California,
Los Angeles

Karen Casey
Florida Atlantic University

Dean Champion
Minot State University

Ellen Chayet
Criminal Justice Research and Policy
Analysis, Palisades, New York

Derral Cheatwood
University of Baltimore

Chau-Pu Chiang
California State University—Stanislaus,
Turlock

Greg Clark
McNeese State University

William Collins
Olympia, Washington

John Conley
Buffalo State College

Thomas F. Courtless
George Washington University

Amy Craddock
Carrboro, North Carolina

Heather Craig
Little Rock, Arkansas

Harry Dammer
Niagara University

Jill D'Angelo
American University

Laura Davis
California State University, San Bernardino

Rolando V. del Carmen
Sam Houston State University

Elizabeth L. DeRieux
Fifth Circuit Court of Appeals, Tyler,
Texas

George E. Dickinson
College of Charleston

Alexis Durham III
University of Tampa

Mark D. Dyrdahl
University of North Dakota

Carolyn Eggleston
California State University, San Bernardino

Randy J. Farrar
U.S. District Court, Eastern District,
Tyler, Texas, and University of Texas

Keith Farrington
Whitman College

Charles B. Fields
California State University, San Bernardino

Steve Fischer
Odessa, Texas

Timothy Flanagan
Sam Houston State University

Edith E. Flynn
Northeastern University

Marilyn Chandler Ford
Volusia County Branch Jail,
Daytona Beach

James G. Fox
State University College, Buffalo

Laurence A. French
Western New Mexico University

Richard H. Fulmer
Millersville University

Thom Gehring
California State University, San Bernardino

Don Gibbons
Portland State University, Oregon

Daniel Glaser
University of Southern California,
Los Angeles

Lynne Goodstein
Pennsylvania State University

Gary Green
Minot State University

Peter Gregware
New Mexico State University

Ruth-Ellen M. Grimes
California State University, Fullerton

Kenneth C. Haas
University of Delaware

Frank Hagan
Mercyhurst College

Bahram Haghighi
University of Texas—Pan American

Donna C. Hale
Shippensburg University

Michael A. Hallett
Middle Tennessee State University

David Halley
Police Department, Roseville,
California

Mark Hamm
Indiana State University

Alan T. Harland
Temple University

Barbara Hart
University of Texas, Tyler

Cynthia Baroody-Hart
San Jose State University

Craig T. Hemmons
Sam Houston State University

Rodney Henningson
Sam Houston State University

Crystal E. Hevener
Millersville University

Thomas J. Hickey
Roger Williams University

William T. Hogan, Esq.
Washington, D.C.

Louis Holscher
San Jose State University

Wendelin Hume
University of North Dakota

James Inciardi
University of Delaware

Chuck Jeffords
Texas Youth Commission, Austin

Robert Jerin
Appalachian State University

Byron Johnson
Morehead State University

Elmer Johnson
Southern Illinois University

Wes Johnson
Sam Houston State University

Richard S. Jones
Marquette University

Don Josi
Irvine, California

David B. Kalinich
Northern Michigan University

Raymond G. Kessler
Sul Ross State University

Peter Kratcoski
Kent State University

Wesley Krause
San Bernardino County Probation

Charles S. Lanier
University at Albany,
State University of New York

Edward J. Latessa
University of Cincinnati

Richard Lawrence
St. Cloud State University

Jan Lindsey
Texas Youth Commission, Austin

Daniel Lockwood
Clark Atlanta University

Rick Lovell
University of Wisconsin

Elizabeth McConnell
Valdosta State College

Malcolm McCullough
New York State Department of Health,
AIDS Institute, Albany

Marilyn McShane
California State University,
San Bernardino

Doris L. MacKenzie
University of Maryland,
College Park

Kathleen Maguire
University at Albany,
State University of New York

Sue Mahan
University of Central Florida,
Daytona Beach

Harry Marsh
Indiana State University, Terre Haute

Alida V. Merlo
Indiana University of Pennsylvania

Deanna Meyer
St. Cloud State University

Reid Montgomery Jr.
University of South Carolina

Richard Morgan
Captain, Washington State Penitentiary,
Walla Walla

Laura Moriarty
Virginia Commonwealth University

Joann Morton
University of South Carolina

K. S. Murty
Clark Atlanta University

Laura Myers
Sam Houston State University

C. Michael Nelson
University of Kentucky

Barbara Owen
California State University, Fresno

Michael J. Palmiotto
Witchita State University

Beth Pelz
University of Houston

Joan Petersilia
University of California, Irvine

Alexander W. Pisciotta
Kutztown University

Joycelyn Pollock
Southwest Texas State University

Paige Ralph
Lake Superior State University

Fran Reddington
Central Missouri State University

Sue Titus Reid
Florida State University, Tallahassee

Edward Rhine
Field Services, Georgia Board of Pardons
and Paroles, Atlanta

Philip W. Rhoades
Texas A&M University, Corpus Christi

John W. Roberts
Office of Archives, Federal Bureau
of Prisons, Washington, D.C.

Julian B. Roebuck
Sul Ross State University

Joseph W. Rogers
New Mexico State University

Joseph Rowan
Juvenile and Criminal Justice International,
Inc., Roseville, Minnesota

Jeffrey Rush
Jacksonville State University

Robert Rutherford
Arizona State University

Michael G. Santos
M.A. Hofstra University

Edward Schauer
Northeast Louisiana University

Thomas W. Seaman
Lynchburg College

Dale Sechrest
California State University, San Bernardino

Francis Sheridan
New York Department of Correctional
Services, Albany, New York

David Shichor
California State University,
San Bernardino

Ira Silverman
University of South Florida

Clifford Simonsen
Criminology Consultants International,
Camana Island, Washington

Risdon Slate
Florida Southern College

Richard Sluder
Central Missouri State University

Beverly A. Smith
Illinois State University

John Smykla
University of Alabama

Jonathan Sorensen
University of Texas—Pan American

Rick Steinmann
Lindenwood College

Stan Stojkovic
University of Wisconsin, Milwaukee

Dennis A. Sweeney
Juvenile Probation, City and County
of San Francisco

Morris A. Taylor Jr.
St. Louis University

James Tesoriero
New York State Department of Health,
AIDS Institute, Albany

Amy Thistlethwaite
University of Cincinnati

Lawrence F. Travis, III
University of Cincinnati

Patricia Van Voorhis
University of Cincinnati

Michael S. Vaughn
Georgia State University

Carol Veneziano
Southeast Missouri State University

Louis Veneziano
Southeast Missouri State University

Sandra Wachholz
St. Thomas University, Fredericton,
New Brunswick, Canada

Carl P. Wagoner
California State University,
San Bernardino

Jeffery Walker
University of Arkansas, Little Rock

David Ward
University of Minnesota

David Weisburd
Rutgers University

Michael Welch
Rutgers University

Wayne Welsh
Temple University

Marian H. Whitson
East Tennessee State University

Frank P. Williams III
California State University,
San Bernardino

L. Thomas Winfree Jr.
New Mexico State University

Betsy Witt
Bemidji State University

Bruce Wolford
Eastern Kentucky University

John Wooldredge
University of Cincinnati

John P. Wright
University of Cincinnati

Kevin Wright
State University of New York, Binghamton

Thomas A. Wright
University of Nevada, Reno

Vernetta Young
Howard University

Chronology of American Prison History

1773 Connecticut converts copper mine to underground prison, called Newgate, in Simsbury

1787 The Pennsylvania Prison Society is founded

1790 Philadelphia's Walnut Street Jail, one of the country's first penal institutions, opens

1793 Mary Weed takes post as principal keeper of Walnut Street Jail, serving until 1796

1819 Auburn prison in New York opens, using silent, or congregate, system

1825 Auburn-style prison (Sing Sing) opens at Ossining, New York

1829 Eastern Penitentiary opens, designed by John Haviland, at Cherry Hill

1870 American Prison Association publishes its guidelines as the *Declaration of Principles*

1873 First separate women's prison opens: Indiana Women's Prison, Indianapolis

1874 Fort Leavenworth prison opens for military offenders

1876 Nation's first reformatory opens under the direction of Zebulon Brockway at Elmira, New York

1891 Congress approves Three Prisons Act to build three Federal penitentiaries (USP Leavenworth, USP Atlanta, and McNeil Island, a former territorial jail, now a Washington state prison)

1901 The first separate reformatory is built exclusively for women at Bedford Hills (Westfield), New York

1906 Federal prison at Leavenworth opens

1914 Thomas Mott Osborne is appointed warden of Sing Sing Prison in Ossining, New York

1927 First woman serves as a federal warden: Mary Belle Harris, at Federal Institution for Women, Alderson, West Virginia

1929 Hawes-Cooper Act passes, placing restrictions on the sale of prison-made goods

1930 Federal Bureau of Prisons is established

1930 First training school for federal prison guards opens in New York City

1933 Alcatraz becomes a federal penitentiary

1935 Ashurst-Sumners Act passes, prohibiting interstate shipment of prison-made products

1965 Prisoner Rehabilitation Act signed by President Johnson

1971 Riot at Attica, New York

1971 First African American to serve as a federal warden: Lee Jett, Federal Corrections Institution, Englewood, Colorado

1974 Robert Martinson publishes his controversial article on rehabilitation ("What Works: . . . ")

1977 *Dothard v. Rawlinson* strikes down minimum height and weight requirements for officers

1980 New Mexico Prison riot at Santa Fe

1980 The Civil Rights of Institutionalized Persons Act is passed

1987 Cuban detainees riot in federal facilities in Georgia and Louisiana

1993 First female director, Federal Bureau of Prisons: Kathleen Hawk

A

Accreditation

Up until the implementation of official standards, prison officials had little assistance in gauging the quality of their facility or the performance of their staff. In the late eighteenth century, the Philadelphia Prison Society constructed guidelines for the treatment of prisoners that included the separation of male and female inmates, the separation of children from adults, the implementation of a classification system, and the basics of prison industry. More recommendations and reforms followed. In 1870, the American Prison Association published its guidelines as the *Declaration of Principles*. Since that time, numerous commissions and councils have addressed the requirements of modern penal institutions and have developed model legislation, programs, and standards.

The acceptance of national professional standards or uniform policies has evolved into a recognized program of national accreditation, a process of peer review or review by outside audit teams. The major organization granting accreditation is the American Correctional Association (ACA). A similar program specific to the accreditation of medical services in corrections is conducted by the National Commission on Correctional Health Care (NCCHC).

The first American Correctional Association manuals of professional standards were published in the 1940s. The standards were revised periodically through 1966. The standards, which were principally for correctional institutions, were used by some agencies, but there was no objective method for verifying compliance. In the years that followed, the courts became more concerned about the deteriorating conditions of prisons and began a

period of active intervention. As a result, prison administrators expressed a need for the existence of some type of performance criterion. The President's Crime Commission published standards in 1967 as part of its work, but no plan for implementation was included. In 1969, the Ford Foundation provided a grant to the American Correctional Association to study the desirability and feasibility of establishing an accreditation process that would address the concerns of prison administrators, prisoners, legislators, and the courts. That study both identified the need for new standards and published a plan for the review, evaluation, and measurement of compliance with the standards, documented in an "accreditation plan for corrections."

In 1970, national goals and standards for correctional institutions were published by the National Advisory Commission on Criminal Justice Standards and Goals. Those standards addressed prison and jail conditions but again provided no plan for implementation, other than recommending a state-by-state effort to create, adopt, and apply similar standards. In 1974, the Law Enforcement Assistance Administration (LEAA) awarded a grant to the American Correctional Association to establish a Commission on Accreditation for Corrections (CAC). Several corporations and private funding sources participated in that effort. The existing standards proved insufficient for use in accreditation because of their overly comprehensive nature, lack of specificity in many areas, and narrow focus on prisons and jails. CAC staff recommended that the grant include the development of a comprehensive set of standards to cover all components of correctional services. An extensive program of drafting, field testing, revising, and approving thousands of standards was begun, addressing the entire field of corrections—prisons, jails, parole boards, probation and parole services, and community residential centers for both adults and juveniles.

The first manual of standards was published in 1976, containing 452 different standards. Ten manuals were produced by 1979 and all were revised by 1983. In 1978 the first accreditation awards were made to a parole board and four halfway houses. The first adult correctional institution achieved accreditation in 1978, the first jail accreditations were in 1980, and the first juvenile agency accreditations were awarded in 1981. Since accreditation is for a three-year period, the first reaccreditations were awarded in 1981. Over one thousand agencies in the United States and Canada have received or are involved in accreditation with the ACA.

Of all the standards, only about 10 percent are mandatory and must be met to achieve accreditation. Mandatory standards generally apply to conditions that ensure the health and safety of staff and inmates. Many mandatory standards simply direct compliance with local laws, such as building, fire, and sanitation codes. Other standards reflect implications or directives from the courts on constitutional issues such as rules, discipline, visitation, and mail privileges.

The original plan stipulated that correctional accreditation was to be performed by an independent commission, the CAC. That was the case from early 1979 through 1986. Although fees were charged for accreditation, they were not sufficient to cover the costs of administration, and placing the CAC within the ACA kept costs down. The commission members had always been elected by the membership of the ACA, which is still the case; the CAC operates independently in its decision-making about accreditation. The ACA has always had a Committee on Standards, which has the responsibility for developing the standards for approval by both groups. Accreditation certificates are awarded by the commission and presented by the ACA.

A similar accreditation effort has been undertaken for medical services. The NCCHC was established in 1983. It maintains nationally recognized standards that are similar to those of the ACA. That is the case because the American Medical Association, which began the process, worked with CAC staff during the initial development of the standards. By February of 1992, there were 301 jails, 75 prisons, and 31 juvenile correctional facilities accredited by the NCCHC (Briscoe and Kuhrt 1992).

A 1983 survey of the staff of accredited state and federal agencies found that 85 percent of the 566 respondents saw accreditation as a good management tool. About two-thirds felt that accreditation had helped staff members in organizing and following policies and procedures, all of which might eventually lead to improvements in conditions and programs. Of the agencies surveyed, more than half agreed that being accredited would help them better defend against lawsuits. Most respondents said that accreditation had better prepared them for emergencies and that it had resulted in a safer, cleaner, and more healthful environment for inmates and staff (Farkas and Fosen 1983; Czajkowski et al. 1985). The impact on prison conditions, however, was questionable. Over half (57 percent) of the respondents were undecided or believed that there was no change in the number of violent incidents since accreditation; only 36 percent indicated that there had been fewer violent incidents in their facility. Forty-one percent did not see a drop in grievance or compensation claims by offenders. About 90 percent of all respondents found no improvements in programs such as visitation (91 percent), recreation (85 percent), meaningful work assignments (92 percent), or education (87 percent). A similar survey conducted in early 1989 revealed similar opinions about the value of accreditation, emphasizing improvements in management and staff performance, better fire safety, and increased funding (Washington 1989). There have been no findings regarding improved conditions or programs, in institutions or in the community.

A 1990 national survey of prison wardens and superintendents (McShane and Williams 1993) found that fewer than half of the respondents (46 percent) felt that accreditation guidelines had any influence on their personal management style. Factors such as budget constraints, legal requirements, the quality of staff, and overcrowding had more impact on their management routines. Some state legislators have cited the difficulty of meeting the standards, fearing the cost and the potential for inmate lawsuits. While compliance with the standards is sometimes seen as both expensive and difficult, their acceptance has nevertheless been quite high.

There is growing evidence of support for standards and accreditation in the courts and in some state legislatures, although court acceptance of the standards and the accreditation process is far from universal. As Miller (1992) states, "Courts have not adopted ACA standards as their primary yardstick for evaluating practices and conditions. In fact, they often establish standards significantly different from . . . [those of the] ACA." Other concerns regarding accreditation, both within and without the field, relate to accreditation fees, the time involved, the massive paperwork demands, and the depth of accreditation. Is it a paper process with too little emphasis on the quality of performance? Are the standards specific enough to make a difference? Is its use as a management tool creating a better working environment for staff and improving services to inmates?

Other criticisms focus on how the standards impinge upon the director's or warden's authority. Also, there are cases in which an agency's current policy or procedure is superior to that required by the standards, and clearly not a violation of the offender's rights or good practice. In fact, the policy may be supported by internal audit findings. Administrators may question the authority of the standards to intercede.

Criticism of accreditation has also come from outside the field. The major concern is that the process needs to be more open and that increased public involvement is necessary. Criticism is often linked to "what the courts will do" or what the constitutional minimum for performance may be. Similar concerns have been expressed by the American Civil Liberties Union's National Prison Project, which states that many of the standards fall short of common constitutional guarantees in several areas and that the standards simply represent the status quo in corrections.

Questions have been raised about whether the correctional facilities and community agencies being certified really meet the highest standards of performance. Judgments of the usefulness of the standards often depend on who is making the assessment. To the corrections practitioner, the standards are generally seen as realistic and challenging; to the reform-minded, they may appear weak and ineffective, perpetuating poor performance and injustice. The standards are adequate within the framework of what appears to be possible at present; they still,

however, may not reflect the highest standards of good practice. Current standards can be supported by well-implemented internal program review and internal audit mechanisms, and improved local and national standards can also be developed through that process.

There is a growing literature on performance review in corrections. A study undertaken by Logan (1993:2) details specific "empirical indicators" in eight major areas, or "dimensions." Review of these indicators against organizational criteria is necessary to identify which areas of performance should be subject to review, and in order to develop review criteria. The eight indicators are security, safety, order, care, activity (programs), justice (fairness), (living) conditions, and (efficient) management; there are also a variety of "subindicators."

A procedure that encompasses both performance review and compliance measurement is program review or internal audit, a technique developed in business and industry that is relevant to all organizations concerned with quality assurance. It has already proven effective in the corrections profession and warrants further evaluation. As part of its program review process, the Federal Bureau of Prisons uses an automated key indicators/strategic support system that provides management with access to a great deal of information on organizational operations. It is an outstanding tool for strategic planning and the application of quality control principles. The data serve as indicators by allowing the user to observe and analyze system changes, such as levels of crowding and the distribution of inmates with regard to security and custody requirements (Saylor 1989). It is expected that program review/internal audit procedures will become part of ACA accreditation procedures in the near future.

The future of accreditation in corrections will be as good as the administrators who embrace it. Corrections cannot operate on intuition or experience alone, a fact that became apparent in the era of court intervention. National standards and accreditation, which required an agency's self-evaluation prior to the external audit, caused many departments of correction to initiate systematic internal reviews. That was, and still is, an excellent starting point; further development and participation, however, is needed.

Dale K. Sechrest

See also AMERICAN CORRECTIONAL
ASSOCIATION

Bibliography

American Correctional Association (1966). *Manual of Correctional Standards*. College Park, Md.: American Correctional Association.

Briscoe, K., and J. Kuhrt (1992). How accreditation has improved correctional health care. *American Jails* 6(4): 48–52.

Czajkowski, S. M., P. L. Nacci, N. Kramer, S. J. Price, and D. K. Sechrest (1985). Responses to the accreditation program: What correctional staff think about accreditation. *Federal Probation* 49(1): 42–49.

Farkas, G. M., and R. H. Fosen (1983). Responding to accreditation. *Corrections Today* 45(7): 40, 42.

Fosen, R. H., and D. K. Sechrest (1983). Standards and accreditation. *Corrections Today* 45(2): 26.

Logan, C. H. (1993). *Criminal Justice Performance Measures for Prisons*. Washington, D.C.: National Institute of Justice.

McShane, M. D., and F. P. Williams III (1993). *The Management of Correctional Institutions*. New York: Garland.

Miller, R. (1992). Working relationship—Examining standards' role in court decisions. *Corrections Today* 54(3): 58, 60.

Reimer, E. G., and D. K. Sechrest (1979). Writing standards for correctional accreditation. *Federal Probation* 43(3): 10–15.

Reynolds, E. (1992). An auditor's view of accreditation. *Corrections Today* 54(3): 44–46.

Saylor, W. G. (1989). Quality control for prisons managers: The key indicators/strategic support system. *Federal Prisons Journal* 1(2): 39–42.

Sechrest, D. K., and E. G. Reimer (1982). Adopting national standards for correctional reform. *Federal Probation* 46: 18–25.

Washington, J. (1989). Accreditation opinion poll update. *Corrections Today* 51(5): 160–61.

Administration

Today's prison manager is responsible for planning, directing, controlling, and communicating not only with staff and inmates but also with related government agencies, state officials, and the general public. That public interaction may mean talking to the families of inmates who are worried about incarcerated loved ones, special interest groups that want certain problems or concerns addressed, the news media, or angry local residents with complaints about traffic around the prison.

To solve all of the daily problems that arise in a prison, management relies on modern technology, formal as well as informal rules and regulations, and a hierarchy of authority. While each individual prison within a state has its own management unit, the units all report to a centralized state system headquarters, usually referred to as a department of corrections. Likewise, each of the federal prisons in this country reports to a regional headquarters that in turn reports to the director of the Federal Bureau of Prisons. The director reports to the U.S. Attorney General, who is the head of the Department of Justice.

As there is no universally accepted vocabulary of management, there is no standardized language of correctional management. Among the states, and among state agencies, there is much variation and misinterpretation in titles, structures, and functions. For example, the chief executive of the state department of corrections may be called director, commissioner, superintendent, or secretary. The head of each individual facility or prison unit can be called a warden, director, assistant director, superintendent, or administrator.

The History of Prison Management

Prisons have historically been plagued by an unprofessional image. There are several reasons for that. First, prisons were located in rural, even remote, areas of farmland. Employees drawn from those regions were often undereducated and unsophisticated. The conflict of cultures that developed between the city-reared inmates and the country-reared guards usually resulted in power struggles and brutality. Another problem was that no training took place, and that guards had little understanding of the broader goals of penology. Salaries were low. In the 1840s, a guard in Missouri might earn $130 per year; one hundred years later, in Louisiana, the earnings were about $130 per month. An even greater problem, however, was that in many locations few if any guards were hired at all. In some systems, the largest and toughest prison inmates were selected to supervise and control the others.

Finally, one of the most damaging policies in prison operations was the use of management positions as gifts of political patronage. In many states, the job of running a prison was given as a reward to political supporters or as a gift to family members and friends. As a result, managers often had no qualifications or prior experience. Another consequence was that wardens or prison superintendents traditionally held office for only short periods of time. A short tenure often disrupts prison operations, destabilizes other employees, and impedes the progress of planned reforms.

In the past, prisons operated as closed systems. Leaders were promoted from within the ranks and little information was passed to the outside concerning daily operations. The prison resembled a paramilitary organization, using rank as authority and passing limited information through a chain of command. Guards were expected to follow orders with little explanation and no questions asked.

While the paramilitary model is still popular today, there now is more emphasis on training officers to make better decisions, rather than simply to follow orders. Concerns about liability and staff morale have meant improving communications between officers and their supervisors and more staff participation in decision-making. Corrections programs are also now viewed more as open systems with continuous interaction with the outside, including the news media, the courts, state legislatures, the governor, public interest groups, and corrections boards or commissions.

Prison Management Today

Prison Management as a Profession

Over the years, prison management has been professionalized. Public criticism arising over scandals, and the incorporation of administrative practices from the business world, have created demands for educated, trained, and accountable leadership that operates according to accepted norms within the field. Today's manager may belong to a number of professional organizations and spends more time interacting with the public and with political leaders. Professional organizations sponsor workshops and training seminars, issue opinion statements on current legislation, and compile standards for the operation of institutions

in the form of accreditation criteria. Up until the implementation of accreditation standards, prison officials had little help in gauging the quality of their facility or the performance of their staff. Most modern corrections officials view accreditation as an effective management tool (although it may not be widely used). Other management tools include departmentally sponsored reviews, investigative services such as internal affairs, and an open line of communications between inmates, staff, and management.

Profile of Management

With prison management now recruiting more women and minorities, the profile of management has become more diverse. Both the riot at Attica and the civil rights movement of the sixties and seventies exposed the racial inequities between prison inmates and officers. Many departments, including the Federal Bureau of Prisons, embarked on campaigns to recruit more minorities into the corrections field.

In 1989 there were approximately forty women in charge of men's prisons. Approximately a dozen states have appointed women as commissioner or director of their department of corrections.

The Organizational Structure of Management

The organizational structures of prisons have grown both horizontally and vertically, to meet the demands of size and increased accountability. The complexity of prison organizations today means that they cannot be run, as in the past, on the authority of one leader. Rather, the organizational chart reflects a wide variety of technical assistants working in such areas as law, finance, public relations, government relations, treatment, industry, and classification.

The modern prison organization is structured into subsystems that perform various internal functions. Production and technical subsystems provide direct operations. Officers and supervisors, managed by the warden, deal directly with the inmates, maintaining security and control. Support subsystems obtain the materials necessary for the officers to do their work and for the inmates to receive necessary services. Support workers include finance officers who procure supplies and distribute the payroll, along with clerical, medical, and psychiatric staff. Maintenance subsystems ensure the proper distribution of staff throughout the department. Recruitment and personnel experts as well as training staff ensure that new officers will be available to replace any who may leave.

Adaptive subsystems allow the organization to respond to changing conditions. These include research departments, legal experts, and planning offices that all help to meet the evolving needs of the prison and keep it in compliance with standards and codes. For example, the Federal Bureau of Prisons has an Occupational Safety and Environmental Health Program, which is designed to guarantee a safe and healthful environment for officers. Safety managers at each facility are concerned with all aspects of safety and environmental health, and inspections make up an important part of the safety manager's routine. Inspections cover food service operations, living units, vehicles, and the prison hospital. Proper use of equipment is a major concern, especially in industrial operations carried out by Federal Prison Industries (UNICOR).

Finally, managerial subsystems exist to coordinate and control the entire operation. Management is ultimately responsible for the allocation of resources within the system, the development of goals and programming to meet them, and the conduct of employees.

Centralization Versus Decentralization

One controversial area for prison administration is the degree to which each individual prison can make its own decisions or policies in day-to-day operations. This is referred to as decentralization. Prisons originally operated as independent units and wardens were considered the kings of their own empires, but that situation was perceived as leading to corruption, mismanagement, and inconsistent performance. Centralization, on the other hand, seemed to provide greater uniformity in policies and more monitoring of day-to-day activities. Often located far away at a central headquarters, however, officials found it impractical, costly, and time-consuming to keep close track of activities at the various facilities around a state. Prison employees often developed an "us-against-them" view of the officials from headquarters, who often did not seem to understand their daily problems. Still, for legal control purposes and for maintaining equitable distribution of resources, a centralized model has been preferred in many areas of public administration.

While there has been steady movement toward centralization over the last fifty to seventy-five years, recent shifts in correctional philosophy are bringing about a tolerance for decentralization in many management areas. That increased tolerance may be the result of several forces:

1. *A trend away from mega-institutions and toward smaller facilities:* The current trend of building smaller facilities has increased the number of facilities and resulted in the spread of power over additional layers of authority. These layers of authority may be geographical or based on the characteristics of the inmate population. Facilities with special inmate populations, such as AIDS patients, the mentally ill, or the elderly, see themselves as different from other units and in need of separate policies, procedures, staffing, and resources.

2. *Administrative interest in the concept of unit management:* Unit management has been defined as the leadership of small, self-contained (self-administered) sections or units within the confines of a larger facility. The units are formed by the creation of housing areas of fifty to one hundred inmates who spend the majority of their time together in a confined area. According to Farmer (1988), the groups are preferably supervised by a group-specific, multidisciplinary management team. The team is normally composed of at least a unit manager, a caseworker, a secretary, a correctional counselor, a correctional officer, an educator, and a psychologist or other mental health worker. The Unit Management teams have discipline, classification, and programmatic authority, and are guided by sets of common policies and procedures.

3. *DOC top administrators' being hired from outside of corrections, with backgrounds in political, legal, or business areas:* The expansion and sophistication of corrections systems has meant that administrative structures have experienced horizontal growth. The complexity of management operations calls for leaders with a wide variety of legal, business, and personnel skills. It is not uncommon to find top administrators with little, if any, background in corrections. In fact, a 1987 study of jail management in Maryland recommended that the department

hire a deputy administrator with expertise in planning, budgeting, financial management, and record keeping. Similarly, Texas appointed a director of corrections whose employment history was in public finance. The strategy in cases like these is that subordinates, more experienced in corrections, will provide these technical experts with the information they need with which to make appropriate correctional decisions. Because top executives are now less experienced in corrections than in the past, and because they rely on their staffs, they are more likely to delegate authority to operate independently in routine institutional matters.

4. *The increased legal liability of wardens:* In many cases, the courts have found wardens and top administrators responsible for the violations of the rights of inmates on their units. For that reason, wardens have a strong interest not only in how policies are carried out, but also in how policies can be formulated to minimize or prevent liability.

5. *Competition among individual prison units for limited state resources:* Only recently have individual departments within systems had to compete against each other for state resources. As facilities are developed for distinct inmate populations, and thereby become differentiated, their needs change. Units that take on medical responsibilities or higher security levels will perceive a need for additional funds, as well as for separate policies or exemptions from traditional policies. Such exceptions are viewed as necessary for their specialized populations.

As the education and experience level of unit administrators increases, so will their expectations for autonomy within the institution. For officials at state headquarters, the desire for decentralized decision-making is not only a threat to their authority but also to the legal simplicity of uniform policies and procedures.

Regional Management

The establishment of regional management systems may offer a compromise between centralized and decentralized systems. Like many large private businesses, some large prison systems rely on regional management as an intermediary step between control by headquarters and the autonomous control of a single prison unit. For example, the Federal Bureau of Prisons (BOP) has adopted a regional organization to bring management support closer to its field locations. Each region conducts audits and management reviews, answers operational questions, and attempts to standardize procedures for its members. Regions are often geographical, as in the Texas Department of Corrections, where a supervisor from the north, south, central, and western regions reports directly to the director of the Department of Corrections.

Management Tasks

There are many challenges for managers in corrections today. First, they must be sensitive to public opinion without operating at its whim. Facing serious overcrowding problems and restricted budgets, managers must devise creative strategies for maintaining adequate services and conditions that meet constitutional requirements. Prison administrators must be aware of all current regulations governing the hiring, management, and supervision of employees, as well as the standards of health care and general welfare that pertain to their inmates.

One of the difficulties in being a prison manager is that many of the aspects of the job are simply out of one's control. Many people do not understand the factors that may make one prison "better" than another, "safer," or "less expensive." That may lead to unfair criticism when people compare one facility with another. Prison architecture, the level of crowding, the inmate-to-staff ratio, and the limits of the budget are factors that administrators must deal with daily, yet they are also things that they cannot alter: forces outside the prison system, or from the past, have created them.

Management Styles

There is considerable debate over the best management style for operating prisons. Up until the 1960s, the most common management style was rooted in authoritarian dominance. The style most appropriate for today's institutions, however, is a controversial issue. Prisons, like other areas of public administration, have borrowed heavily from private business for techniques and policies. While some of those lessons are merely fads that come and go, it is clear that prison administrators are looking for answers that will apply from facility to facility and will last over time. Like managers in private business and in other areas of public administration, prison officials are faced with the problem of how to budget money and other resources, how to integrate the existing workforce with personnel who meet today's changing employee profile, and how to best use and adapt technological advances.

Many reformers have argued that a more democratic style of leadership, allowing staff and even some of the inmates some degree of participatory management, would be best. That was attempted by Thomas Murton at Arkansas in 1967 and by Howard Gill at Norfolk in 1927. To some degree, it was also the underlying theme at Walla Walla during the early 1970s.

Some people argue that true participatory management is not suited to prisons because of the high degree of risk involved with most inmate populations. Indeed, work inside an institution has traditionally been viewed as being performed by less mature workers who do not require a high degree of skill or technical expertise. As corrections has developed into a more legally and technologically sophisticated operation, however, the skill requirements for officers have steadily increased.

There is some consensus that the style of management that administrators use with inmates is not the same style that will be effective with staff. It is believed that styles of management will vary with the level of security in a certain institution or the types of inmates held there. Most managers employ strategies such as walking around the facility, speaking with inmates and staff directly about their concerns, and taking a "hands on" approach to many details of daily operations.

The Future of Corrections Management

The limited attempts at expanding management information systems and improving staff/management relations may become more popular and may even become standard practices. The popularity of private sector techniques such as total quality management (TQM) may mean that management will become more consumer oriented, periodically surveying staff as well as inmates to ensure meaningful feedback that may identify problem areas early and avoid confrontations later. Technological improvement in on-line datasets will allow managers access to more information in daily decision-making. Management training is becoming more popular and more readily available. All of these factors may contribute to reduced liability and fewer potential lawsuits.

Marilyn D. McShane
Frank P. Williams III

See also WARDENS

Bibliography

Archambeault, W. (1983). Management Theory Z: Its implication for managing the labor intensive nature of work in prison. *Prison Journal* 62: 58–67.

Benton, F. W., and C. Nesbitt, eds. (1988). *Prison Personnel Management and Staff Development*. College Park, Md.: American Correctional Association.

Cohn, A. (1987). The failure of correctional management—The potential for reversal. *Federal Probation* 51: 3–7.

Farmer, J. F. (1988). A case study in regaining control of a violent state prison. *Federal Probation* 52: 41–47.

McShane, M. D., and F. P. Williams III (1993). *The Management of Correctional Institutions*. New York: Garland.

Simonsen, C., and D. Arnold (1994). Is corrections ready for TQM? *Corrections Today* 56(4): 164, 166, 168, 169.

Stojkovic, S. (1986). Social bases of power and control mechanisms among correctional administrators in a prison organization. *Journal of Criminal Justice* 14: 157–66.

Administrative Segregation

Administrative segregation is a general term used in institutional corrections that refers to restrictive housing units, cell blocks, or facilities specially designed for disruptive inmates. It is a high maximum-security classification level that typically involves inmates living in single cells, the reduction or complete elimination of group activities among inmates, strengthened measures to control contraband, the use of additional security measures and equipment, and programs and services that are either not available or are restructured and brought to the inmates' housing areas.

Prisoners assigned to administrative segregation units spend most of each day in their cells. They frequently do not have work assignments; they are escorted out of their cells for periodic recreation, medical appointments, family and attorney visits, and scheduled meetings with correctional committees, such as the classification committee or the disciplinary committee. While some correctional systems refer to this highly restrictive classification as administrative segregation, other systems use different terminology; the Washington Corrections Center in Shelton uses the term intensive management.

Although placement of a prisoner in administrative segregation is a response to that prisoner's failure to abide by disciplinary regulations, segregation is typically considered an administrative placement; that is, it is not a punishment. Inmates classified into this restrictive status have been evaluated as being unable to live safely among even maximum security inmates.

Types of Prisoners Assigned to Administrative Segregation

Prison administrators assign inmates to an administrative segregation classification because their behavior is so disruptive that they are security risks to other inmates, the staff, or the facility itself. Some prisoners are assigned because they are escape risks. The restrictive living conditions and limited movement in administrative segregation significantly reduce the opportunities to escape or to threaten the security of others.

A national survey of the disruptive maximum security population was conducted in 1988 by the National Institute of Corrections. A questionnaire was sent by researchers to fifty state correctional agencies, the District of Columbia, and the Federal Bureau of Prisons. Thirty-five agencies responded. At the time of the questionnaire, disruptive inmates constituted 3.8 percent of the overall prisoner population and 54.8 percent of the maximum security population. Approximately 25 percent of the disruptive inmate population had a history of escape or attempted escape, compared with 11 percent of the general population inmates.

Respondents identified murder and hostage-taking as the two actions of primary importance in determining administrative segregation status, followed closely by deadly assault, and the manufacturing, possessing, or smuggling of firearms, explosives, incendiary devices, or poison gas. Other types of behavior that often result in a prisoner's being assigned to administrative segregation include aggravated sexual assault, sodomy, organizing or instigating a riot, work stoppage, or slowdown, and participating in the distribution, smuggling, or manufacture of drugs. In response to the growing problem of prison gang violence, many correctional systems also assign gang leaders to administrative segregation. A few states, such as Texas, house all confirmed prison gang members in segregation.

Another and different type of prisoner that may be housed in administrative segregation are inmates needing protective custody, not because they are disruptive but because their safety is threatened by other inmates. Their security needs may be so great that they must be single-celled and made ineligible for work. Although not in the same housing areas with disruptive inmates, some protective custody prisoners are completely segregated from the general population and live highly restrictive lives.

A major criticism of administrative segregation is that far too often it is used by administrators to house disruptive inmates who suffer from severe mental disorders. Instead of receiving appropriate mental health care, these mentally disabled, troublesome prisoners are managed in administrative segregation, even though for some of them, the isolation in segregated housing can be detrimental.

Management of Administrative Segregation Prisoners

Most correctional systems concentrate all of their segregated disruptive inmates in one or a limited number of facilities, to eliminate duplication of services and programs and to enhance the development of specialized management techniques and staff training. Another advantage of concentration is that it helps create a safer and more orderly environment in prisons that do not house disruptive inmates.

In addition to concentrating their segregated prisoners in a limited number of facilities and housing them in single cells, correctional systems use a number of other methods to manage the disruptive population. Administrative segregation inmates are transported to and from their cells with an officer escort. The inmate is in handcuffs and perhaps in waist or leg restraints. Inmates are usually handcuffed whenever they are out of their cells, except during recreation and visits. Prisoners may be required to take their recreation alone or in small groups during limited time periods.

Correctional officers who work with disruptive inmates often wear protective vests and have additional training in the safe and effective use of physical force, batons, and chemical agents. Videotape records of the use of force are made whenever possible. Officers may be equipped with body alarms and two-way radios. Administrative cell blocks may be fitted with closed-circuit television and paging systems. Depending on the design of the housing unit, additional staffing is usually required. A well-designed administrative segregation unit or cell block includes recreation areas, medical stations, and meeting rooms that are located close to segregated prisoners so that movement is curtailed and contact with general population inmates is avoided.

The length of time a prisoner spends in an administrative segregation classification will vary according to the policies of the correctional system. It will also depend on the number of beds available in restrictive housing and the demand for those beds at any particular time. Some systems have specific written criteria for determining when an inmate should be released to a less restrictive classification. The most common considerations for release include a prisoner's number of rule infractions while segregated and their severity and recency, the amount of time served in segregation, the number of previous segregated confinements, the reason for classification to segregation, the inmate's cooperation with staff, general adjustment, and gang affiliation.

The United States Penitentiary at Marion, Illinois, is an example of an entire prison that houses disruptive inmates. Marion is the Federal Bureau of Prison's highest-security institution (Level 6). Prisoners who have been disruptive in other federal facilities or who were sent from state systems as a result of serious disciplinary problems are concentrated in the Marion facility. After Marion was shifted to Level 6 in 1979, the increase in seriously disruptive inmates resulted in a significant increase in violence. Gradually, the bureau found it necessary to implement tighter control measures. In 1980, all industrial operations were transferred from Marion and the movement of inmates was further restricted. All maintenance work assignments were eliminated. After a fatal assault on two officers, the serious injury of two other officers, and the murder of a prisoner, all in 1983, an indefinite state of emergency was declared at Marion, which continues at this time.

General population inmates, as they are defined at Marion, have very limited recreation and are restricted to their cells, where they take meals. General population inmates who maintain a clear record are eligible for transfer to the intermediate level, where inmates are fed in small groups and are afforded greater privileges and more recreation. The pretransfer unit is a transitional phase before transfer to a less secure facility; it resembles a more traditional penitentiary environment. Prisoners must spend a minimum of twelve months in general population and a minimum of six months in both the intermediate and pretransfer levels.

Legal Issues Surrounding Administrative Segregation

The prisoners' rights revolution that began in the late 1960s has also had an impact on the manner in which correctional systems manage disruptive inmates. Two-thirds of the respondents to the 1988 National Institute of Corrections survey reported that they are involved in litigation pertaining to disruptive inmates. One-fourth reported that they are under court orders affecting the management of disruptive inmates, and one-third are under consent decrees.

In general, courts have upheld the right of officials to segregate inmates who are threats to the order and security of institutions. Judges have ruled that segregation does not violate the Eighth Amendment's prohibitions against cruel and unusual punishment.

The constitutionality of the living conditions in segregation has also been examined in numerous cases. Courts have examined such conditions as the level of hygiene and sanitation, the adequacy of heating, ventilation, plumbing, and lighting, the inmates' opportunity for recreation and other activities, the size of the cells, the use of closed-door cells, and the noise level. Judges have considered each challenge to the legality of living conditions on a case-by-case basis, considering whether any one or a combination of conditions violates the Eighth Amendment.

A class-action lawsuit challenged the living conditions at the Marion federal facility following a lockdown that was initiated in 1983 (*Bruscino v. Carlson*, 1988). Charges included allegations of physical and verbal abuse of inmates by officers, the abuse of strip and digital searches, abuse of physical restraints and chemical agents, lack of recreation, limited visiting privileges, severe restrictions on religious rights, lack of jobs for inmates, and limited access to the courts. The court ruled that the totality of conditions did not violate the Eighth Amendment and the Seventh Circuit Court of Appeals affirmed.

There is little consistency in the courts' rulings concerning the length of time officials may legally segregate prisoners. In *Hewitt v. Helms* (1983), the United States Supreme Court stated that administrative segregation status cannot be used by administrators as a pretext for indefinitely confining an inmate. Lower courts have differed considerably, however, in determining when the length of a particular confinement violates the Constitution. As long as two years has been held constitutional, and thirty days has been held unconstitutional. The decisions seem to depend on the living conditions in segregation and the reasons for the confinement (*Graham v. Willingham*, 1967; *Knuckles v. Prasse*, 1971; *Hutto v. Finney*, 1978).

The other major constitutional issue concerns the process by which inmates are initially classified to administrative segregation. In *Hewitt v. Helms*, the Supreme Court decided that the Constitution's due process requirements do not apply to inmates transferred to administrative segregation because segregation is a status that any prisoner can expect at some point during confinement. Prisoners are not entitled to due process protections under the Fourteenth Amendment alone, as they have no constitutional right to remain in general population. The court went on to say, however, that states may create a right to due process by enacting statutes, regulations, or policies that restrict the discretion of prison officials to place an inmate in segregation. If a state has enacted guidelines or criteria concerning the circumstances under which an inmate can be segregated, that inmate has a right to a notice of transfer and a limited opportunity to present a case against that transfer. The institution is required to follow the regulations it has enacted.

In response to the litigation, many correctional systems provide prisoners with notice and an opportunity to contest their placement in the restrictive administrative segregation environment. In addition, most jurisdictions periodically review an inmate's segregated status, to make certain that the inmate continues to meet the criteria for placement and to provide inmates with assessments of their behavior.

Summary

Administrative segregation is a valuable management tool with which to deal with inmates who require a high level of security, whether they are a threat to others or are in serious danger from others. Its disadvantages include the expense of maintaining segregated housing areas that are specially equipped with extra security devices and are intensively staffed. Also, the inmate population is often difficult to manage. Because of the restrictive nature and the potential for abuse of administrative segregation, inmates are usually provided with significant due process protections.

Barbara Belbot

See also DISCIPLINE

Bibliography

Adams, K. (1983). Former mental patients in a prison and parole system: A study of socially disruptive behavior. *Criminal Justice and Behavior* 10: 358–84.

Buchanan, R., C. Unger, and K. Whitlow (1988). *Disruptive Maximum Security Inmate Management Guide*. Washington, D.C.: National Institute of Corrections.

Henderson, J. D. (1990). *Protective Custody Management in Adult Correctional Facilities*. Washington, D.C.: National Institute of Corrections.

Hodgins, S., and G. Cote (1991). The mental health of penitentiary inmates in isolation. *Canadian Journal of Criminology* 33: 175–82.

King, R. D. (1991). Maximum-security custody in Britain and the U.S.A.: A study of Gartree and Oak Park Heights. *British Journal of Criminology* 31(2): 126–52.

Olivero, J. M., and J. B. Roberts (1990). The United States federal penitentiary at Marion, Illinois: Alcatraz revisited. *New England Journal on Civil and Criminal Confinement* 16: 21–51.

Toch, H. (1982). The disturbed disruptive inmate: Where does the bus stop? *Journal of Psychiatry and the Law* 10: 327–49.

Cases

Bruscino v. Carlson, 854 F.2d 162 (7th Cir. 1988)
Graham v. Willingham, 384 F.2d 367 (10th Cir. 1967)
Hewitt v. Helms, 459 U.S. 460 (1983)

Hutto v. Finney, 437 U.S. 678 (1978)
Knuckles v. Prasse, 435 F.2d 1255 (3rd Cir. 1971)

AIDS

AIDS (Acquired Immune Deficiency Syndrome) represents the final stage in a spectrum of disease caused by infection with HIV (Human Immunodeficiency Virus). HIV assaults and impairs the immune system, exposing the sufferer to a broad variety of unusual illnesses that rarely occur in people with healthy immune systems.

The original Centers for Disease Control (CDC) national case definition of AIDS was as follows:

> an illness characterized by evidence of HIV infection and the presence of one or more "indicator" diseases to include: certain opportunistic infections and illnesses, which take advantage of an individual's compromised immune system such as pneumocystis carinii pneumonia (PCP), toxoplasmosis of the brain, cytomegalovirus, and other viruses and bacterial infections, certain opportunistic cancers like Kaposi's Sarcoma, and central nervous system disorders which also affect the brain and cause a variety of neurologic complications (National Academy of Sciences, 1988).

As of 1 January 1993, the CDC expanded this case definition of AIDS to include individuals over twelve years of age with a CD4+ (T-cell or T4 lymphode cell receptor) count lower than two hundred cells per cubic millimeter of blood, recurrent pneumonia within a one-year period, tuberculosis of the lungs, or cancer of the cervix, when accompanied by HIV infection.

While a case definition is important in order to track the epidemiology of AIDS in the nation, the Presidential HIV Commission in 1988 concluded that the term AIDS was obsolete and that the term HIV infection more correctly defined the problem, thereby focusing on the full course of HIV infection rather than concentrating on the later stages of the disease.

HIV Transmission

There are two known types of HIV: HIV-1, associated with the majority of AIDS cases in the United States, Europe, and Africa; and HIV-2, which is found primarily in West Africa. HIV belongs to a class of viruses called retroviruses. Evidence continues to indicate that there are three primary modes of HIV transmission: sexual contact, with the exchange of genital secretions (that is, semen or vaginal and cervical secretions); intravenous drug use by means of contaminated needles or syringes; and perinatally, through the passage of HIV from infected mother to child, either across the placenta, during delivery, or by breast feeding.

Prior to 1985, the receipt of blood and blood products (blood transfusions) was a major route of transmission, but, because of stricter safeguards regarding blood donation, that is now considered a secondary means of transmission. Transmission occurs less commonly when an uninfected individual is exposed to the transplanted tissue or body organs from an HIV-infected donor. Although rare, HIV transmission can also occur through occupational exposure. The health-care profession is the only place where occupational transmission of HIV has been documented to date. Cases of HIV seroconversion following occupational exposure reflect a low but ever-present risk. Studies have shown seroconversion rates of zero to less than one percent among health-care workers with documented percutaneous injuries (needle-stick or puncture wound), sustained contact with nonintact skin, and mucous membrane exposure to blood or body fluids from HIV-infected individuals.

Stages of HIV Infection and Disease

In order to more accurately define HIV infection and AIDS, the CDC has described a four-stage process, based on the presence or absence of various symptoms.

Stage I—Acute HIV Infection

Soon after the initial infection with HIV, there is a short period of HIV replication in the body. The manufacture of HIV antibodies by the body's immune system normally begins to occur as a means of defense to counter the HIV replication. Within two to twelve weeks of exposure and in conjunction with antibody production, acute response symptoms to HIV infection may appear. Symptoms last from two to fourteen days and include fever, swollen glands, poor appetite, and general weakness. These symptoms are often misdiagnosed as mononucleosis. Although some people get quite ill and require medical attention, others may have few or no discernible symptoms. The immune systems of all HIV-infected people respond with HIV antibody production. Within a one- to three-month period, the HIV antibodies begin to circulate in the bloodstream and become detectable. This process is defined as "sero-conversion." HIV antibodies are detected via serological testing, and individuals are considered HIV seropositive when they have two positive Enzyme Linked Immunosorbant Assay (ELISA) tests for HIV antibodies, confirmed by a more reliable Western Blot test. Public health officials recommend that HIV seroconverted individuals take appropriate behavioral precautions in order to prevent transmission of the virus to others.

Stage II—Asymptomatic HIV Infection
After acute infection, HIV enters into a period of relative inactivity. Individuals in this stage are referred to as HIV asymptomatic. This stage can last from a few months to several years, with the possibility that some will never develop symptoms at this stage. Tuberculosis (TB), sexually transmitted diseases (STDs), other viruses, alcohol and substance abuse, and aging are conditions that challenge and may further weaken the immune system's ability to hold HIV in check. These cofactors can hasten the progression from asymptomatic HIV infection to symptomatic HIV disease.

Stage III—Symptomatic HIV Infection
Stage III begins when individuals exhibit mild to severe medical conditions and clinical symptoms caused by their HIV infection, but have not yet exhibited any of the formal case definition categories of AIDS. In the past, a more common yet unofficial term used to describe such a category was AIDS-Related Complex (ARC). Leading public health officials advocated the abolishment of that term because of its ambiguity in regard to the life-threatening aspects of the disease at this stage. Persistent Generalized Lymphadenopathy (PGL), which is a painless swelling (two centimeters or more in size) of lymph nodes in two or more sites on the body excluding the groin, that persists for more than three months, is the most accurate indicator of this stage of HIV infection. Other indicators include the non-AIDS manifestations of oral (thrush) and vaginal (candidiasis) yeast infections, cervical dysplasia (the abnormal growth of cervical cells), and

chronic, recurrent bouts with herpes simplex virus and Human Papillomavirus (HPV) or genital warts.

Stage IV—AIDS
AIDS is diagnosed when three elements exist: (1) HIV infection; (2) resulting immune suppression; and (3) one or more of the indicator diseases. AIDS indicator diseases include HIV Wasting, HIV dementia, a variety of opportunistic infections caused by four categories of microorganisms, (parasites, viruses, fungi, and bacteria) and the cancers and lymphomas associated with AIDS. Individuals with advanced, severe, clinical illness, whose immune systems are nearly depleted, may lose detectable HIV antibodies as a terminal event. The terminal stage of HIV infection is relatively short and normally lasts only about one year, during which time untreated patients rapidly and invariably progress toward death.

Correlation between HIV/AIDS in Prisons and Injecting Drug Use
Hearings conducted by the National Institute of Corrections (NIC) Advisory Board in 1993 included correctional officials and administrators representing every region of the nation. Prison health care was identified as the most critical current and future issue within the profession. Although there are many important issues related to the correctional health-care crisis, the key contributing factor to the crisis has been AIDS and the correlation between preincarceration injecting drug use (IDU) and HIV infection.

At the start of the decade, twenty-four percent of new AIDS cases in the United States were attributed to IDUs. The concentration of substance abusers in our nation's state and federal prisons is high. A 1991 national survey of over 700,000 inmates in state correctional facilities found that 79.4 percent acknowledged having used drugs. Twenty-five percent admitted the use of cocaine or crack, and 10 percent admitted using heroin or other opiates in the month prior to their imprisonment. Another 25 percent acknowledged IDU at some time during their lives (Snell 1993; Harlow 1993). A previous survey found that 30 percent of those reporting IDU admitted to sharing needles (National Institute of Justice [NIJ] 1990). The large percentages of inmates admitting IDU and the sharing of injection paraphernalia were reflected in the findings of the National Prison

Project, where IDUs represented the majority of inmates with AIDS.

An example of the relationship between IDU and HIV infection exists in New York State. The Rockefeller Drug Laws, implementing determinant sentencing for drug offenders in the late 1970s, affected the New York State Department of Correctional Services (NYSDOCS) by the 1980s and 1990s. The state inmate population grew to fifty-nine thousand in 1991 from twenty thousand in 1979. The increase of court commitments to prison for drug offenses increased the percentage of the state inmate population's IDU (estimated to be as high as 85 percent), which further increased the percentage of HIV-infected inmates. The chief medical officer for the NYSDOCS reported that by the fall of 1989 approximately one inmate per day was dying of AIDS-related illnesses. In 1992, the NYSDOCS estimated that one out of every eight inmates in New York prisons were HIV infected (Glaser and Greifinger 1993).

Nationally, the state and federal prison population increased from 329,821 in 1980 to 823,414 in 1991, primarily the result of a nationwide policy of mandatory minimum sentencing for drug offenses, such as the National Drug Control Strategy (NDCS), implemented in 1989. The dramatic impact of such policies are reflected by the AIDS incidence rate in the prison population, rising from 181/100,000 in 1990 to 362/100,000 in 1992/1993 (Hammett et al. 1993). Additionally, the Federal Bureau of Prisons estimates that by 1995, 70 percent of all new federal court commitments will be for drug offenses (up from forty-seven percent in 1991). Thus, the ongoing "get tough" policy on drugs, with stricter sentencing, will have a great impact on American prisons into the twenty-first century, with a proportional increase in AIDS cases and mortality.

AIDS Policy in American Prisons

Policy concerning AIDS in United States prisons varies greatly according to the jurisdiction in which the prison resides. Policies and procedures regarding education, training, counseling and testing, confidentiality, and health care, continue to be formulated as knowledge about HIV/AIDS increases. AIDS policy and management in the penal setting are two dimensional, in that they represent both criminal justice and health concerns.

HIV/AIDS prevalence surveys of inmates provide data that is helpful in making decisions regarding manpower, personnel, and resources in regard to HIV prevention, detection of HIV/AIDS, special housing and security needs, medical care, treatment, and psychosocial services. Surveys of specific inmate cohorts can later be repeated to measure the effectiveness of programs and to help officials evaluate strategies for preventing HIV infection. Seroprevalence surveys also provide public health officials with useful data about HIV infection rates and the evolution of the AIDS epidemic.

AIDS Epidemiology in American Prisons to Date

In November of 1981, the first confirmed case of AIDS among United States prison inmates appeared in a New York State Department of Correctional Service's facility; just six months after the CDC announced the existence of the disease. By the end of March 1993, only the states of West Virginia and South Dakota had not reported an AIDS case within their correctional systems. The total number of AIDS cases reported by the other forty-eight states and the Federal Bureau of Prisons was 8,525. Of those, there have been 2,858 inmate deaths from AIDS, 39 percent of which occurred after 1990 (Hammett et al. 1993). In 1989, the percentage of cumulative AIDS cases in United States prisons began to exceed the increases in AIDS cases in the general population (Hammett and Moini 1990). Further seroepidemiological surveys established that HIV infection rates in prisons exceeded the general population by as much as five or six to one (Lurigio et al. 1991). The 1992/1993 NIJ/CDC survey reflected an AIDS incidence rate in prison that was twenty times higher than that of the 1992 U.S. general population (362 cases per 100,000 versus 18 cases per 100,000, respectively) (Hammett et al. 1993).

Most of the cumulative AIDS cases in prisons have occurred in urban centers of a million or more residents along the Atlantic coast. The Middle Atlantic states of New York, New Jersey, and Pennsylvania account for 50 percent of the total cumulative inmate AIDS cases; 20 percent have occurred in the South Atlantic region, consisting of Delaware, Maryland, the District of Columbia, Virginia, West Virginia, North Carolina, Georgia, and Florida (Hammett et al. 1993). Although the distribution of AIDS cases was uneven—29 percent of state and federal systems account for 90 percent of the cases reported in the NIJ/CDC survey—it is important to note that the Middle Atlantic region's share of inmate AIDS cases decreased from 75 percent in 1985, while that of all other regions nationwide increased during that time (Hammett et al. 1993).

Forty-four percent of the infected inmates in the NIJ/CDC survey were black, 42 percent were Hispanic, and 14 percent were white (Hammett et al. 1993). Considering that African-Americans and Hispanics constitute approximately 70 percent of our nation's reported drug abusers and are also proportionally overrepresented as inmates within our criminal justice system, those figures are not surprising.

The best estimate of the overall HIV seroprevalence rate in American prisons is 2.2 percent, as reported by the U.S. Department of Justice (Harlow 1993). There is great state-by-state variance in this figure, however. A nationwide study conducted in ten correctional systems with moderate to high rates of HIV infection assessed 10,944 prisoners and found the seroprevalence rate ranging from 2.1 to 14.7 percent. Nine of the ten correctional facilities reported higher rates of HIV infection for women (Vlahov et al. 1991).

Prevention of HIV Transmission Through Education

Although the discovery and initial findings on AIDS led to considerable public panic, by 1993 much of the initial reaction to the epidemic appeared to have dissipated. Many of the original concerns of correctional administrators—such as intraprison transmission by homosexual contact or by the sharing of needles (acknowledged to occur within prisons, Nacci and Kane 1983)—have proved unfounded. Longitudinal research on both federal and state inmates via serological studies has established that HIV transmission within the prison is likely to be rare, at less than 0.5 percent (Vlahov et al. 1991). Today, leading public health officials and researchers still advocate education as the best method to combat the spread of HIV infection. As discussed, the groups from which the American penal population is drawn are at high risk for HIV/AIDS. That population consists of individuals who have had little or no access to health care. For many young adults, the prison is the dominant social institution in their lives, and it can offer an excellent setting for HIV prevention, education, counseling, testing, and effective medical intervention.

HIV/AIDS Education in the American Penal Setting

A recent survey of state correctional departments in the U.S. found that forty-eight states have some type of AIDS education for inmates. Forty-five of those state correctional agencies have AIDS educational programs upon intake, with twenty-two of those also conducting AIDS education upon release. The majority of states (80.9 percent) implemented their programs between the years 1985 and 1989. In rank order, their main reasons for doing so were: (1) to enhance institutional safety for both inmates and staff, (2) to meet their commitment to public health, (3) to improve the prison environment, and (4) to protect the institution from inmate litigation (Martin et al. 1993).

Education is now recognized as the foundation to all HIV prevention efforts in the nation, but it takes on even more significance with inmates. Because our nation's correctional facilities contain such large concentrations of acknowledged IDUs, the AIDS education given to this captive population is key in fostering behavioral changes aimed at reducing HIV transmission. Because IDUs in the general population are difficult for AIDS educators to reach, those in prison are more likely to benefit from AIDS education. The education received by inmates, and particularly drug injectors, is likely to be remembered upon release. AIDS education and training within the correctional setting also help to alleviate concern about the transmission of HIV to either inmates or staff.

HIV/AIDS education in the nation's prisons reinforces a commitment to public health by realizing that it is not solely a criminal justice issue. HIV/AIDS education is important public health information that every citizen should have, and prisoners should not be overlooked. In fact, litigation against the correctional departments of Alabama and Connecticut has been initiated by inmates to ensure that those departments provide adequate AIDS education.

In order for HIV education to be considered truly preventive in the prison setting, it must be up to date and scientifically accurate, appropriate for the educational and cultural level of the inmates, and presented in all the languages necessary to reach the prison population. The content of the educational material should include the modes of HIV transmission, the signs of HIV infection and progression, the implications of the HIV antibody test, the symptoms and signs of AIDS, HIV infection control procedures and confidentiality requirements, and information on assistance for those inmates testing positive for HIV. The education should be mandatory and ongoing for both staff and prisoners (Dubler et al. 1990). HIV/AIDS education is often presented both before and after HIV antibody testing.

HIV Testing in American Prisons

The advent of a blood test for HIV antibodies in 1985 ignited intense national debate concerning HIV testing. The debate centered on the moral and legal issues of mandatory testing used as a tool for policy rather than for medical purposes. Advocates of mandatory testing argue that, by testing everyone, identified HIV seropositives will have the necessary access to life-prolonging treatments, and behavioral changes can be stressed in an effort to protect society as a whole. Civil rights proponents point out that mandatory testing violates an individual's right to privacy, and that those identified as HIV positive may be subjected to such discriminatory practices as quarantine. A further argument against mandatory testing is that a false sense of security may be created, because those with negative test results may not yet have seroconverted (it can take up to six months after infection for HIV antibodies to be detected).

In the nation's general population, voluntary HIV counseling and testing is the norm, with the exception of mandatory testing for U.S. military personnel and for foreign nationals applying for permanent resident status. Because prison inmates tend to demonstrate high HIV infection rates and because inmates have diminished privacy rights under the constitution, however, many lawmakers and correctional administrators have advocated mandatory testing among prison populations. Opinion polls have found that the public overwhelmingly supports mandatory HIV testing of prisoners. The order for mandatory testing for the Federal Bureau of Prisons came in 1987 from President Reagan. In 1993, NIJ/CDC survey results indicated that sixteen state correctional systems had policies requiring all inmates to be screened for HIV (Hammett et al. 1993).

A number of state and federal systems also have voluntary testing that is available to inmates upon request. Approximately 80 percent of the prison systems in the United States employ that method as their primary type of HIV testing (Hammett et al. 1993). Other testing methods used by prisons include targeting risk groups, routine testing of all but those inmates who refuse the test, testing of inmates if clinical manifestations of HIV/AIDS surface, and the testing of inmates who may have been exposed to blood, mucus, or other body fluids, commonly referred to as "incident" testing (Hammett et al. 1993). HIV testing can also originate in the judicial system, and court-ordered HIV testing has occurred in the state correctional departments of Arizona, California, Kansas, and Washington (Lillis 1993).

Regardless of the testing policy adopted by individual prison systems, public health officials deem the following elements crucial to any HIV screening program: (1) pretest counseling focusing on the significance of the test; (2) HIV/AIDS education stressing risk-reduction behaviors; (3) referrals for any medical needs; (4) confidentiality measures, especially regarding test results; (5) support for HIV seropositive inmates, to include medical, mental, and social services; and (6) HIV counseling and education following testing for all inmates, to encourage behavioral changes (Freudenberg 1989). These elements give prison inmates the opportunity to personally benefit from HIV screening within the correctional setting and, more important, to meet their moral obligations to the other prisoners.

The public health model of HIV prevention has had and will continue to have an impact on correctional facilities in this nation. The NIJ/CDC survey indicated that over four hundred correctional institutions have their HIV counseling and testing conducted either by local or state public health departments (Hammett et al. 1993). In 1992, the Centers for Disease Control, via funding lines known as Cooperative Agreements for HIV Prevention Projects, urged departments of health nationwide to work together to provide HIV prevention programs. In 1993, the CDC mandated that all state or local health department requests for such funding include (among others in the criminal justice system) all inmates. This assistance comes as a welcome relief to the nation's correctional system, where the cost for testing and treatment of inmates with HIV/AIDS continues to rise. A report issued in mid 1993 found that 76 percent of the state correctional systems in this nation reported that their health care budgets had increased in the past year and that, on average,

10 percent of the total correctional budget was now allotted for health care (Lillis 1993).

Correctional Policy and the Special Needs of HIV-Infected Inmates

The establishment of HIV/AIDS counseling and testing programs in correctional facilities has done much to alleviate the crisis atmosphere that first surrounded the AIDS epidemic in American prisons. These education and risk-reduction programs provide inmates with information about their HIV serostatus and identify the prisoners who require treatment. Yet HIV and AIDS still pose several serious and unique challenges to correctional administrators. The coming decade will see many more changes aimed at meeting the special needs of the HIV-infected inmate. Specific issues that require attention include the special needs of women infected with HIV, housing and security for inmates with HIV/AIDS, AIDS focused psychological and social services, and medical care and treatment for the inmate with HIV/AIDS.

Female Inmates

Women constitute only 7 percent of the nation's state and federal prison population, but the percentage increase in female commitments between 1980 and 1990 was almost double that of men (a 202.2 percent increase for women compared with a 111.6 percent increase for men). Correctional administrators have been building new women's facilities at record rates. They must keep in mind the necessary requirements for the HIV-afflicted female inmate when constructing new facilities. Incarcerated women have higher rates of HIV seroprevalence than do men, 2.5 to 14.7 percent versus 2.1 to 7.6 percent (Vlahov et al. 1991). That is attributed to higher rates of intravenous drug use among female prisoners, as large numbers are incarcerated for drug crimes or prostitution. Among the special needs of female inmates with HIV/AIDS is access to drug treatment, especially for the female prostitute who is often also an IDU. Women's AIDS education in the prison should stress safe sex via the use of condoms with spermicide, and should include discussions of the potential for IDU lesbians to infect their partners through sexual transmission. Prison HIV/AIDS programs for women must also include such issues as the perinatal transmission of HIV and the availability of HIV testing and counseling for pregnant inmates (Freudenberg 1989).

Housing and Security

As the number of inmates with HIV/AIDS grows, correctional administrators in the nation are increasingly faced with the issue of where to place them. In the beginning of the AIDS epidemic, segregation policies in prison were favored in order to protect uninfected inmates from HIV-infected inmates, who were considered contagious. There has been a shift in policy over time, however, and HIV-seropositive prisoners now tend to be mainstreamed into the general prison population. The NIJ/CDC survey found that 42 percent of state and federal systems had some sort of segregation policy for HIV-infected inmates in 1985, but that the percentage had decreased to just 8 percent in 1993 (Hammett et al. 1993). The new approach to the special housing for prisoners with HIV/AIDS appears to be a case-by-case approach, one contingent on the stage of the inmate's disease. In 1985, 35 percent of the systems favored the case-by-case approach; in 1993, that method was used by 92 percent of the state and federal prison systems (Hammett et al. 1993).

The demise of segregation as an AIDS policy within prisons has come about for several reasons. One important reason is that segregation policies can compound the problem of prison overcrowding for correctional administrators. Sentencing practices in the 1970s and 1980s helped to create an overcrowded penal system by the time AIDS was discovered. The creation of separate HIV/AIDS units within prisons put further demands on the already limited space available for inmate populations.

Certainly, the great majority of HIV asymptomatic prisoners do not require special housing. The need for special housing or hospice services occurs at the termination of the disease, when full-blown AIDS is present. The shift in policy toward a case-by-case approach has ensured that correctional resources can be targeted for effective HIV prevention programs, the purchase of life-sustaining medicines, and the development of special AIDS wards or long-term medical care facilities.

Consideration of AIDS-afflicted inmates on a case-by-case basis has resulted in the emergence of early-release policies by prisons, allowing terminally ill inmates to die at home. This compassionate approach by the penal system toward the dying inmate is workable, provided that necessary health care is available after release. Many inmates are poor and may not have access to medical care outside prison walls. It is therefore imperative that prison officials make sure that they are not releasing a dying inmate into a precarious situation; the case-by-case approach is the best way to ensure a humanitarian and dignified death.

Health Care, Medical Treatment, and Psychosocial Services

Once a correctional system has identified an inmate as HIV infected, it has a duty, imposed by the Constitution, to protect the prisoner and provide adequate medical care (see *Estelle v. Gamble*, 1976, wherein the U.S. Supreme Court held that "deliberate indifference to serious medical needs" violates the Eighth Amendment). Ideally, penal institutions should provide this health care in the least restrictive environment, given security or custodial needs. Health care should begin immediately after the notification of a positive test result. The HIV counselor has an obligation to inform the inmate of the significance of a positive test and to refer the inmate to medical, psychological, and social services. The medical staff should respond with the treatment appropriate for the particular stage of the disease and should work toward preventing further transmission. An early diagnosis of HIV by prison medical staff is crucial to the development of the most comprehensive treatment plan for the inmate.

Treatment for HIV infection involves trying to manage the disease with prophylactic and therapeutic drugs in the hope of increasing the life expectancy of the inmate. It is important to note that early treatment with zidovudine (AZT), thought to prevent the onset of AIDS by asymptomatic HIV-seropositive patients, has recently been questioned by the "Concorde Study" (Aboulker and Swart 1993). That type of drug is very expensive and requires intensive therapy to administer, thereby having a large impact on correctional health care budgets nationwide. Because of the expense, most inmates are not given AZT until they meet Federal Drug Administration (FDA) eligibility criteria [a CD4 (T4) cell count below 500] (Hammett and Moini 1990). The NIJ/CDC survey found that the treatment is available to HIV-infected inmates within 98 percent of the nation's correctional facilities. Approximately 80 percent of the prisons in the survey also offer the antiretroviral drug ddI and Bactrim/Septra or aerosolized pentamidine to treat pneumocystis carinii pneumonia (PCP) (Hammett et al. 1993).

Treatment needs differ by gender; for example, women with AIDS are more likely to develop PCP but rarely develop Kaposi's Sarcoma (KS), which is much more frequent among men. Additionally, pregnant inmates with HIV infection should be monitored closely, as they are more susceptible to opportunistic infections during their pregnancies (Lawson and Fawkes 1993). Research findings from a new study, yet to be corroborated, have found that the risk of perinatal transmission may be cut drastically by administering AZT to HIV-infected women in the weeks immediately preceding delivery.

The need for psychological and social support services for those suffering with AIDS is compounded by the prison environment. At the very least, individual psychological therapy should be available for inmates to help them deal with the anger, denial, and fear that generally follow the notification of a positive test result. If group therapy is available, it can be used to help them deal with the stigmatization that many HIV-infected inmates experience in the penal setting. Inmate-run group therapy has been derived from HIV peer counseling programs like the AIDS Counseling and Education (ACE) program at the Bedford Hills women's prison in New York. Substance abuse programs offered by prisons can help to address the needs of addicted HIV-infected inmates and are extremely important in preventing further transmission of HIV. Lastly, religious support through pastoral counseling is valuable to those prisoners facing death.

The Legal Aspects of AIDS in American Prisons

Litigation concerning HIV/AIDS issues in correctional facilities began to appear in the nation's courts in the mid to late 1980s. The majority of cases were inmate initiated, questioning the constitutionality of AIDS policies in state correctional systems. The litigation has been based primarily on the constitutional prohibition against cruel and unusual punishments (Eighth Amendment), protections against the taking of life, liberty, or property without due process (the Fourteenth Amendment), and the equal protection clause (the Fourteenth Amendment).

Inmate litigation has challenged the adequacy of medical care in prisons and alleged negligence on the part of correctional health care staff (for example, *Botero Gomez v. U.S., Harris v. Thigpen, Hawley v. Evans, Maynard v. New Jersey* and *Weaver v. Reagan*). HIV-infected inmates have brought cases questioning the right to segregate them from the general prison population and the legality of subjecting them to mandatory HIV testing (for example, *Cordero v. Coughlin, Dunn v. White, Harris v. Thigpen, Judd v. Packard, Powell v. Dept. of Corrections*). Uninfected inmates have challenged penal systems on their failure to protect them from HIV-seropositive inmates and have asked for mandatory testing and segregation (for example, *Feigley v. Fulcomer, Glick v. Henderson, Jarrett v. Faulkner, Myers v. Maryland Division of Corrections,* and *Traufler v. Thompson*). Cases have arisen regarding the disclosure of inmates' HIV serostatus (for example, *Doe v. Coughlin, Harris v. Thigpen,* and *Woods v. White*). HIV-infected inmates have petitioned the court for access to denied programs (for example, *Casey v. Lewis* and *Farmer v. Moritsugu*). Cases have also come forth alleging the failure of correctional systems to protect inmates, correctional staff, and medical personnel from assault by seropositive inmates (for example, *Cameron v. Metcuz, Doe v. State of New York,* and *United States v. Moore*) (Belbot and del Carmen 1991; Hammett et al. 1993).

Some of these cases are under appeal, and definitive resolutions around these legal issues could be years in the making. Most inmate-initiated AIDS litigation has been resolved, without full trials, in favor of the correctional systems or their administrators. The courts have generally found that the AIDS policies of correctional institutions are based on a legitimate penological interest and have not violated prisoners' constitutional rights. Regardless, many of the legal problems associated with prisoners infected with HIV/AIDS have just recently emerged, and other issues have not yet been resolved. In view of the rapidity of changes in the field (for example, the advent of AZT therapy), correctional administrators, health care providers, and legal staff should make an effort to stay abreast of developments in AIDS case and statutory law.

Summary

HIV infection and AIDS, which inevitably results from it, pose a tremendous health threat to all of society. Even before the outbreak of AIDS, the American prison system was facing severe overcrowding compounded by a lack of funding and a history of inadequate medical care. In conjunction with HIV/AIDS, which now presents itself in large numbers of prisoners requiring specialized treatment and care, the problem has created a health care crisis within penal institutions of this nation. Add to that the projected rise in HIV-seropositive inmates in the next decade and the continuing threat of inmate litigation, and it appears that the correctional health care crisis will continue for some time. The medical and custodial needs of HIV/AIDS inmates will be one of the most important considerations for correctional administrators well into the twenty-first century.

Malcolm L. Lachance-McCullough
James M. Tesoriero

See also HEALTH CARE

Bibliography

Aboulker, J. P., and A. M. Swart (1993). Preliminary analysis of the Concorde trial. *Lancet* 341: 889–90.

Belbot, B. A., and R. V. del Carmen (1991). AIDS in prison: Legal issues. *Crime and Delinquency* 37: 135–53.

Centers for Disease Control (1990). *HIV/AIDS Surveillance Report*. Rockville, Md.: National AIDS Clearinghouse.

Centers for Disease Control (1992). Guidelines for the performance of CD4+ T-cell determinations in persons with human immunodeficiency virus infection. *Morbidity and Mortality Weekly Report* 41 (no. RR-8): 1–17.

Centers for Disease Control (1992). HIV prevention in the U.S. correctional system, 1991. *Morbidity and Mortality Weekly Report* 41(no. RR-22): 389–97.

Centers for Disease Control (1993). Revised classification system for HIV infection and expanded surveillance case definition for AIDS among adolescents and adults. *Morbidity and Mortality Weekly Report* 41 (no. RR-17): 1–19.

Coughlin, T. A. (1988). AIDS in prison: One correctional administrator's recommended policies and procedures. *Judicature* 72: 63–66, 70.

Dubler, N. N., C. M. Bergmann, and M. E. Frankel (1990). Management of HIV infection in New York state prisons. *Columbia Human Rights Law Review* 21: 392–96.

Freudenberg, N. (1989). Prisoners. In *Preventing AIDS: A Guide to Effective Edu-*

cation for the Prevention of HIV Infection. Washington, D.C.: American Public Health Association.

Glaser, J. B., and R. B. Greifinger (1993). Correctional health care: A public health opportunity. *Annals of Internal Medicine* 118(2): 139.

Hammett, T. M., and S. Moini (1990). *1989 Update: AIDS in Correctional Facilities: Issues and Options*. Washington, D.C.: U.S. Department of Justice.

Hammett, T. M., L. Harrold, M. Gross, and J. Epstein (1993). *1992 Update: AIDS in Correctional Facilities, Issues and Options*. Washington, D.C.: U.S. Department of Justice.

Harlow, C. W. (1993). *HIV in U.S. Prisons and Jails*. Bureau of Justice Statistics Special Report. Washington, D.C.: U.S. Department of Justice.

Lawson, W. T., and L. S. Fawkes (1993). HIV, AIDS, and the female offender. In *Female Offenders: Meeting Needs of a Neglected Population*. Baltimore, Md.: United Book.

Lillis, J. (1993). Dealing with HIV/AIDS–positive inmates. *Corrections Compendium* 18(6): 1–3.

Lurigio, A. J., J. Petraitis, and B. Johnson (1991). HIV education for probation officers: An implementation and evaluative program. *Crime and Delinquency* 37: 125–34.

Martin, R., S. Zimmerman, and B. Long (1993). AIDS education in U.S. prisons: A survey of inmate programs. *Prison Journal* 73: 103–29.

Nacci, P. L., and T. R. Kane (1983). The incidence of sex and sexual aggression in federal prisons. *Federal Probation* 47(4): 31–36.

National Academy of Sciences, Institute of Medicine (1988). *Confronting AIDS: Update 1988*. Washington, D.C.: National Academy Press.

National Commission on Acquired Immune Deficiency Syndrome (1991). *Report: HIV Disease in Correctional Facilities*. Washington, D.C.: The Commission.

National Institute of Corrections (1993). *Advisory Board Hearings Report*. Washington, D.C.: U.S. Department of Justice, Prisons Division.

National Institute of Justice (1990). *Drug Use Forecasting: 1988 Drug Use Forecasting Annual Report*. Washington, D.C.: U.S. Department of Justice.

Snell, T. L. (1993). *Correctional Populations in the United States, 1991*. Washington, D.C.: Bureau of Justice Statistics.

Vlahov, D., T. F. Brewer, K. G. Castro, et al. (1991). Prevalence of antibody to HIV-1 among entrants to U.S. correctional facilities. *Journal of the American Medical Association* 265: 1129–32.

Cases

Botero Gomez v. U.S., 725 F.Supp. 526 (S.D.Fla. 1989)

Cameron v. Metcuz, 705 F.Supp. 454 (N.D.Ind. 1989)

Casey v. Lewis, 773 F.Supp. 1365 (D.Ariz. 1991)

Cordero v. Coughlin, 607 F.Supp. 9 (S.D.N.Y. 1984)

Doe v. Coughlin, 696 F.Supp. 1234 (N.D.N.Y. 1988)

Doe v. State of New York, 588 F.2d 698 (N.Y.S. 1992)

Dunn v. White, 880 F.2d 1118 (10th Cir. 1989)

Estelle v. Gamble, 429 U.S. 97, 97 S.Ct. 285, 50 L.Ed.2d 251 (1976)

Farmer v. Moritsugu, 742 F.Supp. 525 (W.D.Wisc. 1990)

Feigley v. Fulcomer, 720 F.Supp. 475 (M.D.Pa. 1989)

Glick v. Henderson, 855 F.2d 536 (8th Cir. 1988)

Harris v. Thigpen, 727 F.Supp. 1564 (M.D.Ala. 1990)

Hawley v. Evans, 715 F.Supp. 601 (N.D.Ga. 1989)

Jarrett v. Faulkner, 662 F.Supp. 928 (S.D.Ind. 1987)

Judd v. Packard, 669 F.Supp. 741, 742 (D.Md. 1987)

Maynard v. New Jersey, 719 F.Supp. 292 (D.N.J. 1989)

Myers v. Maryland Division of Corrections, 782 F.Supp. 1095 (D.Md. 1992)

Powell v. Department of Corrections, 647 F.Supp. 968 (N.D.Okla. 1986)

Traufler v. Thompson, 662 F.Supp. 945 (N.D.Ill. 1987)

Weaver v. Reagan, No.88-2560, (8th Cir. September 25, 1989)

Woods v. White, 689 F.Supp. 974 (W.D.Wis. 1988)

U.S. v. Moore, 846 F.2d 1163 (8th Cir. 1988)

Alcatraz Federal Penitentiary

Alcatraz Prison, the Rock, was known as one of the most secure and isolated federal penitentiaries of the twentieth century. The stark, rocky island was created over fifteen thousand years ago, at the end of the last ice age, by melting glaciers, which separated the island in San Francisco Bay from any other land by more than a mile. It is believed that the first humans to ever set foot on Alcatraz were the Native Americans of the San Francisco area, who would sail to the island looking for eggs produced by the vast number of birds that made their home there. Alcatraz did not receive its name, however, until 1775, when Juan Manual Ayala, a Spaniard commissioned to survey the harbor, observed the nesting pelicans on the island and named it "Isla de Los Alcatraces," or "Island of the Pelicans."

The Early Years

In 1850, California had become a state and the gold rush was in full bloom. The U.S. Army determined that Alcatraz Island would make an excellent location for a military fortress and lighthouse to protect the settlers and the abundant gold found in the bay area. Construction of the fortress known as the Post of Alcatraz began in 1853, and the army's first objective was the building of batteries of cannon around the island. Although the cannon are long gone, several of the bunkers remain on Alcatraz today.

The lighthouse was completed in 1854 and became the first operational lighthouse on the West Coast. The original lighthouse was in operation for fifty-five years before being replaced in 1909 by a more modern version. In 1970 the lighthouse was destroyed by fire, although the tower remained and since 1963 has been fully automated.

In the 1850s, the army built the Citadel at the top of the island to house military personnel. Guardhouses were also constructed, resulting in the first jail on Alcatraz. It housed soldiers with disciplinary problems and Californians sympathetic to the Confederate cause.

By the 1860s Alcatraz held over one hundred prisoners, and the number increased to more than four hundred by the 1870s. Because the Fort of Alcatraz had been designed as a fortress, the increasing prison population caused both manning and housing problems for the army. Soldiers had to be removed from their posts to guard the prisoners, and additional housing was needed to manage the growing population. By 1880, the Post of Alcatraz had been transformed into a military prison.

The conditions for prisoners were appalling. Each inmate was required to "carry the baby," a 24-pound ball that was chained to his leg. The ball was too heavy to drag behind, requiring each prisoner to pick it up and carry it around with him.

By 1907, the U.S. War Department decided to make Alcatraz a permanent military prison, and conditions for the prisoners improved significantly. The top floors of the Citadel were torn down and new cell houses were constructed. Much of this new construction was completed by the inmates. By 1915, the prison was officially opened as a military disciplinary barracks housing five hundred military prisoners. The new philosophy of the prison focused less on retribution and more on rehabilitation. Alcatraz served in that capacity for the next nineteen years and, during that time, the army continued to add new buildings to the island.

The Federal Penitentiary

Alcatraz Island became a federal penitentiary in 1933, when the Department of Justice took over authority of the island. J. Edgar Hoover and the Department of Justice had been looking for a new federal prison in which to house the most dangerous criminals and troublemakers in the federal prison system, "the worst of the worst." At the time, organized crime was flourishing because of Prohibition and the Depression. The media sensationalized these crimes, making such criminals as Al Capone and "Machine Gun" Kelly appear as frightening villains who must be safely locked away. Alcatraz prison would accept the "troublemakers" or "escape artists" from other federal prisons who interfered with the rehabilitative goals of those institutions.

The first warden of Alcatraz Federal Penitentiary, appointed in 1933, was James Johnston. Warden Johnston supervised the complete refurbishing of the island prison to ensure that it was tight enough to hold notorious escape artists, to deflate "big shots," to disrupt prison gangs (whose leaders would be sent there), and to control those who defied rules and abused privileges. Every modern innovation was used, including full-body metal detectors. All areas were enclosed with cyclone and barbed wire, and sewer and utility tunnels were blocked; the soft-steel cell was replaced with tool-proof steel.

A

Alcatraz Federal Penitentiary opened in 1934. The first prisoners were thirty-two soldier-inmates left over by the military. Next came inmates from McNeal Island in Washington. Most of Alcatraz's inmate population came from other prisons, although there were some exceptions: Morton Sobell was one. He was convicted of espionage along with Julius and Ethel Rosenberg in the 1950s. The Rosenbergs were executed, and Sobell went directly to Alcatraz to serve his sentence.

Alcatraz developed into a "test" prison, one that would deal with a small population of "hardcore" inmates. The directive of the prison was not to rehabilitate inmates but to force them to conform. The staff-to-inmate ratio on Alcatraz was one to three, ensuring maximum control. Each prisoner occupied a five by nine foot cell, and all he could expect were food, shelter, clothing, and medical care. Inmates were informed upon entering the prison that they were there to serve time only; there was no pretense of rehabilitation. Each inmate was issued a book of rules and regulations upon arrival and was locked in his cell for approximately thirteen hours each day. Privileges could be earned by "conducting yourself properly," which included good conduct and a good work record. Inmates who earned the privilege could acquire a job in the laundry or carpentry shops where they were expected to work five days per week, eight hours per day. The exercise yard was a privilege available to qualified inmates on Saturdays, Sundays, and holidays. Activities included baseball, handball, and table games. In later years, movies were shown twice per month. Inmates were not allowed to have money. Additionally, cigarettes or any other contraband was also forbidden for use as "jail money." Caps could not be worn in the cell house.

The food on Alcatraz was said to be the best throughout the prison system. When Warden Johnston refurbished Alcatraz, he had tear gas canisters installed in the ceiling above the dining room tables. There was a protected area next to the dining room that was manned by an officer who could release the canisters automatically if a disturbance developed. Meals were served three times per day and inmates were given twenty minutes in which to eat. Inmates were allowed to take all they could eat within the allotted time.

A library existed on Alcatraz when it opened as a federal prison, and by 1960 it contained fifteen thousand books. Each inmate was allowed three library books, a Bible, a dictionary, and a maximum of twelve study books and twenty-four pamphlets in his cell at one time. In addition to library privileges, prisoners in good standing could also play musical instruments or paint in their cells.

During the first years after Alcatraz opened as a federal prison, inmates were not allowed to speak with each other, or to have visits during the first three months after arrival. In later years, quiet talking between inmates was allowed and each inmate was permitted one visit per month.

Those prisoners who were unable to conform with the rules and regulations of Alcatraz were sent to the Isolation Unit on D-Block, known as "the hole." A stay in the Isolation Unit of D-Block meant a complete loss of privileges and total isolation for a maximum of nineteen days. There was no light, sound, or human contact, and most inmates found this punishment almost unbearable.

No inmate was ever released directly from Alcatraz. The administration had decided that, to lessen tensions between the prison and the citizens of the bay area, prior to each inmate's release he would be transferred to another federal prison. Prisoners were informed when they arrived at Alcatraz that transfer to another federal institution would occur only if they could show a better than average conduct record for several years.

The population of Alcatraz consisted of hardened inmates who had not adjusted well in other prisons. Many of them were famous criminals who had ended up at Alcatraz after causing trouble at other federal facilities. This resulted in an increasingly elderly population of long-term inmates with extensive prior records and growing medical problems. The administrators of Alcatraz solved the problem by transferring those inmates to other facilities. Robert Stroud, the "Birdman," was transferred from Alcatraz in 1959 to a federal medical facility in Springfield, Missouri, when his health began to deteriorate. Interestingly, Stroud had cared for canaries at Leavenworth Penitentiary but never had any birds when he was transferred to Alcatraz in 1942. Another famous inmate, Al Capone, served only five years at Alcatraz before being transferred to Terminal Island Federal Prison when the syphilis he suffered from reached advanced stages. "Machine Gun" Kelly was transferred to Leavenworth in 1951 because of a heart condition.

During the Alcatraz Federal Penitentiary era, thirty-six men tried to escape in fourteen separate attempts. Five are still missing, six were shot and killed, two drowned, two were later executed, and twenty-one were recaptured. To even attempt an escape from Alcatraz was an exceptional feat. The security measures combined with the prison's location made an escape almost impossible. Bay water temperatures range from 45 to 50 degrees Fahrenheit, and the currents surrounding the island move at four to eight miles per hour (three to five knots) and extend out from the island for two hundred yards. Within the current is an extremely dangerous undertow caused by Alcatraz's position in the channel. Six guard towers watched over the facility at all times, and inmate counts were taken at frequent and unpredictable intervals throughout the day.

The most famous of the escapes was made by Frank Morris, John Anglin, and Clarence Anglin, and portrayed in the movie *Escape from Alcatraz*. By chipping out the rotted plaster around the vents at the rear of their cells, the three men managed to escape by placing dummy heads in their bunks. It is believed that they may have had a boat pick them up, or they may somehow have managed to float to shore at San Francisco or Angel Island. Or they may have drowned. At any rate, they were never seen again.

The Closing of Alcatraz

The cost of maintaining high-risk inmates, coupled with the massive deterioration of the prison, resulted in its closing in 1963, just one year after Frank Morris's escape. The cost of transporting the necessities to run the prison (water, food, and supplies) made Alcatraz's budget almost twice that of other federal prisons. Additionally, the absence of a formal rehabilitation program in the midst of the public outcry in the 1960s for reform led to political pressure to close the prison. Attorney General Robert Kennedy announced the closing of Alcatraz, which officially took place on March 21, 1963.

Alcatraz was transferred to the authority of the General Service Administration of the U.S. government in 1964. Several options were considered, including making the island into a University for Native Americans or a casino, or selling it to oil millionaire Lamar Hunt for $4 million. Mr. Hunt was planning to develop a combination space museum, apartment and condominium complex, and mall, but he withdrew his offer because of public pressure. By the late 1960s, no decision had been made concerning the disposition of the island.

In 1969 a group of American Indians moved onto the island, citing an 1868 treaty with the federal government that allowed nonreservation Indians to claim land that the government had taken for forts or other uses and later abandoned. In actuality, the first takeover had occurred five years earlier when a group of Sioux Indians held Alcatraz for four hours before the acting warden, Richard J. Willard, threatened them with felony charges.

Alcatraz became a major symbol of resistance and hope for the Native Americans, who were aided by extensive news media coverage. The goal was to establish a cultural, spiritual, and educational center on the island; Richard Oakes was a prominent leader and spokesman for the group. The beginning of the end of the occupation occurred when Oakes's thirteen-year-old daughter, Yvonne, was killed after falling down three flights of stairs in the officers' quarters. Soon after, Oakes left the island and the remaining groups split into increasingly dissentious factions. Drugs, alcohol, and fighting added to the eventual breakdown of the island society, and in May of 1970 a fire destroyed a number of buildings on Alcatraz. On June 11, 1971, twenty U.S. marshals removed anyone still left on Alcatraz and the island was once again put into the authority of the General Services Administration.

In 1972, administered by the National Park Service, Alcatraz Island was made a part of the newly formed Golden Gate National Recreation Area. The island is now an international biosphere reserve that displays a wide array of birds, flowers, trees, and tide pools surrounding the island. Additionally, 750,000 people visit Alcatraz each year, and the Park Service continues to pursue its goal of maintaining and restoring the historic buildings on Alcatraz. Ironically, the Bureau of Prisons currently provides inmate labor from other federal prisons in the area to repair prison buildings and do landscaping work on the island.

Laura Davis

See *also* FEDERAL BUREAU OF PRISONS

Bibliography
Fortunate Eagle, A. (1992). *Alcatraz! Alcatraz!* Berkeley, Calif.: Heyday.

Hurley, D. J. (1987). *Alcatraz Island Memories*. Petaluma, Calif.: Barlow.

Hurley, D. J. (1989). *Alcatraz Island Maximum Security*. Petaluma, Calif.: Barlow.

Madigan, P. J. (1956). *Institution Rules and Regulations*. San Francisco: Golden Gate National Parks Association.

Films

A La Carte (producer) (1992). *Secrets of Alcatraz*. San Francisco: Golden Gate National Parks Association.

Alcohol Treatment Programs in Prison

The relationship between alcohol use and crime is well established. There are crimes that, by their definition, involve alcohol use: possession of alcohol by a minor (about half of those aged twelve to seventeen admit to this offense), drunkenness (for which about three-quarters of a million people are arrested annually), and driving under the influence of alcohol (for which more than one million people are arrested and as a result of which about twenty thousand accidental fatalities occur annually).

Other criminal acts are committed by persons who are under the influence of alcohol. Excluding the offenses mentioned above, about a third of jail and prison inmates admit to having been under the influence of alcohol at the time of their offense. Slightly more than two-fifths of jail and prison inmates convicted of homicide, rape, or assault admitted to committing their crime while alcoholically intoxicated, as did about a third of robbery and property offenders. The average amount of alcohol ingested by these inmates immediately prior to their offense was almost nine ounces of ethanol, the equivalent of about three six-packs of beer or two quarts of wine. About a seventh of incarcerated offenders admit to ingesting illegal drugs along with alcohol.

There are two competing hypotheses that attempt to explain the strong relationship between alcohol and crime. The dominant hypothesis is the disinhibition hypothesis, which states that alcohol intoxication causes aggressive behavior because alcohol breaks down cognitive filters that normally prevent such aggression. Thus, this approach posits that a person who is under the influence of alcohol may violate laws that would not be violated if the person were not intoxicated. From a correctional treatment standpoint, this hypothesis implies that if alcohol-abusing criminals can stay sober, they will remain law-abiding. This is the treatment approach that prevails in American prisons.

The second, and more recent, approach to explaining the relationship between alcohol and crime is the low self-control hypothesis, which states that both alcohol use and criminal behavior are symptoms of a personality tendency toward immediate gratification. This hypothesis also states that one's propensity for immediate gratification is generally stable from early adolescence through adulthood. Persons who want immediate gratification will seek it through both intoxicating substances and crime (stealing gives one immediate money and violence gives one immediate revenge). Rather than expecting criminals to refrain from crime simply by keeping them away from alcohol, the low self-control hypothesis asserts that one's entire personality must be altered in order to discourage criminal behavior. That is a much more difficult, if not impossible, task for correctional specialists; the general tendency toward low self-control is said to be rarely alterable after adolescence.

Prison Programs

Many criminals with an alcohol problem have participated in some kind of treatment. About three-fifths of drinking inmates have been in at least one alcohol-abuse program during their lifetimes, and about a fifth of drinking inmates join alcohol treatment groups while they are in prison.

Prison alcohol treatment programs differ from other programs in several respects. First, prison programs seek to prepare inmates to stay sober once they leave prison; programs outside prison seek to focus on the present. Second, prisoners do not have access to alcohol, although they do have limited opportunities to drink their own "homebrew," made from bread, juice, and scraps of fresh produce, alcoholic beverages smuggled in from outside, and over-the-counter products such as mouthwash and hair tonic. Alcoholics outside prison are not denied access to drink. Third, participating in an alcohol program outside of prison is voluntary (except as a condition of parole or probation), whereas prison alcohol programs are often perceived by inmates as necessary to gain early release. Thus, although program participation is supposedly voluntary, correctional administrators indirectly coerce many inmates (through promise for parole) into programs in which they otherwise would not participate. Such participation is known as "programming out," and it is done for the wrong reason—getting out of prison rather than self-help.

The most prevalent prison alcohol treatment program is Alcoholics Anonymous. A.A. was founded outside of prison in 1935 by "Dr. Bob" and "Bill W." By 1993 there were more than eighteen hundred such groups in correctional facilities throughout the United States and Canada. Each has a local arrangement with an A.A. chapter outside the prison. According to a recent survey by A.A., institutions participating in A.A. have an average of 1.25 groups per facility; some facilities have as many as ten groups. Prison administrators report that attendance at A.A. meetings is "voluntary" at 90 percent of the institutions.

The conditions under which an inmate group functions are at the discretion of the institutional administrators. Prison A.A. chapters pose only a slight inconvenience to the functioning of an institution. Visits by outside A.A. sponsors are minimal after the prison group becomes established. As with any treatment program in prison, however, correctional officers will have to accommodate the movement of inmates to and from A.A. meetings, which may pose custody problems. Optimally, A.A. prison programs should operate unconnected to religious groups or other therapies or rehabilitation programs.

According to A.A. prison literature, the program consists of a fellowship of men and women who attempt to solve a common problem and help others do the same. The only requirement for membership is a desire to cease drinking. Its primary purpose is to achieve sobriety for its members and other alcohol abusers. The basic approach of A.A. is to create an *esprit de corps* of mutual caring, thus enabling the participants to realize that their problems are not unique. While A.A. in prison has been likened to "milieu therapy" because of a prevailing attitude fostering the goals of A.A., the program setting is actually much less controlled than in milieu therapy. Because of the similar experiences of members and their mutual support, however, participants are unlikely to fool each other; a sort of "honesty milieu" does exist. This peer review/role-model aspect of A.A. has been imitated by several substance abuse programs.

The core of A.A. is its famous "12 Steps." With the help of a higher force that is individually interpreted by each participant, these steps move one from confronting the problem through changes in behavior and to restitution to those previously harmed. The steps culminate in a spiritual awakening and continuing personal introspection that keep one sober. There is a generally monotheistic emphasis in A.A., but there is no affiliation with a particular religion. Thus, the spirituality in A.A. is compatible with the teachings of the spectrum of religions represented in American prisons, Christianity, Judaism, or Islam. A.A. subsidiary programs in prison include Al-Anon (for families of alcohol abusers) and Ala-teen (for youngsters with drinking problems). Some incarcerated alcohol abusers have also participated as paraprofessionals in youth counseling programs, with the prisoners speaking about the problems associated with drugs and alcohol; examples have included Florida's "Operation Reach Out," California's "Prison Preventers," and New Jersey's "Lifers' Program."

Other alcohol treatment programs have been established in prisons. Many of them practice what might be called a responsibility-privilege system, in which the inmate progressively assumes more privileges according to the degree of responsibility for personal behavior that is demonstrated. Group and individual counseling are mainstays of such programs, particularly "reality therapy" (developed by William Glasser in 1965). Rather than using mental health labels like "neurotic," "personality disorder," or "psychotic," reality therapy simply considers the individual to be irresponsible. This type of counseling should sequentially lead inmates to: (1) face the consequences of their antisocial behavior; (2) examine why they choose to act that way; and (3) stop the behavior. As in A.A., the most important aspect of reality therapy is that excuses for behavior are unacceptable.

Maintaining Alcohol Treatment Continuity into Community Release

Because alcohol is seen by correctional specialists as an integral part of the decision to violate the law, every effort is made to maintain an inmate's sobriety after release into community supervision. Thus, alcohol treatment is often mandated in conditions of parole for alcohol-abusing criminals. Rather than wait until the prisoner is released, it is best to coordinate alcohol treatment in the community prior to parole. A.A. cautions that inmates who do not report immediately to a local chapter after their release are less likely to continue in A.A. Forms of aversive therapy can also be used as conditions of release, including the mandated ingestion of disulfiram, or antabuse (which causes an adverse physical reaction when mixed with alcohol). Aversive therapy is not always successful, however, because parolees often fail to ingest antabuse regularly and because some persons go on drinking anyway.

Community correctional specialists should practice both patience (long-term dependence on an altered state of mind is not easily changed) and confrontation (to force the client to be responsible). Additionally, community corrections specialists should try to keep clients from returning to the same environment in which the offender drank prior to prison. Parolees may have their parole revoked on technical grounds if they fail to maintain sobriety, and that threat alone may be sufficient to keep some from reverting to destructive drinking habits. If one believes in the disinhibition hypothesis, sobriety may be all that is necessary to keep a criminal alcohol abuser from further transgressions. If one believes in the low self-control hypothesis, however, removing alcohol from an offender's life will not by itself change the propensity for criminal behavior.

Evaluating Prison Alcohol Treatment Programs

Most evaluations of alcohol treatment address programs administered in the community (for probationers, parolees, and noncriminals) and in nonprison institutional settings (such as hospitals and clinics). There appears to have been no study that has rigorously evaluated a prison alcohol program. A rigorous and scientific evaluation is the only way to determine which prison alcohol treatment programs are best. In the classic scientific experiment, the success of the group receiving the treatment is compared with that of a similar group that did not receive the treatment (the control group). Alcohol treatment programs in prisons, however, introduce several specific problems for the classic experiment.

The first problem is that community follow-up treatment for alcohol is an integral part of the inmate's total rehabilitation program. It becomes necessary, then, for the evaluator to be able to differentiate between the effects of the

in-prison alcohol program and those of the community alcohol program. To do so, the evaluator must look at the recidivism rates of four groups (rather than the two outlined in the classic experiment): (1) the Treatment Group (those who receive both the prison alcohol program and the community alcohol program); (2) Control Group #1 (those who receive the prison alcohol program only); (3) Control Group #2 (those who receive the community alcohol program only); and (4) Control Group #3 (those who receive no treatment). By comparing the recidivism rates of these four groups, the evaluator will be able to isolate the effects of the overall treatment plan (combination of prison and community programs) from the effects of the individual components of the plan.

The people in each of the four groups must be exactly similar according to two dimensions. First, they must be alike in the degree to which alcohol abuse was a factor in their criminality prior to entering prison, because the theoretical underpinning of offering alcohol treatment programs to these inmates is the strong relationship between their alcohol use and their criminal behavior. Determining the extent of that relationship for a particular individual is a difficult task, but it is even more difficult to equalize the factor across all four groups. Subjects who are placed in the four groups must be more than simply criminals who use alcohol; they must be criminals whose alcohol abuse led them to crime.

The second dimension by which persons in the four groups must be equalized is in their general propensity to commit crimes that are unrelated to alcohol use. If the four groups are not equivalent in these ways, the success rates of the groups will be affected by their differing propensities to commit crime rather than only the differences in the treatments that the four groups receive. It will be very difficult for the evaluator to be certain that known predictors of crime (such as age, sex, other substance abuse, crime specialization, and previous failure on parole) are equally distributed across the four groups. Persons in the four groups should also be equalized in terms of the amount of time they have spent in prison for their current offense, to control for nonrecidivism caused by deterrence. Last, the evaluator must equalize the four groups in terms of the conditions the subjects experienced in prison (particularly prison rehabilitation programs that do not relate to alcohol abuse, such as education and job training), to control for nonrecidivism resulting from those factors. While a near-perfect equalization of the four groups across all of these categories is necessary for a sound experimental design, the task is almost insurmountable for the evaluator, and it may never be achieved.

The drinking behavior of the four groups can be tracked after their release, although the commission of further crimes is more important to the overall treatment goal. Members of the four groups must receive equal amounts of community supervision, such as equal numbers of contacts and equal conditions of release. Those in the Treatment Group (who participate in both prison and community programs) and in Control Group #2 (who participate in community programs only) will be the only ones to receive additional alcohol treatment after release, and that treatment must be the same for both groups. When the success rates for the four groups are finally tallied, the evaluator must be certain that individuals in all groups were deemed failures for actions of equal severity (such as conviction for a new crime, chronic drunkenness, or other technical violations of parole).

Gary S. Green

See also DRUG AND ALCOHOL USE IN PRISON, REHABILITATION PROGRAMS

Bibliography

Alcoholics Anonymous (1987). Memo to an inmate who may be an alcoholic. New York: Alcoholics Anonymous.

Alcoholics Anonymous (1992). It sure beats sitting in a cell. New York: Alcoholics Anonymous.

Alcoholics Anonymous (1993). A message to correctional facilities administrators. New York: Alcoholics Anonymous.

Armor, D., M. Polich, and H. Stambul (1978). *Alcoholism and Treatment*. New York: John Wiley.

Bureau of Justice Statistics (1993). *Survey of Prison Inmates, 1991*. Washington, D.C.: U.S. Government Printing Office.

Gottfredson, M., and T. Hirschi (1990). *A General Theory of Crime*. Palo Alto, Calif.: Stanford University Press.

Rossi, J., and W. Filstead (1976). "Treating" the treatment issues: Some general observations about the treatment of alcoholism. In W. Filstead, J. Rossi, and M. Keller, eds. *Alcohol and Alcohol Problems*. Cambridge, Mass.: Ballinger.

Welte, J. W., and B. A. Miller (1987). Alcohol use by violent and property offenders. *Drug and Alcohol Dependence* 19: 313–24.

A

American Correctional Association

The largest private organization in corrections is the American Correctional Association (ACA), a nonprofit organization committed to evaluation and research as well as the formulation of correctional policies and standards. The ACA has existed for over 130 years, creating national policies related to the effective operations of adult and juvenile correctional facilities, local detention centers, and probation and parole departments. It represents the field of corrections at the federal, state, and county levels. As such, it is the largest organization of its kind.

The ACA consists of twenty-three thousand members and sixty-seven affiliated organizations representing states and professional specialties. The membership of the ACA consists of practitioners, academics, agencies, and organizations involved in all parts of the corrections field. The official magazine of the ACA is *Corrections Today*.

Historical Background

The original name of the organization was the National Prison Association (NPA). The NPA was established in 1870 under the leadership of Rutherford B. Hayes, the first president of the association. In spite of the fact that the idea of penal reform was unpopular at the time, Hayes led a reform effort that included E. C. Wines, W. W. F. Round, Z. R. Brockway, Roeliff Brinkerhoff, and Frank Sanborn (Pippin 1989).

The Association's first meeting was held in Cincinnati, Ohio, in 1870. That meeting was suggested by Enoch Cobb Wines, then secretary of the New York Prison Association and a student of penology (Keve 1991). Wines had become an effective voice for reform within that state agency, and he wanted to expand the idea of reform to the national level. There were over 130 delegates from twenty-four states, Canada, and South America at the Cincinnati Congress (Pippin 1989). Wines invited Hayes, then governor of Ohio, to serve as presiding officer at the meeting.

One year before the meeting, Wines and Hayes had corresponded over prison issues. In his State of the State message to the Ohio legislature in 1868, Hayes had publicized the concept of the indeterminate sentence of the Irish system. Wines included that segment of Hayes's speech in his 1869 report. With Wines's support, Hayes's recommendations were adopted by the Ohio assembly.

A number of issues were discussed at the Cincinnati meeting in 1870, including indeterminate sentencing, graded classification, promotion of an international meeting on penal reform, executive pardons, jails, and hygiene (Pippin 1989). As a result, a declaration of principles was developed. The declaration stated that "moral regeneration" was possible through the penitentiary. These principles became the accepted guidelines for corrections in the United States and Europe. There was a subsequent revision of the principles in order to reflect advances in theory and practice. In 1982 the principles were expanded, but the basic ideals have not changed significantly since the original ones were established in 1870 (Keve 1991).

After Wines died in 1879, the NPA became inactive (Hayes became president of the United States in 1877). The organization was revived in 1883, two years after Hayes's term as president had ended. Hayes became president of the NPA in 1883 and continued in that post until his death in 1893. His status as a criminal lawyer and former president added tremendous credibility and publicity to his crusade. As a result, he was able to voice unpopular issues and bring them before the public. In addition to stressing the need for reform practices, Hayes emphasized the idea that crime originated from social and personal causes. There is no doubt that the revitalization of the NPA was solely the result of his efforts (Pippin 1989).

After Hayes's death, Roeliff Brinkerhoff became president of the NPA, serving until 1897. Brinkerhoff was actively concerned about social and political issues. He became knowledgeable about prison problems when, on his own initiative, he visited prisons in other states (ACA Committees Caucus 1992). Brinkerhoff was probably the most effective supporter of a new federal role in corrections. He advocated a nonpartisan administration of prisons even though that was an unpopular view at the time. He ultimately was not very successful in his opposition to political patronage.

The National Prison Association subsequently became the American Prison Association. As a result of changing perspectives on punishment and on the goals of crime control, in 1954 the name of the American Prison Association was changed to the American Correctional Association.

Other historical meetings of the ACA include the Williamsburg conferences of 1971 and 1986 (Keve 1991). The 1971 conference addressed questions related to inmate rights and the need for new directions within the changing correctional environment. The 1986 meeting served as a review of the first twenty-one ratified and completed policies of the association. Members of the association met to create a strategy for the dissemination and acceptance of the policies by all systems in the country.

Correctional Standards and Accreditation

One of the major accomplishments of the ACA has been the development and ongoing evaluation and modification of standards for juvenile and adult correctional facilities, local detention centers, and probation and parole departments (Travisono 1990). The ACA published its first standards nearly fifty years ago. In 1968 the association established an accreditation process through the use of those standards. A standards committee was created with representation from correctional practitioners, the courts, and other criminal justice agencies.

The ACA's standards and accreditation program establishes nationally recognized standards for the field. The program has served to create, implement, and evaluate standards for juvenile and adult facilities; establish the Commission on Accreditation for Corrections as well as the procedures for evaluating the achievement of goals; and publish policy guidelines and operating manuals (Travisono 1990).

In 1987, the Commission on Accreditation for Corrections (CAC) was realigned with the American Correctional Association (Cerquone 1987). The membership of the ACA felt that there was a need to firmly establish the CAC within the ACA. This merger has permitted greater efficiency in the monitoring of accreditation costs, greater efficiency in the accreditation process itself, and a more effective and accurate balancing of the commission's budget.

Accreditation involves a series of reviews, evaluations, surveys, and audits designed to ensure that correctional facilities comply with the national standards created by the American Correctional Association. The accreditation process allows a facility's management the opportunity to identify the strengths and weaknesses of the facility, identify goals, learn how to implement new policies and procedures, establish guidelines for daily operations, learn how to construct defenses against frivolous lawsuits, learn how to increase community support, and increase professionalism and morale among staff.

As the ACA Standards Committee revises standards, it examines court decisions in which judges have made references to existing standards. The purpose is to examine how standards are actually interpreted and applied in practice. The committee recognizes that standards do not exist in a vacuum, so this evaluation serves to inform the committee on problems of clarity in existing standards and difficulties with implementation (Miller 1992).

The first review of the relationship between court decisions and standards came in 1986. The authors of the report concluded that "specific findings of courts should not be used as the foundation for the development of professional standards" (Miller 1992). The review indicated that standards should not simply be evaluated one at a time without considering the entire correctional setting and the interactions between existing policies, how one policy affects others, and the necessity of using discretion in a correctional environment. Examining one standard at a time without considering the entire picture can be misleading. As a result, the latest standards recognize these restrictions and the interactions between different groups and standards.

In 1990, the ACA examined the ways standards have been used by the courts (Miller 1992). The conclusions were as follows:

1. Courts often consult ACA standards when determining standards of behavior in a correctional setting.
2. Courts sometimes cite ACA standards when deriving a court standard or when arriving at a decision.
3. Courts sometimes use ACA standards and accreditation as part of a court order or consent agreement.

Because of the evolution of case law, the evaluation and revision of correctional standards is an ongoing project for the ACA. The continued focus on court decisions is necessary in order to identify changes in judicial views of corrections and to make certain that the ACA standards meet court-established minimums (Miller 1992).

The ACA's Standards and Accreditation Division currently hopes to increase the number of cities, counties, and states that participate in the process of accreditation (Travisono 1990). It also hopes to reduce the number of required standards to a more manageable level.

Future issues being researched by the ACA's Standards and Accreditation Division include the creation of new standards for jail facilities with fewer than one hundred inmates, the development of individual certification, and the development of correctional unit certification. Over time there has been an increase in the number of juvenile facilities interested in achieving accreditation, although the number of adult facilities interested in accreditation has remained constant.

Correctional agencies have recently turned to peer group review for ongoing evaluation. As a result, the accreditation of correctional agencies has reached an all-time high (Travisono 1990). Over 1,140 correctional facilities and programs have engaged in the accreditation process since it began in 1978. Active participants in the process include 80 percent of all state departments of correction as well as numerous facilities operated by the Federal Bureau of Prisons, the U.S. Parole Commission, and the District of Columbia.

Correctional administrators who have engaged in the accreditation process have noted an improvement in management practices and an increase in staff accountability and credibility. They also claim that the accreditation process helps to create safer and more humane environments for both officers and personnel. It also provides measurable criteria for improving correctional programs, personnel, and facilities. ACA standards are also used by state and federal courts to determine whether confinement conditions are humane.

Professional Affiliates
The ACA is supported by its many professional affiliates. These affiliate organizations range from associations of correctional administrators to associations concerned with prison food, health, and educational services (Tyler and Smalley 1989). They are national organizations dedicated to serving specific groups of professionals in the field. The ACA adopts a broad approach to corrections, but the individual professional affiliates are highly focused. The purpose of each affiliate is to serve as a resource to the members of its group.

Examples of affiliates include the North American Association of Wardens and Superintendents, the Association of Paroling Authorities, the American Probation and Parole Association, the American Correctional Health Services Association, the Correctional Accreditation Manager's Association, the American Institute of Architects, and the American Jail Association (one of ACA's larger affiliates).

The process of becoming an ACA affiliate takes approximately a year and a half. In order to qualify, professional associations must be represented in twenty-five states, must have at least 125 members, and must be approved by the ACA's Committee on Membership and Chapter/Affiliate Relations (Tyler and Smalley 1989). Exceptions can be made for membership size, as in the case of the Association of State Correctional Administrators and the Parole and Probation Compact Administrators, which enroll one administrator per state. Current memberships of the ACA affiliates range from fifty to twenty-five thousand.

A requirement of affiliation is that each organization's constitution and bylaws be similar to the ACA's. Most affiliates operate on a volunteer basis, with officers and a board of directors, but some affiliates are large enough to hire staff members and an executive director (Tyler and Smalley 1989).

Some professional affiliates apply for grant money to supplement the organization's income (Irving 1992). Foundation grants have become more popular over the years as the availability of federal funds has decreased. For example, the Edna McConnell Clark Foundation is currently being administered by the National Council on Crime and Delinquency (NCCD). NCCD seeks to develop alternatives to incarceration, stimulating community-based programs for crime prevention.

The Association for Correctional Research and Information Management (ACRIM) is another foundation dedicated to correctional research. It funds studies predominantly related to correctional management. ACRIM has served to create an information exchange for the correctional field at large.

A few of the ACA's professional affiliates were founded as volunteer organizations. Examples include Volunteers of America and the Salvation Army. These organizations include professionals not involved in corrections who work in communities influenced by correctional issues. Another example is the Prison Fellowship, an organization set up as a ministry organization to aid inmates and their families.

There are also several affiliated organizations that are international in scope. Founded in 1946, the Correctional Education Association (CEA) is one of the ACA's largest affiliates. The CEA's twenty-seven hundred members are located in Australia, Canada, England, Germany, New Zealand, and the United States.

The ACA also includes affiliates that focus on women and minorities. For example, the Association on Programs for Female Offenders (APFO) was created to examine and assist programs for female prisoners. The National Association of Blacks in Criminal Justice (NABCJ) was founded fifteen years ago. Today, it has more than three hundred members and thirty-nine state and local chapters across the United States (Tyler and Smalley 1989).

Many of the affiliated organizations work inside institutions. An example is the National Correctional Recreation Association (NCRA), the purpose of which is to promote professional programs and services to aid inmates, as well as to enhance leisure opportunities and skills. NCRA also attempts to improve institutional life by providing a safer, healthier environment, and teaches inmates about the use of leisure time after their release from prison.

The American Correctional Food Service Association (ACFSA) has been an ACA affiliate since 1970. ACFSA began a certification program for food service professionals. The program has increased professionalism in correctional food services and has also encouraged the interdisciplinary exchange of information and ideas. The ACFSA has also established standards of excellence in food service and has recognized achievements in food service.

Policy Development

One of the biggest challenges to the ACA and to the corrections field in general is the development of effective and realistic policies that can be implemented relatively easily (American Correctional Association 1991). In 1981, the ACA Policy/Resolutions Committee was charged with the task of developing a Public Correctional Policy Proposal. After the proposal was adopted, the ACA's president established a Public Correctional Policy Advisory Committee composed of outstanding practitioners. The committee's membership included judges, academics, and leading figures from community-based services as well as local and state departments of corrections.

Public correctional policies on twenty-one major issues were ratified between 1983 and 1985. Recognizing that there were additional issues that needed to be addressed, the ACA Executive Committee adopted the policy development process as a permanent function of the association. The responsibilities of the ACA Advisory Committee on Resolutions and Policy included an ongoing identification of major issues in corrections and the designing of policy statements for consideration.

The policy development process has continued since 1986. In addition, the committee has been heavily involved in the review of existing national correctional policies. For example, in 1991 several policies dealing with community corrections were passed by the ACA Board of Governors and the Delegate Assembly during the 1991 Congress of Correction (Keve 1991). These policies included the following:

1. Seeking authority and funding (public and private) for community programs and services.
2. Developing and ensuring access to residential and nonresidential services that address offender and community needs.
3. Educating the public and offenders about the reasons for community programs and services, how the selection process for these programs operates, and in the idea that these programs constitute punishment.
4. Developing a system to monitor an agency's performance regarding the enforcement of standards and professional practice.
5. Recognizing that the public will be more likely to accept a program that contains elements such as victim restitution, community service, conciliation programs, and adequate supervision of the offender.
6. Seeking input from citizen boards and volunteers regarding community corrections issues.

The policy development process is based on the belief that major issues and their ramifications must be identified, and that public policy decisions must have direction (American Correctional Association 1991).

Research and Practice

Some of the many research topics explored by the ACA include crime prevention, the threat of AIDS in correctional settings, and prison gangs (ACA Committees Caucus 1989). Furthermore, the ACA's Women's Task Force has taken on many challenges, including sexual harassment, issues regarding women officers in male facilities, and domestic violence (ACA Committees Caucus 1990).

In addition to research, the ACA is heavily involved in efforts to educate correctional practitioners. Corrections personnel at all levels require a variety of skills for planning, conducting, and evaluating correctional programs. The ACA conducts training workshops that provide on-site training and educate practitioners about individualized programs that will meet the specific needs of an institution and the members of its population.

The ACA also provides technical assistance for correctional industries personnel through the Correctional Industries Information Clearinghouse (CI-Net). CI-Net offers a computer network, a quarterly newsletter, seminars, and a videotape library.

The ACA also provides juvenile justice administrators with a national forum, a newsletter and resource materials, technical assistance, private sector options for juvenile corrections, regional juvenile justice workshops, research in juvenile detention drug testing, and information on cultural diversity programs. Current projects of the ACA's Contracts Department include training and technical assistance for juvenile corrections, a study of cost-effective confinement for prisons and jails, correctional development services for the U.S. Department of the Navy Corrections System, evaluation of the Model State Prison Industry/Drug Rehabilitation Project, and the development of correctional standards for jails with populations of fifty or less (ACA Committees Caucus 1988, 1989; Huskey 1988).

Membership and Annual Meetings

Membership in the American Correctional Association continues to increase (ACA Committees Caucus 1988). Campaigns have been designed to expand membership within specific groups, such as probation and parole officers, juvenile case workers, and minorities.

The ACA sponsors two annual meetings, the Congress of Correction in August and the winter conference in January. These are interna-

A

tional meetings that provide opportunities for discussions of current issues in the field. The meetings include lectures, seminars, workshops, and exhibits addressing all aspects of corrections (Cerquone 1988).

In the years to come, the ACA will continue to address issues related to crowding in correctional facilities, problems in attracting qualified staff, the need for more rigorous training at all service levels, and the growth of laws that will increase prison populations and community caseloads (ACA Committees Caucus 1989).

John Wooldredge

See also ACCREDITATION

Bibliography
ACA Committees Caucus (1988). ACA annual report shows growth in membership and programs. *Corrections Today* 50(6): 24–26.
ACA Committees Caucus (1989). ACA moves to new heights for the '90s. *Corrections Today* 51(6): 90–92.
ACA Committees Caucus (1990). ACA Women's Task Force enjoys growth and success. *Corrections Today* 52(4): 18.
ACA Committees Caucus (1992). Two dynamic leaders of the National Prison Association. *Corrections Today* 54(1): 96.
American Correctional Association (1991). *Public Policy for Corrections*. Waldorf, Md.: St. Mary's.
Cerquone, J. (1987). CAC realignment with ACA complete. *Corrections Today* 49(1): 86.
Cerquone, J. (1988). Corrections yesterday. *Corrections Today* 50(1): 70–82.
Huskey, B. L. (1988). Tracking critical issues in corrections. *Corrections Today* 50(1): 40.
Irving, J. R. (1992). Supporting a vital process. *Corrections Today* 54(3): 62.
Keve, P. W. (1991). *Prisons and the American Conscience*. Carbondale, Ill.: Southern Illinois University Press.
Miller, R. (1992). Standards and the courts: An evolving relationship. *Corrections Today* 54(3): 58–60.
Pippin, K. (1989). Rutherford B. Hayes. *Corrections Today* 51(5): 112–16.
Travisono, A. P. (1990). Standards: A true reflection of ACA's membership. *Corrections Today* 52(4): 4.
Travisono, A. P., and M. Q. Hawkes (1995). ACA and prison reform. *Corrections Today* 57(5): 70–73.
Tyler, V. R., and E. A. Smalley (1989). The ACA's diverse professional affiliates. *Corrections Today* 51(2): 185–88.

Angola (Louisiana State Penitentiary)

Angola, the Louisiana State Penitentiary, is the largest medium-maximum security prison in the United States. Located sixty miles north of Baton Rouge in southwest Louisiana and situated on eighteen thousand acres of floodplain along the east bank of the Mississippi River, Angola occupies an area of twenty-eight square miles. Bordered on three sides by the Mississippi and to the northeast by the Tunica Hills, Angola is often referred to as the "Alcatraz of the South" because of its naturally secure location.

Angola is home to approximately five thousand male inmates, ranging in age from seventeen to eighty-three, and 1,845 staff members. Two-thirds of the inmate population are serving life sentences in a state where life means life. Angola also houses Louisiana's death row population. Capital punishment in Louisiana is administered by lethal injection. As of December 1993, Louisiana has executed twenty-one inmates since the death penalty was reestablished in 1983.

The first penitentiary ever constructed in Louisiana was established in Baton Rouge. Completed in 1834, the facility was modeled after the traditional Auburn design, with small, one-man cells. Inmates spent their nights in solitary confinement and their days at work stations producing assorted leather, cotton, and woolen products. Prior to that time, the state had housed both men and women, as well as children, in the deplorable conditions of the New Orleans Jail (the same jail that was decried by the visiting French statesman Alexis de Tocqueville).

Prior to the Civil War, Louisiana leased its inmate population to various private businesses. The primary motive behind the convict-lease system was profit, and no efforts were made to reform or rehabilitate the prisoners. The leased inmates were hired primarily to perform physical labor on plantations and farms. Inmates worked under harsh conditions and were subjected to regular floggings by landowners. As many as three thousand inmates died under the convict-lease system.

The state abandoned the convict-lease system for a brief period during the Civil War. The program was reinstated in 1868, however, to make up for a labor shortage resulting from the abolishment of slavery. At that time there were 222 prisoners, most of whom were black and under the age of twenty-five (Carleton 1971). In addition to performing labor on private farms and plantations, inmates were required to work on such public projects as railroads and levees.

The land occupied by Angola was purchased by the state in 1901 from the heirs of former inmate lessor Samuel L. James, with the intention of constructing a prison on the site. The original purchase included the eight thousand-acre Angola cotton plantation, as well as three smaller sugarcane plantations and four levee camps. One of the first camps built at Angola, and one of the most notorious, was the Red Hat Camp, designed to hold Angola's most dangerous inmates. Angola existed as the only state-operated prison for most of this century.

During the early part of the twentieth century, maintaining custody over the inmate population was the only concern of correctional administrators. The first classification system divided prisoners into four classes according to their ability to perform physical labor. Farming has always been and still remains the primary industry at Angola. It was also during this time that Henry L. Fuqua, general manager of the penal system, turned over the responsibility of supervising the prisoners to a select group of inmates (Carleton 1971). These "convict guards" were armed and authorized to administer punishment at their own discretion.

In the 1930s, 194 prisoners escaped from Angola in an attempt to flee the abusive working conditions and brutal corporal punishment. In response, the institution sought to improve its safety measures by constructing heavily armed guard towers and by increasing the number of bloodhounds used for tracking the escaped convicts (Foster, Rideau, and Wikberg 1989).

For most of Angola's history, the abuses associated with the penitentiary were either not known or were not the concern of the general public. That all changed in 1951, when thirty-seven inmates at Angola severed their left heel tendons in protest of the working and living conditions (Butler and Henderson 1990). The incident brought numerous reporters and special-interest groups to the facility, shedding light on the abuses of the system. The problems that were identified included the use of armed inmate guards and untrained civilian personnel, and a lack of formal, written policies and procedures. As a result, several of the old camps were dismantled and new guidelines were instituted, but not before Angola was named "America's worst prison" by *Collier's* magazine (Carleton 1971).

The United States Supreme Court intervened in 1975 by declaring the facility at Angola unconstitutional. A court order forbidding Angola to accept any more inmates forced the institution and the state legislature to address some of the problems; many more, however, remained.

Angola today is confronted with the same challenges encountered by prisons across the United States. Increases in the crime rate coupled with a sentencing philosophy based on retribution and deterrence have had an effect on both the number of incarcerated criminals and the lengths of their sentences. Louisiana alone has tripled its prison population during the past twenty years and prison construction is at an all-time high.

Louisiana State Penitentiary is currently divided into the main prison and six outcamps. Industries include a license tag plant, a silk screen shop, a mattress factory, a broom and mop factory, and a telephone disassembly plant. The law library at Angola includes three main libraries and three outcamp libraries. The prison subscribes to all of the standard legal volumes necessary to assist inmates with their legal needs. Louisiana has shifted away from the rehabilitation-oriented programs found in its institutions during the 1960s and 1970s to a renewed interest in security and in providing inmates with a broad range of work and recreational opportunities.

Angola offers its inmates a wide variety of sports and recreational activities, including organized baseball, football, volleyball, and basketball. Each October, the prison sponsors a rodeo that the prison magazine calls the "wildest show in the South." Close to two hundred inmates perform in the event before some five thousand spectators. In addition, inmates are permitted to participate in various clubs and organizations, such as the Angola Jaycees and the American Boxing Association. The first organization formed at Angola was the Sober Group of Alcoholics Anonymous back in 1953 (Foster, Rideau, and Wikberg 1989).

Angola's prison magazine, the *Angolite,* has received national recognition. It was the

A

first prison magazine to receive the Robert F. Kennedy journalism award and the George Polk award. Published bimonthly, the *Angolite* is circulated to more than one thousand subscribers across the United States and Canada. As editor of the *Angolite* since 1975, Wilbert Rideau turned the magazine into a major contributor to the struggle for prison reform. Rideau himself has been called "the most rehabilitated man in American prison today," yet he has served more time than the vast majority of prison inmates (Butler and Henderson 1990).

Inmates at Angola also operate the only prison radio station licensed by the Federal Communications Commission. *KLSP* broadcasts from noon until midnight, seven days per week, over a thirty-mile listening range. The station consists of outdated equipment donated by local church groups and record albums donated by former prisoners; it is supported by funds received from inmate blood donations. *KSLP* offers the inmates at Angola musical entertainment, as well as news updates, legal advice, and religious programming.

Over the years, Angola has served as home for some well-known inmates. Famous entertainers such as blues singer Leadbelly, Freddie Fender, and Charles Neville have all served time at Angola. James Smith, former president of Louisiana State University, was sent to Angola after being convicted of tax evasion and embezzlement. Framed for the murder of a north Louisiana couple, four-time world champion steer wrestler Jack Favor was sentenced to Angola in 1967, only to be retried and acquitted for the same offense nine years later (Butler and Henderson 1990).

Angola's infamous and chaotic history, combined with its many unique attributes, is an informative subject for examination. Angola has had, and will continue to have, a significant impact on corrections in America.

Amy B. Thistlethwaite

Bibliography

Butler, A., and C. M. Henderson (1990). *Angola: Louisiana State Penitentiary, A Half-century of Rage and Reform.* Lafayette, La.: Center for Louisiana Studies, University of Southwestern Louisiana.

Carleton, M. T. (1971). *Politics and Punishment: The History of the Louisiana State Penal System.* Baton Rouge, La.: Louisiana State University Press.

Foster, B., W. Rideau, and R. Wikberg (1989). *The Wall Is Strong: Corrections in Louisiana.* Lafayette, La.: Center for Criminal Justice Research, University of Southwestern Louisiana.

Rideau, W., and R. Wikberg (1992). *Life sentences.* New York: Times Books.

Architecture

Quaker Influence and the First Penitentiaries
Contemporary prison architecture reflects most of the same concerns that have guided prison design for the past two centuries—the need to carry out the wishes of the citizens and their elected representatives to punish criminals, to deter potential criminals, and to try to change the conduct of lawbreakers for the better, all at the same time. The first penitentiary in America, the Walnut Street Jail in Philadelphia, was initially a facility for holding minor offenders. There was no separation of the inmates by sex, age, seriousness of crime, or length of criminal career. In 1790, however, various reforms were introduced by the Quakers that called for the separation of witnesses and debtors from convicted criminals, the segregation of men from women, imprisonment "at hard labor," and the construction of a block of solitary confinement cells to house "more hardened offenders." This later feature became known as "the penitentiary."

The state of New Jersey opened a penitentiary in 1799. It had an inscription over the entrance that illustrated the influence of the Quakers, who believed that the purpose of imprisonment was "labor, silence, penitence." In 1826, the first prison that reflected the influence of the English social reformer Jeremy Bentham was constructed in Pennsylvania. Bentham's design called for a huge dome made of metal and glass with cells arrayed on the outer edges. In the middle was a central tower from which guards could look into every cell and at every walkway. Bentham's plan was put into stone in the Western Penitentiary at Pittsburgh in 1926, but its ninety solitary-confinement cells were too small to allow prisoners to engage in the hard labor that was required of them. In 1933 the original design was abandoned in favor of a plan calling for larger cells, implemented in the Eastern State Penitentiary at Philadelphia. That prison was constructed with rows of cells, some four and some two levels high, that radiated out from a central rotunda like spokes from a wheel.

The earliest American prisons thus had rehabilitation as one of their goals, even though the reform occurred in a harsh and punitive setting. The cells were large, 11 feet 9 inches long by 7 feet 6 inches wide by 16 feet high, with a separate door that allowed access to a small exercise yard surrounded by a stone wall. Prisoners were allowed one hour of solitary exercise each day, just as today's federal court judges have mandated for prisoners locked up in disciplinary segregation units. Each convict worked alone in his cell on a variety of tasks, from shoe making and weaving to carpentry and brush making. Prisoners who worked on general maintenance tasks outside their cells wore hoods or masks to ensure their isolation. When religious services were held the other solid door to each inmate's cell was opened, leaving the inner grill door locked; a curtain was run down the center of the cell block so that no inmate could see his fellow prisoners in the cells across the way. Ministers conducted services from a point in the hall at which even they remained out of sight.

The design of Eastern State Penitentiary and the rules that governed prison life were based on the Quaker assertion that during their days, weeks, and months in isolation, free from all worldly distractions, prisoners would seek solace in the Bible, reflect upon their sins, and repent.

As so often is the case in criminology, theory produced undesired results. Critics pointed out that some prisoners became insane, that the work produced by individual workers in individual cells was not cost effective, that the prisoners were clever in finding ways to communicate with each other, and that overcrowding was forcing the staff to place more than one man in a cell, destroying the whole notion of isolation.

The Auburn and Pennsylvania Prison Systems
Meanwhile, in the state of New York, a new system of organizing, controlling, and treating criminals was installed in 1819. Under the Auburn Prison plan, inmates were allowed out of their cells to work together in silence during the day but were locked up in individual cells at night. Auburn was designed with rows of cells five tiers high, backed up to each other. Any light or air that came into the small 7 x 3^1/$_2$ x 7-foot cells came through the barred windows of the outer walls of the cell house. While inmates got some relief from the close confines of their cells in the workshops, Auburn authorities also began the practice of locking up "the most heinous offenders" in solitary confinement.

The Auburn and Pennsylvania prison designs, which emphasized control and the rehabilitation of prisoners by silent labor by day and solitary confinement at night (enforced by flogging, bread and water diets, the removal of bedding, and other harsh punishments), provided the model that most American states used in constructing their prisons and determining the regimes within them well into the twentieth century. Even when, in the 1870s, prison reformers began to urge that prisons and prison staff turn to rehabilitation as the main purpose of imprisonment, the new policies and practices that followed were generally implemented in the old prisons. A typical penitentiary at the end of the nineteenth century and in the early decades of the twentieth could be easily identified by a wall, usually thirty feet high with guard towers at the corners and over the gates, that surrounded a massive cell house with back-to-back rows of cells stacked three, four, or five levels high. The economy of confining many hundreds or even thousands of prisoners in what came to be called "fortress" prisons carried the day in prison construction. Perhaps the best—or worst—example of that type of massive prison is the penitentiary at Jackson, Michigan. It is still in use, and as many as six thousand inmates at a time have been locked up inside.

Alcatraz: Prototype of the "Last Resort" Penitentiary
The number of inmates returning after committing new offenses made it clear to both the prison administration and prison reformers that the harshness of prison life was not having the effect of deterring further misconduct. Thus, the nation experienced a crime wave in the 1920s and 1930s related to the failure of Prohibition and the rise of gangsters, calls were heard to lock up the hoodlums in an escape-proof prison simply for purposes of punishment and incapacitation. There was no presumption that the inmates would be better off for the experience. In August of 1934, the Federal Bureau of Prisons sent the first "habitual intractable" offenders to a newly remodeled former military prison on an island in San Francisco Bay.

Alcatraz incorporated some important features of American penology. First, it represented the recognition that, in any prison system, a relatively small number of inmates—something like 1 percent or fewer of the inmate population—were so disruptive and posed such serious management problems that whole prisons had to be devoted to controlling them. The solution was to identify and remove the worst offenders from federal prisons across the country and concentrate them in one small, super-maximum-security penitentiary; the "putting all the rotten apples in one barrel" theory.

Alcatraz held only some 275 inmates at any one time, all in individual cells, on an island thoroughly separated from the rest of the world. Part of Alcatraz's perimeter security system, therefore, was the cold, fast currents of San Francisco Bay. Another part of the system involved limiting inmate activity by locking the prisoners up from 4:50 each afternoon until breakfast the next morning, and a third element was assigning some 150 guards, lieutenants, and other custodial personnel to watch this small group of prisoners closely. Despite the fact that Alcatraz had a limited function and housed only a handful of federal prisoners, it quickly became highly publicized and controversial, because it was established with no pretense at rehabilitation. The prison consisted of only one building, which contained two cell blocks back to back, and a separate "special treatment unit" to isolate even further the worst of the island's troublemakers and escape artists.

Prison architecture and the regimes within them are symbols of governmental authority and of the core presumption of deterrence that is an element of criminal penalties. But prisons like Alcatraz have always had the problem of punishing or appearing to punish so severely that public sympathy can be developed for the offenders within—even when those offenders are some of the nation's most notorious lawbreakers. The sight of an island fortress called "the Rock" not far from a highly populated urban area, combined with horror stories from inmates and sensational speculation by the press, who were always barred from visiting, created a public relations headache for the Bureau of Prisons that lasted for thirty years.

The end of Alcatraz coincided with the growth of the "medical model," which began to influence California policy and practice in the late 1950s and early 1960s. The theory that each offender was the product of arrested or imperfect psychological development and disadvantaged social conditions gave the Federal Bureau of Prisons, which saw itself as a national leader in penology, the justification it needed to abandon Alcatraz. The bureau was then able to jump on the "corrections" bandwagon, which disavowed punishment as a means of changing the behavior of offenders and clearly rejected the notion that some lawbreakers were "hopeless incorrigibles."

New Purposes for New Prisons

The federal prison at Marion, Illinois, opened in 1964 as a replacement of sorts for Alcatraz. Therefore it featured a structure that was designed along the familiar telephone pole style of architecture, which called for cell houses, workshops, recreational facilities, chapels, and social service and dining areas to extend from each side of a long central corridor. Marion was programmed to provide the same educational, vocational, and counseling services found in other federal prisons. Rehabilitation of the most serious and persistent offenders was reestablished as a goal of imprisonment, even in maximum security penitentiaries.

In California, the ever-present concerns about the cost of prison operations and overcrowding came under the influence of the new treatment philosophy. California Mens Colony, East, in San Luis Obispo, put into concrete all of these elements. It was composed of four six-hundred-man quadrangles, each with its own housing, dining, recreation, and social service areas. A core of central services was delivered to the entire population of twenty-four hundred inmates, including a hospital and chapels, a disciplinary segregation unit, and industrial operations. The prison walls were painted in pastel colors to get away from the old prison grey, and its "L" shape, or "over-under" cell construction, was designed to prevent later overcrowding by making it impossible to replace one bed in a cell with a double bunk.

Psychologically based treatment programs prevailed, with inmates meeting in groups with other residents in their housing area. Each quadrangle was composed of two buildings of three floors, constructed in an "L" shape, with some floors further subdivided by grills into fifty-man units to accommodate that variety of group counseling called "community living."

But Mens Colony, Marion, and most of the other prisons in America were soon beset by new problems—problems that became life-threatening for inmates and staff. The civil rights movement and racial confrontations in cities and towns across the country produced the inmate rights movement, but had the unintended consequence that prisoners began to divide themselves up along lines of race and ethnicity. Verbal confrontations became threats, which became physical confrontations. At the same time that violence was increasing, evaluations of the effectiveness of the psychologically based programs that constituted the heart of the medical model—the offender has a problem, the experts diagnose it, apply treatment, and then, through the indeterminate sentencing system, release the patient/client/resident when his problem has been corrected—proved to be disappointing.

In California, Minnesota, and other states, the penal pendulum swung back to the traditional purposes of imprisonment: the punishment and isolation of serious offenders. Treatment, it was now argued, was best accomplished with offenders in the community. Imprisonment was to be used as a last resort for those convicted of crimes of violence or property offenders who had repeatedly failed on probation or in community corrections programs.

The Prototype of a "New Generation" Prison: Oak Park Heights

With racial and ethnic conflict a major consideration and confinement in most state and federal prisons reserved for violent offenders who would be sent to prison for long periods, American penologists began to consider new designs in prison construction and the remodeling of old buildings. The most notable prisons in the first category produced what came to be called "new generation" prisons, of which Oak Park Heights in Minnesota is the best example. This "correctional facility," with a name that suggests a housing development or a senior citizens' complex, was constructed to provide maximum security and maximum separation of different types of inmates. Yet it differed from the standard penitentiary look of Folsom Prison in California; Attica in New York; Jackson, Michigan; Walla Walla, Washington; Leavenworth, Kansas; Joliet, Illinois; Canon City, Colorado; and the other fortress prisons that Americans had become so accustomed to seeing in the movies.

Oak Park Heights features no gun towers; it is, in fact, built into a hillside, earth sheltered, and largely invisible to the surrounding commu-

nity. Its roughly circular design calls for eight forty-eight-man units that are completely self-contained and separated from each other, with all units connected by a security "spine" of two corridors—one for inmate movement and one for staff. Each unit has its own dining, recreational, and laundry facilities, with several units containing industrial operations and several others devoted to education or chemical dependency and sex offender treatment. A separate mental health unit and a "control unit," the new term for the solitary confinement area of the prison, used to isolate prisoners for reasons of misconduct, serve all units.

Oak Park Heights and other new modular construction designs provide many options to prison managers who wish to break up cliques or gangs, to conduct shakedown (search) operations, or to discipline one unit while allowing normal business to be carried on in other units. The two tiers of cells in each unit face a control room surrounded by security-glass windows through which an officer can observe traffic in and out of every inmate's room and activities in the dining, recreation, and laundry areas—in short, all interactions between inmates and between inmates and staff.

The Return to the Alcatraz Regime

The Federal Bureau of Prisons, however, had no new-generation prison with which to deal with the problems its inmates began to pose at Marion, Illinois. In late October of 1983, after dozens of assaults on inmates and staff culminated in the murder of two officers in separate incidents on the same day and the twenty-sixth inmate killing occurred on the following day, federal officials instituted a "lockdown" that remains in effect at Marion to this day. All congregate activity ceased and inmates remained in their individual cells for twenty-three hours a day, leaving them only in handcuffs and leg chains for their hour of solitary exercise. All services, including confession, communion, counseling, and correspondence courses, were conducted through cell bars. The busy, tense, action-packed days of an open movement penitentiary ended with the reestablishment of the maximum punishment, minimum privilege regime from "the Rock."

The press renamed Marion the New Alcatraz, and the familiar controversies about the nature and degree of the deprivation and restraints on the inmates quickly reappeared. After the inmates tested the constitutionality of

A

the lockdown on the grounds of cruel and unusual psychological punishment and lost, however, what the Bureau of Prisons called "indefinite administrative segregation" soon became a feature of American prison life. Officials from state prison systems visited Marion to learn about its highly controlled regimen, and by the early 1990s some thirty-six states had moved to build new maximum security "facilities" or to remodel units within existing prisons to accommodate "the Marion Model." Some of these new prisons added the lockdown regime to the modular design of Oak Park Heights. Several of these prisons—Pelican Bay in California and New York's "maxi-maxi" prison at Southport—have experienced inmate protests and challenges in federal courts regarding the constitutionality of variations they have instituted, in design and programming, from the Marion model.

Correctional Complexes

The latest development in prison architecture is to be found in the new federal "correctional complexes," the first of which opened in 1994 in Florence, Colorado. The Florence complex is composed of a minimum-security prison featuring dormitory living, a medium-security prison with double bunked cells, a maximum-security penitentiary designed roughly along the Oak Park Heights modular design, with each inmate locked up in a single cell and all units facing the interior of the prison, and the federal government's replacement for Marion, called "administrative maximum." Admin-max consists of nine units for some 480 prisoners. All cells are of 110 square feet and are designed for single occupancy; congregate activities will be limited to pretransfer and "intermediate" units. Apart from the pretransfer unit, each inmate's cell contains a steel shower stall, eliminating the need for staff to escort inmates in handcuffs and leg chains to and from common shower areas as they do at Marion and other older prisons. Recreation will be in small exercise areas surrounded by walls and covered with heavy wire screens, one man at a time. A special series of "suites" provide a vestibule between a barred grill and a solid steel door into which the inmate can be passed by remote control with access on one side to a small private exercise cage and on the other to a no-contact visiting booth. These suites testify to the government's wish to house extremely high-risk prisoners (Mafia kingpins, drug czars, celebrity spies, informers, and perhaps the killers of prison staff) in the most secure and isolated environment that the federal courts will allow.

American prison architecture over two centuries has thus changed in form but not in function. At least that is so for the segment of the offender population requiring maximum punishment or maximum control.

Incapacitation: The Goal that Prisons Have Achieved

Prisons have never succeeded in achieving the goal of rehabilitation through punishment (some of it extremely harsh) or through psychologically based treatment programs, and their deterrent function also seems questionable, at least for some segment of the population. If they did deter crime, today's young offenders would not engage in the kind of conduct that ends in their being put away in the life-threatening conditions that prevail in so many state and federal prisons. Prisons have, however, always been good at incapacitation.

Today's penitentiaries are surrounded by layers of razor ribbon wire, electronic monitoring devices that detect movement and sound, and antihelicopter devices. Prisoners are kept in small, separate units in which they are locked securely and kept apart from others who might aid or participate in the very few plots that actually result in attempts to escape. The business of "corrections" goes on in prisons of lower security, including prisons for women, but even more so in "community corrections." Imprisonment today, as it did two hundred years ago, primarily means separation from the free world. It means, especially in high-security prisons and in disciplinary segregation units, opportunities for reflection, penitence, and for the aging process to work its magic in curbing both criminal behavior and prison misconduct. The word "penitentiary" still fits.

Prisons for Women

The first female offenders to be sent to prison were confined in separate sections of men's prisons. But female felons have always been few in number compared with men, have not engaged in riots or taken hostages, and rarely try to escape. With security so much less an issue and prisoner populations so much smaller, separate prisons for women over the past decades have been built without the cell houses, walls, gun towers, or disciplinary segregation units that characterize prisons for men. Both past and present women's prisons feature rooms rather than cells, a campus rather than a yard, fences for perimeter security (although in some women's "facilities" housing or residence buildings themselves substitute for fences), and resemble more a college campus than any penitentiary for men.

David A. Ward

See also ALCATRAZ, AUBURN SYSTEM, EASTERN STATE PENITENTIARY

Bibliography
American Correctional Association (1983). *Design Guide for Secure Adult Correctional Facilities*. College Park, Md.: American Correctional Association.
Barnes, H. E. and N. K. Teeters (1951). *New Horizons in Criminology*. Englewood Cliffs, N.J.: Prentice-Hall.
British Home Office (1985). *New Directions in Prison Design: Report of a Home Office Working Party on American New Generation Prisons*. London: Her Majesty's Stationery Office.
Johnston, N. (1973). *The Human Cage: A Brief History of Prison Architecture*. New York: Walker and Company.
Nagel, W. G. (1973). *The New Red Barn: A Critical Look at the Modern American Prison*. New York: Walker and Company.

Argot

All cultures and subcultures have specialized languages, referred to as slang, by which they communicate in a short-hand fashion. Prisons are certainly no exception to this rule. Argot is a more distinctive version of slang, in which the purpose of the specialized language is to conceal the meaning of the communication from others. Usually, those who use argot are participants in a similar way of life or livelihood. Actually, the term *slang* itself originally meant the same as the word *argot* and came from the language of criminals and beggars; as *slang* came into more popular usage, it lost this distinctive meaning.

There have been many descriptive studies of life behind prison walls for men. These studies generally focus on prison conditions, prisoner characteristics, and the general nature of prison culture. One of the first studies of prison culture was by Fishman (1934), in which he indicated that prisoners developed their own unique language or argot that was relevant only to them. Fishman used the term subculture, a smaller system containing its own special language, status structure, and rewards and punishments, to characterize his observations of the unique social arrangements among prisoners.

Prisoner argot is neither universal nor static, but continuously evolving. Prisoner argot is "composed of slang brought in from the outside, criminal argot, including the language of drug addiction also brought in from the free world, terms unique to prison life in general, and words and expressions that relate to a particular prison" (Cardozo-Freeman 1984, 471).

Functions of Prisoner Argot

Prisoner argot provides a number of functions. According to Little (1982), prisoner argot functions on the emotional level, venting the release of pent-up emotions such as anger, frustration, and anxiety in a way that maintains social space while minimizing tensions. Busic (1987, 8) notes that "the use and need for euphemism is nowhere more apparent than within a prison population. In this highly specialized subculture, the psychological need to disguise and transform unpalatable realities becomes critical." In addition, humor is a constant in prisoner argot. The use of humor enables prisoners to cope with their sentences and to lessen the seriousness of reality in order to make it bearable.

Secondly, prisoner argot functions on a communicative level, transferring information amid an assortment of other signals. Learning prisoner argot enables prisoners to communicate with each other in a language unfamiliar to others. Maurer (1973) notes that criminals must have a secret language in order to conceal their plans from their victims or from the police. In addition, many concepts exist for which there are no terms in the vocabulary of the ordinary citizen. The same holds true once criminals are incarcerated.

Finally, prisoner argot functions on a social level to accent the relationship among individuals and groups of individuals. According to Little (1982), the inmates have a system of classifying members into a status hierarchy that reflects the values of their society. Prisoners, then, reassert their membership in the prison subculture by using inmate argot.

Commonly Used Prison Argot

Slang Term	Meaning
Hack	Correctional officer
Fish	New, inexperienced inmates
Snitch, Rat	An inmate who provides informations to prison staff (tattletale)
Hooch	Prison-made liquor
Hooter	Marijuana cigarette
Mota, Smoke, Reefer	Marijuana
Chiva	Heroin
The Hole	Segregation unit
Punk, Hoke, Bitch	Male homosexual
Home, Homey, Holmes	A friend or companion
Homeboy	An inmate from the same hometown
Hold Thang	An inmate who has been incarcerated for many years
Short-timer	An inmate with only a short time of his sentence remaining
Down	Length of time served: "I have down for 20 months."
Shank, Shiv	A sharp, prison-made weapon
Pipe	An unauthorized object to be used as a weapon
Leg Rider, Riding the Leg, or "Get off his leg"	One who goes out of his way to do special favors for staff. Similar to a dog "hunching" his master's leg
Trembler	One who is afraid of the prison environment
Cellee	A cellmate
Fall Partner	One who is convicted on the same case. A codefendant
Cop Out	An inmate's written request to staff
In Chain	Traveling with cuffs and leg irons
Diesel Therapy	Being transferred on the prison bus
A Shot	An incident report for a violation of prison rules

Source: Michael Welch (1995). *Corrections: A Critical Approach*. New York: McGraw-Hill.

Elements of Prisoner Argot

There are four elements of prisoner argot (Fox and Stinchcomb, 1994, 392):

1. Mockery of the system ("goon squad")
2. Superficial resignation to authority ("play for the gate")
3. Inmate social hierarchy ("right guys" vs. "straights")
4. Adherence to the inmate code (don't "snitch")

The first two elements are related to meeting the psychological, emotional, and communications needs of prisoners (Little 1982). They are also a reflection of the values that are held by the prisoners. Much of the literature on inmate subcultures has focused on the last two elements, the inmate code and argot roles.

Argot Roles and the Inmate Code

Social roles (argot roles) are created and played by prisoners to reduce the deprivations associated with incarceration and to create a form of social cohesion in prison. Argot roles represent the beliefs and attitudes of prisoners and provide an interpretative framework upon which the social world of the prisoner can be understood. Sykes (1958) describes a multitude of argot roles found in the prison.

1. *Rats* and *center men*, who hope to relieve their pains by betrayal of fellow prisoners
2. *Gorillas* and *merchants*, who relieve their deprivation of goods and services by preying on their fellow prisoners, taking their possessions by force or threat of force
3. *Wolves*, *punks*, and *fags*, who engage in homosexual acts either voluntarily or under coercion to relieve their sexual deprivation
4. *Real men*, who endure the rigors of confinement with dignity, as opposed to *ballbusters*, who openly defy authority
5. *Toughs*, who are overtly violent and "won't take anything from anybody"
6. *Hipsters*, who talk tough but are really all "wind and gumdrops"

This system of normatively interlocked roles emerged to allow inmates to cope with the exigencies of living in prison.

The "convict code" of conduct is most often presented as a sort of countercultural adherence to an alternative set of norms, thus implying a corresponding rejection of the conventional code espoused by prison staff and administration. Sykes and Messenger (1960) identified the informal norms, or inmate code, of the prison culture:

1. Don't interfere with inmate interests
2. Never rat on a con
3. Do your own time
4. Don't exploit fellow inmates
5. Be tough; be a man; never back down from a fight
6. Don't trust the hacks (guards) or the things they stand for

It has been suggested that the inmate's need to alleviate the deprivations and frustrations of prison life give rise to the inmate code or system of values. This code acts as a guide for inmates in their relations with fellow prisoners and prison officials, with the dominant goal being group cohesion.

Richard S. Jones

See also PRISONIZATION

Bibliography

Busic, J. E. (1987). Time and life. *Verbatim: The Language Quarterly* 14(2): 8–9.

Cardozo-Freeman, I. (1984). *The Joint: Language and Culture in a Maximum Security Prison*. Springfield, Ill.: Charles C. Thomas.

Clemmer, D. (1940). *The Prison Community*. New York: Holt, Rinehart.

Fishman, J. (1934). *Sex in Prison*. New York: National Liberty Press.

Fox, V. B., and J. B. Stinchcomb (1994). *Introduction to Corrections*. Englewood Cliffs, N.J.: Prentice-Hall.

Little, B. (1982). Prison lingo: A style of American English slang. *Anthropological Linguistics* 24: 206–44.

Maurer, D. W. (1973). *The American Confidence Man*. Springfield, Ill.: Charles C. Thomas.

Sykes, G. (1958). *Society of Captives*. Princeton, N.J.: Princeton University Press.

Sykes, G., and S. Messenger (1960). The inmate social system. In R. Cloward, ed. *Theoretical Studies in the Social Organization of the Prison*. New York: Social Sciences Research Council.

Ashurst-Sumners Act

The concept of work in the prison is as old as the penitentiary itself. Both the Eastern and Auburn systems required inmates to work as a part of their rehabilitation. The Auburn system was more conducive to collective work, however, and the development of the first prison factory at Auburn in 1824 solidified the early place of inmate labor. The eventual triumph of the Auburn system over the Eastern model ushered in an era of industry in prison that was to be the norm for many years. The original goal of inmate labor was to "habilitate" or "rehabilitate" the inmate to a work ethic that was perceived to be lacking in the person, leading to criminality. By the time prison industry reached its peak around the turn of the century, however, the concern for the rehabilitative efforts of the inmates had waned. The focus then turned more toward the economic requirements of a self-supported prison, or to assist in rebuilding efforts in the South after the Civil War.

In the late 1800s, the American Federation of Labor began a campaign to prohibit industry in prison. Their first victory was won in 1887 with the passage of legislation that forbade contracting with any federal prison for inmate-made goods. With the onset of the Depression, labor groups and businesses became even more vehemently opposed to industry in prison. Labor groups opposed prison industry because it reduced jobs in the free marketplace. Businesses opposed it because many felt that they could not compete with enterprises that used prison labor. Led by New York, which was the first state to impose restrictions on the use of contract prison labor and ultimately abolished it in 1894, many states began to create laws limiting the use of prison industry and prison labor. Federal regulation strengthened state opposition to prison labor with the passage of the Hawes-Cooper Act in 1929, requiring that prison products adhere to the regulations of any state to which they were shipped. When business and labor claimed that the Hawes-Cooper Act was not strong enough, Congress took steps to further restrict prison industry by signing the Ashurst-Sumners Act into law on 24 July 1935.

The purpose of the Ashurst-Sumners Act was to prohibit interstate shipment of prison-made products to states where sales of such goods were prohibited by law, and to require the marking of products shipped to any other places. The wording of the act as originally enacted is as follows:

Section 1. *Unlawful shipment of prison-made goods.* It shall be unlawful for any person knowingly to transport or cause to be transported . . . merchandise manufactured, produced, or mined wholly or in part by convicts or prisoners (except convicts or prisoners on parole or probation), or in any penal or reformatory institution, from one State . . . into any State . . . where said goods, wares, and merchandise are intended by any person interested therein to be received, possessed, sold, or in any manner used, either in the original package or otherwise in violation of any law of such State. . . . Nothing herein shall apply to commodities manufactured in the Federal penal and correctional institutions for use by the Federal Government.

Section 2. *Goods to be marketed.* All packages containing any goods, wares, and merchandise manufactured, produced, or mined wholly or in part by convicts . . . when shipped or transported in the interstate or foreign commerce shall be plainly and clearly marked, so that the name and address of the shipper, the name and address of the consignee, and nature of the contents, and the name and location of the penal or reformatory institution where produced wholly or in part may be readily ascertained on an inspection of the outside of such packages.

The intent of the Ashurst-Sumners Act was to protect those states which had passed legislation pursuant to the Hawes-Cooper Act from receiving prison-made goods. The Ashurst-Sumners Act did not completely satisfy the concerns of business and labor, however. Even though the Supreme Court had upheld the constitutionality of the Hawes-Cooper Act in *Whitfield v. Ohio* 297 U.S. 431 (1936), the desire of the supporters of the Ashurst-Sumners Act to ensure its fulfillment was so great that the Webb Kenyon Act and the "Hot Oil Act" were also put forth as protection from judicial intervention. When the concerns of business and industry still were not quelled, the Ashurst-Sumners Act was amended in 1940 with the passage of the Sumners-Ashurst Act to completely prohibit the interstate shipment of prison goods, regardless of the laws of the state to which the goods would be shipped. The Sumners-Ashurst Act is presently codified in law as 18 U.S. C § 1761.

The effect of the Ashurst-Sumners Act was felt for several decades. Beginning in 1976, however, federal legislation began to erode the protections of the act. In that year, the Law Enforcement Assistance Administra-

tion began the "Free Venture" experiment, which provided funding to Connecticut and eventually to six other states to undertake limited prison-industry projects. In 1979, the act was further eroded with the passage of the Justice System Improvement Act (also called the Percy Amendment). The Percy Amendment expanded the number of prison industry projects but required that conditions be met, such as paying the inmate the prevailing wage, voluntary participation by inmates, taxed wages, withdrawal of expenses from wages, and consultation with unions concerning the impact on free-market jobs. The Percy Amendment was later expanded by the Comprehensive Crime Control Act of 1984, also called the Prison Industries Enhancement Program, to allow for up to twenty projects.

As more and more states began to realize the advantages of modern prison industries, the willingness to further loosen restrictions on such activities grew. The words of Chief Justice Warren Burger that prisons could become "factories with fences" became the battle cry of prison-industry proponents. Finally, with the passage of the Federal Crime Control Act of 1990, the expansion of the Prison Industries Enhancement Program effectively neutralized much of the effect that the Ashurst-Sumners Act had had in eliminating prison industry. Several states followed this legislation with laws designed to allow private business involvement in prisons. In fact, the renewed interest in prison industry has grown to the point that several states have entered into cooperative efforts to place prison-made goods in the open market. Recently, attempts have also been made to use cheap prison labor to make American-made goods competitive in heavily controlled import markets, such as electronics.

While many support the return of prison industry on a political, economic, or humanitarian basis, there has been little research supporting the goals of modern industry in prison. The reappearance of prison labor was often predicated on the return of the work ethic concept, thereby replacing the failing notion of rehabilitation as a primary goal of incarceration. Research, however, has not demonstrated the efficacy of that change. In the studies that have been conducted to date, most find no significant difference in recidivism between industry-trained inmates and those not exposed to such activities. Furthermore, the expectation that inmates would be hired by the joint-venture companies has not been realized. Some companies have actually prohibited the employment of prison-industry workers.

Prison industries were founded on the concept that prisoners could be made productive members of society by instilling them with a proper work ethic. Such noble concepts were soon replaced by the desire of correctional officials to operate self-sufficient prisons. The Ashurst-Sumners Act was established in a time when the nation was more concerned with the employability of its citizens and the stability of its businesses than the reform of prisoners or the self-sufficiency of a small correctional system. The effect of the Ashurst-Sumners Act prevailed for many years, until growing prison populations began to threaten state budgets. That concern quickly overcame any prior uneasiness and the pendulum swung toward prison industry again.

Jeffery T. Walker

See also HAWES-COOPER ACT, INDUSTRY

Bibliography

American Correctional Association (1986). *Study of Prison Industry—History, Components, and Goals.* Washington, D.C.: National Institute of Corrections.

Auerbach, B. (1988). *Work in American Prisons: The Private Sector Gets Involved.* Washington, D.C.: National Institute of Justice.

Callison, H. G. (1989). *Zephyr Products: The Story of an Inmate-Staffed Business.* Laurel, Md.: American Correctional Association.

Cullen, F. T., and L. F. Travis III (1984). Work as an avenue of prison reform. *New England Journal on Civil and Criminal Confinement* 10: 45–64.

Flanagan, T. J., and K. Maguire (1993). A full employment policy for prisons in the United States: Some arguments, estimates, and implications. *Journal of Criminal Justice* 21: 117–30.

Flynn, F. (1950). The federal government and the prison labor problem. *Social Science Review* 24 (March, June): 19–40ff.

McKelvey, B. (1936). *American Prisons.* Chicago, Ill.: University of Chicago Press. (Reprinted Montclair, N.J.: Patterson Smith, 1968).

Sexton, G., F. C. Furrow, and B. J. Auerbach (1985). The private sector and prison industries. *Research In Brief.* Washington, D.C.: National Institute of Justice.

Attica

With the exception of the Indian massacres in the late nineteenth century, the state police assault that ended the four-day Attica prison uprising was the bloodiest encounter between Americans since the Civil War (Preface, New York Special Commission on Attica 1972 [also known as the McKay Commission]). Attica, in the fall of 1971, was a quiet farming community located in the western tier of New York state, approximately thirty miles east of Buffalo. Since 1931, Attica had also been the location of the last great Big House prison, a re-designed Auburn-style facility with immense walls, conical guard towers, and stacked tiers of one- and two-man cells. By the late 1960s and early 1970s the prison housed mainly poor, urban, minority-group offenders. The staff, especially the correctional officers (COs), were largely white and of rural origins. Only one of the 398 COs was Puerto Rican and none were black. On the other hand, nearly two-thirds of the more than twelve hundred inmates were Puerto Rican or black. That mix was to prove explosive, as neither group had much in common with the other.

Attica has two meanings for students of corrections, as a riot itself and as a symbol of correctional change and inmate rights. For many, the major significance of Attica is the 1971 prison riot. As a consequence, it is important to place the riot in its proper context. The Attica riot occurred after the 1967 race riot at San Quentin prison, after the bloody police riot at the 1968 Democratic National Convention, after public revelations about the 1968 My Lai massacre in Vietnam, and after the 1970 killings of students by the National Guard at Kent State University. Violence in the name of a political agenda was not unusual. Therefore, it is interesting that during the summer of 1971 there were a number of peaceful protests at Attica, including a successful work strike by inmates. (Unless otherwise noted, what follows is derived from the Official Report of the New York Special Commission on Attica, 1972.)

Leaders of previously antagonistic groups, such as the Puerto Rican Young Lords, the Black Panthers, and the Black Muslims, gained greater political awareness, submerged their differences, and united in a peaceful effort to effect change at Attica. The new inmate solidarity frightened officials. Warden Vincent Mancusi responded by trying to transfer the demonstration leaders as "troublemakers," but he was prevented from doing so by the new Commissioner of the Department of Correctional Services, Russell G. Oswald. Oswald met with inmate representatives at the prison, but he was called away on a personal emergency before any agreement could be arranged.

On 8 September a CO tried to discipline two inmates who appeared to be sparring and a confrontation ensued, but the incident ended with no action taken by the vastly outnumbered COs. That evening, COs appeared and took the two inmates from their cells. A noisy protest arose that night and was renewed when inmates gathered for breakfast the next morning. Suddenly a melee broke out, some COs were taken hostage, and a riot ensued. Prison officials had no plan nor had they been trained to deal with such an emergency. Within minutes inmates took control of the four main cell blocks and seized forty hostages. COs were beaten, and one of them died as a result of his wounds. Three inmates alleged to be "snitches" were executed by retaliating rioters.

The Black Muslims, who had not taken part in the initial uprising, stepped in to protect the remaining hostages during negotiations (Clark 1973). An inmate negotiating committee was formed, although, as the subsequent Attica Commission observed, the prison policy was not to negotiate with inmates. Indeed, when Commissioner Oswald returned to Attica he found that the police were unprepared to retake the prison. By the time sufficient forces had gathered, negotiations were, by default, underway, and Oswald chose to continue them in the hope of preventing bloodshed. At the request of the inmate committee, several outside observers were permitted to enter Attica, including notable reporters, lawyers, and politicians. Negotiations were spontaneous and disorganized. The inmates had two major sets of demands: The first were deemed the "Practical Proposals" and included the usual demands, ranging from better food and improved health care to religious freedom. The second set, the so-called "Five Demands," were far more political and included general amnesty and transport to a "non-imperialist country" (Weiss 1975).

Oswald agreed to most inmate demands for improved conditions. Negotiations broke down over the issue of complete amnesty for the inmates, however, because a CO had died from his injuries. Another difficult issue was the inmates' insistence that Governor, later Vice President, Nelson Rockefeller come to Attica. Rockefeller expressed the opinion that to give in to that particular demand, let alone the other four, would undermine the basic tenets of society. At the same time, Oswald gave the negotiators a "double-barreled" message: Amnesty, the key demand, was "nonnegotiable," and the rebellion had to be ended quickly to avoid an armed attack on the prison (Wicker 1975, 193). Indeed, it was the mixed messages from Oswald that, in the minds of some observers, including Tom Wicker (1975), drove the riot to its inevitable and bloody conclusion.

On the morning of 13 September, in a poorly planned and uncoordinated nine-minute assault, heavily armed state police and corrections officers retook the prison. In the resulting carnage ten hostages and twenty-nine inmates were killed by the assaulting forces. An additional three hostages, eighty-five inmates, and one trooper were wounded in the assault. Adding the one CO and three inmates killed in the initial stages of the riot meant that a total of forty-three had died, the largest number ever killed in a United States prison riot.

In the aftermath of the Attica rebellion, the McKay commission prepared an official report (New York Special Commission on Attica 1972) and several books appeared, some written by participants (Badillo and Haynes 1972; Clark 1973; Oswald 1972; Wicker 1975). Despite the diversity of authors, one assessment is constant: The inmates at Attica made a serious error in judgment. They failed to realize that, to prison officials, the lives and safety of the COs were only slightly more important than the lives and safety of the inmates. In the end, no concern for the lives of inmates or correctional officers prevented state officials from making their point: The state is sovereign, and rebellious prisoners must not challenge that sovereignty.

Besides Attica the riot, there is Attica the symbol. That is, the riot became a watershed in correctional change and prisoner rights (Unseem and Kimball 1989). The rehabilitative optimism of the 1950s and 1960s was tempered in the fires of Attica. The riot "crystallized doubts about the purposes of imprisonment in America" (Unseem and Kimball 1989, 11). Bert Unseem and Peter Kimball observe that the riot occurred at about the same time as other important social changes were taking place. Those included the following: (1) By the mid-1960s, federal courts had chipped away at the "Hands-off Doctrine," increasing inmate entitlements; (2) Largely as a result of civil protests and social unrest, Congress created the Law Enforcement Assistance Administration to help quell the rising disorder throughout society; and (3) There was a decline in public confidence in government and other institutions. In many respects, the riot signaled the decline of rehabilitation, a downturn hastened in 1975 by the Martinson Report, which was read by many critics of American corrections to mean that "nothing works," including prison rehabilitation programs.

It is not surprising, therefore, that the riot was read in different ways by different groups of people. To some, the escalation of conflict in prisons was one more element in the rising tide of disorder that was threatening to overwhelm the forces of stability and order. To others, it seemed that American society was on the brink of some sort of major transformation. The Attica riot was an unmistakable symbol of these possibilities (Unseem and Kimball 1989, 18). Given the currently overcrowded state of our prisons, these words have added meaning for the 1990s and beyond.

There is an interesting legal postscript to the Attica riot. On 27 February 1991, the United States Court of Appeals for the Second Circuit allowed *Al-Jundi v. Mancusi* (F.2d [#902297][2/27/91]), a class-action prisoner suit filed in 1974, to go to trial. This $2.8 billion suit alleged that the top supervisory personnel at Attica, including Commissioner Oswald, Warden Mancusi, Deputy Warden Karl Pfeil, and State Police Commander John Monahan, were liable for the injuries, pain, and suffering of Attica's 1,281 prisoners, including those who died. These officials had made claims of qualified immunity, meaning that they were simply performing their duties as employees of the state and should not be held civilly liable for any consequences that flowed from these lawful actions. But the Second Circuit rejected these arguments (see Deutsch, Cunningham, and Fink 1991 for a complete discussion of the legal elements of this case and legal blocking motions by the defendants).

The case went to trial on 30 September 1991 in Buffalo, New York. The jury decision was rendered in early February of 1992. The verdict was mixed: Deputy Warden Pfeil was found liable on two claims of having overseen brutal reprisals against inmates. Claims against Commissioner Oswald were rejected, and the jury was divided and thus failed to reach a verdict on Mancusi and Monahan (*New York Times,* 5 February 1992; *New York Times,* 6 February 1992). Two weeks later, the state entered motions to set aside the verdict. One of the most violent chapters in the history of American correctional uprisings continues to be a source of legal controversy more than twenty years after it began.

There is no doubt that prisons across the United States learned many valuable lessons from the events at Attica. Policies on hostages, negotiations, and even signs of impending riots were all documented and made a part of officer and staff training. While many criticized the use of outside political observers, negotiators, press, and clergy, their presence may have contributed to the lack of violence inside the institution during the inmate takeover.

L. Thomas Winfree

See also RIOTS

Bibliography
Badillo, H., and M. Haynes (1972). *A Bill of NO Rights: Attica and the American Prison System.* New York: Outerbridge and Lazard.
Clark, R. X. (1973). *The Brothers of Attica.* New York: Links.
Deutsch, M. R., D. Cunningham, and E. M. Fink (1991). Twenty years later—Attica civil rights case finally cleared for trial. *Social Justice* 18: 13–25.
Gould, R. E. (1974). The officer-inmate relationship: Its role in the Attica rebellion. *Bulletin of the American Academy of Psychiatry and the Law* 2: 34–45.
New York Special Commission on Attica (1972). *Attica.* New York: Praeger.
New York Times (1992). Unanswered in Attica case: High level accountability. February 5, B5: 1.
New York Times (1992). Jury renders mixed verdict in Attica case. February 6, B1: 5.
Oswald, R. G. (1972). *My Story.* Garden City, N.Y.: Doubleday.
Unseem, B., and P. Kimball (1989). *State of Siege: U.S. Prison Riots, 1971–1986.* New York: Oxford University Press.
Weiss, R. P. (1975). The order of Attica. *Social Justice* 18: 35–47.
Wicker, T. (1975). *A Time to Die.* New York: Quadrangle.

Auburn System

Developed between 1821 and 1824 at Auburn Prison in New York, the Auburn system denied inmates communication with one another, demanded that they labor in industrial workshops, and imposed harsh discipline. The combination was widely hailed at the time for overcoming prison disorder and forcing inmates to pay through labor for their own keep.

Time of Great Change

After the War of 1812, New York experienced a period of canal building, migration from New England, the temporary elimination of the competition of English industry, and the beginning of its own industrialization. Erosion of traditional and familiar ways increased public concern about criminality and other nonconformity.

The industrial revolution added new machinery to the factory system, opening new opportunities for the close control, supervision, and discipline of factory employees. Factory rules differentiated tasks, specified standards for work performance, and punished deviations from predetermined production schemes. The Auburn system took advantage of the similarities between the factory and the prison in their social controls.

Meanwhile, New York was playing a part in the invention of the penitentiary. In 1796, its legislature joined a movement toward limiting capital crimes to murder and treason, substituting imprisonment for corporal punishment of noncapital crimes, and authorizing the construction of state prisons. The movement in Europe and America raised unprecedented difficulties for managing penal institutions. Jails had confined offenders only temporarily until execution, exile, transportation, corporal punishment, galley servitude, or fines could be carried out. When penal confinement itself had become a final disposition, wardens had to exhibit executive and managerial skills in providing the necessities to prisoners and in controlling them over an extended time.

Reactions to Newgate's Failure

Although the New York Legislature had authorized state prisons in Albany and Greenwich Village, only Newgate Prison in Greenwich Village was constructed and opened, in November of 1797. Its small capacity soon resulted in grave overcrowding and a generous use of pardons to make room for new admissions. Newgate received an unwieldy combination of adult male felons, female offenders, juvenile delinquents, and the criminally insane. The diverse population, congregate quarters, and overcrowding resulted in gross disorder, arson, and sabotage. During an inmate revolt in 1799, guards opened fire when hostages were seized. In 1800, the military had to break up a riot.

Under pressure of public doubts about imprisonment, the legislature tried to create a better basis for prison industries and the control of inmates. Convicts were to work only on the raw materials supplied by private contractors, who would pay a fixed labor charge and sell the products. The contract system would minimize the fiscal risk to the state. In lieu of excessive pardons, prison inspectors (a board of private citizens) could reduce a prison term by a quarter for good behavior and a satisfactory production record. Earnings in excess of the cost of a convict's support were reserved for the released prisoner and his family.

The legislature legalized flogging but specified that no more than thirty-nine blows would be inflicted, upon supervision of two inspectors. The use of stocks and irons was authorized to reduce prison intake; larceny of items worth twenty-five dollars or less was made punishable by fine or imprisonment in a county jail.

The Auburn System Emerges

A law in 1816 authorized another prison in the town of Auburn. In spite of Newgate's unhappy outcome, the south wing was constructed with two-man and congregate cells. In 1819, William Brittin, the first warden, began the north wing with solitary cells. Inmates destroyed by arson most of the north wing in 1821, but he persevered by rebuilding the cells. The north wing and its five tiers set an architectural style that was the fashion for American prisons for a century. The cells were 7.5 by 3.8 by 7 feet, back to back, a shell within the building, facing inward, with barred doors. They were damp in the summer, icy in winter, with the only light and air from small, heavily barred niches in the outside wall.

In 1821 a legislative commission recommended three classes for Auburn inmates. The most hardened would be in constant solitary confinement in the north wing. A less dangerous grade would be in solitude three days a week and otherwise work in groups. The "least guilty and depraved" would work in shops six days a week. The first class was based on the Pennsylvania system developed by the Quakers. The convict would be in a single cell for the entire imprisonment to separate him physically and psychologically from criminals, prevent his identification by other prisoners to minimize criminal contacts after release, and to press him to become penitent. Reforming character was the purpose, but, if he requested work to relieve the solitude, it would be granted as a privilege.

Favorably inclined to the Pennsylvania system, the Auburn authorities placed eighty hardened convicts in constant confinement in the north wing. Not allowed work, they were forbidden to lie down in the daytime and were so treated until their sentences expired. Many of them suffered physical and emotional harm. One man sprang through the opened cell door and jumped from the fourth tier. Stovepipes broke his fall. Another sliced his veins with a piece of tin. A third convict lost an eye by beating his head against the wall. Half of the deaths at Auburn in 1823 were among the experimental group. In 1823 the governor pardoned twenty-six of them and released the others from constant solitary confinement. One pardoned convict committed a burglary the first night of freedom; twelve men were eventually reconvicted. The experiment was terminated in 1825; the threefold classification plan was abandoned.

The Auburn system emerged after Auburn Prison was established; a commission of the legislature found the system in place in 1825. In referring to it, Beaumont and Tocqueville (1964, 42–43) mentioned Governor Clinton, Greshom Powers, John Cray, and Elam Lynds. Perhaps it was an example of serendipity rather than deliberate invention. The founders of the Auburn system seemed to have been trying to preserve the prison as a social institution, rather than seeing themselves as innovators.

Regimentation, Silence, Flogging

In place of the chaos of Newgate and the failure of solitary confinement at Auburn, regimentation became the usual policy of American prison administration well into the 1930s. Powers (1826, 4) suggested the regimentation by describing the lockstep in Auburn's early stage:

> The convicts silently marching to and from their rest, meals and labor, at precise times, moving in separate corps, in single file, with a slow lockstep, erect posture, keeping exact time, with their faces inclined

The Auburn System was named after the structure and management style of the New York State Prison at Auburn. Photo courtesy of the American Correctional Association.

toward their keepers (that they may detect conversation), all give to the spectator some similar feeling as those excited by a military funeral; and the convicts, impressions not entire dissimilar to those of culprits when marching to the gallows.

The inmates were expected to labor diligently and not leave their place in the workshop without permission. They could not look up from their work or gaze at spectators. They were not "to laugh, dance, whistle, sing, run, jump, or do anything that will have the *least tendency* to disturb or alarm the prison" (Powers 1826, 3).

They were made to appear grotesque in black-and-white striped uniforms and shaved heads. Visits and correspondence were forbidden, but the public could pay a twenty-five-cent fee to observe inmates at work through a narrow window in the wall, without the inmates' being aware. Inmates were compelled to address the keepers with polite terminology without receiving respect in return.

The public favored harsh discipline as the answer to Newgate's chaos and general concern about crime; Warden Elma Lynds became a folk hero as a disciple of stern punishment. The public venerated his "common sense" and scorn for philosophical reflection and book learning. He told Beaumont and Tocqueville (1964, 163):

> I consider the chastisement by whip the most efficient and, at the same time, the most humane which exists; it never injures health, and obliges the prisoners to lead a life essentially healthy. . . . I consider it impossible to govern a large prison without a whip. Those who know human nature from books only, may say the contrary.

Prison Labor and Contracting

By congregating inmates in workshops under strict discipline, the Auburn system qualified the prison for efficient adaptation to the factory system and for contracting with private entrepreneurs. With the isolation of men in solitary cells, the Pennsylvania system was unsuited for such adaptation.

The contractor had to agree to a certain number of inmate-workers, risking having an excess of workers if business declined. Prisoners had a reputation for shirking, sabotage, and inferior work skills. Initially, prison officials feared that the contractors would stimulate prison unrest if permitted to communicate directly with inmates. The prison officials were pressed to accept contractors, however, so that the promise of profit from prison labor could be realized. To entice contractors, Auburn Prison had to offer low labor rates and allow contractors to transmit work instructions directly to the prisoners.

The contractors did not have to pay rent on the prison building; also, water power usually was free. The labor force was subject to discipline, but, as Melossi and Pavarini (1981, 129) point out, industrial work led to different methods of motivating prisoners. Usual disciplinary supervision monitors outward compliance with prison regulations. The threat of punishment—strongly present in Auburn's approach—had been used frequently for that purpose. But in prison industry the attitudes and motives of the inmate-worker affect the form and timing of his participation in the work. Rewards are more likely to encourage effective participation, and that psychological principle helps explain the subsequent modification of Auburn's harsh discipline.

Auburn prison did not report a profit from industry until 1829, and the failure to include all the costs of inmate labor raises doubt that genuine profit ever was gained. Reliable information on the value of the products was not provided, although the contractors usually did appear to gain substantial profits. Other controversial issues were raised between 1825 and 1845: the favoring of certain entrepreneurs in awarding contracts, the fierce opposition of various groups of workingmen to the competition of prison labor, and mounting objections to alleged cruelty in the disciplining of inmates to maintain production rates.

The Ultimate Impact of Auburn

Within fifteen years of their appearance, the Auburn system was acclaimed in America and the Pennsylvania system in Europe. Auburn became a model of a finely functioning "social machine" for controlling prisoners and a guide for prison regulations, daily routines, and design of cell blocks. Its economic advantages attracted American adherents. In the nineteenth century, some three dozen prisons were constructed in the Auburn design.

The Pennsylvania scheme kept inmates in perpetual solitude, requiring larger cells and higher construction costs. It prevented adaptation to the factory system and denied access to possible profits. In its rejection of economic considerations and its commitment to a primitive version of the rehabilitation philosophy, the Pennsylvania system forecast the twentieth-century advocacy of treatment for inmates, after prison industry declined and widespread idleness became an increasing problem.

In 1910, Lewis (1967, 88) found unremitted industry, the prevailing silence, small cells, and a gloomy environment surviving at Auburn Prison. The pioneering spirit had been lost by 1848, as the defects of the system became increasingly apparent. The rigorous disciplinary standards had deteriorated. The lockstep, shaved heads, and striped uniforms gradually disappeared. Public support for the industrial prison eroded, especially those elements found originally in Auburn Prison— brutal flogging, contracting labor, and giving high productivity rates priority over humanitarian values. Yet elements of Auburn's philosophy continue to be expressed by members of the security units of prisons. They linger in the architecture of older prisons, and justify the employment of inmates in prison industries under new circumstances more likely to gain their commitment.

Elmer H. Johnson

See also ARCHITECTURE, EASTERN STATE PENITENTIARY

Bibliography

Barnes, H. E. (1930). *The Story of Punishment*. Boston, Mass.: Stratford.

Beaumont, G. de, and A. de Tocqueville (1964). *On the Penitentiary System in the United States and Its Application in France*. Carbondale, Ill.: Southern Illinois University Press. (Originally published 1833).

Crawford, W. (1969). *Report on the Penitentiaries of the United States*. Montclair, N.J.: Patterson Smith.

Hall, B. (1829). *Travels in North America in the Years 1827 and 1828*, Vol. 1 of 3. Edinburgh, Scotland: Cadell and Co.

Hall, H. (1869). *History of Auburn*. Auburn, N.Y.: Dennis Bros. and Co.

Lewis, O. F. (1967). *The Development of American Prisons and Prison Customs, 1776–1845*. Montclair, N.J.: Patterson Smith. (Originally published 1922).

Lewis, W. D. (1965). *From Newgate to Dannemora: The Rise of the Penitentiary in New York, 1796–1848*. Ithaca, N.Y.: Cornell University Press.

Melossi, D., and M. Pavarini (1981). *The Prison and the Factory: Origins of the Penitentiary System*. Glynis Cousin, trans. London: Macmillan.

Osborne, T. M. (1916). *Society and Prisons*. New Haven, Conn.: Yale University Press.

Powers, G. (1826). *Brief Account of Construction, Management and Discipline of the New York State Prison at Auburn*. Auburn, N.Y.: Doubleday.

Rothman, D. J. (1971). *The Discovery of the Asylum: Social Order and Disorder in the New Republic*. Boston: Little, Brown.

Wines, F. H. (1910). *Punishment and Reformation: A Study of the Penitentiary System*. New York: Thomas Y. Crowell.

B

Sanford Bates (1884–1972)

Sanford Bates was the first director of the U.S. Bureau of Prisons. In addition, he occupied top administrative positions in three state correctional systems. His struggle to improve prison and parole during the thirty-five years that he served as director of state and federal prison systems was founded on his belief that offender rehabilitation provides society with the best protection from crime. Along with public service, his career included work as an attorney, educator, author, and consultant.

Bates was born on 17 July 1884 in Boston, Massachusetts, the son of Samuel Walker Bates and Sarah G. (Sanford) Bates. He attended English High School, where he received the Franklin Medal and five scholarship prizes. After graduating from high school in 1900, Bates enrolled in Northeastern University in Boston, where he acquired his LL.B. degree *cum laude* in 1906. He received an honorary LL.D. degree from Northeastern in 1937 and an honorary L.H.D. from Rutgers University in 1954. Sanford Bates married Helen S. Williams on 3 October 1908. Two children were born of their union. He was eighty-eight years old when he died on 8 September 1972.

After serving as street commissioner of Boston for a few months during 1918, Bates accepted his first prison administration appointment as commissioner of penal institutions for Boston. Persuaded by Bates's effectiveness as director of Boston's city institutions, Governor Calvin Coolidge solicited him to become commissioner of the state department of correction in 1919. Bates accepted the invitation, and over the next ten years, until June of 1929, he sponsored many reforms, including a revised parole system, university extension courses, new pris-

on industries, a state wage for prisoners, and a merit pay system for prison employees. He supported legislation for examination of county prisoners by the state department of mental diseases and helped establish two institutions for defective delinquents and the first U.S. prison crime-prevention bureau.

In June of 1929 he moved to Washington, D.C., to become superintendent of the five federal prisons. His title became that of director when the U.S. Bureau of Prisons was established on 14 May 1930. From the beginning, Bates strongly supported legislation that embraced "a convinced policy of reform and rehabilitation." He served as director of the bureau from 1930 to 31 January 1937, under both Presidents Herbert Hoover and Franklin D. Roosevelt. During that period, over fifteen new institutions, including Alcatraz, were added to the federal system. Libraries as well as medical and social-work facilities were started. Pre- and in-service training programs were developed for prison employees.

From 1937 until 1940, Bates was executive director of the Boys Clubs of America, Inc. He left that position to head the New York parole system for the next five years. Beginning in 1945, he served as commissioner of institutions and agencies for New Jersey. Over the next nine years, Bates led in establishing a model parole system and an experimental center for predelinquent adolescents.

After retiring in 1954, Bates lectured and consulted on issues dealing with penology and public administration. He chaired the board of directors of the Federal Prison Industries, Inc., until his death.

Bates's book, *Prisons and Beyond* (1936), was a standard reference in corrections. In it he outlined prison reforms effected under his leadership. There, too, he discussed requisites for good penal and parole systems, such as the following:

On prison administration:
"A prison system so contrived as to aid in the reformation of its inmates offers ultimately the best protection to society."

On prisoner treatment:
"A warden who rules his prison with fairness, firmness, justice and impartiality can usually maintain discipline even among the most incorrigible of men."

On prison labor:
Inmate labor yields benefits in penal economy, discipline, and morale. Prison industries and the use of inmate labor on public outdoor projects should be encouraged.

On parole:
An imperative addition to prison reforms is an effective parole system. Bates argued that early release on parole inspires inmates to good behavior in prison. Parole can deter offenders from returning to crime and help them return to society.

On politicians:
Politicians seeking favors constitute one of the most serious obstacles to good penal management. "In my own career there was hardly a period when I was not being subjected to the pleas, threats, or pressures of politicians who demanded that I should subvert the public's welfare to benefit their own petty, and sometimes sordid, schemes."

Bates edited the *United States Prison Service Study Course* (Bureau of Prisons, 1936). He wrote two of the ten lessons: lesson one, "Outline of Course," and lesson two, consisting of two parts, "Protection as a Penal Policy" and "History and Scope of Federal Penal Administration." The book was distributed to all federal prison officers.

Bates was elected president of the American Prison Association in 1926 and appointed to the executive committee of the American Crime Study Commission (1928–30). He was named sole U.S. commissioner on the International Prison Commission in 1932. He became president of the Washington Council of Social Agencies (1934–35) and trustee for the National Training School for Boys (1929–33).

Bates was president of the American Parole Association from 1940 to 1943. He chaired the national advisory commission on prisoners and parolees to the selective service system in 1944, advised the War Department in 1944, and belonged to the Army Clemency Board in 1945. He directed the American Public Welfare Association from 1933 to 1938 and from 1946 to 1947, and was vice president of the National Conference on Social Work in 1945. He was trustee for the Vineland Training School and the National Probation and Parole Association. He was president of the New Jersey chapter of the American Society of Public Administrators in 1948 and of the American Association of State Parole Compact Administrators in 1949.

He belonged to the United Nations Commission on Crime Prevention in 1951, and was one of three American delegates to the U.N. Congress on Prevention of Crime and Treatment of Offenders in 1955. He attended the International Prison Conferences held in London (1925), Prague (1930), and Berlin (1935), serving as chairman of the American delegation at the latter. Bates was president of the International Penal and Penitentiary Congress from 1946 to 1951.

In 1942, Bates became the first recipient of the Herbert C. Parsons Memorial Award. He was also honored by the Queen of Holland in 1950 and the Institute of Criminology of Argentina in 1952.

Bates practiced law in Boston until 1929. He was admitted to practice before the United States Supreme Court in 1933 and to the New York bar in 1940. He advised the American Bar Foundation in penology and headed a survey of probation, sentence, and parole initiated by that organization in 1955. He was vice-president of the Institute of Criminal Law and Criminology.

He was elected to the Massachusetts House of Representatives (1912–14), the state senate (1915–16), and served on the Massachusetts constitutional convention (1917–18) and the Republican state committee (1917). He also taught at the New York School of Social Work, Teachers College, Columbia University, and the New York University graduate school.

The Newton Gresham Library of Sam Houston State University, Huntsville, Texas, is the repository of the Bates Papers. Included in that collection are his private correspondence, articles, reports, and speeches. The collection also contains his personal memorabilia and a large number of his books, magazines, professional and trade journals, and newsletters.

Rodney Henningson

See also FEDERAL BUREAU OF PRISONS

Bibliography
Bates, S. (1936). *Prisons and Beyond*. New York: Macmillan.
Bates Papers (no date). Newton Gresham Library, Sam Houston State University, Huntsville, Tex.
Bureau of Prisons (1936). *United States Prison Service Study Course*. Washington, D.C.: Department of Justice.
The trouble with prisons is politics. *Saturday Evening Post* 227(May 14, 1955): 22.

Bedford Hills Correctional Facility

History

Bedford Hills Correctional Facility originally opened in 1901 as the New York Reformatory for Women, with a total capacity of 264 women. Today, the facility has the capacity to confine 782 women.

The first superintendent of Bedford Hills was Katherine Bement Davis, an avid reformer and active suffragist from the Progressive Era who promoted the cottage system and encouraged academic, industrial, and recreational programs for women. Davis was also instrumental in establishing the Laboratory of Social Hygiene, which opened in 1911 on the grounds of the reformatory. It was there that Jean Wiedensall, a psychologist hired by Davis, conducted investigations into the feeblemindedness of criminal women. Inmates were compared with working mothers and students and were found to have less formal education, although the majority of inmates did have average or above average intelligence (Freedman 1981; Rafter 1985).

Current Status

Bedford Hills is one of seven prisons in New York State that house female offenders. Bedford is located approximately seventy miles from New York City on two hundred acres in the rolling hills of Westchester County. Bedford Hills is the only maximum security insti-

tution for women and functions as a general confinement facility as well as a reception center. Women who are committed to the New York Department of Correctional Services (DOCS) are initially sent to the central processing facility located in a separate wing at Bedford for orientation. At the reception center new inmates are subjected to medical, psychological, and educational evaluations. The women are then classified and assigned to the appropriate facility.

Although designated a maximum-security institution, Bedford has the appearance of a campus, with red brick buildings constituting the majority of structures on the grounds. The facility is surrounded by razor-wire fences and, in 1990, a new front gate was constructed that includes a guard tower for armed guards. The majority of housing is cell-block style; the inmates live in private quarters. Additionally, Fiske honor cottage houses twenty-four women who have earned the privilege of less restrictive confinement. Fiske is a self-governing unit that allows the women to set up their own rules and regulations subject to administrative approval.

Bedford Hills also has a Psychiatric Satellite Unit (PSU) located on prison grounds. Women who are suffering from mental health problems are transferred to the Satellite Unit to be stabilized before being returned to the general population. Women with less severe emotional problems who are not yet prepared for the general population are confined in the Intermediate Care Program (ICP). The Intermediate Care Program is part of the mental health wing and provides a less structured environment for women than that in which the general population are placed.

A female superintendent runs the facility and has been in charge since 1982. Historically, all the staff have been women, with the exception of a few men. Today, however, men are fully integrated into the staff. There are more than three hundred security staff at the institution and approximately two hundred civilian staff.

According to 1994 data from the New York State Department of Correctional Services, Bedford Hills houses 725 of the 3,500 female prisoners in New York State. The women confined at Bedford have been convicted of crimes ranging from larceny to murder. Over half of the women are confined for violent felonies, with a third convicted of murder or manslaughter. Approximately one-third of the women are serving sentences of ten, twenty, or twenty-five years to life. The typical inmate at Bedford is black or Hispanic, thirty-three years old, and a single mother of young children; she has been committed from the New York City area. It has also been estimated that a substantial number of the women entering Bedford Hills are HIV positive (Potler 1988).

Programs

Bedford has many inmate-centered programs that are very successful. It was the first women's prison to establish a children's center. The children's center consists of several different elements: the playroom, the nursery, the infant center, and the parenting center. The children's center manages several special programs that allow children extended time with their mothers. Both the Summer Visiting Program and the Weekend Program make use of volunteer host families who provide food and housing to inmates' children for several days or a week at a time. The nursery allows women who were pregnant upon their arrival the option of keeping their babies with them for the first year. At the end of the first year, the baby is placed with relatives or in foster care until the mother's release. The infant center provides day care to the nursery babies. Inmates who work in the infant center can pursue federal certification as child care workers. Bedford also participates in the Family Reunion Program, allowing inmates the opportunity to participate in a forty-five-hour visit with family members in a trailer located on prison grounds.

In addition to family-centered programs, there are volunteer tutoring programs, career awareness programs, and counseling groups dealing with violence against women. Women are also involved in Alcoholics and Narcotics Anonymous, and several women have established an AIDS self-help group.

Other programs at the prison include building maintenance, commercial arts, cosmetology, data processing, drafting, food service, radio/television repair, and tailoring and sewing. Women can continue their educations by participating in adult basic education (ABE) and high school equivalency programs (GED). There are also college programs in which women can earn Bachelor's degrees and in some cases, Master's degrees (Ryan 1984).

Conclusion

Bedford Hills is a unique institution in many ways. Most states have only one prison for women, and they are typically designated medium-security facilities. Further, those prisons tend to be located in rural areas (Pollock-Byrne 1990). In contrast, Bedford is a maximum-security institution located in a state with several prisons for women. Consequently, the women housed at Bedford are more violent than would be found in most other state prisons. Moreover, Bedford is situated near a large metropolitan area.

The location of Bedford has been integral to the success of many of its programs, especially the family-centered programs. Because the majority of women are from the New York City area, the prison's location makes it easy for their families to visit. Furthermore, Bedford relies heavily on volunteers to sustain its visitation programs. The pool of potential volunteers is large, given the location of the facility.

Bedford's family-centered programs have served as models for prison programs across the nation. When the children's center first opened, the director, Sister Elaine Roulet, was inundated with requests for information from both men's and women's prisons. Although many prisons have started similar programs, Bedford remains the standard for innovative family-centered programs.

Karen Casey

See also DAVIS, KATHERINE BEMENT

Bibliography

Fletcher, B. R., L. D. Shaver, and D. Moon (1993). *Women Prisoners: A Forgotten Population.* Westport, Conn.: Praeger.

Freedman, E. B. (1981). *Their Sister's Keepers: Women's Prison Reform in America 1830–1930.* Ann Arbor, Mich.: University of Michigan Press.

Harris, J. (1988). *They Always Call Us Ladies: Stories from Prison.* New York: Scribners.

Pollock-Byrne, J. (1990). *Women, Prison and Crime.* Pacific Grove, Calif.: Brooks/Cole.

Potler, C. (1988). *Aids in Prison: A Crisis in New York State Corrections.* Albany, N.Y.: New York State Commission of Corrections.

Rafter, N. H. (1985). *Partial Justice: Women in State Prisons: 1888–1935.* Boston: Northeastern University Press.

Ryan, T. (1984). *State of the Art Analysis of Adult Female Offenders and Institu-*

tional Programs. Washington, D.C.: National Institute of Corrections.

James V. Bennett (1894–1978)

James Van Benschoten Bennett was a leading American penal reformer and prison administrator who served as director of the Federal Bureau of Prisons (FBOP) from 1937 to 1964. In the 1920s, Bennett helped bring about a dramatic reorganization of the federal prison system. Later, as FBOP director, he implemented numerous innovations in prison administration and programming and acquired an international reputation as an outspoken advocate of "individualized treatment" for rehabilitating offenders.

Bennett was born in Silver Creek, Chautauqua County, New York, on 28 August 1894. He grew up in New York, Vermont, and Rhode Island, as his father, an Episcopalian clergyman, traveled from parish to parish. He graduated from Brown University in Providence, Rhode Island, in 1918, and earned a law degree from George Washington University in Washington, D.C., in 1926. During World War I, he was an aviation cadet in the Army Air Corps.

In 1919, Bennett was appointed to the U.S. Bureau of Efficiency (forerunner of the Office of Management and Budget). He studied the management techniques and personnel practices of federal agencies and eventually became the bureau's chief investigator. The turning point in Bennett's career came in 1926, when the director of the Bureau of Efficiency offered him the choice of undertaking an investigation of either the Veterans Administration's supply-procurement system or the prisons operated by the U.S. Department of Justice. As Bennett later wrote in his memoirs, "I chose prison."

The United States Federal prison system in the mid-1920s was small, consisting of only three penitentiaries and two reformatories. While nominally part of the Justice Department, the prisons operated almost independently, with little central direction. The prisons were severely underfunded and desperately overcrowded. Wardens were political appointees, staff were poorly trained, housing conditions for inmates were unhealthful, brutality was a serious problem, and inmate idleness was rife. Bennett condemned conditions in federal prisons as inhumane and unsuited to the task of rehabilitating offenders.

In his report, submitted in 1928, Bennett called for the establishment of a "coordinated system of Federal correctional institutions," that is, a centralized bureau that would operate federal prisons. The bureau he envisioned would have greater access to resources, be empowered to construct more humane prisons to house the burgeoning inmate population, and would have a mandate to devise innovative programs that would promote better inmate management and encourage rehabilitation. Bennett's report also urged the establishment of specialized facilities to treat narcotics offenders.

James V. Bennett (1894-1978) Director of the Federal Bureau of Prisons for almost three decades. Photo courtesy of the Office of Archives, Federal Bureau of Prisons.

Subsequently, a special committee of the U.S. House of Representatives conducted an investigation of federal prisons, and Bennett was assigned to work with the committee. In extensive testimony to the committee, and in the committee's final report, which he drafted in 1929, Bennett repeated his recommendation for a prison bureau.

Bennett's call for a federal prison bureau that would emphasize rehabilitation programs and maintain better living conditions coincided with a renewed national interest in prison reform and more effective law enforcement. Assistant Attorney General Mabel Walker Willebrandt, who already had introduced several important federal prison reforms in her own right, was a strong proponent of creating a centralized prison system. In 1929, she selected the Massachusetts Commissioner of Corrections, Sanford Bates, to be U.S. Superintendent of Prisons and directed him to set up such a system. At Bates's urging, Bennett helped draft several pieces of legislation that would put into effect the various recommendations he had made for prison reform—including the law to establish the FBOP. In 1930, that law was enacted and the FBOP went into operation. Bates was named FBOP director, and he immediately chose Bennett to be one of the new bureau's assistant directors.

Bennett served as assistant director from 1930 to 1937. His most significant achievement during that period was the creation of Federal Prison Industries, Inc. (FPI), in 1934. A crucial factor in alleviating inmate idleness, FPI was a government-owned corporation that employed inmates to produce goods for sale exclusively to the federal government. To avert the opposition from business and organized labor that had scuttled so many previous prison labor programs, FPI was prohibited from competing on the open market, and business and labor leaders were appointed to FPI's board of directors. FPI's profits were used to subsidize the educational and recreational programs for inmates that Bennett valued. Bennett also worked closely with Bates and the FBOP's other assistant directors, Austin MacCormick and William Hammack, to implement many of the other recommendations he had made in 1928 and 1929. The FBOP cracked down on corporal punishment of inmates, rooted out corruption and political patronage, introduced classification programs for inmates, erected a series of new prisons to ease overcrowding, developed procedures enabling inmates to register grievances, and entered into a partnership with the U.S. Public Health Service to establish a prison hospital and two narcotics treatment facilities.

Bennett was appointed FBOP director in 1937, following Bates's retirement. As director, he expanded upon reforms implemented during Bates's administration and introduced many others in an effort to make prison conditions more humane and to help facilitate rehabilitation. He pushed for better educational and vocational training programs, encouraged the use of psychological counseling, group therapy, work release, and study release, worked to increase community participation in rehabilitation efforts by involving civic orga-

nizations and self-improvement groups in prison programs, and liberalized mail regulations and visiting privileges. In the late 1930s and early 1940s he opened special institutions for juvenile delinquents, and in 1950 he helped win congressional approval of the Youth Corrections Act, which provided for special sentencing procedures for youthful offenders and authorized the FBOP to develop diagnostic services and rehabilitation programs for them. In 1958, his campaign for greater equity in federal sentencing helped bring about the Celler-Hennings Act, empowering the FBOP to make sentencing recommendations to judges and to participate with judges and others in periodic seminars designed to reduce sentencing disparities. In another important advance, begun as a pilot project in 1961, the FBOP opened three halfway houses that were among the first in the United States and that helped trigger the development of the community corrections field. Late in his administration, Bennett sought to ensure that his reforms "were battened down in federal law" by championing the Federal Prisoner Rehabilitation Act, which was finally passed in 1965, shortly after his retirement.

As the FBOP expanded, Bennett continued a trend started under Bates to move away from the massive cell-block architecture characteristic of such penitentiaries as Leavenworth and Atlanta and toward less imposing forms of prison design. Traditional steel-barred cells were retained for inmates requiring a high level of security, but at the same time a system was devised offering diversified housing that ranged from minimum-security camps to maximum-security penitentiaries. That was done to reflect the emerging classification system intended to place inmates in settings commensurate with their security needs and rehabilitation prospects. Smaller housing units or cell blocks, open dormitories and individual cubicles, decentralized compounds, spacious facilities for industrial and educational programs, and expanded recreational areas, Bennett believed, could help create a less oppressive atmosphere that would be more conducive to rehabilitation. Bennett's showplace prison was the Federal Correctional Institution at Seagoville, Texas—a campuslike facility featuring Georgian-style "cottages" rather than cellblocks—that he praised as the "prison without bars." He used Seagoville as a laboratory in which to introduce and refine progressive correctional methods, and it became the prototype for the modern medium-security prison.

For lower-security prisons to run smoothly, the FBOP had to operate higher-security prisons for those intractable inmates who would have disrupted rehabilitation programs and threatened institutional safety elsewhere. The most secure institution in Bennett's day was the U.S. penitentiary at Alcatraz, California. Bennett was always uncomfortable with Alcatraz as a highly visible symbol of retributive justice, and as early as 1939 he sought to replace it. But he also recognized that it was essential to concentrate the prison system's worst troublemakers in a secure environment. Calling himself the "talent scout for Alcatraz," Bennett carefully reviewed the case of every inmate assigned there and closely monitored activities at the island prison. A two-day riot at Alcatraz in 1946 that cost the lives of two correctional officers and three inmates was by far the most violent episode anywhere in the FBOP during Bennett's tenure. In the late 1950s he successfully battled for congressional authorization to build a new maximum-security prison, and in 1963 he was able to close the aging and notorious Alcatraz.

If Bennett had a reputation as an advocate of rehabilitation, he was just as well known as a shrewd administrator. He codified a uniform policy structure for all FBOP institutions to observe, imposed a systematic process by which headquarters staff could oversee and audit operations in each prison, completed the process begun by Bates to convert FBOP employees to civil-service status, and enhanced staff development through a system of awards, training programs, and merit promotions. He insisted upon economizing to get the most out of FBOP's modest appropriations, and he used several devices to improve communications within the FBOP as a way of making management of the bureau more cohesive and consistent. His fame as a public administrator was so great that while he was FBOP director he also received assignments to help organize the Social Security Board and the Office of Price Administration, and he served as an advisor to the War Department, the Civil Service Commission, and other federal agencies.

Bennett cultivated support for the FBOP by maintaining a high profile as director, writing and speaking extensively on prison reform and crime control. He forged alliances on Capitol Hill and fought hard to defend his programs, occasionally clashing with Federal Bureau of Investigation Director J. Edgar Hoover, who was disdainful of Bennett's emphasis on rehabilitation, and with Hoover's allies in Congress.

Hoover, in fact, played a key role in the most serious political challenge that Bennett ever faced. As a Democrat, Bennett was vulnerable when his party relinquished control of the White House in 1953 for the first time since he had become director. Trying to undermine Bennett at that critical moment, Hoover launched an investigation into possible irregularities at a federal prison. At about the same time, Senator Homer Ferguson intimated that Bennett was "soft on communism," an accusation that was amplified by the widely read conservative newspaper columnist Westbrook Pegler. Incoming Republican Attorney General Herbert Brownell considered the attacks on Bennett to be groundless, however, and Brownell reappointed him.

In 1964, Bennett retired as FBOP director. He remained active in the field of corrections by speaking and writing on prison issues, representing the United States at a United Nations conference on crime held in Japan in 1970, and serving as vice chairman of the American Bar Association's Section on Criminal Law. He also became a prominent and vocal supporter of gun control legislation, served as president of the National Association for Better Broadcasting, helped rewrite the Maryland state constitution as a member of the Maryland Constitutional Convention in 1968, and was a delegate to the 1972 Democratic National Convention.

Bennett's rehabilitation-oriented approach came to be known as the "medical model" of corrections. Bennett claimed that it was responsible for a drastic reduction in recidivism among federal inmates, and a Ford Foundation–sponsored study completed in 1964 seemed to validate his contention. By the 1970s, however, the medical model was being challenged by scholars and politicians who argued that rehabilitation programs did not work. Despite the attacks, rehabilitation programs were never abandoned; rather, expectations for them changed. They became part of a larger corrections model that sought to provide self-improvement opportunities to inmates who wished to take advantage of them. The new model, however, rejected the notion that rehabilitation could be compelled and held that punishment and deterrence were no less important than rehabilitation as prison goals. Although the medical model faced controversies, Bennett's impact on American corrections—constructive programming, more humane conditions, improved administration, and greater professionalism—was a decisive one.

Bennett was married for forty-eight years to Marie Ettl, who died in 1967. The couple had one son and two daughters. In 1971, Bennett married Olympia Stone. He died in Bethesda, Maryland, on 19 November 1978.

John W. Roberts

See also BATES, SANFORD; FEDERAL BUREAU OF PRISONS; MACCORMICK, AUSTIN

Bibliography

Bennett, J. V. (1970). *I Chose Prison.* New York: Alfred A. Knopf.

DiIulio, J. J., Jr. (1991). *No Escape: The Future of American Corrections.* New York: Basic Books.

Glaser, D. (1964). *The Effectiveness of a Prison and Parole System.* Indianapolis, Ind.: Bobbs-Merrill.

Keve, P. W. (1991). *Prisons and the American Conscience: A History of U.S. Federal Corrections.* Carbondale, Ill.: Southern Illinois University Press.

Roberts, J. W. (1994). Grand designs, small details: The management style of James V. Bennett. *Federal Prisons Journal* 3(3): 29–39.

U.S. Senate, Subcommittee on National Penitentiaries of the Committee on the Judiciary (1964). *Of Prisons and Justice: A Selection of the Writings of James V. Bennett.* Washington, D.C.: 88th Congress, Second Session, 16 April.

George J. Beto (1916–1991)

To the inmates at the Texas Department of Corrections he was known as "Walking George"; to corrections professionals across the nation he was regarded as "the chief architect of the country's safest prison system" and the "author of the 'control model' of prison management." To the public at large he frequently was jokingly introduced as "the most sued man in Texas." Whatever may have been said, there was little dispute that during Dr. George Beto's tenure as director of the Texas prison system in the 1960s and early 1970s, the Texas Department of Corrections achieved a reputation as the best prison system in the nation, a reputation due largely to the philosophy and management style of its director, Dr. George Beto.

George Beto, college professor and Lutheran minister, appeared an unlikely candidate to run a prison system full of hardened criminals. The son of a Lutheran minister, Beto was born in Hysham, Montana, in 1916. After graduating from Valparaiso University in Indiana and later a Lutheran seminary, Concordia Theological Seminary in St. Louis, he began teaching at Concordia Lutheran College in Austin, Texas. Ten years later he was promoted to the presidency of the college, a position he held from 1949 to 1959. While at Concordia he earned a Master's degree in history and a doctorate in education from the nearby University of Texas.

His first official involvement with the criminal justice system came in 1953, when he was appointed to the Texas Prison Board by Governor Allen Shivers. Beto was a prison board member during six of the thirteen years in which reformer O. B. Ellis upgraded living conditions in Texas prisons from among the nation's worst and transformed the prison's agricultural and livestock operations into a profitable enterprise. As a board member, Beto had a front-row seat to this transformation and was, himself, instrumental in a number of reforms providing inmates with improved educational and religious opportunities. Most notably, Beto was instrumental in introducing the General Education Development (GED) program into the state prison system. That program enabled inmates to obtain a high school equivalency degree while serving their time in prison. Beto served in this volunteer capacity for six years before being called by the Lutheran Church to serve as president of Concordia Theological Seminary in Springfield, Illinois.

It was while in Illinois that Beto renewed a friendship with a man who would leave an indelible mark on his philosophy and ideas about prison management. That man was Joseph E. Ragen, director of the famous Illinois Stateville Penitentiary and author of *Inside the World's Toughest Prison.* Ragen had a national reputation for running his prison with military-like discipline and attention to detail.

At Ragen's urging, Beto was appointed to the Illinois Parole Board by Governor Otto Kerner. As a parole board member, Beto's frequent contact with the inmates of Stateville, as well as Warden Ragen, provided him with an up-close opportunity to deal directly with individual prisoners and to study Ragen's management style.

The unexpected death of O. B. Ellis in 1961 left the Texas prison system without a director. Within two hours of Ellis's death, George Beto received a telephone call in Illinois from Texas Prison Board Chairman H. H. Coffield asking him to become the new director of the Texas Department of Corrections. Beto initially declined the offer but finally accepted when the position was expanded to include the duties of Chief of Chaplains. While Beto had no professional work experience or training in prison management, he had established an enviable reputation in the field of corrections through a decade of intense involvement with prison issues, first as a member of the Texas Prison Board and later as a member of the Illinois Parole Board.

On assuming the directorship of the Texas Department of Corrections, Beto stated that it was his plan to continue and expand the work of O. B. Ellis. As Beto was soon to discover, however, there were fundamental issues of prison management still to be addressed. While a great deal had been accomplished under Ellis, the fact remained that inmates were still "managed" with the use of physical coercion, much as they always had been; as a result, they lived in an atmosphere of fear, violence, and brutality.

One of the most pressing questions facing Beto, as it does any prison administrator, was how to establish order in an environment where those being guarded are in greater numbers than those doing the guarding. Beto was convinced that order, discipline, and control were essential to a prison if it were to provide inmates with a safe environment and opportunity for rehabilitation. He believed that prisoners were in prison because they lacked the necessary internal controls to function in a law-abiding manner, and therefore the controls must be externally imposed. Beto believed strongly that each inmate is personally accountable for his own crimes, as well as for his own rehabilitation. Prison was not responsible for rehabilitating the inmate, but rather for providing him with a safe, productive, and humane environment while he paid his debt to society and took advantage of opportunities to better himself if he so chose.

This philosophy was clearly reflected in Beto's approach to prison management, which would later become known as the "control model." The control model involved the strict enforcement of discipline and the tight regulation of the inmate's daily routine, down to how he buttoned his prison uniform. Prisoners were required to work in the prison's agricultural or industrial operation and attend the prison school. Prison guards were to be obeyed immediately and addressed as "boss" or "sir." Prisoners who complied with these rules and worked hard received "good time" deducted from their sentences; those who disobeyed received additional work assignments or time in solitary confinement.

Dr. George Beto (1916–1991), former director of the Texas Department of Corrections.

Beto's philosophy of prison management was challenged soon after he became director. Inmates and prison employees alike quickly discovered that under what appeared to be a mild exterior was an iron will and a rock-solid conviction in control, order, and discipline. Shortly after he had taken over at the Texas prison system, a group of inmates staged a "buck" (refusal to work). Beto gave his wardens a first-hand demonstration of his management philosophy. After spending a few minutes reasoning with the inmates with no results, Beto commanded the unit wardens to mount horses, placed weapons in their hands, and ordered the inmates to begin hoeing the fields immediately. Within minutes the prisoners resumed work and the news of the confrontation spread rapidly throughout the prison system, quickly putting to rest any doubts about the toughness of the new administrator.

Beto's views of personal accountability extended beyond the prisoners and included his staff and himself. He paid careful attention to detail and would not tolerate poor food or dirty prison conditions. He believed that frequent on-site contact with prisoners and staff was essential to effective prison management. The inmates nicknamed him Walking George for his frequent habit of showing up unannounced in the prison cell blocks and yards to see firsthand how things were running and to talk with the prisoners and guards. During these visits, prisoners were allowed to give him uncensored letters requesting a favor or reporting a complaint. Beto would follow up on each and every letter. As a result, he developed a strong informal network of information that further enhanced his ability to keep track of what was going on throughout the system.

While Dr. Beto is perhaps best known as the author and architect of the control model, he was also responsible for a number of other improvements in Texas prisons. Beto revolutionized education in Texas prisons. He convinced the state legislature to create the first nongeographic school district located within a prison system. The Windham School District began by offering basic academic courses and was expanded to include vocational training and college-credit courses. In an effort to provide soon-to-be released inmates with basic living skills, he established the first prerelease program, and later he initiated the first Adult Basic Education program for inmates. Dr. Beto upgraded the system's chaplaincy program and instituted the system's first work furlough program. He also was responsible for racially integrating the Texas prison population and for hiring the first black correctional officers in the prison system.

Beto worked hard to build on the accomplishments of his predecessor to make the prison system as self-sufficient as possible. Ellis had created a successful agricultural program that supplied the prison system with most of its food. Beto expanded the agricultural program and then convinced the Texas legislature to allow the prison to sell industrial products made in the prison to other state agencies and qualified tax-supported industries. Prison industries were developed that included a bus repair shop, a tire recapping plant, a coffee roasting plant, garment factories, a dental laboratory, a wood shop, a license plate factory, and a records con-

version office. Industrial sales rose from less than $1 million when the program was created in 1964 to over $60 million by 1991. Not only did these industries generate considerable revenue, but they also trained thousands of inmates in skills that could lead to employment once they were released from the system.

In spite of these improvements, numerous lawsuits were filed during his tenure, giving rise to joking references to George Beto as the "most sued man in Texas." While the majority of these suits were writs of habeas corpus, filed to remedy some alleged error or violation at the trial court level, some were serious legal challenges to Texas prison authorities' tight control over prisoners. One of the most notable lawsuits was *Cruz v. Beto*, in which the Supreme Court held that Texas prison authorities could not prohibit a Buddhist inmate from worshiping and proselytizing. Another lawsuit that made it all the way to the Supreme Court was *Novak v. Beto*, in which the adequacy of diet while in solitary confinement was challenged but upheld. That case also helped clarify the conditions under which inmates often referred to as jailhouse lawyers could represent other inmates in legal proceedings.

The most significant challenge to the Texas prison system was emerging just as Beto was stepping down as prison director. *Ruiz v. Estelle*, filed in 1974, would prove to have a far-reaching impact on the future of the Texas prison system and Beto's control model. The Ruiz lawsuit and the lengthy legal proceedings that followed focused on a number of prison issues. Perhaps the most significant was the use of inmate guards, otherwise known as building tenders, a practice that both Ellis and Beto had retained from the earlier, prereform days. While both men had expressed reservations about the practice's potential for abuse and had considered abolishing it, neither man did. Both felt that the building tender system improved the prison's efficiency and both were convinced that abuses of the system could be avoided by careful supervision. Dr. Beto's high degree of personal involvement and his independent channels of information enabled him to exert greater control over the building tender system than did either his predecessor or successor. As the prison population grew larger, however, and the prison administration more decentralized, especially under Beto's successor, James Estelle, the building tender system began to deteriorate, giving rise to increased abuse of inmates by their anointed peers.

While many remain strongly divided over the merits of the Ruiz case and the changes it ultimately brought, few would question the fact that, under the leadership of Dr. George Beto, Texas prisons earned a national reputation based on an enviable record for order, efficiency, and inmate safety.

Beto's career brought him considerable recognition in the field of corrections, and in 1969 and 1970 he was asked to serve as president of the American Correctional Association. He was recognized as a distinguished alumnus at both Valparaiso University and the University of Texas.

After retiring from the Texas Department of Corrections, Beto accepted a professorship at Sam Houston State University, located just a few blocks down the street from the prison's central administrative offices. Beto had been one of the driving forces behind the creation of Sam Houston State University's Criminal Justice Center, which was designed to educate and train future criminal-justice professionals. On two occasions he served as the center's interim director, once in 1977–78 and later in 1985–86. In honor of his service to the Criminal Justice Center and to the field of corrections, in 1990 the center was renamed the George J. Beto Criminal Justice Center.

During the nineteen years that he was at Sam Houston State University, Beto continued to influence the field of corrections. In 1976, a U.S. district judge ordered massive changes in the Alabama prison system, and Dr. Beto was asked to serve as one of two court-approved consultants to oversee the restructuring of the system. As a result of that effort, Alabama prisons ended overcrowding, expanded educational and vocational programs, built work-release centers, and improved medical care. Other prison systems in Europe, Japan, Egypt, and Fort Leavenworth, Kansas, also requested Dr. Beto's assistance in evaluating their facilities.

From 1975 to 1987 Beto served as a board member of the Texas Youth Commission, the state's juvenile corrections agency. For the last four of those years Beto served as chairman. Up until the time of his death, on 4 December 1991, Beto was still in service to the ideals and beliefs that he had forged over a lifetime, serving as both chief of chaplaincy services and board member emeritus for the Texas Youth Commission.

Charles Jeffords
Jan Lindsey

Bibliography

Crouch, B., and J. Marquart (1989). *An Appeal to Justice: Litigated Reform of Texas Prisons.* Austin, Tex.: University of Texas Press.

DiIulio, J., Jr. (1987). *Governing Prisons: A Comparative Study of Correctional Management.* New York: Free Press.

George J. Beto, criminal justice legend dies. *Texas Journal of Corrections* 18(1): 7 (1992).

Wilson, J. Q. (1989). *Bureaucracy: What Government Agencies Do and Why They Do It.* New York: Basic Books.

Boot Camps

In 1983, departments of corrections in Oklahoma and Georgia opened prison programs that were modeled after military boot camps. Offenders were required to arise early in the morning and participate in a full day of work, physical training, and military drill and ceremony. The programs attracted a great deal of attention and soon other state departments of corrections were initiating similar programs in their jurisdictions. In less than a decade, thirty states had opened programs for adult felons in state prisons. Local jurisdictions also started boot camps in jails, and many jurisdictions were considering developing programs for juvenile delinquents. The programs became known as shock incarceration programs or, more commonly, boot camp prisons.

The boot camps were similar to earlier shock probation programs in that offenders in the boot camps were required to spend a short time in prison prior to release on probation or parole. They differed from those earlier programs in that the offenders were separated from other prisoners and that there was a strong military-style atmosphere in the boot camp prisons and a rigorous schedule of daily activities.

Boot camp participants are required to adhere to strict rules, and they are swiftly punished for misbehavior. They are allowed only a few personal possessions, no televisions, and few visits from outside.

Rigorous Daily Schedule

In the typical boot camp program, offenders arise early each morning to participate in physical training. Following that, they have a short period of time for bathing and dressing, and

Marching drills at the Boot Camp at Valdosta Correctional Institution.
Photo courtesy of Valdosta Correctional Institution and the American Correctional Association.

then they are required to clean their living quarters and to practice military drill and ceremony. They march as a unit to breakfast, where they must stand at attention while awaiting their turn to be served. They are forced to eat rapidly without talking and to return to their dormitory to prepare to begin work for the day. Work requires hard physical labor, such as clearing land or cleaning community parks. Following a full day of work, inmates are again required to participate in physical training and military drill. After a quick dinner they attend various therapeutic activities, such as academic education, counseling, drug treatment, or life-skills training.

Throughout the day inmates are carefully observed by the correctional officers, who are referred to as drill instructors. When speaking to staff, inmates must refer to themselves as "this inmate" and they must proceed and follow each sentence with sir or madam, as in "Sir, yes sir."

Depending upon the program, offenders spend between 90 to 180 days in the boot camps. Those who do not complete the programs are dismissed prior to graduation and are considered program failures. Offenders who successfully complete the boot camp are released from prison. There is often an elaborate "graduation" ceremony in which the graduates demonstrate the military drills they have practiced. Many

programs encourage family members to attend this final ceremony.

Drill instructors report that they receive letters from graduates telling them that the graduate appreciated their help when they were in the boot camp. The drill instructors who had previously worked in traditional prisons say that this is very different from the way offenders felt about them in other prisons.

Boot Camps

All boot camp prisons have some core characteristics in common. One is a military atmosphere in which offenders are required to participate in physical training and military-style drill and ceremony. Furthermore, participants are separated from offenders who are not in the program. Apart from these core components, however, boot camp prisons differ dramatically.

Most, but not all, programs limit participation to young offenders who have been convicted of nonviolent crimes like drug possession, burglary, or theft. Furthermore, most programs target offenders who do not have an extensive past history of crime. Many states will not allow offenders to participate if they have been previously incarcerated.

Some programs emphasize therapeutic programs while others focus on hard work and physical training. For example, New York boot camp inmates spend more than five hours each day in academic classes, drug treatment, counseling, or group meetings. In comparison, offenders in the original Georgia boot camp were given only a short period of prerelease counseling. They spent most of their time in physical training, drill, and work.

The boot camps with therapeutic programs also differ in the type of rehabilitation that the inmates receive. Some programs focus on academic education while others focus on drug treatment or counseling, in an attempt to change the offenders' criminal attitudes and thinking.

Community Supervision

Boot camps also differ in the type of follow-up surveillance, or "aftercare," the offenders receive after they are released. Offenders who successfully complete boot camp programs are released to the community, where they are supervised by probation or parole agents. Depending upon the boot camp, offenders may receive intensive supervision, supervision at levels determined by their assessed risk, or no additional supervision at all. In Illinois, they are electronically monitored for the first three months after release.

Some program officials have worried about the difficulty offenders will have when they return to the community. For that reason, offenders are furnished with aftercare programs that not only provide intensive supervision but also help in making the transition from prison back to the community. These aftercare programs may offer the offenders vocational counseling, academic education, drug treatment, or short-term housing.

Placement Decisions and Prison Crowding

Boot camps also differ in who makes the decision to place offenders in the programs. Some programs receive offenders directly from the court. The judge may sentence the offender directly to the boot camp prison, or sentencing may be delayed to see how the offender does in the program. In these states, "net-widening" (that is, including new individuals who would not have been previously considered for such serious processing) may occur because the judges may be searching for options other than prison for offenders they might otherwise have placed on probation. If that is the case, the programs may widen the net to send more offenders to prison. In such situations, the boot camps may increase the need for prison beds.

Offenders in other boot camps are sentenced by the judge to a term in prison. The department of corrections evaluates offenders and decides who is eligible to enter the boot camp. Prisoners who enter the boot camp and successfully complete the program are released early. Those who refuse to enter the boot camp or who are dismissed must stay in prison until they are eligible for parole. Thus they spend more time in prison than they would have in the boot camp.

Offenders usually do not want to go to the boot camp, because it requires hard work. Some will agree to go, however, if the program will shorten their sentence. Instead of doing a year or two in prison, they will be required to spend only 90 to 180 days in the boot camp prison, and then they are released. From that perspective, the boot camp is a mechanism that enables the department of corrections or the parole board to release offenders from prison early.

Abuse and Inmate Rights

Offenders who enter the boot camp prisons are often asked to sign a paper saying that they have volunteered for the program. They are given information about the program and about the difference between a boot camp prison and a traditional prison. The first day of the boot camp involves a difficult intake process in which drill instructors confront the inmates. Inmates are given rapid orders about the rules of the camp: when they can speak, how they are to address the drill instructors, and how to stand at attention. They have their heads shaved (men) or are required to wear short haircuts (women) when they first enter the camp. It's a stressful time for most inmates.

One big difference between boot camp prisons and other prisons is that the drill instructors in the boot camps use summary punishments. These are immediate sanctions for misbehavior, such as doing twenty push-ups or running laps around a track. What counts as misbehavior can be such minor things as not looking at the drill instructor or speaking without saying "Sir, yes sir."

The drill instructors have such complete control over the inmates that there is concern that some instructors may abuse their authority and injure inmates. Administrators also worry that the inmates could be accidentally injured during the hard physical labor or physical training.

B

Rapid Growth

Boot camp prisons continue to grow in size and number. There are many reasons for the growth. Boot camps appear to have a certain "face validity"—they feel right to the public. They are consistent with a history of sending young men with problems to military schools or into the military to "become men." In addition, the boot camps are attractive to the news media. The public responds well to the image of young criminals being yelled at by a tough drill sergeant.

Furthermore, policy makers and those involved in the criminal justice system see boot camp prisons as a possible solution to some of the serious problems confronting the corrections system. Boot camps are one of the few alternative sanctions that are viewed as being tough on crime. The public appears to approve of them. At the same time, boot camps hold the promise of reducing prison crowding.

But boot camp prisons are controversial. Some people who have examined the camps are concerned that inmates' rights will not be observed and that the inmates are being coerced into something that is not good for them. Critics say that the summary punishments and the yelling by the staff may be abusive. Graduates may leave the boot camp prison angry and damaged by the experience. Furthermore, critics argue that military boot camps are designed to make a cohesive fighting unit. That is not what prisons are designed to do.

Advocates of the boot camps say that the program addresses the inmates' lack of discipline and accountability. They also argue that there is a strong positive relationship between the offenders and the drill instructors, and that the boot camp is better than a traditional prison because boot camp inmates work on their problems.

Goals

According to a survey of correctional officials, the major goals of the boot camp programs are to change the attitudes and behavior of offenders and reduce prison crowding. Most programs want offenders to be able to obtain employment, reduce their use of alcohol and illegal drugs, be better parents, and, in general, be more involved in constructive social activities. Officials also want to reduce the recidivism rate of the boot camp participants. Some programs are also interested in promoting positive public attitudes, and improving control and management in prison.

Research on the Success of the Programs

Some research has been completed examining the effectiveness of the boot camps in achieving their goals. Research on the attitudes of the boot camp inmates indicates that they leave the camps believing that the experience has been positive and that they have changed for the better. They report positive relationships with the staff, and that they are drug-free and physically healthy.

When their behavior during the first year back in the community is examined, however, there is no evidence that they perform any differently than those who have spent a longer period of time in prison. They participate in the same number of positive social activities (attending drug treatment, keeping a job, or going to school) as the parolees who spent a longer time in prison. Also disappointing is the fact that the same percentage of boot-camp graduates return to criminal activities as do other parolees. Their recidivism rates are very similar.

Thus, there is no support for the idea that boot camps will significantly reduce recidivism or promote socially desirable activities. This research was done using a comparison-groups-design that controlled for differences among groups but did not use random assignment to boot camp or prison. The researchers who completed these studies say that more studies should be done, particularly if new studies are able to make use of random assignment.

Because the programs appear to have some positive effects on offenders' attitudes, the programs may initiate some changes in individual offenders. These changes, however, may not be great enough to enable the offenders to overcome the problems that confront them when they are returned to the community. Their friends may be gang members or drug users who draw them back into crime. Furthermore, they may have difficulty finding employment. Thus even an offender who wants to change may find it very difficult.

The second major goal of boot camps is reducing prison crowding and the associated costs. Research has examined the impact of boot camps on the number of beds needed by a prison system. If a sufficient number of offenders complete the program and are released early from prison, the programs have the potential to reduce prison crowding. The program is used as an early release mechanism, and offenders are permitted to earn their way out of prison because they are willing to work in the boot camp. That is acceptable to many prison systems because most of the boot camp participants are young, nonviolent offenders who do not have a history of involvement in criminal activity. By releasing these offenders early, the prison system saves bed space and money.

Many programs, however, select participants from among those who would otherwise be given a sentence of probation. In those cases the boot camps widen the net to include more offenders in prison, and the prison system requires additional beds.

The Future of Boot Camp Prisons

Although there is some controversy about the boot camp prisons, they are still a popular alternative sanction. Advocates of the programs have been disappointed that the research has not shown boot camps to have a significant impact on recidivism. On the other hand, these offenders do as well as others who have been kept in prison longer. And there is hope that boot camps can be used to reduce prison crowding, or at least to enable jurisdictions to release nonviolent offenders from prison to make room for violent offenders who must be imprisoned for a longer period of time.

Doris Layton MacKenzie

Bibliography

MacKenzie, D. L. (1990). Boot camp prisons: Components, evaluations, and empirical issues. *Federal Probation* 54: 44–52.

MacKenzie, D. L., and D. G. Parent (1992). Boot camp prisons for young offenders. In J. M. Byrne, A. J. Lurigio, and J. Petersilia, eds. *Smart Sentencing: The Emergence of Intermediate Sanctions.* Newbury Park, Calif.: Sage.

MacKenzie, D. L., and A. Piquero (1994). The impact of shock incarceration programs on prison crowding. *Crime and Delinquency* 40(2): 222–49.

MacKenzie, D. L., and C. Souryal (1991). Boot camp survey: Rehabilitation, recidivism reduction outrank as main goals. *Corrections Today* 53(6): 90–96.

Zebulon Brockway (1827–1920)

Zebulon Brockway is identified as a leader in the dynamic reformatory movement of the latter years of the nineteenth century. Along with prison reformers Enoch Wines, Gaylord Hubbell, and Franklin Sanborn, he was influenced by the Irish prison system, condemned the congregate prison system, and advocated the philosophy of reformation of offenders as opposed to punishment. Brockway was an inspired, hard-working man who has been referred to as "the greatest warden America has produced."

In 1848, at the age of twenty-one, Zebulon Brockway began his career in penology as a clerk at Wethersfield Prison in Connecticut. In 1852 he became superintendent at Albany Municipal and County Almshouse. There he founded the first county hospital for the insane. Later, as a prison warden, he adopted the philosophy that offenders were similar to mentally ill people in that they need treatment and cure.

In 1854, at the age of twenty-seven, he became superintendent of the Monroe County Penitentiary in Rochester, New York, where he began to experiment with ideas on making prisons more humane and rehabilitative. He devoted his energies to youthful offenders, as the widely held belief was that they offered the greatest possibility for reformation. In 1861 he moved to Detroit to head the Michigan House of Correction, which housed young offenders between the ages of sixteen and twenty-one, and introduced his new educational methods. In his autobiography he claimed that he instituted inmate self-government there.

Brockway's early philosophy was that the single immediate purpose of incarceration was to protect society against crime but that the ultimate goal was to reform the offender. He created education, training, and reformation programs that he made available to all offenders. While in Detroit, Brockway converted a women's shelter into a women's prison and thereby created the forerunner to women's reformatories in America. Women were placed in the facility based on their good behavior.

Zebulon Brockway's fame was established, however, when he became superintendent of the newly established Elmira State Reformatory in New York in 1876. There he finally had the opportunity to put the theories he had formed into practice in a totally new institution that was hailed as a great innovation in the field of penology. Elmira was originally built for adult felons, but youthful offenders from sixteen to thirty-one serving their first term in prison soon constituted the population, because Brockway was unsuccessful in advancing his theories of reformation for older, more experienced offenders. He attempted to reform the common prac-

B

tices of the time, which relied exclusively on brutal ity and humiliation, and as a result of which prisoners were discharged from prison with shaved heads and in poor health. For twenty-five years he worked to make Elmira a model institution through the development of educational instruction and training for trades. He placed heavy emphasis on military-style discipline, physical fitness, and education.

Under Brockway, the prison atmosphere tended to be repressive, especially for those inmates who were being punished. At Elmira, the whip, a paddle with nails in it, and solitary confinement in dark cells in which inmates were handcuffed to the wall were all used regularly. Other institutions that attempted to emulate the Elmira program often reverted to those practices. Little attention was given to the social aspects of behavior or the need to teach skills of cooperation and collective responsibility. But the contrast between Brockway's Elmira and other less progressive institutions of the era was still great.

The most important aspect of Brockway's methods at Elmira was indeterminate sentencing, a system originally based on a zero-to-five-year range and designed to give incentives to the inmate to qualify for release as early as possible. Prison authorities were given great discretion to determine when, or if, a prisoner had become reformed and thus qualified for release. Three grade levels were used, wherein each inmate was considered second grade when he arrived at Elmira. If he earned nine marks each month for six months he could be moved up to first grade; six more months in that grade earned him release on parole. Points were earned by completing school assignments, participating in vocational training, religious programs, and prison industry labor, and by general good behavior. If the inmate did not cooperate or caused difficulties by quarreling, disregarding the rules, demonstrating indifference to progress, a lack of self-control, or dishonesty, he would be moved to a grade three. In order to move back up to grade two it was necessary for the inmate to compile three months of satisfactory behavior. Then the climb back toward qualifying for release would begin again.

Brockway's indeterminate sentences and grading system, which rewarded inmates for progress, led to the first real parole system in the United States. The program was actually a conditional release system that required each released inmate to report regularly to volunteers known as guardians. By 1901, his model was being copied by many state prison systems.

Brockway's reported successes at Elmira were widely praised. His own reports and writings claimed a success rate over 80 percent. He was recognized by his contemporaries as a leading figure in the field of penology, and today his strong emphasis on the reformation of offenders places him among the most notable of prison wardens in the checkered history of American corrections.

In 1900, Brockway retired. He served in various charitable and public offices until his death in 1920. He was a charter member of the National Prison Association, the forerunner of the Annual Congress of Correction, serving as president in 1898. In 1912 his autobiography, *Fifty Years of Prison Service*, was published.

Patrick R. Anderson

See also ELMIRA REFORMATORY

Bibliography

Barnes, H. E., and N. K. Teeters (1943). *New Horizons in Criminology: The American Crime Problem*. New York: Prentice-Hall.

Bates, S. (1938). *Prisons and Beyond*. New York: Macmillan.

Clear, T. R., and G. F. Cole (1994). *American Corrections*. 3rd ed. Belmont, Calif.: Wadsworth.

McKelvey, B. (1936). *American Prisons*. Chicago: University of Chicago Press (Reprinted Montclair, N.J.: Patterson Smith, 1977).

Building Tenders

Building Tenders (BTs) have been a part of American prisons since the late nineteenth century. A building tender was an inmate who, in return for some direct or indirect benefits, assisted correctional officials in controlling the inmate population. Historically, the BT has served in various roles within the prison system. At some times the BT had absolute control over inmates, while at others he served under the tight and watchful eye of both the correctional officer and the warden. Regardless of the style of supervision imposed by the BT over prisoners, the central element associated with inmate control was force; in some cases, that force was brutal.

The degree to which inmate control was given to the BT was dependent upon many factors. For example, prior to the mid-1900s there were times when the prison population was far in excess of the ability of the staff to manage. In addition, institutions were understaffed and underfunded. To deal with a growing inmate population under conditions of scarcity meant that informal practices were necessary to control the prison. Thus BTs became an essential element in supervising prisoners. In Louisiana there were only nineteen paid guards through 1952, and the more than two thousand inmates were regularly supervised by inmates. This convict guard force, numbering as many as six hundred at a time, was even given shotguns and rifles and orders to shoot anyone who attempted to escape. While the practice of using inmates to maintain order certainly saved money, it also contributed to brutality and the low morale in such institutions as Angola (Carleton 1971). Among the prisoners, BTs became respected and feared at the same time. They were both keeper and kept in a world that thrived on fear and intimidation as the primary elements of prisoner management.

To guarantee both prisoner and staff safety, information on the activities of troublesome prisoners required that clear lines of communication be created among the BTs, other pivotal inmates, and the guard staff. Early on, BTs served as collectors of information on the doings of the inmates. With that information, BTs were able to maintain a tenuous control over the prisoner population in a way that was consistent with the goals of the prison staff, most directly the guards in the housing "tanks." For their services, BTs were given better work assignments, promises of increased "good time," and, most important, they received the protection and support of the guards and other prison officials.

Although BTs were used in many states, particularly in the South, the most well known were perhaps in the Texas prison system. Being a BT prior to 1950 in the Texas prison system meant that one had absolute control over a segment of the inmate population, increased privileges, and total support and direction from those formally in charge of the prison. There was little formal control over the BTs or the BT system. That element of the prison system, however, was to change, beginning in the late 1940s.

With the appointment of O. B. Ellis as director of corrections in 1947, and later under George Beto in 1962, the Texas BT system came under more formal control by prison officials. Both Ellis and Beto stressed the importance of maintaining greater control over BTs. They believed in being selective as to who became a BT and about the conditions under which BTs operated. Through a system of greater supervision and control, the role and authority of BTs became more circumscribed. Ellis and Beto emphasized gaining tighter control over the prison, and they focused on the role of correctional staff in the direct supervision of prisoners (DiIulio 1987).

Between 1950 and 1980, BTs became firmly entrenched in both the informal and formal systems of inmate supervision in the Texas prisons. It was during that time that BTs became recognized as legitimate authority figures among prisoners. According to Crouch and Marquart (1989, 92), BTs were organized in a three-tier system. The first tier was composed of the "head" building tenders. They reported directly to the prison staff and ran their cell blocks without interference. The second tier consisted of "rank-and-file building tenders," "turnkeys," and "book keepers." Those inmates ran the tanks and served as a conduit between other inmates and the head building tenders. The final tier of the BT system consisted of "runners," "strikers," or "hit men." They provided menial services, such as supplying prisoners' needs, and did much of the janitorial work required in the cell blocks. In addition, they also maintained a physical presence to back up other BTs if needed (Crouch and Marquart 1989, 93).

More important, the BTs during that time were of direct service to the correctional staff in four specific ways. First, they were an integral part of the "snitch" system found in the prison. It was their responsibility to report unusual and unacceptable behavior on the part of prisoners in the general population. Most important to the BTs was information on any escape plans, work stoppages, or riots. Moreover, the BTs kept the correctional staff aware of homosexual behavior. In this way, the BTs fulfilled their primary objective: keeping peace and order in the cell blocks.

Second, the BTs assisted correctional officers with the day-to-day duties assigned to officers. Maintaining head counts, assisting in the delivery of meals, and protecting the officers during fights with prisoners were all examples of ways in which the BTs functioned as informal correctional officers. They worked directly with correctional staff to process the demands of inmates while meeting the larger goal of security within the institution.

BTs were also used as "mediators" in the prison setting. It was clear that prisoner violence was to be kept under control by the BTs. Often that meant employing coercion on other inmates. More often than not, however, BTs employed methods of negotiation to settle a dispute between inmates. If needed, however, physical violence was used when other methods of social control failed. It was clear that the BTs were in control of the cell block, and that on very few occasions did they report problems to correctional officers. They were expected to handle their own cell blocks.

Finally, the BTs were also considered managers of their cell blocks. That meant dealing with maintenance of the unit, educating prisoners (particularly new prisoners) about the rules of the tank, and then enforcing the rules. It was the enforcement of the rules that all inmates feared. BTs were allowed to employ any means necessary to enforce both the written and unwritten rules of the tank, and that was where physical violence was most likely to occur. BTs were given institutional license to impose the rules as they saw fit. Through fear, intimidation, and physical reprisal, the BTs kept control of the prisoner population while at the same time they met the needs of the prison administration for a predictable and stable prison (Crouch and Marquart 1989, 106).

With such power, the BTs ruled the tanks with impunity. The beatings and violence were considered acceptable institutional practices for inmates who were the most difficult to control. Yet during the early part of the 1970s, legal challenges to the BT system and its management practices were being considered by prisoners, civil libertarians, and the courts. In June of 1972, inmate David Ruiz filed a federal lawsuit challenging the living and working conditions in Texas prisons. A central element to his lawsuit was the role of BTs in the management and supervision of prisoners. Judge William Wayne Justice consolidated Ruiz's case with eight other prison cases into a class action suit against the Texas Department of Corrections (TDC) entitled *Ruiz v. Estelle* (Martin and Ekland-Olson 1987).

This case was to be one of the most controversial prison cases in American history. Judge Justice ordered sweeping changes in the way the TDC managed its prisons. He ordered more correctional officers hired and trained, that prison facilities be improved, and that the TDC restructure its entire approach and philosophy to inmate management. The TDC fought the judge's orders and extended the litigation over fifteen years. After numerous attempts to gain the compliance of the TDC with his orders, Judge Justice ordered that fines totaling $24 million a month be imposed against the TDC to ensure compliance. In 1987, after fifteen years of litigation, the TDC agreed to fully comply with the court's orders. Later, the judge rescinded contempt fines after what he called "remarkable progress" had been made on the part of corrections officials (Martin and Ekland-Olson 1987, xxix).

With the conclusion of *Ruiz v. Estelle*, the BT system came to an end. At the present time, the TDC is working to develop more legal and rational methods of managing and supervising prisoners. The *Ruiz* case had demonstrated how one prison system could be reformed and brought into line with modern correctional practices and legal requirements. As stated by Crouch and Marquart (1989, 237), it is unlikely that the Texas prison system will go back to the old BT system of prisoner supervision. Once institutionalized in a bureaucratic order, legal precedents are difficult to rescind. Yet, as with all social institutions, the law changes, and with these changes must come attendant modifications by those who run correctional institutions. This can be guaranteed only when "outside agencies . . . ensure that prison structures and practices remain in tune with evolving standards of prisoner treatment" (Crouch and Marquart 1989, 238). Future administrators in the Texas prison system will have to work with external groups to ensure that the BT system of prisoner supervision never again becomes an acceptable practice of institutional management.

Stan Stojkovic

See also TRUSTIES

Bibliography

Carleton, M. (1971). *Politics and Punishment*. Baton Rouge, La.: Louisiana State University Press.
Crouch, B. M., and J. W. Marquart (1989). *An Appeal to Justice: Litigated Reform of Texas Prisons*. Austin, Tex.: University of Texas Press.

DiIulio, J. J. (1987). *Governing Prisons: A Comparative Study of Correctional Management*. New York: Free Press.

Martin, S. J., and S. Ekland-Olson (1987). *Texas Prisons: The Walls Came Tumbling Down*. Austin, Tex.: Texas Monthly Press.

Cases

Ruiz v. Estelle, 503 F. Supp. 1265 (1980).

B

C

Chain Gangs

Sentences involving hard work have traditionally been used as both a punishment and a deterrent. Even prior to the building of penitentiaries in this country, statutes of the 1700s called for convicts to perform hard labor around the local city streets and country highways. Citizens were to observe their backbreaking efforts. Prisoners had their heads shaved and they wore "conspicuous multi-colored garb and were chained to their wheelbarrow." Conditions were so degrading that some prisoners expressed a preference for hanging rather than to continue on the chain gang. Citizens would often ridicule and curse prisoners, even throwing things at them while they worked. There were often fights. Sometimes prohibited items were passed to the convicts by sympathetic passersby. Humanitarian groups, such as the Philadelphia Society for Alleviating the Miseries of Public Prisons, sought to have laws passed that would put the errant into a more private, protective, and reforming environment—solitary confinement.

Discipline and hard work, however, followed the offender into the prison and have been the only consistent underlying themes of its operation. The purpose of adapting industrial models to early prisons was not only to offset expenses but also to instill a work ethic through hard labor. The state's frustration at its inability to make prisons profitable and fears about the mounting cost of caring for growing numbers of inmates led, particularly in the South and Southwest, to the leasing out of convicts to private employers.

Leasing all or a portion of the inmate population was begun by Kentucky in 1825, and soon Michigan, Missouri, Alabama, Indiana, Illinois, California, Nebraska, Montana, Wyoming, Oregon, Texas, and Louisiana all leased out inmates during the 1800s. Businesses had inmates building levees, mining, harvesting cotton and sugar cane, extracting turpentine, and working in brickyards and sawmills. Crews of inmates toiled in the sun, chained together at the ankle to prevent their escape. Conditions were brutal, and hundreds of prisoners died from beatings, disease, malnutrition, or in attempting escape. When leasing systems were abandoned because of their corruptness and brutality, state and local governments were once again faced with uncertainty about how to employ their prisoners. As outside businesses and unions spurred legislation to prohibit competition by prison industries, there were fewer options available for meaningful work.

For some states and counties, the answer was to use inmates on public works projects. The era of the automobile meant that inmates might be used to improve public roads. Although in 1923 all states except Rhode Island had specific laws allowing county convicts to be worked on public highways, chain gangs were used mostly in the South. States noted for their use of such inmate labor included Florida, Georgia, Louisiana, Virginia, North Carolina, Arkansas, Texas, Mississippi, and Alabama. Bureaucratic structures were altered to accommodate the need, and the manpower was allocated to fill it. In fact, at a time when North Carolina had over fifty county chain gangs, the legislature transferred the control of all prisoners sentenced to thirty days or less to the State Highway and Public Works Commission.

The assignment of prisoners to chain gangs spans a period of time from about 1910 to 1945. While some states originally sent only blacks to the road camps, there were soon

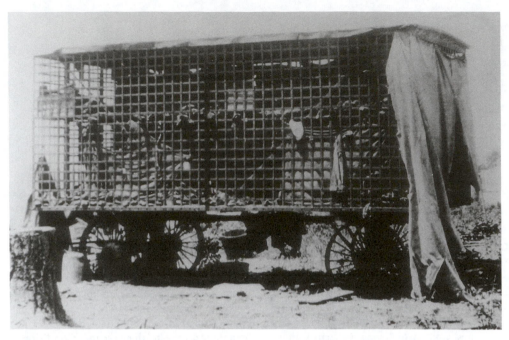

Inmates on the chain gang often slept closely packed in the same wagons they were transported in. Photo courtesy of the American Correctional Association.

separate crews of whites and blacks and eventually integrated units in many counties. Some separated felons from misdemeanants, most did not.

By some accounts, the chain gangs were profitable ventures. Georgia is alleged to have made over $3 million in a four-year period.

Sentences on the chain gang ranged from a few weeks to ten years. Besides constructing roads and bridges, the gangs filled potholes, cleared land, and repaired buildings. Convicts were transported between work sites in caged wagons where they also slept at night. The cages were usually seven to eight feet in width and eighteen feet long. Eighteen men were typically bunked in the cage with a night bucket, a pail of drinking water, and a stove. Most remained chained at night. As any movement would rattle the chains, a prisoner would have to yell "Gettin' up" to the guard and receive permission before rising from bed to use the bucket. The wagons were stuffy and dark when tarpaulins covered the sides in bad weather. Prisoners were likely to remain in the cages from noon Saturday until work resumed on Monday morning.

As one survivor of the Georgia chain gang explained, every meal was the same: a square of corn pone, three slices of fried pig fat, and a dose of sorghum. The only variation was that on holidays there were only two meals instead of three.

Prisoners often wore striped uniforms and were supervised by poorly paid and often sadistic armed guards. In some areas, inmates were promoted to trusties and given the task of tracking escaped prisoners. With the promise of reward money, the trusties shot as many "escapees" as they could. In some instances, escapes were fabricated and unsuspecting convicts were shot for the bounty.

Most of the work of the chain gang was done with a pick and a shovel. In some instances the prisoners were connected by an ankle iron to a chain attached to a belt. Others had both ankles clamped with steel bands with a twenty-inch chain between them. At night the chains could all be connected to a steel rod running the length of the sleeping area. In most cases it took a blacksmith to remove the chains; only a few trusties were without them.

For the prisoners, conditions remained much as they had been under the lease system. Life on the state and county chain gang continued to be brutal and treacherous. Most often out of the public view, convicts were worked from dawn to dusk with little nourishment and constant abuse. Flies and mosquitoes transmitted disease, as did the pits of open sewage and the communal wash basins, towels, and beds. Punishments for not working hard enough included flogging with a heavy leather whip, the sweatbox (a small coffinlike box with a single small air hole), and a diet of bread and water. Some inmates were fitted with iron collars or were forced to torture or beat fellow prisoners. The reputation of the chain gangs for their cruelty was so well known that when Robert Burns escaped from a Georgia crew and fled to New Jersey, that state's governor refused several attempts to have him extradited.

The use of chain gangs in the early 1900s seemed to be a return to the practice in the late 1700s of employing convicts in street labor. Reformists had hoped to end that practice by sentencing convicts to prison and jail. In North Carolina in 1926, the inmate road camp population was more than twice that of the state prison. There are even accounts of drunkards, hitchhikers, and travelers being arrested and forced into labor. The story of a drunken petty criminal who is sent to a chain gang, where he struggles against the oppression and is eventually killed, is the subject of the classic movie *Cool Hand Luke*, starring Paul Newman. Although some of the deaths from whippings drew public rebuke and resulted in scandals that instigated investigations and calls for reform, no meaningful monitoring system was ever developed.

The work available for chain gangs diminished when soldiers returning from war needed the civil-service, construction, and maintenance jobs to provide for their families. Some chain gangs were settled in permanent camps where work was ongoing and some crude buildings were erected. In some jurisdictions, inmate crews from minimum-security camps continued to work on road maintenance through the late 1960s.

Marilyn D. McShane

See also WORK PROGRAMS

Bibliography

Barnes, H. E., and N. K. Teeters (1945). *New Horizons in Criminology*. New York: Prentice-Hall.

Burns, R. E. (1932). *I Am a Fugitive from a Georgia Chain Gang!* New York: Vanguard.

Sellin, J. T. (1976). *Slavery and the Penal System*. New York: Elsevier.

Steiner, J. F., and R. M. Brown (1927). *The North Carolina Chain Gang*. Chapel Hill, N.C.: University of North Carolina Press (Reprinted Montclair, N.J.: Patterson Smith, 1969).

Wilson, W. (1933). *Forced Labor in the United States*. New York: International Publishers.

Chaplains

From their historical roots into the present, prisons have struggled with a mission that incorporates both retribution and reformation. When an Old Testament biblical theme of punishment and retribution is processed within a New Testament perspective of mercy and compassion, a degree of ambiguity is sure to follow (Johnson 1988). Factor into that uncertain mix the current reality of declining resources for prison treatment, education, recreation, and vocational programs, combined with increasing pessimism and fear from a public that often demands longer sentences. The result can easily lead to a diminished hope in corrections, and an increasing acceptance of prisons as little more than human warehouses.

From the 1800s on, before the myriad of mental health and human service specialists evolved, the one person typically standing in the center of such conflict and contradiction was the chaplain or minister (Schrink 1992).

Whether full-time or part-time, today's prison chaplain is supported by a variety of associations and organizations. One noteworthy example is the American Catholic Correctional Chaplains' Association (ACCCA). That professional association encourages competency in three basic areas, the personal, the theological, and the professional. The ACCCA, under the auspices of the United States Catholic Conference Commission on Certification and Accreditation, offers correctional chaplains the opportunity to be professionally certified in their field of expertise. The American Jewish Chaplains' Association provides counseling and support services for Jewish inmates. The Institute for Prison Ministries, which originates from the Billy Graham Center at Wheaton College, distributes books and video tapes on a variety of topics including conflict resolution. The Prison Fellowship, founded by Charles Colson, utilizes Christian volunteers to provide Christian training and support services for prisoners. The Salvation Army sponsors a chaplain of the year award at the annual meeting of the American Corrections Association. Clinical Pastoral Education (CPE), a nationally recognized accreditation body, is an integral part of many seminary chaplaincy programs.

What does a modern correctional chaplain do? There are a number of answers, including work in volunteer programs (such as Alcoholics Anonymous), institutional security, hostage situations, deathbed and funeral services, and issues regarding marriage during confinement, employee injury or death, the death or illness of an inmate's family members, special housing units such as protective custody or for AIDS patients, and the conduct of traditional religious services. A typical correctional facility may house inmates from a variety of religious faiths who may seek ministerial services. Religions may include those of Native American Indians, Protestant Christian churches, Sunnis, Muslims, Roman Catholics, Pentecostalists (Spanish and African-American), Jews, Buddhists, Jehovah Witnesses, and practitioners of Christian Science.

The image of a pastor delivering a weekly sermon from a pulpit does not adequately describe the focus of a typical correctional chaplain. Whether priest, minister, or rabbi, when working in a prison setting little time is spent in the pulpit. "They perform the bulk of their duties quietly, behind the scenes. Each day they offer spiritual hope to inmates who are lonely, depressed, and perhaps forgotten or denounced by loved ones on the outside. Joyful events, events such as weddings, bar mitzvahs, and baptisms play secondary roles in their ministries" (Acorn 1990, 97). While most chaplains in prison ministries believe that they are called to that particular work, many do not see their main purpose as saving lost souls. Rather, they accept their role as helping inmates change their lives to survive the reality of prison (Acorn 1990). Correctional chaplains may have to provide religious counseling and services to inmates whose religious beliefs are quite different from their own. Reverend Sandra Daley states, "The institutional chaplain's role is to be the religious support base for all religions—to manage a program that facilitates fairly, consistently and across the board the exercise of religious freedom for all authorized religions" (Acorn 1990, 98). Besides working with inmates and their families, correctional chaplains may also minister to correctional staff.

Chaplains not only provide vital institutional services, but they are also an important bridge to community involvement in prison ministries. The period between six and nine months after an inmate's release is a critical one for adjustment. J. Michael Quinlin, director of the Federal Bureau of Prisons, suggests three necessary elements to successfully reforming a criminal: (1) a well-run correctional facility; (2) the criminal's own will to change; and (3) involvement by people in the local community (Maxwell 1991). The correctional chaplain spans these three elements with both traditional and innovative services. For example, in Central Florida, Orange County Jail offers an alternative treatment program called "Genesis Building." Chaplains Dan Matsche and Hoby Freeman run a type of "spiritual boot camp" in Dorm A, or, as it is known, the Life Learning Dorm (Ewell-Hunt 1991). Chaplain Zeb Osborne is especially qualified because he himself has been an offender, serving twenty-seven years for various criminal offenses. Although a Christian chaplain, Osborne feels that his role as a servant-minister allows him to provide services to inmates of all faiths (Acorn 1991). The Liberation of Ex-Offenders through Employment Opportunities (LEEO) offers an innovative transitional ministry for offenders. LEEO attempts to integrate religious and secular values by focusing on work, especially with female offenders.

The approach used by LEEO is divided into three parts: (1) liberating the person; (2) liberating the system; and (3) liberating judgment. Issues such as relational power, self-perceptions, closed venues, open systems, and God as a merciful judge whose judgment in the present is for the sake of the future are incorporated in this innovative program (Schloegel and Kinast 1988).

It is ironic that, in an age of declining resources, one of the most important correctional agents, the chaplain, is often viewed as the most expendable. Perhaps the situation is similar to that regarding ministers generally: Those called by God to serve need not be paid like the rest of us, or, in difficult economic times, not paid at all. Nevertheless, the correctional chaplain is both the contemporary helping professional and the ancient time-honored minister who represents humanity in the correctional setting.

Michael C. Braswell
Marian H. Whitson

See also RELIGION IN PRISON

Bibliography

Acorn, L. (1990). The challenges of ministering to a captive congregation. *Corrections Today* 52(7): 97–98, 106.

Acorn, L. (1991). Jacob Hoenig: New York chaplain serves all faiths. *Corrections Today* 53(6): 24–25.

Ewell-Hunt, A. (1991). Jailhouse flock. *Christianity Today* (April 8): 19–20.

Johnson, H. (1988). *History of Criminal Justice*. Cincinnati, Ohio: Anderson.

Maxwell, J. (1991). Getting out, staying out. *Christianity Today* (July 22): 4–36.

Schloegel, J. M. J., and R. L. Kinast (1988). *From Cell to Society*. Grand Rapids, Mich.: W. B. Eeerdmans.

Schrink, J. (1992). Understanding the correctional counselor. In D. Lester, M. Braswell, and P. Van Voorhis, eds. *Correctional Counseling*. 2nd ed. Cincinnati, Ohio: Anderson.

Children of Prisoners

I. Mothers' Issues

There are an estimated 1.5 million children of incarcerated parents in the United States (Center for Children of Incarcerated Parents 1992). Although no official data exist, a recent study by the National Council on Crime and Delinquency (NCCD) conservatively estimates that on any given day in 1991 there were more than 167,000 children nationally whose mothers were behind bars. Approximately three-fourths of those children were under the age of eighteen. Additionally, the number of children of former prisoners may be as much as ten times greater. A study by the Center for Children of Incarcerated Parents in Pasadena, California, found that more than 78 percent of the participants in its Therapeutic Intervention Project (TIP) had a parent who was previously, or is currently, in prison.

When a mother is punished through incarceration, her children are punished as well—by the separation, by the ensuing lack of contact, and in some cases by permanent severance of the parent-child relationship. Unfortunately, there continues to be a glaring lack of awareness of and concern for these invisible victims. The punishment that these children suffer may not be intentional, but that does not diminish its effect. By its very nature, imprisonment has an adverse impact on mother-infant bonding. In most instances, mothers are allowed to spend only several days with their babies after delivery. Essential bonding cannot occur in such a short period of time, and that has serious implications on the future mother-child relationship (McGowan and Blumenthal 1978; Bloom and Steinhart 1993).

Issues Regarding the Children of Inmate Mothers

There is a growing body of medical, psychological, and sociological literature that supports the need to preserve the parent-child relationship. Many experts have concluded that contact between children and their incarcerated mothers is beneficial and that severance of those parental rights may have long-term detrimental effects on children. The harm done to children can be sudden and substantial, and there are immediate and sometimes long-lasting psychological effects. Peer relations and school performance may suffer. The mother-child relationship may be permanently damaged, and the child may be placed at greater risk of future involvement in the criminal justice system.

A number of studies have documented that children of incarcerated parents suffer emotional stress related to the separation caused by a parent's imprisonment (Sack et al. 1976; McGowan and Blumenthal 1978; Stanton 1980; Sametz 1980; Fishman 1982). They often exhibit anxiety, depression, aggression, and learning disorders. More recent research indicates that some children of prisoners may suffer from post-traumatic stress syndrome.

The prevailing literature maintains that children are often traumatized by the arrest and imprisonment of their mothers. Additionally, in many cases, the forced separation from their mothers because of imprisonment is itself a cause of trauma to children.

The Center for Children of Incarcerated Parents reported that children of offenders are "by history and current behavior, the most likely among their peers to enter the criminal justice system." The study found that these children begin to demonstrate emotional reactions to the events of their lives at a very young age. Many express anger, defiance, irritability, and aggression. By preadolescence, these children express such behavior in school through disruption, poor performance, and truancy.

The center's data suggest that there may be three major factors that place these children at greater risk than their peers: (1) they are traumatized by events relating to a parent's crime and arrest; (2) they are more vulnerable as a result of the separation from their parent; and (3) they experience inadequate care because of extreme poverty.

Most children of imprisoned mothers live with relatives, particularly maternal grandparents. Some children, however, are placed in foster homes or institutions. In some cases, siblings are separated by out-of-family placements. These factors may also contribute to future criminality.

Issues and Concerns of Imprisoned Mothers

Since 1980, the number of women imprisoned in the United States has nearly tripled. Over fifty thousand women are currently incarcerated in our nation's state and federal prisons, and approximately 76 percent of these imprisoned women are mothers of at least two children under the age of eighteen.

The average mother in prison is thirty years old, undereducated, and unemployed at the time of her arrest. She is most likely African American or Hispanic, and is more likely than her male counterpart to be the primary caretaker and to have legal custody of her children before entering the criminal justice system. She has a history of substance abuse dating back to her early teenage years, and other members of her family have been incarcerated. She has been the victim of physical, emotional, or sexual abuse. An incarcerated mother is most often serving a sentence for drug law or property violations. She is likely to have committed a crime to pay for drugs or to support herself and her children.

When mothers go to prison, they face tremendous obstacles in maintaining contact with their children, and also in reunifying their families once they are released. During incarceration, mothers tend to suffer emotionally because of their separation from their children. Most incarcerated mothers do not see their children regularly, and they have significantly fewer visits from their children than do their male counterparts. When a man goes to prison, the mother of his children often keeps the family intact, bringing the children to visit him and continuing to provide for the children. In contrast, when a mother goes to prison, the father does not usually assume primary care of the children or maintain the family relationships.

Bloom and Steinhart (1993) found that over 54 percent of the children of imprisoned mothers *never* visited their mothers during the term of incarceration. Women's prisons are usually located in rural areas far from urban centers and are often inaccessible by public transportation. Family members often cannot afford to pay for frequent travel to the prison, or even, in some cases, for collect telephone calls from the mother to her children. In many cases, letters are the most common form of contact between a mother and her family. Additionally, relatives or foster parents may be reluctant to bring children to the prison because of their negative feelings about the criminal behavior of the mother or their views that prisons are bad places for children.

Information about the caretakers of the children of incarcerated women is limited, at best. For the most part, when a mother is convicted her children are placed with relatives or friends. The NCCD data illustrate that most children of incarcerated women were living with relatives (80 percent of the cases). Maternal grandmothers over fifty years old were the most frequent caretakers, followed by other relatives and the children's fathers. More than 7 percent of the children were in foster care.

Nearly 9 percent of the female prisoners reported giving birth while in prison. Of those mothers, 67 percent stated that their infants went to live with relatives. A small percentage of the children were placed in foster care (3.5 percent) or adopted (1.8 percent).

Termination of Parental Rights

Although a mother's incarceration alone should not precipitate the termination of her parental rights, that does occur in some cases, particularly for a mother who is confined for a long time. At least twenty-five states have termination of parental rights or adoption statutes that explicitly pertain to incarcerated parents.

Permanent loss of parental rights during imprisonment can occur in several ways. First, when a child is in the care and custody of the state, or in foster care, the state may bring a judicial proceeding to terminate the parent's rights permanently. Once parental rights have been terminated, the parent loses all right to contact with her child, who can then be adopted without the parent's knowledge or consent.

Second, parental rights may be lost through adoption of children who are not in foster care. For example, if a parent who is not

Providing familiar surroundings for play helps to promote bonds between incarcerated parents and their children during visits. Photo by CVP. Used with permission of the American Correctional Association.

incarcerated has custody of the child and remarries and the new spouse or stepparent wishes to adopt the child, that necessitates terminating the parental rights of the incarcerated parent. Even if the incarcerated parent does not consent to the adoption, termination proceedings can go forward if the parent has had no contact with the child.

Traditional foster care placement is poorly equipped to deal with the growing population of incarcerated mothers who are serving lengthy sentences. It cannot handle the situation of an imprisoned mother who has an ongoing relationship with her child but is unable to resume custody for many years.

Child welfare laws provide for termination of parental rights if the incarcerated mother, who lacks the freedom to maintain consistent contact, has failed to sustain an adequate relationship with her child in foster care (usually for twelve to eighteen months). Child welfare laws also require periodic court reviews of the child's progress in foster care, but an incarcerated mother may have no opportunity to attend these review hearings.

Instead of intervening to permanently sever the bonds between mother and child,

the state should work toward preserving and strengthening family relationships whenever possible. Providing effective reunification services to incarcerated mothers and their children is not an easy task because it involves the coordination of a number of governmental bodies and social systems. Nonetheless, incarcerated mothers whose children are in foster care are entitled to receive reunification services during imprisonment.

Nationwide, correctional policy and programs give only minimal consideration to maintaining the mother-child relationship, and the sad fact remains that no one in the criminal justice system has official responsibility for the children of female inmates. In some states, however, the administrators of prisons for women are increasingly aware of the problems of incarcerated mothers. For example, the superintendent of the Bedford Hills Correctional Facility in New York works closely with organizations that help to maintain such mother-child relationships. There is also some attempt at coordinating visits and support services with child welfare agencies. Current efforts by criminal justice and social service agencies to provide effective services to the children of incarcerated women often do not consider the true costs of the multigenerational aspect of crime. They also often fail to ensure that their programs and services are consistent and coordinated with community services. Such coordination of efforts by state, county, and community-based agencies is essential to improving the programs and services delivered to children of incarcerated mothers.

Innovative Programs for Incarcerated Mothers and Their Children

Programs that encourage contact between mothers in prison and their children are gaining popularity. A range of such programs exist inside and outside of prisons across the nation. Such programs include children's centers, programs that promote prison visits and inmate-family support, and community-based alternatives to incarceration specifically designed for women and their children.

Children's Centers provide environments that encourage the reestablishment and strengthening of the relationship between an imprisoned parent and the child. The centers are usually set up in a separate location, away from the prison visiting area.

The California-based Prison MATCH (Mothers and Their Children) program created a model that combines a supportive, child-centered environment with social service assistance for the family and "parenting" training for the inmate. Jails and prisons across the country have implemented programs similar to Prison MATCH, such as Project REACH in Georgia, the MOLD Program in Nebraska, PACT in Fort Worth, Texas, and PATCH in Missouri.

Community-based programs aimed at maintaining family relationships by promoting prison visits help children stay in touch with their incarcerated parents. Organizations such as Centerforce and Friends Outside in California, and Outside Connection in Kansas, do much to champion visiting support services. Aid to Imprisoned Mothers (AIM) in Atlanta, Georgia, provides an intergenerational model of service that targets imprisoned mothers, their children, and the relatives who care for the children.

New York State has the only prison nursery program in the country that allows mothers to keep their infants with them in prison. The nursery at the Bedford Hills Correctional Facility, the first such program in the United States, houses female inmates who have given birth while in prison. Mothers and their infants can stay together until the child's first birthday, or longer if the mother's release is imminent. The program is closely tied to the Parenting and Children's Center at Bedford Hills.

Since the majority of women in prison are minimum-security, nonviolent offenders, they are good candidates for nonincarcerative programs. Community-based alternatives to incarceration for women and their children offer a healthful, supportive community setting while providing comprehensive services for the mothers and their children. Some programs focus on pregnant, drug-dependent women. For example, Social Justice for Women in Boston created an innovative approach to alternative placement for such women and their infants. The emphasis of the program, named Neil J. Houston House, is on prenatal care, substance abuse treatment, and supportive services for the mothers and their infants.

The California Community Prisoner Mother Program (also known as the Mother-Infant Care Program) is legislatively mandated. Mothers and their young children live in community-based settings where mothers participate in parenting classes, education and vocational training, substance abuse counseling, and life skills preparation.

Conclusion

When mothers are incarcerated they do not automatically relinquish their parental roles, obligations, or concerns. Although they may be separated from their children, they continue to care about their well-being. Ultimately, most reunite with their families.

Consequently, it is of vital importance to maintain the integrity of the family whenever possible. Commissioner Robert Little, child welfare administrator of New York City, believes that we should be developing the strengths of these families rather than focusing on their weaknesses. He states: "We treat families as if they are criminals who have only negatives, but we know that children grow best in the context of the family."

Coordinated efforts should be made by the criminal justice and child welfare systems to ensure that mothers and their children are able to sustain their relationships. Whenever possible, alternatives to incarceration should be considered so that women can maintain their family ties. If we continue to ignore the plight of women prisoners and their children, generations to come will suffer the consequences.

Barbara Bloom

See also CONTACT VISITS, VISITATION, AND WOMEN INMATES

Bibliography

American Correctional Association (1990). *The Female Offender: What Does the Future Hold?* Washington, D.C.: St. Mary's.

Austin, J., B. Bloom, and T. Donahue (1992). *Female Offenders in the Community: An Analysis of Innovative Strategies and Programs.* Washington, D.C.: National Institute of Corrections.

Baunach, P. J. (1985). *Mothers in Prison.* New Brunswick, N.J.: Transaction.

Bloom, B., and D. Steinhart (1993). *Why Punish the Children? A Reappraisal of the Children of Incarcerated Mothers in America.* San Francisco, Calif.: National Council on Crime and Delinquency.

Center for Children of Incarcerated Parents (1992). *Report No. 6: Children of Offenders.* Pasadena, Calif.: Pacific Oaks College and Children's Programs.

Fishman, S. H. (1982). The impact of incarceration on children of offenders. *Journal of Children in Contemporary Society* 15: 89–99.

McGowan, B. G., and K. L. Blumenthal (1978). *Why Punish the Children? A Study of Children of Women Prisoners.* Hackensack, N.J.: National Council on Crime and Delinquency.

Sack, W. H., J. Seidler, and S. Thomas (1976). The children of imprisoned parents: A psychosocial explanation. *American Journal of Orthopsychiatry* 46: 618–28.

Sametz, L. (1980). Children of incarcerated women. *Social Work* 25: 298–303.

Stanton, A. M. (1980). *When Mothers Go to Jail.* Lexington, Mass.: Lexington.

II. Fathers' Issues

Recent estimates indicate that approximately two-thirds of state prisoners and three-quarters of federal prisoners are fathers. According to 1991 U.S. Department of Justice prison population figures, approximately 500,000 men in state and federal prisons have children. Identifying issues of concern to that large population would appear to offer an opportunity for inter-ventions designed to assist prisoners in and after release from prison.

Previous Studies

Most of the existing research in the area of incarceration and family relationships focuses on mothers. And most studies about incarcerated men deal only tangentially with the issue of fatherhood. The primary focus typically is the prisoner's relationship with his family as a whole and how that association is linked with his adjustment to prison life or his eventual rehabilitation. In short, the problems of prisoners as fathers have received little attention from researchers.

There are several notable exceptions to this lack of focus on fathers in prison. Those studies deal with father-child interaction (Lanier 1991), family characteristics and the rearing of children (Hairston 1989; Morris 1967), affective states of incarcerated fathers (Lanier 1993), and programs on child rearing ("parenting") for imprisoned fathers (Hairston and Lockett 1985; Lanier and Fisher 1989, 1990). Still, research on this sizable subgroup of the prison population is largely absent from the literature.

Issues of Concern to Incarcerated Fathers

Notwithstanding the lack of focus on fathers in prison, a wide range of issues concerning fathers in prison have been identified. Those concerns may be legal, economic, practical/environmental, affective/emotional, or involve relationship issues. Many of them are influenced by the length of the parental relationship before imprisonment, the length of the father's prison sentence, and the degree of support from other family members outside prison. Many of the issues of concern to incarcerated fathers are similar to those dealt with outside of prison by divorced or separated fathers who live apart from their children.

Legal Issues. Fathers who attempt to secure their legal rights while incarcerated confront two problems: competent representation and the perception that contact with an imprisoned parent is not in a child's best interest. Still, incarcerated fathers do engage in "visitation contests," challenge adoption proceedings, and litigate foster care issues, especially when the child's mother is dead or also in prison. Fathers in prison also may confront situations in which their partner moves out of state or requests a termination of the father's parental rights.

Economic Issues. Incarcerated fathers generally are dependent on friends and family members outside the prison for economic support. For some, that is a reversal of their previous role as economic provider. Fathers in prison are unable to provide for the basic needs of their families, let alone for transportation or other needs. Some men are forced to watch helplessly as their families turn to public assistance for survival. Other special needs may include the money for family members to travel to the prison for visits or with which to make telephone calls home. Fathers also lack money for birthday, Christmas, and other special gifts for their families.

Practical/Environmental Issues. One of the most difficult situations confronting fathers in prison is explaining to their children about their incarceration. The difficulty may arise from feelings of embarrassment on the part of the father, or from misguided attempts by other family members to protect the children from knowledge of a parent's criminality. In many instances, though, incarcerated fathers have no communication with their children, either because of an intransigent caregiver or because the whereabouts of the children are unknown to the father.

Visiting conditions also prove frustrating to fathers who want to see their children. Visiting often involves waiting on long lines for processing, and there are often no facilities for small children. Visiting rooms themselves are uncomfortable, and often lack toys or other activities designed to engage visiting children. Security concerns may lead to oppressive regulations, such as no running around or no sitting on a parent's lap, and generally create an atmosphere that is inhospitable to children.

Affective/Emotional Issues. Fathers in prison are affected emotionally in a number of ways. Many incarcerated fathers experience depression, anxiety, and lowered levels of self-esteem. Feelings of loss, powerlessness, and sadness, as well as sickness, afflict many men who are separated from their children by the walls of a prison. Many fathers direct their anger and hostility inward, in an attempt to punish themselves for what they have done to their children's lives.

Guilt plagues many incarcerated fathers. Some men feel guilty about the disruption they have caused in their children's lives. Some also feel responsible when their children engage in delinquency or use drugs or alcohol. Many fathers express an awareness that they are responsible for the problems experienced by their children at home, in the community, and at school. Fathers in prison often express guilt over missed opportunities to spend time together with their children before imprisonment, and at not fulfilling their parental role.

Fathers also express confusion over their seemingly contradictory roles as parents and as prisoners. Many never see themselves as parents but rather accept roles more familiar to them, such as those of addicts or criminals. Some fathers in prison long to be responsible parents, yet feel that the prison walls keep them from performing their parental obligations and responsibilities. Fathers also are concerned about the possibility that their children are at home with someone who is emotionally unstable, and about the potential for physical or emotional abuse in the father's absence.

Relationship Issues. Some incarcerated fathers worry about their children's lack of guidance or spiritual upbringing. Fathers also worry about being forgotten by their children, or about being replaced by another person, such as a stepfather. Some worry that their children will want to stop coming to see them, which in turn might lead to their children's alienation from them by the time they are released. Some also are troubled by thoughts that their children might believe that their father abandoned them and worry about losing their children's respect.

Circumstances after release present additional concerns for the incarcerated father. For example, a man nearing release may worry about reentering a family that has become fully independent and accustomed to living and making decisions without him. Others are concerned about losing their spouse or partner. When that occurs, fathers may leave prison to find themselves isolated from their children. Men who participate in parenting programs while in prison also express concern about the imbalance in such education between themselves and their partners.

Programs for Fathers in Prison
There has been no extensive research regarding the attitudes of prison administrators or correctional personnel toward programs for fathers in prison. Some correctional authorities

suggest, though, that fathers' needs can be met within substance abuse or other therapeutic programs that deal in part with the family. It appears that, in large measure, prison officials do not take a direct interest in designing and implementing programs for incarcerated fathers. Most existing programs are developed at the institutional level rather than at the central office level, indicating a lack of awareness on the part of upper-level correctional administrators of the problems faced by incarcerated fathers.

Notwithstanding the decentralized approach to such programs, many strategies currently exist for assisting incarcerated fathers. These programs have been developed by community organizations, academics, prisoners, and correctional employees, acting either alone or together. Many programs function for a specified period of time (such as ten weeks), during which a specific curriculum is completed. Others propose ongoing educational and therapeutic settings in which prisoners with sentences of varying lengths can remain engaged. Generally, most programs consist of a combination of education and therapy (group or individual counseling).

Parents in Prison is a program in the Tennessee State Prison for Men designed to eliminate the potential for child abuse and neglect by prisoners after their release. The leadership of the program is shared among prisoners, community members, and institutional personnel. The program involves home-study courses, structured classroom courses, a monthly special event or rap session, and occasional special projects such as summer picnics or a Christmas banquet. The program involves community members as guest speakers, and focuses on family needs both during and after incarceration.

Project HIP (Helping Incarcerated Parents) is a federally funded collaborative effort involving prisoners, the Maine Department of Corrections, and the Human Services Development Institute at the Southern University of Maine. The long-term goals of the program are to prevent child abuse and neglect and to decrease recidivism. The program includes parenting classes, parent-child workshops under the guidance of child-development specialists, and mutual support meetings. Project HIP serves female as well as male prisoners.

One program for incarcerated fathers, originally developed by prisoners, was adopted by the Family Services Office of the New York State Department of Correctional Services. The program, called the Eastern Fathers' Group, consists of three components: a mutual support group, monthly educational seminars, and a formal parenting course. The program was designed to assist all prisoners, regardless of sentence length, by providing both information and coping strategies developed to help people deal with the loss of family relationships. The program also unites imprisoned fathers with their partners outside prison in joint informational/therapeutic encounters. This program model provides a cost-effective, practical strategy for helping incarcerated fathers.

Another parenting program designed by prisoners is the Parent Occupational Program (POP). This program was designed to strengthen relationships between incarcerated fathers and their children. Another goal of the program is to help prevent child abuse and neglect. Participants take part in a ten-week cycle of parenting classes that covers such topics as child development, parenting skills, and the teaching of values to children. The educational component is supplemented by a support group that meets on alternate weeks for a period of twelve weeks.

PACT (Parents And Children Together) is a parenting program at the Federal Correctional Institute in Fort Worth, Texas, that has been in operation since 1984. Its leadership is composed of prisoners, community members, and institutional staff members, and its primary objective is to prevent future criminality. The three major components of the program are a children's center, which provides a positive atmosphere for father-child interactions; parenting classes, including sessions on employment, self-esteem, values, and family and marriage relationships; and social services assistance, such as help in reuniting families or contacting attorneys for custody matters.

Although never implemented, the proposal for a Prisoners' Parenting Center (PPC) is the most comprehensive and ambitious program model for incarcerated fathers. The PPC was developed by prisoners in New York and was designed to assist in the voluntary socialization and moral development of the offender, while at the same time improving the quality of life for children whose fathers are in prison. The PPC program model includes five essential components to achieve its three goals. The program includes individual counseling by a professionally trained director, regularly scheduled mutual support groups, formal parenting classes, access to parenting-education resources, and highlighted monthly issues. The PPC utilizes both educational and therapeutic techniques in an effort to maximize the assistance available to incarcerated parents.

Fathers in Prison: A Research Agenda

Fathers in prison constitute a large and important subgroup of the prison population. Acquiring information to improve support activities will serve not only the incarcerated father but also his family and correctional personnel. Future investigation should accurately assess the number of fathers imprisoned in state and federal institutions. Additional research could focus on the similarities and the differences between mothers and fathers who serve prison sentences. Differences among parents of various racial and ethnic backgrounds also need to be examined.

Future study should explore what importance fathers in prison attach to their parental role. Research should assess the nature of not only the incarcerated parent's current relationship with his children, but preimprisonment relationships as well. Future research also should examine what impact the length of separation has on the father-child relationship, with particular emphasis on the effects of long-term imprisonment.

Other questions remain unanswered. Tracking the progress over time of both those fathers who remain in prison and those who have been released would help to discern whether a link exists between the father-child relationship, institutional adjustment, and recidivism. Also worthy of attention are prison-based studies that continue to explore the association between the father-child relationship and affective states. Research also could discover how parents deal with issues concerning their children during the period of the father's imprisonment. Another project might involve querying mothers or the children of incarcerated fathers to ascertain the family's ideas about maintaining a relationship with the imprisoned parent.

An attempt to assess the nature and scope of parenting programs for male prisoners also should be undertaken. Such a study should both document current programs for incarcerated fathers (in terms of program goals, components, activities, length, client criteria) in state and federal prisons across the country, and provide a nationwide directory of addresses and contacts for each program. The attitudes of prison administrators and personnel regarding incarcerated fathers is another area worthy of study. The perspectives of prison administrators on the problems confronting imprisoned fathers will be critical in the development and implementation of programs for that population.

Summary

A comprehensive and thorough research agenda would help prison officials manage their incarcerated wards by meeting the special needs of this large population. Focusing on prisoners' parental roles and obligations also would help prison administrators deal with increasingly diverse prison populations, by capitalizing on a common concern that affects a significant number of prisoners. Moreover, support services have been linked to improved prisoner adjustment. Because community services often are available to help support parents in prison, correctional administrators also could benefit by promoting successful programs with relatively little effort and at small expense.

Activities and programs perceived as worthwhile are most likely to make prisoners want to participate, and they offer the best chance for producing positive changes in prisoners' attitudes and behavior. Fathers can obtain help and receive the support they need while in prison. The children of prisoners also can benefit by improved relationships with their fathers. Mothers, by their association, can benefit as well. An increase in support may help strengthen the family unit, and perhaps decrease the potential for problems among the children.

Encouraging incarcerated fathers to focus on their parental roles may increase their potential for personal, reflective decision-making once they are released. Such prisoners may begin to consider the ramifications of their actions not only on their own lives, but on their children's lives as well. An institutional focus on and general approval of the parental role of prisoners, then, may encourage socially constructive values in incarcerated fathers who then can responsibly transmit prosocial attitudes to a future generation.

Charles S. Lanier

See also CONTACT VISITS, VISITATION

Bibliography

Hairston, C. F. (1989). Men in prison: Family characteristics and parenting views. *Journal of Offender Counseling, Services, and Rehabilitation* 14: 23–30.

Hairston, C. F., and P. Lockett (1985). Parents in prison: A child abuse and neglect prevention strategy. *Child Abuse and Neglect* 9: 471–77.

Lanier, C. S. (1991). Dimensions of father-child interaction in a New York state prison population. *Journal of Offender Rehabilitation* 16(3/4): 27–42.

Lanier, C. S. (1993). Affective states of fathers in prison. *Justice Quarterly* 10: 51–68.

Lanier, C. S., and G. Fisher (1989). The Eastern fathers' group: An educational and mutual support program for incarcerated fathers. In S. Duguid, ed. *Yearbook of Correctional Education: 1989.* Burnaby, B.C.: Institute for the Humanities, Simon Fraser University.

Lanier, C. S., and G. Fisher (1990). A prisoners' parenting center (PPC): A promising resource strategy for incarcerated fathers. *Journal of Correctional Education* 41(4): 158–65.

Morris, P. (1967). Fathers in prison. *British Journal of Criminology* 7: 424–30.

Civil Rights of Institutionalized Persons Act

The Statutory Language of the Act—42 USC 1997 (1980)

The Civil Rights of Institutionalized Persons Act authorizes actions for redress in cases involving the deprivation of rights secured or protected by the Constitution or laws of the United States. Included among the institutions are mental institutions, nursing homes, jails, prisons, and juvenile facilities.

The three main components of the act can be summarized as follows:

1. The United States attorney general may institute a civil action in a U.S. District Court against a party he has reasonable cause to believe is violating the act, in order to ensure that corrective measures are taken (42 USC 1997a).

2. Inmates must first "exhaust the internal prison grievance" process prior to personally filing a lawsuit under the act. This permits a federal court to continue an inmate action filed under 42 USC 1983 (commonly referred to as a 1983 federal civil rights action), for a period not to exceed ninety days, so that an opportunity is available to resolve the matter informally through a prison grievance system (42 USC 1997e(a)(1)).

3. It must be certified that state inmate "grievance systems" follow specified minimum standards. The U.S. attorney general or the applicable U.S. district court must determine that state administrative remedies (prison grievance systems) are in "substantial compliance" with the minimum acceptable standards. If not, a court will not permit a ninety-day continuance to resolve a 42 USC 1983 action (42 USC 1997e (b)(2)).

History and Politics

In 1967, the President's Commission on Law Enforcement and the Administration of Justice recommended grievance procedures for prisoners. It argued that offenders "should always have administrative recourse for grievances against officials . . . and the adequacy of this recourse should be subject to review by some outside authority" (Cory 1982b, 23). The 1971 Attica riot was the catalyst for instituting grievance procedures. A 1980 study conducted for the National Institute of Corrections disclosed that approximately three-fourths of the state and local corrections systems questioned had initiated a grievance process after the riot (Cory 1982b, 24). At the time of the act, approximately forty-seven states had already established inmate grievance-resolution systems, and the vast majority of the nation's largest jails had similar procedures. The federal prison system started its grievance process in 1974 (Cory 1982b, 22). It is important to note, however, that the Civil Rights of Institutionalized Persons Act does not pertain to federal correctional institutions (the U.S. Bureau of Prisons), which have their own inmate internal-grievance process.

Prior to the passage of the act, the federal courts and various state attorneys general were concerned about the mounting number of inmate suits filed under section 1983 of the federal Civil Rights Act of 1871 (Cory 1982a). A 1983 action is filed when an individual believes that his constitutional rights have been violated by a state official. For instance, a prisoner may file a 1983 action over inadequate medical care or other conditions of confinement believed to be in violation of civil rights guarantees.

The case of *Patsey v. Florida Board of Regents* traced the legislative history of the act. Normally, exhaustion of administrative remedies is not required as a precondition of maintaining a 1983 action, and the congressional debates involved discussion as to whether it would be appropriate to carve out a narrow exception to that rule. After considerable debate, Congress decided to adopt the limited "exhaustion requirement" of section 1997e in order to relieve the burden on the federal courts. This diverted certain prisoner petitions back through state and local institutions and also encouraged the states to develop appropriate grievance procedures. The "exhaustion requirement" is expressly limited to section 1983 actions brought by an adult convicted of a crime. Congress also hoped that section 1997e would improve prison conditions by stimulating the development of successful grievance mechanisms.

Prisoners' rights advocates objected strenuously to the exhaustion provision, which they felt was "designed to treat prisoners differently from all other citizens in the United States, institutionalized or not." They argued that "granting the attorney general the authority to vindicate the rights of institutionalized persons, and in the same statute imposing an exhaustion requirement on private civil suits by prisoners, is an unnecessary and unacceptable tradeoff" (Cory 1982a, 25).

Attorney General Civil Actions under the Act

The first action brought by the Department of Justice was in 1983, against two Hawaiian state prisons. The suit charged that the conditions at the prisons violated the constitutional rights of the prisoners (citing a "pattern or practice" of ten alleged violation areas) and subjected them to cruel and unusual punishment. The Department of Justice decided to sue after Hawaiian officials denied them access to the two prisons. That 1983 case was only one of twenty-six other investigations of alleged violations of the act that were underway at the time. Subsequently, other actions by the attorney general were brought against the Michigan State Prison system; the Newark, New Jersey City Jail; a Talladega, Alabama jail, and at least one juvenile facility.

Certification of "Prison Grievance Programs" under 1997e

The attorney general conditionally certified Virginia's grievance procedure in late 1982, giving Virginia the distinction of being the first state to conform with the provisions of the act relative to establishing programs that were in "substantial compliance" with the minimum standards (Turk 1983).

The minimum standards of the act (set out at 28 CFR 40) call for the following:

1. An advisory role by both employees and inmates relative to the grievance system.
2. Time limits for written replies to a grievance.
3. Priority processing of grievances of an emergency nature.
4. Safeguards to avoid reprisals against any grievant.
5. An independent review of the disposition of grievances by a person or entity not under the supervision or direct control of the institution.

Lay (1986, 937), a U.S. court of appeals judge, in examining the question of state certification, indicated that "although use of state grievance procedures allows less federal involvement in the administration of correctional institutions and saves states the time and expense of defending 1983 Actions in federal courts, most states feel that obtaining federal approval is either too burdensome or an unrealistic means of resolving grievances within prison walls."

By December of 1985, only Virginia, Iowa, and the Wyoming State Penitentiary had been certified. The attorney general had denied certification to three states, two counties, and one city. Applications from eight other states were pending in 1985 (Lay 1986). A 1990 examination of certification indicated a total of twenty-seven states and the District of Columbia as either obtaining some type of certification (from the attorney general or judicially approved by a U.S. district court) or seeking certification.

Appellate Court Decisions under the Act's "Exhaustion of Remedies" Provision

One commentator addressing the exhaustion of remedies provision suggested, "Arguably, the section 1997e exhaustion requirement was not included to advance the rights of the institutionalized but, in part, was a concession to state officials, who disliked the Attorney General's interference in their corrections systems and wished to limit the occasions on which they would be required to defend their corrections systems in federal court" (*Harvard Law Review* 1991). Irrespective of whether this is an accurate assessment, certainly a number of cases addressing the exhaustion issue have reached the federal courts.

In *Owin v. Kimmel*, the court reinforced the concept that inmates filing 1983 actions would have only to exhaust state inmate "internal grievance systems" when the U.S. attorney general (or applicable U.S. district court) had in fact certified that the prison's administrative remedies are in "substantial compliance" with the act.

In the case of *Rocky v. Vittorie*, the court indicated its desire to "strike a careful balance between recognizing the importance of a federal forum for civil rights suits and facilitating the expeditious resolution of such suits brought by prisoners" by essentially holding that prisoners would not be barred from the federal courts if they, in good faith but unsuccessfully, attempted to exhaust administrative remedies. In other words, the court would not generally hold prisoners to arbitrary "time specific" filing requirements relative to exhaustion of prison remedies.

The case of *Mann v. Adams* established that a state's failure to submit grievance procedures for certification to the U.S. attorney general would not give rise to a prisoner's cause of action. That is, an inmate can not compel a prison to institute a "grievance process" that will be certified as complying with 1997e of the act.

In *Martin v. Catalanotto*, the court clarified its reading of the act's intent relative to 1983 actions. The court stated that "allegations unrelated to conditions of confinement, such as those that center on events outside of the institution, would not appropriately be continued for resolution by the grievance resolution system." Additionally, the court indicated that, where imminent danger to life is alleged, resolution through an inmate grievance process would not be suitable.

The fact that the act applies only to state prisoners was reinforced in the U.S. Supreme Court decision of *McCarthy v. Madigan*. The court concluded, "We find it significant that Congress, in enacting section 1997e, stopped short of imposing a parallel requirement in the federal prison context." The Federal Bureau of Prison's administrative remedy procedure for inmates is set forth under 28 CFR Part 542 (1991).

It is important to note that a state inmate, dissatisfied with the decision made within the certified "Prison Internal Grievance Process," still retains the right to file his 1983 suit in U.S. district court. The inmate, under the act (42 USC 1997e(a)(1)), is merely required to wait until the ninety-day exhaustion compliance period has elapsed.

The 1990 Federal Courts Study Committee Report

The act has been subject to criticism (particularly section 1997e). Turk (1983), a federal district court judge, criticized both the apparent inflexibility of the ninety-day rule under 1997e and 1997e's failure to provide for monetary relief in most tortious situations. Many states, apparently contemplating certification, objected to the "inmate participation" requirement found in 1997e. Some states questioned whether certification would provide any significant benefits, while other states protested that they failed to obtain certification because of the Justice Department's ineffectiveness in processing and acting upon applications for certification (*Harvard Law Review* 1991).

Congress established the Federal Courts Study Committee (See 102 Stat. 4642 (1988)) to survey the "impending crisis" in the workload of the federal courts and to suggest proposals for diminishing that workload (*Harvard Law Review* 1991, 1311). The committee specifically reexamined section 1997e in an effort to determine how the statute could be made more useful in reducing prisoner filings. The committee's 1990 report, recognizing that many states had not sought certification because of objections to the "specific criteria" of 1997e, recommended a fundamental change. The recommendation was that the "substantial compliance" language, employed in assessing whether state prison grievance systems met the statutory minimum standards, be replaced by a "fair and effective" standard. The thinking was that this change would permit the attorney general or applicable U.S. district court greater leeway in granting certification. The proposed "general standard" would also, presumably, persuade more states to seek certification. As of July 1993, Congress had not taken any formal action on the "fair and effective" recommendation.

The attorney general's role in enforcing the act has also been subject to review. Two congressional subcommittees held a joint oversight hearing in February of 1984 on the Justice Department's controversial handling of a suit filed against three Michigan state prisons. The Justice Department was criticized for a lack of diligence in acting on civil rights violations in Michigan prisons.

Proportion of Inmate 1983 Lawsuits since the Adoption of the Civil Rights of Institutionalized Persons Act

One way in which to measure the impact of the act is to assess whether the number of 1983 inmate lawsuit filings in U.S. district courts has decreased as a result of the act's mandated ninety-day continuance provision. A decrease in the number of such actions might indicate that inmates view the internal grievance process as an effective alternative to court litigation.

Whether and to what degree the act has had an impact in reducing 1983 litigation in U.S. district courts is in dispute. An early examination of the process in Virginia by Turk (1983) appears to show a decrease in prisoner filings, while at the same time Turk indicates that other factors may have accounted for the decrease. In Lay's later review of the Virginia experience, however, he cites figures that clearly show that inmates involved in the grievance process were less likely to later pursue the matter in federal court (1986, 943). Lay also describes a letter he received from the Wyoming attorney general, who, commenting on the Wyoming experience, said, "The grievance procedure has significantly reduced the number of inmate complaints that reach the judicial system and has served to provide more expeditious treatment of the complaints filed" (1986, 944).

An editorial in the *Harvard Law Review* argues that an analysis of prisoner filings in certified and uncertified jurisdictions establishes that "insufficient data are available at present to evaluate the workings of the statute in a meaningful fashion" (*Harvard Law Review* 1991, 1312). That source nevertheless reviews filings from 1983 to 1990 and does present several graphs and a chart that outwardly indicate a general downward trend (certainly a substantial decrease in Virginia) in filings by inmates in certified states. The caution is issued, however, that the general findings are "less dramatic" than they appear and that it is too early to "conclude definitively that certification reduces the number of per prisoner filings" (1991, 1314–15).

Conclusion

The enactment of the Civil Rights of Institutionalized Persons Act is an attempt to protect the constitutional rights of individuals in selected institutions. The initial intent of the statute was to enable the attorney general to institute civil actions to ensure that corrective actions would be taken. The role of the attorney general in instituting civil actions, however, appears to have taken on less prominence in recent years. Instead, the focus has shifted to an examination of the "Exhaustion of Remedies" provision (42 USC 1997e) concerning the establishment of certifiable prison grievance systems. A prisoner who files a 42 USC 1983 action is required to have the legal matter continued for ninety days in order that a resolution might be attempted through a certified prison grievance program. The expectation is that a satisfactory resolution through the grievance process will decrease the number of subsequent 1983 filings in U.S. district courts. A dissatisfied prisoner still retains the right to file a 1983 action in a U.S. district court after first participating in the certified grievance process.

Rick Steinman

See also NATIONAL PRISON PROJECT, LEGAL ISSUES (CIVIL RIGHTS)

Bibliography

Cory, B. (1982a). Politics and the Institutionalized Persons Act. *Corrections Magazine* 8(5): 25.

Cory, B. (1982b). Progress and politics in resolving inmate grievances. *Corrections Magazine* 8(5): 20–24ff.

Lay, D. (1986). Exhaustion of grievance procedures for state prisoners under Section 1997(e) of the Civil Rights Act. *Iowa Law Review* 71: 935–74.

Harvard Law Review (1991). Resolving prisoners' grievances out of court: 42 U.S.C. Section 1997(e). *Harvard Law Review* 104: 1309–29.

Turk, J. C. (1983). The nation's first application of the exhaustion requirement of 42 U.S.C. Section 1997(e): The Virginia experience. *American Journal of Trial Advocacy* 7: 1–18.

Cases

McCarthy v. Madigan, 503 U.S. ___, 112
S.Ct. 1081, 117 L.Ed.2d 291 (1992)

Mann v. Adams, 846 F.2d 589 (9th Cir. 1988)

Martin v. Catalanotto, 895 F.2d 1040 (5th
Cir. 1990)

Owin v. Kimmel, 693 F.2nd 711 (7th Cir.
1982)

Patsey v. Florida Board of Regents, 457 U.S.
495, 102 S.Ct. 2557, 73 L.Ed.2d 172
(1981)

Rocky v. Vittorie, 813 F.2nd 734 (5th Cir.
1987)

Classification Systems

Briefly, classification is a sorting-out process
that begins when the individual is first admitted to prison. Classification assigns the inmate
to an institution with the appropriate security
level, designates appropriate housing placements and identifies custody supervision requirements within a given institution, and
makes medical, mental health, vocational, educational, and work assignments based on inmate needs and available resources. This process is usually termed *initial classification*.

After an initial placement, a classification
committee periodically reviews each inmate's
progress in program assignments. The committee also responds to rule violations or any change
in the inmate's situation that would signal a need
for a corresponding change in security, custody,
or programs. These activities constitute the *reclassification* process.

A classification system is a complex enterprise that operates at several levels. First, the
state correctional system creates classification
policy and procedures to meet the philosophy,
resources, goals, and needs of the corrections
department. Second, many states have a centralized classification office that oversees operation of a reception unit for new inmates,
where they stay for several weeks while the
initial classification process takes place. Third,
the unit (or institution) level has classification
committees that make and implement initial
classification decisions and many reclassification decisions (National Institute of Corrections [NIC] 1982).

Classification is clearly a central process in
any prison system. Because of the information
collected on individuals, the classification process provides the best known approach to identify potential risks and program needs, develop

rehabilitation programs, and achieve custody
and security conditions that address those needs
and risks. As a central administrative process,
the classification system is called upon to address a number of issues important to the correctional system. A well-operated classification
system can be an effective means of reducing the
effects of overcrowding, although, of course, it
cannot alleviate overcrowding on its own. In
recent years, though, a number of prison systems have come under court-mandated population limitations, and the individuals released
when capacity is exceeded are normally those
whose classification identifies them as being of
lowest risk to the community.

Classification systems also help identify
facility and program needs. The classification
process can be used to identify emerging situations within the population that need to be addressed, such as substance abuse, AIDS, and
gang involvement. A well-functioning classification system can also help protect the correctional system from litigation by inmates and the
public. Similarly, it helps protect the constitutional rights of prison inmates.

Background and History

Origins and Development of Classification

Rudimentary forms of inmate classification
can be traced back at least to fourteenth-cen-
tury asylums (although the word *classification*
was not coined until much later). For a long
time, classification was no more than separation of broad types of offenders one from another—juveniles from adults, first offenders or
debtors from "hardened" criminals, men from
women, and condemned prisoners from others. Until the late eighteenth century, most
prisons were temporary holding facilities for
those awaiting execution or transport, or were
warehouses for prostitutes, abandoned children, debtors, and other minor offenders. The
purpose of classification was not treatment or
rehabilitation, but simply to facilitate management of the institution.

As theories of criminality and penology
developed in the eighteenth and nineteenth
centuries, the management of offenders also
changed. Early nineteenth-century Quaker reformers in the United States began to isolate
prisoners from each other to allow each person
ample opportunity for introspection. Such religious meditation in a humanitarian environment was intended to rehabilitate the indi-

vidual sufficiently for successful reintegration into society. The enforced isolation, however, drove some prisoners insane, and generally appeared to be of questionable benefit. These prisons were also expensive to construct, because every inmate had a single cell.

After about 1830, corrections officials began to view labor as the definitive method of rehabilitation; concomitantly, classification started to focus on fitness to work. Classification for labor dominated until after the Civil War (and until the early 1900s in the South), when penologists began to be concerned about the reintegration of the offender into the community. The 1870 National Congress on Penitentiary and Reformatory Discipline (precursor to the American Correctional Association, the ACA) adopted principles of classification based on the 1854 Irish system.

Under the Irish system of indeterminate sentences, incarceration began with an initial punishment stage of "separate imprisonment," a reformatory stage wherein the prisoner was trained (or educated) to become a useful member of the community, and a "probationary" stage much like parole. The premier facility for implementation of this approach was in Elmira, New York, under the leadership of Zebulon Brockway. It did not have wide implementation in other systems, though. In 1883, an Alabama penitentiary physician began to record data on inmates' backgrounds. This was the first use of the social history, a document that is still the primary source of information for many types of classification decisions.

By the early twentieth century, interest had shifted to psychological and social issues and away from labor exclusively. Borrowing again, this time from the English Borstal system of minimum-security open institutions for youthful offenders, the American prison system began a new phase of classification philosophy and practice. Individualization and democratization of prison treatment became the paramount concerns. Reformers believed that it was essential to redesign prison environments such that the inmate could develop the skills necessary to return to society.

Psychiatrists supported this change and wanted to take it further. They believed that treatment programs within this new "community model" prison could cure many inmates of their criminality. Moreover, they believed that judges should not set the term of sentence nor decide the best type of institution for a given inmate. Rather, these decisions should be left to the psychiatrists and treatment staff. From that position came expanded use of the indeterminate sentence and development of the diagnostic/reception center.

Intelligence and personality testing had become popular during World War I, and prison psychiatrists made it a major function of diagnostic centers. Use of the inmate social history also expanded. Illinois prisons, influenced by the Chicago School of sociology, considered the inmate's social situation to be as important as his psychiatric condition. This system employed probably the most detailed use of the social history for the time, and in fact had sociologists on staff.

Other states relied more heavily on psychiatric diagnoses. The 1927 New Jersey system, for example, classified inmates into six supposedly different psychological categories. This type of classification system quickly spread to other states. States established professionally staffed reception centers to carry out such diagnoses. In New York, for instance, the reception center at Sing Sing prison admitted new inmates, conducted medical, psychiatric, and educational diagnoses of each individual's needs, and assigned each one to the appropriate placement. Some prisons were designated as industrial centers; some were farms, and others housed the criminally insane and defective. That was not the only system of classification during this period of rapid and sweeping change in prisons. Other states classified prisoners based on their amenability to rehabilitation, with the lower custody levels reserved for those diagnosed as most amenable.

The actual type of classification system was not as important as its mere existence, however. The beliefs of prison reformers and officials during the 1930s and 1940s demanded that the prisoner be treated as an individual, and classification was the method of choice. Clinical prediction techniques used by psychiatrists in mental hospitals were extended to prisons to help design rehabilitation programs. They promised, at least in theory, to identify the violent and potentially violent offenders so that they could be segregated from the general prison population. They also identified those believed capable of rehabilitation. Unfortunately, but expectedly, psychiatrists spent most of their energy on diagnosis, because they knew very little about translating their observations and general recommendations into specific programs for treatment.

Early classification systems focused solely on institutional concerns, primarily security and labor. Later systems emphasized the role of psychiatric diagnosis in managing the prison population. Systems from the 1950s to the 1970s integrated security and treatment. Classification became a two-stage placement process. First, an individual was placed in an institution of the proper security level, based on his danger to the public. Measures of dangerousness were generally based on one's past history of violence and the results of various personality tests administered as part of the classification process. Then one's program needs and suitability were determined, again based on psychological testing and clinical judgment.

Two types of systems are representative of those that existed, although neither was widely used. First is the Quay typology, which divided young male offenders into five categories: inadequate-immature; neurotic-conflicted; unsocialized-aggressive; socialized or subcultural; and subcultural immature. Once diagnosed, inmates could be assigned to counseling programs specifically designed to treat each type of personality.

Second is the RAPS system implemented by the Federal Bureau of Prisons in 1969. The acronym refers to the Rehabilitative potential (in the opinion of the professional staff), the Age (under thirty, thirty to forty-five, over forty-five), number of Prior sentences, and Sentence type and length. Evaluation of these four dimensions determined whether there would be high, medium, or no expenditure of resources above the essential level of service required for each inmate. Members of the "high" category would be reviewed frequently and have first priority on assignments. Those in the "medium" category were reviewed less frequently and had lower priority on available slots in programs. Those in the final category had last priority and were routinely assigned to the labor pool that maintains the institution. This system was designed not only to allocate program expenditures but also to manage the population in a cost-effective manner.

Most jurisdictions used less structured classification systems. Each state typically had its own subjective clinical prediction methods for determining dangerousness and treatment needs. Classification decisions were generally made by a committee made up of representatives from the various facets of the prison (such as medical, work, custody, mental health, and education). Classification committees, however, were not normally responsible for the actual placement or transfer of inmates; security classification frequently bore little relation to where the inmate was actually housed. Placements were often made primarily on the basis of available bed space. If most of the beds were in maximum-custody institutions, then most of the inmates were maximum-custody inmates, regardless of how the committee had classified any individual (Brennan 1987b).

Transition to Current Classification Systems

Just as prison reformers have historically helped shape classification philosophies and practices, the advent of contemporary classification systems is also largely the result of outside influences. Until around 1970, private prison reform organizations were the most active advocates of change. Beginning around 1970, though, federal courts began to intervene. In the 1960s, inmates, perhaps influenced by the success of other groups in demanding civil rights, appealed to the courts to improve prison conditions. These "conditions of confinement" lawsuits led to sweeping changes in prison systems.

The *Holt v. Sarver* cases in Arkansas were the first to identify classification as part of the solution to unconstitutional conditions of confinement. Even though the court did not label the remedy "classification," they required that housing assignments be based on the needs of the population and be designed to reduce the levels of fear and violence within the institution. That implied that a method had to be developed to identify needs and to act on them. These cases established the principle of using a tool that is not a constitutional right itself as a means to remedy unconstitutional conditions.

The first case to order a corrections department to design a classification system was *Morris v. Travisono* in Rhode Island, reiterated later by *Palmigiano v. Garrahy* (also in Rhode Island). The description of classification in that decision set the stage for the development of current classification models and systems. It saw classification as a tool that

is essential to the operation of an orderly and safe prison. It is a prerequisite for the rational allocation of whatever program opportunities exist within the institution. It enables the institution to gauge the proper custody level of an inmate, to identify the inmate's educational, vocational, and psychological needs, and to separate non-violent inmates from the more predatory. . . . Classification is also indispensable for any coherent future planning (*Palmigiano v. Garrahy* at 965).

Not until 1976 in Alabama did the federal court tie classification directly to the constitutionality of prison systems and establish sanctions for failure to establish an equitable classification method. In that case (*Pugh v. Locke*), the judge held that although classification was not a constitutional right per se, it was a major means of bringing the prison system up to constitutionally acceptable standards. Furthermore, the judge required that the classification system consider the needs of the inmates and not respond solely to the needs of the institution or the prison system. A court-ordered research group from the University of Alabama conducted an extensive study of the needs of the population and implemented a classification system that followed the court's order.

Courts have generally held that classification must be rational (*Laaman v. Helgemoe*) and that officials cannot reclassify or transfer an inmate in retaliation for the exercise of a constitutional right (*Jackson v. Cain*). Also, prison inmates have the constitutional right to reasonable protection from assaults. Classification systems are generally seen as the means to identify actually and potentially violent inmates, as well as those who may be likely victims, so that those groups can be separated from each other (*Woodhous v. Virginia; Withers v. Levine*).

These court cases guided prison systems in setting out specific goals and procedures for classification, even if their state was not involved in a lawsuit. Typical classification goals led to the development of policies and procedures that (1) classify each inmate to the least restrictive custody required to protect society, staff, and other inmates; (2) carefully assess and reassess the needs of the inmate while holding the inmate responsible for personal behavior; and (3) provide positive incentives that encourage the inmate to assume more responsibility for personal welfare.

Such goals implied three facets of classification decision-making. First is classification for *programs*. Here an inmate is classified according to needed treatment programs in light of the resources of the prison system and the inmate's situation. Second is classification for *security*. It ascertains the type of perimeter se-

curity necessary to protect the community from the inmate. That is, how much of an escape risk is the inmate? The question is answered both in terms of the likelihood that the individual will actually escape and in terms of the danger to the community if the person does escape. Third is classification for *custody*. Custody refers to the degree of supervision required for the safety of the inmate and those around him, both in housing, work, and program settings (Brennan 1987b).

The hallmarks of the systems developed directly or indirectly in response to court mandates were standardized classification criteria and a minimum of subjective judgments in classification decisions. In addition, reclassification began to take on more importance. Most notably, classification and reclassification criteria began to be based on objectively measurable factors (such as prior incarcerations, length of sentence, number of prison rule violations, and completion of educational programs) rather than on factors that, even though applied to all inmates, were subjectively measured (such as family stability or willingness to change criminal lifestyle).

Cases during the 1980s refined the limits and expectations of classification systems and procedures. Cases typically concerned situations in which classification procedures placed restrictions on inmates (Belbot and del Carmen 1993). Complaints were often related to due process rights or rights to certain types of treatment or liberties within the system. Through various court decisions, the major finding has been that if laws or prison system regulations mandate specific criteria for various procedures or activities (such as placement or holding in segregation, transfer, or work assignment), the state has then created a "liberty interest" that the inmate has the right to expect. If not, a given classification decision will be assumed to be constitutional, even if it is restrictive (*Stephany v. Wagner; Lanier v. Fair; Wallace v. Robinson*).

Current Status of Classification

A classification system encompasses policies, procedures, and models. During the 1980s, many state systems revamped their entire classification systems and implemented "objective" models to replace the clinical models most had used. The National Institute of Corrections (NIC) (1982) set out the following fourteen principles for classification. Many states have adopted them to varying degrees when establishing and operating objective classification systems.

1. *There must be a clear definition of goals and objectives of the total correctional system. A* classification system should be developed to assign inmates in ways that best meet the goals of the prison system.
2. *There must be detailed written procedures and policies governing the classification process.*
3. *The classification process must provide for the collection of complete, high-quality, verified, standardized data. Such* data are essential to making informed classification decisions and are important to monitoring the classification system and in preparing analyses of trends in classification decisions and in population characteristics.
4. *Measurement and testing instruments used in the classification decision-making process must be valid, reliable, and objective.* Many psychometric instruments exist, but many have not been validated for use with correctional populations or for classification purposes. Moreover, instruments developed expressly for classification should be subject to validation.
5. *There must be explicit policy statements structuring and checking the discretionary decision-making powers of classification team staff.*
6. *There must be provisions for screening and further evaluating prisoners who are management problems and those who have special needs.*
7. *There must be provisions to match offenders with programs; these provisions must be consistent with risk classification.*
8. *There must be provisions to classify each prisoner at the least restrictive custody level. A* basic premise of contemporary classification is that every prisoner should be in the lowest custody level suitable for adequate supervision and protection of staff, other inmates, and the community. These custody/security placements should be warranted by the inmate's behavior and not by external concerns.
9. *There must be provisions to involve the prisoner in the classification process. The* ACA has established a standard that calls for such involvement. Provisions should inform the inmate of the classification process and placement criteria for security, custody, and programs, and allow some level of participation in classification committee meetings.
10. *There must be provisions for systematic, periodic reclassification hearings.*
11. *The classification process must be efficient and economically sound.*
12. *There must be provisions to continually evaluate and improve the classification process.* Corrections is not a static enterprise. The characteristics of offenders change over time, as do correctional programs and prison settings. The classification process must be able to respond to these changes. Moreover, evaluation of the process is crucial to operating a sound classification system.
13. *Classification procedures must be consistent with constitutional requisites.*
14. *There must be an opportunity for administration and line staff to be heard when undertaking development of a classification system.*

Contemporary Classification Models

Although most jurisdictions claim to use objective classification systems, their forms vary. Three general types of objective classification have been identified: consensus, equity, and prediction. *Consensus* models have developed because many jurisdictions do not have the necessary resources to collect longitudinal data on which to base classification criteria. One common way to design this type of model is to survey correctional personnel about the factors they perceive as important for achieving the stated goals of classification, usually risk prediction.

Equity-based models seek to restrict factors in the classification decision to legally relevant behavioral characteristics. They usually exclude all information not pertaining to current or prior criminal behavior. The goal is to treat everyone in the same manner, even at the cost of predictive accuracy.

Predictive models use legal, social, psychological, and medical factors to predict in-prison behaviors, such as infractions, escapes, or assaults. Included in this general category are those schemes that have adapted psychometric tests as the sole or major component of the classification decision. These models are not widely used (Brennan 1987a).

Classification models, in practice, tend to combine these approaches. One important facet of all objective systems is the ability to override the indicated classification placement. Clinical judgments and administrative concerns come into play here. Many acceptable reasons exist for overriding decisions, and states have different policies governing such actions. Although classification committees determine the appropriate security, custody, and program placements, they are generally not in control of whether their recommendations are carried out. For example, classification committees cannot place individuals in programs or institutions that have no space. Such recommendations are likely to be overridden by prison administrators.

Surveys in the mid-1980s found that about three-quarters of the prison systems in the U.S. used objective classification models. The most frequently used model was one developed by the NIC and used by 28 percent of the states. Next was the Federal Prison System (FPS) model developed by the Federal Bureau of Prisons (23 percent). An additional 11 percent used a scheme that combined these models. About 13 percent used the Correctional Classification Profile (CCP). The remainder (23 percent) developed their own model or adapted a model developed by another state. Other models have been developed but are not widely used. These include models used for specific populations (such as youthful male offenders) or institutions. Two notable models in this category are those developed by Megargee and Bohn based on the Minnesota Multiphasic Personality Inventory (MMPI) and the Quay Adult Internal Management System (Buchanan and Whitlow 1987).

National Institute of Corrections—Custody Determination Model

In 1980, NIC funded Fisher and Associates to develop a model classification system that could be easily adapted for use in numerous jurisdictions. It was developed through examination of existing systems, consideration of factors found to be associated with institutional behavior, and examination of court mandates. It includes procedures for initial custody designation, needs assessment, and reclassification. It does not consider custody and security separately.

This model makes custody/security assignments based on a numerical score calculated using an instrument that considers the history of institutional violence during prior incarcerations, the severity of the current offense, prior history of violent crime, escape history during prior incarcerations, alcohol or drug abuse history, whether there is a current detainer, prior felony convictions, and "stability" factors—age (twenty-six or older), high school diploma or GED, and employment or school attendance for six months prior to arrest (NIC 1982). This score, while based on principles of equity, also purports to be predictive of the supervision level required to minimize risk to the public and other inmates.

Federal Prison System

In 1979, the Federal Bureau of Prisons (BOP) implemented a new classification system. It was designed primarily to confine inmates in the least restrictive environment possible without jeopardizing staff, inmate, or community safety and to reduce the number of transfers resulting from custody problems. A BOP task force designed the system.

The task force established a list of forty-seven factors potentially important in predicting prisoner behavior. A wide range of BOP staff then ranked the items in terms of their perception of each item's importance to the classification process. The six highest-ranked factors were included in the forms for initial security designation and custody classification: type of detainer, severity of current offense, expected length of incarceration, prior prison commitments, history of escapes, and history of violence. Points are added to arrive at a score that designates the security level of the institution to which the inmate is assigned. Program needs are determined and a classification committee makes referrals after the inmate has been assigned to the proper security level and housing.

Upon reclassification, the committee rescores the security items to determine whether the level is still appropriate. The instrument contains seven items with which to determine the appropriateness of a change in custody: percentage of time served; history of drug and alcohol involvement; mental and psychological stability; most serious disciplinary report in the past year; frequency of disciplinary reports in the past year; responsibility demonstrated by the inmate; and family and community ties.

These items are scored and a custody decision is based on that score.

Correctional Classification Profile

The Correctional Classification Profile (CCP) was developed by the Correctional Services Group (CSG) and has been adapted for use in a number of states. It assesses inmate needs relative to public and institutional risk using eight factors that are weighted to arrive at a score: medical and health care needs; mental health care needs; security and public risk needs; custody and institutional risk needs; educational needs; vocational training needs; work skills; and proximity to residence of release and family ties. Each of these factors is arrived at by consideration of several items. For example, the public risk assessment is made on the basis of the extent of violence on the current offense; the use of a weapon on the current offense; the history of escapes; the history of violence; the current detainer; the time expected to be served; community stability; and whether the current crime is a sex offense. These items are reassessed periodically for purposes of reclassification (Buchanan and Whitlow 1987).

Reclassification

Reclassification systems normally reflect the initial classification system. They have separate scoring schemes, but they use the same rationale. Typically, factors are added to make possible the consideration of behavior in prison. The Correctional Services Group surveyed prison systems in 1986 about the factors used for reclassification. All respondents used major disciplinary violations and over 80 percent included the time left before release and institutional adjustment in making reclassification decisions. Slightly more than half considered program participation and slightly less than half used time in the present security/custody level as factors. The timing of reclassification varies. Six and twelve months are common intervals for review of classification decisions.

Current Issues in Classification

Research on the Accuracy and Validity of Classification Models

All classification models attempt to predict the behavior of individuals to some degree, even though accurate prediction of the behavior of any given individual is extremely difficult. To validate a model, researchers must determine whether it does what it was designed to do. That is, if it was designed to predict individual behavior, it is a valid model if it does so. Perhaps because of the need to devise objective classification methods rather quickly, many current systems were not based on actual observations of inmate behavior, and the factors included were therefore frequently without demonstrated validity. The two most widely used models, FPS and NIC, are examples.

A recent national survey of agencies (Buchanan, Whitlow, and Austin 1986) using "objective" classification systems found that most respondents selected decision-making criteria that they believed to be the best predictors of behavior. The three most prevalent factors used were escape history, detainers, and prior prison commitments. The researchers, however, found only weak to moderate correlations between these and other individual factors and future prison misconduct. These classification models attempt to predict relatively rare events and little variation exists in the dependent variable (misconduct), so a low predictive ability is to be expected.

Rans (1984) measured the validity of several classification schemes in assessing risk. He used several types of institutional as well as post-release misconduct as measures of the validity of a classification model. His and other research also shows that classification criteria have questionable predictive validity.

As Craddock (1988) points out, perhaps the goal of studies of classification is misplaced when it is too closely focused on predicting individual behavior. Objective classification systems were implemented to improve management of the prison population. Clearly, it is important that they treat individuals fairly and adequately assess individual needs, but prediction of an individual's behavior is not their only, or perhaps even their primary, concern. Perhaps the most useful research on classification procedures is work that has examined whether these new models can bring about changes in aggregate measures of inmate conduct (such as rates of rule violations, escapes, or assaults). In fact, a study in three states (Buchanan, Whitlow, and Austin 1986) concluded that objective classification systems enabled correctional authorities to place inmates in lower-level, less expensive custody without increasing the risk to society or to the prison unit.

As of 1991, nineteen states had recently evaluated their objective classification systems.

C

These evaluations went further than evaluating the validity of the model or classification scoring scheme. They generally examined the effect of classification on the prison population as a whole. Most of these evaluations did not focus on issues of behavior prediction, but rather dealt with institutional management issues. Generally, states found that overclassification has significantly decreased. It was determined that from 25 to 40 percent of inmates can be safely housed in minimum custody, compared with much lower minimum custody percentages for older classification systems. Also, adherence to classification policy and procedures has been more successful, and no significant changes in rates of escapes or institutional misconduct have occurred (Alexander and Austin 1992).

Most of the research on classification validity has looked at initial classification placements only. The existence of reclassification processes recognizes that initial classification designations will need to be adjusted. Reassessments reflect changes in risks and the needs of individuals over the course of their incarceration. Studies need to address classification decisions as they change over time and how these changes affect the management of the prison population and the provision of programs (Craddock 1988).

Classification of Women
Historically, discussions of classification were usually either silent about the female population or explicitly dealt exclusively with men. Classification of women inmates may not have seemed a very important issue because most states had only one women's institution, with little variety in housing and often few program placement options. Although most court cases during the 1970s did not discuss classification of women, they generally applied their rulings to the entire correctional population.

As discussed above, classification systems need to develop well-defined goals and base classification procedures on the needs of the inmates, the institution, and the prison system. A 1990 survey revealed two major reasons why practitioners feel that existing classification processes are not well suited to women. The first is an overarching belief that most classification models have no empirical basis and are not valid for either men or women (especially those that focus on risk assessment). Models are likely to be even less adequate for the female population than the male, though, because the

intuitions that go into them are based on beliefs and information about male prisoners. Second, most classification models are designed primarily to keep order and ensure safety within an institution, as well as between the institution and the community. Such practices are likely to overclassify a majority of women (and a minority of men) and jeopardize program efforts. Practitioners have reported that women generally are low security risks but need high levels of treatment. Women's institutions do not usually need to have custody as their prime concern, and it makes sense that their classification models should not focus on custody/security issues. While such considerations are important on a system level, they need to be addressed differently for women (Burke and Adams 1991; Fowler 1993).

Courts have demanded parity between men and women in a number of aspects of correctional treatment (for example, *Glover v. Johnson* and *Canterino v. Wilson*). What seems to be difficult to put into practice, however, is the notion that parity is an outcome and not a process. That is, for there to be parity in classification between women and men, the classification system must aim for the same goals for women as for men. It does not have to take the identical steps, however. In fact, what research has shown is that, in terms of classification, taking the same steps for men and women will definitely not achieve parity, but rather will place women in inappropriate and usually more expensive correctional settings. Indeed, some states have formally adapted their classification systems to women, but no agreement exists about the best approach to the classification of women inmates.

Special Populations
Classification models must address the risks and needs of the entire population. Youths, people with mental illnesses or mental retardation, the elderly, and inmates who do not speak English are examples of special subsets within the overall prison population. The classification system does not create programs and placement options for these and other special groups. The classification system should, however, be able to identify the risks and needs associated with special populations so that the corrections department can plan for them. Assessing risk may be problematic for some special populations, and techniques may not be well developed or agreed

upon. In most cases, methods exist to identify program needs. The classification process must have within it a mechanism for including these assessments when called for.

Future of Classification

Inmate classification has changed dramatically over the past thirty years. As a primary tool for the management of the prison population, classification systems and models must continue to adapt to changes in that population. Recent challenges have included the handling of inmates with AIDS and responding to overcrowding in many institutions.

An effect of overcrowding has been to shorten incarceration periods for some types of offenders. Classification approaches are best suited to relatively longer prison stays. The reception period often lasts several weeks while various processing activities occur. At the end of that period, the prisoner is classified and transferred to the appropriate institution and housing assignment. A number of states report that, because of overcrowding, people are being released much sooner than normal. The length of the reception period can result in individuals not having enough time to complete programs before their release. Often that results in program assignments not being made. Classification officials may streamline the reception period to accommodate the flow of people. More programs may be established for individuals who will be incarcerated for only a few months. As correctional alternatives to incarceration continue to develop, such short-term programs may be coordinated with programs in the community. In addition, classification system personnel may focus on developing better needs assessment mechanisms that can quickly and accurately identify the program needs of individuals.

One related future direction for prison classification is coordination with community supervision agencies to identify individuals appropriate for alternatives to full-term incarceration (such as boot camps, halfway houses, and community corrections). Some recent studies have addressed these issues, such as work on the Level of Supervision Inventory done primarily in Canada (Andrews, Bonta, and Hoge 1990; Bonta and Motiuk 1992).

Such innovations require that the changes in classification models and practices be based on valid measures and techniques. This concern addresses another future direction for classification—the concentrated effort to validate classification systems and models. Several writers have called for support for process and impact evaluations of all classification systems. Fowler (1993) advocates that evaluations pay close attention to two primary areas: issues of equitable classification for women inmates and the handling of special populations; and examination of how well the classification system helps maximize the use of staff and program resources. Not only must measures of the impact of the classification process, model, and system on the characteristics of the correctional population (such as reduction in escapes or overclassification) be included, but also examination of the financial impact of the classification system on the prison system as a whole.

Amy Craddock

See also DIAGNOSTIC AND RECEPTION CENTERS

Bibliography

Alexander, J. A. (1986). Classification objectives and practices. *Crime and Delinquency* 32: 323–38.

Alexander, J. A., and J. Austin (1992). *Handbook for Evaluating Prison Classification Systems*. Washington, D.C.: National Institute of Corrections.

American Correctional Association (1993). *Classification: A Tool for Managing Today's Offenders*. Laurel, Md.: American Correctional Association.

Andrews, D. A., J. Bonta, and R. D. Hoge (1990). Classification for effective rehabilitation: Rediscovering psychology. *Criminal Justice and Behavior* 17: 19–52.

Belbot, B., and R. V. del Carmen (1993). Legal issues in classification. In American Correctional Association, ed. *Classification: A Tool for Managing Today's Offenders*. Laurel, Md.: American Correctional Association.

Bonta, J., and L. L. Motiuk (1992). Inmate classification. *Journal of Criminal Justice* 20: 343–53.

Brennan, T. (1987a). Classification: An overview of selected methodological issues. In M. Tonry and D. M. Gottfredson, eds. *Prediction and Classification: Criminal Justice Decision Making. Crime and Justice: A Review of Research 9*. Chicago: University of Chicago Press.

Brennan, T. (1987b). Classification for control in jails and prisons. In M. Tonry and D. M. Gottfredson, eds. *Prediction and Classification: Criminal Justice Decision Making. Crime and Justice: A Review of Research* 9. Chicago: University of Chicago Press.

Buchanan, R. A., and K. L. Whitlow (1987). *Guidelines for Developing, Implementing, and Revising an Objective Prison Classification System*. Washington, D.C.: National Institute of Justice.

Buchanan, R. A., K. L. Whitlow, and J. Austin (1986). National evaluation of objective prison classification systems: The current state of the art. *Crime and Delinquency* 32: 272–90.

Burke, P., and L. Adams (1991). *Classification of Women Offenders in State Correctional Facilities: A Handbook for Practitioners*. Washington, D.C.: National Institute of Corrections.

Craddock, A. (1988). *Inmate Classification as Organizational Formal Social Control: Implications for Population Management*. Doctoral dissertation. Ann Arbor, Mich.: University Microfilms.

Craddock, A. (1992). Formal social control in prisons: An exploratory examination of the custody classification process. *American Journal of Criminal Justice* 17: 63–87.

Fowler, L. T. (1993). *Classification of Women Offenders*. Columbia: South Carolina Department of Corrections.

Kane, T. (1986). The validity of prison classification: An introduction to practical considerations and research issues. *Crime and Delinquency* 32: 367–90.

National Institute of Corrections (1982). *Prison Classification: A Model Systems Approach*. Washington, D.C.: National Institute of Corrections.

Rans, L. L. (1984). The validity of models to predict violence in community and prison settings. *Corrections Today* 46(3): 51–51, 62–63.

Cases

Canterino v. Wilson, 546 F.Supp. 174 (W.D. Ky. 1982)

Glover v. Johnson, 659 F.Supp. 621 (E.D. Mich. 1987)

Holt v. Sarver, 300 F. Supp. 825 (E.D. Ark. 1969); 309 F. Supp. 362 (E.D. Ark. 1970) *affd.* 442 F.2d 304 (8th Cir. 1971)

Jackson v. Cain, 864 F.2d 1235 (5th Cir. 1989)

Laaman v. Helgemoe, 437 F. Supp., 269 (D. N.H. 1977)

Lanier v. Fair, 876 F. 2d 243 (1st Cir. 1989)

Morris v. Travisono, 310 F. Supp. 857 (D. R.I. 1970)

Palmigiano v. Garrahy, 443 F. Supp. 956 (D.R.I. 1977)

Pugh v. Locke, 406. F. Supp. 318 (M.D. Ala. 1976)

Stephany v. Wagner, 835 F.2d 497 (3rd Cir. 1986)

Wallace v. Robinson, 940 F.2d 243 (7th Cir. 1991)

Withers v. Levine, 615 F. 2d 158 (4th Cir. 1980)

Woodhous v. Virginia, 487 F.2d 889 (4th Cir. 1973)

Co-Correctional Facilities

Co-corrections refers to the incarceration of female and male offenders in the same institution, permitting mixing of the sexes in such activities as meals, recreation, education, and jobs. After a century of separation of the sexes in prisons across the United States, the U.S. Federal Bureau of Prisons opened two co-correctional institutions in 1971. In July, the Robert F. Kennedy Youth Center in Morgantown, West Virginia, opened one of its cottages to adult female offenders from the overcrowded all-women's federal prison at Alderson, West Virginia. Four months later, the bureau acquired a public health facility in Fort Worth, Texas, and opened the first co-correctional facility for adults. Since 1971, at least forty-five correctional institutions across the U.S. have experimented with the coed concept. A number of them have since reverted to single-sex status, including all the co-correctional institutions at the federal level. Today, no more than thirty coeducational facilities exist.

Co-correctional prisons have been suggested for the following reasons:

1. To reduce the dehumanizing and destructive aspects of confinement;
2. To reduce institutional control problems;
3. To reduce predatory homosexuality;
4. To reduce the number of violent assaults;
5. To protect inmates likely to be involved in "trouble" were they housed in a single-sex institution;

6. To provide an additional tool for creating a more normal, less institutionalized atmosphere;
7. To cushion the shock of adjustment for released prisoners;
8. To use space, staff, and programs more efficiently;
9. To relieve overcrowding;
10. To reduce the need for civilian labor;
11. To increase the diversity and flexibility of prison programs;
12. To expand treatment potentials for inmates with sexual problems and to develop positive relationships and coping skills between the sexes;
13. To provide equal access to programs and services for both sexes; and
14. To expand career opportunities for women, previously often boxed into the single state women's institution as correctional staff.

Whether co-corrections fulfilled any of these goals is debatable. Typical of other correctional innovations, there is no tangible evidence of its effectiveness in terms of cost, diversion, programs, or recidivism. Some policy analysts argue that correctional policies like co-corrections fail because they set far-reaching and lofty goals that oversimplify the crime problem and oversell simple solutions. Others, however, argue that co-corrections is a necessary step toward a more comprehensive and graduated sentencing structure, in which punishment more closely matches the crime. For them, restoring just deserts (receiving the punishment one deserves) to the criminal justice system is justification enough for the continued development of co-corrections.

After two decades of co-corrections, we find that evaluation research is conspicuously absent. Nowhere, for example, is there an evaluation of co-corrections using experimental or control groups. Nowhere in the literature do we find the results of a serious examination of co-correctional outcomes, such as which aspects of post-release adjustment are improved by co-corrections, which outcomes contribute to changes in post-release adjustment, and whether post-release adjustment affects recidivism. In spite of these limitations, however, a number of reports seriously question the impact of co-corrections, especially the consequences for women.

In the first decade of co-corrections (1970 to 1980), a number of studies were published in *Coed Prison* (Smykla 1980) that drew attention to the gap between rhetoric and the reality of equal treatment in programs and services for women prisoners in co-corrections. A few of these are discussed below.

Ross, Heffernan, Sevick, and Johnson conducted site visits to ten co-correctional institutions across the U.S. The average ratio of the sexes was five men to one woman. All institutions claimed that education and work programs integrated the sexes but noted that enrollment ceilings, restrictions on movement, the association of some programs with single-sex units, conflicting schedules, lack of staff supervision, and administrative decision-making limited full integration in recreation, dining, inmate organizations, the chapel, and leisure time. Where the researchers found integration limited, women inmates were the ones excluded.

Campbell, warden of the first adult federal co-correctional institution, at Fort Worth, Texas, wrote that one of the main problems at FCI Fort Worth was the way the staff treated women inmates. The former warden said that the ratio of four men to one woman caused staff to indulge women on the one hand while denying them equal opportunities on the other.

Heffernan and Krippel examined patterns of social relationships at FCI Fort Worth and discovered two social roles that exploited women. The first was the commissary companion. Older male inmates paid younger female prisoners to be their companions—to sit with them in the dining room or to be with them elsewhere in the institution. The second was prostitution. The study also found that in spite of the expectation of equal access to programs and services for female inmates, in practice, women had no programs in which they could develop leadership roles and cohesive structures. In short, there was nothing that would provide them with alternative life-styles to replace the ones that contributed to their arrest and incarceration in the first place.

Wilson investigated the ways in which women and men inmates "do time" in a co-correctional institution and found that, while more women than men were involved in academic programs, a higher percentage of men set themselves the goal of earning a college degree. Wilson also discovered differences in requests for vocational education. Women requested training in sewing, upholstery, and cosmetology. Men requested training in meatcutting, air-conditioning repair, waste-water management, welding, and small engine repair. According to

C

Wilson, women inmates in co-corrections were more likely to think of their plans for the future in terms of marriage and babies. Men inmates were more likely to think of themselves as business owners.

Lambiotte studied co-corrections at FCI Pleasanton in California and found that sex-role structures inside the prison duplicated and reflected the social division between the sexes in society at large, both by behavior and behavioral norms and adherence to traditional standards. Women inmates at Pleasanton focused their energies on relationships with men. Men inmates defined the nature of the relationships and controlled the way in which women inmates related to them through labeling, verbal harassment, violation of women's physical space, initiation of relationships, and leadership.

Ross and Heffernan conducted a national assessment of co-corrections and concluded that co-corrections had fewer positive features for women than for men. Introduction of co-corrections in some states meant a reduction in sentencing options for women because the women's prison was used for co-corrections. When men were introduced into a previously all-women's prison they took away the better paying jobs from women, there was an increase in security measures that had not been necessary for the previous all-female population (for example, locking previously open gates and installing mass lighting), and there was a decrease in the number of women's programs.

Another report published in *Coed Prison* by Crawford, former warden of a women's prison, argued that going coed was done to appease male egos and smooth the running of men's institutions. Co-correctional institutions, Crawford argues, are not an appropriate means of reforming the behavior of female prisoners. Women who are institutionalized have generally been exploited by men in their lives. The co-correctional institution may well be a setting for a continuation of that experience. Even if this exploitation is not a material fact, Crawford claims that it will probably be evident in the male inmates' attitudes. The relationship of the male loser and the female loser creates an environment that reinforces negative attitudes. Dependency and insecurity of the incarcerated woman will only continue in the co-correctional setting.

Following the publication of *Coed Prison*, a number of other studies were published in the second decade of co-corrections (1980 to 1990)

that continued to question the promise of equal treatment for women. A few of the studies are reviewed here. In 1983, Chesney-Lind and Rodriguez interviewed sixteen of the twenty-two sentenced women prisoners at the coed Oahu Community Correctional Center in Hawaii. That facility also held eight hundred sentenced men. The typical Oahu woman prisoner was young (twenty-seven), poor, a member of a minority group, a high school dropout, unmarried, and the mother of two or more children for whom she was the sole support. The researchers found that while women prisoners talked of wanting careers that would give them financial independence once released from prison, they maintained traditional and dependent romantic relationships with male inmates, the same type of men who had exploited them on the streets. Over half of the women at Oahu had become romantically involved.

Using institutional records, Chesney-Lind and Rodriguez also reported that male inmates passed drugs to women inmates and expected sexual favors in return. They found that the women failed to participate in academic and vocational programs. They cited the administrative climate created by the disproportionate number of men at Oahu as responsible for the inequality in programs for women and for providing justification for excessive control over women for safety reasons.

In 1984, SchWeber studied the social environment of co-corrections and the extent to which programs available to women were actually used by them. She found that the social environment of co-correctional institutions in New York, New Jersey, and the U.S. Bureau of Prisons was heavily dependent upon the variety of security levels in the facility. The fact that there are relatively few women in prison means that in co-correctional institutions a heterogeneous female population must coexist with a more homogeneous male population; that is, male inmates will usually have the same security levels and be similar in age, while women's security levels and ages vary considerably. This tends to create administrative differences in the treatment of female and male inmates.

Co-corrections is less likely to be based on women inmates' needs than on administrative needs. Indeed, it is an option devised mostly for the more numerous male inmates. Other liabilities for women include restricted movement, pregnancy, and lower-paying job assignments. SchWeber also found that women inmates in co-corrections did not take advantage of educational opportunities. She cited the small proportion of women in prison as one factor that affects the extent of women's involvement in education and vocational training. She found that as the proportion of women in co-corrections increases, so, too, does their enrollment in education. Where there are proportionally larger female populations, the climate of support from the prison administration and staff makes women feel that it is not only safe but also necessary to enroll in academic and vocational education.

In 1986, a survey by Contact Center, Inc., found that thirty-five co-correctional institutions operated within twenty-two states and the U.S. Bureau of Prisons. Survey respondents were asked if female and male inmates participated jointly in food service, recreation, education, and jobs. Three institutions reported no joint participation in any area. The absence of male-female interaction, which generally serves to define the co-correctional program, becomes another forgotten expectation for women. Simply labeling a facility as co-correctional does not mean that the sexes are able to interact or that the institution is producing results favorable to female inmates.

In 1989, Mahan, Mabli, Johnston, Trask, and Hilek compared women's issues at three federal co-correctional and one federal all-women's prison, and the results were disappointing for women in co-corrections. On the average, co-correctional institutions offered seven programs for women inmates compared with twenty-four at the all-women's prison. Women inmates in co-correctional institutions received twice as many infractions per one hundred inmates as women at the federal all-women's facility (2.74 and 1.36, respectively). Finally, the researchers reported that women in co-correctional institutions were more than three times as likely to get pregnant than those at the all-women's prison.

Two studies on co-corrections published in 1990 continued the investigation into the expectation of equal treatment for women in co-corrections. Rafter surveyed state departments of corrections and found that only sixteen states had some type of correctional facility that accepted both sexes, mostly small states in the Northeast and Midwest. Although they held both men and women, these institutions were seldom co-correctional in the sense of a meaningful integration of the sexes. Rafter

wrote that, by 1988, the co-corrections movement of the 1970s was all but dead at the state and federal levels. Co-corrections failed to provide women parity with men. Co-correctional institutions created more options for male prisoners but usually ended up reducing sentencing options for women. Most women prisoners were still assigned to institutions farther from their homes than men. Security was tightened when men were introduced into a formerly female institution. Women (but not men) were barred from work details when there was insufficient supervision. And the burden of avoiding pregnancy fell on women. Rafter concluded that women prisoners have not benefited from either single-sex or co-correctional institutions.

Finally, in 1990, the American Correctional Association reported on the level of interaction between the sexes in six areas in both adult and juvenile co-correctional institutions: shared recreation and leisure activities, shared programs, permission to talk to each other, being served together in the dining room, assignment to the same work crew, and working together in prison industry. Twenty percent of adult, and almost one-half of juvenile, co-correctional facilities permitted interaction in each of the six levels. Of the rest, most permitted talking but none allowed women and men to work together in prison industry.

After two decades of co-corrections, the policy of integrating the sexes has not improved the lives of women, either in prison or after their release. Based on the data, one might conclude that co-corrections will never benefit female prisoners because program design and implementation favor men.

Other researchers, however, are less critical. They say the policy of integrating the sexes should be developed as part of a comprehensive and graduated sentencing structure. They encourage more study and control and call attention to the importance of issues such as staff selection and training, appropriate curricular materials for women and minorities, academic and vocational strategies that encourage women and minorities to participate, and testing and counseling programs to avoid career segregation and stereotyping. The prospects are that co-corrections will continue to survive, if not by design to reform the correctional experience, then by an attitude of indifference toward offenders where nothing succeeds like failure.

John O. Smykla

Bibliography

American Correctional Association (1990). *The Female Offender: What Does the Future Hold?* Washington, D.C.: St. Mary's.

Chesney-Lind, M., and N. R. Rodriguez (1983). Women under lock and key: A view from the inside. *Prison Journal* 63: 47–65.

Contact Center, Inc. (1986). Coed prison's survey finds 35 prisons house both men and women. *Corrections Compendium* 10: 7, 14–15.

Mahan, S. (1986). Co-corrections: Doing time together. *Corrections Today* 48: 134, 136, 138, 140, 164–65.

Mahan, S., J. Mabli, B. Johnston, B. Trask and J. Hilek (1989). Sexually-integrated prisons: Advantages, disadvantages and some recommendations. *Criminal Justice Policy Review,* 3(2):149–158.

Rafter, N. (1990). *Partial Justice: Women, Prisons, and Social Control.* 2nd ed. New Brunswick, N.J.: Transaction.

SchWeber, C. (1984). Beauty marks and blemishes: The coed prison as a microcosm of integrated society. *Prison Journal* 64:3–14.

Smykla, J. O., ed. (1980). *Coed Prison.* New York: Human Sciences.

Commissaries

The prison commissary is the inmate's supermarket. It is one of the few places where those in confinement can spend their money—legitimately—behind prison walls. Inmates acquire money inside most prison systems primarily from two sources. They either earn it through performance pay and bonuses from regular jobs inside the institution, or they receive funds from people outside the prison. In the latter case, the money is deposited into a commissary account against which the inmate can draw. Besides spending money in the commissary, inmates may also purchase certain items from authorized inmate organizations, although that practice is far more limited than commissary purchasing.

Using the Commissary

Each prison operates its own independent commissary. It is the only store in the prison, the only place where inmates are authorized to make purchases. In the federal prison system, inmates are authorized to shop one night each week. Federal registration numbers determine shopping nights. For example, inmates whose five-digit registration number ends with 20 may shop on Monday, while those inmates whose numbers end with 40 may shop on Tuesday.

Shopping in the commissary is a frustrating experience, but one all inmates must endure to obtain their material needs. First, the inmates must wait for their assigned night to shop. Then they must wait for the commissary to open. Movement to the commissary follows the order in which cell blocks are called for meals. Inmates usually forgo the evening meal on their shopping night in order to complete the commissary process as quickly as possible. Such an attitude suggests the lengths to which prisoners will go to lessen the frustration of shopping.

As an example, the commissary at the U.S. Prison (USP) in Atlanta is located about three-fourths of a mile from the nearest housing unit. When inmates are released from their living quarters, there is a mad dash to secure a favorable position in the commissary line. By the time the inmates arrive at the commissary, there may be several hundred other people in front of them. Administrators try different systems to keep the lines peaceful. Some prisons station officers around the line to keep inmates from cutting in; some use a numbering system; still others let prisoners fend for themselves.

At USP Atlanta, the inmate is met at the end of the commissary line with a wall and three windows secured behind thick steel bars. A commissary officer stands on the other side of the windows and communicates to the inmates via a microphone and bull-horn speaker. Working with the commissary officers are commissary workers (inmates), who gather the items for the inmates in line. Once an inmate approaches the window, the officer will ask for the inmate's commissary list.

The commissary list is an individual purchase order that the inmate prepares before going to the window. Every item that the commissary carries is named on the list, along with its price. An inmate wanting to shop simply writes his or her name and registration number on the top of the list, as well as a number indicating the quantity of each item to be purchased. After the list is given to the officer, the inmate commissary workers begin pulling the items from the shelves and placing them in containers for the officer to tally.

After commissary workers gather all of the items on the commissary list, the inmate is called to the window. At that time the inmate gives his identification card (with picture) to the commissary officer. With this card the officer uses the inmate's number to call up the inmate's commissary account on a computer. The officer will then deduct the cost of all items purchased from the inmate's account.

Both correctional systems and individual institutions strictly limit what items will be available for sale in the inmate commissaries. Many items are not sold for fear that they may be fashioned into weapons or used for escape. Then, too, the commissary has only so much space in which it can operate. It stocks only items that the majority of inmates want to purchase. In most systems, inmates may suggest items through an inmate commissary committee, or individually to commis-sary workers. The final word on what is sold, however, lies with the custodial department and the commissary supervisors. Inmate purchases are limited also by a spending policy. The Federal Bureau of Prisons, for example, caps spending at $155 a month per inmate, except during the Christmas holiday season, at which time the monthly limit is expanded to $205.

Typical Items on a Commissary List

The prison commissary at USP Atlanta stocks food and personal items. In the following representative list, items have been included from each category on the commissary list. Prices are cited as of December 1, 1993. Note that they are competitive with free-market prices, even though inmate wages range from $5.25 to around $250 a month.

Stamps, Coins, Phone Time, Photo Tickets (items that do not count against the monthly spending limit). Inmates can purchase up to $15 a week in coins for use in cellblock vending machines and in the visiting room, where they may use the photo tickets. (An inmate who wants a picture to send to his family buys a token for $2.50 in the commissary. The token is given to the inmate photographer assigned to the visiting room, who then takes a picture. Similarly, inmates may purchase credits for making telephone calls.)

Miscellaneous Items. Master locks ($5), alarm clocks ($10.40).

Radios and Watches. M70 Sony Digital ($67.25), Aiwa Mega Bass ($29.15), Ironman digital watch ($32.50).

Clothing. Tube socks ($1.05), gym shorts ($8.15), Reebok running cross training shoes ($90.65).

Toiletries. Mennen Speed Stick ($2.30), Colgate Tarter Control ($2.10), dental floss ($1.45), Pert Plus shampoo ($3.85).

Beverages. Pepsi ($1.90), Maxwell House ($3.75), Tang ($1.55).

Soups. Vegetable soup ($.50), long-grain rice ($.90).

Candies. M&M Peanut ($1.70), cashews ($2.30), deluxe mixed nuts ($2.15).

Ice Cream. Häagen Dazs Carrot Cake Passion ($2.50), Chipwich ($.85), Klondike Bars ($.65).

Cheese and Extras. Refried beans ($2.25), tortillas ($1.60), cheese spread ($1.65).

Cookies. Munchems ($2.15), Chips Deluxe ($2.15), Chocolate Chips ($1.60).

Chips. Nachos ($1.30), potato chips ($1.25), popcorn ($.50).

Meat and Snacks. Olive Oil ($2.90), Spam ($1.65), Jiffy peanut butter ($2.50).

Medicated Products. Good Sense Ibuprofen ($1.85), Good Sense Muscle Rub ($1.50), Good Sense Aspirin ($1.10).

Health Products. Hot Stuff Protein ($35.65), Metabolol Protein ($10.35), multivitamins ($4.75).

Tobacco Products. Dr. Grabow Pipes ($9.55), Marlboro ($1.60), Newport ($1.60).

Yarns. Various colors ($1.55).

Informal Uses of the Commissary

Inmates leave the commissary with large, knit shopping bags filled with edibles and other items for the long hike back to the unit. After a trip to the commissary, the inmates may socialize with each other, eating ice cream or other foods recently purchased. The commissary also is important to inmates for other reasons. It gives them a medium of exchange that they can use to settle debts. For example, inmates may have their clothes pressed by other inmates who work in the laundry. They pay for this service through commissary purchases. Inmates can use the commissary to pay for a wide variety of services provided by other inmates. Likewise, the administration may use the commissary as a tool for discipline. Commissary privileges may be withheld as a form of punishment.

The Commissary Trust Fund
Profits from commissary sales normally go to a commissary trust fund. Within the federal system, a trust was established in 1930, revised in 1932, and approved by an appropriation bill of the U.S. Congress in 1933. The trust has existed ever since [now codified at 31 U.S.C. §1321(a)(22)(1993)]. Originally, in the 1930 trust instrument, three separate "accounts" were created: the Prisoner Trust Fund Account (money belonging to inmates either earned or received from sources outside prison); the Commissary Fund; and the Inmate Welfare Fund. The Inmate Welfare Fund was funded by profits from the Commissary Fund.

In 1932, Circular No. 2244 was issued simplifying the 1930 trust to two "accounts" for appropriations purchases: the Prisoner Trust Fund and the Commissary Fund. The profits (revenues less appropriate expenses) from the Commissary Fund were designated in the 1932 trust for the same inmate welfare purposes as the original trust in 1930. The 1930 and 1932 trust purposes were incorporated into the Trust Fund Management Manual that the Bureau of Prisons operates under today. Profits derived from commissary sales are to be expended solely for the welfare and benefit of all inmates as a whole. Examples of how these funds might be used to benefit inmates include the purchase of recreational equipment or special entertainment. Congress has not authorized any other expenditure of the trust funds.

Summary
The commissary is one of the few opportunities inmates have to purchase items that are important to them during their confinement. Commissary shopping may be frustrating; however, it is also a necessary part of the culture of the prison.

Michael G. Santos

See also CONTRABAND

Bibliography
Bates, S. (1936). *Prisons and Beyond.* Freeport, N.Y.: Books for Libraries Press (Reprinted 1971).
Bureau of Prisons (1990). *The Development of the Federal Prison System.* Washington, D.C.: Federal Bureau of Prisons.
Fleisher, M. S. (1989). *Warehousing Violence: Frontiers of Anthropology.* Newbury Park, Calif.: Sage.

Community Relations
The subject of prisons and community relations is a neglected topic. That is to be expected. People do not see prisons as relevant to their lives. Prisons have been developed to separate individuals from society, and—out of sight, out of mind. While public interest in prisons is growing, the prison has not been able to shake its aura. Even today, the public still reacts with repugnance to the prison.

Prison administrators complain about the prison's reputation and express a need for a more positive image. In actuality, though, prison officials devote scarce effort to community relations. Criminal justice and correctional scholars have not done better. Review any textbook on crime or corrections, consult the specialized journals, and you find that there is scant consideration given to prison-community relations.

Historically, the prison's relationship with the public was virtually non-existent. The term "fortress corrections" proved both a mentality and a philosophy. Fortress corrections can be traced to prisons' rural setting, and their function of separating individuals from society. Far from population centers, prisons were able to operate without interference.

The function of prisons was to separate. Prisons separated not only by walls and distance, but also by life-style and culture. The perils of prison confinement have been invoked for generations to discourage youthful misconduct. At the same time, the prison's actual operations remained shadowy.

Wardens of early prisons saw little benefit in community relations. There was a mutual (although unspoken) agreement between prison managers and the public that what went on behind prison walls was not subject to debate. Prisons did not want scrutiny, nor did the public want to be involved in their operation.

Correctional institutions in the past, however, were studied to a limited degree by outside inspectors. The inspectors, known as Boards of Visitors, served as representatives of the public. They focused on narrow issues. The costs of confinement, the offsetting effects of revenue from inmate industry, and the warden's control of expenses were prominent concerns. The reformative effects of religious instruction and hard work also dominated the boards' reviews.

Legal authorities reinforced the prison as a system unto itself. Until mid-century most courts viewed a prisoner as a "slave of the state." Prisoners lost all rights under law. As such, courts adopted a "hands off" policy toward prisoners' claims. Given that atmosphere, it is not surprising that relations between the community and prison were limited.

This separatist view changed, however, in the late 1960s. The courts began to intervene and regulate prison life. Freedom of expression and speech were extended inside the prison's walls. Inmates' access to the courts, use of mail, visits, media contacts, and religious practices were expanded. Later court decisions addressed the quality of prison life and due process for disciplinary and other institutional decisions.

This shift from a closed system to an open system coincided with events in society. Previously accepted conventions were being challenged in the sixties. The rights of criminal defendants were emphasized and the reach of government appeared to be decreasing.

Not only did citizens challenge societal principles, but they did so in a manner that conflicted with the law, often leading to detention in jails and prisons. Political activism spilled into prisons. Prisoner rebellions, while not new, became media events, intruding on public consciousness. None is more memorable than the national attention generated by the Attica uprising in 1971. The Attica riot led to a state-level inquiry and spawned a generation of researchers concerned with prison issues. It even led to a movie of the same name.

As prisons changed from being closed systems, publicity concerning their inner workings increased. This exposure has not translated into public understanding of prisons. The prison's public image remains shaped by media presentations. Whether one defines media as entertainment or news, both seem to focus on the negative.

The public continues to be exposed to the sensational or unusual: the failings of the prison, such as staff corruption, staff-inmate brutality, inmate escapes, and concerns over rising inmate populations and costs. Such portrayals perpetuate the image of a sadistic and barbaric staff, and undermine an objective analysis of the prison's legitimate function and effectiveness. It is readily apparent that prison administrators need to improve communication to the community.

Negative and sensationalized stories have an unfortunate effect. Correctional staff cringe when abuses are exposed. This leads them either to renew efforts to cultivate community relations or to return to an isolationist posture. The public has a difficult time ignoring sensational reports, be they true or untrue. Thus, the warden's efforts may be met by lukewarm public reaction. A vicious circle may then evolve: redoubled efforts meet with halfhearted response, causing strain. The rebuffed corrections manager becomes hesitant in further public-relations efforts. The ensuing gulf may continue to widen.

Despite these obstacles, many prison managers are able to develop good community relations. Sparking this change are the increasing number of correctional staff who are college educated. The rise in education level translates into openness to innovation, and recognition of the value of public relations.

Along with the rising education level of correctional staff is a push for professionalism. This has led to recognition of the need to communicate the mission of the prison. There is a realization that correctional institutions do not exist in a vacuum. Favorable prison-community relations translate into community confidence. Community support is important when prison tragedies occur. It can offset overreactions to the bad press that follows an escape, a riot, a suicide, or other breach of security.

External pressures are also forcing prison wardens to develop community relations. Crime and corrections occupy a prominent place on the social agenda. Increasing numbers of the adult population are under some form of criminal sanction. It is likely that someone we know—a relative, a friend, a co-worker—is faced with incarceration. When an issue hits close to home, interest increases.

Additionally, when societal controls appear ineffective, traditional institutions of control are even more heavily relied upon. Soaring correctional populations have resulted, pushing prison officials to answer questions about the increasing proportion of tax dollars allocated to prisons. Wardens are faced with accountability issues. What is the return on tax dollars spent for an inmate? What effect does prison have on recidivism?

Public demand to "do something" about offenders accents corrections. Public opinion remains divided on the objectives of prison. Is the prison for punishment (retribution), for reformation (rehabilitation), for incapacitation, or for deterrence? It is crucial that the prison and the community be on the same wavelength, since that influences assessments of how well the prison accomplishes its goals.

Prison-community relations are tested when new prison construction is proposed. First, there is the cost of prison expansion. One estimate places the cost per new prison cell at $75,000 to $100,000. Public support is vital to legislatures that ultimately approve construction funds.

The question of where to build the prison raises intense public emotions. Opponents to the construction or siting of a prison sometimes use the pejorative term "LULU" (locally unwanted land use) to describe prisons. Public outcry against prisons stem from fears about safety, the negative association of having a prison in one's community, and the adverse impact of the prison on local home values.

Another term in such debates is NIMBY, which stands for "not in my backyard." NIMBY refers to individuals who support correctional facilities, but do not want them located near their homes. Interestingly, some towns are now aggressively pursuing prison contracts. A number of once-prosperous towns are now courting new prisons to replace failing industries.

An interesting question is whether towns that already have prisons have more positive prison-community relations than towns that do not. It is logical to expect that where prisons dominate, there are improved prison-community relations. Residents in such towns should have discarded inhibitions about prisons. The resulting economic boon to the town and individual families may create pro-prison attitudes. Moreover, prison officials may be more sensitive and responsive to public opinion because of their preeminent position.

On the other hand, there is some suggestion of unease and distrust between prison officials and citizenry in prison towns. One reason may be that the control exerted by a single industry leads to an undervaluation of the need for community relations. Prison officials sometimes believe that they are asked for too much. The military style of prison management is also apt to carry over to its communications outside the institution. A top-down approach is not conducive to equal interchange. And, because prisons are organized at the state level, decisions are made far from the prison. Despite the local warden's proximity, policies are made at the state level with little regard for the impact on local communities.

A study of correctional officers in a rural prison in upstate New York addressed this issue indirectly. The study suggests that the information exchange in towns with prisons, at the front-line level, is limited. Town residents who do not work at the prison maintain an image of the prison limited by their experience; they do not have a clear image of life behind the prison's walls. Family contact does not significantly change the impact, because family members do not generally discuss their daily work.

During this time, when prison operations are under scrutiny, alternatives to incarceration are being advocated. Yet community-based corrections, whether a work-release facility, a halfway house, or some other intermediate sanction, create their own important prison-community concerns. Not all communities want a halfway house. Additionally, communities that endorse intermediate sanctions in lieu of incarceration need to understand the risks and rewards of that approach.

What exactly is prison-community relations, and how should it operate on the contemporary stage? Prison-community relations start with the simple and passive willingness of prison wardens to respond honestly and openly to media inquiries on matters of public interest, no matter how embarrassing or distressing. The steps in developing a prison-community relations effort begin with the establishment of an open public information policy and a public information officer to meet with the press. The public information officer is more than a news conduit. The effective public information officer serves as an educator about the realities of prisons, their goals, limitations, and internal workings. The public information officer works to correct the often erroneous impressions people have about prisons.

The second stage of prison-community relations involves the opening of the prison to outside groups interested in the salvation and rehabilitation of inmates. A policy that makes use of and encourages volunteers begins to involve important segments of the community, such as churches, universities, and self-help groups in the prison.

A third stage of development of prison-community relations involves the active solicitation of community volunteers and the development of staff positions in the institution devoted to coordinating, training, and recruiting them. Besides their direct benefit to inmates, these contacts serve a secondary community relations role. The prison volunteer interacts with others in the larger community. In the process of these daily interchanges the public is educated about the prison. Volunteers thus serve as independent and unofficial ambassadors for the prison.

The final stage in the development of prison-community relations involves the formation of prison programs in the community. Prison staff and inmates work in an effort to give back to the community that supports them. Inmate work programs provide low-cost labor for municipalities, non-profit agencies, and local charitable efforts.

Allied with this, prison staff become involved in community activities. They reach out to the community to tell the prison's story, and they listen to community concerns in a variety of ways. For example, prison staff speak to neighborhood watch and civic groups about the prison and the correctional profession. They participate in public safety programs, such as fingerprinting children, and donate to goodwill endeavors. In the same vein, some prisons open their programs to community residents. A few correctional institutions have permitted members of the local community to attend educational and vocational programs behind the walls.

All of these functions serve to increase communication between the prison and the community, thereby increasing the chance that the public's understanding of prisons will be improved. The move to an open system has just begun. There is a great deal more to be done to correct the misperceptions fostered by the popular media about prisons, their staffs, and the treatment of inmates.

Marilyn Ford

See also PUBLIC INFORMATION OFFICE AND PUBLIC RELATIONS

Bibliography

Carlson, K. A. (1992). Doing good and looking bad: A case study of prison/community relations. *Crime and Delinquency* 38: 56–69.

Cohen, N. P. (1976). The English Board of Visitors: Lay outsiders as inspectors and decisionmakers in prisons. *Federal Probation* 40: 24–27.

Jacobs, J. B. (1976). The politics of corrections: Town/prison relations as a determinant of reform. *Social Service Review* 50: 623–31.

Krause, J. D. (1992). The effects of prison siting practices on community status arrangements: A framework applied to the siting of California state prisons. *Crime and Delinquency* 38: 27–35.

Lombardo, L. X. (1989). *Guards Imprisoned: Correctional Officers at Work*, 2nd ed. Cincinnati, Ohio: Anderson.

National Advisory Commission on Criminal Justice Standards and Goals (1973). *Corrections*. Washington, D.C.: U.S. Government Printing Office.

Schwartz, J. A. (1989). Promoting a good public image. *Corrections Today* 51: 38ff.

Shichor, D. (1992). Myths and realities in prison siting. *Crime and Delinquency* 38: 70–87.

Zaner, L. O. (1989). The screen test: Has Hollywood hurt corrections' image? *Corrections Today* 51: 64–66ff.

Conjugal Visits

Although American criminologists have been writing about conjugal visits since at least the 1950s, only a modest body of literature on this practice exists. The term refers to the practice of permitting prisoners to visit privately with family members, including wives, children, and parents. As of 1993, nine states permitted some form of the practice (California, Connecticut, Minnesota, Mississippi, New Mexico, New York, South Carolina, Washington, and Wyoming). Conjugal visits are not permitted in federal correctional facilities (Goldstein 1990).

While the practice of allowing such extended family visits is not widespread, it has existed for many decades both in this country and abroad. Even though there is widespread support among prison officials for such visits, most jurisdictions do not offer conjugal visits and are not interested in pursuing such a program. Undoubtedly, what accounts for the infrequency of conjugal visits is the controversy surrounding them.

The Debate about Conjugal Visits

The debate about the merits of conjugal visits probably started in a formal way with the publication of the results of Balogh's (1964) survey of the views of seventy-three American and Canadian prison wardens on the subject. Of the fifty-two who responded, only 13 percent were in favor. Over half (56 percent) were opposed, with a great many respondents undecided or noncommittal.

Among those who favored extended family visits for inmates, several arguments were offered. Some felt that such visits are a right or entitlement rather than a privilege and thus should be made available to all prisoners, although the courts have not upheld that position. Others have argued that conjugal visits reduce homosexuality by alleviating some of the sexual tension that arises for most inmates during an extended prison stay. Conjugal visits are also said to be of value in maintaining family ties in general, and thus promote the prisoner's reintegration into the community. Others maintain that conjugal visits serve as an incentive for good behavior and adjustment and may be considered a form of rehabilitation.

Many arguments also exist in opposition to conjugal visiting. First, such visits have been opposed on moral grounds, with concerns that conjugal visits could lead to prostitution, unwanted children, or other undesirable outcomes, and thus would be opposed by the public. A second argument is based on financial considerations and maintains that conjugal visit programs are too costly to operate, an even more compelling argument now than when it was first made. Another argument reflects administrative concerns, concluding that conjugal visit programs are too unwieldy to administer. Potential administrative problems include the introduction of contraband or other security problems, liability concerns, staff corruption, jealousy by nonparticipating inmates, and the issue of what to do about common-law wives, a problem that may disproportionately affect minority inmates. Finally, it is possible that conjugal visit programs could actually be harmful or burdensome, rather than helpful, to some

inmates or their family members. For example, wives tend to bear the primary responsibility for orchestrating and traveling to the prison for the visit, which can be taxing financially, emotionally, and in terms of energy and time.

The History of Conjugal Visiting

The earliest family visiting program in the United States began in South Carolina during the late 1800s and included common-law as well as legally married wives (Goetting 1982). But the conjugal visit program that has been described in the most detail is the one at the Mississippi State Penitentiary at Parchman (Hopper 1989). Initially an all-black penal farm, in 1918 Parchman began to allow inmates to satisfy their physical and emotional needs by spending time with their wives. In the early days there were no specially designated facilities, and even into the 1970s no formal records of the visits were maintained. In 1940 the inmates themselves began to build special houses for inmate families to occupy during their visits.

Not until 1968 did another state, California, start a conjugal visit program. New York followed suit in 1976, followed quickly by Minnesota (1977), Connecticut and Washington (1980), and New Mexico and Wyoming (1983) (Goetting 1982; Lillis 1993).

In 1980 a task force was appointed within the federal prison system to explore the possibility of permitting conjugal visits in federal correctional facilities. After visiting several such programs at state facilities, it was concluded that it would not be advisable for the federal correctional program to adopt conjugal visits on a large scale, because of administrative and security concerns, negative staff attitudes, lack of access by long-term inmates, and abuses of the program in some states (such as an inmate's marrying a casual acquaintance to qualify for conjugal visits).

Current Practices and Issues

Currently, practices in conjugal visit programs vary by state and facility. In South Carolina, for example, each of the twenty-seven facilities has developed its own program, policies, and procedures. Most states restrict visits to inmates who are low security risks, and some require inmates to be near the end of their sentences and to show evidence of good institutional adjustment. At one new unit at Parchman in Mississippi, conjugal visits are part of a behavioral modification program in which the privilege must be earned.

Today, most conjugal visit programs encourage the participation of relatives other than the spouse, including children, parents, and siblings. Some states restrict extended family visits to weekends, whereas others provide time during the week as well. Visits typically last from twelve to seventy-two hours. Most states provide special facilities, such as trailers or cottages, for reasons of privacy. Typically, a visit involves activities such as cooking meals and eating together, watching television, talking, playing games, and sports—normal family activities that inmates do not have the opportunity to experience (Goetting 1982).

One current issue to affect conjugal visiting is AIDS. The incidence of HIV-infected inmates is high, although three states (New York, New Jersey, and Pennsylvania) account for almost three-quarters of the cases (Bates 1988; Goldstein 1990). Because drug-related confinements continue at a high rate, AIDS is likely to grow as a special management problem for correctional officials. That is likely to be true both for AIDS acquired prior to incarceration as well as HIV infection acquired during confinement. A range of viewpoints exist with respect to whether inmates who are HIV positive should be permitted to have conjugal visits. On the one hand, Bates has argued that conjugal visits can serve as a primary AIDS prevention measure in prison, insofar as such visits serve to reduce sexual activity with other inmates who may be HIV infected. He also recommends restricting conjugal visits to inmates and spouses who are free of infectious diseases (Bates 1988). On the other hand, Goldstein (1990) has argued that depriving AIDS-infected inmates of conjugal visits is clearly discriminatory, since HIV-infected inmates are covered under legislation protecting the handicapped (Section 504 of the Rehabilitation Act of 1973). The lack of consensus on this issue is reflected in state correctional policies on conjugal visits for HIV-infected inmates. California and Wyoming prohibit such visits for HIV-infected inmates, whereas New York, New Mexico, Washington, and Connecticut permit conjugal visits following appropriate disclosure, education, and counseling (Goldstein 1990; Lillis 1993).

Summary and Conclusions

The policy of allowing conjugal visits continues to be controversial, with only a minority of state correctional systems permitting extended family visits. Although most inmates, whether they are eligible for such visits or not, favor conjugal visits, as do potential visitors, correctional officials continue to be concerned about cost, public opinion, and administrative management of such programs. The advent of AIDS has complicated the issue considerably.

Bonnie E. Carlson

Bibliography

Balogh, J. K. (1964). Conjugal visitations in prison: A sociological perspective. *Federal Probation* 28: 52–58.

Bates, T. M. (1988). Rethinking conjugal visitation in light of the "AIDS" crisis. *New England Journal of Criminal and Civil Confinement* 14: 121–45.

Carlson, B. E., and N. Cervera (1992). *Inmates and Their Wives: Incarceration and Family Life*. Westport, Conn.: Greenwood.

Goetting, A. (1982). Conjugal association in prison: Issues and perspectives. *Crime and Delinquency* 28: 52–71.

Goldstein, S. (1990). Prisoners with AIDS: Constitutional and statutory rights implications in family visitation programs. *Boston College Law Review* 31: 966–1025.

Hopper, C. B. (1989). The evolution of conjugal visiting in Mississippi. *Prison Journal* 69: 103–9.

Howser, J. F., J. Grossman, and D. MacDonald (1983). Impact of family reunion program on institutional discipline. *Journal of Offender Counseling, Services and Rehabilitation* 8: 27–36.

Howser, J. F., and D. MacDonald (1982). Maintaining family ties. *Corrections Today* 43: 96–98.

Lillis, J. (1993). Family visiting evolves. *Corrections Compendium* 18: 1–4.

Contact Visits

Visits between prisoners and their guests occur in "contact" or "noncontact" settings. Contact visits take place in settings where there are no physical barriers between the prisoner and the visitor. In noncontact settings physical barriers such as glass or wire mesh prevent physical contact between the prisoner and the visitor. Contact visits have become the norm in prisons across the country. Noncontact visiting is now limited to only the most secure institutions and to small numbers of prisoners who have been classified as high security or safety risks. Unpublished, nationwide, longitudinal survey data gathered by Dickinson show that, between 1971 and 1991, the percentage of prisons across the country that practiced only noncontact visiting declined from 23 in 1971 to 4 in 1991.

In contact-visit settings, the extent of physical contact officially or unofficially permitted varies considerably. The Dickinson survey data reveal that, in 1971, 85 percent of the institutions surveyed allowed prisoners and visitors to embrace; by 1991 the number had increased to 95 percent. The permitted or tolerated behavior may range from a handshake or brief embrace to what might be described as "heavy petting." Until it was closed in 1991, the Virginia Penitentiary in Richmond went so far as to provide separate contact visiting rooms for "family visits" and "adult visits." The rationale was that the child visitor should not be exposed to the behavior that occurs during "adult visits."

Contact visiting has long been regarded as an important factor both in a prisoner's adjustment and for a successful return to the community. Support from one's intimates, such as family and friends, is of major importance to people in prison. The effects of isolation from family are particularly deleterious, whereas good family relations can make coping with prison life easier. The prevailing argument is that contact visits help maintain good relationships with family and friends, and that those relationships will provide valuable support for the offender upon release.

This point of view is founded on social role theory and social support theory (Hairston 1988). Social role theory suggests that contact visiting along with other means of maintaining relationships with family and friends, such as letters and phone calls, allows the prisoner to continue to maintain and function in desirable social roles—such as those of son, husband, father, brother, boyfriend—making it more likely that he will be able to successfully continue in these generally law-abiding roles upon release. Social role theory also asserts that when the desirable social roles are not maintained during incarceration, upon release the former prisoner is more likely to see himself, and to be seen by others, as an "ex-con." "Ex-con" roles are more likely to lead to renewed criminal behavior.

Social support theory argues that the presence of the social network that can be provided by family and friends and maintained in part through contact visits protects prisoners from stressful situations within prison and also protects the former prisoner from situations that might lead to criminal recidivism. This widely held view and its underlying theories tend to be supported by a growing body of research.

The importance of and support for contact visiting within the corrections community is so significant that the American Correctional Association (ACA) includes contact visiting among its standards for institutional accreditation. While the ACA includes contact visiting among its nonmandatory standards, institutions are required to meet 90 percent of the nonmandatory standards to be accredited.

The ACA standard specifies that institutions maintain written policies, procedures, and practices that provide prisoners with visiting facilities that permit opportunities for physical contact and informal communication. The degree of informality in visiting facilities and practices, however, should be consistent with the overall security requirements of the institution.

Contact visiting within the nation's prisons is not free of problems or critics. As is often the case with practices introduced into prisons to promote adjustment and rehabilitation, the practices are viewed as threats to the security and safety of the prison. The often heard arguments are that contact visiting provides an avenue of access for contraband such as drugs, that it provides a source of hostages if prisoners are so inclined, that it creates opportunities for escape, and that the requirements on the overworked prison staff are too great.

The practice of contact visiting, as is the case with other prison practices that seem to contain inherent tensions between adjustment and rehabilitation on the one hand and security and safety on the other, is structured to try to meet the goals of both camps. As with most compromises, neither set of goals is fully realized.

The presence of contact visiting itself is a concession to the proponents of rehabilitation. Supporters of the practice argue that it is too restrictive and underutilized as currently practiced in many institutions. Representatives of that point of view often argue that visiting should be maximized by increasing the visiting schedule, extending the length of visits, permitting more visits and visitors, making visiting areas more comfortable and informal, relaxing rules governing cameras and tape recorders, relaxing dress codes for visitors, and reassessing rules governing displays of affection

(Schafer 1989). Others argue that while contact visits may help inmates maintain contact with family and friends, current practices have limited success because close supervision and lack of recent contact often make the visits stifled and awkward (Carlson and Cervera 1991).

Prison officials responsible for security and safety no doubt insist that contact visiting itself creates threats to safety and security and that the prevailing rules are necessary to attempt to minimize the risks. The rules often involve strip searches of prisoners before and after visits, the right to search visitors, the right to turn away visitors who are not on approved visiting lists or are improperly dressed, restricting the items visitors may bring into visiting areas, and restricting the nature and extent of physical contact between prisoners and visitors (Schafer 1989).

Contact visiting has become an established practice throughout American prison systems and it is likely to remain so. It is also likely that the tension between the practice of contact visiting and the security and safety requirements of the institution will continue and that the implementation of contact visiting will reflect compromises between the two.

Thomas W. Seaman
George E. Dickinson

See also CHILDREN OF PRISONERS, CONJUGAL VISITS, VISITATION

Bibliography

Carlson, B., and N. J. Cervera (1991). Incarceration, coping, and support. *Social Work* 36: 279–85.

Hairston, C. F. (1988). Family ties during imprisonment: Do they influence future criminal activity? *Federal Probation* 52(1): 48–52.

Schafer, N. E. (1989). Prison visiting: Is it time to review the rules? *Federal Probation* 53(4): 25–30.

Schafer, N. E. (1991). Prison visiting policies and practices. *International Journal of Offender Therapy and Comparative Criminology* 35(3): 263–75.

William Conte (1926–)

Dr. William R. Conte is known both for his accomplishments in the field of psychiatry, and for the penal reforms he developed and implemented in the state of Washington in the late 1960s and early 1970s.

Following his graduation from the Vanderbilt University School of Medicine in 1945, Conte embarked upon a diverse and productive career in the fields of medicine, psychiatry, and mental health. In 1959 he went to the state of Washington to become the director of the Division of Mental Health, a position that was part of the state's Department of Institutions. While Conte occupied that position, Washington's three state mental hospitals received accreditation by the Joint Commission on Hospital Accreditation—the first time in state history that all three hospitals had been accredited simultaneously (Conte 1990, 171).

In 1966, Washington State Governor Dan Evans appointed Conte the state's director of institutions, overseeing the Division of Adult Corrections, the Division of Children and Youth, and the Division of Mental Health. Conte's progressive approach to corrections can be seen in his "Philosophy of Corrections" (1970), a paper that articulates both his belief in the need to treat and rehabilitate (rather than merely punish) prisoners and his commitment to preparing inmates for their eventual return to society.

Acting upon the principles in his paper, Conte sent shock waves through the state's prison system in November of 1970 when he introduced a program of far-reaching penal reforms for its adult correctional facilities. Among the reforms that Conte mandated were the extension of telephone and visiting privileges, a liberalizing of disciplinary procedures, expanded educational opportunities, the establishment of a furlough program, and the implementation of a "resident government council." The latter was a political structure to be composed of freely elected inmates, designed to provide inmates with some degree of self-governance in prison.

Because of these dramatic changes in its correctional philosophy and practice, Washington state was seen by many as a leader in the area of prison reform in the early 1970s. Although Conte's reforms were designed for implementation in all of the state's major adult correctional facilities, they received the most attention at the Washington State Penitentiary, in Walla Walla. That occurred for two reasons: First, the Washington State Penitentiary had traditionally been the largest and most visible correctional institution in the state. Second, that facility experienced an unusually large amount of disruption in the decade immediately following the implementation of Conte's reforms—a relationship that was anything but coincidental, in the eyes of many. Whatever its eventual fate, however, in the early 1970s the penitentiary in Walla Walla functioned as "a laboratory for what some observers consider the boldest experiment in recent penal history" (Tyrnauer 1981, 37).

This is not to suggest that all constituents were supportive of or enthusiastic about these new developments. Many of the administrators and correctional staff members objected to giving up so much of their control over the inmates. As described by one author, "The sudden switch from a traditional custody-oriented philosophy to one that focused on treatment created enormous resistance at all levels" (Cardozo-Freeman 1984, 7). Prison officials and staff were hostile to these reforms both because they felt—rightly or wrongly—that the reforms had been developed and implemented without consulting them, and also because they believed that the reforms would ultimately prove unworkable in a maximum security institution like theirs.

Of all of Conte's reforms, the implementation of the Resident Government Council (the RGC) was, by most accounts, both the most innovative and the most controversial. As conceptualized by Conte, the RGC was to consist of eleven inmates, elected by the inmate population, each of whom would serve for a term of six months. The purpose of this council was to give "residents a forum to express themselves and at the same time to learn something of what it means to participate in legal, formal, and proper representative expression of their interests and concerns" (Conte 1990, 87). It was, in short, designed to be "a learning experience . . . not just a governing one."

The RGC, and Conte's reforms more generally, came under increasing criticism at the Washington State Penitentiary as observers saw inmates gaining more and more control of the prison and as violence increased dramatically within its walls. In proposing this innovative idea, Conte had intended to help develop a sense of responsibility within the members of the inmate population. In actuality, however, the RGC gave those inmates who were so inclined the opportunity to see just how far they could expand their control over their fellow inmates, and over the penitentiary more generally. Thus, what originated as an experiment in inmate rights and responsibility gradually deteriorated into a social system of inmate dominance and manipulation.

Indeed, in the eyes of its critics, it was the existence of the RGC that was most responsible for bringing about the increased levels of gang activity, drug abuse, and violence that the penitentiary experienced in the 1970s. The situation was exacerbated by the fact that the prison superintendent, Bobby (B. J.) Rhay, had opted to formally recognize various inmate clubs that were, in principle, based upon shared hobbies and special interests. In fact, however, these clubs served to separate the inmate population into a network of criminal groups that "vied with one another and with the RGC for dominance in the penitentiary" (Tyrnauer 1981, 39; Camp and Camp 1988). Drugs became increasingly available in the penitentiary as inmate clubs grew more organized and established drug ties on the outside. Relatedly, the amount of violence within the institution also increased as a result of drug use, the competition for control of the lucrative drug trafficking market, and a general desire on the part of inmates to seize as much as possible of the power that had suddenly become available within the institution.

The Resident Government Council at the Washington State Penitentiary was dismantled in 1975 following a violent hostage-taking incident and a brief takeover of one wing of the institution. A new Resident Council, with fewer rights than the RGC and a very different underlying philosophy, was established by Superintendent Rhay. The inmate clubs still retained their power, however, and they continued to compete, often violently, both with each other and with the correctional staff. In 1978 and 1979, the tension and disorder within the institution increased to unprecedented levels, and a number of inmates and several correctional staff were killed in a series of violent incidents (Stastny and Tyrnauer 1982, 102–8). Finally, in the summer of 1979, Superintendent Robert Spalding (who had been appointed the previous year) began the process of "reclaiming" the institution, by abolishing most of the remnants of Conte's reforms and reestablishing control over the prison through a series of structural and philosophical changes implemented during the next several years.

There continues to be disagreement over the exact cause of the failure of the Resident Government Council, and Conte's reforms more generally, at the Washington State Penitentiary. As described by one analyst:

The prisoners attribute it to administrative sabotage. Conte blames it primarily on the increasingly powerful officer's union and the reluctant cooperation of administrators. Ex-Superintendent Rhay and most of the custodial staff hold [Donald] Horowitz [who headed the Department of Social and Health Services' legal staff during this period] and Conte responsible for going too far, too fast with what they considered a fundamentally unworkable scheme. Some of the professional treatment staff felt that it was a good program, but it had never been given a chance or an adequate budget (Tyrnauer 1981, 41).

Somewhat ironically, perhaps, Conte was not in a position to oversee and monitor the success of his reforms for the major portion of their existence. In January of 1971, the Department of Institutions became part of a new, larger state agency, the Department of Social and Health Services. Conte served as the deputy secretary of that department until he resigned in July of 1971, in his words, "because the conditions created by the Legislature in DSHS were politically motivated and thus made it impossible to succeed in effecting the reform movement [that he had begun]." Upon leaving state service, Conte pursued a private psychiatric practice in Tacoma, Washington. Conte retired in 1985 but continues to live an active life in the state of Washington.

Sarah Barbo
Keith Farrington

See also WALLA WALLA

Bibliography

Camp, C., and G. M. Camp (1988). *Management Strategies for Combatting Prison Gang Violence. Part II. Combatting Violent Inmate Organizations at the Washington State Penitentiary at Walla Walla: A Case Study*. Washington, D.C.: National Institute of Justice.

Cardozo-Freeman, I. (1984). *The Joint: Language and Culture in a Maximum Security Prison*. Springfield, Ill.: Charles C. Thomas.

Conte, W. R. (1970). A philosophy of corrections. *Perspectives* (Spring): 1–8.

Conte, W. R. (1990). *Is Prison Reform Possible? The Washington State Experience in the Sixties*. Tacoma, Wash.: Unique Press.

Stastny, C., and G. Tyrnauer (1982). *Who Rules the Joint? The Changing Political Culture of Maximum Security Prisons in America*. Lexington, Mass.: Lexington.

Tyrnauer, G. (1981). What went wrong at Walla Walla? *Corrections Magazine* 6: 37–41.

Contraband

Contraband is typically defined as any substance or material not authorized to be in possession of an inmate. Regulating "contraband" is a significant part of the prison security function. In addition to regulating inmate activities, the goods and services available to inmates are also severely restricted. Ironically, prisoner motivation to buy and sell contraband is, in part, a response to the highly regulated prison environment in which limits are placed upon inmates' autonomy and goods and services. In short, inmates attempt to expand their autonomy and the availability of goods and services for which they have a need by developing a marketplace for contraband goods and services.

A list of contraband items is routinely provided to inmates in prison. The following is an abbreviated list of contraband items from a prison in the Midwest:

1. Any weapon, including tools, instruments, or objects that could readily be used as a weapon, unless specifically authorized
2. All fermented alcoholic beverages
3. All dangerous drugs, narcotics, or restricted medications
4. State-owned equipment, tools, supplies, or materials unless authorized
5. All unauthorized clothing
6. All animals or pets
7. All food items not served in the dining room or purchased in the resident store
8. All forms of currency or money not authorized by the prison administration, or prison scrip belonging to another inmate
9. Obscene photographs or pornographic literature

A number of activities are also banned. Many of these activities promote the availability of contraband items. Such activities include loan sharking, in which inmates lend to other inmates money or forms of prison scrip at high rates of interest. Also banned is the practice of inmates acting as prostitutes to sell homosexual sex to other inmates. Often prostitution rings will form, with a group of prostitutes acting under the management of inmates who act as procurers (pimps) and who provide protection for the prostitutes. Jailhouse lawyers—inmates adept at doing legal work—have traditionally existed in institutions, but until recently that activity was banned. Currently, inmates may assist other inmates in legal matters but may not charge. Inmates with good reputations as jailhouse lawyers often charge large sums of money for their services, however.

Inmate laundry is a major task in every prison, and the operation is handled by the prisoners. The more enterprising inmates working in the laundry will charge others for starching and creasing their clothing, a service not otherwise available. Inmates gamble frequently among themselves. Typically, inmates will create an underground bookmaking organization to take bets on sporting events. Inmates will also manufacture "spud juice," an alcoholic beverage made from potatoes, sugar, or other foods stolen from the food service. Spud juice may be made for personal consumption or sold to other inmates in the contraband marketplace.

Contraband goods and services are usually available to inmates in almost all prisons; the amount of contraband will vary depending upon the needs of the inmates and the level of control exerted by correctional staff. Most individuals not familiar with the workings of a prison may find this surprising, and may think of prisons as highly controlled institutions in which activity is regulated twenty-four hours a day. That is true for the few prisons—referred to as maximum-security institutions—that manage volatile or violence-prone inmates. In maximum-security institutions, inmates are kept in their cells almost twenty hours a day and are tightly supervised during their few hours outside their cells. Maximum-security prisons are more expensive to construct and operate than medium- or minimum-security prisons, however. The vast majority of prisons are medium- or minimum-security institutions, in which inmates are given some degree of freedom in their activities. That is necessary because inmate labor is used to perform the services necessary to run the prison system. Inmates provide some clerical assistance, institutional maintenance and repair, food service, laundry work, and a number of other activities. Also, inmates in

most systems make office furniture—desks, chairs, filing cabinets—for state and federal offices. Inmates are also encouraged to attend classes, treatment programs, religious services, and the like. They receive free time for recreation and time in which to congregate outside of their cells in the central area of prison referred to as the yard. All of these activities give inmates some degree of freedom.

Providing inmates with responsibilities and allowing them some freedom also permits them to congregate into social groups and form gangs. That, in turn, allows inmates to share information on beating or circumventing prison security or locating inmates who are dealing in contraband. The freedom inmates have to move about and congregate increases the difficulty for corrections staff trying to keep track of their activities. One officer may be required to supervise between forty and two hundred inmates, depending upon the budget of the correctional system or institution. Hence, inmates who are motivated to deal in contraband have the opportunity to do so.

Correctional officers who work in institutions where inmates have some degree of freedom understand that they cannot totally control or eliminate all contraband. Hence they place a high priority on controlling contraband they view as dangerous. Officers, for example, will make every effort to keep weapons out of the hands of inmates. Officers will conduct random cell searches or frequently search inmates with a history of possessing weapons. Cell searches will occasionally be announced in advance, and inmates will be given an opportunity to throw contraband out of their cells onto the cell block floor prior to the search. Stories abound of the sound of homemade knives and other weapons falling to the floor during such security exercises.

On the other hand, officers will give what they consider less harmful forms of contraband a lower security priority. Officers, for example, will be less concerned about low-level production of "spud juice" for personal consumption, possession of unauthorized cooking utensils or clothing, or even possession or use of marijuana in some instances.

Most contraband is manufactured or acquired within prisons. For example, weapons can be manufactured in prison machine shops or factories from metal products or tools. Inmates are adept at turning harmless objects into weapons. A hair comb can be sharpened by rubbing it on concrete, and a tooth brush can be sharpened to a point or split and retaped with a razor blade inside. It is a long-standing tradition for inmates to steal potatoes and fruit from the inmate dining hall to brew "spud juice." In many prisons inmates will buy large quantities of goods, such as tobacco, candy, potato chips, and other snacks, from the inmate commissary and resell them in the evening hours after the commissary is closed. The price for these items is usually double the original purchase price, but the service provides a convenience for inmates.

Contraband that cannot be manufactured or acquired inside a prison is smuggled into prisons by a number of avenues. Illegal drugs such as cocaine, heroin, or marijuana are usually in high demand among inmates, creating a profitable market for anyone who can provide the inmates with such drugs. Commercial alcoholic beverages, such as bourbon or scotch, are popular with higher-status inmates. On rare occasions, guns are found in prisons. These are a few examples of contraband that is smuggled into prisons for sale in the contraband marketplace.

Prisons are almost always sealed off from the world by tall stone walls or razor-wire fences. The few entrances into prisons are manned by corrections officers who inspect individuals and vehicles that enter prisons in an effort to prevent unauthorized items from entering. Again, it would seem impossible to successfully smuggle contraband into any prison. There are, however, many methods that inmates have devised to breach security.

Occasionally, prison personnel get caught up in the contraband trade and smuggle items into prison for inmates. That is especially true for illicit drugs. As an example, an officer at a prison in the Midwest routinely stopped for breakfast at a restaurant owned by the mother of an inmate. He would pick up a cache of cocaine and deliver it to the inmate. The inmate, in turn, would sell it to other inmates in the contraband marketplace. In another instance, a prison employee was caught attempting to smuggle a large plastic bag of marijuana into prison. In both cases, the employees were receiving substantial sums of money for delivering the drugs.

Prison personnel who smuggle contraband may be corrupt to begin with. Some who get caught up in smuggling, however, are tricked or coerced into doing the bidding of inmates. Enterprising inmates may solicit small favors from officers or other staff. If the staff member complies, and the favor, small as it may seem, violates prison policy, the inmate can use that against the employee and ask for more favors. If the employee doesn't comply, the inmate will threaten to inform on the employee, putting the employee's job in jeopardy. For example, a gullible employee may have what looks like a good rapport with an inmate. The inmate may ask the employee to hand carry a letter to his wife, claiming that an officer in the mail room is maliciously throwing away all of his correspondence. If the employee complies, the inmate will then request that a letter from his wife be carried into the prison. If the employee complies with that request, the inmate now may assert that the letter brought in contained drugs and that the employee has become a member of the inmate's drug ring. If the employee balks, the inmate will threaten to inform the prison authorities and produce the evidence of the employee's complicity. In effect, the employee is threatened with possible prosecution for selling drugs, a charge that carries draconian punishment.

Prison visits can also be an avenue for smuggling contraband. Most visiting is done under high security. Inmates talk to their visitors through screens or over telephones while facing each other through plate-glass windows. Many other institutions, however, provide inmates and their families an opportunity to meet in a more relaxed setting in which they can sit around a table. During such a visit, the inmate is usually allowed to make limited physical contact with visitors, a practice called "contact visitation." Contact visits reduce security. Giving contact visits to inmates for good behavior, however, is a valuable tool in obtaining compliance. Some inmates will take advantage of the privilege by having visitors bring contraband to them. Inmates will secure contraband in their clothing or body cavities or swallow certain items, such as balloons with small amounts of drugs in them, and retrieve them later. Corrections staff are required to search inmates thoroughly before and after visits, including a strip and body cavity search. Some inmates, however, manage to get past the system and successfully smuggle contraband. The relatives of inmates are usually allowed to provide inmates with a few amenities, such as clothing or condiments. If those items are not carefully inspected, the items may become vehicles for smuggling contraband.

Historically, all inmate correspondence—incoming and outgoing—was censored by pris-

C

on personnel. Censorship of inmate mail has now been severely restricted by court decisions, although custodial staff may inspect correspondence before passing it on to inmates to prevent unauthorized items from reaching inmates. One ploy used by inmates has been to have a small amount of cocaine or heroin placed under the stamp. Also, letters have been found to have been soaked in liquefied drugs, making the paper itself a consumable drug.

With some restrictions, books and magazines can be mailed directly to inmates from publishers. It is assumed that books mailed directly from commercial publishers cannot be tampered with and will be free of contraband. Hence, books mailed to inmates packaged by a commercial publisher may be given to the inmate without inspection. Friends of an inmate may order books from a publishing house, however, and have them mailed to their home address. The inmate's friends can hide contraband in the book, send it back to the publisher, and ask that it be mailed to the prisoner.

Selected inmates are assigned to work details and allowed to travel with some freedom in and out of their institutions. For example, inmate mechanics may be assigned to repair prison vehicles that are outside the prison perimeter. Inmates are given these assignments only after careful screening. Some of the inmates holding these positions will attempt to bring unauthorized goods into their prison. In one instance, a prison tow truck that an inmate mechanic was driving back into the prison was searched and twenty pints of bourbon were found under the seat. Also, commercial vehicles make routine deliveries to prisons, and the goods they deliver must, at some point, enter the prison. Contraband can be hidden in the goods being delivered or in some niche on the delivery truck.

Correctional officers are usually vigilant in their attempts to control the flow of contraband into prisons, especially contraband that they consider a danger to the security of the institution. Officers will conduct random inmate and cell searches, search, or "shakedown," entire cell blocks, and provide inmates with opportunities to give up contraband without risk of punishment. Some institutions have implemented random urinalysis to detect drug use by either prisoners or staff. One maximum-security institution in the Midwest reported that, for a twelve-month period, all random drug tests of inmates and staff were negative, suggesting that few or no illegal drugs were being smuggled into that institution.

Perhaps the greatest aid to corrections officers is information from inmates who are seeking favors from the staff or who have some personal interest in seeing a fellow inmate apprehended. For example, inmates who sell contraband often inform on competitors to protect their market. In spite of the vigilance of prison administrators and staff, a contraband market exists in almost all institutions. Inmates demand certain unauthorized goods and services, and other enterprising inmates attempt to supply what's wanted for the purpose of making a profit.

The exchange and possession of contraband can have both positive and negative consequences for a prison. On the positive side, inmates who are successful in buying and selling contraband generally avoid causing problems and make every effort to give the appearance of following rules and regulations. Inmates who are making substantial profits will typically try to protect the order and stability of the prison or their cell area to avoid having their enterprise discovered or disrupted. In effect, such inmates—often referred to as "merchants" or "politicians"—share the institution's need for order. In poorly managed prisons, merchants or politicians may be the major source of institutional security.

There are many harmful consequences of contraband. Obviously, weapons in the possession of inmates is a danger in itself. Inmates who are unable to barter for or purchase the contraband they desire may resort to theft or extortion to obtain contraband goods from other inmates, or they may resort to criminal behavior to obtain the funds needed to purchase what they want. That, in turn, may increase violence among inmates and increase their need for weapons. In the prison drug trade, assaults, killings, or gang wars may develop over turf or market territory. Prison gangs that successfully deal drugs may become powerful and impossible to manage. Because of the enormous amount of money that may be generated from illegal drug sales, staff may become corrupted.

The methods and schemes by which inmates create contraband are endless. Prison authorities and correctional staff engage in an ongoing effort to control the supply of contraband within prison populations. In turn, inmates constantly develop new and sometimes ingenious methods of smuggling contraband. Contraband will very likely remain part of any prison system and a constant challenge for correctional staff.

David B. Kalinich

See also DISCIPLINE

Bibliography
Hill, M. O. (1984). Permanent confiscation of prison contraband: The Fifth Amendment behind bars. *Yale Law Journal* 93: 901–17.
Kalinich, D. B. (1980). *The Inmate Economy.* Lexington, Mass.: Lexington.
Sexton, P. S. (1985). Contraband control and the use of X-rays in the prison environment. *Pacific Law Journal* 16: 409–30.

Corporal Punishment

Corporal punishment is defined as any physical pain inflicted on the body, short of death, by any device or method. It has been used in corrections in the United States both as a sentence and as a disciplinary procedure. Colonial Americans, in an effort to preserve order, imported the same means of punishment that had been used in their homelands.

Corporal Punishment as a Sentence

Methods of Punishment
As a sentence once imposed for noncapital criminal offenses, corporal punishment included whipping, stretching on the rack, various forms of mutilation (tongue cut out, hands cut off, ears cropped, ears nailed to the pillory), burning hands, branding with a letter on fingers, arm, or face, "ducking," and confinement in the stocks and pillories. The stocks held the offender while sitting down, with head and hands locked in the frame, whereas the pillory held the offender while standing. Branding usually involved the imprinting of letters representing the crimes offenders had been convicted of: for example, a "T" for thievery, "B" for blasphemy, or "A" for adultery. By most accounts, whipping was the most common form of corporal punishment. The number of lashes was dependent upon the nature of the offense as well as the criminal career of the offender. In Massachusetts, whippings were generally restricted to a maximum of forty stripes.

History
These punishments were used in the North and the South, for both male and female, black and white, young and old. In some jurisdictions, however, there was a lower age limit for severe corporal penalties. Also, in some instances the specific corporal punishment was combined with a fine or prescribed as an alternative to a fine. In the case of repeat offenders, the severity of the punishment increased. For example, Caldwell (1947) reports that for the first offense a person convicted of burglary or robbery in colonial Delaware would be branded on the forehead. The penalty for the second offense included both branding and a severe whipping.

Concern over the treatment of convicted criminals led to the development of the penitentiary as an alternative to corporal punishment. Laws substituting imprisonment for corporal penalties were first introduced in the late 1700s. The immediate result was a reduction in the use of corporal punishments. In Massachusetts, corporal punishment was abolished de jure in 1826. In Connecticut, it disappeared in 1830. By the turn of the nineteenth century, most states had completely rewritten their criminal codes to outlaw corporal punishments. Its total abolition, however, was gradual. Corporal punishment survived in the Northern states until the early 1800s and in the South until after the Civil War.

Branding was practiced in both Maryland and Massachusetts until 1829. Maryland authorized whipping for wife-beaters, although it was rarely used. Delaware, however, continued whipping as a punishment for serious crimes. According to Caldwell (1947), in 1945 the laws of Delaware prescribed lashes for twenty-four different crimes. Delaware abolished the pillory in 1905, but the whipping post remained until the 1970s, when it was removed from the penitentiary.

With the passage of time these penalties came to be used mainly against blacks. More specifically, Caldwell (1947) reports that in Delaware there were differences by race as well as by gender in the severity of corporal punishments imposed. Delaware abolished the whipping of white women convicted of larceny in 1855, but the whipping of all women, black as well as white, was not abolished until 1889.

In those states that had outlawed the use of corporal punishments there were periodic efforts to restore them. According to Hirsch (1992), between 1816 and the early 1820s there was a "crisis of confidence in the penitentiary." As early as 1816 there were efforts to restore public punishments in Massachusetts. In 1881 there were attempts to reestablish the whipping post in Arkansas.

Corporal punishment has reemerged as an issue. In the early 1980s Newman (1983) argued for a return to corporal punishment, maintaining that properly administered it is less destructive, less costly, and more effective than incarceration. Newman advocated electric shock as the preferred method of punishment. In 1989 a bill was introduced in Delaware to bring back public whipping as a punishment for those convicted of dealing in hard drugs.

The recent caning of Michael Fay in Singapore for spray-painting cars has once again stimulated debate on the pros and cons of corporal punishment as a correctional sentence. The final sentence—four strokes with a rattan cane—was carried out amidst appeals from the president of the United States.

Public opinion polls have provided conflicting reports. A *Los Angeles Times* poll reported that Americans were divided evenly over the caning in Singapore, whereas another poll indicated that most Americans disapproved of the caning. The clear conclusion was that Americans as a group were dissatisfied with efforts to fight crime and that they see tougher punishment for criminals as the answer.

A number of politicians and religious leaders have called for a change in the approach to punishment. A St. Louis alderman, a California assemblyman, and members of the Louisiana house have all introduced legislation that would legalize public caning for graffiti writers and vandals. The bill introduced in California would punish juvenile graffiti vandals with up to ten "whacks" with a wooden paddle. This punishment would be carried out by a parent. The former mayor of New York City and a rabbi in Houston voiced support for the move to corporal punishments for criminals.

Corporal Punishment as a Disciplinary Procedure

Methods of Punishment

The use of corporal punishment as a disciplinary procedure in correctional institutions began with the advent of the penitentiary in the late 1700s and continued into the 1900s. Many institutions permitted these punishments. The types of punishments included the traditional ones of whipping, the cross, the ball and chain, the gag, "carrying water," and treadmills.

History

Corporal punishment has been used to discipline juveniles and adults, men and women. The New York House of Refuge, which opened in 1825, stipulated that those who violated the rules were subject to be lashed. Rothman (1971) reviews the diary of the superintendent, which indicated the use of the whip and the paddle for such rule violations as talking and practicing disobedience. Women in Southern prisons were disciplined the same as men. In the late 1800s, female lessees, mostly black, were not only whipped the same as men but in the presence of male lessees.

Reports of severe corporal punishments were released shortly after the development of the penitentiary. Similar reports have been released throughout the history of the penitentiary. Bowker (1980) reports that brutal treatment of offenders in the North decreased substantially by the 1930s but that in some Southern prisons such treatment was evident as late as the 1970s. These reports of brutality included penal farms, prison camps, the convict lease system, and other alternatives to the penitentiary in the South. Although the legal limit for whippings was fifteen lashes per day, reports indicated many instances of whippings involving a considerably larger number.

According to Keve (1986), Virginia passed legislation prohibiting the use of corporal punishment in adult institutions in 1946, but the practices continued in the juvenile facilities until an administrative directive ordered an absolute stop to whipping in 1973. At that time legislation was also passed that expressly prohibited the whipping of female convicts.

Contemporary Abuses

Although corporal punishment had been used in the Arkansas system for some time, it was not authorized formally until 1962. In Arkansas, whipping was officially the primary disciplinary measure. An inmate could be whipped with a five-foot leather strap ten times a day. Officials in Arkansas also introduced a number of other methods of discipline, which included inserting needles under the fingernails, crushing knuckles and testicles with pliers, hitting the inmate with a club or blackjack or kicking him in the groin, mouth, or testicles, use of the "Tucker Telephone," and use of the teeter board. For the Tucker Telephone, the offender is stripped naked and strapped to a table. Electrodes are attached to his big toe and his penis and electrical charges are sent through his body until just before the prisoner becomes unconscious (Murton and Hyams 1969).

As a result of the *Talley v. Stephens* and the *Jackson v. Bishop* cases, corporal punishment of inmates as well as the use of alternative methods of punishment were outlawed. Shortly thereafter the court ruled that the entire Arkansas state prison system was unconstitutional because of the cruel and unusual punishments inflicted on the inmates. Reports from Louisiana, Mississippi, Virginia, New York, Kansas, Georgia, and Florida indicated that official use of corporal punishment for disciplinary purposes resulting in abuse was not restricted to Arkansas.

Although the disciplining of prisoners by the use of corporal punishment has been legally removed from the federal prison system and most every state's penal system, the practice still persists. As recently as 1993, former inmates of the Onondaga County jail in New York sued for cruel and unusual punishment over the practice of being hung by their handcuffs from cell bars and shackled to their beds.

Summary
Debate over the efficacy of corporal punishment in prison has been waged since its introduction. Reports of the brutal manner in which corporal punishment, both as a sentence and as a disciplinary procedure, was used against criminals, especially women and children, led to early calls for its elimination. Reports of the brutal and racially discriminatory manner in which it was imposed led to post–Civil War calls for its end. Policies and proposals that have prohibited the use of corporal punishment in the home and in the school have furthered the demise of corporal punishment. It would appear that corporal punishment has virtually disappeared. Events in the very recent past, however, suggest that this is one debate that will remain with us for some time.

Vernetta D. Young

Bibliography
Barnes, H. E. (1972). *The Story of Punishment*. 2nd ed. Montclair, N.J.: Patterson Smith.

Bowker, L. H. (1980). *Prison Victimization*. New York: Elsevier.

Caldwell, R. (1947). *Red Hannah: Delaware's Whipping Post*. Philadelphia: University of Pennsylvania Press.

Hirsch, A. (1992). *The Rise of the Penitentiary: Prisons and Punishment in Early America*. New Haven, Conn.: Yale University Press.

Keve, P. (1986). *The History of Corrections in Virginia*. Charlottesville, Va.: University Press of Virginia.

Murton, T., and J. Hyams (1969). *Accomplices to the Crime: The Arkansas Prison Scandal*. New York: Grove Press.

Newman, G. (1983). *Just and Painful: A Case for the Corporal Punishment of Criminals*. New York: Free Press.

Rothman, D. (1971). *The Discovery of the Asylum*. Boston: Little, Brown.

Cases
Jackson v. Bishop, 404 F.2d 571 (1968)
Talley v. Stephens, 247 F. Supp 683 (E.D. Arkansas 1965)

C

Correctional Officers

I. History
Prison reformers of the nineteenth century sought to enhance the rehabilitation process by improving conditions within the penitentiary. Proper supervision of inmates was one area of concern. As Dorothy Dix (1845, 21) cautioned, "I would never suffer any exhibition of ill temper, or an arbitrary exercise of authority. The officers should be equally subject to rules and discipline as the prisoners." Ironically, the first training academy for correctional officers was not opened until almost one hundred years later.

Experts and visitors touring the early American prisons were unimpressed with the quality of supervision. As Kate O'Hare explained (1923, 161):

Prison jobs have become the dumping-ground for the inefficient and unfit relatives and political hangers-on of the professional politicians. These human misfits and failures are thrust into prison jobs because as a rule, they are too worthless for other employment . . . industrially unfit and generally illiterate, human scrubs, mentally defective, morally perverted and very often of much lower type than the prisoners whom they handle.

The correctional officer force, from the earliest institutions until the late 1940s and even later in some states, was untrained, unprofessional, and received their positions on the basis of political patronage. Most prisons were located in remote areas, where employees were undereducated and unsophisticated. Salaries were exceptionally low, and guards usually had to buy their own weapons and uniforms. A 1937 study by the Attorney General's Office found that guards worked an average of forty-eight to eighty-four hours per week. The routine of locking and unlocking doors, the continual counting of inmates, and the supervising of inmates entire days in the hot sun caused the officers to suffer what some experts referred to as a "lock psychosis." Many still sought the jobs, particularly during hard economic times. Benefits included low-cost or free meals as well as laundry service, access to prison-made goods, and state housing.

Yet for many years some prison systems, particularly in the South, hired few guards. Their small guard forces were supplemented by inmate trusties. Early prisons operated as closed institutions, with little public or governmental interference, and brutality by both guards and trustie supervisors was common. When scandals arose over the deaths of prisoners that resulted from beatings or torture, a few employees may have been discharged or reprimanded, but few if any formal changes were likely to result. In 1943, Barnes and Teeters wrote that the "average matron in a reformatory is sex-starved, soon becomes embittered at her worldly fate and takes out her revenge on the helpless inmates" (1943, 596).

As far back as the 1920s, psychologists warned that there was too much "social distance" between the prison staff and administration. The low status of the guards was viewed as stress-producing. Often manipulated by the prisoners, officers felt themselves as much imprisoned as those they guarded.

Though training schools for prison guards have been used in other countries since the late 1830s, the first was opened in this country only in 1930 in New York City. Federal Bureau of Prisons Director Sanford Bates asked Jessie O. Stutsman to design a three-month training program for correctional officers. The philosophy of the school was to control prisoners not with force but with intelligence and leadership. Courses in the academy included the history of crime and punishment, a study of the present crime situation, types of penal institutions and their functions, the prisoner and his background, prison discipline, and classification and segregation. Professional organizations developed to set performance standards and to enhance the image of the occupation. Over the years, the American Correctional Association, employee unions, and state civil-service regulations all contributed to raise the caliber of recruits and to improve pay, working conditions, and the monitoring of professional conduct.

Marilyn D. McShane

See also BUILDING TENDERS, TRUSTIES

Bibliography

Barnes, H. E., and N. K. Teeters (1943). *New Horizons in Criminology.* New York: Prentice-Hall.

Dix, D. (1845). *Remarks on Prisons and Prison Discipline in the United States.* Reprinted 1967, Montclair, N.J.: Patterson Smith.

O'Hare, K. R. (1923). *In Prison.* New York: Alfred Knopf.

Schade, T. (1986). Prison officer training in the United States: The legacy of Jessie O. Stutsman. *Federal Probation* 50(4): 40–46.

II. Selection and Training

Until recently, the role of the correctional officer has been principally one of "turnkey": that is, strictly custodial in nature. Little attention was directed to the issues of recruitment, selection, training, or continued education.

The past thirty-five to forty years of research and correctional activity have created an increasingly complex, although somewhat contradictory, body of knowledge. In a 1947 article, Lundberg referred to the selection process of prison guards as little more than a meaningless exercise. As recently as 1981, Toch wrote, "The correctional officer is a residue of the dark ages. He requires 20/20 vision, the IQ of an imbecile, a high threshold for boredom and a basement position in Maslow's hierarchy" (1981, 20). On the other hand, another view has it that the correctional officer can be the single most important authority in terms of control of the inmate population. Effective inmate treatment programs are improved by the training and professionalism of the correctional officer.

To appreciate and understand the unique role of the correctional officer in the American workforce, one must first have a basic understanding of the dramatic changes that have occurred in penal philosophy during the growth of this nation. Prisons have gradually become less severe and more humane "correctional institutions." Since the 1950s humanitarian reforms designed to lessen the pain of imprisonment and provide constructive inmate "programs" have replaced the more repressive penitentiary setting. Over time, the negative and stereotypical connotations associated with corrections employment have been offset by substantial pay increases and a professionalized work environment. Increased training and organization within the field has brought status and readily marketable skills to the workforce.

Throughout these periods of change, the role of the correctional officer has had to change with the times. Traditionally, correctional officers have been white men from rural areas or small towns. Many of these COs had very limited educations and a history of unemployment. Officers frequently began their careers in their middle to late twenties after having tried a variety of other occupations. Many were retired military personnel. Correctional officers frequently reported an interest in police work and may have chosen corrections because it appeared somewhat related. A primary employment motivation factor for many was job security. The correctional system provided the promise of steady work with little fear of layoffs. The officers frequently were not able to identify with corrections as a profession. The common tendency was to view their work as "just another job" (Lombardo 1981).

The traditional image of the correctional officer is changing in many areas. Change has been the result of a number of factors: (1) more highly trained individuals seeking employment in corrections; (2) correctional systems, such as the Federal Bureau of Prisons and many state organizations, that start most employees out as COs; and (3) pressure from various groups to expand the hiring of both women and minorities. Another factor that has resulted in the changing profile of the correctional officer has been the increasing demands of the job. As corrections has developed as a field of study and an active component of the criminal justice system, so has the level of professionalism among correctional officers. Extended periods of education are becoming more important as selection criteria and requirements for promotion. Successful careers in corrections clearly require greater commitment to professionalism than was necessary as recently as fifteen years ago. Though entry-level requirements are still comparatively low in some places, advancement often requires higher education.

Institutional changes and improvements have created a new opportunity and job definition for the modern correctional officer. The very dynamics created by the rehabilitative model of today's correctional institutions require an overall improvement in officer performance together with a basic understanding of the behavioral sciences. Today's correctional officer is the primary agent for promoting health, welfare, security, and safety within correctional institutions. Through direct interaction with accused and adjudicated offenders, the professional correctional officer is the essential catalyst of change within the correctional process.

Recruitment and Selection

Many applications for work in corrections are prompted by advertisements by civil-service commissions that an examination will be held for an entry-level position. In many other cases, interested persons may approach the personnel officer at the prison. Who is hired depends heavily on the philosophy of the personnel officer, warden, or committee doing the hiring. The selection process is generally acknowledged as a key event in the operational effectiveness of a state or local correctional agency. All jurisdictions necessarily differ in a variety of ways regarding personnel selection. Nevertheless, basic principles exist for the development of an efficient, effective, and fair selection process that results in the appointment of those individuals with the best skills, knowledge, and abilities.

Among the most important components of the selection process is a written job analysis that includes each position's duties and responsibilities, their relative importance, the frequency with which they are to be performed, and the minimum level of proficiency necessary to perform each job.

A job-related, useful, and nondiscriminatory selection process is dependent upon a number of professionally and legally accepted administrative practices and procedures, including informing candidates of all parts of the selection process at the time of formal application, a written directive establishing selection criteria for positions where lateral entry is permitted, written procedures governing the reapplication, retesting, and reevaluation of unsuccessful candidates, and timely notification of candidates at all critical points in the process.

Generally, the first step in the selection process is the administration of a comprehensive written exam. If written tests are used, they must meet the professional and legal requirements of validity (job-relatedness), utility (usefulness), and minimum adverse impact (fairness). Following the successful completion of the written exam, oral interviews of eligible candidates are conducted using uniform questions, evaluation criteria, and rating procedures.

A written background investigation of successful candidates, conducted by trained personnel, is generally recognized as one of the most useful and relevant components of the selection process. Correctional careers require that individuals be of good moral character and not have been convicted of any felony or misdemeanor offenses that involve "moral turpitude." An offense involving moral turpitude is usually interpreted to mean misdemeanor theft or similar, less serious crimes that may suggest an untrustworthy character.

In addition to a criminal record check, the background investigation should include the verification of a candidate's qualifying credentials and the verification of at least three personal references. Some agencies require psychological examinations, a polygraph, or voice stress examinations as an additional investigative aid. Although the use of psychological testing is questioned by some (Wahler and Gendreau 1985), Benton (1988) found that 24 percent of the states do use psychological testing to screen entry-level candidates.

Prior to the final offer of employment, occupational qualifications such as general health, physical fitness and agility, emotional stability, and psychological fitness are measured and interpreted by trained personnel using valid and nondiscriminatory procedures. A probationary period (ranging from six to twenty-four months) and completion of entry-level training is required of all entry-level correctional officers.

Knowledgeable, highly skilled, motivated, and professional correctional personnel are essential to fulfill the purpose of corrections effectively. Improved recruitment and selection standards of entry-level correctional officers can make a positive contribution to the overall function and operation of the organization. Carlos Sanchez, chief of selection and training for the California Department of Corrections, questions the current minimum standards for entry-level officers. According to Sanchez (1989, 166), "We should raise our expectations and require a higher competency level for employment. . . . The writing ability of a large segment of our applicant group is deplorable. . . . We should increase our focus on attracting college-trained applicants."

Chief Sanchez is not alone in his assessment. In a 1992 questionnaire survey of state personnel officers by the Robert Presley Institute of Corrections Research and Training, a majority of the respondents favored "some college up to a minimum associate of arts degree" as a prerequisite for entry-level correctional officers (Sechrest and Josi 1992). Results from the same study, however, indicate that the minimal educational standard for employment as a correctional officer "was less than a high school diploma for 13 states (25.5 percent), a GED or high school diploma in 22 states (43.1 percent), and a high school diploma or more for 16 states (31.4 percent). . . . In two-thirds of the states (35, or 68.6 percent), a GED or less would be sufficient education to become a correctional officer" (1992, 8).

Pre-service and In-service Training
Training has often been viewed as one of the most important responsibilities in any correctional agency. Training serves three broad purposes. First, well-trained officers are generally better prepared to act decisively and correctly in a broad spectrum of situations. Second, training results in greater productivity and effectiveness. Third, it fosters cooperation and unity of purpose. Furthermore, agencies are now being held legally accountable for the actions of their personnel and for failing to provide initial or remedial training.

To carry out their security and supervision responsibilities, correctional officers need to understand their agency's correctional philosophy and their institution's regulations and procedures. They must be security technicians, experts in their search, supervision, and inmate management skills. They must know the limits of their responsibility and authority, as well as how to work as team members with other staff members. Finally, they must understand the judicial and legislative decisions that affect what they do. To impart all of these important facts, well-developed training programs are necessary.

Poorly trained officers with no prior experience are a threat to themselves and to others. New officers with no prior training have no idea of the proper role or job responsibilities of correctional officers. And yet most new correctional officers have no prior experience in working with inmates, and almost none have any training that applies to the prison setting.

The professionalization of training in corrections has followed a long and tortuous path. In many respects, the field of corrections has been slow to recognize the value of training and the impact it can have on the total organization (Carter 1991). That is why training is so critical. In fact, in the late 1970s, the American Correctional Association (ACA) Commission on Accreditation specified the first training standards. ACA not only identified specific standards for new officers but also established requirements identifying essential training topics and the number of hours for preservice orientation, academy, and in-service training.

According to ACA standards, new officers should receive forty hours of preservice orientation training. At a minimum, the preservice training should familiarize the new correctional officer with the overall mission and purpose of the organization as well as present an overview of the correctional occupation. An additional 120 hours of academy-type training is recommended during the first year of employment and forty hours of in-service training each successive year.

Academy training is provided to new correctional officers in virtually all correctional settings. The Federal Prison System has training centers in several institutions in various places around the country. Many states have correctional academies similar to those developed by police departments. In 1990, the Center for the Study of Crime, Delinquency and Corrections (CSCDC) conducted a survey of personnel training in state prison systems. Of the states reporting (thirty-two), twenty-one had established independent academies that served corrections exclusively. Eight states described an academy model that serves multiple state agencies, and the remaining three programs serve single institutions (Carter 1991).

In the paramilitary academy setting, new recruits learn the law under which they function, rules of the institution, elementary personality development, methods of counseling, defensive tactics and use of firearms, report writing, inmate rules and regulations, inmates' rights and responsibilities, and basic first aid and CPR techniques. Most jurisdictions require continuous inservice training, generally involving a specific minimum number of hours of lectures and instruction in each quarter of the year.

Survey results conducted by *Corrections Compendium* (1990) indicate that virtually every state requires at least a minimum of 120 hours of preservice (academy) training for correctional officers. Many states significantly exceed this requirement. More than 50 percent of the states reported a minimum of forty hours of in-service training required annually of employees. Some states required more, others less, and some did not specify.

Post-Secondary Education

A primary goal of education is to instill in individuals the desire to continue learning throughout life. The world in which the corrections professional functions is continually changing. New discoveries are made, new laws passed, new judicial rulings issued, and new technology is developed. The consequences of continuing education are positive. It encourages growth and development for the new correctional officer and stimulates the development of new procedures for accomplishing correctional goals.

The importance of education cannot be overstated. Cherniss and Kane (1987) refer to several studies that support a positive association between continued education and job satisfaction as employees progress up the occupational and organizational career ladder. Other studies have supported the idea that education reduces burnout and stress (Brown 1987).

Correctional officers who avail themselves to a program of continued education have the unique opportunity to gain a more thorough understanding of society. In doing so it is hoped that they will be able to communicate more effectively, helping to reduce prison violence and improve understanding and effective correctional management techniques. A reduction in prison violence may well reduce officer-related compensation claims and, albeit indirectly, reduce employee turnover. Additional education will enable the officer to effectively engage in the exploration of new ideas and concepts within the organization. The importance of education is underscored when one considers competition for promotion and other professional and career development.

The application of all relevant knowledge requires that individuals seek continuing education and training opportunities in their primary fields and in related areas. Continuing education and training must be multidisciplinary in their approach (Lawrence 1984). Both training and education are critical. Each has a different role, and each should be a continuing process. Education concentrates on the development of theoretical knowledge, which allows one to understand processes and to make decisions in ambiguous situations. Training, on the other hand, is designed to impart specific skills that have direct application in more concrete situations. Education is an important prerequisite to career development and progression. Training is essential for minimal performance of duty.

Personnel are the most important factor in any operation dealing with people. While finances and budgets are basic to any operation, personnel implement the operation, and their performance determines the effectiveness of any operation, including correctional institutions. Consequently, recruitment and selection, preservice/in-service training, continued education, and all personnel policies are vital to the effectiveness of the institution.

Don A. Josi

Bibliography

Benton, N. (1988). Personal management: Strategies for staff development. *Corrections Today* 50(August): 102–8.

Brown, P. W. (1987). Probation officer burnout: An organizational disease/an organizational cure: Part II. *Federal Probation* 51(September): 17–21.

Carter, D. (1991). The status of education and training in corrections. *Federal Probation* 55(June): 17–23.

Cherniss, C., and J. S. Kane (1987). Public sector professionals: Job characteristics, satisfaction, and aspirations for intrinsic fulfillment through work. *Human Relations* 40: 125–36.

Corrections Compendium (1990). Survey: Correctional officers, part II—Requirements, training. *Corrections Compendium* 15(10): 15–21.

Lawrence, R. (1984). Professionals or judicial servants? An examination of the probation officer's role. *Federal Probation* 48(December): 14–21.

Lombardo, L. (1981). *Guards Imprisoned.*
New York: Elsevier.

Lundberg, D. E. (1947). Methods of selecting prison personnel. *Journal of Criminal Law and Criminology* 38: 14–39.

Morton, J. B., ed. (1991). *Public Policy for Corrections.* 2nd. ed. Laurel, Md.: American Correctional Association.

Sanchez, C. M. (1989). Attracting and selecting a top-notch staff: The California experience. *Corrections Today* 51(7): 58,166.

Sechrest, D. K., and D. A. Josi (1992). *National Correctional Officers Education Survey.* Riverside, Calif.: Robert Presley Institute of Corrections Research and Training.

Sechrest, D. K., and E. G. Reimer (1982). Adopting national standards for correctional reform. *Federal Probation* 46(6): 18–25.

Toch, H. (1981). Is a "correctional officer" by any other name a "screw"? *Criminal Justice Review* 3(2): 19–35.

Wahler, C., and P. Gendreau (1985). Assessing correctional officers. *Federal Probation* 49(1): 70–74.

III. Career Opportunities

There is good news for job seekers in the field of corrections: Its growth rate earned it the distinction of being listed by the U.S. Bureau of the Census as one of the ten fastest growing occupations in American society. Corrections employment enjoyed an annual growth rate of nearly 8 percent for the past decade. The unfortunate persistence of the crime problem holds the enigmatic promise of still greater corrections employment opportunities for the future, as the American criminal justice system scrambles to provide custody, care, and supervision for its approximately million and a half incarcerated offenders. In 1990, the United States held in custody 282 sentenced prisoners per 100,000 residents. That number increased to 343 per 100,000 residents in 1993. Overall, there was an increase of 157 percent between 1980 and 1990. Every state has been affected by the upswing of incarceration. Prison construction alone totaled $37 billion during the last decade; similar figures are projected for the decade of the nineties. Figure 1 suggests the enormousness of the service and custody needs of offenders in federal and state prisons, local jails, and juvenile residential and nonresidential programs. Close to 62 percent of all adult inmates are

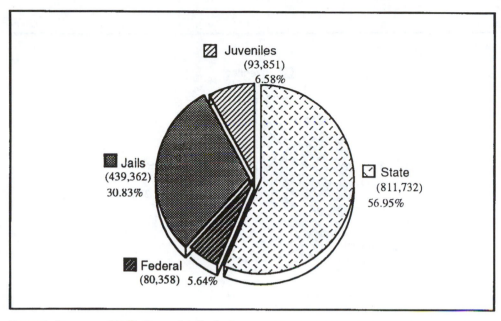

Figure 1. Incarcerated Offenders and Offender Status—1994 (N=1,425,303). Sources: Maguire and Pastore (1994); Camp and Camp (1994).

housed in state and federal prisons. Local jails hold an additional 30 percent. Juveniles, constituting about 8 percent of all offenders, are confined in residential facilities or are assigned to nonresidential programs.

The growth of the inmate population has its counterpart in employment patterns. Figure 2 shows the distribution of all employees in institutional corrections in the United States at the beginning of 1993. The responsibility for looking after the approximately 1.5 million prisoners falls to the swelling ranks of correctional professionals in hundreds of agencies.

Approximately 500,000 employees work in institutional corrections. About 60 percent are employed in state facilities; 5 percent work in federal prisons; local jails employ 27 percent, and juvenile facilities account for the remaining 8 percent. These figures do not include the thousands of inmates housed in private correctional facilities. Staffing needs reflect sentencing policies. Every state is affected by the growth patterns, and response to the burgeoning prison population comes in the obvious form of new prisons and staff. In the six years between 1984 and 1990, the number of state and federal prison employees increased by 70 percent. A similar growth rate is predicted for the decade of the nineties.

Societal Changes and Employment Prospects

Changing employment prospects in institutionalized corrections are traced to crime rates and shifts in population characteristics of the United States. First and foremost, increased inmate populations are a function of rising crime rates; both the magnitude of the increase and the rate of growth present special challenges and opportunities for administrators and staff at all levels of institutional corrections. Second, demographic trends occurring in the larger society include minority population growth, higher rates of employment for women, a graying population, and overall increases in education. Recent employment patterns in institutional corrections reflect these trends. Female and minority state prison employment is increasing at a faster rate than that of their white male counterparts. Candidates for positions are older, more experienced, and bring higher levels of education to their positions.

Third, increased pressure for professionalism is evident in mandated court actions, accreditation standards of institutions, and increased concern for professional ethics. Fourth, despite the recent shift toward a more retributive punishment philosophy, American prison policy continues to incorporate rehabilitative ideals. "Correcting" is very much alive in insti-

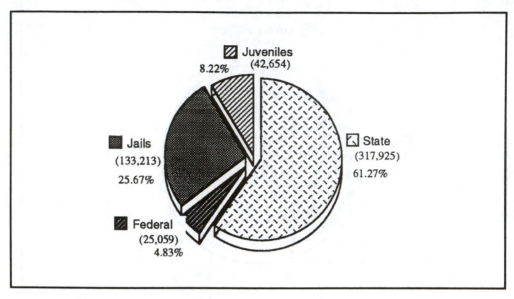

Figure 2. Employees in Institutional Corrections—1994 (N=518,851). Sources: Maguire and Pastore (1994); Camp and Camp (1994).

tutional corrections. The qualities of effective officers include "alertness, sensitivity, fairness, objectivity, and reasonable reactions." Finally, advances in technology, the privatization of prisons, and improvements in treatment and counseling techniques have opened up new and more specialized positions in institutional corrections.

Job Categories and Qualifications
The jobs available in institutional corrections are generally grouped into four categories: custody and surveillance, institutional support, treatment, and administration. About three out of every four employees in 1,361 federal and state correctional facilities for adults, and a similar ratio in 3,316 local jails, perform custody and surveillance duties. Included in this first category are frontline corrections officers who oversee the day-to-day activities of inmates, supervise work details, observe recreational activities, enforce institutional policy, and tend to the care, custody and protection of inmates. Despite modern structures and advancements in surveillance technology, the ratio of officers to inmates has remained steady over time. In 1979 state prisons employed one correctional officer per 4.6 inmates. This ratio dropped to one per 3.9 in 1990, and rose

slightly to one officer per 5.1 inmates in 1993. The increase reflects crowded conditions in most correctional facilities. The ratio of inmates to staff is frequently cited as an important predictor of stress levels for inmates and staff.

Institutional support staff conduct prison services that include the acquisition, distribution, and use of institutional resources. Support staff make up roughly 15 percent of all institutional corrections employees. Treatment personnel—about 16 percent of all state staff—provide a range of educational, case management, and counseling services. Administrative staff, constituting about 3 percent of all state employees, oversee such functions as interpreting institutional policy and supervising employees. Within each of the job categories are numerous specialties that permit a wide range of career possibilities.

Qualifications for all entry-level positions in federal and state correctional institutions include U.S. citizenship, a minimum age of twenty-one, good physical condition, a security check, and either demonstrated work experience in a related field or a college diploma. Corrections employees are regulated by civil-service requirements, and most institutions require a probation period of at least six months. Over twenty states indicate a preference for candidates with associate's or bachelor's degrees. A few states list among their qualifications a preference for employees with previous military or security experience. In 1991, thirty-seven states reported that the education level of corrections officers exceeded the required qualifications for their institutions. For the same year, the demographic profile of federal staff revealed that 63 percent had some college education. Finally, one recent study shows that 30 percent of the officer forces in several states have enrolled in post–high school/college programs.

Career Progression and Promotion

Many studies of corrections staff paint a bleak picture of career selection and advancement. Is corrections a choice of last resort? Are boredom and low morale endemic? Are turnover rates high? Do officers who stay on the job have any chance for promotion? Recent studies of corrections staff show improvement in all these concerns. Turnover is stable at about 11 percent a year, and increasing numbers of officers bring associate's or bachelor's degrees when they apply. Staff boredom and low morale are risks in a career that involves caring for troubled offenders. Frontline officers, however, report more autonomy and variety in prison positions than previously reported.

Opportunities for promotion at all levels are excellent for the next two decades as the baby-boomers near retirement, new prisons open, and smaller facilities permit more specialized and autonomous roles for staff. The career path for a corrections officer generally consists of a series of promotions through a system of ranks that begins at the corrections officer I level and progresses through the ranks of sergeant, lieutenant, captain, and superintendent (or assistant to the captain and superintendent). Criteria for promotion include job experience, written examinations, and, in many states, interviews with review panels. Corrections officers frequently seek additional training and education that enable them to move laterally into institutional treatment positions. As an "emerging profession," institutional corrections are beginning to require increased educational qualifications, the implementation of national accreditation standards that promote professional ethics, expectations of high job-performance standards, and the monitoring of performance.

The applicant qualifications listed for corrections officers apply also to applicants for technical support positions and treatment staff positions. Some of the more technical positions in institutional support, and all treatment positions in juvenile and adult corrections, have the same educational qualifications as human services positions in the private sector. The typical career path for the treatment employee begins with a four-year program in criminal justice or a related social-science major. In 1991, Anderson's *Directory of Criminal Justice Education* reported that 1,041 educational institutions offered one or more criminal justice degrees. That is a 10.5 percent increase since the 1986–87 directory was published. New job titles are constantly being introduced in treatment and support that require specialized education and training. For example, those who may be employed to work specifically with older offenders, offenders who are mentally ill or mentally retarded, or with sex offenders need a type of education and training that is interdisciplinary. That is particularly true in juvenile and community corrections. Promotions are made on the basis of seniority and written and oral examinations.

Conclusions

The field of corrections is broad enough to allow a large number of persons with varying educational backgrounds, interests, and skills to carve out satisfying careers. There are opportunities to work in the community and in institutions, and to serve adults and juveniles through various agencies and widely different types of interaction. While the majority of careers in corrections involve direct contact with offenders in a supervisory or counseling role, there are also positions in administration, training, research, evaluation, and education. Promotion and advancement is possible within institutional corrections on the basis of experience, education, and continued training. Current patterns of growth promise a bright future for candidates for prospective corrections positions.

Robert B. Blair
Peter C. Kratcoski

Bibliography

Camp, George M., and Camile Camp (1994). *The Corrections Yearbook, 1993*. South Salem, N.Y.: Criminal Justice Institute, Inc.

DeLucia, R. C., and T. J. Doyle (1990). *Career Planning in Criminal Justice*. Cincinnati, Ohio: Anderson.

Kratcoski, P. C., ed. (1994). *Correctional Counseling and Treatment*. 3rd ed. Prospects Heights, Ill.: Waveland.

Lombardo, L. X. (1989). *Guards Imprisoned: Correctional Officers at Work*. 2nd ed. Cincinnati, Ohio: Anderson.

Maguire, Kathleen, and Ann L. Pastore, eds. (1994). *Sourcebook of Criminal Justice Statistics, 1993*. Washington, D.C.: United States Government Printing Office.

Stinchcomb, J. D. (1990). *Opportunities in Law Enforcement and Criminal Justice Careers*. Lincolnwood, Ill.: VGM Career Horizons.

Williamson, H. E. (1990). *The Corrections Profession*. Newbury Park, Calif.: Sage.

IV. Subculture

The early sociological literature on correctional officers was informed and directed by the work of Gresham Sykes (1958). In his seminal book, *The Society of Captives,* Sykes presented a picture of the prison guard as an individual who had to complete multiple demands. Guards were held responsible for their cell blocks—that they be kept clean and remained orderly and free from disturbances. Recognizing that they were outnumbered by the prisoners that they had a pathetic system of rewards and punishments to use, and no sense of obligation on the part of inmates to comply with their orders, guards entered into informal relationships with pivotal inmates to maintain order and control in the prison.

Guards, in addition, had to deal with the formal expectations of prison administrators, who were requiring that they follow a well-defined rule book and semirational policies and procedures. On many occasions these rules were ineffectual in keeping control of the inmate population. In response, guards entered into "symbiotic relationships" with key inmates to ensure the stability of the prison. Quite ironically, through such informal adaptations on the part of guards, we see that both the needs of the prisoners and administrators were met, since both valued, more than anything else, the security and stability of the prison.

Much of the early research on correctional officers focused on these informal relationships between keeper and kept. Beginning, however, in the early 1980s and continuing through the 1990s, we start to see other dimensions in which the correctional officer subculture was to be understood. There are three major lines of inquiry that have guided research on the officer subculture since the 1980s. The first was to provide a more adequate description of the prison guard.

In the 1980s, professional organizations, such as the American Correctional Association and the American Jail Association, demanded that more attention be paid to the prison guard. Starting with the title of "guard," these professional associations asserted that such a word was no longer adequate to describe the multiple functions performed by correctional staff. Instead, they argued that the word be discarded for the more accurate title of "correctional officer." To these professional organizations and others in the corrections field, the term "guard" was offensive and demeaning to the men and women who worked in prisons. Moreover, these professional organizations recommended that more systematic research be generated on the nature and functioning of correctional officers. As a result, research on who became correctional officers and where they came from formed a new agenda for criminologists and criminal justice practitioners to pursue.

The research indicated that many correctional officers were politically conservative (Athens 1975) and took up corrections work because of the lack of other employment opportunities (Crouch and Marquart 1980). Such a view of correctional officers was not flattering, nor was it instructive to researchers and correctional professionals who wanted to know more about how officers performed their functions. As such, a second avenue of research developed. This research focused on the determinants of correctional officers' attitudes.

Much of that research examined the factors that either directly or indirectly influenced the officers' attitudes. It was believed that by understanding the source of these attitudes efforts could be developed to reinforce proactive behavior among correctional officers, as well as address any problem areas identified. In this way, more positive policy prescriptions could be made to professionalize correctional officer work. This research explored attitudes among correctional officers by examining two specific areas.

First, research attempted to identify individual factors that affected correctional officers' attitudes, such as age, race, and educational level. As with the research done on prisoners, there were no conclusive findings on the relationship between individual variables and attitudes among correctional officers (Cullen, Lutze, Link, and Wolfe 1989). The research indicated that officers were pretty much a disparate group of individuals, with many factors affecting their attitudes. This position was further supported by evidence developed when looking at organizational determinants.

Organizational factors, such as length of service, shift worked, frequency of contact with inmates, role conflict, and job stress, were a second area examined by researchers. These factors also did not produce consistent findings that would predict attitudes among correctional officers. The research indicated the importance of diversity and differences among correctional officers and that they may not have an identifiable subculture, as early researchers had suggested. Such a finding questioned the value of viewing correctional officers as a monolithic group. Rather, what was more valuable was to examine the unique character of correctional officer work and why some officers responded to a particular set of circumstances in one way while others responded in a completely different manner.

This is where the third area of research on the correctional officer subculture developed. Based on the work of many scholars (Toch 1977; Lombardo 1981; Klofas and Toch 1982; Johnson 1987), the final view of the correctional officer subculture expanded on the theme of diversity. Klofas and Toch (1982, 238) argued that much of what was attributed to officers as subcultural beliefs were in reality not the attitudes found among them. Their research identified a number of subgroupings among officers, each having unique themes and issues, that challenged our understanding of officer subculture as being simply procustodial and against prisoners.

Klofas and Toch (1982, 239) suggested that correctional officers, like other professional groups, tended to view themselves incorrectly concerning their attitudes toward their clients. More often than not, according to Klofas and Toch, correctional officers believed that their attitudes were not widely held by most correctional officers, and that many believed most officers were anti-inmate and in opposition to the treatment goals of the prison. Borrowing from the work of Kauffman (1981), Klofas and Toch argued that what was present among correctional officers was "pluralistic ignorance."

Pluralistic ignorance is defined as the process of self-stereotyping one another into a particular world view about the work setting. With regard to correctional officers, this process meant holding an erroneous belief that a majority of correctional officers held anti-inmate attitudes and that those who were supportive of inmates and treatment programs were actually in the minority. By misperceiving the attitudes of others, correctional officers were misinterpreting how strong the subculture actually was and further alienating themselves from each other as correctional professionals.

Klofas and Toch (1982, 247) posited that the correctional subculture was actually very diverse and made up of a number of values and beliefs supportive of a number of subcultural types. These types were "Subcultural Custodians," "Supported Majority," and the "Lonely Braves." The Subcultural Custodians fulfilled the image of being against prisoners and held antitreatment attitudes. They were the smallest group among correctional officers. The Supported Majority was the largest group, and they held attitudes that were supportive of prisoners, the professionalization of correctional officer work, and treatment programs for prisoners. The Lonely Braves were officers who felt they were being overwhelmed by the conservative and primarily custodial attitudes of the Subcultural Custodians. They felt that they were alone and unable to express any support for efforts to improve the conditions of inmates. The Lonely Braves and the Supported Majority, however, made up over 60 percent of the correctional officers surveyed.

These findings suggested to Klofas and Toch (1982, 250) that the traditional understanding of the guard subculture as being procustodial and anti-inmate was inaccurate. Instead, correctional officers held a number of attitudes, values, and beliefs, most of which were supportive of prisoners and programs to help them in the rehabilitation process. Additionally, they recommended that more research be conducted on the development of the correctional officers' subculture. Such a subculture was much more complex than originally understood. Much of the research of the late 1980s and early 1990s started to question the ways in which correctional officers understood their work worlds.

Beginning with the work of Johnson (1987), research on the correctional officer subculture became more multidimensional. Johnson (1987,

119) suggested that the correctional officer subculture be understood in terms of two dimensions: the public agenda and the private agenda. The public agenda is more stereotypical and is consistent with the antiprisoner sentiment identified by early research, while the private agenda is more oriented toward a human service perspective on correctional work. The private agenda is supported by research which has shown correctional officers to be fairly heterogenous and diverse. As stated by Johnson (1987, 122), "There is no evidence that guards as a group are distinctively prejudiced or authoritarian, or indeed share any personality type at all." This is not to suggest that there are not officers who are pessimistic in their attitudes toward prisoners and hold largely security and custodial concerns. There are such officers, yet the research has found these types of officers to be around 25 percent of the total group.

The private view of correctional officers reinforces the idea that most correctional officers have more interest in their work beyond their purely custodial functions. In the private view, their work is defined under a broader category of human service. Under that definition, correctional officers serve the role of being both advocate for and supervisor over the prisoners. A central concern for the officer, under the human service model, is that prisoners are able to adapt and cope with prison life in a mature way (Johnson 1987, 153). This view of correctional officers is beneficial to both the inmate and the officer. Not only are inmates' concerns addressed under such an approach, but in addition the officer can enhance his/her own level of personal and professional development. In the words of Johnson (1987, 154), a human service role "make(s) the officer's job richer, more rewarding, and ultimately less stressful."

The public agenda and the private agenda of correctional officers present differing perspectives on the correctional officers' subculture. It is probably accurate to conclude that officers are neither mindless brutes nor devout social workers. Instead, the correctional officer subculture represents an amalgam of interests, concerns, and positions that reflect the diversity of the group. To suggest that correctional officers are a monolithic group, therefore, is completely inaccurate. Future research will have to explore how such diversity can be employed by correctional officials to meet the primary objectives of prison facilities. With a more complete awareness of the correctional officer subculture, we are able to develop more reasoned and rational correctional policy today and into the future.

Stan Stojkovic

Bibliography
Athens, L. (1975). Differences in the liberal-conservative political attitudes of prison guards and felons. *International Journal of Group Tensions* 5(3): 143–55.
Crouch, B. M., and J. W. Marquart (1980). On becoming a prison guard. In B. M. Crouch, ed. *The Keepers: Prison Guards and Contemporary Corrections.* Springfield, Ill.: Charles C. Thomas.
Cullen, F. T., F. E. Lutze, B. G. Link, and N. T. Wolfe (1989). The correctional orientation of prison guards: Do officers support rehabilitation? *Federal Probation* 53(March): 33–42.
Johnson, R. (1987). *Hard Time: Understanding and Reforming the Prison.* Monterey, Calif.: Brooks/Cole.
Kauffman, K. (1981). Prison officers' attitudes and perceptions of attitudes: A case of pluralistic ignorance. *Journal of Research in Crime and Delinquency* 18: 272–94.
Klofas, J., and H. Toch (1982). The guard subculture myth. *Journal of Research in Crime and Delinquency* 19: 238–54.
Lombardo, L. (1981). *Guards Imprisoned: Correctional Officers at Work.* New York: Elsevier.
Sykes, G. (1958). *The Society of Captives.* Princeton, N.J.: Princeton University Press.
Toch, H. (1977). *Living in Prison: The Ecology of Survival.* New York: Free Press.

V. Stress

Dr. Hans Selye, a pioneer of stress research, defined stress as a nonspecific response of the body to any demand made upon it. He revealed that the only way to avoid stress is to die. Reportedly, more than fourteen hundred physiological changes, such as dilation of pupils, hyperventilation, increase in blood sugar level, rise in blood pressure, and an increase in heart rate, occur during the initial stage of a stressful event. Each individual is said to come equipped with a limited amount of adaptive energy for dealing with life crises. Once that energy is depleted no more can be obtained, and individuals become subject to illness and death. Humans are likened to springs with a certain amount of resilience to bounce back; if too much bouncing occurs, the spring may break (Cheek 1984).

Sources of Stress
Stressors (those things that cause stress) for correctional officers have been identified as the characteristics of corrections work (such as danger, lack of predictability), factors external to work (such as feeling trapped in a job, living on a low salary), inadequate training, absence of standard policies, lack of communication with superiors, and little consultation in decisions (Philliber 1987). The uniform serves to set the correctional officer apart, making one readily identifiable as an authority figure, differentiating the keeper from the kept. It may even serve to conjure up feelings of ambivalence to authority from the general public.

The courts have also been identified as a stressor in the correctional arena, as correctional officers are often said to be affected by issues surrounding overcrowding, and officers often feel handcuffed in dealing with inmates—afraid that they might violate an offender's civil rights and face legal repercussions. Making decisions can be stressful, but it is the level at which the decisions are made and the potential harm from bad decisions that increase the potential for stress. The stakes are higher when one has responsibility for people rather than things.

Inmate contact has been found to be unrelated to stress or burnout in correctional officers (Adwell and Miller 1985). The focus of corrections research has often been on inmates and their struggle to adapt to confinement. Much of the early stress research in the criminal justice system concentrated on inmates as well, instead of employees, so researchers were surprised to learn that correctional officers have significantly higher blood pressures than inmates. It has been found that correctional officers have more problems with fellow correctional employees than they do with inmates. The administration has been identified as a stressor in the literature on policing, probation, and corrections. Administrative stressors have been identified as the primary source of correctional officers' stress, overriding both job demands and the dangerous nature of the job (Whitehead and Lindquist 1986). In particular, the traditionally paramilitary organizational structure of criminal justice agencies—with emphasis on auto-

cratic leadership styles—has been cited for creating and perpetuating employee stress, turnover, and absenteeism.

The Effects of Stress
The effects of stress on correctional personnel can be devastating. Consider that it has been reported that the average life span of correctional officers is fifty-nine years, while the national average is 75. The divorce rate is purportedly twice the national average, and high rates of alcoholism and suicide are found among line officers. Correctional officers have been found to be more prone than the general public to heart attacks, high blood pressure, and ulcers (Cheek 1984). While correctional officers appear to suffer a greater than average number of stress-induced ailments, they are often quite hesitant to acknowledge the impact of stress on their lives. Some argue that this denial of stress on the part of correctional officers is made in an effort to preserve a macho image (Philliber 1987).

Beyond human costs, stress in the workplace can manifest itself in a number of ways. High turnover, reduced productivity on the job, high rates of absenteeism and use of sick leave, as well as inflated health-care costs and disability payments, have all been found to be associated with stressful working environments. It has been estimated that 40 percent of job turnover is stress-induced. This proves particularly poignant when one considers that the national, annual average turnover among correctional officers is 16.2 percent, with some states experiencing annual turnover rates as high as 40 percent (Jurik and Winn 1987). High absenteeism and job turnover are cited as two of the most readily identifiable measures of the amount of burnout in a working environment. Each time an employee quits, the time and money invested by the agency in training that individual are lost.

Stress affects health, and healthy employees are much more cost-efficient than unhealthy ones. It is clearly to an organization's benefit to strive to keep stress in the workplace under control.

Methods for Reducing Stress
Terry (1983) identified three means of alleviating stress. These are eliminating the stressors, increasing the individual's stress-coping ability, and providing a stressed individual with help. The first approach is considered to be the most

effective method for reducing stress, but it has received the least emphasis.

Traditionally, stress-alleviating techniques on the part of criminal justice agencies have focused on the individual suffering the stress. Such interventions have generally come in the form of stress management workshops or seminars and occasionally in employee assistance programs. Stress is often addressed within the context of in-service training programs or perhaps in some form of employee-family counseling. The focus is often on proper diet, appropriate levels of physical exercise, and positive coping skills. Sessions may frequently end with participants practicing various relaxation and desensitization techniques together in a group.

Traditional stress-reduction techniques focus on the correctional employee, rather than on ways of preventing stress on the job, such as organizational overhauling. Such an approach might be called "bailing out the boat without plugging the leak." It has been maintained that it is senseless to identify "bad people" in terms of their reactions to stress. Instead we should be attempting to identify and examine the "bad situations in which good people function. Imagine investigating the personality of cucumbers to discover why they had turned into sour pickles without analyzing the vinegar barrels in which they had been submerged" (Maslach 1982, 10).

In 1973, the National Advisory Commission on Criminal Justice Standards and Goals in Corrections recommended that participatory management should be implemented in correctional institutions across the country. It was argued that giving criminal justice employees control over their working environments can serve to reduce stress, as lack of control over one's job has been found to be a predictor of both physiological and psychological stress for correctional personnel. Stress reactions by both staff and inmates are heightened by the traditional, rigid, mechanistic organization of prisons. A highly structured, coercive, and conflict-ridden organization alienates the workers exposed to it, creating distrust and psychological distance between the managers and the subordinates. "Creating work environments in which officers feel valued and respected for the highly complex and demanding nature of their work will necessitate allowing them greater opportunities to participate in decisions directly affecting them" (Weiner 1988, 301, 305).

Employee participation in decision-making is repeatedly advocated as a stress reducer in the criminal justice literature. Correctional officers have been found to feel less alienated and be more likely to implement creative and innovative approaches to goals of prison order when they believe that their superiors value their ideas and seek their participation in decision-making. The more open the style of management is perceived to be, the more healthful the social climate. The question becomes, Why cannot those who regularly confront a problem be involved in the decisions about how to solve the problem? (Duffee 1989). Democratic managers, as opposed to authoritarian managers, are associated with high employee morale and job satisfaction. Democratic managers are typically open, less stress-inducing, and more prone to encourage worker participation in the decision-making process than their authoritarian counterparts.

When the attitudes and values of individual members of an organization are largely in accord with the organization's attitudes and values, and when organizational positions are matched appropriately with the personalities and skills of their holders, an organization is said to be well managed. A participative management style is viewed as the means of achieving that state, but it has never really been tried in criminal justice circles (Archambeault and Weirman 1983). Even with all of the support for employee participation in decisions that affect them, inmates are the ones with an established history of being involved in participatory prison management.

Employee turnover in the correctional setting is typically reduced by identifying personality profiles of the employees and then hiring according to those profiles. The use of such profiles ignores factors at the organizational level that may contribute to employee turnover in otherwise qualified individuals (Jurik and Winn 1987). While people should work in the line of employment that best suits their personality, instead of changing people to fit environments perhaps we should change organizations to fit people. Intervention on the job and in the work setting is the most effective and efficient means for combating stress.

Not all situations lend themselves to participation for the resolution of problems or stress. Both individual and organizational means should be employed to help employees better handle their stressors. Organizational means, however, have been underutilized. Participatory management in correctional institutions may serve as one significant means for lessening both occupational and physical stress levels of correctional employees. Organizational costs, such as employee turnover and abuse of sick leave, can possibly be reduced through such mechanisms. Stress is costly and should be attacked by any means necessary (Slate 1993).

Risdon N. Slate

Bibliography

Adwell, S., and L. E. Miller (1985). Occupational burnout. *Corrections Today* 47(7): 70, 72.

Archambeault, W. G., and C. L. Weirman (1983). Critically assessing the utility of police bureaucracies in the 1980s: Implications of Management Theory Z. *Journal of Police Science and Administration* 11: 420–29.

Cheek, F. E. (1984). *Stress Management for Correctional Officers and Their Families.* College Park, Md.: American Correctional Association.

Duffee, D. E. (1989). *Corrections Practice and Policy.* New York: Random House.

Jurik, N. C., and R. Winn (1987). Describing correctional-security dropouts and rejects: An individual or organizational profile? *Criminal Justice and Behavior* 14: 5–25.

Maslach, C. (1982). *Burnout: The Cost of Caring.* Englewood Cliffs, N.J.: Prentice-Hall.

Philliber, S. (1987). Thy brother's keeper: A review of the literature on correctional officers. *Justice Quarterly* 4: 9–37.

Slate, R. N. (1993). *Stress Levels and Thoughts of Quitting of Correctional Personnel: Do Perceptions of Participatory Management Make a Difference?* Ann Arbor, Mich.: University Microfilms.

Terry, W. C., III (1983). Police stress as an individual and administrative problem: Some conceptual and theoretical difficulties. *Journal of Police Science and Administration* 11: 156–64.

Weiner, R. I. (1988). Management strategies to reduce stress in prison: Humanizing correctional environments. In R. Johnson and H. Toch, eds. *The Pains of Imprisonment.* Prospect Heights, Ill.: Waveland.

Whitehead, J. T., and C. A. Lindquist (1986). Correctional officer job burnout: A path model. *Journal of Research in Crime and Delinquency* 23: 23–42.

C

VI. Turnover

Corrections is a high-growth industry. The *San Francisco Chronicle* reported, "Under the recently passed 'three strikes and you're out' law, the state's [California's] present inmate population of 122,232, including 7,755 women, is expected to more than double by the year 2000 to 250,000, about the same as the number of residents in Anaheim" (18 April 1994, A7). California will construct three more prisons in the spring of 1994, with six additional facilities proposed. Even at that high growth rate the new prisons are projected to be immediately filled to 140 percent of capacity.

As the number of prisons and prisoners grows, so does the need for qualified and experienced staff. In 1990, there were over 155,363 correctional officers employed in state and federal prison systems. Across the U.S., approximately 17,500 new personnel were hired in 1993 by departments of corrections, about 350 per system.

Almost every state spends more on personnel than all other expenditures combined. Given the expense of recruiting, hiring, and training each new person, it is important that good employees, once hired, be retained. Turnover is most expensive if employees quit within the first twenty-four months of work. In most cases, however, there is a lag time between one person's leaving and another's being selected, hired, and trained to fill that position. The process can cost anywhere from $10,000 to $20,000 per new officer.

Voluntary and Involuntary Turnover

Turnover is often associated with measures of management effectiveness. Annual total turnover rates as high as 40 percent have been reported in the correctional field, although the average is about 14.5 percent for correctional officers (Davis 1990). State prison administrators have the highest rate of attrition of all prison employees. This attrition has its price—management turnover and its effect on prison operations is often reported as a precipitating factor in riots and scandals.

While statistics on employee turnover abound, most sources fail to distinguish between voluntary and involuntary turnover, often reporting only a total turnover figure. Much research, however, confirms the need to distinguish between voluntary and involuntary turnover to identify more accurately the potential causes, consequences, and costs.

The need to distinguish among different types of voluntary turnover has also been noted. It is important to distinguish between those correctional employees who voluntarily leave their jobs but stay in the same occupation (which is called intraoccupational turnover) and those who leave both their jobs and the occupation (interoccupational turnover). When an employee leaves, the decision is often either a measure of the job's desirability or a reflection of the alternatives available in the job market.

When economic conditions are poor and unemployment is high, turnover should be low, provided that a satisfactory work environment exists. If turnover is high despite limited outside alternatives, then one begins to suspect problems with the nature of the job or the nature of the employee. A 1990 study of correctional administrators asked why employees left their jobs. The reasons given were low pay, better outside opportunities, unhappiness with the geographic area, the nature of the job (poor working conditions, long hours, stress from overcrowding, or offender aggressiveness), and the nature of the employee (not cut out for the work) (McShane et al. 1991).

Factors Involved in Prison Employee Turnover
While many factors contribute to correctional employee turnover, one needs initial comment. Confusion exists regarding the proper goals of correctional institutions. To many people, the primary goal of correctional institutions is to isolate from the rest of society those individuals who have committed crimes. At the same time, however, these institutions are responsible for "correcting," or rehabilitating, inmates. Confusion over what the institution is ideally supposed to do and what it actually does may affect the employees adversely, contributing to role conflict and role ambiguity.

The impact of role conflict and role ambiguity on correctional employee stress has received much attention. Of late, this research has focused on the degree of fit between the individual employee and the work environment and its relationship to job stress. The notion of a lack of fit has been systematized in Person-Environment (P-E) Fit Theory, which argues that an incongruent relationship between individual and organizational demands leads initially to job stress and subsequently to increases in absenteeism and voluntary turnover. Thus, the well-being of both the individual and organization suffers when there is a mismatch between the characteristics or demands of the job and those of the employee.

Work situations in corrections typically do not afford many employees the opportunity to use the full range of their talents. Correctional work settings are, by necessity, characterized by extensive rules, regulations, and procedures that employees report fail to take advantage of their skills and abilities and that create a highly stressful environment. P-E Fit Theory suggests that a better understanding of correctional employee turnover can be achieved through examination of how employees cope and adjust.

Recent research has identified several coping strategies, including problem-focused; avoidance; wishful thinking; minimizing threat; seeking emotional support; blaming self; and growth orientation. Consistent with P-E Fit Theory, growth orientation has been found to predict employee turnover. Growth orientation measures the extent to which individuals value opportunities to learn and grow, to be creative, and to use the full range of their talents. In a sample of correctional workers, it was found that employee growth orientation was lowest in the No Turnover group, moderate in the Intraoccupational Turnover group, and highest in the Interoccupational Turnover group. Following P-E Fit Theory, these results show turnover as a potentially positive individual adjustment strategy when a job does not utilize growth capabilities. Other research has indicated a positive relationship between growth orientation and job performance for a sample of criminal justice workers.

Research examining the relationship between voluntary turnover and employee job performance has produced unclear and conflicting results. While the turnover rate among correctional workers is alarmingly high, a literature review reveals little research on the job performance of correctional employees who subsequently leave their jobs voluntarily. That is, little research exists on the type of worker that corrections loses to job turnover. Even though much research exists in management and organizational behavior regarding the relationship between voluntary turnover or intent to leave a job and employee job performance, the results have been unclear and conflicting. For instance, the "perceived alternatives" turnover model assumes a positive relationship between performance and voluntary withdrawal. This model implies that high performers will be more likely to resign from their jobs than low performers because they have more alternative employment opportunities.

Alternatively, the "contingent rewards" turnover model posits a negative relationship between performance and voluntary turnover based on the theory that many organizations attempt to retain more proficient employees by rewarding them. Conversely, little is done to retain the poorer performers, and thus they are encouraged to leave. Some research has found support for a positive relationship between turnover and performance.

Decreasing Turnover
It is often argued that the reward systems in many correctional organizations do not promote retention of the better employees. For example, many departments do not provide job enrichment, accelerated promotional opportunities, educational incentives, or merit pay raises. It is a common practice for correctional employees in the same job classification who are rated "average" on their annual evaluations to receive the same pay as those who receive "excellent" evaluations. Often there are few or no procedures for rewarding the better performers in correctional organizations.

In another study involving correctional workers, Wright (1991) found that all employees obtaining a performance rating of "excellent" subsequently resigned. These results suggest that some organizations choosing the "most able" applicants may be using a less-than-optimal selection strategy. Specifically, they may be choosing individuals who become dissatisfied with their work and quit.

One solution to high employee turnover may involve the improvement of selection, training and development, and placement criteria to make possible the hiring and subsequent development of competent employees who will stay with the job. Such improvement is imperative in the current correctional environment, in which the prisons of the future will be packed with inmates who have ever fewer opportunities for self-help and rehabilitative programs (because of "three strikes and you're out" laws).

The aim of preventive management is to promote individual and organizational health. Research on preventive management has identified several organizational-level methods, such as task redesign, participative management, flexible work schedules, career development, design of physical settings, role analysis, goal setting, social support, and team building (Quick and Quick 1984). While the nature of correctional work necessitates caution in the application of certain methods (such as task redesign and the design of physical settings), other methods, such as career development, social support, and team building, bear further investigation.

Career development is one method for modifying the demands of work. The primary purpose of career development is to encourage employee growth. That is accomplished through various employee self-assessment procedures and an analysis of opportunities within the organization. Correctional organizations can thus provide the mechanisms through which employees assess their own needs, interests, skills, and abilities.

Maximum benefit is obtained when an employee's self-assessment is coupled with an opportunity analysis. An opportunity analysis identifies the range of organizational and occupational roles available for the employee. More specifically, correctional organizations would not only formally establish career paths but would also be proactive in the creation of job opportunities to foster employee growth and development. Alternatively, the continued failure of corrections to provide preventive management methods, such as career development opportunities, will only result in employee frustration and increased voluntary employee turnover.

Thomas A. Wright
Dennis A. Sweeney

Bibliography
Benton, F. W., E. Rosen, and J. Peters (1982). *National Survey of Correctional Institution Employee Attrition*. New York: Center for Public Productivity.
Davis, S.P. (1990). *National Survey of Correctional Officers*. Lincoln, Nebr.: Contact.
McShane, M., F. Williams, K. McClain, and D. Shichor (1991). Examining employee turnover in corrections. *Corrections Today* 53(5): 220–25.

Quick, J. E., and J. D. Quick (1984). *Organizational Stress and Preventive Management*. New York: McGraw-Hill.

Wright, T. A. (1991). The level of employee utilization and its effect on subsequent turnover. *Journal of Applied Business Research* 7: 25–29.

Wright, T. A. (1993). Correctional employee turnover: A longitudinal study. *Journal of Criminal Justice* 21: 131–42.

Wright, T. A., and D. G. Bonett (1991). Growth coping, work satisfaction and turnover: A longitudinal study. *Journal of Business and Psychology* 6: 133–45.

Wright, T. A., and D. Sweeney (1990). Correctional institution workers' coping strategies and their effect on diastolic blood pressure. *Journal of Criminal Justice* 18: 161–69.

Crowding

I. Introduction

By the first day of 1993 there were approximately 900,000 people incarcerated in state and federal prisons in the United States. California alone accounted for 110,000. Since 1980, the prison population has increased by 168 percent. Prisoners with sentences of over one year are incarcerated at a rate of 329 per 100,000 people in the U.S. Geographically, the South has the highest incarceration rate of all regions. Of all states, Louisiana has the highest incarceration rate (478 per 100,000 state residents), but it is closely followed by Oklahoma (477 per 100,000) and Nevada (461 per 100,000). African-American men are imprisoned (3,109 per 100,000) at a rate that is four times that of black men in South Africa (729 per 100,000).

The tremendous increase in prison population is not an accident; it has resulted from continuous growth over the last two decades. Neither prison construction nor the availability of bed space to accommodate the growing prison population has kept pace. It is not surprising that overcrowding has been one of the key issues in prison lawsuits. The Government Accounting Office reported that for the fiscal year 1992–93, twenty-five state correctional systems requested funds for eighty-five new facilities that would add over fifty-six thousand new prison beds. Texas alone asked for over $600 million to finance the construction of twenty-five thousand new beds.

Causes of Overcrowding

One of the major reasons that prisons have become overcrowded is that crime-control strategies and legislative changes have favored longer sentences. These approaches have taken several forms that, employed together, have incarcerated more people for longer periods of time with less possibility for early release. This is obvious because commitments to prison have grown in disproportionately greater numbers than increases in the population, the number of crimes, the number of arrests, or the number of convictions. In most states, several if not all of the following changes have occurred:

1. The creation of new offenses that can result in prison terms or the revocation of probation or parole, sending offenders from the community back to prison. Some examples are the laws against stalking, or laws that make it a felony to intentionally transmit AIDS.

2. The institution of penalties that now make prison terms mandatory for some offenses that before did not usually result in incarceration, such as DWIs and certain drug convictions. Judges can no longer use discretion in deciding which punishment the offender should receive. A finding of guilty means that incarceration for a set term is automatic. These same laws prohibit probation for certain offenders. For example, in California, legislation has restricted or eliminated the possibility of probation for arson, specific sex offenses including child molestation, and residential burglary.

3. The lengthening of prison terms associated with some convictions, particularly if certain weapons (aggravated crimes) or victims (children, elderly, handicapped) were involved, or if certain quantities of drugs were present. These special circumstances are said to enhance the seriousness of the crime.

4. The passage of habitual felon laws in which life sentences are possible for offenders convicted of a third similar felony. Previously, only the maximum sentence allowed for that particular felony was permitted. The life sentence is a cumulative punishment for what the courts call a "criminal career."

5. The passage of laws under which felons may be given sentences of life in prison

without parole. Previously, all prisoners, after a designated time, became eligible for parole, regardless of whether or not they were actually granted the release.

6. The modification of existing parole eligibility requirements so that offenders must serve more time before becoming eligible. Some states have switched eligibility for review from one-fourth of the sentence to one-third, one-half, or more.

7. The alteration of "good time" statutes so that prisoners accumulate less time for good behavior each month. Thus it takes longer to acquire credits toward parole eligibility or discharge of the sentence.

One example of legislation that has increased prison sentences and virtually eliminated probation and parole is the 1986 Anti-Drug Abuse Act. The result has been that the federal inmate population in 1993 was at approximately 144 percent of the system's capacity. In 1986 the average time served for drug offenses was twenty-three months. In 1994 the average time served was seventy-two months. In July of 1993 the Federal Bureau of Prisons (FBOP) housed 78,661 inmates; the projection for 1997 is 106,174. The bureau had seventy facilities in 1989, but it was building forty-seven new prisons by 1995 at a cost of about $3 billion dollars.

The Cost of Overcrowding

Although no exact cost can be directly associated with overcrowding, we can look at present expenses incurred in prisons and anticipate their increase as the system takes on more and more inmates. Currently, taxpayers spend between $30,000 to $50,000 per inmate per year to maintain the federal and state correctional systems. That includes not only operating costs but also the cost of new construction. Depending on the level of security and the region of the United States, it costs anywhere from $30,000 to $130,000 to build each new bed space. The average cost was somewhere around $56,000 in 1992. Four out of every five capital outlay dollars in construction, however, go for building expenses other than the housing area itself. This includes the laundry, dining area, central kitchen, warehouse, parking lots, and administrative offices.

Construction costs are only the down payment of a prison's cost to society. The Federal Bureau of Prisons explains that operating a prison over its practical lifespan costs about fifteen to twenty times the original construction cost. Cost per inmate per day varies from state to state and then within each state from prison unit to prison unit. Units with greater security or large medical and psychiatric treatment services will, of course, be more expensive to build and operate. The major operating expense is personnel, usually accounting for an average of 75 percent of an agency's total operating budget.

The Effects of Overcrowding

The results of overcrowding are serious deprivations in the quality of life for everyone in a correctional institution. Even though we have built hundreds of new prisons and expanded existing facilities in the last ten years, the average amount of space per inmate has decreased by over 10 percent. Stretching resources beyond their capacity is something the courts watch carefully when monitoring prison conditions. Overcrowding may be measured in shortages of basic necessities, such as space, sheets, hot water, clothing, and food. Vocational, educational, and recreational programs may become seriously overloaded. Medical services and supplies may be insufficient, posing health risks. Throughout the system, high inmate to staff ratios lead to poor supervision and scheduling difficulties, which result in less inmate activity and greater safety risks for both employees and prisoners.

The nature of a crowded environment may itself have serious effects on the health and well-being of inmates. The noise and lack of privacy associated with crowding may contribute to emotional stress and the development of mental health problems. Studies have shown that crowding may increase the number of disciplinary infractions per inmate. Inmates in densely populated units may suffer from higher blood pressure. It has also been concluded that, as density of population increases, so does the rate of mortality in inmates over forty-five years of age (Paulus 1988). Common in overcrowded conditions are increases in the spread of colds, sexually transmitted diseases, and other infectious diseases. Many studies have claimed that the rate of psychiatric commitments and suicides increases for inmates in crowded living areas. Research has also linked higher subsequent rates of criminal behavior to inmates from institutions that were overcrowded. Increases in violence, particularly staff and inmate assaults, are also associated with overcrowded conditions. It is argued that living too close together heightens tempers and aggression, leading to confrontations.

Central to the relationship between overcrowding and violence is the notion of space. The distances we perceive of as important for maintaining social contact and comfort have been designated our "personal space" or "buffer zone." When people position themselves closer than we feel necessary, we might refer to them as "invading our space." In casual social interactions, Americans normally remain 48 to 144 inches apart. People who have difficulty relating to others may require even more space in order to feel comfortable. Studies seem to indicate that violent inmates have even greater personal space needs than nonviolent offenders.

In most settings, cellmates interact a great deal and have little privacy, which may cause their space to become an extension of themselves that is crucial to their well-being. In order to maintain their individuality, inmates may delineate boundaries that will provide them with an imaginary but psychological separateness. In most prisons where there are many inmates with personality disorders and emotional difficulties, crowding may produce symptoms of stress.

Interestingly enough, surveys of inmates have shown that open dorms are the least desirable housing arrangement. Besides having higher levels of inmate to inmate and inmate to staff aggression, interracial violence, racial antagonism, and illness, open dorms increase the inmates' perception of crowding (McCain et al. 1976; Cox et al. 1984; Leger 1988).

Only recently has research begun to explore the effects of crowding beyond those on individual inmates, groups of inmates, and the programs and services they receive. Information is still needed on the effect of crowding on the staff, on management strategies, on budgeting and governmental responses, on facility and equipment durability, and on the cost of operations under varying strategies to reduce overcrowding.

Solutions to Overcrowding

There are three basic strategies employed to reduce overcrowding. One involves reducing the number of people going into prison, another is to increase the number of people coming out of prison, and the third calls for the expansion of bed capacity or the building of more prisons.

Front End Strategies. Front end strategies are attempts to limit the number of people entering prison. One approach to reducing the number of prison-bound offenders is the notion of selective incapacitation. Selective incapacitation is based on the premise that a few serious offenders are responsible for a majority of the crimes. Therefore, it would be most economical and practical to allocate the limited bed space to those high-rate offenders. Proponents of selective incapacitation argue that it would probably produce the same reduction in crime as the rival philosophy of collective incapacitation, which advocates incarcerating all offenders eligible for prison sentences.

The primary problem with selective incapacitation is that of prediction. Many criminologists assert that it is too difficult to ascertain who is a serious offender and who therefore needs to be incarcerated. For many theorists the use of risk-assessment tools to predict who should be released is dangerous and potentially unfair.

Along with the notion of selecting only certain offenders for incarceration is the idea of selecting others for diversion. Probation and shock probation are sentences that can greatly reduce prison populations. Alternative sentences could also include community service, restitution, education and treatment programs, and electronic monitoring. Certain groups of offenders may be most appropriate for diversion, such as drug offenders and DWI offenders, who may be directed to therapy centers. There, as inpatients, the offenders receive treatment as well as custodial supervision.

Another way to reduce the prison population is to enforce population caps or ceilings. Many states are already under court order to maintain a set capacity. This limitation is usually expressed in terms of a percentage of the total bed spaces. For example, if an institution is given a ceiling of 95 percent, it must stop admitting new prisoners when 95 percent of the beds are filled. If more beds are acquired, the population may grow, still adhering however to the 95 percent capacity. When the established capacity is reached, admissions stop, and administrators then take one new inmate for each one released.

Prisoners awaiting beds create overcrowding in jails that causes considerable friction between cities or counties and the state. Overcrowded and underfunded local jails simple do not want to support state prisoners. Some local governments have demanded reimbursement from the state. In the past, the state has offered financial subsidies to counties for each prisoner who is given a community corrections alternative instead of being sent to state prison.

Back Door Strategies. Back door strategies may also be employed to reduce overcrowding. That involves increasing the number of offenders released from prison. Halfway houses and other early-release programs, such as furloughs and work or education releases, assist inmates in their transition back into society. Another back door strategy is the concept of simply increasing the number of paroles or early releases. On occasion, emergency release mechanisms have been employed to reduce crowding by a specific number of prisoners as a one-time event. To do this officials create an award category, a certain number of days' credit for inmates who are already close to their release date. Their pending release is simply moved up to serve an immediate need. This often occurs when judges issue orders to reduce crowding immediately or face fines, the installment of population caps, or the closing of the facility.

Still other approaches include sending inmates with outstanding warrants or pending charges back to the places where those charges originated once they are parole-eligible. That may even mean sending incarcerated illegal aliens into the custody of the Immigration and Naturalization Service for deportation hearings. According to the Federal Bureau of Prisons, there are currently over ten thousand illegal aliens in the federal prison system. Most could be deported. Those inmates take up prison space that it would cost the government $426 million to construct. In March of 1994 the Federal Bureau of Prisons returned eighty-six incarcerated Mexican citizens and received eleven U.S. citizens who had been incarcerated in Mexico. The transfer program is considering repatriating another eight thousand Mexicans held in federal prisons in this country. The government claims that doing so will save millions of dollars. It is anticipated that another 330 American prisoners will be returned from Mexico during this process.

New Construction. New construction strategies, the third means of reducing overcrowding, involve either expanding existing facilities or constructing new ones. Increasing available housing through renovation or new construction is controversial, not only because of its philosophical implications but also because of the expense.

Proponents of new construction argue that incarceration, as punishment, is here to stay. Because there is public support for prisons, we have a responsibility to build adequate facilities. That would allow prison administrators to perform their duties in a constitutionally prescribed manner. In addition, they reason, new facilities should be built to replace the dilapidated relics of the past that do not function efficiently or safely. In 1988, approximately 35 percent of prisoners were living in institutions built more than fifty years ago, and 12 percent were in facilities built before 1888. Regardless of the size of the prison population over the next few years, many antiquated facilities will have to be replaced by more modern institutions.

Opponents of prison construction argue that if we continue to build we will just continue to fill up any space that is created. In other words, some believe that availability alone drives up incarceration rates. Overcrowding today is simply a result of an attempt to warehouse all of our social problems. One study claimed that if present sentencing trends continued, Texas, California, and Florida could build one new five-hundred-bed facility each month and still never reduce their overcrowding (Cory and Gettinger 1984).

Experts claim that most nonviolent offenders do not need to be incarcerated and that it is a waste of resources to do so. Estimates are that 30 percent of the average prison population is made up of nonviolent property offenders who would possibly do well in diversion programs in the community.

Another argument against new construction is that we should not build more prisons because they do not work, they drain community resources, and they do not rehabilitate. Opponents of incarceration say the decision to build should consider lost opportunity costs. That is the cost of not doing other things with the land and resources that were used to build the prison. Opportunity costs usually indicate that money spent on prison is money not spent on education, police and fire departments, public health, human services, and libraries. As it is often remarked, "For every one person who goes to prison, two people do not go to college."

Marilyn D. McShane

See also JUDICIAL INTERVENTION, SITE
SELECTION AND CONSTRUCTION OF PRISONS

Bibliography

Cory, B., and S. Gettinger (1984). *A Time to Build?* New York: Edna McConnell Clark Foundation.

Cox, V. C., P. B. Paulus, and G. McCain (1984). Prison crowding research: The relevance for prison housing standards and a general approach regarding crowding phenomena. *American Psychologist* 39: 1148–60.

Gaes, G. (1985). The effects of overcrowding in prison. In M. Tonry and N. Morris, eds. *Crime and Justice: An Annual Review of Research*, Vol 6. Chicago: University of Chicago Press.

Klofas, J., S. Stojkovic, and D. Kalinich (1992). The meaning of correctional crowding: Steps toward an index of severity. *Crime and Delinquency* 38(2): 171–88.

Leger, R. G. (1988). Perception of crowding, racial antagonism, and aggression in a custodial prison. *Journal of Criminal Justice* 16(3): 167–81.

McCain, G., V. C. Cox, and P. B. Paulus (1976). The relationship between illness complaints and degree of crowding in a prison environment. *Environment and Behavior* 8: 283–90.

Paulus, P. B. (1988). *Prison Crowding: A Psychological Perpective.* New York: Springer-Verlag.

Ruback, R., and T. S. Carr (1993). Prison crowding over time: The relationship of density and changes in density on infractions of rules. *Criminal Justice and Behavior* 20(2): 130–48.

Vaughn, M. S. (1993). Listening to the experts: A national study of correctional administrators regarding prison overcrowding. *Criminal Justice Review* 18(1): 12–25.

II. Court Rulings

The law relating to jail and prison overcrowding can be understood best by examining its development through four stages. These stages are similar to the stages through which the law on the rights of prisoners generally has passed.

The first stage, prior to the late 1960s, was a period during which the courts adopted a hands-off approach to cases in which inmates challenged the administration of a particular prison. During that period, courts were not receptive to lawsuits by inmates who argued that overcrowding is unconstitutional.

During the 1960s, the hands-off approach was replaced by a more interventionist approach by the courts in cases dealing with the rights of prisoners, including cases regarding overcrowding in prisons. The sixties saw a dramatic increase in the number of people sentenced to jail or prison terms. In order to accommodate this increase, many jails and prisons added second or third bunks or even floor mattresses to cells that had been designed to house only one inmate (a practice referred to as double-celling).

In many instances, double-celling occurred in antiquated institutions and resulted in appalling conditions of confinement. Consequently, in the late 1960s and 1970s, during the second stage in the development of the law on jail and prison overcrowding, inmates often convinced courts that the overcrowded conditions of confinement to which they were exposed were so harsh that they violated the inmates' constitutional rights.

In most of these cases, the courts found that (1) double-celling is unconstitutional; (2) operating a jail or prison with more inmates than it was designed to house (its rated capacity) is unconstitutional; or (3) the Constitution requires that inmates be provided some minimal amount of square footage of living space.

The third stage in the development of the law on overcrowding began with the decision of the United States Supreme Court in *Bell v. Wolfish* in 1979. In *Wolfish,* the Court held that double-celling seventy-five-square-foot cells in the Metropolitan Correctional Center (MCC) in New York City did not violate the constitutional rights of pretrial detainees confined in those cells. Two years later, the Supreme Court held in *Rhodes v. Chapman* that double-celling sixty-three-square-foot cells in the Southern Ohio Correctional Facility (SOCF) did not violate the constitutional rights of convicted felons confined in those cells.

These two Supreme Court cases are extremely important for several reasons. First, they established the constitutional standards to be applied in such cases. Convicted defendants are subjected to punishment when they are sentenced to incarceration in a prison. Under the Eighth Amendment to the Constitution, they may not be subjected to "cruel and unusual punishments." The *Chapman* case indicated that cruel and unusual punishment occurs when the overcrowded conditions "either [inflict] unnecessary or wanton pain or [are] grossly disproportionate to the severity of the crimes warranting imprisonment." That standard has been breached if conditions deny inmates "the minimal civilized measure of life's necessities."

The Court found that the SOCF inmates were not subjected to cruel and unusual punishment because they had suffered no harmful effects from their overcrowded conditions. Their double-bunked cells were well-heated and ventilated, and most inmates had access to day rooms with televisions, card tables, and chairs during the hours that they were not sleeping in their cells. The prison provided adequate food. Noise was not excessive, inmates were allowed contact visits, medical and dental needs were being reasonably met, a number of recreational and educational opportunities were available to most inmates, and double-bunking had not increased the frequency of violent behavior in the prison.

Because pretrial detainees have not yet been convicted of any crime, the "cruel and unusual punishment" clause of the Eighth Amendment does not apply to them. The *Wolfish* case, however, establishes that under the due process clauses of the Fifth Amendment (which apply to federal jails and prisons) and the Fourteenth Amendment (which applies to state prisons and local jails), pretrial detainees may not be punished at all.

According to *Wolfish*, overcrowded conditions constitute punishment if they (1) exist because of an intent to punish on the part of corrections officials; (2) are not rationally related to some governmental purpose other than punishment; or (3) are excessive in relation to that alternative purpose. The Court held that the double-bunked cells at the MCC did not punish pretrial detainees because the overall conditions at the jail were good, inmates were required to spend only seven or eight hours a day in their cells, and inmates usually spent fewer than sixty days in the jail before being released or sentenced to incarceration at another institution.

Wolfish and *Chapman* are also important because in each case the Supreme Court stressed that problems of prison administration are quite complex and require the special expertise of legislative and executive officials for an appro-priate solution. The clear message was that federal courts had become too inclined to second-guess the difficult decisions made by corrections officials and should intervene only when overcrowding had created conditions of confinement that were especially egregious.

The final significance of *Wolfish* and *Chapman* is that they rejected the bases on which lower courts had been deciding overcrowding cases. They made it clear that double-celling is not unconstitutional per se, that institutions could be operated constitutionally even with populations substantially above the rated capacity, and that the Constitution does not require a certain amount of square footage of living space for each inmate.

In spite of the Supreme Court's admonition to lower courts to assume a lower profile in overcrowding cases, research conducted in the years following *Wolfish* and *Chapman* suggested that lower courts continued to rule in favor of inmates with great frequency. In fact, the courts issued rulings in favor of inmates in forty-eight of the sixty-five reported cases in lower courts from 1979 through 1986.

The fourth (and current) stage in the development of the law on overcrowded conditions began in 1991 with the Supreme Court's decision in *Wilson v. Seiter*. During the first three stages, lower court cases on overcrowding citing the Eighth Amendment had typically been resolved solely on the basis of whether the conditions had been bad enough to be considered cruel or unusual. *Seiter*, however, established that in addition to that objective component, inmates must also prove that in creating these conditions government officials had acted with deliberate indifference to the needs of inmates (a subjective component).

Prior to *Seiter*, lower court cases had typically examined overcrowded conditions as a whole in determining whether the Eighth Amendment had been violated. In making such a determination, the courts had usually described in detail the conditions and then concluded that they were so serious that they constituted cruel and unusual punishment, without clearly identifying a specific basic human need that had been denied.

In *Seiter*, the Court appears to have rejected that approach. Instead, it indicated that there can be no violation of the cruel and unusual punishment clause unless the conditions deprive inmates of "a single, identifiable human need such as food, warmth, or exercise."

It is still too soon after the *Seiter* decision to gauge its effect on overcrowding cases. It seems likely, however, that the establishment of a state of mind requirement will make these cases more difficult for inmates to win. As pointed out by the dissenting justices in *Seiter*, since "[i]nhumane prison conditions often are the result of cumulative actions and inactions by numerous officials inside and outside a prison . . . it is far from clear whose intent should be examined."

In addition, the dissenters recognized that perhaps "prison officials will be able to defeat a[n] . . . action challenging inhumane prison conditions simply by showing that the conditions are caused by insufficient funding from the state legislature rather than by any deliberate indifference on the part of the prison officials."

Whether these predictions are accurate or not, only time will tell. It is clear, however, that the law on jail and prison overcrowding is a dynamic area of the law that is likely to receive more attention from the Supreme Court in the near future.

Jack E. Call

Bibliography

Call, J. E. (1988). Lower court treatment of jail and prison overcrowding cases: A second look. *Federal Probation* 52(2): 34–41.

Cole, R. B., and J. E. Call (1992). When courts find jail and prison overcrowding unconstitutional. *Federal Probation* 56(1) March: 29–39.

Rosenblatt, P. M. (1991). The dilemma of overcrowding in the nation's prisons: What are constitutional conditions and what can be done? *New York Law School Journal of Human Rights* 8: 489–520.

Thornberry, T. P., and J. E. Call (1983). Constitutional challenges to prison overcrowding: The scientific evidence of harmful effects. *Hastings Law Journal* 35: 313–51.

Cases

Bell v. Wolfish, 441 U.S. 520, 99 S.Ct. 1861, 60 L.Ed.2d 447 (1979)

Rhodes v. Chapman, 452 U.S. 337, 101 S.Ct. 2392, 69 L.Ed.2d 59 (1981)

Wilson v. Seiter, 501 U.S. 294, 111 S.Ct. 2321, 115 L.Ed.2d 1 (1991)

D

Katherine Bement Davis (1860–1935)

Katherine Bement Davis was born in Buffalo, New York, in 1860 to parents she described as reformers. She taught school for ten years after graduating from high school and before going on to earn a degree at Vassar. Katherine attended the University of Chicago on a political economics fellowship and received a doctorate. She returned to Vassar to teach for several years. In 1901, Davis was appointed to run Bedford Hill, the first female reformatory, in Westfield, New York. She was superintendent of the facility for thirteen years.

By all accounts she was a pioneer reformer in penology, particularly as regards female offenders. As female offenders were moved from men's prisons, Davis introduced the cottage system as the architecture of the female facility. Unlike the warehouse-style prisons being built for men, the cottage, she believed, was more in keeping with the personality and temperament of women.

With funding from grants and foundations, Dr. Davis was not only able to hire a psychologist, but also to perform routine psychiatric assessments for incarcerated women. She was a proponent of criminal theories that saw the offender as feebleminded, of subnormal intelligence, a "defective-delinquent." An advocate of the medical model, she was concerned about the number of prostitutes, their lack of education and skills, and their high rates of disease. Fines for prostitution, she argued, were counterproductive, as they usually placed the female offender further in debt to her male pimp. Davis was successful in persuading John D. Rockefeller, Jr., to build a Laboratory of Social Hygiene directly across from the reformatory, establishing one of the first institutes for studying female criminality. Later a small hospital was also built on the grounds, although it was in operation only a few years before funding ran out.

Inmates were required to take academic classes and to learn trades, and they were encouraged to work and to engage in recreation outdoors. Davis even wrote an article entitled "The Fresh Air Treatment for Moral Disease." The women carried out most farming chores, which were said to have a positive effect on all who participated, including those suffering from mental illnesses. A nursery was established within the reformatory in which new mothers could reside with their children for up to two years.

Dr. Davis introduced many programs in art, music, and drama. She saw to it that the women attended travel lectures, picnics, and birthday celebrations. Each New Year's Day she hosted a reception in her quarters where twenty-five to thirty girls attended and were served tea. One of her most widely cited policies was the honor cottage. To encourage good behavior, those in the highest classifications were eligible for election to the "honor cottage," in which the residents formed their own rules and participated in self-government. According to one observer, "The matron of the house has general oversight, but the girls in the honor cottage have as much freedom as a girl at a good boarding-school. The cottage is made as attractive as possible with ferns, pretty furniture, individual sleeping rooms, a pleasant sitting-room, and a sewing room where they make their own clothing" (Gillin 1926, 658).

Katherine Davis also supported early parole and preferred that the women be released into country environments rather than to the city, where bad habits and temptations awaited.

Dr. Davis became the first female corrections commissioner, during which time she recruited Mary Belle Harris to run the workhouse on Blackwell Island. Davis later became a cabinet member of New York City and chairwoman of the city's parole board. She died in 1935.

Marilyn D. McShane

See also BEDFORD HILLS CORRECTIONAL FACILITY; HARRIS, MARY BELLE

Bibliography

Gillin, J. L. (1926). *Criminology and Penology*. New York: Century.

Harris, J. (1990). *They Always Call Us Ladies*. New York: Zebra.

McKelvey, B. (1936). *American Prisons*. Chicago: University of Chicago Press (Reprinted Montclair, N.J.: Patterson Smith, 1968).

Morton, J. (1992). Looking back on 200 years of valuable contributions. *Corrections Today* 54(6): 76–78, 80, 82, 84–87.

Death Row

Although the total population of death row inmates across the country is very small, death row is a high-security classification that is considered resource-intensive. In most prison systems, death row inmates are housed in separate wings and do not mix with the general inmate population for any reason. Recent litigation by death row inmates has challenged this practice, however, as they bid for incorporation into the general population and access to the full range of services and programs provided there.

The separation of death row inmates is historical, legal, and practical. Theoretically, a person sentenced to death is not officially sentenced to the department of corrections, in which prisoners all receive a term of years. In many states, death row inmates technically remain under the jurisdiction of the county that sentences them, although they are housed and cared for by the state. Because of these custody differences, death row inmates are usually not given regular prison numbers—another factor that may add to their sense of isolation in prison.

Death row inmates are considered a high risk for escape and therefore are placed in maximum-security areas. These inmates are also considered a high risk for violence, because it is thought that they have no incentive to avoid engaging in high-risk behaviors. Checks and counts may be conducted more often in these units, and death row inmates are prohibited from possessing a greater number of items than is normal for the general prison population.

The Death Row Population

As of mid-1994 there were 2,870 prisoners on death row in prisons in this country and another six on death row in the armed forces. Forty of the inmates were women. The condemned population is approximately 51 percent white, 40 percent black, and eight percent Hispanic. Thirty-six states currently have a death penalty, as does the federal government. A majority of those under the sentence of death are held in the South. Texas, California, and Florida have the largest death row populations, approximately 330 each. Two hundred and sixty-five new death penalty inmates were received in 1992. Over one hundred death row inmates had their sentences overturned during that year. Two had their sentences commuted, and seven died from other causes. The average age of prisoners sentenced to die is 35. The average stay on death row is nine years, although Kentucky recently reported having a prisoner on death row for 32 years. According to the Bureau of Justice statistics of those prisoners leaving death row in 1991, 14 were executed, 48 had their sentences commuted to life in prison, 59 were awaiting new sentences or retrials, seven died from natural causes and two had capital charges dropped.

Death penalty states executed 38 prisoners in 1993. Texas has executed the most prisoners (78) since 1976; Florida ranks second with 33 executions. In fact, 10 percent of all persons executed in the United States since 1976, when the death penalty was reinstated, were convicted in Houston.

Life on Death Row

The routine of death row is often a cycle of eating and sleeping. Most death row inmates are locked in their eight by ten cells for twenty-three hours a day. Many do arts and crafts, read, write, and draw. Any time allotted for recreation is spent in small, fenced cages, separated from the rest of the prison. Movement within the prison, even to a recreation area, may require that the inmate be handcuffed, put into restraints, and escorted by officers. Many of the inmates receive psychological services and counseling for stress and anxiety. Some do not believe that they will be executed. Almost all do not want to die. Because all death sentences are automatically appealed, many wait anxiously for positive news from the courts. Loved ones on the outside try to keep them optimistic and active.

Although in early American prisons executions, by design, took place adjacent to the cells of the other condemned prisoners, that is not the case today. A short time before the death date, prisoners to be executed are moved to a separate area, sometimes even a separate building away from death row. When someone is executed, death row becomes an eerie and depressing place. Staff and inmates alike strain to cope with the loss and its effects on the others, and with the sudden news and administrative attention that accompanies an execution.

Few prison systems provide additional training for staff members working on death row. Some facilities provide counseling for execution teams and death row staff to help them adjust to the difficulty of the assignment. One system provides an extra pay incentive for correctional officers working with condemned inmates.

Management Issues

Litigation has brought changes to death row populations over the last ten years. Because death row inmates are involved in ongoing appeals, they have strong interests in access to law libraries as well as in frequent and extended visits with attorneys. Serving an average of five to seven years prior to execution also means that inmates have an interest in participating in prison programs and occupying their time with meaningful interests and pursuits. For this reason inmates are now often allowed limited access to special work assignments. Some states have entered into legal agreements to allow more time out of the cell for visitation, religious, recreational, and work activities. In a few institutions, death row inmates with good conduct records have been allowed to take meals in the dining hall and even to work there. When surveyed, wardens stated that the determination to allow a death row inmate access to the general prison population would depend on institutional adjustment, the findings of a psychological evaluation, and staff recommendations.

Because the population of those awaiting execution has increased, some inmates are placed two to a cell. Although death row inmates do not appear to be any more likely to be involved in incidences of violence, escape, or disciplinary infractions, they do have a higher than average rate of suicide or attempted suicide.

Executions

The management of executions is another area of concern for prison administrators. When a death warrant is signed, officials must coordinate visits for family, clergy, and lawyers before the execution, specifications for news media access and the assembly of witnesses, last meal details, communications with executive offices and the courts over possible commutations, appeals, and stays, medical personnel, transportation, and assessment of institutional impact. Arrangements must also be made with area law enforcement for local security. Written policies exist in most facilities based on experience and sensitivity to individual circumstances.

Charles B. Fields

See also EXECUTIONS

Bibliography

American Correctional Association (1989). *Managing Death-Sentenced Inmates: A Survey of Practices*. Washington, D.C.: St. Mary's.

Flack, K. (1993). In Florida: A look at day-to-day death row operations. *Corrections Today* 55(4): 74.

Greenfield, L., and J. Stephan (1993). *Capital Punishment 1992*. Washington, D.C.: Bureau of Justice Statistics.

Jackson, B., and D. Christian (1980). *Death Row*. Boston: Beacon.

Johnson, R. (1989). *Condemned To Die: Life Under Sentence of Death*. Prospect Heights, Ill.: Waveland.

Johnson, R. (1990). *Deathwork*. Pacific Grove, Calif.: Brooks/Cole.

Radelet, M., M. Vandiver, and F. Berardo (1983). Families, prisons and men with death sentences: The human impact of structured uncertainty. *Journal of Family Issues* 4(4): 595–96.

Wunder, A. (1994). Living on death row. *Corrections Compendium* 19(12): 9–21

Detainers

A detainer, in general, is a writ or instrument issued by a competent authority in one jurisdiction authorizing prison officials in another jurisdiction to keep a prisoner in their custody. Thus, it is a type of warrant filed against a person with the purpose of ensuring availability to the authority that has placed the detainer. With the passage of the Interstate Agreement on Detainers (IAD) this procedure has been formalized by statute and court decisions interpreting its provisions.

Most detainers are based on outstanding criminal charges, or additional sentences already imposed against the prisoner. A detainer may also be placed when an escaped prisoner, probationer, or parolee commits a new crime and is imprisoned in another state. The Immigration and Naturalization Service also issues detainers to prison authorities stating that the INS may seek to deport prisoners at the end of their sentences.

Closely related to detainers are writs of *habeas corpus ad prosequendum*. In use since the early nineteenth century, these writs enable a state to take temporary custody of a prisoner confined within another jurisdiction and indict, prosecute, and sentence such a prisoner. It is issued by order of a federal district court judge, and it raises issues for both the "sending" and "receiving" states. Although detainers and *ad prosequendum* writs operate in the same manner to some extent, detainers raise other concerns, especially since the passage of the IAD.

Detainers are distinct from extradition. The latter applies, generally, to situations in which a person is charged with a crime in one state while being imprisoned, or held during criminal proceedings, in another state. By agreement between the governors of the two states, a prisoner may be extradited before the conclusion of the proceedings or the term of his sentence expires, if the other state also wishes to prosecute the individual, on the condition that he will be returned as soon as the prosecution is terminated. Both extradition and detainers apply to federal and state prisoners.

The criminal justice agency filing the detainer requests that the institution either hold the prisoner for the agency or notify the agency upon the imminent release of the prisoner. Wardens of institutions holding prisoners who have detainers on them have invariably recognized the legality of these warrants and have notified the other jurisdiction of their impending release.

There are a number of damaging effects of detainers on prisoners. Although only a fraction of all detainers ultimately result in a conviction or further imprisonment, the consequences of a detainer may lead to "punishment" separate from any additional charges. Mandatory maxi-

mum-security classification, exclusion from vocational rehabilitation programs, and ineligibility for parole have all been applied by some jurisdictions to prisoners with detainers. More specifically, inmates may also be (1) deprived of an opportunity to obtain a sentence to run concurrently with the sentence being served at the time the detainer is filed; (2) ineligible for trustee status or referral to an honor farm; (3) ineligible for preferred living quarters, such as dormitories, or transfer to an institution for youthful offenders; (4) barred from preferred prison jobs that carry higher wages and that may entitle the prisoner to additional good time credit; and (5) ineligible for work-release or study-release programs.

The effect on prisoners is one of stress and anxiety, because they are hindered in the overall rehabilitation process. Since the legal basis for a detainer was rarely examined in the past, a prisoner often suffered loss of privileges and parole because of a charge for which there may have been insufficient proof for a conviction. Thus, prosecutors used detainers to exact punishment, without having to try to charge, in cases that they felt might not result in conviction. In short, detainers have often had a negative effect, leading prisoners to become embittered, thereby increasing the chances of recidivism and defeating the objectives of the correctional system. Because of the uncertainty of their future, prisoners with outstanding detainers sometimes lose interest in rehabilitative, educational, and other institutional opportunities.

Prior to the IAD, when a prisoner with a detainer finished his sentence or was declared fit to return to society, he was delivered to the authorities who filed the detainer to stand trial for old offenses, be they two, five, or ten years old. If a trial ensued, it was under stale circumstances. Delays in prosecution may jeopardize a prisoner's defense, because memories fade and witnesses disappear. If convicted, a prisoner could serve time for an offense for which, arguably, he had already made a partial payment to society. This raised serious concerns related to the constitutional right to a speedy trial, and led to dismissal of charges in some instances.

Because of the long-standing problems associated with detainers, the IAD was enacted and adopted into law. The agreement is a compact among forty-eight states, the District of Columbia, Puerto Rico, the Virgin Islands, and the federal government. First drafted in 1956 by the Council of State Governments, it was adopted by

Congress in 1970. As of 1993, only Louisiana and Mississippi had not enacted the IAD.

The Interstate Agreement on Detainers

The IAD itself does not define a detainer, so courts have adopted the definition found in the legislative reports accompanying the agreement. According to those reports, a detainer is a notification filed with the institution in which a prisoner is serving a sentence advising prison officials that he is wanted to face pending criminal charges in another jurisdiction. A major goal of the IAD is to create a good rehabilitative environment for prisoners serving sentences in one state by facilitating the speedy disposition of charges pending against them in another state. Secondly, the IAD establishes a mechanism that guarantees the speedy disposition of detainers to ensure that any filed for frivolous reasons are quickly disposed of. Finally, the ease with which states may obtain persons incarcerated in other jurisdictions for disposition of criminal charges is a great improvement over more cumbersome extradition procedures.

Because it is a congressionally sanctioned interstate compact within the Compact Clause, U.S. Constitution, article I, section 10, clause 3, the IAD is a federal law subject to federal construction. The disposition of unresolved detainers through the agreement produces sentences of determinate length, so that in-prison programming and rehabilitation can freely occur. Once pending criminal charges in another state are disposed of, a prisoner is more likely to be chosen for a wide variety of programs and in-custody benefits. In sum, the certainty of known sentences and the procedural simplicity of the IAD benefit both prisoners and the government, and they have been principal motivators in its widespread acceptance. By providing swift and certain means for resolving the uncertainties and alleviating the disabilities created by outstanding detainers, the IAD resolved many of the problems previously associated with the use of detainers. It did so in a manner that complies with the fundamental right to a speedy trial under the Sixth Amendment.

The IAD sets out two procedures for the speedy disposition of charges pending against prisoners in another state. The first, contained in article III of the agreement, mandates that prison authorities notify a prisoner of any detainers placed against him, and inform him of his right under the IAD to demand a speedy trial on the indictment, or information, or complaint giving rise to the detainer. Once the prisoner makes such a request, the state issuing the detainer must begin the trial within 180 days. Any request for final disposition made by a prisoner pursuant to the IAD is deemed to be a waiver of extradition with respect to any charge or proceeding contemplated by such a request, and a waiver of extradition to the receiving state to serve any sentence there imposed upon him, after the completion of his term in the sending state. The second procedure, described in article IV, allows prosecuting officials in the state issuing the detainer to obtain temporary custody of the prisoner upon written request to appropriate authorities in the incarcerating state. The requesting state must bring the prisoner to trial within 120 days of such removal and must not return the prisoner before completing the trial. If a court determines that a requesting state has failed to comply with any of the above conditions, it must dismiss the indictment, information, or complaint with prejudice.

The terms of the IAD apply exclusively to prisoners who are actually serving their sentences, and not to pretrial detainees. It also does not apply to those who have been convicted but not yet sentenced. This is consistent with the basic purpose of the IAD, which is to prevent interference with institutional care and rehabilitation. It is not possible to interrupt something that has not yet started. The Supreme Court in *Carchman v. Nash* has also ruled that the IAD does not apply to prisoners with detainers based on probation or parole violations. It also does not apply to those adjudged to be mentally ill or escaped, convicted felons. Thus, the agreement is limited to those detainers charging a prisoner with a criminal offense. In addition, the IAD limits the prosecution of prisoners to the charges in the detainer that formed the basis for the prisoner's temporary custody in the receiving jurisdiction.

For all purposes other than those for which temporary custody is exercised, prisoners remain in the custody of and subject to the jurisdiction of the sending state. Hence any escape from temporary custody may be dealt with in the same manner as an escape from the original place of imprisonment. The state receiving custody of a prisoner under the IAD is responsible for the prisoner and must pay all costs associated with the transfer, including the cost of housing the prisoner in an appropriate facility.

A number of issues arise related to the operation of the IAD. Major areas that have been litigated are the application and waiver of the speedy trial provisions, and formal notice of a detainer. In *Fex v. Michigan* the U.S. Supreme Court held that the 180-day time period under the IAD for bringing a prisoner to trial on out-of-state charges does not commence until the prisoner's disposition request has actually been delivered to the court and prosecutor of the jurisdiction that lodged the detainer against him. Thus, the 180 days do not begin when the prisoner transmits his request to prison officials, but when prison officials have delivered the request to the jurisdiction filing the detainer.

The IAD sets forth a number of requirements for obtaining a continuance beyond the time period within which a trial must be held. To succeed, a party seeking a continuance must demonstrate good cause, and the length of the continuance must be reasonable and necessary. The IAD also governs that period when a prisoner is unable to stand trial, as, for example, when a prisoner is physically or mentally unfit. If a state fails to try a prisoner before sending him back to the other jurisdiction, it loses its right to obtain future temporary custody of the prisoner based on the charges in the detainer. The mandatory language and stringent penalties that the IAD sets out requires states to adhere strictly to the compact's provisions. That is to protect prisoners from the negative consequences of delays and long-standing detainers. When a prisoner is the source of the delay that pushes a trial beyond the required time limit, however, the speedy trial provisions of the IAD will be waived.

Since the IAD is statutory and does not involve a constitutional right, a waiver of rights under the IAD need not be knowingly and intelligently made. For instance, a prisoner can waive his speedy trial rights under the agreement by seeking repeated continuances or by allowing a trial date beyond the 180 days without being aware of the right he is waiving. The Sixth Amendment right to a speedy trial, by contrast, requires a knowing, intelligent, and voluntary waiver by the prisoner. That could occur when a prisoner decides not to seek a trial on pending charges in another jurisdiction, even though he is aware that a detainer is in place against him. In sum, a prisoner can waive his rights under the IAD if he is made aware that a detainer has been placed against him, even if he is not aware that his decisions are pushing the trial date beyond the time period required in the statute.

A formal detainer must be filed before a prisoner may invoke the speedy trial provisions of the IAD, and prosecutors, wardens, and prisoners must all comply with the specific notice requirements in the IAD. For example, when a prisoner sends a letter directly to a prosecutor in another jurisdiction requesting that he be tried on pending charges, there is no compliance with the IAD notice requirements, which stipulate that, after a detainer has been filed, the prisoner must send a request for trial through the warden. Thus the IAD requires prosecutors, wardens, and prisoners all to comply with notice requirements. Finally, a prisoner must exhaust his available state remedies, including invoking provisions of the IAD related to speedy trial, before filing for federal habeas corpus relief.

In conclusion, detainers have a number of negative consequences for prisoners, but the provisions of the IAD allow the states, the federal government, and prisoners to resolve pending criminal charges quickly.

Louis M. Holscher

See also INTERSTATE COMPACT AGREEMENT

Bibliography

Abramson, L. W. (1979). *Criminal Detainers*. Cambridge, Mass.: Ballinger.

Bates, S. (1945). The detained prisoner and his adjustment. *Federal Probation* 9, 3: 16–18.

Clark, T. R. (1986). The effect of violations of the interstate agreement of detainers on subject matter jurisdiction. *Fordham Law Review* 54: 1209–30.

Dauber, E. (1971). Reforming the detainer system: A case study. *Criminal Law Bulletin* 7: 669–717.

Gobert, J. J., and N. P. Cohen (1981). *Rights of Prisoners*. Colorado Springs, Colo.: Shepard's/McGraw-Hill.

Necessary, J. R. (1978). The interstate agreement on detainers: Defining the federal role. *Vanderbilt Law Review* 31: 1017–54.

Wexler, D. B. (1973). *The Law of Detainers*. Washington, D.C.: U.S. Government Printing Office.

Wexler, D. B., and N. Hershey (1971). Criminal detainers in a nutshell. *Criminal Law Bulletin* 7: 753–76.

Cases

Birdwell v. Skeen, 983 F.2d 1332 (5th Cir. 1993)

Burrus v. Turnbo, 743 F.2d 693 (9th Cir. 1984)

Carchman v. Nash, 473 U.S. 716, 105 S.Ct. 3401 (1985)

Fex v. Michigan, 122 L.Ed.2d 406 (1994)

Flick v. Blevins, 887 F.2d 778 (7th Cir. 1989)

United States v. Currier, 836 F.2d 11 (1st Cir. 1987)

United States v. Mauro, 436 U.S. 340, 98 S.Ct. 1834 (1978)

Determinate Sentences

In all fifty states, one or more of three entities—the legislature, the judiciary, and an administrative or executive agency charged with oversight of early conditional release from institutions—determine the amount of time to be served by an inmate in a correctional institution. Thus, there may be three decision-makers involved in such decisions: the legislature, initially responsible for creating sentencing options and setting sentencing terms by statute; the judiciary, whose judges have the authority to choose from among the sentencing options provided by the legislature; and an administrative or executive release authority, usually a parole board, which may release an inmate conditionally prior to completion of the sentence originally imposed.

In some states, legislatures have adopted the determinate sentencing model for felonies. Most misdemeanor sentencing in the United States is determinate in nature: for example, 30 or 90 or 180 days in custody. Determinate sentencing, sometimes called flat, or fixed, sentencing and occasionally presumptive sentencing, invokes a fixed term of imprisonment. It is to be distinguished from mandatory sentencing, in which sentences for particular crimes, from which a judge may not deviate, are set by the legislature. Mandatory sentencing statutes generally prescribe a minimum period of incarceration for offenders whose crime and prior record fall within specific categories. Most commonly, they are employed for violent and serious offenses, perhaps crimes in which a firearm was used, some drinking and driving statutes, and, increasingly, for certain drug offenses. They are often justified on the basis of their perceived deterrent value.

In the determinate sentencing model, a statute establishes the length of time to be served for each crime. Thus, a robbery conviction may carry a single possible penalty, perhaps imprisonment for ten years. Discretion is allowed neither the judge at sentencing nor correctional officials nor parole boards in determining when an inmate is to be released. Although a judge imposes the determinate sentence, it is actually the legislature that has determined the penalty.

In contrast to the determinate sentencing model, in which sentences are established by the legislature, there are also judicial and administrative models of sentencing. In the judicial model the judge decides the length of the sentence within a legislatively established range, such as from five to ten years' imprisonment for robbery. In the administrative sentencing model, the legislature establishes a wide range of prison terms for a particular crime, such as a sentence of from one year to life imprisonment for robbery. Such a sentence is imposed by the judge after conviction, and the decision to release the inmate is made later by an administrative or executive agency of state government, usually a parole board.

Determinate sentencing requires a clearly defined hierarchy of penalties that are codified in state law, and in which specified terms of imprisonment are associated with each criminal offense or category. The occasional use of "presumptive sentencing" as a synonym for determinate sentencing is based upon the fact that the legislature and the law, not an individual judge, determine what the punishment for a particular crime ought to be; that is, a penalty has been set that is presumed to be most appropriate for the offense. Determinate sentencing, then, carries a direct relationship between the offense committed and the sentence imposed, all of which is fixed by law.

Determinate sentencing may not be quite as inflexible as the definitions would suggest. Those states that have a presumptive or determinate sentence for a given offense generally allow for "aggravating" or "mitigating" factors to be considered by the sentencing judge. Aggravating and mitigating factors indicate a greater or lesser degree of culpability on the part of the offender, and the sentencing judge may take one or more of those factors into consideration in imposing a sentence. Consideration of such factors may permit some minor variance between the sentence imposed and the presumptive or determinate sentence prescribed.

Aggravating factors call for a longer sentence and may be based upon prior criminal convictions, injury to victims, or the use of a weapon. Mitigating factors may include such things as cooperation with investigating officers and the prosecution, payment of restitution, or an offender who generally had been of good character prior to the offense. Regardless of the nature of the aggravating or mitigating factors, however, possible adjustments to the determinate sentence are quite limited.

Supporters of determinate sentencing recognize three fundamental sentencing principles: proportionality, equity, and social debt. Proportionality refers to the belief that the severity of sanctions should bear a direct relationship to the seriousness of the crime. Equity in sentencing means that similar crimes should be punished with the same degree of severity, regardless of the general social or personal characteristics of offenders. The equity principle needs to be balanced against the notion of social debt. If there are two offenders, one of whom has a criminal record and the other of whom does not, the criminal record of the first offender implies a higher level of social debt, where all else is equal. Greater social debt requires a more severe punishment or perhaps a greater degree of treatment.

These general principles were amplified upon in the writings of Andrew von Hirsch, who generated a renewed interest in determinate sentencing by arguing for a sentencing model called "just deserts." Von Hirsch noted:

> A desert rationale's central principle is that of commensurate deserts: the severity of punishments should be proportionate to the seriousness of the offender's criminal conduct. The commensurate-deserts principle rests on the condemnatory implications of punishment. Punishment is a censuring institution. It treats the act as reprehensible and the actor as someone to be blamed for the act. The more severe the penalty, the greater the resulting reproof. That is why the severity of punishments should fairly reflect the degree of blameworthiness of the offender's criminal behavior.
>
> A desert rationale makes the penalty depend chiefly on the seriousness of the crime of conviction, with only a modest adjustment for the previous criminal record. The seriousness of crime, in turn, depends on two factors: the harmfulness of the conduct and the culpability of the actor.

Just deserts—a major building-block and intellectual foundation for determinate sentencing—and determinate sentencing itself are founded on the proposition that punishment must be based on the seriousness of the offense and the culpability of the perpetrator. Other sentencing aims—including crime control, general and individual deterrence, incapacitation, and rehabilitation—are not excluded, as long as they do not alter the severity of the penalty. Just deserts and determinate sentencing are a return to retributive principles articulated centuries ago in Mosaic law and its *lex talionis* (retaliation law), which required a measured societal response to wrongdoing. Simply stated, the punishment for a crime should be comparable to the harm inflicted, as in "an eye for an eye."

The move toward determinate sentencing was driven both by liberals and conservatives in the 1970s and 1980s. Energized by rising crime rates and the apparent failure of the rehabilitative ideal, conservatives demanded a get-tough approach to crime. Liberals, who previously had supported indeterminate sentencing and its guiding principle, rehabilitation, reconsidered their positions as they learned of the abuses of discretion nationwide, including significant disparities in sentencing and parole decisions, many of which were tied to such extralegal factors as individual judges, race, socioeconomic status, age, sex, jurisdiction, and type of defense counsel. From a political point of view, determinate sentencing made extraordinarily good sense in that it provided elected and appointed officials at every level of government the opportunity to be "tough on crime."

In the mid 1970s, Maine became the first state to adopt determinate sentencing; its judges sentenced offenders to prison terms of fixed length. All offenders thus sentenced served their entire sentence, less any "good time" accrued while in prison. The state parole board was abolished. Other states followed this pattern, including California, the state that had pioneered the indeterminate sentence. By 1985, all fifty states and the District of Columbia had considered or enacted legislation to change their indeterminate sentencing structures, some by giving guidelines to parole boards, others by using determinate sentences, and others by using sentencing guidelines that narrowed judicial discretion.

States employing determinate sentencing typically abolish parole and parole boards, for under the determinate system they are unnecessary because release is not discretionary. Although prisoners can earn some time off their sentences for good behavior, called "good time," that is not a parole decision.

Several states have established sentencing commissions with the authority to develop and modify sentencing guidelines. In 1984, the United States Sentencing Commission was established and it delivered its federal judiciary guidelines in 1987.

There are, of course, many who are critical of the just deserts, determinate sentencing approach, even though it appears to have been successful in minimizing disparities in sentencing. The criticisms of scholars, practitioners, and politicians center upon the following points:

1. Determinate sentencing is too simplistic and is based upon a primitive concept of culpability.
2. Determinate sentencing rejects the rehabilitative ideal—the idea of change—and ignores the fact that rehabilitation may have been condemned on the basis of flawed evaluations. Determinate sentences leave little incentive for offenders to participate in institutional programs that may contribute to their own positive changes. Indeed, determinate sentencing does not acknowledge that values, attitudes, and behavior can change or be changed.
3. Determinate sentencing reduces the discretion of judges substantially but leaves extraordinary discretionary power with prosecutors. There is the possibility that disparity will be greater, although of a different type. With discretion removed from judges and with longer penalties imposed by legislatures, prosecutors may be more reluctant to prosecute. Indeed, juries may be more reluctant to find defendants guilty. Further, with longer, mandatory sentences, defendants may be less likely to plead guilty and more likely to insist on trials, thus increasing the burden of overcrowded court systems.
4. Determinate sentences contribute to the increasingly serious problem of prison overcrowding. Current data confirm the overcrowding of state and federal correctional systems and institutions.
5. Determinate sentencing does not achieve the goal of decreasing the crime rate by deterring crime. Although it is clear that

those incarcerated for longer periods are not out on the streets committing crime, the total effect on the crime rate is insignificant. Further, it is not clear that determinate sentencing affects the rate of recidivism once the inmates who are serving longer sentences are released.
6. Determinate sentencing is insensitive to the social problems that lead a large proportion of offenders to crime.

Robert Carter

See also INDETERMINATE SENTENCES

Bibliography

Benda, B., and D. Waite (1988). A proposed determinate sentencing model in Virginia: An empirical evaluation. *Juvenile and Family Court Journal* 39(1): 55–69.

Griset, P. (1991). *Determinate Sentencing: The Promise and the Reality of Retributive Justice.* Albany, N.Y.: State University of New York Press.

Pillsbury, S. (1989). Understanding penal reform: The dynamic of change. *Journal of Criminal Law and Criminology* 80: 726–80.

Tonry, M. (1988). Structuring sentencing. In M. Tonry and N. Morris, eds. *Crime and Justice: A Review of Research, Vol. 8.* Chicago: University of Chicago Press.

von Hirsch, A. (1986). *Doing Justice.* Reprint. Boston: Northeastern University Press.

Developmentally Disabled Offenders

The prisons and jails of the United States began as the only secure detention option available in most communities. In some areas that remains the case today. As the nation has moved toward a system of deinstitutionalized care for adults identified as developmentally disabled and those suffering from mental health problems, state and local correctional agencies have become the providers of last resort for many offenders with significant developmental limitations.

Although the term "developmental disabilities" is usually reserved for individuals demonstrating pervasive impairments in several areas of development, it is often used to describe individuals who demonstrate disabilities affecting their behavior and learning. The prevalence of these disabilities is much greater within correctional agencies than in the general population. Incidence studies for such disabilities among prisoners frequently have included over 40 percent juveniles. The average prevalence of such disabilities in adult correctional programs is lower (8 to 10 percent). This may be due to the absence of legal mandates to identify offenders who require special education and related services, which are provided for youth with disabilities under the age of twenty-two.

The most common disabilities among the prisoner population include mild to moderate mental retardation, learning disabilities, and emotional and behavioral disorders. In these conditions, the ability to learn is reduced by cognitive deficits, difficulties in processing language-related information, and the inability to socialize appropriately. These disabilities are not easily recognizable. They may involve such problems as underdeveloped social skills and poor comprehension of questions and warnings, both of which increase the likelihood that offenders with disabilities will be imprisoned. Individuals with more severe disabilities, on the other hand, are more readily identifiable and therefore are more likely to be diverted to other services and agencies prior to adjudication.

Statistics regarding the incidence of disabilities among the prison population are difficult to obtain, because, in the past, efforts were not made to identify or serve such prisoners. Prior to the passage of legislation that mandated appropriate educational and other services for individuals under the age of twenty-two, no incentives or sanctions were available to compel correctional programs to attempt to meet their needs. Even following federal and state legislation mandating such services, prevalence studies have been affected by the lack of qualified diagnostic personnel, identification procedures, and appropriate programs, as well as by disincentives inherent to federal mandates (such as penalties for failing to serve offenders with disabilities appropriately). As the public education system has increased its efforts to identify and serve students with disabilities, estimates of the prevalence of disabilities among prison populations have also risen, especially for juvenile offenders. For example, up to 60 percent of juvenile offenders have been found to have been previously identified as having disabilities and as having received special education programs in the public schools.

Public schools are required to conduct comprehensive assessments of students who are suspected of having disabilities prior to placing them in special education programs. Typically, those procedures consist of an intelligence test, measurements of academic performance, and such other measurements of learning and behavior as may be required to determine individual needs.

Correctional education programs serving school-age youth (up to twenty-two) likewise are required by law to identify students with special education needs. In juvenile institutions, which almost universally offer educational programs, similar identification procedures are followed, and special education services must be made available to all students with disabilities. Although most state and federal departments of correction report that they never have custody of persons with a history of mental disorders prior to their incarceration, the basis for that claim is the absence of prisoners previously adjudged incompetent, insane, guilty but mentally ill, or an "abnormal offender" rather than previous enrollment in a public school special education program. For educational purposes, however, those inmates should also be identified as having a disability, and a full range of educational and related services should be provided to meet their needs. Offenders placed in adult prisons are less likely to enroll in educational programs. Nevertheless, if educational programs for adult offenders are available, special education services are required for all students with disabilities under the age of twenty-two who have not completed high school.

In prison, offenders with disabilities are likely to face problems not encountered by other inmates. For example, offenders with mental retardation are less frequently placed on probation or in other diversionary, noninstitutional programs. They have more difficulty adjusting to prison routines, are less likely to participate in rehabilitation programs, and are more frequently the objects of practical jokes and sexual harassment. Their failure to understand and comply with routines, directions, and to advocate effectively for themselves contributes to their more often being denied parole and serving longer sentences than other offenders sentenced for the same crimes. Individuals with emotional or learning problems face many of the same adjustment problems.

The most significant federal legislation addressing the needs of these offenders has been in the area of education. The Education of the Handicapped Act (P.L. 94-142) and its amendments (most recently, P.L. 101-476, the Individuals with Disabilities Education Act of 1990) and Section 504 of the Vocational Rehabilitation Act of 1973 (P.L. 93-112) have provided the foundation for court interventions in the operation of correctional agencies in behalf of these special populations. Significant litigation has occurred regarding the provision of educational services to individuals with disabilities, particularly as the statutes apply to prisoners under the age of twenty-two. Courts also have intervened with regard to the conditions of confinement for offenders with disabilities. The Texas case of *Ruiz v. Estelle* was one of the most comprehensive attempts by the federal judiciary to intervene in the operations of a correctional agency in behalf of offenders with disabilities. That litigation established the first statewide correctional screening process for the identification of offenders with mental retardation, as well as programming specifically designed for inmates with that disability.

The Americans with Disabilities Act (P.L. 101-336) has expanded and strengthened the federal mandate that offenders with disabilities be provided equal access to a full range of services both within the correctional setting and throughout society. Although the mandates for serving these special populations are clear, many correctional agencies have failed to provide appropriate services for them.

The services that correctional agencies have provided to these populations include special housing, programs, custody, education, work, and transitional assistance. Prisoners with disabilities can be subjected to abuse and manipulation unless special provisions are made for their care. In Georgia, South Carolina, and several other states, special programs have been developed for that purpose. Those programs provide secure housing and programs for vulnerable inmates, as well as educational opportunities in "life skills" to help reintegrate them into the general prison population.

The fact that offenders with disabilities are victimized by other inmates and staff, as well as the lack of qualified professional staff to adapt regular programs for their needs, may limit the access of these prisoners to "mainstream" educational, vocational, and recreational programs. In-service training for correctional staff in the needs of offenders with disabilities is becoming more widely available, however, thereby improving their opportunities. The growth of special education programs for offenders with disabilities has led to a growth in educational services and placements. These include regular educational and vocational classes, Chapter I programs, consultative models (in which regular teachers receive assistance from special educators), part-time resource rooms (in which offenders receive specialized assistance in subjects they find difficult), and self-contained special classes. Correctional special education programs have been developed in many adult and juvenile correctional facilities. The essential components of an effective correctional special education program have been identified:

1. Assessments of the deficits and learning needs of offenders with functional disabilities
2. A curriculum that meets students' individual needs
3. Vocational training opportunities that are specifically tailored to the needs of people with disabilities
4. Transition services that effectively link the correctional education program to a student's previous education, as well as to the educational and human services needed to support the offender after release
5. A comprehensive system for providing a full range of education and related services to offenders with disabilities
6. Effective training in correctional special education to improve the skills of current teachers, as well as to develop skills in teachers currently in training and to attract new special educators into careers in corrections

Federal statutes related to disabilities and special education have provided the basis for litigation, as well as for changes in administration and programs. That has resulted in a greater recognition within correctional settings of the needs of these special populations. In most jurisdictions, the efforts to address the needs of offenders with disabilities have focused primarily upon educational services.

Bruce I. Wolford
C. Michael Nelson
Robert B. Rutherford

Bibliography
Coffey, O. D., N. Procopiow, and N. Miller (1989). *Programming for Mentally Retarded and Learning Disabled Inmates:*

A Guide for Correctional Administrators. Washington, D.C.: National Institute of Corrections.

Leone, P. E., R. B. Rutherford, and C. M. Nelson (1991). *Special Education in Juvenile Corrections*. Reston, Va.: Council for Exceptional Children.

Nelson, C. M., R. B. Rutherford, and B. I. Wolford (1987). *Special Education in the Criminal Justice System*. Columbus, Ohio: Merrill.

New York Department of Correctional Services (1985). *Source Book on the Mentally Disordered Prisoner*. Washington, D.C.: National Institute of Corrections.

Cases

Ruiz v. Estelle, 503 F. Supp. 1265 (S.D. Texas, 1980), cert. denied, 103 Ct. 1438

Diagnostic and Reception Centers

Diagnostic and reception centers are generally separate units within correctional institutions, or separate facilities, where newly admitted prisoners undergo an intensive classification process consisting of assessment, evaluation, and orientation.

Early Classification Developments

The history of classification is deeply entwined with the history of corrections, therefore tracing the development of prison diagnostic and reception centers must begin with an examination of classification as a whole. Classification, or the differentiation of the prisoner population for a variety of management or treatment purposes, preceded the creation of America's first prisons. As early as 1787, the Philadelphia Society for Alleviating the Miseries of Public Prisons recommended that first-time offenders be separated from hardened criminals, that the sexes be segregated, and that liquor and other vices be prohibited in the nation's workhouses and jails.

Classification was clearly in evidence in 1829, when the Eastern State Penitentiary was built in Philadelphia. The concepts of separating convicts from society as well as each other and reforming them through silence, meditation, and hard work were basic elements of the early American fortress-style prisons.

The Birth of Modern Prison Classification

Dissatisfaction with the lack of inmate reform and prison overcrowding in both Auburn- and Pennsylvania-style prisons led to the birth of the Reformatory Movement during the latter part of the nineteenth century. America's first reformatory, Elmira, introduced a new inmate classification or grading system. Inmates received "marks" for good behavior and lost them for misconduct. The accumulation of a specified number of marks could ease institutional restrictions and even lead to earlier parole release. By the first half of the nineteenth century, the majority of states had established reformatories. With the passage of time, the mark system changed to one of ranking or grading inmates in response to their behavior. Inmates earning a place on this "honor" system enjoyed small privileges and were thus able to make their life in prison a bit more tolerable.

By the beginning of the twentieth century America's prisons had evolved into complex institutions, with prison industries and inmate labor the dominant concern. Responding to the needs of the day, classification efforts focused primarily on the assignment of prisoners to either maximum- or medium-security housing, based on the likelihood that they might try to escape, cause disciplinary problems, or inflict injury on staff, other prisoners, or themselves.

The 1930s saw the confluence of three major developments, the results of which revolutionized prison classification. First, criminological and psychological thinking on the causes of crime changed dramatically. Second, American penal policy changed from focusing on punishment through imprisonment to using prisons for correction and rehabilitation. Third, the end of World War I, coupled with the advent of the Great Depression, brought severe restrictions on prison industries, driven by massive national unemployment coupled with the demands of America's labor unions to preserve jobs for law-abiding citizens. The combined pressures of these changes forged the development of a host of educational, vocational, and rehabilitational programs in prisons. These new programs, in turn, created a need for the coordination of the various treatment and training programs. Also, inmates had to be assigned to the programs on the basis of their needs and perceived deficiencies. Thus correctional systems looked to prison classification units for the determination of differential care and the handling of offenders. As such, classification became the main tool for assessing the needs of prisoners and for assigning them to housing and program activities.

Classification Process and Structure

In the United States, prison classification procedures are administered by (1) physically separate diagnostic centers or depots that usually serve as reception and diagnostic centers for several correctional institutions and, occasionally, as statewide units; or (2) relatively independent diagnostic units attached to host institutions; or (3) classification teams or committees, which continue to work with inmates for the duration of their stay in the prison system.

The process of classification itself falls into three distinct phases: initial classification, reclassification, and prerelease assessment for community or parole release. Most but not all correctional departments conduct the initial classification process in special reception or diagnostic centers. Many of the larger departments have regionalized their reception centers to accommodate the recent, unprecedented growth in the number of inmates and prisons in their systems. Regionalization increases the efficiency of the system and reduces the need to transport inmates over long distances.

The Functions of Reception and Diagnostic Centers

Modern reception centers differ significantly from their earlier versions. Reflecting a new reality in corrections, including the abandonment of the medical model in their program approaches, most centers have changed their names from diagnostic to reception and evaluation (R and E) centers. In a similar vein, a major reorientation of mission and programs has taken place. Whereas earlier diagnostic centers were noted for their perfunctory assessment of inmates, a lack of coordination with the institutions to which inmates were assigned, inaccurate data, and the absence of evaluation of their activities or effectiveness, today's R and E centers oversee an inmate's progress from entry into the prison system to reentry into the community.

Unlike regular prison units, reception and evaluation centers are highly specialized facilities in which the efforts of professionals are focused on the newly admitted offender in an atmosphere reflecting the goals of modern corrections. Reception and evaluation centers provide intake processing and high-security detention for newly admitted inmates. Among the key functions performed are records development, orientation to the correctional system, and a detailed inmate classification and assessment of the prisoner's needs.

Records development includes the creation of dossiers by tapping into existing criminal justice databases. Law enforcement agencies, court systems, and state and national databases are contacted to develop a complete criminal history for each offender.

Orientation is provided to inmates in group sessions and individually. Its purpose is to explain the intake process, present an overview of the department of corrections, and explain the rules and regulations of the department, the rights and obligations of the inmate, and the disciplinary process should rule infractions occur. A comprehensive orientation process is particularly important for first offenders. Anxious and fearful, they may have unrealistic expectations regarding prison life. A caring staff will offer sage advice, formally and informally, on how to adapt to prison, with all its bureaucratic and organizational demands. It will also advise the new "fish" to stay clear from the exploitations of repeat offenders, to whom the uninitiated are particularly vulnerable.

The heart of the R and E process is the offender assessment. It includes the determination on the inmate's overall needs and requirements. At a minimum, the assessment process would include the following:

1. A medical evaluation conducted by professional medical staff, during which inmates all receive a complete medical examination and standard laboratory tests to determine their physical condition and medical needs;

2. An intake interview, during which caseworkers review the social and criminal histories of each inmate in clinical interviews to obtain information such as employment history, family background, criminal history, vocational and educational objectives and abilities, as well as substance abuse problems. The clinical interviews are also designed to determine the particular strengths and weaknesses of the inmate and form the basis for the formulation of an individual program plan designed to address the needs of the inmate; and

3. A complete psychological and educational attainment assessment, during which inmates are given a standard battery of psychological and academic tests by trained psychologists and caseworkers. The final component of the R and E

assessment involves the development of an admission report for each inmate, formulated by the caseworkers. It contains a summary of the inmate's life history, an assessment of special physical, psychological, and social needs, the inmate's individualized program plan, and other information deemed necessary to assist staff at the inmate's assigned institution in the formulation of management, program, and housing decisions.

Focus on Risk Assessment in Classification
With the completion of the evaluation process, the R and E center provides its inmates with an initial security classification and assigns them to a correctional institution. But before the inmate is transferred, the better developed programs will provide yet another critical service. Reflecting modern correction's growing and justifiable concern over institutional, inmate, and public safety, many R and E centers also provide objective evaluations of individual offenders' risks. Today's evaluations are very different from the highly subjective classifications used as late as the 1970s. Driven by court rulings and inmate-initiated litigation, prison systems have succeeded in developing validated, objective classification and screening systems on the basis of which risks and needs are ascertained by means of clearly defined criteria and weighted scoring systems. Most systems consider the following factors of great importance in risk assessment:

1. Severity of the current offense
2. Sentence length
3. Detainers or "holds" from other jurisdictions
4. History of escapes or attempted escapes
5. History of violence
6. Number of prior convictions
7. Current age
8. Whether alcohol or drugs are associated with the current offense
9. Mandatory time to be served before parole eligibility or release

Most departments also include such factors as the special notoriety of a particular offense and the court-recommended treatments for offenders in the highest risk classification.

In contrast to previous practice, in which reception and diagnostic processes could take three or four months, most R and E centers complete their assessments within fourteen to twenty-one days of the inmate's arrival at the center. Once the process is complete, inmates are given an opportunity to review and discuss the summary admission report with a staff member or a classification coordinator. They are then transferred to their assigned correctional institution.

Given modern, computer-driven management information systems, the well-formulated R and E process does not stop with the transfer of the inmates to their assigned institutions. Many such programs have institutionalized a systematic exchange of information between the R and E center and the prison facilities they serve. The information includes periodic classification updates, data on program participation, inmate adaptation, and so forth. In today's prisons, periodical reclassification has become the norm. During this process, an inmate's custody and security level is reviewed, as are institutional assignment, job performance, and program participation. Changes in custody and security levels continue to be based on an objective evaluation of the inmate's criminal history and institutional adjustment. As before, risks and needs are determined through objective, validated, weighted scoring systems. The results, coupled with the reclassification reports, help determine the changes, if any, in an inmate's security classification.

The Advantages of a Centralized Intake Process
Today, most correctional systems find themselves operating under the combined strains of overcrowding, inadequate funding, and the constant threat of inmate litigation. Prison reception and evaluation processes are not only labor intensive but also require the employment of highly educated, competent, and therefore costly professional staff. The personnel required for evaluation and assessment includes social workers, caseworkers, psychologists, psychiatrists, and physicians and related medical personnel, as well as information specialists, statisticians, and actuaries. As a result, their use at a central facility (or in regional centers), significantly lowers costs for prison systems, which have been perennially plagued by low levels of funding and austerity programs. Most modern R and E centers have been able to overcome the serious limitations of earlier centers. To the degree that they remain a part of periodical reclassification pro-

cedures and provide continuing information and evaluations on prisoners, they can provide critically needed services at lower cost than other approaches.

Edith E. Flynn

See also CLASSIFICATION SYSTEMS

Bibliography

Alexander, J. A. (1986). Classification objectives and practices. *Crime and Delinquency* 32: 323–38.

American Correctional Association (1993). *Classification: A Tool for Managing Today's Offenders*. Laurel, Md.: American Correctional Association.

Buchanan, R. A., K. L. Whitlow, and J. Austin (1986). National evaluation of objective prison classification systems: The current state of the art. *Crime and Delinquency* 32: 272–90.

Clements, C. B. (1984). *Offender Needs Assessment: Models and Approaches*. Washington, D.C.: National Institute of Justice.

Clements, C. B. (1986). *Offender Needs Assessment*. College Park, Md.: American Correctional Association.

Flynn, E. E. (1975). Problems of reception and diagnostic centers. In *Correctional Classification and Treatment*. Cincinnati, Ohio: Anderson.

Flynn, E. E. (1978). Classification systems. In *Handbook on Correctional Classification*. Cincinnati, Ohio: Anderson.

Solomon, L., and C. Baird (1982). Classification: Past failures and future potential. *Classification as a Management Tool: Theories and Models for Decision-Makers*. College Park, Md.: American Correctional Association.

Diet and Food Service

Food is one of the basic necessities of life, and in prison it becomes even more important because meals are one of the few enjoyable activities for inmates. It is not surprising that bad food is the primary target of inmate complaints and lawsuits and has been a factor in most inmate riots and disturbances. Prison food service is faced with a set of major challenges, including the diverse tastes and special dietary needs of inmates, providing an abundance of food within budgetary constraints, and minimizing inmate lawsuits.

Prisons and jails have adapted their food service operations to meet these challenges. Today, most institutions employ qualified food service administrators. Food preparation is guided by standards either voluntarily imposed by state correctional departments or mandated by court decisions that are often influenced by American Correctional Association standards.

Menu Planning

Prison menus must be planned so that they meet basic nutritional requirements, provide varied and appealing meals, and stay within budgetary constraints. Most correctional systems use some type of "cycle menu," covering a certain time period, at the end of which the menu is repeated. This provides a nutritionally adequate menu that includes popular menu items, avoids undue repetition and monotony, and keeps down average daily food costs. Nationally, daily food cost averages $3.13 per day, ranging from a low of $1.01 in Montana to a high of $7.00 in Hawaii.

Health trends outside prison have influenced prison menus. Recently, many facilities have begun to serve less red meat and fewer starches, and more fish, sandwiches, broiled foods, and vegetables, such as broccoli and brussels sprouts. Food service administrators have also recognized that the stressful nature of prison life demands a more than adequate diet. While inmates may be offered a fully nutritious meal, they may eat only the dessert and three pieces of bread. That fact, as well as the availability of foods unfamiliar to inmates, underscores the need to educate them in the benefits of good eating habits (Boss 1986).

Court rulings have required jails and prisons to provide inmates with special diets as prescribed by physicians or dentists, and to accommodate, where possible, the dietary restrictions of legitimate religious groups. The issue of providing meals that meet religious dietary requirements or special meals for religious celebrations is related to the right to free exercise of religion. The federal courts have allowed regulation of religious exercise based on legitimate institutional needs (such as security or expense). They continue to be split over both the degree to which prison authorities can impose restrictions and the need to substantiate their justifications (Boston 1990).

The two diets most frequently requested are vegetarian and nonpork, to meet the dietary restrictions of Jews, Muslims, and members of

Inmates begin food preparation long before dawn each day. Photo courtesy of Szabo Correctional Services, used with permission of the American Correctional Association.

some other religions (Ayres 1988). To accommodate these requirements, many correctional facilities label or mark with an asterisk foods that contain pork and serve those foods in such a way as to prevent their touching other foods. Other jurisdictions provide at every meal an alternative menu that offers a substitute non-meat entree that meets the nutritional requirements for those vegetarians who do not eat eggs or dairy products and those whose religions require dietary restrictions.

Food Preparation and Meal Service

According to ACA standards, inmates should be provided with at least three meals a day, of which two are to be hot, at regular meal times during each twenty-four-hour period, with no more than fourteen hours between the evening meal and breakfast. To break the monotony of prison life, a different schedule may be instituted on weekends and holidays (Ayres 1988).

Food should be prepared under sanitary conditions for health reasons and because, unlike restaurants, in prison the workers are also customers and will be quick to pass the word

if unsanitary conditions exist (Boss 1986). That can easily spark a disturbance. Also, the emphasis that inmates place on food makes variation, flavor, texture, appearance, palatability, and temperature all-important. No one likes to eat food that is under- or overcooked, dry, or unappetizing.

Most prisoners, except for those restricted to their cells, are fed in large dining areas that often hold 250 to 500 inmates. In newer prisons, these dining areas provide an informal setting where inmates eat four or six to a table. Another trend in newer facilities is decentralized dining, under which inmates are fed in day rooms, cell blocks, or small satellite areas. That reduces the number of inmates congregated in one location at a given time, enhances security, and minimizes the number of security personnel required, although it does require more supervisors. Under this arrangement, food is delivered in insulated trays, in heated carts, or in bulk in hot/cold carts, or by "retherm" systems.

Retherm systems are mobile units that are used to reheat food either in bulk or in serving trays. Heated food is placed in the retherm unit, cold food is placed in another cart, and both are rolled to cell areas or decentralized dining rooms. Some fifteen to thirty minutes after the retherm unit has been plugged into a source of electricity, hot food, cold food, and beverages are ready for delivery to inmates. This type of system can also be used in kitchens where there are adjacent dining areas.

While overcrowding has resulted in the reduction and even the elimination of some prison activities and services, food preparation cannot be substantially reduced. At some overcrowded prisons, cooking may start early in the morning and food may be served all day, which means that there is no break from one meal to the next. That places incredible stress on food service operations.

A more efficient solution is to adopt the cook-chill method of food production, which allows large quantities of food to be cooked and stored in advance. The cook-chill method, a type of cook-to-inventory system, prepares food according to inventory levels using standardized recipes. It is based on maintaining predetermined amounts (par levels) of menu items on hand at all times. For example, if the par level for chili is 400 gallons and only 150 gallons exist in storage, 250 additional gallons would need to be prepared. Food prepared today may be served next week. This takes the pressure off cooks to prepare food for each meal.

With states considering building additional living units at existing prisons (sometimes doubling their capacity) to meet the need for more bed space, these food preparation systems can become even more cost-efficient. As long as storage is sufficient, existing kitchen facilities can meet food service needs simply by adding a second eight-hour shift.

There is no doubt that the food service in correctional institutions is an extremely important function. With riots, lawsuits, and inmate strikes all associated with poor food, prison administrators would be wise indeed to pay constant attention to food preparation.

Ira J. Silverman

Bibliography

American Correctional Association (1990). *Standards for Adult Correctional Institutions*. College Park, Md.: American Correctional Association.

Ayres, M. B. (1988). *Food Service in Jails*. Alexandria, Va.: National Sheriffs' Association.

Boss, D., M. Schecter, and P. King (1986). Food service behind bars. *Food Management* (March): 83–87, 114, 120–36.

Boston, J. (1990). Case law report: Highlights of most important cases. *National Prison Project Journal* 5(4): 9–16.

D

Disabled Inmates

The study of people with disabilities and their rehabilitation has rapidly increased in American society since the mid-1950s. Academic programs in this area have been established in universities. Agencies and services for the disabled have been developed, and occupational specializations have focused on the care of those with mental or physical disabilities. Professionals in a variety of agencies have become concerned with the problems of the disabled. There is little research, however, concerning individuals with disabilities in prison.

It has become increasingly apparent that people with disabilities face a number of social and psychological difficulties. These problems include stigmatization of the disabled and social barriers to friendship and intimacy. Traditionally, individuals with disabilities were excluded from the mainstream of society in education, employment, and social activities. These problems could be overwhelming, particularly when combined with other conditions.

For example, convicted felons must cope with a variety of obstacles, especially obstacles to future employment. The stigma of a felony conviction in conjunction with the problems of a disability could constitute insurmountable difficulties for the disabled inmate. Prison administrators and treatment staff thus need to develop research and treatment with which to teach inmates to cope with these special problems.

Perhaps the most significant event in the integration into mainstream society by people with disabilities was the passage of the Americans With Disabilities Act (ADA) on 26 July 1990 (ADA 1990). It is generally conceded that the ADA is probably the most sweeping civil rights legislation passed since the enactment of the Civil Rights Act of 1964 (Rubin 1993). The ADA was designed to grant full citizenship to Americans with disabilities and to entitle them to equal opportunity and access to mainstream America.

The ADA was based on the belief that people with disabilities have traditionally been

TABLE 1

Basic Terminology of the ADA

Disability	(1) A mental or physical impairment that substantially limits a major life activity; (2) a record of having such an impairment; or (3) being regarded as having such an impairment.
Impairment	A physiological or mental disorder.
Substantial Limitation	When compared to the average person, persons with a disability are: (1) unable to perform a major life activity; (2) significantly restricted on how or how long they can perform the activity; or (3) significantly restricted in terms of being able to perform a class or broad range of jobs.
Major Life Activity	Basic functions that the average person in the general population can do with little or no difficulty, such as walking, seeing, hearing, breathing, speaking, procreating, learning, sitting, standing, performing manual tasks, working, or having intimate sexual relations.

isolated and segregated, and that this discrimination took many forms, including:

1. architectural, transportation, and communication barriers;
2. overprotective rules;
3. exclusionary standards;
4. fewer services, programs, activities, benefits, jobs, or other opportunities; and
5. outright exclusion from certain places and privileges.

While Title I of the ADA addresses employment aspects of the law, and probably has little if any applicability to inmates with disabilities, Title II of the ADA requires government entities to make their facilities accessible to all, which includes the delivery of services and programs to people with disabilities. As such, Title II of the ADA applies directly to correctional facilities housing inmates with disabilities. Before examining the possible ramifications of the ADA on correctional facilities, it is necessary to first define some basic terms and then to provide estimates of the number of inmates with disabilities.

According to the ADA, a person with a disability is someone who (1) has a physical or mental impairment that substantially limits one or more major life activities; (2) has a record of such an impairment; or (3) is regarded as having an impairment. In order to determine whether someone is disabled for the purposes of the ADA, it is essential that certain key concepts be thoroughly understood. Table 1 contains a list and short explanation of some of the key words and phrases commonly used in the ADA to describe its requirements and the obligations of those covered by the law.

There has been little research concerning the number of prison inmates with disabilities (Veneziano, Veneziano, and Tribolet 1987). The available research indicates that most prison systems do not keep this information in a form that can be easily retrieved. Most of the studies that have been conducted have concentrated on a particular disability.

In one of the first studies of inmates with disabilities, Veneziano, Veneziano, and Tribolet (1987) surveyed all of the prison systems at the state and federal level, asking for information on inmates with the following five types of disability: visual deficits, mobility/orthopedic deficit, hearing deficit, speech deficit, and psychological disability.

The results of that survey indicated that a very small percentage (less than 1 percent) of prison populations had visual, mobility/orthopedic, hearing, or speech deficits (Veneziano, Veneziano, and Tribolet 1987). As more than one-third of the jurisdictions that responded reported that such information was unknown or unavailable for one or more of the categories, it was felt that these results should be treated as underestimates.

The results of the survey with regard to psychological disabilities were very much different from the results for physical disabilities. Estimates of mental retardation, learning disabilities, and mental illness varied widely from jurisdiction to jurisdiction, from less than 1 percent to over 60 percent (Veneziano, Veneziano, and Tribolet 1987).

In an attempt to obtain more current results, the above survey was recently replicated. As can be seen from Table 2, the results of the more recent survey were largely consistent with those of the previous survey. Fewer than 1 percent of the inmates had visual, mobility/orthopedic, hearing, or speech deficits, results consistent with another recent survey (Long and Sapp

TABLE 2

Percentages of Inmate Populations With Disabilities

Physical Disabilities

visual deficit	0.2 percent
mobility/orthopedic deficit	0.3 percent
other major health problems	14.2 percent
cancer	0.2 percent
cardiovascular disease	3.4 percent
diabetes	3.1 percent
epilepsy	0.9 percent
hypertension	6.6 percent

Communicative Disabilities

hearing deficit	0.2 percent
speech deficit	0.06 percent

Psychological Disabilities

learning disability	10.7 percent
mental retardation	4.2 percent
psychotic disorders	7.2 percent
other psychological disorders	12.0 percent

1992). While somewhat larger percentages of inmates were categorized as having other major health problems, it is not entirely clear that all of these inmates would be considered disabled under the ADA.

The more recent survey again showed greater numbers of inmates with psychological disabilities. From 2.9 to 20 percent of inmates were estimated to have one or more of the four subcategories of psychological disorders. With the exception of the results for learning disabilities, that is consistent with the findings from other studies.

For example, Waltus et al. (1988) found that the prevalence of psychological disorders among prisoners in state, federal, and military prisons varied little, from 7 to 10 percent. Swetz et al. (1989) reported that 23.7 percent of the inmates surveyed had received psychological services one or more times during their incarceration. In a comprehensive study of learning deficiencies among inmates, however, Bell et al. (1983) found that 42 percent of the inmates tested had a learning deficiency, and that 82 percent of those with learning deficiencies were classified as learning disabled.

There has been little research concerning the services available to inmates with disabilities. Long and Sapp (1992) found that access to programs and facilities for the physically disabled in prison was very limited. Veneziano,

Veneziano, and Tribolet (1987) developed a list of services that might be provided to the disabled inmate, based on a review of the literature. That list of services is contained in Table 3.

In both the original and a more recent survey, correctional health care administrators from each prison system were asked to indicate whether these services were provided to inmates, either those with or those without disabilities.

The respondents indicated that many of the services listed in Table 3 were provided to all inmates. For the most part, no distinction was made between disabled and nondisabled inmates; usually, the services were either available to all inmates, or they were not available at all.

The vast majority, over 90 percent, reported that they provided screening and evaluation services with respect to medical, optometric, and dental examinations, as well as educational evaluations. Less than one-half provided hearing evaluations, and about one-third speech evaluations. With respect to program services, over 90 percent of the respondents stated that they provided optometric and dental services, and inpatient and outpatient medical care to all inmates. About one-half indicated that they provided annual physical examinations to inmates.

Most jurisdictions, again slightly over 90 percent, stated that they provided elementary and high school education to inmates. Fewer jurisdictions reported that they provided college courses (68 percent), and 25 percent indicated that they had some form of postgraduate education. About 90 percent had psychiatric hospitalization in some form, with 75 percent providing chemotherapy, individual, and group therapy. With respect to speech and hearing services, two-thirds offered audiological services, but less than 20 percent offered speech therapy. Recreational services were offered by 90 percent of the jurisdictions to nondisabled inmates, with 66 percent indicating that they provided such services to disabled inmates. Three-quarters provided vocational training programs and social services for some inmates, with 50 percent providing more basic adult living skills training.

About 50 percent of the responding jurisdictions indicated that they provided special housing for handicapped inmates. About 70 percent provided special work assignments. All institutions provided religious services to all inmates. Many jurisdictions offered prerelease services (75 percent), but generally no distinc-

TABLE 3

Proposed Services to Be Provided to Inmates

I. Screening and Evaluation Services
   A. dental evaluation
   B. educational evaluation
   C. medical evaluation
      1. blood tests
      2. laboratory tests
      3. physical exam
   D. psychological evaluation
      1. intellectual evaluation
         a. group intelligence test
         b. individual intelligence test
      2. personality evaluation
      3. psychiatric evaluation
   E. optometric evaluation
   F. speech evaluation
      1. hearing
      2. speech
   G. social evaluation

II. Program Services
   A. dental services
   B. educational services
      1. elementary
      2. high school (or GED)
      3. junior college
      4. college
      5. postgraduate education
      6. special education
   C. medical services
      1. physical exam
      2. inpatient (hospitalization) care
      3. outpatient care

   D. mental health services
      1. chemotherapy
      2. individual therapy
      3. group therapy
      4. psychiatric hospitalization
   E. optometric services
      1. corrective lenses
      2. optometric exam
   F. speech, hearing and language services
      1. audiological exam
      2. hearing aids
      3. sign language
      4. speech therapy
   G. social services
   H. recreational services
      1. arts and crafts
      2. organized sports
   I. vocational services
   J. adult living skills training
   K. special housing for the disabled
   L. special work assignments while imprisoned
   M. religious services
   N. prerelease services
      1. job counseling
      2. job placement
      3. social services
      4. transitional services
   O. aftercare (follow-up) services

tions were made between disabled and non-disabled inmates. Finally, about 50 percent of the responding jurisdictions reported that they provided aftercare services, with again no distinction made between disabled and non-disabled inmates.

The results of the few studies indicate that small numbers of inmates have physical handicaps. The numbers are probably underestimates, however, as the actual figures are not known in many jurisdictions. It should also be noted that not all jurisdictions provide screening and evaluation services with respect to some disabilities, and thus cannot be certain as to whether or not they have inmates with undetected disabilities. With respect to speech and hearing disabilities, for example, Veneziano, Veneziano, and Tribolet (1987) found that many jurisdictions do not screen for these problems and therefore could not be certain about the number of inmates with such difficulties.

The results with respect to psychological disabilities were less clear cut. Estimates of psychological disorders, mental retardation, and learning disabilities differed significantly, with some jurisdictions indicating very low rates and others indicating that substantial proportions of their populations had such disabilities. The problem is at least partially one of definition. The research indicates that estimates of psychological disorders, mental retardation, and learning disabilities vary greatly because there are widely divergent ideas of what those terms mean (Denkowski and Denkowski 1985).

The literature examining the prevalence of disabilities among inmates in prison systems in the United States, therefore, indicates that there are some disabled inmates, but precise counts are not available. A case can thus be made for more systematic screening and evaluation and improved computerized information systems, so that inmates with disabilities can be more accurately identified and treated. Security problems, such as exploitation and victimization of these potentially more vulnerable inmates, could also be avoided if more accurate data were available.

With respect to program services, studies indicate that at the present time correctional facilities provide few mechanisms for screening, flagging, and treating disabled inmates. Although a variety of evaluation services and programs are available to at least some inmates in the majority of states, it appears that special services that specifically address the problems faced by disabled inmates are found in only a small number of states. In a few jurisdictions, some program services are not provided to any inmates.

In summary, there are inmates in prison with disabilities who have special security and treatment needs. Exact numbers are not known. The reliability of the data is in question because of differences in the definition of disabilities and differences in the screening and evaluation of disabilities. The research indicates that disabled inmates are not singled out for treatment, and that little is known about the scope of their difficulties, during or after the time they spend in prison. A variety of programs appear to be offered in the majority of prison systems, but not necessarily in a consistent fashion. There appears to be a need to systematize evaluation and treatment of inmates with disabilities, given the difficulties they are likely to encounter in prison and after release.

This is especially true in light of the recent passage of the ADA. Title II of the ADA does require that government entities, such as correctional facilities, achieve accessibility in their facilities, as well as in the delivery of services and programs to the disabled. While this does not mean that criminal justice agencies must "retrofit" their existing buildings (Rubin 1993), it does mean that new construction or alterations to existing buildings must comply with the ADA. Failure to comply with the provisions of the ADA may provide inmates with disabilities another source of lawsuits against prison systems.

Louis Veneziano
Carol Veneziano

See also HEALTH CARE

Bibliography

Americans With Disabilities Act (ADA), 42 USC, Section 12101. Washington, D.C.: U.S. Government Printing Office.

Bell, R. et al. (1983). *The Nature and Prevalence of Learning Deficiencies among Adult Inmates*. Washington, D.C.: National Institute of Justice.

Denkowski, G., and K. Denkowski (1985). The mentally retarded offender in the state prison system: Identification, prevalence, adjustment and rehabilitation. *Criminal Justice and Behavior* 12: 55–70.

Long, L., and A. Sapp (1992). Programs and facilities for physically disabled inmates in state prisons. *Journal of Offender Rehabilitation* 18: 191–204.

Rubin, P. N. (1993). The Americans with Disabilities Act and criminal justice: An overview. *Research in Action*. Washington, D.C.: National Institute of Justice.

Severson, M. (1992). Redefining the boundaries of mental health services: A holistic approach to inmate mental health. *Federal Probation* 56(3): 57–63.

Swetz, A. (1989). The prevalence of mental illness in a state correctional institution for men. *Journal of Prison and Jail Health* 8: 3–15.

Veneziano, L., C. Veneziano, and C. Tribolet (1987). The special needs of prison inmates with handicaps: An assessment. *Journal of Offender Counseling, Services, and Rehabilitation* 12: 61–72.

Waltus, G., H. Mann, M. Miller, L. Hemphill, and M. Chlumsky (1988). Emotional disorders among offenders: Inter- and intrasetting comparisons. *Criminal Justice and Behavior* 15: 433–53.

Discipline

All prisons and jails must create mechanisms to maintain order and safety. Prison discipline takes many forms. These include rigid rules that encompass all aspects of conduct, institutional policies concerning movement and access to specific areas, procedures that regulate the importation of goods into the prison, regulations covering visiting, telephone, and mail, and many others. Prisons construct elaborate and comprehensive regimes in support of the objective of a well-ordered and disciplined society of convicts.

The great debate among the early designers of penitentiary systems in the United States was essentially a conflict about the best way to achieve prison discipline. The Pennsylvania system featured solitary confinement at all times during the entire sentence. The proponents of the Pennsylvania model argued that complete isolation from the contaminating influence of other inmates best served the interests of prison discipline and reform. The architects of the Auburn-style congregate prisons, in contrast, permitted group labor during the day but required isolation in single cells at night. Moreover, all forms of communication among prisoners were strictly forbidden, whether at work, during meals, or while moving within the institution. As David J. Rothman observed, "To both advocates of the congregate and the separate systems, the promise of institutionalization depended upon the isolation of the prisoner and the establishment of a disciplined routine" (1971, 82).

During most of their history, American prisons have relied on a system of rewards and punishments to maintain order. In the earliest American state prisons, from the 1820s through the Civil War, isolation, silence, hard labor, and cruel corporal punishments were the primary instruments of prison discipline. By the middle of the nineteenth century, American penologists had begun to experiment with a number of reward-based sanctioning systems. These systems included the concept of custody-grading, a scheme in which the prisoner could move through stages of confinement where the intensity of supervision was reduced, certain privileges could be earned, and the amount of trust granted to the inmate was gradually increased.

The reward-based behavioral control system was enhanced in the 1870s with the adoption in American reformatories of the indeterminate sentence, discretionary release authority, and good time systems. These developments permitted inmates to influence, through their prison behavior, the amount of time that they would actually serve. Simultaneously, these methods, which were first developed in the New South Wales (Australia) and Irish prison systems, provided prison administrators with a powerful technique with which to control inmate behavior. In addition to working toward lower-custody housing, better work assignments, improved commissary and recreational privileges, and other benefits, inmates' good behavior would result in "good time credits" deducted from the sentence. Conversely, viola-

tion of prison rules could result in the denial of these privileges, time in solitary confinement, or the reduction of good time credits. The latter penalty is in most respects the most severe, because it increases the time spent in confinement prior to release. Early release is the foremost goal of virtually all inmates.

The Prison Justice System

In many respects, the prison justice system mirrors the characteristics of the larger criminal justice system. The uniformed correctional staff perform a policing function within the prison. In some prisons, correctional officers are referred to as "the police" by inmates. The inmate rule book and the disciplinary procedure manual serve as the penal code and the criminal procedure code of the prison. Like a state penal code, the inmate rule book defines certain behavior as violations of the "law" of the prison, and specifies a range of penalties that may accompany a finding of guilt. The disciplinary procedure manual delineates the process through which allegations of violations are adjudicated and penalties imposed.

Like their counterparts outside prison, correctional officers exercise broad discretion in enforcing the institutional rule book (Poole and Regoli 1980). No prison could manage the adjudication of every minor rule violation that might be charged. Moreover, writing up large numbers of "tickets" may be taken as evidence of an officer's inability to handle inmate conduct in a competent manner.

The categories of behavior that are proscribed in most inmate rule books are broad, so the officer's characterization of the offense may depend on the context in which the offense occurred. For example, verbal jousting between staff and inmates may be acceptable on a one-on-one basis, but an inmate's verbal harassment of an officer in a crowded yard might be "written up" as insolence, harassment, or a similar offense. An American Bar Association survey of institutional rule books in forty-four jurisdictions found that the written rules are "so vague and indefinite that it is difficult to differentiate between what may be permissible conduct and what might constitute a violation" (ABA 1974, 12). Prison rule books contain many of these "wastebasket categories" (Johnson 1966), such as disrespect toward staff, in which the offender's demeanor may play a critical role.

Inmate rule books typically classify infractions according to seriousness, and provide for differential processing of violations. For example, minor infractions (which may result in a reprimand or loss of privileges for a brief time) may be adjudicated by a sergeant or lieutenant, while more serious violations may require a proceeding before an institutional "court." Many facilities provide for prehearing detention (analogous to serving time in jail prior to trial) pending adjudication of the charge. The institutional "court" is variously referred to as the disciplinary hearing, adjustment hearing, or superintendent's proceeding.

In the larger criminal justice systems, many studies have documented the attrition of cases as they pass through the stages of the criminal justice system. Some cases are declined for prosecution by the district attorney, others are dismissed at the initial appearance before a magistrate, and still others are turned back by grand juries or not sustained in the preliminary hearing. In sharp contrast, studies of case processing in the prison justice system show that nearly all cases charged are found guilty. In fact, some researchers have concluded that rather than being an adjudicatory process, the prison justice process is primarily dispositional in nature (Harvard Center for Criminal Justice 1972). That is, once a disciplinary infraction is charged, the primary decision made by disciplinary committees is the meting out of punishment.

The fact that few disciplinary charges are dismissed (and few are reduced via plea bargaining) may simply indicate that correctional officers are selective in writing "tickets." An alternative view is that disciplinary courts, which are staffed by correctional agency employees, are reluctant to dismiss charges because of the belief that the inmate "must have done something" to warrant the officer's formal intervention. Also, reluctance to dismiss charges may reflect the view that such dismissals will undermine prison discipline and the authority of correctional staff. Kassebaum, Ward, and Wilner observed that dismissal of a disciplinary charge "implies that the reporting staff was wrong. For the morale of the rank and file correction officers, such inferences cannot be permitted" (1971, 53).

Like the sentencing judge, the disciplinary committee or hearing officer has a broad range of sanctions to choose from, and discretionary authority to choose among these alternatives. These sanctions range from a simple reprimand with an accompanying entry in the inmate's file, to cell or work assignment changes, payment of restitution, confinement to cell (called "keep lock" in some systems), loss of good time credits, or a combination of sanctions. Referral of the case for outside prosecution is also an alternative for serious crimes, but relatively few prison crimes are referred to prosecutors. Twenty years ago the American Bar Association found that there was little correspondence between the severity of prison rule infractions and the penalties available in prison rule books, but revisions of institutional rules in recent years has made the penalty structure more commensurate with the severity of the infraction. Flanagan (1982) studied sentencing in prison disciplinary hearings and found the same factors that are associated with sentencing outcomes in the criminal justice system—severity of the offense and the prior disciplinary record of the offender.

Who Violates Prison Rules?

Offenses against prison rules are not uniformly distributed among prisoners. A nationwide survey of state prison inmates conducted by the Justice Department in 1986 found that 53 percent of inmates had been charged with a rule violation (Stephan 1989). Moreover, the average number of rule violations per inmate per year was 1.5. The Justice Department study did not distinguish between serious violations, such as assault, and minor violations. The study found that younger inmates, prisoners held in maximum security facilities, recidivists, men, and inmates who used drugs prior to imprisonment were more likely to violate prison rules than were other prisoners. Some studies have reported that blacks are more likely to be involved in prison rule violations, while others have found no race-based differences in infraction rates (Flanagan 1983). Additional research has focused on psychological inventories, crowded conditions, and other factors as predictors of prisoner behavior.

The Justice Department survey also found that 94 percent of prisoners charged with rule infractions were found guilty, and that solitary confinement or segregation and loss of good time were the most frequently imposed punishments. Other penalties, in decreasing order of frequency, included confinement to cell or quarters, loss of entertainment or recreational privileges, loss of commissary privileges, reprimand, extra work, loss of job assignment, loss of visiting privileges, higher custody level within the facility, and transfer to another facility.

D

Legal Issues in Prison Discipline

Prior to the 1970s, courts typically took a "hands off" approach to the operations of prisons. In nearly all facets of prison administration, including the disciplinary process, judges deferred to the expertise and good faith of correctional administrators. Jones and Rhine observed that "a central justification for the 'hands off' doctrine was a fear on the courts' part that interfering in prison administration would undermine prison discipline and order" (1985, 48). Under that view, "Prison officials had unlimited discretion to summarily enforce the myriad rules and regulations . . . and to mete out punishment without regard for an inmate's innocence or guilt" (1985, 51).

The "hands off" perspective gave way in the 1970s, as courts became willing to examine correctional policies and practices. The landmark Supreme Court case on prison discipline was *Wolff v. McDonnell* (1974). The court in *Wolff* reasoned that inmates charged with a serious infraction of prison rules have a clear "liberty interest" in the outcome of disciplinary hearings. Further, the *Wolff* majority found that such interests are protected by the due process clause of the Fourteenth Amendment of the U.S. Constitution. At the same time, the court recognized the interest of the state in operating safe, secure, and orderly prisons. In attempting to reach a balance of these interests, the Court

specified the following as the requisite ingredients of the disciplinary due process hearings: 1. Advance written notice of the charges against the prisoner must be given to him at least 24 hours prior to his appearance. . . . 2. There must be a written statement by the fact finders "as to the evidence relayed and the reasons for the disciplinary action." . . . 3. The inmate facing disciplinary proceedings "should be allowed to call witnesses and present documentary evidence in his defense when permitting him to do so will not be unduly hazardous to institutional safety or correctional goals." . . . 4. Counsel substitute (either staff, or where permitted, a fellow inmate) should be allowed where an illiterate inmate is involved, or where the complexity of the issue makes it unlikely that the inmate will be able to collect and present the evidence. . . . 5. The prison disciplinary board must be impartial (Jones and Rhine 1985, quoting *Wolff v. McDonnell*).

Researchers who have examined the impact of *Wolff* and subsequent decisions on the prison disciplinary process conclude that judicial intervention in this area of correctional management has been beneficial. Jones and Rhine studied the disciplinary process in New Jersey prisons and concluded, "In contrast to the situation before *Wolff*, where disciplinary processes were loosely structured, and governed by substantial, and often unreviewable discretion, prison disciplinary systems are now much more formal, rational and legal in structure" (1985, 103).

Conclusion

The challenge of operating safe, secure, and orderly prisons has never been greater than in the 1990s. Correctional issues such as overcrowding, longer sentences, increasing frequency of mental health problems among inmates, and gang membership make maintenance of prison discipline a herculean task. Moreover, evolving constitutional standards and greater access to courts mean that correctional administrators can be sure that every policy, procedure, and decision is likely to be challenged in administrative or judicial appeals. The structure of prison rules and the procedures for rule enforcement can assist prison officials in socializing offenders to the limits on their behavior and to the process of rewarding good behavior and sanctioning misconduct. When conducted professionally, the prison disciplinary process is a critical component of humane prisons in which people can live and work.

Timothy Flanagan

Bibliography

American Bar Association (1974). *Survey of Prison Disciplinary Practices and Procedures*. Washington, D.C.: American Bar Association.

Flanagan, T. J. (1982). Discretion in the prison justice system: A study of sentencing in prison disciplinary proceedings. *Journal of Research in Crime and Delinquency* 19: 216–37.

Flanagan, T. J. (1983). Correlates of institutional misconduct among state prisoners: A research note. *Criminology* 21: 29–40.

Harvard Center for Criminal Justice (1972). Judicial intervention in prison discipline. *Journal of Criminal Law, Criminology and Police Science* 63: 200–28.

Hewitt, J., E. Poole, and R. Regoli (1984). Self-reported and observed rule breaking in prison: A look at disciplinary response. *Justice Quarterly* 1: 437–47.

Johnson, E. H. (1966). Pilot study: Age, race and recidivism as factors in prisoner infractions. *Canadian Journal of Corrections* 8: 268–83.

Jones, C. H., Jr., and E. Rhine (1985). Due process and prison disciplinary practices: From *Wolff* to *Hewitt*. *New England Journal on Criminal and Civil Confinement* 11: 44–122.

Kassebaum, G., D. A. Ward, and D. Wilner (1971). Prison Treatment and Parole Survival: An Empirical Assessment. New York: John Wiley.

McShane, M. D., and F. P. Williams III (1990). Old and ornery: The disciplinary experiences of elderly prisoners. *International Journal of Offender Therapy and Comparative Criminology* 34: 197–212.

McShane, M. D., and F. P. Williams III (1991). An analysis of prison disciplinary processes as they relate to prison overcrowding. In S. Letman, ed. *Prison Conditions and Prison Overcrowding*. Dubuque, Iowa: Kendall/Hunt.

Poole, E. D., and R. M. Regoli (1980). Race, institutional rule breaking and disciplinary response: A study of discretionary decision-making in prison. *Law and Society Review* 14: 931–46.

Rothman, D. J. (1971) *Discovery of the Asylum: Social Order and Disorder in the New Republic*. Boston: Little, Brown.

Stephan, J. (1989). *Prison Rule Violators*. Bureau of Justice Statistics Special Report. Washington, D.C.: U.S. Department of Justice.

Cases
Wolff v. McDonnell, 418 U.S. 539 (1974)

Dorothea Lynde Dix (1802–1887)

Dorothea Lynde Dix was born to Joseph and Mary Bigelow Dix on 4 April 1802 in Hampden, Maine. Her father was the third son of a prominent Boston family. There is little known about Dorothea Lynde Dix's mother. She is described as much older than her husband and his family believed her social standing inappropriate for a member of their household. Before his marriage, Joseph Dix had studied theology at Harvard University. After his marriage, he left Harvard and became an itinerant Methodist minister. Because of his calling, he was frequently absent from home for long periods. While he was gone, Dorothea and her mother completed tract stitching of his sermons that were sold to supplement Joseph Dix's meager earnings.

Dorothea Lynde Dix's paternal grandparents were very fond of her and she looked forward to her visits to Boston. She was especially close to her grandfather, who died when she was seven. Dorothea was impressed with her grandmother's management of the large household and her benevolence to those less fortunate. There is scant information about Dix's early education. She was probably taught reading and writing by her parents, or attended a village school in Hampden.

Dorothea's early life in Hampden was one of poverty. At the age of twelve she left Hampden to reside in Boston with Grandmother Dix. After two years with her grandmother, Dorothea went to Worcester to live with her great aunt where she started a school for small children. For three years she taught basic reading and writing, manners, customs, and sewing, as well as morals and religion. In 1819 she returned to Boston to prepare herself further as a teacher. In 1821 she opened her first school in Orange Court, her grandmother's home. Later she started an academy but closed it in 1836 because of personal illness. Over the next several years she served as governess to the children of William Channing, the Unitarian leader. It was during this period that her commitment to Unitarian principles was solidified. She also wrote several books, including one for children.

In 1841, at the request of a Harvard divinity student, Dix agreed to conduct a Sunday Bible class for women prisoners at the Cambridge jail. Upon discovering the squalid conditions in the jail, including the confinement of the insane with criminals, Dix was compelled to work for change in the care and treatment of the mentally ill. From 1841 to 1843 she visited every jail, almshouse, and workhouse in Massachusetts. Her reports were instrumental in the enactment of laws in Massachusetts that provided for adequate space for the insane in Boston and Worcester.

From June 1843 to August 1847, Dix traveled an astounding 30,000 miles visiting prisons and poorhouses. Her travels took her from Canada to the Gulf of Mexico and from the

East coast to as far west as the Mississippi River (Brooks 1957, 34). She worked extensively from 1848 to obtain federal government support for the care of the insane. From 1856 to the outbreak of the Civil War in 1861, she obtained more financial aid for benevolent purposes than any who had preceded her (Brooks 1957, 69). Until her death in 1887, Dix was actively involved in the founding of insane asylums and hospitals.

Although Dix is renowned for her work in improving conditions for the insane, she was also concerned about the problem of crime and the institutionalization of criminals. She believed that deviant behavior was a product of the environment and recommended that resources be provided to improve the living conditions of inmates in prison (Rothman 1971).

In 1845 her *Remarks on Prisons and Prison Discipline in the United States* was published. The book was based on her four years of personal study and observation of correctional institutions located primarily in the northern and middle states of the United States. Through visits and correspondence with prison officials she gained insights into the physical aspects of the prisoners' lifestyle including diet, water, clothing, ventilation, heating systems, health care, and punishment. Dix described the reformation of the criminal including the moral, religious, and general instruction provided to inmates in prisons. She also visited houses of refuge for juvenile offenders, jails, and correctional institutions for women. In her report, she elaborated on the use of the Auburn and Pennsylvania systems, addressing the advantages and disadvantages of each. Her report "anticipated many reforms later adopted by penologists, including the education of prisoners and the separation of offenders" (Marshall 1971, 488).

Over forty years of Dorothea Dix's life was devoted to improving the plight of those individuals institutionalized in asylums, prisons, and jails in the United States. Her endeavors to improve the conditions of the mentally ill, as well as those of the criminal, were recognized during her lifetime. Because of her work, many mental hospitals were founded in America and abroad. Her study of American correctional institutions was instrumental in changing both the way prisoners were treated and the focus of American corrections. In the end, perhaps she is best remembered for her devotion and dedication to reforming institutions responsible for the physical care and treatment of the mentally ill and criminally incarcerated.

Donna C. Hale

Bibliography

Dix, D. L. (1845). *Remarks on Prisons and Prison Discipline in the United States.* Boston: Munroe and Francis.

Marshall, H. E. (1971). Dorothea Lynde Dix. In *Notable American Women 1607–1950: A Biographical Dictionary.* Cambridge, Mass.: Belknap.

Marshall, H. E. (1937). *Dorothea Lynde Dix: Forgotten Samaritan.* Chapel Hill, NC: University of North Carolina Press.

Rothman, D. J. (1971). *The Discovery of the Asylum: Social Order and Disorder in The New Republic.* Boston: Little, Brown.

Wilson, D. C. (1975). *Stranger and Traveler: The Story of Dorothea Dix, American Reformer.* Boston: Little, Brown.

Double Celling

Double celling, sometimes referred to as double bunking, is the practice of housing two inmates in a prison or jail cell that was designed to accommodate only one. Since the construction of the first prisons in the United States, it has been a widely accepted principle that most inmates should be housed in individual cells. Accordingly, the vast majority of early prisons were designed with single cells. One reason for this practice was the belief that inmates should spend part of their time in silent penitence, contemplating their wrongs. Other justifications were more pragmatic. Inmates housed in single cells would be isolated from the corrupting influence of their fellow prisoners. They would be unable to organize to engage in prohibited activities, and there was a general belief that offenders were imprisoned partly because of their difficulties in getting along with others. In effect, housing inmates in individual cells permitted prison officials to exert greater control over them.

Regardless of the justification, the single cell concept has often been sacrificed when prisons have become overcrowded. When corrections officials have been faced with the reality of too many prisoners and too few beds, a common response has been to double cell inmates. Early prisons were occasionally forced to resort to the practice of placing two or even more inmates in a single cell, and it became common when prison populations began to swell dramatically in the 1970s.

Because double celling has potentially harmful effects, various standards and guidelines have been established governing this practice. Standards established by the American Correctional Association and advisory guidelines issued by the U.S. Department of Justice both call for single cells to be of no less than sixty square feet for inmates who spend no more than ten hours each day confined to their cells. If inmates are confined more than ten hours a day, the guidelines suggest single cells no smaller than eighty square feet. Despite standards and guidelines, it is estimated that about one-quarter of all inmates in state prisons share cells. Moreover, prisoners who are double-celled each have an average of thirty-four square feet. These figures suggest that many inmates are housed in crowded and cramped conditions.

Given this situation, an inevitable question arises: Is double celling a violation of the Eighth Amendment's prohibition against cruel and unusual punishment? Court decisions suggest that just because a facility provides less square footage than is required by standards does not mean that conditions are unconstitutional. Instead, courts consider the "totality of conditions" on a case-by-case basis in determining whether double celling amounts to cruel and unusual punishment. For instance, some of the factors courts weigh include the adequacy of staff, sanitation and cleanliness, the quality of medical services, access to recreation, meals and food services, work programs, and the amount of time inmates are confined to their cells during waking hours.

The most prominent U.S. Supreme Court case in this area, *Rhodes v. Chapman*, illustrates the approach used. In the *Chapman* case, inmates at a Southern Ohio prison filed suit over double celling. But the Court ruled that double celling was not unconstitutional at this facility for several reasons: The prison was relatively new, well maintained, and had several workshops, gymnasiums, schoolrooms, day rooms, and other areas for inmate activities. Cells were fairly comfortable, heated, well ventilated, and most had windows that inmates could open and close. Also, inmates were allowed considerable time outside their cells. In effect, the Court concluded that because of the general conditions at the prison, double celling did not amount to cruel and unusual punishment. The Court did not issue a blanket approval for double celling, but noted that determining the constitutionality of the practice hinges upon many factors.

The practice of double celling has ramifications at many different levels. At perhaps the broadest level, one must question the moral, ethical, and philosophical implications of subjecting prisoners to crowded conditions that are often cruel and inhumane. The incarceration of offenders represents one of society's most important and sensitive obligations. It might thus be argued that society bears a moral obligation to ensure that the prison experience causes no further physical, mental, or spiritual damage to offenders. Although prison conditions need not be "comfortable," they should reflect "evolving standards of decency that mark the progress of a maturing society."

In terms of the administration of prisons, the effects of double celling can be calamitous. A simple example illustrates the mathematical realities of double celling. A prison designed with one thousand single cells that is forced to house fifteen hundred inmates means that one thousand inmates will be subjected to double celling. Such a situation places incredible strains on virtually every aspect of prison operations. First, prison security becomes a concern. Prison staffing rarely keeps pace with increases in the inmate population. Whenever facilities become overcrowded, security measures like shakedowns, pat searches, and controlling inmate movement assume a greater level of importance. The irony of the situation is that because overcrowding places greater work demands on officers, they have even less time for attending to security matters. It is also worth noting that studies suggest that prison overcrowding is related to increases in assaults, disciplinary infractions, and disturbances.

Second, double celling and overcrowding can also affect environmental conditions in the prison. Maintaining clean and sanitary conditions becomes problematic. Plumbing, water, and sewer systems may be taxed. Noise may rise to irritating, or even intolerable, levels.

Third, inmate access to programs and services is affected by double celling and overcrowding. When correctional facilities become heavily strained by overcrowding, providing inmates with basic necessities like bedding, clothing, and even food becomes problematic. Double celling and overcrowding also mean that inmates often have problems gaining access to institutional programs such as medical treatment, recreation, visiting, religious services, education, and work.

A fourth administrative question is whether inmates who are double celled should be permitted to choose their cellmates, or whether prison officials should control cell assignments. In either case, double celling forces both inmates and administrators to consider such issues as race and ethnicity, smoking, gang affiliation, sexual orientation, and the potential for exploitation.

A final administrative issue lies in the "hidden" costs of double celling and overcrowding. One of the most frequently litigated prison issues is overcrowding. Attorneys' fees and damage awards in these cases can amount to millions of dollars.

Beyond administrative issues, inmates are personally affected in many ways by double celling. For one, inmates face greater health risks in overcrowded conditions. Crowding exacerbates the transmission of disease, ranging from tuberculosis to colds to outbreaks of scabies. Not surprisingly, studies show that overcrowding is associated with an increase in the number of illness complaints made by inmates. Crowding and double celling may also contribute to mental health problems. Some studies have found that inmates living in crowded conditions have feelings of helplessness and have increased fears about their inability to control their environment. Overcrowding increases inmates' fears, anxieties, and apprehensions.

It is unlikely that the double celling of inmates will be discontinued in the near future. Projections suggest the need for adding at least one thousand new prison beds each week to simply keep pace with the current rate of incarceration. Unable to meet these demands, the vast majority of prisons in the country will continue to employ measures like double celling to handle a seemingly endless stream of prisoners.

Richard D. Sluder

See also CROWDING

Bibliography

Gaes, G. G. (1985). The effects of overcrowding in prison. In N. Morris and M. Tonry, eds. *Crime and Justice, An Annual Review of Research*. Vol. 6. Chicago: University of Chicago Press.

Innes, C. A. (1986). *Population Density in State Prisons*. Washington, D.C.: Bureau of Justice Statistics.

Paulus, P. B. (1988). *Prison Crowding: A Psychological Perspective*. New York: Springer-Verlag.

Cases
Rhodes v. Chapman, 452 U.S. 337 (1981)

Drug and Alcohol Use in Prison

The relationship between the use of alcohol and other drugs and criminal activity have been well documented. Research suggests that drinking can influence the occurrence of violence. This connection, however, is embedded in a complex web of such interacting variables as the circumstances, the drinker's cognitive "set," socio-cultural norms, and political and moral values (Collins 1981). With respect to cocaine, heroin, and other illicit drugs, the connections are more direct. Although drug use does not necessarily initiate criminal careers, it tends to intensify and perpetuate them. That is, street drugs tend to freeze users into patterns of criminality that are more acute, dynamic, unremitting, and enduring than those of other offenders (Inciardi 1981; Tonry and Wilson 1990).

Because of drug-related crime and the "war on drugs" of the 1980s and early 1990s, increasing numbers of drug users have been coming to the attention of the criminal justice system. This has been demonstrated by the Drug Use Forecasting (DUF) program, sponsored by the National Institute of Justice, which routinely conducts urinalyses among arrestees. DUF reports indicate that as many as 60 percent test positive for cocaine, and up to 80 percent in some cities test positive for at least one illicit drug (Wish 1991). Furthermore, it has been reported that perhaps two-thirds of those entering state and federal penitentiaries have histories of substance abuse (Leukefeld and Tims 1992). Given this concentration of alcohol and drug users in prisons, it is not surprising that substance abuse is common.

The Prevalence of Drug Use in Prisons

Although most observers assume that alcohol and drug use is widespread in prisons, only minimal research has been conducted on the prevalence and patterns of such use. Not unexpectedly, systematic study of these phenomena are fraught with difficulties. Much of what is known comes from the random urine checks that occur in the vast majority of prisons. The data, however, reflect a mixed picture. For example, a sample of 640 Wisconsin inmates showed that 26.9 percent tested positive for at least one illegal drug (Vigdal and Stadler 1989). In Delaware, only 1 percent of 2,192 randomly collected urine samples were positive for unauthorized drugs (Inciardi, Lockwood, and Quinlan 1993). Between July of 1989 and June of 1990, 565,500 inmates from almost 90 percent of state and federal prisons were tested for one or more illegal drugs (Harlow 1992). In state facilities, 3.6 percent were positive for cocaine, 1.3 percent for heroin, 2.0 percent for methamphetamine, and 6.3 percent for marijuana. In federal facilities, fewer than 1 percent were positive for cocaine, heroin, or methamphetamine, and 1.1 percent were positive for marijuana.

Drug screening in prisons likely underestimates the actual prevalence of drug and alcohol use. Because of the prison grapevine, there are few secrets inside penitentiary walls, and word of an impending drug test spreads rapidly. In an interview survey of residents in a prison-based drug treatment program in Delaware, 60 percent reported having used drugs in prison prior to entering the program (Inciardi, Lockwood, and Quinlan 1993).

Drugs of Choice in Prison

Based on urine surveillance data and inmate surveys, it would appear that the most commonly used drug in prison is marijuana, followed by cocaine and alcohol. The use of LSD, PCP, and methamphetamine appears to be minimal. Crack is smoked in some prisons, by means of soda cans fashioned into crude crack pipes. The making and drinking of "jailhouse wine" is not uncommon. Although individual recipes vary, the main ingredients are fruit, sugar, and bread, all of which are obtained during meals. Fruit juice is mixed with sugar and placed in a jug. Bread or potatoes (in a cloth container) are added for fermentation.

Although intravenous drug use in prison is not widespread, it nevertheless occurs. Among those who inject drugs, the sharing of injection equipment is common, thus increasing the risk of spreading HIV. Also common is the sharing of injection drugs, and the potential for viral contamination as the result of "frontloading" and "backloading"—techniques for distributing a drug solution among a group of people (Inciardi and Page 1991). In frontloading, the drug is transferred from the syringe used for measuring by removing the needle from the receiving syringe and squirting the solution directly into its hub. The intercontamination of drug doses through the mixing and frontloading of "speedball" (heroin and cocaine) is common. Because heroin is "cooked" (heated in an aqueous solution), whereas cocaine is not during its preparation for injection, separate containers are used for the mixing process. Those who share speedball draw the heroin into one syringe and the cocaine into another. They remove the needle from the cocaine syringe and discharge the heroin into it through its hub. Half the speedball mixture is returned to the syringe that originally contained the heroin. If either syringe contains viruses at the start of such an operation, both are likely to contain them afterward (Inciardi and Page 1991).

Backloading involves essentially the same process, but the plunger, rather than the needle, is removed from the receiving syringe. Frontloading seems to be the preferred method, with backloading a substitute when syringes with detachable needles are unavailable. Since hypodermic syringes are closely controlled in prisons, makeshift injection equipment is manufactured from available materials. The most common "works" in the penitentiary is an eye dropper, with the glass or plastic end sharpened to an angular point. Backloading is accomplished by removing the squeeze bulb.

Drug Smuggling and Trafficking

Most drugs are brought into prisons by either visitors or correctional officers, and the methods are quite numerous. For example, drugs may be concealed in visitors' clothing and handed to an inmate during visits. Frequently, the drugs are put in cellophane, a balloon, or a condom and held in the visitor's mouth. The balloon is transferred to the inmate during a kiss. Usually the inmate swallows the entire balloon and retrieves it after it has passed out of the body. There are other ploys. For example, visitors have been known to remove the ink cartridge from a ballpoint pen and fill the pen with heroin or cocaine. During the visit, the inmate trades pens with the visitor. Although inmates are searched after visits, in many institutions the searches entail only brief pat-downs.

Some correctional officers have been found to be smuggling drugs and drug paraphernalia into the prisons, hidden in sports equipment, hollowed-out books, jockstraps, bras, garment linings, and photographic equipment. Drugs are sold in prisons by corrupt correctional officers or inmates. A few officers have reputations for selling drugs, a fact that is regularly communicated through the prison grapevine. Occasionally, an officer approaches the inmate to offer drugs, but more frequently an inmate who wants to "make a buy" makes that fact known to the officer.

Drugs are often sold by the inmates themselves. Inmates who receive drugs in prison typically keep a portion and sell the rest. Inmates usually sell only to people they know, to decrease the chance of discovery. The average price for a "toothpick" marijuana cigarette in 1992 was $3.00 or $4.00, or the equivalent in cigarettes. A jug of jailhouse wine may be exchanged for a carton of cigarettes. It is estimated that the cost of drugs in prison is three to five times that on the street. Most drugs in prison are similar to or of better quality than those on the street. Some inmates feel that if one is going to take the risk of bringing drugs into prison, one might as well bring in the best.

Conclusions

Two theories have been put forth to explain prison drug use. The "deprivation model" suggests that, upon entering prison, inmates are faced with major social and psychological problems resulting from the loss of freedom, status, possessions, security, autonomy, and personal and sexual relationships. Drug use, then, is one way of adapting to these "pains of imprisonment." The "importation model," on the other hand, suggests that the behavior of prisoners is not a direct function of the conditions of confinement, but one of preprison socialization and experience. As such, prison drug use is a continuation of preincarceration behavior. An accumulation of evidence suggests that while some prison drug use may be explained by the deprivation model, the vast majority of those who use drugs in prison did so prior to confinement (Thomas and Cage 1977; Wish 1991).

There has been an increased interest in implementing treatment programs in prisons for drug-involved offenders (Inciardi 1993). Such programs should be comprehensive, and participants should be segregated from the rest of the prison population. This separation serves two purposes. First, it isolates the program and the clients from the prison culture of manipu-

lation, mistrust, violence, and drug use, creating an environment in which sensitive issues can be addressed. Second, separation creates an environment in which changing negative behavior and attitudes can be a continuous process.

James A. Inciardi

See also ALCOHOL TREATMENT PROGRAMS IN PRISON, DRUG TREATMENT

Bibliography

Collins, J. J., ed. (1981). *Drinking and Crime.* New York: Guilford.

Harlow, C. W. (1992). *Drug Enforcement and Treatment in Prisons, 1990.* Washington, D.C.: Bureau of Justice Statistics.

Inciardi, J. A., ed. (1981). *The Drugs/Crime Connection.* Beverly Hills, Calif.: Sage.

Inciardi, J. A., ed. (1993). *Drug Treatment and Criminal Justice.* Newbury Park, Calif.: Sage.

Inciardi, J. A., and J. B. Page (1991). Drug sharing among intravenous drug users. *AIDS* 5: 772–73.

Inciardi, J. A., D. Lockwood, and J. A. Quinlan (1993). Drug use in prison: Patterns, processes, and implications for treatment. *Journal of Drug Issues* 23: 119–29.

Leukefeld, C. G., and F. M. Tims, eds. (1992). *Drug Abuse Treatment in Prisons and Jails.* Rockville, Md.: National Institute on Drug Abuse.

Thomas, C. C., and R. J. Cage (1977). Correlates of prison drug use: An evaluation of two conceptual models. *Criminology* 15: 193–209.

Tonry, M., and J. Q. Wilson, eds. (1990). *Drugs and Crime.* Chicago: University of Chicago Press.

Vigdal, G. L., and D. W. Stadler (1989). Controlling inmate drug use: Cut consumption by reducing demand. *Corrections Today* 51(3): 96–97.

Wish, E. D. (1991). Drug testing and the identification of drug abusing criminals. In J. A. Inciardi, ed. *Handbook of Drug Control in the United States.* Westport, Conn.: Greenwood.

Drug Treatment

Historically, critics have argued against the collective incarceration of violent criminals with vagrants, drug addicts, and alcoholics. Many claimed that the poor, often veterans of war, were discriminatorily penalized for their addictive vices. Some argued that separate work camps should be established for the petty offenders and addicts, while others argued that they should not be incarcerated at all. In 1962 the U.S. Supreme Court stated that addiction itself is not a crime, and that persons cannot be incarcerated simply because of their "status" as a drug addict (Robinson v. California).

Drug Offenders

Drug abuse has consistently been linked to high rates of criminal activity. In a national study conducted in thirteen major cities, from 44 to 87 percent of those arrested were using illegal drugs. The Bureau of Justice Statistics reports from a national survey that just over 30 percent of all prisoners admitted that they were under the influence of drugs at the time of their offense, and 17 percent admitted that they committed the offense to get money for drugs. At this time, 50 percent of federal prisoners are convicted of drug-related offenses. In 1990 in California, 35 percent of prison admissions were drug related, up from 17.6 percent in 1985.

In 1991, the National Institute of Justice reported that a majority of persons charged with serious property offenses and most kinds of violent crime tested positive for illegal drugs at the time of their arrest. Research also indicates that the most serious and frequent offenders are those most heavily involved with drugs. According to the National Institute of Justice, female arrestees are more likely than men to test positive for drugs. Current prison overcrowding and high rates of revocation of early release seem to indicate a pattern in need of successful intervention programs.

The determination that a client needs drug treatment is often made early in the criminal justice process, as in the presentence investigation report. By using interviews, specimen tests, or standardized questionnaires, the professional making the assessment tries to determine the level of involvement the offender has with alcohol or drugs. Measures of "how much" and "how often" are used to distinguish among the categories of use, abuse, and dependence. The decision to place an offender in treatment during incarceration is usually made by intake assessment teams in the reception center or later by a counselor at the facility to which the inmate is assigned.

The needs of the drug abusing offender in treatment are many. Some may have acquired serious criminal records related to substance abuse, including the use of weapons and violence in the commission of crimes, leading to longer periods of incarceration with no parole or early release. Chronic unemployment and a lack of education and skills are characteristic of this population. Many have serious health problems, ranging from vitamin deficiencies to AIDS. Substance abuse may have caused or worsened health problems that are compounded by poor eating and sleeping patterns. And people with a history of substance abuse may have permanently damaged relationships with family and friends. They may receive no visitors or funds for commissary use, and may suffer from depression and isolation.

In addition, many offenders have been involved with the courts several times prior to being sentenced to prison. Most have been placed in some type of community based treatment program as a condition of probation. Often, inmates have dropped out of or have been terminated from several different types of programs. Prior failures at treatment may make clients resistant to new intervention strategies or have less confidence in their ability to succeed.

Treatment Programs

In 1961, California established a separate facility, a rehabilitation center within the Department of Corrections for the treatment of drug addicts. The 1966 Narcotic Addict Rehabilitation Act required federal prisons to offer drug treatment to addicts who had violated federal laws. Initially, drug treatment programs were offered only on special units at certain facilities within a prison system. Addicts also often received counseling or group therapy along with those with other types of problems and needs. As the numbers needing drug treatment grew and as experts became more inclined to direct patients to specific drug treatment sessions, programs appeared at many institutions. By 1978, the federal prison system was operating thirty-three drug treatment units. Although many programs today have been severely limited by budget cuts, attempts have been made to involve not only those inmates under court order to receive treatment but also those who volunteer. Still, only about 11 percent of federal inmates are involved in drug abuse programs while incarcerated. A survey of forty-five states (277 prison facilities) in 1991 determined that about one-third of all inmates participated in some type of drug treatment program. Most had been involved in group counseling; others were in self-help programs, and some received in-patient services.

Some intensive treatment programs are located in separate facilities adjacent to the prison or in nearby secured treatment centers. Officials sometimes voice concern that inmates may volunteer for such programs only because they represent a diversion from the normal prison routine.

Treatment programs vary in philosophy, approach to recovery, and length of time spent in treatment, which may vary from one to six months. They also vary in the intensity of services (live-in versus one visit per week for hourly sessions). Some programs are self-help, some use group therapy, educational videos, relaxation techniques, or medicines to combat addiction.

Counselors or other clinical professionals must make decisions about which type of treatment program would work best for a particular offender. Programs usually have basic underlying assumptions about offenders and addiction that stem from different theories.

Disease theories are based on the medical model, which views addiction as a sickness that must be "cured." In order for patients to become "well," they must gain control over their illness. Proponents of this approach focus on withdrawal of the drug or alcohol from the system. Addicts are viewed as patients and treated in a medical setting by medical professionals. Many experts believe that patients have a genetic predisposition or tolerance for addictive substances, and family history is an important area of examination.

Progression theories concentrate on the process of becoming addicted. Proponents maintain that casual use with less serious substances leads to greater use of more dangerous drugs. Some substances, such as beer or marijuana, are seen as an initiation, from which the experimenter progresses in degrees. Users experience a pleasurable high that they seek to increase, until they reach a dependency identified as addiction.

Sociological theories explain drug use by looking at the structure of society in general and the specific social environment of the substance abuser. Important variables in these theories include such characteristics as poverty, opportunity, age, race, education, and neighborhood. Treatment may focus on changing the socio-economic opportunities available to the offender, changing the environment, and perhaps even the peers with whom the addict socializes.

Psychological theories address the personal needs and emotional traits of each client. Weaknesses in self-esteem and adjustment problems from childhood may be studied in personality analysis. Some theories may be behavioral in orientation. That is, they view an addict as receiving some type of psychological reward or gratification from drug use. Attempts are made to alter an addict's behavior through modification of the interpretation of stimulus and response. Other psychological theories might try to uncover subconscious anxieties related to the need for drugs.

Learning theories combine the influence of both the individual's personality and social environment in contributing to addiction. From this perspective, substance abuse is a learned behavior that fulfills not only personal needs but some group relations as well. Peer influence is instrumental, particularly in terms of gangs or status pressures. To the addict, such learned behavior is successful in what seems to be important spheres. Substance abusers concentrate on them even to the point of being unsuccessful in many other aspects of their lives. The methods of taking drugs or drinking are learned, as well as the rituals and accessories that develop around the drug or alcohol subculture.

On the average, prison treatment programs provide fewer services for shorter periods of time than similar programs on the outside. Outside programs are more likely to involve family, more likely to provide follow up referrals, and more likely to include components such as job counseling, education, and vocational training.

In prison the most common program formats are group therapy, self-help (Narcotics Anonymous), and drug education programs. Educational programs can be presented in short segments; they reach rather large audiences at a lower cost than other methods. Education programs, however, have been criticized for using scare tactics or for not acknowledging the realities that make drug use attractive to those with troubled lives. Educational programs may be more successful when directed at very young populations who do not yet use drugs or those with whom therapists can conduct early intervention. That profile does not describe most incarcerated offenders.

Other program arrangements have also been attempted in prison treatment:

Methadone Maintenance: One historically significant attempt to implement gradual withdrawal from drug addiction is the use of methadone maintenance. In a program of methadone maintenance, patients are supplied daily doses of methadone, which eliminates painful withdrawal from heroin. It may also produce a cross-tolerance with heroin that prevents abusers from experiencing a "high" from further heroin use. Although most convicted felons are "detoxed" by the time they finish the often lengthy criminal justice process, prison programs may continue methadone treatment for those who have been involved in it prior to incarceration.

Therapeutic Communities: A therapeutic community is a separate supportive treatment environment based on a twenty-four-hour learning experience guided by peers and staff. The routine is rigid, with highly structured rules. Participants rely on mutual support, punishments, rewards, confession, and catharsis for recovery. The primary tool is group therapy, and sessions can be confrontive (breaking down denial) and educational (role playing, rehearsing, and evaluating responses and interactions). Although the success rates for those who complete the program are high, a significant number of participants who undertake the treatment drop out or are processed out.

Aftercare or follow-up: The purpose of treatment during incarceration is to prepare the inmate for eventual release back into the community. Most programs recommend some type of monitoring during the early period of release to ensure support, encouragement, and incentives for a drug-free life. Aftercare may mean that the offender returns for counseling, attends the meetings of a support group, or submits to periodic drug tests. Testing positive for drugs may trigger revocation of parole and result in reincarceration.

Treatment Results

The reported successes and failures of treatment programs can be very misleading. To some experts, simple attendance at and completion of a treatment program is a success. It has been argued that evaluation of drug and alcohol treatment within institutional settings may not be valid because a critical part of the recovery process is the ability to abstain from drinking and taking drugs when they are readily available. Others, however, argue that drugs are available to some degree and that continued use may occur even in treatment.

Upon parole, continued drug use may result in reincarceration. In 1990, drug-related parole violations in California accounted for 32 percent of returns to prison. Several studies have linked substance abuse treatment while incarcerated with later success on parole. Unfortunately, many programs do not follow up on their participants to evaluate their success. Additional services such as job training and placement may be necessary for rehabilitation.

Four programs that had relatively low rates of recidivism were reviewed in 1989. The characteristics they seemed to share included offering a wide range of activities, teaching practical life skills, using nontraditional correctional employees who were realistic about the program goals, and both formal and informal mechanisms for continued contact with participants after release. It was also noted that successful programs tended to select participants who had been heavily involved with drugs, who had serious criminal records, and who perhaps had "hit bottom" and were ready to improve their lives (Chaiken 1989). One example was the Stay'n Out program, a therapeutic community operating in New York's Department of Corrections. Inmates completing the program appeared to have a lower percentage of arrests than inmates who attended other treatment programs or who volunteered but attended no programs while incarcerated. Spending more time in treatment also appeared to be related to lower arrest rates and successful completion of parole.

Eliminating Barriers to Effective Programs

Several barriers to effective drug-treatment programming have been identified by Chaiken. They include changes in program priorities, constraints on resources, staff resistance, and, finally, inmate resistance.

As is often typical in the rapidly changing political climate of corrections, priorities often shift. Overnight, existing programs may be replaced with the latest fad in treatment or punishment. This is particularly true when state or federal funds are suddenly made available to implement a new approach. Currently, it is possible for corrections departments to receive large sums of money for implementing programs, hiring staff, and evaluating results yet never be held accountable for producing what was promised.

The shift to new strategies makes it difficult to evaluate the success of previous efforts or to have comparison groups to analyze them by. Program staff may change just when they had established trusting relationships with inmates and staff. Constraints on resources often mean that cheaper programs are used to serve greater numbers of offenders in place of perhaps more effective programs that are limited to fewer participants. Staff as well as inmate resistance can sabotage any new program. Program staff must win and maintain the confidence of both staff and inmates by anticipating concerns, by providing clear explanations of goals and methods, and by keeping lines of communication open throughout the process. Staff especially look to ensure that a program is as concerned about security as they are, placing no one at unnecessary risk. Inmates are concerned about confidentiality and with attempts to make programs fit their individual needs.

Wesley Krause

See also ALCOHOL TREATMENT PROGRAMS IN PRISON, DRUG AND ALCOHOL USE IN PRISONS, REHABILITATION PROGRAMS

Bibliography
Abadinsky, H. (1989). *Drug Abuse*. Chicago: Nelson Hall.
Anglin, M. D., and Y. Hser (1990). Treatment of drug abuse. In M. Tonry and J. Q. Wilson, eds. *Drugs and Crime*. Chicago: University of Chicago Press.
Chaiken, M. R. (1989). In-prison programs for drug-involved offenders. Washington, D.C.: National Institute of Justice.
Hamm, M. S. (1990). Addicts helping addicts to help themselves: The Baltimore City Jail Project. In R. Weisheit, ed. *Drugs, Crime and the Criminal Justice System*. Cincinnati, Ohio: Anderson.
Hamm, M. S. (1993). Implementing prison drug war policy: A biopsy of the wallet. In P. Kraska, ed. *Altered States of Mind*. New York: Garland.
Lyman, M., and G. Potter (1991). *Drugs in Society*. Cincinnati, Ohio: Anderson.
Stewart, S. (1994). Community-based drug treatment in the Federal Bureau of Prisons. *Federal Probation* 58(2):24–28.
Wallace, S., B. Pelissier, D. McCarthy, and D. Murray (1990). Beyond nothing works: History and current initiatives in BOP drug treatment. *Federal Prisons Journal* 1(4): 23–26.

Cases
Robinson v. California, 370 U.S. 660, 82 S.Ct. 1417, 8 L.Ed.2d 758 (1962)

Due Process Rights of Prisoners

The due process rights of prisoners—that is, the legal safeguards afforded to each prisoner with regard to privileges and punishments—have evolved substantially over the past century. To some legal experts, the most significant changes in the definition of due process rights took place in the 1970s.

Throughout most of the nineteenth century, courts maintained a "hands off" policy in dealing with prisons. Confinement was often severe and prisoners had little right of redress. An 1871 Virginia case (*Ruffin v. Commonwealth*) affirmed previous policy by declaring that "prisoners are slaves of the state."

It was not until a federal court decision in 1945 (*Coffin v. Richard*) that changes began. There it was decided that "a prisoner retains all rights of an ordinary citizen except those expressly taken from him by law." Such forfeited rights commonly included the right to vote or hold office and restrictions placed on parolees, such as on drinking alcohol or associating with other felons.

By the early 1970s other cases were decided that resulted in greater rights for both probationers (*Gagnon v. Scarpelli*) and parolees (*Morrissey v. Brewer*). Today, those accused of new crimes or about to have their freedom revoked are entitled to counsel, or at least someone who can assist them, as well as a fair hearing before an impartial board.

Robert McDonnell, a Nebraska prison inmate, felt that it was time to see if these rights would be extended behind prison walls. He challenged the prison disciplinary committee's lack of procedural protections in a case that was decided before the U.S. Supreme Court on 26 June 1974. That decision, known as *Wolff v. McDonnell*, established minimal due process rights that included the following:

1. The right to notice of the charges at least twenty-four hours before the hearing;
2. The opportunity to call witnesses and present evidence, but no real right to cross-examine adverse witnesses;

3. A written statement of the findings;
4. The right to an impartial board, although, as courts decided later, this board could consist solely of prison officials.

The Court stopped short of declaring that there was a right to counsel however, claiming, "The insertion of counsel into the disciplinary process would inevitably give the procedures a more adversary cast and tends to reduce their utility as a means to further institutional goals" (94 S.Ct 2981). It did hold that when an inmate is illiterate, or the issues too complex, an inmate may seek the help of another inmate or of qualified prison staff, and that is usually referred to as a council substitute.

In the years since the *Wolff* decision, certain portions of the ruling have been debated and challenged. For instance, *Wolff* established that prisoners have a reasonable right to notice of any charges that may be brought against them. Relying on *Wolff*, inmates accused of using illegal substances claimed that they should be able to examine the results of their drug tests before their hearing. In *Harrson v. Sahm*, however, a federal court backed the prison's defense that test results went beyond mere notice, and that providing results was inconsistent with an orderly administration of the correctional center. Prisons in almost all states not only follow state laws that prohibit possession of drugs, but also prohibit what is known as "status offenses"—being under the influence of an illegal substance. Some states, such as West Virginia (Prison Administrative Rule 1.21), punish inmates for "Refusing Drug or Alcohol Screening."

Another often litigated prison due process issue has been the right of inmates to call witnesses at disciplinary hearings. In *Wolff* the court held that "the inmate should be allowed to call witnesses and present documentary evidence in his defense if . . . it will not jeopardize institutional safety or correctional goals." Most prison policies, however, limit the number of witnesses that may be called and give the hearing officer the right to refuse any requests for witnesses that might threaten the security or orderly operation of the building. Alabama, for example, allows an inmate to list three witnesses and then makes a determination whether they are relevant. Ohio and Rhode Island allow a "reasonable" number, while Georgia uses an investigator to interview and summarize witness statements that are later provided to the committee. The committee then determines which witnesses are necessary. California does not limit the number, but allows three reasons for denying witnesses. These reasons are endangerment of the witness, irrelevancy, and unavailability.

The rules determining whether a prisoner has a right to cross-examine a hostile witness are neither uniform nor clear. Florida is the exception. Its rules (DOC 33-22.007) mandate that "the inmate shall not be permitted to cross-examine witnesses." Connecticut leaves it up to the discretion of the officer, and, although Texas allows questions of all witnesses, it requires the inmate to place the questions in writing beforehand. These questions can then be asked, but only by a representative counsel substitute. Kentucky (Corrections Policy 15.6) allows cross-examination "unless doing so would be unduly hazardous to institutional safety." This point, whether cross-examination of hostile witnesses by inmates is hazardous to institutional safety, has been often debated. Prisons feel that inmates would lose respect for the officers if they could cross-examine them on equal ground. Pennsylvania (Administrative Directive E-3) allows the inmate a reasonable opportunity "to ask relevant questions of any witness who has testified against him unless the witness objects."

Among the states allowing the broadest rights to cross-examination are Maine and West Virginia. California, under Title 15 3315 E (e), is also clear about granting inmates this right. It mandates that "under the direction of the person conducting the hearing the inmate has the right to ask questions of all witnesses called."

Another issue of contention is the impartial disciplinary committee. The *Wolff* decision did not offer specifics as to committee makeup or size. Questions arose as to whether the committee had to be composed of nonprison personnel, to what extent the members could have actual knowledge of the incident, and how many members are necessary.

In *Willoghby v. Luster*, a federal district court ruled that the right to an impartial committee does not require the committee to add outside personnel, but it does exclude anyone involved in the investigation. *Patterson v. Coughlin* defined an impartial committee as one that does not prejudge the evidence. In that case a correctional officer did not allow the inmate to bring witnesses to an alleged fight, later claiming that he would not have believed them anyway. The inmate won his case.

D

There is no requirement concerning the number of hearing officers, and courts have allowed a single officer to conduct a hearing. This has been affirmed as recently as 1990, when the use of a single hearing examiner was upheld at the Federal Correctional Center at Lewisberg in *Proffitt v. United States*. Most states use a committee, although Idaho, Maryland, New Mexico, Pennsylvania, Utah, New York, and Michigan use only one examiner. In the latter two states, the examiner is a licensed attorney.

Of all the prison due process issues decided over the past twenty years, perhaps the most important was the right to counsel for inmates. During the tenure of the Warren Supreme Court, the right to counsel had been expanded to include any defendant who might face either loss of liberty or a large fine. After the United States Supreme Court decided *Gagnon v. Scarpelli* in 1973, allowing attorneys in cases of probation revocation, it was questionable whether representation would be further extended to prisoners in disciplinary hearings. Anticipating such a move, Minnesota, as part of a consent decree to terminate litigation, allowed attorney representation for its inmates. The right to an attorney was part of the *Wolff* litigation as well, although the court rejected mandatory counsel in favor of counsel substitutes (who are not lawyers) for cases in which the inmate needs assistance.

Currently, only Arizona, Kansas, Louisiana, Massachusetts, Minnesota, and South Dakota allow inmates to have counsel. Rhode Island does not generally allow attorneys, although the warden has discretion to permit them. Maryland allows attorneys only on appeal. The rest of the states use counsel substitutes that are usually other inmates or prison staff.

Whether a counsel substitute is required depends on the state. Oregon's policy is typical. In that system, counsel substitute is mandated if the inmate lacks the capacity to understand the charges. Officials have decided that any inmate with an IQ of under 73 automatically qualifies, as well as inmates whose understanding of English is questionable, and cases in which the issues are complex.

As we examine *Wolff* in the mid-1990s, it now seems as though the parameters of prison due process are clearly established. Nevertheless, there are new prisoners and new prison lawsuits every day, and although the vast majority of these cases are dismissed without serious consideration, some of these claims will eventually shape the future of prisoners' due process rights.

Steve Fischer

See also LEGAL ISSUES

Bibliography

Schafer, N. E. (1986). Discretion, due process, and the prison discipline committee. *Criminal Justice Review* 11(2): 37–46.

Cases

Coffin v. Richard, 132 F2d 445 USCA 6th (1945)

Gagnon v. Scarpelli, 411 US 778, 93S.Ct 1756, 36 L.Ed.2d 656 (1973)

Harrson v. Sahm, 911 F2d 37 (1990)

Morrissey v. Brewer, 408 US 471, 92S.Ct. 2593, 33 L.Ed.2d 484 (1972)

Patterson v. Coughlin, 905 F2d 564 USCA 2 NY (1990)

Proffitt v. United States, 758 F Supp 342 E.D. VA (1990)

Ruffin v. Commonwealth, 62 VA 90 (1871)

Willoghby v. Luster, 717 F Supp 1439 DC Nev (1989)

Wolff v. McDonnell, 418 US 539, 94S.Ct. 2963, 41 L.Ed.2d 935 (1974)

E

Eastern State Penitentiary

The Pennsylvania System

Eastern State Penitentiary (ESP) was America's first attempt at humanely rehabilitating criminals. Inspired by the Quaker philosophy of nonviolence, ESP admitted its first prisoner on 29 October 1829. The greatest praise given John Haviland, ESP's young architect, was that he "captured a philosophy in stone." Modeled after European prisons described by John Howard, ESP had a central rotunda with seven radiating cell blocks. This hub-and-spoke design was replicated in approximately three hundred prisons worldwide.

ESP was designed to be a place where criminals would be isolated from all outside influences, reflect on their past and future, learn a trade, receive moral guidance from selected prison visitors, and thus come out of the "gloomy fortress" a better person. The system, called "Separate and Solitary Confinement at Hard Labor," was the brainchild of the Philadelphia Association for Alleviating the Miseries of Public Prisons, founded in 1787 (now the Pennsylvania Prison Society). The legislature approved the concept in 1818, and construction began in 1821. Opponents argued that work would lessen the punishment felt by prisoners, and should be a privilege rather than routine. The "Hard Labor" language was not added to sentencing statutes until 1828. Built two miles outside the city limits in an orchard (thus its nickname—Cherry Hill), it is now surrounded by deteriorating row houses.

An excerpt from the 1834 report of the trustees of ESP best captures the system's theoretical base:

The Pennsylvania System is emphatically a mild and humane system. Let us look for a moment at the condition of the majority of those who became subject to its regulation. We find them living a hurried and thoughtless life of hourly excitement, and shuddering at the possibility of a pause which could let in (to them, the demon) reflection. . . .

Where do we place them and how do we treat them? They are taken to the bath and cleansed of outward pollution, they are newclad in warm and comfortable garments, they are placed in an apartment infinitely superior to that they have been accustomed, they are given employment to enable them to live by their own industry, they are addressed in language of kindness, interest is shown in their present and future welfare, they are advised and urged to think of their former course and to avoid it, they are lifted gently from their state of humiliation; self-degradation is removed, and self-esteem is induced. Pride of character and manliness is inculcated, and they go out of prison unknown as convicts, determined to wrestle for a living in the path of honesty and virtue. Is not that humane?

Other correctional reform efforts of the early nineteenth century also intended to remove offenders from the corrupting influences of society, specifically the debauchery of the congregate prisons of the day. The New York (Auburn) system accomplished separation through intensive supervision, with harsh and frequent corporal punishments. Elam Lynds, perhaps that system's most famous practitioner

Aerial view of Eastern State Penitentiary as it appeared in 1935.
Photo courtesy of The Library Company of Philadelphia.

and the first warden of Sing Sing, considered it necessary to "break the spirit" of each offender before proper (respectful, obedient, Christian) behavior patterns could be established.

Complete separation of all prisoners was never actually accomplished at ESP. Some prisoners worked in maintenance and service activities, and prisoner labor required interactions over training and supplies. For reasons of administrative incompetence, institutional necessity, and human nature, the system was never fully implemented, but the principle of isolation had a powerful impact on those who experienced it.

The relative efficacy of the New York and Pennsylvania systems was a matter of intense debate, and one of the major issues was the number of discharges for "insanity" from ESP. Opponents contended that lack of human contact drove prisoners crazy. Excessive masturbation was cited as the leading cause of insanity (and other illnesses) in official ESP reports. To the average person, insanity as a result of the "treatment" was the issue on which the two systems most differed. Differences in the cost of construction and the ease and cost of operation were of most concern to legislators and experts. Statistics, charges of abuse and corruption, and vicious personal insults were hurled against both systems, and there was public interest in the details of prison operation scarcely imaginable in today's "lock them up and throw away the key" atmosphere.

In 1842, Charles Dickens visited ESP and exacerbated the insanity debate when he published his *American Notes and Pictures from Italy*. His comment on the practice of "rigid, strict and hopeless solitary confinement" was this: "I hold this slow and daily tampering with the mysteries of the brain to be immeasurably worse than any torture of the body; and because its ghastly signs and tokens are not so palpable to the eye and sense of touch as scars upon the flesh . . . I denounce it as a secret punishment."

As virulent as the Auburn/Pennsylvania debate was, it was other issues—overcrowding and the development of the reformatory—that finally ended this era of penology after the Civil War.

The Twentieth Century

As early as 1831, legislation authorizing additional cells had required modifications in Haviland's original design (8 x 12 x 10–foot cells, each with a private outdoor exercise yard), and a second floor without the exercise yards was added to the fourth through seventh cell blocks in 1838. No new cell blocks were added until overcrowding required double celling in 1866. Three blocks opened in 1877, two (one with three levels) in 1911, and two more in the 1920s. Official policy gradually followed institutional reality as separation became both physically impossible and theoretically unacceptable.

Vocations (cigar shop, weave shop, maintenance and construction work, kitchen tasks, and so forth) were increasingly done together. There was an institution band and orchestra as early as 1900 and a baseball league by 1911. (Instructions were given against cheering so that people outside would not hear prisoners "at play.") None of these practices were legal until 1913, when the legislature dropped "separate and solitary" from the sentencing statutes.

As an urban institution whose "treatment plan" relied on outsiders from the very beginning, ESP attracted students, researchers and professionals in medicine, psychiatry, religion, psychology, and sociology from all of Philadelphia's universities, hospitals, and community programs. It was also a place where Philadelphians worked. Staff and inmates' common backgrounds produced a shared, active definition of acceptable and unacceptable behavior impossible to achieve in more rural areas.

ESP's openness also led to innovation. Entertainment and inspirational radio broadcasts by prisoners aired nationwide around 1930. Medical and psychiatric treatment programs burgeoned in the 1920s. A failed attempt at inmate self-government cost Warden Robert McKenty his job in 1923. Plastic surgery was performed beginning in the late 1940s. AA was started in 1960, and Billy Graham held a televised revival service from ESP on 3 August 1961.

ESP also had the usual prison problems. Willie Sutton and seven others tunneled out in 1945. In 1926, inmates and staff were convicted of counterfeiting coins. Al Capone ran his criminal syndicate from an ESP cell for nine months in 1929 and 1930. In 1923, the chapel had to be turned into an emergency hospital to treat all the inmates suffering from drug overdoses. Of the hundreds of suicides that occurred, the last and probably the most dramatic took place in August of 1969, when inmate Norman Maisenhelder stood on the roof for two hours before stabbing himself before a group of inmates and staff. There were riots at ESP in 1934 and 1961.

By the mid 1960s ESP was a modern treatment institution, with a Ph.D. psychologist as superintendent. Guards and treatment staff co-led therapy groups; and inmates in the pre-release program on Eight Block wore civilian clothes. Chess, sports, and debate teams came into the institution for competitions, and inmates could study anything from art to yoga. ESP was the institution of choice for many "old time" prisoners because it was the most personal, flexible and "comfortable" of all the state's prisons. It was also the last resort for prisoners unable to adjust at other state penitentiaries, and the institution with the best psychiatric services for mentally ill inmates. ESP's proximity to families for visiting purposes was another major attraction.

Beginning in 1915, there were six different legislatively funded attempts to close ESP before it finally happened in 1970. Although used as a political symbol of everything thought to be old and wrong in the 1960s, its history and its humaneness were palpable inside the walls. The actual closing of ESP was less about reform, however, than part of a dispute between the city and the state. When Philadelphia reneged on a promise of land for a new prison, the state closed ESP and filled empty cells elsewhere. Lost in the closing was an idealism rarely found in penitentiaries—then or now.

Richard H. Fulmer
Crystal E. Hevener

See also PENNSYLVANIA PRISON SOCIETY, AUBURN SYSTEM

Bibliography

Atherton, A. (1987). Journal retrospective, 1845–1986: 200 years of Prison Society history as reflected in *The Prison Journal*. Prison Journal 67(1): 3–37.

Barnes, H. E. (1927). *The Evolution of Penology in Pennsylvania: A Study in American Social History*. Reprinted Montclair, N.J.: Patterson Smith, 1968.

E

Fulmer, R., and C. Hevener (1993). Eastern State: Queen of the penitentiaries. *The PAPPC Quarterly* 53(3): 14–16.

Teeters, N. K. (1937). *They Were in Prison: A History of the Pennsylvania Prison Society, 1787–1937*. Chicago: John C. Winston.

Teeters, N. K., and J. Shearer (1957). *The Prison at Philadelphia, Cherry Hill: The Separate and Solitary System of Penal Discipline, 1829–1913*. New York: Columbia University Press.

Films

Kirn, H. (producer and director) (1987). *Let the Doors Be of Iron*. Philadelphia: Hal Kirn and Associates.

Educational Programs

Connections with the Local Schools

The Common School movement of the mid 1800s led to the formation of an American public school system. Efforts to refine and improve public education began almost immediately, in response to the changing nature of the United States. A group of prominent urban school reformers addressed local public school issues before World War I. Among them was educator David Snedden. His work was based on the principles he collected from reformatory school practice. Snedden investigated juvenile correctional education and identified models for use in other school settings. Originally, Snedden and other urban school reformers were interested in reformatory schools because they provided "laboratories" in which compulsory attendance was possible. The reformers aspired to implement or enforce compulsory education for children nationwide, to solve the problem of roving bands of street children who created havoc.

Soon, however, the reformers found additional reasons to study correctional education. Snedden assumed that programs that could succeed in the most restrictive educational environment would flourish elsewhere. In his 1907 book, *Administration and Educational Work of American Juvenile Reform Schools*, he reported on pioneer models of vocational (especially trade and industrial), physical, and military education ("shock incarceration"), and summarized how public school educators could learn from correctional teachers. Many of these models became the antecedents of local school practice.

At the 1938 American Association of School Administrators conference in Atlantic City, approximately two thousand people attended the session on "Reduction in Crime through Improved Public Educational Programs and the Educational Rehabilitation of Prison Inmates," although there was room only for seven hundred. Improvised loud speakers were installed in the corridors, lobbies, and adjoining rooms. Articles about the unprecedented level of interest appeared in *Harper's Magazine* and *School Executive*. At the next year's conference in Cleveland, the correctional education session brought in over eight thousand people.

Public school educators know that their colleagues in institutions address the same problems they themselves find so frustrating. In a coercive setting, those problems are even more difficult than in public schools. Correctional educators work with students who have dropped out, been pushed out, or have experienced repeated failure in the local schools. Such students are often embittered and apathetic or alienated, and they often have a history of violence and poor self-esteem. There is an extremely high incidence of learning and emotional difficulties (43 percent) and drug-related problems (75 percent) in confined populations. In addition, many students lack study skills.

Training schools, reformatories, and prisons are often bleak and seem antithetical to the educational mission. Outside observers expect that these conditions would impede student learning. Yet most correctional education programs are successful, according to traditional measures of learning. In 1980, that fact prompted the U.S. Education Department to establish a Correctional Education office in Washington, D.C. "Programs that can succeed in this most difficult setting can be replicable in less restrictive environments. Toward this end, correctional education should be viewed as a laboratory for testing relevant models that can be disseminated to other contexts" (Gehring 1980).

The Systematic Development of Individualized Instruction

Aristotle taught students individually and "little red schoolhouse" teachers used individualized activities, but the individually prescribed instruction (IPI) method was systematically applied and subsequently perfected at correctional and reformatory schools. John Howard had advocated individualized classification in England in the 1780s. Prison reformers championed individualization because it could result in meaningful treatment programs and the reformation of criminals.

IPI has been closely linked in theory to the medical model of corrections: The offender's needs are clinically diagnosed, remedial programs are prescribed, and progress toward a "cure" is monitored. The IPI method we know today started as a correctional education innovation and was later adopted by local public schools. Consider these events:

1. The New York law that established Elmira Reformatory, drafted by Zebulon Brockway, required that school records be maintained on each individual student.
2. In 1929, Austin MacCormick wrote on the systematic individualization of instruction in his book *The Education of Adult Prisoners* (1931).
3. The history of IPI was reviewed by New York City's associate superintendent of schools, William Grady, in 1939: "The pioneers in . . . classification and individualization of personality were the prisons rather than the schools. My hat's off to the prisons" (APA 1930, 61).
4. During the 1960s and '70s, when IPI was accepted widely in the local schools, Dr. John McKee's experiments at Draper Correctional Institution (Alabama) documented its success in correctional education.

The IPI method was designed to address severe basic skill deficits and heterogeneity of correctional populations. It was one by-product of correctional education.

Historical Themes of Correctional Education

Correctional educators operate on the principle that attitudes, ideas, and behavior can be corrected—that humans are capable of transforming their lives. That is what makes correctional education correctional, and links it to prison reform. Historically, advocates of both prison reform and correctional education have shared a common goal: to reform prisons and prisoners. This relationship is not limited to theory. It is expressed in the historic links and shared traditions of prison reform and correctional education.

Chaos: The Early Reform Years

Prisons are a relatively modern phenomenon. The first important decades are known as the reform period. There could have been no prison reform or correctional education until there were prisons, and the establishment of prisons was itself actually a reform. Incarceration was designed as an alternative to punishments such as the death sentence, mutilation, torture, banishment, or heavy fines borne by the criminal's family.

John Howard, John Henry Pestalozzi, and Elizabeth Fry were prominent in early efforts to establish institutions and programs. John Howard was elected sheriff of Bedford, England, about the time of the American Revolution. He wrote a progressive report on how to manage jails. John Henry Pestalozzi implemented Rousseau's educational philosophy and established juvenile institutions to teach Swiss war orphans after the French Revolution and the Napoleonic Wars. Elizabeth Fry advocated individualized literacy instruction, work, and other programs for women throughout Great Britain and Europe during the early decades of the nineteenth century. These early reformers promoted prison reform and correctional education. Nevertheless, the reform period was marked by divergence of opinion and emphasis. If one could put Howard, Pestalozzi, and Fry in a room together, they might actually agree on very little. The period was chaotic.

The North American correctional education movement began in 1789, when clergyman William Rogers first offered instruction at Philadelphia's Walnut Street Jail. The warden was worried that a riot might result from this revolutionary initiative. He required that two armed guards attend the meeting with a loaded cannon aimed directly at the convicts. Everything was peaceful, but the incident is indicative of the ongoing struggle of teaching within prison walls. Despite its unseemly beginning, adult and juvenile correctional education has been on the cutting edge of publicly funded education for most of its approximately two hundred years.

Brief Chronology of North American Correctional Education History

There have been eight major periods of correctional education history in North America. Each has its own identifiable themes:

1. *1789–1875:* Sabbath school period; Pennsylvania (solitary confinement) and Au-

burn (factory model) systems of prison management; correctional education is possible.

2. *1876–1900:* Zebulon Brockway's tenure at Elmira Reformatory, bringing together the themes emphasized by Machonochie (near Australia), Crofton (Ireland), and the Pilsburys (United States); the beginnings of correctional/special education; movement efforts to transform prisons into schools.

3. *1901–1929:* The development of prison libraries, and reformatories for women; democratic patterns of correctional education—William George, Thomas Mott Osborne, and Austin MacCormick; Anton Makarenko's work begins in the Soviet Union.

4. *1930–1941:* "The golden age of correctional education"; MacCormick's programs and professionalization influence: the New York and federal experiments, rebirth of correctional/ special education; Kenyon Scudder begins his tenure as reform warden of an important experimental prison without walls.

5. *1946–1964:* Recovery from the interruption of World War II; the themes of Glenn Kendall's work extend those of MacCormick and set the pace for Cold War correctional education.

6. *1965–1980:* Key improvements and centers of correctional education: the federal influence in education, postsecondary programs, statewide correctional school districts, special education legislation, correctional teacher preparation programs.

7. *1981–1988:* Conservative trend in federal influence and many states; rise of Correctional Education Association influence; continuation of trends from the previous period; Ross and Fabiano's definitive book on progress in Canada and the U.S.

8. *1989–Present:* The current period, with its emphasis on cultures and humanities, developmental education; rise of international cooperation; information access for correctional educators on their history and literature and to promote professional networking.

Most American prison reformers during the years between 1789 and 1875 shared strong religious convictions. They wanted to teach convicts to read so that they could study the Bible and be "saved." Part-time volunteer chaplains organized early correctional education programs according to the "Sabbath school" model, and Sabbath schools were implemented in many Northeastern states. These improvements were analogous to reform efforts on the other side of the Atlantic by Pestalozzi and Fry. They were facilitated by professional networking associations that catered to the needs of prison reformers and correctional educators: the Philadelphia Society for the Alleviation of the Miseries of Public Prisons, the Boston Prison Discipline Society, and the Prison Association of New York.

The Prison Reform Paradigm

Prison reformers knew that they belonged to a single school of thought. Though geographically separated, their work was parallel. Each admired the achievements of Captain Alexander Machonochie at Norfolk Island, a penal colony in the British Pacific. Machonochie established indeterminate sentences, progressive housing, vocational education, and parole during the years 1840–44. He called his system Reformatory Prison Discipline, and announced that it was an alternative to brutality. In Ireland, Sir Walter Crofton declared himself a disciple of Machonochie and implemented Reformatory Prison Discipline in the recently centralized prison system. These Irish developments won the devotion of American prison managers, including Zebulon Brockway. For his entire career, Brockway had prison reform advocates and tough-minded prison managers working together to implement better correctional education programs, a feat that might seem impossible today. The Reformatory Movement (1870 to about 1900) was an effort to change prisons for young adults into schools. At its height, Elmira Reformatory in New York offered training in more than forty vocational trades, as well as elementary, secondary, and even postsecondary education.

During the 1880s and 1890s, Elmira Reformatory superintendent Zebulon Brockway implemented educational programs for the disabled. The labels were different from the ones we apply today: dullards, weaklings, awkwards, the exceptionally stupid in one academic function, incorrigibles, kindergartners, stupids, and so forth. The methods, however, were somewhat parallel to current practice—and in some cases perhaps more advanced. The special education staff included physicians, craftsmen, professors, attorneys, and teachers (Brockway 1912).

Citizenship and Democracy

The subsequent period emphasized democracy, but a brief explanation may be required. Democracy and prisons are generally believed to be mutually exclusive, since prisons are managed with an emphasis on custody and control. History, however, demonstrates many successes in democratically managed prisons. In that tradition, the work of William George, Thomas Mott Osborne, and Austin MacCormick is most significant.

George started a Long Island summer camp for New York City youth in 1895. It soon became a year-round juvenile institution for boys and girls known as the Junior Republic. George encouraged the children to manage every aspect of the institution except the school, which was regulated by state requirements. Finances, personnel, and program development were administered according to the principles of the U.S. Constitution. Wards voted for representatives, senators, and a president who appointed a supreme court to handle disciplinary matters. Thomas Mott Osborne served on the Junior Republic board and was appointed to its supreme court. The republic was made coeducational; its legislature voted to enfranchise girls before the Nineteenth Amendment gave American women the right to vote (George 1911).

A millionaire industrialist and politician, Osborne disguised himself as a prisoner in 1913 to learn firsthand about conditions at Auburn, the prison in his home town. Osborne helped organize the Mutual Welfare League, a democratic, inmate-controlled organization. With the warden's permission, the league managed every dimension of the prison. Disciplinary problems were nearly eliminated, and production in the prison shops increased. By providing daily experiences in democracy and responsible social interaction, Osborne successfully transformed a loathsome maximum-security prison into an uplifting education-oriented institution. He then became the warden at Sing Sing. The inmates there established a flourishing school, the Mutual Welfare Academy. During the First World War, Osborne was appointed warden at the U.S. Naval Prison at Portsmouth, New Hampshire (Tannenbaum 1933).

Osborne trained Austin MacCormick, who based his correctional education theories on those of Brockway and Osborne. MacCormick's book led to the correctional education "renaissance" of the 1930s. He was the first assistant director of the Federal Bureau of Prisons, traveling around the country establishing and expanding prison schools and libraries. For fifty years MacCormick provided leadership at the Osborne Association, one of the nation's most active prison reform organizations. He was the founder of the Correctional Education Association and the first editor of the *Journal of Correctional Education*. World War II interrupted professional development in correctional education, and then the Cold War constrained it.

Cold War Crisis

In the Ukraine after the Russian Civil War and later throughout much of the Soviet Union, Anton Makarenko fostered "Gorky Colonies" to house and educate war orphans and young criminals. He emphasized the civic responsibilities of "the new Soviet man" through social education and many educational activities (Makarenko 1973).

In the United States, Glenn Kendall established New York's first adult reception and diagnostic center at the old Elmira facility. Kendall wrote the definitive book on social education and promoted special education from the mid 1930s to the mid 1960s. In California, reform warden Kenyon Scudder established a prison without walls in 1941 and helped put educators in charge of educational decisions. Scudder staffed the California Institution for Men according to merit—a departure from the prevailing political reward system—thus implementing MacCormick's "Red Barn" theory, that an effective prison can be established in an old red barn if it is staffed correctly. He served as warden until 1956.

The Post–Cold War Culture Period

During the post–Cold War period the emphasis shifted to teams of contributors rather than single heroes. This period is known as the "culture period," because of its emphasis on the ability of cultures to help people stay out of prison. Cultures inform us how to live decently in the community; subcultures tend to focus on drugs, gangs, and violent criminality. Many people work to improve correctional education, but our focus will be on those who have also contributed most to the growing literature.

The first post–Cold War team worked separately on similar themes. Increasing emphasis on humanities instruction took center stage, along

E

with participatory management; cognitive, cognitive-moral, and cognitive-democratic psychologies; and other related themes. Robert Ross of Ottawa responded to Martinson's 1974 declaration that "nothing works" in the rehabilitation of criminals. Ross and Elizabeth Fabiano launched a comprehensive study to identify "what works, and why?" They then wrote the definitive book on the subject, *Time to Think* (1985), with themes that anticipated the post–Cold War period. Ross and Fabiano viewed postsecondary programs at federal institutions around Vancouver as exemplary. Those programs were managed by Stephen Duguid, whose courses in developmental humanities and the social sciences for inmates have been a great encouragement to many correctional educators. Duguid also edited the *Yearbook of Correctional Education* and founded the International Forum for the Study of Education in Penal Systems (IFEPS). In California, David Werner applied parallel systems and managed the Correctional Education Association's Postsecondary Special Interest Group. His *Correctional Education: Theory and Practice* (1990) clearly articulated culture period emphases and has helped many in the field.

The California team of Carolyn Eggleston and Thom Gehring worked with others to organize the Center for the Study of Correctional Education. The center's activities span the areas of teacher preparation and in-service, research, and professional development. The Eggleston and Gehring team worked to make the rich correctional education literature accessible. Their results suggest that professional networking and study can help increase clarity of thought on correctional education issues, thereby helping practitioners feel less vulnerable to institutional constraints.

Overview of the Chronological Perspective
The tradition of progress will continue through coming generations of correctional educators. It may be premature to speculate, however, about what the future will bring. As seen in this brief history, the related fields of prison reform and correctional education have been mutually supportive, generation after generation, expressed in their common history and parallel goals.

The Professional Identity Issue
For more than two hundred years, the history of the correctional education movement has been a record of step-by-step improvement. Clergymen, sociologists, psychologists, novelists, professionals and community volunteers, bleeding hearts and law and order advocates, have connected the intense correctional education context with an understanding of the need to treat prisoners humanely. But the record indicates that correctional educators themselves may be the last to appreciate the importance of their own work.

Institutional teachers have always been slow to identify professionally with the correctional education field. Instead, they identified with the related disciplines: the chaplaincy, higher education, common schools, vocational education. Adult education, social work, and correspondence courses each had their heyday. For decades, particular aspects of the public school model predominated, almost like fads: educational counseling, career, and special education. More recently, shock incarceration, an industrial emphasis, mandatory literacy, and other control-oriented fads have taken center stage. Correctional educators have always accepted the identity of any professional discipline except the one that fits best—correctional education. This phenomenon has been called the "confused identity problem."

The Correctional Education Association (CEA) has launched a vigorous program to provide information and professionwide leadership to overcome this problem, and to consolidate the field. CEA has a staffed, national headquarters near Washington, D.C. Legislative action to improve correctional education services has resulted in some important successes, even during times of budgetary cutbacks. CEA has undergone intensive, participatory self-study, producing resolutions and long-range plans. The association is a network of professionals, complete with its own journal, national newsletter (the *Yearbook*) a host of regional and statewide periodicals, regular conferences, and well-organized special interest groups. CEA is affiliated with the American Correctional Association.

Applying Kuhn's "Paradigm Change Model" to Correctional Education
Introduced by Thomas Kuhn, "paradigm change" is a new way of thinking about how ideas are adjusted in communities. Educators in any setting focus on change; many define learning as "changed behavior," and educational systems always need improvement. That certainly applies in correctional education. Kuhnian

FIGURE 1

Three Phases of Kuhn's Paradigm Change Model

Chaos (1)	Normal Science (2)	Extraordinary Science (3)	New Paradigm (2 again . . .)
Occurs only once	Community accepts a paradigm and begins a period of puzzle-solving; some anomalies surface that the paradigm cannot solve	Anomalies produce crisis ("the rules no longer work"); revolution results	A new period of normal science, under a new paradigm

thought is holistic, developmental, and cooperative—a refreshing shift from the linear, mechanistic, and competitive thinking that has dominated for so long. Kuhn wrote about change in the "hard" sciences (especially physics), but his ideas have been applied to many fields of human activity, including correctional education. Figure 1 displays the main attributes of Kuhn's model.

In his book, *The Structure of Scientific Revolutions*, Kuhn described the chaos that exists in a field before its first paradigm. Chaos is an immature stage of development. It consists of mere categorization of divergent data that predates an accepted way to answer questions. In correctional education, the period of chaos was marked by the contributions of the reform period, especially those of John Howard, John Henry Pestalozzi, and Elizabeth Fry.

Eventually, someone advances a useful theory; if the community embraces it, that theory becomes the first paradigm. It suggests which questions are worth answering and helps solve them. Alexander Machonochie advanced such a theory, and his ideas were developed and applied by Walter Crofton and Zebulon Brockway during the prison reform period of correctional education. Thus began the paradigmatic cycle, ensuring that the field would never again revert to chaos. Normal science begins with the first paradigm, in this case Reformatory Prison Discipline. Normal science is "paradigm driven," dependent upon solutions provided by the paradigm.

Anomalies are problems that the paradigm cannot solve. Soon after the paradigm is installed, they begin to surface. At first anomalies are ignored. Eventually, however, the problems that the paradigm cannot solve become perceived as more important than those it can, which is especially frustrating. It leads to what Kuhn called a crisis, when the rules no longer

seem to work. In correctional education the crisis was initiated by the success of democratic practices in coercive institutions, a totally anomalous concept that appeared absurd but soon demonstrated its effectiveness by promoting good behavior on the part of inmates. The emphasis on citizenship and democracy by George and Osborne, though proven, was too different from conventional wisdom for the field to embrace.

It was MacCormick, in his 1931 book *The Education of Adult Prisoners* and his professionalization initiatives, that translated some of those anomalies into attainable aspirations from which all subsequent developments in the field emerged. But the momentum that MacCormick and those around him fostered ended abruptly with America's entry into World War II.

A crisis existed when the correctional education community perceived that the paradigm-generated rules no longer worked. The Cold War affected correctional education by exacerbating all the school-oriented problems created by World War II. What good are professional rules that cannot solve important problems?

Crisis is the first stage of extraordinary science. In their anxiety, community members grasp for a theory that might solve the most pressing anomalies. The community discards the old paradigm, and another theory is installed as the new reigning paradigm. Kuhn called this a revolution. During the Cold War, correctional educators adopted procedures of control and authoritarianism. They discarded the old prison reform paradigm that aspired to transform prisons into schools and ignored the democratic anomalies. Makarenko and Kendall contributed to the Cold War paradigm; Scudder's work was relatively anomalous.

FIGURE 2

Summary of Correctional Education Paradigm Changes

Period	Main Contributors	Time Period	Contributions	Summary Statements
Reform (Chaos)	John Howard	Period of American Revolution	First state-of-the-art prison reform handbook	Salary Jailers; classify and separate prisoners
	John Henry Pestalozzi	Turn of the nineteenth century	Educated Swiss war orphans	Psychologize education
	Elizabeth Fry	1809-1830s	Advocated individualized education, work	Pennsylvania system; literary (read the Bible, be saved)
Prison Reform (Normal Science)	Alexander Machonochie; Sir Walter Crofton; Zebulon Brockway	1840-1844 American Civil War 1876-1900	Progressive housing, vocational education, indeterminate sentences, parole; other innovations	Reformatory prison discipline; Irish system of prison discipline; the "educational idea of it all"
Citizenship/ Democracy (Anomalies)	William George; Thomas Mott Osborne; Austin MacCormick	1895-1909 1913-1926 1915-1979	Democratic management of institutions by elected wards or inmates, including discipline, with the warden's permission	"Citizenship is our standard"; the New Penology; "better citizens" Adult education for citizenship; socialization
Cold War (Crisis)	Anton Makarenko	1933-mid 1930s	Educated youth for Communism	The New Soviet Man; social education
	Glenn Kendall	1939-1973	Special education; group learning	Diagnosis-prescription method, social education
	Kenyon Scudder	1941-1956, at Calif. Institute for Men	Put educators in charge of education	Prisoners are people; Red barn personnel theory
Culture (New Paradigm)	Ross and Fabiano; Stephen Duguid; David Werner	1980s and 1990s	Education of whole person, personal responsibility, ethical decision-making; international professionalization	Humanities, developmental learning for maturation; participatory management
	Eggleston and Gehring	1980s and 1990s		"New Paradigm"; Center for the Study of Correctional Education

The emerging North American paradigm in correctional education focuses on culture. It subsumes and transcends the current emphases on basic and marketable skills. "Culture period" correctional education takes a "whole student" perspective, using a developmental (as opposed to the Cold War's incremental) approach, to help students grow and mature toward personal responsibility and ethical decision-making. In this effort, the work of Ross and Fabiano, Duguid, and Werner stand out. Eggleston and Gehring helped extend and consolidate the trend. It is probable that additional contributions will be made by correctional educators and writers within this same school of thought, but it is too early to anticipate the nature of their contributions. We live in a period of deep cultural transformation. Paradigm-generated rules are shifting all around us. Even though we may clearly see the general direction of the trend, we do not know what will happen next.

Eventually, a new set of anomalies surface (no paradigm is perfect), and the normal-extraordinary science cycle continues. Figure 2 shows how Kuhnian thought helps explain issues that shaped the development of prison reform and correctional education.

Conclusion

Correctional education has been allied with prison reform, as well as being a modern institutional program. The field has its own history and literature, heros, and proud traditions. There has been a direction to correctional education development: from discordant reform efforts, through the prison reform paradigm, democratic anomalies, the renaissance of the 1930s, the Cold War crisis, to the current culture period. These processes are still unfolding, and the field remains formative, even after more than two hundred years.

Thom Gehring
Carolyn Eggleston

See also BROCKWAY, ZEBULON; EDUCATION OF ALL HANDICAPPED CHILDREN ACT; MACCORMICK, AUSTIN; OSBORNE, THOMAS MOTT; VOCATIONAL PROGRAMS

Bibliography

American Prison Association (1930). *Proceedings of the Sixtieth Annual Congress of the American Prison Association*. Louisville, Ky.: American Prison Association.

Brockway, Z. (1912). *Fifty Years of Prison Service: An Autobiography*. Montclair, N.J.: Patterson Smith (Reprinted 1969).

Gehring, T. (1980). Correctional education and the United States Department of Education. *Journal of Correctional Education* 31(3): 4–6.

George, W. (1911). *The Junior Republic: Its History and Ideals*. New York: D. Appleton.

Kuhn, T. (1970). *The Structure of Scientific Revolutions*. Chicago: University of Chicago Press.

MacCormick, A. (1931). *The Education of Adult Prisoners*. New York: National Society of Penal Information.

Makarenko, A. S. (1973). *The Road to Life: An Epic in Education*. New York: Oriole.

Ross, R., and E. Fabiano (1985). *Time to Think: A Cognitive Model of Delinquency Prevention and Offender Rehabilitation*. Johnson City, Tenn.: Institute of Social Sciences and Arts.

Snedden, D. S. (1907). *Administration and Educational Work of American Juvenile Reform Schools*. New York: Columbia University Press.

Tannenbaum, F. (1933). *Osborne of Sing Sing*. Chapel Hill: University of North Carolina Press.

Werner, D. (1990). *Correctional Education: Theory and Practice*. Danville, Ill.: Interstate.

Education of All Handicapped Children Act

In 1975, Congress passed Public Law 94-142, the Education of All Handicapped Children Act (EHA). The legislation represents one of the most significant federal education efforts, with broad implications for public schooling in the United States. The passage of the EHA came about as a result of grass roots efforts by the parents of disabled students and special education professionals. The arguments used to pass the legislation centered on discrimination against the disabled in public schools inasmuch as disabled students, as a group, were not receiving services adequate to meet their educational needs.

Special education is similar to the corrections classification of "special needs," but it is not exactly the same. Special needs cases may be those identified for special services such as mental health, and may also be eligible for special education services. The classification of special needs might also result from a high risk for escape, or because of enemies in the facility. Those reasons would not make someone applicable for special education, because they are not education related. There is often a great deal of overlap, however, because wards or inmates who need services for specific problems may also require special education.

The EHA was built in part on the 1973 Vocational Rehabilitation Act, which was the basic civil rights act for the disabled. Section 504 of the Vocational Rehabilitation Act dealt specifically with the education of the disabled, but was not as specific as EHA requirements. The EHA requires that disabled children may not be discriminated against in school, and that the school is required to provide special support to help them meet their special learning needs.

The EHA was designed to correct the lack of programs for educationally disabled children and youth aged five through twenty-one in the public schools. It states that disabled students, wherever they are found, must be provided a "free, appropriate, public education" (FAPE). A disabled student's placement in a correctional facility is specifically included under the EHA.

Before the EHA was passed, disabled students were often excluded from public education through placement in trailers, cramped classes, or separate facilities. The FAPE requirement, imposed to solve this problem, requires that disabled students must be educated with other students to the maximum extent possible. In addition, cost to the parents for their education cannot be more than the cost for other students.

The EHA also required that schools actively seek out disabled students. This helps in the early identification of problems. The effort is called "Child Find," and it is designed to solve the problem of disabled students' not being identified and thus not being provided appropriate services.

The federal government committed itself to a process of reimbursing state departments of education for a portion of the additional cost of educating disabled students. Reimbursement was achieved through the provision of "flow-through" funds for local schools from the state education agency.

Evaluation for placement into special education was a major area addressed by EHA. Before its passage, students were often evaluated by one professional using testing instruments that were racially and class biased. Students were placed into special education after limited educational evaluation efforts, and they were not regularly reevaluated to determine if progress had been made. The solution to these problems was the development of multidisciplinary team evaluation. To determine which students are eligible for special education services, at least four professionals must evaluate their strengths and weaknesses. These professionals make up the multidisciplinary team, which must include (at least) an educational evaluator/teacher, a psychologist (who does an individual psychological examination), a medical representative, and a social worker who completes a social history. Others may be called upon for evaluation when necessary, such as speech or language clinicians and occupational or physical therapists. Together, the multidisciplinary team makes a determination concerning the student's placement into special education. The plan must not be limited by what services are readily available but must indicate what the student actually needs.

Eleven categories were established under which students could be found eligible for special education. A student must fit into one or more of the categories to qualify for special education. The eleven categories are specific learning disability, serious emotional disturbance, mental retardation, hearing impaired/deaf, visually impaired/blind, multiply handicapped, communication handicapped, other health impaired, orthopedically handicapped, physically handicapped, and speech impaired.

Placement options for the special education student include such diverse alternatives as a regular classroom with some support, all the way to placement in a residential facility. The student may be placed in a part-day special education program, generally called a resource, or a full-day special education program, termed self-contained. The critical issue here is that a "cascade of educational services" be available, with options that will meet the student's needs. The student is always to be placed in the Least Restrictive Environment (LRE) possible. Emphasis is on placing the student in a less restrictive environment first, then moving on to greater restrictions as needed. Corrections agencies have successfully negotiated this problem with the provision that educationally disabled wards and inmates be placed in the same environment as others. Although the institution may be very restrictive, identified wards and inmates are treated equitably as long as they are not housed in more restrictive areas because of their disability.

The EHA also addressed the problem of a student's being placed in special education and never reviewed for progress. The solution was the development of an Individualized Education Plan, or IEP. The IEP contains a statement of goals and objectives for the disabled student. It is generated from the information collected during the multidisciplinary evaluation. The initial IEP is written after the student is found eligible for special education services, and it must be reviewed every year. After the third year a complete reevaluation must be done, which involves complete retesting.

One critical area addressed by the EHA is an increased role for parents. A lack of parental involvement was seen as a major problem before the EHA was passed. Parents might not know if their child had been evaluated for or placed in special education. Educational records were available to any agency but not to parents. The EHA provides for parental involvement at each stage of the special education process. It includes a system of due process procedures in the case of disagreement about placement or programs. This can conflict with confidentiality restrictions in corrections, but successful accommodation has been possible in most systems.

Although the EHA was designed to be a public school law, it has clear application to corrections. Many of the requirements are difficult to implement in correctional institutions, but litigation in a number of states has verified its application. The most successful state correctional systems have worked closely with their state departments of education in developing special education programs that meet the spirit of the law while addressing institutional restrictions.

Individuals with Disabilities Education Act (IDEA)

In 1990, Public Law 94-142, the EHA, was reauthorized to consolidate changes and to incorporate changes passed in the form of amendments or those identified through litigation. The first change was made in the way eligible students are labeled, from the term "handicapped children" to "children with disabilities." This new label is more consistent with current approaches and ideas about disabilities.

The EHA was initially perceived as applying to school-age children, which overlooked the fact that disabled students need support before and after those ages. In order to adequately serve students with disabilities during school age, attention had to be given to developmental periods before and after those years.

To address the first concern, the IDEA developed programs and regulations for early intervention of disabled infants and toddlers. Early intervention by the school makes an enormous difference in a child's progress. The focus of early intervention programs is in working with families as well as children with disabilities.

A second problem in the earlier legislation was solved by the provision of transition services for students with disabilities aged sixteen or older. States may choose to start transition planning at age fourteen, and many states have done so. Transition services must be a set of activities specifically designed to help the student move into postschool activities. These may include training for employment, postsecondary education, or other training. The efforts must be coordinated and address the student's individual needs and interests, as well as community support options.

A transition plan is to be made part of the IEP for each disabled student. This plan is called the Individualized Transition Plan, or ITP. The ITP is required for all disabled students, including those found in corrections. Correctional systems will be required to go beyond the limited prerelease programs now available and develop transition plans for all identified special education wards and inmates.

Another important aspect of the IDEA legislation is the development of an additional program of support for students identified as "seriously emotionally disturbed" (SED). This area is of particular significance to corrections populations because of the relative overrepresentation in them of students identified as SED. Under EHA, students who were determined to be socially maladjusted were eliminated from the category of serious emotional disturbance. New definitions are more specific and less influenced by subjective opinions.

A final significant area of change under the IDEA deals with the provision that students with severe disabilities be placed in integrated settings. Public school classrooms will for the first time, be integrated to include students with severe disabilities. Although the emphasis on integration is again focused on the public schools, correctional agencies may face similar challenges.

Corrections agencies have been slow to implement P.L. 94-142. Some systems, particularly for adults, have not made any attempts. Both P.L. 94-142 and P.L. 101-476 apply to corrections as well as public schools. Litigation of this issue in corrections has overwhelmingly supported the rights of wards and inmates to special education. The result of this litigation has been that a number of states have been forced to implement special education under federal court order, which is the most expensive and least effective means of implementation. A much more logical approach is to take a proactive role in special education implementation.

Carolyn Eggleston
Thom Gehring

See also EDUCATIONAL PROGRAMS, VOCATIONAL PROGRAMS

Elderly Inmates

Crime is traditionally considered a young man's game and, while that appears accurate, prisons in the United States are housing a growing number of older inmates. According to the U.S. Bureau of Justice Statistics, the number of inmates aged fifty-five and older more than doubled from 1981 to 1990. In a study conducted by the Federal Bureau of Prisons, it was predicted that the federal system, which houses the largest number of older inmates, will have a population increase in those aged fifty and older of from 11.7 percent in 1988 to 16 percent by the year 2005.

There are several factors influencing the number of older people in prison. First, there are more older people in the general population, and they are living longer. According to the U.S. Census Bureau, those aged sixty-five and older make up the fastest growing population group in the U.S., and in the last sixty years, the average life expectancy has increased from fifty-four years to over seventy-five years. At the same time, society's heightened concern about crime and violence has resulted in longer sentences and mandatory incarceration to include life without parole for an increasing number of offenses. Additionally, several jurisdictions including the federal government have abolished parole and limited probation as a sentencing option.

Studies indicate that most prisons are not designed for older inmates and do not adequately meet their needs. Correctional practitioners and policy makers have a growing awareness of the problems older inmates face and are increasingly debating the options that should be available for them.

Definitions of "Older"

There is no uniformly accepted definition of the point at which one becomes "old." The federal government's programs for the elderly designate a range of ages depending on the program, from a low of age forty to a high of age sixty-five. Correctional agencies also do not have a single definition of who constitutes an older inmate. This lack of consistency complicates planning, programs, evaluation, and research for correctional agencies. In a recent administrative guide prepared for the National Institute of Corrections, Morton recommended that correctional agencies and service providers adopt the age of fifty as the starting point for defining older inmates. That age is considered important because heredity, socioeconomic conditions, lifestyles, and the medical care available to many inmates result in their aging prematurely. The starting point must also be low enough to allow correctional agencies to implement early health care intervention and preventive programs for older inmates to help minimize the expense of medical care and other services this group will require.

Chronological age is only one factor in determining who is "old." The complexity of the relationship among various inherited and environmental factors results in wide variations; some inmates may be physically or mentally old at fifty, while others are active and coping well at seventy. Emphasis then must be placed on the individual inmate's level of functioning. Determining this level of functioning requires an assessment of how older inmates are coping mentally and physically and what they are capable of doing to maintain the activities of daily living.

In general, older inmates are more heterogeneous than any other age group. This requires that prison programs for older inmates include individualized assessment, planning, and monitoring to meet the needs of this diversified group.

The Characteristics of Older Inmates

According to Camp and Camp inmates fifty years of age and older constituted 6 percent of the people incarcerated in the United States in 1993. As with general inmate populations, men greatly outnumbered women. The Bureau of Justice Statistics reported that 63 percent of those aged fifty and older were incarcerated for violent offenses including murder and sexual assault. Many had victimized family members and had been using alcohol at the time the crime was committed.

Studies indicate that older offenders can be categorized into at least three groups, based on their criminal history. Each group adjusts to prison in a different way and has varying needs upon release. That in turn affects security, programs, and supervision in the facility.

The first group consists of those who committed their crime after age fifty and are sentenced to prison for what is usually the first time. The crime is often violent and carries a lengthy sentence. Inmates in this group frequently have adjustment problems and are the most likely to be victimized by other inmates. Some will have strong community ties and will be relatively easy to place upon release. Others will have victimized family members and thus lose community support systems.

The second group is made up of career or habitual offenders who move in and out of prison, serving a few years at a time throughout their lives. These are the "old cons," who on the surface appear to make a positive adjustment and have the skills necessary to cope with other inmates. Some studies indicate, however, that, when more closely analyzed, prisoners in this group may have adjustment problems and may fear other, stronger inmates. Many have substance abuse problems, particularly alcoholism, that grow more severe as they age. They may also have other chronic problems, as well as lacking skills required to be successful in society. Their community ties may have been destroyed by alcoholism or other abuses, and their work history is often intermittent, making them difficult to place upon release.

The third group consists of those who received long sentences for serious crimes at an early age and have grown old in prison. Because of the nature of their crimes, they have often spent long periods in secure confinement and are the most institutionalized of the three groups. They may have behavioral problems and a long history of disciplinary infractions. Many will "burn out" as they age and appear to make a positive adjustment in the institution. In reality, many are on the defensive or even offensive and will victimize staff and other inmates if given the opportunity. Maintaining positive behavior and motivating this group over a lifetime in prison can be managed to some degree through the development of career ladders in industry or work assignments that enable them to acquire ever-increasing skills or responsibilities. Participation in such programs will assist in preparation for release, as most in this group will have few community ties, little work history, and limited coping skills for the world beyond the prison. They will be among the most difficult to place.

While there certainly are exceptions, the majority of older inmates from all three groups will be less violent and cause fewer disciplinary incidents than their younger counterparts. Many may be reluctant to participate in activities requiring contact with younger, more aggressive inmates. In general, older inmates tend to suffer more from depression and a sense of isolation than their younger counterparts. In particular, almost all older inmates fear dying in prison.

Since they are few in number and generally do not create problems for staff, older inmates can be easily overlooked and their needs ignored. Discussed below are a number of issues relative to older prisoners that must be addressed by correctional personnel, including mainstreaming, special units, medical care, programs and services, staffing, and older female offenders.

Mainstreaming Older Inmates

Older inmates have differing housing and program needs. The majority of older offenders will be mainstreamed in general-population housing, just as most older people in the community live at home. Mainstreaming helps ensure that older inmates are not denied access to programs and services. It also enables them to be closer to home, maintain community ties, and receive visits from family and friends, who may be elderly themselves and have difficulty traveling.

Correctional personnel have traditionally supported the concept of mainstreaming because older inmates are thought to have a calming, settling effect on younger inmates. Mainstreaming also allows administrators to have several assignment options for placement. That is particularly important because, although older inmates have frequently committed violent offenses, they usually are not considered high security risks. Administrators can mainstream those older inmates who need less supervision in lower cost minimum-security housing and reserve the expensive maximum-security cells for those inmates who pose a higher risk.

There are also legal considerations that mainstreaming can help to resolve. Under the far-reaching Americans with Disabilities Act of 1990, all those, including inmates, who have physical or mental conditions that substantially impair one or more of their life activities, such as walking, breathing, or dressing, must have equal access to all programs and services available to all other inmates. Thus, housing should be modified or designed to meet universal access standards so that individuals who are impaired can reach all areas of the facility. Agencies that do not provide the opportunity for full access by older inmates can be subject to legal action to include federal lawsuits.

For mainstreaming to be successful, older inmates must be observed and assessed on an ongoing basis, because their level of functioning can deteriorate rapidly. They can also easily fall prey to younger, stronger inmates.

E

Mainstreaming also requires correctional personnel to be flexible and to modify policies, procedures, and programs as needed to allow older inmates to develop or maintain their optimum level of functioning. This may involve such things as housing older inmates in clusters on ground-floor units close to dining, medical, or other services. It may also mean providing special diets, clothing, temperature control, mattresses and bedding, handrails in bathrooms, ramps, and other modifications to meet access requirements for older inmates. In some instances, programs and services may need to be brought to housing units, rather than having older inmates travel long distances or be hindered by architectural barriers they might encounter. Designing or modifying facilities and programs to foster independence among older inmates, to help them stay in the general population, is cost effective and provides better community adjustment upon release.

Special Units for the Elderly

There are those older inmates whose physical, medical, mental, or other conditions prevent them from functioning in the general population and who will require placement in a protected environment. That could mean special housing units or, for large numbers of older inmates, special institutions designed or modified to be accessible for and to meet the needs of older inmates. Such units should have clearly defined goals and objectives, so that they do not become overcrowded or house those who can cope elsewhere. Placement criteria should include many factors, including medical and other needs, and agencies should not base admission to special units on age alone.

For those older inmates who cannot function in the general population, special units can be critical to their survival. Moore (1989) found that older inmates have less fear for their safety and are better adjusted when placed in special units. Such units also make possible the development of a range of specialized services and programs, as well as a cost-effective concentration of skilled staff and resources.

Special units or facilities are not widely available for older inmates in state and federal prisons. The National Institute of Corrections in 1985 identified only eleven states that had such units. A 1991 study of thirty-nine states and the Federal Bureau of Prisons reported that fourteen had some type of special unit or housing for older inmates whose functioning was impaired. That same study found that most systems with special units lacked minimum-security options for older inmates and thus were using medium and maximum-security space for frail older inmates who might be safely placed in less secure and less expensive facilities.

Medical Care

One of the most costly aspects of incarcerating older inmates is medical care. Legally, inmates must be provided with medical care that meets the same standards available outside prison. A 1990 study of older inmates in Maryland found that older inmates suffered an average of three chronic illnesses and generated three times the medical expenses incurred by younger prisoners. In 1988, the Federal Bureau of Prisons found that older inmates had higher rates of chronic illness, including cardiac and hypertension disorders, than their younger counterparts. The bureau predicted that by the year 2005 those two illnesses alone will cost more than $93 million to treat. To keep health care costs from continuing to rise, correctional systems will have to take a long-range approach to prevention, intervention, early diagnosis, and treatment.

Aging causes physiological changes that can affect the practices and procedures of correctional facilities. Taste, smell, touch, sight, and hearing all become dulled. Since they take in less sensory information, older inmates may not be able to respond quickly or appropriately to stimuli. These changes occur gradually, and they may not be noticeable to the inmate or staff. This necessitates regular medical examinations as well as routine screening by other staff members, to identify and treat these conditions before they become critical. Activities directed at keeping inmates healthy and improving their lifestyles will slow deterioration to some extent and partially counteract the effects of the debilitating lifestyles that many inmates engaged in prior to incarceration. As one ages, the bones become more brittle and lung capacity decreases, resulting in a loss of oxygen throughout the body, including the digestive system. That reduces stamina, which, in turn, affects work assignments. These and other changes necessitate special diets for older inmates. The kidneys begin to lose mass after age fifty, which can cause frequent urination or incontinence among older inmates. Transportation schedules and proximity to bathrooms are but two of the factors that must be considered.

Medical staff trained to work with older inmates are essential. Older inmates are often uninformed about their bodies or medical treatments, and so staff members must ensure that they understand their condition and learn how they can work with medical personnel. Staff must be particularly sensitive to the effects of medication on older inmates; 25 percent of the older patients in hospitals are there as a result of improperly prescribed drugs ordered by their physicians.

Older inmates with chronic medical problems usually require the availability of medical staff on a twenty-four-hour basis. To the degree possible, correctional agencies should arrange for community placement of seriously ill, chronically ill, and terminally ill inmates. That includes the identification of beds in nursing homes outside prison that can be used for inmates who need skilled nursing care. If the inmates remain under the correctional system's jurisdiction, the agency may have to pay more than the Medicaid rate for a community nursing home bed, but it will still be less expensive and the service more effective than keeping the person in prison. In 1990, Hall found that twenty-two states surveyed had some type of compassionate release program that could be used to place frail, older inmates in community facilities. No evaluation of their effectiveness, however, has been conducted.

Because many older inmates will die in prison, facilities must provide for hospice programs, counseling for terminally ill inmates, and visits by family, friends, and volunteers. The inmate's right to a living will, medical power of attorney, and other legal matters must also be addressed. When death occurs, counseling will be needed for inmates and staff members who worked closely with the deceased. If there is no family to accept the remains, a funeral or memorial service and a dignified burial service should be provided.

Other Programs and Services

Programs for older inmates must provide for individualized assessment and treatment plans. Counseling, leisure time activities, education, and legal services need to be adapted to meet the needs of older inmates. Even disciplinary programs need to be examined, because strategies that encourage younger inmates to participate and behave acceptably may not be effective with sixty-year-olds.

Most older inmates want to be busy and productive. Modifications of full- or part-time work assignments, however, may be necessary to enable them to participate. Where inmates are permitted to earn time off their sentences by participating in work or other activities, older inmates may spend more time in prison than their younger counterparts if denied access to such opportunities. Systems in which access and availability are denied will then be vulnerable to charges of discrimination under the Americans with Disabilities Act and other federal and state statutes.

Successful planning for reintegration into the community and transitional services are of particular importance to older inmates. Morton's 1991 study of forty agencies found a serious lack of specialized prerelease programs for older inmates and a limited use of outside resources to meet their needs. Reentry programs designed for younger inmates will need modification to ensure that housing, continuity of medical care, and other concerns of the aging are addressed. Placing those who have no family to assist them or who may not be able to live independently requires that correctional personnel work closely with the community providers of services to the aging.

Failure to provide effective prerelease services may result in older inmates refusing release or otherwise spending more time in prison because they have nowhere else to go. A recent Maryland study, for example, predicted that 14 percent of the older inmates in that prison system would be homeless if released without prior planning and preparation.

Staffing

Not everyone can work with older inmates. Staff must be carefully screened and selected on the basis of their interest in and ability to relate to older people. They must also be provided with special training in gerontology that begins with an examination of their own feelings about aging. Many will be coping with aging relatives or friends and, given the limited scope of community programs and resources for the elderly, may have difficulty with the perception that older inmates are provided better care than other older people receive.

In addition to developing self-awareness and information about the normal aging process, staff members, through the empathetic training model, can be helped to better understand disabling conditions such as hearing, visual, and mobility impairments. In this training, participants use cloudy glasses to blur their vi-

E

sion, ear plugs to impair their hearing, and bandages, crutches, or wheelchairs to simulate limits on mobility. Through exercises that simulate everyday prison activities, staff members become more sensitive to the barriers and problems faced by older inmates.

Interpersonal communication training specifically directed at interacting with older inmates is another important component of a staff training program. Effective listening, variations in voice tone and pitch, and body positioning are among several important factors that must be taken into consideration when communicating to older persons. Inadequate training can not only impair the staff's effectiveness but can also result in costly legal actions.

Because older inmates require more intensive support and services, they will need a higher staff-to-inmate ratio than the general population. This adds to the cost of incarceration and reinforces the need to maximize the use of community resources and placement for those older inmates who are not a threat to public safety.

Incarcerated Older Women

As of 1990, according to the American Correctional Association, women aged fifty and older constituted some four percent of the women incarcerated in state and federal prisons. Because of mandatory sentencing, the war on drugs, longer sentences, and sentences of life without parole, women as a whole make up the fastest growing group of prisoners. If these approaches to crime control continue, the number of older women in prison will increase.

Incarcerated older women are more likely to be in the general population than in special units. A 1991 survey of state and federal prisons identified only three systems that reported having special units for women, compared with fourteen that had them for older men.

One of the few reported programs designed specifically for older women was the American Association of Retired Persons Women's Initiative Project in the Corrections Center for Women at Purdy, Washington. The project staff emphasize the need for support groups among older women, separate activities geared toward their interests, and dietary and medical services designed to improve their overall health. Of particular concern relative to prison programs was the observation that older women are very passive and need assistance in becoming more assertive and taking control of their lives.

Prison personnel must also be sensitive to physiological and societal differences between men and women in the development and implementation of programs for older women. Although older women are not considered a great threat to society, their economic plight and negative image compound the problems they encounter in reentering the community.

Joann B. Morton

See also DISABLED INMATES, HEALTH CARE, LONG-TERM PRISONERS AND LIFERS

Bibliography

Aday, R. H. (1994). Aging in prison: A case study of new elderly offenders. *International Journal of Offender Therapy and Comparative Criminology* 38: 79–91.

Camp, G. M., and C. G. Camp (1993). *The Corrections Yearbook* 1993. South Salem, N.Y.: Criminal Justice Institute.

Chaneles, S., and C. Burnett, eds. (1989). *Older Offenders: Current Trends*. New York: Haworth.

Hall, M. (1990). *Special Needs Inmates: A Survey of State Correctional Systems*. Boulder, Colo.: National Institute of Corrections Information Center.

McCarthy, B., and R. Langworthy, eds. (1988). *Older Offenders: Perspectives in Criminology and Criminal Justice*. New York: Praeger.

McShane, M., and F. Williams (1990). Old and ornery: The disciplinary experiences of elderly prisoners. *International Journal of Offender Therapy and Comparative Criminology* 34: 197–212.

Moore, E. O. (1989). Prison environments and their impact on older citizens. *Journal of Offender Counseling, Services and Rehabilitation* 13(2): 175–91.

Morton, J. B. (1992). *An Administrative Overview of the Older Inmate*. Washington, D.C.: National Institute of Corrections.

Morton, J. B. (1993). Training staff to work with elderly and disabled inmates. *Corrections Today* 55(1): 42, 44–47.

Elmira Reformatory

For much of the nineteenth century, New York was the national, if not international, leader in penal affairs. Auburn prison gave its name to the "silent," or congregate, labor model of maximum-security prisons for men. Sing Sing was recognized worldwide as a prison for urban criminals, sent "up the river" from New York City. The New York House of Refuge and Rochester's Western House of Refuge, owing much to French and German institutions, became in turn models for the incarceration of male, and later female, delinquents. New York also built the pioneering and most influential institution in America's third penal system—the Elmira Reformatory for young men.

Elmira, built in the upstate community of the same name, became the flagship institution of America's "progressive era" philosophy of rehabilitation rather than retribution and deterrence, for at least certain populations. Beyond its position in New York's penal system, Elmira owed its preeminence to its first superintendent and to the penal history on which it seemed to draw.

That penal tradition included Alexander Machonochie's mark system, which rewarded (with early release) transported felons, largely English and Irish, for their industry, education, and deportment. Adopting Machonochie's marks, Sir Walter Crofton in post-famine Ireland began the so-called Irish system of first separate and then congregate confinement, followed by early release through a mark system, intermediate training prisons (halfway houses), and supervised parole. That Irish, or Crofton, system attracted penal reformers around the world, including participants at the first National Congress on Penitentiary and Reformatory Discipline meeting in Cincinnati in 1870. In reality, the Irish system had a single overburdened parole officer dependent on lay and clerical volunteers, underfunded or nonexistent training programs, no real application to female convicts, and reliance on a stubborn yet charismatic reformer adept at manipulative publicity campaigns (Smith 1980). Those and other problems were to beset Elmira Reformatory, which was seen by most contemporaries and historians as the embodiment of the declaration of principles passed at the 1870 congress (Waite 1993; Gehring 1982).

As Alexander Pisciotta superbly demonstrates in *Benevolent Repression* (1994), Elmira Reformatory lived up to neither its promise nor its own publicity. Institutional records and special investigations reveal a scandal-ridden institution, a rebellious inmate population, and a harsh, even brutal first superintendent, Zebulon Reed Brockway. Beginning in 1848, Brockway had held a series of penal administrative posts

in three different states. His name was to become virtually synonymous with the institution he directed for a quarter century.

Even before hiring Brockway, New York had selected a site, hired an architect, begun construction, and limited the commitment to between sixteen and thirty male first-time offenders. Elmira's first inmates were thirty transfers from Auburn, in July of 1876. For the next four years, those transfers and others from Auburn and Sing Sing completed the main cell house and other structures. Those first years were also marked by escapes and the murder of the first assistant superintendent, before Brockway instituted his three-stage program to shape the inmates, criminals largely from the state's urban, immigrant working class.

Using terms drawn from medicine and education, then emerging as modern professions, Brockway claimed that his program successfully "treated" inmates, who became Christian gentlemen at Elmira, "the college on the hill." Like many other penal reformers, Brockway wanted prison administration recognized as an ordered and humane profession that disciplined society's most disordered elements for their own and the greater good. On the surface, Elmira seemed the embodiment of those hopes.

As a first stage, Brockway personally interviewed new admissions to gather demographic, criminal, and social and moral information on them, before they entered into the second of three inmate "grades." Elmira was supposed to treat the criminals rather than their crimes. The chief "medicine" was in the second grade, which included labor in the iron foundry, factories, farm, or on the maintenance crew. Dinner was followed by formal schooling and occasional speeches by guest lecturers. Sundays meant mandatory church services. Those who earned three marks each for education, labor, and behavior each month for half a year were promoted to first grade; another six months of "nines" could earn parole hearings before Brockway and the five Elmira civilian managers. Under intermediate sentencing, inmates could spend as little as a year in prison before being paroled to homes and jobs they themselves had prearranged. Failure to follow the rules for the third grade, or release, meant revocation of parole and return to Elmira's second grade.

Brockway acknowledged few inmate or parole failures. In part, he could report parole successes because he employed parolees as monitors, who served as guards alongside civilians. Clearly, Brockway carefully shaped Elmira's reputation, and his own, through an astute publicity campaign. The reformatory's press printed Brockway's glowing annual reports (which he circulated widely among reformers and penal administrators) and, from 1883 on, *The Summary*, the inmate newspaper. He lectured extensively and opened Elmira's gates for personally conducted tours. The reformatory's visitors, and there were many, saw various displays of inmate industry and discipline, probably none more impressive at first glance than the military drill.

Beginning in 1888, when the legislature, under pressure from business and labor, temporarily outlawed prison industries, Elmira's inmates were divided into military units led by inmate officers, essentially trustees, and guards. For many reformers, the success of abolition and the Civil War's glorification of sacrifice validated the rehabilitative powers of the military (Smith 1988). Among those who visited were state politicians and administrators, who adopted the Elmira model, including military drill and parole, in ten adult reformatories.

At the same time that Elmira was being enthusiastically copied, an investigation uncovered major problems behind the facade of humane and successful treatment. In 1893–94, the New York State Board of Charities conducted extensive sworn interviews with Elmira's staff and inmates, including parolees and transfers to other prisons. Inmate interviews revealed brutality, ineptitude, neglect, and inmate resistance. The investigators' final report charged that Brockway himself physically assaulted inmates during the admission process and later. Inmates were shackled and hung from the bars of what with grim humor were labeled "rest cure" cells. And inmates responded with violence against other inmates and staff, suicides, and resentment of the mark system, which had been converted into a wage system that required payment for institutional services. The investigation uncovered inadequate medical care, nepotism, perfunctory parole hearings and supervision, and a homosexual ring run by inmate monitors who extorted sexual favors. Brockway vehemently denied the charges and intensified his public relations campaign until the governor appointed a second investigation, whose majority report generally exonerated him. He was able to remain superintendent until 1900, when new managers forced his resignation after finding decaying facilities, high recidivism rates,

staff corruption, and widespread smuggling of contraband.

Brockway's immediate successors, including two physicians, changed Elmira's focus from one of treatment and rehabilitation to custody and treatment. Newly developed psychological tests were used to show that high percentages of the inmates were mental defectives, shaped by heredity or by urban decay, for whom there was little or no hope of reform. This positivistic viewpoint was also behind the building of Elmira's sister institution, the Eastern New York Reformatory. Opened in 1900, Napanoch was to hold defectives, thus eugenically protecting society. Until 1921, Elmira's administrators controlled the two institutions, 120 miles apart. A chief advocate of seeing the mental defective as both the troublesome inmate and the recidivist was Dr. Frank L. Christian, who came to Elmira as physician from Napanoch and later served as superintendent from 1917 until 1939.

From the eve of the Second World War until the mid 1970s, Elmira was led by six superintendents. By the 1930s, the institution had fourteen hundred cells and a Catholic chapel, built by private donations. In 1932, New York established a statewide parole board for all of its penal facilities. In 1945, the state established a reception center adjacent to the reformatory to test and classify men between the ages of sixteen and twenty-one. The two were formally merged in the early 1970s as the Elmira Correctional and Reception Center. The 1970s also saw a mosque, an inmate grievance committee, and community college program established (Beltzer and Spears 1976). Today, as the Elmira Correctional Facility, New York's one-time showcase institution is just another maximum-security prison in the large state system. In truth, it always was.

Beverly A. Smith

See also BROCKWAY, ZEBULON

Bibliography

Beltzer, W., and E. Spears, eds. (1976). *Elmira: 1876–1976 Centennial Acknowledgement of Its History, Programs, and Purpose*. Albany, N.Y.: New York State Department of Correctional Services, Office of Public Relations.

Gehring, T. (1982). Zebulon Brockway of Elmira: 19th century correctional education hero. *Journal of Correctional Education* 33: 4–7.

Pisciotta, A. W. (1994). *Benevolent Repres-*

sion: *Social Control and the American Reformatory-Prison Movement*. New York: New York University Press.

Smith, B. A. (1980). The Irish general prisons board, 1877–1878: Efficient deterrence or bureaucratic ineptitude? *Irish Jurist* 15 (Summer): 122–36.

Smith, B. A. (1988). Military training at New York's Elmira Reformatory, 1888–1920. *Federal Probation* 52 (March): 33–40.

Waite, R. G. (1993). From penitentiary to reformatory: Alexander Machonochie, Walter Crofton, Zebulon Brockway, and the road to prison reform—New South Wales, Ireland, and Elmira, New York, 1840–1970. In L. A. Knafla, ed. *Criminal Justice History: An International Annual*. Westport, Conn.: Greenwood.

Escapes

The concern over inmate escapes involves everyone associated with an institution, from warden to correctional officer to the residents living nearby. Escapes also make good plot lines for movies and television. Despite this wideranging concern, escapes appear to have been overlooked by most writers on corrections. Very little exists in the literature with respect to escapes. Yet, in and around correctional institutions, the concern with escapes seems to take on an almost mystical quality.

For example, in 1865, one of John Wilkes Booth's lieutenants, John Surratt, managed to escape the custody of, and the subsequent dragnet set up by, the War Department. His escape appears all the more interesting given that the crime involved the assassination of President Lincoln and that Surratt's escape (or the decision not to mount an intensive search and investigation) may have been promoted by Secretary of War Stanton. It is also interesting to note that the assassination of Lincoln was one of the first crimes to raise the question of a conspiracy.

Alcatraz, and the Myth of Its Being Escape-Proof

The U.S. federal prison on Alcatraz had a mystique regarding escapes. Alcatraz, the home of some of the most notorious federal inmates of its time, was billed as an escape-proof prison. While we now know that no such institution exists, the idea that Alcatraz was escape-proof helped ease the minds of many in the San Francisco Bay area. The myth also probably contributed to relaxed security on the part of correctional officers at that institution. Despite what others might have believed about Alcatraz, or perhaps because of that belief, many inmates thought that escape was possible. Between 1935 and 1962 there were fourteen escapes involving thirty-six men, of whom only five remain unaccounted for. Most of the other thirty-one died in the attempt. Two of the five unaccounted-for inmates are presumed to have drowned. Other than showing up as characters in a Clint Eastwood movie (*Escape From Alcatraz*), what happened to the other three is not known. Many (including those involved with Alcatraz) believe that they died. There have been reports, however, of letters, and of the sighting of at least one of the escaped prisoners in South America. Despite much investigation, we may never know if anyone ever successfully escaped from Alcatraz.

Prediction of Escapes

It is obvious from prison data that only a small number of inmates attempt to escape, and that most of those are caught and returned to the institution (Herrick 1989). Most escapes occur from minimum- and medium-security facilities. A survey of forty-three correctional systems in 1993 found that there were 802 escapes. With an average daily population of about 653,000 inmates, that averages about eighteen escapes per reporting system. In 1991 there were seventy-two escapes from California prisons; all but twenty-seven were from low-security prison camps. That is a dramatic decline from twenty years earlier, when there were 441 escapes from California prisons.

Very few escapes result in injury or death to anyone involved. The same 1993 survey indicated that only five staff members were hurt in escape attempts, and none were reported killed. Twenty inmates suffered escape-related injuries, and two died. The deaths of three private citizens were also reported for that year (Lillis 1994).

In addition to recording escapes, officials also keep figures on prisoners who "walk away" from a low-security facility, work release assignment, or furlough. In 1993, there were over five thousand reported "walk-aways," or AWOLs, in forty-three prison systems surveyed (Lillis 1994).

We also know that escape risk can be predicted. Whether institutions attempt to do this and, if so, how effective they are is not known. The most common predictive characteristics include race, previous escape history, type of crime

for which the inmate was arrested, prior employment history, and juvenile record (Thornton and
Speirs 1985; Staffer et al. 1985; Murphy 1984).
Although obtaining and adequately assessing a
juvenile record may be difficult, the other characteristics are readily available and easily assessed. Property offenders are more likely to escape than violent offenders. Whether that is
connected to the nature of the crime, rather than
the institution, is a subject for further research.
Most likely, however, it is due to the lower level
of security afforded property offenders.

Escapes and the Surrounding Community

With the current push to build more prisons and
boot camps, the NIMBY (Not In My Back
Yard) syndrome will continue to affect the siting of prisons. Most towns do not want a prison
in their backyard; it is okay for someone else's,
but not theirs. Part of that concern has to do
with escapes. As Carlson (1990) found, however, escapes do not concern all residents in the
same way. In fact, most residents adjust to the
institution and the potential for escapes and
come to see the institution as tolerable and beneficial. Indeed, apart from the movies, there are
few reports of escapees breaking into neighborhood residences. Most escapees want to get as
far away as possible, primarily because the area
immediately surrounding the prison will be the
first and most intensively searched.

Conclusions

Little is known about escapes, especially from
jails, and the subject is therefore ripe for research.
What is known, however, is fairly reassuring and
should probably be communicated to residents
in and around institutions to allay their fears.
Escapes, while a concern, occur fairly infrequently, and, as the corrections population continues to grow, the number of escapes declines.
In the vast majority of cases, escapees are caught
and returned. Moreover, escape risk can be predicted and measures can be taken to reduce the
opportunity for escape. Some states credit the
decline in escape and walk-aways to prison improvements, tightening of furlough rules, restrictions on work release eligibility, and better staff
training. Oregon has created a fugitive unit to
search for its escapees. California, Massachusetts, and Indiana have installed electric "death"
fences around the perimeters of several institutions that will immediately electrocute anyone
coming in contact with the fence.

Jeffery P. Rush

See also ALCATRAZ, SECURITY AND CONTROL

Bibliography

Carlson, K. A. (1990). Prison escapes and
community consequences: Results of a
case study. *Federal Probation* 54(2):
36–42.

Herrick, E. (1989). Inmate escapes 87 and 88.
Corrections Compendium 14(4): 9–12.

Lillis, J. (1994). Prison escapes and violence
remain down. *Corrections Compendium*
19(6): 6–9.

Murphy, T. (1984). *Prediction of Minimum
Security Walkaways*. Lansing, Mich.:
Michigan Department of Corrections.

Staffer, C. E., D. Bluoin, and C. G. Pettigrew
(1985). Assessment of prison escape risk.
*Journal of Police and Criminal Psychol-
ogy* 1: 42–48.

Thornton, D., and S. Speirs (1985). Predicting
absconding from young offender institutions. In D. Farrington and R. Tarling,
eds. *Prediction in Criminology*. Albany,
N.Y.: State University of New York Press.

Executions in the United States

The earliest recorded lawful execution in America was in 1608 in the colony of Virginia. Captain George Kendall, a councilor for the colony,
was executed as a spy for Spain (Espy and
Smykla 1987). Since then, more than fifteen
thousand legal executions have been performed
in the United States under civil authority. The
vast majority of those executed have been men;
only about 2.5 percent have been women. Ninety
percent of the women executed were executed
under local, as opposed to state, authority,
and the majority (87 percent) were executed
prior to 1866. The first woman executed was
Jane Champion in the Virginia colony in 1632
(Schneider and Smykla 1991). Currently, only
about 1.5 percent of death row inmates are
women, and the only woman executed in the
United States since 1968 was Velma Barfield,
who was executed in North Carolina on 2 October 1984.

About 2 percent of those people executed
in the United States since 1608 have been juveniles, that is, people whose offense was committed prior to their eighteenth birthday. The first
youth lawfully executed in America was Thomas Graunger in Plymouth colony in 1642 for
the crime of bestiality (Streib 1988, 251). The
youngest nonslave legally executed in the

United States was Ocuish Hannah in New London County, Connecticut, on 20 December 1786; he was twelve (Schneider and Smykla 1991). The last youth executed in the United States was Dalton Prejan in Louisiana on 18 May 1990 for the crime of "aggravated" murder. About 1 percent of current death row inmates are juveniles.

Prior to the mid nineteenth century, lawful executions in the United States were conducted in public under local authority. These public spectacles were believed to have an educational and deterrent value and sometimes drew thousands of people to the carnival-like atmosphere. The word *gala* aptly describes the atmosphere in which many early executions took place. Beginning in the 1830s, however, a trend toward private executions began, when some state legislatures required executions to be moved inside county jails or prisons. One reason for that move was to escape the mobs that frequently were incited either by botched executions or last-minute reprieves. The first "private" execution (except for a few designated officials and relatives of the condemned) occurred in Pennsylvania in 1834. New Jersey, New York, and Massachusetts conducted executions in private the following year (Bowers et al. 1984, 8), all presumably under local authority. The last public execution occurred nearly one hundred years later in 1937 in Galena, Missouri (Bedau 1982, 13).

The movement from local to state-authorized executions came later. The first person executed under state authority was Sandy Kavanagh, who met his fate at the Vermont State Prison on 20 January 1864. After Kavanagh, however, there were only about two state or federally authorized executions per year well into the 1890s; the rest were locally authorized (Bowers et al. 1984, 43 and 50). In the 1890s about 90 percent of executions were imposed under local authority, but by the 1920s about 90 percent were imposed under state authority (Bowers et al. 1984, 54–55). Today, all executions are imposed under state authority (except for the federal government and the military).

The only period of any length during which there were no executions in the United States was between 1968 and 1977, when an informal moratorium on executions was observed pending the outcome of litigation that challenged the constitutionality of aspects of the punishment itself. (There were also no executions in 1978 and 1980.) The litigation culminated in the 1972 landmark decision of *Furman v. Georgia,* in which the Supreme Court for the first time in its history held that the death penalty, as administered, constituted "cruel and unusual punishment" in violation of the Eighth Amendment. What the Court found to be a problem in *Furman* was that Georgia's death penalty statute gave the sentencing authority (judge or jury) complete discretion to decide whether to impose the death penalty or a lesser punishment in capital cases. A result of that sentencing discretion, according to some of the Court's majority opinions (nine separate opinions were written), was that the death penalty had been imposed arbitrarily, infrequently, and often selectively against minorities. It is important to emphasize, however, that the Court did not rule that the death penalty itself was unconstitutional, only the way in which it was being administered.

The practical effect of the *Furman* decision was that the Supreme Court voided the death penalty laws of some thirty-five states, and over six hundred men and women had their death sentences vacated to a term of imprisonment. By the fall of 1974, however, thirty states had enacted new death penalty statutes that were designed to meet the Court's objections. The constitutionality of those new statutes was quickly challenged, and, on 2 July 1976, the Supreme Court announced its rulings in five test cases. In *Woodson v. North Carolina* and *Roberts v. Louisiana,* the Court rejected "mandatory" statutes that automatically imposed death sentences for defined capital offenses. In *Gregg v. Georgia, Jurek v. Texas*, and *Proffitt v. Florida* (hereafter referred to as the *Gregg* decision), the Court approved several different forms of "guided-discretion" statutes. These statutes, the Court wrote, struck a reasonable balance between giving the jury some guidance and allowing it to take into account the background and character of the defendant and the circumstances of the crime. The most dramatic effect of the *Gregg* decision was the resumption of executions on 17 January 1977, when the state of Utah executed (at his own request) Gary Gilmore by firing squad.

Currently, the statutes of thirty-six states, the U.S. government, and the U.S. military authorize execution as punishment for the most heinous crimes (the District of Columbia and fourteen states do not). Only a little over half of those thirty-six jurisdictions, however, have put someone to death since executions in the United States

E

resumed in 1977. Altogether, about two hundred people have been executed in the United States since 1977. Over half of them have been executed in Texas, Florida, and Louisiana, and nearly 85 percent of the executions have taken place in the southern states of the old Confederacy. Texas alone has executed nearly twice as many people as any other state. What makes these states unique, in the last decade of the twentieth century, is that they are the only jurisdictions among all Western industrialized societies to continue to execute criminals.

As late as the eighteenth century, criminals in the United States occasionally were executed by such barbaric methods as pressing, drawing and quartering, and burning at the stake (Bedau 1982, 15). After adoption of the Eighth Amendment, however, which prohibits cruel and unusual punishments, the only acceptable method of execution for a century was hanging (Bedau 1982, 15). The one exception was in the case of spies, traitors, and deserters, who could be shot under federal law (Bedau 1982, 15). Today, there are five methods of execution authorized in various jurisdictions: hanging, firing squad, electrocution, lethal gas, and lethal injection. Only a few jurisdictions authorize execution by hanging, firing squad, or lethal gas. While as many as ten states allow electrocution, the most common method is lethal injection, authorized by almost half the states.

Oklahoma was the first jurisdiction to authorize execution by lethal injection in May of 1977. The rationale of the Oklahoma legislature was at least in part economic. Repairs to the electric chair, which had not been used since 1966, would be expensive, as would the construction of a gas chamber. Death by lethal injection, on the other hand, was estimated to cost no more than $10 or $15 per "event" (Bedau 1982, 17). Another factor in favor of lethal injection over other methods of execution was the possibility that a condemned criminal would be able to donate bodily organs for medical transplants, something that Gary Gilmore had wished but was unable to do (Bedau 1989, 17). A third rationale for lethal injection is that it is more humane than other methods of execution (Zimring and Hawkins 1986).

The idea of using lethal injection as a method of execution is not a new one. It was first proposed in New York in the 1880s (Bedau 1982, 17; Zimring and Hawkins 1986, 107). The New York legislature rejected lethal injection in favor of electrocution, however, at least in part because of forceful arguments that electrocution was more humane (Bedau 1982, 17; Zimring and Hawkins 1986, 107). In any event, the first person in the United States executed by lethal injection was Charlie Brooks in Texas on 7 December 1982 (Zimring and Hawkins 1986, 120–21).

With the exception of lethal gas, each of the execution methods currently authorized has been challenged on the grounds that it constitutes cruel and unusual punishment in violation of the Eighth Amendment. The Supreme Court, however, has not found any of the following methods or aspects of execution unconstitutional: shooting (*Wilkenson v. Utah*, 1878), electrocution (*In re Kemmler*, 1890), a second electrocution after the first attempt has failed to kill the condemned (*Louisiana ex rel. Francis v. Resweber*, 1947), hanging (*Andres v. U.S.*, 1948), and lethal injection (*Heckler v. Chaney*, 1985). Given wide public support for capital punishment in the United States—about 75 percent of the public currently favors it for first-degree murderers (Gallup and Newport 1991)—it seems unlikely that the penalty will be abandoned anytime soon.

Robert M. Bohm

See also DEATH ROW

Bibliography

Bedau, H. A. (1982). *The Death Penalty in America*. 3rd ed. New York: Oxford University Press.

Bowers, W. J., G. L. Pierce, and J. F. McDevitt (1984). *Legal Homicide: Death as Punishment in America—1864–1982*. Boston: Northeastern University Press.

Espy, M. W., and J. O. Smykla (1987). *Executions in the United States, 1608–1987: The Espy File* (machine-readable data file). Ann Arbor, Mich.: Inter-University Consortium for Political and Social Research.

Gallup, A., and F. Newport (1991). Death penalty support remains strong. *Gallup Monthly Report* (June).

Johnson, R. (1990). *Death Work: A Study of the Modern Execution Process*. Pacific Grove, Calif.: Brooks/Cole.

Schneider, V., and J. O. Smykla (1991). A summary analysis of executions in the United States, 1608–1987: The Espy file.

In R. M. Bohm, ed. *The Death Penalty in America: Current Research.* Cincinnati, Ohio: Anderson.

Streib, V. L. (1988). Imposing the death penalty on children. In K. C. Haas and J. A. Inciardi, eds. *Challenging Capital Punishment: Legal and Social Science Approaches.* Newbury Park, Calif.: Sage.

Zimring, F. E., and G. Hawkins (1986). *Capital Punishment and the American Agenda.* Cambridge, Mass.: Cambridge University Press.

E

F

Federal Bureau of Prisons

On 14 and 27 May 1930, President Herbert Hoover approved two acts establishing the federal prison system. With the power of the federal government (and the federal purse) behind it, the Federal Bureau of Prisons soon became an innovator and leader in correctional management and operations. The Federal Bureau of Prisons is an entirely separate system from the state and local correctional agencies. It is designed to deal only with those who have violated federal laws.

Federal prisoners were originally placed in state and local institutions to serve their sentences. One of the first acts of Congress encouraged the states to pass laws providing for the incarceration of federal offenders in state institutions. Most of the states did pass such laws, and all federal offenders sentenced to one year or more served their sentences in state facilities. Offenders who were sentenced to terms of less than one year or those being held in detention awaiting trial were usually confined in local jails.

In 1870, Congress established the Justice Department. A general agent in the Department of Justice was placed in charge of all federal prisoners in state and local institutions. Later, the general agent became the superintendent of prisons, responsible to an assistant attorney general for the care and custody of all federal prisoners.

State prisons became seriously overcrowded in the period that followed the Civil War. With increasing numbers of both state and federal prisoners, many states became reluctant to take federal prisoners when they could not even care properly for their own. In some states, only federal prisoners from that state were accepted. In 1885, there were 1,027 federal prisoners in state prisons and approximately 10,000 in county jails. By 1895, those numbers had risen to 2,516 federal prisoners in state prisons and approximately 15,000 in county jails.

On 3 March 1891, the U.S. Congress authorized the construction of three penitentiaries, although their funding was not approved until later. The establishment of federal prison facilities was considered necessary because of the states' reluctance to house federal prisoners, the exclusion of federal prisoners from contract labor, and the increasing number of federal and state offenders.

Early Federal Prison Facilities

In 1895, the Department of Justice temporarily acquired the surplus military prison at Fort Leavenworth in eastern Kansas. For the first time, federal prisoners—those transferred from state institutions as well as new commitments—were confined in a federal facility. On 10 July 1896, Congress appropriated funds for the construction of a penitentiary capable of holding twelve hundred inmates, three miles from the prison at Fort Leavenworth. The penitentiary was built by convict labor and the Fort was then returned to the military. The new Leavenworth obtained its first prisoner in 1901, although the facility was not totally completed until 1928.

The United States Penitentiary at Atlanta, Georgia, was built in 1899, and a third penitentiary, located on McNeil Island, Washington, was constructed between 1872 and 1875. The Auburn style of architecture, characterized by multitiered cell blocks and a fortresslike appearance, was adopted in all three penitentiaries.

Between 1900 and 1935, American prisons, including federal institutions, were primarily custodial, punitive, and industrial. Nevertheless, there were significant developments during the early 1900s that brought a larger number of people under federal criminal jurisdiction. The number of offenders incarcerated under those new statutes swelled the federal prison population beyond the capacity to hold them. Largely because of the population increase in the federal prisons, in 1925 Congress authorized a reformatory for "male persons between the ages of seventeen and thirty" that was constructed in Chillicothe, Ohio. (This facility is now an Ohio correctional institution.)

By the 1920s, the number of female prisoners warranted the building of special federal facilities. In 1927, a new five-hundred-bed prison for women opened at Alderson, West Virginia.

In 1929, when overcrowding reached a critical stage in the New York City area, the state and local authorities ordered all federal prisoners removed from the Tombs and the Raymond Street Jail. Responding to this crisis, a federal detention center was built in a newly constructed three-story garage and called the Federal Detention Headquarters.

The Bureau of Prisons is Born
In 1929, Congress created the House Special Committee on Federal Penal and Reformatory Institutions. After extensive deliberations, legislation was drafted, passed, and signed into law by President Herbert Hoover on 14 May 1930, creating the Federal Bureau of Prisons within the Department of Justice. Sanford Bates was appointed by President Hoover to be the first director of the Bureau of Prisons. The selection of Bates signified that the attitude toward penal administration appointments in the federal government had shifted away from political patronage.

Early Growth of the Federal Bureau of Prisons
It was obvious that three penitentiaries, a reformatory for young men and one for women, a jail, and eight camps did not meet the growing needs of the federal prison system. It was decided to build new structures or remodel existing structures to serve as regional jails.

In the early 1930s, the old New Orleans Mint was modified for use as a jail. A new regional jail was opened at La Tuna, Texas, primarily to house the influx of immigration-law violators. A similar institution was opened near Detroit at Milan, Michigan. Another penitentiary was added at Lewisburg, Pennsylvania, and a men's reformatory was constructed west of the Mississippi River at El Reno, Oklahoma. A hospital for mentally ill prisoners (and for those with chronic medical ailments) was opened at Springfield, Missouri. The crime wave of the 1930s, combined with the expanding role of the federal government in crime control, brought the old military prison on Alcatraz Island in California under the control of the Department of Justice.

Recent Developments
Public attitudes toward criminals and society's response to them were influenced by many factors during the 1980s. Chief among those were the increasing number of convicted offenders and the growing problems in administering prisons. Inmate disruptions at Attica and other institutions provided opportunities for the public to reexamine the prison's goals.

After a 1987 uprising by one thousand Cuban inmates held at the federal Oakdale facility in Louisiana and fourteen hundred held at the federal penitentiary in Atlanta, a public outcry was raised. The Cubans, part of the Mariel group of 100,000 refugees admitted into the country in 1980, had taken hostages and overrun both facilities after hearing on their radios that twenty-five hundred "undesirable" (Marielito) Cubans were about to be deported to Cuba. A siege of both facilities went on for eleven days, ending with the release of eighty-nine hostages unharmed. The decision by the Department of Justice to hold no one responsible for the millions of dollars in damage to the institutions was widely criticized. A call for law and order prompted a public debate about crime and criminals similar to the one that had occurred in the 1930s. In response to this public concern, the Bureau of Prisons devised a comprehensive master plan with four objectives:

1. Increasing program alternatives for offenders who do not require traditional institutional confinement, thereby minimizing the negative effects of imprisonment, lessening alienation from society, and reducing costs to the taxpayer;
2. Enhancing the quality of the correctional staff by providing increased training opportunities, better working conditions, and heightened professional challenges to inspire continuous personal growth and satisfaction;

3. Improving present physical plants and incorporating new facilities into the system to increase the effectiveness of correctional programs; and

4. Expanding community involvement in correctional programs and goals because, in the final analysis, only through successful reintegration into the community can the former offender avoid reverting to crime.

A significant development during the 1970s and 1980s was the assignment of responsibility for the planning and management of programs for inmates to treatment teams, under the concept of unit management. Although the staff makeup of the teams varied among institutions, they usually consisted of a caseworker, a correctional counselor, and an educational representative. The functional unit approach, or unit management, was also introduced in place of traditional casework programming. The unit management system provides for semiautonomous unit teams.

The bureau's rehabilitation programs and their increasing sophistication were challenged in the mid 1970s by academicians, researchers, and practitioners who pointed out the poor results obtained from traditional rehabilitation programs. In 1975 the medical model of corrections in the Federal Bureau of Prisons was deemphasized, and in its place was substituted a philosophy of rehabilitation, retribution, deterrence, and incapacitation.

The 1970s found the Bureau of Prisons with more new facilities than it had had at any time since the 1930s. A steady increase in inmate population during the first five years of the decade dictated the acquisition of additional and modernized facilities to reduce overcrowding, create more humane and safe living conditions, and make possible closing the three old penitentiaries at McNeil Island, Washington; Atlanta, Georgia; and Leavenworth, Kansas. Only McNeil Island, however, has since been closed. It was sold to the state of Washington to help solve some of its overcrowding problems. The institutions at Atlanta and Leavenworth still serve the overcrowded federal system.

The Federal Bureau of Prisons experienced as much change in the 1970s as it did in any other time in its history; yet many of the activities of the bureau for the most part remain unchanged. This apparent contradiction could be explained as the result of contradictory demands from Congress, the public, professional correctional personnel, and others who on the one hand wish prisons to be secure and to protect the public and, on the other, wish in some way to reform prisoners.

Organization and Administration
The Federal Bureau of Prisons provides administration at the central office in Washington, D.C., and at five regional offices. The central office comprises the director's office and four divisions: Correctional Programs; Administration; Medical and Services; and Industries, Education, and Vocational Training. Each division is headed by an assistant director. There is also an Office of General Counsel and an Office of Inspections, both of which report to the director.

The five regions are headed by regional directors. They are located in Atlanta, Dallas, Philadelphia, Burlingame (San Francisco), and Kansas City, Missouri.

Inmate Populations Explode
The inmate population of the Federal Bureau of Prisons was 71,608 in 1991. It grew to 78,002 by midyear 1993. Federal court sentencing of offenders to longer terms of confinement for serious crimes and the effort to combat organized crime and drug trafficking greatly contributed to sharp prison population increases in 1992 and 1993. The decline in the rates of some crimes has been minimized or eliminated from federal data, primarily because of shifts in the policy of the Department of Justice in the 1970s and a decision by the Bureau of Prisons not to house juvenile offenders, who made up a large portion of those convicted of auto theft.

Community Programs
Prison space is a scarce and costly resource, to be used in situations where the interests of society must be protected. Because of the continuing record-high prison populations, the use of alternatives to incarceration for nonviolent offenders became essential. A large number of prisoners are confined in Bureau of Prisons contract facilities. Approximately 80 percent of eligible offenders released to the community are regularly released through community treatment centers. Those centers are used for offenders near release as a transition back to the home, job, and community. Time is used to find a job, locate a place to live, and reestablish family ties.

The Community Correctional Center project was implemented in Washington, D.C., in

F

1983. The project uses imprisonment alternatives such as community service, work, and victim restitution when recommended by the U.S. district court. The center is available to federal courts in the District of Columbia, Maryland, and Virginia for sentenced offenders who are not a risk to the community and who may be in custody for up to one year. A second Community Correctional Center was opened in Detroit, Michigan, in September of 1985.

All persons adjudicated under the Juvenile Justice and Delinquency Prevention Act are placed under contract in local and state facilities as well as in such facilities as boys' ranches, group homes, or foster homes. Most adult inmates sentenced to serve less than six months are confined in local jails.

A small number of federal inmates are still housed in state prisons. Those inmates are housed in state facilities primarily for protection purposes, as most have cooperated with the federal government in providing court testimony.

Inmate Classification System

The Bureau of Prisons' inmate classification system has been in effect since April of 1979. Variables such as severity of offense, history of escapes or violence, expected length of incarceration, and type of prior commitments are used to determine an inmate's security level. The system groups the forty-seven institutions into six security levels. Institutions labeled "Security Level 1" provide the least restrictive environment, whereas the "Security Level 6" institution in Marion, Illinois, is the most secure. Security level is determined by the type of perimeter security, number of towers, external patrols, detection devices, security of housing areas, type of living quarters, and the level of staffing.

The Federal Bureau of Prisons is now responsible for carrying out the judgments of federal courts whenever a period of confinement is ordered. The institutions range from minimum to maximum security and employed twenty-four thousand people in 1993. In its growth projections, the bureau plans to have 115 facilities on line by 1995, to provide for the anticipated increase in prisoners. Almost eighty thousand inmates are confined in federal institutions. All sentenced offenders who are medically able are required to complete regular daily work assignments. In addition, all offenders have opportunities to participate in education, vocational training, work, religion, and counseling programs.

The classification system, designed to place offenders in the least restrictive institution possible that is closest to their homes, has proven effective. Security Level 1 inmates account for approximately one-third of the federal inmate population. Only six federal institutions are maximum security. Although Marion was built in 1963 to replace Alcatraz, it did not obtain its level six classification until 1979.

UNICOR: Federal Prison Industries, Inc.

Federal Prison Industries, Inc., with the corporate trade name UNICOR, is a wholly owned government corporation that sells its products and services to other federal agencies. UNICOR's mission is to support the Federal Bureau of Prisons through the gainful employment of inmates in diversified work programs.

Eligible inmates confined in the Federal Prison System are employed by UNICOR. Occupational training is also offered through UNICOR. This includes on-the-job training, vocational education, and apprenticeship programs. There are hundreds of formal training programs in various trades offered by federal institutions. Apprenticeship programs, registered with the U.S. Department of Labor's Bureau of Apprenticeship and Training, exist at about two-thirds of the federal institutions. An active program of plant modernization and expansion of industries began in 1983 and continues in hopes of providing meaningful activity for the growing prison population.

Education and Training

The Federal Bureau of Prisons provides academic and occupational training programs to prepare inmates for employment upon release. Program options are extensive, ranging from Adult Basic Education (ABE) through college courses. Occupational training programs include accredited vocational training, apprenticeship programs, and preindustrial training.

A mandatory literacy program has been implemented for inmates since 1983, requiring all federal inmates to be able to function at a sixth-grade educational level. Those who could not were required to enroll in the ABE program for a minimum of ninety days. In 1986, the standard was raised to an eighth-grade literacy level, the nationally accepted functional literacy level. In 1991, the Crime Control Act of 1990 (P.L. 101-647) directed the Federal Bureau of Prisons to have in place a mandatory functional literacy program for all mentally capable inmates. The bureau voluntarily raised the standard to twelfth grade and required participation for a minimum of 120 days. All promotions in Federal Prison Industries and in institution work assignments were made contingent upon the inmate's achieving literacy.

The Adult Basic Education program has been quite successful. Certificates for completion of the General Education Development (GED) program have been awarded to thousands of inmates. English as a Second Language (ESL) is also provided for all who need it. Projects are funded by UNICOR to provide job training in such fields as computer sciences, business, diesel mechanics, water treatment, petroleum technology, graphic arts, and food service.

Staff training provides every bureau employee with the knowledge, skills, and abilities required to ensure high standards of employee performance and conduct. The staff training network is composed of the Staff Training Operations Office, Washington, D.C.; a Staff Training Academy at the Federal Law Enforcement Training Center in Glynco, Georgia; a Management and Specialty Training Center in Denver, Colorado; and a Food Service and Commissary Training Center at the Federal Correctional Institution in Fort Worth, Texas. All new employees are required to undergo four weeks of formal training during their first forty-five days with the Bureau of Prisons.

Treatment and Other Services

All inmates are afforded opportunities for pursuing their individual religious beliefs and practices. The bureau's full-time chaplains are assisted by religious advisers from the community working under contract, and by community volunteers. Religious activities are among the most well-attended programs in the institutions.

A professional psychology staff provides a wide range of mental health services to inmates and provides psychological evaluations of offenders when requested by federal courts. Bureau psychologists coordinate suicide prevention, drug abuse, and employee assistance programs. They also screen new institutional commitments, and assist in the classification of offenders. Additionally, psychologists provide training to staff and serve on interviewing panels for new employees.

A wide range of medical and dental services are provided to meet the needs of the inmate population. In the majority of cases, medical care is provided within the prison. Community facilities are used to supplement that care as necessary. The primary medical referral centers are located in Rochester, Minnesota; Springfield, Missouri; and Lexington, Kentucky. More limited medical services are available at the Federal Correctional Institution in Terminal Island, California. Psychiatric services are available at the Federal Correctional Institutions in Butner, North Carolina; Lexington (women only); Terminal Island; and at the medical centers in Springfield and Rochester.

The Federal Medical Center in Rochester, Minnesota, was activated in 1985. The facility added 110 medical and surgical beds and 128 psychiatric beds to the system. There are also outpatient beds for medical, surgical, and psychiatric cases. A chemical dependency unit provides evaluation and treatment services for chemically dependent patients. The center also provides medical services to both male and female inmates and obtains medical assistance from the Mayo Clinic, also located in Rochester.

Changes in the "Quality" of Federal Inmates

The Federal Bureau of Prisons was looked upon for years as dealing with just the "cream of criminals." Whether true or not, the times are changing, and the federal system incarcerates many serious and violent offenders today. There is now critical overcrowding across the system and violence in the more secure facilities. In 1984, Congress created the U.S. Sentencing Commission as an independent body, located in the judicial branch of the government. The commission began its work in 1985 and submitted new guidelines that have dramatically altered sentencing practices in the federal criminal justice system and have had a major impact on the correctional administrators in the Bureau of Prisons in the form of a massive increase in the numbers and types of inmates confined in federal institutions, institutions that were already overcrowded.

Clifford E. Simonsen

See also Alcatraz; Bates, Sanford; Fort Leavenworth; Marion Penitentiary; MacCormick, Austin

Bibliography

Federal Bureau of Prisons (1993). *Annual Report*. Washington, D.C.: U.S. Government Printing Office.

Kline, S. (1992). A profile of female offenders in the Federal Bureau of Prisons. *Federal Prisons Journal* 3(1): 34.

Roberts, J. W. (1990). View from the top. *Federal Prisons Journal* 1(4): 27–55.

U.S. Department of Justice (1979). *The Development of the Federal Prison System*. Washington, D.C.: U.S. Government Printing Office.

Films

Since the beginning of the motion picture industry, audiences have been intrigued by the images of prison on film. Characters have gone to prison, come back from prison, and been followed through their terms in prison. In the latter films, plots invariably contained cruel guards and administrators, backbreaking labor, assaults, riots, exploitation, and escapes. Some prison films have been based on actual prison experiences, while others have created imaginary heros and villains, dramatizing the hopelessness as well as the triumph of the human spirit locked behind prison walls. The symbolism of the prison is its separation from society, the unveiling of basic survival instincts, and the primitive struggle of good and evil.

One of the earliest of the well-known prison films, *The Big House* starring James Cagney, told a tragic story of how a relatively minor conviction could lead one down the path to death and destruction. Almost fifty years later, the violence of prison was similarly captured in films like *Bad Boys* (1983) starring Sean Penn.

Infamous prisons such as Alcatraz inspired several films, including *Birdman of Alcatraz* (1962) starring Burt Lancaster and *Escape from Alcatraz* (1979) starring Clint Eastwood. Attica and San Quentin have also prompted their share of films.

Escape has been a popular theme. Steve MacQueen and Dustin Hoffman gave exceptional performances in a biography of the man who escaped from Devil's Island in *Papillon*. A young American escaping from the brutal insanity of a Turkish prison was the subject of a powerful 1978 film, *Midnight Express*. *Mc-Vicar* (1980), starring rock singer Roger Daltry, provided an interesting glimpse of a British prison in the story of a famous escape.

Maverick administrators (such as Robert Redford as Arkansas reform warden Tom Merton in *Brubaker*, 1980) and infamous gangsters have also made for popular legends. In *American Me* (1994), director and star Edward James Olmos tells the story of southern California gang members building a life in prison. Portrayal of the fictional tragic hero in *Cool Hand Luke* (1967) helped showcase the talent of actor Paul Newman, although George Kennedy won the Oscar for supporting actor in that film.

Other notable feature films have included a look at early American territorial prisons in *There Was a Crooked Man* (1970) starring Kirk Douglas and Henry Fonda; *The Glass House,* based on a novel by Truman Capote, with Alan Alda (1972); and *The Longest Yard,* starring Burt Reynolds (1974). While some of those films were relatively accurate presentations of life behind bars, most have been filled with fantasies, fabrications, and illusions based on what a storyline needed or on what a director or writer believed a prison to be. In all, prison films may be like any other genre of theater: mostly illusion, but still worthy of analysis for what they tell us.

Marilyn D. McShane

Force, Use of

Use of force by correctional personnel is most often judged in terms of its reasonableness. An officer's actions are compared with expectations about how much force should be necessary to compel prisoners to act or to stop acting in a certain manner. There are three basic types of force used by correctional officers to gain inmate compliance or to deal with emergencies. Force is usually described in degrees of seriousness: minor use of force, major use of force, and deadly force.

Minor use of force involves any physical contact with an inmate in a confrontational situation. Some jurisdictions require that touching of inmates, however, be reported as a use of force. Such force is applied to control behavior or to enforce an order. For example, an officer might place his hands on the shoulders of an inmate and turn him toward the direction he wants him to move. Minor force becomes major force when:

1. restraints are applied to restore or preserve order. This would not include routine use of restraints, such as when mov-

ing psychiatric patients or when a high-risk prisoner is transported outside the institution;

2. chemical agents, water, batons, or other "instruments of force" are used;
3. any offensive or defensive physical contact is used, including blows, pushes, or come-along holds; and
4. any injury has been sustained.

Major force becomes deadly force whenever firearms are used. According to United Nations directives, firearms may be used only "in self-defense or in the defense of others against the immediate threat of death or serious injury" (United Nations Principles 1990).

One of the most difficult things for an officer to learn is the proper level of force necessary in a variety of emergency situations. Inmate behavior must often be interpreted, and even the most experienced employees can have difficulty reading the signs and using the proper discretion. Normally, minor force may be required when immediate compliance is needed to maintain order and safety, when verbal persuasion is impractical or fails, or when the usual disciplinary sanctions are inadequate. The use of major force, on the other hand, implies that there is some imminent danger of injury. The force then must be applied to maintain or regain control, particularly in the event of a riot or disturbance. Major force might also be used to prevent an escape or serious property damage.

In most systems, some type of written report must be made whenever major force is used. These reports are usually reviewed for appropriateness of conduct, and employees may be disciplined if it is determined that unnecessary or unreasonable force was used. Reports may also indicate areas of difficulty and enable officials to develop policy changes or special training programs.

A reasonable prelude to the use of major force would be an initial attempt to handle a disturbance with minor force. That would imply that the officer had already listened to and attempted to calm the inmate, secured the area, requested additional staff assistance, tried to restrain the inmate, and, in some cases, called for the use of a video camera if one was not already installed in the area. Deadly force may be indicated in order to prevent life-threatening injury, to stop an escape, or to quell a riot when there has been loss of life and serious injury to others.

According to a study based on use-of-force reports in the Texas Department of Corrections, most incidents occur in the main hallways of the prison or in segregation or solitary areas. Force is most often used to enforce an order that an inmate has refused. Also, most incidents take place during the first and second shifts, when movement is at its peak (Sapp and Lopez 1985). A study of Florida prisons revealed that 44 percent of incidents involving the use of force occurred in housing units (Henry et al. 1994). That same study also indicated that most use-of-force incidents were either fights between inmates (36 percent) or the refusal of inmates to obey orders (35 percent). Further, 44 percent complied when force was used, but 42 percent of the inmates physically resisted the use of force.

Most officers are familiarized with use-of-force equipment during training. That includes restraint equipment such as handcuffs, straitjackets, and belly chains; protective equipment such as riot helmets, gas masks, and batons; and control equipment, primarily chemical agents, pepper spray or gas, and stun guns. With regard to the latter, Tennessee has reported several lawsuits resulting from the use of stun guns, but in each instance such use was found to have been appropriate (Bryan 1994). Further, as stated in several court cases, chemical agents may be used to control only the most serious emergencies and may never be used as a punitive measure. There have been some occasions, however, in which the use of force or chemicals (tear gas) in reaction to a disturbance has been found to constitute cruel and unusual punishment.

One issue constantly facing prison administrators is how to improve the institution's response to situations requiring the use of force. A national survey found that 37.9 percent of the respondents felt that the answer was in more and improved training of correctional personnel. Improved correctional technology was mentioned by 31.6 percent, 28.8 percent desired more use-of-force technology, 25.4 percent mentioned additional personnel, and 19.8 percent advocated more interpersonal communications training (Henry et al. 1994).

Legal Aspects of the Use of Force

The concern administrators have about the use of force is further reflected in their investments in training correctional officers on the proper use of force and the development of written policies that explain procedures for reporting use-of-force incidents. Prison officials realize that the courts are likely to view the unnecessary use of force or injuries resulting from such force as cruel and unusual punishment in violation of the Eighth Amendment. That was the case in a lawsuit brought by inmates following the Attica riot. The prisoners claimed in *Inmates of Attica Correctional Facility v. Rockefeller* that the actions of the guards following the resolution of the riot constituted retaliatory brutality:

> Injured prisoners, some on stretchers, were struck, prodded or beaten with sticks, belts, or other weapons. Others were forced to strip and run naked through gauntlets of guards armed with clubs which they used to strike the bodies of the inmates as they passed. Some were dragged on the ground, some marked with an "X" on their backs, some spat upon or burned with matches, and other poked in the genitals or arms with sticks. According to the testimony of the inmates, bloody or wounded inmates were apparently not spared this orgy of brutality.

The standards for determining when the use of force violates an inmate's constitutional rights were first expressed in 1973 in *Johnson v. Glick*. In that case the court considered the following:

1. The need for the application of force
2. The relationship between the need and the application of force
3. The seriousness of the resulting injury
4. Whether the motivation behind the use of force was a good faith effort to maintain or restore discipline or a malicious desire to harm

In addition to these criteria, the court may also look at punishment standards such as those evaluated in *Gregg v. Georgia*. In that case, the Court held that punishment (force) was excessive if it involved the "unnecessary or wanton infliction of pain" or if it was out of proportion to the severity of the crime itself. For example, in *Sampley v. Ruettgers*, the Tenth Circuit Court applied the "unnecessary and wanton infliction of pain" standard to a case of the use of force by a correctional officer. The judges declared that the inmate would have to show a "severe pain" or "lasting injury" before they would find that the force used had violated the Eighth Amendment.

That decision was recently altered by the U.S. Supreme Court in *Hudson v. McMillian*. That 1992 decision made it clear that an injury did not have to be permanent, serious, or significant to constitute cruel and unusual punishment. Hudson was beaten while handcuffed and suffered bruises and cracked teeth. The court decided that the harm caused by the officer was malicious and sadistic and therefore unconstitutional.

The criteria established in *Johnson* and in *Gregg* have also been expanded to interpret the constitutionality of the force used during a prison riot. In *Whitley v. Albers* (1986), the Supreme Court added two additional considerations: the extent of the riot's or disturbance's threat to the safety of prison personnel and other inmates, and the efforts made to lessen the severity of force used. In this case, the Court placed an extremely heavy burden on the inmate plaintiffs to show that the defensive action taken by the officers was unconstitutional. The assumption that the Court made was that during a riot all actions taken by officers are defensive. The Court recognized that in a riot the guards must react, and they do not have the benefit of hindsight that later evaluators do. Therefore not every infliction of pain that in retrospect seems unnecessary will constitute a violation of civil rights. The majority in that five-to-four decision was supportive of the individual officer's judgment and discretionary action in a riot or disturbance. Ironically, the disturbance in this case was precipitated by the inmates' perception that guards were using unnecessary force in escorting a couple of intoxicated prisoners.

Carl P. Wagoner
Marilyn D. McShane

See also VIOLENCE

Bibliography

Bryan, D. (1994). Dealing with violent inmates: Use of non-lethal force. *Corrections Compendium* 19(6): 1–2, 23.

Henry, P., J. Senese, and G. S. Ingley (1994). Use of force in America's prisons: An overview of current research. *Corrections Today* 56(4): 108, 110, 112, 114.

Sapp, A., and P. Lopez (1985). Use of force situations within the Texas Department of Corrections. Paper presented at the annual meeting of the American Society of Criminology, San Diego, California.

United Nations Principles on the Use of Force by Law Enforcement Officials, 8th United Nations Congress on the Prevention of Crime and the Treatment of Offenders, 27 August 1990.

Cases

Hudson v. McMillian, 503 U.S. 1, 112 S.Ct. 995, 117 L.Ed.2d 156 (1992)

Inmates of Attica Correctional Facility v. Rockefeller, 453 F.2d 12 (1971)

Johnson v. Glick, 481 F.2d 1028 (1973)

Sampley v. Ruettgers, 704 F.2d 491 (1983)

Whitley v. Albers, 475 U.S. 312, 106 S.Ct. 1078, 89 L.Ed.2d 251 (1986)

Fort Leavenworth

The Leavenworth area has long been host to many and varied penal institutions. The Oklahoma Territorial Jail was located there even before Kansas was a state. That facility became the first state penitentiary shortly after statehood was achieved in 1861. Fort Leavenworth, the U.S. Army Disciplinary Barracks (USDB) (also known as "The Castle"), was established by congressional action in 1874. It is the oldest federal penitentiary in existence, predating both the Atlanta and Leavenworth penitentiaries by almost twenty-five years.

While established and administered by the U.S. Army, Fort Leavenworth has twice been given to the U.S. Department of Justice (DOJ) to be used as a prison for civilian offenders. The first transfer came in 1895 and lasted until 1906. It was during that time that the DOJ constructed the nearby Leavenworth penitentiary. Prisoners from the fort were marched to the construction site of what would be the first United States penitentiary (USP) for federal (nonmilitary) prisoners ever built. Inmates toiled twelve hours each day with only a short break for lunch, and anyone disobeying an order was chained by the leg to a twenty-five-pound ball. The second transfer of authority came in 1929 and lasted until 1940. Since 1940, Fort Leavenworth has been operated exclusively by the Department of the Army.

One of the main objectives of the prison, established in the beginning and continuing today, was the correctional training of prisoners. Fort Leavenworth holds the distinction of having established the first vocational training program in this country for prisoners. It now encompasses thirteen vocational training shops, including a farm and an award-winning greenhouse. In addition, the USDB provides a variety of educational, recreational, and religious programs for its inmates. Fort Leavenworth is also one of the relatively few penal institutions to achieve accreditation by the American Correctional Association (ACA).

With an inmate capacity of 1,777 (in times of national emergency that number can be increased to 5,000) the USDB is the only maximum-security confinement facility in the Department of Defense. It houses all felony offenders from the U.S. Army, Air Force, Marines, and Coast Guard. The USDB also houses, by special agreement, women and naval officers convicted of felonies (Cohen 1983). Its two-fold mission is to incarcerate people sentenced to confinement under the Uniform Code of Military Justice and to provide correctional treatment and training, care, and custodial supervision to military prisoners so as to prepare them for useful civilian lives.

Unlike civilian institutions, the USDB houses generally older and better-educated inmates; the majority average three and a half years of service in the military. Most inmates are first-time offenders. Military drill, appearance, and discipline are maintained throughout the institution.

The inmates in the USDB have been incarcerated for crimes similar to those for which civilians are imprisoned. Most of the inmates have committed a violent crime, with almost one-half confined for sexually related offenses. Approximately 12 percent of the inmates are incarcerated for drug-related offenses. Somewhat interesting is the small number (approximately 1 percent) of inmates incarcerated solely for military crimes. The commandant explains this situation by saying, "[T]hese individuals happened to be in the military when the crime was committed but the military is not the reason the crime was committed" (Cavanaugh 1983, 49).

There are presently six men on death row in the basement at Fort Leavenworth. Although nine soldiers have been put to death since the Uniform Code of Military Justice was established in 1950, the last execution took place in 1961, when a young private was hanged for rape. The military's use of the death penalty was suspended until 1984, when it was reinstated by President Reagan. Military executions now employ lethal injection.

Jeffery P. Rush

See also FEDERAL BUREAU OF PRISONS

Bibliography

Cavanaugh, C. G., Jr. (1983). Behind the walls. *Soldiers* June: 42–52.

Cohen, R. L. (1983). USDB. *Military Police Journal* 10(4): 18–19.

USDB (undated). *United States Disciplinary Barracks*. Fort Leavenworth, Kansas.

G

Gangs

One of the most significant developments in American prisons in the last two decades has been the emergence of inmate gangs. Committing almost every type of infraction of institutional policy, gang members are five times more likely to be involved in institutional violence than are other inmates. In some prisons, gang members have imported the identity and power of their street gangs. In others, inmate gangs with no prior outside affiliation have developed. Although prisons across the country cannot agree on a common label ("security threat group," or "disruptive group") and many administrators feel politically pressured to deny the existence or true impact of gangs, gangs exist in every prison system and major jail.

In comparison to the quantity of literature addressing street gangs, little attention has been given to inmate gangs. What has been written about prison gangs can be divided into the practically oriented "who they are and what they do" literature of the trade journals such as *Corrections Today*, and the theoretically oriented "why they form" literature, which addresses inmates' social organization. Both types of analysis are necessary in drawing a total picture of the prison gang. This is particularly true in light of the changing nature of prison gangs, which has been documented by many intelligence reports.

Federal, state, and local gang coordinators report that the influx of street gangs into America's correctional institutions is drastically changing the nature and focus of gang activity and management. Organization is expected to be more fluid, activity less predictable, and prevention or interdiction much more difficult.

History

The Gypsy Jokers Motorcycle Club, in the Walla Walla, Washington, state penitentiary in 1950, was the first prison gang on record. The exact date of its origin differs according to different official sources. Today, it is commonly accepted that the gangs in most of America's prisons are either incarcerated members of street gangs or have ties to, or are patterned after, gangs that originated in the California prisons.

John Conrad, the former director of research for the California Department of Corrections, contended that the success of the Black Muslim movement began the erosion of the old order. He argued that inmates with far less worthy goals were shown that inmates could successfully organize and that the prison administration could be challenged. That gave rise to gangs founded on ethnic solidarity or common cultural backgrounds.

John Irwin, a former prisoner at Soledad in California, chronicled the evolution of young, unorganized, juvenile-prison graduates into well-organized, racially radical gangs who controlled the inmate economy. He suggested that the radicalization of the inmate-rights movement by blacks so frightened the white and Hispanic prisoners that racial tensions provided the catalyst for inmate coalitions along racial and ethnic boundaries.

The first organized California prison gang was formed at Deuel Vocational Institution at Tracey, California, in 1957. The Mexican Mafia, or EME, as it was called, was made up of Chicano inmates from the East Los Angeles barrios. In keeping with its goals of self-protection and control of the underground narcotics trade, the organization spread throughout the entire prison system. Their activities soon expanded to include the entire inmate economy and, in 1967, the first gang-ordered murder occurred at San Quentin. In response to a second homicide at San Quentin, unaffiliated rural and valley Hispanics formed the Nuestra Familia (the Family) and confronted the EME in the "war of the shoes." The first violent confrontation of the two gangs was over an inmate's stolen shoes. A violent feud ensued that continues today.

The radical black faction of inmates evolved from the Black Liberation Army (BLA) and its predecessor, the Black Panther Party. The Black Guerilla Family (BGF), formed in 1971, was the inmate counterpart of the "free-world" BLA. Organized around the revolutionary teachings of Mao Tse Tung, its political orientation forbade the taking of drugs and justified the use of extreme violence in the name of the cause. Its ultimate goal was black nationalist revolution within the United States. Several black gangs have formed in other state and federal prisons, and all are based upon the concept of black political power.

Feeling their position and status within the inmate community being threatened by the emergence of the newly assertive black groups, racist Nazi and biker inmates formed the Aryan Brotherhood (AB) at San Quentin in 1968. Based upon an underlying white supremacist philosophy, the goals of the AB were self-protection and profit. The California Aryan Brotherhood has spread to several other state institutions, as well as the Federal Bureau of Prisons, and a few similar, yet unaffiliated, supremacist gangs have developed in other states.

Gangs were first recorded at Stateville in the Illinois prison system in 1969. These were made up of the imprisoned members of such gangs as the Blackstone Rangers, the Vice Lords, and the Latin Kings. The aggressive black and Latin gangs precipitated counterorganizations among white inmates. By 1989, upon leaving the Illinois system, director Michael Lane estimated that "80 to 90 percent of the inmates in the Illinois prison system have some affiliation with street gangs." Lane suggested that incarcerated street gangs used the prison for recruitment and that gangs with ties to the Chicago area spread into several Midwestern states, including Michigan, Iowa, and Wisconsin.

Although gangs originated within the California prisons, they have spread to states adjacent to California and to Mexico. Some experts attribute the spread of prison gangs to the reincarceration of inmates in various prison systems and to the gang management strategy of interstate transfer. That is particularly true within the Texas system. Its three most prominent gangs (the Texas Syndicate, the Mexican Mafia, and the Aryan Brotherhood) are the result of the re-arrest of gang members from California (the Syndicate is an extension of the TS in California) or developed as unaffiliated branches of California gangs of the same name (Texas Mexican Mafia and the Aryan Brotherhood of Texas).

Prevalence

The most current national research into gangs in America's prisons is a study conducted by the American Correctional Association for the National Institute of Justice (ACA 1994). The study found a total of 1,153 different "security threat groups" (STGs, a term used instead of prison gangs) and 46,190 members. Members constitute 5.9 percent of the inmate population in the adult state prison systems, the District of Columbia, and the Federal Bureau of Prisons. Systems with the greatest number of group members are Illinois (14,900, or 48.1 percent); New Jersey (6,000, or 24.4 percent); California (3,384, or 3.2 percent); Texas (2,720, or 5.3 percent); Federal Bureau of Prisons (2,434, or 3.7 percent); and Pennsylvania (2,181, or 9.8 percent). In addition, many smaller prison systems reported that a significant percentage of their inmates are STG members: Wisconsin (17 percent); Connecticut (9.8 percent); Iowa (8 percent); and Tennessee (8.1 percent). Fifteen states either reported no gangs, were unable to assess the number of members, or refused to release their data.

A total of 479 different gangs were identified nationwide. Twenty-nine systems indicated the presence of the Aryan Brotherhood (not to be confused with the Arizona Aryan Brotherhood or the Texas Aryan Brotherhood), twenty-nine systems reported members of Crips, twenty-six reported Bloods, twenty-six reported Skinheads, nineteen reported Black Disciples, eighteen reported Latin Kings; sixteen reported Vice Lords, ten reported the Mexican Mafia (not to be confused with the Texas Mexican Mafia or Mexikanemi), and eight reported the Texas Syndicate.

Security threat groups include some groups commonly viewed as street gangs, whose members are incarcerated at high rates. The prison gangs most tracked, because of their violent behavior, are the Aryan Brotherhood, the Mexican Mafia, the Nuestra Familia, the Black Guerilla Family, and the Texas Syndicate.

Problems with Measurement

At a May 1993 national prison gang workshop, the thirty-nine participants (all of whom were security or intelligence directors for state prison systems or the Federal Bureau of Prisons) spent over two hours attempting to adopt a label for prison gangs that was both accurate and politically acceptable. The morning ended with an agreement to disagree. Very few systems today use the term prison gang. Several feel that the label is too restrictive, as many of their inmates are street gang members. Others feel that the term is too explosive. Consequently, researchers, administrators, and intelligence officers are not always sure that they are measuring and reporting the same phenomena.

In addition, many systems are either unable or unwilling to validate gang organization and activity. Measurement of gang activity is difficult because few states or localities have instituted intelligence or interdiction programs, and many insist that large-scale disturbances labeled by experts as gang-related are not. Few systems have developed formal identification, confirmation, or tracking systems. Therefore a great deal of activity that many view as gang-related is not officially designated as such.

Even in those systems where sophisticated gang intelligence operations have been developed, the primary emphasis for addressing the problem has been placed on upper-level management. The line officer, or the line supervisor, who is normally the first person to note gang activity, is often self-trained and self-motivated. When such officers leave or are promoted, their replacements frequently begin as novices in developing identification and tracking techniques. Consequently, a great deal of information is lost before the new officer learns to recognize gang activity.

The clandestine nature of gangs is another major hurdle to tracking their activities. One of the cardinal rules of all gangs is secrecy. Violation of that rule can, and often does, mean death. A great deal of information, therefore, is provided by inmates who have decided to withdraw from the gang. As most prison gangs require lifetime membership, however, those inmates are placed on protection, and the information they provide becomes less and less

reliable the longer they are out of touch with other gang members.

Gang Profiles and Activities

As previously mentioned, there are five groups that are universally recognized as major prison gangs. Members of those gangs are as much as five times more likely to be involved in a major infraction of institutional rules than other inmates. These infractions include such activities as assaults and homicides, smuggling drugs into the prison, directing narcotics and weapons trafficking from prison, prostitution, gambling, extortion, and murder for hire both within prison and outside. These activities are often interstate enterprises.

Aryan Brotherhood (AB)

Reported to be in over twenty-nine prison systems, the Aryan Brotherhood was formed in the early 1960s at San Quentin, California. The organization is based on white supremacy, self-protection, and control of certain types of drug trafficking within its institutions. The group is organized along military lines with line members, officers, and a leadership council. Membership is based on "blood in—blood out" (one must kill someone to become a member, and anyone trying to withdraw from the gang will be killed). Noted as the most indiscriminately violent of the major prison gangs, the Aryan Brotherhood does not recognize either the Arizona Aryan Brotherhood or the Texas Aryan Brotherhood, although they have been known to tolerate individual members of those groups within the same institution.

Although the AB originally directed most of its violence against black inmates, they are now reportedly more interested in drug trafficking than racial cleansing or retribution for alleged instances of disrespect by black inmates. In that vein, a great deal of AB violence in the last five years has been directed against its own members who have been judged to be errant.

Mexican Mafia (EME)

The Mexican Mafia operates within at least nine state prison systems and the Federal Bureau of Prisons. Their organizational structure is patterned after the Costra Nostra, from which the concept of the Mafia was taken. It consists of a military chain of command, with leadership based in California. Their primary enemies or rivals are the Nuestra Familia, as the Mexican Mafia's membership is primarily urban southern-

California Hispanics. It also adheres to a blood in—blood out doctrine and demands complete confidentiality from its members. The organization is to be placed above all else, including one's own family. Failure to carry out an order can result in death.

The group's primary activity is drug trafficking throughout the Southwest. It operates within the walls of many of America's prisons as well as many communities outside prison. The EME has developed some rather well-defined international drug connections, as well as some significant relationships with the more youthful street gangs. Reports from several major urban areas within the U.S. indicate that the EME has warned several street gangs to curtail the indiscriminate violence that attracts too much attention from police in neighborhoods within which the Mexican Mafia has active drug, prostitution, or gambling enterprises.

La Nuestra Familia (NF)

Primarily composed of rural, northern-California Hispanics, the NF is much more structured than the Mexican Mafia. Rank is achieved by the number of hits (murders) a member makes or is involved in. Governed by a board of directors, the group maintains a "kill on sight" blood war with the EME. The feud between the NF and the EME has been so violent that prison systems normally house the members at entirely different institutions, if possible (some systems maintain only one maximum-security institution). The NF is engaged in much the same type of enterprises as other prison gangs. Although they do not have the extensive drug connections of the EME, Nuestra Familia members are involved in competition for control of drug distribution in prison.

Texas Syndicate (TS)

Composed primarily of Hispanic Texas natives or residents, the TS formed in the mid 1970s in Folsom to protect Hispanic Texas inmates incarcerated in the California system from the violence between the Mexican Mafia and the Nuestra Familia. Once viewed as the most dangerous of all prison gangs, the TS has weathered challenges from the Texas Mexican Mafia and several other prison gangs for control of the illegal narcotics trade within eight state systems and the Federal Bureau of Prisons. Although the majority of its members reside in Texas institutions or Texas communities, leadership remains in California.

A paramilitary-style structure is governed by an extensive set of rules. Membership is for life, and violation of the rules may result in death. The syndicate's reputation for patience in waiting for an opportunity to punish violators is legendary. Many believe that the TS never forgets.

Black Guerilla Family (BGF)

Formed in San Quentin in 1966 by George Jackson, the BGF is a Maoist revolutionary group. Members consider themselves political prisoners and are extremely violent, often assaulting staff. The BGF has been involved in assaults and murders of law-enforcement personnel and armored car robberies. They also share in the prison economy.

The BGF has developed relationships with a number of black street gangs, and many of its current members were members of street gangs prior to incarceration. They are not, however, as organized on the streets as are the other major prison gangs. Their organizational structure consists of a single leader, a central committee, and a loose ranking of soldiers. The BGF is reported to be loosely affiliated with several of the Chicago street gangs.

Gang Management

Gang organization and violence has had a great impact on the day-to-day management of America's prisons. Management strategies have proven costly and, at times, ineffective. Many management plans exist. Some systems have sophisticated programs that have been evaluated and refined, while other systems are still operating in a crisis mode. Recognizing the vital importance of a comprehensive approach to gang organization and activity in prisons, the National Institute of Corrections offers a thirty-six-hour seminar in gang management for correctional administrators. It is one of their most requested presentations. Many other management programs exist, most of which contain the following elements:

Identification/Confirmation

Minimum standards of evidence are established for identifying gang members. They usually include admission of membership, tattoos, informants, and possession of gang constitutions, policies, rules, or correspondence.

Tracking

Prison systems have developed different methods of tracking the movement and activity of gang members. Most, however, have attempted to establish a systemwide reception office that is sent information from designated staff members in individual institutions. The information is then disseminated throughout the system on a need-to-know basis. This official communication network provides constant surveillance.

Segregation
Separating gang members from the general population of the prison is a management strategy that is used by most systems. The assumption is that separation will hamper the spread of gang membership to unaffiliated inmates and also hamper the day-to-day activities of the gangs. Most systems house gang members in high-security units. Gangs are also separated from each other to avoid violence.

Transfer
When possible, many correctional systems transfer gang members from one institution to another to keep them from establishing effective operations. Constant movement is thought to keep gangs off guard. An interstate compact was formed by a number of state legislatures for the purpose of transferring troublesome gang members, in the hope of impeding the gangs' growth and activities. Some transfers, however, have proven to *aid* in gang organization and activity, by extending the gangs' range. For that reason, most interstate transfers have been halted and intrastate transfers have been curtailed.

Enhanced Prosecution
Efforts to prosecute prison gang members have been intensified in many correctional systems. Some (as in Texas) have appointed special prosecutors to address gang activity. Other states, as well as the federal government, are committed to increased prosecution of gang members. This is particularly true in those areas of the country where prison gangs have been able to expand their activities outside the prison. The 1993 federal prosecution of Texas Syndicate members in Houston and the 1994 prosecution of Mexican Mafia members in San Antonio are evidence of this commitment. Several states have also enacted "gang enhancement" statutes, which provide for more severe sentences if criminal behavior is proven to be gang related. Both strategies appear to be having an impact on the nature and extent of gang activity.

Connection to Street Gangs
Federal, state, and local gang coordinators argue that the influx of street gangs into America's correctional institutions is drastically changing gang activity and management. As street gang members are incarcerated within adult institutions, the average age of gang members declines. These younger gang members are more violent and, although they appear to be learning the institutional ropes from the older gang members, intelligence reports indicate that the youths are not being absorbed into traditional gangs. They are, instead, evolving into unique organizations that pose diverse problems for correctional administrators and gang coordinators. The most pressing issue is the lack of information on young street-gang members. Although most have been through state juvenile systems, little is known about them in adult institutions.

The Sociological Perspective
Though the development of inmate gangs cannot be traced to previously organized street gangs in many of our nation's prison systems, their origin can be found in an adaptation process that includes the importation of cultural, racial, and ethnic biases. Inmate social systems foster gang organization through the integration of internal and external factors. In examining inmate gangs, it is important to differentiate between the sociological ingredients that foster the peculiar development of each racial, cultural, or ethnic coalition and those structural elements within correctional organizations that give rise to the projection of these alliances. Students of inmate social organization theory (social structure of the prison) would argue that the structural elements are based on deprivation, or the prisonization process, while the elements that foster the development of differential racial/ethnic affiliations are the result of an importation of preprison attitudes and values.

Many would therefore suggest that inmate behavior such as gang organization and activity is sociologically based on the prisonization and inmate subculture assertions of Clemmer and Sykes, who claim that attempts to adapt to the deprivation of incarceration dominate behavior, or the suggestions of Irwin and Cressey that behavior classified as part of the prison culture is actually an importation of preprison attitudes and experiences. Although those are commonly viewed as contradictory behavior rationales, a realistic view of modern inmate social behavior interprets importation as encompassing the influence of the deprivations of incarceration.

The basic premise of the deprivation model is that the institutional environment produced by the structure of the prison organization results in an inmate culture that is in opposition to custodial staff. The inmate code that develops in response to the rejection of the formal prison behavior code influences behavior in such a way as to allow inmates to adapt to the pains of imprisonment. The deprivation of liberty, heterosexual relations, goods and services, autonomy, and security make confinement so difficult as to require a group rather than an individual adaptation. Implicit in the assumptions of the deprivation model is the conception of prison as a total institution into which one is socialized only after being stripped of all preprison identity and status (Carroll 1974).

Proponents of the importation model argue that social scientists have overemphasized the impact of the internal influences of prison and have failed to recognize the impact of external behavior patterns on inmate conduct. Irwin and Cressey argue that the inmate subculture is not unique to correctional institutions. In order to accurately define prison conduct, a distinction has to be made between the inmate society as a structural response to the problems of incarceration and behavior that determines solutions to those problems. Though they concede that inmate societies result from the internal conditions of prison, they argue that solutions are guided by the latent culture of external experiences.

Indeed, it would appear that importation would best explain the racial tension and subsequent gang organization within many of America's prisons. Yet the importation model is seen by many to be misunderstood as a contradiction to deprivation theory. Carroll (1974) states that such a contradictory view represents an undue polarization when each may represent inmate organization under different conditions. Many researchers support this assertion. It appears the importation model is simply an evolutionary consequence of deprivation theory and that although most major prison gangs can be traced to preprison attitudes and values, conditions within the institutions have greatly influenced when and to what extent gang activity and violence occur. The political and social unrest of the 1960s and 1970s altered the prison structure in such a fashion as to greatly increase the impact of preprison self-identities and subsequently provide fertile ground for inmate gang development.

Mary E. (Beth) Pelz

See also PRISONIZATION

Bibliography
American Correctional Association (1994). *Gangs in Correctional Facilities: A National Assessment.* Washington, D.C.: National Institute of Justice.
Camp, G. M., and C. G. Camp (1985). *Prison Gangs: Their Extent, Nature and Impact on Prisons.* Washington, D.C.: U.S. Department of Justice, Office of Legal Policy.
Camp, G. M., and C. G. Camp (1988). *Management Strategies for Combating Prison Gang Violence.* South Salem, N.Y.: Criminal Justice Institute.
Carroll, L. (1974). *Hacks, Blacks and Cons: Race Relations in a Maximum Security Prison.* Lexington, Mass.: Lexington.
Irwin, J., and D. R. Cressey (1962). Thieves, convicts and the inmate culture. *Social Problems* 10: 142–55.
Pelz, M. E., J. W. Marquart, and C. T. Pelz (1991). Right-wing extremism in the Texas prisons: The rise and fall of the Aryan Brotherhood of Texas. *Prison Journal* 71(2): 23–37.
Pelz, M. E., and C. T. Pelz (forthcoming). *When Brotherhood Leads to Violence: Inmate Gangs in the Texas Prisons.* New York: Garland.

Howard Belding Gill (1890–1989)
Howard B. Gill directed the construction of the Massachusetts Correctional Institution at Norfolk, Massachusetts, and was its first superintendent. No less an authority than the dean of American criminology, Edwin Sutherland, hailed Norfolk at the time as the "most noteworthy achievement in the field of penology in the United States in the last generation."

Gill referred to Norfolk as a "community prison," reflecting his belief that offenders could be rehabilitated in an environment that mirrored the outside world as much as possible. A wall was necessary to guarantee safe custody, but it also made possible the development of a community without undue restraints. Inside Norfolk's walls was a campus-style arrangement of buildings: an administration building, a school, a hospital, a church, a community recreation building, twenty-three residential units (each designed for fifty men living in individual rooms) and several fields for recreation. The day-to-day supervision of inmates was in the hands of house-officers, caseworkers who lived with the inmates. Uniformed guards provided only perimeter security. Prison uniforms were abandoned in favor of ordinary clothing, and inmates did not march to and fro but were merely expected to be at their assignments at the appointed time.

Under Gill, Norfolk was managed through a system of "cooperative self-government." Inmates elected a council, and members of this council served, as equal members, with administrative staff on a wide variety of committees charged with setting policy and managing the various aspects of institutional life. This joint participation and shared responsibility of both staff and inmates set Norfolk apart from earlier attempts at inmate self-government, such as Thomas Osborne's Mutual Welfare League at Auburn and attempts at Sing Sing that had excluded staff.

The policies and procedures that Gill put into practice at Norfolk were not the result of a full-blown plan but rather were developed inductively as need arose. Before his appointment to head Norfolk in 1927, Gill had no experience as a correctional administrator. Born in Lockport, New York, he graduated from Harvard College in 1912 and the Harvard Business School in 1914. For the next decade, he worked as an efficiency expert for several engineering firms in Massachusetts and taught at the Harvard Business School. By virtue of both education and experience, he developed a keen appreciation for the influence of physical space on human behavior.

Immediately prior to coming to Norfolk in 1927 he had been retained by the Department of Commerce and the Department of Justice to study prison industries, an assignment that took him into most of the major prisons in the country. In the course of his journeys, he had been particularly impressed by the District of Columbia Reformatory at Lorton, Virginia, which served as the inspiration for the prison at Norfolk. Within such facilities, he believed it possible to create an organization that provided inmates with the best opportunities to develop a sense of responsibility while simultaneously diagnosing and treating, through social case-

work, the problems that had led them into trouble with the law.

Gill was forced to resign as superintendent of Norfolk in 1934 after several escapes triggered an investigation that, in turn, led to allegations of mismanagement and public outcries against coddling criminals. He went on to Washington, where he served as an assistant to the director of the Federal Bureau of Prisons, working mainly on architectural design and the development and management of correctional industries. Later he was appointed general superintendent of prisons for the District of Columbia. He also founded the Institute for Correctional Administration at American University, one of the first centers to provide professional training for prison managers. Throughout his long career, Gill was a frequent consultant to state correctional agencies, the military, and foreign governments around the world.

The ideas that guided Gill in his administration of Norfolk, and that he later taught, had a powerful impact on American corrections during the 1950s and 1960s. The President's Commission on Law Enforcement and the Administration of Justice (1968, 398–415), for example, recommended that even close-custody institutions should be "collaborative institutions." By this, the commission meant that life in such institutions should be kept as similar as possible to life on the outside, that staff be trained as social workers, and that inmates be accorded some responsibility in the management of the institution. Some of these ideas still persist in less ambitious form, as, for instance, in the concept of unit management. Support for most of them, however, evaporated in the 1970s.

The loss of support for radical prison reform is directly traceable to increased concern over crime in the streets and hardening attitudes toward the treatment of criminals. This shift in public sentiment is itself attributable, at least in part, to the downturn in the economy during the 1970s and the loss of confidence in public institutions following the end of the Vietnam War and the resignation of President Richard Nixon. These events undermined faith in the capacity of correctional institutions to rehabilitate, eroded resources for such programs, and created resistance to accepting offenders back into the mainstream of society.

Similar changes plagued Gill's efforts at Norfolk. His greatest success occurred in the early stages, when he and a small group of inmates were constructing the wall and living in temporary wooden housing. The completion of the wall coincided with the descent of the economy into the Depression of the 1930s. Shortly after the wall was completed, the use of inmate labor in further construction was prohibited. Idleness became a severe problem as the population increased dramatically. Relations between staff and inmates became strained as Gill and his staff assumed more authority in the face of mounting disorder.

Violence and disorder were also widespread in the collaborative institutions of the late 1960s and 1970s. Despite their good intentions, those who sought to humanize prisons along the lines laid out by Gill at Norfolk lacked, as did he, a model of administration that permits a stable balance between security and safety, on the one hand, and conditions that promote the development of individual responsibility and rehabilitation, on the other. Gill would not have concluded that the failure of such efforts proved such a balance impossible, any more than he deemed his work at Norfolk a failure. Ever the optimist and pragmatist, he would have urged continued experimentation.

Leo Carroll

See also NORFOLK PRISON

Bibliography

Commons, W. H., T. Yahkub, and E. Powers (1940). *A Report on the Development of Penological Treatment at Norfolk Prison Colony in Massachusetts*. New York: Bureau of Social Hygiene.

Gill, H. B. (1940). *The Attorney General's Survey of Release Procedures*. Vol. 5. Washington, D.C.: U.S. Government Printing Office.

Gill, H. B. (1962). Correctional philosophy and architecture. *Journal of Criminal Law, Criminology, and Police Science* 53: 312–22.

Gill, H. B. (1965). What is a community prison? *Federal Probation* 29: 15–23.

Gill, H. B. (1970). A new prison discipline: Implementing the Declaration of Principles of 1870. *Federal Probation* 34: 29–33.

President's Commission on Law Enforcement and the Administration of Justice (1968). *The Challenge of Crime in a Free Society*. New York: Avon.

Good Time Credit

Credit-based early release from prison or jail, commonly known as "good time," "gain time," or "time off for good behavior," is used in many correctional systems around the world. In the United States, almost every state has a form of good time that allows inmates to be released before serving their entire sentence. A 1989 survey of laws and policies showed that forty-three of forty-nine responding correctional jurisdictions offered good time. The survey illustrated the variability in good time practices across the country. For example, inmates can reduce their sentences by as few as four and a half or as many as seventy-five days for each month incarcerated.

Good time in the United States was conceived in connection with the reform of the American penitentiary and its problems (Parisi and Zillo 1983). New York enacted the first good time law in 1817. Prison inspectors at a new prison in Auburn were empowered to reduce inmates' sentences by up to 25 percent for good behavior and work habits. The policy was initiated as an alternative to the overuse of pardons, and it reflected the reform orientation of early nineteenth-century penology. These developments also mirror a concurrent trend in European penal systems, such as Alexander Machonochie's mark system for earning release from Norfolk Island penal colony (1840 to 1844), the Irish prison system reforms of Sir Walter Crofton (1850s), and earned release and remission systems implemented by Montesinos y Molina in Italy (1835). Subsequently, following the example of other states, New York introduced an expanded good time policy in 1876 that predated the indeterminate sentence by over ten years. While most states instituted some form of good time over the next century, parole policies came to overshadow credit-based early release. Nonetheless, corrections administrators often retained some form of good time in their prison systems.

At least three contemporary rationales are offered for the use of good time, frequently alongside parole. First, good time is believed to contribute to prisoner reform, by encouraging participation in programs aimed at rehabilitation. As an incentive to good behavior, it also strengthens the social skills necessary for a law-abiding life in the community. Second, the power to grant credits is thought to provide corrections officials with a tool for maintaining institutional control and discipline. The prospect of a reduced sentence in exchange for good behavior encourages better conduct among inmates. And the deterrent value of possibly losing credits is thought to lead inmates to refrain from misbehavior.

Finally, release via good time as a "back-end" solution to prison overcrowding has recently become more important. Credit-based discharges may alleviate population pressures if policies permit correctional administrators to facilitate the use of credits, restrain their revocation, or restore previously revoked credits. This use of good time is particularly important in jurisdictions without discretionary parole release. For example, between 1980 and 1983, the Illinois Department of Correction used existing Meritorious Good Time to achieve early release, at a time when inmate populations burgeoned under efficient prosecutions, determinate sentencing, and the abolition of parole (Austin 1986). Provisions to grant emergency good time credits when court-ordered population ceilings are reached have also been justified using the rationale of population management.

How is Good Time Administered?

Four main forms of credit-based early release (administrative, earned, meritorious, and emergency credits) are used in varying degrees within contemporary prison systems. Administrative good time may be automatically awarded to prison inmates, who are frequently credited with all potential credits they can receive upon commitment to custody. Time served is then affected primarily by credits revoked for misbehavior. Good time, rather than rewarding good conduct, is used to sanction poor behavior. This leads some to call it a disincentive, or punishment, system (Ross and Barker 1986).

Earned credit systems are closer to.the original concept of good time as a reward for positive behavior. Inmates reduce their sentences by participating in prison programs or activities such as education and vocational training or prison industries. Meritorious or special good time credits are awarded to inmates who perform exceptional acts, such as donating blood.

Finally, overcrowded prisons and frequent court-ordered caps on inmate populations have encouraged the use of special emergency credit awards. All inmates meeting specific requirements, such as those close to release or nonviolent offenders, may be granted a block of credits that result in early release. These awards are often enabled under existing administrative good time statutes that vest the discretion for responding to population crises in prison administrators, who are empowered to advance inmates' discharge dates (Austin 1986).

Credit-based early release exists in all types of sentencing systems. In some indeterminate sentencing jurisdictions, its coexistence with parole may render it ineffective as a behavioral incentive. For example, good time may be deducted only from the maximum sentence, while parole eligibility is calculated from the minimum. In those states, good time is not likely to be an effective correctional tool, because the parole date nearly invariably precedes the date of credit-based discharge. Jurisdictions also vary with respect to policy on the forfeiture of credits already accumulated, and on whether good time discharges are accompanied by a period of supervision in the community.

The administration of good time, which involves granting, revoking, and restoring credits, is often complex. Frequently, no formal policy or guidance is available to encourage consistent decision-making. In particular, revocation criteria are often ambiguous. These decisions are usually made by corrections officers and staff in disciplinary hearings, during which infractions of prison rules may be penalized by a variety of sanctions. Lost credits may be restored by a prison authority and typically occurs as the inmate nears release. Restoration of what may amount to a substantial number of days is usually not governed by standards specifying the circumstances and amount of time to be restored (Jacobs 1982).

Treatment Disparity

Correctional autonomy fuels the criticism that good time is a hidden system of discretionary decision-making. Since such decisions are not subject to scrutiny by anyone outside the corrections agency, placing substantial control over time served in the hands of correctional officers may exacerbate or shift inequalities introduced at sentencing (Clear, Hewitt, and Regoli 1978). The use of good time can potentially compromise equality of treatment and fairness. While, in principle, inmates are entitled to minimal due process protection for charges potentially involving a loss of good time (see *Wolff v. McDonnell*), subsequent court decisions have largely eroded that protection.

Good time may be revoked for reasons unrelated to the seriousness of the misbehavior.

Studies of the penalties imposed for disciplinary offenses suggest that their severity is often associated with such factors as race, age, and place of incarceration, as well as the severity of the infraction (Flanagan 1982).

Earned credit systems present a potential for unfairness. Some inmates may be excluded without just cause. And others may be willing to participate but be unable, such as sick inmates and those in protective custody.

In recent years, still other questions have been raised about the fairness of good time policies. For instance, differences exist within many prison systems in the number of credits revoked for particular offenses. In four New York facilities, the percentage of prisoners who lost good time credits for disciplinary reasons ranged from 11 to 46 percent of the cases heard. Penalties also vary from one hearings officer to another. And differences in classification status may entitle some inmates to accrue credits faster than others. That was the case for offenders housed in jails rather than prisons, a situation that recently prompted Virginia to propose reform of its system for awarding credits.

Risk to the Community
One of the original goals for good time, reforming offenders and thus reducing risk to the community, is particularly difficult to measure. While no controlled studies to date have examined whether inmates released through credit-based discharges commit more crimes, significant research does exist on risk to the community posed by special early-release programs. For example, the use of meritorious good time credits in Illinois was found to present only a small risk to public safety. Inmates released early were no more likely to commit crimes than those who were not released early. Austin argues that the program increased the amount of reported crime by less than 1 percent (Austin 1986). Research in Colorado also suggests that public safety is not compromised by early release. Under *People v. Chavez* (1983), substantial good time was awarded to inmates confined in jails prior to sentencing. Recidivism analysis of 150 inmates with resulting accelerated release showed no increased likelihood of re-arrest.

Does good time enhance the rehabilitative potential of prison programs? If inmates elect to participate in a credit-granting program simply for the prospect of a reduced sentence, the rehabilitative benefits of the program may be questionable. "Practicing" good behavior in prison may also affect rehabilitation, however, reinforcing the positive skills necessary for a law-abiding life after release. Serious challenges have been raised about the ability of good time to act as a behavioral modifier (Ross and Barker 1986). True behavior modification programs generally require other incentives, immediately granted and explicitly articulated. These conditions are not met in most good time systems.

Prison Discipline
Does good time help the correctional administrator maintain prison discipline? In Indiana, it was predicted that a change from earned statutory good time to a system of formula-based classes of credit time under sentencing reform would make the prisons more difficult to control. Predatory behavior offenses did not increase, although a rise in more minor offenses was reported. Another study, while primarily evaluating the impact of determinate sentencing on prison unrest in California, suggested that serious violations of prison rules increased despite substantially strengthened good time provisions. California prison officials felt that good time was ineffective as a deterrent to misconduct, because it had only limited potential to reduce sentences. Martin Forst argues that inmates in that instance were unlikely to change their behavior on the basis of promised rewards far in the future.

Population Management
Does good time enable administrators to manage the size of their prison populations? Is good time an effective safety valve? Most research says yes. In Illinois, the use of emergency meritorious good time produced a 10 percent reduction in the size of the projected prison population. In Florida, a nearly universal policy of granting unlimited extra good time credit successfully controlled prison population growth, shortening the average time served from two years to less than one (Austin 1991). A recent simulation of the impact of abolishing both parole and good time on the population in Texas prisons predicted dramatic and immediate increases over a six-year period, which would require the construction of 184,000 new prison beds. While good time awards may permit substantial reductions in an inmate's sentence, however, prosecution, sentencing, and parole policy may ultimately be more important in determining population size.

As compared with other elements of American corrections, little is known about how good time operates and what effects it has upon the criminal justice system, inmates, or the community (Weisburd and Chayet 1989). In view of this lack of solid information supporting good time policies and recognizing their potential for abuse, James Jacobs (1982) suggests that good time be abolished, or at the least strictly curtailed and controlled. He and others have argued that good time operates as an invisible system of prison discretion that has not met its purported goals. Recent "truth-in-sentencing" legislation similarly calls for curtailed or eliminated statutory good time and minimal adoption of earned credits. Nevertheless, good time remains an integral part of correctional systems throughout the United States. Indeed, the current population crisis in corrections, combined with reduced discretion among judges and parole boards, has led to increased reliance upon good time as a tool for reducing sentences. Good time will likely remain a fact of correctional life well into the next century.

David Weisburd
Ellen F. Chayet

See also DISCIPLINE, REHABILITATION PROGRAMS

Bibliography

Austin, J. (1986). Using early release to relieve prison crowding: A dilemma in public policy. *Crime and Delinquency* 32(4): 404–502.

Austin, J. (1991). *The Consequences of Escalating the Use of Imprisonment: The Case Study of Florida*. San Francisco: National Council on Crime and Delinquency.

Clear, T. R., J. D. Hewitt, and R. M. Regoli (1978). Discretion and the indeterminate sentence: Its distribution, control, and effect on time served. *Crime and Delinquency* 24: 428–445.

Flanagan, T. J. (1982). Discretion in the prison justice system: A study of sentencing in institutional disciplinary proceedings. *Journal of Research in Crime and Delinquency* 19(2): 216–37.

Jacobs, J. B. (1982). Sentencing by prison personnel: Good time. *UCLA Law Review* 30(2): 217–70.

Parisi, N., and J. A. Zillo (1983). Good time: The forgotten issue. *Crime and Delinquency* 29: 228–37.

Ross, R. R., and T. G. Barker (1986). *Incentives and Disincentives: A Review of Prison Remission Systems*. Ottawa, Canada: Ministry of the Solicitor General of Canada.

Weisburd, D., and E. F. Chayet (1989). Good time: An agenda for research. *Criminal Justice and Behavior* 16(2): 183–95.

G

H

Mary Belle Harris (1874–1957)

Mary Belle Harris's lengthy career in corrections involved positions as superintendent of the State Reformatory for Women at Clinton, New Jersey; assistant director of the Section on Reformatories and Detention Homes for the U.S. War Department; superintendent of the Federal Institution for Women at Alderson, West Virginia; and member of the Pennsylvania Board of Parole. She championed reform and rehabilitative treatment. Her book, *I Knew Them in Prison,* was acclaimed by such notables as Eleanor Roosevelt, Sing Sing Warden Lewis E. Lawes; and the distinguished correctional administrator and author Austin H. MacCormick.

Mary Belle Harris was born within a decade of the Civil War, on 19 August 1874, in Factoryville, Pennsylvania. The oldest of three children, she was the only daughter of John Howard and Mary Elizabeth (Mace) Harris. Her father, a Baptist minister, became president of Bucknell University, over which he presided from 1889 to 1919. Mary Belle was educated along with her brothers at the Keystone Academy, a Baptist secondary school founded by her father. She began her college work at Bucknell University at age sixteen. By her mid twenties she had gained an A.B. in music, an A.M. in Latin and Classics, plus a Ph.D. in Sanskrit and Indo-European linguistics from the University of Chicago. After her doctorate, she taught in schools in Kentucky and Chicago, worked at the famous Hull House, played the organ in various places, and even published musical compositions of her own creation. Later she went to Baltimore to study numismatics at the Johns Hopkins University and to teach Latin at the Bryn Mawr School.

After a trip to Europe, she met with a friend, New York City Commissioner of Corrections Katherine Bement Davis, and accepted an offer to be superintendent of the Women's Workhouse at Blackwell Island. She was thirty-nine when she took over what was considered to be the worst among twelve institutions under the commissioner.

The workhouse contained 150 cells as well as other facilities. There were about four hundred inmates in those cells and the hospital wards; each cell contained four beds on the floor and two suspended from the upper walls. Approximately sixty of the residents were drug addicts for whom no treatment or segregation was provided, and they were a chronic source of eruption. The overall conditions were deplorable. Chaos, in the form of fights, assaults, insubordination, and enforced idleness, prevailed. The workhouse lacked a classification system, nor did it possess work programs, outdoor recreation, or any form of entertainment. Harris found deadly monotony supervised by an inadequate staff of matrons, some elderly and feeble. The resident physician, just prior to Harris's arrival, had been sentenced to a three-year penitentiary term for selling narcotics to the workhouse women.

From such beginnings, this corrections pioneer would reveal what would become the spearhead of her rehabilitative approach to troublesome individuals: firmness and fairness wrapped in a cushion of caring and genuine friendship. While making certain key decisions, such as transferring clearly psychotic inmates to the state mental hospital, Dr. Harris emphasized open lines for personal communications, not leaving the counseling role to a worn-out staff. She would respond to written notes from women, some desperate; some women sought attention, and she served their needs much as a crisis intervention worker would do today.

Fewer than a hundred of the women were provided work, which consisted primarily of garment-making, mending, laundering, cleaning, and assorted chores. The remaining three hundred had no work once their cells were cleaned in the morning, and they were left to vegetate month after month. Their clothing was atrocious; their shoes had no rights or lefts. The beds had no mattresses, and the bedding consisted only of pillows (without cases) and woolen blankets. There were no knives or forks, only spoons—regardless of menu. Such matters the commissioner and the superintendent gradually altered. They created outside exercise yards. They scheduled regular fresh air walks for every woman, along with flower gardening, and established a separate ward for the drug addicts, who received more individualized treatment. In the process, drug contraband was effectively reduced. The Wassermann test was introduced to help free the institution of venereal disease. Those cases, too, were classified for separate facilities and up-to-date treatment.

Over the resistance of those who viewed card playing as taboo, Dr. Harris countermanded the previous rule that matrons were to destroy cards on sight. Instead, she permitted inmates to play cards on the simple condition that they not fight or gamble. She soon learned the merit of removing troublemakers from their audience as quickly as possible. She accepted the importance of occasional catharsis (screaming) for venting of frustration and anger. Whenever possible she dealt with discipline in the privacy of her office rather than where an inmate might lose face. She would shift cell assignments to increase cellmate compatibility. She sought the support of the New York Public Library, which began contributing books for the women to read, leading to the appointment of an inmate librarian.

Dr. Harris celebrated her first workhouse Thanksgiving by bringing the women into their newly remodeled dining room, repainted in red and white and adorned with window plants and dotted Swiss curtains, all gifts she had solicited. For the first time the women had knives and forks, and from that day forward their meat was served on plates instead of in bowls as stew. Harris acquired a piano and a victrola. Listening, playing, singing, dancing, and attending concerts was a privilege earned.

The next assignment for Dr. Harris was a state reformatory in Clinton, New Jersey, that was located over a three hundred-acre farm. Although the inmate population was far smaller than that of the workhouse, there were no teachers and few officers. In her short term at the reformatory, Mary Belle was able to make many improvements. These included measures of self-government for the women prisoners, a dairy run mostly by inmates, and an exit club for women about to be paroled. She discontinued the stigmatizing practice of dressing runaways in red dresses and cutting their hair in disfiguring fashions.

In late 1918, Dr. Harris took a leave of absence to serve in the War Department's section on Detention Houses and Reformatories for Women as assistant director. She was responsible for women and girls arrested in military camps or bases. The women, many of them homeless and infected with venereal diseases, were assigned to health and rehabilitative facilities. Mary Belle helped to establish cooperative advisory boards composed of prominent local women who could maintain programs after they were initiated.

In 1919, Dr. Harris became the superintendent of the State Home for Girls in Trenton, New Jersey. Upon arrival she found the facility in shambles, with rooms deteriorating or destroyed and many of the staff resigned. She recruited several college students from Bucknell University to help teach and coordinate programs.

Although the teenagers were often violent and disruptive, Harris eventually won over most of the girls, the staff, the community, and even a hostile press. She involved much of her staff in classification, thereby enhancing teamwork, diagnosis, and planning. Among other things, she incorporated a credit card system whereby at the end of each day a girl received her pay or credit loss on the basis of effort, conduct, and work. She instituted an elaborate and formal annual graduation ceremony, with parents and guest speakers to honor each class of departing residents. The facility had a chapter of the Camp Fire Girls, courses in home nursing sponsored by the American Red Cross, and special programs for expectant mothers.

Throughout these years, the Harris treatment philosophy was underscored by these beliefs:

1.   It is unnecessary to have elaborate tests and verified case histories in order to

create meaningful programs for new arrivals. She felt that too many administrators and staff utilized lack of information as an excuse for doing nothing.

2. Although psychiatrists play an important role in human adjustment, for the average run of problems, the less attention paid to a child's peculiarities, the better.

3. Harris pioneered the employment of parolees from her own institution in the belief that this served as a model to others who were being asked to hire them.

4. It was illogical to use any kind of important or essential work, no matter how unpleasant its character, as punishment: it degrades a positive conception of labor and the person doing it.

5. Judges should visit the facilities and be familiar with where they are sending individuals.

6. Residents should be given things to do and learn that they can attain and know success, progress, and achievement.

Mary Belle Harris's last assignment began in 1925, when she was sworn in as the first superintendent of the new federal prison for women at Alderson, West Virginia. Because the facility was not yet completed, Dr. Harris was involved in the planning, contracting, purchasing, and building for the site. She emphasized innovations, opportunity, and program options. For example, instead of erecting a massive surrounding wall, so characteristic of traditional prisons, the institution used its red brick for attractive Georgian Colonial buildings. These were arranged around quadrangles she thought to be both dignified and attractive. She insisted on cottages rather than the offensive cell blocks that she had so detested at the workhouse. These enhanced the classification system that she installed. There was no need for heavily armed guards or many other symbols of coercion. Those were replaced with varied educational and vocational offerings, extensive agricultural and physical activities, a system of inmate self-government, plus clubs, hobbies, special celebrations, contests, ceremonies, dances, and other activities designed to motivate and occupy. The women were offered music and other arts, movies, a library, typing, and religious services; they even engaged in charity affairs for the needy outside prison. In Alderson's early years, it was considered a model institution with relatively few serious disciplinary actions and no escapes.

In March of 1941, at the age of sixty-six, Dr. Harris retired from Alderson after a sixteen-year reign as its first superintendent. She returned to her native state of Pennsylvania, where she served briefly on the State Board of Parole until it was dissolved by the legislature just two years later in 1943. The remainder of her life was spent in a combination of community service, lecturing, writing, and travel. On 22 February 1957, Mary Belle Harris died of a heart attack at the age of eighty-two.

Among her writings, a proper epitaph may be found in the following:

> We must remember always that the "doors of prisons swing both ways"; that most of their tenants are coming back to the community to sit beside us in the street-cars, and beside the children of our families at the movies, with no bars between and no wall around them. Unless we have built within them a wall of self-respect, moral integrity, and a desire to be an asset to the community instead of a menace, we have not protected society—which is ourselves—from the criminal. Whether he deserves it or not, we owe it to ourselves as citizens of an enlightened country to proceed more intelligently in our treatment of the prisoner.

Joseph W. Rogers

Portions of this entry previously appeared in Volume 3, Number 9 (1988) of the *Criminal Justice Research Bulletin,* published by the Criminal Justice Center at Sam Houston State University. They are used by permission.

See also DAVIS, KATHERINE BEMENT

Bibliography

Harris, M. B. (1942). *I Knew Them in Prison.* Rev. ed. New York: Viking.

Moeller, H. G. (1980). *Federal Prison System, Fiftieth Anniversary, 1930–1980.* Springfield, Mo.: Federal Bureau of Prisons.

Parker, J. A. (1985). Women wardens. *CJ International* 1(3): 3–5, 221–24.

SchWeber, C. (1980). Harris, Mary Belle, Aug. 19, 1874–Feb. 22, 1957: Prison administrator. *Notable American Women 1950–1975.* Cambridge, Mass.: Harvard University Press.

H

SchWeber, C. (1980). Pioneers in prison: Inmates and administrators at Alderson,
the Federal Reformatory for Women:
1925–1930, the founding years. *Federal
Probation* 44(3): 30–36.

John Haviland (1792–1852)

John Haviland is best known to criminologists
as the architect of the Eastern Penitentiary in
Pennsylvania, which became the prototype for
the Pennsylvania System of prisons. His contribution to the development of prisons in the
United States and the rest of the world is two-
fold: the physical design of the prison and the
humanitarian aspects of the design, which were
unheard of at the time. Although the Pennsylvania System was not widely adapted in the
United States, certain features of the prison
designed by Haviland remain in our structures
today (Johnston 1973).

Haviland was born on 15 December 1792
in Somerset, England. He studied architecture in
London under James Elmes, who was not only
one of the prominent architects in England at
that time but also the author of a pamphlet on
prison planning. His pamphlet showed a famil-
iarity with the works of John Howard, the leading prison reformer in England, who advocated
cleaner and more orderly facilities for prisoners.
It is believed that Haviland was influenced by
this pamphlet and by John Howard's works in
his later designs for prisons (Johnston 1973).

In 1815, Haviland left England for Russia with the intention of joining the Imperial
Engineers. While there, he met Sir George von
Sonntag, a former Philadelphian, who may
have urged him to travel to the United States.
Haviland decided not to remain in Russia, and
he left for America in 1816. He arrived in
Philadelphia, where he opened a school of architectural drawing. Soon he was commissioned to build private residences, public structures, and churches (Johnston 1973).

In 1821, the Pennsylvania legislature passed
an act authorizing the construction of two penitentiaries, one in Philadelphia and one in Pittsburgh. The legislature was influenced by the
teachings of the Quakers, who were responsible
for the Walnut Street Jail, which incorporated
classification of prisoners, solitary confinement,
and hard labor in its program. The legislature
was also influenced by the Philadelphia Society
for Alleviating the Miseries of Public Prisons,
which advocated individual treatment of prisoners according to the motivation for their crimes
and indeterminate periods of imprisonment, in
addition to classification of prisoners and labor.

The first prison to be built was the Western Penitentiary in Pittsburgh, designed by William Strickland. That structure incorporated
solitary confinement in single cells, with no labor. The prisoners were to reform themselves by
contemplating their crimes and reading religious materials while avoiding the contamination of contact with other prisoners. This plan
proved to be a failure, and by the time preparations for the second prison began in 1829, the
legislature passed an act that required solitary
confinement at hard labor in both of the prisons (Barnes 1968).

Haviland drew up the winning plans for
the Eastern Penitentiary in Philadelphia, and
construction began in 1823 and was finished in
1836. He was also commissioned to tear down
the interior of the Western Penitentiary to make
conditions more healthful for the prisoners and
to facilitate prison industry in each cell. During
this same time (the 1830s) Haviland was involved in the construction of a court building
and detention center in New York City that
later became known as "the Tombs" because of
its Egyptian style. In addition, he was supervising the construction of a state prison in Trenton, New Jersey, and he designed state prisons
for both Missouri and Rhode Island (Johnston
1973).

Haviland's most famous prison, the Eastern
Penitentiary, or Cherry Hill, as it was also
known, was based on a radial design. That was
not an original idea, having been influenced by
previously constructed prisons such as the Ghent
Prison in Belgium, San Michele in Rome, and the
Ipswich County Jail in England, and by the
works of both John Howard (Barnes 1968) and
Jeremy Bentham (Johnston 1973). But Haviland
is credited with making original modifications in
those designs to fit the needs of his prison.

His plans consisted of seven wings of outside cells with inside corridors radiating from a
central office and observation building, with
each cell having its own work space and a small
recreation yard attached. The cells were twelve
feet long, eight feet wide, and ten feet high; the
exercise yard was eighteen feet long and unroofed (Barnes 1968). Four of the wings of the
prison had a second story. The top cells were en-
larged to double the size of the bottom cells to
compensate for the lack of an exercise yard
(Ericksson 1976). Each cell had a flush toilet,

tap water, a bunk attached to the wall by chains, and adequate light, ventilation, and warmth, all of which were considered advances at the time (Johnston 1973). The cells contained a clothes hanger, workbench, stool, pewter mug, a bowl for food, a mirror, broom, sheets, blankets, and a straw mattress to fit on the bunk (Ericksson 1976).

The prison itself was a Gothic, gray structure intended to intimidate the prisoner and the public and to act as a deterrent for both. It was also designed with security as a main goal, from the central observation room where all the cells were visible to the floor paving stones, which were joined together in such a manner so as to be inaccessible to prisoners. The prison was consequently much more secure than most prisons of the time. This penitentiary defined the Pennsylvania System of prison reform, which was later replaced in the United States by the Auburn System (Johnston 1973).

Haviland's work was the object of both criticism and praise. Initially, the Cherry Hill Penitentiary was hailed as a great innovation both in the United States and abroad because of its security design and superior accommodations. It was viewed as an enlightened approach to prison reform and a great improvement over the Western Penitentiary. Representatives from various nations visited the Eastern Penitentiary shortly after it was built and hailed the structure as a success. England, Germany, Belgium, Spain, Holland, Switzerland, Finland, Denmark, Sweden, Austria, Hungary, France, Russia, Japan, and Italy all adopted structures patterned after Cherry Hill or Pentonville, the prison designed by Haviland in England in 1842. Two architects from France, Beaumont and de Tocqueville, noted the advantages of the Pennsylvania System for reformation: "In Philadelphia, the moral situation in which the convicts are placed, is eminently calculated to facilitate their regeneration. We have more than once remarked the serious turn which the ideas of the prisoner in this penitentiary take" (Beaumont and de Tocqueville 1964, 82–83). Thus the radial design was reintroduced to the European continent and newly introduced to the Asian continent. Haviland's influence can still be seen there today in the many radial-design prisons. Also, modern architects and art critics have praised the design of the Eastern Penitentiary (Johnston 1973).

Criticism of the Eastern Penitentiary grew in the United States, however, as prisons became overcrowded and costs increased. In Auburn, New York, the warden, Elam Lynds, introduced solitary confinement at night accompanied by congregate work during the day with a silent system of communications. Cells could be built smaller if a work area and separate exercise area were not required. Beaumont and de Tocqueville (1964) noted that the expense of the Pennsylvania System made it impossible to build an exact duplicate in their country. What became known as the Auburn System eventually was adopted in most of the prisons in the United States. That consisted of cells built in tiers with outside corridors and a central dining room, work area, and exercise yard. Prisoners walked to the various areas in a lock-step formation that allowed no time for idle loitering. A system of silence was enforced wherein the prisoners were not allowed to talk with each other and were allowed to communicate with the guards only through hand signals (Johnston 1973).

Critics of the Pennsylvania System also noted that confining the prisoners to their cells twenty-four hours a day was too restrictive and inhumane. It led to mental breakdowns, as had incarceration in the Western Penitentiary in Pennsylvania, where prisoners were in solitary confinement with no work. Critics in more modern times (the 1960s and 1970s) have concluded that the imposing Gothic structure and punitive nature of the system were not conducive to reform, in light of psychological explanations of criminal motivation. Others feel that religious materials should not be distributed to prisoners unless they request them.

Today, Haviland's influence on American prisons can be seen in structures that are designed in the radial model. These include prisons in Kansas, Washington, California, Texas, and Colorado. All of those prisons are specific radial designs or modifications of the radial design (Johnston 1973).

Despite the criticisms of his prison, Haviland continued to be involved in the construction of prisons. In addition, he also designed many buildings in Philadelphia for public and private use. He submitted plans for state prisons in Arkansas and Louisiana and for the District of Columbia, however, that were not used. By 1839 he was not involved in any major prison projects, and he began soliciting work in England, France, and Mexico. The following year, he was again designing plans for prisons in Pennsylvania, as certain counties were then authorized to build their own penitentiaries.

That year, he began construction of a prison in Harrisburg, followed by prisons in Reading in 1846 and Lancaster in 1849. The prison in Lancaster was completed in 1852, shortly before Haviland's death from apoplexy on 28 March 1852 in Philadelphia. Haviland was survived by a son, Edward, who later designed county prisons modeled after his father's work (Johnston 1973).

Haviland is credited with giving the prison building its first design in plan and elevation. When his designs appeared, progress in prison construction temporarily ceased because prison administrators were occupied with the implementation of his plans. Johnston (1973) argues that his greatest contribution was not the radial design, which might have found its way back to the European continent without his impetus or have been introduced in the United States by another architect, but Haviland's high standards of construction, which can still be seen in today's prisons.

Betsy Witt

See also EASTERN STATE PENITENTIARY, PENNSYLVANIA SYSTEM

Bibliography

Barnes, H. E. (1968). *The Evolution of Penology in Pennsylvania*. Montclair, N.J.: Patterson Smith.

Beaumont, G. d., and A. d. Tocqueville (1833). *On the Penitentiary System in the United States and Its Application in France*. Reprinted Carbondale, Ill.: Southern Illinois University Press, 1964.

Ericksson, T. (1976). *The Reformers: An Historical Survey of Pioneer Experiments in the Treatment of Criminals*. New York: Elsevier.

Johnston, N. B. (1973). John Haviland. In H. Mannheim, ed. *Pioneers in Criminology*. Montclair, N.J.: Patterson Smith.

Teeters, N. K., and J. D. Shearer (1957). *The Prison at Philadelphia: Cherry Hill*. New York: Columbia University Press.

United States Bureau of Prisons (1949). *Handbook of Correctional Institution Design and Construction*. Leavenworth, Kans.: United States Bureau of Prisons.

Vaux, R. (1872). *Brief Sketch of the Origin and History of the State Penitentiary for the Eastern District of Pennsylvania at Philadelphia*. Philadelphia: McLaughlin Brothers.

Hawes-Cooper Act

The Hawes-Cooper Act (H.R. 7729, Public No. 669, now codified at 49 U.S.C. Sec. 11507) was passed on 19 January 1929. It placed a legislative restriction on the marketing of goods made by the "forced labor" of inmates. The Hawes-Cooper Act was the result of an unprecedented level of cooperation between organized labor and business, who collaborated in this instance against the sale, production, and distribution of "convict-made goods." According to government statements, the primary aim of the Hawes-Cooper Act was to "restrict the sale of prisoner-made products on the open market" and to "permit a state, if it so chose, to prohibit the sale of prisoner-made goods, whether made in other states or within their own borders."

The primary rationale for the Hawes-Cooper Act was aptly summarized by the Supreme Court in *Whitfield v. Ohio,* which rejected a challenge to Hawes-Cooper as an unconstitutional burden on interstate commerce: "All such legislation, state and federal, proceeds upon the view that free labor, properly compensated, cannot compete successfully with enforced and unpaid or underpaid convict labor of the prison."

Historical Development

While initially heavily influenced by English penal practices, the Colonial United States had gradually developed its own distinct version of the incarcerative ideal. Specifically, the English practice of "transportation"—the shipping of large numbers of convicts overseas to English colonies to work as indentured servants or in prison labor camps—laid the foundation for the use of prisoners as labor in America. Transportation effectively served to alleviate the surplus labor population within England during the period of its use and provided a cheap source of labor during the establishment of the colonies.

During and before the industrial revolution, three distinct but interrelated factors led to the use of inmates as labor in America. First, Pennsylvania passed a law in April of 1789 that set aside a section of the Walnut Street Jail for convicted felons engaged in hard labor. This action helped to combine ideas about the "reformation" of convicts through religious salvation with the practice of "hard labor" and radically transformed American prison development. Later, the Newgate prison and the famous Auburn prison system were developed on this Walnut Street Jail model, including work plants on the prison premises. Second, and related to the first, an important shift in the working philosophy of prison administrators around the turn of the century helped cultivate the notion that prisoners should work for their spiritual as well as their physical livelihoods. While solitary confinement and strictly imposed silence was initially the preferred disciplinary strategy of prison administrators, increasing public attention to the costs of prisons led administrators to examine ways in which prisons could become "self-sufficient," as well as "reformative." Over time, hard labor and prayer became the dual elements of the disciplinary program of early American prison administrators.

Third, and also related to the other two factors, the industrial revolution itself was generating broad and sweeping changes across both American and European societies. Industrial growth across several sectors of the American economy prompted unique opportunities for prison labor. These developments included more efficient production in the garment industry (with the invention of the sewing machine), technologically improved methods for manufacturing farming implements molded from iron in large prison sweatshops, the discovery of oil (and the corresponding need for barrels, which proved a stable inmate product), and the unique ability of inmates to cheaply produce things like brooms, brushes, shoes, and even cigars. Each of these industries relied on the concepts of division of labor and assembly-line production—both of which were uniquely suited to prisons and their populations.

Impact, Adversaries, and Sponsors

The Hawes-Cooper Act addressed five systems of labor used to employ prisoners at the time of its passage:

1. The "lease system," in which inmates were literally "leased" or rented to individual contractors for their labor, often off-site of the prison itself
2. The "contract system," in which the state kept, fed, and guarded inmates in a prison facility, where the inmates performed their labor
3. The "piece-price system," in which a contractor agreed to pay a price for each piece of material produced
4. The "public account system," in which prison administrators determined the line of production in which to engage inmates and then sold the products of inmate labor on a "piece by piece" basis
5. The "state use or state account system," in which state-run prison production was limited to articles for its own consumption and was not permitted to compete with nonprison labor. In the "state account" system, prisoner labor was commonly, and primarily, used for the benefit of governmental agencies.

At the time the Hawes-Cooper Act was passed, more inmates were working under the "contract" and "piece-price" systems than any other. Several key labor organizations lobbied hard for the restriction of prisoner-made goods in the open market. Those who lobbied the hardest were the American Federation of Labor, the General Federation of Women's Clubs, and the United States Chamber of Commerce. The iron-molding and shoemaking industries were particularly affected by prison labor, as state-financed prison facilities required low maintenance (heat, light, and water bills, for example) and almost no pay for inmates. In short, free-market labor could not effectively compete with the lower-priced products of forced inmate labor. A number of measures had been attempted before the passage of the act to limit the impact of inmate-made goods on the market, including the requirement in some states that these goods contain the stamp "state-prison."

Not surprisingly, many prison personnel were against passage of the Hawes-Cooper Act, for a variety of reasons. The Indiana State Prison warden, in 1929, warned that the Hawes-Cooper bill would idle a large percentage of the inmate population. The Missouri Department of Penal Institutions, in its biennial report for 1927–28 stated: "It is our opinion that the passage and approval of this law strikes a death blow to the manufacturing industries now conducted by the Penal Board at the penitentiary and . . . will result in the state being forced to abandon the employment of convict labor in any profitable enterprise." Finally, the American Prison Association issued a resolution stating, "Whereas, idleness in penal institutions is destructive of the physical, mental, moral and spiritual welfare of their inmates, and . . . whereas penal institutions should be made as nearly as possible self-sustaining, and not be a burden upon the taxpayers of their respective states . . . we are opposed to any and all state and federal legislation that would directly or indirectly interfere with the production, manufacture, transportation, or sale of products of penal institutions."

Several legislative acts came in the aftermath of Hawes-Cooper, including the Ashurst-Sumners Act in 1935, the Sumners-Ashurst Act of 1940, and the Walsh-Healey Act of 1936. The last major legislation on prison labor was the Comprehensive Crime Control Act of 1984, which actually encouraged the expansion of prison industries to defray the rising costs of incarceration during the 1980s.

Michael A. Hallett

See also ASHURST-SUMNERS ACT, INDUSTRY

Bibliography

Gildemeister, G. A. (1987). *Prison Labor and Convict Competition with Free Workers in Industrializing America, 1840–1890.* New York: Garland.

Robinson, L. N. (1931). *Should Prisoners Work?* New York: John C. Winston.

U.S. Department of Justice (1987). *Work in American Prisons: The Private Sector Gets Involved.* Washington, D.C.: National Institute of Justice.

Health Care

It has been only a little over two decades since correctional health care emerged as a topic of special interest. Prior to the early 1970s, the United States courts had adopted a "hands-off" policy regarding the administration of prisons. With the advent of the Attica riots, though, both the courts and health professional associations began to look more closely at the type and extent of health care provided to inmates.

The American Medical Association (AMA) undertook a survey of the nation's jails in 1972 that revealed a number of deficiencies in health care delivery. It launched a remedial program in 1975 to address problems of availability, access, and adequacy. Key components of this early program were the development of standards for health care delivery in jails and prisons, and the initiating of a voluntary accreditation program for facilities that met those standards.

In 1976, the United States Supreme Court added its weight to the reform movement by its ruling in *Estelle v. Gamble.* It established that adequate health care was a right that must be extended to all inmates, not a privilege subject to the discretion of correctional officials. The Court held that failure to provide needed medical care constituted "cruel and unusual punishment" proscribed by the Eighth Amendment. It also established the legal standard of "deliberate indifference to serious medical needs," which is still the standard used today in correctional litigation.

Litigation. Litigation is a fact of life for U.S. prison officials. At last count, forty state prison systems had one or more facilities under a class-action suit or court order to improve general conditions. Such suits generally are brought under Section 1983 of the Civil Rights Act and allege that the inmates' living conditions amount to cruel and unusual punishment. The most common conditions at issue in such suits are crowding and health care.

Accreditation. Litigation is a lengthy and expensive way to improve health services. Many correctional administrators voluntarily seek accreditation of their facilities as a way to decrease litigation. The leading accreditation body for correctional health care is the National Commission on Correctional Health Care (NCCHC). It is a not-for-profit organization that evolved from the AMA's early program. NCCHC's board of directors is composed of representatives named by thirty-seven professional associations primarily in the health care and correctional fields (for example, the AMA, American Bar Association, American Nurses' Association, American Psychiatric Association, and the National Sheriffs' Association).

The NCCHC has separate sets of standards for jails, prisons, and juvenile facilities. It offers accreditation of health services for all three types of facilities. NCCHC's standards cover administrative and personnel issues as well as environmental health, preventive care, routine and emergency health services, and medical-legal concerns. Mental health and dental services are addressed, as well as basic medical care.

The U.S. Supreme Court decided in a 1980 case, *Bell v. Wolfish,* that standards developed by professional associations are advisory and do not necessarily define what is minimally required by the Constitution. In practice, though, both the courts and correctional administrators turn to standards of professional groups such as NCCHC to help them define what constitutes adequate health care.

Components of a Model Health Care System. Every prison needs to have an adequate delivery system in place to identify and respond to inmates' medical, dental, and mental health needs. The primary components of a model delivery system are basic ambulatory care, specialty care, inpatient care, and emergency care.

Every prison should have the necessary resources, such as clinic space and health staff, to provide at least basic ambulatory care on site. All new admissions should be screened on arrival by health staff to identify any immediate health needs and to arrange for appropriate follow-up care. Within a week of the initial screening, a more detailed health appraisal should be conducted and treatment plans developed for those patients with special health needs (pregnancy, chronic illnesses, infectious diseases, mental illness or retardation). Inmates also need a way to acquire health services when problems arise during their incarceration. Most prisons hold sick call five days a week, and health professionals are available to respond to acute medical needs.

Each prison also must make arrangements to provide higher levels of care in advance of need. For instance, inmates with ongoing health problems often require referral to specialists such as cardiologists, internists, psychiatrists, or gynecologists. Additionally, emergencies occur that require ambulance service and hospitalization. Most prisons rely on community health resources to provide those higher levels of care.

Patient Profile. People committed to prisons in the United States are overwhelmingly poor and disproportionately minorities. Many of them have not had access to preventive health care. Further, such practices as use of tobacco, substantial drug and alcohol abuse, multiple sexual partners, poor nutrition, and lack of exercise make them susceptible to a host of serious illnesses and debilitating conditions. For example, studies have shown that inmates have a higher incidence of HIV infection, tuberculosis, high-risk pregnancy, and suicide than do people in the community.

Inmates also utilize health services more often than people in the community. On any given day, it is not unusual for ten percent of a prison population to turn out for sick call. Undoubtedly that is partly due to their increased need, but it is also attributable to other factors unique to prison life. For instance, many prisons require inmates to come to sick call to receive over-the-counter preparations for minor complaints that they would treat themselves on the outside. Additionally, inmates may use the health system to avoid work, to socialize with their friends, or to obtain drugs or other contraband. Differentiating inmates' health "needs" from their "wants" is a major challenge for correctional health professionals.

Organizational Structure. Prison health services are organized differently in different states. In the smaller systems, health staff may report directly to the warden of a given institution. In contrast, many of the larger states have a central office health division with line authority over the unit health staff. While most state prison systems still operate their own health services, contracting out health services to national for-profit firms has increased in recent years.

Privatization is especially appealing to those prison systems that have had difficulty in recruiting and retaining qualified health care staff. The management and operation of the health system then become the responsibility of the contractor. The state is still ultimately responsible for ensuring that the health services provided to inmates are adequate, however. Thus, states that have privatized their health services often establish a contract monitoring section in the central office to ensure that the services provided meet standards established by national organizations such as the NCCHC.

Current Issues. Substantial improvements have occurred in the provision of health services to inmates over the past two decades. The development of standards and the accreditation of prison health systems as well as a certification program for correctional health professionals offered by NCCHC have helped to enhance the field. Most prison systems now have an adequate delivery system in place to address inmates' serious health needs, as a result of either voluntary improvements or litigation.

There are a number of areas, though, where additional improvements are needed:

- Containing health care costs
- Improving the quality of the care
- Improving relationships with custody staff
- Controlling the explosion of infectious diseases
- Fostering data collection and research activities for management and planning purposes

- Increasing the professionalism of providers through continuing education
- Emphasizing a public health approach to providing care

Another challenge will be to coordinate the health care given in prison with that of jails and the community. In this age of general health care reform, the failure of most prisons to consider inmates' prior care results in overuse of health resources in some cases and insufficient use in others. A seamless approach to correctional health care is needed both to provide inmates with the care they need and to make the best use of scarce health resources.

B. Jaye Anno

See also AIDS, Legal Issues

Bibliography

American Bar Association (1990). *Guidelines Concerning Privatization of Prisons and Jails*. Washington, D.C.: Criminal Justice Section.

Anno, B. J. (1992). *Prison Health Care: Guidelines for the Management of an Adequate Delivery System*. Longmont, Colo.: National Institute of Corrections Information Center.

Anno, B. J. (1993). Health care for prisoners. How soon is enough? *Journal of the American Medical Association* 269: 633–34.

Glaser, J. B., and R. B. Greifinger (1993). Correctional health care: A public health opportunity. *Annals of Internal Medicine* 118: 139–45.

Kay, S. (1992). *The Constitutional Dimensions of an Inmate's Right to Health Care*. Chicago: National Commission on Correctional Health Care.

Koren, E. J. (1993). Status report: State prisons and the courts. *National Prison Project Journal* 8: 3–11.

National Commission on Correctional Health Care (1992). *Standards for Health Services in Prisons*. Chicago: National Commission on Correctional Health Care.

Weiner, J., and B. J. Anno (1992). The crisis in correctional health care: The impact of the National Drug Control Strategy on correctional health services. *Annals of Internal Medicine* 117: 71–77.

Cases

Bell v. Wolfish, 441 U.S. 98 (1980)

Estelle v. Gamble, 429 U.S. 98 (1976)

History of Prisons

I. The Jacksonian Era

In industrialized Western societies, imprisonment has become the preferred means of punishment for breaking the law. How and why did imprisonment become so popular, and when and where did this occur? Many different forms of punishment have been practiced in other cultures and in other times. There is no logical necessity that punishment require imprisonment, and punishments have often been much more immediate and violent. Were it not for unique ideas and social conditions that converged in late eighteenth-century and early nineteenth-century Europe and America, a very different legacy might have been born.

Conditions in eighteenth-century American jails closely resembled those of their European predecessors, in which inmates were detained under harsh conditions pending state trial or some form of state punishment, complete with fees for jail-keepers. Prior to the American Revolution, however, incarceration as a form of punishment was rare, while public and corporal punishments were the norm. Chain gangs of convicts, wearing distinctively striped prison clothing and watched by armed guards, were sent to work on public roads. Prisoners, easily identified by their garb, were often the target of verbal and physical abuse by a moralistic public. For serious offenses, public hangings, floggings, brandings, and mutilations were common; for less serious offenses, the stocks and the pillory served as visible reminders of the consequences of breaking the law. Colonists' postrevolutionary concern for basic human rights and their fear of unrestrained governmental power over citizens eventually led to calls for reform.

Colonists attempted various criminal code reforms following the Declaration of Independence, based partially upon their own adverse reactions to earlier European experiences and recent oppression by the British, but also upon the influence of Enlightenment thinkers, who emphasized rationality, individualism, and the limitations of government. Particularly influential in the thinking that fueled the adoption of prisons as punishment were the writings and ideas of John Howard, imported from England. Dr. Benjamin Rush and the socially conscious, reform-oriented Quakers played major roles in the U.S. These reformers were successful in getting large portions of state criminal codes rewritten. Death penalties and corporal punishments for crimes except the most serious were abolished, and fines or periods of imprisonment took their place. At about the same time, the newly created states began to build their own state-run facilities for more serious offenders. City or county jails took charge of less serious offenders and pretrial arrestees, while state prisons took charge of the more serious felons, who previously would have faced corporal punishment or execution.

Generally considered the forerunner of American correctional institutions, Philadelphia's Walnut Street Jail was created in 1790 to house and work convicted felons. Although the jail was actually modeled after similar institutions in Ghent and Gloucester, it surely represented a major innovation in American punishment. It was one of the first institutions anywhere to be built or operated according to any concrete principle of penology. The Quakers, long concerned about the inhumane treatment of convicts and the brutalities of the convict labor system, felt that a more humane, rehabilitative means of dealing with offenders was to subject them to solitary confinement or "penitence." By contemplating their sins, in conjunction with solitary work, offenders might eventually repent and rejoin society. These ideas reflected a dramatic change in thinking about punishment. The emphasis began to shift from punishing the body of the criminal toward methods of instilling discipline and self-control. Punishment began to work on the mind and soul of the offender.

The negative effects of extreme isolation (reports of mental anguish and madness), however, were not anticipated; neither was the rapid flow of inmates that soon inundated the jail. In fact, the director of the Walnut Street Jail resigned in disgust in 1801. In 1820, a committee of the Pennsylvania Society of Friends visited the jail and decided that the current building was unfit. Prisoners were not being adequately segregated according to age, sex, or offense. Overcrowding severely weakened the penal goal of reform, and prisoners were too often idle. Larger and better-planned facilities, rather than abandonment of the "separate" system of confinement, were seen as the solution in Pennsylvania.

State prisons based on the Pennsylvania model were erected in Pittsburgh (Western Penitentiary) and Philadelphia (Eastern Penitentiary).

New penitentiaries in Pittsburgh (1821) and Philadelphia (1829) were intended to serve as examples of a new and improved model of punishment for nineteenth-century America and Europe. Even the architecture, originally designed after Bentham's Panopticon model (Foucault 1977; Rothman 1971) was designed to invoke penitence and moral self-improvement. The design, with several long corridors of cells arranged like spokes around a central surveillance tower or hub, was intended to create the feeling that one was constantly under watch (by guards, literally, but by God, metaphorically). Power was visible, but unverifiable. Even today, as one walks down the long corridors of the decayed Eastern Penitentiary, one is struck by the monastic quality. One notices the two-feet-thick walls and the smallness and isolation of the cells (about eight feet wide by ten feet long), illuminated by a narrow skylight (six feet by five and a half inches) that allows a slender ray of sunshine to enter from the heavens. From high at the end of each of the long, narrow corridors, carefully focused illumination enters through a broad churchlike window, offering hope of salvation from above. Religious metaphor is embodied in the prison's construction.

In fact, members of the Prison Society were represented on the Board of Commissioners entrusted with the planning and construction of the prison. In 1787, Dr. Benjamin Rush outlined his ideas for the physical manifestation of the penitence ideology, eventually realized by architect John Haviland in 1829:

> Let the avenue to this house be rendered difficult and gloomy by mountains and morasses. Let its doors be of iron; and let the grating occasioned by opening and shutting them be increased by an echo from a neighboring mountain that shall extend and continue a sound that shall deeply pierce the soul (cited in Atherton 1987, 6).

The building itself was set high above the rest of the city on a hill. The imposing fortress served as a visible reminder of the consequences of sin. "The design and execution impart a grave, severe, and awful character to the external aspect of the building. The effect which it produces on the imagination of every passing spectator, is peculiarly impressive, solemn and instructive" (Teeters 1937, 178).

The emphasis of these influential reformers was clearly upon rehabilitation, yet they were not so naive as to suggest that jails or prisons could or ever should be pleasant places. The Pennsylvania Prison Society noted that their purpose was:

> not to destroy prisons, not to destroy their just terrors, but to have their discipline so regulated that no bad principles in the man incarcerated shall be made worse, and the whole administration of the penal laws so modified and enforced, that no injustice, no extreme of infliction, and no sentiment of maudlin humanity shall make the prison less than a place in which to guarantee society against violence and fraud, and to ensure to the guilty a just punishment for crime, while that punishment is made to minister to the moral improvement of the convicted offender (quoted in Atherton 1987, 4).

The "separate" system lived up to its name. Because of their previous experience with jails, Prison Society members felt that the greatest obstacle to individual reform was contamination by other prisoners. When a new inmate entered the prison, a hood was placed over his head. He was then led to his cell. Once ensconced therein, the prisoner was expected to accept responsibility for his transgressions and accept God's leadership in his life. The prisoner was aided in this spiritual journey by reading the Bible and other books, but also by visits and instruction by prison staff, chaplains, official visitors of the Prison Society, and the Board of Inspectors.

The visiting program complemented the philosophy of the Prison Society and other reformers: concern for the individual, belief in the process of penitence and rehabilitation, and belief that moral improvement required guidance. Over time, visits by prominent citizens and eventually by professional case workers were added. Some of these visitors (for example, Dorothea Lynde Dix) later initiated pleas to remove women, children, and the mentally ill from the prison.

The prisoner was also encouraged to work at a productive trade (such as carpentry) within the confines of his cell. Each cell was furnished with a small workbench for that purpose. In addition, most of the cells opened outside into a small yard slightly longer than the cell, used for exercise or gardening.

A competing "congregate labor" model of incarceration was initiated at Auburn, New York, at about the same time. The Auburn system was based on strict discipline and hard work. As in the Pennsylvania system, inmates were originally to be confined separately. In contrast, though, inmates at Auburn ate and worked together during the day in a large, factory-like setting. Talking between inmates was strictly forbidden. No communication was allowed between inmates at any time, and they were required to march in a military lockstep fashion, keeping their legs stiff and looking straight ahead at all times. Any violation of rules was met with strict punishment, including whippings.

There was considerable competition between the two models, although the Auburn model eventually prevailed. The Pennsylvania system was criticized as too expensive. Its labor was seen as unproductive, and separate (if not entirely solitary) confinement was seen to cause disorientation and even insanity. In fact, the first criticism quickly became moot, because a shortage of space caused both prisons to begin double-celling only a few years after their openings. The Auburn system, proponents argued, could house more prisoners in less space. Because inmates were allowed outside during the day, the cell was needed only for nighttime confinement. It also allowed for more productive, factory-type labor, which required large groups of inmates working on related tasks. Increased movement of inmates required more and better-trained custodial staff to supervise them, however, as well as improved classification of inmates according to their security risks. The cost savings of the Auburn system may have been illusory (early comparative data are not available), but the attractiveness of perceived economic benefits and supporting beliefs in the rehabilitative value of hard work had much to do with the Auburn system's emergence as the preferred model of incarceration in the United States.

As in England, the advent and expansion of the industrial age in America was accompanied by social upheaval and displacement of people from rural to rapidly expanding cities. While the displacement factor appears to have followed, rather than preceded, the construction of many large prisons in America, it is clear that jail and prison capacities even in the early

1800s only rarely kept pace with quickly growing admissions. By the beginning of the Civil War, most large cities or counties had erected jails, and many states (especially in the North and Midwest) had built one or more large prisons. In little more than seventy-five years, the use of prisons had moved from a radical idea to the preferred model of punishment.

Wayne N. Welsh

See also AUBURN SYSTEM, EASTERN STATE PENITENTIARY, PENNSYLVANIA PRISON SOCIETY

Bibliography

Atherton, A. L. (1987). Journal retrospective, 1845–1986: 200 years of Prison Society history as reflected in the *Prison Journal*. *Prison Journal* 67(1): 1–37.

Fogel, D. (1975). *We are the Living Proof*. Cincinnati, Ohio: Anderson.

Foucault, M. (1977). *Discipline and Punish*. Trans. Alan Sheridan. New York: Pantheon.

Howard, J. (1929). *The State of Prisons in England and Wales*. London: J. M. Dent.

Rothman, D. (1971). *The Discovery of the Asylum*. Boston: Little, Brown.

Teeters, N. K. (1937). *They Were in Prison: A History of the Pennsylvania Prison Society, 1787–1937*. Chicago: John Winston.

II. The Progressive Era

Characteristics of the Progressive Era
The period between 1900 and 1930 is often labeled the "progressive era" because of the reforms that took place in penal institutions across the country. Christian principles, a belief in scientific treatment, volunteerism, and the installation of social science experts in policy-making positions characterizes the progressive era. Progressives of the early twentieth century sought to modernize prisons by abolishing the lockstep and striped uniforms, liberalizing correspondence and visitation policies, and burying once and for all the rules of silence (Rothman 1980). They also sought to redesign the prison by creating communities with outdoor recreation, fund-raising events, and psychiatric services.

This same period has also been referred to as the "industrial period" (American Correctional Association 1983, 97) because many prison systems were increasingly involved in manufacturing and the production of materials useful to the military, the public, and the government. Progressives saw the use of labor as a means of instilling discipline and teaching responsibility. They did not, however, believe in labor as punishment or as a way of making profits for the state.

When the United States became involved in the latter stages of World War I (1914–18), the demand for goods was especially strong. Prison industry was not a new phenomenon at the turn of the century, however. Many prisons, especially in the South, had operated large farms prior to, during, and following the Civil War. Prison labor was cheap and convict leasing agreements were commonplace during that period.

The National Prison Association, subsequently known as the American Correctional Association, was established in 1870, with future U.S. president Rutherford B. Hayes as its first president. This organization originated in a milieu of correctional reforms. The Elmira State Reformatory in Elmira, New York, was established in 1876. Inmate rehabilitation was the new concept of the late 1870s. Although inmate rehabilitation persists today as a goal of prisons, correctional experts and authorities are realistic enough to note that the massive rehabilitative movement in penal reform has fallen far short of its originally conceived aims.

Despite the fact that many prisons in the late 1800s and early 1900s either continued or inaugurated different types of prison industries, many systems operated as warehouses to simply maintain and monitor offenders, who were held in idleness. The coming of the Great Depression meant that many prison systems were neglected. Economic distress also meant years of record high unemployment, and Prohibition meant bootlegging and organized crime. The FBI grew to be a powerful crime-fighting establishment under J. Edgar Hoover, and G-men rounded up "gangsters" considered the most dangerous in the country. Looking for the most secure facility possible, the government adopted the island fortress of Alcatraz as their "escape-proof" prison.

Several writers have been critical of such offender warehousing and the potential problems it creates. A number of prison riots in the 1920s were blamed on inmate idleness, arbitrary rules and punishments, and the failure of rehabilitation. These problems were studied by the National Commission on Law Observance and Enforcement (Wickersham Commission) in

1931. The committee continued to recommend improvements in classification, educational and vocational training, as well as camps and farms for less serious offenders.

Progressive Reformers and the Medical Model
Early twentieth-century prison systems became increasingly influenced by the medical model, a treatment orientation in which criminal behavior was regarded as a disease that could be treated with appropriate therapy or medication. In this instance, "medication" was proper inmate management and therapy as rehabilitative strategies. Two of the early proponents of the medical model of management for prison systems were Katherine B. Davis at the women's reformatory at Bedford Hills (1901) and Thomas Mott Osborne, warden of Sing Sing prison (1914). Osborne's early experiences in corrections included pretending to be a prisoner in the Auburn penitentiary for one week. Thus, he was perhaps the first participant observer in a social research experiment. He wanted to know what it was like to experience confinement and treatment from the perspective of an inmate. Subsequently, Osborne experimented with different methods whereby inmates could manage themselves. These attempts at prisoner self-rule were forerunners of present-day inmate disciplinary councils. Although Osborne's intentions and quest for the rehabilitative ideal were honorable, his critics overwhelmed him with various scandals and resistance and his experiments did not achieve fruition.

Another significant actor in the history of American penology was Howard B. Gill (1889–1989). Gill was appointed by the Massachusetts state legislature in 1927 to construct and supervise an innovative prison facility known as the Norfolk Prison Colony. The Norfolk facility was constructed with inmate labor. Thick walls were constructed to surround a complex of old buildings. The walls were constructed nineteen feet high and up to eighteen feet deep. Bartollas and Conrad (1992) suggest that the depth of these walls was to discourage tunneling by escaping inmates, although two escapes were attempted. Gill wanted to create a rehabilitative colony resembling a small community, wherein inmates could learn to reintegrate themselves into society and acquire various skills to help them lead productive lives after their release.

Gill created one of the first prisoner classification systems. He divided inmates into situational, custodial, asocial, medical, and person-

ality cases. He believed that each type of inmate case could be treated by a physician, psychiatrist, teacher, social worker, counselor, or custodian. Prisoners were divided according to their initial classification, with the least dangerous and most "curable" prisoners receiving the widest array of privileges and freedoms. The most dangerous and least treatable offenders were confined with few, if any, amenities. Gill's experiment was unsuccessful because few officers and experts were available to provide the necessary services. Few persons possessed the skills and the requisite expertise to accomplish Gill's ambitious aims. Furthermore, Gill did not realize that prisoners themselves would devise innumerable ways to undermine his plans. Finally, Gill did not realize that chronic and persistent inmate overcrowding would undermine the best attempts to rehabilitate offenders, regardless of the skills of the staff.

One of the major problems facing American prison reformers like Osborne and Gill was that the public was simply not interested in the system. The public abandoned prisons, ignored them, and gave them no support. When that happened, the void created by lack of public interest was often filled by political control. One of the main consequences of political ties is that wardens or prison superintendents traditionally hold office for only short periods of time. When Osborne resigned from Sing Sing in 1916, he was the eighth man to leave that office in twelve years. A short tenure can disrupt prison operations, destabilize other employees, and impede the progress of reforms.

Efforts at reform were also subverted by the insurmountable costs accompanying improvements and the disfavor that incurred among politicians. Also, the more contemporary penological goal of rehabilitation, because of its associated expenses, was not able to overcome the farm-for-profit image that many officials and even some of the public believed in.

Probation, Parole, and the Indeterminate Sentence
The industrial and progressive era had other prominent features. Besides the attempts at institutional reform noted above, other areas of corrections were undergoing transformation simultaneously. For instance, probation had been pioneered by John Augustus (1784–1859) in 1841 in Massachusetts. In 1878, Massachusetts established the first full-time probation

officers to manage nonincarcerated offenders (Shane-DuBow, Brown, and Olsen 1985, 6). Generally, incarceration was believed to be conducive to further criminality. Thus, any means whereby convicted offenders could be diverted from incarceration were used to "save" them from the criminogenic influences of prisons and jails. By the early 1900s, most states and the federal government had probation departments with probation officers.

Consistent with the strong rehabilitative emphasis of the period between 1900 and 1930 was the dramatic increase in the use of parole. Parole is early release from prison, usually as a reward for good behavior. Massachusetts established parole officers in its prison system in 1884. In fact, by 1900, twenty states had established parole systems for their prisoners, and by 1944 all states had them. The U.S. Board of Parole was established in 1930. Parole's uses are several. It functions as a reward to prisoners for good behavior, alleviates prison overcrowding, and makes possible earlier reintegration into society.

Consistent with the medical model was the belief that a person should be confined and treated until such time as the prisoner is ready to return to society. Because treatment was individualized, the appropriate time for each release would be decided by professionals and correctional administrators. Thus, a sentence would be of an indeterminate length. Good behavior, proper remorse, and a waiting job would ensure offenders an earlier parole.

Both probation and parole have been criticized because of relatively high rates of recidivism. Recidivism is the commission of new crimes by previous offenders. Both probationers and parolees have been convicted of crimes, and rates of recidivism among both populations have been as high as 70 percent in some jurisdictions. These repeat offenders, recidivists, cause the public and others to be skeptical of the rehabilitative efforts of penologists and criminologists. It has been found that intensifying management or monitoring during probation or parole does reduce recidivism. Although recidivism will probably always continue to characterize all probation and parole programs to a degree, they are believed by most to be useful for reintegrating the offender into society and as front-door and back-door solutions to prison overcrowding.

Dean J. Champion

See also BEDFORD HILLS CORRECTIONAL FACILITY; DAVIS, KATHERINE B.; GILL, HOWARD; NORFOLK PRISON; OSBORNE, THOMAS MOTT; PAROLE BOARDS; SING SING PRISON

Bibliography
Adamson, C. (1984). Toward a Marxian penology: Captive criminal populations as economic threats and resources. *Social Problems* 31: 435–58.
American Correctional Association (1983). *The American Prison: From the Beginning—A Pictorial History.* Laurel, Md.: American Correctional Association.
Bartollas, C., and J. P. Conrad (1992). *Introduction to Corrections.* New York: Harper Collins.
Dean-Myrda, M., and F. T. Cullen (1985). The panacea pendulum. In L. Travis, ed. *Probation, Parole, and Community Corrections.* Prospect Heights, Ill.: Waveland.
Rothman, D. (1980). *Conscience and Convenience.* Boston: Little, Brown.
Shane-DuBow, S., A. P. Brown, and E. Olsen (1985). *Sentencing Reform in the United States: History, Content, and Effect.* Washington, D.C.: U.S. Department of Justice.
Sullivan, L. (1990). *The Prison Reform Movement: Forlorn Hope.* Boston: Twayne.

III. Modern Prisons: 1960 to the Present

United States prison systems have changed slowly but significantly since 1960. Changes have been made by administrators within prison systems. Some of these changes have been the result of pressures from the public and from the news media, as well as legislative changes. By far the greatest reform has come as the result of federal court intervention. All of these influences have been in response to the changing size and demographics of U.S. prison populations.

Changing Demographics of Prison Populations

Since 1960, the number and characteristics of prison populations have changed significantly. A 1995 Bureau of Justice Statistics publication, based on 1993 data, reported that the number of federal and state inmates had reached 909,000, a record high, compared with 74,952 in 1960. Although the population remains predominantly male and minority, the sex distribution is changing. The percentage of female inmates (a total of 8.4 percent) has increased two percentage points faster than male inmates. The same publication noted that, in 1989, 29.5 percent of inmates were admitted for drug offenses, compared with 4.2 percent of the 1960 population. Prior to 1984 most of the increase was the result of offenders incarcerated for violent offenses. After that date the increase was due primarily to increases in drug offenses.

The *Survey of State Prison Inmates, 1991,* indicated that between 1986 and 1991 the number of state prison inmates incarcerated for violent offenses fell from 55 percent to 47 percent, while the number incarcerated for drug offenses increased from 9 percent to 21 percent. In 1991 about one-fifth of total state inmates were incarcerated for drug crimes, one-fourth for property crimes, and fewer than one-half for violent crimes. In 1991 female inmates were more likely than male inmates to be serving time for a drug offense (33 percent versus 21 percent), but men were more likely to be serving time for a violent offense (47 percent versus 32 percent).

Sixty-four percent of 1993 state inmates were minorities, up from 60 percent in 1986. Sixty-eight percent were under age thirty-five, a decrease from 73 percent in 1986. Although comparable data are not available for earlier periods, 6 percent of 1991 state inmates were members of gangs. In recent years gang membership in prisons has created internal problems, including increased violence, and it has resulted in numerous lawsuits. Other changes have resulted from the discovery of the human immunodeficiency virus (HIV), which leads to the deadly disease AIDS. In 1991 slightly over one-half of state inmates reported that they had been tested for HIV, and of that group 2.2 percent of those who reported the results of those tests indicated that they were HIV-positive, with the number higher among women than among men.

These changes in the demographics of inmates have created problems for prison systems. The growing number of female inmates has necessitated making additional provisions for housing them, as well as for providing equal opportunities for medical, educational, recreational, and other prison facilities. The smaller number of female inmates in the 1960s meant that they had fewer opportunities to take part in prison programs, a problem that has been highlighted by the inmates' rights movement of the late 1960s and early 70s.

The changes in the size and demographics of prison inmates, along with federal court intervention, has created the need for changes in prison facilities and prison administration as well as the need to make internal changes required for the recognition of inmates' legal rights.

Prison Facilities

Historically, U.S. prisons have been large, secure, and located in rural areas. These fortresses reflected the primary purpose of prisons, which was to remove offenders from society and make certain they did not escape. Michael Foucault has argued that reform was a goal of early prisons, too, and that inmates were expected to be changed individuals when they returned to society.

The security goal of these early prisons was reflected in the walls that surrounded many of them and the guard towers at the four corners of those walls. Some had guard towers inside, with cell blocks surrounding them. The reform goal was reflected in the separation of inmates in some prisons and the enforcement of silence in others. It was assumed that inmates would corrupt each other. Likewise, they should not have much contact with the outside world. Visits were limited, including visits with attorneys. Some prisons, such as Alcatraz, located on an island off the coast of San Francisco, were isolated, making it very difficult for inmates to have visitors.

The pressure of numbers and the growing recognition of inmates' legal rights forced changes in prison architecture as well as prison policies. Prison administrators (often prodded by court decisions) recognized the need for inmates to have contact with others and to be provided with reasonable living accommodations and nutritious food, vocational training, work opportunities, education, recreation, health care (including psychological and psychiatric attention), and access to courts. Newer facilities had to be provided to accommodate these needs as well as the growing numbers. Most U.S. prison systems have not been able to accommodate these growing needs; the result is that most are under federal court orders mandating changes.

Classification of inmates (not common in early prisons) has resulted in the construction of facilities that are not the fortresses that earlier prisons were. Minimum- and medium-security facilities have been constructed for male as well as for female and juvenile inmates. The increasing number of female inmates necessitated constructing new space or converting old facilities to accommodate them. One solution was to designate co-correctional prisons, housing both men and women, but in separate quarters. Some prison systems contracted with other systems to house their female inmates.

These solutions were not satisfactory. While co-correctional facilities allow the system to relieve some of the overcrowding, the physical contact issue has caused problems. Such institutions are no longer in use in the federal system, and only a few exist in state systems. When prison systems contract with other systems to house their female inmates, the result is that many female inmates are incarcerated far from their homes and families, increasing the difficulty of visits with family, friends, and attorneys. In addition, many states do not have the space to offer on a contract basis.

The pressure of numbers has forced the expansion of prisons, the building of new facilities, or the conversion of old facilities. That is expensive, especially when the facilities are required by federal court order to meet certain specifications. In the 1990s, many prison systems are facing a crisis. The public is demanding that more offenders be incarcerated and for longer periods, but state prison systems are resisting the high costs of doing so. Some systems have used temporary facilities, such as tents or barges, while others scramble to convert other buildings into acceptable prison quarters. Private businesses have entered the picture in many prison systems. They may construct new facilities and lease them to prison systems. In some systems prisons and jails are owned and operated by private businesses.

Prison Administration
In previous times, the rehabilitation of inmates was considered important, along with security and safety. Today rehabilitation is less emphasized, and security has become the dominant function. Maintaining security has become more difficult because of changes in administration, along with the recognition of the legal rights of inmates and those of prison personnel.

In the past, prison control was maintained by autocratic wardens who developed and enforced strict rules in hiring, disciplining, and firing staff and correctional officers. The officers in turn maintained control by a show of force against inmates or through the inmate social system, wherein some inmates controlled others in exchange for favors granted by the officers. The system ran smoothly in most institutions. Few rights were granted to inmates, and violence and escapes were kept to a minimum.

The building tender system in Texas is an example of the strict control enforced over inmates. The system prevailed until the initial decision in *Ruiz v. Estelle* (1980). This case placed the Texas prison system under court order, where it remained until December of 1992. Prior to the 1980s, inmates known as building tenders (BTs) were given the power to control other inmates. They performed this function in return for special privileges. The BTs maintained control through the use of intimidation and force.

With the *Ruiz* decision, the Texas system was under court order to address the BT system and a multitude of unconstitutional conditions. The change was slow and frustrating because of the changed relationships between inmates and correctional officers. Inmate violence escalated. Correctional officers found themselves in closer contact with inmates than they had been under the BT system. Inmates had little security in their daily lives, and gangs began to develop at an alarming rate to furnish the protection and security that the BT system had once provided.

While the changes brought on by *Ruiz* seemed to cause many unintended consequences in the Texas prison system, it started a search for the balance between due process rights for inmates and security for the prison. As a result of *Ruiz* and other federal court decisions, inmates may not hold positions of power over other inmates, and prison staff and administrators are less likely to maintain control by physical force. The growing recognition of the legal rights of inmates and of correctional officers, as well as the changing demographics within the inmate population and the legal system, have made traditional prison administration obsolete and in most cases illegal. Today, prison administrators are required to incorporate some elements of due process with regard to their treatment of employees and inmates.

Changes have occurred in the profile of administrative personnel as well. Prison wardens have traditionally been white men. While white men continue to occupy most positions as wardens or superintendents of American prisons, women and minorities have been appointed to those positions, too. For example, Kathleen

Hawk serves as director of the Federal Bureau of Prisons. The appointment of minorities is illustrated by the appointment of Harry K. Singletary, Jr., as secretary of the Florida Department of Corrections.

The appointment of women and minorities as administrators and correctional officers has not been met with enthusiasm by all. Some criticize prison systems for moving slowly in these appointments. Nor has it been easy for women and minorities to deal with the resistance from co-workers in a traditionally male occupation like corrections. Some women have had to deal with the resistance of their male counterparts, some of whom may feel that prisons are unsafe for women and that it is their responsibility to protect female correctional officers. The untraditional methods some women use in their jobs may appear to be dangerous to male officers. Misunderstanding of these differences causes tension and conflict among some co-workers.

The diversity issue is complicated further by the issues of opposite gender searches, pregnancy, and sexual harassment in the workplace. One reaction of correctional administrators has been to provide diversity training on gender-related issues as well as issues regarding race and disabilities, such as those covered by the Americans with Disabilities Act (ADA). The state of Maryland is an example. Supervisory staff attend a seminar on the effects of cultural, racial, and gender diversity. The purpose of these seminars is to demonstrate how diversity can be an asset within the workplace. The Maryland seminar and others like it demonstrate a commitment on the part of corrections' administrators to confront diversity issues.

The internal administration of modern prisons is complicated further by the lack of resources, the resistance of some administrators to the changes brought about by the inmates' rights movement, the pressures of numbers, increased violence within prisons, and the internal conflicts among racial groups as well as the problems created by gangs. Contacts with inmates who are HIV-positive or who have AIDS is another problem for prison administrators and correctional officers. Inadequate staff and correctional officer training make it very difficult for prison administrators to respond adequately to all of these problems.

There have been some positive developments. A degree of professionalism is emerging within correctional administration. More educated personnel are being promoted. Professional organizations have begun developing standards. The American Correctional Association has played a major role in the development of these standards, which serve as guidelines for the operation and management of correctional systems. In the past, either guidelines did not exist or they were so inconsistent that they provided limited assistance in the complex operations of prisons. In addition, many correctional managers are beginning to see the importance of correctional research in solving the problems of the modern prison.

Despite these accomplishments, there is room for improvement. Salaries are low, as has historically been the case. In 1993, the average starting pay was approximately $18,374. The average maximum was $29,684 (Camp and Camp 1993). The average starting pay is only a 5 percent increase from 1990, and the average maximum is only an 8 percent increase for the same time period.

The consequences of low pay are many. Solving the problems faced by modern prisons requires the education and training of all personnel. Many people with college degrees are not willing to work for low salaries. If officers receiving low pay get their education while working, they are likely to use the correctional job as a stepping stone to another occupation. Another consequence of low pay is the likelihood of unethical and illegal practices within the prison. When officers are underpaid, they may be tempted to engage in corrupt practices to supplement their incomes. In addition, a lack of education and training means that officers may not be prepared to cope with temptations, which may lead to unethical and illegal behavior.

Since many correctional officers lack a college education, training is the means to correct improper behavior and instill proper practices. In 1993, the agency average for training new officers was 214 hours, with forty hours of annual in-service thereafter (Camp and Camp 1993). Training efforts are complicated by the harsh and deteriorating nature of correctional institutions. The question is whether the average amount of training time is sufficient to overcome the problems that correctional staff face.

While correctional officers may not be well paid or as educated as they should be, there is some indication that the attitudes of correctional officers are changing. In the past, many correctional officers viewed their jobs primarily in terms of security. There is evidence that today many correctional officers view themselves as providing rehabilitation and human services, as well as order and security within the prison.

Another current issue of prison administration is the need to deal with the issue of special needs populations. Because of increasing medical technology, people are living longer. Inmates are living to be older than in the past, and that presents prison administrators with the problems of housing the elderly. Another special needs population within prisons, as within society, are those with learning, physical, and psychological disabilities. The ADA requires prison officials to cope with many of the problems of these individuals. The problems range from minor to severe.

Another special needs group is the women, many of whom have children. Some may be pregnant when they are incarcerated, and provision must be made for their infants. Still others become pregnant in prison. Some modern prisons are attempting to find solutions to these challenges, even providing special-care facilities within prisons for the infants and small children of inmates.

A more serious condition within the institution is that growing numbers of inmates have AIDS or are members of high-risk groups. AIDS is the leading cause of death among inmates. This poses a major health risk for both inmates and correctional staff. Because detection of this disease is so difficult, the best correctional policy has been to educate and counsel all inmates about the disease and to treat everyone within the institution as a potential carrier. This means taking all necessary precautions with everyone in every situation, whether they are known to have the disease or not.

Another problem is gangs. The emergence of gangs within prison has been a major administrative concern for several decades. Prior to the sixties, organized gangs had not formed within prisons perhaps because of strict racial segregation and lack of contact. Once contact was permitted and growing proportions of youths with street-gang backgrounds were incarcerated, many militant gangs, divided by race, began to form. These gangs parallel their outside counterparts in name and allegiance.

Today many states utilize staff to track and study gang activities within the prison system. Various strategies are employed to prevent gang violence and to reduce the number of inmates recruited into gangs. Profiles and training are often provided to assist officers in recognizing gang symbols, tatoos, and messages.

Recognition of Inmates' Legal Rights

The constant media coverage of crime and the resulting fear of crime have caused the public to place pressure on legislatures to do something about criminals. Longer sentences are demanded, and many legislatures and Congress have succumbed to these demands. But correctional officials face the problem of housing more inmates for longer periods of time without additional facilities, budgets, or staff, and while parole options are being cut.

At the same time, prison officials must comply with federal court mandates concerning inmates' legal protections. The recognition of these rights is the greatest change that has occurred in modern prisons.

Historically, the legal rights of inmates have not been an issue. It was assumed that prison administrators could grant privileges, but that few rights existed. A 1871 federal court opinion declared that the offender "has as a consequence of his crime, not only forfeited his liberty, but all his personal rights except those that the law in its humanity accords to him. He is for the time being the slave of the state" (*Ruffin v. Commonwealth*, 1871). In 1974 the U.S. Supreme Court said, "But though his rights may be diminished by the needs and exigencies of the institutional environment, a prisoner is not wholly stripped of constitutional protections when he is imprisoned for crime. There is no iron curtain drawn between the Constitution and the persons of this country" (*Wolff v. McDonnel*, 1974).

In the 1960s and 1970s, federal courts have decided many cases that have expanded the recognition of inmates' legal rights. In so doing, courts have abandoned their previous hands-off policy. However, courts still defer to prison administrators, who, according to the Supreme Court, "should be accorded wide-ranging deference in the adoption and execution of policies and practices that in their judgment are needed to preserve internal order and discipline and to maintain institutional security" (*Bell v. Wolfish*, 1979). In the 1980s and 1990s, the pendulum appears to have shifted back with a more conservative Supreme Court once again emphasizing the need for institutional security, upholding more restrictive administrative policies.

Federal lawsuits have been filed concerning overcrowding, too. Prison systems are under federal court orders to reduce populations, which generally is accomplished by building more prisons or releasing some inmates early. The latter policy has been criticized bitterly, especially when the media highlights a case where an inmate incarcerated originally for a violent offense commits an additional offense soon after release. Some jurisdictions have reacted to the overcrowding issue by designing alternatives to prisons, such as boot camps for youthful offenders. Others have built new prisons, an extremely costly option. Another alternative has been the conversion of other facilities into prisons.

Conclusion

The most significant changes in the United State prison system over the last few decades have come about as a result of demands and pressures from outside the system itself. Increased use of prison sentences, the inmates' legal rights movement, and the decline in the rehabilitative ideal have placed significant stress on all levels of the correctional system.

The nature and characteristics of inmate populations have changed dramatically with the recognition of many special needs groups. The increase in female offenders has strained criminal justice systems, which struggle to meet their needs. Administrators have had to meet the evolving demands placed on the prison system. Although some current administrators are more professional and better educated than their predecessors, problems remain.

As an organization, prison systems have had to respond in significant ways. While efforts to cope with these issues have been impeded by lack of money and training, solutions have emerged. Many innovative and well-planned responses to complex problems have emerged. Progress in technology and architecture as well as advances in medical care and classification have all improved safety and security.

It is evident that prison operations in the nineties are complex at best. Modernization of correctional practice has been the result of demands and pressures from outside, which, while difficult to handle, have forced innovative minds in the prison system to develop the new practices that will take us into the next century. While the road will continue to be difficult, the last three decades of prison operation point to the advances of the future.

Laura B. Myers
Sue Titus Reid

Bibliography

Bureau of Justice Statistics (1992). *Prisoners in 1991*. Washington, D.C.: U.S. Department of Justice.

Bureau of Justice Statistics (1993). *Survey of State Prison Inmates 1991*. Washington, D.C.: U.S. Department of Justice.

Camp, G. M., and C. G. Camp (1993). *The Corrections Yearbook 1993*. South Salem, N.Y.: Criminal Justice Institute.

Murton, T. (1976). *The Dilemma of Prison Reform*. New York: Holt, Rinehart and Winston.

Nagel, W. B. (1973). *The New Red Barn: A Critical Look at the Modern American Prison*. New York: Walker.

Sykes, G. (1958). *The Society of Captives*. Princeton, N.J.: Princeton University Press.

Cases

Bell v. Wolfish, 441 U.S. 520, 99 S.Ct. 1861, 60 L.Ed.2d 447 (1979)

Ruffin v. Commonwealth, 62 Va. 790, 796 (1871)

Ruiz v. Estelle, 503 F. Supp. 1265 (S.D.Tex. 1980)

Wolff v. McDonnell, 418 U.S. 539, 94 S. Ct. 2963, 41 L.Ed.2d 935 (1974)

Homicide

Donald "Pee Wee" Gaskins was executed at 1:04 AM in the electric chair in Columbia, South Carolina, on 6 September 1991. He was put to death because he killed a fellow inmate on South Carolina's death row on 12 September 1982. Wilton Earle (1992) reports that Gaskins committed "the impossible crime" of killing an inmate on death row with smuggled explosives. "Pee Wee" described the scene in the following manner: "Guards was running all over the place. I couldn't get onto the Row to see things for myself, but at my trial I got to see the pictures of Tyner's body and his cell and there were bits and pieces of him stuck all over the walls and ceiling and floor" (1992, 204).

Inmate Tyner died because Pee Wee was hired to kill him. Murder in prison may be committed for any of several reasons, ranging from racial fights to prison riots.

David Schultz, in his master's thesis about Pelican Bay State Prison, quotes one California inmate's view of prison homicides: "I've been on the yard watching people get shot, watching people die. People on the outside say, ah, that doesn't happen. You weren't there, man."

In a 1990 survey of federal and state prisons, Davis found that, between 1984 and 1989, 411 persons were killed by inmates in prisons in forty states. Twenty-one of the victims were staff members and 390 were fellow inmates.

Murder Behind Bars

Crime occurs everywhere in the United States. Nearly thirty-seven million people have been injured by criminals in the past twenty years. Crime cost the nation more than $19 billion in 1991 alone. If society is dangerous, you can imagine the dangers in prison. Murder is not uncommon.

Prison riots have occurred in the United States since 1774, when a riot took place at a prison in Simsbury, Connecticut. Riots can result in inmate deaths. Fox (1972) theorizes that prison riots are spontaneous. He considers prisons to be time bombs, detonated by spontaneous events like fistfights or gang wars.

One of the most brutal riots in American prison history was the February 1980 riot at the penitentiary of New Mexico in Santa Fe. The thirty-three deaths were all murders of prisoners by other prisoners. The major targets were informers located in cell block four of the prison. W. G. Stone (1982, 123) describes the horror in the following manner:

> Some were killed the easy way, cremated to death by gasoline or paint thinner thrown into their cells along with a lit match or the flames of the torch. Others paid the hard way. One man was held down, convulsing as his executioners hammered a metal rod through his head. When they stopped, the man was dead, blood soaked his face and the hands and clothes of his killers, and the rod stuck out of the other side of his skull.

"State-raised" inmates also tend to be violent inmates, according to Jack Abbott (1991). They have spent many years in prison and have learned that violence is the way to deal with their problems.

Prison gangs are responsible for many homicides behind bars. They use violence as a means to control prison rackets, protect gang members, pursue vendettas against their enemies, and earn prestige in the prison system.

California, as an example, had thirty-five inmate homicides in 1970. Thirty-two of these attacks were by stabbing. There are four major prison gangs in California: two Chicano gangs (including the Mexican Mafia, or EME), the Aryan (Caucasian) Brotherhood, and the Black Brotherhood. Conflicts between the gangs have led to stabbings, rape, blackmail, and exploitation of nonaligned prisoners.

Mandatory "life without possibility of parole" sentences are being used at the state and federal levels for violent offenders. Braswell et al. (1985, 152) report "that prisoners with many years to serve will react in different ways, some will be desperate, some will be hopeless, and many will decide that *they have nothing to lose* by acting on any vagrant impulse." Some lifers may commit violent acts while in prison. One example of this was the 1 April 1986 prison riot at the Kirkland Correctional Institution in Columbia, South Carolina. The riot, according to Catoe and Harvey (1986), started when inmates (mostly lifers) in the most secure area of the prison overpowered a guard. More than $700,000 worth of damage was done to prison dormitories and living areas, including the canteen, library, and educational buildings, all of which were set on fire. The riot ended after four hours when a riot squad armed with shotguns retook the institution.

America is a violent society. FBI reports indicate that the number of juveniles arrested for homicide soared 142 percent from 1983 through 1992. These violent juveniles will be tomorrow's adult offenders, and adult prisoners.

Overcrowding in America's prisons is a cause of stress that can lead to homicide. Braswell et al. (1985, 75) report "that reactions to the stress of crowding may include suspicion, isolation, physical disease, and *intense violence.*"

Attica (New York) and Santa Fe (New Mexico) prisons were both overcrowded at the time of their riots. According to Braswell et al. (1985, 80), the "capacity of Santa Fe was set at 900, but there were 1136 prisoners held there at the beginning of the riot. The capacity of Attica was 1200 but approximately 2225 were being held there when the riot broke out."

Prevention of Murder in Prison

One prevention strategy is to teach inmates how to deal with violence in their facility. Sue Rochman (1991) examined such a program for inmates at New York State's Elmira Correctional Facility. The Elmira workshop is a twenty-two-hour program that involves inmates in activities designed to break down barriers, increase relaxation and fun, build community spirit, examine violence, and explore how violence erupts and how to intervene if it does. Trainers show inmates that the principles of nonviolence can work in their daily lives. For example, in prison society if one inmate takes another inmate's sneakers, the victim usually responds with an assault. This workshop teaches inmates that there are alternatives to assaulting fellow inmates.

The prison environment can influence violent behavior. Herrick (1989) reports that air conditioning may be a factor. For example, thirteen years of Missouri statistics showed a definite and striking seasonal pattern in assaults. Violence increases as summer temperatures soar and decreases as the weather cools.

Segregation units have been used in some states as a way to respond to the problem of prison gangs. Gang leaders and core members are placed in these units for long periods. Ralph and Marquart (1991) report that this tactic was used by the state of Texas when fifty-two murders occurred in their prisons between 1984 and 1985. Ninety percent of the murders were gang-related. By 1991, more than fifteen hundred known gang members were locked in administrative segregation.

The United States Senate (1983) has been arguing for many years over a bill to impose the death penalty for those who murder while serving a life sentence. The impetus for this legislation was incidents at the federal prison in Marion, Illinois, in which prisoners sentenced to life murdered two correctional officers.

Classification can be a factor in the prison environment. The Adult Internal Management System (AIMS) approach, for example, classifies inmates objectively into one of three groups: alphas (who are the most aggressive and may be leaders); betas (who are dependent, often ask for help, and are usually passive but may explode if provoked); and gammas (who are neither aggressive nor dependent, are more cooperative, have less criminal history, and avoid trouble). A life history checklist and a correctional adjustment checklist help prison authorities determine in which of the three categories to place each inmate. Ideally, each group would be housed separately. Furthermore, unit management would be used to ensure that the staff of each unit can do things consistent with the type of inmates assigned to the unit. Unit management combines line correctional officers and case workers in one unit. This approach breaks the barrier between uniformed and nonuniformed staff.

Prison tactical teams are essential for modern correctional systems. These teams can be used as a show of force or to deter violence, and as an effective tool in containing, controlling, and resolving violent incidents. These teams have common characteristics: (1) they are all prepared to do essentially the same job; (2) they are made up of highly trained professionals; (3) they have an uncommon dedication that sometimes means placing their lives in extreme jeopardy; and (4) they must display total discipline.

Reid H. Montgomery, Jr.

See also VIOLENCE

Bibliography

Abbott, J. (1991). *In the Belly of the Beast: Letters from Prison.* New York: Vintage Books/Random House.

Braswell, M., S. Dillingham, and R. Montgomery (1985). *Prison Violence in America.* Cincinnati, Ohio: Anderson.

Catoe, W. D., and J. L. Harvey (1986). *A Review of the Kirkland Correctional Institution Disturbance on April 1, 1986.* Columbia, S.C.: South Carolina Department of Corrections,

Earle, W. (1992). *Final Truth: The Autobiography of Donald "Pee Wee" Gaskins.* Atlanta, Ga.: Adept.

Fox, V. (1972). Prison riots in a democratic society. *Police* 16: 33–41.

Herrick, E. (1989). The surprising direction of violence in prison. *Corrections Compendium* 15(6): 1, 4–9.

Ralph, P., and J. Marquart (1991). Gang violence in Texas prisons. *The Prison Journal* 71 (2) 38–49.

Rochman, S. (1991). Alternatives to prison violence. *Corrections Compendium* 16(6): 1, 6–8.

Stone, W. G. (1982). *The Hate Factory.* Agoura, Calif.: Dell.

I

Illegal Aliens in Prison

The Illegal Immigrant Problem

On 11 April 1994, the state of Florida filed a suit against the U.S. government, demanding $1.5 billion as reimbursement for federally mandated health, education, legal, and welfare services to illegal immigrants. According to the state of Florida, the U.S. government failed to protect borders, thus attracting undocumented immigrants. As a result, Florida paid $884 million in 1993 alone for social services for 345,000 illegal immigrants. California, along with Florida, Texas, New York, and Illinois, also suffers from overwhelming problems with illegal immigrants and is considering a similar lawsuit. The state of California provided $489 million in health care alone to more than 400,000 illegal aliens in 1992.

There are an estimated 320 million illegal immigrants in the U.S., and nearly half of them reside in California. Once rebuffed, most illegal immigrants come back and try again the next day. Hispanics make up about five-sixths of all illegal immigrants. According to the U.S. Commission on Immigration Reform, there are an estimated 500,000 illegal aliens entering the United States every year. In 1993, in Texas alone, the Immigration and Naturalization Service apprehended more than 380,000 illegal Mexican immigrants. It is almost impossible to secure a two thousand–mile border (California, Arizona, New Mexico, and Texas), no matter how much the government enhances the interdiction methods.

Aliens in Prison

According to the Survey of State Prison Inmates in 1991, about 31,300 inmates (about 4 percent of all state prison inmates) were not U.S. citizens. These aliens were from forty-nine countries in North America, South America, Europe, Africa, and Asia. Mexicans account for about half (47 percent) of the population. Cubans account for 10 percent of the alien inmate population, followed by aliens from the Dominican Republic (9 percent), Colombia (4 percent), Jamaica (4 percent), El Salvador (4 percent), Guatemala (2 percent), Trinidad and Tobago (2 percent), the United Kingdom (1 percent), and Vietnam (1 percent).

Nearly all incarcerated aliens are male. More than four-fifths of them are of Hispanic origin, and about half of them are between twenty-five and thirty-four years of age. About a third of imprisoned illegal aliens are married, nearly two-thirds have not completed high school, and four-fifths were employed at the time of their conviction. Approximately one in ten illegal alien prisoners is a non-Hispanic black. About one in twenty-five is a non-Hispanic white, and about one in twenty-five is an Asian or Pacific Islander. Approximately two-fifths of illegal alien state inmates have used drugs during the month prior to their arrest, and about a fifth were under the influence of drugs at the time of their offense. About fourteen thousand illegal aliens were incarcerated for drug offenses (45 percent of all offenses), including seventy-nine hundred for trafficking and sixty-one hundred for possession. Approximately 10,800 aliens were incarcerated for violent crimes (34 percent of all offenses), including homicide, robbery, assault, and sexual assault.

The Problems of Illegal Alien Inmates

Incarcerated illegal aliens confront different problems than do U.S. citizens. Problems such as language, deportation, and immigration status are of concern to aliens. According to McShane (1987), alien inmates also suffer the punitive effects of detention, including the denial of promotions, restriction from certain education and training programs, inability to obtain furloughs and parole, and inequitable treatment from the U.S. criminal justice system. For example, illegal aliens tend to be held in prison longer than other inmates. Another problem is the limited space for detainees. The Immigration and Naturalization Service has only six thousand beds nationwide, but more than one million undocumented immigrants of all nationalities were arrested in 1992.

Other concerns, such as food, nutrition, and family pressures, are also great among these aliens. For example, some Chinese illegal immigrants pay as much as forty thousand dollars each to smugglers who arrange their transportation to the United States. To fulfill the "American dream," those illegal immigrants borrow money from friends and relatives with a promise that they will pay them back. Once they are incarcerated, it is difficult to fulfill their promises.

Illegal aliens worry about what will happen to them once they are released. For example, by being incarcerated, aliens who were originally in the country legally have not only violated their entry agreement but may have remained in the U.S. past the expiration date of their agreement. Deportation is one of the major concerns among all illegal aliens. Most of them are told by smugglers to claim asylum if they are caught. Under U.S. law, claiming asylum prevents the INS from immediately instituting deportation procedures. The reason is that everyone on U.S. soil—even a foreign citizen—has the legal right to full due process under the U.S. Constitution.

Some aliens, however, are not as fortunate. Those aliens, especially juveniles, are bailed out by smugglers and forced to commit illegal activities or become prostitutes. Many of them end up in bondage, or are forced to become gang enforcers or drug couriers. Some may even be killed by the smugglers.

Extradition Procedures

Two options the United States has to deal with alien prisoners are extradition and a convention on the transfer of sentenced persons (a special treaty with selected countries). The United States has extradition agreements with several Latin American countries, including Argentina, Chile, Colombia, the Dominican Republic, Ecuador, El Salvador, Guatemala, Honduras, Mexico, Nicaragua, and Panama. In addition to extradition, the U.S. also has signed a convention on the transfer of sentenced persons with Austria, the Bahamas, Belgium, Canada, Cyprus, Czechoslovakia, Denmark, Finland, France, Germany, Greece, Hungary, Italy, Luxembourg, Malta, the Netherlands, Norway, Spain, Sweden, Switzerland, Turkey, and the United Kingdom.

Extradition (and convention) procedures are not processed expeditiously while aliens are in prison, although it is not uncommon for the INS to actually conduct deportation proceedings in the institutions. The INS seems to have an informal policy that incarcerated aliens can wait while others are processed first. This has created a problem for state penal institutions, where overcrowding is the rule and bed space is at a premium. If aliens were extradited quickly, bed space could be freed up. California, among other states that border Mexico, has raised the issue with the federal government several times.

Summary

Research on illegal aliens in prison is rather scarce. The problems of alien inmates deserve more attention from the criminal justice system and academic experts. New laws are needed to ensure due process and fairness for illegal aliens in prison. Moreover, the American criminal justice system should incorporate international efforts to deal with the problems of illegal aliens.

Chau-Pu Chiang

Bibliography

Bureau of Justice Statistics (1991). *Survey of State Prison Inmates, 1991.* Washington, D.C.: U.S. Department of Justice, Bureau of Justice Statistics.

McShane, M. D. (1987). Immigration processing and the alien inmate: Constructing a conflict perspective. *Journal of Crime and Justice* 10: 171–94.

Indeterminate Sentences

A prison sentence is said to be indeterminate if its duration depends not only on the decision of a court but also on that of a parole authority. Usually this division of responsibility for the penalty is achieved by the court's specifying a minimum and a maximum duration of imprisonment, and a parole board's authorizing the exact date of release within those limits.

In some states indeterminacy occurs even when the court specifies imprisonment for a definite period, called "definite" or "determinate" sentencing. They are in fact indeterminate in states where the law authorizes parole after some minimum time has been served. Thus, a sentence of nine years in prison is an indeterminate sentence of three to nine years in any of the several states that make prisoners eligible for parole when they have served a third of their sentence. Some states, in certain periods of their histories, have allowed parole for any prisoner after some minimum time is served, usually one year, thus making all their sentences indeterminate. In most states, unless a sentence is stated to be life imprisonment without parole, all life sentences are indeterminate; parole may be granted, with the minimum time before parole eligibility varying in different states from seven to thirty years.

An infrequent use of the expression "indeterminacy in sentencing," with which this article is *not* concerned, refers to how little a judge's discretion on punishment is limited. For example, it is indeterminate in that sense if the penalty may be probation, any duration of confinement, restitution, fines, or community service.

In the United States, authority to release on parole, hence to make a sentence indeterminate, is generally traced to New York's Elmira Reformatory, which opened in 1877. It copied earlier "ticket of leave" and "release on license" practices in Australia and Ireland that gave prison officials authority to release well-behaved inmates who had improved themselves by study and work while confined, but on condition that they commit no further offenses for a specified period of time.

Several arguments have been given for making confinement sentences indeterminate, rather than having their duration fixed when imposed. First of all, it facilitates the control of prisoners, since they risk longer confinement by misbehavior. Second, it can give inmates incentives for self-improvement, for example, if their advancement in school work or completion of a vocational training program is required before they can be paroled. Third, it is contended that a prisoner's criminality can be assessed more accurately during confinement than at the time of the trial, when the focus is on the offense more than on the offender. Fourth, it is pointed out that because judges are trained in the law but not in assessing the criminality of an offender, they are qualified to determine guilt fairly but not to decide what penalties are most likely to reduce recidivism, or to deter others from committing crimes.

Indeterminate sentences were adopted in most of the U.S. during the first half of the twentieth century, but were partly or fully replaced by definite penalties in many states in the 1960s and thereafter. One argument for their abolition was that parole gave a politically oriented and often unqualified lay board, in the executive branch of government, what had traditionally been the judicial branch's independent authority to grant or deny liberty. A second argument was that parole boards conduct hearings secretly, without due process, and reach decisions without adequately justifying them. A third argument points out apparently dangerous or unfair parole board decisions, such as early releases after notorious crimes, violent offenses by parolees, or denial or revocation for infractions that were not felonious. Fourth, it is claimed that the risk of recidivism cannot be judged much more accurately after confinement than it can soon after conviction, especially if it is judged by subjective impressions unguided by actuarial risk tables. Finally, it is asserted arbitrarily that punishment should be based only on what the legislature regards as just punishment, and nothing else.

One argument for retention or restoration of indeterminacy is that definite sentences prescribed by law are repeatedly made longer after they are first accepted. That occurs because publicity over any notorious crime soon prompts some legislators to propose higher penalties to show that they are crime fighters, while other legislators and the governor often refuse to oppose such increases for fear of being labeled "soft" on crime. This results in long mandatory sentences that overcrowd prisons, drain state budgets, incarcerate many unadvanced offenders who do not seriously endanger society, and usually do not lower crime rates. Examples include mandatory ten-year minimum terms for possessing even small amounts of illegal drugs, including such widely used substances as marijuana.

Another argument against determinate penalties is that they greatly increase pretrial negotiation of punishment, in which prosecutors offer to reduce the severity of charges if defense lawyers persuade defendants to plead guilty. Such plea bargaining usually occurs in secret. It is unrecorded, it is affected by the prior obligations of the attorneys to each other in other cases, and it reflects attorney workloads. It violates due process standards much more than does most parole board decision-making.

A final argument for indeterminate sentences is that statistical research can produce sentencing and parole guidelines that maximize the probability of protecting society by incapacitating and reforming criminals. These guidelines can set upper and lower limits, but they may also recommend alternatives such as house arrest with electronic monitoring, restitution, community service, academic or vocational training, or day fines. Such decisions can be made by qualified judges and parole board members.

Daniel Glaser

See also REHABILITATION PROGRAMS

Bibliography

Alschuler, A. W. (1978). Sentencing reform and prosecutorial power: A critique of recent proposals for "fixed" and "presumptive" sentencing. In National Institute of Law Enforcement and Criminal Justice. *Determinate Sentencing: Reform or Regression?* Washington, D.C.: U. S. Department of Justice.

Cullen, F. T., and K. E. Gilbert (1982). *Reaffirming Rehabilitation.* Cincinnati, Ohio: Anderson.

Glaser, D. (1985). Who gets probation and parole: Case study versus actuarial decision making. *Crime and Delinquency* 31: 367–78.

Griset, P. L. (1991). *Determinate Sentencing: The Promise and the Reality of Retributive Justice.* Albany, N.Y.: State University of New York Press.

Morris, N., and M. Tonry (1990). *Between Prison and Probation.* New York: Oxford University Press.

Industry

I. History

The development of prison industry in the United States can be traced to the first American prisons, Walnut Street in Philadelphia and Newgate in New York City, established in the 1790s. The existing Walnut Street Jail in Philadelphia was remodeled in 1790 to accommodate thirty solitary confinement cells. A classification system was introduced and the worst criminals were sentenced to solitary confinement and had to earn the right to work. Those not sentenced to solitary confinement were required to work between eight and ten hours per day. A public-account system was used in the first penitentiaries. Under that system the prison carried out all aspects of prison production. The warden was responsible for purchasing materials and equipment, the manufacturing, marketing, and sales. All profits belonged to the state.

Prisoners at Walnut Street worked at carpentry, weaving, shoemaking, tailoring, and the manufacturing of nails. Inmates were compensated for their labor and charged for their board and tools. Wages were scaled to one's abilities and were similar to prevailing Philadelphia wages. Several states followed Pennsylvania's lead. New Jersey in 1798 and Massachusetts in 1805 constructed prisons and provided for inmate employment through a public-account system.

In 1796, New York began construction of Newgate prison in New York City. Absent from Newgate's design were the solitary cells that the Pennsylvania reformers considered central to the classification and discipline of prisoners. Inmates at Newgate were housed in dormitory type rooms designed to accommodate eight. Newgate's first industry was shoemaking, followed by the production of nails, barrels, linen, and woodenware. Inmate labor at Newgate also was organized under a public-account system. During her early years, Newgate was praised for achieving positive results. The industrial program encountered problems as early as 1804, however, when inspectors discovered that shortages of money for supplies had created a debt of several thousand dollars. Newgate had been overcrowded for nearly a decade when rates of civilian unemployment soared in 1815 and 1816 and prison commitments more than doubled. Insufficient resources coupled with steady increases in the prison population led to chronic idleness. As crowding increased, discipline crumbled, and by 1816 the prison was hopelessly in debt. In 1825 an investigative commission reported staggering levels of filth and idleness in the industry shops, and by 1828 Newgate was closed.

The Walnut Street Jail in Philadelphia had reached an equally deplorable condition. By 1800, discipline began to decay as a result of the overcrowded conditions. Production was hindered by inmate congestion in the shops. By 1820, the use of the solitary cells, the central feature of Pennsylvania's approach, was completely abandoned.

Walnut Street and Newgate prisons are the most widely discussed examples of America's first penitentiaries. They were established on the premise that work is therapeutic, reformative, and potentially profitable. Moreover, it was assumed that financial and reformatory advantages would go hand in hand. These early efforts at prison labor failed, however, both in terms of economics and prisoner reformation.

The demise of Walnut Street and Newgate gave way to a second attempt at reform. In 1816, the silent system was established at Auburn penitentiary in New York. In Pennsylvania the separate system was developed at the Western penitentiary at Pittsburgh in 1817 and the Eastern penitentiary (Cherry Hill) at Philadelphia in 1821. The silent and separate systems amounted to competing schemes of prison labor, the characteristics of which divided the New York and Pennsylvania reformers for decades. Both approaches were premised on the rule of enforced silence, but they departed on the crucial issue of how to manage inmate labor.

In the Auburn silent (congregate) system prisoners worked together in silence in industry shops during the day for maximum industrial production; they were separated at night to prevent moral contamination. At Auburn, it was reasoned that so long as silence was maintained there was no danger of moral contamination as a result of inmates working together. Moreover, prisoners must work, and any scheme of separate employment would prove economically unsound.

In contrast, the Pennsylvania system was noted for its complete separation of inmates from each other. So convinced were the Pennsylvania reformers of the need for radical departure from previous methods that, at the new Western penitentiary at Pittsburgh, there was absolute deprivation of work as well as enforced solitude. The practice of solitary confinement without work, however, was rapidly condemned. It was concluded that solitary confinement without labor engenders poor health without producing any reformative benefits over and above confinement with labor. An 1829 law was passed requiring convicts at both the Eastern and Western penitentiaries to perform handcraft labor (usually shoemaking) in their solitary confinement cells.

The Auburn model took hold rapidly. Connecticut, Massachusetts, Maryland, and Ohio imitated Auburn, as did New Jersey and Rhode Island after brief and unhappy experiments with the separate system. Consequently, the Pennsylvania model of complete separation of prisoners stood alone. The widespread adoption of Auburn's model in other states was largely the result of their legislatures' desire to exploit convict labor. Moreover, prisons modeled after Auburn were much less costly to construct than those conforming to the Pennsylvania style.

The movement that gave birth to the Auburn penitentiary emphasized inmate reformation over prisons for profit. Attention to reform, however, soon gave way to the severe punishments and relentless work schedules that were deemed necessary for generating profits. Convict labor at Auburn was contracted out to a variety of local manufacturers. Corruption, graft, and inefficiency soon poisoned the labor program at Auburn, and the public called for harsher discipline and controls. A strict regime of hard work coupled with flogging and clubbing for these who transgressed became the norm.

This speedy move away from interest in convict reform was partially a result of prison officials succumbing to constant pressure from the legislature to render their prison shops profitable. Further, until the brutality associated with Auburn's approach became unavoidably apparent, most prison officials and reformers were comfortable with the contention that strict silence and harsh labor schedules were part and parcel of reformation. These beliefs gave rise to inhumane labor routines and cruel punishments in order to effect the discipline necessary for optimal output.

Inmates at Auburn were employed in a number of industries, the largest of which were the cooper shop and the weaving shop. Auburn also maintained a shoemaking industry, a tailor shop, and a blacksmith shop, all operating through prison contracts with private businesses. The contract system replaced public accounts beginning in the 1820s and prevailed throughout most of the century. Under this system the prison advertised for bids for the employment of convicts, and their labor was sold to the highest bidder. Private contractors entered the prisons and supervised the workshops.

They paid the state a specified price per day for each inmate's labor. By offering the state a steady and reliable source of income, the contract system proved more profitable than the public-account system.

During the 1830s and 1840s prisoners at Auburn also made furniture, steam engines, and boilers, all under prison contractors. At Auburn, prisoners did not receive payment for their labors. As a result of Auburn's industrial efficiency, the prison was turning a profit by 1829, and officials announced that no further appropriations from the state would be needed.

The contract system, however, also brought with it two intractable problems. First, exploitation of prisoners for the mutual profit of the state and the contractors rapidly ensued, and wardens were retained or dismissed according to the fiscal return of their industries. Harsh punishments such as flogging, the gag, the straitjacket, the yoke, and the shower bath (dousing with cold water in winter) were characteristic of the Auburn model. Second, the efficiency of prison production under private contractors resulted in increased competition with free-market laborers.

The years between 1820 and 1840 witnessed a gradual swell of protests from free laborers charging unfair competition from prison production. Laborers argued that prison contracts were not dispersed equitably, that products marketed by prisons created chaotic price deflation, and that former convicts, trained in prison, would flood the labor market upon release, thereby taking jobs from law-abiding citizens.

Initially, legislators were not sympathetic to the cries of laborers because profitable or at least solvent prisons were very appealing from a legislative point of view. But by 1835, the New York legislature reluctantly passed a law to appease laborers. This law provided that prison industries be confined to the production of products only currently available from abroad, that due notice be given for the letting of all prison contracts, and that only those convicts possessing a trade prior to conviction be employed in prison industry. Continued protests from laborers brought a law passed in 1842 that nullified many existing contracts made in violation of the law of 1835 and that once again limited convicts to work in trades they had learned previous to their incarceration.

The New York and Pennsylvania reforms of 1816–18 intended that the silent and separate systems provide environments conducive to reflection and self-improvement. Within five years of its inception, Pennsylvania's model was breeding insanity and poor health while Auburn's was reduced to relying on inhumane practices to spur production. Within ten years both systems were under investigation by legislative commissions and under attack from free laborers charging unfair competition. By most standards, both the silent and separate systems were failures within two decades of their establishment. The prisons were neither conducive to reformation nor able to sustain economic self-sufficiency.

Laws against prison labor that were passed in the 1830s and 1840s crippled production in the penitentiaries, and reports of worsening conditions in the prisons continued. At the close of the antebellum period frustrations were high, and few still believed in the superiority of the Auburn model. By 1860, however, the industrial boom brought to the penitentiaries by Civil War production temporarily revived prison industries.

Post–Civil War Developments in Prison Labor
Prison industries flourished during the Civil War years, boosted by the manufacture of Yankee army supplies at the prison shops. Both the prisons and the contractors realized handsome profits. A depression followed shortly after the war, however, dropping prison production to its lowest point. Prison industry suffered attacks from several fronts during the postwar era. The 1860s and 1870s witnessed a rapid rise in national trade unions, and those young and powerful groups seized the opportunity to renew attacks against prison industries despite low productivity in the prisons. Penologists and state legislatures scrutinized the contract system following charges of inmate abuse and entrepreneurial mismanagement. Both the expanding trade unions and penologists critical of prison contracts simultaneously influenced several state legislatures over the next two decades to end the contract system that had monopolized prison labor since the 1820s.

During the 1870s, the National Prison Association was organized primarily to lobby for the abolition of the contract system and the return to emphasis on inmate labor designed for individual reformation rather than prison profits. At the 1870 meeting of the National Congress on Penitentiaries and Reformatory Discipline, members passed a declaration condemning prison labor contracts. They concluded that the primary objective of imprisonment should be moral and religious improvement.

Investigative commissions that convened in New York in 1866 and 1871 vindicated prison industry of charges of unfair competition but asserted that contracts were economically disadvantageous to the state. These commissions cited such activities as overcharging the state for inmate labor, fraudulent record keeping, and the introduction of contraband to inmates. By 1880, New Jersey, Connecticut, and Massachusetts had also set up commissions to investigate the contract labor system. By the close of the 1870s, labor agitation had succeeded in mounting laws against prison contractors in several states. Ohio, New Jersey, Illinois, and New York responded by instituting the piece-price system that allowed prisons in those states to earn only a portion of their expenses. The piece-price system, a modification of the contract system, allowed inmates to remain under the complete supervision of prison officials, so as not to diminish the rehabilitative effort. Contractors did not enter the prison, they merely supplied the materials, received the finished products, and paid the state a price per piece received.

In New York, the Yates law of 1888 and the Fassett law of 1889 together prohibited contract labor, called for the retention of the piece-price system coupled with the state-use system, required all state institutions to purchase from prisons, restricted the number of inmates in a prison trade to 5 percent of all free men engaged in the trade throughout the state, introduced a labor classification system, and stipulated that wages be paid to inmates. A state constitutional amendment in 1894 banished contract labor in New York and firmly installed the state-use system. Under the state-use system prisoners manufactured products to be sold only to other state agencies, departments, or institutions. In many states, governmental agencies are mandated by law to purchase from prisons.

These New York laws provided the foundation for much of what was to come in surrounding states during the following years. In Massachusetts, all prison contracts were abolished by 1897 and a state-use system adopted. Most other New England prisons remained free of anticontract influences for several more years, largely because they were able to acquire reasonable labor bids and remain self-supporting. Also in 1897, the Muehlbronner Act was passed by the Pennsylvania legislature, abolishing the use of power machinery in Pennsylvania's prison shops. This act all but destroyed prison labor in Pennsylvania for the next thirty years. Michigan was already operating largely on a public-account system and thereby escaped the whirlwind of labor legislation. By 1899 the contract system was forbidden in eighteen states and territories, and by 1911 it was abolished in twenty-six states. The remainder, however, retained the contract system in whole or in part for several more years.

The Lease System and Penal Labor in the South

The lease system was widely used throughout the South during the post–Civil War period and dominated there until well into the twentieth century. Under that system the state temporarily relinquished almost all supervision of its convicts to a lessee. The lessee received the prisoners and housed, fed, clothed, and disciplined them as well as employed them. Lessees were at liberty to employ the inmates within the institution or to transport them anywhere within the boundaries of the state.

Although the leasing of convicts was not strictly a Southern phenomenon, the system is associated with the South because of its widespread and enduring use there. Prior to the Civil War, the South experienced relatively few penal problems. Prisons were small and housed small populations, and there was little organized attempt to employ the inmates. Discipline of the slave population was left to slave owners, who avoided formal imprisonment to avoid the loss of valuable labor. After the Civil War, however, penal problems in the South grew rapidly. Newly freed slaves had to be handled by state authorities, and many Southern prisons were either destroyed during the war or were inadequate to house the growing criminal population. The leasing of convicts was a ready solution to a mounting problem in this war-torn region. By 1878 eleven states were fully committed to leasing their prisoners, and traces of the system lingered in some states until as late as 1923. The leasing of convicts provided revenue to the state several times the cost incurred for each prisoner. The same facets of the system that made it desirable to state governments, however, soon gave way to appalling practices. The profit motive led to excessive and harsh punishments, including flogging, the shackles, and the stocks. These abuses occurred and persisted because state officials satisfied themselves with falsified and incomplete lessee reports on the welfare of convicts, rather than acknowledging a problem that would clearly require the termination of revenue-producing contracts. Moreover, prison populations in most Southern states after the Civil War were between 60 and 80 percent black. Racial bias coupled with economic concerns suppressed objections to the obvious horrors of the system.

The largest purchasers of convict labor were the railway contractors, large lumber and turpentine companies, and coal mining plants. By the turn of the twentieth century, when labor concerns in the North were successfully suppressing competition from prison labor, reformers in the South who attempted to revise or replace the lease system ran up against the stiff political clout of the companies that directly benefited from the leases.

Mississippi was the first state to abolish the lease system, by constitutional amendment in 1890. But the practice continued unchecked at the county level for another two decades. County autonomy proved to be a major obstacle to abolition of the system in many states. By 1908 the federal government took interest in the matter and a series of federal prosecutions of Southern officials and contractors paved the way for uprooting the intractable system. Several states introduced convict farms and road work projects to be managed by state or county officials. But the abuses did not halt. Deaths from overwork were not uncommon among members of road gangs and severe, often fatal, whippings frequently occurred on the farms. These conditions continued until the Depression, when most prisoner work ceased nationally.

Prison Industry in the Twentieth Century
The state-use system gained ground during the first decade of the twentieth century in the Northeast and Midwest, while the South lagged behind, clinging to the lease system. Meanwhile, the public works system took hold in many Western states in the early 1900s. Previously, a handful of Western states dabbled in prison contracts, leasing, and state-use employment. But anticontract legislation initiated by the federal government, prohibiting contract employment for federal prisons, virtually eliminated industries from the territorial prisons. When these new states were formed, their constitutions often prohibited contract labor in prisons. As a result,

there was little organized labor in that region until the onset of public works honor camps early in the twentieth century. The system involved using prisoners to build public buildings, roads, and parks. New Mexico and Colorado introduced the "honor system" in 1903. That involved sending convicts out to work on public roads, often at great distances from the facility, with few or no guards accompanying them. By 1911, Oregon, Washington, Montana, and Utah had established road gangs on the model of New Mexico and Colorado.

Nearly every Western state employed inmates on public works during the first quarter of this century. Many states in other regions also employed convicts on public projects until the onset of the Depression, when that type of work was largely halted. Road work was a success in these states but not the entire solution, because convicts could be employed only certain months of the year. Efforts to enhance penal labor pressed on in those states. By 1923, there was a movement to introduce the state-use arrangement in all states.

The state-use system appeared to be the answer to nearly a century of problems surrounding prison industry. It was designed to appease labor unions, and the approach seemed to favor rehabilitation of convicts as well as to allow for the possibility of profitable prison shops. The state-use system dictates that the manufacture of prison goods be restricted to products that can be consumed by state government agencies, political subdivisions thereof (such as counties), or other nonprofit concerns. Legislators and prison administrators, however, were ill-prepared to handle such a comprehensive change in the inmate labor system. Legislatures were often unable to subsidize the installation of new machinery and equipment adequately, and the management of prison industries under the state-use system was wholly unorganized. The demand for state-use goods was limited and overestimated. Idleness increased at the very time when prison populations were becoming unwieldy. Prison administrators in New York, Pennsylvania, and Massachusetts could no longer rely on a hard day's labor for discipline.

As of 1920, many states had not yet adopted state-use programs and still engaged in either contracts or the piece-price system. As a result, national labor organizations continued to see prison industries as unfair competition. That perception, along with the increasing political influence of free labor concerns, pro-voked a series of federal laws regulating prison industry. In 1929 the Hawes-Cooper Act man-dated that prison goods transported from one state to another be subject to the laws of the importing state, thereby permitting a state to prohibit the sale of prison goods whether made by convicts in other states or locally. In 1935 the Ashurst-Sumners Act was passed, making it a federal offense for carriers to violate state laws promulgated under Hawes-Cooper. Ashurst-Sumners also mandated the labeling of prison-made goods. As a result, most carriers refused to accept prison-made products for interstate shipment.

In 1940 Congress passed the Sumners-Ashurst Act, forbidding the interstate trans-port of prison-made goods for private use re-gardless of whether a state banned importation of prison goods (products manufactured for the federal government or other state govern-ments were exempt). The shift from open markets to state-use markets did not curtail labor opposition. In 1940, the Walsh-Healy Act drastically limited the use of convict labor in projects involving federal government con-tracts. With the market for prison-made goods severely diminished, most remaining entrepre-neurs abandoned the prison factory because it was no longer profitable.

The Depression also dealt a staggering blow to prison industry, knocking out of con-structive employment 80 percent of all prison-ers nationally. The decline of prison industry during the period was dramatic. The Depres-sion, coupled with the series of federal restric-tions, proved to be the fatal blow to prison industry. Not even the temporary release of fed-eral restrictions during World War II could re-vive industry programs.

Labor agitation was not entirely respon-sible for the decline in prison labor during the twentieth century. Early in the 1950s, the treat-ment ethic arrived on the penological scene. It generated a new punishment ideology, rooted in the medical model, that subordinated industry programs to rehabilitative efforts involving vocational training, group therapy, education, and casework-based treatment. At the height of the treatment approach, many states employed fewer than 10 percent of all inmates in prison industry shops, while most equipment and machinery either fell into disrepair or became antiquated. This state of affairs prevailed, largely unchanged, until the mid 1970s.

The Revitalization of Prison Industries
During the 1970s, interest in prison industry was rekindled. By the late 1960s, the two de-cade old rehabilitation model was in serious decline. Changes in correctional philosophy were phasing out the unfeasible medical model. Along with the decay of the rehabilitative ideal were the additional developments of exploding prison populations and the rising cost of con-finement. Prison industry was once again viewed as a way to combat the idleness of a growing prison population as well as of offset-ting the increasing costs of incarceration. Also making possible the rebirth of prison industry was the retreat of labor unions. Because state-use industry employed small numbers of pris-oners, private industry no longer viewed the existing low levels of prison production as a threat.

The federal government became interested in reviving prison industry and in 1977 funded the Free Venture initiative directed toward re-vamping prison industry programs in seven states so that they might operate more like the civilian world of work. These seven pilot pro-grams were designed to foster a realistic work environment and included such things as a full workday, inmate wages based on output, pro-ductivity standards comparable to those of pri-vate industry, transferable job skills, deductions from inmate wages for room and board and restitution, and preparation for release (includ-ing job placement), while also striving for profit-making industrial operations.

In 1979 the Prison Industry Enhancement Act provided for exceptions to the 1940 Sumners-Ashurst Act by allowing the seven pi-lot projects to place prison goods into inter-state commerce and to sell to the federal gov-ernment. The act established conditions under which interstate shipment of prison goods could occur: Inmates working in Free Venture enterprises must receive a wage comparable to those of civilian laborers in the locality. Local union organizations must be consulted prior to initiation of the project, and inmate employ-ment must not displace currently employed civilians. The federal government took the lead in relaxing restrictions on prison industry, and between 1970 and 1985 over twenty states had enacted legislation partially repealing state-use statutes and providing for limited sales by prison industries to the private sector. These efforts set the stage for the revitalization of industry programs in many states and the reentry of the private sector into the arena of prison production, which began in the mid 1980s and continues today.

Kathleen Maguire

See also ASHURST-SUMNERS ACT, HAWES-COOPER ACT

Bibliography

American Correctional Association (1986). *A Study of Prison Industry: History, Components, and Goals.* Washington, D.C.: U.S. Government Printing Office.

Cullen, F., and L. F. Travis (1984). Work as an avenue of prison reform. *New England Journal on Criminal and Civil Confinement* 10 (Winter): 45–64.

Flanagan, T. (1989). Prison labor and industry. In L. Goodstein and D. L. MacKenzie, eds. *The American Prison: Issues in Research and Policy.* New York: Plenum.

Funke, G. S., B. L. Wayson, and N. Miller (1982). *Assets and Liabilities of Correctional Industries.* Lexington, Mass.: D. C. Heath.

Hawkins, G. (1983). Prison labor and prison industries. In M. Tonry and N. Morris, eds. *Crime and Justice: An Annual Review of Research.* Vol. 5. Chicago: University of Chicago Press.

Hiller, E. T. (1914). Labor unionism and convict labor. *Journal of Criminal Law and Criminology* 5: 851–79.

Lewis, W. D. (1965). *From Newgate to Dannemora: The Rise of the Penitentiary in New York, 1796–1848.* Ithaca, N.Y.: Cornell University Press.

McKelvey, B. (1935). The prison labor problem: 1875–1900. *Journal of Criminal Law and Criminology* 25: 254–71.

McKelvey, B. (1936). *American Prisons.* Chicago: University of Chicago Press (Reprinted, Montclair, N.J.: Patterson Smith, 1977).

Miller, M. B. (1980). At hard labor: Rediscovering the 19th-century prison. In T. Platt and P. Takagi, eds. *Punishment and Penal Discipline.* Berkeley, Calif.: Crime and Social Justice.

Mohler, H. C. (1924). Convict labor policies. *Journal of Criminal Law and Criminology* 15: 530–97.

Teeters, N. K. (1955). *The Cradle of the Penitentiary: The Walnut Street Jail at Philadelphia, 1773–1835.* Philadelphia: Pennsylvania Prison Society.

Wines, E. C., and T. W. Dwight (1867). *Report on the Prisons and Reformatories of the United States and Canada.* Albany, N.Y.: van Benthuysen (Reprinted, New York: AMS, 1973).

Wines, F. H. (1919). *Punishment and Reformation: A Study of the Penitentiary System.* New York: Crowell (Reprinted, New York: AMS, 1975).

II. Current Programs in Prison Industry

Society is now witnessing a resurgence of interest in prison industries. The expansion of prison industries is appealing to elected officials and policy makers partly because of the rising costs of incarceration and declining state and federal budgets. Currently there are more than twenty-six prison-based industries in over ten states across a variety of institutions from community-based to maximum-security facilities.

Types of Prison Industries

Prison industries vary significantly from one another. There is no standard or universal model that governs the type of industries found in correctional settings. There are six models of private-sector involvement in prison industries currently operating in the nation. Each of these models has overlapping characteristics but are distinguished by unique aspects.

Employer Model. The private sector firm owns and operates a business that uses inmate labor to produce goods or services and has control of the hiring, firing, and supervision of inmate labor. This is the most common model, in which the business firm makes all the decisions related to personnel, products, wages, and market sales, and bears all the financial risk. The correctional institution is not heavily involved, other than in providing security, but businesses developed under this model do require incentives for their participation.

This model is dominated by small businesses founded by entrepreneurs who employ prisoners directly. If a prisoner does not perform well, the firm has the authority to fire the inmate and hire another. These small businesses sell their products and services on the open market to private sector customers. The types of products and services include cloth bags, data processing, vinyl products, and ceramics.

Large companies are not generally found in this model, but the Howard Johnson and Best

Western motel chains are exceptions. They hire prisoners to serve as reservation clerks and in other service positions. The hotels have the additional responsibility of supervision. During prime tourist season, especially on holidays and weekends, inmate labor is useful to these types of business establishments. The hotel's regular staff enjoy the benefit of having more weekends and holidays off because of their temporary replacement by prison labor. The inmates receive wages comparable to those of the regular employees performing the same functions; this provides an incentive for the inmates to be productive. On the other hand, inmates are taking jobs that would otherwise be offered to the public. The model thus has some limitations, in addition to its benefits.

Investor Model. The private sector firm capitalizes, or invests in, a business operated by a state correctional agency, but it has no other role in the business. The private investor plays the same role that the state legislature played in the late nineteenth and early twentieth centuries by providing the funds necessary to develop and run a prison industry. The wage structure is similar to that of the piece-price system of a century ago in which inmates were paid a rate based on their individual production. One example of this model is the Wahler Company in Arizona, which invested in a furniture plant in one of the correctional facilities. Wahler provided the production equipment in return for a share of the plant's profits. The finished products are sold on the state and public markets in Arizona only. This business agreement appears to be working, but, as with the corporate model, prison products are competing with public-sector goods and services. That in the long run may ultimately lead to the demise of prison industry.

Customer Model. The private sector firm purchases a significant portion of the output of a state-owned and -operated business, but has no other role in the business. The customer model is similar to the investor model prison industry in that both require a limited role for the private-sector firms. The private-sector firm purchases a significant portion of the product produced by the prison, but it has no other functional role in the prison industry. The state assumes the role of owner/operator, with all the attendant responsibilities, risks, and rewards of a private business. The Utah State Prison in Draper operates a print-

ing and graphics shop that employs thirty inmates. The products are sold on open markets to the public and private sectors. Forty percent of the product is purchased by the private sector. Thus the shop's operation resembles that of a private-sector business.

Other state-run businesses produce a range of products that include metal fabrication and furniture and also serve as subcontractors for the production of similar goods. As with the employer and investor prison industry models, the primary goal appears to be profit for the prison and the business, which conflicts with the traditional goals of imprisonment. Also, the products provided by the prison are competing with those in the private sector, which historically has been unacceptable.

Controlling Customer Model. The private sector firm does not own or operate the business, but strongly influences its management because of its role as dominant or exclusive customer. It may also possibly have a role in financing.

In this model, the customer is the primary and critical player in the state-owned prison business. As a sole or almost exclusive customer, the private-sector firm influences the production by providing equipment and management assistance and by purchasing the product. Without this customer, the prison-based business would not survive. This model resembles the wholly owned subsidiary found in the corporate world, such as the firms that produce auto parts. The firms are owned by one of the auto makers, which, in turn, purchases all the products of the parts firms. The difference for the prison industry is that the business is owned by the state, not the primary or exclusive customer. The profits from this model revert to the state.

A current example of this model is the electrical/mechanical assembly shop run by the Minnesota Correctional Industry in Stillwater. This correctional institution employs one hundred male inmates to produce computer disk drives and wire harnesses for the Magnetic Peripherals Corporation (a subsidiary of Control Data Corporation, CDC). CDC provided technical assistance in the development of the plant, and management and technical training. CDC also established production schedules and developed the quality-control standards. Other examples of this model produce such items as shipping pallets and air conditioning components, and some repair computers.

Two other models are mentioned in the field but, to date, there have been no examples of these models in operation.

Managerial Model. The private sector firm manages a business owned by a correctional agency, but has no other role in the business. In this model, the private sector's only role is to manage a current business owned by a correctional agency. The corrections facility contracts with a private firm to manage a prison-based business. The private sector managers serve as full-time employees (consultants) of the prison to ensure that technical knowledge and management expertise are available.

Joint Venture Model. The private sector firm has a role in both the ownership and operation of a prison-based business, sharing the responsibilities with the correctional agency. The joint venture model is similar to the managerial model in that both models are managed by private-sector managers. In the joint venture model, however, the private sector has an investment in the business as well as a managerial role jointly with the corrections facility. All responsibilities, risks, and rewards are shared and terms are specified in a contract. Since the private sector has an investment in the business, the same problems may arise in this model as arise in the corporate and customer models. There are no current examples of this form of prison industry.

Each of these models is different and each offers different resources, responsibilities, and risks for the private sector and the states involved in prison-based industries. Which of these models is chosen will depend on the correctional agency's in-house business management expertise, its capitalization resources and production capability, and its desired level of production, sales, risks, and rewards.

Issues Related to Prison-Based Industries
There are many complex issues surrounding the incorporation of the private sector in prison industries. These issues cover matters of inmates' rights, security, rehabilitative goals, and competition with private markets.

The complexity is compounded by the many federal and state laws governing prison industries that emerged in the 1930s. Most of these laws are restrictive in nature, and they emerged in a political climate that was opposed to prison industry. The reemergence of interest in prison industries in the 1970s resulted in changes in many of the laws. The result is a mixed and, as yet, unclear collection of laws that do not provide direction for a national policy on prison industries.

Twenty-one states have laws authorizing private-sector employment of prisoners. Twenty states either prohibit the private employment of inmate labor or contracting with private firms to produce goods, and only twelve states address the important issue of wage levels for inmates. To compound this confusion, twenty-five states prohibit the sale of prison-made goods on the open market. On the other hand, the federal government has eased some of the restrictions on the distribution and sale of prison-made goods across interstate markets.

Clearly, the emergence of prison industries has not resulted in a clarification of the legal climate that was established under very different circumstances sixty years ago. Inmate wages are specified in only twelve states, with the norm being a minimum wage similar to the established federal level. The issues of unemployment compensation and employee benefits are even less uniform, except that most states do not authorize these benefits.

The existence of private-sector businesses in prisons necessitates changes in institutional routines. Changes in schedules for meals and prisoner counts are needed to allow full workdays. Delivery schedules are changed to facilitate the flow of raw materials and finished products in and out of the prison.

The largest, and maybe the most important, legal issue affected by the inclusion of private businesses in prisons is related to the legal status of inmate workers. In the past, inmates were not legally defined as employees, and prisons were not considered employers of inmate labor. With private businesses now hiring, firing, and paying wages to inmates through a state institution, the legal issues surrounding the definitions of "employee" and "employer" become significant.

Some scholars maintain that prison industries will reduce inmate idleness. Rather than prisoners remaining in their cells day after day, a prison industry provides inmates with an opportunity to get involved in a meaningful task. Inmates can acquire skills that may better prepare them for jobs in the private sector upon their release. In addition, inmates can save money, receive good time or work furloughs, or pay restitution to the prison or victims. Although past prison industries have not been financially successful, new versions are suggested as a remedy to the rising costs of incarceration (Flanagan 1989).

On the other hand, others have argued that the goals of prison industries are too vague. They don't specify their objectives, except for profits, and they don't integrate the work into the punishment, rehabilitation, or social control functions of prisons. A second criticism is that the wages inmates earn in these industries are often so small that the incentive to do a good job is minimal. A third criticism is that privately run prison industries are susceptible to corruption and to abuse of the inmates.

As demonstrated by many of the prison industry models discussed here, the private sector plays a significant role. The development of prison industry is not by any means a new phenomenon in American prison history, but the growth pattern has been cyclical. After a long hiatus, it appears that the number of prison industries is increasing today. In many of the models, profit is the primary goal, a goal that is not a traditional function of imprisonment. As indicated by the above discussion, by encouraging private-sector involvement in prison industries we may be reverting back to the same problems we faced in the nineteenth century. In spite of the popularity of private-sector involvement in prison industries over the past decade, there has been little to no research on these models. In fact, the issues have yet to be clarified. Much more applied research and program evaluation is needed before large-scale and long-term policies can be developed and implemented.

John A. Conley
Jill D'Angelo

Bibliography

Criminal Justice Associates (1985). *Private Sector Involvement in Prison-Based Businesses: A National Assessment.* Washington, D.C.: U.S. Department of Justice.

Flanagan, T. J. (1989). Prison labor and industry. In L. Goodstein and D. MacKenzie, eds. *The American Prison: Issues in Research and Policy.* New York: Plenum.

Logan, C. H. (1990). *Private Prisons: Cons and Pros.* New York: Oxford University Press.

Miller, R., G. E. Sexton, and V. J. Jacobsen (1991). Making jails productive. *Research in Brief.* Washington, D.C.: National Institute of Justice.

Sexton, G. E., F. C. Farrow, and B. J. Auerbach (1985). The private sector and prison industries. *Research in Brief.* Washington, D.C.: National Institute of Justice.

Inmate Self-Governance

Prison inmates have historically evolved collective adaptations to confinement that have been implicitly or explicitly intended to be forms of self-governance—whether or not such adaptations have been formally sanctioned by the prison administration. Among the earliest forms of informal governance structures were those in which inmate "leaders" served as brokers for the interests of the larger prisoner community. These inmate leaders could speak directly to prison guards and wardens without suspicion of their being informers because of established relationships of trust among inmates and because of well-established reputations as loyal "convicts."

One of the earliest forms of formal prisoner governance occurred at the Michigan State Prison in Jackson in 1887. That short-lived experiment in participative management was taken from Thomas Mott Osborne's concept of the Mutual Aid League (Helfman 1950). During the post–World War I period, a similar program was established at New York's Auburn prison. It lasted longer but was eventually ended in 1928 because it had been subverted by a small number of prisoners pursuing personal and special interests.

Today, the most widely accepted and commonly used form of inmate representation has been formalized into inmate liaison committees (or inmate advisory committees). These committees meet periodically with designated prison staff to present problems and to develop solutions to specific issues, such as dissatisfaction with supervision in housing units or the quality of food service, medical services, or recreational and educational programs.

The rehabilitation era of the 1960s spawned the formation of numerous inmate self-help groups, such as Alcoholics Anonymous chapters, drug treatment groups, and other similar organizations. During that decade, these groups were gradually brought under the direct supervision of programs and services management, resulting in a more formalized relationship to the prison administration. The process of the formalization of previously informal inmate organizations not only brought inmate groups more closely under the supervision of prison officials, but it also provided a stronger foundation for inmate achievements and participation in prison decision-making, and it gave participants a new and more acceptable means of achieving status within the inmate community.

During the 1970s, prison reform activists and legal challenges to prison rules and regulations opened the prison environment to a much wider range of groups and organizations, including religious and cultural education organizations formed along racial and ethnic lines. Among the most controversial groups during the prison reform period were the Muslims, who won hard-fought court battles to practice their Islamic faith and to lead a life in prison compatible with their religion.

Similarly, the civil rights movement served as a mechanism that focused greater public attention on the treatment of black inmates, and that served to spawn the emergence of black history and awareness, as well as Native American and Hispanic cultural groups and organizations—many of which were formally linked to parent organizations in the community. These groups had recognized inmate leaders, most of whom were elected through a democratic process approved by prison management.

Contemporary examples of inmate self-governance can be found in various adaptations of the therapeutic community model, as well as in the unionization of prisoner labor. One example using a variation of the therapeutic community model was at the Women's Correctional Facility at Niantic, Connecticut, during the late 1970s; it was called the "Just Community." Prisoners were given power to make a wide range of collective decisions, addressing not only their own welfare in confinement, but also decisions regarding the readiness of inmates for release, furlough, and participation in other therapeutically linked activities. Later, this approach was extended to a part of the male prisoner population.

Male inmates in Stillwater, Minnesota, were organized into a workers' council—a formal union-type structure that gave inmates substantial shared decision-making over a wide range of prison industry operations, such as production, wage scales, safety, and benefits. Inmates worked side-by-side with prison indus-try staff and custodial officers to improve the effectiveness and efficiency of prison industry operations. Inmates were also organized into a statewide prisoners' union that was allowed to elect representatives to meet with top prison officials in the state central office.

One of the most comprehensive scholarly works examining prisoner organizations was published in 1982. This National Institute of Justice–sponsored study (Fox 1982) found that prisoners participate in a wide range of formal prisoner organizations, such as the Jaycees, during confinement in maximum-security prisons. Among the types of organizations observed were special interest, religious, cultural awareness and education, and self-help groups. These organizations had elected leaders and were given considerable opportunity to meet and interact with prison management to discuss their activities and organizational needs. Fox (1982) found that approximately one-third of all maximum-security prisoners were members of at least one formal prisoner organization. This pattern of prison adjustment appeared to be more likely among long-term prisoners—who sought some constructive outlet for their time and interests—and within those prisons that had a more progressive and open approach to discipline and order. The opposite pattern appeared to be associated with tight security. For example, Soledad Prison (CTF-C) was administered under coercive custody and security measures because of the concentration of prison gangs. It consequently had only a small number of prisoners involved in legitimate prisoner organizations.

Fox (1982) found that prisoner organizations served to narrow the social distance between prisoners and prison management. In addition, the more pervasive formal prisoner organizations were within the prison community; the less powerful were traditional underground groups and gangs.

Prison management has several concerns regarding any form of inmate participation in decision-making. Among the most widely expressed concern is that a small number of powerful inmates, such as gang leaders or drug dealers, may seek to control and manipulate the organization to pursue their own interests. Consequently, many inmate organizations are kept under tight control and observation by prison management and custodial staff. Another concern addresses the balance between rights and responsibilities. It is perceived that extending greater privileges, such as being granted participatory decision-making powers, should be accompanied with greater inmate responsibility to maintain compliance to prison rules and to govern the membership. The traditional social roles of prison inmates and the social distance between inmates and staff may have changed, but there remains substantial suspicion within the inmate community about the motives of some inmates and the long-term interests of prison management. For example, if formal inmate organizations are viewed as "giving-in" to the demands of prison management, their acceptance by the larger inmate community will likely decline, and the organization may be seen as operating in the interests of prison management.

The long-term survival of inmate self-governance or participative management initiatives appears to swing on the openness of the goals and objectives of those who are elected as leaders and the willingness of prison management to extend participatory powers to inmates who often have little preparation, education, or training for organizational decision-making.

James G. Fox

See also OSBORNE, THOMAS MOTT; SING SING PRISON; UNIONS

Bibliography

Baker, J. E. (1964). Inmate self-government. *Journal of Criminal Law, Criminology, and Police Science* 55: 39–47.

Baker, J. E. (1974). *The Right to Participate: Inmate Involvement in Prison Administration*. Metuchen, N.J.: Scarecrow.

Burdman, M. (1974). Ethnic self-help groups in prison and on parole. *Crime and Delinquency* 20: 107–18.

Fox, J. G. (1982). *Organizational and Racial Conflict in Maximum Security Prisons*. Lexington, Mass.: Lexington.

Helfman, H. M. (1950). Antecedents of Thomas Mott Osborne's Mutual Welfare League in Michigan. *Journal of Criminal Law, Criminology, and Police Science* 40: 597–600.

Huff, C. R. (1974). Unionization behind prison walls. *Criminology* 12: 145–49.

Kasinsky, R. G. (1977). A critique of sharing power in the total institution. *Prison Journal* 57(Autumn–Winter): 56–61.

Murton, T. (1971). Inmate self-government. *University of San Francisco Law Review* 6(October): 87–101.

Murton, T., and P. J. Baunach (1975). *Shared Decision-Making as a Treatment Technique in Prison Management*. Minneapolis, Minn.: Murton Foundation for Criminal Justice.

Osborne, T. M. (1917). Self-government by the prisoner. In J. S. Jaffrey, ed. *The Prison and the Prisoner: A Symposium*. Boston: Little, Brown.

Scharf, P., and J. Hickey (1977). Thomas Mott Osborne and the limits of democratic prison reform. *Prison Journal* 57(Autumn–Winter): 3–15.

Inmate Supervision: The New Generation Philosophy

For many years in the United States, courts assumed a "hands off" policy in regard to a number of issues surrounding the operation and management of correctional facilities. That is not the case today. Over the last several decades the courts have taken an active role in the administration of correctional facilities. In particular, judges have been concerned about such issues as solitary confinement, corporal punishment, use of force against inmates, inmate rights, and overcrowding. In fact, many facilities and even states have been placed under federal court orders to remedy various conditions deemed cruel and unusual punishment (*Cooper v. Pate*, 1964; *Wolff v. McDonnel*, 1974; *Holt v. Sarver*, 1976; *Estelle v. Gamble*, 1976). The courts' willingness to hear inmate allegations along with the willingness of inmates to pursue litigation have increasingly produced an environment wherein correctional officials have been forced to rethink many correctional practices. According to Zupan (1991), many jurisdictions have constructed new facilities in order to forestall court intervention.

Against this backdrop, one of the most profound innovations in correctional institutions has been the dramatic shift over the last fifteen years to what has been labeled the "new generation philosophy." While this approach represents a significant departure from the traditional methods of inmate supervision, it also encompasses architectural, security, management, and other day-to-day operational and supervisory changes. Also referred to as "podular/direct supervision," this new philosophy of inmate supervision is based on the belief that inmates are rational human beings who will always attempt to manipulate an environment to their advantage. In a correctional facility operated under this new generation philosophy, the environment is structured in such a way that these attempts will be readily detected and dealt with by staff. Podular/direct supervision requires inmates to be grouped in manageable units and housed in a space that facilitates continuous and direct observation and supervision (Zupan 1991).

According to Nelson and O'Toole (1983), this new approach puts staff, rather than inmates, in a position to control the facility. It is accomplished by maintaining open lines of communication between custodial staff and inmates, and between staff members as well. Zupan (1991) claims that a primary purpose of direct supervision is to force officers to move around the modules and to interact with inmates. That encourages officers to view the pod as space that they have assumed "ownership" over. This sense of territory is vital to ensure that officers, rather than inmates, exert control and leadership in the pod. Further, rewards and punishments are structured to ensure compliant inmate behavior.

The new generation approach to supervision of inmates runs counter to the traditional "intermittent surveillance" of inmates, in which correctional officers periodically walk down corridors and observe inmates in their cells. In that intermittent surveillance approach to supervision, the correctional officer and the inmate are separated by cell bars; there is only occasional actual observation and minimal interaction. Direct supervision requires the correctional officer to be present in the pod and to be constantly interacting with the inmates. This philosophy of inmate supervision increases the officer's awareness of what is happening in the pod. As a result, a correctional officer may be able to intervene and head off a situation that otherwise might lead to a fight between inmates. Applied correctly, direct supervision aids the officer in detecting friction between inmates before an incident takes place. In that respect, the new generation philosophy is a proactive rather than a reactive approach to supervision. Consequently, advocates claim that the new generation approach will considerably reduce violence.

Proponents of the new generation philosophy also believe that the number of suicides in correctional facilities can be reduced through this new approach to inmate supervision. Be-cause correctional officers in direct supervision facilities basically reside among the inmates in a pod, it is hoped that they would be much more likely to notice an inmate who is severely depressed about some news in a letter from a family member. The officer could prevent a potential suicide.

Proponents of the new generation philosophy point to a host of significant benefits to be realized from implementation of such an approach. Advocates claim that direct supervision facilities are safer and more humane for both inmates and staff. Through improved architectural design and supervision, stress can be reduced for both inmates and staff. Another major benefit is the cost savings realized in the construction of direct-supervision facilities. Many of the security features associated with traditional institutions are not necessary in the design of a direct-supervision facility.

As Senese et al. (1992) point out, however, relatively little has been reported in the literature about new generation jails and their operation. Farbstein et al. (1989) compared five "direct" and "indirect" correctional facilities through questionnaires, surveys, interviews, and case studies. While far from conclusive, their findings generally support many of the assumptions made by those who favor direct supervision over more traditional approaches such as intermittent surveillance. Similarly, Johnson (1994) reports that, in a survey of administrators in new generation facilities, most respondents indicated that the direct supervision philosophy was responsible for improved staff morale, reduced stress levels for both inmates and staff, and reduced violence.

Lovrich et al. (1991) examined direct supervision facilities to determine what impact this philosophy of management and design had upon turnover and stress. They found that stress and turnover varied across correctional facilities and positions. A number of methodological problems made it impossible to identify factors clearly related to stress and employee turnover. It is important to note that overcrowding in direct supervision facilities appeared to mask whatever benefits one might otherwise have expected.

Jackson (1992) evaluated a new generation jail in California and concluded that in general the new generation jail is safer and more secure for both inmates and staff. Officers at the direct supervision facility, however, report feeling less safe from physical assault.

The research by Senese et al. (1992) may be the only systematic attempt in the literature to study a podular/direct supervision facility and compare it with a traditional correctional facility. Their findings are mixed. Their analysis of infractions led them to conclude that correctional officers are effectively handling the day-to-day problems within their pod (as proponents for direct supervision would expect). On the other hand, there was a significant increase in disciplinary problems (which is inconsistent with the expectations for direct supervision). Logically, however, one might expect officers who are present in the pod at all times to observe more infractions of rules than officers who observe inmates only periodically.

There appears to be growing support among a wide range of correctional administrators for this approach to inmate supervision and management. There is no question that the new generation philosophy of inmate supervision is having a greater effect with each passing year. Many of the nation's new jails, detention centers, and prisons are being designed, built, and operated on the direct supervision philosophy. On the other hand, as Zupan (1993) has indicated, the jury is still out on direct supervision. More research and more systematic evaluations are necessary before we can draw conclusions about the new generation philosophy.

Byron R. Johnson

See also ARCHITECTURE

Bibliography

Farbstein, J., and Associates (1989). *A Comparison of "Direct" and "Indirect" Supervision Correctional Facilities—Final Report*. Washington, D.C.: National Institute of Corrections.

Jackson, P. G. (1992). *Detention in Transition: Sonoma County's New Generation Jail*. Washington, D.C.: National Institute of Corrections.

Johnson, B. R. (1994). Exploring direct supervision: A research note. *American Jails* 8(1): 63–64.

Lovrich, N. P., and Associates (1991). *Staff Turnover and Stress in "New Generation" Jails: Key Implementation Issues for a Significant Correctional Policy Innovation—Final Report*. Washington, D.C.: National Institute of Corrections.

Nelson, W. R., and M. O'Toole (1983). *New Generation Jails*. Boulder, Colo.: Library Information Specialists.

Senese, J. D., J. Wilson, A. O. Evans, R. Aquirre, and D. Kalinich (1992). Evaluating inmate infractions and disciplinary response in a traditional and a podular/direct supervision jail. *American Jails* 6(4): 14–23.

Zupan, L. L. (1991). *Jails: Reform and the New Generation Philosophy*. Cincinnati, Ohio: Anderson.

Zupan, L. L. (1993). The need for research on direct inmate supervision. *American Jails* March/April: 21–22.

Cases

Cooper v. Pate, 378 U.S. 546, 84 S.Ct. 1733, 12 L.Ed.2d 1030 (1964)

Estelle v. Gamble, 429 U.S. 97, 97 S.Ct. 285, 50 L.Ed.2d 251 (1976)

Holt v. Sarver, 442 F. 2d 308 (8th Cir. 1971)

Wolff v. McDonnel, 418 U.S. 539, 94 S.Ct. 2963, 41 L.Ed.2d 935 (1974)

Interstate Compact Agreement

An Interstate Compact Agreement is a formal arrangement used by many different correctional agencies within the criminal justice system. Technically speaking, an interstate compact agreement is "an agreement between two or more states to transfer prisoners, parolees, or probationers from the physical custody or supervisory custody of one state to that of another" (Ferdico 1992). Thus, the Interstate Compact Agreement does not cover the international transfer of offenders, which is dealt with under the International Convention on the Transfer of Sentenced Persons. Additionally, the compact does not pertain to transfers within a state.

History

The development of interstate compacts for adults and juveniles was in response to several problems. Within the adult system, citizens were often put at unnecessary risk before the compact agreement was in place, because felons and other offenders were often permitted, and sometimes forced, to leave the state of conviction without notifying or obtaining supervision in the receiving state (Abadinsky 1991). Additionally, rehabilitation was often compromised because even though many individuals were arrested and convicted in a state far from where they had relatives or other community ties, there was no means for supervising an offender outside the state in which they were convicted.

In the juvenile system during the mid 1950s, many juvenile justice professionals were concerned about three problems directly related to the increased mobility of our society:

1. There were no procedures whereby out-of-state runaways could be returned quickly to their home state;
2. There was no system for continued supervision of juveniles whose families moved to another state;
3. There were no standard procedures to quickly return juveniles who absconded across state lines to their supervising jurisdictions.

Pursuant to the Crime Control Consent Act passed by Congress in 1936, a group of states began formulating the adult Interstate Compact Agreement. The Interstate Compact Agreement was originally signed by twenty-five member states in 1937, and the agreement was fully ratified by all the states in 1951. Today, all fifty states plus the District of Columbia, Puerto Rico, and the Virgin Islands have signed the compact (Cromwell and Killinger 1994). To address the juvenile concerns, the Council of State Governments finished drafting a juvenile interstate compact agreement in 1955. The juvenile compact has since been ratified by all fifty states and the District of Columbia.

Administration

The adult and juvenile interstate compact agreements are quite similar in nature. Both provide an orderly and legal means of granting offenders the privilege of being transferred out of the state in which they were sentenced to a state where they may have better opportunities for rehabilitation, while still protecting society. The compacts also regulate interstate travel by offenders; individuals must obtain a travel pass notifying the receiving state of their upcoming visit.

To be eligible to participate in an interstate compact agreement, the offender must ordinarily be a resident, must be benefited by an available program, and have relatives or employment in the receiving state. Before granting any kind of permission to transfer an offender, the receiving state is given the opportunity to make an investigation into the appropriateness of the proposed placement.

The compact agreement also calls for each participating state to provide a compact administrator. The administrators work with the administrators of other states, as well as with state, county, and municipal justice officials in their own state, to coordinate and implement the terms of the compact. Additionally, all correspondence concerning interstate cases is to be sent through the administrator's office, not directly from one jurisdiction to another, unless an emergency exists.

Advantages

The interstate compact agreement, like other aspects of the criminal justice system, is a mixture of advantages and disadvantages. First let us look at some of its primary advantages.

Administrative. Because the interstate compact agreement has become a formal plan in American corrections, it has been brought under the control of a state administrator's office. In some instances, that could be the director of the Department of Corrections and Rehabilitation, the director of parole or probation, or the director of institutions. This ensures that the administrators of both states are involved in processing the paperwork and procedures regarding the offender. If the request is granted, the receiving jurisdiction will ensure that correct supervision is instituted.

Cost. The interstate compact agreement differs from other components of the criminal justice system in that it does not require the extradition process. Extradition is costly, and the procedures involved are time-consuming. Should a supervision violation occur, extradition is typically waived automatically, and the offender is returned to the original jurisdiction. The offender is bound by the conditions of parole, probation, or incarceration of the receiving state, but is always under the sending state's jurisdiction.

Rehabilitation. Perhaps the greatest advantage of the interstate compact agreement is that it serves to reunite families that have been torn apart because the offender is under supervision in some other state. In their home state, offenders may also have a better chance of finding employment to alleviate some of the financial stress on their families, thereby reducing the probability of recidivism. One of the main goals of the interstate compact agreement is that it be used for rehabilitation rather than punishment. Programs available in the receiving state may further the goal of rehabilitation. For instance, a state that has no accessible drug or alcohol treatment program may turn to a neighboring state with a program that could be of benefit to the offender.

Disadvantages

The following disadvantages may occur with the use of the interstate compact agreement.

Reciprocity. Some states receive more than their share of offenders. In Mississippi, for example, out-of-state placements numbered 1,342, while in the same year Mississippi received only 916 out-of-state offenders. The difference could become a heavy burden on some institutions or states, especially those plagued by high caseloads or crowded institutions. In an already overburdened system, even a small imbalance involving interstate transfers could make a drastic difference.

Policies. Different jurisdictions also have their own policies and procedures. This can create problems, because what is a violation in one state may not be in another. Deciding when the termination, revocation, or completion of out-of-state supervision is warranted is another problem. The difficulty with differing policies lies in the fact that when decisions have to be made regarding an out-of-state placement, the state of original jurisdiction must first authorize such a decision through the appropriate but often time-consuming channels.

Frequency of Use. Though all fifty states have signed the Interstate Compact Agreement, it is not widely used. On average there are 200,000 probationers and parolees whose request to relocate is accepted each year. This count does not include the number of interstate compact transfers of prisoners each year (McShane and Krause 1993).

Time. The time factor may be one of the biggest problems in dealing with interstate trans-fers. Offenders are often counseled to allow at least sixty days for a decision regarding their interstate placement request to be made. The time delay does not allow offenders the possibility of quickly taking advantage of unforeseen treatment or employment opportunities.

Dumping. In the past, some receiving agencies have accused sending states of "dumping." This refers to the practice of sending difficult cases out of state for no reason other than to rid themselves of problem offenders. Such practices may also occur when a state has high caseloads.

Conclusion

Despite many problems with the interstate compact agreements, their use and applicability will likely both continue and increase in the future. Several steps can be taken to improve compact agreements.

One way to alleviate the problems caused by time delays while waiting for acceptance from the receiving state is to automatically assume acceptance as long as the offender has met a standard set of criteria established by the receiving state. Using computers to process requests, as several states are currently doing, will also expedite the process. Finally, training selected staff members in the rules and regulations regarding interstate compact requests will allow for more efficient and timely use of this agreement in the future.

Wendelin M. Hume
Mark D. Dyrdahl

Bibliography

Abadinsky, H. (1991). *Probation and Parole Theory and Practice*. Englewood Cliffs, N.J.: Prentice-Hall.

Cromwell, P., and G. Killinger (1994). *Community-Based Corrections: Probation, Parole, and Intermediate Sanctions*. 3rd ed. St. Paul, Minn.: West.

Ferdico, J. N. (1992). *Ferdico's Criminal Law and Justice Dictionary*. New York: West.

McShane, M., and W. Krause (1993). *Community Corrections*. New York: Macmillan.

J

Jailhouse Lawyers

The term "jailhouse lawyer" refers to an inmate who has studied to become knowledgeable in the law while in prison and who assists others in the preparation of legal documents. Jailhouse lawyers generally have been viewed negatively—clogging the courts with frivolous litigation, producing legal work of poor quality, and exploiting fellow inmates. They can, however, be viewed as engaged in a form of dispute resolution. Their efforts to bring their concerns to the attention of administrators and the public are a much more functional form of expression than rioting. Thomas (1988, 8) views "prisoner litigation [as] a form of resistance to the deprivations of prison life."

Historically, the courts have employed a hands-off policy when it comes to prison administration. Authorities were more or less unrestricted in their choice of policies for controlling the inmate population. Prisoners were viewed as slaves of the state. Consequently, prison regulations forbade inmates from engaging in any type of legal work for themselves or on behalf of others. Individuals were severely punished if they possessed legal materials or law books. To do so was seen as a threat to administrative authority. Inmate "writ writers," as they were called, were viewed as troublemakers by prison administrators.

Access to Courts

In 1941, with *Ex parte Hull* the court held that the state or its officers cannot abridge or impair inmates' access to the court. Significant changes in the guarantee of constitutional rights occurred during the 1960s and 1970s (Jacobs 1979). The most active agent of reform has been the U.S. Supreme Court's upholding the principle of individual rights in the face of governmental power. During that era the Court held that the guarantees of the First, Fourth, Fifth, Sixth, and Eighth Amendments were made binding on the states through the language of the Fourteenth Amendment.

The pivotal cases that seemed to support the notion of "jailhouse lawyering" are *Johnson v. Avery* and *Bounds v. Smith*. These two important cases were concerned with the right of individuals' access to the courts. *Johnson v. Avery* concerned the assistance of fellow inmates in preparing postconviction appeals of imprisonment (preparation of a federal writ of habeas corpus). The court felt that, because jails and prisons are populated by a high proportion of illiterate, undereducated, and poor people, the assistance of jailhouse lawyers was the only way that their constitutional claims would be heard. In addition, many inmates today do not speak, read, or write English and are in need of bilingual services in order to understand their legal correspondence.

In *Bounds v. Smith* the Supreme Court made it clear that the state has a responsibility to protect the inmates' right to access to the courts by providing "meaningful access to the courts" (providing materials for legal research). This has been interpreted to mean that states must provide law libraries or other legal assistance in order to ensure inmates the resources to present claims if their constitutional rights have been violated.

Jailhouse lawyering has been surrounded with a great deal of controversy. Most prison policies, which have been upheld by the courts, emphasize that the jailhouse lawyers can not be compensated for their assistance in any way. The decision in *Johnson v. Avery* is explicit regarding compensation. Most jailhouse lawyers, however, take some form of "gift" in exchange for their legal assistance. This compensation can take many forms in prison. Given the values of the prison world, it is not appropriate to give one's services free of charge. To do so may lead to a person's being taken advantage of or, worse yet, losing face and compromising one's reputation.

Being a jailhouse lawyer is a valued identity in prison. It provides a way to gain power, money, and independence, all highly prized in the prison environment. Being a jailhouse lawyer also provides a positive social identity, hope for release, and a constructive, nonviolent activity during incarceration.

On the other hand, being a skilled jailhouse lawyer is also one way to attract the scrutiny of the staff and administration, many of whom view the practice as disruptive. In *Smith v. Rowe*, a female jailhouse lawyer was punished because of her activities when a new, more restrictive warden took over the Illinois facility in which she was incarcerated. Smith had been working as a law librarian, assisting other inmates in translating legal documents and doing legal research. Accused of possessing contraband, she was placed in a cold, rodent-infested solitary cell for more than twenty-two months with nothing but a bed, dresser, toilet, and sink. The courts held the warden liable for depriving Smith of her constitutional rights and ordered a damage award of $80,700.

Activities of the Jailhouse Lawyer

"Jailhouse lawyering" may involve a variety of actions filed by an incarcerated person over grievances against the criminal justice system. Jailhouse lawyers have specific remedies available to them at both the state and federal levels. They include criminal appeals, administrative appeals and inmate grievances, tort actions, writs of mandamus and prohibition, habeas corpus petitions, and (federal) civil rights complaints (article 42, section 1983). The relief available from these remedies includes release, award of money or damages, and injunctive relief (ordering an institutional authority to cease engaging in a specified act or to undo some wrong). Inmates may also require legal assistance to answer divorce petitions, terminations of parental rights, or problems with immigration, inheritance, social security, and veterans' issues.

In addition to traditional legal problems, female inmates may have other concerns that require legal assistance, such as medical care, equal protection or "parity" claims for educational and vocational programs available to male inmates, and issues regarding children and family. These have generally concerned Fourteenth and Eighth Amendment issues. Medical care for female offenders includes such issues as pregnancy, abortion, and childbirth. The equal protection clause of the Fourteenth Amendment is relevant to the disparities in vocational and educational programs available to male and female inmates. The court has stated, however, that equal protection does not guarantee identical treatment but rather "parity." Issues regarding relationships with children are extremely important in light of the special mother/child bond that is frequently a casualty of women's incarceration.

Jailhouse lawyering appears to function differently for men and women. Generally, it functions for men as a way to do time and conduct a "business." Women have been described as apathetic about prisoner litigation. The pendulum has swung, however; women appear to have evolved as litigants, showing a greater concern for a social and institutional struggle over issues of women's imprisonment.

Cynthia B. Hart

See also LEGAL ISSUES

Bibliography

Alyward, A., and J. Thomas (1984). Quiescence in women's prison litigation: Some exploratory gender issues. *Justice Quarterly* 1: 253–76.

Jacobs, J. (1979). *Individual Rights and Institutional Authority: Prisons, Mental Hospitals, Schools, and Military.* Indianapolis, Ind.: Bobbs-Merrill.

Thomas, J. (1988). *Prisoner Litigation: The Paradox of the Jailhouse Lawyer.* Totowa, N.J.: Rowman and Littlefield.

Cases

Bounds v. Smith 430 U.S. 817 (1977)

Ex parte Hull 312 U.S. 546 (1940)

Johnson v. Avery 393 U.S. 483 (1969)

Ruffin v. Commonwealth 62 Va. (21 Grat.) 790, 796 (1871)

Smith v. Rowe, 761 F.2d 360 (7th Cir. 1985)

Judicial Intervention

In 1992, prisons in over forty states were operating under federal court orders mandating reform of unconstitutional conditions. Such widespread judicial intervention into penal administration is a radical break with precedent. For most of our history, courts took little interest in prisons beyond a recognition of the right of those confined to demand, via a writ of habeas corpus, a hearing before a judge to examine the legality of their detention. In some states, prison inmates were simply "slaves of the state" (*Ruffin v. Commonwealth,* 1871) who retained no constitutional rights. Courts in other jurisdictions, especially the federal courts, might recognize that prisoners retained rights but nonetheless adopted a "hands-off" posture with respect to prisons. They justified this stance by reference to federalism, the separation of powers, and their lack of sufficient penological expertise to make sound decisions.

Over the past half century, however, views of the appropriate role of the courts changed dramatically. In the past, the primary and proper function of the courts was the adjudication of disputes between two parties, and many still hold to that view today (Fuller 1978). Since World War II, however, a more expanded view has emerged. Fiss (1979) describes this function as giving meaning to public values, by which he means that the distinctive role of the court is to protect constitutional rights. Where necessary, courts must restructure state bureaucracies to eliminate threats to constitutional values. To traditionalists who argue that such an expanded role is a usurpation of executive or legislative functions, proponents of the expanded role respond that the courts are the only body capable of intervention when governmental officials fail to uphold their constitutional responsibilities.

The expansion of the judicial role came about in cases involving the citizenship rights of disadvantaged and relatively powerless groups. Racial and ethnic minorities, women, poor people, the mentally ill, gays and lesbians, and other marginal groups have successfully pressed to have their grievances recognized and to be granted admission to the social mainstream. Prisoners linked their plight to this broader civil rights movement and presented their claims in terms such that the federal courts were obligated to hear them.

In 1961, the Supreme Court ended the dispute over the right of federal courts to intervene in state matters when it determined in *Monroe v. Pape* that federal courts have jurisdiction over cases in which state officials, acting under the "color of law," infringe on rights guaranteed by the Constitution. Although *Monroe* was not a prison case, its ruling opened the way for prisoners to challenge the conditions of their confinement. Several years later, prisoners were explicitly brought within its scope in the first modern prisoners' rights case to reach the Court.

Illinois prison officials denied Black Muslim prisoners any opportunity to practice their religion. Inmate Thomas Cooper challenged this prohibition on the grounds of racial and religious discrimination. His original suit was dismissed for failing to state a cause of action, but the Supreme Court proved more receptive to his claim than had the lower courts. In its ruling the Court affirmed that the Muslim prisoners had legal standing to challenge religious discrimination under Section 1983 of the Civil Rights Act of 1871 (*Cooper v. Pate* 1964). Although the substance of the decision was narrow and technical, its implications were enormous: Prisoners retained rights that prison officials had to respect, and the courts had to provide a forum in which prisoners could challenge their keepers. As James Jacobs (1980, 434) has rightly observed, this case sounded the death knell for authoritarian prison regimes.

Leading civil rights attorneys, such as Alvin Bronstein of the American Civil Liberties Union and William Bennett Turner of the NAACP Legal Defense Fund, soon began to devote their full attention to prisoners' rights cases. In this they were joined on the state and local level by countless numbers of younger attorneys working in legal-services projects funded by the federal government's Office of Economic Opportunity and large private foundations as well. This prisoners' rights bar initiated and won cases affecting every aspect of prison operations. In an explosion of litigation in the 1960s and early 1970s, courts recognized the legitimacy of a wide variety of inmates' grievances and ordered major changes in institutional practices and conditions. It was made clear that the state has a duty to protect from harm those it confines and that it must provide them with adequate medical care. Corporal punishment was abolished, as was the arbitrary censorship of mail and publications. Prisoners were afforded minimal due process protections in disciplinary hearings. And to secure these and other rights, prisoners must have meaningful access to the courts.

The high point of the prisoners' rights movement was reached in *Wolff v. McDonnell* (1974, 555), in which Justice White, speaking for the Court, stated clearly that "there is no iron curtain drawn between the Constitution and the prisons of this country." Ironically, this statement came at a time when public support for such liberal causes as prison reform had begun to wane. Civil rights demonstrations, antiwar protests, urban riots, and increasing levels of violent crime sparked widespread fear of a complete collapse of public order in the late 1960s and early 1970s. As part of President Nixon's campaign to restore law and order, being tough on crime was a prime criterion for appointment to the Supreme Court, and legislation was passed that specifically excluded civil rights suits from federal government grants for legal services for the indigent.

While continuing to proclaim the need to provide safe and humane conditions of confinement, the Supreme Court has over the past decade acted to slow the expansion of prisoners' rights. It has introduced new standards that make it more difficult for plaintiffs to sustain their claims, chastised lower courts for becoming too involved in the minutiae of prison operations, and cautioned the lower courts to be more deferential to the expertise of correctional administrators.

Despite a less receptive legal climate in the past decade, the prisoners' rights movement is far from dead. The ACLU's National Prison Project continues to litigate cases across the nation, often in support of the initiatives of local chapters. In the 1990s there are over twenty thousand suits filed by state prisoners and pending in federal courts each year, up from about two hundred in the mid 1960s. Most of these are filed *pro se* (without legal assistance) and are dismissed prior to trial. But with even only a small percentage surviving to trial, the number of litigated cases remains substantial.

A Model of Institutional Reform Litigation

Most prisoners' rights cases are brought as class actions, lawsuits brought by one or a few people on behalf of a larger group of whom the plaintiffs believe themselves to be representative. Rule 23 of the Federal Rules of Civil Procedure authorizes class actions, provided that the plaintiffs can show they are proper representatives of the class, that the type of issues they raise are common to the class, and that they can demonstrate how a remedy can be formed to meet the needs of the entire class. Plaintiffs usually seek injunctive relief, an order that declares current conditions or practices illegal and that requires defendants to change the conditions or stop the illegal practices. As experience has shown that general injunctions are frequently ignored, plaintiffs today usually seek affirmative relief as well, remedial decrees that direct specific changes in conditions and practice to undo the damage suffered by plaintiffs and to prevent it from reoccurring.

Following an extensive study of institutional reform litigation or, as he terms it, remedial decree litigation, Phillip J. Cooper (1988) proposed a model for understanding the dynamics of such cases. The model consists of four phases: trigger, liability, remedy, and postdecree.

Trigger Phase

Cooper's research (1988) led him to conclude that most institutional reform litigation is not the result of carefully planned moves by national groups like the ACLU's National Prison Project. On the contrary, most are relatively spontaneous reactions to longstanding practices or policies that are triggered by some critical event. What defines a particular event as critical and prevents the suit from being rejected by the courts is dependent upon a host of factors at both the local and national levels. Thomas Cooper's decision to file his *pro se* suit against Warden Pate in 1962 was undoubtedly influenced by the successes of the broader civil rights movement, and perhaps by the perception of a weaker prison regime following the resignation of the charismatic Joseph Ragen, who had ruled Stateville with an iron hand until 1961 (Jacobs 1977, 52–65). As we have seen, it was rejected by the lower federal courts for failing to state a cause for action but was viewed much differently by the Supreme Court. That ruling by the Supreme Court created a legal climate in which many more events triggered similar litigation.

Liability Phase

As the term suggests, the purpose of the liability phase is to determine if there has been a violation justifying some sort of remedy and, if so, what the extent of the injury suffered by the plaintiffs is. This phase is largely controlled by the lawyers for the plaintiffs, defendants, and any other parties who may join or be brought into the litigation. Of particular importance at this phase is knowledge of relevant case law and access to expert witnesses. It is in these areas that the experience and skill of national prisoners' rights organizations have been telling, as they have frequently been opposed by young and inexperienced counsel for the defendants.

The liability phase is often lengthy, as it encompasses extended investigation and may involve a variety of legal maneuvers even before a trial. What is perhaps the most widely known prisoners' rights case, *Ruiz v. Estelle* (1980)—a challenge to conditions in Texas prisons—was certified as a class action suit in April of 1974 but did not come to trial until October of 1978. The Department of Justice was brought into the case by the court to investigate the facts alleged in the prisoners' complaints, a maneuver that the state sought unsuccessfully to block. Even before the process of discovery could begin, there were a series of separate hearings resulting in court orders enjoining defendants from harassing inmates cooperating with attorneys for the plaintiffs. The trial itself lasted 161 days, during which time testimony was heard from 349 witnesses and some 1,530 exhibits were entered in evidence (Martin and Ekland-Olson, 1987, xxvi).

As the power of the courts to mandate changes and compel compliance became clear, not to mention the cost of protracted litigation, the proportion of cases going to trial appears to have declined and the proportion settled by consent decree has increased. A consent decree is an order that is negotiated among the parties in which administrators, without admitting liability, agree to change practices or conditions. In 1970, for example, a comprehensive and detailed set of regulations governing the classification and discipline of prisoners in Rhode Island's Adult Correctional Institution was entered as interim order of the federal court (*Morris v. Travisono* 1970). These regulations, while approved and ordered by the court, were the product of negotiation between attorneys for the plaintiffs and defendants.

The Remedy Phase

The negotiation of a consent decree may shortcut or bypass the liability phase altogether, bringing the case directly into the remedy phase. Two processes characterize this phase. First and foremost is the development of a plan to resolve the identified problems. Second, where there has been a finding of liability, there may also be an appeal that, when completed, may significantly affect the remedial plan.

The role courts have played in crafting a remedy and the detail in which it is crafted has varied greatly. In some cases judges have deferred to administrators, simply ordering them to eliminate the offending conditions or practices with little or no guidance about how to do it nor means of assessment. A prime example of this approach occurred in *Holt v. Sarver* (1970). After finding massive violations in Arkansas's two major prisons, the judge mandated general improvements in prison conditions but placed full responsibility for formulating and implementing the remedy on the defendants and refused to become actively involved in monitoring compliance.

The deferential posture of the court in *Holt* was more characteristic of early cases, in which judges naively believed that their orders would be respected and followed simply because they emanated from a court. In later cases, especially those in which the defendants refuse to participate in the development of a plan, courts typically have adopted a more directive role. In *Pugh v. Locke* (1976), for example, after an extensive trial, Judge Frank Johnson unilaterally developed an extremely detailed remedial plan without significant input from either plaintiffs or defendants and appointed a large Human Rights Committee to monitor its implementation. The court of appeals, however, found that the committee and its powers intruded too much into the daily operation of the prison and reversed that part of the order (Yackle 1989).

The basis for the reversal of that portion of Judge Johnson's plan appointing the Human Rights Committee related to the composition and specific powers of that committee, not to the right of the court to use independent agents to assist it. Indeed, it is a long-established principle that courts have inherent equity power to provide themselves with appropriate instruments required for the performance of their duties, and Federal Rule of Civil Procedure #53 provides explicitly for the appointment of special masters to assist judges in complicated cases.

The roles of special masters in prison cases vary depending upon the needs of the case and the discretion of the judge. In some cases, masters have been appointed soon after a determination that an evidentiary hearing upon the plaintiff's complaint is necessary and empowered to hear all or some of the evidence in the case and to make findings of fact based on that evidence. In other cases masters have been appointed after the finding of a constitutional violation, but before the issuance of a remedial decree, to assist the court in the formulation of the decree. Most commonly, however, masters have been employed to monitor compliance with a court's remedial decree.

All three functions were evident in *Guthrie v. Evans* (1986), involving conditions at the Georgia State Penitentiary. Rather than proceed with a formal trial, the judge appointed a special master to hold hearings and submit findings of fact and recommendations. These reports became the basis for extended negotiations between the parties, refereed by a master, resulting in numerous consent decrees. Finally, still another master was appointed to assess compliance with these decrees (Chilton 1991).

The Post Decree Phase
A fourth phase of institutional reform litigation follows the issuance of and remedial order or the entry of a consent decree. During this phase, which is often protracted, the remedy is implemented, evaluated, and compliance of the defendants with the decree is assessed. Along the way the original decree is frequently refined and may, in fact be substantially modified.

Judicial decrees are not self-executing. Courts are dependent upon those who administer the institution to implement the required changes. Ironically, these are often the very administrators responsible for the violations, and frequently they will not or cannot comply with the court's order. Even seemingly simple, straightforward directives, sometimes even after being upheld on appeal, have been simply ignored or implemented in the narrowest possible terms, resulting in further litigation to clarify related issues. The right of Black Muslims in Illinois to attend religious services, to have access to the Quran, and to communicate with ministers was recognized in litigation following the Supreme Court's decision in *Cooper* (1964). Correctional officials, however, continued to deny Muslims the right to wear religious medallions, to have a pork-free diet or to receive Muslim literature. The result in Illinois and elsewhere was years of further litigation on these and other related issues (Jacobs 1977, 59–70, 106–7).

Until 1970, prisoners' rights cases were framed in terms of specific practices or conditions, such as freedom of religion or due process of law. In *Holt v. Sarver* (1970), however, a new concept emerged that at once widened the potential scope of decrees and made their implementation even more complicated. The totality of conditions in Arkansas's two major prisons were found to violate the Eighth Amendment ban on cruel and unusual punishment. By the totality of conditions the court meant that the aggregate of circumstances in a facility might constitute cruel and unusual punishment, even though no single condition by itself is so deficient as to constitute a constitutional violation.

As noted above, Judge Henley's order in *Holt* was quite general. It relied on state officials to formulate and implement the remedy and made no provisions for monitoring progress. Little progress was made in remedying conditions until eight years later, when a compliance coordinator was appointed. By that time the case had expanded tremendously as a result of additional litigation.

In later totality-of-conditions cases, judges typically have fashioned detailed remedies that set standards and deadlines, and have appointed special masters with extensive powers to monitor progress. As they have encountered inertia or resistance, they have been less hesitant to use their resources and powers. Soon after a remedial order was issued in *Palmigiano v. Garrahy* (1977), for example, the special master in that case was instrumental in finding an experienced correctional administrator to provide capable leadership for Rhode Island's Department of Corrections in developing plans and funding for renovations after voters rejected a bond issue. Years later, however, after the state had failed to take any meaningful steps to alleviate serious overcrowding that was jeopardizing the reforms, Judge Raymond Pettine found the state in contempt of court and levied a fine of $189,000, which was used to establish a bail fund.

Similar actions have been taken in other cases. Judge Justice, for example, found the Texas Department of Corrections in contempt of court for failure to implement major provisions of a settlement agreement negotiated as part of the remedy in *Ruiz* and threatened the state with fines as high as $24 million per month. Shortly thereafter, Texas officials decided to move rapidly toward compliance (Martin and Ekland-Olson 1987). In Alabama, Judge Johnson stripped the Board of Corrections of its authority by placing the department in receivership and appointing as receiver a newly elected governor who had publicly committed himself to making changes in the prisons (Yackle 1989, Ch. 7).

Actions such as receivership, contempt citations, and fines have been taken by the courts only in the face of seemingly intractable resistance. For the most part, judges have been patient and flexible, proceeding incrementally toward compliance while refining and modifying the original decree in light of experience and changing circumstances. In his original decree in 1977, Judge Pettine ordered Rhode Island's one hundred-year-old maximum-security prison closed but permitted the state to use it for one year, provided that it was cleaned and made fit for habitation (*Palmigiano* 1977). It was nearly two years before these minimal objectives were met, however, and still a new high-security unit that had been scheduled to open in 1978 had not been completed. In the meantime, the inmate population had begun to increase. Rather than adhere to his original order, Judge Pettine continuously extended the deadlines, permitted structural renovations of one cell block after another, and finally agreed to permit the state to use the prison indefinitely.

The Impact of Judicial Intervention

Evaluating the impact of judicial intervention on prisons is difficult. The most important questions are not whether specific unconstitutional practices or conditions have been eliminated but whether, in the process, the prison or correctional system has been transformed so that the constitutional conditions have been institutionalized. Often, as in totality-of-conditions cases, this question is exceedingly complex, going to virtually every aspect of prison operations. Even in cases involving specific practices or conditions such as hygienic standards or due process guarantees, the evaluation is made difficult because interest is in the long run rather than the short term. But the longer time there is between the intervention and the evaluation, the more difficult it is to attribute any changes to the intervention rather than other events.

Many of the early cases involved unspeakably horrible conditions: inmates forced to live in terribly overcrowded, filthy, vermin-infested facilities; armed inmate trustees supervising other inmates; and official torture, such as electric shocks to the genitals. Public awareness of such conditions produced strong pressure for reform, and the worst abuses and harshest conditions were rather quickly eliminated. The scope of the relief, however, was usually confined to the specific issues presented in the litigation. Despite significant improvements, conditions generally remained poor. Moreover, as these issues presented in the litigation were, more often than not, symptomatic of more fun-

damental problems, it was questionable if the improvements would be maintained (Harris and Spiller 1976).

Where conditions were not so shocking, there was little public pressure for change. Prison administrations across the country, like those in Illinois, noted above, for years resisted extending religious freedoms to Black Muslims on the grounds that doing so would jeopardize security. Similar objections were raised to granting inmates minimal due process guarantees in disciplinary hearings. Six months after the entry of the consent decree in *Morris v. Travisono* (1970), for instance, researchers found that the provisions of the decree had not been implemented to any satisfactory degree owing, in large part, to staff resentment and resistance (Harvard Center 1972).

Being defined as a defendant in a court case was, at least in the early years of intervention, a startling role reversal for correctional administrators and staff. To the shock of being accused of constitutional violations was frequently added bitter frustration at not being able to convince the courts of the wisdom of their administrative practices, and outrage at decisions that, in their eyes, made them seem villains, placed the law on the side of the inmates, and made it impossible for them to maintain order and security. Many experienced administrators and officers retired or quit; others simply retreated from routine performance of their duties. As turnover rates went up, morale plummeted, and violence rose dramatically.

The most dramatic increase in violence occurred in Texas. Prior to the court order, and for some time thereafter, an inmate elite, known as "building tenders," were used by Texas officials to maintain control of the population. Over two thousand new staff were hired as the building tenders were phased out over a two-year period. These new and inexperienced officers, often supervised by superiors with little more experience than themselves, faced a rapidly growing prisoner population resulting from the "war on drugs." Gangs emerged as a dominant force among inmates as traffic in drugs grew and previously repressed racial tension boiled. Weapons possession proliferated, and a system once known for its safety saw rampant violence. In 1984 and 1985, there were over six hundred nonfatal stabbings and fifty-two inmate-on-inmate homicides (Martin and Ekland-Olson 1987; Crouch and Marquart 1989).

The upswing in violence in Texas proved to be a temporary phenomenon, associated with the transition from one system of control to another. In Texas, staffing increased to prescribed levels in 1987 and the new staff, carefully trained in judicially approved rules and procedures, gradually grew confident in applying them. Thousands of gang-affiliated or violence-prone inmates were identified and placed in administrative segregation where, under court sanctioned policy, they could be kept indefinitely. Population pressures were relieved considerably as new units came on line following a massive construction program, and after passage of legislation allowing early paroles and limiting admissions from the largest counties. As the violence subsided, court supervision became more passive. Within the department, decision-making, which had been highly centralized in an effort to secure compliance with the court's orders, was once again decentralized. Now, however, it was structured by written policies and procedures and monitored through extensive reporting systems. Negotiations to terminate the suit began in 1990 and were completed in 1992, nearly twenty years after it had begun.

Resistance to court intervention was probably greater in Texas than elsewhere. The experience in that state demonstrates that determined intervention by the courts can, over the long run, be successful in changing prison conditions and practices even in the face of widespread and intense opposition. Despite local differences, the cases that have been the subject of long-term study suggest that the experience in other states is close to that of Texas. Court intervention is resisted; there follows a period of staff demoralization and increasing violence among inmates. Finally, there is movement toward compliance. In the process, old line wardens are replaced by new administrators with more formal education, and the demands of the court for rational decision-making and accountability result in a centralization of authority and a bureaucratized administrative structure.

The emergence of more professionalized administration has not been limited to those states in which there has been sweeping intervention. Judicial scrutiny has contributed to the development of a movement within corrections to establish national standards. The American Correctional Association, for example, has established an accreditation pro-gram, based on rigorous standards covering all aspects of prison operation. If successful, it may provide a means by which to increase the resources available to corrections, improve conditions, and limit future intervention by the courts.

Leo Carroll

See also LEGAL ISSUES

Bibliography

Chilton, B. S. (1991). *Prisons Under the Gavel: The Federal Court Takeover of Georgia Prisons.* Columbus, Ohio: Ohio State University Press.

Cooper, P. J. (1988). *Hard Judicial Choices: Federal District Court Judges and State and Local Officials.* New York: Oxford University Press.

Crouch, B. M., and J. M. Marquart (1989). *An Appeal to Justice: Litigated Reform of Texas Prisons.* Austin, Tex.: University of Texas Press.

DiIulio, J. J., ed. (1990). *Courts, Corrections and the Constitution.* New York: Oxford University Press.

Fiss, O. (1979). The Supreme Court, 1978 term—forward: The forms of justice. *Harvard Law Review* 93: 1–58.

Fuller, L. (1978). The forms and limits of adjudication. *Harvard Law Review* 92: 353–409.

Harris, M. K., and D. P. Spiller (1976). *After Decision: Implementation of Judicial Decrees in Correctional Settings.* Washington, D.C.: American Bar Association.

Harvard Center for Criminal Justice (1972). Judicial intervention in prison discipline. *Journal of Criminal Law and Criminology* 63: 200–228.

Jacobs, J. B. (1977). *Stateville: The Penitentiary in Mass Society.* Chicago: University of Chicago Press.

Jacobs, J. B. (1980). The prisoners' rights movement and its impacts. In N. Morris and M. Tonry, eds. *Crime and Justice: An Annual Review of Research.* Vol. 2. Chicago: University of Chicago Press.

Martin, S. J., and S. Ekland-Olson (1987). *Texas Prisons: The Walls Came Tumbling Down.* Austin, Tex.: Texas Monthly.

Yackle, L. W. (1989). *Reform and Regret: The Story of Federal Judicial Involvement in the Alabama Prison System.* New York: Oxford University Press.

Cases

Cooper v. Pate, 378 U.S. 546, 84 S.Ct. 1773, 12 L.Ed.2d 1030 (1964)

Guthrie v. Evans, C. A. No. 73-3068 (S.D. Ga. 1986)

Holt v. Sarver, 309 F.Supp. 362 (1970)

Monroe v. Pape, 365 U.S. 167, 81 S.Ct. 473, 5 L.Ed.2d 492 (1961)

Morris v. Travisono, 310 F. Supp. 857 (1970)

Palmigiano v. Garrahy, 443 F. Supp. 956 (1977)

Pugh v. Locke, 406 F. Supp. 318 (1976)

Ruffin v. Commonwealth, 62 Va. 790 (1871)

Ruiz v. Estelle, 503 F. Supp. 1265 (1980)

Wolff v. McDonnell, 418 U.S. 539, 94 S.Ct. 2963, 41 L.Ed.2d 935 (1974)

J

L

Lease System

The practice of putting social outcasts and criminals to work has a long, and sometimes disturbing, history. In ancient Greece, criminals were put to work on both public and private projects. In what may be the first instance of government leasing of labor, state-owned slaves were leased to private mining operators to work in the silver mines in fifth-century B.C. Greece. It was a major operation, with as many as ten thousand laborers at work at Laureion. Conditions in the mines were dangerous and led to many deaths.

Convict labor was also used during the Roman Empire, although generally on state-operated public works. The decrease in the number of slaves resulting from the end of the Roman conquests created labor shortages that made the use of convict labor very attractive.

Convict labor was used on a limited basis during the Middle Ages. Offenders unable to pay financial compensation could be sold into slavery and would be set to work by their owner. Galley slavery came into existence late in the period, and by the seventeenth and eighteenth centuries, galley convicts were sent to work for private employers and were paid for their work at about 20 percent of the prevailing wage (Sellin 1976).

It is important to note that imprisonment in institutions had played only a minor role in the punishment of criminals to that time. Although slaves were incarcerated on the plantations of slaveholders in ancient Rome, imprisonment was not used as a punishment for free citizens involved in serious crimes.

That began to change in the sixteenth century. In 1556 the Bridewell in London opened to confine vagabonds and minor offenders, and to put them to work grinding corn, making nails, spinning fabric, or laboring at other tasks (McConville 1981). Subsequent houses of correction followed this model and were run essentially as private business ventures by the facility keeper. In Amsterdam, in 1556, the Rasphuis opened with some of the same objectives. A private contractor was brought in to manage the weaving shop, and an institution for women, the Spinhuis, opened soon after. Before long, the concept of confining various kinds of deviants and putting them to work began to spread across Europe. Workhouses and houses of correction confined increasing numbers of European offenders.

The Use of Work in America

The same trend occurred in the American colonies. For instance, a 1699 Massachusetts statute "declared that rogues and vagabonds were to be punished and set to work in the house of correction" (Rothman 1971, 26). Other colonies followed suit and houses of correction in the colonies were used to extract labor from a wide range of minor offenders and miscreants.

The mission of the prison was, of course, somewhat different from that of the workhouse. Prisons were generally designed to hold and punish relatively serious offenders for greater periods of time. Such offenders were forced to labor at the very outset of the American prison experience. Newgate of Connecticut opened in 1773 in an abandoned copper mine. The enacting legislation provided that offenders work during the course of their imprisonment. The more famous Walnut Street Jail, which began to accept prisoners for long terms of incarceration in 1790, set its inmates to work under what we now call the piece-price system.

With the rise of the penitentiary system in the late eighteenth and early nineteenth centuries, the focus shifted toward the reform of the offender, but the emphasis on prison labor remained in place. Among other things, toil at hard labor was believed to have a beneficial effect on behavior, and thus was part of the penitential regime.

The Rise of the Lease System

By the end of the first quarter of the nineteenth century, prisons across the nation were putting inmates to work under a variety of arrangements. The main systems in use during this period in history were the piece-price, contract, and lease systems. In the piece-price system, a private contractor pays the prison for each finished piece that is produced through inmate labor. The contractor pays for the raw materials, but inmates remain in the prison and work under the supervision of prison employees. The contract system is similar, in that the contractor pays for raw materials, but supervision of the inmate at work is assumed by the contractor and the fee paid to the state is a per diem amount for the labor of each inmate.

The lease system differs from both the piece-price and contract systems in a number of important respects. The inmates may remain in the prison or they may be removed to a worksite outside the institution. Daily care of the inmate, including feeding, clothing, housing, and discipline, is provided by the private entrepreneur. The state receives a fee that typically is based on the number of inmates handled over an agreed-upon period of time.

The first American leasing arrangement was crafted in Kentucky in 1825. A merchant named Joel Scott agreed to pay the state one thousand dollars per year for the labor of inmates confined in the Frankfort prison. He was awarded a five-year lease, which permitted him to assume responsibility for the entire prison. In the years that followed, new cells, a dining room, a chapel, and new factories were added to the original structure. Both Scott and his successor, T. S. Theobold, were able to turn a profit using inmate labor.

Although the Frankfort experience is regarded as the first "pure" leasing arrangement, it is important to note that hybrids of piece-price, contract, and lease systems were not unusual during the nineteenth century. By the mid nineteenth century, for instance, entrepreneurs operating under the contract system in Illinois and Indiana managed to extend their authority until they had achieved the level of autonomy typical of lessees.

Other states began to emulate the Kentucky plan. The main reason was simple and straightforward: money. Prisons, after all, were relative newcomers to the American system of punishment. One of the great concerns regarding prisons was their cost. A nation accustomed to inexpensive means of punishment, such as execution, banishment, or flogging, was now being asked to bear the expense of supporting offenders. For the first time, taxpayers were being asked to pay for the food, clothing, housing, and supervision of convicts over lengthy periods of time. Naturally, there was resistance, and solutions were sought to decrease the economic burden. Part of the great battle between supporters of the Pennsylvania and Auburn systems of imprisonment revolved around the relative costs of the two systems. In many states, wardens who could not make their institutions economically self-sufficient were soon looking for new employment.

Increases in prison populations at mid century also fueled economic concerns. Melossi and Pavarini point out that the lack of inmate labor and the expense of maintaining the enormous warehouse prisons that had become common at mid century created a crisis for states already bedeviled by other financial obligations. One important analyst of penal history notes that "making a profit became the prime objective of these institutions, and when they failed to realize it some of the states devised plans that in effect turned the prisoners into penal slaves" (Sellin 1976, 141). In their 1867 report on American and Canadian prisons, Enoch Wines and Theodore Dwight reported that the reformation of inmates had been abandoned and that "one string is harped upon, ad nauseam—money, money, money" (Wines and Dwight 1867, 289).

It is worth noting that the newly developing industrial factory system was an increasingly significant part of the American economic landscape. In fact, according to some analysts, the factory provided the model for penitentiary labor enterprises. States tried to organize their prisons in terms of both the architecture and discipline of industrial factories. In some states these efforts met with success. In others, especially in the South, other means had to be found to meet the growing economic demands placed on prisons.

After the Kentucky experiment, several other states tried leasing arrangements. Louisiana, for instance, opened its prison in 1835. Within a single decade inmate populations increased dramatically and the costs of maintaining the institution became unacceptable, despite in-house labor programs. In 1844, the institution was turned over to a private manufacturer on a five-year lease.

Alabama was so pleased to be able to relieve itself of the burden of its penitentiary that it leased it to a private company in 1846 without requiring any payment for the lease. The company assumed responsibility for operating the facility and was able to benefit from the labor of the convicts.

Post–Civil War Leasing Systems

The real increase in interest in leasing came after the conclusion of the Civil War, especially in the South. Southern states were devastated by the war, and in some states the prison buildings themselves had been destroyed. Moreover, before the war prisons had been created to hold deviant whites; slaves had been dealt with in separate ways as part of the plantation system. After emancipation, however, blacks were funneled into the existing penal systems, much to the dismay of those charged with their operation. Prison populations swelled and states facing the enormous costs of postwar reconstruction were overwhelmed (Ayers 1984).

These realities, combined with the longstanding belief that criminals should labor both as part of their punishment and to offset the costs of their captivity, led states to consider bids from private entrepreneurs interested in acquiring inexpensive labor. Some analysts of Southern history see the convict lease system that developed as little more than a recasting of the slave system that had been dismantled by Emancipation. In fact, the Thirteenth Amendment affirmed the legitimacy of slavery as a punishment for crime. Southern states were more than ready to exercise their rights under this Amendment.

One of the first states to lease out its penitentiary after the war was Alabama. In 1866 the state turned over the institution to a contractor, who worked the prisoners in mines and in railroad camps. Eventually, both state and county prisoners were turned over to lessees; they worked for lumber and turpentine companies, as well as for farmers.

In Georgia, the state prison at Milledgeville had been destroyed by the Union forces during the war. In 1868, one hundred convicts were leased to work on the railroads (Ayers 1984). By the end of the 1860s, seven companies were leasing convicts. At the conclusion of the 1870s all state convicts were in the hands of three companies, which had acquired lease terms of twenty years. The state received $25,000 annually for the convicts (Sellin 1976).

Louisiana, one of the earliest states to try leasing, renewed its interest in the practice after the war. The penitentiary at Baton Rouge was leased in 1868 to a lessee who resold the lease to another corporation. Convicts worked on the levees and in the swamps, under the supervision and control of the lessee.

Many other states followed the same route. Within a decade after the close of the Civil War, Mississippi, Louisiana, South Carolina, Alabama, North Carolina, Tennessee, Georgia, and Arkansas placed some or all of their convicts into the hands of private companies. Although many penal reformers and legislators were aware of the potential hazards of leasing, the tremendous fiscal difficulties that states were experiencing resulted in little support for penal systems that drained resources from the public coffers. Moreover, the fact that increasing proportions of prisoners were black did nothing to stimulate public interest in prison conditions, beyond what was necessary to see that the institutions did not burden the taxpayers.

Southern states were not the only ones to adopt the lease system. In the far West, for instance, California, Oregon, Montana, and Wyoming leased their institutions during the latter part of the nineteenth century. In the breadbasket of the nation, Nebraska leased its prison in 1877, agreed to pay the lessee forty cents a day per inmate and to give the lessee all convict labor in return for assuming charge of the inmates (McKelvey 1936, 223). Kansas did likewise.

Prison Conditions under Lease Systems

Conditions in many of these institutions were often quite severe, even by nineteenth century standards:

> What a lessee was interested in was maximum financial profit from his management of the institution. This meant keeping maintenance costs at a minimum by feeding and clothing the convicts as cheaply as possible, hiring guards willing to work for substandard wages or using prisoners in that capacity. It meant working the prisoners from

dawn to dusk and extracting their best efforts by the threat or use of the ever-present whip of the overseer (Sellin 1976, 143).

Even in light of conditions in state-operated institutions, which had been less than humane, conditions in some of the institutions operated by lessees were often shocking. For instance, a Mississippi grand jury investigating conditions under which state convicts were forced to live found that "most of them have their backs cut in great wales, scars, and blisters, some with skin peeling off in pieces as the result of severe beatings. . . . They are lying there dying, some of them on bare boards, so poor and emaciated that their bones almost come through their skin, many complaining for want of food. . . . We actually saw live vermin crawling over their faces. . . ." (Sellin 1976, 148).

A legislative committee investigating conditions on railroad construction sites found that leased convicts "were placed in the swamp in water ranging to their knees, and in almost nude state they spaded caney and rooty ground, their bare feet chained together by chains that fretted the flesh. They were compelled to attend to the calls of nature in line as they stood day in and day out, their thirst compelling them to drink the water in which they were compelled to deposit their excrement" (quoted in Ayers 1984, 193).

Mississippi was not the only state to have difficulties. An investigator appointed by the governor of Alabama found that convicts

> were as filthy, as a rule, as dirt could make them and both prisons and prisoners were infested with vermin. . . . Convicts were extremely and, in some instances, cruelly punished. . . . They were poorly clothed and fed. . . . I verily believe that there were men who had not washed their faces in twelve months. . . . The system is a disgrace to the State, a reproach to the civilization and Christian sentiment of the age, and ought to be speedily abandoned (Sellin 1976, 151–52).

An Arkansas investigation revealed many atrocious practices. In one incident

> a white boy convict, sentenced for a minor offense, was shot down and, after being delivered to the station to be transported

to the hospital, while lying on the platform of the depot in the burning hot sun, his blood trickling down the planks of the platform, many people passed by and saw him. When he cried to passers-by to give him some relief, the warden refused to permit anyone to go near him. He was transported to the hospital and the next day died (Sellin 1976, 161).

Countless investigations and scandals afflicted the lease system throughout the second half of the century, and opposition on humanitarian grounds increased as the twentieth century approached. Some of the investigations of abuses led to the abandonment of the lease system altogether. Leasing in South Carolina began in the 1870s. Within the first decade of operation an investigation found that the convict death rate at two work sites was greater than 50 percent. Such findings led to the speedy termination of all leasing in South Carolina in 1885.

Other states had similar experiences. In Georgia, many investigations revealed serious abuses throughout the decades after the war, yet leasing continued until 1909. Despite the appalling conditions documented in the previously noted 1881 report on Alabama leasing, leasing continued until 1928. In his comparison of Northern and Southern penal practices, McKelvey notes that "while the average death rate of twenty-eight northern prisons was 14.9 per thousand, the average in the South was 41.3 per thousand. The appalling conditions which these statistics reveal were partly the cause and partly the result of the brutal practices of the lease system" (1936, 210).

The End of the Lease System
Eventually, the steady stream of revelations about the harsh conditions convicts were forced to endure led to increasing opposition to the lease system. Not surprisingly, the main obstacle to the abandonment of the system was economic. States did not want to absorb the costs of running their penal systems. Moreover, a leasing lobby arose to protect the interests of those engaged in leasing. In states such as Georgia, state inspectors were also wardens for private companies. Private special interests were at times intertwined with the state's interests. According to Sellin, convict labor "became a windfall for politically powerful lessees who profited from it and therefore resisted its abolition" (Sellin 1976, 162).

What finally brought an end to the leasing system was not simply wholesale revulsion at the inhumane practices that characterized the operation of many lease systems, but the economic objections of both labor and business. Free workers complained that convict labor deprived them of jobs, and in some cases free laborers took dramatic action to end leasing. In Tennessee, for instance, miners revolted and released five hundred convicts who had been set to work laboring in the mines.

Businesses not benefiting from convict labor also objected to leasing. They argued that leasing placed them at a competitive disadvantage because they were forced to hire free labor and thus sustained higher labor costs. The objections of both business and labor proved to be telling, and states began to outlaw or restrict the leasing of convicts. A number of states eliminated leasing before the close of the nineteenth century, and by the end of the first quarter of the twentieth century leasing was essentially finished.

Convict labor was still used, but now under more direct state control, often under state use or public account systems. These systems kept workers under direct state supervision and removed the profit motive that had resulted in so many of the abuses endured by convicts under the leasing system.

Summary

Despite the unhappy early American experience with leasing, the modern correctional privatization movement seeks to bring back the involvement of the private sector into corrections. It is too soon to determine what forms this modern movement will finally assume, or whether private involvement can avoid the difficulties that led to the demise of convict leasing at the end of the nineteenth century. The early American experience does, however, provide guidance that should prove instructional to those contemplating a return to the lease system.

Alexis M. Durham III

See also HISTORY (THE JACKSONIAN ERA), PRIVATE PRISONS

Bibliography

Ayers, E. L. (1984). *Vengeance and Justice: Crime and Punishment in the 19th-Century American South*. New York: Oxford University Press.

McConville, S. (1981). *A History of English Prison Administration*. London: Routledge and Kegan Paul.

McKelvey, B. (1936). *American Prisons*. Chicago University of Chicago Press (Reprinted Montclair, N.J.: Patterson Smith, 1977).

Melossi, D., and M. Pavarini (1981). *The Prison and the Factory: Origins of the Penitentiary System*. Totowa, N.J.: Barnes and Noble.

Rothman, D. (1971). *The Discovery of the Asylum*. Boston: Little, Brown.

Sellin, J. T. (1976). *Slavery and the Penal System*. New York: Elsevier.

Wines, E., and T. Dwight (1867). *Report on the Prisons and Reformatories of the United States and Canada*. Montclair, N.J.: Patterson Smith (Reprinted 1976).

L

Legal Issues

I. Introduction

There are undoubtedly many areas for disagreement between the state and those kept involuntarily within its custody. Most disputes between employees, inmates, and administrators are settled informally; there are also formal means, however, such as grievance procedures, union intervention, and the courts.

Today, a prisoner with a dispute may approach the courts in any one of four ways. First, inmates may file a petition for a state writ of habeas corpus, asking for a hearing on the terms of their confinement. When state remedies have been unsuccessfully exhausted, prisoners may then file a petition for a federal writ of habeas corpus. These cases will generally decide the status of only one individual, without affecting other cases.

Second, like an ordinary citizen, a prisoner may file a civil suit or tort action in local courts against a prison employee for damages caused by wanton or gross negligence or some intentional act of harm. An inmate may also seek criminal charges against an employee who has committed a felony—such as assault, theft, or threat to do harm—against him. The difficulty in such cases would be the prisoner's ability to find a district attorney willing to prosecute. The final option is to sue for violations of state or federal civil rights protections. In federal court, inmates use Section 1983 of the Civil Rights Act, under which a petitioner may ask for injunctive relief as well as monetary damages. Because inmates view the federal government as more sympathetic than the state, Section 1983 is the most common action taken. As the court expressed in *Preiser v. Rodriguez,* the potential for suits is inherent in the nature of the relationship between the inmate and the state. "For state prisoners, eating, sleeping, dressing, washing, working, and playing are all done under the watchful eye of the State. . . . What for a private citizen would be a dispute with his landlord, with his tailor, with his neighbor, or with his banker becomes, for the prisoner, a dispute with the State."

On a daily basis, most of the state's complaints against inmates are handled in routine disciplinary hearings. When serious crimes are committed, such as assaults on staff or other inmates, the state may file criminal charges against an inmate. New criminal convictions may increase the time an inmate spends in prison.

On occasion, employees have filed civil suits against prisoners for injuries that resulted from inmate misconduct. Although most inmates have no money or assets, the suit is often a symbolic victory that remains on the record and against any assets the inmate may acquire in the future.

Perhaps the most expensive and time-consuming lawsuits related to prison are those that employees file against the state, particularly class-action suits involving large numbers of similarly situated employees. Assignments and promotions, terminations, working conditions, and risk on the job are areas of constant litigation. The decisions in these cases often have implications for prison systems across the country as well as other related criminal justice and civil service agencies.

Marilyn D. McShane

Note: Case citations appear at the end of the last section.

II. Historical Background

Judicial involvement in the affairs of prisons is a relatively recent phenomenon. Throughout most of the history of this country, the courts have not been concerned with the operation of prisons or the treatment of prisoners. The judiciary generally adhered to a "hands off" attitude with respect to prisons. They felt that prison administrators had a tremendous task in maintaining security and that the courts lacked the expertise to intervene. Prisoners were also considered "slaves of the state," who had forfeited their rights by virtue of their crimes. This perspective mirrored the prevailing view in American society that prisoners suffered a total deprivation of liberty when entering the doors of the prison.

There were other reasons why the courts refrained from becoming involved in prison issues. One was the notion of separation of powers, a kind of diplomacy that meant one branch of government did not interfere with another. Since prisons were the responsibility of the executive office, the judiciary as well as the legislature were unwilling to be critical. Consequently, great administrative discretion was afforded prison officials, and there was little exercise of the power of judicial review. This was expressed in *Williams v. Steele* when the court said, "[S]ince the prison system of the United States is entrusted to the Bureau of Prisons under the discretion of the Attorney General . . . the courts have no power to supervise the discipline of the prisoners nor to interfere with their discipline."

Another reason cited for the lack of court intervention in prison policy was the federalist principle that certain aspects of state government should not be interfered with by the federal government. As a matter of courtesy, the federal courts were reluctant to stir up any conflict between the two jurisdictions. The states were very sensitive to the federal government's meddling in their affairs.

Finally, the courts were also concerned that if they were regularly involved in cases of prisoner complaints, there would be a flood of litigation on every conceivable issue. To avoid that, they separated themselves from prison matters except in rare cases, when they were faced with "exceptional circumstances" in which beatings, torture, or physical abuse were too blatant to be overlooked.

The judiciary first became involved with the rights of prisoners hundreds of years ago, when the courts started reviewing the propriety of a prisoner's confinement. The signing of the Magna Carta by King John granted Englishmen the right to be set free from prison if they were not provided due process. The role of habeas review initially was limited in scope, although it gradually extended beyond actions of the king. The founding fathers of this country recognized that the need for habeas corpus review was of such importance that it is guaranteed in Article I, Section 9 of the Constitution: "The

Privilege of the Writ of Habeas Corpus shall not be suspended, unless when in Cases of Rebellion or Invasion the public safety may require it." The purpose of habeas corpus review was to prevent indefinite imprisonment without a judicial hearing. The writ did not and today still does not test the correctness on the merits of a decision; rather it focuses on procedural considerations concerning the imprisonment.

The modern era of judicial involvement in prisoner affairs developed during the last half century. What precipitated the court's intervention in the area of prisoner rights was the same series of complex social and philosophical changes that characterized reform movements from the late 1950s through the 1970s. School desegregation, war protest, and the womens' movement were all part of the fabric of developing humanistic reforms. Simply by being a minority group under the regulation of the state, prisoners, as a class, were swept up in the process of redefining the rights and limits of punishment.

Ex parte Hull (1941) is normally singled out as the first case in which the Supreme Court held that prisoners have a right of access to court. The Supreme Court invalidated a Michigan rule that prevented state prisoners from filing habeas corpus petitions unless the petitions were found to be "properly drawn" by the institutional welfare office and the legal investigator of the parole board. The Supreme Court emphasized that the state and its officers could not interfere with a prisoner's right to apply to a federal court for habeas corpus relief (1941, 549).

Johnson v. Avery (1969) was the next important case. Johnson, a state prisoner incarcerated in Tennessee, was a jailhouse lawyer, or "writ writer." In other words, he helped other inmates prepare legal documents, including petitions for a writ of habeas corpus. The prison system had a regulation that prohibited inmates from assisting each other with legal matters. Johnson was subjected to disciplinary action for violating the rule. The Supreme Court granted relief to Johnson, holding that unless and until the state provided some reasonable alternative to assist inmates in the preparation of petitions for postconviction relief, prison officials could not enforce the prison regulation barring inmates from furnishing assistance to other prisoners (1969, 490).

Two constitutional provisions were instrumental in leading the Court to its decision. As mentioned, prisoners have a right to file and pursue writs of habeas corpus. The second reason is based on the concept of equal protection found in the Fourteenth Amendment to the Constitution: "No State shall . . . deny any person within its jurisdiction the equal protection of the laws." A state cannot maintain a regulation that penalizes prisoners who happen to be poor. The Tennessee regulation had the effect of allowing only those inmates who were fortunate enough to have money to proceed to court. Inmates who had the funds to hire an attorney could receive representation, while indigent inmates would have to fend for themselves. The Supreme Court's decision entitled indigent inmates to receive assistance from either attorneys or other inmates.

In *Wolff v. McDonnell* (1974), the Supreme Court extended the right of access to court to civil rights cases. Thus inmates have a right to present civil rights cases to the federal courts, and indigent inmates have a right to receive assistance from others, either attorneys or other inmates, in the preparation and pursuit of relief in civil rights matters.

The most important case by the Supreme Court in this area is *Bounds v. Smith* (1977). The Court specified that inmates have not only a right of access to court, but they also have a right to *meaningful* access to court. Furthermore, prison systems are obligated to provide inmates with the means to obtain meaningful access to court. The state must provide them with the tools necessary to develop and present their claims in the courts. The prison system must also provide inmates with either an adequate law library or legal services. This requirement includes providing inmates with writing utensils, notarial services, and stamps. The state may decide which specific types of assistance to employ in its prisons. Forty-seven states have chosen to implement programs including law libraries, while twenty-three states provide attorneys.

The *Bounds* decision has been the subject of criticism. The dissenting justices sitting on the Supreme Court, such as William Rehnquist, disagreed with the conclusion that the state has an affirmative duty to provide inmates with the means to attain access to court; they argued that the duty is merely negative and prohibits states from interfering "with the individual exercise of such federal rights" (1977, 384). Most of the members of the majority in the *Bounds* decision have retired from the Court and have been replaced by conservatives, who would likely agree with the dissenters in the case, such as Chief Justice Rehnquist. Nonetheless, *Bounds* is still the leading decision concerning an inmate's right of access to court.

Suits by prisoners have emerged as one of the primary sources of litigation in the federal court system. According to the *Annual Report* of the director of the Administrative Office of the United States Court, 46,452 civil suits were filed by prisoners in 1992, which was approximately 20 percent of all civil cases filed in federal court. Both Congress and the federal judiciary have discussed the prospect of curtailing the number of cases filed by prisoners.

Jon R. Farrar

Bibliography

Bronstein, A. J. (1980). Prisoners' rights: A history. In G. P. Alpert, ed. *Legal Rights of Prisoners*. Beverly Hills, Calif.: Sage.

Jones, C., and E. Rhine (1985). Due process and prison disciplinary practices: From Wolff to Hewitt. *New England Journal on Criminal and Civil Confinement* 11(Winter): 44–122.

Manville, D. E. (1983). *Prisoners' Self-Help Litigation Manual*. New York: Oceana.

Potuto, J. (1991). *Prisoner Collateral Attacks: Federal Habeas Corpus and Federal Prisoner Motion Practice*. Deerfield, Ill.: Clark, Boardman and Callaghan.

Schwartz, M. A., and J. E. Kirklin (1991). *Section 1983 Litigation: Claims, Defenses, and Fees*. New York: John Wiley.

Note: Case citations appear at the end of the last section.

III. Habeas Corpus

A writ of habeas corpus is an order issued by a court commanding the person who has custody or control of an inmate to appear in court and show why the inmate is confined. The discussion of habeas corpus law in this section will be limited to the law surrounding proceedings challenging the fact or length of an inmate's incarceration. To initiate a habeas corpus proceeding, a prisoner must file a "petition" or "application" with the court. The petition for a writ of habeas corpus is also referred to as a "collateral attack" on the judgment, or a "postconviction remedy."

The writ of habeas corpus is sometimes regarded as the single most important writ known to constitutional law either in England or in the United States. Article I, Section 9 of the Constitution gives assurance that the "Privilege of the Writ of Habeas Corpus shall not be suspended, unless when in Cases of Rebellion or Invasion the public Safety may require it." Federal courts were authorized by Congress to issue writs of habeas corpus in Section 14 of the Judiciary Act of 1789. It is often referred to as the "Great Writ," because it was so called by John Marshall, when he was the chief justice of the Supreme Court.

Habeas corpus petitions are filed in different locations depending on the type of relief sought. Federal prisoners challenging the legality of their convictions must file their petition in the court where they were convicted under 28 U.S.C. § 2255. On the other hand, federal prisoners challenging the implementation of their sentences (such as time calculation issues) or matters occurring while in custody (such as prison disciplinary proceedings) file the petition in the federal court with jurisdiction over the prison facility where the inmate is incarcerated. The proceeding is filed pursuant to 28 U.S.C. § 2241. A prisoner in state custody challenging his conviction in federal court must file the petition in the federal court having jurisdiction over the county where he was convicted. The petition is brought in federal court pursuant to 28 U.S.C. § 2254. Most states also have statutory procedures by which a state inmate can pursue habeas corpus relief. In such cases, state inmates must initially file their habeas corpus petitions in state court before they can proceed with a challenge in federal court. This is known as the "exhaustion of state remedies" doctrine. In order to exhaust properly, the inmate must "fairly present" all of his claims to the highest state court (*Picard v. Connor*, 1971).

In most cases, a petition for a writ of habeas corpus is used to show an infirmity in the conviction that is of constitutional magnitude. A prisoner must show that a right guaranteed by the Constitution has been violated, such as a conviction obtained in violation of the right against double jeopardy or without due process. On the other hand, a statutory error generally will not provide a basis for habeas relief. Prisoners in state custody commonly make the mistake of deemphasizing a direct appeal in state court under the erroneous belief that the chance of gaining release is greater in federal court.

Federal habeas corpus relief, however, is limited to constitutional issues. Moreover, federal habeas corpus relief is limited to only a small number of constitutional violations. For example, challenges based on an illegal search and seizure generally will not provide a basis for habeas corpus relief. In *Stone v. Powell* (1976), the Supreme Court ruled that where a habeas corpus petitioner claiming a Fourth Amendment violation was given the opportunity for a full and fair hearing in state court, the federal courts would not hear the issue. The primary point of the ruling was that an *opportunity* for a full and fair hearing was sufficient, as opposed to a hearing that was *actually* full and fair. By contrast, inmates may pursue constitutional and statutory errors on direct appeal. The remainder of this article will focus on the primary areas in which habeas relief may be obtained in federal court, along with the obstacles to obtaining relief.

Court statistics show that at least 95 percent of all defendants plead guilty. The majority of habeas proceedings in federal court are from inmates who pled guilty. To obtain habeas relief, the prisoner must show that his plea of guilty was invalid. The test for determining the validity of a guilty plea is "whether the plea represents a voluntary and intelligent choice among alternative courses of action open to a defendant" (*North Carolina v. Alford,* 1970). A prisoner will typically argue that his plea was involuntary because counsel was ineffective. In order to succeed on that basis, the petitioner must show that his attorney's performance was deficient and that the deficient performance prejudiced the outcome of the case (*Hill v. Lockhart,* 1985; *Strickland v. Washington,* 1984). The voluntariness of the plea depends on whether counsel's advice "was within the range of competence demanded of attorneys in criminal cases" (*McMann v. Richardson,* 1970). A defendant who pled guilty upon the advice of counsel may attack the voluntary and intelligent character of the guilty plea only by showing that the advice he received from counsel was not within the range of competence demanded of attorneys in criminal cases (*Tollett v. Henderson,* 1973; *Hill v. Lockhart,* 1985, 56–57).

Inmates also routinely allege that counsel was ineffective in cases in which they pled not guilty but were found guilty by the court or jury. The standard is essentially the same. The habeas corpus petitioner must show that "counsel's representation fell below an objective standard of reasonableness," with reasonableness judged under professional norms prevailing at the time counsel rendered assistance (*Strickland v. Wash-*

ington, 1984, 688). The standard requires the reviewing court to give great deference to counsel's performance, strongly presuming counsel exercised reasonable professional judgment (*Strickland v. Washington,* 1984, 690). The right to counsel does not require errorless counsel; instead, a criminal defendant is entitled to reasonably effective assistance (*Boyd v. Estelle,* 1981; *Rubio v. Estelle,* 1982; *Murray v. Maggio,* 1984). In addition, the habeas petitioner "must show that there is a reasonable probability that, but for counsel's unprofessional errors, the result of the proceeding would have been different. A reasonable probability is a probability sufficient to undermine confidence in the outcome" (*Strickland v. Washington,* 1984, 694). He must "affirmatively prove," not just allege, prejudice.

Insufficient evidence is another major area of habeas litigation. In *Jackson v. Virginia* (1979), the Supreme Court held that in a federal habeas corpus proceeding challenging the sufficiency of the evidence supporting a state conviction, a petitioner is entitled to relief where "no rational trier of fact could have found proof of guilt beyond a reasonable doubt." In applying the standard, "All of the evidence is to be considered in the light most favorable to the prosecution" (1979, 320). The Court added that this "standard must be applied with explicit reference to the substantive elements of the criminal offense as defined by state law" (1979, 324 note 16). "Under *Jackson,* [a federal court] may find the evidence sufficient to support a conviction even though the facts also support one or more reasonable hypotheses consistent with the defendant's claim of innocence" (*Gibson v. Collins,* 1992, 783).

The double jeopardy bar protects against a second prosecution after acquittal, a second prosecution for the same offense after conviction, and multiple punishments for the same offense (*Ohio v. Johnson,* 1984). This principle applies when the prior prosecution was for a lesser included offense (*Waller v. Florida,* 1970). The most common question for the Court's consideration when there are two convictions out of the same incident is whether the two convictions represent multiple punishments for the same offense. The test to be applied to determine whether there are two offenses or only one is whether each offense requires proof of an additional fact or element that the other does not (*Blockburger v. United States,* 1932).

A catch-all provision of the Constitution is the due process clause. Federal courts review habeas corpus petitions for a "constitutional infraction of the defendant's due process rights which would render the trial as a whole fundamentally unfair" (*Lavernia v. Lynaugh*, 1988, 496). "The test applied to determine whether a trial error makes a trial fundamentally unfair is whether there is reasonable probability that the verdict might have been different had the trial been properly conducted" (*Foy v. Donnelly*, 1992, 1317). The standard of review in the context of habeas corpus proceedings is very narrow, and not a broad exercise of supervisory power (*Darden v. Wainwright*, 1986). An example of when relief may be possible is the suppression of favorable evidence to an accused by the prosecution, when that evidence had been specifically requested by the defense and when the evidence is material to guilt, innocence, or punishment (*Brady v. Maryland*, 1963). It must again be emphasized that the role of a federal court is more limited than that of the state court. "An evidentiary error in a state trial does not justify federal habeas corpus relief unless it is of such magnitude as to constitute a denial of fundamental fairness unde the due process clause. . . . Thus, even the erroneous admission of prejudicial testimony does not justify habeas corpus relief unless it is 'material in the sense of a crucial, critical, highly significant factor'" (*Skillern v. Estelle*, 1983, 852).

As previously mentioned, Fourth Amendment issues such as evidence obtained by an illegal search and seizure may not be brought in federal court so long as the opportunity for a full and fair hearing exists in state court (*Stone v. Powell*, 1976).

A major complaint about criminal proceedings, particularly in death penalty cases, is that prisoners may keep a conviction pending in the court system for years. The Supreme Court has recently taken steps to speed the process. Federal rules permit prisoners to bring only one petition for a writ of habeas corpus in federal court. The rule historically has not been enforced, but the Supreme Court now places greater emphasis on the rule, specifying that a "petitioner must conduct a reasonable and diligent investigation aimed at including all relevant claims and grounds for relief in the first federal habeas petition" (*McCleskey v. Zant*, 1991, 1472). In the context of § 2254 proceedings, the Supreme Court has decided that successive petitions will not be decided on the merits except in rare instances:

Unless a habeas petitioner shows cause and prejudice . . . a court may not reach the merits of: (a) successive claims which raise grounds identical to grounds heard and decided on the merits in a previous petition . . . ; (b) new claims, not previously raised which constitute an abuse of the writ . . . ; or (c) procedurally defaulted claims in which the petitioner failed to follow applicable state procedural rules in raising the claims (*Sawyer v. Whitley*, 1992, 2518).

The State has the "burden to plead abuse of the writ . . . the petitioner must then prove cause and prejudice (*Saahir v. Collins*, 1992, 118).

The abuse of writ standards for federal prisoners seeking relief in § 2255 proceedings is identical to that of state prisoners seeking relief in § 2254 proceedings (*United States v. Flores*, 1993). The fact that a habeas corpus petitioner is bringing a successive petition will be excused only if he can show (1) cause for failure to raise the claim, as well as prejudice from the errors that form the basis of his complaint or (2) that the court's refusal to hear the claim would result in a fundamental miscarriage of justice. The latter prong basically means that the prisoner may not obtain relief unless he can show a constitutional violation that probably resulted in his conviction even though he is innocent.

Another major limitation on the availability of relief for state prisoners in a federal proceeding is the contemporaneous objection rule. A prisoner may be barred from raising an issue if the prisoner failed to make an objection at trial, absent a showing of cause and prejudice for the failure to object (*Francis v. Henderson*, 1976). A final limitation concerns the retroactive application of a decision in one case to other trials conducted previously. The Supreme Court has generally ruled that new rules may not be applied retroactively (*Teague v. Lane*, 1989).

Prisoner litigation, including habeas corpus issues, makes up a large portion of the workload in the federal courts. The trend in recent years has been to tighten the availability of relief. The limitations discussed here are products of that trend, and additional limitations will probably be added in the future. Despite the limitations, the "Great Writ" still provides a potent means of invalidating a conviction that transgresses the rights guaranteed by the United States Constitution.

Jon R. Farrar

Note: Case citations appear at the end of the last section.

IV. Civil Rights

Prisoners do not lose all rights when they enter the doors of a prison. They retain rights guaranteed to them by both federal and state laws. Congress and most states have promulgated laws to enable prisoners to enforce these rights in court. This section focuses on federal civil rights litigation.

To succeed in a civil rights lawsuit, a prisoner must show a deprivation of constitutional magnitude. The most commonly used constitutional provisions are as follows:

First Amendment: freedom of speech, religion, freedom of press;

Sixth Amendment: right to be informed of the nature and cause of the accusation and the right to have assistance of counsel;

Eighth Amendment: right to be free from cruel and unusual punishment, which covers such areas as prison conditions, excessive use of force, assaults by other inmates, medical care, among others;

Fourteenth Amendment: right to due process and equal protection of the law.

The primary method by which prisoners bring civil rights claims in federal court is under the provisions of 42 U.S.C. § 1983. In order to prevail, inmates must prove two essential elements. First, prisoners must show that prison officials acted under color of state law, which means that officers derived their authority from their position as corrections officials clothed with state power. Second, inmates must show that officers violated a clearly established statutory or constitutional right.

Section 1983 suits may, for example, be used to sue state, city or county employees who abuse their legal powers and violate a prisoner's constitutional rights (see *Monroe v. Pape*, 1961; *accord, Brown v. Miller*, 1980). A city or county can also be a "person" subject to suit within the meaning of 42 U.S.C. § 1983 (*Monell v. Department of Social Services*, 1978).

Prisoner suits filed under the Eighth Amendment, particularly suits involving the conditions of confinement, have had the greatest impact on jails and prison systems. Inmates have repeatedly prevailed in class action lawsuits concerning the facilities in which they are confined. Most state prison systems and many county jails have been forced to comply with court orders changing their operations.

The standard for determining whether the conditions are cruel or unusual "must draw its meaning from the evolving standards of decency that mark the progress of a maturing society" (*Rhodes v. Chapman*, 1981, 346). Conditions "alone or in combination" may amount to a constitutional violation (1981, 347). The Supreme Court emphasized, in *Wilson v. Seiter* (1991), that the Constitution does not mandate comfortable prisons and that only deprivations denying "the minimal civilized measure of life's necessities" form the basis of an Eighth Amendment violation.

Incidents of deprivation of food or medical care, or gratuitous beatings, standing alone, may be sufficient to amount to a constitutional violation. Other conditions may establish an Eighth Amendment violation "in combination" when each would not do so alone. For example, the Fifth Circuit held that a cold, wet, roach-infested cell, with inoperative toilet facilities was a cause of action (*Bienvenu v. Beauregard Parish Police Jury*, 1983). Similarly, allegations of cold cells with rats crawling all over prisoners state a cause of action (*Foulds v. Corley*, 1987).

In order to state a cognizable claim, a prisoner must also allege facts showing that jail officials acted with a culpable state of mind, in other words, they acted with "deliberate indifference" (*Wilson v. Seiter*, 1991, 2327). Prisoners may occasionally be able to show that the conditions are constitutionally deficient but ultimately fail because they cannot show that the defendants were deliberately indifferent. The rule in *Wilson v. Seiter* may be significant in cases in which a prison official realizes that the conditions are inadequate but he is not provided sufficient funds to remedy the problems. In two more recent cases, however, the Eleventh (*Howell v. Burden*, 1994) and the Third (*Durmer v. O'Carroll*, 1993) Circuit courts of appeals have rejected the inadequate funding defense.

The major cases of the 1970s and 1980s have been class action lawsuits involving prison conditions. In Texas, for example, the entire prison system was examined. The United States District Court for the Eastern District of Texas issued remedial orders concerning almost every facet of the operation of the prison system (see *Ruiz v. Estelle*, 1982).

The most common type of lawsuit involving a single incident concerns excessive use of force. In *Hudson v. McMillian* (1992), the Supreme Court emphasized that the core judicial inquiry in an excessive use of force claim is "whether force was applied in a good-faith effort to maintain or restore discipline, or maliciously and sadistically to cause harm." The Supreme Court in *Hudson* emphasized that a use of force claim, like all Eighth Amendment claims, has subjective and objective components. In other words, a court must consider whether the officials acted with a "sufficiently culpable state of mind" and if the alleged wrongdoing was objectively "harmful enough" to establish a constitutional violation.

Two considerations are important in assessing the situation. The claimant must allege and prove that there was an "unnecessary and wanton infliction of pain." The concept of what constitutes cruel and unusual punishment "draws its meaning from the evolving standards of decency that mark the progress of a maturing society" (*Hudson v. McMillian*, 1992, 1000).

The Supreme Court added the following caveat concerning the nature of the force used in a given situation:

That is not to say that every malevolent touch by a prison guard gives rise to a federal cause of action. (See *Johnson v. Glick*, 1973, 1033, "Not every push or shove, even if it may later seem unnecessary in the peace of a judge's chambers, violates a prisoner's constitutional rights".) The Eighth Amendment's prohibition of "cruel and unusual" punishment necessarily excludes from constitutional recognition *de minimis* uses of physical force, provided that the use of force is not of a sort "repugnant to the conscience of mankind" (*Hudson v. McMillian*, 1992, 1000).

The Eighth Amendment affords prisoners protection against injury at the hands of other inmates. The standard to employ is a subjective test for determining whether prison officials were "deliberately indifferent" to the safety needs of an inmate. "[A] prison official cannot be found liable under the Eighth Amendment for denying an inmate humane conditions of confinement unless the official knows of and disregards an excessive risk to inmate health or safety" (*Farmer v. Brennan*, 1994, 1979).

Medical claims are the next most frequent lawsuit in which inmates invoke the protection of the Eighth Amendment. Deliberate indifference to a prisoner's serious medical needs constitutes an Eighth Amendment violation and states a cause of action under 42 U.S.C. § 1983 (*Estelle v. Gamble*, 1976). The facts as alleged must show "an unnecessary and wanton infliction of pain" (*Whitley v. Albers*, 1986). In order to state a cognizable claim, a prisoner must allege "acts or omissions sufficiently harmful to evidence deliberate indifference to serious medical needs" (*Whitley v. Albers*, 1986). Complaints about unsuccessful medical treatment or disagreements with doctors concerning the medical care provided does not give rise to a civil rights action; neither does negligence. That is, malpractice claims may not be brought under § 1983. The touchstone of a medical claim is that a prisoner had a serious medical need and officials failed to provide medical care because of deliberate indifference.

A state must furnish its prisoners with reasonably adequate food (see *Newman v. Alabama*, 1977). The meals must be well balanced and contain nutritional value to preserve health. The prison system is not, however, required to provide inmates with three meals a day. The fact that food occasionally contains a foreign object or is cold does not amount to a constitutional violation (*Hamm v. De Kalb County*, 1985). Food service officials need not respond to particularized religious dietary needs (*Udey v. Kastner*, 1986).

Besides the Eighth Amendment, other constitutional provisions have played a prominent role in prison litigation. Many suits charge that policies or regulations within the institution impose unwarranted restrictions on guaranteed constitutional freedoms. In *Turner v. Safley* (1987), the Supreme Court held that "[l]awful incarceration brings about the necessary withdrawal or limitation of many privileges and rights," and that "[w]hen a prison regulation impinges upon the inmates' constitutional rights, the regulation is valid if it is reasonably related to legitimate penological interests."

The Supreme Court identified four factors that should be considered in determining the reasonableness of a regulation:

1. Whether there is a valid, rational connection between the prison regulation and the legitimate governmental interest put forward to justify it

2. Whether there are alternative means of exercising the right that remain open to prison inmates
3. The impact accommodation will have on guards and other inmates, and on the allocation of prison resources generally
4. The absence of alternatives is evidence of the reasonableness of a prison regulation.

Currently, a prison policy will probably be upheld if officials satisfy these four factors.

There are a number of issues routinely presented by inmates that do not provide an adequate basis for civil rights suits. Negligence on the part of prison officials does not give rise to civil rights claims (see *Daniels v. Williams,* 1986). It is unresolved whether allegations of gross negligence or recklessness suffice. Deprivations of property by prison officials, even when intentional, do not violate the due process clause of the Fourteenth Amendment, provided that an adequate state postdeprivation remedy exists (*Hudson v. Palmer,* 1984). Finally, prisoners do not have a right to privacy while confined. Jail officials may search inmates' cells at any time (*Block v. Rutherford,* 1984), provided, however, that the search was not for an improper purpose, such as retaliation.

Thus far, the discussion on civil rights has focused on the rights of convicted prisoners as opposed to pretrial detainees. The rights of pretrial detainees are generally protected by the due process clause. The issue for consideration is whether the condition and restrictions of pretrial detention "amount to punishment of the detainee" (*Bell v. Wolfish,* 1979). Pretrial detainees have not been convicted, accordingly they may not be subjected to punishment. The conditions or restrictions will be approved if they are related to a legitimate governmental purpose. It must be stressed that the due process clause provides protection in addition to the provisions previously discussed.

When a state official is confronted with a civil rights lawsuit, there are several defenses. Obviously, one defense is that the incident as alleged did not occur. In such cases, the trier of fact must make its decision after hearing both sides. The primary defense available to a state actor is qualified immunity. The defense of qualified immunity shields government officials performing discretionary functions from liability for civil damages insofar as their conduct does not violate clearly established rights that a reasonable person would have known (*Harlow v. Fitzgerald,* 1982). The doctrine of qualified immunity shields government officials from civil damages liability as long as their actions could reasonably have been thought consistent with the rights they are alleged to have violated (*Fraire v. Arlington,* 1992, 1273, citing *Anderson v. Creighton,* 1987).

[W]hether an official protected by qualified immunity may be held personally liable from an allegedly unlawful official action generally turns on the "objective legal reasonableness" of the action . . . assessed in light of the legal rules that were "clearly established" at the time it was taken (*Anderson v. Creighton,* 1987, 639).

A state actor will be entitled to have a claim against him dismissed if he can show that his actions were reasonable under the clearly established law existing at the time of the incident in question. Prison personnel should endeavor to become acquainted with established law and comply with the rules to avoid liability.

Jon R. Farrar

Note: Case citations appear at the end of the last section.

V. Constitutional Issues in Prison Operations

Although "prisons are not beyond the reach of the Constitution" in that "no 'iron curtain' separates one from the other" (*Wolff v. McDonnell,* 1974, 555), inmates possess fewer rights than do free citizens. Courts weigh the constitutional rights of inmates against the security and safety needs and orderly operation of prisons. While not always winning their cases, administrators who restrict inmate rights in the interest of order and custody are generally afforded great deference and discretion by the courts.

In the 1960s, only a few hundred inmate suits were filed every year in federal courts; in 1993, there were over thirty-three thousand (Dunn 1994). The National Association of State Attorneys General has endorsed a variety of methods to limit inmate appeals while retaining constitutional rights. These efforts include requiring inmates to first go through all available prison grievance procedures before filing a suit, charging a small filing fee, and then screening all cases carefully before they are filed in federal courts (Dunn 1994). One observer characterizes prison litigation today as belonging to a "one-hand-on, one-hand-off" period, in which judi-

L

cial intervention in prison administration, while continuing, is no longer as frequent or as intense (Collins 1993). In most prison cases, inmates raise issues related to the First, Fourth, Sixth, Eighth, or Fourteenth Amendments.

First Amendment Rights

Speech. There are several concerns about the meaning of freedom of speech involving incarcerated populations. Some issues are related to security because of the belief that disgruntled inmates, speaking out on the shortcomings of the state, may incite others to riot. When prisoners are serving long sentences, it is believed that they may feel there is nothing to lose by joining a disturbance. Therefore, inciting a riot, and creating a disturbance have been common disciplinary charges against agitating, vocally critical inmates.

Free speech questions have also surfaced about whether prisoners should be able to profit from interviews or stories and movies written about their crimes. "Son of Sam Laws," named after an infamous serial killer who was the subject of several books and movies, were passed in most states to limit the profits a convicted person might realize from selling the story to the news media. A recent U.S. Supreme Court ruling has reaffirmed the commitment to free speech, but placed restrictions on how those laws may be written.

In *Simon and Schuster v. Members of the New York State Crime Victims Board* (1991), the high court struck down a New York law that required anyone contracting with an accused or convicted person for a depiction of the crime to submit a copy of the agreement to the Crime Victims Board and to turn over any income generated from that contract to the board. The law also provided that the Victim Compensation Board put the money into an account to be paid to any victim who wins a civil action for money damages against any offender.

The *Simon and Schuster* case arose when Nicholas Pileggi wrote a book entitled *Wiseguy* (1985) that detailed the life of an organized crime figure. When the Victim Compensation Board demanded the royalties, Simon and Schuster sued, claiming the law violated the First Amendment. The Supreme Court used a two-pronged test to evaluate the law. First, to regulate the content of a criminal's speech, the state must show a compelling interest. The Court held that although the state has a compelling interest in compensating victims of crime

and in ensuring that criminals do not profit from their crimes, the state does not have an interest in transferring the proceeds of crime from criminals to victims. Second, the state must show that the statute was written specifically enough to meet the interest in compensating victims without being too broad and limiting other types of expression related to the author's thoughts and recollections which may not always be directly related to the crime. In sum, the law was ruled unconstitutional because the statute was not narrowly drawn and because the state failed to show a compelling need to establish policies that may discourage the creation or publication of works of a particular content.

Media Interviews. The Supreme Court has held that the media does not have special access to inmates for purposes of conducting face-to-face interviews. State prisons (*Pell v. Procunier,* 1974) and the Federal Bureau of Prisons (*Saxbe v. Washington Post,* 1974) may prohibit media interviews with specific inmates. In allowing prisons to restrict interviews, the Court said that neither the inmates' nor the journalists' First Amendment rights were violated. Inmates' rights were not infringed because they could communicate with the news media by mail or through representatives. As for the rights of a free press, the Court said that "the First Amendment does not guarantee the press a constitutional right of special access to information not available to the public generally" (del Carmen et al. 1993, 77). These cases did not say, however, that prison officials may completely forbid communication between the news media and prisoners. Such a practice would be unconstitutional, except under emergency situations.

In 1978, the Supreme Court revisited the question of media access to correctional facilities in *Houchins v. KQED,* and reaffirmed the holding that the media have no right of access to inmates and prisons beyond that given to the general public. In that case, TV station KQED asked the sheriff to be allowed to inspect and take pictures of a jail in which an inmate had committed suicide. The sheriff refused the request for an inspection by the TV station, but indicated that the TV crew could join the regularly scheduled monthly tours to which all interested parties were invited. KQED sued and argued that the tours were inadequate because pictures, recordings, and access to individual inmates were restricted. On appeal, the Court disagreed, saying that the Constitution does not give the media more access beyond that given to the general public.

Mail. Inmates are entitled to receive mail, but prison officials may monitor mail correspondence. The Supreme Court first addressed censorship of prison mail in *Procunier v. Martinez* (1974), in which the Court struck down California's mail censorship and attorney-client interview regulations. In addition to banning "the use of law students and legal paraprofessionals to conduct attorney-client interviews with inmates," California had a rule that forbade inmate correspondence that "complained, magnified grievances, expressed 'inflammatory political, racial, religious or other views or beliefs,' or contained matter deemed defamatory or otherwise inappropriate" (del Carmen et al. 1993, 61). In striking down the regulations, the Court set a two-pronged test. First, prisoner mail censorship does not violate the First Amendment if the regulation or practice is used to justify an important or substantial prison interest. Second, the Court said that mail censorship policies must be the least restrictive of the inmates' First Amendment rights. The Court concluded that a prison regulation, policy, or practice that censored prisoner mail for important or substantial penological interests would be unconstitutional if it were not specifically narrow in scope.

It should be noted that the least restrictive means test was abandoned by the court in *Turner v. Safley* (1987), in which the Supreme Court held that prison regulations that infringe on inmates' rights are valid if they are reasonably related to legitimate penological interests. In 1989, the Court applied the criteria used in *Turner v. Safley* in *Thornburgh v. Abbott,* a case involving the censorship of incoming mail. The Federal Bureau of Prisons had a regulation that prohibited publications that were detrimental to the safety, security, and order of the institution, or publications that encouraged criminal activity. In upholding the regulations as reasonable, the Court said that the prison administrators must have broad discretion in managing prison facilities.

Access to Publications. Correctional administrators may prescribe rules that restrict inmates from receiving publications from all sources except the publishers of such materials. In *Bell v. Wolfish* (1979), the New York City Metropolitan Correctional Center allowed pretrial detainees to receive books and magazines only from publishers, book stores, or book clubs. In upholding the rule, the Court reasoned that allowing others to mail inmates personal belongings would increase the flow of contraband into the facility, which would pose a security risk. Moreover, given the threat to institutional safety, the regulation was neither exaggerated nor irrational. A total ban on incoming publications, however, might be unconstitutional.

Religion. The Supreme Court has decided two cases on inmates' rights to religious freedom. In 1972, the Court held in *Cruz v. Beto* that inmates must be given a reasonable opportunity to exercise their religious beliefs. In that case, Texas encouraged participation in the Catholic, Jewish, and Protestant faiths by providing chaplains, Bibles, and Sunday school classes, but failed to offer chapel services or access to a religious advisor for inmates practicing Buddhism. A Buddhist inmate sued, claiming that he was not given a reasonable opportunity to practice his unconventional religious beliefs. The Court agreed, holding that prison administrators must afford equal treatment to inmates of all religions, including those not considered by the majority to be in the mainstream of religious beliefs. Religious groups must be afforded equal access to meeting places, literature, and religious advisors.

In 1987, in *O'Lone v. Estate of Shabazz,* the Court used the *Turner* test and held that prison policies that prevent inmates from exercising religious freedoms are constitutional if they are reasonably related to legitimate penological interests. In this case, prison policies prevented inmates of the Islamic faith from attending religious services. The prison required that inmates who were classified as "gang minimum" work outside the buildings where they were housed and where religious services were held. For security reasons, the prison also prohibited inmates who worked outside from returning to these buildings during the day, thus effectively prohibiting the inmates from attending Jumu'ah, an Islamic religious service held on Friday afternoons. In balancing the inmates' religious freedoms against the institution's needs for security, the Court held that the policies were reasonably related to the safety needs of the facility. By deferring to correctional administrators, the Court enhanced the power of prison officials to restrict religious freedoms in the name of institutional safety and security.

The above freedom of religion cases notwithstanding, a law passed by Congress in 1993 is expected to have a significant impact on future freedom of religion cases in prisons. Known as the Religious Freedom Restoration Act of 1993 (RFRA) and aimed primarily at curbing restrictions on religious freedom outside prison, the law declares that the government "shall not substantially burden a person's exercise of religion . . . except only if it demonstrates that application of the burden to the person (1) is in furtherance of a compelling governmental interest; and (2) is the least restrictive means of furthering that compelling governmental interest." This law applies to everyone in the country, but the absence of a provision exempting prisons from coverage means that prisoners too are protected by the provisions of the act. Attempts were made during consideration of the law to exempt prisons from its coverage; Congress, however, refused to exempt inmates. The provisions of this new law make it difficult for prison administrators to limit the religious freedom of prisoners, unless such limitation is justified under the "compelling governmental interest" test and only if such is "the least restrictive means of furthering that compelling governmental interest." These limitations may be hard for prison administrators to overcome.

Court Access. The Court has decided at least five major cases on inmate access to courts. In *Johnson v. Avery* (1969), the state of Tennessee prohibited inmates from helping other inmates in legal matters for fear that doing so would jeopardize prison security and order. Although the Court agreed with Tennessee that sometimes "writ writers" constitute a menace to prison discipline and impose a burden on the courts because of their unskilled briefs, the Court invalidated the regulation because the state provided no alternative assistance for inhouse lawyers. The Court concluded that writ writers should be allowed to help inmates on legal matters and that prisons cannot ban them out of fear that their activities expose prisons to lawsuits.

Two years later, in *Younger v. Gilmore* (1971), the Supreme Court affirmed a lower court opinion that held that prison law libraries must have sufficient legal materials to provide prisoners with reasonable court access. In that case, prison regulations promulgated by the California Department of Corrections allowed inmates to use only those books that were on a prison-prepared list. The inmates sued, claiming that the restrictions denied them reasonable access to the courts. The case established that the state has a responsibility to furnish inmates with extensive law libraries or provide them with professional or quasi-professional legal assistance.

In another case, the Court expanded on what is meant by furnishing prisoners with meaningful access to the courts. In *Bounds v. Smith* (1977), the Supreme Court held that the constitutional right of access to the courts requires prison authorities to assist inmates in the preparation and filing of meaningful legal papers by providing prisoners with adequate law libraries or adequate assistance from persons trained in the law. In this case, the Court gave some examples of what prisons must do to meet the "meaningful access" requirement:

1. Training inmates as paralegal assistants to work under lawyers' supervision
2. Using paraprofessionals and law students as volunteers or in formal clinical programs
3. Organizing volunteer attorneys through bar associations or in other groups
4. Hiring lawyers on a part-time consultant basis
5. Using full-time staff attorneys in new prison legal assistance organizations or as part of the public defender or legal services offices (del Carmen et al. 1993, 18–19).

The Court has decided that states cannot require indigent inmates to pay a filing fee to have their cases heard in court. In *Smith v. Bennett* (1961), it held that a four dollar filing fee violated an indigent inmate's right to court access. In *Smith,* an Iowa inmate filed a petition for a writ of habeas corpus. The local district clerk refused to docket the petition without the four dollar filing fee, as required by Iowa law. On appeal, the Court said that the Iowa law was unconstitutional because access to the courts must not be determined by a person's ability to pay. This decision assumes renewed significance in view of the movement in some states to control the upsurge in "frivolous" prison cases through the imposition of a filing fee. This can be done, but such fees must be waived for inmates who are indigents and cannot pay the fee.

Not all indigent inmates seeking relief from the Supreme Court have prevailed, however. For example, the Court has rejected claims by indigent inmates who asked for state-appointed counsel for postconviction appeals. Because postconviction proceedings are discretionary and not considered critical to the criminal process, the Supreme Court has held that the state is not required to appoint counsel for indigent prisoners on appeal (*Pennsylvania v. Finley,* 1987). The *Finley* rule was extended to indigent inmates on death row in *Murray v. Giarratano* (1989). In *Murray,* an inmate sentenced to death sued the Virginia Department of Corrections, saying that the state must provide counsel for the inmate's postconviction proceedings. The Court disagreed, saying that neither the Eighth Amendment's prohibition against cruel and unusual punishment nor the Fourteenth Amendment's requirement of due process of law requires the state to appoint counsel for indigent death row inmates seeking postconviction relief. It appears, however, that the recent decision in *McFarland v. Scott* (1994) has modified this position. The Supreme Court held that current statute has created a right to qualified legal representation for defendants with capital cases when they undertake federal habeas corpus proceedings. The right to counsel would begin prior to the filing of the formal habeas petition. This also means that a district court would be able to grant a stay of execution if necessary to allow the capital defendant to secure habeas counsel.

Fourth Amendment Rights

Searches and Seizures. Inmates possess few Fourth Amendment rights in a penal facility. In *Hudson v. Palmer* (1984), the Court held that, because prison cells are not protected under the Fourth Amendment, cells may be searched without a warrant or probable cause. The Court concluded that inmates have no reasonable expectation of privacy in their prison cell. On issues involving the Fourth Amendment, the Supreme Court, as in practically all constitutional rights cases, balances the institutional needs of the prison against the constitutional rights of the inmate. Often, because of safety considerations and the security needs of the facility, prison administrators are allowed to search and seize without the usual requirement of a warrant and probable cause. This means that prison authorities may search an inmate's cell at any time as long as the search does not constitute harassment.

Sixth Amendment Rights

Right to Counsel. Inmates in administrative segregation are not entitled to counsel prior to the initiation of judicial proceedings (*United States v. Gouveia,* 1984). In this case, the issue was whether inmates under investigation for murder who were detained in administrative detention were entitled to appointed counsel before charges are filed. Relying on *Kirby v. Illinois* (1972), the Court said that the Sixth Amendment right to appointed "counsel does not attach until the initiation of adversary judicial proceedings" (del Carmen et al. 1993, 21). The Court added that the right to counsel applies only after formal charges are filed, even if the inmate is in administrative segregation prior to the filing of formal charges. The Court said that giving an inmate the right to counsel at this stage affords inmates more rights than free citizens who, although under investigation but not yet charged, are not entitled to counsel.

Eighth Amendment Rights

Medical Care. After the Supreme Court made the Eighth Amendment applicable to the states in 1962, prisoners brought cases, with increasing regularity, alleging unconstitutional medical care. The courts held that to raise a constitutional claim of inadequate medical care, plaintiffs had to show more than "mere negligence." Before *Estelle v. Gamble* (1976), however, the level of culpability needed to raise a Section 1983 claim was unclear and uncertain. *Gamble* settled that issue, however, when the United States Supreme Court adopted the "deliberate indifference" standard to assess the constitutionality of inmate challenges to prison medical care. Gamble was an inmate in the Texas prison system who injured himself unloading cotton from a truck. Gamble sought medical relief at the prison hospital and was prescribed pain and muscle relaxant medication. The medications lasted three months, but Gamble was dissatisfied and filed suit alleging inadequate medical care.

The Court first said that if a state decides to punish individuals convicted of criminal activity, it is required to treat their medical needs. Because inmates cannot care for themselves, prison officials must provide medical care to relieve "pain and suffering" that serve "penological purpose[s]" (1976, 104). The Court added that "an inadvertent failure to provide adequate medical care cannot be said to constitute 'an unnecessary and wanton infliction of pain' or to be 'repugnant to the conscience of mankind'" (1976, 106–7). In this case, however, the Court held that prison officials had not been "deliberately indifferent" to Gamble's serious medical needs. There was no "deliberate indifference" because Gamble "was seen by medical personnel on 17 occasions spanning a 3-month period" (1976, 108). The Court said that the failure by prison doctors to order an X-ray of Gamble's back perhaps amounted to medical malpractice, but that medical malpractice in itself does not amount to the constitutional standard of "deliberate indifference" as to create liability.

Use of Force. In 1986, the Court for the first time set the legal standard for the use of deadly force to quell a prison riot. In *Whitley v. Albers* (1986), the plaintiff-inmate was shot, without a verbal warning, by prison officials attempting to suppress a riot. In holding prison officials liable, the United States Ninth Circuit Court of Appeals said that the officials were "deliberately indifferent" to the inmate's constitutional rights. The Court disagreed, holding that the correct standard in prison riot cases is "whether force was applied in a good faith effort to maintain or restore discipline or maliciously and sadistically for the very purpose of causing harm" (1986, 1085). To prove a "malicious and sadistic" application of force, the Court said inmates must show "wantonness with respect to the unjustified infliction of harm as is tantamount to a knowing willingness that it will occur" (1986, 1085).

Hudson v. McMillian (1992) set the standard for use of force cases in general, not just in deadly force cases in riot situations, as was the case in *Whitley v. Albers.* In *Hudson,* correctional officials held down and beat up an inmate. A supervisor watched and admonished the officers "not to have too much fun." As a result of the beating, the prisoner suffered minor bruises and swelling of the face, mouth, and lip. The beating also loosened his teeth and cracked a dental plate (del Carmen et al. 1993, 53). As in *Whitley,* the *McMillian* Court rejected the "deliberate indifference" standard and opined that in all use of force cases the inquiry should be "whether force was applied in a good faith effort to maintain or restore discipline or maliciously and sadistically for the very

purpose of causing harm." The *McMillian* Court also held that a prison guard who uses excessive force may be held liable even if the inmate does not suffer serious injury, if such force was used "maliciously and sadistically to cause harm." The decision does not imply, however, that any injury caused by correctional officers in the performance of responsibilities is automatically a violation of the Eighth Amendment prohibition against cruel and unusual punishment. Liability must be judged in light of the "malicious and sadistic" standard set by the Court.

Inmate-by-Inmate Assault. In *Farmer v. Brennan* (1994), the Court unanimously ruled that inmates can win lawsuits against prison officials for inmate attacks if they show that prison officials knew of a substantial risk of harm and recklessly disregarded that risk. In this case, Farmer, in the process of a sex change, was classified as a man and housed in a male correctional facility. Farmer served most of his sentence in protective custody, which isolated him from the general inmate population. After a transfer, however, he was housed in the general inmate population where he was raped and beaten.

In a suit for civil damages, the Court held that officials are liable if they demonstrate "deliberate indifference" to the security and safety needs of inmates. In defining "deliberate indifference," the Court rejected the civil law definition of recklessness in which officials could be sued for failing "to act in the face of an unjustifiably high risk of harm that is either known or so obvious that it should be known" (page 1978). Instead, the Court held that "deliberate indifference" was related to a "finding of recklessness only when a person disregards a risk of harm of which he is aware" (1978–79). *Farmer v. Brennnan* is significant because it helps eliminate ambiguity as to when prison officials can be liable for inmate attacks on other inmates. *Farmer* establishes a compromise between a high level of intent, "malicious and sadistic for the very purpose of causing harm," which is used to hold prison officials liable for excessive force, and a low level of intent, "negligence," which is used to hold prison officials liable for deprivations under state tort law.

Conditions of Confinement. Prior to 1991, it was difficult to determine what standard applied to conditions of confinement cases. Courts assessed whether prison conditions were constitutional under a number of legal standards, including "evolving standards of decency" (*Trop v. Dulles*, 1958), "minimal civilized measures of life's necessities" (*Rhodes v. Chapman*, 1981), "wanton and unnecessary infliction of pain" (*Gregg v. Georgia*, 1976), "deliberate indifference" (*Estelle v. Gamble*, 1976), and "denial of basic human needs" (*Hutto v. Finney*, 1978).

In *Wilson v. Seiter* (1991), the Court attempted to end the confusion by adopting "deliberate indifference" in all prison "conditions" cases. The decision is consistent with all other Eighth Amendment cases in that the "deliberate indifference" standard must be employed. Wilson, an inmate in Ohio, filed a civil rights suit against prison officials, alleging cruel and unusual punishment stemming from poor prison conditions. In rejecting the inmate's claim, the Court said that the Eighth Amendment has both an "objective" and a "subjective" component. To meet the objective component of the Eighth Amendment, inmates must show that prison conditions violate "evolving standards of decency." To meet the subjective component of the Eighth Amendment, prisoners must show that prison officials possessed a culpable mental state amounting to "deliberate indifference." This case is also significant because it makes it difficult for inmates to recover damages from prison officials in "conditions of confinement" cases and sets the standard by which all Eighth Amendment "conditions of confinement" cases are to be judged.

Can inmates in prison be double celled? *Rhodes v. Chapman* (1981) answered yes to that question. In that case, state prisoners in the Southern Ohio Correctional Facility brought suit against state officials alleging that double ceiling inmates violates the Constitution. The prisoners alleged that double celling confined cellmates too closely and was a source of overcrowding. The Court rejected this argument and decided that double celling prison inmates does not, in and of itself, constitute cruel and unusual punishment. There may be instances, however, when because of deprivation of food, medical care, crowding, sanitation, and other factors, the conditions may be so poor as to constitute a violation of the Eighth Amendment cruel and unusual punishment clause. The key to understanding Rhodes is to realize that the prison in this case was described by the Court as "unquestionably a top-flight, first-class facility." It was a relatively modern facility built in

the early 1970s that had larger than average cells and several recreational facilities. The Court would likely have decided the case differently if the conditions of the prison involved had not been as good as they were.

Smoking in Prison. In 1993, the Court held that inmates may have a constitutional right to be free from unreasonable risks to future health problems from exposure to environmental tobacco smoke (ETS). In *Helling v. McKinney* (1993), an inmate in the Nevada State Prison filed a suit claiming that being involuntarily exposed to second-hand tobacco smoke was cruel and unusual punishment. The inmate had been placed in a six by eight cell with a five-pack-a-day smoker. Although not seriously ill when he brought the case, the inmate said that such exposure constituted a threat to his future health. The Court agreed, holding that exposure to unreasonably high levels of ETS may sometimes be cruel and unusual punishment. The Court also said that a "prison inmate [can make out a successful Eighth Amendment claim about] unsafe drinking water without waiting for an attack of dysentery" (1993, 2480). The Court added that "it would be odd to deny an injunction to inmates who plainly proved an unsafe, life-threatening condition in their prison on the ground that nothing yet had happened to them" (1993, 2481). Reaffirming *Wilson v. Seiter,* the Court said that plaintiffs must show both the objective and subjective components of the Eighth Amendment. It is important to note, however, what the Court did not and did say in this case. It did not say that prisoners have a constitutional right to a smoke-free prison environment; what it said was that the Constitution may be violated if it can be shown that exposure to tobacco smoke constitutes a present or future threat to the inmate's health.

Fourteenth Amendment Rights

There are two basic rights under the Fourteenth Amendment, the right to due process and the right to equal protection. Due process basically means fundamental fairness; therefore, any case involving the violation of a due process right implies that fundamental fairness has allegedly been denied. Equal protection denotes that everyone must be treated in the same manner, unless there are justifications for differential treatment. Both rights have been invoked repeatedly in prison cases and have resulted in some leading Court decisions.

Right to Due Process. The most significant case on due process is *Wolff v. McDonnell* (1974), which involved disciplinary hearings. In that case, prison inmates in Nebraska brought suit alleging that the Nebraska prison disciplinary proceedings violated due process because inmates were given only limited rights by prison officials prior to being disciplined. In what was then considered a sweeping decision in favor of prisoners, the Court said that inmates are entitled to due process in prison disciplinary proceedings that can result in the loss of good time credit or in punitive segregation. Specifically, these rights were as follows:

1. Advanced written notice of the charges must be given to the inmate no less than twenty-four hours prior to appearance before the disciplinary committee
2. There must be a written statement by the fact finders as to the evidence relied on and the reasons for the disciplinary action
3. The inmates must be allowed to call witnesses and present documentary evidence in their defense, as long as such will not jeopardize institutional safety or correctional goals
4. Counsel substitute (either a fellow inmate or staff) will be permitted when the inmate is illiterate or when the complexity of the issues makes it unlikely that the inmate will be able to collect and present the evidence for an adequate comprehension of the case
5. The prison disciplinary board must be impartial

These rights, however, are required only in prison disciplinary cases involving serious misconduct, interpreted as cases that can result in solitary confinement or deprivation of "good time" credit.

In another case, *Superintendent, Massachusetts Correctional Institution, Walpole v. Hill* (1985), the Court ruled that prison disciplinary board findings that result in loss of good time must be supported by some evidence in order to satisfy the requirements of due process, hence a finding based on whim or on no evidence at all violates due process. At the same time, the courts should uphold a decision if there is "some evidence" to support a finding. A federal court cannot substitute its conclusion for that of prison disciplinary personnel. Another case (*Baxter v. Palmigiano,* 1976) holds

that inmates are not entitled to counsel or cross-examination in prison disciplinary hearings and that silence on the part of the inmate may be given adverse evidentiary significance by the disciplinary board. This is different from a regular criminal trial, in which the silence of an accused cannot be taken as an indication of guilt, nor can it be commented on by the prosecutors.

In addition to disciplinary proceedings, due process concerns are often raised in the decision to transfer inmates to psychiatric facilities and to medicate them against their will. The question arises as to whether such a change in status and treatment requires a judicial hearing. In *Washington v. Harper* (1990), inmate Harper refused to continue taking his prescribed medication in the form of antipsychotic drugs. The policy at the Washington State Penitentiary provided that if a psychiatrist orders antipsychotic medication, an inmate may be involuntarily treated. Safeguards were in place, however, for such involuntary treatment. These were that the involuntary treatment could be administered only if the inmate suffers from a "mental disorder" and is "gravely disabled" or poses a "likelihood of serious harm" to himself or to others. Moreover, a hearing was provided in which these two conditions are judged to have been met, after which a special committee consisting of a psychiatrist, a psychologist, and a center official, none of whom may currently be involved in the inmate's diagnosis or treatment, can order involuntary medication, but only if the psychiatrist is in the majority. The inmate was given the right to notice of the hearing, the right to attend, present evidence, cross-examine witnesses, and a right to appeal to the center's superintendent. Despite these safeguards, Harper alleged that he had a right to a hearing before a judge prior to being administered antipsychotic drugs against his will. On appeal, the Court sided with the prison system, saying that the due process clause of the Constitution permits the state to treat a prisoner who has a serious mental illness with antipsychotic drugs against his will if he is a danger to himself or others and if the treatment is in his medical interest.

Two years later, the Supreme Court decided a case on involuntary psychotropic medication of a mentally ill pretrial detainee. In *Riggins v. Nevada* (1992), Riggins was awaiting trial on capital murder charges when he started hearing voices. Over Riggins's objection, a psychiatrist ordered antipsychotic medication. Riggins was found competent, tried, convicted, and sentenced to death. The U.S. Supreme Court held that the involuntary medication violated Riggins's liberty interests under the Fourteenth Amendment. The trial court, it was reasoned, failed to make a determination about the need for the medication or of any reasonable, less intrusive alternatives. Once Riggins rejected the medication, the state had a duty to show the need for the medication and its treatment propriety.

Right to Equal Protection. Historically, the right to equal protection has been invoked in prison cases involving discrimination on the basis of race. As early as 1968, however, the Court ruled in *Lee v. Washington* (1968) that racial segregation in prisons is unconstitutional. Since then the Court has not addressed this issue again, perhaps because there is no prison system in the country at present that segregates prisoners on the basis of race. In recent years, however, the right to equal protection has been raised in the context of discrimination on the basis of sex, particularly unequal programs in male and female institutions. Although the Court has not addressed this issue, lower courts tend to declare unconstitutional disparate treatment of male and female inmates unless justified by compelling circumstances. Unequal treatment is unconstitutional and is also proscribed by the Civil Rights Act of 1964.

Visitation. The Court has decided two cases on visitation and has held that inmates do not have unlimited rights to visits, including contact visits. Although not falling under any specific constitutional right, prison visitation has traditionally been considered an integral part of prison life, and prison authorities allow visitation as a matter of sound administrative policy. Its constitutionality, however, is far from established. In *Block v. Rutherford* (1984), the Los Angeles County Central Jail forbade detainees from having contact visits with family members. In granting deference to correctional authorities, the Court held that the "jail's blanket prohibition on contact visits is an entirely reasonable, non-punitive response to legitimate security concerns" (del Carmen et al. 1993, 122). In another case, *Kentucky v. Thompson* (1989), Kentucky had rules governing prison visits that said a "visitor may be denied entry if his or her presence would constitute a 'clear and probable danger to the safety and security

of the institution or would interfere with the orderly operation of the institution'" (del Carmen et al. 1993, 124). After some women were denied visitation without a hearing, inmates filed a class action suit, alleging a due process violation. The Supreme Court held that the mere existence of prison regulations governing visitation does not create a liberty interest that requires a hearing every time someone is denied visitation.

Conclusion

Since the abandonment of the "hands off" policy by the courts in the early sixties, prisoners have come a long way toward establishing constitutional rights while in prison. The selective cases discussed above indicate that the United States Supreme Court has been active in the last three decades in the area of prisoners' rights. The result has been a spate of leading cases that outline prisoners' rights under the United States Constitution.

The rights established by the Court in the above and other cases form the bare minimum of rights enjoyed by prisoners. Lower courts may extend the rights of prisoners beyond those set by the Supreme Court. Such expansion may be based on the state's constitution, state law, judicial orders, consent decrees resulting from prison litigation, and self-promulgated administrative rules. Nothing prevents a state or its prison system from going beyond the minimum set by the courts; what they cannot do is give inmates fewer rights than those the courts say are constitutionally required.

The period of intense prison litigation has peaked. The major "test cases" have been decided, leading precedents have been set, and standards have been prescribed. Although some constitutional issues have yet to be resolved and the extent of their applicability delineated, what remains is basically the refinement of major issues that have already been decided. Some constitutional issues, currently being decided in lower courts, will gradually make their way to the Supreme Court and further sharpen the prison law landscape. A major challenge for prison administrators in the nineties is implementation of court decisions, compliance with court orders, and making sure that issues that have been resolved in previous court cases do not reappear to set the stage for another round of litigation that is usually costly and time consuming. That is a major challenge for any prison system, particularly in an era of burgeoning

L

prison populations and diminishing state resources for corrections.

Michael S. Vaughn
Rolando V. del Carmen

Bibliography

Alexander, R. (1994). Hands-off, hands-semi off: A discussion of the current legal test used by the United States Supreme Court to decide inmates' rights. *Journal of Crime and Justice* 17: 103–28.

Bronstein, A. J. (1985). Prisoners and their endangered rights. *Prison Journal* 65: 3–17.

Collins, W. C. (1993). *Correctional Law for the Correctional Officer.* Laurel, Md.: American Correctional Association.

del Carmen, R.V., S.E. Ritter, and B.A. Witt (1993). *Briefs of Leading Cases in Corrections.* Cincinnati, Ohio: Anderson.

Dunn, A. (1994). Flood of prisoner rights suits brings effort to limit filings. *New York Times,* March 21: A-l, B-12.

Vaughn, M. S., and R. V. del Carmen (1993). Smoke-free prisons: Policy dilemmas and constitutional issues. *Journal of Criminal Justice* 21(5): 151–71.

Note: Case citations appear at the end of the last section.

VI. Prison Crimes

Prisoners who commit crimes while confined in a prison may be prosecuted in criminal proceedings in state or federal courts. All substantive and procedural laws governing criminal prosecution apply to prisoner prosecutions. For example, a prisoner has the same rights to the presumption of innocence, jury trial, and assistance of counsel during the proceedings as those afforded to nonprisoners.

The uniqueness of the prison setting influences some of the prisoner-defendant's rights in a criminal proceeding. Prisoners do not forfeit all constitutional protections when they are convicted and confined in prison. Some of those rights, however, are subject to restrictions and limitations. Maintaining institutional security and preserving internal order and discipline are essential goals that require limitation of prisoners' constitutional rights. Prisoner-defendants lose the benefit of protections afforded other criminal defendants in two areas: *Miranda* warnings and searches.

The Fifth Amendment to the United States Constitution guarantees that a criminal defendant cannot be compelled to be a witness against himself. If law enforcement interrogation overcomes a defendant's will to remain silent by force or coercion, any statement made by the defendant cannot be used to convict him. The Supreme Court in *Miranda v. Arizona,* and subsequent decisions, required that any time an individual in custody is interrogated, he must be given the now familiar *Miranda* warnings: that he has the right to remain silent, and that any statement he does make may be used as evidence against him; that he has the right to the presence of an attorney, either retained or appointed. Because a prisoner is, by definition, in custody, a literal application of the *Miranda* rule to the prison setting would require the reading of *Miranda* rights every time a prison employee questions an inmate about any matter that could uncover illegal activity. While there is no definitive case from the Supreme Court on this point, various circuit courts of appeal have approved the admission into evidence of statements made by prisoners to prison officials in response to interrogation with no *Miranda* warnings. Because the courts have yet to draw a bright line on this question, any incriminating statement made by an inmate in response to questioning might be admissible in a later criminal trial. Because of the currently unsettled nature of the law, however, the risk runs both ways. If a prison official exacts an incriminating statement from a prisoner without first reading his *Miranda* rights, the statement may be inadmissible on Fifth Amendment grounds.

The Fourth Amendment to the Constitution prohibits unreasonable searches of persons, houses, papers, and effects. If the government can convince a judicial officer that there is probable cause to believe that a crime has been committed, the judicial officer issues a search warrant particularly describing the place to be searched and the persons or things to be seized. In certain limited circumstances, the courts have held that a search is reasonable, even without a warrant. In criminal prosecutions, the government, when challenged, must establish that evidence sought to be introduced in a criminal trial was seized pursuant to a valid warrant, or pursuant to a recognized exception to the warrant requirement. If the evidence was obtained in violation of the Fourth Amendment warrant requirement, the evidence is suppressed, meaning that it cannot be introduced at trial. Suppression is a powerful tool available to a criminal defendant, because if some or all of the government's evidence is suppressed, the prosecution may not be able to prove the defendant's guilt.

Prison officials, however, can search a prisoner's living quarters, personal property, clothes, and in most cases even body cavities without a warrant if they suspect a violation of prison rules or pursuant to a general security search or "shake down." The courts have held that such searches are an appropriate security measure and are not unreasonable under the Fourth Amendment. If evidence of a crime is seized during a search, the prisoner has no basis for suppressing the evidence in a subsequent criminal trial, and thus loses another weapon in the criminal defense arsenal.

In order for criminal proceedings to be initiated, a crime must be reported to or witnessed by a law enforcement official. Because state and federal law enforcement officials do not patrol the insides of prisons where they would have the opportunity to witness prison crimes, all prison prosecution is initiated by reports or complaints. Anyone, including another prisoner, a prison visiter, or a prison employee, can make such a report. As a practical matter, few prosecutions result from complaints made by prisoners and prison visitors against inmates. Further, prisons have strict requirements governing employee reporting procedures. An employee who witnesses a crime being committed by a prisoner is required to report that crime to the proper prison authorities. An employee must comply with rules about who must be told, when the report must be made, what form the report must take, and confidentiality of internal prison events. These rules are considered necessary to ensure the safety of employees and inmates, and if ignored by employees, are grounds for dismissal. Consequently, prison officials exercise wide discretion in determining when crimes will be reported and criminal proceedings initiated.

Exercise of that discretion is informed by a wide variety of concerns. Any behavior that amounts to a criminal offense also subjects the offender to prison disciplinary action. Prison officials can choose to discipline the prisoner in an internal proceeding, to report the crime to law enforcement officials for prosecution, or both. Internal disciplinary actions have the advantage of swifter punishments that are specially designed to deter and control bad behavior in the prison setting. They typically include reprimand, restrictions on privileges such as commissary and visitation, extra duty, confine-

ment in a disciplinary cell, and loss or withholding of statutory good time. Disciplinary proceedings are less disruptive and less expensive than formal criminal prosecutions. For these reasons, misdemeanors and less serious felonies are almost never prosecuted. Murder, escape, assault, sexual assault, riot, possession of a controlled substance, and possession of a weapon are the most commonly indicted prison crimes.

Two exceptions to prison official discretion merit mention. Most jurisdictions require that any death of a prisoner be reported for investigation by a grand jury or law enforcement official outside the prison. Murder and manslaughter are therefore regularly reported. Second, reporting prison riots is not discretionary, largely due to involvement by outside law enforcement agencies and the news media. Negotiations with rioting prisoners often include demands for and promises of amnesty from criminal prosecution. Regardless of the public policy arguments on both sides, courts and prosecutors are not bound to honor promises of amnesty made by prison officials during riot negotiations.

In low-population counties or parishes that contain a large state prison, the considerable expense of criminal prosecution can be a significant factor in determining which crimes are prosecuted. The public coffers must provide prosecutors, judges, courtrooms, and appointed lawyers to defend any indigent inmate. When more prisoners are indicted than the local system can process and bring to trial, court dockets become backlogged. Delays mean missing witnesses and violation of speedy trial rules, and they can result in dismissal of the charges. Prosecutors tend to offer the prisoners reduced charges and sentences in exchange for guilty pleas in an attempt to relieve the backlog. Faced with the reality of delayed, reduced, or avoided punishments, prison officials opt for internal discipline in all but the most serious crimes.

Crimes committed on federal property must be prosecuted in federal court. For example, a crime committed by a prisoner in the federal prison facility in Kansas would be prosecuted in the Federal District Court for the District of Kansas, rather than in a Kansas state court. Therefore, criminal prosecutions from federal facilities do not tax the judicial resources of the counties where they are located.

Another factor that officials consider is the disruption caused by prosecutions outside the prison, particularly if the courthouse is some

L

distance from the prison. The defendant is entitled to have his lawyer visit with him and interview any witnesses, including prisoners and prison employees who may have information about the charges. The prosecution, the defense lawyer, and their investigators may need to go through prison records, view the crime scene, and subpoena employee and prisoner witnesses. Transportation, security, sleeping, and eating facilities must be provided for all prisoner witnesses and defendants during pretrial hearings and for the duration of the trial.

Punishment for prisoner prosecutions is governed by the state and federal statutes. Each jurisdiction adopts its own punishment provisions, which vary widely from jurisdiction to jurisdiction. Some charges carry enhanced punishments for crimes committed on prison grounds. For instance, carrying a weapon in a penal institution, or assaulting a prison guard who is performing his official duties may carry harsher punishments under the statute than carrying a weapon in a grocery store or assaulting a bartender. In addition, judges and juries may be less sympathetic to a prisoner-defendant when given the authority to select a punishment within a wide range. Aside from such cases, punishment is the same for prisoner prosecution as it is in any criminal matter.

Elizabeth L. DeRieux

Bibliography

Finizio, S. (1992). [Comment] Prison cells, leg restraints, and "custodial interrogation": *Miranda*'s role in crimes that occur in prison. *University of Chicago Law Review* 59: 719.

LaFave, W. R. (1986). *Search and Seizure, a Treatise on the Fourth Amendment.* 2nd ed. St. Paul, Minn.: West.

Robbins, I. P. (1982). Legal aspects of prison riots. *Harvard Civil Rights, Civil Liberties Law Review* 16: 735.

Ulshen, R. Z., and R. J. Burke (1992). Prisoners' substantive rights. *Georgetown Law Journal* 80: 1677.

Note: Case citations appear at the end of the last section.

VII. Employee Legal Issues

Correctional employees live in a society that increasingly seems to take every dispute, real or imagined, to court. These employees deal daily with inmates who sometimes seem to live to sue them. It therefore is scarcely any wonder that correctional employees increasingly turn to the courts to resolve grievances.

While inmates seek relief primarily from the U.S. Constitution, employees have a much broader array of legal protections available to them. Employees base claims on federal and state constitutional theories, on rights guaranteed by state and federal statutes and regulations, and often on rights won in labor negotiations and defined by collective bargaining agreements.

This entry will review recent developments in only some of the many areas where correctional employees enjoy protections from the law.

Employee Safety

Working in a correctional institution can be dangerous. According to the 1992 *Sourcebook,* while no state or federal prison workers were reported killed by inmates in 1991, over eight thousand staff members were injured in assaults by inmates. That number would be even higher if it included jail staff.

A logical question can be asked in the context of a prison or jail. Inasmuch as the institution has a duty to protect inmates, and staff members can be sued for failure to protect inmates, does the institution have a similar duty to protect the staff? Can a correctional employee sue the employing agency or the head of the institution for "failure to protect" if the employee is injured by an inmate? Employees' rights in this area are at once both greater and fewer than those of inmates.

Civil Rights Suits. Inmates typically file their failure to protect claims under 42 USC Sec. 1983, one of various federal civil rights statutes. In a "1983 action," plaintiffs typically claim that their constitutional rights were violated by the action of a governmental defendant.

Employee claims that try to follow a similar route find rough sledding at best. In overruling a lower court judgment in favor of officers injured or killed in a prison riot, one court of appeals said: "The state must protect those it throws into snake pits, but the state need not guarantee that volunteer snake charmers will not be bitten. It may not throw Daniel into the lion's den, but if Daniel chooses to be a lion tamer in the state's circus, the state need not separate Daniel from his charges with an impenetrable shield" (*Walker v. Rowe,* 1986, 511).

In a more recent case, the employee's claim fared somewhat better (*L. W. v. Grubbs*, 1992). In a sense, the court in *L. W.* said that the state may not trick Daniel into the lion's den or falsely tell the snake charmer that the snake has had its fangs and poison removed. In *L. W.*, a nurse in a prison was raped and terrorized by a sex offender known to be violent. A series of mistakes and errors of judgment by institution officials led the sex offender to be assigned to a job where he would be alone with the nurse. The nurse claimed that she had been told she would not be required to work alone with dangerous sex offenders. Recognizing an exception to the usual rule of no constitutional liability for workplace injuries, the Ninth Circuit Court of Appeals said that if the employee could prove the facts she alleged, she would have a claim, because the state's affirmative conduct put her in danger.

Despite the potentially favorable result in *L. W.*, claims by the employee against the employer based on a constitutional failure to protect theory are not likely to be successful.

Other Sources of Relief. If federal civil rights actions are not a fertile ground for employee failure to protect claims, various state or federal statutes may provide some relief. State workmen's compensation laws typically provide the employee injured on the job with at least limited monetary relief. Workmen's compensation provides the employee with what amounts to no-fault insurance for "personal injury by accident arising out of and in the course of employment." Where this coverage exists, however, the law prevents the employee from suing the employer in state court for damages.

Occupational Health and Safety Act (OSHA). Safety issues in a correctional institution can also be the subject of a complaint under the federal Occupational Health and Safety Act. While OSHA does not provide any direct monetary relief to the injured employee and while employees cannot bring lawsuits directly under OSHA, the law includes a "general duty" clause that requires employers to maintain a workplace free from recognized hazards that are likely to cause serious injury or death to workers (Hood and Hardy 1983, 155). Federal OSHA inspectors (or state inspectors, where OSHA enforcement has been delegated to state agencies) have the power to enter and inspect premises. Citations can be issued that include a proposed penalty and correction date. Ultimately, courts may enforce OSHA penalties and corrective orders.

Equal Employment Opportunities
"Cross-gender" supervision (the supervision of one sex by the other) presents an example of an area in which the rights of inmates and the rights of employees conflict. Most commonly, the conflict is between the inmates' rights of privacy and the rights of the employee to equal opportunity. The institution/employer may find itself caught in the middle of this conflict: accommodating the inmate's privacy concerns may trigger legal claims from the employees, but meeting the employee demands may result in suit by the inmates. New federal legislation, described below, may give some inmates a freedom of religion claim to pit against the interests of the officers.

Case law dealing with female officers supervising male inmates generally supports women working almost all posts and performing nearly all tasks in an institution. Courts have indicated that a male inmate's right to privacy would be violated by female officers regularly observing the inmate in states of undress and using the toilet (*Cookish v. Powell*, 1991). But where the observation is more incidental or restricted by distance, courts have accepted such observation (*Grummett v. Rushen*, 1985). Pat searches of male inmates by female officers have also been approved, assuming the searches are done in a professional manner (*Timm v. Gunter*, 1990; *Grummett*, 1985).

While case law is fairly well developed concerning women working in male facilities, the opposite is not true. It is not at all clear that the female officer cases such as *Grummett* and *Timm* provide strong precedent for the male officer situation. There are very few cases dealing with male officers supervising female inmates. The most recent, *Jordan v. Gardner* (1993), held that a policy allowing male officers to routinely pat-search female inmates inflicted cruel and unusual punishment in violation of the Eighth Amendment because of what the court believed would be the psychological effects on at least some of the women subject to the searches. Experts in the area of abused women testified that women who had been raped or sexually abused in the past could be further traumatized by the pat searches, which were so thorough the court preferred to call them "rub" searches. *Jordan* did not address what other limitations might exist for male officers working in female institutions.

As an aside, *Jordan* is an example of a case in which the institution administrator was facing a lawsuit regardless of what policy he opted for concerning opposite gender pat searches. Prior to implementing the policy allowing such searches, he was receiving considerable pressure from employee groups to permit the searches.

Thus, while there is increasingly clear case law that permits women to perform almost all of the tasks of a correctional officer, what little case law there is regarding men supervising women appears to be more protective of the women. The uncertainty of the law in this area reflects both the lack of litigation concerning male officers in female institutions and the evolving relationships of men and women in American society generally.

The Religious Freedom Restoration Act of 1993 (RFRA), PL 103-141, passed by Congress in November of 1993, may also have an impact on the opposite gender supervision issue to the extent that pat searches are involved. RFRA makes it more difficult for the government to justify any "substantial burden" its actions place on the exercise of religion. Unless the government can show its actions are the least restrictive means for furthering a compelling governmental interest, the actions will be illegal under RFRA.

Some inmates object to being pat-searched by persons of the opposite sex on religious grounds. While claims that such searches violate the First Amendment (freedom of religion) have failed, RFRA will allow the question to be reopened (*Madyun v. Franzen,* 1983). The result of this likely litigation could be that certain inmates will have to be pat-searched by officers of the same sex. In *Madyun,* Muslims argued against opposite gender pat-searches. In *Jordan,* a woman raised the issue as part of her general Christian beliefs, citing Scripture to support her position. The Ninth Circuit opinion in *Jordan* (1992, 1137) did not address the woman's religious claim, although an earlier circuit opinion in the case had reversed the lower court's decision that supported the claim.

RFRA also protects employees' religious beliefs and practices. Actions of employers that burden an employee's religious practices will be subject to examination under the demanding standards of the new law. One area that is likely to be reviewed again will be employee requests for time off for special holy days or to observe the Sabbath. Since these types of restrictions probably have survived legal challenge under the compelling state interest test already, it is more likely that they will survive future legal challenge than many inmate oriented restrictions.

Searches and Urine Testing

Employees have often strongly objected to urine testing requirements, especially a requirement for random testing. Late in 1993, the Ninth Circuit upheld the Federal Bureau of Prison's policy of random testing of all employees working in correctional institutions (*American Federation of Government Employees v. Roberts,* 1993). The court said that the bureau had a strong interest in preventing drug use by prisoners and accepted the bureau's argument that there was a connection between employee drug use and possible drug smuggling. The court indicated that because the testing program detected relatively few drug-using employees, the "call was close" as to whether the government showed a strong enough need for testing to overcome the employee's privacy rights. Nevertheless, the court upheld the program. At least one other federal appeals court has upheld random testing of correctional officers, at least those working in medium- or maximum-custody institutions who had direct inmate contact (*McDonnell v. Hunter,* 1987).

The fact that many correctional employees are subject to random urine testing does not mean they are subject to arbitrary testing. If an employee is selected for testing for "cause," that is, not randomly, the employer will need a "reasonable suspicion" to justify the search. A police officer who was required to submit a urine test without sufficient cause and fired when he refused won over $150,000 in damages (*Jackson v. Gates,* 1992).

The federal Constitution is not the only source of potential protection for officers objecting to urine testing. State constitutions may provide greater privacy protections for correctional employees with regard to urine testing (*Guiney v. Police Commissioner,* 583 N.E.2d 523 Mass., 1991). State statutes may address urine testing. Urine testing may be subject to bargaining under a collective bargaining agreement (*Local 194A v. Bridge Cmsn.,* 1990).

The urine test cases demonstrate the basic formula for other types of employee search issues: Is the government able to demonstrate a strong enough need for a given type of search (urine testing, employee pat-searches, locker searches, and so forth) to overcome the employee's interests in privacy. Given the strong interest correctional institutions have in maintaining security and preventing the flow of contraband to inmates, correctional employees are clearly subject to more types of searches than employees working in other governmental jobs.

Due Process

Employment status is protected in most jurisdictions by civil service laws, and often by the collective bargaining agreement. These two sources of protection may limit the grounds on which an employee may be disciplined or fired and they define the procedures necessary in a disciplinary matter. The due process clause of the Fourteenth Amendment also affords procedural protections. For instance, coercing an employee to resign in a way that is deemed involuntary violates due process. Three county police officers whose resignations were obtained through threats and other coercive means were awarded damages in excess of $250,000 plus attorneys' fees (*Angarita v. St. Louis County,* 1993).

Americans with Disabilities Act

The Americans with Disabilities Act (ADA), 42 USC Sec. 12101-12213 does not apply exclusively to corrections, but it will certainly have an impact on correctional employees and institutions. ADA prohibits discrimination against a "qualified person with a disability" in every aspect and step of the employment process, from application to retirement.

The term "disability" is broadly defined under ADA. The requirements of the law and its implementing regulations go far beyond such things as providing wheelchair ramps or grab bars in toilets. Unlike other civil rights laws that only prohibit discrimination but do not create affirmative duties for the employer, ADA requires the employer to make reasonable accommodations for the "known physical or mental limitations of an otherwise qualified individual" who is a job applicant or an employee.

Some of the requirements of ADA are very specific. For instance, the law prohibits the employer from requiring a job applicant to take a medical examination or answer questions about medical issues until after a conditional offer of employment has been made. In general, the law frowns on absolute standards or re-quirements that would disqualify a person from a job or a particular position. Instead, the law requires a specific inquiry about the individual and the essential functions of a job: What skills and abilities does the job require? Can the disabled person do the job, either regardless of the disability or with some reasonable accommodation by the employer?

In a simple example, a wheelchair-bound person applying for a position in a control room cannot get to the control room because it is three steps above the main floor. Once in the room, the person can do everything the job requires. A reasonable accommodation might be to install a ramp or lift to allow the person access to the control room.

Employees who feel that they have been discriminated against because of a disability may file a complaint with the Equal Employment Opportunities Commission. EEOC may investigate the complaint and try to resolve it through negotiation. If conciliation fails, EEOC may file suit or issue a "right to sue" letter to the complainant. Ultimately, a court may award injunctive relief (such as ordering reinstatement and back pay) and damages. The amount of damages that can be awarded is capped at $300,000 for employers with five hundred or more employees and at lesser amounts for smaller employers.

As an example of the breadth of ADA's protection, a federal appeals court decided in late 1993 that, in some circumstances, severe obesity is a disability (*Cook v. Rhode Island Department of Mental Health,* 1993). That case was decided under Sec. 504 of the 1973 Rehabilitation Act, but ADA mirrors the substantive requirements of that law, so the result would be the same under ADA.

Other Statutes Protecting Employees

Persons working in corrections, like all other employees, enjoy the protections of various state and federal laws governing the workplace. In addition to the ADA, correctional employees will be litigating claims about medical leave under the new Family and Medical Leave Act. Claims about overtime, when it must be paid and to whom, will continue to be litigated under the Fair Labor Standards Act. Claims of discrimination on the basis of race, creed, color, sex, religion, and national origin will be the subject of lawsuits under Title VII of the Civil Rights Act of 1984. Various state law claims will be pursued.

Conclusion

Disputes between employers and employees are as old as the concept of work for hire. Historically, the employee had little power and no place to receive a hearing, let alone relief, about a dispute. First with the growth of unions and now more and more through various types of state and federal legislation directly affecting the workplace, employees are gaining power and finding state and federal forums to pursue disputes. Even in nonunion workplaces, the correctional employee enjoys many legal protections.

William Collins

Bibliography

Equal Employment Opportunity Commission (1992). *A Technical Assistance Manual on the Employment Provisions (Title I) of the Americans with Disabilities Act.* Washington, D.C.: U.S. Government Printing Office.

Hood, J. B., and B. A. Hardy, Jr. (1983). *Workers' Compensation and Employee Protection Laws in a Nutshell.* St. Paul, Minn.: West.

Case Citations for Legal Issues Sections

American Federation of Government Employees v. Roberts, 9 F.3d 1464 (9th Cir. 1993)

Anderson v. Creighton, 483 U.S. 635, 107 S.Ct. 3034, 97 L.Ed. 2d 523 (1987)

Angarita v. St. Louis County, 981 F.2d 1537 (8th Cir. 1993)

Baxter v. Palmigiano, 425 U.S. 308, 96 S.Ct. 1551, 47 L.Ed.2d 810 (1976)

Bell v. Wolfish, 441 U.S. 520, 99 S.Ct. 1861, 60 L.Ed. 2d 447 (1979)

Bienvenu v. Beauregard Parish Police Jury, 705 F.2d 1457 (5th Cir. 1983)

Block v. Rutherford, 468 U.S. 576, 104 S.Ct. 3227, 82 L.Ed.2d 438 (1984)

Blockburger v. United States, 284 U.S. 299, 76 L.Ed. 306 (1932)

Bounds v. Smith, 430 U.S. 817, 97 S.Ct. 1491, 52 L.Ed.2d 72 (1977)

Boyd v. Estelle, 661 F.2d 388, 389 (5th Cir. 1981)

Brady v. Maryland, 373 U.S. 83, 83 S.Ct. 1194, 10 L.Ed.2d 215 (1963)

Brown v. Miller, 631 F.2d 408 (5th Cir. 1980)

City of Cleburne v. Cleburne Living Ctr., Inc., 473 U.S. 432, 105 S.Ct. 3249, 87 L.Ed.2d 313 (1985)

Cook v. Rhode Island Department of Mental Health, 10 F.3d 17 (1st Cir. 1993)

Cookish v. Powell, 945 F.2d 441, (1st Cir. 1991)

Cruz v. Beto, 405 U.S. 319, 92 S.Ct. 1079, 31 L.Ed.2d 263 (1972)

Daniels v. Williams, 474 U.S. 327, 106 S. Ct. 662, 88 L.Ed.2d 662 (1986)

Darden v. Wainwright, 477 U.S. 168, 106 S.Ct. 2464, 91 L.Ed.2d 144 (1986)

Durmer v. O'Carroll, 991 F.2d 64 (3rd Cir. 1993)

Estelle v. Gamble, 429 U.S. 97, 97 S.Ct. 285, 50 L.Ed.2d 251 (1976)

Ex parte Hull, 312 U.S. 546, 61 S.Ct. 640, 85 L.Ed. 1034 (1941)

Farmer v. Brennan, __ U.S. __ , 114 S.Ct. 1970, 128 L.Ed. 2d 811 (1994)

Foulds v. Corley, 833 F.2d 52 (5th Cir. 1987)

Foy v. Donnelly, 959 F.2d 1307 (5th Cir. 1992)

Fraire v. Arlington, 957 F.2d 1268, 1273 (5th Cir. 1992)

Francis v. Henderson, 425 U.S. 536, 96 S.Ct. 1708, 48 L.Ed.2d 149 (1976)

Gibson v. Collins, 947 F.2d 780 (5th Cir. 1991), *cert. denied,* 113 S.Ct. 102 (1992)

Gilmore v. Lynch, 319 F.Supp 105 (N.D. Ca. 1970)

Gregg v. Georgia, 428 U.S. 153, 96 S.Ct. 2909, 49 L.Ed.2d 859 (1976)

Grummett v. Rushen, 779 F.2d 491, (9th Cir. 1985)

Guajardo v. Estelle, 580 F.2d 748 (5th Cir. 1978)

Guiney v. Police Commissioner, 582 N.E.2d 523, 411 Mass. 328 (Mass. 1991)

Hamm v. De Kalb County, 774 F.2d 1567 (11th Cir. 1985)

Harlow v. Fitzgerald, 457 U.S. 800, 102 S.Ct. 2727, 73 L.Ed.2d 396 (1982)

Hay v. Waldron, 834 F.2d 481, 486 (5th Cir. 1987)

Helling v. McKinney, 509 U.S. __, 113 S.Ct. 2475, 125 L.Ed.2d 22 (1993)

Hill v. Lockhart, 474 U.S. 52, 106 S.Ct. 366, 88 L.Ed.2d 203 (1985)

Houchins v. KQED, 438 U.S. 1, 98 S.Ct. 2588, 57 L.Ed.2d 553 (1978)

Howell v. Burden, 12 F.3d 190 (11th Cir. 1994)

Hudson v. McMillian, 503 U.S. 1, 112 S.Ct. 995, 117 L.Ed.2d 156 (1992)

Hudson v. Palmer, 468 U.S. 517, 104 S.Ct. 3194, 82 L.Ed.2d 393 (1984)

Hutto v. Finney, 437 U.S. 678, 98 S.Ct. 2565, 57 L.Ed.2d 522 (1978)

Illinois v. Perkins, 496 U.S. 292, 110 S.Ct. 2394, 110 L.Ed.2d 243 (1990)

Jackson v. Cain, 864 F.2d 1235 (5th Cir. 1989)

Jackson v. Gates, 975 F.2d 648 (9th Cir. 1992)

Jackson v. Virginia, 443 U.S. 307, 99 S.Ct. 2781, 61 L.Ed.2d 560 (1979)

Johnson v. Avery, 393 U.S. 483, 89 S.Ct. 747, 21 L.Ed.2d 718 (1969)

Johnson v. Glick, 481 F.2d 1028 (2nd Cir. 1973)

Jordan v. Gardner, 986 F.2d 1521 (9th Cir. 1993)

Kentucky v. Thompson, 490 U.S. 454, 109 S.Ct. 1904, 104 L.Ed.2d 506 (1989)

Kirby v. Illinois, 406 U.S. 682, 92 S.Ct. 1877, 32 L.Ed.2d 411 (1972)

Lavernia v. Lynaugh, 845 F.2d 493 (5th Cir. 1988)

Lee v. Washington, 390 U.S. 333, 88 S.Ct. 994, 19 L.Ed.2d 1212 (1968)

Local 194A v. Bridge Cmsn., 572 A.2d 204 (N.J. App. Div. 1990)

L.W. v. Grubbs, 974 F.2d 119 (9th Cir. 1992)

Madyun v. Franzen, 704 F.2d 954 (7th Cir. 1983), cert denied, 104 S.Ct. 493 (1983)

Mathis v. United States, 391 U.S. 1, 88 S.Ct. 1503, 20 L.Ed.2d 381 (1968)

McCleskey v. Kemp, 481 U.S. 279, 107 S.Ct. 1756, 95 L.Ed.2d 262 (1987)

McCleskey v. Zant, 499 U.S. 467, 111 S.Ct. 1454, 113 L.Ed.2d 517 (1991)

McDonnell v. Hunter, 809 F.2d 1302 (8th Cir. 1987)

McMann v. Richardson, 397 U.S. 759, 90 S.Ct. 1441, 25 L.Ed.2d 763 (1970)

Miranda v. Arizona, 384 U.S. 436, 86 S.Ct. 1602, 16 L.Ed.2d 694 (1966)

Monell v. Department of Social Serv., 436 U.S. 658, 98 S.Ct. 2018, 56 L.Ed.2d 611 (1978)

Monroe v. Pape, 365 U.S. 167, 81 S.Ct. 473, 5 L.Ed.2d 492 (1961)

Murray v. Giarratano, 492 U.S. 1, 109 S.Ct. 2765, 106 L.Ed.2d 1 (1989)

Murray v. Maggio, 736 F.2d 279 (5th Cir. 1984)

Newman v. Alabama, 559 F.2d 283 (5th Cir. 1977)

North Carolina v. Alford, 400 U.S. 25, 91 S.Ct. 160, 27 L.Ed.2d 162 (1970)

Ohio v. Johnson, 467 U.S. 493, 104 S.Ct. 2536, 81 L.Ed.2d 425 (1984)

O'Lone v. Estate of Shabazz, 482 U.S. 342, 107 S.Ct. 2400, 96 L.Ed.2d 282 (1987)

Pell v. Procunier, 417 U.S. 817, 94 S.Ct. 2800, 41 L.Ed.2d 495 (1974)

Pennsylvania v. Finley, 481 U.S. 551, 107 S.Ct. 1990, 95 L.Ed.2d 539 (1987)

Picard v. Connor, 404 U.S. 270, 92 S.Ct. 509, 30 L.Ed.2d 438 (1971)

Plyler v. Doe, 457 U.S. 202, 102 S.Ct. 2382, 72 L.Ed.2d 786, reh. den., 458 U.S. 1131 (1982)

Preiser v. Rodriguez, 411 U.S. 475, 93 S.Ct. 1827, 36 L.Ed.2d 439 (1973)

Procunier v. Martinez, 416 U.S. 396, 94 S.Ct. 1800, 40 L.Ed.2d 224 (1974)

Procunier v. Navarette, 434 U.S. 555, 98 S.Ct. 855, 55 L.Ed.2d 24 (1978)

Rhodes v. Chapman, 452 U.S. 337, 101 S.Ct. 2392, 69 L.Ed.2d 59 (1981)

Riggins v. Nevada, 504 U.S. ___, 112 S.Ct. 1810, 118 L.Ed. 2d 479 (1992)

Rubio v. Estelle, 689 F.2d 533 (5th Cir. 1982)

Ruiz v. Estelle, 679 F.2d 1115 (5th Cir. 1982), opinion amended in part and vacated in part, 688 F.2d 266 (5th Cir. 1982), cert. denied, 460 U.S. 1042 (1983)

Saahir v. Collins, 956 F.2d 115 (5th Cir. 1992)

Sawyer v. Whitley, 505 U.S. ___ , 112 S.Ct. 2514, 120 L.Ed.2d 269 (1992)

Saxbe v. Washington Post, 417 U.S. 843, 94 S.Ct. 2811, 41 L.Ed.2d 514 (1974)

Simon and Schuster v. Members of the New York State Crime Victims Board, 502 U.S. 105, 112 S.Ct. 501, 116 L.Ed.2d 476 (1991)

Skillern v. Estelle, 720 F.2d 839, 852 (5th Cir. 1983), cert. denied, 469 U.S. 873 (1984)

Smith v. Bennett, 365 U.S. 708, 81 S.Ct. 895, 6 L.Ed.2d 39 (1961)

Stone v. Powell, 428 U.S. 465, 96 S.Ct. 3037, 49 L.Ed.2d 1067 (1976)

Strickland v. Washington, 466 U.S. 668, 104 S.Ct. 2052, 80 L.Ed.2d 674 (1984)

Superintendent, Massachusetts Correctional Institution, Walpole v. Hill, 472 U.S. 445, 105 S.Ct. 2768, 86 L.Ed.2d 356 (1985)

Teague v. Lane, 489 U.S. 288, 109 S.Ct. 1060, 103 L.Ed.2d 334 (1989)

Thornburgh v. Abbott, 490 U.S. 401, 109 S.Ct. 1874, 104 L.Ed.2d 459 (1989)

L

Timm v. Gunter, 917 F.2d 1093 (8th Cir. 1990)

Tollett v. Henderson, 411 U.S. 258, 93 S.Ct. 1602, 36 L.Ed.2d 235 (1973)

Trop v. Dulles, 356 U.S. 86, 78 S.Ct. 590, 2 L.Ed.2d 630 (1958)

Turner v. Safley, 482 U.S. 78, 107 S.Ct. 2254, 96 L.Ed.2d 65 (1987)

Udey v. Kastner, 805 F.2d 1218 (5th Cir. 1986)

United States v. Flores, 981 F.2d 231 (5th Cir. 1993)

United States v. Gouveia, 467 U.S. 180, 104 S.Ct. 2292, 81 L.Ed.2d 146 (1984)

Waller v. Florida, 397 U.S. 387, 90 S.Ct. 1184, 25 L.Ed.2d 435 (1970)

Walker v. Rowe, 791 F.2d 507 (7th Cir. 1986)

Washington v. Harper, 494 U.S. 210, 110 S.Ct. 1028, 108 L.Ed.2d 178 (1990)

Whitley v. Albers, 475 U.S. 312, 106 S.Ct. 1078, 89 L.Ed.2d 251 (1986)

Williams v. Steele, 194 F.2d 32 (8th Cir. 1952)

Wilson v. Seiter, 501 U.S. 294, 111 S.Ct. 2321, 115 L.Ed.2d 271 (1991)

Wolff v. McDonnell, 418 U.S. 539, 94 S.Ct. 2963, 41 L.Ed.2d 935 (1974)

Younger v. Gilmore, 404 U.S. 15, 92 S.Ct. 250, 30 L.Ed.2d 142 (1971)

Life without Parole

A life-without-parole sanction is a legal provision that specifies that the remainder of the criminal's natural life will be spent in prison. The life-without-parole sanction gained popularity as people realized that a normal life sentence, even a "natural life" sentence, does not necessarily mean that the offender will be behind bars for life. Almost every state has a provision in its laws so that an offender sentenced to life becomes eligible for parole after a set number of years, or can accrue "good time" credits and thus be released. Further, in most states the governor, sometimes in concert with a board, may commute a prisoner's sentence or may pardon an individual. In those states, a governor could pardon a prisoner with a life sentence outright, or could commute a life-without-parole sentence so that the individual would then be eligible for parole.

The sentiment among the public during the 1980s and into the 1990s for a sentence that would put some offenders away for their full natural lives was so strong, however, that states increasingly wrote laws that did away with parole for some offenders, or that bypassed the authority of governors or parole boards to ever release such offenders. Because there are a number of variations in life-without-parole laws, it is difficult to be precise about exactly how many states have a life-without-parole sanction available. A number of states have passed laws that establish life-without-parole sentences. Other states have provisions in their parole or probation laws that create the possibility of a life-without-parole sentence by making individuals with specified sentences ineligible for consideration for release of any kind. And in some states there are life-without-parole laws under which the offender does not become eligible for parole until twenty, thirty, or forty years of the sentence have been served. While these may be called life-without-parole laws, they do not actually guarantee that the offender will remain in prison for life. As of 1990, there were thirty-one states that had clear provisions for a life-without-parole sanction in their laws. In those states the offender cannot be considered for parole no matter how many years have been served.

Also, since some states have provisions for commutation or the possibility of other forms of release besides parole, it is impossible to determine precisely how many inmates are serving a true life-without-parole sentence. As of 1990, however, there were a minimum of three thousand inmates in the United States serving life-without-parole sentences, and possibly as many as ninety-five hundred if one counts states in which every inmate convicted of first degree murder is theoretically doing life without parole.

There are two fundamental types of life-without-parole statutes. One addresses the problem of habitual offenders or career criminals, while the other reflects a just-deserts morality toward the most serious criminal offenders. In the vast majority of the states with such statutes, the sanction may be applied for a single crime, most commonly first degree murder, rather than for any pattern of criminal behavior. Since the majority of these statutes apply to first degree murder, they are referred to as capital offender statutes. As of 1990, approximately thirty states had some variation on a life-without-parole sanction for capital offenders. The laws are quite similar, with minor variations in each state. In six states the life-without-parole provision is found among the legislated duties and responsibilities of the parole board or parole commission. These laws restrict the authority of the parole board to consider parole or early release in specified capital cases.

The penalty may be an alternative to capital punishment or to a normal life sentence, depending upon the circumstances of the offense and offender. In capital offender cases in states where life without parole is available, there are four basic models. In states with a system that Julian Wright calls a triple tiered approach, the offender may be sentenced to life, life without parole, or death (Wright 1990, 540–41). In one variation on the double tiered approach the options are life without parole or death. In states with capital punishment, then, life without parole may either be an alternative to be considered by the court after weighing the circumstances of the case, or may automatically be imposed if the death penalty is not given.

In states without capital punishment, in the second variation on the double tiered approach, the options are life without parole or life. In the single tiered approach the only option available is life without parole, and the sanction is automatic if an offender is found guilty of first degree murder, of specific forms of murder, or of murder occurring under specific circumstances. Only lesser degrees of homicide or the specific recommendation for mercy by the jury (depending upon the state) can allow for parole.

Fourteen states have habitual offender statutes that address the problem of the career criminal through a life-without-parole sentence. Although the specifics vary, these statutes have three elements in common. First, an offender must have been convicted of from two to four prior felonies. Second, at least one of those prior felonies is commonly required to have been a violent offense. Third, the offender must have served a period of incarceration for one of the prior offenses. If these conditions are met, then the offender is eligible to be sentenced to life without possibility of parole for any offense, whether it is violent or not.

The question has been raised in the courts whether placing someone in prison without any chance for parole is constitutional. When applied to capital offenders, the courts have held that this form of punishment is constitutional. When applied to career criminals, however, there is a question of proportionality. The courts have held that life without parole for a habitual offender guilty of housebreaking is constitutional, but for a habitual offender whose most recent offense was a bad check the sentence was held to be dis-proportionate to the crime and, therefore, unconstitutional (Wright 1990, 535–38).

The life-without-parole statutes are written so that the possibility of release through parole or expiration of sentence (possible in some cases because of provisions for "good time") is eliminated. In some instances, even the possibility of work-release or educational furlough is excluded. Forty-eight states, however, have granted some form of commutation power to the executive, and legislative action that rules out the opportunity for release under these circumstances may challenge the constitutional powers of clemency held by the executive by these states. Susan Martin has noted that changes during the 1970s and 1980s restrained the use of commutations by governors. In at least one state, Alabama, the governor is not allowed to commute life-without-parole sentences or pardon any criminal offenders. Pending legislative action, a life-without-parole sentence in Alabama is irreversible.

This sanction will have a significant impact on the correctional system. In the short run, the major problem will be with security and the possibility of the "superinmate." It is possible that an inmate serving life-without-parole and thus with no hope of release and nothing to lose could become what Stewart and Lieberman called "superinmates, prone to violence and uncontrollable" (1981, 16). Correctional officials disagree on whether this would be a real problem. When these inmates are young, they may be more dangerous because they may be willing to take more chances to escape. That would seem logical, because they are individuals whose crimes were judged to be particularly violent or heinous. It appears, however, that prisons are able to handle these offenders well within the framework of their normal procedures. Some of these individuals may prove to be particularly dangerous, but as a group those serving life-without-parole sentences do not yet appear to be unusually dangerous or violent in prison. Also, these inmates realize that their life will be spent in prison, and so they may be more "institutionalized" and thus prone to cause less trouble than other inmates.

But the long-term problem for corrections is with the growth and aging of this population. In the future, prisons will not be dealing with life-without-parole inmates who are young, vicious, and dangerous, but who are burned-out and ill old men and women. Strains will be placed on the health care facilities, the prison, the staff, and on the general social and psychological state of the inmates and the staff working in these prisons. Research on aging and the elderly in prison indicates that about 25 percent of all elderly inmates need almost constant medical attention, and that about 95 percent of an elderly prison population requires medication. Someone in correctional departments with large populations of life-without-parole inmates has to begin to think in terms of maximum-security convalescent homes.

If the life-without-parole sentence is widely used, these offenders will also contribute to prison overcrowding in the long run. In 1987, of all the murderers who received a death sentence or a sentence of life, 1.5 percent received a life-without-parole sentence. Because everyone else, including those receiving a "life" sentence, will be released sooner or later, the percentage of life-without-release prisoners as a percentage of the total inmate population will continue to increase, even if the percentage of commitments they represent remains constant. The Bureau of Justice Statistics estimates that of all persons sentenced to life, 77 percent will actually be released within ten years (because of parole or other provisions). But while there will be turnover among these "normal lifers," those serving life-without-parole will stay on, and their proportion relative to the rest of the population will increase as more are added each year. If over two-thirds of the normal lifers are out by ten years after sentencing, an increasing proportion of the "lifers" remaining in the institution will be life-without-parole inmates. After forty years, as these inmates near age sixty-five and over, each 1.5 percent originally sentenced to a life-without-parole term will have come to be approximately 8.7 percent of the life sentence population in prison.

Derral Cheatwood

See also Long-Term Prisoners and Lifers

Bibliography

Cheatwood, D. (1988). The life-without-parole sanction: Its current status and a research agenda. *Crime and Delinquency* 34: 43–59.

Martin, S. (1983). Commutation of prison sentences: Practice, promise, and limitation. *Crime and Delinquency* 29: 593–612.

Steward, J., and P. Lieberman (1981). What is this new sentence that takes away parole? *Student Lawyer* (October): 14–17, 39.

Wright, J. H. Jr. (1990). Life-without-parole: An alternative to death or not much of a life at all. *Vanderbilt Law Review* 43: 529–68.

Long-Term Prisoners and Lifers

While there is no universal criterion for defining long-term prisoners, researchers typically regard those incarcerated for at least five to ten years, as well as those serving life, life-without-parole, and death sentences, as long-term prisoners. The long-term inmate population in the United States has been characterized as a "growth industry" (Flanagan 1985). A 1990 *Corrections Compendium* survey of state, federal, and Canadian correctional systems revealed that the number of inmates serving life sentences increased 45 percent between 1988 and 1990, a significantly higher rate of growth than for the prison population as a whole. In 1991, about one in eleven inmates, 9 percent of the prison population, was sentenced to life imprisonment or death.

Inmates serving long-term sentences make up increasing proportions of the United States prison population (Flanagan et al. 1990). There are several reasons for this disproportionate increase in long-term offenders in the United States prison system. Most notably, state and federal jurisdictions have enacted mandatory sentencing laws for habitual offenders and drug law violators, resulting in their being imprisoned for longer periods of time than they would have been in previous years. In addition, public demand for longer sentences, enhanced law enforcement, prosecution efforts directed at career criminals, and changing judicial attitudes in sentencing have all led to the imposition of longer sentences (Flanagan et al. 1990).

The greater proportion of long-term offenders in a prison system that is increasing generally in size means an increase in both their absolute and relative numbers. Moreover, given the reasons for these increases, the composition of the long-term group has changed as well. Because a wider range of cases have become eligible for extended prison terms, some researchers speculate that it is becoming increasingly composed of younger, more criminally experienced and more violent inmates (MacKenzie and Goodstein 1985).

In the past, the traditional lifer population included a high proportion of homicide offenders who tended to have no history of criminal behavior prior to the commission of their crimes. In contrast, habitual offenders, who are increasingly entering the ranks of the long-term offender population, by definition have previous criminal histories and had less stable and prosocial lifestyles. In a New York study examining characteristics of long-term offenders over a twenty-five-year period, Flanagan et al. (1990) found that more recent long-term offenders are "more serious," with more prior adult convictions and substantially more extensive histories of preprison drug use.

Crimes and Sentences

Contemporary long-term prisoners have extensive criminal records. Nearly 85 percent of New York state's "very long-term prisoners" (who have served more than ten years) had prior adult convictions in 1989, up from 35 percent in 1956 (Flanagan et al. 1990). More than half of life-sentenced prisoners serving time in state prisons had served time in a correctional facility for a prior offense; a fifth had been incarcerated as juveniles (Bureau of Justice Statistics 1993).

Offenses for which long-term prisoners are incarcerated tend to be among the most serious. In 1989, New York state's population of very long-term inmates was composed primarily of homicide offenders (80 percent), with robbery (5 percent), rape (5 percent), and other offense categories (less than 1 percent each) making up the balance (Flanagan et al. 1990). The top four average sentence lengths (in months) imposed in United States district courts were: kidnapping (175.2), murder (156.5), robbery (101.1), and drug trafficking (86.1). The average time served by violent offenders in 1991 was 66 months (Bureau of Justice Statistics 1993).

The penalty of death has been available to courts in thirty-six states and the federal system since its reinstatement in 1976 by the United States Supreme Court. Due to the extensive litigation surrounding capital cases, prisoners condemned to death generally spend long years in prison awaiting execution, thus also qualifying as long-term offenders. The death penalty is retained for the most serious offenses, including first-degree murder, treason, kidnapping when the victim is killed, and aircraft piracy. At year-end 1989, 2,250 prisoners were under a sentence of death.

Coping with Long-Term Confinement

The prospect of spending a significant portion of one's life behind bars and removed from one's community, family, and friends conjures up images of social isolation, deterioration, and assimilation to a world of violence and victimization. Indeed, early writings on the long-term offender focus on the "devastating impact" (Wormith 1984) of long-term imprisonment. A consequence of long-term incarceration that involved confusion, clouding of consciousness, and amnesia was identified in 1898 by Ganser and coined the "Ganser Syndrome" (cited in Wormith 1984). This debilitation due to institutional life has also been described as "barbed-wire disease" or "metapsychosis" (Vischer 1919, cited in Taylor 1971).

Rather than falling prey to the dire consequences of long-term imprisonment described by early theorists, most long-term offenders cope relatively well with their situation, according to more recent work on long-term imprisonment. Most do not suffer from mental, physical, or emotional deterioration; in fact, many actually show signs of improvement during their long prison stays.

The physical health of long-term prisoners remains stable (Rasch 1977) or, in some cases, improves as a result of superior medical care, improved diet, and detoxification from chemical substances. Tests measuring intellectual ability "yielded no convincing proof of a definite intellectual deterioration during the course of long imprisonment" (Rasch 1977, 216; Banister et al. 1973). Researchers studying personality and emotional factors have found no generally adverse effects of long-term incarceration on factors such as anxiety, depression, self-esteem, and psychosomatic illnesses (MacKenzie and Goodstein 1985). Indeed, one study (Zamble 1992) measured significant decreases in a variety of measures of emotional dysphoria, including depression, anxiety, and guilt feelings. Nor do long-term prisoners appear to alter their responses to prison life or their attitudes toward home, marriage, the law, police, and prisons (Heskin et al. 1974).

Long years of residence in correctional institutions obviously define the realities of long-term prisoners in ways distinguishable from their short-term counterparts. It is pointless for long-termers to focus upon resuming their lives following release from prison; they must come to terms with the fact that the institution is the setting in which their lives will unfold. They must develop strategies for maintaining contacts with family and friends on the outside or learn to accept the diminution of contact over time. They must navigate the complex world

L

of the correctional institution in an attempt to locate meaningful work and social support among other inmates and staff.

The most difficult time adjusting to prison life for the long-term offender apparently comes early on in the incarceration. While that period is difficult for most inmates, those anticipating shorter prison stays are relatively better able to adjust to prison life, exhibiting less depression and fewer psychosomatic symptoms than those anticipating long-term imprisonment.

Following a period of difficult adjustment, most prisoners with long sentences develop strategies for coping with prison and for shaping meaningful, or at least tolerable, lives. One strategy appears to be selective affiliation with other long-term prisoners. Long-termers seek out others for social and emotional support and, in some cases, protection. In addition, long-term offenders frequently form formal "lifers' clubs" that function to provide social networks and as service and advocacy organizations.

Women long-term prisoners, admittedly a small number, constituting only 4 percent of lifers (Herrick 1988a; Bureau of Justice Statistics 1993), manifest some distinctive patterns of interaction. Defined by society as those primarily responsible for child rearing, women suffer particular trauma at their separation from their children. More than male long-termers, women are preoccupied with their children's welfare, albeit it from a distance, and with opportunities for visits. Women long-termers also seem to suffer the severity of their problems increasingly as they serve more time in prison. "They suffer realistically because they cannot interact with their loved ones, social stimulation is lacking, they miss men and social life, they want more to do and they wish they could get an interesting job" (MacKenzie et al. 1989, 236).

Differences in men's and women's adjustment to long-term imprisonment may be accounted for by structural factors caused by the relatively small numbers of women long-termers in any one prison. Opportunities for locating friends among this population are limited, thereby creating more social isolation. Women's prisons, frequently the sole institution for women in the state, tend to be geographically remote, precluding visits by families or transfers to prisons closer to home.

In an important longitudinal study of men's adjustment to long-term imprisonment, Zamble (1992, 414) reported that inmates with long sentences tend to have a deliberate policy of "withdrawing from the flow of institutional social activity," preferring instead to concentrate on solitary activities such as studying, hobbycraft, or watching television. On the other hand, they are not social isolates, as evidenced by the fact that they also tend to cultivate one or two close friendships with other long-termers.

Zamble's (1992) research challenged the conventional wisdom that lengthy sentences tend to destroy men's families. In contrast to others, who have emphasized the difficulty of public visits, increasingly strained relations, and the death of family members during long-term incarceration (Cobden and Stewart 1984), Zamble's work (1992, 415) suggested that "outside contacts did not decrease systematically over time in prison." Indeed, there was a significant increase from the beginning of the term in the number of visits received, as families move to be closer and inmates establish institutional conduct records allowing them extended family visits. Results of a 1987 survey in *Corrections Compendium* indicate that long-term prisoners in three-quarters of United States correctional systems may be released on furloughs and that the vast majority (over 90 percent in all but three states) were successful.

Finally, long-term prisoners manifest a desire to benefit from their extensive time in prison through acquiring new skills and further education, to "use time constructively rather than simply serving time" (Flanagan 1981, 218).

Management Concerns and Strategies

Prison environments and experiences appropriate for prisoners who will spend much of their lives behind bars are distinct from those geared for short-termers. As Toch (1984, 514) wisely notes, "Freedom for the long-term inmate is decades away and is thus not a meaningful behavioral goal, and life without goals is an exercise in eventlessness and monotony. The challenge is that of building highlights into imprisonment, things to aim for and achieve and to take pride in when achieved."

The increase in the number of lifers and long-term offenders in the prison system will tax administrators enormously in terms of facility capacity and services. Structuring meaningful work and training opportunities is a high priority in the development of programs for long-term offenders. One aspect of this is continuous reassessment of changing educational and vocational needs. A skill or trade that is relevant one day may be obsolete twenty-five years later (Flanagan 1985). Toch (1977) offered the concept of "prison careers" to emphasize the developmental nature of work opportunities for long-termers. Some recommend giving specialized training so that long-termers can assume supervisory positions in prison industries and education or as consultants to arbitrate disputes between prisoners and staff, evaluate programs, and counsel peers.

Changes in sentencing policies dealing with violent and repeat offenders have resulted in long-term prisoners who do not fit the traditional model of the criminally inexperienced, cooperative homicide offender. This may have implications for placement of long-termers. A more diversified population of long-termers with substantial numbers of violent, difficult to manage inmates will call into question long-standing prison practices that have made possible the concentration of long-term offenders. While many prisoners and administrators may prefer housing long-term inmates in discrete units within existing prisons, that model may be contraindicated for some.

For all long-term inmates, considerations of quality of life for the many years these individuals will spend in prison is tantamount. Flanagan (1985) argues for the importance of reducing the "secondary sanctions" of imprisonment; Palmer (1984) advocates "naturalizing" the prison through creating "softer," more homelike environments. Many writers stress the importance of visits with family and friends throughout the long-termer's sentence. In general, then, those concerned with long-term offenders emphasize the need to provide them with opportunities to live meaningful, comfortable, and fulfilling lives while they are removed from the community.

Release from Life Sentences

In the article "Dangerousness and the Tariff: The Decision-Making Process in Release from Life Sentences," British researchers conclude that

> the decision to recommend release or continued detention depended upon two main criteria: whether or not the man was "safe" to return to the community and whether or not, in the American terminology, he had served enough "time for the crime." In other words, the decision was made along the dual axes of "dangerousness" and "the tariff." Most lifers lost the label of "dangerousness" at approximately the ten year point in their sentence; whereas the recommendations for meeting the requirements of justice, the "tariff," fell largely between years seven and twelve (Maguire et al. 1984, 258).

Most inmates serving life terms in U.S. prisons become eligible for parole at some point (Herrick 1988). As of 1 January 1987, parole was possible for inmates serving life sentences in twenty-one states (Cheatwood 1988). Parole eligibility, however, varies considerably among states. As of 1988, ten U.S. states required commutation of a life sentence before parole eligibility, some only for offenders convicted of first-degree murder, others only for life-without-parole sentences. The amount of time a lifer must serve before parole eligibility varies considerably from state to state. For example, prisoners in Georgia convicted of first-degree murder are eligible after serving seven years, while similar offenders in Missouri must serve fifty years (Herrick 1988a, 1988b).

Release from life sentences in each state is dictated by legislation that may include sentencing enhancements. For example, in South Carolina a lifer can be ineligible for parole because of a repeat violent offender statute; in Colorado, certain murder offenses are not eligible for parole. In a 1992 Bureau of Justice Statistics survey, thirty-one states reported having a sentence of life without parole.

Lynne Goodstein

Bibliography

Banister, P. A., F. V. Smith, K. J. Heskin, and N. Bolton (1973). Psychological correlates of long-term imprisonment: I. Cognitive variables. *British Journal of Criminology* 13: 312–23.

Bureau of Justice Statistics (1993). *Survey of State Prison Inmates*. Washington, D.C.: U.S. Government Printing Office.

Cheatwood, D. (1988). Life-without-parole sanction: Its current status and a research agenda. *Crime and Delinquency* 34: 43–59.

Cobden, J., and G. Stewart (1984). Breaking out: A perspective on long-term imprisonment and the process of release. *Canadian Journal of Criminology* 26: 500–10.

Davis, S. P. (1990). Survey: Number of lifers up 45 percent in two years. *Corrections Compendium* 15: 1, 8–16.

Flanagan, T. J. (1981). Dealing with long-term confinement: Adaptive strategies and perspectives among long-term prisoners. *Criminal Justice and Behavior* 8: 201–22.

Flanagan, T. J. (1985). Sentence planning for long-term inmates. *Federal Probation* 49: 23–28.

Flanagan, T. J., D. D. Clark, D. W. Aziz, and B. P. Szelest (1990). Compositional changes in a long-term prisoner population. *Prison Journal* 80: 15–34.

Herrick, E. (1988a). Number of lifers in U.S. jumps nine percent in four years. *Corrections Compendium* 12: 9–11.

Herrick, E. (1988b). Survey: Lifers eligible for parole in most states. *Corrections Compendium* 12: 9–13.

Heskin, K. J., N. Bolton, F. V. Smith, and P. A. Banister (1974). Psychological correlates of long-term imprisonment: III. Attitudinal variables. *British Journal of Criminology* 14: 150–57.

MacKenzie, D. L., and L. Goodstein (1985). Long-term incarceration impacts and characteristics of long-term offenders. *Criminal Justice and Behavior* 12: 395–414.

MacKenzie, D. L., J. W. Robinson, and C. S. Campbell (1989). Long-term incarceration of female offenders: Prison adjustment and coping. *Criminal Justice and Behavior* 16: 223–38.

Maguire, M., F. Pinter, and C. Collis (1984). Dangerousness and the tariff: The decision-making process in release from life sentences. *British Journal of Criminology* 24: 250–68.

Palmer, W. R. (1984). Programming for long-term inmates: A new perspective. *Canadian Journal of Criminology* 26: 439–57.

Rasch, W. (1977). Observations on physio-psychological changes in persons sentenced to life imprisonment. In S. Rizkallan, R. Levy, and R. Zauberman, eds. *Long-term Imprisonment: An International Seminar*. Montreal: University of Montreal.

Taylor, A. J. W. (1971). Social isolation and imprisonment. *Psychiatry* 24: 373–76.

Toch, H. (1977). *Living in Prison*. New York: Macmillan.

Toch, H. (1984). Quo Vadis? *Canadian Journal of Criminology* October: 514.

Wormith, S. J. (1984). The controversy over the effects of long-term incarceration. *Canadian Journal of Criminology* 26: 423–37.

Zamble, E. (1992). Behavior and adaptation in long-term prison inmates: Descriptive longitudinal results. *Criminal Justice and Behavior* 19: 409–25.

Zamble, E., and F. J. Porporino (1988). *Coping, Behavior, and Adaptation in Prison Inmates*. New York: Springer-Verlag.

M

Austin Harbutt MacCormick (1893–1979)
Austin Harbutt MacCormick, the son of a Presbyterian minister, author, college professor, college administrator, consultant, and warden, was a pioneer in correctional reform for over fifty years. MacCormick, described in one newspaper as "almost frail looking" but a "bundle of nervous energy," was born in Ontario, Canada, in 1893 and moved to the United States with his parents later that year. He graduated from Bowdoin College in Brunswick, Maine, in 1915. His graduation essay focused on prison reform and was heavily influenced by the eminent penologist Thomas Mott Osborne.

In 1915, Paul Douglas, an author writing on the history of Maine, sought out MacCormick to assist him in an investigation of the state's prisons. Following the example of Osborne, young MacCormick had himself committed to the state penitentiary as a forger. He spent a week in prison establishing close relationships with several "lifers" as his cronies, gaining inside knowledge about the operations of prisons and the prisoner subculture. Upon his release, he wrote an exposé in the *New York Herald Tribune* that rocked the local political establishment and brought national attention to prison conditions.

In the fall of 1915, MacCormick enrolled in Columbia University and was awarded an M.A. in education in 1916. Following his graduation he married and returned to Bowdoin College, where he served as an instructor. In 1917, MacCormick was recruited by Osborne to assist him in an investigation of the Naval Prison at Portsmouth, New Hampshire. Following their established mode of investigation, they had themselves committed voluntarily for desertion. Their investigation revealed that the facilities at Portsmouth were inadequate and unreasonably brutal.

Following the completion of their investigation, the United States became involved in war and MacCormick joined the Navy. Shortly thereafter, he was assigned as an executive officer to assist Osborne, who had been appointed commander of the naval prison in Portsmouth, New Hampshire. This event created a special bond between the two men, and they became life-long friends and associates. Osborne spent many hours with MacCormick both on and off duty, discussing politics and sharing theories. Osborne was a frequent visitor to the MacCormick house who entertained the couple by playing the piano and reciting poetry. In many ways, Osborne became MacCormick's spiritual father.

Between 1917 and 1921, MacCormick worked with Osborne to put their progressive penal philosophies into action. They believed that prisoners should be actively involved in shaping their own punishment and treatment, and they experimented with inmate self-governance programs. During MacCormick's tenure, an honor system was established among prisoners, outdoor recreation was allowed for the first time, and special efforts were made to return prisoners to naval duty. In fact, when a prisoner was returned to duty he participated in commencement exercises and was escorted back to his ship by a prison band. Their success in returning prisoners was unprecedented.

After MacCormick's retirement from the military in 1921 he returned to Bowdoin College, where, at the rank of professor, he served as the alumni secretary. During that time he taught, became a polished after-dinner speaker, and collaborated with an old friend and colleague, Paul Garret, on several investigative projects. Together they conducted the first survey of prisons west of the Mississippi River, publishing those results in the *Handbook of American Prisons* in 1926. During this investigation, MacCormick developed a special interest in prison education. A grant from the Carnegie Corporation enabled him to further his research interests and led to his investigation of education in prison. In 1931, his findings were published in *The Education of Adult Prisoners*. This work and the *Handbook of American Prisons* are today considered classics and have stimulated significant change in the administration of prisons.

In 1934, MacCormick was recruited by Mayor LaGuardia of New York City to regain control of the city's penitentiary, Welfare Island. Welfare Island was known as a "gangsters' country club" where narcotic smugglers, vicelords, and other "underworld" figures controlled prison operations, reveling in costly food and drink while other inmates received too little food and had little or no protection from the cold. On the day that Commissioner MacCormick raided the Welfare Island prison he boldly walked into the main mess hall alone, unprotected, surrounded by more than 800 prisoners. Luckily for MacCormick, his move was seen by the inmates as an expression of his bravado and in time they came to respect him even more. This single event enabled him to establish lines of communication with the inmates, break the lines of control established by the vice lords, and regain control of the penitentiary.

In 1937, the outdated prison on Welfare Island was abandoned and prison operations were moved to a new and modern prison on Rikers Island. Commissioner MacCormick capitalized on this change and implemented a number of innovations designed to improve the control of prisoners, minimize danger to correctional officers, and improve the quality of life within the prison. Segregation of prisoners, classification procedures, and medical and educational services were some of the strategies he relied upon to improve the prison's efficiency, effectiveness, and integrity.

During MacCormick's tenure as the New York Commissioner of Corrections, he served as president of the American Prison Association (1938–39) and received both national and international attention for his reform efforts. When he retired in 1940 he was hailed by the newspapers as "one of the greatest prison executives in the United States" and praised for his "great contribution to modern, honest, and humane prison administration."

Following his retirement, MacCormick became executive director of the Osborne Association. The Osborne Association was formed to study crime and prison life and to make informed suggestions to both policy makers and administrators to improve formal responses to crime. The association, created in honor of MacCormick's mentor, Thomas Mott Osborne (1859–1926), maintained an employment and relief bureau for released prisoners, conducted surveys of juvenile and adult institutions, and served as a resource for program evaluation and assessment. As executive director of the association, Osborne visited most of the nation's institutions and provided advice about their operations. He is also known for his role in correcting inhumane conditions in Texas work camps (1944).

During World War II, MacCormick served as a consultant to the secretary of war and served on the War Department's advisory boards on parole. He also served as vice-chairman of the War Department's clemency board. His work on these boards reflects his earlier orientation toward rehabilitation and the reintegration of the convicted soldiers to active duty. In 1951, in an attempt to attract young people to humane correctional administration, MacCormick joined the School of Criminology faculty at the University of California at Berkeley.

Austin Harbutt MacCormick's life brought him in touch with criminals, correctional officers, correctional administrators, heads of state, presidents, corporate executives, volunteers, researchers, students, academicians, and the working public. Though MacCormick's appearance was said to have been less than charismatic, he had the ability to communicate with people from all walks of life. MacCormick's greatest successes occurred out of the public's view, behind prison walls; they appear to have been the product of his unique understanding of prison life and the prisoner psyche. He was said to have talked with more prisoners than any other single person in the country, and he could talk with prisoners in a personal way without ever losing his authority. His reforms reshaped America and have left an indelible mark on American corrections.

W. Wesley Johnson

See also FEDERAL BUREAU OF PRISONS; OSBORNE, THOMAS MOTT

Bibliography

Barlett, A. (1934a) The four eyed kid: Austin MacCormick. *New Yorker,* May 26: 24–27.

Barlett, A. (1934b). Welfare Island raid aids prison reform: Commissioner MacCormick's "new broom" assault on the corruption of New York's gangster-ruled penitentiary. *Literary Digest,* February 3: 5–6.

Barlett, A. (1940). M'Cormick to quit corrections post. *New York Times,* January 12: 15.

Barlett, A. (1951). Austin H. MacCormick. In *Current Biography*. New York: H. W. Wilson.

Richard A. McGee (1897–1983)

Richard A. McGee was born in Chisago County, Minnesota, on 11 September 1897. He was raised in Minnesota, one of nine children. McGee was an excellent student and graduated from high school at the age of fifteen. He continued his education at the University of Minnesota and received his Bachelor of Arts degree in 1923. He went on to get his Master of Arts degree in education at the University of Minnesota in 1928.

Shortly after getting his Master's degree, McGee held a variety of jobs. In 1931, the Great Depression caused McGee to seek a job as a personnel manager trainee for a public utility corporation. As the Depression worsened, McGee was laid off and became unemployed for the first and only time in his life.

McGee's correctional career began by accident. Jobs were scarce and McGee had to settle for a job as a supervisor of education at the federal penitentiary in Leavenworth, Kansas. When the new federal penitentiary opened in Lewisburg, Pennsylvania, in late 1932, McGee transferred to that institution.

After a few years, despite a position with an up-and-coming prison bureaucracy, McGee felt the need for a change in his career. He sought the challenge of a leadership role in a diverse and unsettled environment, which is what he experienced as the warden at Rikers Island penitentiary. McGee was appointed to organize, open, and manage the new penitentiary for short-term offenders in New York City. When it opened in 1936, it became the main jail in New York City. This position was to become one of the toughest jobs McGee would ever embark on. The year before McGee's appointment, there had been scandals at the old Welfare Island penitentiary that the Rikers Island facility replaced. For years, prisoners who had money or influence received desirable work assignments and ate officer's food instead of inmate food. They were also allowed to remain out of their cells until late at night and would obtain clothing from the outside.

During his administration at Rikers Island, McGee eliminated the prisoner abuses that occurred at the old Welfare Island facility. McGee saw to it that all inmates received the same privileges regarding clothing, commissary, recreation, and cell equipment. He also established a classification program whereby a short case history of inmates was created to help the jail staff with assigning prisoners to work and other programs. With his background in education McGee felt that it was important to educate prisoners, so he promoted vocational education programs and established a library in the jail.

While McGee was the warden at Rikers Island, he helped form the National Jail Association in 1938 (the National Jail Association later merged with the American Jail Association, and the organization is now known by the latter name). The purpose of the association was to improve the conditions of local jails throughout the country. With his work in the association, McGee began a lifelong commitment to improve the conditions at jails and prisons for both prisoners and staff.

In 1941, McGee was ready for a new challenge. He wanted to take on more responsibility. His chance came in December of 1941. One week before the bombing of Pearl Harbor, McGee became head of the Washington State Division of Institutions. At the time, the Division of Institutions consisted of fourteen diverse facilities that included prisons, mental hospitals, and schools for the blind, deaf, and retarded. Although there were problems in the whole system, the state's four correctional institutions were the most troubled.

In his new job, McGee dealt directly with the governor (which proved to be a valuable experience). He also learned to deal with the state budget system at a time when money was scarce because of World War II. Though McGee had successes at the head of Washington's institutions, his greatest contributions to corrections during this time of his career came when he became president of the American Prison Association. Through that position, McGee had the foresight to look to the future of corrections. He believed that future leaders of the corrections profession should be college educated. He also felt that the correctional field must work diligently with individual offenders.

In the early 1940s, the prison system in California was fragmented with individual wardens who made up their own policies, procedures, and programs. Wardens were often picked for political reasons and many were incompetent. Prison staffs had little or no training and many officials were corrupt. When Earl Warren became governor of California in 1943, he introduced a prison reform bill. Corrections was seen as a part of the "spoils system" used by politicians, and they were not ready to give way to reform. Warren expected an uphill battle for his reform bill.

One morning, Warren received a call from Charles Dullea, who was the chief of police of San Francisco at the time. He told the governor that the police had seen two notorious criminals, who were supposed to be serving time in Folsom prison, spending time with some women in a hotel in San Francisco. Chief Dullea asked Warren what should be done about the men. Warren, seeing a chance to use the scandal to promote his reform bill, told Dullea to arrest the men with as much publicity as possible.

After the incident, Governor Warren immediately called the legislature into a special session to bring to light the scandalous conditions of the prisons. In January of 1944, the state legislature passed the Prison Reorganization Act, thus creating the California Department of Corrections. A short time later, Warren named McGee the new director of the Department of Corrections.

McGee immediately set out to professionalize the corrections field. He worked closely with the state personnel board in developing an employee classification system that included salary scales, a definition of duties, minimum qualifications, and so on. He also established well-organized training programs for correctional officers and strove to give correctional officers peace officer status.

In an effort to reform the prisons themselves, McGee reorganized the staffs at San Quentin, Folsom, and the Institution at Chino in such a way that the wardens had under them a business manager, an assistant warden in charge of custody and discipline, an associate warden in charge of individual training and treatment, and a manager of institutional indus-

tries. With the reorganization, McGee also established new policies that developed a set of rules and regulations covering all phases of institutional operations. Later McGee transformed the correctional facilities into specialized institutions that could house inmates that had special requirements for incarceration and rehabilitation.

McGee also sought to improve prison conditions. Most of the facilities were old and beginning to deteriorate. McGee updated the structures as funds became available. He established a centralized record system on the inmates and created prison industries to employ and train inmates. Furthermore, McGee improved the food served to the inmates and provided medical and psychiatric treatment for those who needed it.

McGee served seventeen years as the director of the California Department of Corrections. In 1961, Governor Brown promoted McGee to the new cabinet-level post of administrator of the Youth and Adult Corrections Agency. In that new position, McGee headed both the Adult and Youth Authorities.

McGee retired from public service in 1967, but that did not slow his drive to improve the corrections field. In 1959, McGee had established the Institute for the Study of Crime and Delinquency (later known as the American Justice Institute). This nonprofit organization used private funding to conduct studies to improve the criminal justice system. McGee was the first president of the organization and served on the board of directors until his death. A good public speaker, McGee advocated many reforms to any criminal justice organization or political group that would listen. McGee also wrote several books and many articles on corrections issues.

Richard A. McGee was one of the greatest administrators in the history of American corrections. Many of his ideals are the cornerstones of correctional philosophy today.

David Halley

Bibliography

Conrad, J. P. (1981). *Justice and Consequences*. Lexington, Mass.: Lexington.

Conrad, J. P. (1991). Personal Interview. October 11.

McGee, R. A. (1981). *Prisons and Politics*. Lexington, Mass.: Lexington.

McGee, R. A., Jr. (1991). Personal Interview. September 30.

Warren, E. (1977). *The Memoirs of Chief Justice Earl Warren*. Garden City, N.Y.: Doubleday.

Marion Penitentiary

The Federal Penitentiary at Marion is touted as the nation's most secure facility and home to the most dangerous federal prisoners. It was built in 1963 as a replacement for the less practical facility at Alcatraz. The inmates from Alcatraz were not sent there, however; all were assigned to other units within the federal system. Marion initially opened as a facility for younger offenders.

Built inside a national wildlife refuge in southern Illinois, the unimposing structure was marked by guard towers and rolls of coiled razorwire that cascaded from the fences. The perimeter was outfitted with new electronic intrusion-detection systems and employed armed mobile patrols. Interior security had state-of-the-art, remote-controlled gates and closed-circuit television. Inmates were to be placed alone in a cell. The cells had concrete fixtures with stainless steel toilets. The interior structural design allowed for an open compound in which inmates could move about more or less unrestrictedly.

The most difficult and notorious federal prisoners did not arrive until 1979, when the facility was designated as the only level six federal facility. Wardens from other facilities were allowed to send their most difficult and violent offenders. Many were gang members who had killed other inmates or who had assaulted an officer while incarcerated. Some states contracted with Marion to keep prisoners they had been unable to control or protect.

It was not long before the prison took on the violent character of the inmates who were shipped there. Between 1980 and 1983 a series of work stoppages occurred that resulted in the removal of industrial operations. There were also fourteen escape attempts, ten group uprisings, fifty-eight serious inmate-to-inmate assaults, thirty-three attacks on staff, and nine murders. Two officers were killed in one day in separate incidents. The warden declared a state of emergency and called in a tactical team of officers from Leavenworth to help restore order. Inmates were locked in their cells for approximately twenty-three hours per day. Meals were delivered, as were the limited goods available from the commissary. In some areas, inmates were handcuffed when they left the cell for a shower and escorted by three guards. The "lockdown" continued for years. An inmate's appeal to the Supreme Court over these conditions was declined.

This highly restrictive routine has become a way of life for some Marion inmates, particularly those demoted into the institution's special Control Unit. Cells are searched often and body cavity searches are common. For others, Marion has developed a system in which privileges can be earned and inmates can gradually earn promotions into work and housing plans that allow more time out of their cells. Inmates can also earn the right to participate in limited programs and personal activities. The goal is for most inmates to eventually be transferred to lower security facilities.

Today there are approximately 335 inmates housed at the main Marion penitentiary, less than 1 percent of the federal prison population. The average prison sentence is forty years. A small group of special cells in the basement are used to sequester long-term inmates whose widely publicized crimes involved threats to government security (spies like Jonathan Pollard or John Walker, Jr.) or whose connections make them high risks for escape attempts assisted by family or friends outside (drug lords or illegal weapons dealers for foreign countries).

The Concentration Model

Marion represents what penal philosophy refers to as a "concentration model," meaning that all of one type of inmate are sent to one facility. That facility serves the system by addressing the special needs of that population. Concentration models are believed to be more efficient in that the facility develops expertise in handling that specific group rather than having the group's members dispersed throughout the system in small numbers. Staff and inmates at other facilities feel safer knowing that the most predatory and assaultive inmates will be shipped out. The threat of being sent to such a high-security unit may act as a deterrent for inmate misconduct at lower level facilities.

Under a dispersion model, each prison must dedicate resources to meeting the demands of all types of inmates. High-risk inmates are usually put in solitary or administrative segregation until they have served a punitive term or have demonstrated that they can adapt to the general-population rules.

The disadvantages of a concentration model, particularly when a facility is designated for violent and disruptive inmates, is that the facility develops a negative reputation. Inmates may feel that there is nothing to lose and may continue to act out. At the end of the line, there are no further threats to use in modifying a prisoner's behavior. Some feel compelled to live up to the reputation that they are "the worst of the worst." Staff morale is also affected by the negative reputation of the facility. Much like the prisoners, many staff members feel compelled to develop an aggressive exterior and live up to the tough image of those who guard the "worst of the worst."

The Federal Bureau of Prisons is in the process of developing a new super-maximum-security unit in Florence, Colorado. New architectural features and technological advances will allow this facility to incorporate more security with fewer physical restraints. Cells will have individual showers, so that prisoners will not have to be escorted to the showers, thus enhancing both staff and inmate safety. It is expected that Marion will be used as a more traditional maximum-security prison in the future.

Marilyn D. McShane

See also FEDERAL BUREAU OF PRISONS

Bibliography

Dickey, C. (1990). A new home for Noriega? *Newsweek,* January 15: 66–69.

Earley, P. (1992). *The Hot House.* New York: Bantam.

Holt, R., and R. Phillips (1991). Marion. *Federal Prisons Journal* 2(2): 28–36.

Medical Experiments

The use of prisoners for medical experiments is a phase of American prison history that tells us as much about society's attitudes toward prisoners as it does about prisoners' willingness to take part in any activity that might hold some type of reward, regardless of the danger. In the period from the 1930s through the late 1970s, thousands of inmates participated in hundreds of medical experiments throughout the United States. It has been reported that as many as forty-two institutions participated in continuing major research efforts. It has also been estimated that prisoners were used in the testing of at least 85 percent of all new drugs invented (Gettinger and Krajick 1979).

In most cases the experiments were carried out by large drug manufacturing companies, although from time to time local physicians or researchers working on grants for research institutes or the government were also involved. In the beginning, there were no guidelines or regulations for medical experiments or experimental drug tests, and there was no supervision by agencies such as the Food and Drug Administration. Later, the FDA set up guidelines governing medical research in prisons, requiring that all experiments be approved and monitored by an independent institutional review board.

Traditionally, inmates have always looked for ways to better their prison life. Perhaps the stark deprivations of life behind bars make prisoners particularly susceptible to the benefits of participation in research. Many inmates had no money for cigarettes or toiletries, simple items that made their existence tolerable, and most experiments paid between one and five dollars per day. The price was usually set in terms of the pain or inconvenience, rather than the actual medical risk involved. For example, prices for participation in Upjohn and Parke Davis experiments in the 1970s in Southern Michigan State Prison ranged from twenty-five cents for a fingertip blood sample to twelve dollars for a spinal tap. In 1976, seventy-four participating inmates earned over $32,520, an average of about $439 each.

Money was not the only incentive for participation. Other possible benefits included moving to more spacious living areas with television and exercise rooms, the use of phones, and more visiting privileges. Subjects were also provided with cigarettes, books, and good food. Many simply enjoyed the medical attention and the interest paid to their health.

Most prisons had some type of program in which inmates could earn money or good time credit for donating blood. In many cases, inmates donated as often as allowed. Up until the early 1980s, inmate records at the Texas Department of Corrections still reflected "blood time," good time credit earned through donating blood. Although prison officials continually stressed that the state does not promise anything for their participation, inmates held the perception that cooperation in the drug experiments would look good on their records and might even favorably influence their parole outlook.

From a medical standpoint, inmates made subjects that were very easy to control. They were basically healthy, had regular diets, were relatively free of alcohol or drugs, and were unlikely to wander off or lose interest in participating. Although inmates were volunteers and often signed consent forms, there is some doubt as to whether they were all capable of making an informed consent (that is, could understand the papers pushed before them), or whether the promise of gifts made that consent coerced.

The Three Phases of Drug Testing

Historically, drug testing took place in three phases. In Phase I a drug is given to one hundred or so subjects who are normal, healthy, with no obvious signs of any disease. Researchers simply monitor the effect of the drug on the body, tracking its absorption and its bioavailability and measuring any side effects or toxic reactions. Prisoners were often used in this type of research, including early experiments on LSD.

Phase II testing used small groups of patients, or those purposefully infected with the disease or condition. In many prison research cases, the medical problem had to be created or induced. For example, during WW II the government was seeking a drug to protect Allied soldiers from malaria. A project was begun at the penitentiary at Stateville, Illinois, in which hundreds of prisoners were exposed to hungry disease carrying mosquitos. Infected inmates endured fevers, chills, and the aches of the disease as they were measured, probed, wired, and watched as the disease ran its course. While some received medications, others were nonmedicated for comparison purposes. Some received treatment only in the latest stages of the illness, to test the effectiveness of the medications at different phases. This particular experimental project was in operation for over twenty-five years.

In Tuskegee, inmates were injected with syphilis to test drugs at all stages of the disease. Half, the control group, were left untreated, and others were given medicine only in the advanced stages of infection so that researchers could study the drugs' effect on the most serious cases. In 1962, two hundred inmates in Ohio were injected with cancer cells by researchers associated with the Sloan Kettering Cancer Center, funded by the National Cancer Institute and the American Cancer Society. At that time researchers were still unsure whether cancer could be transmitted from one person to another and wanted to see if cancer cells would be rejected or would grow in otherwise healthy tissue. The director of this project was later put on probation by the New York State Board of Regents for conducting these same experiments on his regular (outside) patients without their knowledge.

Phase III drug testing involves giving the medication to large groups of ill people who live under normal everyday circumstances out in society. That is the final step in the testing process, and it allows researchers to see the way the drug functions under routine conditions. Obviously, inmates would not be used in this final phase.

Benefits for the Institution

In addition to the benefits received by the inmate participants, institutions also received substantial rewards or compensation for cooperation with the drug companies. When Eli Lilly experimented on its early forms of Darvon with inmates at Indiana State in 1972, the prison received a dishwasher, a remodeled hospital, high school supplies, and library and gym improvements.

At the Oregon State Penitentiary, a group of inmates volunteered for bilateral testicular biopsies. In these experiments, researchers were testing the effects of steroids and sex hormones on sperm production and reproductive health. Experimental subjects had tissue removed from their testes and examined, before and after the administration of the chemicals. In return, the prison received pharmacy services and some emergency medical equipment.

Not all relationships with outside researchers were positive. In the early 1960s, Timothy Leary, the famous drug guru from Harvard University, was experimenting with psilocybin, a narcotic similar to LSD in hallucinogenic properties. Leary believed that the drug could reduce criminal tendencies, and so he administered it to inmates at the Concord State Prison in Massachusetts. After extensive testing, the program was canceled because state officials believed that Leary was creating internal tensions and inciting inmates to rebel. Leary was eventually fired from the university when his extensive personal experimentation with hallucinogenic drugs and his advocacy of such use became public.

Ethical Issues and the Demise of Drug Experiments

Medical experiments conducted during the Cold War, when this country feared nuclear attack, have only recently been uncovered in detail. In addition to prisoners, the homeless, mentally ill, and unhealthy poor were often subjected to secret tests involving highly radioactive substances. Even some researchers expressed concern about the tests' being a possible violation not only of their Hippocratic oaths but also of the Nuremberg Code of 1947, which issued standards for informed consent. In a 1963 memo one radiologist (Healy 1994) explained that "I'm for support at the requested level, as long as we are not liable. I worry about possible carcinogenic effects of such treatments."

Many of the experiments conducted on inmates were extremely dangerous and caused serious permanent damage. Between 1963 and 1973, 131 prisoners in Washington and Oregon had their genitals irradiated by X-rays or their testicles dangled in irradiated water in order to study the effects of radiation on reproduction. These experiments were funded by the Atomic Energy Commission, a forerunner of the Nuclear Regulatory Commission. Inmate participants were paid five dollars per month. After these tests the men were directed to receive vasectomies to "eliminate the possibility of defective offspring"; several of the participants changed their minds at that point, however, and did not have the vasectomy.

Around that same time a physician in Alabama conducted a plasma separation experiment in which blood samples, minus the plasma, were injected back into the donors. This process was repeated up to sixteen times per month on some inmates. Unfortunately, the project was conducted in such unsanitary conditions with unsterile equipment that over five hundred cases of serum hepatitis resulted. Three inmates died from this experiment, and yet no formal complaints were ever filed.

Because the research experiments did not track participants over a long period of time or conduct later follow-ups, it is difficult to say exactly how much permanent physical damage was caused by these projects. Prison records and experimental data were often destroyed, and former prisoners are characteristically difficult to locate once released.

Legal and societal changes over the last twenty years have greatly reduced, if not eliminated, medical testing in prisons. The negative publicity attached to lawsuits and federal investigations convinced states to abandon such activities and to formulate policies against it. Concern over the coercive implications of participation, legal liabilities, and sophisticated government regulation of testing procedures discouraged related practices. By 1980, the Department of Health, Education and Welfare had stopped funding medical research projects that proposed using prisoners. The Federal Bureau of Prisons and other federal agencies ceased participation. And the American Correctional Association established a ban on medical research with prisoners as a criterion for obtaining accreditation.

In addition, inmates today are less likely to be considered suitable subjects for routine medical testing. Compared with the general population, prisoners have significantly more health problems and higher rates of risk for HIV and AIDS, particularly those with histories of intravenous drug use.

Marilyn D. McShane

Bibliography

Bettag, O. (1957). Use of prison inmates in medical research. *American Journal of Correction* 19(3): 4–6, 26–29.

Gettinger, S., and K. Krajick (1979). The demise of prison medical research. *Corrections Magazine* 5(4): 4–14.

Healy, M. (1994). Science of power and weakness. *Los Angeles Times,* January 8, Section A: 1, 12.

Krajick, K., and F. Moriarty (1979). Life in the lab: Safer than the cellblocks? *Corrections Magazine* 5(4): 15–20.

Mills, M., and N. Morris (1974). Prisoners as laboratory animals. *Society* 11(5): 60–66.

Mentally Ill Prisoners

Throughout American history, society has struggled to develop practical as well as humane treatments for the mentally ill. Treatment has evolved much like the strategies for handling criminals, swinging from institutionalization to community treatment, from medication to isolation and an assortment of popular therapies. Though only some of the mentally ill are actually criminals and only some of those have a history of violence, the mentally ill are viewed as difficult to understand, expensive to manage, and unpredictable in behavior.

History

In the early nineteenth century, Americans began institutionalizing a number of groups of people, including criminals, the insane, orphans, delinquents, and the chronically unemployed. Many jurisdictions had limited resources, however, and often incarcerated these different populations together in one facility. After touring prisons in the early nineteenth century, reformer Dorothy Dix commented that there was great inconvenience in dealing with the insane inmate, an "unhappy class of prisoners in all prisons" (Dix 1845, 42). Detailing the particularly vile and inhumane conditions suffered by the insane, she concluded that they could not receive the appropriate and peculiar care that their conditions demanded while in prison. Her impassioned pleas to the legislature of Pennsylvania were soon followed by a law establishing a separate institution for the insane, who were then removed from prison.

For the most part, then, criminals were sent to prisons, the insane went to hospitals, and a few institutions were even specifically established for the criminally insane. In 1855 the first psychiatric hospital for criminals opened as the State Lunatic Asylum for Insane Convicts near the state prison at Auburn, New York. While most states separated youths from adults and the noncriminal from the criminal, mentally ill offenders most often remained incarcerated in regular state penal institutions.

The rise in the number of mentally ill appearing in prisons in the 1970s was spearheaded by the massive releases of patients from state hospitals under the Community Mental Health Act. While this deinstitutionalization movement was seen as a reform, it did not provide the mentally ill with adequate alternative community services. As a result, many simply wandered the streets. Often, their irrational behavior drew police attention and brought them into the criminal justice system. Thus a number of people previously serviced by the mental health system were left untreated until they committed some offense that would result in their being sent to prison.

At that time there were also laws and court decisions that created stricter criteria for committing someone to a mental institution and that limited the time a person could be held without a case review. As the mental institutions discharged their chronic patients they achieved great cost savings. They could maintain low operating costs by making it difficult to get in. Many of the original nineteenth-century facilities were in such poor condition that they had to be closed permanently. The lack of alternative facilities in which to confine those deemed dangerous or disturbed left judges with few sentencing choices except prison.

Today there appears to be a public mandate for punishment that is less likely to view mental illness as mitigating the necessity for incarceration. Many fear that psychiatric hospitals will release violent offenders too soon and, as a result, many offenders receive long prison terms instead. The use of prison as a "dumping-ground" for the mentally ill (Toch and Adams 1987) comes at a time when prison populations are already at an all-time high. As Toch and Adams (1986) explain, correctional systems were unprepared for the influx of patient-prisoners and soon realized that they had neither the staff nor the resources to accommodate that special population.

Identifying the Mentally Ill

In a national prison survey, officials have estimated that the number of inmates who suffer from mental illness ranged from 1 to 40 percent of the population. The wide disparity in estimates may be caused by differing conceptions of mental illness and varying criteria for defining mental disabilities. As one writer explains:

> For long I was puzzled by the strength of the observation made by the psychiatrists . . . that all prisoners suffered from mental disease. The inclusive "all" meant all those prisoners treated by the psychiatrists and no others. . . . They worked in prison settings either on an hourly, part time basis seeing only those inmates considered by staff as presenting acute signs and symptoms requiring an emergency response, like attempted suicide or a violent berserk episode. The inclusive "all" also meant the appearance of signs of mental illness that is so apparent on entering a prison and seeing angry, suspicious glances, hostile muttering and the disturbing shuffling gait. Because the medical and psychological histories of prisoners were so scant and uninformative—as well as hopelessly unreliable—it is well nigh impossible to even crudely assess whether psychiatrists making the inclusive "all" observation were looking at an adaptive consequence of incarceration or an underlying cause of incarceration (Chaneles 1986).

Most states have defined mental illness in their statutes governing mental health programs and civil commitment procedures. A typical description might be worded like New York's, in which mental illness is "an affliction with a mental disease or mental condition which is manifested by a disorder or disturbance in behavior, feeling, thinking or judgment to such an extent that the person afflicted requires care, treatment and rehabilitation" (Mental Hygiene Law §1.03).

Many officials will admit that they do not have an accurate count of the number of mentally ill within their correctional systems. According to Walters et al., most studies reveal serious psychopathology in 5 to 10 percent of incarcerated inmates. More than half could be diagnosed as having some type of psychiatric problem, most commonly a personality disorder. In fact, mentally disturbed prisoners have been cited as the number one health problem behind bars. Quite commonly, because of their difficulties they are less likely to be granted early releases such as parole and are more likely to serve longer sentences than inmates with similar criminal histories who are not mentally ill. They have also been categorized as a group that, once released, returns to prison at an unusually high rate (Toch 1982, Wiehn 1982).

Ironically, the mentally ill are often sent to prison because they have failed in other treatment and residential settings and judges see no place else to send them. In light of what one report calls their "demonstrated incapacity to negotiate life," prison appears to be a humanitarian choice, inasmuch as they will get a bed, three meals and, it is hoped, some supervision (Toch and Adams 1987). What may be overlooked, however, is that prison is also a hostile and potentially dangerous place, where the weak are easily abused and exploited. It is a place where a great deal of competence and savvy are necessary just to survive. Supervision is often insufficient to protect the mentally ill inmate fully or to assist him in learning to cope and adjust. In a study of New York prisons, Hans Toch noted that inmates with a history of emotional disturbance were more often victimized while incarcerated than were more emotionally stable inmates.

Another reason that mentally ill offenders may be incarcerated is their potential for violence. Though notably difficult to make predictions about (Monahan 1984), aggressive psychiatric patients have been profiled as being more likely than other psychiatric patients to be young, to be male, to suffer from organic mental syndrome or substance abuse disorder, to have shorter lengths of illness (which might be related to their youth), to suffer depression, and to have difficulty in delaying gratification (Kay et al. 1988). It is not suprising that this profile also fits the description of many other prison inmates.

Significant research has been done on the effect that mental illness has on inmate disciplinary problems. As one might predict, inmates with a history of hospitalization for mental illness prior to incarceration were more likely to engage in violations of prison rules (Adams 1981). Patterns of disruptiveness included violence more often among the emotionally disturbed than other inmates. In addition, the disciplinary violation rate for schizophrenics and antisocial personalities was higher than that for other disturbed inmates (Toch and Adams 1986).

Inmate psychiatric patients appeared in another study to have higher rates of the types of rule infractions that could be associated with severe personality disturbances. These inmates had higher incidences of charges of causing a disturbance, damaging state property, using vulgar language, refusing to obey an order, and staff assault than did nonpsychiatric inmates. Although the psychiatric inmates had more staff assault charges, they did not have a higher rate of inmate assaults. This finding may indicate that there is more actual conflict between psychiatric patients and staff, or that there is a greater tendency for staff to interpret the inmate's behavior as threatening or assaultive. Either way, the problem appears to lie in the role relationship between officers and psychiatric inmates and is not characteristic of the psychiatric patient's interactions with other inmates (McShane 1989). A typical staff assault by a psychiatric inmate might be reported as follows:

> Two officers responded to a disturbance and found the prisoner "going into very abnormal behavior." The Disciplinary Report states: "Inmate _____ just kept running on about someone coming to get him and kill him." The officers tried to escort him to pre-hearing detention. During the escort an altercation occurred in which one officer was hit in the nose and one officer was hit in the leg (Thirty-ninth Monitor's Report to the Special Master in *Ruiz v. Estelle* 1986, 80).

It is not suprising that correctional officers who are not well trained in the management of psychiatric patients will have a physically and emotionally difficult time dealing with these special-needs inmates. In many departments, specifically selected officers attend extensive additional training before being assigned to a mental health unit. Many are still unprepared for the stress of working in the conflicting roles of security and treatment. Compounding the problem is the likelihood that the number of mental health staff is insufficient and that current treatment practices are inadequate.

Treatment

Mental health treatment in most corrections systems takes the form of individual and group counseling and the use of psychotropic medication. Psychotropic drugs, such as antipsychotics (tranquilizers), and antidepressants (neuroleptics), modify mental activity and consequently alter behavior. Two of the most commonly used behavior-altering drugs are brand-named Haldol and Thorazine.

Long-term use of these or other antipsychotic or neuroleptic drugs may cause crippling and often irreversible damage to the central nervous system. That condition, called tardive dyskinesia, results in face and body movements that are violent and uncontrollable, as well as facial tics, teeth grinding, and jerking of the arms and legs. Associated with high doses of psychotropic drugs over periods of time as short as a year, the symptoms were observed almost twenty years ago, soon after the drug became popular. The effects were first dismissed as the "crazy movements of crazy people" (Pye and Potter 1980).

Still, the drugs have been so successful in reducing violence in psychotics, reorienting schizophrenics to reality, and reducing disabling hallucinations that their use has continued and increased. Psychiatrists often prescribe additional medication designed to lessen the negative side effects of the primary drugs. For example, Cogentin may be given with Haldol to decrease the possible adverse effects.

In monitoring psychiatric services within the Texas Department of Corrections as part of an ongoing civil rights lawsuit, the Special Master's Office filed this report:

This prisoner entered TDC in 1982. The diagnostic work-up indicates a history of periodic contact with a psychiatrist for "atypical depression." He was treated on and off with minor tranquilizers. . . . In December 1985 the unit psychiatric services staff began to note significant deterioration. The patient advised that he was unable to maintain control when metal detectors were used because the metal detectors caused the "mines" in his head to blow up. An entry in the medical record by a licensed vocational nurse reports that the inmate claimed his toilet was trying to "suck him up." The unit physician treated the prisoner in February 1986 for "delusional behavior" and placed him on Haldol and Cogentin. Shortly thereafter the prisoner was evaluated by the unit psychologist, who reported that the prisoner believed he was at the rodeo to meet his family, who he stated were going to take him home. Security reported that the prisoner had barricaded himself in his cell, but when questioned the prisoner reported that he had "no problems." A diagnosis of schizophreniform disorder and anti-social personality was made by the psychologist. . . . The unit psychologist is of the opinion that lock-up "just got to him." His condition has continued to deteriorate. On June 26, 1986, the unit psychologist met with the State Classification Committee to request that this prisoner be released from segregation. Contrary to the psychologist's recommendation, the committee decided to leave the prisoner in administrative segregation. (Thirty-Ninth Monitor's Report, November 1986, 79–80).

The case above illustrates not only the powerlessness of the pyschologist, but the frequency with which diagnoses and evaluations change. To Toch (1982, 335), that is often dependent upon who is doing the report. In one case he notes that a prison psychiatrist, perhaps eager to transfer an inmate off the unit and into a hospital setting, would write "paranoid schizophrenia" and ship the inmate to treatment. Six weeks later a hospital psychiatrist wrote, "No diagnosis or condition on Axis I; anti-social personality disorder," and shipped the inmate back. As one prison employee confided, "The mental health system drugs them up . . . gets them sufficiently passive, and sends them back to prison, where they don't give them their medication. Then they decide they have 'regressed' and they send them back to mental health." Toch notes that this shuttling back and forth is characteristic of treatment given to offenders who are both disturbed and disruptive. In a sense, they have failed both at being a prisoner and at being a patient.

One approach to helping inmates cope with their mental health problems would be to provide education on the causes, symptoms, and treatment of various mental illnesses. The theory behind such programs is that the more an inmate learns and understands about his problems the greater is the likelihood of cooperation in treatment. One Atlanta facility held special workshops that included lectures, discussions, video presentations, and the opportunity to compete for prizes in games that tested retention of the material covered.

Mental Health Professionals in Prison
Psychologists and psychiatrists working with inmate populations are often put in the position of having to explain and defend a mentally ill person's behavior to security staff. Often times mental health professionals are asked to give testimony for disciplinary hearings that might mitigate an inmate's guilt. The specialists argue that this puts them in an awkward position in later treatment if the inmate associates them with the outcomes of disciplinary actions or blames them for punishment received. The association is not an unrealistic one, for therapists are often consulted for their recommendations concerning the level of punishment. For example, in Texas, a psychiatric treatment team member must approve all disciplinary actions on clients before they may be brought to hearing. There is a specific process that allows the psychologist to veto any punishment that might be detrimental to the inmate's progress. Needless to say, that option is seldom if ever invoked.

A survey of psychologists employed throughout the criminal justice system found that those working in correctional institutions were the most personally troubled by ethical dilemmas. They cited as problems that affected treatment such things as the power authorities hold over inmates, the high priority of custody and punishment, and the coercive link between treatment and release. Many psychologists felt that therapy should be geared toward helping the inmate prepare for discharge with goals that focus on adjustment to society. They acknowledged, however, that the administration pressures them to assist in the "housekeeping" of the institution, ensuring that inmates are compliant and docile. Mental health professionals were also concerned that the use of behavior modification techniques by untrained staff had led to serious abuses. Many of the professionals surveyed complained that psychological services were institutional control wrapped in the "ceremonial robes of treatment" (Clingempeel et al. 1980, 137).

Constitutional Issues in Mental Health Treatment
The legal issues arising in mental health care are concerned with the obligation to provide treatment and, conversely, the inmate's right to refuse treatment. When courts evaluate the duty to furnish mental health services, much like medical-care standards established in *Estelle v. Gamble*, they are concerned about a deliberate indifference to a serious medical need. In cases like that, the failure to provide treatment would have to rise to such an emergency, or risk, level that the custodian's neglect would constitute a violation of the cruel and unusual punishment clause of the Eighth Amendment.

Assessment of mental health conditions and necessary treatment, however, are often extremely subjective. The most that might be appropriate for some patients is "recommended" rather than "essential" treatment. In cases like those, it is not clear that the courts find rehabilitation constitutionally necessary. As Collins (1988, 46) explains: "The duty may be to provide short-term care to relieve an acute psychotic episode, but not to provide treatment addressing the inmate's long-term mental health needs. (This is not to suggest that such treatment is unwise or inappropriate, but only to note that providing such care is more a question of policy than of legal necessity.)"

Mental health care for the psychiatric patient in prison may be handled by the courts in much the same manner as care for mentally retarded inmates. The ongoing nature of their problem may be significant in determining how much the prison should be obligated to do. Judges would be reluctant to require that service providers attempt to cure conditions that might be organic, chronic, or untreatable.

The expectation of the courts that the prisons be able to handle mental health emergencies would be satisfied by clear written policies, readily accessible treatment professionals and programs, and adequate referral mechanisms. In many instances, courts may not find liability where harmful incidences could not be anticipated or prevented. Still, they will examine a facility's policies and procedures to see, in general, how well equipped the system is to react to such cases. Courts would assess the general ability of the staff to recognize problems and react to them, and to see that a patient receives appropriate and expeditious treatment. If it could be established that there was an ongoing pattern of indifference to inmates' serious mental health needs, incompetence in service delivery, or a failure to properly train staff to react to such emergencies, then the prison or staff may be found liable. The finding that a mental health delivery system is deficient may result in orders for relief requiring that the services be upgraded. Personal damage awards of "astronomical proportions" may also be assessed against the prison in these cases (Collins 1988, 50).

The Right to Refuse Treatment

In 1980, the U.S. Supreme Court held in *Vitek v. Jones* that prisoners were entitled to the same due process protections as others when facing involuntary commission to a mental hospital. Also, like patients outside prison, inmates have the right to refuse treatment. As explained by Collins (1988, 48): "Only in relatively extraordinary circumstances may this due process-protected right be overcome. The only justification clearly accepted by the courts for involuntary medicating an inmate is protection of safety or security. Even then, this is only in emergency situations or where the need is "manifest." In other words, there is an immediate threat of violence that cannot be avoided through less restrictive means."

In a survey of psychologists involved in the criminal justice system, 85 percent believed that inmates should have the right to refuse medication, treatment, and rehabilitation in general. While most gave a "definite yes," some had qualifications to their agreement (Clingempeel et al. 1980).

Even though there is agreement among the judiciary that some type of due process must take place before a patient can be involuntarily medicated, they do not agree on just what type of procedure is necessary.

In *U.S. v. Charters* (829 F.2d 479, 4th Cir., 1987) the court required judicial approval, while the court in *Bee v. Greaves* (744 F.2d 1387, 10th Cir., 1984) said that neither a judicial hearing nor an adversary process was needed. Instead, there had to be a professional medical judgment, applying accepted medical standards, which evaluated all relevant circumstances. These circumstances included the nature and gravity of the safety threat, the characteristics of the inmate, and the likely effects of the drugs. Alternatives less restrictive than antipsychotic drugs had to be considered and used, if appropriate (Collins 1988, 50).

In analyzing the *Bee* decision, Collins is quick to point out that it was a highly unusual ruling and should not be considered as establishing a precedent. In fact, he suggests that it is far more reasonable to assume that in order to forceably medicate a prisoner, the court would require:

at least an adversarial administrative hearing resembling a prison disciplinary hearing. The court might even require a full-blown judicial hearing conducted according to the jurisdiction's civil commitment laws.

If an administrative hearing is approved, the inmate likely will be entitled to assistance of some sort (perhaps even legal counsel). This is because, by definition, the inmate is suffering from some form of mental illness that very likely would make it unrealistic to expect him or her to present an adequate defense at the hearing.

Conclusions

For the time being, the mentally ill will continue to be sent to prison and the administration will be obligated to provide treatment, even if only in some emergency capacity. Experts recommend that all correctional staff be given some training in working with the mentally disturbed. Instruction on the challenges of working with the mentally ill will not only give the staff confidence, but may also provide them with an opportunity to derive satisfaction out of the rehabilitative aspects of their job.

Training is also an economic and legal necessity. Administrators could incur liability from "failure to train," which is one type of negligence. Should an emergency result in injury or death, the litigation and damages awarded could be more costly than the preventive investment in training.

Marilyn D. McShane

Bibliography

Adams, K. (1981). Former mental patients in a prison and parole system: A study of socially disruptive behavior. *Criminal Justice and Behavior* 10: 358–84.

Cameron, J. (1988). Balancing the interests: The move towards less restrictive commitment of New York's mentally ill. *New England Journal on Criminal and Civil Confinement* 14: 91–106.

Chaneles, S. (1986). On the mental health of prisoners. *Journal of Offender Counseling and Rehabilitation* 11: 1–5.

Clingempeel, W. G., E. Mulvey, and N. Repucci (1980). National study of ethical dilemmas of psychologists in the criminal justice system. In J. Monahan, ed. *Who is the Client?* Washington, D.C.: American Psychological Association.

Collins, W. (1988). Medicating the jailed mentally ill. *Corrections Today* 50(7): 46–50.

Dix, D. (1845). *Remarks on Prisons and Prison Discipline in the United States.* 2nd ed. Montclair, N.J.: Patterson Smith (Reprinted 1967).

Kay, S., F. Wolkenfeld, and L. Murrill (1988). Profiles of aggression among psychiatric patients. *Journal of Nervous and Mental Disease* 176(9): 539–48.

McShane, M. D. (1989). The bus stop revisited: Discipline and psychiatric patients in prison. *Journal of Psychiatry and Law* 17: 413–33.

Monahan, J. (1984). The prediction of violent behavior: Toward a second generation of theory and policy. *American Journal of Psychiatry* 141: 10–15.

Pye, M., and E. Potter (1980). Dangerous side-effects of neuroleptic drugs. *International Journal of Offender Therapy and Comparative Criminology* 24: 290–92.

Toch, H. (1982). The disturbed disruptive inmate: Where does the bus stop? *Journal of Psychiatry and Law* 10: 327–49.

Toch, H., and K. Adams (1986). Pathology and disruptive behavior among prison inmates. *Journal of Research in Crime and Delinquency* 23: 7–21.

Toch, H., and K. Adams (1987). The prison as dumping ground: Mainlining disturbed offenders. *Journal of Psychiatry and Law* 15: 539–53.

Toch, H., and K. Adams (1989). *The Disturbed Violent Offender.* New Haven, Conn.: Yale University Press.

Wiehn, P. (1982). Mentally ill offenders. In R. Johnson and H. Toch, eds. *The Pains of Imprisonment.* Prospect Heights, Ill.: Waveland.

Cases

Bee v. Greaves, 744 F.2d 1387 (10th Cir., 1984)
Estelle v. Gamble, 97 S.Ct. 285 (1976)
Vitek v. Jones, 445 U.S. 480 (1980)

Mutilation

Definition of Self-Mutilation

In most psychiatric and sociological reports, mutilation is a clinical concept usually defined as a self-inflicted injury to parts of one's own body. Most descriptions cover any of a wide range of behaviors that produce injury, regardless of the intent. Even early psychological profiles of the mutilator include depression, hostility, self-hate, overwhelming guilt feelings, pessimism, and thoughts of suicide. Most mutilators use some type of sharp instrument to cut or stab themselves, although they may also burn or hit themselves or ingest a wide range of foreign objects.

Historical Perspective on Self-Mutilation

Although early accounts of self-mutilation in prison are undocumented, many incidents appear to have been related to the stress of long hours and brutal work conditions in the fields and factories of the early institutions, particularly in the prison farms of the South. The physical and mental abuses suffered by the inmates forced to labor on hoe squads led not only to sickness and death but also to outbreaks of self-mutilation. The motivation to injure and even cripple oneself was seemingly as much a protest as it was a direct attempt to escape the fields.

In the 1930s, mutilations and maimings in the Texas Department of Corrections were not uncommon. Occasionally, inmates would cut off parts of a hand or foot to keep from working; others chose heel stringing, cutting the Achilles tendon running from heel to calf. When this tendon is severed, the foot flops uncontrollably; lack of adequate medical treatment, as was often the case, made the condition permanent.

Prison folklore has many accounts of inmates nicknamed for this self-inflicted injury. While at one of the most notoriously tough prison farms in Texas, Clyde (of Bonnie and Clyde fame) Barrow is said to have cut off a toe in hopes of being transferred from the very rural site to a prison close to a larger town. Unsuccessful in obtaining a reassignment, he served all but one month of a two-year sentence on the farm.

Similar occurrences took place in Louisiana as late as 1951. That year a small group of prisoners, claiming serious abuses including unsanitary conditions, malnutrition, violence, and threats of death from officials in a work camp, each cut a heel tendon with a razor in order to get to a hospital. Once there, they hoped to get word to the news media about the brutal conditions at the farm. Fearing that there would be no intervention from outside and concerned about being returned to the unit, where they would face punishment, the inmates managed to obtain a razor and cut their other heel tendon. They also sent word back to the camps for other inmates to cut their heels. In all, thirty-seven inmates participated in the heel-stringing. As one inmate later explained:

> It didn't hurt much, just a little sting, but when that tendon let loose and flew up your leg, you could sure feel that. . . . They hauled us over to the hospital. We didn't have no doctor then. Mrs. Mary Margaret Daugherty was the nurse; without her, we was dead. She was the only doctor we had back then; without that nurse, we'd have been crippled. She reached up in there and pulled that tendon down, then sewed it back together. We smuggled letters out to the *Shreveport Times* and the New Orleans *Picayune* to tell them what was going on . . . .

Dreading a scandal from the heel-stringing incident, Louisiana Governor Long appointed a thirty-four-member citizen committee to investigate Angola prison. Though the committee concluded that the heel slashing was a result of long-term physical, mental, and emotional brutality, their calls for reform were ignored throughout the governor's term of office.

In 1968, Beto and Claghorn explained the high level of mutilation for Latin Americans and the low level for blacks in terms of religion and self-concept.

> The Baptist Negro has a closer, more personal relationship with his God. The Latin American's God is more formal and, consequently, he is frightened of Him. . . . His God is one who dictates law and administers punishment. Unfortunately, unlike the Negro, he does not see his God as a loving, forgiving God. . . . The Latin American, feeling remorse for his crimes or present situation, but having no means of communication with his God, believes that cutting himself will serve his punishment (1968, 27).

Administrative Views on Self-Mutilation

In the past, administrators viewed mutilators as manipulative troublemakers, a label that continues despite advances in our psychological understanding of self-destructive behavior. Today, there are only small amounts of field labor being done, and most officials simply employ administrative restrictions on any inmate who refuses to work. It is also likely that a significant number of the cases of mutilation are related to mental and emotional health problems and self-destructive tendencies. Still, there is the prevailing notion that self-mutilators are manipulators who should be punished. In most prison systems the self-mutilators are punished, and no one attempts any psychological explanation for their behavior or, more than superficially, invests in treatment.

For prison officials, traditional classification schemes may be as simple as dividing inmates into groups that work and those that do not. Therefore, a prisoner's mental illness is also defined by the extent to which the prisoner is incapable of work: Everyone who is fit to work is probably not mentally ill. This all-or-nothing approach often prevents any consideration of the mutilation as a pathological expression or a form of mental illness. For that reason a majority of self-inflicted injuries are unrecorded or doctored and forgotten, written off as part of the unpredictable nature of inmates themselves. The staff often do not take these episodes seriously and view it as childish attention-getting.

A majority of the inmates, some experts claim, are trying to escape from gangs or bad debts—hoping that they will be transferred from an environment in which they feel threatened or to get a better job or housing assignment. One factor that may influence the rate of mutilation is the department's transfer policy. If the unit makes it clear that they will not transfer inmates who mutilate themselves, there would be less incentive to do so for purposes of assignment.

Psychiatric Perspectives

According to many current studies, the most common psychological diagnosis of the mutila-

M

tor is that of personality disorder. In the prison setting, however, such a diagnosis is appropriate for a majority of the inmates, so that symptom appears to occur in the "average" prisoner.

Some psychiatric professionals claim that only about one-quarter of those who mutilate themselves do so because they have a major psychiatric disorder. Some inmates claim to cut because it releases tensions and provides self-reinforcement. These inmates may be in a fugue state, and in an attempt to bring themselves back to reality, to feel something, they injure themselves and experience a quick rush or high. It is also possible that the mutilation is a warning sign that the inmate's mental health is deteriorating and that punishment and solitary confinement are only making the illness worse. In one study, an inmate cut off his thumb while in a delusional state. Punished with 180 days' special housing and 365 days' loss of good time credit, it was less than a week before the inmate was committed to a psychiatric hospital.

An important factor may be the seniority or rank that the prisoner has earned in housing and privileges, especially good time credit earned. For the most part, only those inmates with lower status levels are found in solitary and segregation. Again, the tendency to commit mutilation may be related less to the actual placement in restrictive custody than to the loss of status and the punishment that preceded it. In one study it was found that the single most important factor in predicting whether an inmate self-mutilated him or herself was the severity of disciplinary reports the prisoner had recently received. It is possible that giving a serious punishment to an inmate who is known to be depressed and a potential mutilator without taking precautions may constitute cruel and unusual punishment. Such cases may represent actions of "deliberate indifference" to a known condition or need. Wrongful injury or death suits may even be filed in behalf of a patient as a result of wanton neglect of the patient's mental health needs.

Findings from Research on Self-Mutilation

In several studies of inmates who mutilate themselves it has been found that most of the injuries were on the arms, hands, and wrists. Only small percentages were on the neck or on the legs and feet. Research has indicated that mutilators are most often white, younger than the rest of the prisoner population, and likely to have a history of cutting themselves. Many already had scars on their wrists and forearms when they were admitted to prison. Also, young mutilators tend to make more cuts than older ones. One study found that self-harm appears to develop in late adolescence and continues in a chronic and repetitious pattern. Another study found that mutilators alleged to have a manipulative motive were more likely to have a history of self-injury than those whose acts appeared to be suicide attempts.

Admittedly, there is much administrative pressure on mental health employees to find inmates "fit to work" when they examine mutilators. If not, they are expected to be able to justify expensive and limited inpatient services which in most textbooks are not indicated for the average personality disorder. The timing of the mutilations, the politics of psychiatric assessments, and the manifestations of other clinical symptoms as well as the interpretation and reaction of the staff to the inmate's behavior all seem to be critical to the definition of the problem.

Marilyn D. McShane

Bibliography

Bennum, I. (1983). Depression and hostility in self-mutilation. *Suicide and Life Threatening Behavior* 13: 71–84.

Beto, D., and J. Claghorn (1968). Factors associated with self-mutilation within the Texas Department of Corrections. *American Journal of Corrections* 30: 25–27.

Franklin, R. (1988). Deliberate self-harm. *Criminal Justice and Behavior* 15: 210–18.

Johnson, E. H. (1973). Felon self-mutilation: Correlate of stress in prison. In B. Danto, ed. *Jail House Blues*. Orchard Lake, Mich.: Epic.

Jones, A. (1986). Self-mutilation in prison. *Criminal Justice and Behavior* 13: 286–96.

Lloyd, C. (1990). *Suicide and Self-injury in Prison: A Literature Review*. London: Her Majesty's Stationery Office.

Ross, R., and H. McKay (1979). *Self-Mutilation*. Lexington, Mass.: D. C. Heath.

Schaffer, C., J. Carroll, and S. Abramowitz (1982). Self-mutilation and the borderline personality. *Journal of Nervous and Mental Disease* 170: 468–73.

Simpson, M. (1980). Self-mutilation as indirect self-destructive behavior. In N. Farberow, ed. *The Many Faces of Suicide*. New York: McGraw Hill.

N

National Prison Project

The American Civil Liberties Union's National Prison Project (NPP), a nonprofit organization funded by the ACLU Foundation, originated in 1972 in the aftermath of the Attica prison riots. The project is designed to safeguard adult and juvenile offenders' Eighth Amendment rights to be free from cruel and unusual punishment.

The National Prison Project also serves as a resource center for American corrections law. The project publishes the *National Prison Project Journal,* which focuses on important contemporary issues in American corrections. Topics discussed in the *Journal* include juvenile justice and detailed reports on AIDS in prison. Past issues of the *Journal* have also considered the recent development of "super-maximum" prisons, prison crowding, women in prison, private ownership of prisons, and the role of special masters in prison litigation.

National Prison Project staff members also draft model legislation affecting prisoners' rights and advise state legislatures about potential alternatives to incarceration. In addition, project attorneys prepare model pleadings, briefs, and memoranda, and help to train other attorneys and law students in prison reform litigation techniques.

The National Prison Project's primary emphasis, however, is Eighth Amendment litigation in federal court. Executive Director Alvin J. Bronstein heads the project, which has eight full-time staff attorneys and a regular caseload of twenty to twenty-five active cases. The project staff is also assisted regularly by attorney-associates throughout the country.

So far, the National Prison Project has attained sweeping systemic reform of prison conditions in Alabama, Colorado, New Mexico, Oklahoma, Rhode Island, South Carolina, and Tennessee. The project has also successfully challenged punitive "behavior modification" programs in several states, including Connecticut, Georgia, Kentucky, Hawaii, Virginia, and Arizona, as well as in the federal prison in Marion, Illinois. The NPP also pioneered the use of court-appointed special masters to oversee penal reforms during litigation.

One important case litigated by National Prison Project attorneys, in which a court relied heavily on a special master, occurred in Rhode Island. In *Palmigiano v. Garrahy,* approximately 650 prisoners and pretrial detainees at a Rhode Island correctional institution brought a class action lawsuit challenging the conditions of their confinement. The inmates, represented by the NPP's Alvin Bronstein, maintained that the Rhode Island prison system violated the Eighth and Fourteenth Amendments to the United States Constitution.

Specifically, the inmates claimed that they were subjected to constitutionally intolerable conditions of confinement. Those conditions included: filth, unsanitary living quarters, unsanitary food services, dangerously inadequate medical care, nearly total idleness, and intolerable levels of prison violence.

Following a lengthy trial, United States District Court Judge Raymond Pettine held that conditions at the prison violated the Eighth Amendment's cruel and unusual punishment clause. Judge Pettine issued a remedial order to rectify the problems and also held that, if the state failed to comply with his order, he would close the state's existing prison facilities because they were unfit for human habitation.

The court also appointed a special master to supervise its remedial order. In July of 1985, the special master filed a report indicating that the state's medium security facility, and the intake center that houses pretrial detainees, were severely crowded. In May of 1986, Judge Pettine issued an order banning double-celling and placing population limits on both facilities.

In January of 1990, the state filed a motion to modify the court's orders dealing with prison crowding. After a hearing on the state's motion, Judge Pettine held that the state was in contempt of court and he imposed sanctions. Later that year, the state opened two new prison facilities which, to some extent, alleviated the crowding in the Rhode Island prison system.

In November of 1992, Rhode Island's governor, Bruce Sundlum, issued an executive order creating a Prison System Advisory Commission. The commission's report to the state legislature developed a statutory scheme to permanently address crowding issues within the Rhode Island prison system. In 1993, the law was passed by the Rhode Island legislature and negotiations for a final settlement of the case are presently concluding.

To summarize, the National Prison Project has exerted a major impact on American corrections. By vigorously litigating prisoners' Eighth Amendment claims, the project has consistently attempted to enforce the constitutional protection against cruel and unusual punishment.

Unfortunately, the contemporary American political climate has demanded a "get tough on crime and criminals" approach to criminal justice policy. That attitude has resulted in politically popular but overly simplistic solutions to the complex problem of crime in society, including the widespread passage of determinate sentencing laws. Such policies will inevitably lead to heightened levels of prison crowding and inhumane treatment in American prisons. Thus, there is every reason to believe that the National Prison Project will continue to play a vital role in the movement to reform American corrections.

Thomas J. Hickey

Bibliography

Berger, A. B. (1992). An unsatisfying attempt at resolving the imbroglio of Eighth Amendment prisoners' rights standards. *Utah Law Review* Spring: 565–99.
Bronstein, A. J. (1985). Prisoners and their endangered rights. *Prison Journal* 65: 3–17.
Chilton, B. S., and D. C. Nice (1993). Triggering federal court intervention in state prison reform. *Prison Journal* 73: 30–46.
Conrad, J. P. (1985). The view from the witness chair. *Prison Journal* 65: 18–25.
Donahue, W. A. (1991). The new agenda of the ACLU. *Society* 28, 2: 5–14.
O'Manique, J. O. (1992). Development, human rights and law. *Human Rights Quarterly* 14: 383–408.
Rudovsky, D. (1973). *The Rights of Prisoners: The Basic ACLU Guide to a Prisoner's Rights.* New York: Discus.
Ryan, M. (1992). The Woolf Report: On the treadmill of prison reform? *Political Quarterly* 63: 50–57.

Cases

Bell v. Wolfish, 441 U.S. 520, 99 S.Ct. 1861, 60 L.Ed.2d 447 (1979)
Palmigiano v. Garrahy, 443 F. Supp. 956 (D.R.I. 1977)
Rhodes v. Chapman, 452 U.S. 337, 101 S.Ct. 2392, 69 L.Ed.2d. 59 (1981)

Newgate Prison

Although the use of confinement to punish serious offenders began in earnest during the eighteenth century in Europe, the concept of incarcerating offenders for long periods of time as a punishment for their crimes is a relatively recent development in America. Prior to the 1770s, with few exceptions, serious offenders usually received fines, corporal punishment, death, or banishment, but they were not incarcerated as a form of punishment. Jails were designed to hold only defendants awaiting trial and minor offenders serving relatively short sentences. The purpose of punishment during this era was not crime control, but rather a reflection of the Puritan ethos of equating crime with sin. Since it was believed that humans were born in sin, punishment was in accordance with God's law. This Puritan view on crime was abandoned, however, during the latter part of the eighteenth century. It was during that period that priority was given to altering the behavior of criminals, thus giving rise to institutions designed to carry out that goal.

Most introductory criminal justice texts proclaim the Walnut Street Jail in Philadelphia (1790) to have been the first prison in the U.S. According to Durham, however, Newgate Prison preceded the Walnut Street Jail by almost twenty years. In the spring of 1773, the Connecticut General Assembly explored the possibility of converting an abandoned copper mine in Simsbury into a prison for serious offenders. In October of that year, the assembly approved the purchase of the mine and then later converted the mine into a prison. In December of 1773, Newgate Prison accepted its first inmate. It was closed during the 1820s because of rising costs, its failure to achieve the mandates of the legislature, and the opening of a new state prison modeled after the Auburn system.

Newgate Prison was originally designed to confine five categories of serious offenders: robbers, burglars, forgers, counterfeiters, and horse thieves. Later on, murderers, prisoners of war, and political prisoners were housed at Newgate. The sentences ranged from less than two years to the offender's natural life. Newgate, an underground correctional facility, was described as a "dungeon with continually dripping water and foul air" by one of its former residents. It was, however, relatively free from the insects and associated disease that infested aboveground facilities. Moreover, the temperature inside the caverns was moderate year round. It was described as "extremely favorable to the health and longevity of the occupants" by an observer. Security was a major problem for this underground correctional facility from the very beginning. The first inmate committed to the facility escaped within three weeks of his admission. All of the convicts sent to the facility broke free within the first six months of operation.

More important than its unusual physical structure was the fact that Newgate Prison was among the first institutions (if not the first) designed to incarcerate offenders as a form of punishment. This break with traditional types of punishment reflects the change in philosophy that occurred during this era. But why the change in thinking at this point in time? After all, prisons are expensive enterprises. The traditional forms of punishment required little expense or manpower. They also provided opportunities for what Erikson terms "boundary maintenance," which means that examples of inappropriate behavior are punished in such a manner as to define and reinforce the boundaries between acceptable and unacceptable acts in a community. Alexis Durham examined the advent of Newgate Prison in light of the four dominant penological theories, which are presented below.

Rothman: Social Disorder and Penal Discipline

According to David Rothman, the development of incarceration as a general solution to deviance could be explained by concern over the growing social disorganization that resulted from an influx of immigrants and migrants from rural to urban areas. He believed that the appearance of the penitentiary and other institutions, such as mental institutions, almshouses, and asylums, reflected the perceived breakdown of traditional norms associated with this new social order.

High levels of social mobility, however, were not evident in Connecticut in the 1770s. Moreover, the day-to-day operations of Newgate were not designed to restore the order and discipline of the Colonial era. Therefore, the conditions associated with the rise of social control institutions in the nineteenth century do not seem to apply to Newgate Prison.

Foucault: The Extension of State Power

According to Michel Foucault, corporal punishment sometimes resulted in martyrdom, thus becoming the focal point for a resistance movement bent on undermining the state's authority. The movement away from punishing the body (corporal punishment) toward punishing the mind (incarceration) offered the opportunity to limit threats to the state's power while simultaneously expanding that power by including a wider variety of punishable offenses. Newgate Prison, however, did not appear to serve this function, because a small number of select offenders (five categories) were incarcerated there.

Ignatieff: Industrialization and Social Disorder

Michael Ignatieff stated that the development of the prison was a response to the perception that social solidarity was deteriorating. He opined that increases in unemployment, vagrancy, crime, and public disturbances resulted in the creation of formal mechanisms of social control, such as the police and prisons. In the 1770s, however, the citizens of Connecticut were more concerned about their relationship with England and did not experience large-scale labor problems, vagrancy and petty crime, or unemployment. Thus, it appears that those social conditions were not the impetus for the establishment of Newgate Prison.

Economic Determinism and the Origin of the Prison

The untapped labor potential of offenders did not go unnoticed by governmental officials. The enabling legislation for Newgate Prison provided that inmates were to be profitably employed. Little effort was expended by the Connecticut legislature, however, to ensure financial success. The proceeds from inmate labor never replaced the need for government funding. Thus economic incentives also do not appear to have been the impetus for the creation of Newgate Prison.

So why did prisons evolve at this time? Perhaps no single theory can explain the rise of the penitentiary. On the other hand, perhaps Newgate Prison's legacy is a reminder that anomalies do occur that seem to defy our best attempts at theoretical explanation. Thus a general pattern may exist, as predicted by the theories outlined above, but exceptions to the pattern also occur.

Durham presents a convincing argument that Newgate Prison in Connecticut was an anomaly. The prison contained may features of "modern" prisons, such as common work and recreation areas where inmates could congregate. That was in stark contrast to the "silent system" and solitary confinement of the Eastern Penitentiary in Philadelphia. Newgate was supported by state funds, which was also a departure from the practice of leasing inmates to private enterprise, a policy designed to generate revenue. What Newgate lacked was a clear philosophical basis for its existence and strong support by influential contemporary penologists. What the prison did have was a mixed mandate from the legislature, which wanted a secure institution with low operating costs.

Perhaps the real lesson from the experiences at Newgate Prison is that any institution without a clear mandate grounded in the prevailing philosophy of the times may experience a limited and difficult existence. Some institutions have been fortunate to have both, as was the case with the Auburn system of prisons. Other institutions have had to·create their own mandate, often engaging in what Harold Becker terms "moral entrepreneurism." Obviously, more study of the sort undertaken by Durham is needed to better understand the function of criminal justice agencies in a political context.

Michael B. Blankenship
Chau-Pu Chiang

Bibliography

Durham, A. M. (1989). Newgate of Connecticut: Origins and early days of an early American prison. *Justice Quarterly* 6: 89–116.

Durham, A. M. (1990). Social control and imprisonment during the American Revolution: Newgate of Connecticut. *Justice Quarterly* 7: 293–323.

Erikson, K. T. (1966). *Wayward Puritans: A Study in the Sociology of Deviance*. New York: John Wiley.

News Media

The news media, which encompasses the newspapers, radio, television, and magazines, was of little concern to correctional administrators prior to 1970. Correctional facilities were closed and secretive, and few "outsiders" were privy to what went on behind their walls and fences. That resulted in very little research or interest in relations with the news media on the part of correctional officials. That was to change during the 1970s and 1980s. A review of the literature discloses thirty-one publications pertaining to the news media, and sixteen of those were published during the period 1980–84.

Three factors played key roles in "opening" correctional operations to the news media and, thereby, to the public. One factor was the "activist" nature of the courts during the 1960s and 1970s. Another factor was a growing social activism during that same period of time, in which the "rights" of inmates were a prime consideration. Thus, correctional administrators were besieged by the news media on a number of issues, including overcrowding, riots, furloughs, early releases, executions, inmate treatment, and living conditions. Finally, while legislation like the Privacy Act protects staff and inmates from disclosure of some personal information, the Freedom of Information Act of 1966 has given the news media great access to all types of previously inaccessible governmental documents.

Nature of the Relationship

The traditional approach for correctional administrators had been to avoid the news media. Avoidance became harder, if not impossible, as a result of court and public involvement during the 1970s and 1980s. Many correctional administrators, however, met this forced "openness" with the news media in a distrustful manner and with a lack of cooperation. That has been to the disadvantage of correctional administrators as regards most correctional issues.

The overriding aspect of the corrections/news media relationship is one of give and take.

The news media will either provide the public with the official view, promulgated by the administrator or a designated public information office, or they will provide news from other sources that may, or may not, adequately or accurately address the issue at hand. Thus, it is imperative that administrators establish a rapport and spirit of cooperation with members of the news media.

A cooperative approach by the correctional administrator can have positive effects. Two former correctional administrators, Joseph E. Ragen and Richard A. McGee, had successful relationships with news media personnel. The news media were allies of both men on a number of occasions. When conflict with the news media did arise, those administrators were able, in most instances, to minimize the adverse effects of the conflict by virtue of the positive relationships they had cultivated with editors and reporters.

Developing News Media/Corrections Relationships

How can correctional administrators develop a relationship with the news media that is open and mutually cooperative? The following six elements should be a part of every correctional administrator's attempt to establish a successful relationship with the news media.

1. *Tell the truth.* Truth is the key to establishing and maintaining a positive relationship with the media. A lack of truth, or the perception thereof, can create distrust of the corrections systems and its personnel. In today's society, failing to tell the truth may generate more adverse publicity than telling the truth.
2. *Know publishers, editors, and reporters.* Many times a personal relationship can save both sides embarrassment. It may result in the news media's delaying its report in the best interest of the correctional institution. It can also result in better, more comprehensive, information for news reports.
3. *Do not play favorites.* This concept is simple. Treat each and every news media representative equally. Make sure all news outlets receive the same information at the same time. That can be accomplished through news conferences or the distribution of written news releases.
4. *Establish a clearly stated public relations policy.* It is essential that policy guidelines be promulgated for the correctional system and all its personnel. All corrections personnel should be trained and held accountable for complying with the policy.
5. *Promulgate programs and concepts, not personalities.* It is important to educate the public on correctional programs and concepts. For example, explaining the furlough program and the concept behind it could create greater public acceptance than presently exists. The public might better understand it as an attempt to maintain family relationships and ties, rather than the misperception that it is another method of coddling criminals.
6. *Designate an information official.* It is often suggested that a professional information officer be hired, but with today's reduced budgets that may not be possible. In lieu of a professional, the administrator or a designated person should deal with the news media. That way the views and opinions of the correctional administrator can be disseminated without the confusion or deliberate undermining that may occur as a result of hidden agendas on the part of some correctional personnel.

Conclusion

A discussion of corrections/media relationships leads to three inescapable observations for correctional administrators. First, the news media will report on correctional issues with or without the cooperation of correctional administrators. Therefore, it would seem to be in the best interests of the administrator to establish a spirit of cooperation with media representatives. Second, crime and how we deal with convicted offenders are a media staple. Thus it is imperative that administrators provide a truthful representation of correctional operations and concepts to the public. Honest mistakes generally have little news value. Most media representatives, however, will pursue real or perceived dishonesty and subterfuge with interest and vigor. Third, since media access and reporting on correctional issues are inevitable, it is essential to establish and enforce a public information policy. That can help to ensure efficacy in dealing with the news media on correctional issues and a minimum of misrepresentations or errors in news articles and reports.

Harry L. Marsh

Bibliography

Dulaney, W. L. (1970). The news media and corrections. *Federal Probation* 34(2): 63–66.

Jacobs, J. B., and H. A. Brooks (1983). The mass media and prison news. In J. B. Jacobs, ed. *New Perspectives on Prisons and Imprisonment*. Ithaca, N.Y.: Cornell University Press.

Marsh, H. L. (1986). The media and correctional administrators: The time for mutual cooperation and understanding has come. *Criminal Justice Research Bulletin* 2(4): 1–4.

McGee, R. A. (1981). *Prisons and Politics*. Lexington, Mass.: Lexington.

Turnbo, C. (1994). News at eleven. *Federal Prisons Journal* 3(3): 47–50.

Norfolk Prison

The State Prison Colony at Norfolk, as the Massachusetts Correctional Institution at Norfolk was formerly known, was established by the legislature in 1927. Norfolk is located approximately twenty-five miles southwest of Boston. The prison was designed and constructed under the personal direction of Howard Gill, the first superintendent. It opened officially in 1931.

The land, including a circular piece known as the "oval" and some of the original buildings, was part of the former state hospital, which had been abandoned. Norfolk was built largely by inmate labor. On 1 June 1927, twelve inmates were transferred from the state prison at Charlestown to begin the construction. Superintendent Gill decided to use inmate labor for economic and rehabilitative reasons. The Commonwealth saved money and the inmates learned a trade that would lead to employment and facilitate their return to society. The inmates built the massive concrete wall that still surrounds the institution today. Topped by three lines of barbed wire, the wall extends nineteen feet above the ground and four and a half to eighteen feet below the ground, and encompasses thirty-five acres of land.

The influx of inmates to construct the prison and the accompanying lack of security that characterized their living quarters created somewhat of a dilemma for Superintendent Gill. Norfolk had two fundamental rules: no escapes and no contraband. Superintendent Gill attempted to reduce the likelihood of escapes by enlisting the cooperation and support of staff and inmates. An inmate council was established to deal with escapes and contraband.

The council evolved and ultimately consisted of fifteen inmates, representing each of the housing units. The council attempted to resolve difficulties and to work through problems effectively and fairly. The staff was similarly organized, and the two groups met weekly with the superintendent. No guards or other members of the custodial unit were invited to participate on the council. The superintendent believed that the custodial staff should be responsible for security only, and that less formal inmate contact should be avoided. The council decided a range of issues concerning, for example, construction problems, education, and entertainment. The council had only advisory powers, however, and the final decisions were made by the staff.

The inmate council concept helps to illustrate Gill's penal philosophy: The prison was a community surrounded by a wall. Although having a concrete wall surrounding the prison was atypical for a medium-security institution, the physical security was deemed necessary for the public's protection and to facilitate treatment programs. Inside the wall, inmates moved freely from dormitory to classroom to recreation. There was none of the marching or the uniforms that had characterized earlier institutions. The inmates were expected to be at their appropriate assignments in the same way as were individuals on the outside.

Architecturally, Norfolk is a series of buildings that were originally designed to house approximately 150 inmates each. These buildings are further divided into three units, each housing fifty inmates. Inmates eat, sleep, and participate in some group activities in the dormitory, but they work, attend vocational and educational classes, and participate in other programs outside the unit during the day. Two house officers (whose role most closely approximated that of case workers) were responsible for each group of fifty inmates within the unit. They were responsible for assisting and counseling inmates and helping to implement individual plans for inmate reform. Despite the proximity of the two other units in the same building, there was no interaction between units.

Norfolk is distinguished from other prisons of the early twentieth century in its architectural style and its treatment philosophy. For Gill, these two elements were inseparable. The Norfolk Plan, according to Gill, involved four components: inmate classification, a group system of housing and supervision, community organization on the basis of joint responsibility, and individual treatment programs. The treatment was fairly straightforward: Provide inmates with a decent routine, restore them to normal living conditions, and reduce their criminality. Inmates were given an indeterminate sentence, with the actual date of their release being decided by prison officials. In comparison with the dehumanizing aspects of other prisons and the plethora of rules and regulations most inmates were accustomed to, Norfolk was unlike any other institution of its time.

Although the projected capacity of the State Prison Colony at Norfolk was twelve hundred, it was anticipated that the growth and expansion would be gradual and that it would occur as facilities were developed and appropriate inmates were selected. The population at the institution, however, increased rapidly. In January of 1931 there were 168 inmates, and by January of 1934 there were 551 inmates. Although the influx of inmates partially alleviated the overcrowding at Charlestown, it posed a variety of problems. The facilities were not equipped to handle the inmates, and some of the transferred inmates were rebellious. The informal and personal contacts that had existed at Norfolk since its inception were now replaced with the more formal and impersonal contacts that occur in larger institutions. Suddenly, the institution had a new cadre of inmates who were unable to participate in prison construction. The use of inmate labor to construct the prison ended in 1933, when the third dormitory building was completed. In 1934, the state secured a federal grant that mandated the use of outside contractors and laborers. Inmates were unable to participate in programs as the superintendent had envisioned and they had anticipated. Not surprisingly, the number of inmate disciplinary actions increased.

In April of 1934, Gill was removed as superintendent. His termination was preceded by a series of events that were politicized and sensationalized (see the entry on Howard Gill). Gill continues to be recognized as a progressive who clearly made a mark in the evolution of corrections. Although later prisons did not incorporate all of his concepts, he significantly influenced

community-based residential programs. His model of a community that provides inmates with responsibility, self-esteem, and leadership opportunities continues to characterize a number of programs for both offenders and victims.

The State Prison Colony at Norfolk officially changed its title in the mid 1950s to the Massachusetts Correctional Institution at Norfolk. Today, Norfolk continues to embody some of its original design and treatment components. Offenders are not sentenced to Norfolk directly by the courts. Through the classification process, the staff determines which inmates are appropriate for the level of security and treatment programs at Norfolk, and then transfers inmates to the institution. MCI-Norfolk is currently the largest facility in Massachusetts. It is still characterized as a medium-security community prison.

Alida V. Merlo

See also GILL, HOWARD

Bibliography

Barnes, H. E., and N. K. Teeters (1951). *New Horizons in Criminology*. 2nd ed. New York: Prentice-Hall.

Carnevale, A. (1993). *Programs at MCI Norfolk*. Springfield, Mass.: Executive Office of Public Safety.

Commons, W. H., T. Yahkub, and E. Powers (1940). *A Report on the Development of Penological Treatment at Norfolk Prison Colony in Massachusetts*. New York: Bureau of Social Hygiene.

Gill, H. B. (1931). The Norfolk State Prison Colony at Massachusetts. *Journal of Criminal Law and Criminology* 22(May): 107–12.

Gill, H. B. (1962). Correctional philosophy and architecture. *Journal of Criminal Law, Criminology and Police Science* 53(3): 312–22.

Gill, H. B. (1970). A new prison discipline: Implementing the Declaration of Principles of 1870. *Federal Probation* 34(2): 29–33.

McKelvey, B. (1936). *American Prisons*. Chicago: University of Chicago Press (Reprinted Montclair, N.J.: Patterson Smith, 1977).

N

Thomas Mott Osborne (1859–1926)

Thomas Mott Osborne, businessman, philanthropist, and later warden of Sing Sing and Portsmouth Naval prison in New Hampshire, could be thought of as the father of adult prison reform. He was born in Auburn, New York, and flourished as one of the pillars of that community. The Harvard University graduate retired from business with considerable wealth and later held many important civic positions. He served as mayor of the city of Auburn, New York, from 1903 to 1905, and he was a member of the board of education for nine years. Additionally, he served as a member of the Public Service Commission of the Second Division from 1907 to 1909 and achieved further distinction by being appointed chairman of the State Commission on Prison Reform in 1913. He was known for being a disruptive force to political schemes and was a formidable foe of Tammany Hall and all of its disciples.

In 1913, the same year that he was appointed chairman of the State Commission on Prison Reform, Osborne was determined to fully understand the prison experience as part of his attempt to reform the punishment philosophy of penologists of his era. He took the unprecedented step of allowing himself to be incarcerated as an inmate at Auburn prison for one week. He used the alias Tom Brown, and on 29 September 1913 he entered the prison as inmate No. 33,333X. The day before his incarceration he addressed the prisoners in chapel and explained his intentions. The only other person who knew his true identity was the warden—the guards were not informed. This experience provided Osborne not only a first-hand look at the gross and sometimes inhumane realities of prison life, it also convinced him of the need for immediate reform.

Osborne believed that the most effective way to implement prison reform was to have inmate self-governance. Much of this idea he borrowed from his friend William Reuben George (1866–1936), founder of the George Junior Republic, who adopted a self-governing disciplinary approach for juvenile offenders between the ages of sixteen and twenty-one. The Junior Republic was a self-contained community organization in which boys and girls were considered citizens and empowered to maintain order for their community. Osborne had been president of the board of trustees of the George Junior Republic for fifteen years at Freeville, New York. It was George's suggestion to Osborne that a similar form of self-government for adult prisoners might also be feasible.

Having now observed, mingled, and lived with inmates, he was convinced that only by training prisoners in the duties and responsibilities of citizenship could they ever hope to become productive citizens. He reasoned that a model democracy, similar to the one at the George Junior Republic, was the only logical course of action to be taken for true prison reform and inmate rehabilitation. Osborne named this new initiative the Mutual Welfare League. This penological experiment called for inmate self-government and posed a significant break from the traditional penology of the era. The institutional rules were in the hands of the prisoners, primarily a body of delegate inmates elected by other convicts based on their representation of the many work shops and gangs. Although this represented a radical change in penology, the Auburn warden, Charles F. Rattigan, and Governor Sulzer of New York endorsed the idea, and in 1914 the concept of prison democracy was launched.

The Mutual Welfare League was almost an overnight success and soon achieved national attention. Penologists and criminal justice scholars were watching it with great interest and admiration. As a result of the league's success, on 1 December 1914, Osborne was appointed warden of Sing Sing prison. He had been advised by friends against taking the position because of the intense political corruption that was known to exist there; it was feared that Osborne might become involved in a political jostling match. One of the Sing Sing inmates, however, had sent him a telegram saying, "For God's sake, take the wardenship. All the boys are anxious to have you." After receiving this telegram, he felt compelled to assume the leadership at Sing Sing as its new warden.

As soon as Osborne arrived at Sing Sing, he began to implement the Mutual Welfare League just as he had done at Auburn. The superintendent of prisons, John B. Riley, believed, however, that Osborne was doing no more than coddling the prisoners. That set the stage for a protracted and vigorous disagreement between the two men. As early as 4 August 1915, an article in the *New York Tribune* entitled "Osborne Must Go by Tuesday or be Ousted" appeared, placing the league in a tenuous position. On 26 December 1915, Osborne was indicted by the grand jury of Westchester County for perjury and neglect of duty. Various charges were filed against Osborne, among them "permitting unauthorized prisoners into the death house; failure to exercise general supervision over the government, discipline, and police of the prison; for breaking down the discipline and thus encouraging crimes; and finally that he did not deport himself in a manner as to command the respect, esteem, and confidence of the inmates of the prison." In spite of these serious allegations, he refused to resign. He instead requested a leave of absence so that he could fully defend himself of the charges levied against him, and he requested that his old friend Dean George W. Kirchwey of the Columbia University Law School be appointed interim warden. Dean Kirchwey had been responsible for the creation of the state commission on prison reform, of which Osborne had been chairman, and was originally appointed by New York Governor Sulzer. Dean Kirchwey had an outstanding reputation and was appointed temporary warden.

Thomas Mott Osborne returned to Sing Sing on 16 July 1919. He had been fully vindicated, and the league had survived under the leadership of Dean Kirchwey. Additionally, Osborne had proved that the league could survive under any competent and intelligent warden. He was reinstated as warden, but resigned exactly three months later. Osborne reasoned that politicians and his official superiors were determined to discredit his reform efforts. His resignation was hastened when the superintendent of prisons issued an order that "no long-term convict should be allowed outside the prison walls."

In 1917, Osborne was appointed head of the Portsmouth Naval Prison. He retired in 1920. It was there that he spent the happiest years of his life and influenced the founding of the National Society of Penal Information, which later became the Osborne Association in his honor. Osborne, an intelligent and articulate philanthropist, worked with the likes of Franklin D. Roosevelt, Assistant Secretary of the Navy Orlando F. Lewis, secretary of the Prison Association of New York and an authority on penology, and Charles F. Rattigan, warden of Auburn prison.

Although Osborne's innovative reforms strived for true rehabilitation, they were never fully accepted. The Mutual Welfare League continued intact at Auburn prison until 1929. In that year a series of sensational riots destroyed the efficacy of the league. As a result, in 1931 the new warden significantly changed the administration of the league, revoking self-governance.

Similar problems erupted at Sing Sing. The league barely survived and was reduced to a mere shell of its original design. When Osborne left, the new warden, William H. Mayer, revoked many league privileges and some of its most important members were transferred to other institutions. The league also was terminated at Portsmouth Naval prison in 1921, in part because of a change in political party and ideology. When President Harding assumed office he appointed a new secretary of the Navy to replace Roosevelt, and the old regime was reinstituted.

The Mutual Welfare League eventually became extinct, although remnants of the league continued to exist in limited form. Osborne's league was successful primarily because of his personality and leadership style. One of the central criticisms of the league had been that it applied to unreformable and well as reformable inmates. The critics believed that unreformable convicts should be ruled decently but firmly in a separate institution. Osborne refused to accept that notion and was convinced that he and others who thought like him could transcend difficulties posed by recalcitrant inmates. After his death, however, the importance of the league declined rapidly. Other institutions that attempted similar inmate organizations were the State Prison Colony, Norfolk, Massachusetts; the United States Industrial Reformatory, Chillicothe, Ohio; the United States Penitentiary, Leavenworth, Kansas; the Maryland State Penal Farm, Roxbury, Maryland; Annandale Farms, New Jersey; and several leading institutions for women. Although similar attempts at inmate self-government have been made, perhaps professor Thorsten Sellin's elucidating observation is still true today, that self-government is

the most promising, yet ill-fated movement in correctional education. That it will be more widely used in our penal institutions as a means of resocialization there is not the slightest doubt, but since it is an eminently delicate training instrument, which requires for its successful employment fine psychological insight and broad pedagogical understanding on the part of institutional executives and their staffs, the greatly increased use of self-government will have to wait until the level of administrative work has been generally raised."

Morris Taylor

See also INMATE SELF-GOVERNANCE, SING SING PRISON

Bibliography

Bacon, C. (1974). *Foundations of Criminal Justice: Prison Reform*. New York: AMS.

Bates, S. (1938). *Prisons and Beyond*. New York: Macmillan.

Haynes, F. E. (1939). *The American Prison System*. New York, NY: McGraw Hill.

Lewis, O. F. (1922). *The Development of American Prisons and Prison Customs*. New York: Prison Association of New York.

Osborne, T. M. (1916). *Society and Prisons: Yale Lectures on the Responsibility of Citizenship*. New Haven, Conn.: Yale University Press.

P

Panopticon

Panopticon (from the Greek meaning "all see-ing") was a concept coined by Jeremy Bentham (1748–1832) in his book *Panopticon* (1787). The unique, utopian, and imaginative quality of Bentham's proposal has given it a special place in the early history of criminological thought. Bentham was a genius, having graduated from Oxford University at the age of twelve. Even though he had earned a master's degree in law at Oxford, he was far more interested in practical public policy and particularly reform of the criminal justice system.

Bentham was heavily influenced by the writings of Cesare Beccaria (1738–94) and the Scottish philosopher David Hume (1711–76). With Beccaria he founded the classical school of criminology, which was noted for its emphasis on reform of the then-unpredictable penal system and advocated a more rational system of criminal justice. From Hume he gained an emphasis on utilitarianism, a philosophical emphasis on the greatest good for the greatest numbers. Bentham has been called an advocate of "utilitarian hedonism," or "felicific calculus," or "penal pharmacy." The classical theorists viewed individuals as acting out of free will and as being motivated by hedonism (pleasure-seeking). Individuals were viewed as rational actors who govern their behavior by considerations of pleasure and pain. Punishment graduated to the seriousness of the act was viewed as a means of rational deterrence. Unlike Beccaria, Bentham recognized mitigating circumstances such as poverty and mental illness. Along with Beccaria, Bentham felt that in order to deter potential criminals the system of punishment or discipline must be rational, sure, swift, certain, and graduated to the seriousness of the offense.

The Panopticon, or "Inspection House," was envisioned as a circular prison with a glass roof that featured a central guard house (tower) from which the inspectors or guards could observe all of the cells, located around the outer perimeter. Each cell was separated from the others. While strategically positioned venetian blinds would prevent the prisoners from observing the guards, the guards would have an unobstructed view of the prisoners. Prison regimen included isolation, strict discipline, reflection, moral instruction, and industry. The latter involved contract labor to offset the cost of incarceration. Bentham also envisioned a series of speaking pipes linking the inspection house with all cells. He expected that the total power, observation (inspection) and work training (discipline) would be achieved through architectural design.

Bentham's plans called for the Panopticon to be run by private contractors, who, as entrepreneurs, would develop capitalistic prison industries (similar to workhouses) whose proceeds would pay for the operation of the facility. Economy was the watchword in his plans, down to the reliance on only a few inspectors or guards. Bentham had hoped himself to be a contractor for a Panopticon in England, but unfortunately it was not approved by the Parliament.

Although the English rejected Bentham's ideas, some of his plans were used in the first national English prison, built at Milbank on Thames (1817), and later at Pentonville (1842). Results, however, were poor. Experiments with variations of the Panopticon were also tried in the United States. The first was in Pittsburgh in 1826 with the opening of Western State Penitentiary. It featured a solitary system of confinement and some architectural elements of a Panopticon, but within ten years the prison was redesigned due to the impracticality of the scheme.

In the twentieth century, an Illinois state prison at Stateville (built between 1916 and 1924) used elements of Bentham's design. The architectural appearance was described as similar to that of large silos. That design was also quickly abandoned and judged to be unworkable. Part of the problem at Stateville apparently was that the inmates were able to observe the guards far too readily, thus defeating one of Bentham's essential elements (Hawkins and Alpert 1989). Bentham's Panopticon was in many ways ahead of its time. His plans presaged television monitors, listening devices, speakers, and electronic monitoring.

Bentham's penal philosophy reflected an emergent rehabilitative ideal—that prisons should be used not for corporal punishment but to reform ("discipline") inmates. He hoped that the disciplined work regimens learned by prisoners while in the Panopticon would aid in their reformation upon release. His strong emphasis on the redeeming possibilities of learning disciplined work habits found Bentham extending his Panopticon plans not only to prisoners but also to groups such as the poor and mentally disabled. Massive pauperization during the early Industrial Revolution created a rootless "dangerous class" who threatened the public peace.

Another reformer of the period, Ebenezer Howard, in 1898 proposed that a series of new towns, or Garden Cities of Tomorrow, be built to ring London in order to resettle the burgeoning population and to reform society by combining the best of the city (industry) and the country (healthful living). Also, during the 1790s, Bentham proposed "Panopticon Hills," a series of "houses of industry" in which experiments could be conducted to improve the livelihood of the downtrodden. The poor, orphans, unemployed, unwed mothers, and retirees were welcomed to become educated, trained, and to flourish in small manufacturing centers amidst farms. Although other planned utopian communities would be developed in the late nineteenth century, nothing ever came of Bentham's proposal.

While his utilitarianism and rehabilitative themes never replaced the retributionism that preceded them, the twentieth century did bring about a movement from corporal punishment to incarceration as a correctional strategy. Perhaps, in the last analysis, Bentham's Panopticon was never given a fair test, as it never was built in the pure architectural form that he had prescribed. But his futuristic flight of imagination guarantees that it forever will occupy a special place as a curious slice of the history of criminal justice and corrections.

While Bentham never realized his dream of a Panopticon, his creativity and eccentricity would continue to make a mark long after his death. At the time of his death, he requested that his skeleton be dressed in usual attire and displayed at University College (London). His fully dressed skeleton even attended faculty assemblies and was duly noted by speakers at the gatherings.

Frank E. Hagan

See also STATEVILLE

Bibliography

Bentham, J. (1787, 1791). *Panopticon: Or, The Inspection House.* 3 vols. Dublin, London: T. Payne.

Hawkins, R., and G. P. Alpert (1989). *American Prison Systems.* Englewood Cliffs, N.J.: Prentice-Hall.

Howard, E. (1965). *Garden Cities of Tomorrow.* Cambridge, Mass.: MIT Press.

Parole Boards

The Development of Parole

Revolutionary innovations in prison management during the mid-nineteenth-century provided the impetus for the eventual development of parole (Cavendar 1982). Alexander Machonochie, superintendent of the Norfolk Island Prison Colony from 1840 to 1844, wrote the first of these innovations in response to the brutalities he witnessed in the administration of the Australian penal colonies. As superintendent, he argued that a prisoner should be taught self-discipline and personal responsibility by successfully moving from highly regimented to less restricted stages of freedom. The last stage, resulting in release, came to be known as a "ticket of leave." It was the final step, from which prisoners would be discharged without supervision or constraint.

Sir Walter Crofton, who in 1854 became chair of the board of directors of the Irish prison system, borrowed and expanded many elements of Machonochie's system. Of most significance for parole, he developed the concept of strict supervision while on a ticket of leave. Offenders released from prison were expected to submit monthly reports and to avoid association with known criminals. Surveillance of the released convicts was provided by the police or by prisoners' aid societies.

The principles and methods devised by Machonochie and Crofton were widely discussed by prison reformers in the United States, who were concerned with an apparent increase in social disorder and disillusioned by the seeming ineffectiveness of congregate prisons. Their discussions set the stage for fundamental reform in correctional practice when the newly formed American Prison Association (later to become the American Correctional Association) held its first National Congress on Penitentiary and Reformatory Discipline in 1870 in Cincinnati, Ohio.

The congress adopted a new and more humanitarian approach to prison management in its widely circulated "Declaration of Principles." Among other things, the declaration called for the "moral regeneration" of offenders through the use of a reformatory system premised on the indeterminate sentence and provision for parole. With the appointment of Zebulon Brockway as superintendent of the Elmira Reformatory and the passage of enabling legislation in 1877, parole was given official birth in the United States.

It is ironic that despite the commitment to offender reformation and the promise of Elmira, the years between 1870 and 1900 may very well have been the most brutal in the history of American corrections. Within that context, the early practice of parole often served functions unrelated to offender reform. In some states, parole legislation was enacted to relieve governors of the time and trouble associated with the review of petitions for executive clemency. In others it was used as a safety valve to reduce prison crowding. In most states, it was championed by wardens who viewed it as an effective tool for maintaining order and control inside prison walls.

Nonetheless, the concept of parole was seeded during this time. If at this point parole was valued more for its contributions to prison management than to offender reform, its role and functions were significantly redefined during the "progressive era."

The Progressive Era, Rehabilitation, and Parole

The progressive era evolved during the first quarter of the twentieth century. Characterized by an ardent commitment to broadscale societal reform, the ideological legacy of progressivism on criminal justice proved to be substantial. In terms of parole, the first several decades of the 1900s saw the speedy passage of parole statutes in nearly every state and jurisdiction across the country. By 1927 only three states—Florida, Mississippi, and Virginia—were without a parole system.

Parole quickly became the principal means of releasing inmates from confinement. Yet despite the spread of parole it was from the start the most controversial and most unpopular of the reforms recommended by the progressives (Rothman 1980). Often viewed by the public as an act of leniency and an indefensible method for turning "hardened criminals" loose before the full service of their term, opposition to parole was at times strident and uncompromising.

The progressives argued that an effective system of parole was dependent upon a reformatory method of prison governance. The decades that followed, however, reflected the era of the "big house," with an emphasis on firm discipline and hard labor. During the 1930s and 1940s remedial, or treatment-oriented, programs were still an exception to the rule. It was not until after World War II that the "big house" was replaced by the "correctional institution." Although this transition represents more of a change in degree than in kind, it was accompanied, if not fueled, by the rise of the "rehabilitative ideal."

The rehabilitative ideal exercised an ideological hegemony over the field of corrections well into the 1960s. As it evolved, the rehabilitative ideal was inextricably bound to a system of indeterminate sentencing, prison-based treatment programs, and discretionary parole release. Under its auspices, indeterminacy in sentencing in tandem with parole acquired a newfound legitimacy. The presence of a parole board—composed of experts in behavioral change—presupposed the capacity to discern that moment during confinement when an offender was rehabilitated and thus suitable for release.

The dominance of rehabilitation in the vocabulary of American penologists was reaffirmed by the President's Commission on Law Enforcement and Administration of Justice (1965–67). At the time of the commission's work, more than 60 percent of adult felons were released on parole. Though it found problems in the practice of parole, the commission argued that a strong parole system was an essential component in the fight against crime.

Shortly after the president's commission completed its work, the core ideas of its reform-oriented agenda—the rehabilitative ideal, indeterminacy in sentencing, and parole—were subjected to withering criticism by both liberals and conservatives alike. During the early 1970s the problem of crime, if not law and order more generally, emerged for the first time as a serious concern in public opinion polls. While conservatives attacked the criminal justice system as ineffectual and soft in its response to crime, liberals challenged a sentencing and parole system that they viewed as abusive and unfair.

To understand how parole boards have responded to the criticisms that were raised, it is necessary to begin with a review of the current structure of parole.

Current Structure of Parole Systems

Paroling authorities or parole boards are located within the executive branch of government. Though small in size relative to other criminal justice agencies, the scope and consequences of their decisions—statutory and administrative— are enormous. Their actions determine the actual period of time many offenders spend behind bars or under supervision once released.

Parole boards play a key role within the overall parole process. The parole process refers to three principal components: release, supervision, and revocation. Though interdependent in most jurisdictions, these functions are performed by separate agencies: parole boards and parole field services.

Parole boards have the statutory responsibility for deciding when an inmate may be released from confinement and whether parole should be revoked if the offender fails to comply with the conditions of supervision. Their jurisdiction, however, reaches far beyond release and revocation.

While there is some variation across the country, many boards have the authority to rescind an established parole date, issue warrants and subpoenas, grant final discharges, and restore offenders' civil rights. In addition, most boards have the statutory authority to either recommend or grant a pardon or commutation of sentence. Pardons and sentence commutations are forms of executive clemency. With respect to the latter, in states with the death penalty the board often plays a role in determining whether to permit an execution to go forward or to reduce a capital sentence to life imprisonment.

In a majority of states, supervision is carried out by parole field services. These agencies are usually housed in the department of corrections, although in ten jurisdictions they are located under the board. Field service agencies are responsible for enforcing the conditions of parole. If an offender commits a crime or otherwise violates parole rules, the agency may initiate revocation proceedings and refer the matter to the board for a final decision.

Parole Boards and Corrections

Just as the administration of field services is usually independent of the board, in most jurisdictions paroling authorities operate independently of correctional departments. Despite their independence, the work of each directly affects the other. This impact is most apparent in three main areas: institutional support during the preparole and hearing process, the maintenance of prison order and control, and the management of correctional resources.

In most if not all states, the department of corrections provides office space, files, and other logistical support leading up to and during parole board hearings. The extent of cooperation and communication that occurs between prison officials, board members, and paroling authority staff who are housed within correctional institutions is critical to the smooth operation of the parole process.

Well into the progressive era, wardens and superintendents were some of the most enthusiastic advocates of parole. Like their colleagues from an earlier period and for the same reasons, many correctional administrators today support parole release because they believe that it contributes to order and stability within the prison.

The impact of parole board practices is perhaps most significant in relation to the management of correctional resources. An expansive release policy assists a state in maintaining a certain equilibrium with respect to prison population levels. Accelerated parole releases have at various times served as a "safety valve" at the back end of the correctional system.

Likewise, shifts in parole revocation practices may also produce a discernible change in the size of the prison population. As several jurisdictions, such as California, have found, an increase in the number of parolees returned to custody as "technical" violators without a new sentence may greatly exacerbate an already serious prison crowding crisis.

The recognition has only recently begun to spread that changes in revocation policy may contribute to significant growth in the prison population. In large measure, that reflects the fact that when attention is focused on parole, it is often riveted on what is the most controversial component of the parole process—the decision to release.

Release on Parole

Through the 1960s, parole release decisions were usually made with few outside constraints. Parole boards were given broad discretion to determine when an offender was ready for release—a decision limited only by the constraints of the maximum sentence imposed by the judge. There were few standards governing the decision to grant or deny parole. Parole boards were considered an integral part of an indeterminate sentencing system that emphasized rehabilitation as the central purpose of imprisonment.

In response to growing criticism of the indeterminate sentencing and the nearly unbridled exercise of discretion, some parole boards began to experiment with parole guidelines (Gottfredson, Wilkins, and Hoffman 1978). The gradual adoption of parole guidelines represented an attempt to bring greater structure and rationality to the decision to release. The first and best-known guideline project was initiated by the U.S. Parole Commission (then the U.S. Board of Parole) in 1972. Other boards followed suit shortly thereafter. An ACA Parole Task Force survey conducted in 1988 found that twenty-three jurisdictions reported using formal guidelines for release (Rhine et al. 1991).

There is no one common definition for such guidelines. In some states a "matrix" approach is used, while in others various factors (aggravating and mitigating) influence the release decision. Studies of different states' experiences with parole guidelines, however, have concluded that structuring the release decision through guidelines provides for a measure of equity (by reducing both sentencing and parole disparities), greater consistency and fairness, and more accountability (Tonry 1987).

Many states that use parole guidelines also include a structured assessment of prisoners' risk. Predicting which inmates may be returned

safely to the community has always been a primary concern of parole boards. Although some states use risk instruments in the absence of parole guidelines, where guideline grids have been adopted, they combine the risk assessment and the severity of the offense to determine the time to be served.

While there has been considerable movement toward standardizing parole release, there has also been an attempt to open the parole process by providing notice and allowing for comment from groups that were previously excluded. Though it varies by state, many parole boards have formal procedures for soliciting comments from victims, prosecutors, law enforcement personnel, and judges. Once the hearing has been completed, the victims and others may be notified of the board's decision and the date of release, if parole has been granted.

Parole release has become a more complicated and at times more sophisticated process than it was before the advent of parole guidelines. To some extent, the adoption of such guidelines, combined with the opening of the parole process, has served to legitimize parole board decision-making. Nonetheless, parole boards still retain the ultimate authority to deny parole, if specific circumstances occur that cannot be incorporated into their decision-making procedures.

The Revocation of Parole

There is no constitutional right to parole merely because a state provides for its possibility (*Greenholtz v. Inmates of the Nebraska Penal and Correctional Complex*, 1979). As recognized by the courts, there is a fundamental distinction between granting something of value an inmate does not have (release from confinement), and removing a tangible benefit bestowed by the government that a parolee currently enjoys (conditional freedom). This distinction has special relevance to parole revocation.

Through the 1960s, parolees had virtually no legal standing to question the actions of parole officers who pursued revocation or the board's final decision to revoke parole. Parole then (and now) could be revoked for new criminal charges or for technical parole violations. The situation has changed dramatically, mainly because of the landmark Supreme Court decision *Morrissey v. Brewer* (1972).

Rooted in the "prisoners' rights movement" in correctional law, the decision in *Morrissey* determined for the first time what due process guarantees were applicable in parole revocation proceedings. In its ruling, the Court stated that the revocation of parole must incorporate two stages.

The first stage requires that a reasonably prompt preliminary hearing be held by an impartial decision-maker to assess if there is probable cause to believe that the parolee has violated the conditions of supervision. If probable cause is found, a full revocation hearing must be held that accords the parolee the following due process protections: a written notice of the alleged violation; disclosure of the evidence; an opportunity to be heard in person and to present evidence as well as witnesses; a qualified opportunity to confront and cross-examine adverse witnesses; judgment by a detached and neutral hearing body; and a written statement of the reasons for revoking parole and the evidence relied on in reaching the decision.

Though *Morrissey* did not extend the right to representation during such hearings, the issue was addressed one year later in *Gagnon v. Scarpelli* (1973). In *Gagnon,* the Court ruled that the decision to extend legal counsel to probationers or parolees facing possible revocation should be made on a case-by-case basis by the state officials responsible for administering field services.

Morrissey stands as the constitutional benchmark against which revocation practices must be assessed. According to a recent survey, nearly all paroling authorities have established formal procedures governing the revocation process that comport with the requirements of due process (Rhine, Wetter, and Runda 1994).

The decision to revoke parole rests ultimately with the parole board. Though they have various options short of returning a parole violator to prison, in most jurisdictions the board's response to parole violators is completely unstructured. Recall, however, that how parole boards respond to such violators may carry significant consequences with respect to prison crowding.

In response to this issue, several parole boards have begun to develop explicit policies to structure or guide revocation decisions. Revocation is considered only one—albeit the most serious—of a number of possible responses to parolee violations. The types of options most often considered represent cost-effective, intermediate sanctions that offer alternatives to reimprisonment. Some of the better known of these sanctions include home confinement, electronic monitoring, day reporting programs, and placement in a residential program or a halfway-back correctional facility.

The trend toward greater structure in parole revocation decision-making, as well as the growing reliance on intermediate sanctions when responding to parole violators, represents a rather recent development. It is notable that the focus on the revocation of parole has grown in prominence at the same time that the legitimacy of discretionary parole release has been seriously challenged. This reflects the still-unfolding impact of the sentencing reform movement.

Sentencing Reform and Parole

The years since the 1970s have witnessed the collapse of indeterminacy as the reigning paradigm in sentencing; it had manifested a remarkable durability for over four decades in criminal justice. In many states, the philosophy of sentencing has shifted from rehabilitation and a focus on the offender to a "just deserts" rationale that stresses retribution and the nature of the offense. Under the banner of sentencing reform, the statutory changes that have been adopted reflect a fundamental shift to greater determinacy in sentencing.

Though no one model predominates across the states, the newly adopted sentencing structures focus on tailoring punishment to the nature of the crime and the criminal record. They downplay rehabilitation and treatment programs. The challenge to indeterminacy in sentencing has been coupled with an assault on parole as well.

Since its inception, the practice of parole has been subjected to criticism (National Commission on Law Observance and Enforcement, 1931). From the progressive era through the late sixties, numerous commissions and studies found that the practice of parole was seriously flawed. Yet there was a strong belief that, while practices were in need of reform, the concept itself was sound. During the 1970s, many of the same criticisms were made. The demise of the rehabilitative ideal and the stirrings of determinate sentencing reform, however, gave these criticisms new meaning. To many, the problems of parole were viewed as symptomatic not of a disparity between theory and practice, which could be overcome, but of an inherently flawed concept that should be abolished (von Hirsch 1976; von Hirsch and Hanrahan 1979).

The sentencing reform movement has exerted a more far-reaching impact on parole than on any other component of the criminal justice system. With Maine in the forefront, six states either eliminated or severely limited parole release between 1976 and 1979: California, Colorado, Illinois, Indiana, Maine, and New Mexico. Between 1980 and 1984 another five states followed suit: Connecticut, Florida, Minnesota, North Carolina, and Washington.

Likewise, at the federal level, the Comprehensive Crime Control Act of 1984 created the U.S. Sentencing Commission. The legislation abolished the U.S. Parole Commission, which is scheduled to be phased out in 1997.

In a relatively short period of time, the sentencing reform movement has produced a significant diminution of parole boards' discretionary authority to release. Between 1977 and 1990, the percentage of inmates granted conditional or parole release declined from 71.9 percent to 40.5 percent. Conversely, those released to mandatory supervision jumped sharply, from 5.9 percent in 1977 to 29.6 percent in 1990 (Bureau of Justice Statistics 1991). "Mandatory releasees" leave prison when the calendar time they have served plus good-time or other credits equals their maximum sentence.

The impact of sentencing reform on parole continues. Since 1990, discretionary parole release has been abolished in Arizona, Delaware, and Kansas. North Carolina, which placed severe restrictions on its parole commission in 1981, recently abolished the commission altogether. The discretionary authority to grant parole is under close scrutiny and vulnerable to significant change or curtailment in Georgia, Ohio, Oklahoma, Pennsylvania, and Virginia.

Though the long-term impact of structured sentencing reform will be profound, it remains the case that nearly 75 percent of the states rely on traditional discretionary parole release in their decision-making (Rhine, Wetter, and Runda 1994). Likewise, some states that at one point abolished discretionary release have recently restored their parole boards (Colorado and Connecticut). Rhode Island in 1993 adopted comprehensive changes in its sentencing policies that have expanded the jurisdiction of the parole board. Florida, which adopted structured sentencing in 1983 and revised guidelines in 1994, abolished and then restored the parole function under a new name, the Control Release Authority.

Conclusion

Parole is experiencing a period of major transition, the outcome of which is not yet clear (Bottomley 1990). Within the United States, it was first introduced at a specific stage in correctional history in response to specific pressures and needs (Simon 1993). The practice of parole has often served a loosely defined set of purposes, and its legitimacy eventually became dependent on an acceptance of the rehabilitative ideal and indeterminate sentencing.

The incessant politicization of crime control policy and the marked loss of faith in the capacity of sanctions to diminish criminal behavior have contributed to the growing popularity of determinate sentencing reform. Concerns for greater fairness and equity, as well as the elevation of retribution and incapacitation as the primary goals of sentencing, pose a serious challenge to parole. In some states, prison crowding will continue to derail efforts to abolish parole. Unless there is a fundamental shift, however, toward a sanctioning philosophy that seeks to balance incapacitation, rehabilitation, just punishment, and fairness, the influence and legitimacy of parole boards will continue to wane in the years ahead.

Edward E. Rhine

Bibliography

Bottomley, A. K. (1990). Parole in transition: A comparative study of origins, developments, and prospects for the 1990s. In M. Tonry and N. Morris, eds. *Crime and Justice: A Review of Research*. Chicago: University of Chicago Press.

Bureau of Justice Statistics (1991). *Probation and Parole 1990*. Washington, D.C.: U.S. Department of Justice.

Cavendar, G. (1982). *Parole: A Critical Analysis*. Port Washington, N.Y.: Kennikat.

Gottfredson, D., L. T. Wilkins, and P. B. Hoffman (1978). *Guidelines for Parole and Sentencing*. Lexington, Mass.: Lexington.

National Commission on Law Observance and Enforcement (Wickersham Report) (1931). *Report on Penal Institutions, Probation and Parole*. Washington, D.C.: U.S. Government Printing Office.

Rhine, E. E., W. R. Smith, R. W. Jackson, P. B. Burke, and R. LaBelle (1991). *Paroling Authorities: Recent History and Current Practice*. Laurel, Md.: American Correctional Association.

Rhine, E. E., R. E. Wetter, and J. C. Runda (1994). *The Practice of Parole Boards.* Lexington, Ky.: Association of Paroling Authorities International.

Rothman, D. J. (1980). *Conscience and Convenience: The Asylum and Its Alternatives in Progressive America.* Boston: Little, Brown.

Simon, J. (1993). *Poor Discipline: Parole and the Social Control of the Underclass, 1890–1990.* Chicago: University of Chicago Press.

Tonry, M. (1987). *Sentencing Reform Impacts.* Washington, D.C.: National Institute of Justice, U.S. Department of Justice.

von Hirsch, A. (1976). *Doing Justice: The Choice of Punishments.* New York: Hill and Wang.

von Hirsch, A., and K. J. Hanrahan (1979). *The Question of Parole: Retention, Reform or Abolition?* Cambridge, Mass.: Ballinger.

Cases

Gagnon v. Scarpelli, 411 U.S. 778 (1973)

Greenholtz v. Inmates of the Nebraska Penal and Correctional Complex, 442 U.S. 1 (1979)

Morrissey v. Brewer, 408 U.S. 471 (1972)

Patuxent Institution

The state of Maryland's Patuxent Institution opened in January of 1955, operating under the provisions of the state's recently enacted "Defective Delinquency" statute. Those who drafted the statute (Article 31B of the Maryland code) patterned it after sexual psychopath laws then in force in several states. They were optimistic that this new law could be employed effectively to deal with a "borderline" class of adult offenders considered the most difficult to treat and the most dangerous to society. At that time, these offenders were medically diagnosed as psychopaths or sociopaths. It was a population for whom the traditional or "classical" criminal law and procedure together with ordinary incarceration were found to be inadequate for both the protection of society and rehabilitation. Thus, Maryland's legislators stretched the legal concept of sexual psychopathy so that it included a broad category of mentally disordered, yet legally sane, offenders. The breadth of coverage may be seen in the original statutory language, which defines the defective delinquent as one who:

by the demonstration of persistent aggravated antisocial or criminal behavior, evidences a propensity toward criminal activity, and who is found to have either such intellectual deficiency or emotional unbalance, or both, as to clearly demonstrate an actual danger to society so as to require such confinement and treatment, when appropriate, as may make it reasonably safe for society to terminate the confinement and treatment (Article 31B, §5, *Annotated Code of the Public General Laws of Maryland*, 1951, 1977, 1989).

The certainty that the framers of the original legislation felt regarding the ability of psychologists and psychiatrists to carry out the tasks assigned them at Patuxent Institution was spelled out in the original recommendations for passage of the statute:

A fundamental problem, however, is whether medical science has progressed to where we can segregate such a class of defective delinquents and handle its treatment with reasonable assurance of accomplishing the purpose of the legislation. We believe that experience elsewhere has demonstrated that this is possible. Also, we have consulted a distinguished group of Maryland psychologists and psychiatrists and their composite opinion is included herein. . . .

In many ways the Maryland plan for handling this complicated problem is the best that has yet been projected. If put into effect, it will bring the State into the forefront of penological advance. . . . [T]here is a real opportunity for scientific knowledge to be advanced in a field comparable to the scourge of cancer, so far as its effect upon the welfare of society is concerned (Commission to Study Medico-Legal Psychiatry, *Report to the Governor and General Assembly of Maryland*, Annapolis, Md., 28 December 1948).

Arguably, Patuxent Institution represented the clearest example in American correctional history of the application of positivist principles laid down in what has been called the Lombrosian Legacy. This legacy may be summarized as follows: Effective control of crime requires the scientific study of individual offenders to assign them to appropriate treatment categories.

As the Patuxent staff went about its business of receiving, examining, and treating, releasing some and holding others in confinement, it was, in effect, adhering to that legacy. The "scientific" techniques they employed consisted of an array of psychiatric and psychometric examinations and tests. As a result of those tests, some state offenders were diagnosed as defective delinquents, others were not.

Those diagnosed as defective delinquents were returned to court for a commitment hearing that was civil in nature. If the court concurred in the diagnosis, the offender was formally committed to the institution for an indeterminate period, regardless of the length of his original sentence.

Much of the concern expressed in the past regarding Patuxent Institution's ability to perform satisfactorily centered on two vital questions: (1) Was its staff accurately able to predict the future dangerousness of those admitted for diagnostic examination? (2) Could the staff identify those in its committed population who were "ready" for release? Readiness was most often defined strictly in terms of the patient's capacity for living in the community and the staff's ability to provide support services for as long as required to maintain the patient out of the institution.

The statute contained a section that provided an indeterminate sentence for those committed as defective delinquents. The staff, as well as those who wrote this section into the law, considered that essential to stimulate inmates to change, as well as an important safeguard for the community when offenders did not change or could not be changed.

At the same time, the law permitted the staff to release early those offenders who were considered to present little risk to the community. The carefully structured release process, together with the provision of "outpatient" services through the institution's own staff resources, was a remarkable departure from traditional correctional practice. The statute gave the institution its own paroling authority (through an Institutional Board of Review) that included release decisions and the supervision of parolees (called outpatients).

The result of all this careful attention to detail, however, left the institution isolated from the general public and the rest of the state's correctional system. Its decision-makers failed to take into account changing societal standards with regard to the balancing of punishment and "treatment" for serious crimes, especially in terms of the length of incarceration. In the United States today, imprisonment has become the favored punishment for serious offenders. Prison populations have been exploding for the past several years, and statutory sentencing laws increasingly call for mandatory and longer prison terms. In such statutes, treatment objectives are absent.

The Patuxent staff and its review board also failed to take into account the increasing demand for the recognition of victims' interests when prison inmates are considered for release. That failure was dramatically brought to the attention of the public and lawmakers when two patients with violent histories of multiple murders and rape were released during the 1988 presidential campaign. No one in the community was consulted about these releases. The decisions were reached in the closed atmosphere of the institution and its board of review. Anger over the failure to take victims and the community into account was heightened because the persons to be released spent only a relatively short period in confinement for the most heinous of crimes.

For these failures, which might be considered collectively as a consequence of professional elitism, Patuxent Institution paid a high price. Major legal changes took away its cherished autonomy; its reputation as a cutting-edge treatment facility has virtually been destroyed. The lessons to be found in the Patuxent experience ought to be learned by others in the correctional field. In the current climate, the public was bound to revolt against what was regarded as a flagrant violation of its rights and safety.

In the final analysis, there were two fundamental problems that this prison ultimately was unable to solve, and that failure brought about its demise as a unique facility in American corrections. The first was its statutory requirement to predict future dangerousness in its offender referrals. Making of accurate predictions is now generally regarded as impossible by the mental health community. The second problem never to be satisfactorily solved lay in the inherent conflict between the two missions assigned to Patuxent Institution: delivering treatment to its population, and the indefinite confinement of those who did not respond to treatment.

Patuxent Institution at the present time is a very different prison than it was when it opened in 1955. All commitments must be certified as treatable. That is, they must be found by the staff to be amenable to the programs available in the institution. In addition, it is extremely difficult, if not impossible, to admit offenders with life sentences. Inmates can no longer be kept indefinitely; they must be released upon serving their judicially prescribed sentences. Finally, severe restrictions have been placed on the review board's authority to grant furloughs and paroles. The current statute provides that one voting member of the board must be a member of a victims' rights organization.

Thomas F. Courtless

See also REHABILITATION PROGRAMS

Bibliography
Boslow, H. M. (1959). The Maryland defective delinquent law. *British Journal of Delinquency* 10: 5–13.
Carney, F. L. (1974). The indeterminate sentence at Patuxent. *Crime and Delinquency* 20: 135–43.
Contract Research Corporation (1977). *The Evaluation of Patuxent Institution: Final Report.* Belmont, Calif.: Contract Research Corp.
Courtless, T. F. (1989). The rehabilitative ideal meets an aroused public: The Patuxent experiment revisited. *Journal of Psychiatry and Law* 12: 607–26.
Hodges, E. (1971). Crime prevention by the indeterminate sentence law. *American Journal of Psychiatry* 128: 291–95.
Legislative Council of Maryland (1950). *Research Report No. 29.* Annapolis, Md.: Legislative Council of Maryland.
Wilkins, L. T. (1976). Treatment of offenders: Patuxent examined. *Rutgers Law Review* 29: 1102–16.
Zenoff, E. H., and T. Courtless (1977). Autopsy of an experiment: The Patuxent experience. *Journal of Psychiatry and Law* 5: 531–50.

Pennsylvania Prison Society

The Pennsylvania Prison Society is the contemporary version of the Philadelphia Society for Alleviating the Miseries of Public Prisons (founded by Dr. Benjamin Rush on 8 May 1787). The original and continuing philosophy of the society, which changed its name in 1887 to the Pennsylvania Prison Society, is to work for the improvement of prison facilities and treatment of offenders.

For over two centuries, the society has worked as an advocate for prisoners, prison reform, and the humane treatment of anyone incarcerated or released from prisons in Pennsylvania. Among their accomplishments over the years have been the use of indeterminate sentences, establishment of prison visiting rights, the removal from prisons of the criminally insane to mental hospitals, the use of separate facilities for women, having children removed from adult facilities, improving county jails, providing counseling to prisoners and former prisoners, and providing professional training for staff.

Currently, the society is still active in prison reform and offender advocacy in Pennsylvania. The society continues to lobby for the elimination of capital punishment, the reduction of crowding in prisons and jails, the establishment of earned good time, the expansion of alternatives to incarceration, and other correctional reforms. The society runs an early release program, an arts and humanities program, a volunteer visiting program, client services, and a project that requires community service from offenders. It also offers financial assistance for the education of prisoners, former prisoners, and criminal justice students, along with other special projects.

Another society function is to disseminate information through periodical publications. Beginning in 1845, with the publication of the *Journal of Prison Discipline and Philanthropy,* since 1921 called the *Prison Journal,* and through an official newsletter, *Correctional Forum,* topics of special interest in the field of criminal justice and corrections are examined. The *Prison Journal* expanded its scope in 1992, and it is now a refereed journal edited at Temple University's Department of Criminal Justice but still affiliated with the society.

The society is funded by its members, the United Way, direct public support, grants, and governmental programs. With a combination of paid staff, volunteers, and student interns, the society seeks to influence the operations of the correctional system in Pennsylvania and those who come into contact with it. The society has a membership of about six hundred people from all walks of life. Objectives and goals for the society are developed by a board of directors that consists of approximately thirty people who meet ten times a year. The society continues today as an advocate for the humane treatment of prisoners, the improvement of prison conditions, and the welfare of discharged prisoners.

Robert Jerin

See also EASTERN STATE PENITENTIARY; PHILADELPHIA SOCIETY FOR ALLEVIATING THE MISERIES OF PUBLIC PRISONS; RUSH, BENJAMIN

Pennsylvania System

Prisons, reformatories, and custodial institutions for juvenile offenders have been a feature of the American landscape for well over a century, as have mental institutions, state-operated residential facilities for the mentally or physically handicapped, and other "asylums" (Rothman 1970). Incarceration of adult lawbreakers became particularly widespread in the United States beginning about 1975, as the nation embarked upon a "prison binge" (Irwin and Austin 1994).

It would be a mistake, however, to assume that imprisonment has always been a prominent form of punishment (Gibbons 1992, 462–66). As other contributors to this encyclopedia have indicated, during the long and complex history of punishment, myriad different sanctions have been employed at one time or another. Offenders have been tortured, subjected to social humiliation such as the stocks and pillories, banished and transported to other countries, or made to suffer financial penalties. In addition, while it can fairly be said that prisons and penitentiaries are an American invention that arose in the early years of American history, they were preceded by workhouses and other prisonlike facilities in Europe. Finally, the growth of American prisons was a slow, rather than an abrupt, process. Several decades passed between the creation of the first American prison prototype, the Walnut Street Jail in Philadelphia, and the construction of state and federal prisons and reformatories.

The first large prison erected in the United States was the Eastern Pennsylvania prison at Cherry Hill, opened in 1829. It has usually been identified in penological histories as the centerpiece of the "Pennsylvania system" sponsored by American Quakers. That system has also been termed the "solitary" system, because its developers' intent was to incarcerate prisoners in solitary confinement. The Pennsylvania system had a major competitor in the United States, the Auburn, Sing Sing, or silent system, so-named because it initially involved the imprisonment of persons who worked together but who were enjoined not to speak.

The term "Quaker" was originally a derisive term for members of the Society of Friends, a leftwing branch of Puritanism that arose in England in the seventeenth century. Beginning in the mid-1600s, Quakers began to immigrate to America in some numbers, and they dominated the West Jersey and Pennsylvania Colonial areas prior to American independence. Appalled by the brutal punishment of lawbreakers that was common at the time, they urged that corporal punishment be replaced by imprisonment. Their advocacy of imprisonment arose out of humane motives, rather than from an interest in inflicting greater pain.

After the Declaration of Independence, Quaker influence led the Pennsylvania legislature in 1790 to mandate that imprisonment at hard labor become the preferred method of punishing offenders. The Philadelphia Prison Society was a key organization behind this development. Benjamin Franklin, as well as Dr. Benjamin Rush, one of the signers of the Declaration of Independence and a famous physician and social reformer, also played a major role in these events, as did Pennsylvania Supreme Court Judge William Bradford.

The Walnut Street Jail in Philadelphia, which has sometimes been called "the cradle of the penitentiary" (Teeters 1955), had formerly been a city jail, but in 1790 it was remodeled and converted into a small-scale version of what has come to be known as the Pennsylvania prison style. A new building structure was added to an existing one within the yard of the old jail. That two-story structure consisted of sixteen one-person cells in each of two stories and was intended for "more hardened offenders." Available descriptions of the cell block paint a grim picture of the conditions of solitary confinement, for the light entering the single window in each cell was extremely meager, the cells had few if any furnishings, and the massively thick walls made communication with other prisoners impossible. In addition, prisoners had virtually no physical or verbal contact with the jail officials. Most of the inmates were idle rather than employed or otherwise occupied. It bears repeating, though, that the Quaker designers were motivated by humane rather than punitive sentiments. In their view, solitary confinement would be beneficial to convicted criminals. Cut off from harmful associations with other offenders, they would be led to meditate upon "the error of their ways," with the result that they would refrain from further lawbreaking upon release.

The Pennsylvania system came to full flower in 1829 in the form of the Eastern Penitentiary of Pennsylvania at Cherry Hill, on the outskirts of Philadelphia. That prison was designed by John Haviland, an English-born architect who has often been identified as the father of classic prison architecture.

The guiding philosophy around which the Eastern Penitentiary was designed was that of the solitary confinement of all inmates at "hard labor," which was viewed as contributory to the reformation of the prisoner rather than as added punishment. The penitentiary was surrounded by a high wall. The prison itself was specifically designed to provide solitary confinement for all prisoners. Historian Harry Elmer Barnes (U.S. Bureau of Prisons 1949, 28) has provided a good description of this penitentiary:

> Haviland built within the secluded rectangle of his prison walls a seven-spoked structure, only one of the "spokes" or radial wings being more than one story high. From a central rotunda, reached by a broad path from the handsomely battlemented gate house, these spokes radiated almost to the prison walls with their similarly crenelated guard towers at each corner. Every one of these spokes was a cell house of outside cells, each cell house having a central corridor which gave access to the long row of cells on either side.

By outside cells, Barnes meant that the outside wall of each cell was created from or was part of the outside wall of the cell house itself. (These cells differed from those in the Auburn/Sing Sing-style prisons constructed around the United States, particularly in the nineteenth century, in that in those, the inside cell blocks or tiers constituted, in effect, a building-within-a-building.) The cells in the Eastern Penitentiary measured about eight by twelve feet and were unusually large by the standards of the day. Each of the cells had a door that led to a high-walled, unroofed yard in which the inmate engaged in solitary exercise.

As in the Walnut Street Jail, prisoners in Eastern Penitentiary were kept in solitary confinement in their cells, save for an hour each day that they spent in the exercise yard (only alternate yards were used at the same time, so as to deter inmates from communicating with each other). Solitary confinement was relieved somewhat, however, in that inmates had some contacts with guards and also with members of the Philadelphia Prison Society, who often visited the prison and exhorted prisoners to reform themselves.

Inmates in the Eastern Penitentiary engaged in work in their cells, laboring at spinning, weaving, shoe making, and other tasks. Work was regarded by the designers of the Pennsylvania system as salutary rather than punitive, for they held that it would contribute to the self-reflection engaged in by prisoners.

Did the Pennsylvania system produce the results intended by its designers, that is, did it lead to reformation on the part of incarcerated criminals? Prison reformers and other critics have often argued that it did not, and that many prisoners were driven to insanity by the conditions of solitary confinement, or, alternatively, that many of them became even more hardened criminals upon release. Hard evidence that would support such claims, however, is not to be found.

Although some architectural elements of the Pennsylvania system were incorporated in a few other American prisons, including the New Jersey state prison designed by Haviland, neither the architecture nor philosophy of the system was widely adopted in this country. The Pennsylvania system lost out in the competition with the Auburn/Sing Sing silent system and the prison design associated with it, probably in large part because of the higher costs of constructing and operating solitary institutions. The Pennsylvania system was completely abolished in that state in 1913.

On the other hand, a number of European observers came to the United States in the early 1800s to scrutinize these two competing prison systems, with many of them returning to Europe to praise the Pennsylvania system. Interestingly, Charles Dickens was not one of the admirers. He argued in *American Notes* and elsewhere that the Pennsylvania system was insufficiently punitive and that he much preferred "to see the determined thief, swindler, or vagrant sweating profusely at the treadmill or the crank" (Ackroyd 1990, 377). A number of prisons constructed in Europe in the 1800s did incorporate some elements of the Pennsylvania system.

Don C. Gibbons

See also ARCHITECTURE, EASTERN STATE
PENITENTIARY, WALNUT STREET JAIL

Bibliography
Ackroyd, P. (1990). *Dickens*. New York:
Harper/Collins.
Barnes, H. E. (1968). *The Evolution of Pe-
nology in Pennsylvania: A Study in
American Social History*. Montclair,
N.J.: Patterson Smith (Reprinted.)
Foucault, M. (1979). *Discipline and Punish:
The Birth of the Prison*. New York: Vin-
tage.
Gibbons, D. C. (1992). *Society, Crime, and
Criminal Behavior*. 6th ed. Englewood
Cliffs, N.J.: Prentice-Hall.
Irwin, J., and J. Austin (1994). *It's About
Time: America's Imprisonment Binge*.
Belmont, Calif.: Wadsworth.
Rothman, D. J. (1970). *The Discovery of the
Asylum*. Boston: Little, Brown.
Teeters, N. K. (1955). *The Cradle of the Peni-
tentiary: The Walnut Street Jail at Phila-
delphia, 1773–1835*. Philadelphia: Penn-
sylvania Prison Society.
U.S. Bureau of Prisons (1949). *Handbook of
Correctional Institution Design and
Construction*. Washington, D.C.: U.S.
Bureau of Prisons.

The Philadelphia Society for Alleviating the Miseries of Public Prisons

The Philadelphia Society for Alleviating the Miseries of Public Prisons was founded in 1787 by the physician Benjamin Rush, a signer of the Declaration of Independence, along with thirty-six other doctors, clergymen, and other upstanding citizens of Philadelphia. Including in its early membership some of the most prominent figures in Philadelphia, including Benjamin Franklin, the society emerged as a reaction to accounts of the degrading and potentially counterproductive treatment of prisoners at the time. In his paper *An Inquiry into the Effects of Public Punishment upon Criminals and upon Society*, Dr. Rush had drawn attention to a 1786 law under which convicts were led out of the Walnut Street Jail to perform hard labor "tethered like cattle . . . their heads shaved, carrying in their wheelbarrows, balls and chains riveted to their ankles, and dressed in bizarre distinctive dress of multi-colors" (Teeters 1962, 7–8).

Within a few years of its formation, lobbying via a series of position papers, or "Memo-

rials," resulted in the society's helping to persuade the Pennsylvania legislature to repeal the "wheelbarrow law." In its stead, the society fervently promoted the now notorious practice of solitary confinement at labor known as the "Pennsylvania System of Prison Discipline." Better described as a system of "separate" confinement, the Pennsylvania system advocated by the society was one in which prisoners were to be confined at all times and for all purposes, including labor, in single-person cells, isolated from contaminating contact with each other. They were, however, to be exposed to the reforming influences of their keepers, chaplains, the Board of Inspectors, and members of the society who, by an 1829 law, were granted access to the prisons as "official visitors."

Rooted in faith in the possibility of reformation of offenders through repentance and acceptance of God's guidance, the noble intent and reasoning behind the society's advocacy is visible in its first memorial to the legislature in 1788:

> The Punishment of Criminals by "hard Labor publicly and disgracefully Imposed" as Indicated in the Preamble to the Law, your Petitioners wish the House would be pleased to revise; being fully Convinced, that Punishment by more private or even *solitary* Labor, would more successfully tend to reclaim the unhappy Objects: as it might be Conducted more Steadily and uniformly, and the kind and Portion of Labor better adapted to the different Abilities of the Criminals; the Evils of familiarizing young minds to vicious Characters would be removed; and the Opportunities of begging Money would be prevented. . . .
>
> Your Petitioners also would wish to Recommend to the Attention of the House, the very great Importance of a Separation of the Sexes, in the public Prisons. . . . And that some more effectual Provision be made for the Prohibition of Spirituous Liquor amongst the Criminals, the use of which tends to lessen the true sense of the Situation and prevents those useful Reflections, which might be produced by Solitary Labor and Strict Temperance (Teeters 1937, 447).

Half a century later, Eastern State Penitentiary, the most enduring legacy of the system of "separate confinement at labor," and America's first penitentiary designed and operated to that end, was built in Philadelphia. Although many of the innovative architectural features of Eastern State were emulated throughout the world, the Pennsylvania system itself, despite the society's ardent support and defense of it throughout most of the nineteenth century, was not. New York's Auburn system of congregate labor offered an alternative approach that found favor in many jurisdictions. Even in Philadelphia, beset with crowding problems forcing double-celling almost from the outset, Eastern State was never completely able to match theory to practice. Closed by the state in 1975, the facility has fallen into serious disrepair resulting from vandalism and neglect. Today the society, known since 1887 as the Pennsylvania Prison Society, is a central figure in efforts to preserve Eastern State, open it to the public, and establish it as a center for correctional scholarship. It is arguably one of the most historically significant sites in the country.

Alan T. Harland

See also EASTERN STATE PENITENTIARY; PENNSYLVANIA PRISON SOCIETY; RUSH, BENJAMIN

Bibliography

Atherton, A. L. (1987) Journal retrospective—1845–1986: 200 years of Prison Society history as reflected in the *Prison Journal. Prison Journal* 67(1): 1–37.

Teeters, N. K. (1937). *They Were in Prison: A History of the Pennsylvania Prison Society 1787–1937.* Chicago: John Winston.

Teeters, N. K. (1962). The Pennsylvania Prison Society: 175th anniversary issue. *Prison Journal* 42 (Spring): 1ff.

Prerelease Programs

Prerelease programs are designed to help offenders reintegrate into the community upon their release. Programs include assisting inmates with employment, providing contacts in the community, counseling on personal matters, and assessments for parole boards. A typical prerelease program might:

1. provide information and instruction on on-the-job safety, emphasize loyalty to the employer, and develop skills for business and industry
2. provide job opportunities and employment aids
3. stress the importance of being on time
4. provide training for a driver's license
5. discuss insurance, legal problems and contracts, basic financial management, buying a car, Social Security and Medicare benefits, community agency assistance, and the importance of establishing and maintaining credit
6. emphasize family responsibilities and conflict resolution in marriage
7. warn against the use of alcohol, drugs, and cigarettes (Bartollas and Conrad 1992).

The origin of prerelease programs can be traced to the 1960s, when the Corrections Task Force of the President's Commission on Law Enforcement and Administration of Justice recommended the use of community-based corrections for all but hard-core offenders. Reintegration was the philosophy upon which community-based corrections would be based. The task and challenge of the reintegration model, according to the commission, was to keep offenders in the community and to help them reintegrate into community life (President's Crime Commission 1967).

The reintegration model depended upon the community as the center of treatment. In this model, offenders would be offered a wide range of reentry programs, including prerelease instruction, work release, educational release, and home furloughs. If it were necessary to confine offenders in correctional institutions, they would be brought into the decision-making process that determined their prison programs (President's Crime Commission 1967).

The prerelease programs that developed throughout the nation in the 1970s generally took on one of three formats. First, some prisons excused inmates from work in prison industries or from academic or vocational programs in order to attend prerelease classes within the prison complex. Second, some prisons transferred inmates ready for prerelease programs to facilities outside the main prison compound. Third, some inmates who were ready for release were transferred to prerelease guidance centers in the community, where they received the benefit of work release, home furlough, and formalized prelease instruction.

The Sam Houston State University Institute of Criminal Justice and Contemporary Corrections drew several conclusions from a 1973 national survey of prerelease programs:

1. Prerelease preparation should begin as early as possible in the sentence, and inmates should know in advance the purpose and intention of this program.
2. A sound program rather than the appeal of special privileges should persuade inmates to participate.
3. Organized with realistic goals in mind, the prerelease program should be part of the total treatment process.
4. Counseling programs should be oriented toward present adjustment and problems rather than underlying personality conflicts.
5. Participants selected by staff should be chosen individually rather than by predetermined or arbitrary standards.
6. Employee-employer rather than custodian-inmate relationships should exist between staff members and inmates.
7. Every effort should be made to enlist the participation and support of the community; family contact should eventually be encouraged.
8. Work release ideally should be included in prerelease programs (Frank 1973).

Studies of the effectiveness of prerelease programs report mixed results. In one systematic study, participants in five-week prerelease programs were tested on a number of items before and after instruction. Although 69 percent felt that the course had been beneficial, the data showed little change in the respondents. The researchers concluded that because the program sought to meet the needs of the inmates as a group rather than as individuals, it failed to meet any one inmate's particular needs (Frank 1973). Another study reported that apparently well-planned prerelease programs in California and Minnesota also had little effect on participants (Holt and Renteria 1969). Yet researchers did find that programs in Massachusetts and Maryland had reduced recidivism (Buckley 1972).

By the beginning of the 1980s, the "get-tough-with-criminals" mood that had started in the mid 1970s had dramatically reduced the number of formal prerelease programs, as well as work release and home furloughs, from both prison and community-based settings. It seemed that correctional strategy across the nation had shifted toward a reluctance to release inmates from correctional confinement for such programs as work release, educational release, or home furloughs. With that reluctance also came a deemphasis on formalized prerelease instruction.

The present prerelease program of the California Department of Corrections is probably the most innovative in the United States. It provides a three-week, full-time training program for inmates who are within fifteen to forty-five days of release. In this program, inmates are given training in maintaining positive attitudes and the skills needed to find and keep a job, to establish sound money managements, to improve communication skills, and to seek and receive community and parole resources. Following the evaluation of the inmates' needs, they are given a list of five objectives to be achieved within thirty days of being paroled, and the names and addresses of five public or private agencies that can be called upon for assistance. Inmates further participate in a mock job interview and acquire a California driver's license.

Two other noteworthy prerelease programs in the 1990s are Ohio's Lebanon Correctional Institution and Colorado's Canon City complex. The prerelease program in Lebanon is housed in a facility a short distance from the main prison. A similar arrangement is found at the Canon City complex, where a separately administered prerelease unit housing eighty inmates has been in operation since 1983.

It has been a long time since the glory days of prerelease programs. Here and there a formalized type of prerelease instruction takes place, but, like rehabilitative programming, it has little support from correctional administration, staff, or even inmates. An evaluation of prerelease instruction even in its heyday, of course, must be guarded. Overall, high expectations for a brief prerelease program in a prison setting appears to be unrealistic. The best justification for their continuation is that some inmates do find prerelease programs helpful.

Clemens Bartollas

See also REHABILITATION PROGRAMS, VOCATIONAL PROGRAMS

Bibliography
Bartollas, C., and J. P. Conrad (1992). *Introduction to Corrections*. 2nd ed. New York: Harper/Collins.
Bronick, M. J. (1989). Relieving subpopulation pressures. *Federal Prisons Journal* 1(2): 17–31.

Buckley, M. (1972). Enter the ex-con. *Federal Probation* 36 (December): 24–30.

Frank, B. (1973). Graduated release. In B. Frank, ed. *Contemporary Corrections*. Reston, Va.: Reston.

Holt, H., and R. Renteria (1969). Prerelease program evaluation: Some implications of negative findings. *Federal Probation* 33(June): 42–44.

LeClair, D. P., and S. Guarino-Ghezzi (1991). Does incapacitation guarantee public safety? Lessons from Massachusetts' furlough and prerelease programs. *Justice Quarterly* 8: 9–36.

President's Commission on Law Enforcement and Administration of Justice (1967). *Corrections*. Washington, D.C.: U.S. Government Printing Office.

The President's Commission on Law Enforcement and Administration of Justice, Task Force Report: Corrections

The social and political climate of the 1960s was uncertain and rapidly changing. The burgeoning civil rights movement and resistance to the Vietnam War added to the public's frustration with the government. Public opinion polls reflected the growing fear of crime. In 1965, for the first time, crime was rated the nation's most important problem by respondents to the Gallup poll. It was within this historical context that President Johnson launched his "war on crime" by creating the President's Commission on Law Enforcement and the Administration of Justice. Hundreds of recommendations from the commission were compiled by numerous task forces. These recommendations were summarized in a general report entitled *The Challenge of Crime in Free Society* (1967). The report ushered in a new era in American criminal justice. The systems approach, as developed by the commission, had a widespread influence on the study and practice of criminal justice.

The task force report on corrections actually resulted in a change of approach from treatment to reintegration. The integration approach, suggested by the task force, followed from members' beliefs about the causes of crime. They believed that community disorganization and lack of opportunity impeded the influence of traditional institutions on individuals. Efforts to improve the situation of the offender should not be focused solely on the individual offender, as in the rehabilitation philosophy, but instead should involve the entire community. In its report, the task force stated that the main task of corrections was to include "building or rebuilding solid ties between offender and community, integrating or reintegrating the offender into community life, restoring family ties, obtaining employment and education, securing in the larger sense a place for the offender in the routine functioning of society" (1967, 7).

Just as the reintegration perspective followed logically from the commission's premise regarding the cause of crime, the main form of treatment was also implicit—the expanded use of community-based corrections. Rather than treating prisoners in isolated institutions, the commission suggested that keeping offenders in the community or reintegrating them into the community upon release and offering them a variety of opportunities would prevent further criminality. Specific recommendations made by the task force were aimed at sustaining community ties and absorbing offenders into the community. If the lines between institutions and communities were to be effectively blurred, however, the role and function of both community-based and institutional corrections had to change.

In community-based treatment, the first change had to occur within the existing framework of probation and parole. Under an expanded system, probation and parole officers would act more as brokers than counselors, matching offenders up with services in the community while attempting to enlist the assistance of community institutions. Caseloads were to be varied, based on the offender population served, but were not to exceed thirty-five clients. The number of officers would have to be increased and the services of volunteers solicited. A whole new genre of community-based treatment programs were also recommended, so that offenders could be diverted from institutions whenever possible. The task force also recommended the gradual release of those institutionalized through furlough programs, locally based halfway programs, and mandatory supervision of all released offenders.

Institutional corrections also needed a complete overhaul. The task force suggested that a fundamental move be made away from the depersonalized operations of traditional institutions. In their place, a collaborative model was to increase communications between custodial and treatment staff, and also diminish the distinctiveness of their roles. Custodial officers would have an expanded treatment role under the new model, while treatment staff would be more involved in the daily management of the institution. This would require upgrading personnel, which could be made possible by offering better working conditions, increased salaries, and advanced educational opportunities.

The task force recommended that inmates be given more of a voice in institutional decision-making, as well as in the treatment process (for example, through group counseling). Rather than treating inmates in a standardized manner, they would be handled fairly, but differentiated in treatment strategies. That would allow prisoners to take full advantage of treatment opportunities, ranging from increased educational and vocational programs to meaningful work, thus increasing their chances of successful reintegration.

Such individualized treatment would require improving the intake and classification of offenders. The task force suggested that small institutions be built in cities to serve as intake and prerelease centers and community-based treatment centers. Local jails were also included in the plan, being integrated with state correctional institutions. Juveniles and those awaiting trial would be separated from convicted offenders in these institutions.

Many of the task force's recommendations, such as the collaborative model of decision-making and state control over local jails, have not really been achieved. Some recommendations became irrelevant when the correctional pendulum swung back to a punitive approach. Stojkovic (1994) states that, along with the changing philosophy in corrections, an increased number of prisoners, overcrowding, and limited resources have forced correctional administrators into crisis management. Under such conditions, little more than warehousing of prisoners has been taking place. Nonetheless, recommendations made by the correctional task force have led to improvements in the delivery of correctional services, better classification procedures, and the increased use of community-based corrections.

Jonathan Sorensen

Bibliography

President's Commission on Law Enforcement and the Administration of Justice (1967). *The Challenge of Crime in a Free Society*. Washington, D.C.: U.S. Government Printing Office.
President's Commission on Law Enforcement and the Administration of Justice (1967). *Task Force Report: Corrections*. Washington, D.C.: U.S. Government Printing Office.
Stojkovic, S. (1994). The President's Crime Commission recommendations for corrections: The twilight of the idols. In J. Conley, ed. *The 1967 President's Crime Commission Report: Its Impact 25 Years Later*. Cincinnati, Ohio: Anderson.

Prisonization

During the 1950s and early 1960s, prison sociologists attempted to examine the effects of incarceration on prisoners. Consequently, the concept of "prisonization" developed. According to Donald Clemmer in the classic *The Prison Society* (1958, 299), prisonization is "the taking on in greater or less degree the folkways, mores, and customs, and general culture of the penitentiary." Because imprisonment engenders a common institutional experience among inmates, prisonization is best understood as a socialization or assimilation process in which inmates internalize the norms, values, and informal rules (that is, the inmate code) of the prison community or the inmate culture.

The process of prisonization begins with a transformation of prisoners' status by altering their identity from what it had been on the outside to that of a prisoner. Indeed, this transformation occurs immediately. Upon their admission to prison, inmates are forced to accept the role of inferiors in the prison hierarchy. Just as significant, numbers replace names, institutional uniforms replace street clothes, and institutional routine replaces personal routine. Through the adoption of prison rules and regulations, inmates surrender much of their personal autonomy.

Though the institutional order is rigid, prisoners develop ways to express themselves that symbolize the prison experience. One aspect of prisonization is the inmate language or argot. Even inmates who do not use this slang quickly learn its meaning. Inmate slang is a feature of prison society that reflects its dogma and ideology. It permits inmates to share the prison experience, and, in some situations, it serves to enhance inmate solidarity.

Inmate Solidarity

A dominant theme in the prison community is solidarity. Through solidarity, inmates can partially alleviate the pains of imprisonment (isolation, loneliness, and boredom) and make the experience less degrading. Solidarity also creates a meaningful social group that may serve to restore the inmate's self-respect and sense of independence. Inmate solidarity is often reinforced by the inmate code—a list of rules that symbolize inmate solidarity in the face of conventional values and goals and the prison staff. Internalizing the inmate code is a crucial element of prisonization. The inmate code delineates normative boundaries in the prison community, thereby enhancing inmate solidarity.

Compliance with the inmate code mirrors the degree of inmate solidarity. Inmate codes promote strong normative imperatives, and noncompliance is met with sanctions ranging from ostracism to violence. Nevertheless, violations of the inmate code are commonplace in prison. Obviously, one cannot expect full compliance from those who disobey society's rules. Inmates may violate the inmate code in several ways, and Sykes and Messenger (1960) have constructed an inmate typology based on noncompliance. Note that the inmate code and the inmate typology rest heavily on exaggerated images of masculinity by promoting "macho" behavior and condemning weakness, including homosexuality.

The Inmate Typology

Sykes (1958) and Sykes and Messenger (1960) point out that there is no evidence that inmate values are embraced with equal intensity. As a result of various forms of noncompliance to the inmate code, different social roles emerge among inmates. Consequently, the interrelationship among these social roles contributes to the inmate social system. The following types or roles are expressed in prison argot. The first type exists as a model, or ideal type, by which inmates are measured, because it represents the highest level of conformity to the inmate code.

The Right Guy. Also known as the "real con" or the "real man," the right guy is the inmate who enthusiastically embraces the inmate code. He remains loyal to inmates and never lets others get him down no matter how difficult prison life becomes. The right guy is

Major Categories of the Inmate Code

1. Don't Interfere with Inmate Interests:
   Never rat on a con.
   Don't be nosey.
   Be loyal to your class—the cons.
2. Don't Lose your Head:
   Play it cool and do your own time.
3. Don't Exploit Inmates:
   Don't break your word.
   Don't steal from the cons.
   Don't sell favors.
   Don't be a racketeer.
   Don't welsh on debts.
4. Don't Weaken:
   Don't whine.
   Don't cop out (cry guilty).
   Don't suck around.
   Be tough, be a man.
5. Don't Be a Sucker:
   Be sharp.

(From Sykes and Messenger 1960)

dependable and always keeps his promises. As an ideal type, the right guy functions as the baseline character, or moral center, among inmates.

Rat or Squealer. The rat (also known as a snitch) provides inside information about other inmates to the staff, and, in doing so, is vehemently despised. As we shall see in later sections, the rat is often the victim of brutal revenge attacks by other inmates.

The Tough. The tough is a highly volatile and aggressive inmate who is always willing to fight, even over minor issues and sometimes without a reason at all.

The Gorilla. The gorilla is more predatory than the tough, and attempts to exploit other inmates by force.

The Merchant or Peddler. The merchant violates the inmate code by engaging in rackets by selling goods that are in short supply. He frequently participates in trickery and scams.

The Weakling or Weak Sister. The weakling is characterized by not being able to be tough and withstand the pressures of incarceration.

The Wolf, Fag, and Punk. This category draws distinctions among certain forms of homosexuality. The wolf seeks homosexual relations because of his inability to cope with the deprivation of heterosexual relations. The fag plays the passive role in a homosexual relationship because he "likes" it, or "wants" to, and the punk is coerced or bribed into a passive role.

The Rapo or the Innocent. Inmates who are always claiming their innocence or professing that they got a "bum rap" fall into this category. Such complaints grow tiresome to other inmates.

The Square John. The square john embraces outside values, not inmate values, and aligns himself closely with officialdom.

Conditions of Prisonization

Whereas all inmates are exposed to prisonization, not every inmate becomes prisonized. In fact, Clemmer (1958) noted that there are degrees of prisonization. Several factors determine the extent to which inmates are prisonized. For example, prisonization depends on personality; relationships with people outside prison; whether prisoners become affiliated with prison primary or semiprimary groups; being assigned to a work gang; and whether prisoners accept the dogma or codes of prison culture. Furthermore, age, criminality, nationality, race, and regional conditioning are also important.

Clemmer constructed the following list of factors that may compel an inmate to complete the prisonization process:

1. A sentence of many years; thus, a long subjection to the conditions that promote prisonization
2. A somewhat unstable personality made unstable by an inadequacy of "socialized" relations before commitment, but possessing nonetheless a capacity for strong convictions and a particular kind of loyalty
3. A dearth of positive relations with people outside the walls
4. A readiness and a capacity for integration into a group that emphasizes relations primarily with other prisoners
5. A blind (or almost blind) acceptance of the dogmas and mores of the primary group and the general penal population
6. A chance placement with others of a similar orientation
7. A readiness to participate in gambling and abnormal sexual behavior.

Two major models shape the debate on prisonization: the deprivation and the importation models. The deprivation model acknowledges the pains of imprisonment as presented by Gresham Sykes in the classic *Society of Captives* (1958), including the deprivation of liberty, the deprivation of goods and services, the deprivation of heterosexual relationships, the deprivation of autonomy, and the deprivation of security. By its very nature, prison deprives inmates of basic needs; that in turn creates frustration, pressure, and strain. Hence, prisonization serves to alleviate feelings of deprivation and the pains of imprisonment.

According to the importation model, however, the pressure created in prison has less to do with deprivations and more to do with the characteristics of inmates. Prisoners import ideas, attitudes, and behavior from their outside lives as street criminals into the prison. Though there is a debate as to whether prisonization can be attributed to deprivation or importation, the most reasonable perspective borrows from both models. Clearly, inmates both experience deprivation and also import their own characteristics into prison.

Prisonization may generate some positive effects, such as inmate solidarity. At the same time, however, it also produces negative effects by reinforcing convict attitudes, beliefs, and values. As a consequence of these negative effects, Clemmer (1958) equated prisonization with criminalization. Moreover, because prisonization leads to the rejection of conventional values, Clemmer argued that it also impedes reform and rehabilitation.

Research on Prisonization

The concept of prisonization, albeit a popular one, has been subject to extensive scrutiny by penologists. In sum, the critique of prisonization stems from three critical approaches (Hawkins 1976). The first line of criticism addresses Clemmer's assumption that the degree of prisonization is determined by the length of confinement; hence, the longer the sentence, the higher the degree of prisonization. The most significant finding that challenges this linear proposition was revealed by Stanton Wheeler (1961), who reported a curvilinear, or

U-shaped, pattern. That is, inmates experience a cyclical fluctuation during their incarceration, from holding conformist attitudes to antisocial attitudes, then returning to conformist attitudes upon nearing completion of their sentences. Since inmates are prisonized and deprisonized, the overall impact of the inmate subculture was found to be relatively short. These findings were supported by subsequent research by Garabedian (1963) and Glaser (1964).

The prisonization thesis also is criticized for failing to take into account that informal groups vary within the larger institution with respect to their characteristics, behavior, and functions. Moreover, the orientation of the institution itself contributes to these patterns of behavior. That is, treatment-oriented institutions tend to promote cooperation between informal leaders and prison staff, which in turn facilitates rehabilitation (Grusky 1959). Conversely, custodial prisons increase deprivations for inmates, thereby contributing to hostile, antisocial attitudes toward the prison staff (Berk 1966).

The final criticism of prisonization returns to the debate between deprivation and importation theories. It has been argued that what is understood as prisonization resulting from deprivation is actually a form of antisocial behavior that is deeply rooted in the inmate's criminal history. John Irwin and Donald Cressey (1962) note that what is often called inmate culture stems from beliefs, attitudes, and lifestyles imported from the outside. James Jacobs (1974) supported this position by illuminating the process by which street gangs import their organizational roles and ideologies into the penitentiary. It should be noted, though, that the prison environment serves to strengthen the subcultural identity among inmates. In sum, it is difficult to assume that the mere process of incarceration leads to what Clemmer describes as prisonization, because prisons vary according to orientation, size, and security level. Perhaps what best resembles prisonization in the classic sense, however, is the assimilation that occurs in repressive maximum-security penitentiaries.

Prisonization and Women's Prisons

Though early observations of prisonization emerged from research in men's prisons, it is important not to overlook the socialization patterns that occur in women's institutions. The social world in women's prisons resembles that of men's prisons insofar as women inmates also form close bonds with each other. Whereas men's institutions are characterized as harsh, coercive, and punitive environments, however, prisons for women tend to be less oppressive and, most important, less violent. Nevertheless, women, like men, also experience the debilitating effects of incarceration, the loss of freedom, and other deprivations—most notably, the lack of emotional support. Moreover, women are more likely to suffer the consequences of being separated from their children, which compounds the guilt, depression, and low self-esteem that women experience while imprisoned.

Because women's institutions differ from men's prisons, which are characteristically more violent and feature an underground drug market as well as various gang activities, the effects of prisonization are also different. For example, the subcultures that develop in men's prisons serve to protect against victimization by other inmates. In contrast, subcultures among women prisoners promote emotional support for each other.

One aspect of the women's subculture that is sometimes related to emotional support is homosexuality. In comparison to male prisoners, homosexuality among women inmates is more often consenting. In men's prisons, however, homosexuality tends to take the form of rape or commerce (prostitution), which reflects the dynamics of power in a coercive environment. By contrast, women tend to bond more closely to one another emotionally, and homosexuality generally reflects their need for intimate involvement.

As with men's prisons, institutions for women also feature social roles, argot, and an inmate code. Esther Heffernan (1972) identified three dominant social roles among female prisoners: the "square," the "cool," and the "life." They closely resemble Irwin and Cressey's typology (the "square," "thief," and "cool"). The "square" is typically a middle-class woman sentenced to prison for a first offense involving embezzlement or situational homicide. She does not have a criminal orientation and views herself as otherwise respectable. The "square" resists the effects of prisonization by identifying more with the staff than with fellow inmates. The "cool" straddles the line between prisonization and convention. She generally attempts to make her stay pleasurable while avoiding trouble. The "life" is a hardened criminal who overly identifies with the prison subculture by

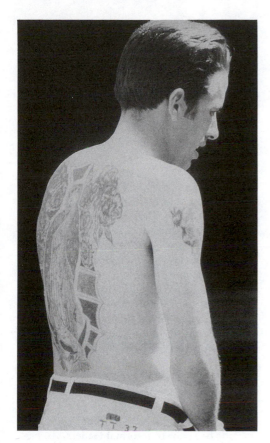

For many inmates, adaptation into the subculture means acquiring tattoos that often reflect one's values and identity. Photo by James A. Bolzaretti.

making it a way of life. She has a strong criminal orientation and frequently violates institutional regulations.

Female inmates may also assume the role of the politician (one who works well with the staff) or the outlaw (one who relies on violence or the threat of violence to get her way) (Simmons 1975). Women inmates may also become snitches, inmate cops, jive bitches, boosters, and several roles associated with homosexuality (Giallombardo 1966).

The primary features of the female inmates' social world are the pseudofamily and the complex network of friendships and homosexual liaisons that develop among the women. While men tend to form gangs, women in prison gravitate to social relationships that resemble families, cliques, or dyads. A pseudofamily is best characterized by a set of roles that include father and mother figures who care for their daughters. In some cases, an ex-

tended family may emerge, in which women assume the roles of grandparents, aunts, and uncles. The pseudofamily appears to draw on the stereotypical, idealized family, whose various roles are enthusiastically embraced. For example, the mother functions as a warm, caring, and nurturing family figure. The father figure will often display masculine characteristics by adopting a short hair style, men's clothing, and acting authoritatively. Some pseudofamilies, however, do not have a father figure and are structured around two women who live as partners. Perhaps even more common, though, are women who serve as a mother figure to several mostly younger female inmates (daughters) without an elaborate family structure or rigid role playing.

Institutional staff often recognize these families, and internal order is sometimes established by rewarding the mother figures for controlling problem inmates. For example, at the request of a staff member, an (inmate) mother may calm down an unruly (inmate) daughter. The degree of control or influence, however, depends on the level of commitment of a particular inmate to the pseudofamily. Inmates who have recently entered the prison are often highly committed to the pseudofamily. Furthermore, if the inmate has few family contacts outside of prison, or if she is serving a lengthy sentence, she is more likely to turn to the pseudofamily for support. The same holds true for those who are serving brief sentences, or have a lot of contact with family outside of prison. Moreover, the degree of commitment to a pseudofamily is further determined by the quality of family life the inmate experienced before incarceration. If the inmate had an abusive family life, she sometimes will seek a better experience in the form of a pseudofamily.

It is important to note that as women's prisons began to introduce more family programs, visits, and furloughs in the late 1970s and 1980s, the need for pseudofamilies was dramatically reduced. Today, many women's prisons encourage inmates to maintain strong family ties outside the institution. Consequently, their strong emotional needs are often met through these external ties.

Because the socialization process in women's prisons is modeled after the family, it is difficult to equate this form of prisonization with criminalization (although an exception to this would be the "life"). Clearly, the pseudofamily in women's prisons mitigates the pains of imprisonment in ways that are generally prosocial, not antisocial.

Policy and Programming
Policy and programming continue to be influenced by ideas concerning prisonization. Moreover, such intervention relies on formal as well as informal mechanisms of control. Although corrections administrators recognize the negative aspects of gang activities (violence, weapons, drugs, and other forms of contraband), they also acknowledge the positive aspects of gangs. Prison staff often co-opt gang leaders in an effort to maintain internal order. For instance, prison staff will encourage gang leaders to control unruly inmates in exchange for favors and privileges. Unfortunately, that type of exchange bolsters the power of gang leaders to the detriment of all. Subsequently, if gang leaders become too powerful and use their influence to challenge the prison staff, administrators often transfer them to another institution where they will yield considerably less power.

In terms of programming, a criticism expressed by correctional administrators is that gang members do not "program." That is, they do not enroll and participate in counseling and rehabilitation programs. The reason for this prohibition among gang members is that counseling is regarded as an individual activity, while the purpose of a gang is to convert imprisonment into a group experience. One exception, though, are programs that offer education. Many gangs value self-improvement such as reading and earning high school equivalency diplomas. Indeed, gang leaders often encourage members to help each other with study and other academic tasks.

Policy also extends to other aspects of programming, most notably attempts to prepare inmates to enter the community upon their release. Work release, educational release, furlough, and other programs take into consideration the negative effects of incarceration. These programs are based on the assumption that every inmate undergoes at least some negative transformation, even though the term prisonization is not always used to describe the process.

Summary
In sum, Clemmer's contribution to penology clearly has had a lasting impact on the field. Indeed, the concept of prisonization has been uncritically accepted by many prison experts.

Despite criticisms, many studies focusing on the effects of incarceration and institutional adjustment continue to rely on the notion of prisonization—whether the concept is stated or merely implied. Other components of prisonization and socialization, such as inmate codes, argot, and social roles, also remain vital subjects in penology.

Michael Welch

See also ARGOT

Bibliography
Berk, B. B. (1966). Organizational goals and inmate organization. *American Journal of Sociology* 71: 522–34.

Clemmer, D. (1958). *The Prison Society*. New York: Rinehart.

Garabedian, P. G. (1963). Social roles and processes of socialization in the prison community. *Social Problems* 11: 139–52.

Giallombardo, R. (1966). *Society of Women: A Study of Women's Prison*. New York: Wiley.

Glaser, D. (1964). *The Effectiveness of a Prison and Parole System*. New York: Bobbs-Merrill.

Grusky, O. (1959). Organizational goals and the behavior of informal leaders. *American Journal of Sociology* 65: 59–67.

Hawkins, G. (1976). *The Prison: Policy and Practice*. Chicago: University of Chicago Press.

Heffernan, E. (1972). *Making it in Prison: The Square, the Cool, and the Life*. New York: Wiley.

Irwin, J., and D. R. Cressey (1962). Thieves, convicts, and the inmate culture. *Social Problems* 10: 142–55.

Jacobs, J. (1974). Street gangs behind bars. *Social Problems* 21: 395–409.

Simmons, I. (1975). *Interaction and Leadership among Female Prisoners*. Unpublished dissertation. Ann Arbor, Mich.: University Microfilms.

Sykes, G. (1958). *The Society of Captives*. Princeton, N.J.: Princeton University Press.

Sykes, G., and S. L. Messenger (1960). The inmate social system. In R. A. Cloward et al,. eds. *Theoretical Studies in Social Organization of the Prison*. New York: Social Science Research Council.

Welch, M. (1995). *Corrections: A Critical Approach*. New York: McGraw-Hill.

Wheeler, S. (1961). Socialization in correctional communities. *American Sociological Review* 26: 697–712.

Privacy

The issue of privacy in prison raises many legal, social, and administrative concerns. Privacy was recognized as a right as early as 1890, and its place in the litany of human needs is readily apparent. Privacy has been variously defined as the right to one's personality, or the right to preserve one's human dignity, individuality, and self-determination.

The absence of privacy has been a cornerstone of the "total institution" structure of prisons. The prison is a place where, either by design or effect, human dignity is attacked, one's individuality is negated, and one retains limited avenues for self-determination. Human dignity is degraded when an inmate is regularly subjected to genital and anal searches or continuously subjected to surveillance and monitoring. One's individuality is negated when self-identity related possessions and clothes are denied or subjected to periodic search and seizure; clothes and "personal" items are standard issue and clearly marked as belonging to the institution. Self-determination is minimal in an environment where one cannot decide when to sleep or when to get up, what to eat or when to eat. One's name may be of less importance than one's assigned number, which serves to differentiate the inmate from perhaps thousands in the prison.

An inmate is seldom left alone either by officials or other inmates. In dormitories or cell blocks, noise levels can be intense, constant, and discordant from the many TV sets and radios. The inmate subculture includes high levels of violence, and thus the inmate is subject to harassment by other inmates, leading to a high probability of rape. As Goffman (1961) put the matter, "The boundary that the individual places between his being and the environment is invaded and the embodiments of self profaned."

The overcrowding of prisons and jails intensifies the lack of privacy. Multiple bunking has been instituted in cells originally designed for one person, and inmates have been stuffed into gymnasiums, television rooms, libraries, and hallways. Such prison overcrowding encourages the formation of cliques and gangs in each cell or dormitory and limits official observation, providing increased opportunity for old-timers to take advantage of newcomers, especially through sexual exploitation.

Early studies of mice and rats in crowded conditions demonstrated severe physiological and behavioral pathology. Research on inmates in crowded prisons has similarly shown an association between crowding and increased rates of disease, death, suicide, self-mutilation, inmate assaults, disciplinary infractions, and psychiatric commitments. The effects of overcrowding are related primarily to increased social density, which means increased loss of privacy.

An inmate, confronted with such lack of privacy, seeks to gain some semblance of control by creating a space, or "niche," within the larger prison. In "defense of the boundaries of self," an inmate may create a "space" by draping a towel or blanket (usually in violation of prison rules) from an upper bunk bed or from cell bars. Many will focus their prison activities toward eventually acquiring bunk space in smaller rooms or cells. Inmates may seek some relative privacy by requesting access to the prison chapel or law library. Others take solitary walks in the prison yard, or retreat into the space provided by earplugs or by earphones and loud music. The inmate culture may also create its own informal but enforced privacy rules, such as requiring that an inmate not look into another's cell while passing by or not entering another inmate's cell uninvited. As a last resort, some may actually seek out the protective isolation of disciplinary or administrative segregation. Unfortunately, that almost total seclusion may produce considerable psychological damage.

The following are some of the most important privacy-related issues in prisons.

Mixed-Gender Staffing

Many prison administrators have faced significant pressure to hire correctional officers of both genders, primarily to include women correctional officers in men's prisons in order to provide women equal opportunity to career advancement. Such requests have often been met with objections from some prison officials, who argue that the employment of both genders in a prison intrudes on the inmates' privacy. Critics of that idea suggest that the argument is a subterfuge for discrimination against the employment of women in maximum-security institutions.

The available research on the supervision of male prisoners by female officers suggests that some positive outcomes may occur, such as "normalizing" an environment in which male prisoners are less "macho" and better behaved, especially as male prisoners report a relatively low level of privacy invasion. Male supervision of female inmates is more problematic, as female prisoners typically adapt to institutions differently and demand more privacy and individuality than their male counterparts.

Mixed-Gender Observation

While many prison facilities continue to allow observation of inmates' genitals and bodily functions by officials of the opposite gender under normal prison conditions, a few states have prohibited such practice, as taking away the inmate's last "residuum of personal dignity." In practice, many facilities with mixed-gender staff have instituted special robes, sleepwear, modesty half-screens in showers, and privacy doors on toilet stalls.

Cell and Body Searches

The Supreme Court, in *Hudson v. Palmer* (1984), said that inmates have no privacy interests in their cell, leaving inmates with the unlikely recourse of seeking state tort damages if their property is destroyed or stolen by correctional officers. Body searches may entail greater invasions of privacy than cell searches. Even so, the courts have generally taken a "hands off" attitude toward such administrative decisions. For example, the courts have validated automatic body cavity searches of pretrial detainees after contact with their attorneys. Yet some privacy protections remain over how, and by whom, such searches may be performed. State courts have placed some limitations on the number of people observing the body search and have prohibited prison officials of the opposite gender from performing genital or anal searches on inmates in nonemergency situations.

Communications

Inmate conversations with others in the institution have never been considered private, and will become less so with the increasing used of electronic surveillance measures. While some measure of privacy is afforded inmates in their communication with attorneys, court personnel, and occasionally religious leaders, all other communication with people outside the institution is subject to official intrusion.

AIDS

One area of personal privacy recently recognized by the courts has been in response to the increase of AIDS and HIV among prison populations. While the courts have generally given prison officials discretion to segregate infected inmates, they have prohibited unauthorized disclosure of an inmate's AIDS status to prison staff or other inmates. This prohibition on disclosure has precluded indirect information disclosure, such as practices that placed inmates in special "hygiene suits" or marked their personnel files with special stickers. Similar restrictions have been placed on the unauthorized disclosure of other medical information.

Peter Gregware

See also LEGAL ISSUES

Bibliography

Alpert, G., and B. Crouch. 1991. Cross-gender supervision, personal privacy, and institutional security. *Criminal Justice and Behavior* 18: 304–17.

Cox, V., P. Paulus, and G. McCain (1984). Prison crowding research. *American Psychologist* 39: 1148–60.

Goffman, E. (1961). *Asylums*. New York: Doubleday.

Ibrahim, A. (1974). Deviant sexual behavior in men's prisons. *Crime and Delinquency* 20: 38–44.

Johnson, R. (1987). *Hard Time: Understanding and Reforming the Prison*. Monterey, Calif.: Brooks/Cole.

Schaeffer, M., A. Baum, P. Paulus, and G. Gaes (1988). Architecturally mediated effects of social density in prison. *Environment and Behavior* 20: 3–19.

Small, M., and M. Scalora (1991). Assessing mental injury claims arising from privacy invasions. *Forensic Reports* 4: 337–52.

Private Prisons

In the 1970s, America declared a "war on crime." A "war on drugs" followed in the early 1980s. These policies led to a dramatic increase in the size of the prison population. During the decade between 1980 to 1990 the number of inmates in state and federal prisons grew from 315,947 to 738,894 (an increase of 133.9 percent), and the incarceration rate (prisoners per 100,000 population) increased from 139 to 292. In 1992 the prisoner population reached

885,593 and the incarceration rate 329. Currently, the U.S. incarcerates the highest number of people per capita in the world. As a result, the cost of incarceration has skyrocketed. In 1984, total state expenditures on correctional institutions was about $6 billion; in 1990 they were approaching $20 billion, an increase of 223 percent.

The large scale and rapid increase in incarceration resulted in prison crowding and serious financial problems. In 1988, thirty-nine states were under some kind of court order to limit their prison population unless they could increase their prison capacity. Often these orders brought an early release of inmates, a practice that clearly runs contrary to the prevalent "get tough" crime policies. In that situation there was a need to seek out alternative solutions to the problem. One that received considerable attention was prison privatization. In the early 1980s, thirty-eight states in the U.S. had some kind of contract with private companies to supply various correctional services. This trend coincided with President Reagan's administrative attempts to privatize many public services that traditionally were the sole responsibility of the government. These policies were supported by the American tradition of distrust of government and the strong belief in the efficiency of private enterprise.

In the early 1980s, private corporations started to operate entire prisons. In 1991, a census of private prisons in the U.S. indicated that forty-four correctional facilities were operated by fourteen companies, housing about 13,400 inmates (Thomas and Foard 1991). Two of those companies operated 50 percent of the private institutions; the other twelve operated one to three facilities each. There are several issues involved in the privatization of prisons, including conceptual, legal, contract-related economics, quality, and personnel issues.

Historical Background

Private involvement in the administration of punishment is not a new phenomenon in Western, especially English-American, tradition. In England, jails were operated by private entrepreneurs during the Middle Ages. Beginning in the thirteenth century, the crown gave the right to private citizens to manage jails in order to relieve itself of the responsibility. In some cases the right was sold, in other cases it was bestowed upon minor royal servants in lieu of a pension. The jailers made their living by extracting fees from prisoners for various services. Eighteenth-century records show that often special accommodations, including wine and women, were provided for those who could afford it. Most of the income came from selling beer, liquor, and tobacco to the inmates. Those who could not afford to pay had to work for the jail keepers, who often hired them out to work for others. In addition, payment for the incarceration of poor prisoners was made by the magistrates. Those payments were considerably below those paid by the well-to-do inmates. It was known to the authorities that the system was liable to abuse, but they accepted it because of its practicality. This practice created great differences between the treatment of those prisoners who could pay for services and those who could not.

The lucrativeness of operating jails was known, and in many instances, the office was subject to sale and purchase. Some families were involved in the occupation for generations. The abuses of this system were evident. The famous eighteenth-century penal reformer John Howard demanded the abolition of private fees in jails and government payments for the jailers. The fee system was abolished toward the end of the eighteenth century.

In America during the Colonial period, local jails were used mainly for detention and only on rare occasions held convicted prisoners. Generally, the jails were crowded and in poor condition. Escapes were frequent. The jailers were paid by the counties, but corruption was widespread, and many jailers embezzled public funds, extracted bribes from prisoners, sold whiskey to them, and physically abused them.

Penitentiaries

Toward the end of the eighteenth century, the penitentiary was born in the United States. Soon two competing types emerged. The Pennsylvania system was based on solitary confinement. Later, labor was introduced to the solitary cells, primarily to provide inmates with something to do. Prisoners were credited with "fair pay" and debited for their upkeep. In 1819 the Auburn (New York) penitentiary was opened. In that institution prisoners slept in separate cells, but during the day they worked and ate together under a strict rule of silence. Auburn soon became the leading model for prisons in America. One of its major attractions was that it lent itself to modern industrial production. Thus, the modern prison that developed during the industrial revolution fit into the system of mass production, which in turn provided ample opportunity for private involvement in prison industry.

It was not uncommon for manufacturers in the 1800s to contract with the prison for industrial production. The manufacturers supplied the materials, supervised the work, and paid for the finished goods. The Auburn penitentiary, for example, was not only self-supporting financially, but was even producing surplus revenue for the government. In some prisons, inmates were hired out to work outside the institution for private contractors. These arrangements gained widescale official and public support because many believed that in this way offenders could be punished, the community could be protected, potential offenders could be deterred, and all these results would come about without financial burden for the government. The entrepreneurs often made themselves a handsome profit. The contract system was the most widespread practice. In some prisons the industrial production was contracted out to several contractors, limiting the influence of any one of them. The contractors could interact with prisoners only to instruct them on the job.

The lease system, in which a private contractor operated the whole prison, was adopted in some states, mainly in the expanding frontier areas. The first such arrangement is traced to the state prison in Frankfort, Kentucky. In 1825, Kentucky, in a financial crisis, leased the prison to a businessman for five years for an annual rate of one thousand dollars. In several states, inmates were leased by private contractors to work outside the prison. Often these convicts were treated brutally; many of them escaped.

After the Civil War there was a great impetus in the South to expand leasing, because of the need to replace the liberated slaves with a cheap labor force with which to rebuild the devastated economy. The majority of Southern prisoners were black, and they were often kept by the private lessees in worse conditions than the slaves had been. This practice was discontinued at the end of the nineteenth century during an economic depression, when few contractors were ready to lease convicts.

Conceptual and Legal Issues

Punishment is a legally imposed deprivation or suffering. A core question concerning privatization is whether a private entity should profit from the punishment of lawbreakers. Support-

ers of privatization make a distinction between the sentencing of those who are found guilty in committing a crime and the actual administration of punishment.

Accordingly, the claim is made that the punishment remains under governmental authority, which supervises execution by a private party. In regard to the constitutionality of this arrangement, the federal courts have allowed the delegation of power to private contractors. The issue is more a concern of the states, because about 92 percent of inmates are in state prisons. State laws on the delegation of power, however, are confusing. Several states have therefore legislated laws that authorize the delegation of correctional functions to private parties.

One of the concerns is that, while formally the private company operating the prison is only administering the sentence and should not influence it, informally it does have an impact on the punishment, by setting and enforcing minor institutional rules. While disciplinary hearings are conducted by governmental personnel, the disciplinary write-ups by employees of private companies may influence the conditions of confinement and even the date of release, by determining the "good time" earned by inmates.

Similarly, reports and evaluations of institutional behavior prepared by the staff may influence parole decisions. There is also the potential problem raised by critics that private companies have a financial interest in keeping the prison full at all times; therefore, they might overstate negative disciplinary reports when there is a decline in the prison population. So far, however, there had been no evidence of that during the 1980s and 1990s, when the prison population was growing rapidly.

Legal Liability

Legally, the government is responsible for what is happening in the prison. A private company's executive has stated this vividly: "The state can contract out duties, but it cannot contract away responsibility" (Fenton 1985, 44). Many state agencies would be ready to delegate legal liability to private companies, together with the management of the prison. As it stands, however, while the government does not have full control over the operations of private prisons, it does carry the ultimate liability. In that respect the government serves as a "safety net" for the private contractors. The issue is important in light of the large number of civil rights suits brought by inmates against the prison system. The fact that the government carries the ultimate liability may provide more security for the inmates in private prisons, because the company is liable to the government and thus in turn is liable before the courts (Logan 1990). This underlines the importance of the contract between the government and the private company and the effectiveness of its monitoring, as a safeguard against potential legal and financial problems for the state.

Issues of Contract and Monitoring

Contracting for the operation of prisons with private companies follows the contracting out of various governmental services such as garbage collection, data processing, building, and automobile maintenance. There are various services in many prisons that are contracted out (laundry, medical services, vocational and educational training, and so forth). The privatization of management of entire prisons, however, is qualitatively different from the provision of certain specific services.

A clearly written contract is a key element in the success of private prison operations. One issue is the term of the contract. Contracts are usually written for one to three years, in order not to commit money for the next budget period, to enable the government to change contractors, or to make changes in the contract. Short-term contracts are problematic for the contractors, because it is difficult to plan for such a short period.

The companies have an interest in long-term contracts, because of the up-front investments involved in privatization. A longer contract may be beneficial for the government as well, because changing contractors may involve a serious administrative and financial burden. The longer contract may also induce contractors to make more improvements to facilities or programs. And a longer contract may prevent bad publicity arising from frequent changes. Sometimes, changing contractors may be difficult because there are not many private prison companies available, and the government may not be in a position to take over prison operations after it becomes dependent on private providers. Thus, the advantages and disadvantages of both the short- and the long-term contracts have to be weighed when contracting is considered. The contract has to be flexible enough that its early termination is possible by either side if a valid and legitimate reason arises.

Monitoring Private Contracts and Facilities

Effective monitoring of prisons, private and public alike, is important. Prisons are not visible institutions, and the public rarely gets a glimpse of them except on occasions of unusual violence such as escapes or riots. There is a need to ensure that prisons follow operational guidelines not only because of the legal responsibility of the government, but also because in a democratic society inmates must be treated decently and according to the law. In addition, monitoring must make sure that private contractors operate in compliance with the contract.

Rigorous monitoring of private prisons may be expensive, because governmental agents must be on the premises. Also, the contracting agency may find little interest in monitoring, because the agency itself selected the firm and it may receive bad publicity if improprieties are discovered. On the other hand, the monitors may have little incentive to demand conditions beyond the minimum legal standards.

One possible way to make monitoring easier is to include in the contract incentives for positive performance in the form of bonuses or fines. It is likely that private contractors would respond to financial incentives.

An underlying concern of correctional privatization, that has implications for monitoring as well, is the entrenchment of correctional firms (Gentry 1986). To exercise effective monitoring, it is essential that the government have a backup ability and not be at the mercy of a handful of companies only. Therefore, it would be important that a free market evolve with the emergence of more private companies competing for the prison business. That would allow authorities to switch from one company to another if they are not satisfied with the services, or if they can find a less costly provider.

Another potential problem relates to the division of authority between the management of the private prison and the officials in charge of monitoring. "Unless care is taken to define the respective roles of public and private managers, two organizations are responsible, but neither may be clearly accountable" (Mullin et al. 1985, 75).

This kind of monitoring may confuse the chain of command in the prison, since lower-level state officials placed in the institution will have to approve decisions made by private executives and managers. "In the summary of this issue it is important to state that:

To a large extent, the effectiveness of monitors . . . will depend upon the levels of sanctions that they can ultimately mobilize and the degree of critical autonomy that they can maintain from the organization being monitored" (Matthews 1989, 4).

Economic Issues

The major attraction of private prisons is economic. The claim is that private prisons can do the same job public prisons do, but less expensively. This can be accomplished, according to supporters, by the introduction of sophisticated private management techniques, more productive staff deployment and staff reduction (because they are not restricted by civil service regulations and union contracts), and by more effective and flexible procurement, which can cut expenses considerably. These companies can not only operate less expensively, they can also construct facilities faster and less expensively than government agencies can.

So far, there have been conflicting reports regarding the cost comparisons between public and private prisons. Some estimates indicate that private facilities are more cost effective, while others claim that private institutions are more expensive because of hidden costs that are hard to calculate. There are also those who find the cost comparisons inconclusive.

Cost estimates for government-run prisons are usually understated, because the operation often benefits from the services of other agencies. For example, education departments may run classes and government hospitals may care for sick prisoners. There may be hidden costs for the government in the operation of private prisons as well. Those may include monitoring expenses; legal work involved in the preparation of contracts; costs that may accrue in unusual circumstances, such as the bankruptcy of private prison companies; maintenance of public services used in emergencies, such as in riots, fires, and natural disasters; and tax benefits given to companies and their investors. The major areas of cost comparisons are construction financing, the construction itself, and prison operations.

Construction Financing

In many states, the traditional method to raise money for prison construction is to issue bonds upon the voters' approval. During the 1980s, in the midst of an economic boom, the public tended to approve bond proposals. With the downturn of the economy, some proposals were turned down. In certain states, because of the legal debt ceiling the government could not take on any more financial obligations.

Private corporations may raise money through private sources. Often, the government and the private firm enter into a lease-purchase agreement according to which the governmental agency becomes a tenant in a facility owned by the company. At the end of an agreed-upon period, the ownership is transferred to the government. Payments under this arrangement are considered a part of the operating cost, thus the debt ceiling is not applicable. A major advantage of this arrangement is that the funds are raised much faster than through conventional methods. Private financing is usually costlier than public financing, because the government in general can obtain loans at lower interest rates than private companies can. This has to be included in the cost analysis.

Construction of Facilities

Private firms claim that they can site and build prisons faster and less expensively than the government does. The largest private company, Corrections Corporation of America (CCA), states that its construction price is only 80 percent of the government's cost (Logan 1990). Generally, it takes between two and three years to site and build a prison (maximum-security prisons may take five years). Some contractors, however, have designed, financed, and built a facility in six months (Logan 1990). Comparisons should be made on the same kind of institution. Also, the quality of construction is important. New materials and new methods of building should be carefully evaluated (Sechrest et al. 1987).

Prison Operations

According to the private companies, they can deliver the same services less expensively than the government does through "the side-stepping of government bureaucracy in building and operating prisons, better staff motivation, the utilization of modern management techniques, and increased flexibility in the hiring and firing of employees" (Borna 1986, 328).

Labor Costs

Corrections is a labor intensive industry. Between 60 and 80 percent of the cost is labor related. In order to operate prisons less expensively than the government does, and to make profit on them, private companies must cut their labor costs. They do so in various ways: paying lower salaries, providing fewer fringe benefits, limiting promotions, reducing staff, and providing less training.

Advocates of privatization claim that labor cost-cutting is achieved mainly through flexible staffing, using more electronic surveillance, and substituting profit sharing for fringe benefits (Crants 1991). Critics, on the other hand, believe that labor cost-cutting may result in reduced safety and security in prisons. Also, staffing formulas are often fixed in the correctional standards and labor contracts, making them hard to change.

It has also been suggested that differences in the managerial approach between the public and the private sectors affect prison costs: "Profit-and-loss incentives differ fundamentally from budget-driven bureaucratic incentives. Entrepreneurs are competitively motivated to provide maximum satisfaction at minimum cost. In contrast, bureaucrats are rewarded not so much for efficiency, but in direct proportion to the size and total budget of their agencies" (Logan 1990, 86).

Flexibility

Private companies are more flexible and can take advantage of more opportunities to cut costs than can public agencies. They can purchase supplies from any business that offers the best price. Their purchasing does not have to go through complex bureaucratic channels, and they are not bound by contracts with specific suppliers, as governmental agencies are. Using their centralized purchasing power, they can buy supplies nationwide and look for the best prices.

The public sector is known to be wasteful. For example, surplus money remaining in public institutions at the end of the budget year must be spent. If there are savings, the next year's budget may be smaller. Thus, prudent money management is penalized rather than rewarded. Consequently, there is no incentive for cost control. Private companies do have an interest in cutting expenses, because every dollar saved increases their profit. It is not ensured, however, that any part of the savings will be transferred to the government. There is also the question of whether substantial cost-cutting would lower the quality of incarceration.

Per-Diem Payments

The most often used formula of payment for correctional services is a specified sum per day.

One concern is that private firms will have an interest in keeping the prisons filled to capacity in order to receive maximum payments. That could result in lobbying efforts to promote policies of imprisonment and to abandon programs aimed at early release (Anderson et al. 1985).

The government must guarantee a certain occupancy level, below which the per diem rate goes up in order to provide the contractor with a "safety net" against losses. The addition of each inmate in private prisons adds the same amount to the expenses. In public prisons, however, the addition of an inmate will increase the total cost only marginally and can decrease the per capita cost. This may be a factor in the overcrowding of public prisons.

Quality of Service

Private companies contend not only that they can operate prisons less expensively than governmental agencies do, but that at the same time they can provide better quality of service. In the context of prisons, some refer to quality of service in terms of the quality and quantity of food, the variety of programs, and the professional background of staff. Others use indicators such as the condition of the buildings, escape rates, security and control procedures, the physical and mental health of the inmates, and the extent of recidivism.

The few available studies aimed at exploring the quality of services in private prisons seem to agree that the services are either at the same level as, or better than, those in public facilities. It will have to be seen whether this pattern will continue when larger and higher security institutions are privatized.

There is a need for continuous scrutiny of all penal institutions. In private prisons, it is a concern that the profit motive not override other considerations in the operation of the facility. Cutting costs, whether or not it results in the decline of quality, provides an opportunity to increase corporate profits, and it may be too tempting for some firms not to follow this policy.

Rehabilitation of offenders can be considered as a matter of quality of service, both for the inmates, in helping them to become a part of mainstream society, and for the community, as a way of correcting antisocial behavior. This emphasis on rehabilitation as a major goal of corrections has declined sharply since the early 1970s, but the public's desire for some efforts to rehabilitate offenders still exists. As mentioned, private companies do not have an incentive to implement successful rehabilitation programs. In fact, it may be a disadvantage for them, as the programs could lead to earlier release of inmates and sometimes to a loss of income. A clear set of criteria for rehabilitation included in the contract and tied to the amount of profits that the company can make could have some positive results in this matter.

Management and Personnel Issues

Corrections is labor intensive. Therefore, staff-inmate ratios and staff training have an important role in determining the cost of incarceration and the quality of services. Employees influence the quality of life in a prison through the level of order maintained. The training and personal characteristics of the staff are important to the general atmosphere in prison.

A considerable number of private prison workers are recruited from the unskilled labor force, and many of them work only part-time (Weiss 1989). Some of them are retired state correctional officers and retired military personnel. Private correctional workers often have fewer professional qualifications than public prison staff. For example, it was found in a California study that a private company that operated work furlough projects, community correctional programs, and INS detention facilities required no formal training from its line employees and paid the minimum wage to its new workers.

While that is not necessarily the case with every private company, there seems to be a pattern of lower pay, fewer benefits, and lower staffing formulas than in public prisons. Critics question whether well-qualified staff can be hired for such low pay. Private companies claim that they follow the correctional standards set by the American Correctional Association (ACA). Others suggest that certain private companies provide better and more effective training for their workers than public agencies do (Crants 1991). It is also claimed that effective personnel management can cut operating costs without cutting salaries. "Adequate and appropriate staffing, better working conditions, and more efficient procedures improve productivity and morale, decrease absenteeism and turnover and reduce expensive reliance on overtime" (Logan 1990, 81).

Alan M. Schuman, director of the Social Service Division in the superior court of the District of Columbia, points out that lower wages and fewer fringe benefits in private prisons lead to the hiring of less qualified personnel and a high turnover rate. "Many of the best qualified private sector staff eventually apply for public sector probation positions that offer more job security and higher salaries. The high turnover rate must impact the quality of services that are provided; a factor that should be considered in cost analysis" (Schuman 1989, 32).

To alleviate staff problems, some companies, like the CCA, provide a stock option plan for "key employees" that usually does not include custodial personnel. There is also an Employee Stock Ownership Plan for all employees. Such plans are devised to substitute for the fringe benefits that are not provided by the companies. The effects of these programs will have to be evaluated.

Studies of Private Prisons

There have been relatively few studies of private prisons. The Silverdale facility in Tennessee, operated by the CCA, has been evaluated several times. Logan and McGriff (1989) compared the operational cost of that institution with the estimated cost if it were operated by the same agencies that ran the facility before privatization. An annual savings of at least 3 to 8 percent was shown. The authors claimed also that the services were better under private management, mainly because there were two full-time managers instead of one—the warden and the government monitor.

Another study of the same facility focused on the inmates' perceptions of the quality of services (Brakel 1988). Generally, inmates gave more positive than ambivalent or negative ratings to the services in the private facility. There were negative ratings concerning recreational opportunities and release procedures. Release procedures and good time credits, however, were handled by public authorities and not by the CCA. Six inmates were able to compare the prevailing situation in Silverdale with the conditions when it was operated by the county. Out of twenty-eight comparisons, twenty-four were favorable to private and four to county administration. This study had some major methodological problems. The most obvious was that the questionnaires were distributed by the prison chaplain to inmates in a manner that was "random in all respects except that they [inmates] were known by him to be reasonably articulate" (Brakel 1988, 180). This procedure hardly can be considered unbiased, random, and scientific.

Another study compared three private facilities (one of them Silverdale) with three public institutions. One of the comparisons was made between two secure juvenile institutions (Sellers 1989). The researcher had made three on-site visits and had interviewed administrators and staff members. The main findings of this study showed that in private facilities more programs were generally available to the inmates than in public ones, and that the cost in private institutions was substantially lower than in public facilities, mainly because the latter had higher staff-inmate ratios. The study concluded that the main motive for prison privatization is financial. It was recognized that some firms may deliberately submit low bids in order to obtain contracts (low-balling). For the long run, however, it was projected that eventually the competition among contractors will keep costs down. Another positive effect of privatization suggested by this evaluation was that its efforts have created more options for the public sector.

The fact that several studies focused on the Silverdale facility raises the question whether there is anything unique about this institution. It is noteworthy that these studies fail to mention that in 1986 there was a riot in this facility. The inmates demanded better food, more adequate recreation, and generally better treatment. A police SWAT team was called in to restore order.

The Urban Institute has conducted an evaluation of two private facilities, one in Kentucky and the other in Massachusetts, and compared them with two public institutions in the same states. In Kentucky, two minimum security prisons were compared. The private prison scored higher in the quality of programs and the delivery of services. The per diem cost in the private facility was 10 percent higher, but if the construction costs had been included the public prison would have cost 28 percent more. In Massachusetts, two secure juvenile institutions were compared. The quality of services was somewhat better in the private one, but there were no significant differences in the cost (Hatry et al. 1989).

Two other evaluations were reviewed by Thomas and Logan in a paper presented to the American Society of Criminology at its 1991 meeting. One of them compared the quality of incarceration in a privately operated female prison in New Mexico with the same prison a year earlier, when it was operated by the state,

and with a federal women's prison. The study found that the private prison outperformed the state and federal institutions in six out of eight measures of quality. In a separate analysis, however, it was found that, while the staff survey and the official records showed a higher quality of confinement in the private prison, inmates favored the conditions in the state prison. This divergence of opinions should be examined further. In terms of expense, the private facility cost 12.8 percent less than the state prison.

The Texas State Auditor's office issued a report in 1991 on four five-hundred-bed prisons contracted out to two private firms. The report indicated that private companies operate facilities 10 to 15 percent less expensively than the State Department of Corrections could.

There is a need for more studies to assess the consequences of prison privatization. The Government Accounting Office has concluded that private prisons have not yet been shown to have a substantial advantage over public prisons and, therefore, it did not make a recommendation for the privatization of prisons in the federal system.

Conclusions

The major push toward privatization of prisons came with the unprecedented growth of the inmate population during the 1980s, in the wake of the "get tough" crime control policies and the great increase in the cost of criminal justice.

This development should be seen in the framework of the American tradition that favors small government and free competition. There is a widely held public opinion that private sector management is more efficient than public sector management and that workers in private organizations work harder, are more motivated, and do a better job than workers in the public sector. The terms "bureaucracy" and "bureaucrat" have come to epitomize society's negative attitude toward governmental organizations and their employees.

Similar attitudes are held toward prisons, which often show a poor record in terms of violence, riots, waste, and abuse of prisoners. Along with the lure of cost savings, they contribute to the support for private prisons. Prisons are expected to protect society by keeping violent and harmful inmates incarcerated, but at the same time they must house them safely. The public perception of inefficient management, violence, lack of rehabilitation, physical deterioration, and inept staff, coupled with growing cost, results in a negative attitude about prisons. Many feel that "the situation cannot become worse" and that "it is worth it to try anything" to improve prison conditions. These attitudes provide fertile ground for the privatization of prisons, an idea that not only promises lower costs but also better services.

There are, however, some pitfalls with this policy. Privatization tends to support the crime control policies of the 1980s. It promotes the idea that massive incarceration can win the "war on crime" and that the major task is to make incarceration less expensive and more flexible. It also diverts attention from alternatives to the growing trend of incarceration. On the other hand, the idea of prison privatization has helped to focus on the problems of public prisons and on needed reforms both in those institutions and the correctional system as a whole. A continuous effort to introduce more effective methods of operation and more flexible administration, with the cooperation of employee unions, could help to alleviate some of the problems of public prisons.

As noted, punishment is largely a moral issue. It involves judgments of what is right and what is wrong. In the debate about privatization, however, there is an overemphasis on pragmatic considerations, mainly cost, and a considerable neglect of ethical and theoretical issues. There is already a great deal of private involvement in the penal process and in corrections. The key question is where should the line be drawn in privatization? One opinion is that the operation of entire prisons should not be delegated to private entities because the administration of punishment is inherently a public function. An opposing opinion holds that while the determination of punishment has to be made by public authorities, its administration can be delegated to private parties, who may do a better job in terms of cost and even in terms of quality.

In a social climate of increasing public concern about violent crime and such legislation as "three strikes, you're out," there is a strong likelihood that the prison population will continue to increase, and that that will fuel the development of privately operated prisons.

David Shichor

Bibliography

Anderson, P., C. R. Cavoli, and L. J. Moriarity (1985). Private corrections: Feast or fiasco? *Prison Journal* 45(2): 32–41.

Borna, S. (1986). Free enterprise goes to prison. *British Journal of Criminology* 26(4): 321–34.

Brakel, S. J. (1988). Prison management, private enterprise style: The inmate's evaluation. *New England Journal of Criminal and Civil Confinement* 14(2): 175–244.

Crants, R. (1991). Private prison management: A study in economic efficiency. *Journal of Contemporary Criminal Justice* 7(1): 49–59.

Fenton, J. (1985). A private alternative to public prisons. *Prison Journal* 65(2): 42–47.

Gentry, J. T. (1986). The Panopticon revisited: The problem of monitoring private prisons. *Yale Law Journal* 96: 353–75.

Hatry, H. P., P. J. Brounstein, R. B. Levinson, D. M. Altschuler, K. Chi, and P. Rosenberg (1989). *Comparison of Privately and Publicly Operated Corrections Facilities in Kentucky and Massachusetts.* Washington, D.C.: Urban Institute.

Logan, C. H. (1990). *Private Prisons: Cons and Pros.* New York: Oxford University Press.

Logan, C. H., and B. W. McGriff (1989). *Comparing Costs of Public and Private Prisons: A Case Study.* Washington, D.C.: National Institute of Justice.

Matthews, R. (1989). Privatization in perspective. In R. Matthews, ed. *Privatizing Criminal Justice.* London: Sage.

Mullen, J., K. J. Chabotar, and D. M. Carrow (1985). *The Privatization of Corrections.* Washington, D.C.: National Institute of Justice.

Schuman, A. M. (1989). The cost of correctional services: Exploring a poorly charted terrain. *Research in Corrections* 2: 27–33.

Sechrest, D. K., N. Papas, and S. J. Price (1987). Building prisons: Pre-manufactured, prefabricated, and prototype. *Federal Probation* 51(1): 35–41.

Sellers, M. P. (1989). Private and public prisons: A comparison of costs, programs, and facilities. *International Journal of Offender Therapy and Comparative Criminology* 33: 241–56.

Thomas, C. W., and S. L. Foard (1991). *Private Correctional Facility Census.* Gainesville, Fla.: Center for Studies in Criminology and Law, University of Florida.

Weiss, R. P. (1989). Private prisons and the state. In R. Matthews, ed. *Privatizing Criminal Justice.* London: Sage.

Protective Custody

The use of protective custody (PC) is one of the ways prison administrators attempt to isolate and protect those inmates most likely to be victimized. Protective custody is a restricted housing area that usually is made up of maximum-security single cells located within the larger prison setting. In most cases, there are only a limited number of cells available. PC is often referred to as a "prison within a prison."

While in most cases protective custody must be requested by the inmate, jurisdictions vary in their policies for granting such assignments. In a survey of the states, 37 percent responded that they grant most PC requests, although it is difficult to judge what proportion of expressed fears are truly valid (Pierson 1988). Inmate requests come from those with known enemies, sex targets, informants or "snitches," those with gambling debts, and inmates whose low intelligence and poor social skills make them vulnerable in the general population. Drug trafficking and gang activity also increase requests for assignments in protection.

A number of states require inmates to provide some factual basis for their PC request, such as the types of threats they have received, the names of aggressors, and details concerning the circumstances. Computer-based data systems should allow staff to verify the location of known enemies or cases in which one inmate testified or gave information against another. In most instances, an inmate will be placed in PC if there is reason to believe that there is life-threatening danger. A formal hearing may be held before a committee and a report filed. Periodic reviews are held on all inmates in PC so that those appropriate for reassignment may be moved out.

The use of protective custody housing is problematic for administrators. While they may be held liable for injuries to an inmate who is denied protection, the courts have also made it clear that protective custody status cannot result in lower quality treatment, as it might in a punishment status (solitary confinement or administrative segregation). Recent litigation trends are to require costly single cells for PC and to ensure that the privileges, services, and work opportunities of PC inmates are equivalent to those of the general population. There is also concern about the psychological harm of living in isolation for long periods of time, dependent upon protection and being constantly reminded of one's fears of the general population. Inmates who leave PC also suffer from the stigma of having been there, if other inmates find out where they have been.

Many large state prison systems and the federal system attempt to transfer inmates at risk of harm to other wings or other facilities first, where they may not be in any danger. With few exceptions, most states have a greater number of protection-based transfers than assignments to protective custody wings. Smaller states, however, with only a few facilities, do not have such options. In one case, a federal court ordered a state to place an inmate in federal custody because they could not ensure his safety anywhere within the state system (*Walker v. Lockhart*).

Assignments to protective custody do not guarantee an inmate complete safety. On occasion, gangs have attempted to place a member in PC under false pretenses in order to conduct an execution or retaliatory attack.

Current trends in prison architecture have featured smaller pods or housing units that are self-contained, allowing almost all routine activities to take place without the inmate's having to leave the secured area. Inmates order commissary items that are delivered to the cell. Hot carts deliver warm meals efficiently, and access to visiting areas does not involve routes through highly trafficked areas of the prison. This means that many maximum-security areas can accommodate inmates seeking protection, although the goal would eventually be to reintegrate as many inmates as possible into lower, less labor-intensive security.

Charles B. Fields

See also ADMINISTRATIVE SEGREGATION

Bibliography

Henderson, J. D. (1992). Managing protective custody units. *Federal Prisons Journal* 3(2): 43–47

Lockwood, D. (1977). Living in protection. In H. Toch, ed. *Living in Prison: The Ecology of Survival*. New York: Free Press.

Pierson, T. A. (1988). Use of protective custody: How different systems respond. *Corrections Today* 50(4):150, 152, 154.

Seymour, J. (1977). Niches in prison. In H. Toch, ed. *Living in Prison: The Ecology of Survival*. New York: Free Press.

Seymour, J. (1982). Environmental sanctuaries for susceptible prisoners. In R. Johnson and H. Toch, eds. *The Pains of Imprisonment*. Beverly Hills, Calif.: Sage.

Cases
Walker v. Lockhart, 713 F.2d 1378 (8th Cir. 1983)

Public Information Office and Public Relations

The Public Information Office or Officer (PIO) in corrections serves two broad functions. First, the PIO is the primary information channel between corrections and taxpayers (often through the news media), the legislature, other professional organizations, other criminal justice agencies, inmates' families, and staff members' families. Corrections public information must be accountable to and must accommodate the information needs of each of these groups.

The second function, equally important, is to satisfy the public relations needs of the correctional agency itself. Correctional administrators have recognized the need to educate, even persuade, the public, the news media, and the legislature about correctional needs, philosophy, and practices. The corrections PIO provides an effective mechanism for accomplishing both these functions.

In spite of the pivotal role that the PIO plays in today's prison system, the development of public information policy and practices is relatively new in the long history of corrections. In the pre–*Cooper v. Pate* days, the courts as well as the public and news media maintained a "hands off" policy. The fortress concept of corrections consisted of more than high walls, razor wire, and pickets set in nearly unreachable rural areas. The concept extended to its philosophy and the mentality of its personnel. Providing information to the public was not a consideration. In fact, to do so would have been interpreted as a threat to security. Even the progressive *Task Force Report: Corrections* (1967) by the President's Commission on Law Enforcement and Administration of Justice made no reference to public information or to public relations for corrections.

In the late 1960s and 1970s, however, the courts decisively penetrated the correctional fortress. Correctional administrators found themselves forced to supply information, not only to the court, but also to a demanding legislature and a voracious public. The news media even insisted that the First Amendment guaranteed them access to information. Many correctional administrators, used to operating in semiseclusion, reacted defensively to these demands and resisted supplying information unless doing so was court mandated. A myriad of correctional rules and regulations helped administrators evade requests from the news media. It is not surprising that correctional administrators with little previous exposure to the news media and no training in public information regarded the press as an adversary and were fearful of providing information to the public.

Experts saw the situation differently. District Judge Marvin Frankel, in *Sobell v. Reed*, ruled in 1971 that "whatever may once have been the case, it is not doubtful now that the Constitution and notably the First Amendment reaches inside prison walls." One of the leading correctional authors of the time, Vernon Fox (1972), urged a proactive position with the news media. "In no case can the administrator afford to offend the news media. . . . The administrator who discusses his problems and limitations openly, together with an explanation of his objectives will get help from the news media" (1972, 367).

The urgent need for public relations became evident in the 1960s and 1970s. With the civil rights revolution, correctional administrators were desperately seeking additional legislative support and funding to comply with court orders. But, simultaneously, the news media were bombarding the public with negative and in some cases horrifying stories about prison conditions. Predictably, in the absence of a balanced perspective, corrections lost much public support. Legislators found themselves caught between reelection and the need to increase taxation to fund much-needed prison improvements.

Some correctional administrators begin to see the applicability of public relations to corrections. The power of organized promotion had been evident, through the welfare work and sale of war bonds in the First World War, the Depression, and national politics during the Second World War. In industry, public relations had emerged as a strategy with which to combat the criticisms levied against big business and monopolies in the early twentieth century. Industry adopted widespread PR tactics to elevate its reputation and to cause the consumer to think that big business was concerned with issues more lofty than making money.

Corrections had similar needs. Public relations could assist not only in obtaining resources for corrections but also in reestablishing the credibility of the profession. The public had a one-sided view of corrections, and that image was terrible. Heretofore, citizens had been almost totally uninformed about corrections, and now their primary source of information was unsympathetic television and newspaper coverage. Violations of civil rights, inhumane conditions, and brutal riots had supplied the news media with great features but not with a balanced view that included a positive view of corrections.

Recognizing the power of the press, some correctional administrators attempted to manipulate or to falsify information releases. They were quickly exposed. Other administrators attempted to curry favor with the news media and the public by acquiescing to almost all demands for information. That approach also backfired. Neither the news media nor corrections had the background or training to be able to recognize what information should be public and what should remain confidential. For example, the McKay Commission Report criticized Commissioner Oswald for allowing news access to the Attica negotiations. The inmates played to the news media, and negotiations were more for show than real.

PIO training and assistance came from the Law Enforcement Assistance Administration (LEAA) and from the American Correctional Association (ACA). An ACA Committee on Publicity searched for successful public relations programs within corrections to share with other correctional agencies. Unfortunately, they found few programs to share (Sharp 1973, 30). In 1978, the Correctional Data Analysis Systems project, funded by LEAA, was designed to assist correctional agencies in data management. In response to the court and legislative requirements, corrections had started producing voluminous reports but found itself unable to manipulate that data and respond quickly to individual requests for information (Friel et al. 1982).

In spite of improved administrative stability and fewer court interventions, the need to supply public information and maintain public relations has increased. The February 1989 issue of *Corrections Today* was devoted to public information and emphasized the importance of the PIO. A survey of correctional public information officers in 1988 reaffirmed the in-

creased need for accurate, informative news stories (Yurkanin 1989).

Today, public opinion regarding the mission of corrections remains ambiguous. Scarce resources and increasing costs have intensified the confusion and created a mood of despair. The media's portrayal of corrections is still negative, further contributing to a dismal public perception. Problems and exceptions sell copy, and, with such a large, complex enterprise, it is not difficult to discover problems. The impact of public perceptions on correctional politics cannot be overstated. As Petersilia (1991, 24) says, "[Correctional] policies appear driven by public opinion, fear, and political hype."

The job of balancing the view of corrections to include the positive aspects of corrections, its needs, and its successes falls to PIO (with the support and direction of the administration). Unlike the police, corrections has no Joseph Wambaugh to romanticize its work. No television shows elevate the correctional officer to hero status (Schwartz 1989). Nor has Hollywood glamorized prisons. In fact, negative publicity can come from the highest levels. In the 1988 presidential campaign, most professionals in corrections knew that the advertisement about Willie Horton (the inmate who fled while on furlough and raped a woman) was intentionally misleading, but they said nothing (Schwartz 1989).

Koehler, the commissioner of the New York City Department of Corrections in 1989, advocated an aggressive, open approach, meeting with the news media regularly. He suggested that the public information system regularly provide the press with interesting material, information, and stories. That type of approach provides more than just information. First, regular contact between the correctional agency and the press promotes understanding and rapport between the news media and workers in corrections. Second, providing regular, comprehensive information, as opposed to crisis updates, will provide a perspective that balances problems with successes (Koehler 1989, 16–17). Koehler added, "We cannot permit corrections to be viewed in isolation. We cannot even permit corrections to be viewed only as one element of the criminal justice system. We must insist that we be viewed in the context of all the social problems and issues that our inmates and systems manifest" (1989, 17). The correctional PIO, with the support of the administration, is the key to assisting other components of the criminal justice system, and the public, understand the correctional mission.

Barbara L. Hart

See also NEWS MEDIA

Bibliography

Fox, V. (1972). *Introduction to Corrections.* Englewood Cliffs, N.J.: Prentice Hall.

Friel, C. M., H. J. Allie, B. L. Hart, and R. L. Pennel (1982). *Correctional Data Analysis Systems.* Washington, D.C.: U.S. Government Printing Office.

Koehler, R. J. (1989). Like it or not: We are news. *Corrections Today* 51(1): 16–17.

Petersilia, J. (1991). The value of corrections research: Learning what works. *Federal Probation* 55(2): 24–26.

Schwartz, J. A. (1989). Promoting a good public image—Effective leadership, sound practices make the difference. *Corrections Today* 51(1): 38–42.

Sharp, P. E. (1973). Directline. *Journal of Corrections* 35(Jan.–Feb.): 30.

Yurkanin, A. (1989). PIOs rate news media in recent survey. *Corrections Today* 51(1): 80.

R

Racial Conflict

Racial and ethnic minorities have always been disproportionately represented in American prisons. As far back as 1833, Gustav de Beaumont and Alexis de Tocqueville, visiting to study the newly invented penitentiary system for the French government, observed that "in those states in which there exist one negro to thirty whites the prisons contain one negro to four white persons." De Beaumont and de Tocqueville's observations, as suggested by the proportions, pertained only to free blacks in Northern and border states. Most African Americans at the time were slaves and were seldom placed in prison. Masters punished the transgressions of their property as they saw fit.

After the Civil War, slavery was reproduced in the form of the convict lease system. Crime rose as freed slaves roamed the countryside with no legitimate means of support. Moreover, the prisons were used as a way to control former slaves. By 1870, more than 90 percent of the convicted felons in the South were black. The few white prisoners were kept in centralized facilities. Black convicts were rented to plantation owners and businessmen, for whom they worked under unspeakably brutal conditions. In any given year, some 20 to 40 percent of them died (Ayres 1984, 197).

Continuing revelations of atrocities brought the convict lease system to an end around the turn of the century. Several Southern states then went into the plantation business themselves. Black and white inmates were typically segregated into separate work camps on these vast estates. Up until twenty-five years ago, for example, the Tucker Prison Farm housed white inmates in Arkansas while the Cummings Farm housed its black inmates.

Outside the South, the policy in most prisons has been, until recently, to segregate inmates by race within the same prison. The New York State Special Commission on Attica, for instance, reported that that prison had been administered on a segregated basis until the mid 1960s. Black and white inmates were assigned to separate cell blocks and different work assignments. They played in separate athletic leagues and even went to different barbers.

Applying the logic of *Brown v. Board of Education* (1954), which had found that racially segregated schools are inherently unequal and thus unconstitutional, a number of federal courts between 1963 and 1974 declared racially segregated prisons to be similarly unconstitutional. The early cases arose in Southern states that maintained completely separate prisons. Only one of those cases went to the Supreme Court, however, and the Court disposed of it in three sentences, finding the lower court's decisions "unexceptional" (*Washington v. Lee*, 1966). The brevity of the decision leaves unclear what desegregation of the prison means. Can, for example, prison officials take into account inmates' expressed preferences for segregation or must they pursue a policy of maximum feasible integration? That and other questions have not been addressed by the Supreme Court, but lower court decisions since 1966 have generally mandated policies of maximum feasible integration (Jacobs 1983, Ch. 4).

It has, thus, been only in past quarter century that black and white prisoners have been incarcerated together. That this should happen at a time when the entire structure of race relations in the country as a whole is undergoing fundamental change is scarcely coincidental. In turn, the changing structure of race relations has been a major factor contributing to the crisis in corrections over the same time. As one observer of long-term trends in corrections has observed, in the contemporary prison "racial politics set the background against which all prisoner activities are played out" (Jacobs 1983, 79).

Race Relations in Prisons for Men

Among Inmates

Until 1970, researchers detailing the social organization of the prison ignored race and ethnicity. Donald Clemmer, in his pioneering study *The Prison Community,* notes that about one-fourth of the inmate population at Menard at the time of his study were black, but he nowhere discusses race relations. Similarly, Sykes, in his classic study of the New Jersey State Prison in Trenton (*The Society of Captives,* 1958), observes that the "inmate population is shot through with a variety of ethnic and racial cleavages which sharply reduce the possibility of continued mass action," but he ignores these cleavages in his analysis.

Despite such passing references, most scholars at the time conceptualized the prison as a total institution, existing in complete isolation from the surrounding society and impervious to its influence. Inmates' pre-prison identities presumably were systematically stripped from them upon admission and they became socialized into new identities that were defined both in terms of the prison's formal structure and a shared inmate code. It was upon these prison identities that scholars focused their attention.

The naivete of this conception was clear even in the late 1950s, as Black Muslims began to proselytize black prisoners and challenge the authority of white prison officials. In hundreds of lawsuits, Muslims protested religious discrimination, censorship, and disciplinary practices. More often than not, these suits met with success, but their impact went far beyond the issues. In bringing the courts into the prisons, the Muslims sounded the death knell for prison despotism. In the process, other prisoner groups became politicized, racial tension intensified, and the prison became balkanized (Jacobs 1983, 36–38, 63–67).

Avoidance and Segregation. Race relations among prisoners is characterized by extreme segregation and avoidance. In some systems, officials continue to segregate inmates along racial lines by using surrogate variables such as residence, risk, or gang affiliation in making assignments to particular institutions and to cells and jobs within the institution. Even where administrative policy is maximum feasible integration and race is explicitly taken into account to achieve racial balance, however, administrative pressure is eroded by inmate preferences for self-segregation. Groups of contiguous cells, areas in the cell blocks, industrial buildings, and recreational facilities become identified with particular cliques and used only by them (Carroll 1988; McDonald and Weisburd 1992).

In this pattern of segregation and avoidance, the social order of the prison resembles the "ordered segmentation" characteristic of multiethnic slums. Racial and cultural differences and the fact that many peers are known to share disreputable characteristics produce in residents a high degree of suspicion and mistrust of one another. In the absence of trust, people withdraw into small territorial groupings segregated first by race and ethnicity and then by sex and age.

Most African-American inmates of Rhode Island's maximum security prison in the early 1970s were found to have several "partners." Some of these partnerships were imported from the community, "homeboys" or "crime partners," while others, "jail-house partners," developed in the prison. Partners sought to live and work near one another, and regardless of the origin of the relationship, they were expected to support and protect one another. In consequence, virtually the entire black inmate population was bound together by an interlocking structure of diffuse relationships of mutual aid and obligation (Carroll 1988, Ch. 5).

Gangs. Racially homogenous, age-graded cliques like partnerships are the building blocks of street gangs, and gangs are a dominant feature of life in many of the larger prison systems. A recent national survey indicated that there are prison gangs in thirty-two states and in the federal prison system.

One of the oldest prison gangs is the Mexican Mafia. It was organized at the Deuel Vocational Institute in 1957 by Chicano youths from East Los Angeles to protect themselves from attack, but soon moved into the drug trade. Several years later, as the Mexican Mafia attempted to monopolize drug trafficking in California prisons, it came into conflict with other Chicanos, mostly from small towns in northern and central

California. They formed another gang, *La Nuestra Familia*. At about the same time, George Jackson was establishing the Black Guerilla Family in San Quentin, and members of white motorcycle gangs formed the Aryan Brotherhood.

Whereas California prison gangs developed within the institutions, those in other states have been imported into the institutions. Jacobs, in his book *Stateville,* has documented how four street gangs developed in Stateville Penitentiary following a crackdown on street violence in the late 1960s. Those four gangs—the Black P. Stone Nation, the Vice Lords, the Devil's Disciples, and the Latin Kings—quickly came to dominate the inmate economy, and their leaders were consulted in formal decision-making.

For years Texas officials used an inmate elite known as "building tenders" to maintain security and control in that state's prisons. These building tenders essentially constituted a "white con power structure." When the building tender system was abolished by order of a federal court some people believe a gang structure similar to that in California emerged to fill the vacuum. A Mexican Mafia developed among Latinos from the large cities. White motorcycle gang members formed both a Texas Mafia and an Aryan Brotherhood, while African-American prisoners organized several gangs, the Mandingo Warriors, the Interaction Organization, and the Seeds of Idi Amin.

Conflict and Violence. The level of violence in prison is exceedingly high. The rate of homicide in prisons is about three times the rate in the nation as a whole, and it is estimated that as many as 70 percent of inmates may be assaulted every year. Much of this violence crosses racial and ethnic lines. Small racially and ethnically differentiated cliques prey upon each other in virtually all prisons, and in the larger systems gangs struggle to control the inmate economy.

Incarceration poses a threat to the sexual identity of young men, and many respond to that threat by sexual aggression against others. Research during the 1970s found that most of that aggression was interracial, disproportionately involving black aggressors and white victims (Carroll 1988). As this pattern of sexual domination of whites by blacks occurs even in prisons where blacks are a minority, it cannot be explained by the overrepresentation of African Americans in prisons. More important factors seemed to be racial antagonism, perhaps intensified by incarceration, greater exposure of black inmates to an urban subculture of violence, and the greater cohesion and solidarity of black inmates resulting from their shared political perspectives and subculture. In more recent years, however, researchers have not found race to be a defining characterisitc of either aggressors or victims, but have not offered any explanation for the apparent change (Tewksbury 1989; Chonco 1989).

Sexual aggression is only one dimension of racial conflict and violence in prison, however. There exists within every prison an illegal economy through which inmates seek to meet their desires for everything from tailored clothing to drugs. Struggles to control these rackets have produced much of the conflict and violence in recent years. Jacobs has documented how gangs in Stateville took control of the inmate economy by force, destroying the "old con" power structure in the process. Many long-time black and Hispanic prisoners secured protection by affiliating themselves with the gangs as "advisors." White inmates, however, were subject to extortion, assault, rape, and constant harassment, and eventually white gangs emerged to protect their members from these predations.

For years, prisons in California experienced all-out warfare as rival gangs struggled to control the rackets. Violence became so widespread that officials began to take into account gang affiliation in the classification process. A similar wave of violence seemed to follow the dismemberment of the semi-official building tender system in Texas. Ninety-three homicides, most of them gang-related, occurred in Texas prisons between 1980 and 1986 as emerging gangs sought to recruit members and eliminate competitors.

Gang violence appears to have subsided in recent years for a number of reasons. Power has been consolidated as alliances have formed among gangs, and leaders have negotiated agreements that divide control of the rackets and provide mechanisms for settling future disputes. Such agreements tend to be tenuous, however, and official policies have probably had an even greater impact. Prison officials now attempt to identify gang members and place them in administrative segregation, where they are kept indefinitely. Such policies may, however, buy racial peace at the price of greater segregation and potential discrimination.

R

Staff and Inmates

At the time of the Attica riot in 1971, nearly two-thirds of the inmates were black and another 10 percent were Puerto Rican. There were, however, only two minority employees on a staff of over five hundred. Following the riot, prison administrators around the country began active programs to recruit African-American and Latino officers in the hope that having minority staff members would reduce racial tensions. Far from easing tensions, however, the infusion of minorities appears to have introduced it among the custodians.

Skin color and language are not the only ways in which minority staff members differ from their white co-workers. They are also younger, better educated, and more likely to have grown up in large metropolitan areas. Yet the recency of their hiring places them disproportionately in lower level positions, a fact that, if nothing else, increases the social distance within the administrative hierarchy. In the eyes of white wardens and superior officers, minority staff members are uncommitted to the job, identify too much with inmates, and are responsible for much of the contraband. White officers resent them because of what they feel is reverse discrimination (Fox 1982; Owen 1985). For their part, minority staff members believe themselves to be discriminated against. In one study, over half the nonwhite officers interviewed complained that the racial attitudes of their co-workers were a serious problem for them on the job (Jacobs and Grear 1977).

Most of the time, this racial tension among the staff remains hidden, but occasionally it erupts into open conflict. In both California and New York, for example, correctional officers' unions have engaged in partially successful litigation to block the implementation of affirmative action promotion programs. Minority officers, in turn, formed separate associations pledged to fight discrimination in both the correctional departments and the unions (Irwin 1980, 22; Jacobs 1983, 146).

Despite the mistrust, suspicion, and tension separating the races, the attitudes and beliefs of minority officers appear to be quite similar to those of their white co-workers (Jurik 1985). Why officers should be so similar in their attitudes despite such differences in their backgrounds is an open question. It may be that the constraints of the job are such that all officers develop a similar "working personality." Another possibility, however, is that recruits whose attitudes are greatly at variance from the norm are screened out during the six- to nine-month probationary period common in most correctional systems (Jacobs and Grear 1977).

Discrimination. Whether, and to what extent, there is discrimination against nonwhite inmates is a question about which there is little research. Moreover, for a number of reasons, it is a difficult question to answer; thus, the conclusions drawn by researchers tend toward ambiguity. A recent study of a Northeastern prison, for example, found no clear-cut pattern of racial segregation in cell assignments such that white and nonwhite prisoners are isolated from one another. For the most part, what segregation there was seemed to result from the personal preferences of the inmates. There was, however, some evidence of preferential treatment of whites, in that they were somewhat overrepresented in the better cell blocks (McDonald and Weisburd 1992).

Most of the research on discrimination concerns discipline. In Rhode Island in the early 1970s, an anomic custodial force was threatened by the radicalism and solidarity of the black inmates. Fear led the white officers to keep black inmates under closer surveillance, but also led the officers to be more cautious in confronting them. Black inmates thus were placed on report more frequently than were whites but received lighter penalties. Nonetheless, black inmates felt themselves to be the objects of discrimination because they compared themselves with a white inmate elite who was immune to punishment for even the most blatant misconduct (Carroll 1988, Ch. 5).

While some studies have reported no racial differences in regard to disciplinary infractions (see, for example, Ellis et al. 1974), these conclusions must be regarded with skepticism, as they rely solely on official statistics. Other studies that have combined official reports with self-reports do find evidence of discrimination. In general, they find that while black inmates report no more infractions than do white inmates, they receive a greater number of disciplinary reports (Poole and Regoli 1980; Wright 1989). Racial differences in the number of reported infractions, moreover, are greater for infractions in which the officers have more discretion, such as disobeying an order, than for more objective offenses, such as assault. There is also some evidence that past bias may amplify current discrimination. Poole and Regoli (1980) found that black inmates had poorer prior institutional records, in part the result of bias, and that prior record influenced punishment for current offenses only for blacks.

A Note on Prisons for Women

Much less is known about life in prisons for women than in prisons for men. From what is known, however, race relations appear to be devoid of the hostility and conflict found in the men's prisons.

Women adapt to prison differently than men. Where the social order of men's prison is a segmental one in which cliques are formed and allies created through conflict, that of prisons for women is familial. Women seek to cope with the rigors of imprisonment through the formation of intimate, dyadic relationships in which the participants offer each other affection and support. Often, though not always, these relationships involve sex, and not uncommonly the dyads are linked into elaborate extended families (Giallombardo 1966).

It has long been noted that these dyads tend, disproportionately, to be interracial. For example, five of the seven dyads diagrammed by Giallombardo (1966, 174–84) involve blacks and whites, as do nearly 75 percent of the relationships in the larger pseudofamilies depicted. Consistent with these observations, Kruttschnitt (1983) found a Minnesota Institution for Women to be characterized by a high degree of integration. While some racial tension did exist, it was mainly between the overwhelmingly white staff and the minority inmates who felt discriminated against. Despite this tension, the vast majority of women of all races maintained close interracial friendships.

Leo Carroll

See also VIOLENCE

Bibliography

Ayres, E. (1984). *Vengeance and Justice: Crime and Punishment in the 19th-Century American South*. New York: Oxford University Press.

Carroll, L. (1982). Race, ethnicity and the social order of the prison. In R. Johnson and H. Toch, eds. *The Pains of Imprisonment*. Beverly Hills, Calif.: Sage.

Carroll, L. (1988). *Hacks, Blacks and Cons: Race Relations in a Maximum Security Prison*. Prospect Heights, Ill.: Waveland. (Originally published 1974).

Chonco, N. (1989). Sexual assaults among male inmates: A descriptive study. *Prison Journal* 69: 72–82.

Ellis, D., H. Grasmick, and B. Gilman (1974). Violence in prison: A sociological analysis. *American Journal of Sociology* 80: 16–43.

Fox, J. G. (1982). *Organizational and Racial Conflict in Maximum Security Prisons*. Lexington, Mass.: Lexington.

Giallombardo, R. (1966). *Society of Women: A Study of a Women's Prison*. New York: Wiley.

Irwin, J. (1980). *Prisons In Turmoil*. Boston: Little, Brown.

Jacobs, J. B. (1983). *New Perspectives on Prisons and Imprisonment*. Ithaca, N.Y.: Cornell University Press.

Jacobs, J. B., and M. Grear (1977). Dropouts and rejects: An analysis of the prison guard's revolving door. *Criminal Justice Review* 2: 57–70.

Jurik, N. C. (1985). Individual and organizational determinants of correctional officer attitudes toward inmates. *Criminology* 23: 523–39.

Kalinich, D. B. (1986). *Power, Stability and Contraband: The Inmate Economy*. Prospect Heights, Ill.: Waveland.

Kruttschnitt, C. (1983). Race relations and the female inmate. *Crime and Delinquency* 29: 577–92.

McDonald, D. C., and D. Weisburd (1992). Segregation and hidden discrimination in prisons: Reflections on a small study of cell assignments. In C. A. Hartjen and E. E. Rhine, eds. *Correctional Theory and Practice*. Chicago: Nelson-Hall.

Owen, B. (1985). Race and gender relations among prison workers. *Crime and Delinquency* 31: 147–59.

Poole, E., and R. Regoli (1980). Race, institutional rule breaking and disciplinary response: A study of disciplinary decision-making in prison. *Law and Society Review* 14: 931–46.

Tewksbury, R. (1989). Fear of sexual assault in prison inmates. *Prison Journal* 69: 62–71.

Wright, K. (1989). Race and economic marginality in explaining prison adjustment. *Journal of Research in Crime and Delinquency* 26: 67–89.

R

Cases

Brown v. Board of Education, 347 U. S. 483
  (1954)
Washington v. Lee, 263 F. Supp. 327 (M.D.
  Ala. 1966), *aff'd per curiam*, 390 U.S.
  333 (1968)

Recidivism

Reducing recidivism, an offender's return to crime, is one of the most important goals of the criminal justice system. Police, courts, and corrections are all designed to reduce the reoccurrence of criminal behavior. Defining and measuring recidivism are thus central to answering the question "How well are we doing?" It has been said that recidivism rates are to the criminologist what the Geiger counter is to the geologist (Korn and McCorkle 1966, 24). In other words, they are the most objective overall basis we have for evaluating the performance of justice agencies.

Recidivism data not only serve as our major evaluation tool, they also are the primary means by which we increase our understanding of the causes and correlates of criminal behavior, project the demand for criminal justice services, and study the dynamics of the criminal career. It is much easier to observe criminal behavior among known offenders than to observe this behavior for the population at large, because criminal activity in the general population is assumed to be relatively rare. In fact, many (if not most) criminal justice programs and policies have resulted from the analysis of recidivism data— usually showing that some population has a particularly high risk for criminal activity or that some current policy is not working effectively.

For example, the well-known Philadelphia birth cohort study analyzed police records of all males born in 1945 who lived in Philadelphia between the ages of ten and eighteen (Wolfgang et al. 1972). The study found that 6 percent of this birth cohort had five or more record police "contacts" (arrests) before the age of eighteen, and that these "chronics" accounted for over half of all recorded delinquencies in the entire group. This study, based entirely on recidivism data, was the first to empirically document the existence of "career criminals." It led to the establishment of special laws and ultimately led police and prosecution units to focus on recidivists.

Recidivism studies have also been instrumental in developing the U.S. Parole Board's Salient Factor Score (now used nationally to determine eligibility for parole release). It has provided the basis for objective classification systems for parole and probation, and it guided states and the federal government in devising sentencing guideline systems (Petersilia 1987).

Recidivism data are also the primary source used to develop understanding of the causes and correlates of criminal offending. For example, by identifying the factors associated with recidivism, we have developed hypotheses on the causes of crime. We have discovered that intensive drug use and unemployment are related to an increase in recidivism, and conversely that gainful employment or a stable marriage contribute to decreased recidivism. Such information has provided the empirical basis for developing programs to reduce recidivism.

Recidivism data also drive the development of laws. Consider the very popular "three-strikes-and-you're-out" bills (requiring lifelong sentences for three convictions of certain types of crimes). Those laws were initiated as a result of the publication of recidivism data indicating that offenders released from prison on parole continued to commit heinous crimes.

Despite the recognized importance of recidivism for criminal justice policy and practice, it is difficult to measure because there is no uniformly accepted definition for the term. While "recidivism" generally refers to the reoccurrence of criminal behavior following a given event, it is not clear exactly how reoccurrence should be defined. Should it be a new arrest, new conviction, or new imprisonment that counts as evidence of new criminal behavior? Over what time period? Should misdemeanors be included, or just felonies? What about technical probation and parole violations? Indeed, the literature is replete with suggestions regarding correct definitions, optimal methods of counting, and the most valid sources of information (for examples, see Maltz 1984). What has resulted is a research literature that contains vastly different conventions—different outcomes, different time periods, and different methodologies. Thus recidivism data reported in one study are seldom comparable to the data in another.

The importance of the recidivism concept for criminal justice, and the incomparability of existing definitions, led the National Academy of Sciences' Panel on Rehabilitation to urge the adoption of a standardized national definition. They believed that such conventions would assist policy makers and program managers to

TABLE 1

Components in Measuring Recidivism

1. Study Population
   Juveniles or adults
   Prior record, demographics, current crime
2. Starting Event
   Arrested
   Granted probation/parole
   Entry to program
   Exit/completion of program
   Release from jail/prison
3. Type of Recidivism Event
   Revocation
      Technical or new crime
   Formal charge
   Conviction
   Incarceration
      Jail or prison
4. Seriousness of Recidivism Offense
   Felony or misdemeanor
   Type of crime
   Type of technical violation
5. Follow-up Time Period
   Length of follow-up period (1, 2, or 3 years)
   Street time controls (subtract time in jail/prison)
   Distinguish formal community supervision from "free"
6. Data Sources
   Self-reports
      Surveys or interviews
   Official record data
      Local (police, court), state (prison, state rap sheets), or federal (FBI)
7. Number of Times an Offender Will Be Counted
   Once (the first instance of recidivism; measures time to failure)
   Multiple (same transaction, events in single day coded as "most serious")
   Multiple (different transactions)
8. Policy Variables
   Laws (e.g., mandatory prison)
   Programs (e.g., ISP)
   Practices (e.g., divert misdemeanors)

compare the success or failure of programs across diverse settings and populations, and in the long run increase our understanding of crime prevention (Waldo and Griswold 1979). That recommendation has not been followed, although Texas and Oregon recently proposed adopting standardized definitions of recidivism for all of their criminal justice agencies (Hill 1993; Fabelo 1991).

Most now agree that it is not as important to have a common definition, or to adopt a single one, as to report multiple recidivism measures that are clearly identified and rigorously measured. Since we currently know so little about the causes of crime, it may be premature to adopt a single definition. But everyone agrees that we must clearly identify the characteristics of the sample being studied, report the recidivism rates over similar time periods when comparing populations, and describe the instances of recidivism and the biases in the data being used. It is also clear that answering the question "Did they recidivate?" with a yes or no answer is simplistic. Recidivism studies that discuss the time of the "event," the duration, and how subsequent crimes compared with one another (in a criminal career) are much more informative. Even without a common definition, it seems imperative that future recidivism studies define how the key components have been operationalized. The remainder of this entry identifies the issues that one needs to consider in operationalizing recidivism.

Issues to Consider in Operationalizing "Recidivism" Rates

In general, recidivism rates are usually calculated as the proportion of all offenders who have entered or exited some justice system intervention (probation, prison) who "fail" within a specified follow-up period. Recidivism rate is thus equal to the number of offenders placed under community supervision, completing program, or released from custody (a) during time period (x) with unfavorable outcome (y) within (z) number of months or years.

But, as noted above, the components of this equation are not well defined. Which recidivism events will be included as an "unfavorable outcome" ("y" in the definition above)? Will all arrests be counted, or only felonies? What about technical violations? Will multiple arrests be counted, or only the first arrest? Will the total time period be defined in terms of calendar time, "street time" (when the offender was free in the community and thus at risk for committing crime), or some combination of the two? These and many other decisions are critical and can dramatically affect the recidivism rate. For example, in a study of probation outcomes, Petersilia and Turner (1993) reported that recidivism rates could have legitimately ranged from 10 to 90 percent over the one year follow-up period, depending on exactly how the recidivism rate was calculated.

There are a number of important considerations in calculating a recidivism rate. The most important of these are summarized in Table 1, with a brief discussion of these elements below. The author recommends that all future recidivism studies consider each of these issues, and, most important, publish how each issue was resolved and measured. In this manner, we may begin to produce recidivism studies that are comparable.

Study Population

Who comprises the study sample—for example, juvenile or adults? For the specified population, what are their demographic, prior criminal record, and current crime characteristics? These factors are important because certain preexisting characteristics (such as age or prior criminal record) are known to correlate with recidivism, regardless of any justice system intervention.

The Starting Event

The event that initiates the follow-up period must be stated explicitly (such as release from prison, granting of probation, completion of a treatment program), because doing so ensures that all members are starting at a similar point in the process. These "starting events" may be in the juvenile or adult justice system.

Type of Recidivism Event

It is critical that the particular type of recidivism event be specified, although there is no agreement on which type of event is the best measure of recidivism. Some have argued that recidivism is best measured closest to the event (at arrest), since later events take us further away from the offense itself and so many arrests fail to result in conviction—leading to an underestimation of recidivism. But others argue that convictions are a more appropriate measure, since many arrests are unfounded and the definition of arrest differs so widely from one jurisdiction to another. Some have taken a middle ground by including as recidivism only arrests that were followed by a formal charge or some other prosecutorial action. That measure is more accurate than arrest data alone, as it avoids the errors caused by including in the recidivism rates those offenders arrested but never charged. Those data, however, are often difficult to obtain.

Seriousness of Recidivism Offense

This refers to the type of crime involved, either classified as a felony or misdemeanor, or the specific type of crime (drugs, burglary, robbery). An important and often overlooked distinction here is between revocation and a new arrest. Revocation is the result of a violation in the rules of probation or parole supervision. Revocation can occur because of a new offense or as the result of an administrative or "technical" violation such as failure to pay or to perform community service. Revocation rates are separate from recidivism and apply only to offenders under formal supervision.

Follow-Up Time Period

This specifies the total follow-up period as well as other factors that are taken into account during the study. It is generally agreed that a three-year follow-up time frame is ideal. Research has shown that most of those who will recidivate will do so during that time. It is also useful to collect the data such that one-, two-, and three-year calculations can be performed. In fact, if possible it is useful to collect the data corresponding with each recidivism event, so that survival rate analysis (which tracks the pace of recidivism) can be conducted. With survival analysis, one is able to examine whether there are specific and identifiable "critical periods" during which offenders are likely to recidivate, or whether some subgroups within a sample of offenders are more likely to do so than others.

It is critically important to specify whether the recidivism rates have controlled for street time, that is, have removed from the total time period the months during the follow-up, when the offender was unable to commit crimes because he was incarcerated. If at all possible, street-time information should be obtained and taken into account when reporting the recidivism rates, because it can make a major difference in the rates. For example, if one is comparing a probation program involving intensive supervision with a routine probation program, the data may show that 45 percent of those on routine probation had a new arrest during the follow-up period, whereas only 25 percent of those on intensive supervision did. One might conclude that the ISP program was more successful at reducing recidivism, when the fact is that the ISP offenders were quickly sent to prison for technical violations and spent almost the entire follow-up period incarcerated (that is, they were removed from the population "at risk" for recidivism).

It is also important that follow-up time periods specify when the offender was on and off formal probation and parole. Many recidivism studies track offenders for a specified number of years, say three. Often the offenders were on probation or parole for a subset of the follow-up period, but when the offender was off and on supervision is seldom specified. This omission makes it nearly impossible to assess the effect of probation and parole on recidivism. Future recidivism studies should incorporate this (relatively easy to obtain) data.

Data Sources

This specifies whether the data were collected from official records (and what type) or were self-report interviews or surveys (self-report versus official, and the nature of the official records). Data derived from official measures contain a number of limitations, as do self-reports. Official records reflect patterns of differential law enforcement, methods of gathering and reporting statistics, and a community's punishment preferences. Self-reports, on the other hand, are often of questionable validity.

Number of Times the Offender Will Be Counted

When measuring recidivism over a period of time, offenders can be counted either once (the first instance of recidivism) or many times (the total number of instances over the entire follow-up period). Multiple counting reflects "criminality," while counting the first event reflects the time to first failure. But another factor is also important: How are multiple recidivism events that happen on a single day (or a single transaction) to be recorded? For example, a police rap sheet will often show several charges on a single arrest, or the clearance of several arrests on a single day. Is each to be counted separately, or are all events in a single transaction to be counted as one type (usually the most serious)? The answer can significantly affect the number of multiple recidivism events per offender.

Policy Variables

This is often the most neglected and potentially most important factor affecting the measurement of recidivism. Researchers should be aware, and explicitly state, any extraneous factors that may affect the recidivism data they are reporting. For example, parole officers use wide discretion in responding to technical violations by parolees. The decision whether to respond formally or informally to such violations varies by region or even among local parole offices within regions. These policies, programs, or laws may influence reincarceration rates and recidivism measures as much as, or more than, criminal behavior. It is important to understand that the recidivism measures we have available are not accurate indicators of the offenders' criminal behavior, but are proxy measures that reflect the response of the criminal justice system combined with the offenders' behavior.

Conclusion

Before undertaking a recidivism study or calculating a rate, one should go through and review each of the components in Table 1, specifying exactly the dimensions that will be used in calculating the recidivism rates. (In a sense, it can be viewed as a checklist for those undertaking recidivism research, reviewing it, or comparing or reporting it.) Discussing the various components also forces one to consider what is and, equally important, what is not being included in the specific recidivism rate being reported.

Joan Petersilia

Bibliography

Fabelo, T. (1991). *Uniform Recidivism and Revocation Rate Calculation.* Austin, Tex.: Criminal Justice Policy Council.

Hill, J. (1993). *The Measurement and Reporting of Recidivism in the Oregon Department of Corrections.* Draft memorandum. Salem, Oreg.: Oregon Department of Corrections.

Korn R. R., and L. W. McCorkle (1966). *Criminology and Penology.* New York: Holt, Rinehart and Winston.

Maltz, M. D. (1984). *Recidivism.* Orlando, Fla.: Academic.

Petersilia, J. (1987). *The Influence of Criminal Justice Research.* Santa Monica, Calif.: RAND Corporation.

Petersilia, J., and S. Turner (1993). Intensive probation and parole. In M. Tonry, ed. *Crime and Justice: An Annual Review of Research.* Vol 17. Chicago: University of Chicago Press.

Waldo, G., and D. Griswold (1979). Issues in the measurement of recidivism. In L. Sechrest, S. White, and E. Brown, eds.

The Rehabilitation of Criminal Offenders: Problems and Prospects. Washington, D.C.: National Academy of Sciences.

Wolfgang, M., T. Sellin, and R. Figlio (1972). *Delinquency in a Birth Cohort.* Chicago: University of Chicago Press.

Recreation Programs

Recreation programs in prison can be traced back to some of the earliest American prisons. On 4 July 1864, warden Gideon Haynes of the Massachusetts State Prison at Charlestown allowed the inmates to assemble together after chapel services. The inmates were taken to the yard where they were informed that they would have one hour's time to enjoy themselves as they wished. The inmates, who had been forced into routines of silence for so long, were overwhelmed. It was reported that they shouted and cried, shook hands, embraced each other, and danced about. This experiment in recreation was copied by the warden at Joliet a few years later. It was not long before holiday recreation was expanded to include Sundays and regular baseball games (Gillin 1926, 418).

It has been suggested that recreational programs in our nation's prisons yield important benefits for offenders. The U.S. courts have emphasized the importance of both meaningful exercise and recreation programs for prisoners. Recently, U.S. District Judge William Wayne Justice, known for his reform of the Texas prison system, has made it clear that reform should include issues specific to recreational programs (*Dallas Morning News,* 1994).

A recent survey of Texas prisons by John Sharp (1994), comptroller of public accounts, revealed continual problems in the area of recreation. These problems pertain to restrictions placed on the use of existing equipment. Another issue in Texas that may mirror the national situation is that officers supervising recreational facilities are often reassigned without warning, making recreation temporarily unavailable to inmates. The same survey points toward the success of other states in achieving meaningful recreational programs. Sharp (1994, 124) states: "The U.S. Bureau of Prisons and many state systems, including those of Oklahoma, Michigan, and Florida, have policies to maximize the use of recreational programs. These programs fill in time not devoted to structured programs of education, work, and vocational training, in positive, constructive ways. As a management tool, such practices lessen boredom, assaults and other violations by inmates." Concomitantly, an examination of programs at the federal correctional institution (FCI) in Ft. Worth, Texas, buttresses Sharp's observation about the federal prison system. FCI includes structured and nonstructured events including flag football, softball, basketball, weight-lifting, and board games.

At FCI-Ft. Worth, an inmate wellness program has been instituted. The supervisor of the wellness program is responsible for screening, body assessments, fitness and nutrition, and counseling. These activities are consistent with the mission statement of the Federal Bureau of Prisons (FBOP). The FBOP mission statement reads as follows: "Recreational programs in the Federal Bureau of Prisons are intended to keep inmates constructively occupied; to promote wellness as a personal goal for all inmates; to increase physical fitness . . . and . . . contribute to personal and institutional stability through maximum participation in formal and informal programs" (FBOP 1993).

Recreation as Prevention

In the summer of 1969, twenty-five riots occurred in response to poor housing, crowded living conditions, competition for jobs, and racial tensions caused partly by the lack of recreational facilities. It is believed that the dearth of recreational programs and opportunities (in the inner city) had an impact upon rioting that occurred many years ago. The argument has it that had there been recreational outlets, rioting might not have occurred on such a wide scale. As assistant superintendent of a halfway house in the state of Florida, this writer observed the benefits of a well-planned recreational program. Recreational programs add an important dimension to the lives of the residents. An added benefit is reduced tension and suspicion, coupled with a lessening of petty squabbles among program participants. The benefits of planned recreational activities for adult offenders should be apparent.

Exercise versus Recreation

There is also a debate, and a misunderstanding, over two concepts, exercise and recreation. Exercise relates to physical health and hygiene. Exercise helps reduce deterioration of the cardiovascular system and abates atrophy of the muscles. Consequently, the absence of physical exercise may lead to a need for increased medical services, resulting in additional costs to the taxpayer. Ironically, if some news headlines are accurate indicators, there may be growing resentment from taxpayers who are convinced that a right to exercise results only in inmates with bulging muscles. One such article in *Time* magazine (Hull 1994, 47) raised the following question: "Why are taxpayers in Milwaukee and elsewhere subsidizing what could be considered the largest health club chain in the nation, allowing tens of thousands of otherwise scrawny murders, muggers, and rapists to transform themselves?"

The issue in Milwaukee County is so volatile that politicians have voted to ban weightlifting from the institution. One sponsor of the ban, Roger Quindeld (Hull 1994, 47), states: "Allowing these guys to bulk up in prison is so stupid. Do we really want stronger criminals? I'd rather buy them computers and then let them do calisthenics." The implication is that these inmates, when released, will be stronger and better able to commit crimes of violence on America's streets. In other words, physically strong offenders will be able to wreak havoc and commit twice the number of heinous crimes. There is, however, no literature to support this notion. Most inmates upon release "shrivel up" and spend less time weight-lifting. The notion that muscle-flexing allows offenders to commit heinous crimes and rob banks is simply another myth perpetuated by an uninformed public.

Related to the notion of exercise is recreation. There is a twofold purpose to correctional recreation: (1) to relieve the daily tensions created by incarceration, and (2) to develop both existing and new leisure skills. Simply put, recreational programs offer opportunities that are fun, cerebral activities, transcending the sweat and grind of weight rooms in prisons.

Welch (1991, 146) makes a cogent case for prisons with well-developed recreational programs. Welch notes that Oklahoma "has one of the largest and most effective arts programs in the United States, with some classes at all 15 state institutions and at least 3,000 inmates who participate out of a population of 10,250." One serendipitous effect of an arts/recreational program is the reduction of undesirable behavior. These activities fill time, reduce tension, and educate. Not only do planned programs like art divert inmates from destructive thoughts, they relieve tensions as well. Welch (1991, 148) states: "By teaching self expression, communication and a way to think creatively, they become therapeutic."

Conclusion

Tragically, there is much controversy over such an important yet apparently little-appreciated concept. Recreation, weight-lifting, and leisure programs have a meaningful place in most correctional settings. Weight-lifting yields benefits that include stress reduction, improved self-esteem, and positive use of idle time. Proponents of leisure activities (such as arts or painting) suggest that, although these programs are more cerebral than physical, they also function as an outlet for aggression. Specifically, these programs help divert attention from undesirable behavior within the institution. The current "get tough" attitude toward criminals and the recent attention to the use of weights in prison should not be allowed to discount the advantages or obscure the important health, medical, spiritual, and physical benefits to be derived from recreation.

Robert L. Bing III

See also REHABILITATION PROGRAMS

Bibliography

Dallas Morning News (1994). Judge rules prison rec areas are top priority. (June 4): A-39.

Federal Bureau of Prisons (1993). *Program Statement*. Washington, D.C.: U.S. Department of Justice.

Federal Bureau of Prisons (1994). *Institution Supplement*. Washington, D.C.: U.S. Department of Justice.

Federal Medical Center (1994). Description of recreational programs at Federal Medical Center. Ft. Worth, Tex.: Federal Medical Center (formerly FCI-Ft. Worth).

Gillin, J.L. (1926). *Criminology and Penology*. New York: Century.

Hitchcock, H. (1990). Prisons—Exercise versus recreation. *Journal of Physical Education, Recreation and Dance* 61(August): 84–88.

Hull, J. (1994). Building a better thug. *Time* (April 11): 47.

Sharp, J. (1994). *Behind the Walls: The Price and Performance of the Texas Department of Criminal Justice*. Austin, Tex.: Comptroller of Public Accounts.

Welch, R. (1991). Arts in prison: Tapping inmates' creativity offers hope, improves security. *Corrections Today* 53(5): 146–52.

Reformatory

The opening of the Elmira Reformatory in Elmira, New York, in July of 1876 marked the birth of the American reformatory-prison movement. Under the direction of Superintendent Zebulon Brockway, Elmira introduced a number of innovations that set America's "third penal system" apart from the traditional cornerstones of the nation's correctional system, adult prisons, and juvenile reformatories. More important, Elmira—and the adult reformatories that followed—introduced a new approach to thinking about crime and treating criminals that transformed late-nineteenth and early-twentieth century corrections and laid the foundation for many current programs, policies, and debates.

Brockway's "Elmira system" was, in theory, grounded upon the notion of treatment and benevolent reform. Male, first-time offenders between the ages of sixteen and thirty were committed on indeterminate sentences (for example, one to five years) and exposed to a new regimen of reform that was based upon prison science and the medical model. Brockway's multifactor positivist approach to the causes of crime rejected the prevailing notion that criminals were free, rational, and hedonistic actors who deserved punishment. Brockway's version of the "new penology" viewed criminals as unique individuals whose behavior is determined by a variety of complex psychological, biological, social, and economic forces. Academic and vocational education, labor, religion, recreational activities, military drill, an elaborate mark and classification system, and parole were used to correct the roots of deviance.

There was a wide disparity, however, between the promise and practice of the world's most acclaimed penal experiment. Inmates who resisted the Elmira system and failed to act, as Brockway put it, like "Christian gentlemen" were subjected to extraordinarily harsh punishments, including whippings with a leather strap, months of incarceration in a dark dungeon on bread and water, and other forms of deliberate psychological torture. Other components of Brockway's Elmira system were also ineffective, including the acclaimed indeterminate sentencing and parole systems. Escapes, violence, gangs, drugs, predatory sex, arson, and suicide were persistent problems. The Elmira Reformatory, much like the institutions that preceded it, was designed to instill lower-class offenders with the Protestant ethic—the habits of order, discipline, and self-control—and fit them into their "proper place" in the social, economic, and political order as obedient, lower-class workers. Elmira was a brutal prison.

The keepers of Elmira—pursing personal and organizational interests—launched a carefully crafted public relations and marketing campaign in the early 1880s that claimed that their new approach to prison science was marvelously successful. Declining faith in traditional adult prisons and juvenile reformatories, coupled with increasing fear of crime and social disorder, masked the reality of the Elmira system and laid the foundation for the spread of the adult reformatory movement. Adult reformatories for men opened in Michigan (1877), Massachusetts (1884), Pennsylvania (1889), Minnesota (1889), Colorado (1890), Illinois (1891), Kansas (1895), Ohio (1896), Indiana (1897), Wisconsin (1899), New York–Napanoch (1900), New Jersey (1901), Iowa (1907), Washington State (1909), Oklahoma (1910), Kentucky (1910), Connecticut (1913), and the District of Columbia (1916). By the close of the "progressive era," over twenty reformatory-prisons for men and women had opened in the United States.

These institutions did not, however, blindly copy the Elmira system. Reformers modified the Elmira system to reflect and serve the specific needs and interests of their states. The nation's second adult reformatory, the Michigan House of Correction and Reformatory, was the ideological and programmatic antithesis of Elmira. It accepted felons and misdemeanants without restrictions on age. Indeterminate sentencing, parole, and other key components of the Elmira system were rejected. Punishment and profit-oriented labor aimed at deterrence were the focus of Michigan's version of the new penology. The nation's third reformatory-prison, the Massachusetts Reformatory, introduced an eclectic approach. Massachusetts reformers, like their Michigan counterparts, accepted misdemeanants and felons, irrespective of their age and prior offense history. They adopted Elmira's goal of reform, however, and implemented key treatment programs, including indeterminate sentencing and parole. By the late 1880s there were, then, three types of adult reformatories: New York's version, which stressed "treatment" and "reform"; Michigan's "punishment and profit" approach; and an eclectic version developed in Massachusetts.

The keepers of the adult reformatories adopting each of the three competing systems confidently announced, much like Brockway, that their institutions were enormously successful and that they had, indeed, discovered the elusive elixir to dispel deviance and disorder. These claims of success spurred the diffusion of the new penology. By the close of the nineteenth century, juvenile reformatories and adult prisons across the United States and around the world enthusiastically embraced Elmira's penal philosophy (rehabilitation), theory of crime causation (multifactor positivism), diagnostic methods (medical model, prison science), correctional vocabulary ("hospital," "patients," "students"), and treatment programs (academic and vocational education, labor, religion, indeterminate sentencing, mark and classification system, military drill, recreation, biogenic treatments, parole). The American reformatory-prison movement had, quite simply, sparked a revolution.

The fame of the adult reformatory system, however, was short-lived. Disputes between proponents of the Elmira, Michigan, and Massachusetts systems left the reformatory-prison movement without a central core and focus. The national mood favoring a return to punishment—coupled with the uncomplimentary findings of a number of investigations and mounting criticisms from practitioners and academicians—revealed that there was a wide disparity between the promise and practice of the America's third penal system. By the close of the progressive era, reformatory-prisons were no longer viewed as a "reform panacea," and faith in the new penology declined. Few adult reformatories opened in the United States after 1920, and many existing reformatory-prisons, including Elmira, became adult prisons. Adult prisons and juvenile reformatories once again emerged as the cornerstones of the American correctional system.

The adult reformatory movement, without question, had a profound effect upon late-nineteenth and early-twentieth century American corrections. The opening of these institutions contributed to the discovery of a new class of criminal: the "dangerous" youthful offender. Reformatory-prisons expanded the state's network of social control by providing a place of incarceration for intermediate-level offenders (those who were too old to be sent to juvenile institutions but whose offenses did not merit incarceration in adult prison). The spread of prison science enhanced the status of professional penologists, contributed to the rise of scientific criminology, and altered the social contract between criminals and the state.

But America's third penal system has also had a profound impact upon contemporary approaches to crime, delinquency, and social control. Many current programs, policies, and debates (such as, to punish or reform? indeterminate or fixed sentencing? abolish or expand parole?) can be traced to the "reforms" introduced by the reformatory-prison movement. Modern correctional institutions continue to incarcerate the "dangerous classes": lower income blacks and Hispanics. Contemporary correctional institutions, like Brockway's Elmira and other reformatory-prisons, promise benevolent reform but deliver benevolent repression.

Alexander W. Pisciotta

Bibliography

Brockway, Z. R. (1912). *Fifty Years of Prison Service: An Autobiography.* Montclair, N.J.: Patterson Smith (Reprinted 1969).

McKelvey, B. (1936). *American Prisons.* Chicago: University of Chicago Press. (Reprinted Montclair, N.J.: Patterson Smith, 1977).

Pisciotta, A. W. (1982). Scientific reform: The "new penology" at Elmira, 1876–1900. *Crime and Delinquency* 29: 613–30.

Pisciotta, A. W. (1994). *Benevolent Repression: Social Control and the American Reformatory-Prison Movement.* New York: New York University Press.

Rafter, N. H. (1990). *Partial Justice: Women, Prisons and Social Control.* 2nd ed. New Brunswick, N.J.: Transaction.

Smith, B. A. (1988). Military training at New York's Elmira Reformatory, 1888–1920. *Federal Probation* 52: 33–40.

Rehabilitation Act of 1973

The Rehabilitation Act of 1973 (P.L. 93-112) was designed as an expansion of and replacement for the Vocational Rehabilitation Act. The Rehabilitation Act was "to develop and implement through research, training, services, and the guarantee of equal opportunity, comprehensive and coordinated programs of vocational rehabilitation and independent living." The act created the Rehabilitation Services Administration and expanded funding mechanisms for training, counseling, and placement of those eligible for work; for research on both handicapping conditions and methods of providing services; and for the goods or services necessary to assist handicapped individuals to become employable. To qualify for funds, state governments were required to create a statewide, comprehensive plan for vocational rehabilitative services.

The overall cost of the funding provisions and the expansion of the federal bureaucracy seemed to be the main issues of those in opposition to the legislation. Those issues led to a pocket veto of a 1972 version of the act and a failure to override the veto of a version in early 1973. Some opposition was based on the act's intended expansion from the earlier law's focus on improving employability of the handicapped to a broader-based provision of services.

While the originally defined targets of the legislation were individuals whose physical or mental disabilities were such that it formed a substantial handicap to employment and for whom rehabilitation services could improve employability, the intent of the legislation was broader. An amendment to the act in 1974 (P.L. 93-516) changed the definition of handicapped toward the broader focus by expanding beyond the employability issue. The 1974 amendment defined as handicapped "any person who (1) has a physical or mental impairment which substantially limits one or more of such person's major life activities, (2) has a record of such an impairment, or (3) is regarded as having such an impairment." Major life activities included walking, seeing, hearing, speaking, and learning, as well as working. The law considered handicapped anyone with specific conditions such as an amputation, a vocal, auditory, or visual impairment, cancer, heart disease, diabetes, cerebral palsy, muscular dystrophy, multiple sclerosis, mental illness or retardation, or drug or alcohol addiction.

The broadened focus of the act was intended to extend rehabilitative services to a larger number of individuals. Another provision of the act, however, limited that potential. State plans were required to place a primary emphasis on those individuals with the most serious disabilities. The cost of rehabilitative services increases with the severity of the disability. This priority matched the limited funds available to those in greatest need, but thereby limited the total number of handicapped the funds could serve.

The Rehabilitation Act of 1973 was also a civil rights act. Speeches made in support of the act upon its introduction in both houses of Congress stressed the need for American society to be opened to full participation of the handicapped, who were viewed as having been forgotten and pushed aside, suffering from isolation, discrimination, and maltreatment. The act was to bring to the handicapped equal protection and treatment. It established handicap as a basis for civil rights protection.

To those ends, Section 501 required all federal agencies to create affirmative action plans for hiring handicapped citizens. All buildings owned, occupied, or financed by the federal government were to provide for access by the disabled. Of greater significance were sections 503 and 504. The former required all employers with federal contracts of $2,500.00 or more to engage in affirmative action to hire and advance qualified handicapped workers. Section 504 prohibited discrimination against otherwise qualified handicapped individuals in any program receiving federal financial assistance. Under Section 504, employers were prohibited from basing decisions on an individual's disability alone. An assessment of the individual's talents and qualifications in regard to the job must be made. Further, employers must make reasonable accommodation for the handicapped as long as such accommodation does not create an undue burden on the employer.

The civil rights effect of the act have been limited by an absence of federal effort in a conservative era. Governmental agencies were slow to write regulations. Enforcement of the antidiscrimination provisions was weak or nonexistent. The act's provisions appeared to apply to prison inmates, substance abusers, AIDS sufferers, and those eligible for drug testing. Little actual use of the Act has been made in those areas, however.

Where prisoners were concerned, the act appeared to mandate specialized rehabilitative training for the handicapped and structural changes in facilities to accommodate their disabilities. Additionally, handicapped applicants for correctional employment would receive greater consideration, and, if necessary, facilities would be adapted to allow greater access.

The Congress, partially in response to the failures and limitations of the Rehabilitation Act, recently replaced and expanded many of its provisions. The Americans with Disabilities Act of 1990 (P.L. 101-336), while leaving some of the earlier act's provisions in place, has become the primary civil rights act for the disabled.

Philip W. Rhoades

See also REHABILITATION PROGRAMS,
VOCATIONAL PROGRAMS

Bibliography

Baum, E. M. (1984). Handicapped prisoners: An ignored minority? *Columbia Journal of Law and Social Problems* 18: 349–79.

Cook, T. (1983). The substantive due process rights of mentally disabled clients. *Mental Disability Law Reporter* 7(4): 174–85.

Harvard Law Review (1984). Employment discrimination against the handicapped and section 504 of the Rehabilitation Act of 1973: An essay on legal evasiveness. *Harvard Law Review* 97: 997–1015.

Khan, A. (1990). The application of section 504 of the Rehabilitation Act to the segregation of HIV-positive inmates. *Washington Law Review* 65: 839–81.

Robbins, A. (1993). Employment discrimination against substance abusers: The federal response. *Boston College Law Review* 33: 155–209.

Shumaker, G. M. (1986). AIDS: Does it qualify as a "handicap" under the Rehabilitation Act of 1973? *Notre Dame Law Review* 61: 572–94.

Rehabilitation Programs

The desire to reform convicted offenders has a long tradition in American correctional policy and practice. From the late eighteenth century to the present, politicians, correctional professionals, religious leaders, scholars, and prison inmates themselves have participated in ongoing reform movements and experiments, all designed to change lawbreakers into prosocial, self-supporting individuals. David Rothman's (1980) chronicle of these trends shows us that the history of correctional rehabilitation practice has been a turbulent one, fraught with idealism and ill-conceived ideas, in which even the best innovations are challenged by hostile political climates or administrative disorganization.

History of Institutional Rehabilitation

Throughout most of American history, correctional policy makers have positioned rehabilitation among the most important correctional goals. Treatment has appeared in many forms, and clearly many ideas have proven ultimately to be unfounded. The earliest institutional treatment models, for example, placed heavy reliance on the qualities of institutional life combined with spiritual contemplation as a source of individual reformation. The earliest penitentiaries were founded under a Quaker influence, supporting either solitary confinement or a congregate model that nevertheless imposed total silence upon prisoners. It was assumed that in both systems inmates would be isolated from evil influences and subjected to strong discipline and uninterrupted contemplation. The outcome, presumably, would be a responsible citizen who had seen the error of his ways. More realistically, the practice of solitary confinement produced many instances of mental illness before its use was abandoned. Historians have referred to this period as a time in which harshness was too quickly assumed to be discipline, an abusive discipline that did more to break spirits than it did to reform them.

A more positive approach was envisioned shortly after the Civil War and put into practice in 1876 at the Elmira Reformatory for youthful offenders in New York. That program used principles that today would be recognized as related to those of operant conditioning. Borrowing from earlier Australian reforms implemented by Alexander Machonochie and Sir Walter Crofton's prison "mark" system, reformers planned a model in which inmates could earn transfers to less secure prisons and ultimately their release through good behavior and work performance. Points could also be earned for good school performance.

The reformatory system is also known for the contemporary introduction of the indeterminate sentence and postrelease supervision or parole. Indeterminate sentences afforded correctional professionals the opportunity to predicate a release decision upon an inmate's satisfactory rehabilitation. In that sense, one's sentence became individualized according to the time needed to reform, within the limits of a maximum term.

The Elmira Reformatory, and others built shortly afterwards in other states, should also be noted for their educational and other programs designed to facilitate change. With the advent of deliberate programming, one sees a notable transition in correctional policy toward the planning of change-oriented interventions and more active engineering of the change process, as opposed to the idea that inmates, themselves, would see the need to change while correctional agencies assumed a passive role.

Even more intensive efforts at planned change appeared from 1900 to the 1920s, when progressive reformers seized upon the new clinical approaches offered by emerging social and psychological sciences. The general social optimism of the times encouraged public education and the belief that social ills, including crime, could be prevented. Science, particularly social, medical, and psychological sciences, also asserted that causes could be identified, diagnosed, and ultimately treated. The field of criminology during those years was characterized by the work of the positivists, researchers who found the roots of crime to be in biological, "atavistic," traits and psychological ills, rather than in the rational choices made by offenders. The offender, in other words, was ill.

This perspective emphasized individual, clinical treatments that first sought to diagnose the causes of crime and then treat them. The medical model, as this philosophy and approach came to be known, was seen in community corrections, newly formed juvenile courts, and in correctional institutions. Cullen and Gilbert (1982) conclude that the progressives' greatest impact was in the development of a less adversarial and more rehabilitative ideology. For adults, the medical model envisioned prison hospitals equipped with diagnostic centers and psychiatric treatment approaches. Medical and clinical staff would replace custodial staff.

While later years did see the arrival of more treatment staff in the form of social workers, educators, and psychological and psychiatric staff, the penitentiaries and juvenile correctional facilities did not become hospitals. Moreover, the level of public investment in the treatment enterprise never achieved sufficiency. Finally, the therapeutic value of some treatment-oriented programs was questionable. Rothman (1980) concludes that the psychiatric approach of the times appeared more invested in diagnosis and classification than in the design of change-oriented programs. Nevertheless, the goals of individualized treatment, classification, and community corrections, and the substitution of humane, reform-oriented programs for punishment, dominated correctional policy throughout the first half of the twentieth century. And rehabilitation, according to Cullen and Gilbert (1982), enjoyed unchallenged status as *the* correctional priority until mid century.

Toward the end of this period, rehabilitation enjoyed an additional impetus from two presidential crime commissions and resulting legislation that provided state and federal seed money for many new crime prevention and treatment initiatives. These promotions, however, were short lived. The medical model and indeterminate sentencing were being challenged on moral grounds as unjust and inhumane, especially when imposed on unwilling participants. Conservatives were lamenting a high crime rate and asserting that deterrence and incapacitation, the "get tough" approaches to crime, were more effective. In the mid 1970s, a review of the treatment evaluation literature by Robert Martinson (1974) concluded that rehabilitation had achieved "no appreciable effect on recidivism." Politically, the report was well timed. With it, policy-makers could now add effectiveness to the above list of concerns. The Martinson report was indeed supportive of the subsequent swing to a far more conservative crime agenda. Over the next twenty years there were a move away from indeterminate sentencing toward determinate or presumptive sentencing models or sentencing guidelines; a drop in money available for new demonstration programs; and cuts in many existing correctional treatment budgets. American prisons became frighteningly overcrowded, growing in population by 168 percent from 329,821 in 1980 to 888,593 in 1991, largely on the promises of politicians to get "tough on crime."

Notwithstanding these changes, correctional agencies did not totally give up on rehabilitation. Treatment in juvenile institutions continued to be a priority. A growing drug problem required new strategies for dealing with drug and alcohol addictions. Treatment research and evaluation efforts continued and began to show move favorable results. These also pointed to a host of effective program models (Gendreau and Ross 1987; Palmer 1992). While current use of treatment and rehabilitation technology is not what it should be in actual practice, most rehabilitation scholars conclude that a good deal has been learned over the past decades about specific strategies that work.

Definition of Rehabilitation

For most, rehabilitation is synonymous with interventions or treatment. Sometimes *rehabilitation* might more accurately be called "habilitation." "Habilitation," in this sense, refers to the correctional offender whose criminal behavior is the result of not having received the skills or personal qualities needed to live a life free of crime. Whether we are speaking of habilitation, rehabilitation, treatment, or intervention services, we are referring to distinct correctional programs that, according to Palmer (1992), are designed to: "a) change or modify the offender or help him (her) to modify himself (or herself), or to b) change or modify life circumstances and improve social opportunities." Such methods should "utilize, develop, or redirect the powers and mechanisms of the individual's mind and body in order to enhance the ability to cope and grow" (1992, 2–3). Palmer excludes from his definition any correctional options that try to "reduce, physically traumatize, disorganize or devastate the mind or body by means such as dismemberment or electroshock techniques" (1992, 3). He includes measures that try to "affect the individual's future behavior, attitudes toward self, and interactions with others by focusing on such factors and conditions as the individual's adjustment techniques, interests, skills, personal limitations, and/or life circumstances" (1992, 3). It is important to note that such programs are planned interventions. Often the term rehabilitation refers to a clinical intervention, but for the purposes of this entry, we also include planned educational or vocational interventions.

It is also important to identify what is not included in this definition of correctional rehabilitation. Occasionally, correctional options are put forward as measures for reducing future crime, but, on close examination, there is no component of the option that actively plans such a change and nothing in the program is specifically targeted to individual criminogenic factors. Halfway houses, by themselves, for example, do not constitute "treatment" unless they offer treatment programs. This definition excludes other custody, control, and punishment options that contain no additional treatment components. This distinction between treatment and control and custody may be a confusing one for policy-makers and others, because one seldom hears of any new correctional option put forward without some promises that it will either solve the crime problem or reform the offender. Boot camps, for example, have been touted as short-term treatment programs for first-time offenders, particularly drug-offenders. But the military regimen has little basis in any treatment model, and often no interventions are specifically targeted to the drug problem. In a similar vein, intermediate sanctions such as intensive probation, house arrests, and electronic monitoring serve a custody and control function rather than a treatment one.

Types of Correctional Rehabilitation Programs
Consistent with the above definition, rehabilitation may occur in mental health and substance abuse, educational, or vocational programs. Some might also include spiritual programs, although very little research has been devoted to the use of religious programs as vehicles for rehabilitation. We must also differentiate rehabilitation that is offered in juvenile facilities from that offered in facilities for adults. Typically, one would expect to find more mental health, psychotherapeutic, and educational programs in an institution for juveniles. Moreover, such institutions are required to educate youths until the age of eighteen. In adult institutions, a much higher proportion of the staff are assigned to serve custody and security functions than treatment (Bartollas 1985).

Mental Health and Counseling Programs
Mental health programs comprise a diverse array of strategies. In rare instances, an institution might provide in-depth psychotherapy for seriously troubled inmates. Such approaches would deal with internalized conflicts, anxieties, phobias, depression, uncontrollable anger, neurosis, and other serious mental health problems, stemming perhaps from early abuse, trauma, abandonment, or dysfunctional family life. Strategies known as "here and now" treatment models, however, are far more common approaches to treating or counseling prison inmates. As the phrase suggests, "here and now" programs assist clients to deal with current issues in their lives, such as how poor attitudes might influence work performance. Here and now strategies include behavioral programs, social learning approaches, and cognitive therapies. All of these are discussed briefly below, but may be examined in more detail elsewhere (see Lester et al. 1992).

Here and now approaches are preferred for a number of reasons. They cost much less than in-depth psychotherapy and do not require highly skilled clinicians. Correctional personnel with a bachelor's or a master's degree, for example, can be trained to use Reality Therapy and behavioral approaches. Moreover, the here and now strategies are more apt to deal with observable behavior than with the more abstract, sometime subconscious processes that are the subject of psychoanalysis. Finally, the here and now strategies work well in group settings, and most correctional counseling occurs in groups.

In-depth psychotherapy employs or borrows from the tenets of psychoanalysis, the strategies developed by Freud and considerably modified by his followers. In its most intense form, psychoanalysis employs insight therapies that endeavor to alert clients to the sources of present-day conflicts and difficulties. According to Redl and Toch (1979), the various techniques used in these approaches afford clients the opportunity to make past problems come alive in the present to be "rehearsed, sorted out, coped with and (ultimately) set aside" (1979, 184). To ignore these past traumas or sources of difficulty is to allow them to continue to influence our behavior in the present in the form of nonrational processes such as defense mechanisms, some of which predispose individuals to criminal or delinquent behavior.

Of course, not all offenders are appropriate for such therapies. Even setting aside matters of cost and inefficiency, these are insight therapies that require verbal, insight-oriented clients. In addition, not all inmates will present the types of problems that are amenable to indepth psychotherapy. Redl and Toch write, "The psychoanalytic perspective adds little to what we know about businessmen who cut their losses by burning down stores. It may tell us much, on the other hand, about fires that are set in response to feelings of powerlessness, inadequacy, boredom, frustration, self-hate, and loneliness" (1979, 192). The latter example, however, prompts an important question. If we don't address the past, then what? Often clients who are amenable to in-depth therapy present extremely serious problems, such as violent behavior in the form of reaction formations or displaced aggressions, or phobias, psychosomatic ailments, and extreme anxiety. It is not at all certain that the less intensive approaches that are discussed in the following sections can address these more serious issues. Indeed, although stopping short of advocating the most expensive forms of psychotherapy, Palmer (1992) notes that some correctional inmates have internal problems that must be confronted through therapies that address internal processes. Unfortunately, the realities of high costs and tight budgets often mean that the needs of seriously disturbed offenders cannot be met.

Behavioral treatment programs are far more common. In fact, one such program, the token economy, can be seen in various forms in many, if not most, juvenile correctional institutions. Token economies work from the tenets of B. F. Skinner's operant conditioning theory: we repeat behaviors that are rewarded and avoid those behaviors that result in punishments. In this way, programs can shape prosocial behavior, discipline, or other "operants" by rewarding approximations of the behavior and ultimately the behavior itself.

The reward system in token economies is highly structured. If we want an adolescent to do homework for one hour per evening, for example, we must consistently reward such behavior, and the reward must be given shortly after the demonstration of the behavior or operant we are attempting to foster. In token economies, youths are usually informed of a series of behaviors that staff expect to see while in the institution, such as good social skills (no fighting and cooperation with others), cleanliness (having one's bed made by 7:00 A.M.), good study habits, performance of assigned chores, and adherence to a daily schedule. On a frequent and regular basis, an accounting is made of whether the youth has behaved as desired. Points are awarded for doing so, and the youth can accumulate points and exchange them for primary reinforcers, such as a day's outing (under supervision), extra television time, or recreation time. On the same principle, points can be subtracted, or punishments administered (such as "time outs"), for not following rules or for acting out.

Token economies are typically for the entire facility. An important function of the program is to phase out the reward system, so that the youth is not dependent on it. Part of the phasing out process can also involve graduating to other levels of supervision within the institution that are less structured and offer more freedom. Promotion to a less restrictive level of supervision, however, must be earned. Moreover, subsequent levels offer the rewards less frequently. Ultimately, the rewards are phased out altogether, and the hope is that prosocial behavior, good study skills, and other good behavior will have their own intrinsic rewards.

Token economies are also popular for the fact that they assist personnel in their efforts to manage the institution. Many of the operants have to do with cleaning the premises and adhering to schedules, which benefit the correctional facility as well as the inmates. In fact, experts warn treatment planners against a tendency to focus on those that help the institution to run effectively while not attending to those that will be meaningful to the clients upon their release.

The behaviorists recognize that clients do not necessarily have to receive rewards and punishments themselves in order to learn, since humans also learn vicariously by observing the experiences of others. Social learning theories introduce the notion of the role model, who, if perceived as attractive, similar, and well rewarded, will influence the behavior of observers. Programs that follow from that theory provide for a process of modeling appropriate behaviors, and an opportunity to practice them. Arnold Goldstein and his colleagues at Syracuse University, for example, have produced a skills development model. They list approximately fifty skills that they are attempting to foster in delinquents and predelinquents. Each skill is broken down into component behaviors. "Dealing with anger," for example, first teaches youngsters to recognize when they are angry. Staff then teach the youths a series of coping strategies and alternatives to acting out the anger (Goldstein et al. 1989). Sometimes the social learning programs also provide rewards for the learning of desired behaviors. Social learning treatment models have been extremely varied, ranging from teaching good social skills, to vicarious learning from prosocial youth (engineering the peer group dynamics), to confronting procriminal attitude systems.

Programs based in social learning theory have many correctional applications and can be used in both community and institutional settings, with youth and adults, and with family members. Many of the skills-based programs operate from the notion of "habilitation," in which skills are taught to individuals for the first time. Often these are skills that are absolutely essential to life in these complex times. Without them, individuals are indeed predisposed to failure.

Social learning programs (also called cognitive-behavioral models) have also been viewed as a way of interrupting the bad influence of delinquent peers. Building from the realization that offenders have learned from criminal peers, some programs have attempted to provide positive peer groups. Positive peer cultures, milieu therapies, guided group interaction, and other social approaches seek to develop environments in which inmates are exposed to prosocial models and a fair application of rules. Often such programs hold discussion circles in which group members identify and confront each other's procriminal attitudes and world views. To the extent that such processes confront thinking patterns, the treatment strategy might also be termed a cognitive or cognitive-behavioral model.

Cognitive programs operate on the notion that one's thinking strategies, including one's attitudes, world views, beliefs, and values, can sometimes generate troublesome behavior. In fact, certain procriminal thinking patterns serve to rationalize behavior that would otherwise be unacceptable. In doing so, they "free" offenders to behave in ways that hurt others.

An example of a cognitive approach is seen in the work of Stanton Samenow (1984). Building from earlier work (Yochelson and Samenow 1976), Samenow identifies many criminal "thinking errors," such as a refusal to accept responsibility or a denial of the concept of injury to others. In his criminal personality group interventions, staff and ultimately inmate peers are trained to recognize these thinking errors and to call them to the attention of the inmate who demonstrates them. A good deal of teaching and modeling may proceed from this diagnostic stage. From there, inmates can be taught appropriate anger management and negotiating skills, or extremely constructive interactions may take place around the notion of empathy. Inmates learn that not everyone shares their views and that more prosocial, empathic, and responsible perspectives can be taken on the subject at hand.

Reality Therapy is another cognitive-behavioral approach that has enjoyed a good deal of popularity as an approach for dealing with offenders. Expanding from the writings and work of William Glasser (1965), Reality Therapy works on the notion of instilling responsibility for one's behavior. This approach ignores past influences on one's present situation and focuses instead on one's responsibility to change one's life in the "here and now." An often overlooked component of Reality Therapy is the task of getting offenders to recognize two key needs: their need to feel worthwhile to themselves and others, and their need to love and to be loved. Alerting individuals to these needs builds a context for responsibility, since irresponsibility often interferes with one's meeting these needs.

The cognitive and cognitive-behavioral treatment models are popular treatment strategies for some of the same reasons that the behavioral programs are. They are efficient to administer. They lend themselves to group treatment strategies. Correctional staff can be trained to use the approaches, and the change strategies target observable, stated thoughts, attitudes, and values.

Group Counseling and Treatment approaches can be applied in group settings as well as individual ones. In fact, most treatment approaches in corrections are group counseling programs, necessitated by the large prison populations and the limited number of treatment personnel and limited resources. This is not necessarily a disadvantage, because group treatments offer more than just economy. Indeed, group cohesiveness and peer influence can be vehicles for change in themselves. Moreover, group approaches afford an opportunity for social interaction that cannot take place in individual counseling situations. The opportunities for modeling, identification of important issues, dialogue, working through, and other key therapeutic events are greater in group settings than they would be in an individual session.

Self-Help Groups add additional advantages. Self-help groups are common in prisons, ranging from Alcoholics Anonymous and Narcotics Anonymous to the Seventh Step prisoner self-help movement. While these groups should not be viewed as therapy groups, they are often therapeutic and can be a crucial supplement to group or individual counseling. Key to their success is their unique ability to provide support, sponsorship, and an unparalleled means for dealing with the social stigma. In these settings, participants are introduced to others, like them, who can model a way to recovery, growth, and rehabilitation.

Notwithstanding their value, however, it has been an unfortunate practice to equate self-help groups with treatment. Of course that is tempting, because the self-help programs are not merely cost effective, they are usually free.

Therapy/Treatment for Specific Problems

Against this basic outline of prison mental health programs, it is not uncommon to implement therapeutic strategies for dealing with specific types of prisoners or problems, particularly criminogenic ones. Many prisons, for example, have implemented sex-offender programs. Often these are cognitive behavioral models that confront offenders' distorted orientations toward their victims, their use of vio-

lence, and their ability to control anger. The most successful models, however, employ principles of operant and classical conditioning. Intensive follow-up components, in which offenders are required to repeat therapies at regular intervals, have been crucial to their success (Maletsky 1991).

With studies showing that 40 to 80 percent of prison inmates evidence serious substance abuse histories, it is even more common for institutions to provide drug and alcohol treatment programs. Treatment models are varied. In large part, that is because there is no consensus on the causal dynamics of substance abuse. Addiction is viewed, for the most part, as emanating from complex and intertwined biological, familial, psychological, and cultural factors.

Generally, most institutions employ psychotherapeutic (group counseling approaches) and the therapeutic community models. These two types of programs are then supplemented by self-help groups such as Alcoholics Anonymous, Narcotics Anonymous, and Cocaine Anonymous. Group counseling programs address attitudinal, relationship, familial, behavioral, and other factors associated with addiction, although approaches can vary according to needs. Borrowed from mental illness programs, the therapeutic community approach to addiction was first implemented during the late 1960s and has since spread to many state correctional systems. These programs build from social learning models. Treatment rests heavily upon the notion of reducing hierarchical institutional relationships while at the same time increasing inmates' responsibilities for the management of their residential units. Development of healthy social relationships, occasional personality restructuring, and the formation of new, economically productive lives are stressed. Therapeutic community programs have been found to be widely successful in both community and institutional settings. Success is more likely for those programs that provide relapse prevention components. This involves recognizing the symptoms of relapse and having the opportunity to return to treatment if these symptoms appear (Gendreau and Ross 1987).

Sources disagree whether total abstinence is a necessary outcome of addiction "recovery." Canadian prison programs, for example, found success in their controlled drinking models designed to foster moderate use of alcohol (Gendreau and Ross 1987).

Prison Education Programs

A brief review of the education and competencies of prison inmates speaks strongly of the need for prison educational programs. Bell et al. (1984), for example, observe that 42 percent of the incarcerated adult population function below a sixth grade academic level. Over half of the inmate population appear to lack basic reading skills. Many would qualify for special educational programs, particularly those for the learning disabled.

Notwithstanding these rather compelling statistics and the fact that academic and vocational education has long been identified as an important goal of correctional agencies and correctional professional organizations, the state of educational programs in American prisons is not a commendable one. Adult populations are largely underserved and program effectiveness is questionable.

Yet most prisons provide educational programs. The most common ones address academic deficiencies. Adult basic literacy programs, or Adult Basic Education programs, for example, endeavor to promote literacy and address basic academic deficiencies. Such programs may be self-paced and require the use of programmed materials rather than classroom instruction. Outside volunteers or inmate volunteers often facilitate student instruction. For those who have attained competency in basic academic skills but have not graduated from high school, General Education Diploma (GED) classes are available in most adult correctional settings. For adults, participation in these programs is usually voluntary and part time.

Both the GED model and the basic education models are sometimes criticized for their failure to stress important life skills and competencies. The GED, for example is a test-driven model that certifies rather than educates. This criticism extends to other areas of prison education. Vocational education programs are faulted for their failure to teach inmates marketable job skills, those that would prepare inmates to enter the work force. Vocational programs include but are not limited to computer training, barbering, cosmetology, electronics, welding, air conditioner repair, mechanics, painting, secretarial services, textiles, printing, meat cutting, plumbing, and others. Many of these fields have become much more technical in recent years, and correctional agencies cannot afford to keep up

with these advances and the machinery needed to train inmates in their application. Thus, the vocational educational programs are often outmoded. Women's programs are faulted for emphasizing traditional women's jobs such as cosmetology, food preparation, and clerical services, although there are several exceptions. This criticism recognizes that many women are single parents who need better paying jobs, that is, nontraditional careers. Finally, careers requiring licenses or apprenticeships are not well suited to prison, because prison terms are often too short to meet a typical apprenticeship period.

Post–high school educational programs are sometimes extended to prison inmates in the form of correspondence courses, televised instruction, release to attend college during the day, or a small number of college courses offered in the prison through a cooperative arrangement with a college or university located nearby (Bartollas 1985).

The Question of Effectiveness

Recent correctional history shows us that treatment endeavors can be toppled quickly by those who question their effectiveness. Moreover, when their doubts are voiced in the context of an unfavorable political climate, the results can be devastating. Yet one of the favorable outcomes of the discouraging setbacks to correctional rehabilitation has been approximately two decades of research designed to check the accuracy of the unfavorable reviews by Martinson and others.

Clearly the most valuable contribution to our knowledge in this area comes from the advent of meta-analyses, in which the results of many studies are statistically aggregated and assessed as one sample. Across these studies, findings typically show that effective programs reduced recidivism rates by approximately 20 percent. Generally, 25 to 35 percent of the experimental treatment programs studied achieved positive results (Palmer 1992). The meta-analyses, along with several extensive reviews of the literature, also identify the treatments most likely to succeed. These include behavioral, cognitive behavioral, life skills, family intervention, and some multimodal approaches (see Garrett 1985; Gendreau and Ross 1987). At the same time, a cross-study identification of treatments that produce no effects or detrimental effects is also emerging. According to Palmer (1992), these include individual and group therapy or counseling, probation and parole enhancements, confrontation (deterrence or shock) strategies, delinquency prevention (area-wide strategies), and nonsystem diversion.

The meta-analyses also show us that the treatment modality is only one of the factors that differentiates a successful intervention from an unsuccessful one. Programmatic characteristics also have an impact. These characteristics include:

1. Whether the program is well-matched to its clients
2. Dosage, or how much of an intervention is received
3. Therapeutic integrity
4. Administrative management style
5. Provision of a relapse prevention component
6. Whether the program was designed according to a theoretical model (see Palmer 1992).

Of the above list of factors, "therapeutic integrity" warrants special note. One of the unfortunate realities of rehabilitation programs is the high number of failures to operate programs according to their original program design. This occurs in a number of ways. A program, operating on limited funds, for example, may not be able to hire staff who are qualified to administer the treatment model. Staff may refuse to follow the treatment plan, or there may be no treatment plan. Unfortunately, an evaluation study of such a program would show that the treatment had not worked, when in fact, the treatment had never been administered. Indeed, many treatment failures have really been treatments that were never administered.

Sources put forward cautious optimism, recognizing that there are still many evaluation studies that have not produced favorable results. "Success" in this sense means relative success. A 20 percent success rate appears to represent the best that we can achieve, with the best programs found to date. Furthermore, there are no "magic bullets," or programs that will work for all types of offenders (Palmer 1992). To put this in a another context, however, sound rehabilitation programs even at this rather modest success rate are more successful than other correctional strategies, such as incapacitation and deterrence.

Contemporary Correctional Policy and Rehabilitation

In an unfavorable, punishment-focused political climate, the relative success of rehabilitation appears to go unnoticed. Politicians quell the public's fear of crime with promises of yet stricter incarceration policies, more police officers, and occasional digressions into the latest correctional fad. Our most recent fad, the boot camp, mollified the public in spite of a series of evaluations that failed to show favorable recidivism results. State and federal legislative calendars overflow with legislation proposing untested and unexamined solutions to the crime problem.

Sadly, this singular focus on punishment is not purely representative of public sentiment. While it is true that the public favors "get tough" policies, support for rehabilitation is also strong. A series of surveys conducted over the past decade show that indeed the public is punishment oriented, but, the surveys also show incontrovertibly that the public expects treatment-oriented programs to accompany incarceration (Cullen et al. 1990; McCorkle 1993). "Get tough on crime" in other words does not mean to "warehouse" or to ignore treatment and education.

Patricia Van Voorhis

See also ALCOHOL TREATMENT, DRUG TREATMENT, EDUCATIONAL PROGRAMS, VOCATIONAL PROGRAMS

Bibliography

Allen, H., and N. Gatz (1974). Abandoning the medical model in corrections: Some implications and alternatives. *Prison Journal* 54(Autumn): 4–14.

Bartollas, C. (1985). *Correctional Treatment: Theory and Practice.* Englewood Cliffs, N.J.: Prentice-Hall.

Bell, R., E. Conard, and R. Suppa (1984). The findings and recommendations of the national study on learning deficiencies in adult inmates. *Journal of Correctional Education* 35: 129–37.

Cullen, F. T., and K. E. Gilbert (1982). *Reaffirming Rehabilitation.* Cincinnati, Ohio: Anderson.

Cullen, F., S. Skovron, J. Scott, and V. Burton (1990). Public support for correctional treatment: The tenacity of rehabilitative ideology. *Criminal Justice and Behavior* 17: 6–18.

Dinitz, S. (1979). Nothing fails like a little success. In E. Sagarin, ed. *Criminology: New Concerns*. Beverly Hills, Calif.: Sage.

Garrett, C. (1985). Effects of residential treatment on adjudicated delinquents. *Journal of Research in Crime and Delinquency* 22: 287–308.

Gendreau, P., and R. R. Ross (1987). Revivification of rehabilitation: Evidence from the 1980s. *Justice Quarterly* 4: 349–408.

Glasser, W. (1965). *Reality Therapy*. New York: Harper and Row.

Goldstein, A., B. Glick, M. Irwin, C. Pask-McCarty, and I. Rubama (1989). *Reducing Delinquency: Intervention in the Community*. Elmsford, N.Y.: Pergamon.

Lester, D., M. Braswell, and P. Van Voorhis (1992). *Correctional Counseling*. 2nd ed. Cincinnati, Ohio: Anderson.

McCorkle, R. (1993). Research note: Punish or rehabilitate. *Crime and Delinquency* 39: 240–52.

Maletzky, B. (1991). *Treating the Sexual Offender*. Newbury Park, Calif.: Sage.

Martinson, R. (1974). What works? Questions and answers about prison reform. *Public Interest* 35(1): 22–54.

Palmer, T. (1992). *The Re-Emergence of Correctional Intervention*. Newbury Park, Calif.: Sage.

Redl, F., and H. Toch (1979). *The Psychoanalytic Perspective*. In H. Toch, ed. *Psychology of Crime and Criminal Justice*. New York: Holt, Rinehart, and Winston.

Rothman, D. (1980). *Conscience and Convenience: The Asylum and Its Alternatives in Progressive America*. Boston: Little, Brown.

Samenow, S. (1984). *Inside the Criminal Mind*. New York: Times Books.

Yochelson, S., and S. Samenow (1976). *The Criminal Personality, Vol. 1: A Profile for Change*. New York: Jason Aronson.

Religion in Prison

Legal Overview

In the First Amendment of the United States Constitution it is stated that "Congress shall make no law respecting an establishment of religion, or prohibiting the free exercise thereof." Because of that amendment, state and federal correctional institutions provide inmates with certain legal rights concerning the practice of religion. Among these rights are the opportunity to assemble for religious services, attend different denominational services, receive visits from ministers, correspond with religious leaders, observe dietary laws, and obtain, wear, and use religious paraphenalia. These rights, however, must not supersede the security considerations of the prison.

Many of the leading court cases that provide current guidelines for the practice of religion in American prisons were decided during the 1960s and 1970s. Until then, legal issues related to religious inmates were rarely brought before the courts. Among the most important cases during this period were *Fulwood v. Clemmer* (1962), *Cooper v. Pate* (1964), and *Cruz v. Beto* (1972). In the *Fulwood* (1962) case, the U.S. district court for the District of Columbia ruled that correctional officials must recognize the Muslim faith as a legitimate religion and not restrict those inmates who wish to hold services. In *Cooper* (1964) the courts recognized that prison officials must make every effort to treat members of all religious groups equally, unless they can demonstrate a reason for doing otherwise. In the first prisoner-religion case to reach the Supreme Court, it was ruled in *Cruz v. Beto* that it was discriminatory and a violation of the Constitution to deny a Buddhist prisoner his right to practice his faith in a way comparable to that of other prisoners.

In 1977, a federal court ruled in *Theriault v. Carlson* that the First Amendment does not protect so-called religions that are obvious shams, that tend to mock established institutions, and whose members lack religious sincerity. That case was important as being one of the first cases to shift the tide away from decisions in favor of inmates' religious rights. In recent years, courts have ruled more favorably on the side of correctional authorities. For example, in *O'Lone v. Estate of Shabazz* (1987), it was ruled by the Supreme Court that depriving an inmate of the right to attend a religious service for "legitimate penological interests" is not in violation of the First Amendment.

Historical Background

The influence and practice of religion in the correctional setting is as old as the history of prisons. Religion in prison probably began with religious men who themselves were imprisoned. Bible stories of prisoners include those of Joseph and Jeremiah in the Old Testament, and John the Baptist, Peter, John, and Paul in the New

Testament. Beginning in the days of Constantine, the early Christian Church granted asylum to criminals who would otherwise have been mutilated or killed. Soon thereafter, imprisonment under church jurisdiction became a substitute for corporal or capital punishment. In medieval times, the Roman Catholic Church developed penal techniques such as the monastic cell, which later served as a punishment place for secular criminal offenders. As late as the eighteenth century, the Vatican prison served as a model design for Europe and America (Garland 1990).

Early settlers of North America brought with them the customs and common laws of England, including the pillory, the stocks, and the whipping post. During the eighteenth century, isolating offenders from fellow prisoners became the accepted correctional practice. It was thought that isolation encouraged offenders to become penitent over their sins—thus the term "penitentiary." West Jersey and Pennsylvania Quakers were primarily responsible for many of the prison reforms. They developed the idea of substituting imprisonment for corporal punishment and combining the idea of the prison with the workhouse. The prototype of this regime was the Walnut Street Jail in Philadelphia.

Even during the nineteenth century, when daytime work was initiated by the Auburn System, solitary confinement at night was still the norm in correctional practice. The forced solitary confinement was thought to serve the same penitential purpose as the older penitentiary. Educational reform also assisted in the growth of religion in prison. Because of the limited budgets of correctional institutions, chaplains were often called upon to be the sole educators in many American prisons. The "schooling" often consisted of the chaplain standing in a dark corridor with a lantern, extolling the virtues of repentance (Evans 1978). At present, many of our older correctional institutions are being refurbished or destroyed and replaced with facilities designed for better observation and security. Yet the initial influence of religion on the philosophy and design of the penitentiary will surely remain.

Religious Groups and Programs in Prison
The practice of religion is commonplace in most jails and prisons throughout the United States. Worship is either individual or within the structure of organized religious denominations or

Organizations Serving Religious Inmates and Correctional Staff

> Aleph Institute, Surfside, Fla.
> American Correctional Association, Laurel, Md.
> Bill Glass Ministries
> Christian Prison Ministries
> David Ministries
> Federal Bureau of Prisons, Religious Services Department
> International Prison Ministries
> Kairos Prison Ministry
> Liberia Religiousa Distribuidora, Inc., Miami, Fla.
> Match-2
> Mike Barber Ministries, Houston, Tex.
> Moorish American Publishing Co., Mt. Clemons, Mich.
> Nation of Islam
> Native American Prison Ministry Project, Denver, Colo.
> Prison Fellowship, Va.
> Spanish Evangelical Literature Fellowship Inc., Ft. Lauderdale, Fla.
> Tahrike Tarsile Qur'an, Inc., Elmhurst, N.Y.
> The Program for Female Offenders
> Victory Ministries, San Antonio, Tex.

programs. Nearly all state and federal correctional institutions provide support for the four traditional religious denominations—Catholic, Protestant, Muslim, and Jewish. The forms of religious practice vary from prison to prison and state to state. Among the variations of the four denominations in prison are Moorish Temple, Nation of Islam, Black Hebrew Israelite Nation, Native-American, Buddhist, Rastafarian, Curanderism, Santeria, Espiritismo, Jehovah Witness, Christian Scientist, and Third Order Franciscans.

Religious programs conducted by these groups differ according to the beliefs of the group, inmate interest, time and space available in the prison, the competence of the religious staff, and the support of the correctional authorities. It is not uncommon for a large prison to have many religious services on a daily basis. For example, a typical Sunday could include Bible study, Protestant and Catholic services, Islamic Ta'Leem, Jewish Faith Meeting, Spanish Gospel Group, and a Prison Fellowship support group.

The main responsibility of the religious representatives (chaplains, volunteers, spiritual advisors) is to provide pastoral care to inmates and institutional staff. In the past, common duties were to provide religious services, to counsel troubled inmates, and to advise inmates of "bad news" from home or from correctional authorities. More recently, the role of faith representatives has been expanded to include coordinating facilities, organizing volunteers, facilitating religious furlough visits, contracting for outside religious services, and training correctional administrators and staff about the tenets and rituals of nontraditional faith groups.

Reasons for Inmate Religious Involvement

It is difficult to determine why prisoners become involved with religion while incarcerated. Religious belief and practice are individual matters, and the psychological complexities of living in prison make such a determination even more difficult. In research conducted in the correctional setting, however, it has been found that inmates practice religion while in prison for various personal and pragmatic reasons (Dammer 1992).

In some cases inmates gain direction and meaning for their life from the practice of religion while in prison. They feel that God, or Yahweh, or Allah provides a direction in life, one that is better than their present psychological or physical condition. Religion also provides hope for the inmates—hope to reform from a life of crime, and from a life of imprisonment. Some inmates even feel that being incarcerated is the "Will of God" and that full acceptance of this will is essential to being faithful in one's religious belief.

An important reason why inmates become involved with religion is to improve their own self-concept. Lack of a positive self-concept is a common problem with correctional inmates, who may suffer from guilt related to failures in life, remorse over criminal acts, or from the pain of a dysfunctional family background. Because the core of many religious beliefs includes acceptance and love from a higher being, and from members of the faith group, inmates often feel better about themselves if they practice religion while incarcerated.

Other inmates use the practice of religion to promote a personal behavioral change. Because of the rules and discipline that the serious practice of religion requires, inmates learn to become more controlled. An increase in self-control can help an inmate avoid confrontations with other inmates and staff and assist them in complying with prison rules and regulations. Inmates appear to gain a certain peace of mind from the practice of religion. Having this peace of mind is important for the psychological survival of inmates because they are often facing a long time in prison.

Correctional inmates may also become involved with religion to gain protection, to meet other inmates, to meet volunteers, or to obtain special prison resources.

For Protection

Inmates choose religion for protection because they feel that to be safe while in prison they need a group to protect them. Without such protection, inmates believe that they may be subject to physical confrontations and economic or sexual exploitation. Inmates who practice religion for this reason assume that the religious group will provide the protection necessary to avoid such difficulties.

The role of religion as protection is often entangled in other prison issues like race, past criminality, and sexual preference. It is believed by many inmates and staff that protection may be the main reason why African-American inmates become members of the Muslim faith while incarcerated. The same can be said for many of the white inmates who become members of the Protestant, Catholic, or Jewish denominations. Others believe that if a male inmate has been incarcerated for a certain sex offense (child molestation or sexual assault of an older woman) he will be stigmatized as a deviant among deviants. The label used to describe those who committed such crimes is "skinner." The "skinner" is the least respected of all the inmates and is subject to verbal and physical abuse. Inmates of this type may become involved with religion while incarcerated because religious involvement allows them some respite from the fear of attack. They feel that religious services are a "safe haven." Male homosexual inmates have been said to attend religious services for the same reasons.

Religious services can also be a safe place for those with (HIV) AIDS. In some prisons, inmates with AIDS are treated with disdain and cruelty by the others. In religious services, the inmate can receive much-needed psychological assistance from chaplains. Inmates with (HIV) AIDS may find religious services to be the only place where they can interact with other inmates in a positive fashion.

To Meet Other Inmates

Religious services are an important meeting place for inmates because the opportunity to attend is usually available to all inmates in the general prison population. Inmates value the opportunity to meet other inmates for many reasons, but two are noteworthy. First, like most people, inmates enjoy regular social interaction with friends and groups of people with similar interests. Becoming involved in religion while in prison can provide a means of feeling accepted. Second, some inmates meet at religious services for the purpose of passing contraband. The contraband passed can be food, candy, written messages, cigarettes, drugs, or weapons.

To Meet Volunteers

For many of the Catholic and Protestant weekly services and programs, civilians often volunteer time to visit the prison and assist in religious instruction. In men's institutions, because the inmates' interactions with women is limited to contacts with an occasional visitor or one of the few female staff members, they look forward to coming to religious services to meet female volunteers.

To Obtain Prison Resources

Other inmates become involved with religion to gain free access to special resources that are difficult or costly to obtain while incarcerated. These may include food and coffee, holiday greeting cards and books, and musical instruments. For example, during many of the special religious services, coffee, cookies, and donuts are offered. Similarly, certain religious groups receive special food privileges during certain religious holidays. All inmates can receive these goods and privileges if they attend certain religious services or show a minimal interest in being a member of a specific religious group. The resources gained from religious involvement can also include individual favors from the chaplain, who can sometimes provide phone access or written recommendations for parole or transfer. Because of institutional rules about use of the telephone, inmates who need to telephone for emergency reasons may find access limited. The inmates' only other option is to use the phone of a staff member. Chaplains are the most likely choice because they are often sympathetic to the needs of the inmates and have a phone in their office. Inmates may also feel that the religious representative may be a good person to ask for a letter of reference before a parole board hearing or to request a transfer to another institution.

How the Practice of Religion is Viewed by Inmates and Correctional Officers

The most common belief about the practice of religion in prison is that many inmates "find religion" for manipulative purposes. It is believed that inmates hope that prison administrators and parole authorities will view their religious practice as an attempt to become moral, prosocial, and law-abiding citizens, resulting in earlier parole release. For decades, correctional literature and the popular media have cultivated that belief.

Correctional officers often support this "religion for early parole" viewpoint. They base their belief on their personal experience with inmates who have professed to be religious but who have then acted to the contrary, or who are repeat offenders returning to the prison. Also, correctional officers support this view because they are influenced by their own subculture. This subculture, like other cultures, has certain beliefs that are accepted as truth and passed among the officers. The belief about inmates' finding religion for early parole has been transmitted through generations of correctional inmates, officers, and staff.

Inmates' opinions of religion in prison are quite diverse. Some believe, like the correctional officers, that inmates practice religion while in prison only to influence the chaplain or warden for a positive recommendation to the parole board. Others feel that fellow inmates participate in religious programs for a "psychological crutch." These skeptics feel that religion serves to support individual inmates who are weak or need assistance in dealing with the difficulties of prison life. They claim that the practice of religion may enhance self-esteem and good feelings, but only because those involved cannot find those things without a crutch.

Not all inmates, correctional officers, and staff think negatively of the intentions of religious inmates. Because serious religious involvement promotes self-discipline, introspection, and concern for others, many feel that inmates can acquire a number of positive characteristics from the practice of religion in prison. The positive characteristics include peace of mind, positive self-concept, and improvements in self-control and intellectual abilities. We can conclude that there are many reasons why inmates become involved with religion while incarcerated; to determine their religious intentions is a difficult task.

The Future of Religion in Prison

With the continuing growth of the American correctional system and the trend toward making prisons more secure, it is likely that the face of religion in prison will soon change. When budget cuts are made in prison rehabilitation programs to accommodate increased security, the role of religious programs will be expanded. Representatives of the various faiths will be asked to develop and implement programs aimed at reducing racial conflict and improving multiculturalism. As counseling programs are trimmed, support for those with (HIV) AIDS will fall to the religious programs. With job requirements becoming more complex, correctional officers and staff will surely turn to religious leaders and volunteers to help them deal with the psychological stress of working in prison. Programs aimed at the successful reintegration of inmates back into the community will need the assistance of religious personnel to find employment and promote positive family relationships.

Harry R. Dammer

Bibliography

Dammer, H. R. (1992). *Piety in Prison*. Ann Arbor, Mich.: University Microfilms.

Evans, K. (1978). Reflections on education in the penitentiary. In W. Taylor and M. Braswell, eds. *Issues in Police and Criminal Psychology*. Washington, D.C.: University Press of America.

Garland, D. (1990). *Punishment and Modern Society*. Oxford, Mass.: Clarendon.

Hamm, M. (1992). Santeria in federal prisons. *Federal Prisons Journal* 2(4): 37–42.

Johnson, B. (1984). *Hellfire and Corrections*. Ann Arbor, Mich.: Microfilms International.

Smarto, D. (1987). *Justice and Mercy*. Wheaton, Ill.: Tyndale House.

Research in Prison

Consideration of research concerning prisons, particularly research in prison settings, involves broad realms of examination and the coincidence of a variety of potentially useful perspectives in coming to a detailed understanding of relevant information and issues. Obviously, this entry is not intended to provide a comprehensive discussion of research in prison. Rather, it presents an overview and emphasizes selected aspects relevant to research in prison—ones that we think can contribute to developing a fundamental basis for asking questions about why things happen the ways they do in corrections.

Research Inside Prison

The history of U.S. prisons is rather short and not at all glorious. While some efforts to examine prisons from the inside did take place during the nineteenth century, the sorts of efforts we now generally associate with "research" did not enter prisons in significant ways until well into the twentieth century.

Several dimensions of research predominate in the development of information or knowledge from studies inside prisons. One main dimension involves examination of prison social structure. Across and along this dimension are studies concerning formal and informal aspects of prison organization, particularly emphasizing inmate social systems. There have been many notable studies and much branching out as researchers have explored many prison-related concerns. These include assimilation into prison society; degree of prisonization and effects on allegiances as well as conformity to staff expectations; development and effects of inmate social roles; differential responses of inmates to prison environments; the adequacy of a functional approach to understanding inmate adaptions (i.e., whether or not prison social systems are largely the products of the prison); the adequacy of an importation approach to understanding prison social systems (i.e., whether or not prison social systems are largely the products of the backgrounds, attitudes, associations inmates bring with them into prisons); and the potential for integrative explanations regarding prison social systems, amalgamating the functional approach and the importation approach perhaps even with other viewpoints to facilitate understanding and investigation. Within these examinations, researchers variously have focused on topics such as: inmate sexual behaviors, drug related behaviors of inmates, contraband systems, adaptations to the pains of imprisonment, and many other specifics.

A second dimension of research inside prisons involves guards/correctional officers and their work. A number of researchers have produced studies of various sorts examining the individual backgrounds of officers (e.g., looking at age, race, gender, experiences of officers) and how these correlate with attitudes toward prisoners; examining potential organizational determinants of officer attitudes (e.g., role conflict, shift worked, job stress, frequency of inmate contact, perceptions of danger, among others) and effects on work performance; and examining performance of work and perceptions of performance of work, as well as factors which may affect these.

Another dimension has involved the administration of prisons, describing and examining from a number of perspectives factors and conditions related to development of an understanding of what is necessary for effective and appropriate prison management. Such research has centered on identifying and analyzing the mix of context, approaches, and personalities important to understanding prison management and to drawing inferences about what constitutes appropriate and effective prison management.

Effects of incarceration and conditions of incarceration are additional, tangential dimensions of research inside prison. Among the many efforts, researchers have centered attention and studies on: a constellation of legal issues regarding prison conditions and confinement; planned and unplanned effects of incarceration; violence in prisons; effects of incarceration on physical health of inmates; effects of incarceration on psychological well-being of inmates; special aspects of incarceration such as "solitary confinement" or "administrative lockdown," long terms of confinement, confinement of those judged to be mentally ill; and other particular emphases.

Many studies have been devoted to work fitting along a dimension of concern with activities and rehabilitation efforts inside prisons. For example, research attention has been directed to the implementation and effects (intended and unintended) of education programs, vocational programs, therapeutic programs, recreational activities, religious activities, and associational activities (i.e., participating in organized groups such as JayCees and many others within the prison). What works and what does not work, what might work and what might not work, are issues which have provided platforms for research and for controversy concerning research regarding efforts to orient prisoners to law-abiding lifestyles.

There is more to research inside prison. The efforts mentioned above are simply a beginning, suggesting a map of the territory to be explored when considering research inside prison. One would want to continue to provide overlays and detail to such a map.

Research Outside Prisons, Concerning Prisons

Research outside prisons, concerning prisons, comprises several dimensions. Research on possible general deterrent effects provides emphasis to a set of studies regarding prison. Research concerning the effectiveness of punishment and of prison programs/efforts as related to recidivism and life after prison includes a large array of emphases and studies employing a variety of designs. Studies regarding efforts to "reform" prisons and studies concerned with the history of "reform," politics of "reform," and other closely related topics are evident. Studies on the history of incarceration and punishment, history of particular prison systems, development of alternatives to imprisonment, and directly related questions may be seen as a dimension of research centering attention on the role for prisons in society—perhaps asking the question, "What are prisons for?" As with research inside prison, there is more we could mention. The point here is that one begin to understand the scope and nature of research done outside prisons, concerning prisons.

Research From Many Sources, Much Variety

Prison-oriented research is conducted by a variety of investigators and is initiated by a variety of persons, groups, and organizations with diverse, sometimes competing, interests. Research projects may be carried out by practitioners working in prisons, by researchers working for Departments of Corrections (DOC) or the Federal Bureau of Prisons, by researchers working for other agencies or organizations, by academicians and others who have basic research interests, by academicians and others who have applied research interests, among others. Research may be initiated (and research questions, as well as the ways in which research is carried out, may be shaped) by administrators of DOC, the Federal Bureau of Prisons, or other state and federal agencies, by leaders of large and small foundations interested in prisons and corrections, by vested interest policy groups, or by reform-oriented interest groups and other interest groups of many sorts.

Moreover, the research takes many forms, in design and in implementation. Cataloguing the body of prison oriented research by method or type would be a very large task. Keep in mind, though, that there is a broad range of studies, from less rigorous to more rigorous, encompassing qualitative, quantitative and hybrid designs, and much research-based information regarding prisons has been produced.

Use of Research

Most of us expect research information to be authoritative and valuable, and most of us hold a common image that the findings of research will influence decision-making and policy-making directly, shaping significantly or even dictating decision outcomes. As shown above, there has been much research, and there exists a rather large constellation of findings from research regarding prisons.

During the past decade, the use of imprisonment as a strategy for dealing with felony offenders has grown enormously in the United States (the number of people in prison on a given day in America has more than tripled since 1983). With over one million people in prison, there would seem to be great reason for policy-makers and decision-makers to utilize findings available to them in their deliberations about incarceration as a societal strategy, about policies regarding prisons and imprisonment, about the actual operations of prisons, and other important issues.

To inquire as to whether or not policy-makers and decision-makers do so (or to inquire as to whether research information significantly affects decision outcomes) is to ask questions requiring a complex examination. To provide a starting point only, there are several issues to consider.

As shown above, there is much research information available "out there," in many places, regarding prisons. Much of this research information is produced for general consumption by anyone interested in research findings regarding prisons. Some of this research information is produced to address specific questions generated by persons interested in particular prison or prison related situations, but even that information is usually available to those who search for it.

The fact that research findings are in existence in no way ensures their use for policy-making and decision-making in the real world. Quite often, the research findings are inconclu-sive. That is, the findings from a study or studies may not provide a clear answer or may not provide usable practical policy-making and decision-making. Research studies may actually generate controversy and result in less certainty about what to do, rather than producing greater clarity about what to do. Understanding this and considering the complex realms of policy-making and decision-making (which we cannot address here) is only the very beginning to asking questions about the use of research findings.

Beyond that beginning, one must consider the ways in which research information could be used, whether one is concerned with use of research information by certain persons over time or use for addressing a discrete problem or set of problems at a particular time, and a host of critical operational concerns related to what constitutes significant use, how to measure use, and so on. There is a rather large body of research on the use of research information, although only a small amount focused on corrections is available. Those persons who contribute to this body of research, asking all sorts of questions, recognize that a large array of conditions and factors may be important in whether or not a particular set of findings (or a general set of information) may be seen as valuable and may be used.

Those who ask about research use recognize that policy-makers and decision-makers:

1. May make decisions and policies based directly on research findings and recommendations
2. May digest and consider research information and use it to better understand issues or achieve greater clarity in thinking about problems
3. May gather and use research information as ammunition or a bargaining advantage to assist in supporting their own favored positions, in diminishing the favored positions of others, and in supporting requests, such as requests for resources
4. May make little or no effort to secure and consider research information, either for particular types of issues or perhaps as a matter of preference across issues
5. May choose to ignore or not use research information even when it is available to them and is relevant to issues at hand.

A very brief sampling of considerations, conditions, and factors that might be important in what policy-makers and decision-makers choose to do about research information includes:

1. The cost of searching for and securing relevant research or information, perhaps having to fund a study to obtain relevant information
2. The methodological quality of the research information available
3. The nature of the issues to be addressed (research efforts sometimes cannot adequately answer questions, for a number of reasons)
4. The adequacy, effectiveness, and timeliness of communication of research results (is the information understandable, in time for a decision where deadlines force attention, and so on)
5. The nature of political constraints and political acceptability related to issues under consideration
6. The individual characteristics and orientations of the policy-makers and decision-makers themselves
7. An array of variables associated with the organizational context for decision-making and policy-making, the cumulative effects of previous decisions, and the role of research information in relation to other forms of information.

Simply put, there is much to think about in trying to get a handle on the nature and scope of research regarding prisons, and the overlays to our map of the territory to be explored become more intricate if we want to think about use or potential use of research findings regarding prisons.

Future for Prison Research

America's prison population is expanding rapidly, with little indication of abatement through the decade of the 1990s. Imprisonment is a dominant strategy for dealing with felony offenders, and it is not likely that reliance on this strategy will decrease through the 1990s. Regarding prison research, it is clear that the types described above (and other efforts) will continue. Particular research emphases may be cast in high relief (for example, research on the effects of crowding and, with issues surrounding AIDS, research concerning health effects, among others). The need for research of all types will grow. For the future, particular attention must be directed to research on change and how to accomplish beneficial change relevant to imprisonment. As well, particular attention must be directed to understanding the role for research as an input to the very important decisions to be made about imprisonment in America.

Rick Lovell

Bibliography

Lovell, R., and D. Kalinich (1992). The unimportance of in-house research in a professional criminal justice organization. *Criminal Justice Review* 17: 77–93.

Lovell, R., and S. Stojkovic (1987). Myths, symbols and policymaking in corrections. *Criminal Justice Policy Review* 2: 225–39.

Weibel, W. W. (1975). Social constraints in the conduct of evaluation research. In E. Viano, ed. *Criminal Justice Research*. Lexington, Mass.: Lexington.

Williams, F. P., M. D. McShane, and D. Sechrest (1994). Barriers to effective performance review: The seduction of raw data. *Public Administration Review* 54: 537–42.

Riots

The potential for violence is ever-present in prisons, but the most feared type of prison violence is a riot. Unlike other prison violence, riots involve a seizure of control by inmates over part or all of the prison, violence against guards or other prisoners, and demands for administrative changes in the prison.

Today, most facilities distinguish between riots and disturbances. The differences are usually the number of inmates involved, the type of activity inmates engage in, and the amount of damage. The tendency is for prisons to label most incidents as disturbances, because the term is less sensational. For example, in 1993 there were over 186 disturbances in twenty-one systems surveyed and only seven of those were classified as riots. What may be a disturbance in one area, however, may be classified as a riot in another. According to Lillis, in Connecticut a gang fight involving three hundred inmates and causing $101,000 worth of damage was classified as a riot. At Leavenworth, a racial fight involving 427 inmates that caused significant damage to the auditorium, chapel, and industry buildings was classified as a disturbance.

A Historical View

The first prison riot in the United States occurred in 1774, and riots have erupted with frequency throughout the country ever since. Some three hundred prison riots have been reported in this country in the past two centuries.

Two of the bloodiest and most violent riots in American prison history were that at the Attica State Correctional Facility in New York in 1971 and the riot at the Penitentiary of New Mexico in Santa Fe in 1980. At Attica, ten hostages and twenty-nine inmates were killed in the recapture of the institution, and there were reports that one officer and three inmates were killed by inmates during the riot. In the Santa Fe riot, thirty-three inmates died at the hands of other inmates. Although hostages were brutalized, none of them died. The 1993 riot at the Southern Ohio Correctional Facility in Lucasville was the longest prison takeover in the United States. Nine inmates and one officer were killed in the eleven-day siege by inmates at Lucasville. The three riots illustrate the various origins and causes of prison riots.

Riots, like collective violence, are sometimes spontaneous outbursts, but in other instances they may be planned. An organized group of inmates at Attica, bound by racial solidarity and political consciousness, initiated that riot in 1971. Some believe that the riot reflected the social climate of the late 1960s. It has been called a political protest against the white oppression experienced by the mostly black inmates. In contrast, the New Mexico riot of the 1980s was a spontaneous, disorganized outburst, with inmates killing and brutalizing fellow inmates. For the most part, prisoners at Santa Fe acted individually or in small groups. No strong leadership emerged. The Lucasville riot of the 1990s was also spontaneous, but inmates quickly established a system of social order and eventually negotiated a peaceful end to the uprising. In spite of the differences between these three riots, there were striking similarities in prison conditions in Attica, Santa Fe, and Lucasville prior to the riots.

The presence and threats of violence tend to receive little attention outside of prisons until the violence erupts in the form of highly publicized riots. Then inmate groups often capitalize on news media attention to air their grievances or to make demands for administrative changes in the prison. The role of the news media has grown progressively more critical and controversial in the past twenty years. At Attica, inmates were interested in newspaper coverage. They requested that reporters known to be sympathetic to prison reform come and observe their situation. Tom Wicker of the *New York Times* became famous for the book, *A Time to Die,* that he wrote after his experiences there. In Santa Fe prison, rioters demanded national television network coverage of their conditions. Graphic footage of the carnage that aired on the news made the riot the subject of international attention. At Lucasville, the role of the news media was even more interactive. According to some, a thoughtless announcement by a State Corrections Department spokeswoman that inmate demands were "self-serving" and "petty" and that their threats were "standard" was responsible for the death of the only hostage killed in the riot. News media interviews were traded for hostages. News media representatives agreed to videotape the surrender to ensure that no violence ensued. These examples show that over the decades the role of the news media in prison riots has become more complex.

Causes of Prison Violence

Researchers have approached the problem of prison violence from a number of perspectives: sociological and organizational theories; individual inmate characteristics; institutional factors; and external environmental conditions.

From a sociological perspective, DiIulio suggests that prison disturbances are the result of either too much control or a dangerous lack of it. Theorists once indicated that tight controls would be the best defense against violence in prisons. During the 1960s, control was not emphasized so much as personal freedom and creativity. Prisons were seen as oppressive instruments of a racially discriminating and vengeful society. By the 1990s, however, ideas about restrictions are returning, the issues of discrimination and oppression having given way to concerns for crime control and getting tough. The tension between control and lack of control continues to be an issue in the administration of corrections.

Overcrowding

Overcrowding in prison raises the tension level. Further, it restricts prisoners' privacy in the living units and limits their opportunities for participation in work and recreational and educational programs. Before the 1970 riot, Attica prison held 2,225 inmates in a facility designed for 1,200. In Santa Fe, 1,136 inmates were jammed into a facility designed for 900. At Lucasville, double-celling was in effect to handle 1,820 maximum security inmates in a prison designed for 1,540 in single cells. Inmates at Attica, Santa Fe, and Lucasville were idle most or all of the day. The lack of programs and space contributed to the restlessness and boredom.

Crowding interferes with prison classification procedures. Desperate attempts to house inmates in crowded facilities make it nearly impossible to keep different types of inmates separated. Housing aggressive, violent offenders with nonviolent prisoners raises the tension level and the potential for prison violence. In such conditions even nonviolent inmates may become aggressive out of self-defense. Constant competition for scarce resources adds to the tension.

Both the American Medical Association and the American Public Health Association consider sixty square feet of living space to be the minimum for adequate living. Nearly every prison in the country far exceeds its maximum capacity, however, and inmates are often double- or triple-celled. Factors other than crowding must affect the tension levels and violence in prisons, because many overcrowded prisons do not have riots. Studies examining whether prison crowding triggers violence report inconclusive results. Factors such as the level of prison security and the age of the prisoners are also important considerations.

Racial Antagonism

The proportion of racial and ethnic minorities in prison is considerably greater than in the general population. The close living quarters and general tension in prison add to racial antagonism, particularly when blacks equal or outnumber whites in many prisons. Prisons in some regions of the country have disproportionately large numbers of Hispanics and Native Americans. Racial tension in prison is heightened when inmates segregate themselves and group together along racial or ethnic lines, primarily for self-protection. White inmates suddenly become the minority group in prisons where a large percentage of the prison population is black or Hispanic. Researchers have found that as inmates have a greater perception of crowding, their antagonism toward racial groups also increases.

In the Attica riot, the Black Muslims played a significant leadership role. At Santa Fe,

Hispanics were in the majority, most of the blacks escaped the riot, and whites were both preyed upon and predators. In Lucasville, Black Muslims again played an important role; the White Aryan Brotherhood was also organized and involved. But in this case hostages also took on some of the racist characteristics of their captors. Two white officers had visible lightning bolt tattoos signifying their white supremacist beliefs long before they were taken hostage in the riot. A black officer put on the garb of a Black Muslim while he was a hostage.

Environmental Factors

There are a number of environmental and situational characteristics in prisons that may invoke violence. Kratcoski studied inmate-to-guard violence rates and found these factors to be important: (1) location where the assault occurred; (2) shifts when assaults occurred; (3) presence of other staff members when assaults occurred; (4) assaults on officers occurring after a threat was issued. In federal institutions, nearly three-fourths (71 percent) of all assaults on officers occurred in the detention unit. For state institutions, the high-security unit also reported the highest rate of assaults on officers, but the assault rate overall was more evenly distributed. The highest percentage of assaults occurred during the day shift, when inmates have the least restrictions put on them. Researchers have found that violence toward staff is more likely to occur in areas where inmates are active but not engaging in highly structured activities. Violence toward other inmates is likely in areas where they congregate. Self-inflicted injuries are the only type of violence likely to occur inside an inmate's cell. Inmate aggression directed at correctional officers is more apparent on disciplinary floors, even though restricted movement is enforced, while aggression directed at other inmates is less likely in such restrictive environments.

Administrative Factors

Long-standing problems in prison administration and management contribute greatly to unrest. Frequent turnover (at all levels), inadequate staff training, and dangerous breaches of security are major factors in upsetting the stability of a delicate system. While a number of the causes of riots and disturbances are beyond the control of correctional staff, several precipitating factors can be traced directly to poor management practices, including lack of communication and inad-

Correctional officers in riot gear at the 1987 Cuban detainee riot at the Atlanta Federal Penitentiary. Photo courtesy of the Office of Archives, Federal Bureau of Prisons. Provided by the American Correctional Association.

equate personnel. The field of corrections is characterized by frequent administrative turnovers. Some degree of turnover is normal and to be expected. Excessive turnover stemming from political agendas, however, often prompts major changes in correctional philosophy and tends to result in periods of instability in prison systems. Poor lines of communication serve to further aggravate the vague lines of authority and responsibility, the absence of clearly defined regulations, and the general indecisiveness among administration, especially regarding legitimate inmate grievances. At Attica, Santa Fe, and Lucasville, living conditions and lack of adequate programs were frequently cited as inmate complaints that went virtually unheard. More important, however, were the reports of harassment and the documented cases of excessive use of force against prisoners before the riots. While rumors and warnings of violence persisted, preventative measures were not initiated. At the least, emergency preparation for riots should have been implemented, but the staff were not adequately trained for emergencies.

At many facilities, staff members are highly inexperienced. Unseasoned correctional officers are quickly hired to fill vacant spots left open by frustrated line personnel who found the job low paying, unrewarding, and stressful. Since 1981, the American Correctional Facility Commission on Accreditation for Corrections Standards has required that new correctional officers receive 160 hours of training during their first year and forty hours each year thereafter. Few prisons, however, meet this standard.

The staff cannot be blamed, though, for physical mechanisms in prisons that break down at the time of a riot. At Attica, a faulty weld in a metal gate that was supposed to hold back the onslaught of prisoners gave way, allowing prisoners access to most of the prison. At Santa Fe, administrators depended on "shatter-proof" glass to hold back the barrage of inmates in a riot, but it broke in minutes. At Lucasville, inmates were able to collect master keys from hostages. One key opened most of the doors on an entire cellblock in a matter of moments. These examples show that dependence on mechanical measures cannot take the place of a well-trained, alert staff.

The importance of administrative issues in the tension that leads to prison riots cannot be overlooked. Administrative instability and lack of a consistent approach to prison policy in New York contributed to the riot at Attica. The New Mexico Department of Corrections was also unstable, and the lack of leadership at the upper levels was matched by a long-standing clique of middle and lower level managers at the prison who were frequently cited for corruption. In Ohio, the warden at the Lucasville facility was said to have been an outstanding leader at the time of the riot, but the middle and lower levels of administration at the prison were not being adequately handled, so the warden's policies were seldom carried out.

In each of the three state system, New York, New Mexico, and Ohio, goals of security were in strong conflict with goals for rehabilitation. Inmates felt this goal conflict personally as confusion, inconsistency, lack of predictability in their daily affairs, and unmet expectations.

Braswell, Dillingham, and Reid list inhumane treatment, unprepared line officers, and lack of consistent administrative policy as major precipitators to the violence that erupted at Attica and Santa Fe.

Individual Factors

Prisoners in Attica, Santa Fe, and Lucasville were relatively young, violence-prone, and inadequately classified. The American Correctional Association notes that inmates are typically young, unmarried men who are often the product of dysfunctional families. Furthermore, they are uneducated or undereducated and uncommitted to socially acceptable goals. Young people are more prone to violence, perhaps because of greater physical strength and lack of social commitments. In addition, many inmates adopt attitudes of machismo or join a gang as protection against sexual assaults.

Gang Violence

Gang violence in prisons is widespread, often organized along racial, ethnic, or geographic lines, and is commonly provoked by racial antagonism. Gangs in prisons began surfacing around the early 1970s, primarily for protection. In the last decade, however, gangs have also organized themselves to obtain and maintain control. Membership in gangs often requires violence as an initiation process; once an inmate is in, getting out is another occasion for violence. Gang-related activities seem to invite violence. Many inmates are killed in what are believed to be gang-related incidents in prisons each year.

But the role of gangs in prison violence is not a direct one. In some cases, gangs are believed to keep order in prisons. Often it is not in the best interest of prison gangs to promote violence. When gangs control the market in contraband and the flow of information, they may act as a stabilizing influence in order to protect their own highly profitable social order.

When prisons erupt in riots, the role of gangs is even more complex. At Attica, for example, the inmates who claimed membership in the Black Muslims kept order and prevented attacks on hostages and other inmates. At Santa Fe, on the other hand, there were no well-established gangs, just factions and groups of "home-boys." In the Santa Fe riot, the inmate-to-inmate violence was out of control. The Lucasville riot involved an unlikely coalition between Black Muslims and Aryan Brothers, who worked together to organize and carry out the riot and to keep order during the long eleven-day siege that followed.

Social Structure

The social structure within prisons often provokes violence and incidents that may escalate to riots. Israel Barak-Glantz believes that the causes of prison disturbances fall into four categories: (1) solidary-opposition social system (the natural desire to challenge authority); (2) racial, political, and ideological tensions; (3) relative deprivation; and (4) prison as mixed-goal institutions (treatment versus custody). They use a 1981 Michigan prison riot to illustrate these categories. First of all, the delicate social system was upset by legislative measures that sought needed changes in the living conditions of inmates. While the intention was respectable, it was defeated by the public, giving the prisoners little hope of seeing better conditions by that route. The loss of hope for better living conditions, with no future changes in sight, also disrupted the stability of the social system. Furthermore, mixed goals became apparent after a major shift in administration from a security- and custody-oriented warden to a treatment-oriented warden. It was not necessarily the shift in goals, but the failure to carry out expected changes that was behind the riot. Line officers and middle management were not aware of, or largely ignored, new policies because of habit or disagreement. Therefore, a power vacuum took over the institution. The triggering mechanism seemed to be an unauthorized shakedown and the potential threat of an unauthorized lock-down. The prisoners' perceptions of desperation may have made them feel as if there was little to lose.

Some experts believe that riots are endemic to prisons. Fox describes prisons as time bombs that are spontaneously ignited. He divides the typical prison riot into five phases. First some undirected violence erupts, followed by the recruitment of inmate leaders who develop new policies. At that point, there is interaction with prison officials and attempts to determine alternatives for resolution. At some point, there is a prisoner surrender (voluntary or coerced) and, finally, there are investigations and, ideally, administrative changes. In a similar vein, Smith believes that prison riots are triggered by some unresolved conflict and that inmates can respond in four ways: bargaining, withdrawal, combat, and mediation. Smelser proposes a theory of collective behavior and emphasizes six determinants that increase the likelihood of a prison riot: structural conduciveness; tension; spread of a generalized belief; precipitation factors; mobilization and organization for action; and, finally, operation of mechanisms for social control. Smelser's six determinants highlight the importance of the environment as a whole as well as the collective behavior that results behind the walls for understanding prison riots.

Braswell, Dillingham, and Reid suggest that riots are most likely a combination of these three theories: Fox's triggering event, Smith's conflict alternatives, and Smelser's overall environmental preconditions.

Costs of Prison Riots

Public apathy in regard to the conditions in corrections is likely to be a cause of administrative breakdown, which in turn may lead to conditions conducive to violence. Attica, Santa Fe, and Lucasville suffered from fiscal and budgetary problems, probably stemming from a general lack of interest from the public and legislature. In many people's minds, convicted offenders deserve any form of punishment they receive. The false assumption behind this reasoning is, of course, that only the inmates pay. It should be recognized that correctional officers and other staff members who are attacked, taken hostage, and in extreme cases beaten, sodomized, or killed, are public servants performing a service in the name of justice and the duty of protection. Furthermore, many facilities embrace the theory of rehabilitation, and offenders who become tense and violent in prison will be no better in

society when released. As human beings, convicted criminals have certain fundamental rights, among them fair and impartial treatment.

Braswell, Dillingham, and Montgomery classified the costs of prison riots into three categories: loss of life, loss of property, and loss of time. In addition to the immeasurable physical and psychological cost to both victims of violence and their families, the monetary cost to taxpayers from violence, particularly riots, is astronomical. Preliminary figures put the cost of rebuilding after the Lucasville riot at more than $15 million. The cost of the Santa Fe riot was estimated to have been at least $28.5 million; the riot at Attica cost an estimated $3 million.

Loss of time both during and after a riot constitutes a great deal of expense in administrative and personnel resources, in addition to the cost of assistance from various outside agencies. Additional costs for maintaining the facility, developing new programs, and adding more staff and improving training must be paid through funding from state and federal governments and ultimately the taxpayers, who are often unwilling to contribute until they see themselves as forced to do so after violence has erupted.

Prevention of Prison Violence

What have we learned from these brutal eruptions of violence and from the theories that attempt to explain riots? All prison riots point to needed changes and improvements in prison administration and operations. Saenz and Reeves note that the New Mexico riot in particular offered specific lessons. First, they emphasize that violence is an ever-present threat where many of the most incorrigible offenders are incarcerated together. Second, corrections management needs to be stabilized; reduced turnover promotes consistency. Third, information gathering techniques need to mature beyond the use of snitches. Fourth, adequate staffing and training programs must be implemented. Fifth, riot contingency plans must be ready for emergencies.

Effective prevention and intervention can reduce opportunities for aggression. Providing ombudsmen to mediate disputes, an improved classification system, greater restrictions on movements inside prison, and a responsive staff are all improvements important for preventing riots.

Prevention of yet more overcrowding might be accomplished by fewer mandatory sentencing practices, alternatives to incarceration, and improved budgetary planning. In addition, a better educated public would learn the importance of funding for prison construction and program improvements.

Another preventative strategy against violence in prisons involves establishing formal inmate grievance procedures. To prevent riots, inmate grievances must be taken seriously. In addition, programs that promote active, purposeful goals channel unspent energy in a useful manner. Highly qualified individuals must be recruited for work in corrections and extensively trained if riots are to be prevented. Retention of quality personnel requires adequate salaries, benefits, and good working conditions.

Administrators also alleviate some tensions by making themselves visible and available to both staff and inmates. Correctional facilities greatly benefit from an alert and well-trained professional staff. Prepared staff can anticipate tension, predict causes of strain, and alleviate some of the pressure. The American Correctional Association notes that quality personnel should possess the following basic skills: knowledge of the common causes of riots, understanding of minority concerns, and knowledge of the rights of inmates. Well-trained officers are aware of potentially explosive situations such as unusually large congregations of prisoners, gang-related threats or minor assaults, and security breakdowns. They take quick, responsive action to prevent further problems.

It is clear that prison violence is not new and is not inevitable. Certain precautions can prevent large-scale riots and reduce the day-to-day violence behind the walls. Confusion, uncertainty, and general resistance to new policies are precursors to trouble. Administrative policies and communications should be clear and precise. Legislators and the public should be aware of the potential for violence in prisons and the cost in taxpayer dollars and public safety. Consistency among policy-makers and better correctional management can and do reduce the potential for prison riots. While the possibility of riots and disturbances exists continually in some prisons, they are avoidable with proper prison administration.

Sue Mahan
Richard Lawrence
Deanna Meyer

See also VIOLENCE

Bibliography

American Correctional Association (1981). *Causes, Preventive Measures, and Methods of Controlling Riots and Disturbances in Correctional Institutions.* College Park, Md.: American Correctional Association.

Barak-Glantz, I. (1985). "Anatomy of another prison riot." In Braswell, M., S. Dillingham, and R. Montgomery, eds. *Prison Violence in America,* 47–71. Cincinnati, Ohio: Anderson.

DiIulio J., Jr. (1987). *Governing Prisons: A Comparative Study of Correctional Management.* New York: Free Press.

Fox, V. (1972). Prison riots in a democratic society. *Police* 16: 33–41.

Kratcoski, P. (1988). The implications of research explaining prison violence and disruption. *Federal Probation* 52: 57–62.

Lillis, J. (1994). Prison escapes and violence remain down. *Corrections Compendium* 19(6): 6–21.

Saenz, A., and T. Z. Reeves (1989). Riot aftermath. *Corrections Today* 51: 66–67, 70, 88.

Smelser, N. (1973). The theory of collective behavior. In South Carolina's Department of Corrections (Collective Violence Research Project) *Correctional Institutions: A Search for Causes.* Columbia, S.C.: State Printing Co.

Smith, A. (1973) The conflict theory of riots. In South Carolina's Department of Corrections (Collective Violence Research Project) *Correctional Institutions: A Search for Causes.* Columbia, S.C.: State Printing Co.

Wicker, T. (1975). *A Time to Die.* New York: Quadrangle/New York Times Books.

Benjamin Rush (1747–1813)

Benjamin Rush, doctor, statesman, and early promoter of prison reform, was born in Byberry, Pennsylvania. His father, a gunsmith, moved the family to Philadelphia when Rush was two. Rush's father died two years later, when Benjamin was four, leaving his mother with seven children. She sold the gunsmith's shop and opened a general store that she ran successfully for many years. From 1759 to 1760 Rush attended the College of New Jersey, which would later become Princeton University. Then, at the age of fifteen, Rush decided to go into medicine. He went to live as an apprentice with one of the most successful doctors in Philadelphia. Rush also spent three years in London continuing his medical career before returning to Philadelphia. He started his own medical practice in 1769 and also began teaching chemistry at the College of Philadelphia.

Rush began his involvement in politics and public issues shortly after his return to Philadelphia. He wrote papers on slavery, patriotism, and many medical issues. Rush was the first person in American history to propose to the government a plan for a statewide education system. In 1776, Rush was elected to Philadelphia's Committee of Inspection and Observation. Working to enforce the resolves of Congress, this committee regulated the price and supply of such scarce supplies as salt. If they found a ship to be transporting contraband cargo, the committee would often impound it and imprison the owners. The Inspection Committee also played a role in the fight for an independent America; by a close margin, the state representatives voted in favor of independence. At that time, new delegates were elected to represent the state and Rush was chosen. Rush resigned from his post as physician-surgeon of the army and took his seat in Congress.

In 1786, new penal legislation was instituted in Pennsylvania. The legislation mandated limited use of the death penalty and reduced the amount of corporal punishment that was used. Although the changes in penal law were at least partially the work of some progressive reformers of the time, Rush was one of the first to speak publicly against the changes. While attending a meeting of the Society for Promoting Political Inquiries (which met in the home of Benjamin Franklin), Rush presented two primary concerns he had about the punishment of offenders. First, Rush believed that punishment should not be a public event and, second, that the only purpose of punishing offenders was to reform them. Rush thought that all offenders could be reformed if they were punished in a manner that encouraged penance.

In 1787, the Philadelphia Society for Alleviating the Miseries of the Public Prisons was established. It would later become the Pennsylvania Prison Society. Attending the first meeting was Benjamin Franklin, a number of Quaker reformers, and Benjamin Rush. Although Rush was a Presbyterian, he has often been associated with Quakers in America and the prison reforms they supported. The society lobbied the state government for changes in prison administration, the rules of prison labor, and changes to the penal code. The first project taken on by the society was to improve the Walnut Street Jail. Rather than solely confining the inmates as punishment, the reformers also wanted the offenders to engage in meditation and have moral instruction. They supported solitary confinement, in which the inmates were separated from each other and isolated from all contact with the outside world. The jail was referred to as a "penitentiary" because it was where inmates were to do penance for their crimes. Members of the society would sometimes visit the prisoners to assist in their moral instruction.

The idea of solitary confinement was tested on a larger scale with the construction of the Eastern State Penitentiary. The Pennsylvania system of corrections was abandoned by 1900 because of its harmful impact upon the prisoners. Many offenders when isolated for extended periods of time suffered extreme psychological damage, some of them going as far as to commit suicide. The Pennsylvania system was replaced with the Auburn system, which allowed inmates to work together during the day and be isolated only at night.

Benjamin Rush was one of the foremost physicians in the United States. He was a friend of Thomas Jefferson's and John Adams's, and he signed the Declaration of Independence. Rush had married Julia Stockton in 1776 and they had thirteen children, nine of whom lived to adulthood. As his family grew, Rush began to spend less time involved in politics and prison reform. He worked at the Pennsylvania Hospital and took special interest in the treatment of the mentally ill after one of his sons was classified as insane. Rush wrote one of the most famous books on the diseases of the mind, and, as his fame increased, the number of students taking his university classes also grew. Although some of his political colleagues accused him of abandoning his responsibility to the causes he had supported, Rush merely responded that his family had grown to require more of his time. Rush died in 1813 at the age of sixty-five.

Paige H. Ralph

See also PHILADELPHIA SOCIETY FOR ALLEVIATING THE MISERIES OF PUBLIC PRISONS

Bibliography

Bacon, M. H. (1969). *The Quiet Rebels: The Story of the Quakers in America*. New York: Basic Books.

Hawke, D. F. (1971). *Benjamin Rush: Revolutionary Gadfly*. Indianapolis, Ind.: Bobbs-Merrill.

James, S. V. (1963). *A People among Peoples: Quaker Benevolence in Eighteenth-Century America*. Cambridge, Mass.: Harvard University Press.

McKelvey, B. (1936). *American Prisons*. Chicago: University of Chicago Press. (Reprinted Montclair, N.J.: Patterson Smith, 1977).

S

San Quentin Prison

The popular image of the prison is the "Big House." San Quentin State Prison, at the tip of Marin County, California, fits this image well. An imposing structure, built in the mid 1850s, this prison has all the features of the classic fortress prison. The three-tiered cell blocks, the cells fronted by iron bars, the large exercise yard, and the guard towers and gun rails all contribute to the overall feeling that this is indeed a place for punishment.

In the early days of California's history, just after the state itself was formed, felons were held in old Mexican jails and barges that were scattered around the state. In 1851, General Vallejo and his partner, Major James M. Estell, were given a contract by the newly formed state to house the state prison convicts. Later that year, Estell leased the 268-ton bark *Waban* for service as a prison ship. On 7 July 1852, land at San Quentin Point was purchased. By 1854, the first cell block was erected. As in most prisons of the time, the cell blocks in San Quentin were built by convict labor. According to Barbara Yaley and Tony Platt, an investigation committee examined the new prison and found that it was "no paradise for scoundrels" and "a very real penitentiary—a place for suffering and expiation."

Prison Labor

At San Quentin, prisoners were a primary source of both labor and profit. Convict workers were leased out to private businesses, for the profit of the lessors, or to local governments for public works projects. Many of the roads in the northern part of the state were built by convict labor under this system. There is also evidence that the prison, under the supervision of Vallejo and Estell, was beset by corruption and profiteering.

By 1858, the state of California took control over the prison as the legislature reacted to public criticism of the private management. In that year, an inspection team found that "of now over 500 convicts, 120 were barefoot, most were in rags, sick and infirm inmates neglected, food inadequate, and the cells filthy" (Ashcroft 1993, 16).

As prison labor continued to be used for both private and public works, there was significant criticism about the unfair competition presented by cheap convict labor. By 1871, most of the prison labor was put to work in the prison's factories, manufacturing such items as bricks, jute sacks, furniture, and shoes. Labor groups continued to object to the use of the prison workforce labor, which resulted in decreased use of prison labor in products sold on the outside. In the 1990s, prison labor is used in the operation of the facility; its products are available only to state agencies, including other prisons. A few industrial programs exist under the supervision of the Prison Industry Authority.

Women at San Quentin

Although the prison now holds only men, women were housed in the prison before 1933. Women were then moved to a new prison in Tehachapi, and, in the 1950s, to the new women's prison in Corona, the California Institution for Women. Although there is little record of life for the women of San Quentin, conditions were difficult, with few activities. There is some evidence, documented in hearings held in 1856, that the prison guards were accused of "cohabiting and drinking with female inmates" (Ashcroft 1993, 33). Now housed in separate facilities throughout the state, women receiving the death penalty will return to San Quentin to be put to death.

Changes at San Quentin

Life at San Quentin was harsh for most of the prisoners. Inedible food and physical punishments characterized prison life from its inception. Escapes were also a problem, prompting many of the local residents to complain about the lack of security. By 1904 prisoner classification began, initiating a process through which prisoners were separated by offense, criminal history, and other variables. The 1930s and 1940s saw the development of educational and vocational programs, a practice that continues today. Clinton Duffy became the warden of San Quentin during that era. In the 1950s, the Department of Corrections began to incorporate a version of rehabilitation based on the indeterminate sentence system and a policy of individualized treatment. In the 1960s prisoners began a period of unrest, much of it based on racial divisions and perceptions of injustice. By the 1970s, many prisoners began adopting a political ideology, which in turn led to a less stable prison culture among the inmates. By the 1980s and into the 1990s, two key features characterized life in California prisons: racial divisions, often represented by gang membership, and crowding. San Quentin itself no longer houses the most violent of California's prisoners. It serves as a medium-security facility and a reception center.

21 August 1971

San Quentin is also famous for a controversial event on 21 August 1971. George Jackson, an inmate convicted of robbing a gas station and who had a long record of prison problems, was held in the adjustment center, the "prison within the prison," designed to hold the prison's disruptive inmates. Many have argued that the adjustment center was also punishment for political activities, particularly those of black and Latino inmates. The facts remain: On 21 August 1971, George Jackson and another inmate were found running outside of the AC, and three officers were found with their throats cut. In all, three officers and three staff members died that day at San Quentin. Further details can be found in *Soledad Brother* and *American Saturday*. The incident, however, served as a rallying point for many involved in the period's black movement.

The Gas Chamber

In addition to its early historical significance, San Quentin is also the site of the gas chamber, in which about three hundred men and women have been put to death since 1893. Capital punishment was established early in the prison's history, through the California Criminal Practices Act of 1851, and reincorporated in the California Penal Code on 14 February 1872. Prior to 1893, sheriffs of the local counties handled executions. In 1893, San Quentin was designated the site for executions. Hanging was the method of execution. The gas chamber was built in 1938, with the last hanging occurring in 1942. As of the spring of 1994, there are about four hundred men and women awaiting death in the gas chamber (the four women are held at a separate institution in Central California).

San Quentin Today

Prison labor is no longer contracted to the outside community, but most prisoners work or participate in educational programs. The nature of the population has also changed. San Quentin today no longer serves as the most secure facility in the state. As the prison population in California continues to climb, San Quentin has been replaced by newer, larger, and more controlled institutions. The aging buildings, the inadequate housing design, and new ideas about prisoner management have combined to downgrade the institution to a medium-security prison. San Quentin continues, however, to have a significant place in the history of California and its prison system. Ideas about prison labor, humanitarian treatment, the death penalty, and other issues critical to understanding punishment in modern society have been played out within its walls and continue to shape correctional policy and the question of punishment and rehabilitation.

Barbara Owen

Bibliography

Ashcroft, L. (1993). San Quentin, its early history and origins. *Marin County Historical Society Magazine* 17(Spring): 1ff.

Davidson, R. T. (1974). *Chicano Prisoners: The Key to San Quentin.* New York: Holt, Rinehart and Winston.

Duffy, C. (1950). *The San Quentin Story.* Garden City, N.J.: Doubleday.

Howard, C. (1981). *American Saturday.* New York: R. Marek.

Jackson, G. (1979). *Soledad Brother.* New York: Coward McCann.

Lamott, K. (1960). *Chronicles of San Quentin: Biography of a Prison.* New

York: David McKay.

McKenna, C. (1987). The origins of San Quentin, 1851–1880. *California History*, 66:49–54.

Nichols, N. A. (1991). *San Quentin Prison: Inside the Walls*. San Quentin, Calif.: San Quentin Museum Press.

Owen, B. (1988). *The Reproduction of Social Control: A Study of Prison Workers at San Quentin*. New York: Praeger.

Searches

I. Introduction

Searches are performed to prevent weapons or other prohibited items from being brought into or circulated within a prison. These items include anything not allowed on prison grounds or in the possession of staff or inmates. Perhaps a simpler definition of such contraband is anything other than the limited number of items that prisoners are specifically allowed to possess. Examples of contraband include weapons, recreational drugs, alcoholic beverages, and unauthorized clothing that may be used to aid in an escape. In some prisons, however, the definition may also include glue, matches, and chewing gum. Prisoners, staff, visitors (including family members), attorneys, clergy, and volunteers are all subject to routine or random searches.

Searches may be conducted with handheld or walk-through metal detectors. Dogs trained to scent drugs are also used to search individuals and areas for contraband drugs. A "clothed body search" is a manual and visual inspection of all body surfaces, hair, clothing, briefcases, and similar items. This search includes visual inspection of ears, mouth, and nasal cavities. A "frisk search," or "pat down," is a brief manual and visual inspection of body surfaces, hair, clothing, and similar items. The removal of coats, jackets, shoes, and socks may be required for a frisk search. Frisk searches are normally conducted when inmates return from a worksite outside their housing area, particularly if their jobs give them access to any type of tool that may be smuggled out.

A "strip search" requires removal of all clothing and jewelry and includes inspection of mouth, ears, nasal cavities, and inspection of vaginal and rectal cavities. The person being searched is required to bend over and spread the buttocks and, if a woman, spread the lips of the vagina to permit inspection. All cloth-ing and articles removed from the person being searched are also inspected. Regulations often call for strip searches to be conducted in a location that affords limited privacy for the inmate. Strip searches are often conducted following a contact visit.

A "body cavity search" goes beyond the strip search, as physical intrusion into the body cavities will take place. These searches are conducted by qualified medical personnel and are used only when less intrusive methods would not be adequate. When the courts examine cases to see if such searches violate civil rights, they are concerned with the manner in which the search is conducted, where it occurs, and who conducts the search.

Prisoners are usually subjected to random frisk and clothed body searches. Visitors and staff will routinely be subjected to screening devices and frisk searches when entering and leaving prisons. Strip searches and body cavity searches are conducted only if prison authorities have reasonable suspicions based upon facts and rational inferences from those facts that a person is probably in possession of contraband. They may also be performed on the basis of an official warrant. In prisons with both male and female staff, strip and body cavity searches are performed by staff members of the same gender, except in emergencies. Body cavity and strip searches are tightly controlled and usually need authorization by the prison superintendent or a designee.

Inmates may swallow contraband and retrieve it later after defecating. For example, one method of smuggling is to swallow a small balloon of drugs to retrieve later. If an inmate is suspected of having swallowed such an item, the inmate can be placed in isolation, under watch for a period of time determined in consultation with medical staff, to retrieve the contraband upon defecation.

Inmate cells may be randomly or systematically searched. Officers may look for something specific in one inmate's cell, or they may conduct a "shakedown" search of an entire cellblock. Stolen items or drugs found in cells may be used as evidence against inmates without the benefit of a search warrant. It is not unusual for both inmates in a cell to be charged when prohibited items are confiscated because of the difficulty in determining who "possessed" them.

In general, inmates have no privacy rights against searches of their cells by authorities, as would free citizens in their homes (*Hudson v.*

Palmer). Although cell searches may be conducted without the inmate present (*Block v. Rutherford*) many institutions make it a policy to have the inmate present whenever possible to reduce accusations of lost or damaged property.

While searches assist staff in maintaining security and control, they are often viewed by inmates as acts of oppression and degradation. Malicious or sadistic personal or cell searches lead to antagonism between inmates and staff and may even cause disturbances and generate lawsuits.

David Kalinich

See also CONTRABAND, LEGAL ISSUES

Cases
Block v. Rutherford, 468 U.S. 576, 104 S.Ct. 3227, 82 L.Ed.2d 438 (1984)
Hudson v. Palmer, 468 U.S. 517, 104 S.Ct. 3194, 82 L.Ed.2d 393 (1984)

II. Strip Searches

A strip search is one in which the clothing is removed and the clothing and body (including cavities) are thoroughly examined (Rush 1986). There are two types of strip searches: visual inspection of body and cavities, and physical intrusion into a body cavity for the purpose of discovering objects concealed there. The first type, visual inspection of a naked body, is conducted routinely by prison staff when an inmate first checks into the jail, returns from a furlough, or after contact with outside visitors. The second type, physical intrusion, is occasionally conducted, preferably by medically trained personnel, when there is reasonable suspicion that an inmate is concealing drugs, contraband, or weapons.

The Attitudes of Staff and Inmates

Staff members usually feel positively about strip searches of inmates for health and safety reasons. As one senior officer expressed it:

> I feel strip search is a very important phase in processing an inmate, before he is placed in a housing zone and after contact with outside visitors. I feel that it should and must be done to make the jail safe. I have no problem with looking at naked bodies, because I feel it is for my safety and my duty. . . . During the search I look for money, weapons, drugs or anything the

Inmates returning from work in the field each day must be strip searched before re-entering the building. Photo by James A. Bolzaretti.

inmate may be trying to hide and take to the housing area. I also check for skin condition, rashes, discoloration, etc., which may be a sign of a medical problem that the medical staff needs to know about (personal interview, March 1994).

But there is nothing nice about a strip search in the view of inmates. To them, it is demeaning, dehumanizing, undignified, humiliating, harassing, terrifying, unpleasant, embarrassing, and repulsive. One inmate described:

> Like you go to your visits and you're having a very good time, you know, your mom's coming up, and there's this man sitting there looking at you. Now, as soon as your visit is over you're going to get stripped. This man is going to look in your asshole. He sees you right there. It is impossible for you to put anything there, but yet he is going to tell you to strip, bend over, and spread your cheeks. Now, that kills the visit. I don't care how nice the man is, no man is going to look up my ass. That is just another way of harassing you. . . . And then, if you're in the box, they not only do it there but when you go up here,

they do it again. . . . They're always looking for a time to harass. They think they can rule (Toch 1977, 100).

Some consider it a dehumanizing event. One former Los Angeles gang member said, "I was made to strip and go through the degrading motions. One last stab at my humanity" (Shakur 1993, 329).

Purpose and Function

The main purpose of strip searches is to maintain internal prison security. Strip searches of prison inmates are constitutional as long as they comply with the provisions of the Fourth Amendment, which afford protection against unreasonable searches and seizures. Determining whether a search is reasonable in its circumstances and proper in its manner, however, has been a continuing challenge for courts. There is also a controversy regarding whether or not strip searches should be conducted indiscriminately and without regard to probable cause. For example, Chapter 35 of California case law prohibits, prior to placement in the general jail population, strip and visual body cavity searches of persons arrested and detained for minor offenses, unless the offenses involved weapons, controlled substances, or violence, or there is probable cause to believe that an inmate is concealing a weapon or drugs.

Procedures and Techniques

All strip searches are expected to follow some general guidelines:

1. The search should be conducted by officers of the same gender as the individual being searched
2. Officers of the opposite gender should not be allowed in the room where the search is being conducted, except in cases of overriding security concerns
3. Privacy from outside observation must be guaranteed
4. Officers conducting the search should refrain from touching or making any references to the individual's body while conducting the search to preserve the individual's dignity
5. Strip searches should never be conducted randomly or at the whim of an officer, but rather pursuant to specific guidelines established by the agency (Summers 1991).

Techniques for conducting strip searches of both men and women seem to be somewhat similar. First, they are taken to a closed area where there are persons of the same gender. Then they are visually searched, including body cavities. One senior female staff member explained the strip search of female inmates:

All clothes are removed and given to me to place them in a storage bag. Inmates get completely naked. As they are undressing, I am visually looking over the body—ears, armpits, breast, navel, hands, nails, groin, and feet. Then, inmates are asked to open their mouth wide and lift their tongue up. Females with large breasts are asked to raise their breasts. Females are given a jail comb to comb all of their hair forward, then all backward. Females are asked to directly face me, extend arms to the ceiling with palms, facing forward, hands wide open, and legs spread far apart. Keeping this position they bend knees and give three hard coughs. This is done again with them facing away from me, so that the back of the body can be visually checked. They are asked to raise their feet so the soles are checked. They are then told to bend forward, while still facing away from me, and take their hands and spread their buttocks open. Lastly, the inmate is showered, sprayed, and placed in county clothes (personal interview, March 1994).

Strip searches of male inmates involve similar techniques. Malcolm Braly, an ex-convict, described his experience:

When they (prisoners) had all been photographed, the sergeant ordered them to strip down and throw their coveralls into a canvas laundry basket, and their shoes, socks, and underwear into a cardboard box next to it. . . . The sergeant stepped in front of the counter and began to instruct the first of the now naked men. "Lift your arms." He looked at the armpits. "Run your fingers through your hair. All right, open your mouth. Wider. Okay, skin it back. Lift your balls. Turn around and bend over. Spread your cheeks. Okay, lift your feet. The right. Now the left. Okay, get a blue coverall over there, and put on a pair of those cloth slippers (Braly 1967, 34).

Sometimes these searches include "wiggling tongue" and "giving big coughs" (Shakur 1993, 320).

Training Conducted on Searches
The prisons usually conduct policy and procedure classes once a year. The policy and procedures of conducting searches, including strip searches, are explained during these classes and the actual training is given while processing inmates by a senior staff member.

Komanduri S. Murty

Bibliography
Braly, M. (1967). *On the Yard*. New York: Penguin.

Rush, G. E. (1986). *The Dictionary of Criminal Justice*. 2nd ed. Guilford, Conn.: Dushkin.

Shakur, S. (1993). *Monster: The Autobiography of an L.A. Gang Member*. New York: Atlantic Monthly Press.

Summers, W. C. (1991). Conducting strip searches. *Police Chief* 58(5): 54–56.

Toch, H. (1977). *Living in Prison: The Ecology of Survival*. New York: Free Press.

Security and Control

I. Perimeter Security
In corrections, the goal of a perimeter alarm or security system is to keep people from escaping. Four principal actions are involved in a comprehensive system. The first stage is to delay any attempted escape by means of a physical barrier, such as a wall or fence. The second component is the actual detection of the intruder by the detection system sensors. This detection leads to the third stage, the alerting of security staff. The final level is the response of the security staff to the situation, which may include CCTV monitoring and recording as well as physical investigation of the alarm. All four actions must be considered when planning a perimeter intrusion system.

In designing and selecting a system, one should look at the broad aspects of the perimeter alarm system. Design considerations, program concerns and implementation, as well as maintenance requirements must be taken into consideration. Conditions such as type of terrain, environmental effects, zone length, shape of fence line, and possible methods of defeating the system must also be taken into account in order to provide the technology most suited for the situation.

This review should not be left up to engineers or consultants only. The corrections department should have its own staff involved in the design, development of specifications, analysis of bids, and evaluation of the service providers' expertise to ensure that the final product is one that will meet the security needs of the facility.

In addition to the hardware requirements, attention must be paid to the maintenance requirements of any system. Staff must have adequate training and skills to ensure proper testing and maintenance of the system. Certain systems have greater maintenance requirements than others, and repair time varies in the event of failure. Departments should also scrutinize the availability of factory service representatives and replacement equipment. The cost of installation and the expected life cycle of the system must also be figured in the selection process.

Secure perimeters are much more than simple alarm systems. There are many interactive components. Locking systems, intrusion alarm systems, fire alarm systems, and other products necessary for the day-to-day operation of facilities must be evaluated continuously.

One method of evaluation is empirical. Historically, prisons have experimented to determine what works and what doesn't work, and many products have not changed substantially over the years. In the high technology area of intrusion alarm, access control, and security glazing, however, the state of the art changes almost daily. In order to remain current, representatives from all operational areas of a prison must participate in the evaluation of new security products.

Methods of product evaluation include field trips, site and facility visits, presentations by manufacturers, and the testing of new products and systems. One example of New York State's "hands on" program of evaluation was the installation of four different perimeter intrusion alarm systems at a maximum-security prison in upstate New York to determine which worked best. Conditions included severe weather changes, rain, snow, ice, uneven terrain, irregular perimeters, and varying soil types. The data obtained enabled the department to evaluate which systems were suitable for which environments.

The Product Evaluation Committee reviewed, from a program and cost basis, the suit-

Towers or pickets allow guards a view inside the prison compound as well as the surrounding outside areas. Photo by James A. Bolzaretti.

ability of detection systems and other types of expensive, high-technology equipment. Some of the evaluaton findings are explained below.

The fence mounted sensor is a terrain-following system in which movement of the fence activates an alarm. The advantages of this system are early detection, that no perimeter space is required, and that it is easily installed at a relatively low cost. Some of the disadvantages are that poor fence installation can cause false alarms, as can rain and wind.

The taut wire fence system is another terrain-following system based on wires connected to a tilt switch that activates an alarm when the wire is deflected or stretched. The advantages of this system are early detection, the creation of a man-barrier as well as a detection device, a low false alarm rate, and that the equipment is not seriously affected by environmental conditions such as rain and wind. One of the disadvantages of this approach is the high installation cost and the high level of maintenance required on the fence.

A balanced capacitance sensor system uses balanced sensing cable equally spaced on the left and right side of the protected object to trigger an alarm. This arrangement has a low false alarm rate, as the cable must be touched or approached closely to activate. This system is used in such places as roof tops, or along selected areas of fencing, and it is not designed for use as a perimeter system.

A seismic sensor system has a terrain-following buried sensor that listens for disturbances. This system is difficult to install and maintain, however, and it is not recommended for cold regions or those that get heavy snow. In addition, a discrimination array line is required to screen out nearby seismic activities, such as heavy traffic or thunderstorms.

Microwave sensor systems operate on line of sight. An alarm occurs when a person passes between the receiver and transmitter, disturbing the volumetric field. These systems have a high probability of detection and provide excellent coverage when installed on flat, smooth perimeters. Although alignment and sensitivity checks must be done, the set-up is relatively low maintenance. The disadvantages are that the system is not suitable for hilly terrain, and that vegetation and snow must be kept clear between sensors.

Infrared sensor beam systems use a line-of-sight principle similar to microwave, although the typical cost for a zone is greater. These systems are used mostly on short distances (such as truck sallyports). Sensors are stacked on poles to provide zones of varying height. Environmental conditions like rain, fog and falling snow do not impede its operation. Snow accumulation and vegetation, however, will create difficulties for the system.

Electric-field sensor systems are based on penetration of the volumetric field created by interaction of the field and sense wires, which are mounted on galvanized poles. The major advantage of this package is that the terrain-following system has a high probability of detection. The system requires attentive maintenance to ensure proper tuning and that vegetation in the area be strictly controlled.

Ported coaxial cable sensor systems consist of two buried cables that emit (leak) an electromatic field. The alarm is activated by disruptions in the field that meet the predetermined criteria (of mass, velocity, and duration). Advantages of this arrangement are that it is adaptable to most terrain, and that it is not affected by wind (if moving objects such as trees or brush are not in field). Potential problems are that heavy rain and the pooling of water affect the field, and that repairs to buried cable are difficult.

Video motion detection sensor systems respond to changes in the video signal provided by a CCTV camera caused by moving objects. The combination of a monitoring and a detection system in one package reduces cost. A control room has immediate assessment of each alarm. This system has a high alarm rate, however, because of environmental conditions such as fast changes in light levels caused by clouds. Moving objects, such as swaying trees, can also affect the system if they are in view of the camera. While new programming algorithms have reduced these problems, the system still remains a high alarm technology when used outdoors.

Francis Sheridan

II. Internal Security

Standards for security inside a correctional facility have been established by recommendations of the American Correctional Association, the Commission on Accreditation for Corrections, the National Institute of Corrections, and by rules established by the various state departments of corrections. Maintaining prison security inside a facility is a complex task. Policies and procedures must be established and closely adhered to.

There are various security levels among prisons, from maximum security to the community correctional facility (which could be a facility with no perimeter security system or with a private residence). This section deals with prisons that are concerned with security. In a security-conscious prison, inmates are housed in single cells that are secured by heavy-duty doors, windows, locks, and other necessary equipment. Such a facility requires that frequent searches for weapons and contraband be conducted. Inmates who are moved out of their cells are closely guarded within the facility. Handcuffs, leg irons, and waist chains are used when correctional officers transport inmates. Prisoners leaving work areas or passing through different sections of the prison are required to pass through metal detectors. Also, as many as five correctional officers in addition to restraints may be required to transport a dangerous prisoner.

Professional prison administrators responsible for the internal security of the prison are expected to establish written security control policies and procedures. These procedures are published in an operational manual available to all prison personnel. Security control policies and procedures should be reviewed at least once a year. The security control manual contains material on inmate classification, building inspection, inmate counts, key control, tool control, inmate searches, and emergency procedures. Operational procedures prohibit correctional personnel from entering high-security areas without the availability of immediate assistance. Inmates are under visual surveillance and control twenty-four hours a day, every day of the year. To enforce the vigilant supervision of inmates, correctional officers constantly stay within hearing distance of inmate living areas, so as to deter misbehavior and disorders. Being close by, correctional officers can respond quickly to emergencies.

There are several operating procedures that can assist in maintaining prison security inside the facility. These procedures, as established by policy, are extremely important in preserving security. They are guidelines that need to be followed. Various security policies and procedures will be discussed.

Inmate Classification

Inmate classification is a process that attempts to identify hardened and dangerous prisoners. The classification process assists in pinpointing inmates who are dangerous to others or who

Information Used in Security Classification

Name	Homosexual
Age	Segregation needs
Offense	Violent/nonviolent
Gender	characteristics
Date of birth	Violent offender
Race	Habitual offender
Defendant ID#	Security risk
Prior record	Escape risk
Personal history	Mannerisms, etc.
Social history	Relevant individual
Handicap alert	characteristics; for
Medical alert	example, visible
Mental alert	signs of gang
Suicide alert	membership

represent serious escape risks. Violent inmates must be segregated from other inmates.

Key Control

Keys are vital to the security and orderly running of a prison. Key control is an extremely important part of security. A system of control must be established that indicates the location of every key and lock in the institution at every hour of the day or night. There must be constant security of all keys at all times.

A correctional supervisor will be responsible for the supervision of the key and lock control policies. The key control officer will have functional responsibility for the implementation and daily operation of the key and lock control procedures. The key control officer will report any changes in location of any lock or duplication of any key that the correctional supervisor approves.

Four cross-index files of the "Working Key Board" and "Back-up Key Board" should be maintained in the key control office or some other locations within the prison. A key inventory list should be maintained in the key control office that includes the following: key code and lock number; door or room number; back up board number; working board number; location of door, room, or lock; officer to whom key is permanently issued; number of keys on back-up board and working key board; emergency key ring number.

A numerical listing or card file consecutively numbered by key hook number of the Working Key Board must be maintained in the key control office and the control room where the board is located. It must indicate the following: working board key hook number; number of keys on key ring; what each key fits; back-up key hook number; and emergency key ring number. Key control requires that a numerical listing or card file, consecutively numbered by key hook or the Back-up Key Board, be maintained by the key control officer. The location of the Back-up Key Board indicates the following: backup board key hook number; number of keys on hook; key code number; what the assigned key fits; working board location and key hook number; and emergency key ring number.

Finally, a numerical listing or card file consecutively numbered by door number and location should be maintained in the key control office and the control room where the board is located, indicating the following by building and areas within buildings: door or room number; what the key fits; working board key hook number; number of keys on key ring; backup board key hook number; emergency key ring number. The Back-up Key Board should be maintained by the key control office. The Back-up Key Board should contain a hook designated for each institutional key. Duplicate keys to the same hook should be placed on a ring, tagged with the hook number and number of keys, and stored in the back of the key cabinet drawer. Replacement keys should be obtained from the Back-up Key Board for placement on the working key rings as needed by the key control officer.

Any changes in location of any lock or duplication of any key has to be authorized by the correctional supervisor in charge of that detail. The key control officer makes all necessary changes in all cross-index files. Only one key ring should be assigned to each hook on the Working Key Board. All keys have to be stored in the key control office and a master count of key blanks should be maintained by the key control officer.

A current inventory of all keys and key blanks is maintained. All changes affecting the inventory in any way must be authorized by the correctional supervisor in charge of keys. The Working Key Board and Back-up Key Board should have enough hooks to accommodate all key rings and keys. Each hook on the board should be assigned a number or a number and letter. Every hook on the Working Key Board should be filled at all times, containing either a set of keys or a key chit stamped with the name of the staff member who has been assigned the keys. A metal tag, showing the number of keys and the hook number, should be attached to

Inmates wait outside their cells during count until everyone has been accounted for. Photo by James A. Bolzaretti.

each key ring. Correctional officers assigned to the control center are required to check the key board as soon as they report to duty, ensuring that they account for each key ring and make a logbook entry indicating the same. Restricted-use keys should be placed in one area of the key board for easier control. This area on the Working Key Board should be a specific color, such as blue, to designate a restricted issue key. These key rings must be signed out for on the Inventory Control Log each time they are pulled and returned.

All prison employees should be provided with key chits on which their name or an assigned number is imprinted. Chits are used as receipts for all keys assigned to employees. The warden has to authorize in writing the assigning of keys on a twenty-four hour basis. Inmates are never allowed to have security keys in their possession. Emergency key rings are to be maintained in order to have available access to any part of the prison. The warden assigns specific prison personnel who are authorized to be issued emergency keys. Specific policies need to be adopted for specific restricted areas such as the armory, pharmacy, and records office.

Polices need to be developed explaining how prison personnel are to handle keys, detailing the reporting of lost keys or misplaced keys, and who specifically has the authorization to duplicate a key. Key control is extremely important to the internal security of a prison, and prison employees must be extremely careful to keep control of their keys.

Tool Control

For internal security of a prison, tool control must be strictly enforced. The purpose of tool control is to prevent escapes, assaults, the manufacturing of weapons, and to keep tools in good repair. Policies are established to regulate the purchase, storage, inventory, use, issuance, and replacement of all tools. Tools are classified as hazardous or nonhazardous. Hazardous tools are a threat to personal safety. All other tools should be considered nonhazardous.

All tools are inventoried as being either hazardous or nonhazardous. At least three copies of the inventory list should be completed, with one going to the assistant warden responsible for prison security, one to the maintenance supervisor, and one to the tool shop. The warden in charge of security should, at a minimum, conduct a complete audit of each inventory on a quarterly basis. Inventories should also include equipment and tools used by civilian contractors working inside the prison.

Every tool must be marked with an identifying symbol, indicating the unit or department that is assigned the tool. Symbols are etched on the tool. Tools that cannot be etched must be kept in a locked storage when not being used. The storage of tools is determined by the warden in charge of security, who should take into consideration the design of the prison. The best device for storing tools is the shadow board. Each tool has its silhouette or hanging device. Shadow boards should be secured from inmates. Tools such as files, metal cutting blades, and hacksaws should be stored outside the prison perimeter. When a tool has been removed from the shadow board it should be replaced with a tool chit.

Armory

The armory should be a part of the front entrance but outside the perimeter security. The armory should be easily accessible to prison staff in case of an emergency but inaccessible to inmates. Firearms, ammunition, and chemical agents are stored in the armory. A correctional officer is assigned to the armory and has the responsibility to keep an accurate account of firearms, ammunition, and chemical agents. He keeps the inventory and makes certain all equipment operates effectively. The armory officers follow the policy of requiring all personnel who enter the armory to sign a log book stating the date and time they entered, the date and time they left, and the purpose for entering the armory. Only the warden should authorize any firearms being brought into the prison. Individuals wanting to enter the prison should check their firearms and ammunition into the armory.

Only the warden or a designee can authorize firearms, chemical agents, or weapons inside the prison. The policy providing for weapons brought into the prison is in the policy manual.

Inmate Count

A key aspect of managing inmates is accountability. Prison personnel must account for all inmates during every minute of the day. They must know where inmates are at all times. Prison managers have the responsibility of establishing policies and procedures on how to account for all inmates. Procedures have to be established for formal counts, census checks, and emergency counts.

There should be at least one formal count during each shift, at the end of the work day, and one after lockup. The end of the work day count guards against inmates hiding and the possibility of escape. The lockup count refers to all inmates being secured in their cells for the night. This count, the end of the day count, may require that all inmates stand by their cell doors to be counted. This procedure will ascertain that all inmates are present. All inmates have to be counted simultaneously, and no inmate is allowed to leave the assigned area during the count. A report of each count is provided to the shift supervisor, who then verifies the count with the control center.

Census counts are frequent but irregular counts made by a correctional officer to verify that all inmates are present. Typically, these counts are made while inmates are working, engaging in daily activities or in recreational or some other activity. For inmates on work detail, a count is made when they assemble for work, at frequent intervals during the work period, and when the work detail is dismissed at the end of the work period. Census checks are to be noted by the correctional officer on the station log. Any discrepancies should be reported and the shift supervision notified if necessary.

Emergency counts are counts made at other than regular times. Emergency counts should be taken if there is good reason to believe that an inmate may be missing, or as a check after a major disturbance. When an emergency count is conducted, all inmates are returned to their cells.

Facility Inspections

Security inspection of prison facilities covering every part of the prison should, at the minimum, be done weekly by prison administrators. It must be done daily, however, by shift supervisors. Visual inspections should be conducted to determine the following: sanitation problems, broken welds, malfunctioning or broken doors, jams, or locks, contraband, steel filing, condition of plumbing, vents, and masonry. Inspections should also include any evidence of tampering or weakness. Correctional officers must make security checks and observations of all inmates in their living units periodically. More frequent checks and observations must be made for inmates who are violent, mentally disturbed, or who demonstrate bizarre or suicidal behavior.

Inmate Searches

Frequent inmate searches are conducted to control contraband, to detect hazards to health and safety, to recover stolen or missing property, and to prevent disturbances and escapes. Inmate searches should be conducted in a manner to avoid unnecessary force, embarrassment, or indignity. An entire unit should be shaken down and thoroughly searched weekly. After each shakedown a report should be written. There should also be frequent unannounced searches of inmate cells. Other areas of the facility are to be searched as often as necessary to ensure the safety and security of the facility.

There are three types of searches that correctional officers perform. The first, the "pat search," is often used in the daily security routine of the facility. The search is often performed poorly. The pat search should be done at irregular, random times and at any time there is probable cause to believe that inmates might possess contraband. Second, the "strip search," requires that prison personnel be properly trained. The inmate should be informed that a strip search will occur. Inmates are touched only enough to conduct a comprehensive search of the person. A strip search may be necessary when it is suspected that an inmate possesses contraband or that he is involved in some kind of internal disturbance. The correctional officer conducting the strip search should be of the same gender as the inmate. Third, the "body cavity" search, requires that a witness be present. Visual inspection of inmate body cavities is conducted whenever there is a suspicion that the inmate is carrying contraband or other prohibited material. The body cavity inspection is done by trained personnel of the same sex as the person being searched, and in privacy.

Use of Force

Procedures have to be implemented that restrict the use of physical force that is necessary to control an inmate. The use of force must be justified on the grounds that the correctional officers are defending themselves or others, protecting property, or preventing an escape. The use of physical force must meet the statutory authority provided a correctional officer.

Correctional officers, when dealing with unruly inmates, should follow specific steps:

1. Attempt to convince the inmate to cooperate

2. Warn the inmate of the consequences of noncooperation
3. Call for backup personnel in an attempt to persuade the inmate through a show of force
4. If the inmate initiates aggressive, physical, attacking behavior, attempt to control the inmate by use of physical takedown restraint techniques or use physical force of the type sufficient to bring the inmate under control

Correctional officers, if unable to gain control of the situation, should retreat and obtain adequate backup to control the situation.

Deadly force may be used only when it appears necessary for officers to protect themselves, fellow officers, or others from an immediate threat of death or other serious bodily injury. Deadly force may also be used in the prevention of a crime in which the suspect's actions place persons in jeopardy of death or serious bodily injury. In addition, it may be used to apprehend a felon fleeing from a crime involving serious bodily injury or the use of deadly force, or when there is a substantial risk that the person whose arrest is sought might cause immediate death or serious bodily injury to others if apprehension is delayed.

Instruments of Restraint

Instruments of restraint such as handcuffs, leg chains, leather restraints, and straitjackets are often used for medical reasons at the direction of the medical officer. These restraints are also used as a protection against self-injury, injury to others, or property damage, where there exists approval from the prison administration. Restraints should be used only for the amount of time absolutely necessary and not for punishment.

Restraints should never be used about the head or neck or in a way that causes physical discomfort. The restraint should not inflict pain or restrict the blood circulation or breathing of the inmate. Also, drugs should never be used as a restraint solely for security purposes. Restraints are often used when an inmate has become disruptive or threatening to staff, inmates, or others. When the correctional officer gains control and the inmate continues to resist, restraints such as handcuffs may be used. In applying restraints, only the force necessary to gain control may be used. Whenever possible, several correctional officers should assist in applying restraints, to minimize the possibility of injury.

Reporting Incidents

Prison personnel are required to write a report following any incident resulting in physical harm or that threatens the safety of a person in the prison or the security of the institution. The reporting officer should provide a complete record of the incident, including the names of all persons involved and witnesses. Incident reports are reviewed by the warden or a designee.

Conclusions

Prison security inside the facility is extremely important for preserving control and order. The deputy warden in charge of security has the responsibility of developing and publishing a security manual that contains details on how to implement security policies. The security manual contains information on inmate classification, counts, facility inspection, firearm and chemical control, key control, tool control, and emergency procedures. The manual is reviewed periodically, with changes made when needed.

Michael J. Palmiotto

Bibliography

American Correctional Association (1981). *Standards for the Adult Detention Facility*. College Park, Md.: American Correctional Association.

Henderson, J. D., and W. H. Rauch (1987). *Guidelines for the Development of a Security Program*. College Park, Md.: American Correctional Association.

Sentences, Excessive

In the past quarter century, the United States has imprisoned more people than any other Western nation. Moreover, American prison sentences as authorized by statute are among the longest in the world and are getting longer. Since the 1980s, Congress and the state legislatures have responded to crime and illegal drug use by enacting tough new sentencing laws. An increasing number of states have passed laws abolishing or sharply limiting parole eligibility and laws that establish harsh minimum-mandatory sentencing for a broad range of offenses. Many states have also enacted so-called "habitual offender" or "three-strikes-and-you're-in" statutes that mandate extraordinarily lengthy prison sentences, often with no possibility of parole, for those who are convicted of three or more offenses arising out of separate incidents.

Since the 1910 case of *Weems v. United States,* the Supreme Court has recognized that punishments that are disproportionate in their severity to the crimes committed can sometimes be held to violate the "cruel and unusual punishments" clause of the Eighth Amendment. Paul Weems was an American working in the Philippine Islands (which at that time permitted the U.S. Supreme Court to decide questions involving rights that were included in both the Philippine Bill of Rights and the U.S. Constitution). Weems had been convicted by a Philippine court of falsifying an official document—an offense from which neither he nor anyone else stood to profit. Nevertheless, he was sentenced to *cadena temporal,* a form of punishment that began with twelve to fifteen years of imprisonment, during which time he was forced to perform hard and painful labor while chained at his ankle and wrist. After his prison term ended he would still not be truly free, for he would *permanently* lose such basic civil rights as the right to own property, the right to marital and parental authority, and the right to be free from government surveillance. Finding a punishment to be cruel and unusual for the first time, the Supreme Court declared that "[s]uch penalties for such [minor] offenses amaze those who . . . believe that it is a precept of justice that punishment for crime should be graduated and proportioned to offense." The justices concluded that future efforts to apply the Eighth Amendment should take into account the nature of the crime, the purpose of the law, and the severity of the punishment.

For nearly three-quarters of a century, it remained unclear whether the Supreme Court (or any court) could reduce or overturn a prison sentence solely on the grounds that the length of the sentence was disproportionate to the severity of the crime and thus violative of the cruel and unusual punishments clause. To be sure, the *Weems* decision had established that the Eighth Amendment prohibits imposition of a sentence that is grossly disproportionate to the offense. But the majority opinion in *Weems* had consistently referred to the harshness of both the length of the imprisonment and its "accompaniments"—the permanent loss of the right of privacy and of marital and parental authority. Thus it could be argued that *Weems* applied only to "imprisonment plus" punishments and not to the length of imprisonment in and of itself.

Rummel v. Estelle (1980)

In 1980 this issue was squarely presented to the Court for the first time. In *Rummel v. Estelle,* the justices addressed the question of whether the Eighth Amendment had been violated when the State of Texas imposed a sentence of life imprisonment on a defendant who had been convicted on three separate occasions of non-violent felonies involving property losses of less than $230.00. William Rummel had a previous conviction for making fraudulent use of a credit card to obtain $80.00 worth of goods or services (for which he was sentenced to three years in prison) and a prior conviction for passing a forged check in the amount of $28.36 (for which he received a four-year sentence). Under Texas law, both offenses were classified as felonies, and in 1973 Rummel was convicted of a third felony. After accepting payment in return for his promise to repair a broken air conditioner, he failed to complete the job and was convicted of obtaining $120.75 under false pretenses. The prosecution pointed out that the law provides a mandatory life sentence for anyone convicted of three separate felonies, and the trial judge had no choice but to impose a sentence of life imprisonment.

Rummel appealed, arguing that like the punishment imposed in the *Weems* case, his sentence was so grossly disproportionate to his offenses as to constitute cruel and unusual punishment. But on 18 March 1980, the Supreme Court by a single vote rejected Rummel's claim and upheld his life sentence. Writing for the majority, Justice Rehnquist began by asserting that the *Weems* holding was of little usefulness in assessing the constitutionality of Rummel's sentence. The *Weems* Court's finding of dispro-portionality, he argued, "cannot be wrenched from the extreme facts of that case; the trivial-ity of the charged offense, the impressive length of the minimum term of imprisonment, and the extraordinary nature of the 'accessories' in-cluded within the punishment of *cadena tempo-ral.*" According to Justice Rehnquist, the only other case in which the Court had upheld an Eighth Amendment proportionality challenge was *Coker v. Georgia,* a 1977 decision invali-dating a death sentence imposed on a man con-victed of the rape of an adult woman. *Coker,* however, was of limited assistance in deciding the constitutionality of the punishment meted out to Rummel, "[b]ecause a sentence of death differs in kind from any sentence of imprison-ment, no matter how long. . . ." Thus, although the Court had overturned a death sentence (*Coker*) and a sentence of "imprisonment plus accessories" (*Weems*) as disproportionate to the crimes committed, it had never struck down a sentence of "pure imprisonment" on dispro-portionality grounds.

Judicial history did not settle the issue, how-ever, for as Justice Rehnquist conceded, "This Court must ultimately decide the meaning of the Eighth Amendment." Justice Rehnquist also conceded that only three states—Texas, West Virginia, and Washington—authorized manda-tory life sentences upon the commission of a third felony, and that Rummel's claims that he would have received a more lenient sentence in any of the other forty-seven states appeared to be true. According to the majority, however, this was no reason to invalidate either the Texas law or Rummel's life sentence, for such distinctions among the states "are subtle rather than gross" and would require the Court to make complex judgments that are traditionally left to legisla-tures. "A number of States impose a mandatory life sentence upon conviction of four felonies rather than three. Other States require one or more of the felonies to be "violent" to support a life sentence. Still other States leave the impo-sition of a life sentence after three felonies within the discretion of a judge or jury."

Such comparisons among the states be-come even more complex, added Justice Rehn-quist, when considering the many differences among the states in calculating parole eligibil-ity for prisoners serving a life sentence. Texas, for example, was said to have "a relatively lib-eral policy of granting 'good time' credits to its prisoners, a policy that historically has allowed a prisoner serving a life sentence to become eli-gible for parole in as little as 12 years." Justice Rehnquist acknowledged that there is no "right" to parole and that it would be unfair to treat Rummel's life sentence as if it were equiva-lent to a twelve-year term. Nevertheless, he ar-gued, the Court's assessment of the constitu-tionality of Rummel's punishment could not ignore the possibility that Rummel might not actually be imprisoned for the rest of his life. This was because "the possibility of parole, however slim," served to distinguish the Texas law from a recidivist statute such as Missis-sippi's, which provided for a life-without-parole sentence if an offender is convicted of three felo-nies including at least one violent felony.

The *Rummel* majority opinion seemed to take the position that a court is *never* justified in overturning a legislatively enacted punishment of "pure imprisonment," regardless of the length of the sentence. But in a one-sentence footnote, Justice Rehnquist acknowledged a remote possibility that a court might be justified in upholding an Eighth Amendment challenge to an extraordinarily lengthy prison sentence "if a legislature made overtime parking a felony punishable by life imprisonment."

The four dissenting justices were led by Justice Powell, who challenged the majority's contention that the cruel and unusual punishments clause did not fully extend to "pure-imprisonment" sentences that are grossly disproportionate to the offense. According to Justice Powell, the notion that the principle of proportionality is somehow less applicable to noncapital sentences than to death sentences "finds no support in the history of Eighth Amendment jurisprudence." The majority, he explained, had interpreted *Weems* too narrowly. A careful reading of the *Weems* opinion reveals no reason to believe that the Court did not intend to apply the principle of proportionality to extraordinarily lengthy prison sentences.

Justice Powell was equally critical of Justice Rehnquist's treatment of *Coker v. Georgia*. In holding that the rape of an adult woman may not be punished by the death penalty, the *Coker* majority had stated that *any* punishment is unconstitutionally excessive "if it (1) makes no measurable contribution to acceptable goals of punishment and hence is nothing more than the purposeless and needless imposition of pain and suffering; or (2) is grossly out of proportion to the severity of the crime." Nothing in the *Coker* opinion, declared Justice Powell, suggests that the prohibition of grossly disproportionate punishment applies only to death penalty cases.

The most important principle to emerge from the *Coker* analysis, Powell argued, is the understanding that "Eighth Amendment judgments should not be, or appear to be, merely the subjective views of individual justices." Instead, the Court's decisions in this area "should be informed by objective factors to the maximum extent possible." That is why the *Coker* Court analyzed the contemporary attitudes of state legislatures (finding that Georgia was the only state authorizing the death penalty for rape) and the actual behavior of sentencing juries (finding that Georgia juries imposed a death sentence in less than 10 percent of rape cases) before concluding that death is a disproportionate punishment for the crime of rape. A similar analysis

should have been employed by the majority in Rummel's case, argued Justice Powell, and the fact that Congress and forty-seven state legislatures have not adopted such an extraordinarily stringent habitual offender statute should have weighed heavily in favor of invalidating the Texas law. If such a proportionality analysis had been done, Justice Powell concluded, it surely would have found that a mandatory life sentence for a series of nonviolent offenses that led to less than $230.00 in property losses crosses any rationally drawn line separating lawful from unlawful punishments.

Hutto v. Davis (1982)

In spite of Justice Powell's efforts, *Rummel* arguably established that legislatively mandated prison terms, regardless of length, could not be subjected to an Eighth Amendment proportionality challenge. After all, the only exceptions—cases similar to one in which an offender receives life imprisonment for overtime parking—were highly unlikely ever to materialize in American courts. This reading of *Rummel* was affirmed by the Supreme Court two years later. In *Hutto v. Davis* (1982), the Court refused to interfere in the case of a Virginia man who was sentenced to forty years in prison (as authorized by Virginia law) for possessing and distributing approximately nine ounces of marijuana. Five justices joined in an opinion emphasizing that "*Rummel* stands for the proposition that federal courts should be reluctant to review legislatively mandated terms of imprisonment . . . and that successful challenges to the proportionality of particular sentences should be exceedingly rare."

The *Davis* majority acknowledged that a forty-year sentence for possessing and distributing less than nine ounces of marijuana may strike some as a disproportionate punishment, but as *Rummel* had stressed, the excessiveness of one prison term as compared with another is a subjective determination that should be made by the legislative branch of government. Justice Powell, who had written the dissenting opinion in *Rummel,* issued a concurring opinion in *Davis,* but he did so "reluctantly" and only because the *Rummel* decision "is controlling on the facts before us." Justice Powell made it clear that he still viewed *Rummel* as having been wrongly decided and that he regarded Davis's forty-year prison sentence as unjust and disproportionate to the offense. He also noted, however, that Davis's drug-related offenses were more serious than Rummel's "trifling" offenses and that "Davis had been unable to show—by means of statutory comparisons—that his [sentence suffered] from a greater degree of disproportionality than Rummel's did." Consequently, the doctrine of *stare decisis*—the longstanding principle that courts should rarely, and only with the greatest care and consideration, reverse their settled precedents—left him with little choice but to vote to uphold Davis's sentence.

Interestingly, Justice Brennan, joined by Justices Marshall and Stevens, issued a stinging dissent that not only described *Rummel* as incorrectly decided, but rebuked the majority for "a serious and improper expansion of *Rummel*." According to Justice Brennan, *Rummel* did not establish that it was improper to engage in a proportionality analysis in extreme cases and "this case *is* one of those 'exceedingly rare' cases in which a sentence should be invalidated on Eighth Amendment grounds." Davis's forty-year sentence, he declared, was far more severe than sentences meted out to drug offenders in Virginia and in other states, and, by upholding it, the Supreme Court had abdicated its role as the ultimate guarantor of Eighth Amendment rights.

Solem v. Helm (1983)

Justice Brennan was on the losing side in *Davis,* but, a year later, he found himself in a majority that for the first time made it clear that a legislatively authorized prison sentence, by itself, can be a cruel and unusual punishment. In *Solem v. Helm* (1983), the Court considered a case with circumstances that were similar, but not identical, to those that had been before the Court in *Rummel*. In 1979 Jerry Helm was convicted for passing a bad check for $100.00. Ordinarily, the maximum sentence for that crime would have been a prison term of five years and a five thousand dollar fine. Helm, a thirty-six-year-old alcoholic and bad-check artist who had spent many of the previous fifteen years behind bars, was sentenced to life imprisonment without possibility of parole under the South Dakota habitual offender statute. Helm had six prior felonies—three third-degree burglaries and convictions for drunk driving, grand larceny, and obtaining money under false circumstances. Immediately after accepting Helm's guilty plea on the bad-check charge, the trial judge sentenced Helm to life imprisonment without the possibility of parole. Pointing out

that Helm had just pleaded guilty to his seventh felony, the judge explained: "I think you certainly earned this sentence and certainly have proven that you're an habitual criminal, and the record would indicate that you're beyond rehabilitation and that the only prudent thing to do is lock you up for the rest of your natural life."

On 28 June 1983, the Supreme Court, by a single vote, determined that Helm's life-without-parole sentence violated the Eighth Amendment's prohibition against cruel and unusual punishments. Justice Powell, the author of the *Rummel* dissent and the *Davis* concurrence, wrote for the five-justice majority stressing the fundamental distinction between a life sentence without parole and a life sentence with the possibility of parole.

Justice Powell made it clear that appellate courts were still obligated to grant "substantial deference" to the paramount authority of legislatures and sentencing courts. Nevertheless, "no penalty is per se constitutional." In cases in which a sentence may be so disproportionate as to raise a legitimate Eighth Amendment claim, the reviewing court should apply "a combination of objective factors" to identify those "admittedly rare cases" in which a sentence of imprisonment is so grossly disproportionate to the offense as to constitute cruel and unusual punishment. Justice Powell listed three objective factors that appellate courts should examine in order to determine whether a particular prison sentence is constitutionally disproportionate: (1) a comparison of the gravity of the offense and the harshness of the penalty; (2) a comparison of the defendant's sentence with the sentences imposed on other criminals in the same jurisdiction; and (3) a comparison of the defendant's sentence with sentences imposed for the same crime in other jurisdictions.

Relying upon these kinds of objective criteria, Justice Powell maintained, would demonstrate that the Court's Eighth Amendment decisions were not simply the subjective views of a majority of the justices. He stressed that although comparing the severity of different crimes is the kind of line-drawing that is usually left to legislatures and trial judges, appellate courts are also quite capable of drawing distinctions between different crimes based on the culpability of the offender and the harm done to the victim and to the community. Courts have no choice but to engage in such judicial line-drawing when deciding whether certain laws or policies violate provisions of the Constitution.

Next, Justice Powell applied the three-pronged proportionality test to the life-without-parole-sentence that had been imposed on Jerry Helm. First, comparing the gravity of Helm's trigger offense—passing a bad check for one hundred dollars—with the harshness of his punishment—life imprisonment without parole—revealed that Helm had received the most severe sentence then authorized in South Dakota for "one of the most passive felonies a person could commit." It was true, Justice Powell acknowledged, that Helm was charged not only with passing a bad check, but also with being a habitual offender, a status that clearly made Helm deserving of a stronger penalty than a first-time offender would receive. It was also true, however, that all of Helm's prior crimes were nonviolent, relatively minor property offenses, and he had received a "far more severe" sentence than the sentence received by William Rummel, who "was likely to have been eligible for parole within 12 years of his . . . confinement." Thus, the first prong of the three-part test suggested an obvious imbalance between Helm's crimes and his punishment.

The state fared no better in the second part of Justice Powell's proportionality analysis. Comparing Helm's sentence to those prescribed for similar or more serious offenses in South Dakota, the majority discovered that state law mandated a life-without-parole sentence for only a few crimes—murder, and on a second or third offense, treason, first-degree manslaughter, first-degree arson, and kidnapping. Criminals committing these offenses, Justice Powell observed, "ordinarily would be thought more deserving of punishment than one uttering a 'no-account' check—even when the bad-check writer had already committed six minor felonies." According to Justice Powell, the record showed that no one else in South Dakota was serving a life sentence on the basis of comparable crimes.

Finally, when Justice Powell compared Helm's sentence with those imposed for the commission of the same crime in other jurisdictions, he found that Helm could not have received such a severe sentence in forty-eight of the fifty states. The only other state in which Helm could have received a similar life-without-parole sentence was Nevada, where a life-without-parole sentence was merely authorized, not mandatory, for minor offenses such as Helm's. The record indicated that the Nevada law had never been applied to crimes as trivial as Helm's.

Concluding that all three components of its proportionality analysis weighed heavily in Helm's favor, the Court next dealt with the state's contention that this case was essentially the same as *Rummel v. Estelle,* in that the possibility of parole for Rummel was matched by the possibility of executive clemency for Helm. This argument was false, Justice Powell explained, because the possibility of parole is far greater than the possibility of executive clemency. As a matter of law, the parole system is governed by detailed standards and procedures that make it reasonably possible to predict when a parole might be granted. Parole is a regular stage in the rehabilitative process, and "[assuming] good behavior, it is the normal expectation in the vast majority of cases." Executive clemency, on the other hand, is an ad hoc exercise of gubernatorial power without any standards. The possibility of commutation is nothing more than a hope.

Whereas Texas had a relatively liberal parole policy that typically allowed life-term inmates to become eligible for parole in only twelve years, South Dakota historically granted executive clemency in very few cases. Indeed, the record disclosed that only one South Dakota life sentence had been commuted since 1975. Furthermore, a commutation merely made a prisoner eligible for parole; there was no guarantee that he or she would be paroled, and the South Dakota parole system was far more stringent than the Texas system in *Rummel.* The Court, therefore, was not overruling the *Rummel* precedent, but distinguishing it. The *Helm* case, unlike the *Rummel* case, presented the Court with a sufficiently stabilized sentence on which to base a full-fledged proportionality analysis that showed that Helm's sentence was grossly disproportionate to his crimes and thus was prohibited by the Eighth Amendment.

Chief Justice Burger, joined by Justices Rehnquist, White, and O'Connor, wrote a harshly worded dissenting opinion. Their principal point was that the *Rummel* and *Davis* decisions had conclusively resolved that proportionality review was not appropriate in length-of-sentence cases because the Eighth Amendment "reaches only the *mode* of punishment and not the length of imprisonment." Chief Justice Burger asserted that the essentially arbitrary lines between various sentences of imprisonment must be drawn by legislatures, not by courts. The majority's decision to extend proportionality review to sentences of imprisonment, he charged, was a "bald substitution of [the majority's] subjective moral values for those of the legislature."

Harmelin v. Michigan (1991)

For eight years, the line drawn in *Helm* remained relatively clear and unchanged. But on 27 June 1991, the Supreme Court ended its 1990–91 term by announcing a major decision that muddied the waters considerably. In *Harmelin v. Michigan* (1991), a five-justice majority stopped short of an outright reversal of *Helm*. The Court, however, clearly modified the *Helm* holding and weakened the Eighth Amendment as a shield against disproportionate prison sentences. The case was brought to the Court by Ronald Harmelin, an unemployed forty-six-year-old Air Force veteran who had no previous criminal record. When Harmelin failed to make a complete stop at a red light in the early morning hours of 12 May 1986, two police officers stopped him, searched him and his car, and found two bags containing 672.5 grams of cocaine. Harmelin later admitted that he was a drug addict who had been hired by a drug dealer to transport the cocaine. In many states, a first-time offender who had been caught with a comparable amount of cocaine (approximately $1^1/_2$ pounds) might have faced probation, a relatively short prison sentence, mandatory drug treatment, or some combination of these penalties. But Harmelin had been arrested in Michigan and he was charged under a 1978 statute—the toughest of its kind in the nation—that mandated a sentence of life imprisonment without parole for anyone convicted of possessing 650 grams or more of cocaine or other controlled substances.

After a bench trial, Harmelin was convicted of possessing 650 or more grams of "a substance containing cocaine," and was sentenced—as the Michigan statute mandated—to life imprisonment without the possibility of parole. The Michigan Court of Appeals affirmed both the conviction and the sentence, and the Michigan Supreme Court denied leave to appeal, enabling Harmelin to seek relief from the United States Supreme Court. The Supreme Court granted certiorari in May of 1990, making it clear that the sole issue to be resolved was whether Harmelin's sentence amounted to cruel and unusual punishment in violation of the Eighth Amendment. Harmelin's attorney offered two arguments in support of Harmelin's claim. First, she asserted that his sentence was "significantly disproportionate" to his offense.

Second, she challenged the mandatory element of the Michigan statute, asserting that the sentencing judge had no choice but to impose the life-without-parole sentence and thus was precluded from considering any mitigating factors, such as Harmelin's military service and his lack of a prior criminal record.

On 27 June 1991, a sharply divided Court rejected both of these claims, holding that Harmelin's sentence "cannot be considered constitutionally disproportionate" and that the mandatory nature of his sentence alone did not contravene the Eighth Amendment. *Harmelin v. Michigan* produced a five-to-four decision, but the majority split as to its reasoning. First, in an opinion written by Justice Scalia and joined by Chief Justice Rehnquist, the primary argument was that the Eighth Amendment contains no proportionality principle that applies to the length of prison sentences. *Solem v. Helm,* in Justice Scalia's opinion, had been incorrectly decided and should be overruled. Since *Helm* "was scarcely the expression of clear and well accepted constitutional law," it should be discarded and replaced with the "correct" understanding that had been expressed in *Rummel v. Estelle* and *Hutto v. Davis*: "[F]or felonies . . . punishable by significant terms of imprisonment in a state penitentiary, the length of the sentence actually imposed is *purely* a matter of legislative prerogative." Justice Scalia conceded that proportionality review may sometimes be permissible in capital cases.

Indeed, Justice Scalia rejected all three parts of the *Helm* proportionality analysis, contending that the Constitution does not require the State of Michigan to follow the prison-sentencing policies of other states. He reserved his harshest criticism for the first prong of the three-part test, observing that there are no historical or textual standards for determining which offenses are inherently grave, and that certain crimes will always be treated differently by different jurisdictions. Thus, while the state of Massachusetts punishes sodomy ("not more than 20 years" in prison) more harshly than assault and battery ("not more than $2^1/_2$ years" in prison), many states do not even classify sodomy as a crime. Similarly, in Louisiana, "one who assaults another with a dangerous weapon faces the same maximum prison term as one who removes a shopping cart from a [grocery-store parking lot]." This kind of line drawing, Justice Scalia asserted, is best done by the elected officials who are familiar with the particular problems in their communities.

The *Helm* majority, according to Justice Scalia, had exaggerated the significance of the *Rummel* footnote acknowledging that a proportionality principle might come into play "if a legislature made overtime parking a felony punishable by life imprisonment." This "fanciful" example of an extremely disproportionate punishment—an example that "[is] certain never to occur"—was not meant to open the door for proportionality challenges to allegedly severe prison sentences; it was meant to convey the point that courts are not empowered to invalidate lawfully imposed prison sentences on the basis of a judicially created proportionality analysis.

As further evidence for this position, Justice Scalia pointed to the precise wording of the Eighth Amendment, which specifically prohibits "excessive fines," but says nothing about the excessiveness of other types of criminal penalties. The fact that the Eighth Amendment prohibits "cruel and unusual" punishments but not "excessive" or "disproportionate" punishments demonstrates that the framers of the Constitution did not intend to ban disproportionate punishments, but rather cruel *methods* of punishment "which are not regularly or customarily employed." Justice Scalia added that the phrase "cruel and unusual" did not contain the principle of proportionality, because "[a]s a textual matter . . . a disproportionate punishment can perhaps always be considered 'cruel,' but it will not always be (as the text also requires) 'unusual.'" In other words, the Eighth Amendment explicitly forbids "cruel *and* unusual punishments, not cruel *or* unusual punishments."

Although they agreed that Ronald Harmelin's life-without-parole sentence must be upheld, the remaining three members of the *Harmelin* majority did not subscribe to the Scalia-Rehnquist view that the Eighth Amendment contains no proportionality principle permitting courts to review lawfully imposed but allegedly excessive prison sentences.

In a concurring opinion in which Justices O'Connor and Souter joined, Justice Kennedy contended that the Eighth Amendment contained "a narrow proportionality principle" that applied to capital and noncapital cases alike. The Eighth Amendment, he explained, does not require "strict proportionality" between the crime and the sentence; "it forbids only extreme sentences that are 'grossly disproportionate' to the crime." As the "least common denominator" viewpoint of the five justices who constituted the *Harmelin* majority, the Kennedy-O'Connor-Souter concurring opinion now represents the Court's "official position" on the existence of a proportionality principle. As of 27 June 1994, the last day of the 1993–94 term, the Court had announced no new rulings on Eighth Amendment proportionality issues.

Justice Kennedy also pointed to studies showing a direct nexus between illicit drugs and other crimes, including a recent report estimating that 60 percent of the murders in Detroit were drug-related. Such studies, he admitted, "do not establish that Michigan's penalty scheme is correct or the most just in any abstract sense. . . . But they do demonstrate that the threat posed to the individual and society by possession of this large an amount of cocaine . . . is momentous enough to warrant the deterrence and retribution of a life sentence without parole." Accordingly, there was no need to compare Harmelin's sentence with other sentences in Michigan or in the other forty-nine states. All that was necessary was to perform the first part of the three-part test—a general comparison of the gravity of the crime and the severity of the sentence—and that was enough to convince Justices Kennedy, O'Connor, and Souter that Ronald Harmelin's sentence was not grossly disproportionate to his crime and thus did not violate the Eighth Amendment.

Although the majority justices did not agree on a single rationale for sustaining Harmelin's sentence, there was one issue upon which all five agreed: that the mandatory nature of the sentence did not in and of itself amount to cruel and unusual punishment. Justice Scalia, writing on behalf of all five majority justices, relied upon a literal interpretation of the Eighth Amendment, emphasizing that a punishment must be *both* cruel and unusual to fail constitutional muster. "Severe, mandatory penalties may be cruel," he conceded, "but they are not unusual in the constitutional sense, having been employed in various forms throughout our Nation's history." Justice Scalia pointed out that all of the Court's holdings requiring an individualized sentencing hearing, during which the defendant has an opportunity to present evidence of mitigating circumstances, had come in death-penalty cases. This, he maintained, was another example of the "death is different" doctrine. "[T]here is no com-

S

parable requirement outside the capital context, because of the qualitative difference between death and all other penalties."

Interestingly, although Justices Kennedy, O'Connor, and Souter joined in this part of the Scalia-Rehnquist opinion, Justice Kennedy's concurring opinion did not entirely rule out the possibility that a mandatory prison term might under certain circumstances violate the Eighth Amendment. Justice Kennedy expressed his general agreement with Justice Scalia's approach to this issue, but he also stated that he would prefer to reserve to the Court the power to strike down mandatory prison sentences "in the most extreme circumstance." He added that there was no need to decide this question now, as Ronald Harmelin's sentence, though severe, did not fall into this category of exceptional cases.

Surprisingly, the four dissenting justices were led by Justice White, who had voted with the majority in *Rummel* and *Davis,* and with the dissenters in *Helm.* Justices Stevens and Blackmun joined Justice White's dissent, while Justice Marshall noted in a brief dissenting opinion that he agreed with Justice White in every respect "except insofar as [he] asserts that the Eighth Amendment does not proscribe the death penalty." Justice Stevens, joined by Justice Blackmun, also issued a separate dissenting opinion, one that expressed agreement with Justice White and stressed that Ronald Harmelin's sentence was *both* cruel and unusual.

Justice White dismissed Justice Scalia's historical arguments with the observation that "the Eighth Amendment as ratified contained the words 'cruel and unusual,' and there can be no doubt that prior decisions of this Court have construed these words to include a proportionality principle." According to Justice White, it was disingenuous of Justice Scalia to contend that the Eighth Amendment limits excessive fines but not excessive prison sentences. Justice White also attacked the Scalia-Rehnquist view that the words "cruel and unusual" provide proportionality protection only in death-penalty cases. He categorized this position as nothing more than a pretext for disregarding clear precedential support for a proportionality requirement in length-of-sentence cases.

The dissenters also took issue with the Kennedy–O'Connor–Souter opinion, commenting that "[w]hile Justice Scalia seeks to deliver a swift death sentence to *Helm,* Justice Kennedy prefers to eviscerate it, leaving only an empty shell." Justice White refuted Justice Kennedy's conclusion that a proper proportionality review could consist of only the first part of the *Helm* three-part test. How was it possible, he asked, to assess in an objective manner the proportionality of a crime and its punishment without looking at the penalties for other crimes in the jurisdiction where the sentence had been imposed, as well as the sanctions imposed for the crime in other jurisdictions?

Justice White proceeded to analyze Harmelin's sentence by applying all three components of the *Helm* balancing test. In his view, the first *Helm* factor—an assessment of the gravity of the offense and the severity of the punishment—clearly weighed in favor of Harmelin's appeal. Justice White did not dispute Justice Kennedy's concerns about the harmful consequences stemming from the possession of illicit drugs, but he maintained that a constitutionally proportionate sentence must be tailored to the defendant's *personal* responsibility and moral guilt. Noting that life imprisonment without parole is the most severe punishment authorized by the state of Michigan (which has no death penalty), Justice White asserted that the mere possession of drugs, even in a relatively large quantity, is simply not comparable to first-degree murder, rape, or other violent felonies that may warrant a state's ultimate penalty.

Turning to the second *Helm* criterion, the dissenters pointed out that in Michigan, mandatory life-without-parole sentences are reserved exclusively for only three offenses: (1) first-degree murder; (2) manufacturing, distributing, or possessing 650 grams or more of narcotics with the intent to manufacture or distribute the narcotics; and (3) mere possession of 650 grams or more of narcotics. It seemed odd and arguably irrational, Justice White commented, to punish the mere possession of a quantity of an illegal drug as severely as the possession of the same amount of the same drug with the intent to distribute or manufacture the drug. And surely, he added, our society had reached a consensus that first-degree murder—the deliberate taking of a human life—was deserving of a harsher punishment than was the mere possession of a banned substance. Furthermore, in Michigan very serious crimes directed against the persons and property of others—second-degree murder, rape, and armed robbery—do not carry the same harsh mandatory penalty that is meted out to first-time drug offenders such as Ronald Harmelin. These comparisons clearly demonstrate that Harmelin "has been treated in the same manner as, or more severely than [other Michigan] criminals who have committed far more serious crimes."

As for the third part of the *Helm* test—the sentences imposed for the same crime in other jurisdictions—the dissenting justices emphasized that not one of the remaining forty-nine states, or the Federal Sentencing Guidelines, punishes possession of this amount of cocaine as severely. The Michigan penalty for Ronald Harmelin's offense was by far the harshest in the country. Only one other state (Alabama) provided a mandatory life-without-parole sentence for a first-time offender convicted of drug possession; there, however, the defendant must be convicted of possessing *10 kilograms* or more of cocaine. Justice White summarized the dissenters' view succinctly: "Application of *Helm*'s proportionality analysis leaves no doubt that the Michigan statute at issue . . . is unconstitutionally disproportionate in that it violates the Eighth Amendment prohibition against cruel and unusual punishment."

Conclusion

Today it is clear that the Eighth Amendment prohibits not only barbaric or torturous punishments but also those that are disproportionate to the crime committed. The Supreme Court has gradually expanded the scope of the Eighth Amendment proportionality principle first to unusual (or "imprisonment plus") punishments (*Weems*), then to capital punishment (*Coker*), and finally to allegedly excessive prison sentences (*Helm*). *Harmelin v. Michigan*—the most recent in this line of cases—holds, however, that the Eighth Amendment guarantee against disproportionate prison sentences is extremely narrow and will be applied only in those "exceedingly rare" cases in which the length of the sentence is "grossly disproportionate" to the gravity of the offense.

The standards for proportionality review articulated in *Harmelin* and the decision itself—upholding a mandatory life-without-parole sentence for cocaine possession—will make it extraordinarily difficult for prisoners to mount a successful proportionality challenge in the federal courts. Although *Harmelin* weakened the *Helm*-created proportionality test, the line drawn by the *Rummel* and *Helm* decisions remains intact. A state may constitutionally impose a sentence of life imprisonment with the possibility of parole on an offender convicted of a series of nonviolent felonies, but not a life-without-parole sentence. What about the constitutionality of the various "three-strikes-and-you're-in" laws that recently have been passed in several states and are currently under consideration in Congress and at least two dozen state legislatures? Based on the *Rummel-Davis-Helm-Harmelin* precedents, it seems likely that the Supreme Court would uphold a law that would impose a mandatory life-without-parole sentence on a three-time felon so long as the law stipulated that each of the three crimes was a serious or drug-related felony and that at least one was a violent felony. Each case would have to be decided on its own merits, however.

It is also important to realize that unlike federal courts, state courts are not strictly bound to follow the precise dictates of the *Harmelin* decision. Under what is generally called the "judicial federalism" doctrine, it is now well established that a state court is free as a matter of state law to extend greater civil-liberties protection to its own citizens than the U.S. Supreme Court has found to exist under the federal Constitution. Thus, the U.S. Supreme Court will not overturn a state supreme court decision that clearly and expressly is based on the state constitution so long as the decision expands, rather than undermines, federally guaranteed rights. So far, there has been no rush by state courts to invalidate legislatively authorized prison terms on grounds of excessiveness. There are two recent decisions, however, that constitute noteworthy exceptions to the general judicial reluctance to review the length of prison sentences.

First, in *State v. Bartlett* (1992), the Arizona Supreme Court held that even under the austere standards of *Harmelin*, a forty-year sentence without any possibility of early release was a grossly disproportionate punishment for a man convicted of two counts of sexual conduct with minors. Stressing that the facts revealed that the defendant, who had no prior criminal record, had engaged in consensual sexual intercourse with two girls who were just under fifteen years of age, the Arizona Court concluded that a forty-year sentence was one of those "exceedingly rare" sentences that are barred by the Eighth Amendment.

Second, on 16 June 1992, the Michigan Supreme Court struck down the very law that the U.S. Supreme Court had upheld in *Harmelin*. In *People v. Bullock*, the Michigan Court held that the mandatory penalty of life imprisonment without parole as imposed on defendants convicted of mere possession of 650 grams or more of cocaine constituted a violation of the "cruel *or* unusual punishments" clause of the Michigan constitution. By a four-to-three margin, the court ruled that even though the U.S. Supreme Court had determined in *Harmelin* that the "cruel and unusual punishments" clause of the United States Constitution provided only a very narrow proportionality guarantee, the "cruel or unusual punishments" provision of the 1963 Michigan constitution was intended to give the people of Michigan greater protection against disproportionate sentences. The *Bullock* majority added that "this Court . . . has long followed an approach more consistent with the reasoning of the *Harmelin* dissenters than with that of the *Harmelin* majority."

In what surely was welcome news for Ronald Harmelin, Ruth Bullock, and 160 other Michigan prisoners sentenced under the "650 gram" law, the Michigan Supreme Court ordered that those sentenced under the law must be considered for parole after ten years. Ironically, the Michigan court did not act on another Michigan law, one that provides a mandatory twenty-year prison sentence for anyone convicted of possessing 225 to 650 grams of cocaine. The court acknowledged that it may have created an "arguable incongruity" in Michigan law, but concluded that this issue could not yet be addressed because "the validity of the penalty for possession of 225 to 650 grams is not before us in this case."

It can be concluded that after over eighty years of court decisions on the question of what constitutes an excessive prison sentence, there still is no clear answer. It is, however, settled law, at least for now, that the Eighth Amendment contains a proportionality principle that applies to "grossly disproportionate" prison sentences. But the precise contours of this principle remain unclear and will have to be decided on a case-by-case basis by the federal and state courts.

Kenneth C. Haas

See also LEGAL ISSUES

Bibliography

Baker, T. E., and F. N. Baldwin, Jr. (1985). Eighth Amendment challenges to the length of a criminal sentence: Following the Supreme Court "from precedent to precedent." *Arizona Law Review* 27(1): 25–74.

Forer, L. G. (1994). *Rage to Punish: The Unintended Consequences of Mandatory Sentencing*. New York: W. W. Norton.

Gallo, C. (1981). *Rummel v. Estelle*: Sentencing without a rational basis. *Syracuse Law Review* 32(3): 803–40.

Hackney, G. D. (1992). A trunk full of trouble: *Harmelin v. Michigan. Harvard Civil Rights-Civil Liberties Law Review* 27(1): 262–80.

Keir, N. (1984). *Solem v. Helm*: Extending judicial review under the cruel and unusual punishments clause to require "proportionality" of prison sentences. *Catholic University Law Review* 33(2): 479–515.

Legum, B. C. (1983). Down the road toward human decency: Eighth Amendment proportionality analysis and *Solem v. Helm. Georgia Law Review* 18(2): 109–36.

Schwartz, C. W. (1980). Eighth Amendment proportionality analysis and the compelling case of William Rummel. *Journal of Criminal Law and Criminology* 71(4): 378–420.

Theodore, M. H. (1992). *Harmelin v. Michigan*: Is Eighth Amendment proportionality in jeopardy? *New England Journal on Criminal and Civil Confinement* 18(1–2): 231–58.

Cases

Harmelin v. Michigan, 501 U.S. ___, 111 S. Ct. 2680, 115 L.Ed.2d 836 (1991)

Hutto v. Davis, 454 U.S. 370, 102 S.Ct. 703, 70 L Ed.2d 556 (1982) (per curiam)

People v. Bullock, 440 Mich. 15, 485 N.W. 2d 866 (1992)

Rummel v. Estelle, 445 U.S. 263, 100 S.Ct. 1133, 63 L.Ed.2d 382 (1980)

Solem v. Helm, 463 U.S. 277, 103 S.Ct. 3001, 77 L.Ed.2d 637 (1983)

State v. Bartlett, 171 Ariz. 302, 830 P.2d 823 (1992)

Weems v. United States, 217 U.S. 349, 30 S. Ct. 544, 54 L.Ed. 793 (1910)

Sex Offender Programming

Incarcerated sex offenders pose a special treatment problem for a number of reasons. First, the terms "sexual offense" and "sexual offender" are legal and not clinical concepts. Second, we must distinguish between those who are convicted of sexual offenses and those who subsequently commit sexual offenses while incarcerated for other, nonsexual offenses. A third, related factor, is the prison environment itself.

Sexual offenses are legal labels defined by statute along with corresponding punitive sanctions for those convicted of those offenses The clinical reasons associated with sexual offenses, where applicable, are defined in the *Diagnostic and Statistical Manual*.

The manual is an international classification system for major clinical syndromes. It is based on the *International Classification of Diseases*. Sexual sadism and impulse-control disorders are examples of these clinical classifications. Commonly associated clinical conditions include substance abuse and the V-codes—conditions not attributable to a mental disorder that are a focus of attention or treatment. Adult antisocial behavior, childhood or adolescent antisocial behavior, marital problems, parent-child problems, other specific family circumstances, and other interpersonal problems are examples of V-codes that are likely to be associated with sexual offenses.

Those convicted of sexual offenses are usually classified according to the nature of their offense. These offenses, in turn, are divided between rape (coercive sexual assault) and molestation (the seduction of children or those not deemed legally competent to give consent to sex). Rape is often viewed as the sexual expression of aggression and for that reason alone it can wreak havoc with its victims, both psychologically and physically. Molestation, often termed "child molestation," involves one or more of the following interactive processes: seduction, enticement, persuasion, manipulation, deception, and entrapment. The victims usually are under the offender's control. Here, the potential for lasting psychological damage is of concern to society, the criminal justice system, and clinicians alike. Sexual offenders, regardless of type, generally fall into two clinical categories—those fixated, or driven, with their sexual deviance, and those whose sexual offense is due to regression. Regression, one of the basic defense mechanisms defined by Sigmund Freud, is considered to be a transitory reaction to a stress-reaction. In these instances, we term this a "sex-stress situation."

Sex-stress situations are common within total institutions such as prisons and secure psychiatric facilities. This is known as the "phenomenon of incarceration." Gresham Sykes addressed this phenomenon some thirty years ago. Sykes noted that because of the unnatural prison milieu, inmates suffer from four basic sociocultural deprivations. These deprivations, in turn, can have serious psychological consequences for the inmate. These deprivations include access to goods and services, heterosexual relationships, personal autonomy, and personal security. These stressors often lead to sex-stress situations and homosexual liaisons that would not otherwise exist among these individuals outside prison. Thus, when looking at the treatment of sexual offenders, it is imperative to determine the type of offender and the circumstances under which the sexual deviance occurred.

Treatment Considerations

The literature on sex offenders can be divided into two parts, that which addresses the causes of sexual deviance and that which looks at potential treatment methods. Obviously, most clinical concern is focused on what is termed the fixated offender, whether molester or rapist.

Research within the last thirty years has eliminated any single biological factor, in itself, as the definitive cause of sexual aberration. There is still considerable interest in the role of the extra male sex chromosome (XYY) coupled with the impulse control disorder among male sex offenders. We realize now, however, that the XYY configuration is not a sufficient causal factor by itself. Socialization is another factor that plays a role in our sexual orientation and subsequent behavior—realized or imagined. Berlin cited the case of a botched circumcision of an infant who was subsequently penectomized, sexually altered, treated with estrogen, and reared as a girl. "Thus, although she is a woman with an XY rather than a XX chromosomal karyotype, as a consequence presumably of how she has been raised, she feels herself to be a woman and she finds men to be sexually appealing (1986, 17)."

Another element of the socialization process is the relationship between sex offenders, notably pedophiles (both molesters and rapists), and their own role as adult victims of childhood sexual assault. Groth warns that the often cited data concerning adult victims are flawed. Instead of 90 percent of the offenders and 20 percent of the victims being male the real figure is more likely to be 75 percent of the offenders and 50 percent of the victims. Women account for closer to 25 percent, rather than the 10 percent often cited, of the number of perpetrators, and women more likely represent 50 percent of the victims rather than the 80 percent once believed. Another interesting figure Groth's research produced is that only about 30 percent of battered children go on to become battering adults. It is important for the clinician to keep that in mind, especially in light of the recent controversy over "reconstructed memory" (false memory syndrome).

What are the factors that are most likely to contribute to the cycle of abuse? Most researchers would agree on these three:

1. Persistent abuse by the same offender over time
2. Multiple abuse by many abusers
3. Intense sexual trauma occurring in isolation, with no one available to help in processing the trauma

Interestingly, these factors can be initiated in prison itself, hence providing a breeding ground for sexual offenders among inmates who did not have a history of sexual abuse and sexual offenses. This is yet another dilemma of incarceration. On the other hand, society has a right to be protected from dangerous sexual offenders.

One common element for classification as sexually deviant is the presence of the clinical features of intense sexual urges coupled with sexually arousing fantasies. Groth also noted that a number of factors seem to be associated with male sexual offenders (rapists). These central features seem to be a lack of a warm relationship with their fathers, viewing women in subservient roles, and a history of psychological or physical abuse while children at the hands of adult men.

When considering treatment effectiveness within prisons or secure psychiatric institutions, it is difficult, as French points out, to form conclusions based on institutional behavior and treatment responsiveness. "Treatment, especially within a correctional setting, can compound the issue by masking environmental stimuli that may contribute to the sexual behaviors (1991, 1195)." We now realize that it is a mistake to judge treatment success solely upon behavioral appearances of how clients respond to talk therapy, their perception of women or children, or some other associated feature such as church or AA attendance.

Another treatment consideration, according to French, is that of sex as an associated clinical feature that may surface, for the first time, as a result of the phenomenon of incarceration: "In these situations stressors associated with the phenomenon of incarceration tend to exacerbate sex-related clinical features linked to untreated mentally ill inmates (1992, 1197)." The link here seems to exist between sex-stress features of incarceration and a number of major clinical syndromes including post-traumatic stress as a reaction to prison rape or sexual adaptations and adjustment disorders, especially those with a depressive-anxiety mix. Impulsive sexual aggression is not an uncommon means for venting these frustrations of incarceration. Prison stress can also exacerbate certain associated features of psychotic inmates, notably hypersexuality. This is a common feature of acute schizophrenia, schizoaffective disorders, atypical psychosis, and manic-depressive disorders. The latter has been a serious problem within incarcerated populations within the past twenty years with the de-institutionalization of mental hospitals and facilities for the mentally retarded. Those who are not afforded community based treatment, or refuse it, often end up being treated within the criminal justice system.

A unique treatment for the dangerous (fixated) male sexual offender, regardless if he is a rapist or molester, is the use of the synthetic female hormone progesterone. Depro-Provera and Provera influence the sex drive by decreasing the male libido through suppression of testosterone and luteinizing (fantasy hormone) hormones. Berlin, a pioneer in this technique, noted that this form of chemical castration is superior to surgical castration not only because it is reversible but also because surgical castration does not lower the effects of luteinizing hormones, which are, for the most part, the root of deviant sexual fantasies. Again, it must be realized that chemical castration is not the answer for all dangerous sexual offenders. Moreover, it is not a cure in itself, even for those sexual offenders who respond well to treatment.

What is the ideal treatment formula? Clinical psychopharmacological interventions, psychotherapy directed at the sexual offense itself coupled with psychotherapy for any associated conditions (substance abuse, interpersonal relationship problems, antisocial behavior), and lifelong monitoring. Today, twenty-two states have sex offender registration laws. More states are expected to follow. On the legal front, what is needed is for all convicted sexual offenders to be entered into a national network in which courts, schools, churches, children's organizations, and police departments can check the background of employees or potential employees.

When it comes to psychotherapy, Groth outlined certain conditions that correctional therapists need to apply with sexual offenders.

1. There is no confidentiality between the client and therapist because of the severity of the nature of sexual offenses
2. All prior arrests and convictions must be made available to the correctional treatment team
3. The client must admit guilt and not blame it on associated features (it was the drugs or alcohol; I am an adult victim of sexual abuse, etc.). Clients who refuse to do so are classified as "refusing treatment" regardless of how many other religious, support, or so-called treatment sessions or groups they attend. And for that to have meaning, there need to be significant "response costs" (greatly restricted privileges) for the client-inmate.

Groth estimates that it takes at least a year of psychotherapy for the sexual offender to reach the level of "empathic guilt" (insight into the feelings of one's victims instead of feeling sorry for oneself).

The New Hampshire Department of Corrections has been a pioneer in the field of treating dangerous sexual offenders. Berlin introduced his chemical castration to this population in the early 1980s. More recently, the Sex Offender Psychosocial Re-Educational Program, based on Groth's treatment concepts, was implemented. The program goals are:

1. To reduce the likelihood that the individual who has committed a sex offense will commit another
2. To enable the individual who has committed a sex offense to accept responsibility for his behavior
3. That the individual who has committed a sex offense understand that vigilance about himself and his behavior is a task that he must be willing to face every day of his life from now on.

These goals are implemented through eight program modules within the correctional environment:

1. Family life and sexuality
2. Addictions: sex offender group
3. Sex offender clinical group
4. Completers group (ongoing maintenance group for those sex offenders who have completed the program but remain incarcerated)
5. Alcohol or drug addiction
6. Anger management
7. Religion, values, and behavior
8. Optional extended training (additional clinical treatment within a secure clinical milieu—Summit House)

A treatment program for sexual offenders within correctional or secured psychiatric environments needs to have three interrelated components: clinical psychopharmacological interventions; psychotherapy that addresses the sexual offense; and lifelong monitoring once the offender is released from custody.

Laurence French

Bibliography

Berlin, F. S., and E. K. Krout (1986). Pedophilia: Diagnostic concepts, treatment and ethical considerations. *American Journal of Forensic Psychiatry* 7: 13–30.

Cooper, A. (1986). Progestrogens in the treatment of male sex offenders. *Canadian Journal of Psychiatry* 31: 73–79.

Earls, C., and V. Quinsey (1985). What is to be done? Future research on the assessments and behavioral treatment of sex offenders. *Behavioral Sciences and the Law* 3: 377–90.

French, L. (1992). Characteristics of sexuality within correctional environments. *Corrective and Social Psychiatry* 38: 5–8.

French, L., and J. Vollmann, Jr. (1987). Treating the dangerous sexual offender: A clinical/legal dilemma. *International Journal of Offender Therapy and Comparative Criminology* 31: 61–69.

Groth, A. N., and F. J. Oliveri (1989). Understanding sexual offense behavior and differentiating among sexual abusers. In S. Sgroi, ed. *Vulnerable Populations*, vol. 2. Lexington, Mass.: Lexington.

McFarland, L. (1986). Depro-Provera therapy as an alternative to imprisonment. *Houston Law Review* 23: 801–19.

Sapp, A. D., and M. S. Vaughn (1991). Sex offender rehabilitation programs in state

S

prisons: A nationwide survey. *Journal of Offender Rehabilitation* 17: 55–75.

Spitzer, R. (1987). *Diagnostic and Statistical Manual* (3rd ed., rev.). Washington, D.C.: American Psychiatric Association Press.

Whitfield, R. (1987). Treatment of male sexual offenders in a correctional facility. *Journal of Offender Counseling* 8: 2–16.

Sexual Exploitation in Prison

Sexual aggression in institutions extends beyond rape or attempted rape. Sexual harassment and sexual advances are also major causes of stress and violence. According to one prison expert, they are potentially the most dangerous type of conflict in prison. Sexual aggression can cause serious problems for correctional officials. Victims can be severely harmed both physically and emotionally. Fear often instigates violence between aggressors and potential victims. Staff can also become involved in lengthy and costly lawsuits for failure to protect weaker inmates from predators. In several states, male staff members have also been charged with sexually exploiting female prisoners, in some instances involving wide-scale sex rings. Measures to prevent or at least reduce the amount of sexual violence seem costly and restrictive.

Estimating the Frequency of Sexual Assaults
Estimates of the number of inmates sexually assaulted in prison range anywhere from 1 to 28 percent of the total population. Perhaps the best way for investigators to determine the number of rapes occurring in any system is by thoroughly interviewing random samples of prisoners. In the federal system, for example, when that was done researchers from the Bureau of Prisons found the rate to be 0.6 percent of 330 men. In the New York State Department of Correctional Services, it was 1.3 percent of 76 men. Such social science researchers have found the rate of prison rape to be much lower than claimed by popular writers on the topic, who have guessed at the rate without using proper victimization surveys.

One way to estimate the rate might be to look at the *Survey of Inmates of State Correctional Facilities, 1986*, a random survey carried out by the Bureau of Justice Statistics of the U.S. Department of Justice. The survey scientifically estimated the characteristics of the entire prison population of the United States based on a large representative sample. Although this study was not explicitly designed to measure prison victimization, it did ask 10,687 male prisoners if they had "ever been both physically and sexually abused after the age of 18." Of these, 130 answered "yes," giving an estimated rate of 1.2 percent. One could assume that most of this victimization had occurred when the men were in jail or prison, because the rape of men in the general population is exceedingly low.

Higher estimates of sexual violence have been found in several state studies. A 1982 study in the California system found that 14 percent of the inmates admitted to having been assaulted. Another New York study found that 28 percent of the prisoners acknowledged having been attacked (Getlin 1994).

One activist, an ex-offender who was sexually assaulted in prison, has formed a nonprofit organization called Stop Prison Rape. He estimates that there are more than a quarter million sexual assaults on inmates each year in American correctional facilities. He claims that the figures reported in surveys are low because most inmates are reluctant to admit that they had been victimized in such a manner (Getlin 1994). Absent a carefully designed study, the rate in any particular institution, at any point in time, must remain in question. Consequently, we have no way of accurately determining a national rate.

Profiles of Sexual Predators
Sexual aggressors are generally violent men and boys who have used threats and force with weapons against weaker victims long before they entered institutions. Most are serving time for violent predatory crimes such as robbery. In the few institutions in which researchers have thoroughly examined the problem, where whites have been in the minority, most aggressors have been African American and most victims have been white.

Aggressors can be categorized as "gorillas" or "players." Gorillas overwhelm their victims with physical force or threats, often wielding improvised knives and clubs. Players see themselves in the role of a pimp, and try to fast-talk their prey first. If that fails, they use force. Several aggressors often attack single victims, carefully planning the event to circumvent prison security.

Sexual aggressors in prison have been heterosexuals on the street. They view their behavior in confinement as a continuation of their former approaches to women. They do this by viewing the objects of their attacks as women, placing them in female roles.

While there is a good deal of academic speculation about the causes of prison and jail rape, aggressors themselves see a compelling sexual drive behind their behavior. Viewing their acts as caused by the sexual deprivation that is part of a sentence to prison, they argue that they, ultimately, are the real victims.

Profiles of Victims

For potential victims, the threat of an impending attack may cause fear. Consequently, they may respond violently, in public, to project an image as tough, violent men whom predators searching for the weak should avoid. They may also wish to communicate to others that they are decidedly heterosexual.

Other times, believing that verbal approaches are a certain precursor to rape, some targets will make preemptive strikes at opportune moments. Fearful men whom aggressors have approached with threats or the use of force also use violence to defend themselves. These events unfold, of course, in a social setting that discourages potential victims from seeking official help because they fear retaliation.

In the initial stages of a rape attack the victim may also become violent. Then the situation can quickly escalate to high levels of violence as both parties become angry and the parties arm themselves with homemade weapons.

Unfounded myths add to the intensity of targets' reactions. In actuality, the frequency of rape is far lower than is thought by newly arriving prisoners. Most initial approaches are unsuccessful. Very few victims undergo changes of sexual orientation or become the permanent sex partners of protective aggressors. In truth, victims' violence and the restrictive lives they live afterward generally prevent similar events from happening later. While the crisis resulting from attack can have grave psychological consequences, these do not include changes in sexual behavior or attitudes.

The Effects of Sexual Victimization

The psychological impact of fear and anger can result in a crisis, as targets sometimes find the problem unsolvable. Occasionally self-injury or suicide can follow. Fear also can result in isolation and the avoidance of activities. Nonviolent or weak men may be unable to confront tough aggressors who often are members of groups. Those adhering to the convict code will be reluctant to be seen as "snitches." The remedies the institution offers may be unacceptable: solitary confinement in a protection unit, transfer to another prison too far for frequent home visits, or requiring that victims give over the names of aggressors before they can be helped.

Because of the unsolvable nature of the problem, sexual approaches, harassment, and attacks can be the cause of severe stress in confinement. Anger and fear increase. Unable to withdraw from the situation, targets may cut their wrists or attempt to hang themselves, for one of three reasons. The first and most common is "fate avoidance." Here, the man in crisis attempts to end his life to avoid what he perceives to be certain victimization in the future. A strong belief in imminent and successful sexual attack causes the target to avoid this fate through suicide.

A second category of suicide is "self-classification." Here a man who sees overwhelming obstacles to his request for a transfer to a safe place through normal channels seeks to be moved by a suicide attempt which he hopes will be serious enough to impress officials but not serious enough to kill him. He hopes that the event will earn him a move to a hospital, mental health facility, or at least to the sympathetic ear of a counselor or a psychologist.

The third category is "self-deactivation." Here, actual or perceived sexual victimization adds to a sad and dreary number of accumulated life experiences that may include other consequences of criminal conviction such as loss of job, car, house, wife, and children. This added indignity tips the balance toward not wanting to go on. Just why some men who are the object of advances can view these events as a severe failure has much to do with typical working-class and convict views about self-image and public presence. A man in the position of a target, who has always viewed himself as a man, suddenly must cope with the painful knowledge that others are viewing him as a woman or, what may be even worse from his perspective, as a homosexual, for this is how aggressors understand their behavior.

Strategies for Reducing Sexual Victimization

One primary solution to the problem is protecting the safety of vulnerable inmates through the "special classification" of potential victims when they enter prison. The men most at risk are smaller than others, whites, if that racial group is in the minority, as it often is, and often from small towns and rural areas lacking criminal subcultures that may provide group support for "homies" while confined. Social isolates are especially at risk, and often that includes those with histories of mental disturbance or retardation. It is also possible to use psychological tests such as the Prison Preference Inventory to identify those most likely to have fear-related crises.

Custody staff should observe and gather intelligence on known aggressors. Officers should see to the surveillance of all areas where inmates congregate. The harsh and expensive security measures in correctional facilities are often as necessary for the protection of inmates as they are for preventing escape. Privacy may appear humane; out of the need for inmate safety, however, it is often taken away so that supervising guards can always observe inmates. Because aggressors always exist in prison and jail populations, rape is usually the result of inadequate security. Well-run correctional facilities following contemporary professional standards generally prevent most sexual assaults nowadays, even though increases in populations have led correctional systems to house more prisoners in open dormitories. At times, however, clever aggressors inevitably learn to circumvent security procedures, or these procedures break down temporarily.

"Target hardening" has been a solution to the problem for many years. The same message is given by prisoners and staff to new arrivals who may be at risk: "Do your own time"; "don't respond to friendly overtures"; "don't get involved with others." Such solutions, unfortunately, blame potential victims for what might happen to them and also cut new arrivals off from supportive associations that they may need for survival and to cope with the unfamiliar, lonely, and frightening setting in which they find themselves. Such messages also tend to exaggerate and intensify the perception of prison as a dangerous and fearful place. Such thoughts themselves become a cause of violence in confinement.

Another aspect of target hardening comes from advising potential or actual targets to arm themselves or to become violent so that others will leave them alone. This is one way that confinement teaches men to solve interpersonal disputes with private violence, possibly with lasting consequences for long-term behavioral and attitudinal change.

Liability for Failure to Protect Against Sexual Assault

The common observation concerning sexual assault in prison is that a potential victim has limited options: fight, flee, or submit. To this list, one author has added a fourth and relatively new option: sue. Inmates who suffer sexual assault in prison may bring civil (tort) suits against their custodians. In such litigation, the plaintiff seeks monetary compensation for the pain and suffering caused by the prison system's failure to protect him.

A lack of adequate protection against sexual assault may also be grounds for a civil rights suit. In *Stokes v. Delcambre,* an inmate filed suit against a sheriff and deputy after he was beaten and sexually assaulted by other inmates in a Louisiana jail. In awarding $380,000 in compensatory and punitive damages, the court pointed out that the deputy was deliberately indifferent to the fighting that was taking place, and that he "should have known" that he had an obligation not to detain an inmate in a manner that made it likely that the inmate would be beaten or sexually assaulted.

In a Missouri case argued before the U.S. Supreme Court, it was held that individual acts of violence rather than the usual patterns of violence would be all that would have to be established to win a claim. Though punitive damages are rare in inmate civil rights cases, the Court found it appropriate when "the defendants' conduct is shown to be motivated by evil motive or intent or when it involves reckless or callous indifference to the federally protected rights of others" (*Smith v. Wade*). In this case Wade, an inmate in a first offenders facility, was harassed, beaten, and sexually assaulted by two cellmates. In deciding that the guard, Smith, knew or should have known that Wade was at risk, the jury awarded the plaintiff twenty-five thousand dollars in compensatory and five thousand dollars in punitive damages. According to Levin (1985, 22), such a decision should have a "cautionary effect on corrections officials. Prison officials who view inmates as potential plaintiffs might be more inclined to prevent situations conducive to assault."

Fear of impending sexual assault has also been cited by defendants facing criminal charges for escape. Most courts hearing cases in which the prisoner claims to have fled because of duress will allow such a defense if the situation meets the criteria outlined in *People v. Lover-*

camp. That is, a prisoner "(1) must face a specific threat of death, forcible sexual assault or substantial bodily injury in the immediate future, (2) must have no time to complain to authorities and no prior history of frivolous complaints, (3) must have no time or opportunity to resort to the courts, (4) must commit no violence against prison personnel during the escape, and (5) must report immediately to prison authorities upon escaping" (Levin 1985). Interestingly enough, Lovercamp was a female inmate harassed by a number of lesbian inmates and one of the few defendants to use the rape/ duress defense successfully.

Given the problem of sexual assault, the possibility of spreading sexually transmitted diseases and the responsibility of correctional systems to avoid the risk of violence, the prevention of violence through nonviolent methods should be a top priority, along with carrying out adequate procedures for inmate safety and psychological survival.

Daniel Lockwood

See also VIOLENCE

Bibliography

Bartollas, C., S. J. Miller, and S. Dinitz (1976). *Juvenile Victimization*. Newbury Park, Calif.: Sage.

Davis, A. (1968). Sexual assaults in the Philadelphia prison system and sheriff's vans. *Trans-Action* 6: 8–16.

Getlin, J. (1994). I'm still fighting. *Los Angeles Times*. May 20: E1, E4, E5.

Jones, R. S., and T. J. Schmid (1989). Inmates' conceptions of prison sexual assault. *Prison Journal* 76: 53–61.

Levin, M. (1985). Fight, flee, submit, sue: Alternatives for sexually assaulted prisoners. *Columbia Journal of Law and Social Problems* 18: 505–30.

Lockwood, D. (1980). *Prison Sexual Violence*. New York: Elsevier-North Holland.

Siegal, D. (1992). Rape in prison and AIDS: A Challenge for the Eighth Amendment Framework of *Wilson v. Seiter. Stanford Law Review* 44(6): 1541–81.

Cases

People v. Lovercamp 43 Cal App. 3d 823, 118 Cal Rptr 110 (1974)

Smith v. Wade 461 U.S. 30, 103 S.Ct. 1625 (1983)

Stokes v. Delacambre 710 F.2d 1120 (1983)

Sing Sing Prison

In the nineteenth century, convicted felons in New York City often heard the words, "You are being 'sent up the river'!"—that is, to Sing Sing Prison, thirty-three miles north of New York City in Ossining, New York. The "Bastille on the Hudson" perches 170 feet above the Hudson River and is among the best known and most notorious prisons in the world. The massive stone structure was originally named Mt. Pleasant Prison but was quickly nicknamed "Sing Sing" for the town in which it is located. In 1970 the name was changed from Mt. Pleasant to Ossining Correctional Facility, and in 1985 it was again changed, this time to Sing Sing Correctional Facility.

Sing Sing was built in 1825–26 on 130 acres formerly called the Silver Mine Farm and owned by John Fleetwood Marsh. It cost the State of New York a mere seventy thousand dollars to erect the 482 by 44 foot, four-tiered building. The poorly ventilated, damp cells are small (7 feet by 3 feet 3 inches by 6 feet 7 inches), and arranged back-to-back, consistent with the Auburn system of enforced silence. The infamous warden, Captain Lynds of Auburn, was recruited to build Sing Sing. He handpicked one hundred convicts from Auburn Prison (near Syracuse, New York) because they were used to his heavy-handed discipline and were "broken," and therefore docile. In the spring of 1825, these one hundred shackled men were taken from Auburn to Ossining, first by canal and then by the Hudson River, to build the new prison that was to replace Newgate Prison in New York City.

Prisoners had not before built their own prison. The convicts were lodged in the fields during the construction, and there were some concerns about security. Lynds's rigid discipline and silence were enforced by officers with guns, and these officers could "inflict stripes" on prisoners (whip them) without reporting it to superior officers. The prisoners mined the stone for the prison on the state land. Sing Sing was no doubt the model for early movie makers who showed prisoners, dressed in striped uniforms, picking and hammering in the prison mines. By May of 1826, all of the prisoners from the old Newgate prison were transferred to Mt. Pleasant Prison, and by October of 1828 the main building was finished. One hundred years later, in 1928, a building housing a kitchen, hospital, and chapel was constructed. Mt. Pleasant Prison was the first prison constructed with no wall (although it has one today). Instead, the prison design created an enclosed courtyard, commonly referred to today as the "yard."

In 1839 the Mt. Pleasant Female Prison opened at Sing Sing. This was the first separate facility for women in the United States. It was in operation until 1877, when women were sent to county jails until the women's prison was constructed at Auburn in 1893. Women were transferred out of Sing Sing in 1877 because of overcrowding, and also because of complaints that women who could not serve their time at Sing Sing and thus remained in county jails were not stigmatized as dramatically as women who did their sentence at Sing Sing. Therefore, all female felons in New York served their state sentence in county penitentiaries from 1877 to 1893.

Immediately upon its opening, the state sought ways to make Sing Sing profitable. Because stone cutting by prisoners had been profitable in nearby New Hampshire and Massachusetts, it was determined that Sing Sing would mine the marble on the property. The proximity to the New York City market, the Hudson River for transportation, and the free labor of convicts made Sing Sing an ideal prison industrial site. By 1828 the state had commissioned cut stone for many contracts in New York City, for the courthouse in Troy, and the city hall in Albany. Further, the state was entering into contracts with outsiders for convict labor. By 1831, however, the labor organizations in New York City began criticizing the prison industry for underselling them. The state was selling marble below market price and hiring out convicts at low wages, prompting petitions to the legislature to end the prison industry system. The public, however, liked the system. For prisons to be self-sufficient and to instill rigid discipline and hard work was appealing. Organized labor won some concessions. Convicts were restricted to working at trades they knew before coming to prison. Complaints from labor and the unveiling of atrocities at Sing Sing eventually brought about the demise of the prison labor system there.

From the day it opened, Sing Sing was the target of criticism. Lynds's harsh Auburn system was not universally admired. In 1830 a respected commissioner of prisons in New York, Samuel M. Hopkins, charged that Lynds was guilty of cruelty and maladministration. Hopkins called Lynds an "absolute dictator" who was completely unconcerned about the welfare of the prisoners. Although a "select" committee of the New York Senate exonerated Lynds of wrongdoing, the investigation was the beginning of the end of the Auburn system. In 1834 Lynds resigned as warden of Sing Sing, replaced by Robert Wiltse, who ran Sing Sing as a "virtual slave camp." Wiltse was replaced in 1840 by David Seymour, who relaxed the harsh regime only to be criticized for being too lenient. He was also blamed for prison unrest during that time. Captain Lynds returned in 1844 and brought back his strict discipline: silence enforced with the lash. Punishment at Sing Sing was notoriously harsh under Lynds. For example, it was reported that as many as three thousand lashes per month were given, women were "gagged," straitjackets were used on disruptive prisoners, and bread and water diets were common.

Concerns about prisoners and prison conditions at Sing Sing were mounting. In 1844 John W. Edmonds, chairman of the New York Board of Inspectors, called for a meeting of those interested in prison reform. Out of this grew the New York Prison Association. Initial concerns focused on released prisoners who were set free with a "bare pittance." These grew to more general concerns about prisoners and prisons. One association member, Friend Isaac Hopper, helped prisoners find homes and jobs upon release, laying the groundwork for parole agents' work.

Throughout the remaining years of the nineteenth century and into the twentieth century, Sing Sing was the target of much criticism. Perhaps because of its proximity to New York City, it received constant attention from the New York press, especially from the *New York Times*. Sing Sing was continuously described as "overcrowded," and this overcrowding was often blamed for its many escapes: "news of attempts at escape, successful and unsuccessful, of the difficulties of maintaining discipline, and of a great many other incidents connected with the crowd at Sing Sing . . ." (*New York Times*, 18 November 1869). It was also subject to concern about torture in the prison: "The trapeze . . . consists of two thin tarred ropes run over a pulley. . . . The ends of these ropes are fastened to the thumbs of the convict who is to be punished. . . . The victim is lifted off his feet . . . and dangles in mid-air" (*New York Times,* 13 November 1869). One commissioner appointed to investigate conditions in 1913 was quoted as saying, "I said in my Sing Sing report that 'stories of torture of prisoners in the Middle Ages sound like descriptions of luxuries in comparison with tales that have been told me of the lives some of the prisoners in Sing Sing live. . . .'" (*New York Times*, 26 July 1913). The considerable public attention eventually led to major changes in the prison.

Not surprisingly, capital punishment had a place at Sing Sing as well. In 1889, New York State contracted with Harold Brown, the inventor of the electric chair, to build three electric chairs using alternating current, the method advocated by George Westinghouse. One of the chairs was to be housed at Sing Sing (the others were to be at Auburn and Clinton, near Plattsburg, New York). Thomas Edison, who was initially opposed to capital punishment, claimed that Westinghouse's alternating current was "more dangerous" than direct current. In a bizarre twist, Edison then claimed that his direct current method of execution was better. On 2 February 1882, the Edison method of execution was tested at Sing Sing by strapping Charles McElvaine to a chair with his hands plunged into vats of salt water. The current was passed through the salt water and into McElvaine, slowly torturing him to death. The outcome was that Westinghouse's alternating current was "more dangerous," in that it was quicker and more effective. All executions in New York State were conducted at Sing Sing from 1914 to 1963, when the last execution was performed. No doubt the most famous executions to occur at Sing Sing were of Julius and Ethel Rosenberg for espionage in 1953. In 1969 the location for all future executions in New York was moved from Sing Sing to Green Haven Prison.

Continued attention to Sing Sing opened the door to reform attempts in addition to the formation of the New York Prison Association. In 1896 Mrs. Maud Ballington Booth founded the Volunteer Prison League in Sing Sing. The goal of that group was to encourage prisoners to pray and read the Bible daily, to use clean language, to adopt cheerful habits, and to obey prison rules. For accomplishing this, prisoners received a certificate. Sing Sing had an inmate newspaper, the *Star of Hope*, during the early years of the twentieth century. The Golden Rule Brotherhood was founded in 1913 by Sing Sing warden Thomas McCormack. This association gave convicts the chance to use the prison yard "as they saw fit" on Saturdays and Sundays. Without question the most revolutionary change in Sing Sing was initiated by Thomas Mott Osborne, who became warden in 1914.

Osborne gained notoriety as a prison reformer at Auburn when he lived among the prisoners to learn about prison life. Osborne was a vocal and harsh critic of the Auburn prison system. At Auburn he established the first democratic organization of prisoners, the Mutual Welfare League. His work at Auburn brought him to the attention of the governor and superintendent, and in 1914 he was asked to become warden at Sing Sing, where he helped to establish a Mutual Welfare League. Perhaps because of his quick and dramatic reforms, Osborne was frequently criticized. The prisoners seemed to prefer Sing Sing under Osborne to any other prison. Prisoners at Sing Sing regarded it as punishment to be transferred to the less crowded Auburn, and the transferred prisoners were seemingly chosen at random with no say from Osborne. This practice led to considerable unrest at Sing Sing: "Warden Osborne blames the unrest and the two recent escapes on this fear . . . which he says destroys the effect of all his theory that deserving inmates shall be rewarded and that the undeserving shall be punished" (*New York Times*, 3 July 1915). Osborne had enemies in the state who wished him to be fired: "Superintendent Riley is a prison manager of the old school and has never looked kindly upon what he regards as the 'pink tea' methods of Mr. Osborne. . . . Superintendent Riley thinks he could run the prison department . . . without the services of the millionaire art connoisseur and prison reformer" (*New York Times*, 15 July 1915). The next year Osborne resigned under pressure from political enemies in the New York State prison system.

During Osborne's reform era at Sing Sing, his efforts were aided, albeit for a short period, by psychiatrist Dr. Bernard Glueck, who founded a medical/psychiatric clinic at Sing Sing in 1916. This new era of "clinical criminology" was financed by the Rockefeller Foundation, and Glueck and other clinicians organized the National Committee for Mental Hygiene based largely upon their work with prisoners at Sing Sing. Glueck introduced a comprehensive exam of all inmates received at Sing Sing during the administrations of Osborne and later Kirchwey, a friend of Osborne's. Glueck argued that Sing Sing should be used exclusively as a classification and distribution prison. Glueck and clinical colleagues further argued that clinical evidence could and should be substituted for the legal system of determining an inmate's sentence. Their work led to the use of psychiatric consultants by courts and, most importantly, to the classification of prisoners. Gleuck's work had a significant impact on how New York and other states operated prisons during the remainder of the twentieth century. Punishment gave way to individualization of prisoners through classification and ultimately rehabilitation. Lewis E. Lawes, warden at Sing Sing in the 1920s and 1930s, oversaw much of the rehabilitation movement at Sing Sing.

During the general nationwide prison unrest of the 1960s, Sing Sing saw some action as well. A prison strike at Sing Sing in 1966 was successful in pressuring the state legislature to adopt more lenient disciplinary procedures.

Sing Sing is nearly 175 years old. It has been a continuously operating maximum-security prison since 1826, when prisoners built its first cells. Today Sing Sing is classified as a maximum-security prison for men twenty-one years and older. Sing Sing also includes medium-security general confinement, a detention center for men sixteen years and older, a diagnostic and treatment center, and a satellite mental health unit. As of mid 1994, Sing Sing housed approximately 1,750 inmates; its capacity is 2,200. Sing Sing is among the State of New York's largest prisons, outsized only by Clinton and periodically by Attica. Maximum-security inmates are housed in single cells, while medium-security general confinement inmates have dormitory-style housing.

Lisa A. Callahan

Bibliography
Lewis, O. F. (1922). *The Development of American Prisons and Prison Customs (1776–1845)*. Albany, N.Y.: J. B. Lyon.
McKelvey, B. (1936). *American Prisons*. Chicago: University of Chicago Press. (Reprinted Montclair, N.J.: Patterson Smith, 1977).
Trombley, S. (1992). *The Execution Protocol: Inside America's Capital Punishment Industry*. New York: Crown.

Site Selection and Construction of Prisons
The political reality of our nation's "get-tough" policy against crime is an ever-increasing incarceration "snowball," resulting in severe overcrowding within our state and federal correctional systems. Since 1973, prisoner incarceration in this country has more than tripled. Construction has not been able to keep pace with the increased rates of incarceration. Since 1987, the California prison system alone has opened ten new facilities, with an additional ten slated to open before the end of the century. Even with this enormous increase in available bed space, the California Department of Corrections anticipates a maximum population in excess of 150 percent of capacity.

Increasing prison populations, and the associated overcrowding, make prison siting a major issue for the criminal justice system. Governments are finding it increasingly difficult to find locations for future prisons that do not come under a barrage of local criticism. Correctional institutions are often considered locally undesirable land uses (LULUs) by nearby residents, who would rather they be located elsewhere. Ballot initiatives in support of correctional facility construction traditionally fare quite well. The same constituency that supports additional funding, however, generally rejects construction within their community. This "not in my backyard" (NIMBY) philosophy reflects an appropriate community concern, but it is seldom evaluated against the potential benefits of having such facilities in the area.

The American Correctional Association has two fundamental guidelines regarding correctional facility siting:

1. The institution should be located in a place near inmate families and near metropolitan areas, to facilitate family visits and access to courts, medical resources, and other necessary services.
2. Site selection should make optimum use of existing resources and strive to develop and maintain community support.

It has even been argued that institution siting is the most important factor in prison development, affecting the community, the correctional institution, and the inmate alike. The institution must be integrated into the community, providing jobs for residents, stimulating the local community both economically and socially, while maintaining security and safety.

Selection Criteria
According to the Federal Guidelines for Prison Site Selection, the primary objective of the site selection and acquisition process is an overriding concern for environmental issues and pub-

lic acceptance. Neither can be overlooked or underestimated if agency officials are to gain the cooperation of the host community.

The first issue to trigger the acquisition process at the federal level is identification of enough inmates in a specific area to justify a new facility there. After a region has been designated, the bureau advises state chambers of commerce, regional economic development associations, and state departments of corrections that it is interested in considering potential sites.

The bureau's comprehensive plan for evaluating potential sites includes development suitability, hazards avoidance, availability of special resources, and the endorsement of local officials. It also includes such basic factors as adequate space (approximately 200 to 250 acres with adequate visual buffers along the outer boundaries), location within fifty miles of a large population center (of fifty thousand people or more), an accredited, full-service hospital within a one-hour drive, a nearby fire department, nearby higher education facilities, accessibility to public transportation and major highway systems, and adequate public utilities.

Community Response

Locating correctional institutions in or near cities has met with uneven community response. Formerly, when prisons were deliberately built in the most sparsely populated areas, there was no need to consult or negotiate with local residents. Today, a range of opinion is to be expected. Some communities have competed with each other to have a regional correctional facility built in their area; others have flatly rejected the prospect.

One of the most difficult and potentially adverse events in the site selection process is premature disclosure of a proposed project, resulting in negative community reaction. With caution and diplomacy, the agency or department should discuss its plans with community leaders as a first step. If the reaction is favorable, an intensive public information effort follows. Communities frequently organize a local task force early in the process to mobilize support for the prison proposal. It is not uncommon for opposing groups to organize similarly. This increased community awareness and involvement often leads to controversy and misunderstanding.

When a public education program is launched in a community, it stresses the potential economic benefits. Fears are allayed by let-ting community groups tour existing institutions similar to the one proposed for their area, giving them a chance to talk with staff and meet with local community groups.

Environmental Consequences

The greatest environmental concern is a new correctional institution's effect on the quality of life in the host community. Environmental issues must be properly monitored and presented for public review in an easily understood format. Most communities want to know whether a new institution will:

1. Jeopardize the town's safety and security;
2. Adversely affect property and housing values near the institution;
3. Adversely affect city schools and other community services;
4. Burden local law enforcement agencies;
5. Consume an inordinate amount of the community's water supply and sewage capacity;
6. Intrude visually on neighboring properties;
7. Give the town a negative "prison town" reputation.

Security and Safety

Near prisons, community contact with visitors or inmates on work-release programs or community-service furlough can affect the residents' feelings of security, which are often based neither on experience nor fact. Rather, some citizens have an image of prisons, encouraged by the news media, that exaggerates both the frequency and threat of prison escapes as well as of increased crime within the surrounding area. In fact, analysis of current research into communities with and without correctional facilities indicates that crime rates near correctional institutions were *lower*, when there was a difference at all (Rogers and Haimes 1987).

As part of the overall marketing plan, the developmental agency should emphasize to community leaders the low incidence of escapes. In some cases, a certain amount of public relations work may be necessary, combining emotional appeal with rational argument.

Property Values

There is often a general feeling that having a correctional institution in an area makes property less desirable and lowers property values. So many factors are involved, from architectural to political, that a general relationship between prison construction and nearby land values cannot adequately be made. The correctional agency should maintain an open dialogue with community residents, their representatives, and local real estate experts to balance any devaluation concerns against the region's need for a correctional facility.

Psychological Impact
A fear of change or the unknown is associated with a sudden influx of people in the area. Fear of change is most frequently related to a prison subculture or community stigma, in which a community comes to be associated with undesirables involved in drug trafficking or violent crimes. The prison may be seen as a place of fear, hostility, and tension. Some citizens feel that offenders, coming and going, some on temporary-release programs, would not live up to community standards of behavior.

Existing research indicates that these fears are greater than any objective measurement of the impact of a prison on the local community in explaining resistance to potential siting (McGee 1981). Nearly all prison neighbors studied reported no direct impact on their families.

Effect on Local Institutions
Do prisons place unconscionable demands on existing resources, creating burdens on the local community? For police, concerns include hiring competition for potential officers and police response to prison escapes. Police in nearby communities, however, often find that the benefits of the prison outweigh any potential burdens. Increased traffic and demands for public services and environmental resources, however, are sometimes associated with LULUs.

Economic Impact
The principal economic concern is that benefits to the local community will be limited. If there are only a few local expenditures, or they are of limited size, local gains are offset by increased expenditures to ensure public safety and by increased "community infrastructure" costs, yielding an increase in taxes. Recent studies would not support this conclusion. The benefits stemming from nearby prisons, in the form of increased earning, income, and employment, are substantial. Besides the temporary construction jobs associated with the building a new

facility, two hundred staff positions for each four hundred inmates are typically generated by an institution. For the most part, these jobs are filled by local residents.

Conclusion
To expect a community to spontaneously embrace a correctional institution in its midst is somewhat unrealistic. It is up to responsible leadership to explain the need and to develop understanding and support. Public confidence in correctional management is more important than the probability of escape or the potential benefits a correctional facility may bring to an area. If these facilities are to gain public acceptance, the public must be assured that the security of the institution is adequate for the type of inmates and that the facility is managed well. The local community cannot establish confidence in an isolated institution or facility; such confidence can be established only through association. Correctional institutions are accepted best when they become an integrated part of the community.

By presenting the institution as a necessary humanitarian project and as an economic asset, planners and community leaders can muster the needed support. Stressing the institution's rehabilitation purpose (through job training and placement) can help align community residents with this aim. If the correctional facility is seen as mainly punitive-custodial, even the humanitarian spokesmen of the community may oppose it.

Data on escapes are considered to be favorable by most in corrections. These facts and other related issues can be discussed with community leaders to reach a decision on location that is based upon correctional policy, past experience, and a realistic assessment of future community trends.

Don A. Josi

Bibliography
Carlson, K. A. (1992). Doing good and looking bad: A case study of prison/community relations. *Crime and Delinquency* 38: 56–69.

Eynon, T. G. (1989). Building community support. *Corrections Today* 51(2): 148, 150–52.

Federal Bureau of Prisons (1987). *Federal Guidelines for Prison Site Selection*. Washington, D.C.: U.S. Government Printing Office.

Grieco, A. L. (1978). New prisons: Characteristics and community reception. *Quarterly Journal of Corrections* 2(2): 55–60.

Houk, W. B. (1987). *Acquiring New Prison Sites: The Federal Experience*. Washington, D.C.: National Institute of Justice.

Ince, M. (1988). *Impact of a Correctional Facility on the Surrounding Community*. Washington, D.C.: American Planing Association.

Krause, J. D. (1992). The effects of prison siting practices on community status arrangements: A framework applied to the siting of California state prisons. *Crime and Delinquency* 38: 27–55.

McGee, R. A. (1981). *Prisons and Politics*. Lexington, Mass.: D.C. Heath.

McShane, M. D., F. P. Williams, and C. P. Wagoner (1992). Prison impact studies: Some comments on methodological rigor. *Crime and Delinquency* 38: 105–20.

Rogers, G. O., and M. Haimes (1987). Local impact of a low-security federal correctional institution. *Federal Probation* 51(3): 28–34.

Sechrest, D. K. (1992). Locating prisons: Open versus closed approaches to siting. *Crime and Delinquency* 38: 88–104.

Shichor, D. (1992). Myths and realities in prison siting. *Crime and Delinquency* 38: 70–87.

Singer, N. M. (1977). Economic implications of standards for correctional institutions. *Crime and Delinquency* 23: 14–31.

Snitch

A snitch is an informer, an inmate who reports the activities of other inmates to prison authorities. Synonyms are "rat," "fink," and "stool pigeon."

Prison Subcultures and Inmate Codes

The existence of inmate subcultures, codes, and snitches has been noted in all prisons. One aspect of prison subculture is an inmate code that, like the code of criminals outside prison, forbids informing. Conformity or nonconformity with the inmate code is reflected in prison argot. One of the most commonly stigmatized argot roles is that of "snitch." In general, the snitch is hated and despised by those who adhere to the inmate code and may be the object of violent reprisal. The norm against snitching is elastic, varying according to institutional

custom and structure and the motive and status of the offender.

Although prison staffers frequently rely on snitches, many staffers dislike snitches, perhaps because of a broader cultural norm against informing on one's peers.

Functions of Snitches

For prison officials the snitch is a source of information that enhances their control and makes the informer an agent of control (Stojkovic 1986; Marquart and Crouch 1984). Inmates inform for a variety of reasons: revenge, to harm competitors, to gain favor or privileges, or to prevent harm to themselves. Inmates who reject the inmate code and identify with the administration feel that it is their duty to inform (Johnson 1961).

Snitching weakens inmate solidarity and the secrecy necessary for inmates to carry out unauthorized activities. For many inmates, aggression and hostility toward snitches strengthens in-group solidarity, provides a drain or outlet for frustration, and helps define the boundaries of proper inmate conduct. The snitch can also provide an explanation of, and scapegoat for, unpleasant circumstances (Johnson 1961).

Snitches and Prison Riots

Inmates have been known to warn officials or favorite staff members, especially teachers and counselors, of an imminent riot or disturbance. Frequently these warnings go unheeded (Roebuck and Smith 1993; Morris 1983, 13–27).

Excessive reliance on and abuse of snitches by prison administrations has been cited as a source of tension contributing to riots, including the brutal 1980 Santa Fe, New Mexico, riot. There, prior to 1975, snitching by inmates was voluntary, and the administration did not aggressively recruit informants. Subsequent curtailment of prison programs and other changes led to a breakdown in the old snitch system. Beset by a shortage of information and increasing escapes and violence, the administration initiated an aggressive, coercive snitch system. Some inmates were threatened with transfers, loss of privileges, and so forth. Inmates were also coerced into informing by the threat of "hanging a snitch jacket" on them. This involved threatening to leak false information to other inmates that the individual was a snitch. Inmates who did cooperate were frequently given immunity from discipline, which enabled them to victimize other inmates. The increasing use of these and other coercive tactics and other conditions led to a breakdown in the old inmate system of social control that had helped minimize stress and violence. This breakdown and other factors eventually led to the riot (Morris 1983, 86–90; Colvin 1992, 151–75).

The Texas Building Tender System
Although informants are generally scorned and live in fear, such was not the case in Texas prisons, where a "building tender" (BT) system was once used. Older, aggressive, and feared inmates were selected by staff to assist in keeping order and providing information. In return, BTs and their assistants were offered special privileges and immunities. BTs developed their own cadre of informers. Because of their personal attributes and *de facto* authority to use force on other inmates, BTs and their associates were able to avoid the open scorn, stigma, and violence that informants usually suffer. BTs and their aides operated openly and rationalized their deviation from the inmate code by labeling ordinary prisoners "scum" and "losers." Although the BT system helped maintain order in Texas prisons, there were frequent abuses and the system was dismantled under federal court order in 1982. Some believe that the dismantling and other reforms left an information and power vacuum that the state was unwilling or unable to fill. This power vacuum, they theorize, was filled by violent individuals and gangs with a resultant increase in reported violence (Marquart and Roebuck 1985; Marquart and Crouch 1984).

Snitching in Women's Prisons
Much less is known about snitching in women's institutions. In general, snitching is more widespread. It is deemed a less serious transgression, and inmate sanctions against informers are less severe. In some institutions, the norm against informing may not exist (Giallombardo 1966, 106–15).

Snitching and Prison Administration
At least in theory, the administration's dependency on and ability to use snitches should be inversely proportional to the strength of the inmate code and the utility of the prison's other avenues of control and intelligence.

Although the snitch system is widespread, it is frequently criticized. It reportedly corrupts or weakens the authority of prison guards, cre-ates a class of privileged inmates who abuse others, and creates tension and distrust (Kalinich and Pitcher 1984; Johnson 1961, 130–32; Morris 1983, 89). Many penologists, however, still recommend the prudent use of snitches. Coercion, deals with (and extra privileges for) informants, and excessive reliance on inmates for intelligence are, however, not recommended (Kalinich and Pitcher 1984, 49–50; Vandivier 1989).

Courts have validated the use of information from snitches in prison disciplinary hearings. In *Wolff v. McDonnell,* the U.S. Supreme Court held that due process does not require that the identity of informants be revealed to the accused inmate.

Because of possible retribution, informants frequently request, or are placed in, protective custody along with other vulnerable prisoners. In riots, suspected snitches are prime targets. For instance, during the 1980 New Mexico prison riot, inmates forced their way into the protective custody unit and brutally murdered twelve inmates (Colvin 1992, 186–89).

Conclusion
There has been no systematic, large-scale research on snitching. Most of the literature involves studies of particular institutions and summaries or analyses thereof.

Some form of snitching has been noted in other countries, (Akerstrom 1989; Priestly 1980), and it may be a universal mode of adjustment for some confined in what Goffman terms "total institutions," (that is, mental hospitals, concentration camps).

Raymond G. Kessler
Julian B. Roebuck

See also Argot, Building Tenders

Bibliography
Akerstrom, M. (1988). The social construction of snitches. *Deviant Behavior* 9:155–67.
Akerstrom, M. (1989). Snitches on snitching. *Society* 26(2): 22–26.
Clemmer, D. (1940). *The Prison Community*. New York: Holt, Rinehart and Winston.
Colvin, M. (1992). *Penitentiary in Crisis: From Accommodation to Riot in New Mexico*. New York: State University of New York Press.
Giallombardo, R. (1966). *Society of Women*. New York: Wiley.

Johnson, E. H. (1961). Sociology of confinement: Assimilation and the prison rat. *Journal of Criminal Law, Criminology, and Police Science* 51: 528–33.

Kalinich, D. B., and T. Pitcher (1984). *Surviving in Corrections: A Guide for Corrections Professionals*. Springfield, Ill.: Thomas.

Marquart, J. W., and B. M. Crouch (1984). Coopting the kept: Using inmates for social control in a southern prison. *Justice Quarterly* 1: 491–509.

Marquart, J. W., and J. B. Roebuck (1985). Prison guards and snitches. *British Journal of Criminology* 25: 217–33.

Morris, R. (1983). *The Devil's Butcher Shop: The New Mexico Prison Uprising*. New York: Franklin Watts.

Priestly, P. (1980). *Community of Scapegoats: The Segregation of Sex Offenders and Informers in Prisons*. Oxford, Mass.: Pergamon.

Roebuck, J. B., and R. A. Smith (1993). The Atlanta riot: A study in identity and stigma management. In N. K. Denzin, ed. *Studies in Symbolic Interaction*. Greenwich, Conn.: JAI Press.

Stojkovic, S. (1986). Social bases of power and control mechanisms among correctional administrators in a prison organization. *Journal of Criminal Justice* 14: 157–66.

Sykes, G. (1958). *The Society of Captives*. Princeton, N.J.: Princeton University.

Vandivier, V. (1989). Do you want to know a secret? Guidelines for using confidential information. *Corrections Today* 51(4): 30, 32, 73.

Williams, V. L., and M. Fish (1974). *Convicts, Codes and Contraband: The Prison Life of Men and Women*. Cambridge, Mass.: Ballinger.

Cases

Wolff v. McDonnell, 418 U.S. 539, 94 S.Ct. 2963, 41 L.Ed.2d 935 (1974)

Stateville

In reaction to the unilateral criticism of the "old state prison" at Joliet, the Illinois state legislature secured sixty-five acres in 1907. The site of the new facility was to be Lockport, a mere six and a half miles northwest of Joliet and forty miles southwest of the city of Chicago. In both concept and construction, the new facility was to mirror the growing mood of reform in turn-of-the-century penology. Accordingly, a three-man panel was dispatched abroad for the sole purpose of research and study of the world's most prominent prisons. The panel became much enamored of the design of English utilitarian philosopher Jeremy Bentham. The most distinctive feature of his plan was a revolutionary departure from the more conventional Auburn and Philadelphia models. What he had envisioned was the Panopticon (from Greek *panoptes*, "all-seeing"), namely a single surveillance tower presiding at the center of a circular cellhouse.

The pragmatic benefits of the panoptic design are substantial. Conceivably, manpower needs could be met by a lone guard. By virtue of the design, a guard located in the tower is afforded a 360-degree field of vigilance. Every cell could be viewed, every inmate accounted for, thanks to copious lighting from both the roof and the back windows of individual cells. Further, the one guard could operate the necessary security mechanisms from within the tower.

The philosophical implications of the Panopticon are equally weighty. Metaphysical historian R. Andre Wakefield has somewhat lyrically characterized the panoptic model as "so many invisible tendrils of conscience." The idea is to inculcate compliance in the inmate by subjecting him to constant surveillance. The effect is inexorably theatrical. The focal point is no longer singular and central. The stage inverts itself along the visual radii drawn from the tower to each cell. The inhabitants of the galleries then become the principal players in the isolated dramas transpiring in individual cells.

On 9 March 1925, Stateville opened its doors for operation. The four Panopticons, or "roundhouses" as they are more commonly known, were connected by corridors to the central hub, the dining hall. Each roundhouse boasted an overall capacity of 248 cells and four galleries, or tiers, with sixty-two cells. Because of financial constraints, administrators decided to forgo the construction of the last two roundhouses in favor of the "longhouse." Unit B is reportedly the largest rectangular cellhouse in the world, containing six hundred cells divided into two units between B-East and B-West. The roundhouses were in full operations until the late 1970s, when three were demolished and replaced by the "K" design of units H and I. After extensive renovation, unit F began functioning again in 1982. It is the sole remaining Panopticon in the world.

Since it first opened its doors, Stateville has witnessed an impressive parade of academicians. Scholars have been in the vanguard of policy and program development on behalf of the institution. Even before the prison opened its doors, academic and general reform interest were responsible for establishing the Illinois Division of the State Criminologist. The first to assume the post was Herman Adler, professor of psychiatry at Harvard Medical School. The criminologist's contributions to prison life were merely advisory. He was to chronicle social histories, perform psychological evaluations, and conduct psychiatric interviews in an effort to provide comprehensive recommendations submitted to the state parole board.

The contribution of the University of Chicago, first represented by Professors Burgess and Sutherland in their service with the Clabaugh Commission in 1928, was auspicious. Through their evaluations of parole and sentencing policy, they were able to bring into being the state's Office of the Sociologist-Actuary in 1933. The main duty of the position was the systematic derivation of parole prediction tables. This post would be occupied by the renowned sociologist Lloyd Ohlin in the years to come.

Norval Morris, dean of the Center for Studies in Criminal Justice, aided in writing the 1970 Illinois Unified Code of Corrections. The code mandated specific reforms in adult and juvenile corrections. Salient features of the code included provisions for staff training, research, and the compilation of written records, all in conjunction with securing a greater extent of "due process" rights for inmates.

At least one academia-Stateville collaboration produced controversy. The joint project was the development of the Special Unit Program in 1971. The SPU sought to intensify the maximum-security classification by segregating the most intractable of inmates in one splinter program, which billed itself as "maximum treatment–maximum security." It looked to garner support from liberals and conservatives alike. The treatment overtones appealed to the liberals, whereas the extensive precautions in security appealed to conservatives. After hiring Dr. Karl Menninger as a consultant, correctional administrators proceeded with plans and converted a dilapidated cellhouse in Joliet into the location for the experi-mental SPU. Construction of the unit required state-of-the-art technology and security measures. A mobile guard cage allowed correctional officers to patrol the unit free from fear of assault. Once the unit commenced operations, however, positive reaction from all quarters was not forthcoming. Inmates inaugurated the first six months of SPU's operation with violence and destruction. Legal interest groups were no more enthusiastic. They questioned the constitutionality of the program. At the heart of contention was the program's attempts to prescribe severe behavior modification techniques. Under the direction of the ACLU, the class-action *Armstrong v. Bensinger* was filed in federal district court in 1972. Subsequently, the court ruled that assignment to SPU could not be realized under the pretense of "therapy" as it was foremost a punitive sanction. Nevertheless, the court declined to deem placement in SPU as constituting "cruel and unusual punishment."

As a palpable result of over three decades of staggering litigation, the nature of the penitentiary's highest administrative office has changed drastically. The patriarchies of the "old bosses" have long since evanesced, only to be replaced by a highly curtailed fraction of the original authority. The warden's position is more legalistic and bureaucratic at present. Nowhere is this better chronicled than through the last significant intervention by an academic at the prison. Four years of in-depth casework culminated in James B. Jacobs's definitive 1977 work, *Stateville: The Penitentiary in Mass Society.*

Thus, the last twenty years have seen a variety of managerial styles, ranging from the "human relations" model of the mid 1970s, through "crisis" management of the 1980s, to current-day "unit" management. This prolonged drift in the philosophy of the chief administrative officer acutely parallels the alarming turnover in the job itself. That particular phenomenon has served to contrast the advent of each incumbent with that of Joseph P. Ragen.

Joe Ragen was the charismatic warden of Stateville and Joliet for twenty-five years. He was a man of modest education (ninth grade) and modest background (he had been a rural county sheriff prior to his debut in prisons). He assumed control of the post–Depression penitentiary in 1936, when its population burgeoned to 3,900. He was by all accounts an old-style disciplinarian, who regularly exercised his dominion in even the minutiae of daily operations. His belief was that if he emphasized the ordering of details, the larger issues would follow suit naturally. He inspired both loyalty and disdain from staff and inmates. He maintained that inmates were entitled to decent food, shelter, and security. Anything beyond that was a privilege that had to be earned. His guiding principle regarding treatment was work. Prison industries in concert with jobs in operations and maintenance composed his rehabilitation component. Critics charged that his job programs were thinly disguised featherbedding or busywork.

Yet it is worthwhile to note that for the balance of Ragen's regime, prison population hovered around twice maximum capacity. Socially, it was an utterly different climate. Lengthy sentences were the norm. In the late 1950s, nearly 40 percent of sentences were for more than twenty years. Inmates tended to view power and status through job and cell assignments. The warden was granted much latitude in carrying out his functions. His superior, the director of public safety, was his supervisor in name only.

Nonetheless, it is astounding to consider that over his twenty-five years as acting warden, Ragen compiled a nearly flawless record: no riots, one escape, one inmate and two guards killed. These results did not come without controversy. Ragen tolerated no dissent. Those who challenged or defied his authority were promptly placed in segregation. Thomas X. Cooper, leader of Stateville's Black Muslims, was "salted away" in segregation for ten years for his ardent protestations. (Cooper achieved national notoriety in 1962 for his landmark case against Ragen disciple Frank Pate. In *Cooper v. Pate,* Cooper alleged civil rights abuses stemming from his status as a practicing Muslim.) Ragen buttressed his own legacy by hand-picking, grooming, and promoting up through the ranks those he favored. For more than twenty years after Ragen's departure, Assistant Warden Vernon Revis continued the "old boss" custody-oriented philosophy.

Present-day Stateville is rife with problems endemic to most correctional facilities. After a turbulent decade in the 1970s, administrators concentrated their efforts on at least stanching gang participation. As much as 90 percent of the prison population is estimated to have a gang affiliation. The daily population has been steady, averaging just over two thousand for the last ten years. Correctional officers' benefits have improved, and their jobs have become more stable since their entrance into AFSCME in 1966. The institution has found a measure of stability in its ACA accreditation, first granted in 1985 and renewed thereafter at three-year intervals. Another stabilizing factor has been the 1991 appointment of Warden Salvador A. Godinez. By everyone's account, Warden Godinez's style is personable, and he reintroduces a modicum of charisma into interactions with staff and inmates. Interestingly enough, Warden Godinez purports to bring to his post a resource that no preceding warden has been able to lay claim to: that he is the first chief administrative officer from the "streets of Chicago," just as the majority of Stateville's inmates are.

Ironically, these assets may prove to be of little use. In an occupation where longevity can be measured in terms of a few years, unforeseen vicissitudes (or DOC hierarchical whimsy) have the last word in career outcomes. Warden Godinez summarizes well in saying, "You're only as good as your handling of the latest crisis."

William Hogan

See also PANOPTICON

Bibliography
Jacobs, J. B. (1977). *Stateville: The Penitentiary in Mass Society.* Chicago: University of Chicago Press.

Suicide

The Frequency of Suicide in Prison
Next to AIDS, suicide is the leading cause of unnatural deaths in prisons. Homicides rank third, and then natural deaths far outnumber any of the other remaining causes of death (G. Camp, C. Camp 1992). Although the incidence of completed suicides in prison is approximately double that found in the community, suicide is far more frequent in jails than in prisons. One study found that an inmate is 6.5 times more likely to commit suicide in jail than in prison. Rates for jail suicides were 156 per 100,000 persons in jail, compared with 24 per 100,000 in prison (Moran 1988).

In 1993, forty-three prison systems across the United States reported one hundred inmate suicides, which is an increase over the ninety-one in 1992 but is down from the 136 reported in 1988. Texas, with one of the largest systems in the country, reported seventeen suicides in 1993, while ten systems reported none. The number of attempted suicides also increased, with 1,849 in 1993 as compared with 1,661 in 1992 (Lillis 1994).

Factors Related to Suicide

According to some writers, prison suicide may be linked to the authoritarian, regimented environment of the institution. Other reasons are loss of control over one's life; separation from family and friends; victimization by stronger inmates; the trauma to "first-timers" of being incarcerated; the fear produced by movies and television; rampant idleness in many facilities; the dehumanizing aspects of incarceration, such as communal hygiene facilities.

Staff should also be aware of the psychological damage inflicted on inmates who are raped and sexually abused in prison. Potential victims of rape are often thin, small, naive and appear effeminate. The potential victim should be cautioned not to accept favors from other inmates, as that may lead to "paying back" sexually.

Suicide or attempts at suicide may be motivated by feelings of hopelessness or helplessness. In prison, there are generally a lack of stabilizing and support services. When an inmate believes that no one cares, the suicide option seems the best one. Only one day, one week, or one month later, when the situation producing the depression is no longer there, the idea of suicide passes. Intervention can come from staff help, support by peers, or a resurgence of strength the prisoner develops. Often the suicidal person wavers between the desires to live and to die.

Identifying Suicide Risks

Some suicide attempts, particularly by young prisoners, are caused by bad practices of staff. The desire to "get even" will trigger a suicide attempt. Inmates know that to staff, the most disturbing incident in prison life is an unnatural death. Strange as it may seen, the suicide for revenge, or "I'll show you" suicides, are not uncommon.

The following are the most common signs or risk indicators for potential suicide in prison:

1. Any pronounced mood or behavioral change
2. Receipt of bad news, such as divorce or the death of a loved one
3. A history of mental illness or chemical dependency

4. A terminal illness, such as AIDS
5. Rape or threats of sexual assault
6. Being incarcerated for the first time or facing a very long sentence
7. A family history of suicide
8. Too much or too little sleep
9. Increase or loss of appetite or weight
10. Talk about death or preoccupation with death and suicide

Suicide Prevention

Efforts to prevent suicide can include screening of all incoming inmates, architectural manipulation of the environment, mental health intervention, and staff awareness training. Experience has shown that most potential suicides can be detected at admission by trained screeners. Specific questions are often asked to uncover risk factors, such as, "Have you ever thought about or attempted suicide?" "Is this the first time you've ever been incarcerated?" and "Do you now or have you ever had any serious medical or mental problems?" Nurses or specially trained correctional officers do most of the intake screening at diagnostic or in-processing centers. Special consideration may be given to high-risk inmates so that their housing and work assignments are in low-stress environments, and they are referred to appropriate treatment programs.

Because as many as 90 percent of all prison suicides result from hanging, bars are a dangerous element around potential victims. Some prisons have made old cells suicide-resistant by removing easy-access protrusions or objects to which a noose can be attached. Since many suicides involve a metal bed, some prisons have installed concrete slab beds. Closing off bars from floor to ceiling with detention screen with openings of one-eighth inch and spot welding the screen over air grilles are two of the best means of deterring suicide attempts. The Texas Department of Corrections, like many prison systems, has designated special observation rooms that do not contain any bars, exposed electrical outlets, or fixtures on which a patient could harm himself. These rooms also contain a window through which an observer can see the entire room. Checks are made as regularly as every fifteen minutes.

While constant monitoring by staff is the most successful method of suicide prevention, few prisons have the manpower. Instead, some have tried using selected and trained inmates as "buddy companion watchers." This concept has been used for over fifty years by mental hospitals, and by the Federal Bureau of Prisons since 1982. It is also used in the New York City Department of Corrections, Alaskan correctional institutions, the Mobile (Alabama) County Jail, Rhode Island correctional facilities, and the Iowa Medical and Classification Center. As in the self-help program of Alcoholics Anonymous, "buddy watchers" derive many benefits from helping others, including greater self-esteem. Further, other inmates do not victimize or harass the buddy watcher but instead respect him. Use of inmates as "buddy watchers" significantly reduces the negative inmate code of silence and creates a more positive inmate-staff relationship, and thus a "cooler" institution. There has never been a known lawsuit from using inmates in this capacity.

Many prisons use closed-circuit television (CCTV) for monitoring suicidal inmates. Several problems, however, have been noted with this means of prevention. Equipment often breaks down; blind spots, poor reception, and poorly lighted cells limit viewing of all activities. Officers who watch the CCTV monitor for more than one hour without a break often suffer from monitor hypnosis—they often do not see what they are looking at.

The national standards do not require CCTV but instead require two-way audio communication between the control unit and the inmate living quarters. The officer is more likely to detect a suicide attempt by hearing it than by seeing it, as hanging victims often make gasping noises and flail their arms and feet.

Management strategies for prevention of suicides are thought to be at least 90 percent effective. Prevention programs are more likely to be successful, however, when there are positive working relationships among not only custody and correctional staff and program personnel (especially medical, mental health, and classification) but also among the inmates. It has been found that at least one quarter of the suicides in prison were known of beforehand by fellow inmates who followed the "code of silence" and did not pass the knowledge on to staff.

Experts do not recommend that an inmate at risk for suicide be placed in isolation, as three quarters of completed suicides occur while the inmate is alone. In most policies on suicide prevention, the inmate is not removed from the general inmate population. Because suicide tends to be a very private act, it rarely occurs in the company of others, except when everyone else is asleep. In addition, suicidal prisoners should not be stripped naked, as that may only make them more depressed. An indestructible gown has not yet been developed, and paper gowns can be used to fashion a noose. A noose can also be made by braiding rolls of toilet paper into a rope, soaking it in water, and allowing it to dry. Suicides also occur from stuffing the nose and mouth with cloth or toilet paper.

One problem in responding to potential suicides has been security policies cautioning officers not to enter some inmates' cells without the backup of another officer. Prisoners may die or suffer brain damage if they have to wait for first aid, specifically CPR. Officers must often make quick judgments about whether an inmate is faking the suicide in order to draw them into the cell or whether it is a genuine attempt to die.

It is important to identify staff who lack the skills to respond to the dangers of suicide, because the failure to respond may subject the institution to wrongful death and negligent injury lawsuits. A profile of correctional and health care staff who fail to prevent a suicide has been developed from surveys of actual cases. In many instances, these staff members displayed an "I-I-Me-Me" rather than a "We-Teamwork" attitude, a lack of confidence and self-respect, cynicism, sarcasm, unnecessary use of force, arrogance, and prejudice in carrying out their duties. Suicide experts agree that if only one worker cares and shows it, that positive attitude will likely prevent a suicide. The "I-Me" staff member, however, who is usually hard and rejecting, can foster suicide attempts.

Joseph R. Rowan

Bibliography

Albanese, J. (1983). Preventing inmate suicides. *Federal Probation* 47(2): 65–69.

Anno, B. J. (1991). *Prison Health Care: Guidelines for the Management of an Adequate Delivery System.* Chicago: National Commission on Correctional Health Care.

Camp, G., and C. Camp (1992). *The Corrections Yearbook—Adult Corrections.* South Salem, N.Y.: Criminal Justice Institute.

Charle, S. (1981). Suicide in the cellblocks. *Corrections Magazine* 7(4): 6–16.

Lillis, J. (1994). Prison escapes and violence remain down. *Corrections Compendium* 19(6): 6–9.

Moran, T. (1988). Inmate suicides difficult to prevent, experts agree. *Houston Chronicle.* July 6, B: 1.

National Commission on Correctional Health Care (1987). *Standards for Health Services in Prisons.* Chicago: National Commission on Correctional Health Care.

Rowan, J. R. (1991). *Suicide Prevention in Custody.* Laurel, Md.: American Correctional Association.

T

Technology

Critical in the operation and management of today's correctional institution is the interaction of technology and human beings. Over the past fifteen years, technological innovation has spawned a proliferation of new devices that have had a dramatic impact on prisons. While the number and type of devices used in prison operations are vast, they can generally be categorized into seven areas: perimeter security, locking systems, internal-external surveillance, internal security, fire safety, communications, and management information systems.

Perimeter Security

The area in which technology has played the greatest role in prisons today is perimeter security. When you say "prison" to most people, the first image that comes to mind is a high wall with towers, each with armed guards. While the prison of the past certainly fit that description, most prisons built during the past fifteen years or so have replaced the gun tower with electronic gadgetry that both guards the perimeter and also allows for re-deployment of staff. For example, staffing a tower is an around-the-clock function that requires about four full-time officers per week, per tower. Electronic perimeter systems can allow for direct supervision by removing officers from towers and making them available for assignment to housing units and elsewhere inside the prison gates. The major technological innovation in the area of perimeter security has been in the use of electronic security systems. Such systems include microwave, motion detectors, electronic alarms, and infrared devices. Each type of system detects movement through the disruption of a "steady state signal." Some systems are designed to be used with roving perimeter vehicles, while others can include towers. Most electronic perimeter systems perform well and, in general, correctional personnel feel positively about them. Electronic perimeter systems are not inexpensive (the average cost is about $225,000), but, as mentioned above, they can permit a more efficient use of staff.

All electronic perimeter systems are affected by the weather and environment. Wind, lightning, snow, birds, and animals all have an effect on these systems. The results are often termed false alarms, but in fact they are the result of an intrusion into the system. Part of the solution is designing and selecting a system that is compatible with the environment. For example, motion detectors are a problem in areas with ground motion or seismic activity. Microwave systems are affected by heavy snows. Proper calibration helps reduce some of these alarms, but the most important factor is accepting the fact that an electronic perimeter system will average several "false alarms" a day. Most correctional administrators accept this as part of the system, and view it as a way of checking that the system works.

Locking Systems

Locks are an important part of an institution. They are expensive to install, maintain, and replace, and they are constantly in use. Remember, a prison is used 365 days a year, year in and year out. To a large degree the safety of the inmates and staff depends on the locking system. Today, the old single key lock or bar lock has been replaced by electronic or pneumatic locking systems in about 80 percent of prisons built within the past fifteen years. Electronic or pneumatic locking systems make the job of correctional officers easier by allowing them to operate many locks from a single location, and to check the status of locks by referring to an indicator panel as opposed to manually testing each door. Officers appreciate the fact that automated locking systems relieve them of much of their "turnkey" function. General problems include broken keys, jamming, false panel lights, malfunctioning panels, and unavailability of replacement parts. Some of the problems stem from using inappropriate locks, such as medium-security locks on maximum-security cells. As with any electronic device, weather, especially lightning, can short-circuit locking systems.

Internal/External Surveillance

Watching inmates within an institution, as well as controlling who and what comes into a prison, is a critical element in prison operation and security. Internal/external surveillance equipment includes closed circuit television and listening devices. Generally, the higher the security level of a prison the more likely it is that internal surveillance equipment will be used. Surveillance equipment is usually used at the institution's entrance, rear sally port, and visiting areas. Some prisons also monitor housing units, hallways, and recreation areas.

Internal surveillance equipment is not without problems. Poor illumination, blind spots, and inadequate lighting are the rule rather than the exception in most prisons. In addition, external cameras are effected by the weather, and equipment can be easily tampered with if placed in areas where inmates can reach it.

Internal Security

Internal security equipment includes metal detectors, magnetic scanners, and X-ray or fluoroscope machines. About 90 percent of prisons use some sort of internal security equipment, with the most common being metal detectors.

The reliability of internal security devices within prisons is mixed. X-ray machines appear to work reasonably well, as do handheld metal detectors. But the results from walkthrough metal detectors are disappointing; they do not work well in prisons. Their failure is usually attributed to the large amount of metal surrounding the units (prisons, after all, are filled with metal). It should also be mentioned that many of the walk-through metal detectors used in prisons are of lesser quality than the high-priced, state-of-the-art detectors

found in most airports. Cheap, low-quality equipment is often purchased because of state bidding regulations.

Communications Systems

Communicating in a prison is vital for safety and day-to-day operation. Communications systems include walkie-talkies, radios, person-down alarms, pagers, public address systems, and phones. Overall, the majority of these systems seem to work well in prisons, and most correctional personnel are satisfied with them.

Problems with communications systems include inadequate range, interference with signals caused by geographic or structural barriers, and battery failure.

Fire Safety

Fire safety is a high priority in prison. Not only are inmates often locked in cells, but fire can bring early warning of a prison disturbance or riot. The fire safety systems include smoke detectors, sprinkler systems, air packs, fire extinguishers, heat sensors, and electronic alarm panels. Fire systems are expensive (the average cost is about $210,000) and need to be constantly maintained. When these systems fail it usually requires that the entire system be replaced. There are also problems with false alarms, short circuits caused by lightning, and faulty smoke detectors. In many cases, smoke detectors have been tampered with by inmates or poorly located. Many so-called "false" alarms are actually caused from smoke or dust. Lounges, work and shop areas, laundries, and kitchens are some of the most common areas for alarms. They are also the areas where fire is most likely to occur. It is important that the staff not lose confidence in the system or ignore it. The results can be catastrophic.

Management Information Systems

Computers have invaded most workplaces, and the prison is no exception. Computers or management information systems are used for a wide variety of tasks that involve information. There are basically two types of management information systems found in prisons: centralized mainframe systems, and stand-alone personal computers. The centralized systems are usually state controlled networks accessed via terminals.

A great variety of functions are performed by these systems. Almost all prison management information systems are used for inmate

T

Sophisticated surveillance and monitoring systems are built into strategically located control booths. Photo courtesy of Secure-Tech, Inc., Rocklin, California.

counts, inmate tracking, and for recording intake and release information. Other uses include planning and evaluation, payroll and commissary accounts, and tracking medical records. Other functions performed by various MIS include such tasks as inventory, inmate classification, and parole eligibility.

Many of the problems encountered with MIS are not technological problems, but rather resource problems. Not being able to hire adequate staff or purchase modern equipment is more a problem of funding than technology. Other problems with management information systems are not so much technical in nature as they are problems with managing these systems. Correctional officials need to be more aware of how such information systems can improve their operations, as well as the implications that increased automation has for the overall operation of their systems, if they are to gain maximum advantage from a management information system.

A number of general conclusions can be made with regard to the use of technology in prisons. First, while its impact has been generally positive, the changes produced by technology have been incremental rather than dramatic. Technology has not been shown to produce major changes in staff size, staff composition, or in the operation of prisons. Second,

technology needs to be adapted to the prison environment. Those who know technology and those who know prisons need to work together more closely if new technology is to be successfully integrated. Planning is also critical. If a particular system cannot meet the needs of the institution, then it is probably wiser not to purchase it, rather than attempt to adapt an inappropriate tool to the job. Finally, the staff who operate and maintain the equipment must be well trained and knowledgeable in its limitations and capabilities.

Several points can be made about the future of technology in correctional institutions, and in fact all areas where technology has entered the workplace. First, technology will not replace people. Well-run, well-managed institutions adopt technology successfully. It helps make these institutions more efficient and easier to manage. It will not solve the problems of poorly run institutions. In the broad range of correctional institutions, technology appears to be making the correctional task easier and more efficient, but it is only a tool, not the solution to our problems.

Edward J. Latessa

See also SECURITY AND CONTROL

Bibliography

Latessa, E. J., R. W. Oldendick, L. F. Travis, S. B. Noonan, and B. E. McDermott (1988). *Impact of Technology on Adult Correctional Institutions*. Washington, D.C.: National Institute of Corrections.

Travis, L. F., E. J. Latessa, and R. W. Oldendick (1989). The utilization of technology in correctional institutions. *Federal Probation* 53(3): 35–40.

Treatment Plans

For those men and women who are lucky enough to one day leave prison, the treatment plan is the blueprint for guiding their successful resettlement into the community. Properly formulated, treatment plans can help prisoners receive the counseling, education, and training needed for their reintegration. Improperly formulated, they can do more harm than good. A properly formulated treatment plan is based on eight essential principles drawn from theoretical penology, the growing evidence on the effectiveness of correctional treatment, and the existing knowledge base on offender classification systems.

Principle 1: *There must be an underlying theoretical premise for the treatment plan.*
Effective plans are based on the theory of criminal rehabilitation, not on theories of punishment or deterrence (see Cullen and Gilbert 1982).

Principle 2: *Not all prisoners need a treatment plan.*
While certain treatment programs are effective in reducing recidivism for some prisoners, other treatment programs are not. The goal is to identify which treatment is most effective for the individual inmate. All treatment plans are therefore individualized. The most effective treatment plan is the one targeted for hard-core, high-risk offenders, those who commit such crimes as armed robbery, assault, arson, rape, or grand theft. Low-risk offenders include those who have committed such offenses as burglary, theft, drug use or sales, or larceny.

Principle 3: *The matching of a prisoner to a treatment must be based, first and foremost, on the offender's criminogenic needs.*
Some prisoners may need to change their attitude toward conventional employment. Others may

need to change their attitude toward women. Still others may need to change their attitudes toward drugs, alcohol, criminal peers, or authority figures. Criminogenic needs are important because they serve as the primary treatment goals. When these goals are met (or, when needs are diminished), prisoners will stand a better chance of succeeding when released from custody.

Principle 4: *Criminogenic needs must be based on a systematic risk-needs assessment.*
This assessment must relate not only to the prisoner's history (prior convictions, age at first arrest, and so forth) but also to current behavior and attitudes as a prisoner. Those factors are important because criminogenic risks and needs are dynamic; they are always changing. Examples of such an assessment device include the Level of Supervision Inventory (see Andrews and Bonta 1994), the Wisconsin classification system (Baird 1981), the Community Risk/Needs Management Scale (Motiuk 1993), and the Renovex substance abuse program (Harem 1993).

Principle 5: *Treatment goals must be written in a language that is comprehensible by the prisoner.*
The treatment plan is not a college research paper. It is meant solely to help offenders get their lives back together. Keep in mind that the average prisoner has no more than a high school education.

Principle 6: *Treatment goals must be measurable.*
That is, each treatment plan must contain numerical or substantive indicators of the prisoner's progress toward the reduction of criminogenic needs. Examples include hours completed in a counseling program, educational degrees or certificates earned, and written evaluations by the treatment staff.

Principle 7: *Treatment plans must contain incentives to move prisoners toward their treatment goals.*
These incentives, or reinforcement contingencies, must be designed with assistance from the prisoners. The incentives provide the basis for a working contract between the prisoner and the prison administration. As prisoners move toward their goals, they are incrementally rewarded each step of the way with such dividends as greater access to library, recreational, and re-

ligious activities; greater access to personal property, such as radios, books, magazines, and such musical instruments as guitars and harmonicas; and, most important, increased access to improved housing.

Principle 8. *Treatment plans must be typed, copied, and distributed to the prisoner and every member of the prisoner's treatment team.*
Members of the treatment team include housing unit managers, caseworkers, counselors, teachers, work supervisors, and chaplains. Team members must create a file for each inmate's treatment plan, and firmly but fairly enforce the reinforcement contingencies. For their part, prisoners must place the treatment plan on their cell house wall and think of it as a potential ticket out of prison.

Mark S. Hamm

See also REHABILITATION PROGRAMS, VOCATIONAL PROGRAMS

Bibliography

Andrews, D. A., and J. Bonta (1994). *The Psychology of Criminal Conduct*. Cincinnati, Ohio: Anderson.
Baird, S. C. (1981). Probation and parole classification: The Wisconsin model. *Corrections Today* 43: 36–41.
Cullen, F. T., and K. E. Gilbert (1982). *Reaffirming Rehabilitation*. Cincinnati, Ohio: Anderson.
Harem, N. S. (1993). Implementing prison drug war policy: A biopsy of the wallet. In P. B. Kraska, ed. *Altered States of Mind*. New York: Garland.
Motiuk, L. L. (1993). Where are we in our ability to assess risk? *Forum on Corrections Research* 5: 14–19.

Trusties
Trusties are inmates of a jail or prison who have been entrusted with certain custodial or other responsibilities relating to the operation of the institution. In most cases, these are duties that would otherwise be preformed by correctional officers or staff. Trusties may have special privileges and liberties and more freedom of movement than regular inmates. Usually given as a reward for good behavior, trusty status can, in some jurisdictions, result in a reduction of sentence length.

While most prisons have some mechanisms whereby inmates assume certain quasi-custodial roles, the trusty system represented a dramatic departure from the traditional staff–inmate relationship. These roles eventually became institutionalized with the formal prison structure and offered a legitimate way for an inmate to enhance his status; in effect an inmate in legal definition only.

Historically, the trusty system developed in the post–Civil War prisons of the deep South. The economy was primarily agrarian and inmates were leased to private concerns, such as railroads, construction companies, plantations, and turpentine camps. Under that system, the private lessor worked the prisoners as well as fed, clothed, and disciplined them. So many flagrant abuses arose that the system was abolished and was replaced by the contract system. Under that system, private contractors engaged the state for the labor of the convict, which was performed near the prison.

With the demise of the contract system, penal plantations and prison farms emerged. These institutions were severely understaffed and underfunded and, because the "subcultural ethos" of the rural South emphasized a castelike social structure (with recently freed slaves at the bottom), that same social structure could be observed in the Southern prisons. The structure and design did not conform to that of the typical prison of the time. The inmates were instead housed in semiautonomous institutions and were given the responsibility of farming the area around the prison.

One of the major problems of the penal plantation was how to ensure inmate cooperation with institutional goals and values. A threat and exchange system developed, and certain inmates were given jobs normally performed by lower-ranking staff members. Those inmates chosen for the position were sometimes given a small income, relieved of certain custodial requirements, allowed free access to most sections of the prison, and given separate quarters. Some were even permitted conjugal visits with their wives.

Despite widespread use of the trusty system, particularly in Southern prisons, not until the 1960s was much attention devoted to the practice. In the 1970s, with the advent of federal court intervention, the trusty system was critically examined and evaluated for the first time. The prison systems in two Southern states, Mississippi and Texas, best illustrate the development and evolution of the trusty concept and the conditions that led to its demise.

The Mississippi State Penitentiary (Parchman) was originally organized around a series of semiautonomous camps, built and maintained by inmate labor. There was a rigid hierarchy among inmates. Occupying the lowest strata were the gunmen, regular convicts who composed most of the manual labor force at the institution. At the next level were the half-trusties (half-pants, or legs, in prison jargon), inmates who were permitted to work unsupervised and occupied better living quarters. At the top were the trusties, those inmates who were selected by the staff and who constituted about 20 percent of the inmate population.

The trusties not only guarded other inmates but also occupied positions of authority throughout the institution. Within the trusty ranks, there were additional classifications, depending on the particular position held. For up to twelve hours a day, the hall boy was responsible for all inmates within the fence, kept the inmate count, locked and unlocked all doors and gates, and even served as host to visitors to the prison. The clerk was second trusty. He assisted the hall boy and was vested with similar authority. Other trusty positions included the dog boy (keeper of the bloodhounds), the line shooter (who kept custody of gunmen in the field), and the shack shooter (who kept the arsenal and shot would-be escapees). All of the trusties were armed. Trusties were officially confined to the yard at night but, during daylight hours, could come and go with complete freedom, sometimes even hunting, fishing, or horseback riding. For their services, trusties received fifty-five days' commutation of sentence yearly and were allowed an annual ten-day leave.

In 1972, a class action suit (*Gates v. Collier*) was filed in response to conditions and practices at the Mississippi State Penitentiary. Although the case involved many issues, the fact that armed trusties were in charge of guarding other inmates emerged as one of the many important concerns. As a result of the suit, the vast majority of the state's inmates are now housed in two large facilities and the plantation system was dismantled.

In contrast, the Texas Department of Corrections consists of several large, maximum-security institutions, where extensive farming and industrial operations exist. Historically, Texas emphasized the control model of correc-

tions, wherein certain inmates were in charge of supervising and controlling the rest of the inmate population. The late George Beto, director of the Texas Department of Corrections from 1962 through 1972, believed that if the institution were to be safe, clean and cost-effective, a way had to be found to neutralize the effect of these inmate leaders.

Beto felt that rather than allowing the most violent and aggressive inmates to exercise control, exemplary inmates should be selected for the position of trusty and they should be given special official status:

> In any contemporary prison, there is bound to be some level of inmate organization, some manner of inmate society. . . . The question is this: who selects the leaders? Are the inmates to select them? Or is the administration to choose them or at least influence the choice? If the former, the extent of control over organized and semi-organized inmate life is lessened; if the latter, the measure of control is strengthened (quoted in DiIulio 1987, 112).

While these inmates held a number of different official titles (for example, floor men, wing porters, wing tenders, orderlies, count boys), they were generally referred to as building tenders. Inmates were used because of the inadequate number of custodial staff. In 1979, when understaffing was a major problem, almost 10 percent of the inmates were classified as building tenders. In general, at least one building tender was assigned to each tier in each wing of the institution. In most prisons in the Texas Department of Corrections system, there were more building tenders on duty at some times than correctional officers. They tended to serve longer sentences for more violent crimes than inmates in the general population.

Although the official use of the position of building tender was discontinued by statute in 1972, the primary duties of these inmates did not change. In *Ruiz v. Estelle*, a class action begun in 1972 and culminating in 1985 in the implementation of a consent decree, several aspects of confinement in the Texas Department of Corrections were challenged, including overcrowding, health care, discipline, access to the courts, and security and confinement. As a result of *Ruiz*, the building tender system was abolished in the Texas Department of Corrections.

Charles B. Fields

Bibliography

Clemmer, D. (1958). *The Prison Community*. New York: Rinehart.

Cloward, R. (1960). *Theoretical Studies in Social Organization of the Prison*. New York: Social Science Research Council.

DiIulio, J. J., Jr. (1987). *Governing Prisons: A Comparative Study of Correctional Management*. New York: Free Press.

DiIulio, J. J., Jr. (ed.) (1990). *Courts, Corrections, and the Constitution*. New York: Oxford University Press.

McWhorter, W. L. (1981). *Inmate Society: Legs, Half-Pants and Gunmen, A Study of Inmate Guards*. Saratoga, Calif.: Century Twenty-One.

Sykes, G. M. (1958). *The Society of Captives*. Princeton, N.J.: Princeton University Press.

Cases

Gates v. Collier, 349 F. Supp. 881 (N.D. Miss., 1991)

Ruiz v. Estelle, 679 F. 2d 1115 (5th Cir. 1982)

T

U

Unions

I. Correctional Officers

The unionization of correctional officers has emerged out of the general push toward unionization of civil service employees. Correctional officers were about the last group of public servants who formed unions. Today, almost all states have a correctional officers' union. Like other criminal justice agents, correctional officers are legally prohibited from striking. Only seven states have recognized the right to strike by correctional officers' unions.

The movement toward unionization of correctional work originates from three prime sources. First, provisions for increasing inmates' access to the courts and growing recognition of inmates' rights during 1960s and 1970s seemed to restrict correctional officers' authority and created a sense of powerlessness among them. This judicial activism made for a challenging occupation. In the 1970s and 1980s, in particular, correctional officers were frequently the subject of inmates' law suits. The need to respond to this legal pressure and the perception of a gradual loss of correctional officers' authority produced a need for unification.

Second, correctional officers today are much more heterogenous than they were two decades ago. A vigorous recruitment of minorities and women during the last two decades eradicated the well-known "good old boy" image and diffused the well-established correctional officers' subculture. In the 1960s, there were only a few hundred correctional officers in each state. Today, because of greater emphasis on incarceration, the construction of new institutions and the recruitment of the required staff the number of correctional officers has greatly increased. The formation of correctional officers' unions appeared necessary to protect their interests.

Third, the increasing pressure of inmate litigation severed the interests of correctional officers from those of supervisors and correctional administrators. Unlike many organizations, in which external threat commonly strengthens the subcultural norms and unifies the employees, litigation produced an unprecedented alienation between administrators and correctional staff. Consequently, correctional officers were faced with as much pressure from administrators as from prison inmates, if not more so. The formation of correctional unions, therefore, was a legal first step in regaining strength with which to deal with correctional supervisors.

Since their inception in 1970s, correctional officers' unions have produced mixed results. On the positive side, the unions have been an essential bargaining tool in improving work conditions, promotions, pay, fringe benefits, safety, workers' compensation, and in gaining accreditation of correctional institutions by the American Correctional Association. In particular, concern for safety and secure working conditions has been at the forefront of bargaining issues, and that emphasis has been a significant factor in empowering the unions. In many respects, the formation of correctional officers' unions has resulted in regaining employees' lost rights while balancing the effects of recent court decisions concerning inmates' constitutional rights.

Unionization also has been an essential tool for correctional officers in dealing with correctional supervisors and administrators. The unions have been particularly effective in establishing administrative guidelines for recruitment of new officers, assessing minimum qualifications, revising training curricula, setting the probationary period, and other labor-related concerns. The unions have represented correctional officers' interests in employee drug testing, vacation time, work-related stress, and staffing ratios. Probably the most significant impact of the correctional officers' unions has been the legal representation of correctional officers in work-related matters. In the past, correctional officers could be dismissed without due process of law and with little remedy or right to appeal. Today, because of the support and representation of their unions, correctional officers have gained tremendous power in the employee disciplinary process.

A goal of correctional officers' unions, like other labor and public employee unions, is to partake in administrative decision-making. An example is the Walla Walla state prison, where the union gained administrative action on behalf of a group of correctional officers. The officers were concerned about safety in a workshop run by an inmate bikers' club and claimed that the members were making weapons while repairing their bikes. The union forced the warden to close down the workshop.

Recently, the goal of correctional officers' unions has been stretched beyond simple participation in administrative decision-making. Many unions have been increasingly involved in politics through heavy lobbying and offers of support to political candidates. For instance, in 1990, the correctional officers' union in California provided a major boost to Republican gubernatorial candidate Pete Wilson by spending nearly one million dollars to help put him in office. In that campaign, the union's political action committee contributions to political candidates were topped only by those of the California Medical Association. The union's political contribution in California has already paid off, as Governor Wilson has demonstrated a commitment to increasing salaries, to creating safer correctional environments, to the construction of new prison facilities, and by signing a tougher crime bill.

The formation of correctional officers' unions has also produced some negative results, and gains have not necessarily been made in all expected areas. In 1981, for example, research by Lombardo recorded a sense of powerlessness among correctional staff in Auburn prison during the period of time in which the institution had an officers' union. Similarly, in a 1982 survey of correctional officers in five maximum-security institutions, Fox found a visible feeling of powerlessness among correctional officers in dealing with both supervisors and inmates. Ironically, all surveyed institutions had correctional officers' unions.

Probably the most damaging aspect of unionization in correctional work is the possibility of a strike by correctional officers. Even though a majority of states have prohibited correctional officers' unions from striking, unlawful strikes have still been promoted by several unions. For instance, a massive 1979 strike by over seven thousand New York correctional officers crippled correctional work in thirty-three state institutions. The strike cost taxpayers one million dollars per day, as National Guards replaced the striking correctional officers. In that event, the court held that the union was in violation of law and imposed a heavy fine on the union. The union leaders were sentenced to jail terms for contempt of court.

Rom Haghighi

Bibliography

Christianson, S. (1979). How unions affect prison administration. *Criminal Law Bulletin* 14: 243–47.

Fox, J. G. (1982). *Organizational and Racial Conflict in Maximum-Security Prisons.* Lexington, Mass.: D. C. Heath.

Lombardo, L. X. (1981). Occupational stress in correctional officers. In S. Zimmerman and H. Miller, eds. *Corrections at the Crossroads.* Beverly Hills, Calif.: Sage.

Potter, J. (1979). Guard's unions: The search for solidarity. *Corrections Magazine* 5, 3: 25–35.

Smith, B., and A. Sapp (1985). Fringe benefits: The hidden costs of unionization and collective bargaining in corrections. *Journal of Police and Criminal Psychology* 1, 2: 33.

II. Inmates

The adequacy of inmate labor conditions has been a source of concern and debate since the middle of the last century. Historically, there have been few mechanisms in place with which inmates could express grievances they may have had about their workplaces. Since the early 1970s, however, inmates in various states have experimented with and, in some instances, have successfully established inmate labor unions.

Broadly stated, inmate labor unions consist of coalitions of inmates who have voluntarily come together to improve their labor conditions within correctional facilities. These unions provide offenders with an opportunity to engage in formal bargaining with correctional personnel over work-related grievances. The individuals who belong to inmate unions believe that collective action is necessary for obtaining labor rights.

Although the objectives of these unions have varied somewhat, in general their demands have focused on the establishment of fairer wages, worker's compensation, safer working conditions; and meaningful vocational training. Inmate unions have identified the establishment of fairer wages as a priority because prison employment has traditionally offered minimal or no pay. They believe that inmate wages are unjust and that they do not provide prisoners an opportunity to save money for their release. Various unions have argued that inmates should receive the prevailing minimum wage for their labor (DeGraffe 1990).

The introduction of safer work conditions, and worker's compensation if an offender is injured, are also seen as important union goals. Most states have denied inmates any compensation if they are hurt while performing their work assignment. While labor safety conditions are thought to have improved over the last three decades, critics suggest that the well-being of inmate employees is still often secondary to prison security concerns. As such, inmate unions have sought to ensure maximum safety work standards for prisoners.

Finally, inmate unions have also called for the introduction of meaningful vocational training. While many have argued that prison employment and vocational training can contribute to the rehabilitation of offenders, all too often these programs fail to provide offenders with real, marketable skills. A significant number of prison labor systems are plagued by the fact that they use outdated equipment and production techniques. Many have also been criticized for training prisoners for jobs that have no equivalent position or an excess of workers outside prison. Responding to these concerns, inmate unions have worked to bring about improved and expanded vocational training programs.

Historical Development of Inmate Unions
The historical roots of inmate unions are thought to rest in inmate self-government programs that were introduced by various social reformers and penologists in the late nineteenth and first half of the twentieth century. Perhaps the best known early self-government program was the Mutual Aid League that Thomas Osborne founded in 1913 at New York State's Auburn prison. Introduced during America's progressive reform era, the league was open to all inmates and functioned as a democratic body governed by rules that had been established by the inmates themselves. Members of this league were provided with an opportunity to manage their educational programs, inmate labor, and disciplinary procedures for prison infractions. Osborne firmly believed that by fostering responsibility, inmate self-government could contribute to the rehabilitation of criminals.

Although Osborne's program won the support of various penologists, it was in existence only for a few years. The early inmate self-government initiatives that were introduced by people like Osborne were often inadequately structured and frequently faced opposition from prison personnel. Since many of these programs were highly dependent on the support of those who founded them, the founder's departure often led to the death of the program.

The inmate advisory councils that appeared in various states during the first half of the twentieth century were another undertaking designed to engage inmates in self-government. These councils were established to promote communications between prison personnel and inmates. The inmates who sat on these councils were elected by their fellow inmates. Council members were generally provided with an opportunity to express their opinion about recreational, entertainment, and holiday programs. Although touted as having a broad range, in reality these councils were generally in a position to advise on only a narrow range of prison activities. They were viewed by some prison personnel as "gimme groups" (Baker 1964).

These early inmate programs did, nonetheless, establish a precedent for the inmate unionization movement, which is premised on the belief that inmates can and should be involved in self-governing functions. This movement began in the late 1960s in conjunction with the grass-roots political activism of that period. Inmates, like many other groups, were affected by the intense political energy of the 1960s and early 1970s. It was a period in which many questioned the structure and policies of the American government and its institutions. Inmates joined this broad social movement and, among other things, formed labor unions in an attempt to work collectively to improve their workplace rights and to redress the labor conditions they saw as oppressive (Berkman 1979).

One of the earliest unions to form was the Ohio Prisoner's Labor Union, which was introduced in 1973. Among its many goals, this union sought to establish worker's compensation, meaningful apprenticeship and training programs, and a minimum wage for inmate labor. During the early 1970s, it claimed to have the support of over 60 percent of the inmate population in that state.

Inmate unions with similar goals appeared throughout the 1970s in states such as California, Massachusetts, Michigan, New York, and North Carolina. These unions were formed by politically oriented prisoners, but they received a significant amount of support from individuals and groups outside correctional facilities. Labor unions, clergy, and left-wing activists, for example, have all worked in behalf of the inmate unionization movement (Huff 1974).

Many unions formed in the 1970s, however, were in existence for only a few years and were unable to achieve the goals they had established for themselves. They encountered strong resistance from correctional personnel and the courts, and when political grass-roots activism in the larger American society waned, the inmate unionization movement weakened as well. Without the political energy and the outside support of various social activists, it was difficult for the unions to sustain themselves (Berkman 1979).

There are, nonetheless, a number of inmate unions still in existence advocating better inmate labor conditions. The Prisoner's Rights Union in California, for example, has sought to establish more satisfactory workplace environments for inmates. Established in 1970 and open to all California inmates, this union strives to protect and enhance the civil and human rights of the imprisoned and their families. While it does not specifically identify itself as a union, it does address labor concerns (Prisoner's Rights Union 1994).

Strong inmate unions can be found in most of the Scandinavian countries. In many instances, these unions have successfully introduced better inmate labor conditions. In Sweden, for example, the inmate union known as KRUM is credited with obtaining wages for inmates equivalent to those outside prison and for bringing about safer and more meaningful inmate training and employment programs.

Like the California Prisoner's Union, KRUM addresses a wide range of inmate issues. It does, however, identify labor concerns as an important priority. Advocates of inmate unions have studied the union movement in Sweden and the activities and structure of KRUM to discern why it has been so successful. This is an important undertaking, for they believe that there are many benefits associated with inmate unions like KRUM (DeGraffe 1990; Ward 1972).

Potential Benefits Associated with Inmate Unions

Advocates of inmate unions suggest that these organizations can be beneficial to both inmates and to correctional institutions. For inmates, one obvious benefit is that unions provide offenders with a forum through which they may bargain collectively for better working conditions. These unions can bring about safer and more rewarding workplaces. In addition, various scholars argue that inmate unions can contribute to the rehabilitation of offenders. They suggest that participation in formal union bargaining and decision-making can conceivably foster a sense of self-respect, dignity, and responsibility among those offenders who are active members of inmate unions. Inmates may maintain these positive attributes upon release from prison and, therefore, more successfully reintegrate themselves into society.

It has also been suggested that unions may contribute to rehabilitation by their advocacy of meaningful inmate vocational training. The average offender enters a penal institution with limited education and marketable skills. Vocational training during incarceration could provide inmates with skills with which to acquire a good job after their release from prison. Unions can negotiate for training programs that would foster such skills.

Finally, some believe that inmate unions could contribute to rehabilitation by pressing for fairer inmate wages. A real wage for inmate labor can enable prisoners to meet some of the financial costs of prison life (such as toiletries or reading material) and to save money for their release. Both of those opportunities are presumed to aid adjustment outside prison.

The benefits of inmate unions to correctional institutions are also thought to be quite substantial. Supporters of inmate unions argue that one of the most important advantages of these organizations is that they provide a peaceful means by which to resolve conflicts. Through collective bargaining, inmates and correctional personnel may be able to address grievances that have not been adequately dealt with by legislative or judicial bodies. Inmate unions may curtail violence and thereby serve as a useful mechanism for the resolution of conflict within correctional institutions.

Resistance to Inmate Unions

Although those who support inmate unions contend that they can be advantageous to inmates and the correctional facilities in which they are housed, the inmate unionization movement has encountered resistance from courts and correctional administrators. Directors of state corrections have typically opposed the formation of inmate unions on the grounds that they may threaten the security and custody needs of their institutions. Various administrators have expressed a concern that union activity might create friction between prison personnel and union members and, in turn, between union inmates and nonunion inmates. Some suggest that this might lead to serious prison disturbances and to work stoppages of services essential to the maintenance of an institution.

A number of administrators also fear that the general public may not support the concept of inmate unionization. They contend that establishing inmate unions might generate a public backlash. The public, they note, could become disgruntled with prison policies and withdraw its support for a variety of prison programs and initiatives (Huff 1974).

Some observers contend, however, that the concerns of correctional administrators about inmate unions may be overstated. They argue that if unions were able to usher in realistic employment, training, and collective bargaining opportunities, those achievements might produce a more stable and peaceful prison. They also point out that inmate union activities in various European countries have not resulted in serious prison disturbances.

The opinions and fears of correctional administrators about inmate unions have, nonetheless, been afforded a high degree of deference by the Supreme Court. In *Jones v. North Carolina Prisoner's Labor Union, Inc.* 97 S. Ct. 2532 (1977), for example, the Court held that the restrictions that North Carolina prison administrators had placed on activities of an inmate union were rationally related to reasonable prison security objectives and, therefore, did not violate the First Amendment and equal protection rights of the inmates who were union members.

In this instance, the North Carolina Department of Corrections had prohibited inmates from soliciting for union membership, holding union meetings, or receiving bulk union mail. The Court deferred to the opinion of prison officials who argued that such activities posed a threat to the security and harmony of correctional facilities. The Court did not prohibit the existence of inmate unions per se, but it did make it clear that restrictions can be placed on inmate union activities if they are reasonably related to legitimate penological objectives.

Future Considerations

Given the difficulties that inmate unions have encountered from correctional personnel and the courts and the relatively conservative political climate in the 1990s, it is difficult to predict the future of inmate unionization in the United States. It is clear, however, that it faces many obstacles.

One new challenge to inmate unions may be the correctional privatization movement. Critics of this development suggest that in an effort to reduce labor costs, private corporations may make every effort to discourage employee unionization within correctional facilities. If this practice does emerge as a trend within privatized prisons, it may be exceptionally difficult for inmates to establish unions of their own.

The general decline in the labor movement in the United States is also thought to pose a threat to the inmate unionization movement. In 1968, 28 percent of all American workers were unionized. By 1986, that figure had fallen to 18 percent. This decline may mean that inmate unions will have fewer opportunities to receive support from the outside labor movement.

The inmate unionization movement may be somewhat strengthened in the near future, however, by what appears to be an emerging interest in engaging larger numbers of inmates in prison labor. Factors such as prison overcrowding and prisoner idleness have focused new attention on prison labor. If larger numbers of inmates are involved in prison employment in the future, then individual protests about labor conditions may turn into collective statements. This trend could usher in a call for greater inmate self-government within the workplace.

Sandra Wachholz

Bibliography

Baker, J. E. (1964). Inmate self-government. *Criminal Law, Criminology, and Police Science* 55: 39–47.

Berkman, R. (1979). *Opening the Gates: The Rise of the Prisoner's Movement*. Lexington, Mass.: Lexington.

DeGraffe, L. J. (1990). Prisoner's unions: A potential contribution to rehabilitation of the incarcerated. *New England Journal of Criminal and Civil Confinement* 16: 221–40.

Huff, C. R. (1974). Unionization behind the walls. *Criminology* 12: 175–93.

Prisoner's Rights Union. (1994). *Information Bulletin*. Sacramento, Calif.: Prisoner's Rights Union.

Ward, D. A. (1972). Inmate rights and prison reform in Sweden and Denmark. *Journal of Criminal Law, Criminology and Police Science* 63: 240–55.

V

Violence

One of the most common themes in literature, films, and news media accounts of prison life is violence or the threat of violence. Juveniles are threatened with the promise of future victimization if their delinquent activities result in incarceration. New staff are trained to respond to as well as to prevent violent situations, and the families of those incarcerated worry about their loved ones surviving the daily exposure to prison violence.

It is important that prison violence be kept in proper perspective. Only a small proportion of the inmates in prison are responsible for a majority of the disciplinary problems. Also, not all disciplinary problems are serious or involve violence.

Historically, administrators and reformers have been concerned about separating the violent from the nonviolent offender. Currently, about 30 percent of all individuals entering prison have been convicted of a violent offense and the current prison population serving violent crime convictions is approximately 47 percent. That does not mean, however, that these persons are most likely to engage in violent behavior within the institution. Many persons convicted of serious crimes adapt well to prison, while many of those causing disturbances and assaults in prison are serving shorter drug- or property-crime sentences. Disciplinary problems can be caused by either violent or nonviolent offenders, and these incidents may also be categorized as violent or nonviolent acts.

One measure of both the degree of order and the quality of prison life is the amount of violence. Violence may take the form of riots, disturbances, rapes, fights, assaults, and homicides. Destruction of property is also considered a form of violence within the institution. Officers may be threatened by inmates, doused with urine, or stabbed with a homemade weapon. Inmates may be killed by other inmates or assaulted by staff. Suicides and mutilation constitute acts of violence against the self.

When violence increases in prisons, management and security policies are often scrutinized and blamed. Wardens are often replaced and more restrictive guidelines put into effect. Whole cell blocks may be put in lockdown status, in which no activities take place outside the cells and cold food is brought in. Cells are searched and weapons confiscated. Officers feel considerable stress to contain and prevent violent incidences, and relations with inmates are strained.

Historically, the violent nature of prisons and their inability to accomplish rehabilitation led reformers to search for alternatives such as probation and community sanctions, so that less serious offenders could avoid the harm of incarceration.

Analysts often compare the safety in the streets to that in prisons. At various times, newspapers have boasted that certain state prison systems are safer, having lower homicide or assault rates than certain large cities in the same area. It is critical to realize, however, that not everyone out on the street is at the same risk. While young males have the highest victimization rates in society, they are also overrepresented in prisons, so it is not surprising that prisons are characteristically violent.

The amount of violence reported by any institution may vary by the type of incident, the degree to which prisoners report victimizations, and the institution's need to minimize or accentuate the problems inside. For example, riots or disturbances often bring pressure for additional funding and staffing, or new security equipment for trouble-plagued institutions.

Measuring Prison Violence

Because of the different definitions of crimes committed in prison, it is difficult to compare the actual amount of violence in institutions. Some may track only incidents that were witnessed by a staff member or assaults that were written up as disciplinary infractions, and some may track only victims treated in medical units. Some institutions may attribute much of the violence to gangs; some may not bother to classify events by motivation. A Corrections Compendium survey of prison violence was conducted in forty-one states and the Federal Bureau of Prisons for the years 1992 and 1993. It was determined that 127 inmates had suffered violent deaths in 1992 and that there were 149 in 1993. Overall, the number of violent deaths has decreased over the last ten years despite increases in incarceration rates.

Inmates are almost twice as likely to assault other inmates as they are to assault staff. The actual ratio is probably much higher, because many inmate assaults are unreported, while few staff assaults would be. Inmates often feel that it is useless to report victimizations and fear reprisals if they do. In 1993, the Corrections Compendium survey reported over eight thousand inmate-to-inmate assaults, an average of 193 per system. Forty-seven inmates were killed by other inmates.

In 1992, the number of assaults on staff was less than half the number reported in 1991. The 1993 Corrections Compendium survey reflected forty-eight hundred inmate assaults on staff, approximately 112 per system.

There are many explanations for violence in prison. Some reasons focus on the character of the inmates, others examine the nature of the institutions.

Violence and the Nature of Inmates

Past research on prison violence has focused on the type of inmate who commits violent acts, assuming that an inmate's disposition accounts for violent behavior. Theorists may argue that the internal controls of inmates are weaker than those of others in society and that if the prison's external control is imperfect, violence will occur. Theories often link violence to values and behavior that the inmate brings into the prison setting. These influences include street fighting, racism, and sex-role behavior, particularly the "macho," or manliness, of defending one's honor or reputation. Theories of male aggression are supported by the fact that men are much more likely to be incarcerated for a violent offense than women. Critics argue that this reasoning allows for "attribution error," or the tendency to attribute causes of behavior to the personality of the individual even in the face of contradictory evidence such as the presence of situational factors.

The individual characteristics of the offender are also central to an understanding of prison violence. Age is a significant variable, with younger inmates more eager to prove themselves by toughness and fighting. According to some experts, younger inmates have more opportunities to be aggressive, are more likely to be instigated into aggression by their peers, and are more often rewarded with praise and respect. Because of their immaturity, young inmates are less aware of and less likely to view the possible punishments they face as costly. In addition, some suggest that custodial staff are more likely to tolerate the aggressive behavior of the younger prisoners.

The violent inmate's background may include drugs, gangs, and mental health difficulties. They may also have spent time in other prisons or juvenile detention facilities where they have acquired the skills of survival that often dictate striking first. It is not uncommon for attacks to occur when people believe that they have been insulted or threatened in some way.

Attempts to predict which inmates may be violent are not highly scientific or effective. Prisoners who are predatory and engage in sexual assaults on weaker inmates may be different from the inmate who carries out assassinations ordered by gang leaders. Initial classification systems use prediction devices such as personality tests or records screening to score inmates on their risk potential when they arrive. Prior violent behavior is the best predictor of future violent behavior that experts know of. Based on these scores, inmates may be assigned to more secure facilities and housing areas. In periodic reviews, these inmates may be promoted to less restrictive environments if they have not caused problems. Likewise, those who are initially assigned to lower level security may be demoted to more secure assignments if they prove that they cannot adjust to the general population.

Violence and the Prison Environment

Theories that focus on the character of institutions examine the nature of prisons and see inmates reacting to an unreal environment. In places of deprivation, prisoners are cast into a struggle for the limited power and possessions available. The prisoner's inability to control privacy and space increases stress. Poor architectural design, the availability of weapons, and limited staffing create places and opportunities in which victimization can occur. Inadequate classification or overcrowding lead to a mixing of weak and exploitive inmates. Undereducated and poorly trained correctional officers or inexperienced administrators lead to inadequate inmate supervision and control. It may even mean the corruption of officers or intimidation of staff by the more powerful inmates.

Research has been conducted that indicates that specific types of violence are more likely to occur at certain times of the day, certain places within the institution, and during certain types of activities. For example, Steinke (1991) found that violence toward staff was more likely to occur in areas where inmates were engaged in a loosely structured activity such as dining, recreation, or showers, and that inmates were more likely to be alone when aggressive toward staff. Violence against other inmates was more likely to occur where inmates were allowed to congregate and less common in single-celled housing areas. While in some instances the presence of others served to deter violence, it seemed to enhance tendencies toward violence in other cases. Some research has associated violence with levels of heat and the summer months, while other studies have found that older prisons with less surveillance because of the architecture are more violent. The degree of overcrowding has also been correlated with violence. Still other studies associate more experienced correctional officers with lower levels of violence in institutions.

The Cost of Prison Violence

There are many direct and indirect costs associated with prison violence. Obviously, the most serious are loss of life and physical and psychological injury. Staff may be placed on worker's compensation or permanently disabled. Loss of property and damage from fires, riots, and disturbances create overwhelming expenses. Other costs following a violent incident include paperwork, clean-up, and overtime. There are also the expenses of disciplinary hearings, or even criminal trials, transfers to other units, and the placement of inmates in more costly, solitary housing.

Fear of violence may keep some inmates, particularly older inmates, from participating in meaningful programs or recreation. They may prefer to isolate themselves in their cells rather than risk confrontations. Fear of victimization may lead to medical problems as well as psychiatric illness.

Theories have also been developed that argue that violence is normal and even useful in the prison environment. Given the backgrounds of those incarcerated and the unnatural conflict orientation of the institution, it is not unexpected that there is violence. In fact, many wonder why there is not more. It can be argued that power struggles, the resulting awards of status, and position in the social hierarchy result in order, and even stability, in the prison subculture, which are essential to its structure and survival. It is also asserted that violent incidents allow inmates to blow off steam or experience releases in the otherwise constant tension of incarcerated life. In a life engineered so that inmates have no control over or effect on events, striking out against another or one's self is not only expression, but also confirmation that they still have some degree of power. As one lifer explains, "Prison deprives those locked within of the normal avenues of pursuing gratification of their needs and leaves them no instruments but sex, violence, and conquest to validate their sense of manhood and individual worth. And they do, channeling all of their frustrated drives into the pursuit of power, finding gratification in the conquest and defeat, the domination and subjugation of each other" (Rideau 1992). Many administrators believe that it is more practical to talk in terms of controlling and regulating violence than eliminating it altogether.

Responses to Prison Violence

Historically, prison officials rarely recorded incidences of violence or their response. From unofficial stories and reports, however, we know that retaliation and brutal punishments were common. Today, accurate logs are kept on all incidents, including witness statements, photographs, and tapes. Official reports are monitored by administrators, evaluated, and used in training.

One aspect of training involves sensitizing officers to the telltale signs of trouble "brewing" within the institution. In general populations, requests for unit transfers, or protective custody, increases in mental health problems, increases in the number of grievances and disciplinaries filed, accumulations of contraband, hording of commissary items, and rumors of retaliation may all indicate impending violence. Decreases in attendance at programs or activities are also important barometers of violence.

Physical controls such as the use of force and restraints may be employed by officers in contact with inmates. Many prison systems have special teams that are highly trained in the technical and legal aspects of successful emergency response. Other systems have tried and abandoned such teams because of the need to train all officers in these skills because of the unpredictable nature of such emergencies. The existence of elite teams of tactical response may undermine the confidence and morale of regular officers, who are the first on the scene of most prison disruptions.

Legally, prison administrators have an obligation to protect inmates and staff from violence. Liability may be incurred when officials knew or should have known of a potentially violent situation and no corrective action was taken. This may include failure to protect informants from retaliation or vulnerable inmates from sexual assaults, understaffing high-risk areas, failing to secure tools that could be used as weapons, and lack of training for officers in how to respond to a disturbance.

Attempts to Reduce Prison Violence

Strategies for reducing the amount of prison violence range from segregating violence-prone inmates to improving building design to provide greater surveillance. Special management units (SMU), special housing units (SHU), or restricted housing units (RHU) are the names commonly used for entire facilities or wings dedicated to the control of violent prisoners. These are all maximum super-security units that have many controls built in specifically to limit the prisoners' access to people and things that may result in additional harm. All cells are constantly monitored with audio and video surveillance. Inmates are released one at a time from cells by remote control to the shower or recreation area. Partly punishment for serious offenses committed in prison, partly preventive, special housing is used when prisoners have demonstrated that they cannot adjust to the general population. Because these units are resource intensive, the goal is to control the inmates' behavior and then move them progressively with reward privileges through various phases until they can be reintegrated into the general population. Officials in the Pennsylvania Department of Corrections claim that 85 percent of those reassigned from the RHU to the general population are successfully reintegrated (Beard 1994).

Some prisons have developed special programs for teaching inmates conflict resolution and new techniques of stress management. Cognitive theories suggest that poor judgment and reasoning cause inappropriate responses such as threats and violence. Education and counseling strategies attempt to alter inmates' attitudes and prevent future violence by teaching communication skills and more successful approaches to problems solving.

In general, population units' contemporary architectural designs stress open living spaces with enhanced surveillance. The new style of direct supervision has officers within, instead of outside, the population, so that they can more carefully control activities. Their presence seems to deter acting out. Many experts recommend that the officers' role be expanded to emphasize the rehabilitative aspects of inmate-staff relations. Besides increasing job satisfaction, better supervision may reduce the opportunities for predatory behavior.

Some would argue that solutions should be developed at each individual prison given its unique population and environment. Data-collection systems should track information on each incident of violence and be analyzed for trends and solutions. Classification systems should seek to develop the most effective screening devices and assessment procedures for accurately predicting violence among inmates. Bowker (1982) also recommends the use of ombudsmen to resolve tension-producing problems between inmates and administration; a normalization of prison industry programs to include better wage incentives; facilitation of family visits; and initiation of conjugal visiting programs.

Marilyn D. McShane

See also DISCIPLINE, GANGS, HOMICIDE, RIOTS, SEXUAL EXPLOITATION IN PRISON

Bibliography

Beard, J.A. (1994). Using special management units to control inmate violence. *Correc-*

tions Today 56(5): 88–91.

Bowker, L. H. (1980). *Prison Victimization.* New York: Elsevier.

Bowker, L. H. (1982). Victimizers and victims in American correctional institutions. In R. Johnson and H. Toch, eds. *The Pains of Imprisonment.* Prospect Heights, Ill.: Waveland.

Braswell, M., S. Dillingham, and R. Montgomery, eds. (1985). *Prison Violence in America.* Cincinnati, Ohio: Anderson.

Ekland–Olson, S. (1986). Crowding, social control, and prison violence: Evidence from the post–Ruiz years in Texas. *Law and Society Review* 20: 389–421.

Fleisher, M. S. (1989). *Warehousing Violence.* Newbury Park, Calif.: Sage.

Larsen, N. (1988). The utility of prison violence: An A-causal approach to prison riots. *Criminal Justice Review* 13(1): 29–38.

Love, B. (1994). Program curbs prison violence through conflict resolution. *Corrections Today* 56(5): 144, 146–47.

McCorkle, R. (1992). Personal precautions to violence in prison. *Criminal Justice and Behavior* 19(2): 160–73.

Rideau, W. (1992). The sexual jungle. In W. Rideau and R. Wikberg, eds. *Life Sentences: Rage and Survival Behind Bars.* New York: Times Books.

Roberg, R., and V. Webb (1981). Violence in prison: Its extent, nature and consequences. In R. Roberg and V. Webb, eds. *Critical Issues in Corrections.* St. Paul, Minn.: West.

Scharf, P. (1983). Empty bars: Violence and the crisis of meaning in the prison. *Prison Journal* 63(1): 114–24.

Steinke, P. (1991). Using situational factors to predict types of prison violence. *Journal of Offender Rehabilitation* 17: 119–32.

Wright, K. N. (1991). The violent and victimized in the male prison. *Journal of Offender Counseling Services and Rehabilitation* 16: 1–25.

Visitation

Visitation in prison has been a part of the penal tradition since the early years of its existence. As far back as 1790, with the establishment of the Walnut Street Jail, prisoners who remained well behaved were allowed to have close members of their families visit them for about fifteen minutes once every three months. Brief conversations took place through a thick grill and were restricted by close supervision of the guards.

In other early penitentiaries, such as the Auburn and Pennsylvania systems, isolation of the inmates was enforced, so that visitation was strictly prohibited except in certain circumstances. For example, the prison in Philadelphia allowed only an extremely small number of relatives or friends to visit an inmate's cell, and prison officials carefully screened the visitors to make sure "there could be no doubt in their virtue." The visitation process came under such strict scrutiny because prison officials wanted to keep the convicts ignorant of external affairs. Thus, all exchanges of correspondence with the outside world, even newspapers, were banned. Just as prison administrators wanted the prisoners ignorant of outside affairs, they also wanted the outside world ignorant of internal affairs. Prison officials, therefore, did their best to sever all ties with the outside world, whether it was family or the press.

Visitation restrictions such as these continued into the 1830s in many prisons. In New York's facility, for example, inmates were strictly prohibited from any visitation with relatives. In the 1840s, though, policies on visitation became somewhat more relaxed. For example, at Sing Sing prison, inmates were allowed to send one letter every six months and receive a single visit from relatives at some point during their sentence. Most other states followed by enacting similar regulations.

The 1840s brought more reform, as prison administrations began allowing the public to tour and observe the prison facilities for a fee. By charging a fee, prisons were able to generate revenue while allowing the outside community to see a limited amount of the prison facilities. This system of accepting money for prison tours was later discontinued because it was felt that allowing people to tour the prisons and observe the inmates was not an aid to the moral and reforming influences of the prison.

Today, all prisons have some kind of visitation system, because it is believed that receiving visits from families and friends and keeping ties with the outside community are essential to the rehabilitation of the prisoners. Research has suggested that those prisoners who receive visitors have a lesser chance of returning to prison than those who do not. Additionally, studies have shown that those inmates who had no vis-

V

its during their incarceration failed parole at a greater rate than those who had frequent visits from family and friends (Holt and Miller 1972). Studies have also shown that those prisoners with "active" family interests during their imprisonment are more successful in completing parole than those who reported no family interest (Glaser 1964). In essence, it is believed that, because most prisoners will return to society at some point, communication with the outside world is essential to the inmate's transition back into the community.

Support for visitation was expressed by the National Advisory Commission on Criminal Justice Standards and Goals in 1973, when they urged that visitors be encouraged rather than just tolerated. This sentiment was reaffirmed by the Commission on Accreditation for Corrections in 1981, when it linked contact visits to accreditation and called for fewer restrictions on visits if possible.

Types of Visitation

There are several types of visits that occur in prisons, the two main types being closed (noncontact) and contact. Closed visits prohibit any contact from occurring between the prisoner and visitor, ensuring that no exchange of contraband will occur. Usually, prison policy restricts visitors to speaking to the prisoners through a screen. In some prisons, the inmate and visitor may be separated by bulletproof glass and must talk to each other by telephone. These types of visits are also closely monitored by guards.

Contact visits, the type used in most prisons, are visits that are a bit more "free," in that the prisoner and visitor are able to communicate without a screen or glass and are usually allowed to touch. Generally, these visits occur in an open visiting area where there are places to congregate. The areas may also contain picnic tables or playgrounds for the children. Prisons that lack the space to provide these types of facilities often use gymnasiums, classrooms, or anywhere else the prison has extra room. Administrative policies governing contact visits may or may not allow the prisoner and visitor to touch, embrace, or kiss. Inmates who are extremely dangerous may be able to communicate with the visitor without a glass or screen but must remain in shackles and handcuffs. Prison guards are constantly overseeing the visitation area and are prepared to reprimand those prisoners and visitors who violate the rules.

Conjugal visits are particularly controversial in that they allow the spouse of a prisoner to visit for a specified period of time, during which the two are alone on the prison grounds without guards overseeing the visit. The couple is usually given access to a room for their private use. A few state institutions have programs regulating this type of visit, but the majority of the penal institutions do not. Mississippi was the first state to allow this type of visitation, dating back to the early 1900s. Other states, however, did not begin to endorse it until the late 1960s. Even with the approval of a few states, such as California, New York, and Florida, it still meets with much controversy in this country. Proponents of conjugal visiting view it as a way to keep the family together and to discourage homosexuality from occurring in the prison. Others, however, disapprove. They believe that it puts too much emphasis on the physical aspect of marriage, is unfair to unmarried prisoners, and decreases the intensity of the punishment.

Some states have changed the name of conjugal visits to "Family Weekends" or "Family Reunion Programs." This has been done to reduce the focus on sex and allow the prisoner's entire family to visit for the weekend. Activities for these weekends can include camping in areas designated for the prisoners and their families, or prisons may provide a room, building, or trailer specifically for the inmate and the inmate's family to use for the weekend.

The results of a 1987 survey showed that opportunities for private and extended family visits were more widely available than they had been in 1976. And the number of visits per inmate has increased since 1987. For example, in 1976 only two states permitted conjugal visits; by 1987, that number had increased to twenty-three institutions in eight states. Furthermore, 35 percent of the institutions responding to the 1987 study indicated that they permitted daily visits for the inmates, and 20 percent stated that prisoners could receive four to five visits per month.

A Right or Privilege?

In the past, visitation was widely viewed as a privilege that officials could grant or deny on the basis of the prisoner's behavior. In the 1970s, however, the prisoner's rights movement led some penologists to believe that courts would consider visitation a right of the prisoners. That did not occur, however, as judicial decisions at all levels of the court have continued to rule that there is no constitutional right to prison visitations. Although visitation is considered a privilege, it has been strongly suggested by the American Correctional Association (ACA) that prison officials encourage visitors rather than tolerate them.

One of the early cases involving visitation was *Walker v. Pate* (1966). In that case, the circuit court held that prison officials can prohibit a visit by the spouse of a prisoner if the spouse has a criminal record. Another court declared, in the case of *Rowland v. Wolff* (1971), that the relatives of a prisoner can be prohibited from visiting by prison officials on the basis of an informant's statement that they had smuggled contraband into the prison.

The question of visitation's being a right or a privilege was first acknowledged in the case of *Lynott v. Henderson* (1980). In that case the court upheld a prison regulation stating that visitation privileges could be extended to friends or other nonfamily members if prison officials believe that it is a genuine friendship and that the prisoner would profit from the contact.

It seems from these cases that visitation is a privilege that prison officials can expand or restrict according to circumstances. Although there have been numerous cases involving visitation, courts have not definitively determined whether it is a right or a privilege. The difference is great. If visitation is a right, prison officials cannot prohibit prisoners from having visitors because of their behavior. If, however, it is a privilege, officials have the authority to deny visits to inmates. Visitation is an important issue that has not been clearly defined.

Conjugal Visitation

Issues concerning conjugal visits have also been frequently debated. Two leading cases concerning conjugal visitation were *Payne v. District of Columbia* (1958) and *Tarlton v. Clark* (1971). In both of those cases, conjugal visitation was declared not to be a constitutional right. In *Payne,* a federal appellate court held that such visits are not constitutionally required. The Fifth Circuit Court of Appeals ruled in *Tarlton* that a prisoner's claim to a right of conjugal visitation "would not come up to the level of a federal constitutional right so as to be cognizable as a basis for relief in the federal court."

Another case concerning conjugal visits was *Polakoff v. Henderson* (1973), in which an inmate and his wife sued the Atlanta Federal Penitentiary based on alleged deprivations of his First, Eighth, and Fourteenth Amendment rights. They claimed that the prison's denial of their rights of consortium constituted a prohibition against free exercise of religion. They also claimed that they were suffering physically and mentally because of the denial of those rights. Mrs. Polakoff alleged that her right to equal protection under the law was violated, in that other women were not deprived of rights inherent in the marriage contract. Mr. Polakoff claimed that his rights of equal protection under the law were violated because other similarly situated prisoners were granted conjugal visits.

In *Polakoff,* the district court ruled in favor of the correctional administration. The district court stated that the state can neither favor nor inhibit religion but must remain neutral at all times. Additionally, Mrs. Polakoff's claim of Fourteenth Amendment rights violation failed because the court found no discrimination against her, because many other prisoners' wives are not allowed conjugal visits. In regard to Mr. Polakoff's claims that another institution allowed conjugal visits, the court stated that not every penitentiary must have the same policies for visitation.

In short, courts at every level have declared that conjugal visitation is a privilege and not a right. Prison administrations may permit conjugal visits at their own discretion. On the basis of the cases that have gone to court, no person or prisoner has a right to conjugal visits.

Media Visitation

Visits by the press and news media have also been issues of concern. *Pell v. Procunier* (1974) was a leading case, in which the U.S. Supreme Court answered the claim by four prisoners and three journalists that the prisons' policies prohibiting journalists from specific personal interviews with inmates violated their freedom of speech rights. The Court found no support in the Constitution for a duty of the government "to make available to journalists sources of information not available to members of the public generally." The Court clarified its position later that year in *Procunier v. Martinez* (1974). It stated that, as long as restrictions on interviews did not target content, "reasonable limitations" would be seen as falling within the appropriate rules and regulations to which inmates are necessarily subject. Regarding the press, the Court ruled that interviews are not a news media privilege because such interviews are not generally available to all members of the public.

In another case, *Saxbe v. Washington Post Company* (1974), the news media challenged the federal prison's policy of prohibiting personal interviews between newsmen and individually designated inmates. The Court stated, relying on the decision in *Pell,* that the regulation did not violate any First Amendment rights because it "does not deny the press access to sources of information available to members of the general public." It is simply a particular application of the general rule that nobody can enter the prison and pick an inmate to visit, unless that visitor is a lawyer, member of the clergy, relative, or friend of the inmate.

Legal Assistance

A final aspect of visitation that has been brought to the courts is nonattorney legal assistance. Those types of visits are for people associated with attorneys, such as attorney assistants. Most attorneys have assistants who help them gather the information they need for their cases; that includes meeting with their clients. If prison policy restricts attorney assistants from visiting inmates in prison, it could prolong the case because attorneys are usually working on several cases at once. Without the help of assistants, they cannot see every client. Whether prison policies allow visitation by attorney assistants is therefore an important issue.

In *Souza v. Travisono* (1974), the circuit court stated that prison officials may not arbitrarily limit access to nonattorney legal assistance, but that they may place reasonable regulations on those visitations. They may regulate the time, place, and manner of visits to further the governmental interests of security, order, or rehabilitation.

Security

A primary concern of prison administrators is the fear that illegal contraband may be brought into prison by visitors. Security, therefore, is an overriding factor when considering how much contact be allowed between the inmate and the visitor. The ACA recommends that all visitors be searched by a scanning device or frisked when entering the prison grounds and that all prisoners be frisked or strip-searched when leaving the visiting area. Visitors, however, cannot be subjected to a body cavity search. If it is believed that the visitor is concealing contra-

band in an area that cannot be searched, the only recourse of prison officials is to deny admission for visitation.

Generally, prison staff have policies by which visitors and prisoners must abide. An ACA rule states that, before the visit occurs, all visitors must be registered as guests and identified, checked to determine that they have been approved for visitation, and advised of all the prison visiting rules by having the rules placed in an area that will be seen by everyone. Violation of the rules on the part of the prisoner may result in the prisoner's not being allowed to have visitors for a certain period of time. When a visitor breaks the rules, that visitor may not be permitted to return to visit for a specified time.

The type of visits, closed or contact, varies according to the type of security at the institution as well as the administrative policies of the facility. In most high-security prisons prisoners are considered to be extremely dangerous. Therefore, only closed visits are allowed, so that officials will not have to be concerned about contact between the inmate and visitor and the possibility that contraband will enter the prison. In institutions with lower security, prisoners are considered less threatening; contact visits are usually allowed, but with close scrutiny by the guards.

Other Issues Concerning Visitation

All visits are met with controversy. Many feel that the distance some visitors and families must travel is unfair because many prisons are located in rural areas far away from the urban areas where large numbers of prisoners come from and where most of their families live. That makes travel and the cost of transportation a burden for many families. As a result, most families in this situation cannot visit whenever they desire but only when they have the transportation to get there or the money for transportation. A 1994 study indicated that wives were least likely to be able to afford the cost of visiting (Shafer 1994). In response, some private agencies have instituted programs to subsidize the cost of visits and to provide hostels where families who travel long distances can rest, eat, and freshen up during visits. In some jurisdictions, the prison system itself, or some other governmental agency, assists families with transportation.

Also, the length of the visit is controversial, as each institution sets limits on the amount of time visitors may spend. Length of visits vary with the number of inmates within the institution and the amount of space it has for visitors. Visitors may travel a great distance to see an inmate for two hours. One study comparing policies in 1971 and in 1981 found that, over time, more visits per month were permitted and for longer periods per visit (Dickinson 1984).

Another concern is the areas in which visits are held. Many prisons were not built with a specific area for visits. This may result in uncomfortable visiting conditions because prison officials have to make room in areas where space is available.

While most correctional systems have increased the amount of space allocated to visiting, as institutional crowding and staff shortages continue, many prisons have been forced to offer each inmate fewer and shorter visiting opportunities.

With the exception of conjugal or family visitations, visits are in an open area where there is virtually no privacy for the family and friends. Also, conversations are not private, as guards are constantly scrutinizing the visitation area and therefore are able to hear conversations.

Heather Craig

See also CONTACT VISITS, CONJUGAL VISITS, CHILDREN OF PRISONERS

Bibliography

American Correctional Association (1965). *Manual of Correctional Standards*. New York: American Correctional Association.

Dickinson, G.E. (1984). Changes in communication policies. *Corrections Today*, 46(1): 58–60.

Glaser, D. (1964). *The Effectiveness of a Prison and Parole System*. Indianapolis, Ind.: Bobbs-Merrill.

Holt, N., and D. Miller (1972). *Explorations in Inmate-Family Relationships*. Research Report No. 46. Sacramento, Calif.: California Department of Corrections.

Krantz, S. (1983). *Corrections and Prisoners' Rights in a Nutshell*. 2nd ed. St. Paul, Minn.: West.

Shafer, N.E. (1989). Prison visiting: Is it time to review the rules? *Federal Probation*, 53(4): 25–30.

Shafer, N. E. (1994). Exploring the link between visits and parole success: A survey of prison visitors. *International Journal of Offender Therapy and Comparative Criminology*, 38(1): 17–32.

Cases

Lynott v. Henderson, 610 F.2d. 340 (5th Cir. 1980)

Payne v. District of Columbia, 253 F.2d. 867 (D.C.Cir. 1958)

Pell v. Procunier, 417 U.S. 817, 94 S.Ct. 2800, 41 L.Ed.2d 495 (1974)

Polakoff v. Henderson, 370 F.Supp. 690 (N.D.Ga. 1973)

Procunier v. Martinez, 416 U.S. 396, 94 S.Ct. 1800, 40 L.Ed.2d 224 (1974)

Rowland v. Wolff, 336 F.Supp. 257 (D.Neb. 1971)

Saxbe v. Washington Post Company, 417 U.S. 843, 94 S.Ct. 2811, 41 L.Ed.2d 514 (1974)

Souza v. Travisono, 498 F.2d. 1120 (1st Cir. 1974)

Tarlton v. Clark, 441 F.2d. 384 (5th Cir. 1971)

Walker v. Pate, 356 F.2d. 502 (7th Cir. 1966)

Vocational Programs

Although there have been work and industry ventures in even the earliest American prisons, vocational programs are more likely to be associated with periods of rehabilitative emphasis. Teaching inmates a skill and preparing them with good work habits was part of reform thinking that often included educational programs. Today, vocational programs are linked to work release and apprenticeships as well as the ability to obtain certifications, licenses, and other professional credentials.

Ever since we began to study recidivism and correlates of criminality, steady employment has been associated with success on parole and the prevention of further lawbreaking. Correctional administrators believed that teaching the offender a trade was a critical step in breaking the cycle of unemployment and crime.

Although prison industry has been limited by legislation that makes it difficult to produce competitive goods for sale, vocational programs have been able to train inmates in various occupational skills without necessarily jeopardizing outside markets and raising the ire of local unions.

Early Vocational Training

One of the pioneers in vocational programs was Zebulon Brockway at Elmira Reformatory. Individualized assessment and placement were keys to success in vocational planning. In the 1930s, one New York prison system had courses in agriculture, commercial art, barbering, carpentry, construction, estimating, loom repair, masonry, electricity, mechanical drawing, navigation, tailoring, marketing, bookbinding, machine shop practice, shorthand, advertising, salesmanship, and cartooning. World War II provided a chance to integrate hundreds of new vocational programs into the prison as were needed by the defense industry and support services.

Scope of Vocational Training Today

Vocational education in prison is guided by standards developed by the American Correctional Association as well as guidelines from outside vocational education associations. New York reports that over six thousand inmates are involved in their programs, which include forty standardized vocational programs, 350 instructors, and a supervisor for every six vocational teachers. Also, the Ohio State University Center for Vocational Programs has been very active in correctional education.

In other institutions, inmates learn heating and air conditioning repair, horsemanship training, dental laboratory skills, microfilming, cabinet making, and business computer applications. In Nevada inmates restore rare antique cars for shows, a time-consuming and exact science for twenty-four inmates trained by restoration supervisors. Two inmates have since left the prison and have obtained permanent jobs with the car collection in Las Vegas. Although the inmates selected for this program have auto-mechanics, bodyworking, and electrical-metal backgrounds, the opportunity to develop the skills necessary to restore the priceless vehicles has elevated their self-esteem and craftsmanship to levels they never imagined.

Another tedious occupation few on the outside have mastered is the transcription of music, math, and literature into Braille. In the Louisiana prison system, specially trained inmates have been certified in these services and provide a valuable resource for the blind.

Unfortunately, there are many factors limiting the ability of institutions to provide effective vocational training today. Many programs feature outdated skills in occupations that offer very few opportunities, such as television repair and furniture upholstering. Prisons often operate on the path of least resistance, leaving a program in place simply because it has always

been there and has been successful in the past. Outdated programs may also be retained because the staff are trained and in place to teach in a particular trade and it is not feasible to retrain or reassign them. Also, expensive equipment may have been donated or purchased for the trade school, so the prison may be reluctant or unable to purchase new materials. This has made it particularly difficult to initiate nontraditional training programs for women.

Consequently, much of the equipment that inmates train on is outdated and years behind the state of the art used in companies across the United States. Many newly released inmates are disappointed to find that the techniques and methods they learned in fields like computing or drafting are obsolete. In Georgia, however, officials attempted to anticipate a growing need for solar heating and cooling units and began training prisoners in the maintenance and repair of the equipment. In 1981 the program claimed that 80 percent of the trained inmates were able to find work in solar-related businesses. Georgia also attempted to put the moonshining experiences of inmates to work at producing ethanol distilled from corn and sugar cane stalks. The state anticipated converting many of its vehicles to the gasoline substitute product.

Some critics have complained about the training of prisoners in high-risk occupations such as asbestos removal, hazardous waste processing, and even firefighting. Historically, it may have seemed appropriate to expose prisoners to danger because most were facing death sentences anyway, but today there are constitutional concerns about worker safety and protections from potential abuse because inmates are often not free to choose work assignments nor covered by worker's compensation benefits.

On the other hand, some have argued that high-risk jobs bring excitement and attractive salaries, aspects very important to many former prisoners. The oil well firefighting program at one prison prepared inmates to work on offshore rigs where conditions were confining and controlled but not unlike those at the institutions inmates had once adjusted to.

With overcrowding pushing most institutions past their capacity, there are not enough vocational training programs to service the number of inmates who need them. It has also been argued that assignment practices are often political, and the most in need are not always placed in training. Also, training is often dependent upon the length of time a person has left

Vocational training and work programs provide many positive incentives for those incarcerated. Photo by Hennepin County Adult Corrections Facility. Used with permission by the American Correctional Association.

to serve. Some programs require that inmates have served a portion of their sentence before enrolling, although many programs also require a significant amount of time to complete, thus eliminating many short-term inmates from participation. This is disheartening because those who need the skills to obtain jobs upon release are often passed over for those serving lengthy sentences.

Lack of resources means not only more applicants than a program can service but also shortages of staff to oversee learning and supervision. In addition, because of financial limitations, programs are not properly able to test inmates for aptitudes and interests so that assignments can be guided by meaningful information. Although a wide range of tests are available to ensure proper placement in occupational fields, they are rarely administered. First come, first served is often the way participation is determined.

Discrepancies Between Vocational Programs for Men and Women

There are many differences over what is really vocational education, what is on-the-job training, and what is just plain work. Many so-called vocational programs do not really have an educational component. Others simply involve "practice" at manual labor skills that provide the upkeep of the institution and its services under the titles of housekeeping, laundry, painting, food service, landscaping, and horticulture.

Women's advocates express concern that many of the vocational opportunities are perpetuations of stereotypical "pink collar" roles for women, such as hairstyling, flower arranging, and nurses' aides. These jobs are often the lowest paying on the outside. It is only recently that women have had access to a wider range of nontraditional vocational training programs such as heavy equipment operation, welding, and computer maintenance.

In addition, women are often in need of vocational counseling as well as actual job training and placement. Many have unrealistic expectations about the careers they are interested in and how long it takes to prepare for them.

Barriers to Successful Career Transitions

One problem with vocational training in the past has been that it often prepared inmates for careers for which there were barriers in the outside world. Some jobs would eventually require employees to be bonded, which is difficult for former offenders, while others, like barbering, had strict licensing requirements that often excluded people with a history of criminal convictions. From the 1980s on, however, many of these restrictions have been removed and most occupations remain open to those with a criminal conviction, unless proscribed by the specific nature of the offense (such as child molestation or embezzlement).

Another potential barrier to a successful career outside of prison is parole or early release restrictions on where the offender may reside. Not being able to move to another state or jurisdiction may make it difficult to procure positions or promotions when called upon to do so. Today, most parole agencies attempt to resolve these conflicts by transferring supervision jurisdictions if the receiving party will agree.

Promising Programs and Strategies for the Future

The use of video and interactive video transmissions to teach and train larger numbers of inmates in vocational skills may be a reality soon. It is hoped that successful vocational programs will be accredited by national professional organizations and will lead to certificates, licenses, and other recognized credentials. The programs will be linked with job providers on the outside who will make employment contacts with inmates prior to release. More than learning one specific skill, the inmates will be taught the methods of adapting to technology and tools so that even if equipment changes over time, they will have the ability to adjust and continue to perform in that field.

Thom Gehring
Carolyn Eggleston

See also EDUCATIONAL PROGRAMS, INDUSTRY

Bibliography

Boston, G. R. (1986). Seeds of hope. *Corrections Today* 48(7): 104.

Hershberger, S. (1987). Vocational education: Preparing for life outside. *Corrections Today* 49(5): 128, 130–32.

Lattimore, P., A. D. Witt, and J. R. Baker. (1990). Experimental assessment of the effect of vocational training on youthful property offenders. *Evaluation Review* 14(2): 115–33.

Mitchell, A. (1981). Dawn of solar training. *Corrections Magazine* 7(5): 41–44.

Nelson, P. (1985). Marketable skills. *Corrections Today* 47(5): 70.

Schumacker, R., D. Anderson, and S. Anderson (1990). Vocational and academic indicators of parole success. *Journal of Correctional Education* 41(1): 8–13.

Simon, R. J., and J. Landis (1991). *The Crimes Women Commit: The Punishments They Receive*. Lexington, Mass.: Lexington.

Storck, C. (1985). Standardizing vocational education. *Corrections Today* 47(5): 44–45.

Zumpetta, A. (1988). Full-time vocational training in corrections: Measuring effectiveness vs. appearance. *Journal of Correctional Education* 39(3): 130–33.

Volunteers

I. Citizens

Volunteers have enjoyed a long and varied history in American corrections. There are reports of community reform groups offering support to prisoners as early as the 1700s. In 1776, for example, the Philadelphia Society for Assisting Distressed Prisoners brought food and clothing into Colonial prisons, only ceasing that activity when the city was invaded by British forces in September of 1777. The revised penal code of 1786 replaced the sanction of capital punishment for many types of crimes with long-term incarceration and hard physical labor. Shortly after, in 1787, Quakers and reformists created the Philadelphia Society for Alleviating the Miseries of Public Prisons, a society that brought community members back into Colonial prisons. The society expressed concern about the use of hard labor and questioned it as an effective means of dealing with prisoners. This historical precedent was imitated in several major American cities.

Historically, early volunteers not only sought to provide for prisoners' needs that were not met in prison, but also to address an array of humanitarian concerns. That centered on the spiritual as well as physical needs of the incarcerated. With the emergence of social services, many of the services of the early correctional volunteers and reformers were provided for elsewhere and the movement of outside groups coming into the prisons seemed to lose momentum. The practice of "volunteers" or community groups or members coming into prisons declined between 1920 and the 1950s (Winter 1993). Many of today's national correctional volunteer agencies, however, have their roots in the early Colonial prison reform movements.

Rebirth of Volunteerism
The 1960s saw the emergence of a nationwide volunteer movement that included many disciplines, including criminal justice and corrections. Many credit Judge Keith J. Leenhouts of Royal Oak Court in Michigan for the reemergence of volunteers in criminal justice and, more specifically, corrections, in 1959. The judge did not have either precourt investigation or probation duties provided for his court, a void he filled by using volunteers from the community. By 1972, the U.S. Department of Justice published results of a national survey and concluded that "volunteers today constitute a significant work force in the criminal justice system as individuals and in groups. At present estimates, the citizen volunteer outnumbers paid workers in the system four or five to one. Exclusive of law enforcement agencies, and above the misdemeanant court level, approximately 70 percent of criminal justice agencies have some sort of volunteer programs" (Scheier et al. 1972, iii). A Lou Harris (1969) survey, however, found that 67 percent of correctional agencies did not have a volunteer program, and those that did had no screening, training, placing, or evaluative tools in place. Furthermore, the resurgence of the volunteer movement in the United States through the 1980s still found the presence of volunteers in the justice system "the exception rather than the rule" (Winter 1993, 20).

Volunteers in Corrections: The Debate
There is a recurring historical theme that questions the place of volunteers and community members in prison and community-based correctional programs. In 1972, the National Advisory Commission on Criminal Justice Standards and Goals stated, "Implementation of Community Corrections requires citizen involvement on an unprecedented scale. In fact, the degree of citizen acceptance, involvement, and participation in community-based corrections will decide not only the swiftness of its implementation but also its ultimate success or failure." The 1969 Harris survey also, however, examined the attitude of correctional administrators toward their volunteers and concluded that "correctional administrators remain divided on the value of the volunteer for the correctional agency as well as on the question of the most appropriate role and function of the volunteer in the correctional program" (Harris 1969, i). This remains an issue today (Winter 1993).

It is not difficult to imagine that correctional administrators would have valid concerns about the use of volunteers in their programs, especially in a secure setting. Questions would focus on such issues as liability, safety, and responsibility of the volunteer and the agency, the rights of the volunteer, prisoner privacy, the training and screening of volunteers, and introducing volunteers to the often unknown world of the prison and its culture.

Services that Volunteers inside Prison Can Provide
Though the use and need for volunteers in the criminal justice system, and particularly in the prison setting, has been an area of debate, there are many good reasons for having volunteers in a prison setting. Volunteers in prisons can

1. Bring in extra staff members with different and varied skills, and bridge the isolation to the outside community that prisoners can experience
2. Strengthen community relations
3. Serve as a neutral liaison between prisoners and paid staff
4. Provide services at little cost
5. Be used as a measure of community concern and citizen response to prison-related issues.

Volunteers across the country can and are helping inmates develop decision-making skills and find employment after release; helping support inmates' families; collecting resources; teaching inmates to read and write; and offering support, encouragement, and hope.

In addition, volunteers are dealing with the specific needs of female prisoners. In 1813,

Elizabeth Fry was particularly concerned about the conditions women faced in London's Newgate prison. She was deeply affected by the newborn children she saw, and the conditions they faced within the prison. Her concern resulted in the creation of the Association for the Improvement of the Female Prisoners in Newgate. Mothers in prison and their special needs have long been a concern of administrators. Today, in the Maryland Correctional Institution for Women in Jessup, the Girl Scouts of Central Maryland sponsor a Girl Scout Troop for daughters of incarcerated women (Moses 1993). In the Taconic Correctional Facility in Bedford Falls, New York, volunteers provide female inmates with many of the services offered male inmates in addition to acting as nursery volunteers; health care volunteers address the specific health care needs of female inmates (Gladwin 1993).

As an example of the effective use of volunteers in the prison system, in 1992 the National Office of Citizen Participation (NOCP) was created in the Federal Bureau of Prisons. The mission the NOCP is to coordinate volunteer services in federal prisons nationwide. The NOCP works with the Federal Bureau of Prisons chaplaincy and education departments to develop liaisons with agencies that provide a ready pool of volunteers—colleges and universities, community aid programs, and social service organizations and clubs. There are presently four thousand volunteers in the federal prison system. They provide a number of traditional volunteer services, including visitation and support, mentoring activities, religious and social services, and recreational and educational activities. These volunteers also provide a vital link between prisons, staff, inmates, and the community (Hawk 1993).

Concerns about Volunteer Programs

While volunteers are welcomed and even sought in the federal and some state prisons, the creation and administration of an effective volunteer program is not an easy task. Many programs fail, and there are often hidden pitfalls on the road to a successful volunteer program. Fortunately, this is a problem area that is being addressed in the literature, and the steps to building a successful program can be found and followed. Before creating a program, it is wise to examine the oft-cited problems in volunteer programs that can cause a program to fail—sometimes before it has even begun.

Problems that may arise before, during, or after the creation or implementation of a volunteer program might include the following:

1. High turnover rates of volunteers
2. Poor record-keeping
3. Poor volunteer management
4. Lack of employee cooperation as a result of the staff's fear that volunteers will somehow undermine their position or make it more difficult
5. Inadequate recruitment, screening, and training of the volunteers
6. The belief that the volunteer program administration itself does not cost money
7. The failure to provide the program with the support and personnel it needs to be successful.

Newer concerns include the civil rights of volunteers and liability of prison administrators if harm comes to volunteers. Questions arise regarding confidential information, the use of ex-convicts in a prison setting, and the responsibilities of administration in the recruiting, hiring, training, and supervision of volunteer employees. Questions of physical danger to volunteers and the liability of the prison system are also timely. Despite the concerns and problems of using volunteers in a prison setting, good management and planning can overcome all of these long before they materialize into serious problems for prison officials.

Administration of an Effective Volunteer Program

The American Correctional Association has proven itself to be an advocate for the successful use of volunteers in the various correctional forums. ACA has published many helpful books and articles dealing with the subject. One article by Ogburn (1993) specifically provided advice for volunteer administrators who are faced with the challenge of creating a volunteer program. The article presented a successful volunteer program as a series of steps to be followed:

1. Assess the need for a program and determine which tasks are to be given to volunteers
2. Articulate the goals of the volunteer program and write job descriptions for the volunteers

3. Get the staff involved in planning and starting the program—a most important step to ensure future cooperation and harmony
4. Seek volunteers through community organizations
5. Train volunteers about inmates, prison culture, and the institutional environment
6. Train volunteers about security needs, procedures, and their rationale
7. Familiarize volunteers with the institution's mission and impart to volunteers their part in that overall mission
8. Evaluate the effectiveness of the program. One way this can be addressed is by careful documentation of volunteer services. It is also wise to let the inmates, staff, and volunteers themselves be instruments of evaluation
9. Reward volunteers for the job they do. Like any paid employee, a volunteer needs to be treated as a valued member of a team.

It has been suggested that prison volunteer movements wax and wane with the public's awareness of and interest in penal issues. It would only stand to reason that volunteer programs within the criminal justice system and particularly within the prison system will continue to attract citizen attention. There can be, and are, successful volunteer programs that benefit not only the prisoner, but also the community, the volunteer, and the criminal justice system as well.

Frances R. Reddington

See also PHILADELPHIA SOCIETY FOR THE ALLEVIATION OF THE MISERIES OF PUBLIC PRISONS

Bibliography

Gladwin, B. (1993). Taconic warden finds volunteers have much to offer women inmates. *Corrections Today* 55(5): 88–93.
Harris, L. and Associates (1969). *Volunteers Look at Corrections*. Washington, D.C.: Joint Commission on Correctional Manpower and Training.
Hawk, K. (1993). 4000 BOP volunteers are committed to working within the federal system. *Corrections Today* 55(5): 72–75.
Moses, M. (1993). New program at women's prison benefits mothers and children. *Corrections Today* 55(5): 132–35.
Ogburn, K. (1993). Volunteer program guide: Starting and maintaining your program. *Corrections Today* 55(5): 66.
Scheier, I., J. L. Berry, M. L. Cox, E. Shelley, R. Simmons, and D. Callaghan (1972). *Guidelines and Standards for the Use of Volunteers in Correctional Programs*. Washington, D.C.: U.S. Department of Justice.
Winter, B. (1993). Does corrections need volunteers? *Corrections Today* 55(5): 20–22.

II. Inmates

In the Pennsylvania and Auburn prisons of a century ago, prisoners did little else besides serve their sentences. Some institutions prevented their captives from even communicating. Others gave each prisoner a Bible and solitude. Today, prison administrators seek out ways to keep inmates constructively employed with a variety of meaningful work and volunteer experiences.

We now have a long history of offering prisoners opportunities to provide services both inside and outside of prison walls. Some of those services are involuntary. Prisoners are assigned to work in industrial programs, prepare meals for their fellow prisoners, and hold maintenance jobs inside their institutions. Besides these inmate work details, though, some inmates donate their time freely by participating in voluntary programs designed to benefit other inmates in their institutions and the wider community outside of prison walls. Inmate volunteers also hold programs that raise money for outside charities. Prison administrators today involve inmates in a variety of volunteer projects aimed to give prisoners opportunities to the contribute to the community.

Voluntary programs have many advantages. They give prisoners opportunities to serve their communities rather than simply serve time. The beneficiaries of volunteer programs are the recipients of inmate labor and services, but there are other advantages to such programs that may not be as apparent. For one thing, inmates who contribute to projects that enhance surrounding communities boost the image of prisons and ease residents' anxieties over having convicted felons nearby. Community agency administrators also benefit from inmate volunteer services. Prisoners who volunteer on community projects help municipal administrators to conserve financial resources. These civic leaders meet with prison administrators and together develop plans to meet the needs of the community without jeopardizing the security concerns of prison administrators. The broader community benefits from the contributions of the prisoners. The voluntary programs also help administrators manage their institutions by reducing inmate idleness—a critical problem during these times of rising prison populations.

Unfortunately, prison populations increase in America faster than administrators can create meaningful jobs for prisoners. That increases the threat of empty time for the inmates, which many administrators believe can translate into restlessness and perhaps violence. Voluntary programs help fill inmate time and give the inmates opportunities to contribute to projects for which they can see results. Such programs help build prisoner self-esteem. They give the prisoners a sense of community belonging.

Most facilities operated by the Federal Bureau of Prisons have Community Relations Boards designed to bring community leaders together with prison officials to discuss issues of mutual interest. Such meetings have resulted in many projects that would not succeed without inmate volunteers. For example, a group of inmates confined in a Wisconsin state prison volunteer their time to read books on tape for area schools and universities. Local teachers use the tapes to help students who suffer from learning disabilities overcome their difficulties. Also, inmates propose and work out other projects by themselves with the approval and support of staff sponsors. For example, inmates held at the U.S. penitentiary in Atlanta sold pajamas and slippers to their fellow inmates to raise money for local orphanages. Volunteer projects likely will become increasingly valuable as prison and community budgets tighten. Inmate volunteers reduce labor expenses.

The U.S. Forest Service, a public service charged with the awesome responsibility of preserving our nation's forests, suffers from shrinking budgets. It has difficulty providing the machinery and labor necessary to keep our nation's parks and wilderness areas clean. In New Waverly, Texas, the Forest Service gladly accepts help from female volunteers confined at the federal prison camp at Bryan, Texas. The inmate volunteers work in the forest clearing brush, maintaining trails and recreational facilities for the public, and performing various related duties.

New York State, too, uses prisoners to help maintain the natural environment. Through its Rehabilitation of Offenders program, inmate volunteers participate in supervised work to provide services and products to the state's Department of Environmental Conservation Agency. The inmate volunteer crews rake, sweep, paint, clean culverts and ditches, cut hazardous trees and perform other manual labor needed in the maintenance of the state facilities. Inmate volunteers are credited with 85 percent of a complete renovation on a two-story house belonging to the Department of Environmental Conservation. Volunteer inmates also were responsible for rebuilding a large boathouse on Saranac Lake. They helped stabilize an eroding bank of the Schroon River. And these New York volunteer inmates planted approximately eight million trees over a fifteen-year period.

Inmate volunteers at the Federal Correctional Institution in Schuylkill, Pennsylvania, work together with the National Weather Service, which uses the prison as a weather observatory. Inmate volunteers measure and record weather data at least twice each day. The volunteers working on the project also provide information to the Pennsylvania Department of Transportation for Schuylkill County, the agency responsible for maintaining the county's highways.

Reducing costs is not the objective of all volunteer projects though. Some exist to lift the burdens of suffering citizens, like a project at the federal prison camp in Atlanta that uses volunteer inmates to repair the properties of elderly people in the community. In that project, six inmates from the prison camp worked diligently to repair a widow's roof. Other projects exist to bring smiles to those in pain, like projects to help children.

Children appreciate attention from any source. Toys are an especially nice treat that are always welcome, especially when they are suffering. Inmate volunteers at the federal correctional institution in Sheridan, Oregon, recognized an opportunity to bring smiles to children in difficulty. These inmates began collecting scrap wood generated at the institution's furniture factory. Then, with staff approval, they began using this scrap wood to make toys for the children. The local Kiwanis Club in Sheridan works together with the inmate–volunteer group by distributing the donated toys to nearby children's hospitals and other charities.

Besides volunteering their services to the community outside of prison walls, inmates also volunteer their time to work together with prison administrators in a quest to enhance the quality of life inside the prison itself. Swelling prison populations coupled with an overworked staff encourage administrators to welcome inmate volunteers. J. Michael Quinlan, a former Bureau of Prisons director, often spoke about the inmates outnumbering the staff four to one in any institution. Many of these inmates realize that, through their contributions, they can help some of the programs succeed.

One voluntary program active in most all prisons concerns the danger of suicide. Prisons separate people from their family and friends. Some describe life in confinement as a sensation of falling with no control. Prisoners sometimes entertain thoughts of suicide to end their battle with depression.

The suicide-watch program encourages volunteers from the prison community to help the administration ensure that prisoners do not commit suicide during a particularly weak moment. Inmates who volunteer for this program work together with the prison's psychology department, which usually administers suicide-watch cadres. The psychologist in charge designs a training session to inform the volunteers about the dangers of suicide and how it can be prevented. After the training is complete, the volunteers will observe at-risk inmates in assigned shifts around the clock.

Another popular area in the institution for inmate volunteers is the chapel. Inmate volunteers help to fill the spiritual needs of their fellow prisoners. Some of the fastest growing religious groups in the prison system are rooted in Islam. This religion has many factions, and inmates inside the various prisons volunteer to bring its numerous programs to life. Inmates also volunteer to assist in the development of Jewish, Christian, Native American and other worship groups.

Inmate volunteers working with suicide-watch and religious programs develop a sense of satisfaction from helping others. Their efforts directly affect the population in their communities, while at the same time mitigating the difficulties prison administrators face in their efforts to meet inmates' needs. Volunteers in these programs improve their organizational skills and help their fellow inmates. They also provide much-needed assistance to staff members, frequently with no formal recognition for their contributions.

Educational programs are another area in which volunteers make significant contribu-

tions. One study shows that as many as 82 percent of the prisoners held in Orange County, California, are functionally illiterate. Federal Bureau of Prisons data show that fewer than 50 percent of newly arriving prisoners hold high school diplomas. Such figures place a high demand on prison educational departments and create a need for inmate volunteers.

The Bedford Hills Correctional Facility, a prison holding female inmates in New York State, welcomed the assistance of inmate volunteers to help establish a literacy program at that institution. Kathy Boudin, a well-educated inmate, voluntarily assumed the role of an Adult Basic Education teacher. As an inmate volunteer, Boudin found the inmates willing. She designed a curriculum that proved of interest to her students and encouraged them to continue their pursuit of education. One of the highlights of Boudin's program was a play about the impact AIDS has on the incarcerated population that she and the other volunteers from her class wrote and performed. Besides having cultural and artistic value, the play also helped the volunteers and the prison's population understand the dangers and tragedies associated with the AIDS virus. The women's efforts, entitled *Our Play,* helped the participants to develop a growing consciousness of themselves as part of a community, first in the classroom and then in the prison. Boudin's program was also helpful in literacy development.

Prisoners in the federal system, too, see the value of volunteer programs. Most federal prisons offer formal and structured classes for adult basic education and preparation for the high school equivalency examination, but the students' ages vary between eighteen and seventy. Many do not respond as well in a structured classroom as they do with individual tutors. The students may feel embarrassed because of their lack of formal schooling or they may feel uncomfortable because they learn more slowly than the other students in the class. Volunteer tutors reduce these problems because they are able to work with the students individually and at each student's pace. Inmate volunteers who tutor other inmates contribute a great service to other prisoners. The tutors, too, benefit; teaching others to read and write is a satisfying accomplishment. Prisons offer few organized, formal opportunities for such experiences. Volunteers simply create their own.

Some highly literate inmates volunteer to help other inmates with their legal problems.

Such volunteers screen a large volume of their fellow inmates' requests for legal assistance. After determining which issues are most urgent, the volunteers work on sentence computation problems, assist other inmates in gathering their legal papers (for example, transcripts of trial), help prepare appeal documents, work on detainers, and instruct their peers on how to become more literate with legal issues.

As these examples show, inmate volunteers have a role in providing maintenance and emergency services to neighboring communities. They contribute to their own institutions, too, by working on suicide-watch patrols, providing tutoring services, and helping their fellow inmates with legal issues. Still another area in which inmate volunteers have been helpful has been in working with adolescents and juvenile delinquency.

One of the more popular programs, Scared Straight, was formed by volunteer prisoners at the Rahway prison in New Jersey. The volunteers call themselves the Lifer's Group. The group strives to eliminate the myths and romance of prisons by terrifying potential young criminals with tales of prison rape, physical brutality, and the mental torture of captivity.

Another project inmate volunteers at USP Atlanta operate is called Slow Down. Slow Down differs from the Scared Straight program in that it does not endeavor to scare adolescents. Instead, it helps them to understand the ramifications of crime. Through testimonials, the volunteers discuss their experiences with crime and the criminal justice system. They detail the impact their decisions have had on them, on their families, and on the community. Volunteers from Atlanta's federal prison camp attend local schools and other institutions to spread the Slow Down message. The Slow Down program boosts the self-esteem of the participants by allowing them to play a positive role in the community. It also encourages young citizens to pursue alternatives to crime.

Another way prison volunteer programs benefit local communities is by raising money and giving it to causes the volunteers deem worthy. At the U.S. penitentiary in Terre Haute, Indiana, inmates sold T-shirts and beverages at a motorcycle show they sponsored. The event helped the volunteers raise enough money to donate one thousand dollars to Terre Haute's Hamilton Center Prenatal Unit. At the federal correctional institution in McKean County, Pennsylvania, inmate volunteers operate a store unique to federal prisons. The Inmate Benefit Fund sells clothing and other specialty items to the inmate population. In its effort to boost the local economy, the fund sells only products that come from within a fifty-mile radius of the prison. Profits raised from the sales are used to fund educational projects inside the prison. The fund has also donated over fifty thousand dollars to local charities since the program began in 1989. Inmates at the McKean prison also have volunteered to work with the YWCA on projects aimed at helping battered women living in McKean County.

As this discussion demonstrates, inmate volunteer programs provide needed services to the communities inside and outside of prison walls. Like volunteer work outside prison, volunteering inside improves the prison community. As one inmate volunteer said, the projects give prisoners opportunities to develop a sense of brotherhood and enable them to contribute to the lives of others.

Michael G. Santos

Bibliography

Boudin, K. (1993). Participatory literacy education behind bars: AIDS opens the door. *Harvard Educational Review* 63(2): 207–32.

Hendricks, T. (1992). Shock, it works! *The Conservationist* 7(2): 44.

McDonald, D. C. (1986). *Punishment without Walls*. New Brunswick, N.J.: Rutgers University Press.

Federal Bureau of Prisons (1992). *State of the Bureau 1992*. Sandstone, Minn.: U.S. Department of Justice.

Federal Prison System (1979). *The Development of the Federal Prison System*. Leavenworth, Kans.: U.S. Department of Justice.

Wheller, W. L. (1993). Gentle gestures. *Corrections Today* 55(5): 136, 139.

Walla Walla, Washington State Penitentiary

The Washington State Penitentiary (WSP) was the first and is the largest of the fourteen prisons in the Washington State Department of Corrections. It is located in southeastern Washington in the city of Walla Walla on approximately 580 acres of land. There are 553 security staff, 293 support staff, and 33 persons employed by the Division of Correctional Industries, bringing the total employment for WSP to just under 900. The annual payroll for the penitentiary for the fiscal year ending 30 June 1994 was almost thirty-five million dollars, including salary and benefits. The current superintendent of the penitentiary, Tana Wood, is the first woman to head this adult men's correctional facility.

The Washington State Penitentiary occupies a central place in the early sociological literature on prisons. Indeed, much of the formative empirical research on prisons conducted by scholars like Clarence Schrag (1950), Donald Garrity (1956), Stanton Wheeler (1958), and Peter Garabedian (1959) took place at the University of Washington and involved the WSP. Subsequently, the tumultuous period experienced by the penitentiary during the 1970s was described and analyzed in books such as Ethan Hoffman and John McCoy's (1981) *Concrete Mama,* Charles Stastny and Gabrielle Tyrnauer's (1982) *Who Rules the Joint?* and Inez Cardozo-Freeman's (1984) *The Joint.* Most recently, the Washington State Penitentiary has been the basis for a series of studies investigating the economic and social impact of major correctional facilities upon their host communities.

At present, WSP houses approximately twenty-three hundred inmates within four sub-facilities. These subfacilities divide the penitentiary into four separate prisons, representing different inmate classification levels. The department is currently making the transition to a "case management" model, which seeks to identify an individual inmate's needs when the person enters the system, and to allocate departmental resources to meet those needs as the inmate progresses toward release or long-term incarceration.

The Washington State Penitentiary was the first prison built in the state of Washington, and it is one of the oldest prisons in the Pacific Northwest. In the 1860s, following the Civil War, the territory of Washington was faced with growth, as were all of the western territories. Experiencing both an increase in crime and the first pangs of yearning for statehood, territorial residents were becoming self-conscious about their image. Vigilante justice was increasingly unacceptable as civilization crept in, but resources were scarce. Keeping long-term prisoners in county jails was impractical and often dangerous.

The sheriffs of Thurston and Pierce counties approached the territorial legislature with the proposal that they provide a prison for the region's criminals, in exchange for a subsistence fee and the right to the wages of conscripted labor. Located somewhere between the towns of Seattle and Tacoma in a community called Seatco, the sheriffs profited well by cutting the rations of the prisoners and subjecting their charges to a host of substandard living conditions. It was not long before tales of torture and neglect found their way to area newspapers. Reportedly, the sheriffs pocketed the subsistence allowance and materials that had been supplied by the territory and intended for the inmates.

Rail-killed stock and game (often in an advanced stage of decomposition) were common fare for meals. The inmates were provided with one set of clothing, which frequently became reduced to little more than rags.

The keepers of the Seatco prison maintained discipline with corporal punishment and torture. Solitary confinement was rarely used, as it kept the inmate from working and reduced the sheriff's income. Instead, tactics such as the "water treatment"—a pitcher of cold water held high above the restrained inmate and poured directly into his open mouth—were used to punish misconduct such as speaking out of turn. The near-drowning experience would be repeated until several episodes of unconsciousness were achieved. Evidently, this practice achieved the desired contrition, while not preventing the inmate from working.

The city fathers of Walla Walla realized that statehood and the Enabling Act might mean competitive institutions that would force their struggling new enterprises, a hospital, and a college into oblivion. For that reason, they planned and carried out their intentions to secure a prison for Walla Walla—an act that would successfully preclude the siting of a large state hospital or university when statehood came. Stories persist to this day that Walla Walla had a choice of institutions and that city leaders made the "mistake" of choosing a prison over a large state university. Not so. A prison was specifically targeted, solicited, and lobbied for, to the extent that part of the cost of siting the original facility was assumed by the city.

The scandals of the "Seatco Dungeon" detailed above provided the final impetus to relocating the territorial prison, and the Walla Walla lobbyists succeeded in winning it with offers of donated land and community support. Construction began on the prison in September of 1886, and the first inmate arrived in May of 1887. By the turn of the century, the penitentiary held a total of 400 to 450 inmates. The penitentiary's first superintendent was F. W. Paine, who served from May of 1887 to April of 1893.

Although located on the outskirts of the city and enclosed by massive stone walls (constructed of basalt rock from the nearby Columbia River), the penitentiary would come into the public eye from time to time throughout its history—quite often for negative reasons. To quote a document prepared by the Washington State Department of Corrections in the 1960s, "As late as 1930, the National Society of Penal Information criticized 'the overcrowding, the lack of industries and the rigid and repressive discipline' at the Washington State Penitentiary, adding that 'in few prisons in the nation is the overcrowding more serious and in none of them is less done to reduce the evils inherent in such a condition.'"

There were, however, periods of reform and progress interspersed within the penitentiary's early years. One of the most significant was the tenure of Charles Reed (the tenth of the twenty-eight men and one woman who have served as superintendents), who administered the prison between 1907 and 1913 and became well known for his progressive attitude. He abolished the striped convict uniforms that were common for the period and attempted to address the evils of inmate idleness and overcrowding. But Reed's reformist tendencies appear to have been the exception, rather than the rule, during the prison's first half century.

The 1920s brought serious unrest, in large part because of overcrowding and the lack of meaningful work. Riots broke out, and, in one incident, destroyed a significant portion of the prison. Although public attention to these troubles of the penitentiary forced temporary relief, violence would revisit in 1934 on Lincoln's birthday. In an escape attempt gone awry, inmates took hostages. As they attempted to make their way out, the order to cut them down with machine guns was given. Seven inmates and one officer died.

The 1940s were a relatively quiet time at the penitentiary, as it was in prisons across the country. WSP was actually deeply involved in the war effort, sponsoring various forms of public entertainment such as boxing matches, smokers, plays, skits and talent shows, and selling war bonds and war stamps. This practice of providing entertainment within the institution for the local community continued well into the 1960s.

With the end of the war, the fragile equilibrium that had prevailed within WSP was undone, and major prison disturbances took place in 1953 and 1955. The riot of 1955 was particularly noteworthy, in that nearly all of the prison was lost to inmate rioters. There were many hostages, and prison staff were relegated to the almost medieval role of laying siege to a nearly impenetrable castle. The book *The Riot* (Elli 1967), written by an inmate who participated in this disturbance, provides a graphic account of the events, relating how prisoners tried to escape during the siege by tunneling out of the prison theater, and describing how inmates modeled the official roles of their keepers—even to the point of conducting mock counts and enforcing discipline among their peers.

A negotiated end to the 1955 riot was achieved by guaranteeing the ringleaders that they would not be placed in the infamous One Wing, commonly known as the "Growler" (a term referring to the noise made by hungry stomachs that endured a stay there). That portion of the prison was deeply hated by inmates. It was the original cell block, which had not undergone any improvements since it was constructed in 1886, and it still retained extremely small cells with no ventilation, no water, and with "honeybuckets" for toilets. As a condition to ending the riot, the inmate leaders demanded that they not be made to suffer confinement in One Wing.

Following their surrender, Superintendent Lawrence Delmore, Jr., kept his word and had the inmates shipped to the Yakima County Jail, where they were held until a newer cell wing could be renovated to accommodate them. They were then returned to these modified segregation quarters, where they remained for the duration of their disciplinary time.

In February of 1957, Bobby (B. J.) Rhay was appointed superintendent of the Penitentiary, a position that he would hold for two decades. At the time of his appointment, Rhay was the youngest prison superintendent in the nation, and, at the time of his retirement twenty years later, he had served the longest single tenure of any superintendent in the country (Stastny and Tyrnauer 1982, 83). Rhay was "a tough-talking, con-wise Walla Walla native" (Hoffman and McCoy 1981, 5) who himself used firearms on escaping inmates on at least one occasion. Rhay's early administration brought about a stabilizing of conditions within the penitentiary, capitalizing effectively upon "the warden's image as a strong and fearless personality who could mete out punishment as well as mercy" (Camp and Camp 1988, 58).

Between 1963 and 1968, Dr. C. Alvin Paulsen of the University of Washington conducted X-ray experiments on a number of WSP inmates, seeking to determine the relationship between exposure to radiation and sterility. The sixty-four inmates who volunteered for these experiments suffered massive doses of radiation to the testicles and received only a small stipend in return. These experiments later became the source of controversy, as the federal government (the source of funding for the research) failed to publicly acknowledge the dangerousness of the study until the mid 1970s.

The late 1960s and 1970s marked a unique period in the history of the penitentiary, as conditions within the institution changed dramatically. Consistent with the humanitarian philosophies of that period, both within and outside the field of corrections, dramatic reforms were initiated under the leadership of Dr. William Conte and implemented in the Washington State Penitentiary—with mixed results. As a consequence, from the early 1970s to the early 1980s, the Washington State Penitentiary came to be seen in many circles as one of the most progressive and permissive prisons in the country. That image was fostered in part by a photodocumentary that appeared in an issue of *Life* magazine in the late 1970s. It was regarded by others as one of the toughest and most dangerous prisons in the nation. In reality, both views were probably correct.

In fact, the Washington State Penitentiary at this time was a virtual microcosm of events and attitudes in society generally. Freed of many of the restrictions that had been part of basic WSP operating procedure before Conte's reforms, inmates enjoyed a remarkable amount of freedom (Hoffman and McCoy 1981). For example, at any point in the day or evening, hundreds of inmates, groomed to their own personal taste, were likely to be found outside in the prison's Big Yard, doing pretty much as they pleased. Motorcycles built and ridden by the members of the prison's Bikers' Club roared around the prison's main recreation area. Officers were expected to take members of the prison's powerful "Lifers With Hope Club" out of the prison—with no restraints, and in civilian clothes—to their homes or to local restaurants, for a meal and outing. Hundreds of volunteers from local colleges and the community more generally had free access to and liberal contact with the prison's inmates in the Social Therapy Program. Marijuana was openly smoked in "People's Park." And babies were conceived in the prison's infamous visitation area. In many ways, "the Washington State Penitentiary in Walla Walla in 1972 [and for the remainder of the decade] looked more like a college campus from the mid-sixties than a prison" (Tyrnauer 1981, 37).

But these freedoms did not come without a price, and, for WSP, that price was disorder, conflict, and violence. At that time, the following incidents were recorded:

1. The taking of thirteen hostages, two were stabbed in December of 1974
2. A riot on Easter Sunday in 1977 that did major damage to the prison chapel and store
3. The fatal wounding of an officer by an exploding pipe bomb in August of 1978
4. A spectacular (but unsuccessful) escape attempt in December of 1978, in which a number of inmates sought to gain their freedom via a tunnel extending from Lifer's Park to a point beyond the West Wall, only to be turned back by a hail of gunfire from correctional officers who had been tipped off and were awaiting the escapees
5. The fatal stabbing of an officer caught in a conflict between inmates from feuding racial cliques in June of 1979.

The pervasive threat of violence within the institution during the period was demonstrated by the fact that there were three murders in the 1960s and twenty-five in the 1970s (Hoffman and McCoy 1981, 6).

As a result of these conditions, staff morale was exceedingly low and conflict between staff and turnover among employees were extremely high. The resignation rate among officers at the time was reported as high as 70 percent (Stastny and Tyrnauer 1982, 103), and five different people served as superintendent between the time of Rhay's retirement in 1977 and the appointment of Larry Kincheloe in May of 1982. As powerfully summarized by two commentators, "In the space of a decade, WSP's national image had plummeted from that of the best of maximum-security prisons to one of the worst" (Stastny and Tyrnauer 1982, 4).

In June of 1979 the turmoil and violence within the penitentiary led Superintendent James Spalding to lock down the entire institution for a period of 129 days. This began the process whereby the prison was "taken back," and order and security were reestablished. The process was not easy. Spalding dismissed close to fifty correctional officers in the latter months of 1979 for brutality and insubordination. In May of 1980, a U.S. district court judge ruled that "the totality of conditions at Walla Walla is cruel and unusual punishment beyond any reasonable doubt" (Stastny and Tyrnauer 1982, 112–13). An inmate riot in September of 1981 caused over two million dollars worth of damage to the prison's kitchen and dining area. Slowly, however, the prison returned to relative calm by the 1990s.

With only 1,380 inmates in 1988, the state was renting vacant cell space to other state correctional systems. At least partly because of the passage of the Sentence Reform Act in 1984, which had the effect of standardizing and "toughening" criminal sentencing in Washington, the size of the inmate population in the penitentiary steadily increased. Surplus space diminished as the population reached 2,482 inmates in March of 1993. And, although the state has embarked upon an aggressive program of prison renovation and new construction, the Washington State Penitentiary remains "the end of the line" in the state's criminal justice system. The facility houses increasing numbers of violent and habitual offenders, $3^{1}/_2$ percent of whom are serving sentences of life without the possibility of parole and $17^{1}/_2$ percent of whom have been convicted of committing first-degree murder. The state has also passed a new "Three-Strikes-and-You're-Out" law that specifies mandatory life imprisonment for all offenders convicted of three felony offenses.

Most recently, the Washington State Penitentiary was the source of considerable public attention. It was the site, at one minute past midnight on 5 January 1993, of the hanging of child sex abuser and murderer, Westley Allan Dodd—the first execution in the state of Washington in thirty years and the first judicial hanging in the nation since 1965. Dodd's case piqued national interest because he aggressively pursued his own execution and demanded that it be by hanging as opposed to lethal injection (the two means of execution specified by the administrative code of the state of Washington). There are currently ten inmates on death row at the penitentiary. One of them, Charles Rodman Campbell, has just lost a lengthy appeal that argued that being forced to make the choice between dying by hanging or by lethal injection represented a fundamental violation of his personal religious principles.

At present, the Main Institution at WSP serves as an example of an early territorial prison that has been successfully converted into a twentieth-century penitentiary. Behind the original one-hundred-year-old stone wall that still separates the inmates from the world beyond, lies a newly renovated, thoroughly modern prison—the product of over sixty million dollars worth of structural improvements since the early 1980s. And, almost ironically, the Washington State Penitentiary, once infamous for its own violence and intolerable conditions, now finds itself a model for other prison systems.

Richard Morgan
Keith Farrington

Bibliography

Camp, C., and G. M. Camp (1988). *Management Strategies for Combatting Prison Gang Violence. Part II. Combatting Violent Inmate Organizations at the Washington State Penitentiary at Walla Walla: A Case Study.* Washington, D.C.: National Institute of Justice.

Cardozo-Freeman, I. (1984). *The Joint: Language and Culture in a Maximum Security Prison.* Springfield, Ill.: Charles C. Thomas.

Elli, F. (1967). *The Riot.* New York: Coward-McCann.

Farrington, K., and R. P. Parcells (1991). Correctional facilities and community crime rates: Alternative hypotheses and competing explanations. *Humboldt Journal of Social Relations* 17: 17–127.

Hoffman, E., and J. McCoy (1981). *Concrete Mama: Prison Profiles from Walla Walla.* Columbia: University of Missouri Press.

Parcells, R. P., and K. Farrington (1988). Walla Walla, Walla Walla County and the Washington State Penitentiary. In R. M. Lidman, M. E. Poole, and P. A. Roper, eds. *Impacts of Washington State's Correctional Institutions on Communities.* Olympia, Wash.: Washington State Institute for Public Policy.

Stastny, C. I., and G. Tyrnauer (1982). *Who Rules the Joint? The Changing Political Culture of Maximum Security Prisons in America.* Lexington, Mass.: Lexington.

Tyrnauer, G. (1981). What went wrong at Walla Walla. *Corrections Magazine* 6: 37–41.

Tyrnauer-Stastny, G., and C. I. Stastny (1977). The changing political culture of a total institution: The case of Walla Walla. *Prison Journal* 57: 43–55.

Walnut Street Jail

In 1682, William Penn and the Society of Friends produced *The Great Law* for the Commonwealth of Pennsylvania. It embodied the humanitarian principles of the Quakers, sharply differentiating their criminal code from the codes of other colonies. This document called for the recognition of man as a rational, spiritual human being. The Quakers dissented from the English and Puritan beliefs in the need for corporal punishment and the death penalty for many offenses. Their milder representation of justice called for a new American system of reformative discipline. The Walnut Street Jail, commissioned in 1773 by the city fathers of Philadelphia, challenged the old order to recognize man's inhumanity to man and to embrace a benevolent penal philosophy. Throughout its relatively short history, from 1773 to 1835, the jail bore witness to their belief in liberty of conscience and freedom of worship.

The Early Merger of Architectural Design and Penal Philosophy

Robert Smith, a prominent member of the Carpenter's Company, was contracted to design the original structure in 1771. It was a simple, quite ordinary building of rough-hewn stone, constructed to give an air of "solitude and fitness." The design reflected the fundamental Quaker belief in man's ability to reform himself through reflection and remorse. The jail was located at the intersection of Sixth and Walnut streets in Philadelphia. Its unimposing main entrance led into a passageway, through two iron-gated doors, to a hall with eight arched rooms. Two wings ran off the central building, each two stories tall, containing five rooms apiece overlooking a central courtyard.

The Walnut Street Jail was constructed in recognition of the need for a larger and more secure facility, in light of Philadelphia's growth and the parallel increase in crime. Despite the lofty principles of its founding, the new facility simply witnessed a transfer in 1776 of 105 felons, prisoners of war, Tories, and debtors from the old prison. With the American Revolution already underway, the partially completed jail's conditions quickly deteriorated. No systematic reform measures were visible, the prevailing policy at the time being simply to lock the prisoners away.

The Philadelphia Society for Assisting Distressed Prisoners was born in 1776 to address the squalid conditions and suffering. The society canvassed Philadelphia neighborhoods with a wheelbarrow emblazoned with the slogan "Victuals for the Prisoners" and empha-

Walnut Street Jail, Philadelphia, 1773–1835. Photo courtesy of the American Correctional Association.

sized the need for even distribution of charitable goods to avoid the perception of their bringing "a promiscuous feast" to the incarcerated.

A general amnesty was ordered in August of 1776 for all nontreasonous offenders throughout the commonwealth. The remaining population thus included only prisoners of war and capital offenders. In 1777 the British occupied the city, so the jail then housed American rebels. Destitution and starvation continued in the jail during this period.

The British left Philadelphia in 1778, and the jail reverted to control by the patriots and functioned as their military prison for the duration of the War of Independence. Shortly after the war, many American cities were in chaos. Hoodlums roved the streets and the authorities simply housed offenders with no separation by sex, age, race, or offense. The jail became a "promiscuous scene of unrestricted intercourse, universal riot, and debauchery."

The prevailing state attitude after the war endorsed "publically and disgracefully imposed punishment." The Philadelphia fathers, however, were in opposition to this philosophy and were deeply concerned with prison welfare. The Philadelphia Society for Alleviating the Miseries of Public Prisons, founded on 8 May 1787,

had a significant impact on the jail by reinstituting reformation as the primary function of punishment.

The society's work was directly affected by its reliance on the ideas of John Howard, internationally recognized prison reformer. Howard advocated construction of "penitentiary-houses" with individual cells in which the prisoners would work, sleep, and eat. Compatible with Quaker thinking, his conception of solitary confinement was that it promoted introspection and consequent reformation.

Legislative Intervention and the Creation of the World's First Penitentiary

Acts of the General Assembly of Pennsylvania, under the influence of the Philadelphia Prison Society (formerly the Philadelphia Society for Alleviating the Miseries of the Poor), called for reorganization of the jail and ushered in "the glorious decade of progressive penology from 1790–1799." The Act of 27 March 1789 designated the jail as a penitentiary house, harking back to William Penn's original thinking and invoking "a renaissance of judicial philosophy." Follow-up legislation of 5 April 1790 directed construction of a special cell block in the yard for solitary isolation at hard labor for the most serious offenders. The purpose was reformation through reflection and penitence. This cell block then actually became the first penitentiary in the world.

While the acts established the jail as the depository of the most serious offenders in the commonwealth, the legislation reflected the Prison Society's abhorrence of public punishment and belief in "punishment by more private or even solitary labor." The 1790 act instructed judges to sentence offenders whose actions would have previously made them subject to the death penalty (the only remaining capital offenses being premeditated murder and treason) to a period of solitary confinement not to exceed one-half or less than one-twelfth of their overall sentence. Records documenting the use of the cell block for that purpose indicate that fewer than 5 percent of the convicts were sentenced to solitary confinement. The block was used, however, as punishment for serious rule infractions within the prison.

The act of 1790 was the first American adoption of the principle of solitary confinement. The historical origins of the practice may be traced back to the age of Louis XIV, when penitents were secluded in separate cells for living and laboring. When engaged in public worship, these penitents would be placed in separate stalls to ensure their isolation from one another.

It is important to distinguish between the concepts of separation and solitary confinement. We have referred to the solitary confinement of prisoners at the jail in the context of individual punishment and isolation. The overall separation of inmates refers to the philosophical belief that all prisoners should be kept apart from one another—to avoid the failures of the congregate method—but it does not rule out contacts with other people such as ministers and educators.

Later Architectural Mergers with Penal Philosophy

The penitentiary's brick structure, built in 1790, comprised sixteen solitary cells of six by eight by nine feet. The cells confined a prisoner within two iron gratings. They were heated by a passageway stove, lighted by individual windows, and cleanable by stream water. The prisoner was provided a mattress and appropriate clothing and was fed a pudding of maize and molasses. At no time during his stay in solitary was the prisoner allowed out of his cell.

On 4 April 1796 the legislature moved to construct brick workshops to accommodate an increased labor pool. The workshops were built in the jail yard in 1797. In addition, the original two-story central building was adorned with a pediment and topped by a copper weather vane with a gilded key. The entire prison was surrounded by a twenty-foot wall with a wooden overhang designed to dissuade potential escapees from throwing hook and rope devices over the wall.

The jail satisfied the solitary confinement requirement with its sixteen single cells. A common misinterpretation in the literature, however, suggests that the 1790 legislation created the separate system—widely known as "the Pennsylvania system"—at the Walnut Street location. In fact, the inmates lived together in apartments and worked together in the sheds. The strict requirement of no communications was never actually met at the jail. The Pennsylvania system actually began with Eastern State Penitentiary.

Strategies Designed to Implement Legislative Directives

To implement the specific directives, personnel were hired who endorsed the new functional penology. The following changes were made: elimination of graft and preferential treatment; prohibition of alcohol and prostitution; segregation by sex, age, and offense; revamped diet; and guardianship of minors. Prisoners were encouraged to demonstrate successful rehabilitation through good conduct, in return for an early pardon from the governor and possible cancellation of fines. Inmates were also encouraged to inform on one another for violation of rules in return for a pardon, a practice that later added to the jail's demise.

Work Programs and "Keepers"

The legislation called for a "piece-price system" in which contracts were made for specific manufactured articles to be sold at wholesale prices. Tasks were assigned by sex and offense. Men were delegated to such jobs as beating hemp and picking moss. Women were confined to spinning cotton and yarn and to other domestic activities. Inmates were paid one dollar to one and a half dollars per day for skilled labor, from which costs of room, board, clothing, fines, and any equipment damage were deducted. Work began at sunrise in the workshops and ended at dusk when roll was taken and the inmates were returned to their apartments. Silence was then enforced.

Four unarmed male "keepers" acted as guards under the direction of a principal keeper. Elijah Weed was the initial main jailer until his death from yellow fever in 1793. His spouse, Mary Weed, succeeded him as the principal "jaileress" of 280 prisoners—an extraordinary occurrence that suggests that she was probably the first woman prison warden in America.

The inmates were assigned plain, functional prison uniforms, made entirely at the jail. Minor rule infractions resulted in food deprivation that day. Serious transgressions resulted in solitary confinement.

Religious, Educational, and Treatment Programs

To complement the productive labor, inmates were afforded religious and educational services. Religious reading was encouraged and Sunday worship was required. In 1798, a school was established inside the jail to attend to reading, writing, and arithmetic. Both the development of labor skills and educational benefits mirror the rehabilitative philosophy.

An infirmary was available and rounded out the benefits delivered to the prisoners; only pleasurable recreation was disallowed in the jail. While these goods and services were provided to those convicted of specific offenses, those incarcerated as debtors were not afforded these basics and were housed away from the regular inmate population. Further, the debtors were required to pay for their food and lodging. The condition of the debtors' apartment was reportedly pitiful, with frequent episodes of starvation.

Decline, Debauchery, Demoralization

In 1798, an arson destroyed the workshops in the prison yard. The destruction brought about disillusionment. The increased numbers of prisoners coupled with idleness because of the fire resulted in changing attitudes among prison management. Disciplinary problems rose with overcrowding, and escapes and violence increased. The number of destitute vagrants and debtors soared, as did the incidence of disease. Political turmoil created conflicts between Quakers and "common sense" prison board members. Clashes between inspectors and keepers became commonplace.

By 1815, the prison population had swelled to 378. By 1816, the number had risen to 433, a 55 percent increase from Mary Weed's day. Rising costs crippled the jail's budget, and an act of 3 March 1818 called for its sale. The classification system for housing inmates broke down. Violent assaults on keepers rose as inmates armed themselves. These changing conditions culminated in the rebellion of 27 March 1820. The situation was chaotic, as whites fought blacks and corrupt officials turned loose the entire population into the yard. Citizens shot prisoners and the militia was called out. Resolutions were passed after the riot to arm the guards and install alarm bells. Forty-five inmates were sent to solitary in irons, another setback for the previously noninvasive punishment policy.

Between 1820 and the abandonment of the jail in 1835, the failure continued. With no systematic classification system, housing again became integrated across sex, race, nationality, age, and offense categories. The penitentiary housed up to 464 inmates, two-thirds of whom were unemployed. The debtors' colony numbered 180. Low staff morale and the opportunity for corruption skyrocketed, as did disease and mortality.

The End of the Holy Experiment

On 5 October 1835 the state prisoners were removed to the Eastern State Penitentiary, with the remaining county inmates and those awaiting trial sent to the new county jail, Moyamensing, on 19 October. Both this new county facility as well as the new state penitentiary were actually built to follow the separate system philosophy, housing the inmates in individual cells and discouraging inmate interaction.

Evaluators of the Walnut Street Jail cite laziness and corruption for its decline. Nonetheless, the humanitarian aims of "the holy experiment" continue to be applauded, in recognition of human dignity and the rights of man.

Ruth-Ellen M. Grimes

See also PHILADELPHIA SOCIETY FOR ALLEVIATING THE MISERIES OF PUBLIC PRISONS; RUSH, BENJAMIN

Bibliography

Foulke, W. P. (1855). Remarks on the Penal System of Pennsylvania. *Pennsylvania Journal of Prison Discipline and Philanthropy* 10(2).

Irwin, J. (1985). *The Jail: Managing the Underclass in American Society.* Berkeley, Calif.: University of California Press.

Johnston, N. (1973). *A Brief History of Prison Architecture.* New York: Walker and Co.

Pigeon, H. D., et al. (1944). *Principles and Methods in Dealing with Offenders: A Manual for Pennsylvania Correctional and Penal Workers*. State College, Pa.: Pennsylvania Municipal Publications Service.

Takagi, P. (1975). The Walnut Street Jail: A penal reform to centralize the powers of the state. *Federal Probation* 39(4): 18–25.

Teeters, N. K. (1937). *They Were in Prison: A History of the Pennsylvania Prison Society, 1787–1937*. Philadelphia: John C. Winston.

Teeters, N. K. (1955). *The Cradle of the Penitentiary: The Walnut Street Jail at Philadelphia, 1773–1835*. Philadelphia: Pennsylvania Prison Society.

Wardens

Much research exists on the dynamics of prison life for inmates and guards. Early prison works identified the pains of imprisonment and the social order among the "society of captives" within American prisons. In contrast, only a handful of investigations have focused exclusively on the position at the top of the prison hierarchy, the prison warden. The position of warden is an executive or managerial role to which a person is appointed to serve. Historically, these appointments were made by the governor and tied to political favors and rewards. A 1957 study of prison wardens who held office in forty-three states over a fifty-year period (1906–1955) found that the lack of an experienced, professional pool of leaders and the cycle of political elections meant that wardens came and went quickly. Thirty-seven percent of the wardens served two years or less, and more than 60 percent were in office for less than five years. Some wardens came and went from the same job three and four times (Lunden 1957). In Missouri, no warden served more than four years in the period from 1880 to 1920, as they changed with each governor.

While wardens may still be appointed by the governor today, they are most likely to be recommended by the state Board of Corrections or top administrators within the Department of Corrections. For the most part, the position is apolitical, and it does not shift with elections. Wardens are likely to complete entire careers in the corrections system.

Characteristics of America's Prison Wardens

Findings from a national survey of the population of 512 adult prison wardens indicate that wardens' average age is 46.5 years. They have more than sixteen years of education, are predominantly (86 percent) white, have previous military experience (67 percent), and are responsible for the custody of an average of 862 adult inmates within their prisons (see Cullen et al. 1993a). As for juvenile wardens and superintendents, a national survey of all 448 wardens reveals the following profile: average age, forty-five years; percentage white, 78 percent; percentage male, 79 percent; years of education, seventeen; years of correctional experience, seventeen; previous military experience, 29 percent; average number of supervised detainees, 117 youths (see Caeti et al. 1994). One study found that in earlier years all wardens in Illinois had risen through the ranks from the position of correctional officer. Ten years later, few if any of the wardens had followed that career path (Bartollas and Miller 1978).

The Changing Role of Prison Wardens

In the past, prison wardens held ultimate decision-making power in the operation of the penitentiary. The traditional bureaucratic structure of prisons ensured wardens the authority to hire, fire, oversee budgets, and discipline inmates. In the classic study on Stateville prison in Illinois, Jacobs (1977, 29) describes the degree of control exerted by Joseph Ragen, a powerful warden for almost thirty years: "The old boss devoted his life to perfecting the world's most orderly prison regime. He exercised personal control over every detail, no matter how insignificant. He tolerated challenges neither by inmates nor by employees nor by outside interest groups. He cultivated an image that made him invincible to his subordinates as well as to the prisoners."

Prior to the 1960s, prison wardens enjoyed autonomy to run "their prisons" as they deemed appropriate. That is, wardens were typically immune from outside inquiry into the operation of their institutions. Moreover, inmates and staff alike were mandated to adhere to the regime of the all powerful warden.

Today, however, the traditional powers afforded prison wardens have eroded. Wardens today must contend with inmate unions, employee labor unions, prisoners' rights (that is, litigation and prisoner grievances), and judicial intervention scrutinizing the daily operations of the prison. In Texas, for example, inmate litigation (from the *Ruiz* case) led the federal district court to order changes in working and living conditions. Additional court decisions have ordered states to alter classification and disciplinary practices and reduce overcrowding. In this changing climate, wardens no longer can employ an autocratic method of leadership within the prison.

The Institutional Impact of Prison Wardens

Although the nature of a warden's authority has changed over the past several decades, the warden continues to define the correctional "agenda" within prisons. John DiIulio's work on prison wardens (1987, 1991) suggests that wardens' managerial style continues to be the most important factor shaping institutional safety, order, cleanliness, and services to inmates. Thus, wardens remain capable of greatly influencing the nature of their prisons.

Recently, researchers have assessed prison wardens' attitudes toward their occupation and toward the inmates. Studies indicate that prison wardens are concerned primarily with one dominant role—custody. That is, custody and control of the institution take precedence over competing roles such as providing services to inmates and advocating rehabilitation programs. In the end, the warden's job security depends upon successful control of the institution. Escapes, riots, sit-ins, and extreme episodes of violence threaten the tenure of wardens.

Despite the emphasis on custody, studies have examined wardens' job satisfaction and found wardens to be satisfied with their careers as correctional leaders (see Cullen et al. 1993b). Additionally, investigations of wardens' attitudes toward the use of rehabilitation for inmates reveal that treatment programs are supported by most wardens (Cullen et al. 1993a). Contrary to the assumption that wardens desire only punishment for inmates, they do realize the merits of correctional rehabilitation. Future research on prison wardens must address the ability of wardens to adapt to an ever-changing criminal justice community, while maintaining control of the prison facility.

Velmer S. Burton, Jr.
Tory J. Caeti
Craig T. Hemmons

Bibliography

Bartollas, C., and S. Miller (1978). *Correctional Administration: Theory and Practice*. New York: McGraw-Hill.

Caeti, T., C. Hemmons, V. S. Burton, Jr., and F. T. Cullen (1994). An occupational study of juvenile prison wardens and directors. Working paper #2. Huntsville, Tex.: Criminal Justice Center Press.

Cullen, F. T., E. J. Latessa, V. S. Burton, Jr., and L. X. Lombardo (1993a). The correctional orientation of prison wardens: Is the rehabilitative ideal supported? *Criminology* 31: 69–92.

Cullen, F. T., E. J. Latessa, R. Kopache, L. X. Lombardo, and V. S. Burton, Jr. (1993b). Prison wardens' job satisfaction. *Prison Journal* 73: 141–61.

DiIulio, J. J., Jr. (1987). *Governing Prisons: A Comparative Study of Correctional Management*. New York: Free Press.

DiIulio, J. J., Jr. (1991). *No Escape: The Future of American Corrections*. New York: Basic Books.

Jacobs, J. (1977). *Stateville: The Penitentiary in Mass Society*. Chicago: University of Chicago Press.

Lunden, W. (1957). The tenure and turnover of state prison wardens. *American Journal of Corrections*, Nov./Dec.: 14–15, 33, 34.

Enoch Cobb Wines (1806–1879)

Enoch Wines was born in Hanover, New Jersey, on 17 February 1806, and spent his youth on a farm near Shoreham, Vermont. He received his A.B. degree from Middlebury College in 1827, and his A.M. degree from the same school in 1830. He was awarded an honorary D.D. degree from Middlebury College in 1853 and the LL.D. degree from Washington (Pennsylvania) College in 1857.

Known for his optimism, superior organizational ability, and delicate sensibility, Enoch Wines had an early educational career, and a midlife career as a Christian minister and college professor. The last quarter of his life was dedicated to the directing and energizing of the prison reform movement.

Upon his college graduation in 1827, Wines became principal of St. Albans (Vermont) Academy. There he experimented with the development of a classical school. In 1829, he became the schoolmaster of midshipmen aboard the U.S. frigate *Constellation*, where he taught mathematics.

He resigned from teaching and married Emma Stansbury in 1832. Seven sons were born from that union, one of whom, Frederick Howard Wines, like his father, became well known as a correctional theorist, prison reformer, and Presbyterian minister. Shortly after his marriage, Enoch Wines purchased Edgehill Seminary in Princeton, New Jersey, which he ran after the pattern of the German gymnasia. Edgehill Seminary proved to be unsuccessful financially, so in 1838 Wines moved to Philadelphia, where he became the professor of languages at Central High School. He taught at Central High School until 1844, when he purchased a classical school in Burlington, New Jersey. When the school in Burlington developed fiscal instability, Wines left it in 1848 and concentrated upon the study of theology.

Enoch Wines became a licensed Congregational minister in 1849. He served pastorates in Vermont, New York, and Pennsylvania. Concurrent with his last pastorate, 1853 to 1859, Wines served as chair of ancient languages at Washington (Pennsylvania) College. Moving into his final academic position, Wines became the president of the City University of St. Louis in 1859. The university was closed in 1862 because of the outbreak of the American Civil War, and Wines left education to devote full time to the prison reform movement.

Enoch Wines died in Cambridge, Massachusetts, on 10 December 1879. He lived most of his life during the "penitentiary era," yet he helped usher in the "reformatory era," which began on paper in 1870 with the Cincinnati Declaration of Principles and with bricks and programs in 1876. Wines had his mind in both eras, his heart in the new.

The writings of Enoch Wines trace the chronology of interests he displayed during the course of his life. For example, in his early educational career, he published several tracts, "Hints on Popular Education" (1838) and "How Shall I Govern My School?" (1838); and he edited the *American Journal of Education* for a time in the 1840s. *Two Years and a Half in the Navy,* a critique of shipboard education, was published in 1832. His theological training and the beginning of his interest in criminal justice is portrayed in his *Commentaries on the Laws of the Ancient Hebrews; with an Introductory Essay on Civil Society and Government* (1853), suggesting a Biblical origin of the major principles of civil liberty, legal codes, and democratic government. Wines' concepts of the importance of the religious training of inmates is illustrated in his next work, *The True Penitent Portrayed: A Doctrine of Repentance* (1864). With his last two works, *The Actual State of Prison Reform* (1878) and *The State of Prisons and of Child-Saving Institutions in the Civilized World* (1880), the latter published posthumously, we find Wines doing what he did best, that is, advocating correctional reform.

Enoch Wines made many important contributions to the development of correctional philosophy and management. In his thinking, he wed the disciplines of religion, education, and penology in a holistic management and reform model. He believed that the sources of inmate reform were labor, education, and religion. He stated that religion is the most powerful of the reformatory agencies because of its impact upon the human mind.

Wines favored moral control over physical control as penal policy, a philosophy of reformation rather than a doctrine of punishment. He believed that neither severity nor regularity of punishment would correct behavior, but that they would tend to turn the receiver of that punishment from reform. Rather, personal interest shown in the inmate, the building of self-respect, and an attempt to correct would attain better results toward reform. Wines felt that the purpose of a prison should be the reformation of the prisoner.

He suggested the mark system (Irish system) as a basis for the progressive classification of prisoners, favored reductions in sentences based upon good behavior, and worked toward the adoption of indeterminate sentencing. Wines encouraged the centralization of management (statewide) for prison systems, which he felt should include a grading of prisons and classification of inmates. He was global in his thinking, feeling that all persons of good will should join in a plan for the ideal prison system. He believed that intergovernmental collaboration would lend support and influence to the reform movement.

Enoch Wines was strongly opposed to maintaining prisoners in idleness. He believed that the major causes of crime were intemperance in alcohol consumption and the wretched (or the lack of a) home life in cities. His favored treatments for juveniles were religious and elementary education, removal to new scenes that were free of impure influences, agricultural employment, moral training, and supervision by parentlike figures in a familylike setting.

Along with Theodore Dwight, Franklin Sanborn, and Zebulon Brockway, Wines believed that the Irish system was the best prison model known to contemporary penologists, and that it could be adapted to fit American prisons. The Irish system was copied by the above-mentioned reformers in the creation of the New York State Reformatory at Elmira, in 1876, under the leadership of Zebulon Brockway.

In 1865, Enoch Wines and Theodore Dwight did a survey (and tour of inspection) of American prisons. A monumental report followed that was presented to the state of New York at its constitutional convention in 1867. Prison issues had come to the public's attention after the Civil War for two reasons: First, the increased commitments during that era led to prison overcrowding, and second, free workers began to become concerned over competition with prison labor. In the conclusion of their study, Wines and Dwight lamented that no state prison existed in which convict reform was considered the major policy goal. Wines made annual reports to the New York State legislature each year thereafter, and these reports stimulated a widespread reform movement.

Enoch Wines was connected with many correctional institutions and projects between 1862 and 1879. He became secretary of the New York Prison Association in 1862 and served in that position until his death in 1879. He revived the organization financially through appeals to churches and state and local governments.

Wines was possibly the leading figure in the formation of the National Prison Association (later called the American Prison Association and still later the American Correctional Association). He called the first national prison congress together and directed its meeting in 1870. That meeting resulted in the Cincinnati Declaration of Principles (principles that contain many of his thoughts) and the creation of the National Prison Association. He was elected the first president of the National Prison Association and served as secretary of that organization from 1870 to 1879.

As the secretary of each of the National Prison Congresses (meetings that took place in 1870, 1872, 1874, and 1876) Wines helped organize and actively direct reform. In 1941, the congress was renamed the Annual Congress of Correction.

In 1871, Wines served in two additional capacities. He first was appointed as one of three commissioners by the state of New York to study the relationship between prison labor and free labor. Secondly, under his influence, the

United States Congress made a joint resolution that created a U.S. commissioner to gather the countries of the world to an international prison reform congress. As a result, Wines was appointed by President Grant to that position and sent to Europe to arrange for an international prison congress. He called approximately twenty nations together in London for the International Penitentiary Congress in 1872. Wines had designed this congress to be inspirational in intent, thus the ninety agenda topics were not acted upon by resolution but rather carried by the commissioners for consideration in their respective countries. This congress, under Wines's leadership, did however create the International Penitentiary Commission (later known as the International Penal and Penitentiary Commission), which was a permanent organization intended to foster intergovernmental cooperation. Wines chaired this commission in 1874, 1875, and in 1877. After World War II, the tasks of the IPPC were assumed by the United Nations.

Made honorary president of the Second International Congress of Prisons, Stockholm, Sweden, in 1878, Wines was unable to attend because of poor health. He died shortly thereafter. His son, Frederick Howard Wines, was the Illinois delegate at this meeting.

Enoch Cobb Wines is remembered today as the guiding light of the dynamic reformatory movement of the 1860s and 1870s. He is counted as one of the three major actors in penology in the late nineteenth century, the others being Zebulon Reed Brockway and Franklin Benjamin Sanborn.

Also remembered for his success in founding the forerunner of the American Correctional Association (the leader in correctional reform, standards, and accreditation), Wines set precedents in the formulation of correctional standards. In 1982 the ACA reformulated and restated the Declaration of Principles, the ideas and objectives underlying the practice of corrections. The thoughts and life of Enoch Cobb Wines are echoed in this current Declaration of Principles.

Edward J. Schauer

Bibliography

Barnes, H. E., and Teeters, N. K. (1943). *New Horizons in Criminology*. New York: Prentice-Hall.

Bentham, J., and Wines, E. C. (1991). Jeremy Bentham and Enoch Wines discuss the privatization of corrections. *Journal of Contemporary Criminal Justice* 7: 60–68.

Clear, T. R., and Cole, G. F. (1994). *American Corrections*, 3rd ed. Belmont, Calif.: Wadsworth.

Eriksson, T. (1976). *The Reformers: An Historical Survey of Pioneer Experiments in the Treatment of Criminals*. New York: Elsevier.

Malone, D. (1936). *Dictionary of American Biography*. New York: Charles Scribner's Sons.

Wines, E. C., and Dwight, T. W. (1867). *Report on the Prisons and Reformatories of the United States and Canada*. Albany, N.Y.: Van Benthuysen and Sons' Steam Printing House.

Wines, F. H. (1919). *Punishment and Reformation*. New York: Crowell.

Women Inmates

I. History

Historically, women have rarely been sentenced to prison or jail. In 1850, for instance, women constituted only 3.6 percent of the total number of prisoners in thirty-four states (Freedman 1981). In the earliest decades of this country (in the 1600s to the 1700s), there was no classification by sex. Housed together with men in jails, women and children who had no other financial resources sold sexual favors for better living conditions or were sexually abused by other prisoners and keepers. Jails were used only to house debtors and those awaiting punishment. Most jails were run by a keeper and his wife and the prisoners housed there paid for their food and other necessities. Those who could not afford to pay lived in abysmal conditions. There is very little research on female prisoners in the jails of the 1700s. Basically all we know is that there were very few of them and that they were considered not worthy of sympathy.

Eventually, women were housed in separate wings or rooms in facilities for men but were still guarded by male warders. The crimes for which they were imprisoned ranged from murder to public order offenses, typically prostitution. Elizabeth Fry's description of Newgate in England probably accurately described this country's prisons as well. Writing in 1813, she described the "filth, the closeness of the rooms, the furious manner and expressions of the women towards each other, and the abandoned wickedness . . ." (cited in Dobash et al. 1986). Her admonitions to separate women and have women matrons supervise them in such endeavors as education, domestic training, and Bible study eventually had some influence over what occurred in the United States.

Some of the facilities for women had atrocious sanitation and recreational opportunities. For instance, in Auburn prison (New York), the women were housed in one room over the administration building, never allowed out, and had their food brought to them and waste removed once a day (Rafter 1985). The general theme of the time was that women who were deviant enough to be incarcerated were beyond redemption. Society needed to be protected from them, and they were unworthy of sympathy or care. Male warders forced women prisoners to prostitute themselves, and this sexual mistreatment led moral reformers like Sarah Doremus, Abby Hopper Gibbons, and Dorothea Dix to question the practice of men guarding women and the conditions in which female prisoners were kept. The first step was to convince institutions to hire women to guard female prisoners. Maryland hired a female jail keeper in 1822. Connecticut hired a woman to run the prison section for females in 1827, and in 1828 women were hired to run the separate building for female offenders in Ossining, New York. Elizabeth Farnham may be the best known of these women administrators. Hired in 1844 to manage Mt. Pleasant (Ossining), she brought in such refinements as a piano and instituted classes and Bible readings. This liberal view of reform led to her removal after only two years.

The reformers who championed the cause of separate institutions and female matrons to supervise female prisoners should not be confused with suffragettes or equal rights advocates. The argument used to pressure state legislatures to build such institutions was that women were different from and, indeed, morally superior to men. The reformers who ended up as administrators were not feminists in the traditional sense, since they believed in "separate spheres" of influence. The sphere of womanhood included prisons for women but led to those institutions being managed in such a way that the female prisoners were treated like children. The prison was a family with the warden as head mother supplemented by a staff of "matrons."

Private "houses of refuge" were created throughout the 1800s (for example, in New York City in 1825) that sought to reform prostitutes and other offenders through religion, education, discipline, reading, and sewing (Freedman 1981). These facilities were more oriented toward reform than punishment and were actually precursors to halfway houses. Women were sent there by the courts in lieu of a prison sentence, but some women also came in voluntarily as an alternative to street life. Some of the concepts developed in these privately run institutions were adopted later by state reformatories.

In the latter part of the 1800s, several states finally built separate new facilities for women. The first completely separate institution was built in 1873 in Indiana. Although this institution did not follow the reformatory model, others did. The New York House of Refuge was opened in 1881 for female misdemeanants, and Bedford Hills was opened in 1900. The reformatories often employed a cottage architectural style and emphasized feminine skills such as homemaking. Other institutions were more traditional, but all facilities for women were different from those for men. The highly educated women who ran these reformatories could be described as reformers with a mission. Their goal was to help their "fallen sisters" develop the traits of "true womanhood." The attitude toward female prisoners at this time changed from disgust and abhorrence to one of sympathy and compassion. Men were often seen as the cause of the women's deviance and, therefore, female role models could shield them from male influences as well as help to teach them feminine skills. The most reform oriented institutions were reserved for white and young offenders. Women of color and those with multiple offense histories were still sent to the wings or buildings in prisons for men, and those facilities had none of the "homey" elements of the reformatories (Rafter 1985). This was true even though historically (as today) women of color were disproportionately represented in prison.

Interestingly, the early reformatories for women implemented many of the programs associated with the reformatory era before these innovations found their way into reformatories for men. Zebulon Brockway, who was instrumental in the 1870 Prison Congress and later went on to open Elmira Reformatory, had worked with female offenders early in his career and, in fact, had developed many of his concepts concerning graduated release from working with female prisoners. The early programs in women's institutions, such as educational classes, libraries, art and music programs, work release, community visitation programs, and the like, were possible because of a belief that women were less dangerous and more passive than men. It was only after these programs were established in facilities for women that they were "discovered" and implemented in prisons for men.

It appears that the women who ended up in these early reformatories were more sexually deviant than criminal. For instance Lekkerkerker (1931) writes that reformatories housed young women (even as young as twelve or fifteen) convicted of such crimes as "petit larceny, habitual drunkenness or being a common prostitute, of frequenting disorderly houses or houses of prostitution or of any misdemeanor." Other descriptions profiled the reformatory woman as a young, unhardened, misdemeanant. Most were under twenty-five, white and native born. Two-thirds were widowed, divorced, or separated. Most had no prior convictions and their crimes were minor, such as drunkenness or prostitution (Freedman 1981). Some may have been sent by "exasperated mothers or embarrassed husbands" who charged them with sexual misconduct (Rafter 1985).

Throughout the 1900s, women's prisons continued to be built and many were run under modified reformatory models. The female administrators who followed the first wave were more professionals than crusaders, unlike those who originally staffed the institutions and helped create them. They did not view the work as a mission and were more likely to be trained in social work, law, or medicine. In the 1930s a study was done of women's reformatories by a Dutch lawyer. Lekkerkerker (1931) found that women's prisons still carried the legacy of the past in that they had few vocational programs and concentrated on domestic skills. Lekkerkerker also found that more was expected of the matron than the guard, in that the matron was supposed to represent a role model of purity, intelligence, and good will to the female inmates. Matrons often lived on the prison grounds and had almost as many restrictions over their lives as the inmates. Their shifts were long and they had few days off.

Lekkerkerker's description of some Northern reformatories sounded almost idyllic. "The buildings, scattered wide apart, form an attractive whole with the romantic lake, the wood and thicket, the rolling hills and green pasture, which offer the women abundant opportunity for healthy outdoor sports. . . ." In the South, women were even less likely to be incarcerated than in the North. Imprisoned women tended to be women of color or women convicted of violent crimes. Instead of reformatories, prison farms characterized Southern corrections during this time. Unlike male prisoners, however, women were not typically leased out as farm labor. They would perform domestic chores, either in the prison camps or in the homes of prison administrators, and also care for domestic gardens.

Throughout the 1900s most states built a separate facility for women, although it wasn't until the 1970s that every state had one. Those who did not have their own prison either housed their female offenders in wings of men's facilities or contracted with other states to house them. There is a partial list of early prisons and when they were built in Table 1.

Prisons for women today have inherited the legacy of the early reformatories. There are still differences in programs. For example, women's institutions have more domestic programs and programs influenced by sexual stereotypes. The interaction between staff and women is less formal than that found in prisons for men. Also, the physical structure of women's facilities tends to be different. More are built using the cottage architectural style, and they are almost always smaller than penitentiaries for men. The idea that the prison should teach feminine skills still plays a part in the prisons of today.

Joycelyn M. Pollock

Bibliography

Dobash, R., E. Dobash, and S. Gutteridge (1986). *The Imprisonment of Women.* New York: Basil Blackwell.

Feinman, C. (1984). An historical overview of the treatment of incarcerated women: Myths and realities of rehabilitation. *Prison Journal* 63(2): 12–26.

Freedman, E. (1981). *Their Sister's Keepers: Women's Prison Reform in America, 1830–1930.* Ann Arbor: University of Michigan Press.

Lekkerkerker, E. C. (1931). *Reformatories for Women in the U.S.* Gronigen, Netherlands: J. B. Wolters.

Pollock-Byrne, J. (1990). *Women, Prison and Crime.* Pacific Grove, Calif.: Brooks/Cole.

Rafter, N. (1985). *Partial Justice: State Prisons and Their Inmates. 1800–1935.* Boston: Northeastern University Press.

Strickland, K. (1976). *Correctional Institutions for Women in the U.S.* Lexington, Mass.: Lexington.

TABLE 1

Dates of Construction of Women's Prisons

Indiana	1873	Arkansas	1920
Massachusetts	1877	California	1920
New York	1887,	Minnesota	1920
	1887,	Nebraska	1920
	1902	Pennsylvania	1920
New Jersey	1913	Wisconsin	1921
Maine	1916	Delaware	1929
Ohio	1916	Connecticut	1930
Kansas	1917	Illinois	1930
Michigan	1917	Virginia	1932
Connecticut	1918	N. Carolina	1934
Iowa	1918	California	1936

Source: Freedman 1981.

II. Current Issues

Women form a very small percentage of the total incarcerated population in this country. The American Correctional Association reports that only 5.4 percent of prisoners were women in 1991. That figure, however, represents over forty-three thousand women. While the percentage remains small, it is clear that during the late 1980s and 1990s women are increasingly more likely to be incarcerated. Between 1980 and 1989, the number of women prisoners increased by 202 percent, compared with the 112 percent increase for males (Bureau of Justice Statistics 1991). Women's numbers doubled on death row in 1989, and there were fifteen women on death row in March of 1992 (Fletcher et al. 1993).

From an analysis of arrest rates, it does not seem to be true that the increased incarceration of women is due to greater criminality. While arrest rates have also increased in the last decades, they have not been close to the double digit increases of incarceration rates. It is clear that for most felonies, women (and men) are more likely to be incarcerated today than they were twenty years ago. Another way to look at these figures is in the percentage of women incarcerated for violent offenses. Today, the total number of women in prison for violent offenses is lower than it was several decades earlier. This does not necessarily mean that women are committing less violent crime; it does mean that more property offenders are being sent to prison. Another major contributor to women's numbers in prison is drug offenses. Some states report a doubling of the figures of drug offenders in prisons and jails. Steffensmeier (1993) reports that women continue to be arrested for minor property crimes like larceny and fraud while the number of women being sentenced to prison for homicide is going down. The percentage of women incarcerated for homicide has gone down from 17 percent of the total in 1960 to 10 percent in 1990. Part of the decrease is related to a decrease in domestic homicide (Browne reports a 20 percent decrease in domestic homicide). This may be attributed to the rise of legal and other resources available for abused women.

The increased probability of incarceration can most likely be attributed to determinate sentencing laws, strict laws on drug crimes, an increasingly intolerant attitude by the public and judges toward crime and criminals, and even a perception that equal opportunity means equal incarceration. For these reasons, women's prisons are overcrowded, and alternative sentences are less likely to be used for women than they were in the past.

The increase in incarceration has resulted in prisons for women being built at an unprecedented rate. Rafter (1990) writes that in the 1980s, thirty-four women's units or prisons were built, compared with only one-tenth that number in earlier decades. Abandoned hotels, motels, mental hospitals, nurses' dormitories, and youth training schools have been employed to house the burgeoning number of female prisoners. Seventy percent of states are planning to add new facilities for women, at an average cost of twenty-two thousand dollars per bed (ACA 1990). Still, most states have only one or two facilities for women and up to a dozen for men. This means that facilities for women tend to be farther away from their homes, often in the most rural areas of the state. The institution almost always houses all classification levels. Maximum-, medium-, and minimum-security inmates are housed together. Sometimes work release programs are operated out of the facility as well. This makes supervision difficult, as it is impossible to use transfer as a control device.

In a 1990 survey, data were collected on the demographic characteristics of women in prison. Most female prisoners are poor minorities with children. Over half of the women incarcerated are members of minority groups (57 percent). Most are between twenty-five and twenty-nine years old. Thirty-seven percent have never been married or are single parents with one to three children (62 percent). The children are being cared for by mothers or grandparents (48 percent). Most women plan to regain custody of their children (72 percent). Most women came from a single-parent home. Fifty percent have other family members who are incarcerated. Thirty-six percent have been the victim of sexual abuse, usually between the ages of five and fourteen and typically by a male member of the immediate family (49 percent). Another source reports a survey in which fully 88 percent of female prisoners have been victimized by physical or sexual abuse (Chesney-Lind 1992). Close to three-quarters started using drugs or alcohol before they were fifteen (74 percent), and they continue to use either one or the other or both at least once a month, usually to feel better emotionally (39 percent). Almost half used cocaine, and 22 percent used it daily. Forty percent have used speed, and 56 percent have used marijuana, 22 percent daily (ACA 1990). Over a quarter have attempted suicide. Over half dropped out of high school (59 percent), perhaps because of pregnancy (34 percent). Most preprison jobs were service or clerical positions (73 percent) (ACA 1990).

Although one cannot necessarily make any generalizations to a national population, a study in Oklahoma found differences between black and white women. Black women had more children, more siblings, were less likely to be married, were incarcerated at an earlier age, reported less abuse than white women, and reported higher levels of self-esteem. This study also found that white women were more likely to use speed and alcohol and black women more likely to use crack cocaine (Fletcher et al. 1993).

Over half the women incarcerated have been arrested two to nine times starting at the age of fifteen. Close to 40 percent were arrested for property crimes and 22 percent for crimes of violence. Half of the women are serving sentences of two to eight years. Most will serve approximately one-fourth of their sentences. Most women report that the most helpful programs in prison are alcohol programs (94 percent), drug programs (86 percent), and Job Corps (66 percent) (ACA 1990).

Women's prisons often present less forbidding exteriors than prisons for men. All are much smaller than penitentiaries for men, although women's prisons are increasing in size as well as number. Many have minimal perimeter security. Some have been described as looking like college campuses. The "cottage" architectural style—several small residential buildings, either with decentralized or centralized eating and working facilities—is common. Women are often allowed to decorate with personal items, and the harsh appearance of cells may be softened by curtains, family photos, and hand-crafted pillows. This pleasant interior belies the problems one finds there. There is a lack of meaningful training or treatment programs. The loss of family is acutely felt, and anger, boredom, and despair often characterize the lives of the women found within the walls.

Recently there have been attempts to make women's prisons more like prisons for men. For instance, security measures such as razor wire and fences are being added to facilities or incorporated into the new facilities being built. Supervisory personnel who have worked in prisons for men observe that women's prisons are run in a lax manner. There have been attempts to bring them "in line" with procedures characteristic of the prisons for men in the same state. This is occurring despite the fact that escape attempts have always been relatively rare and there are few major disturbances in prisons for women.

Whether women should be treated more like men in prison is a hotly debated issue. On the one hand, women's prisons have long been the stepchild of the system and last in line for scarce resources. Typically there have been fewer vocational and educational programs for women and placements in work and educational release facilities were few or nonexistent. The argument has always been that the small number of female prisoners means that programs and placements for women are much more expensive than what can be offered for male prisoners. Recently, because of court action, administrators of women's prisons have had to increase their program offerings to provide a level of service comparable to that offered men.

On the other hand, the differential treatment that women have been accorded in the past has had its positive points. Visitation has usually been more lenient and comprehensive for women. For instance, several prisons allow weekend visits with children and at least some prisons allow women to keep their babies for some length of time after birth. Most also allow more frequent phone calls for women, recognizing their need to keep in touch with children. Privacy needs have also been recognized and protected. There have been no large outdoor showers, no supervision by males in shower areas, and doors can be found instead of open bars in the cells in many prisons. These favorable conditions are partly the result of smaller numbers, but also of sex-role stereotypes. Because most prisoners are mothers, programs for children are found in almost all prisons. This is not necessarily the case in prisons for men, even though most male prisoners are fathers. An equalization model may mean that women lose some of the special privileges they have received in the past. For example, women may gain the right to vocational programs that are needed in order to make a living and to support a family upon release, but lose the right to have programs for their children during imprisonment since these programs are unique to facilities for women.

One area in which women have traditionally been shortchanged is in medical care. Because women's facilities are smaller, there are typically no extensive medical services available at the prison itself. On-call care is sometimes less than adequate. In this area, women have traditionally received fewer services than men, but their needs may be greater. Gynecological concerns, pregnancy, and years of drug use pose special medical problems. In New York, women filed suit charging that the level of health care services provided to them violated the Eighth Amendment. The court declared that the state had failed to provide female inmates at Bedford Hills with adequate treatment by medical specialists. The suit *(Todaro v. Ward)* was filed in 1974, decided in 1977, and finally implemented in 1978, so that now at least a doctor is to be on call at all times.

Only about a quarter of the prisons in the country use a classification system specifically designed for female offenders (ACA 1990). This is indicative of the neglect women inmates have experienced in corrections. Historically the vocational programs in prisons for women were heavily influenced by sexual stereotypes. Women had access to clerical and cosmetology programs, but little else. Often male inmates in the same state system had access to three or four times the number of programs. The problem with vocational offerings for women inmates have been twofold. First, there are few of them, and second, they are typically geared to low-paying, "pink collar" work. Women, until recently, have been seen primarily as mothers rather than breadwinners, yet most are leaving prison to be the sole support of their children. In several cases, courts have recognized that women deserve equal access to programs that may help them become self-supporting upon release. In Michigan, for instance, women inmates filed suit and the court held *(Glover v. Johnson)* that women had fewer and inferior vocational programs and deserved "substantially equal" programs. The court added that although the programs must be substantially equal they should be based on the needs and interests of women. Courts have generally not allowed states to use the excuse of administrative convenience or cost to justify different treatment of women.

Another problematic issue is the nature of the program. Historically, all vocational programs have been heavily influenced by sexual stereotypes. Thus, auto mechanics and welding might be found in prisons for men and cosmetology and food service in prisons for women. Women have found that prison programs train them for extremely low-paying jobs upon release. Training programs that lead to higher paying jobs in nontraditional areas, such as carpentry, auto mechanics, and so on, are few and far between, although many states are now starting such programs. Interestingly, those states that do have these programs find that they must convince women prisoners of their value. Once it is shown that such programs can lead to better lives, women have been more willing to enter nontraditional areas. Of course, there is the same problem in women's prisons that is found in prisons for men. Programs that require a higher level of reading and mathematical ability are difficult to fill because of the extremely low educational levels of all prisoners, men and women alike. Also, as is typical in prisons for men, many programs have long waiting lists. There are rarely enough vocational training program slots to meet the demand in any prison.

For female prisoners, each day is spent typically in some type of work, school, or program assignment. Programs can be divided into four major categories. First are those activities necessary for maintenance of the facility, such as clerical work, food service, and custodial work. The second category is education. Most educational programs in prisons for men are remedial or basic education. The third category is vocational programs that may lead to either a certificate or qualification in some skill area. The fourth category of activity is treatment programs. While all prisons have basic programs such as Alcoholics Anonymous, the number and effectiveness of drug and other treatment programs in women's prisons could be improved. Women tend to have less idle time than men in prison (because of their smaller numbers it is more feasible to keep them occupied). They also are likely to have more communication with family members, either through visits or letter writing. They are less likely to be involved in organized sports than men and their leisure time is more often taken up with television, cards, and board games.

Drugs are an increasingly influential element in the lives of incarcerated women. Surveys show that women are typically initiated into the drug world by male partners. Over the 1980s women's arrests for drug crimes increased 307 percent (compared with 147 percent for men); 12 percent of women in prison are there for drug crimes (compared with 8.4 percent for men) (Bureau of Justice Statistics 1991). Although some prisons have drug treatment programs, there is a need for more programs and more research as to what constitutes an effective program.

Studies indicate that the loss of the mother role is the most severe deprivation of imprisonment for incarcerated women. Most women in prison have children and most will retain or regain custody. Much of what occurs in any prison revolves around children. Disciplinary infractions often result from frustration related to being unable to mother their children. The presence of children is one of the elements that differentiates a women's prison from prisons for men. Some prisons have allowed newborns to remain with the mother for up to six months. Visitation programs often allow children inside the prison walls beyond the visiting room. While most men have their children cared for by the children's mother, most children of incarcerated women are not cared for by their fathers. This fact alone may be the biggest single difference in the lives of men and women.

Research indicates that the prisoner subculture found in prisons for women is different than that in prisons for men. Women are more likely to form smaller cliques than to group together in gangs. They are more likely to have semistable homosexual dyads or form pseudo-families with make-believe family roles, such as father, mother, and sister. Homosexuality is more open and tied to relationships rather than used as a commodity to buy and sell. One does not find the racial tension in prisons for women that is typical of many prisons for men. Violence is present but it is more spontaneous, more emotional, and less lethal. There is a less extensive black market and weapons are not as elaborate or plentiful as in prisons for men. Drugs can be found, but there is less organization in the marketing of drugs. Drugs do not cause as much violence as in prisons for men (Pollock-Byrne 1990).

Some studies have found that women more often engage in rule breaking. This is probably because women seem to be held to higher standards of behavior, and incidents that may not get written up in a prison for men do result in a "ticket" for women. On the other hand, women do seem to "act out" against each other and correctional staff more frequently in obvious and apparent ways, while men may assail each other in a covert manner. It is difficult to compare such things as rule breaking because the institutions involved are so different. For instance, most prisons for women house all classification levels, while prisons for men house only one or two levels. This means that other variables in addition to the sex of the inmate are influencing the frequency of rule breaking. Other research indicates that women are more likely to attempt suicide or mutilate themselves. This may indicate that prison life is difficult for both men and women, but that at least some women may experience the deprivations of institutional life more severely. From most research, the loss of family can be identified as probably the greatest deprivation for incarcerated women.

Supervision by male officers working in facilities for women has become more frequent in the last several years since women officers have fought for and won the right to work in prisons for men. Ironically, this has seemed to result in the same problems that led to separate institutions for women in the late 1800s, as there have been reports of sexual harassment, rape, and sexual misconduct in those facilities where men supervise women inmates in living units. While there are no studies available that document sexual abuse, there are several ongoing court cases in which women inmates have sued the prison or the officers involved.

Women are more likely to be incarcerated today, and while today they may have access to more types of vocational programs, the slots available are still insufficient to meet the demand. Women inmates may serve their time in a "nicer" prison, at least one that looks more attractive, but the loss of family, the pervasive rules that govern every detail of living, and the proximity of unpleasant and dangerous people, make imprisonment similar for men and women.

Joycelyn M. Pollock

See also CHILDREN OF PRISONERS (MOTHERS' ISSUES)

Bibliography
American Correctional Association (1990). *The Female Offender. What Does the Future Hold?* Washington D.C.: St. Mary's.
Browne, A. (1992). Violence against women. *Journal of the American Medical Association* 267: 3184–89.
Bureau of Justice Statistics (1991). *Prisoners in 1991*. Washington D.C.: U.S. Department of Justice.
Chesney-Lind, M. (1992). Rethinking women's imprisonment: A critical examination of trends in female incarceration. Unpublished manuscript.
Fletcher, B., L. Dixon-Shaver, and D. Moon. (1993). *Women Prisoners: A Forgotten Population*. Westport, Conn.: Praeger.
Moyer, I. (1992). *The Changing Roles of Women in the Criminal Justice System*. Prospect Heights, Ill.: Waveland.
Muraskin, R., and T. Alleman. (1993). *It's A Crime. Women and Justice*. Englewood Cliffs, N.J.: Regents/Prentice-Hall.
Pollock-Byrne, J. (1990). *Women, Prison and Crime*. Pacific Grove, Calif.: Brooks/Cole.
Rafter, N. (1990). *Partial Justice: Women, Prisons and Social Control*. New Brunswick, N.J.: Transaction.
Steffensmeier, D. (1993). National trends in female arrests, 1960–1990: Assessment and recommendations for research. Unpublished manuscript.

Cases
Glover v. Johnson, 478 F. Supp. 1075 (1979)
Todaro v. Ward, 431 F. Supp. 1129 (1977)

Work Programs

Since the establishment of America's first penitentiary at Walnut Street Jail (1790), inmates have been assigned to a variety of jobs in prison, such as support, maintenance, or industry (state-run or privately run). An examination of the history of corrections reveals that a series of whirlwind forces (fueled by government, business, labor, public, and institutional concerns) has contributed to a rise and fall of work programs for inmates.

History of Work Programs in Prison

The origin of inmate labor has a European flavor. As early as the thirteenth century, the English government used every barbaric punishment imaginable in dealing with crimes committed by the destitute. There was little utility in having work programs in prison. With the establishment of workhouses in the mid to late 1500s in England, however, prisoners began to perform hard labor as a condition of their confinement. At the same time, the English penal code remained quite severe. The arbitrary and capricious punishments handed out by the English government were eventually called into question during the eighteenth century. The initial function and structure of our prisons in America are the result of the contributions of such reform-minded individuals as William Penn, Cesare Beccaria, John Howard, Charles Montesquieu, and Francois Voltaire. As America gained its independence from England, the Pennsylvania Quakers established penal institutions (such as Walnut Street Jail, 1790) with work programs centering on hard labor. In essence, capital punishment took a back seat to a work ethic approach.

As prisons were being developed in America, there emerged a debate over the issue of work by inmates. According to the Pennsylvania school of prison discipline, solitary confinement was viewed as the appropriate way of handling inmates. It was believed that solitary confinement would enhance the personal reformation process for each prisoner. Under this Pennsylvania scheme, work performed by prisoners had to be completed in their cells. This discipline system did not allow for the adoption of the more efficient factory modes of production that were emerging in society during the 1880s.

The disciples of the rival Auburn approach advocated that inmates work with other prisoners in factory or farm settings. These "congregate" work programs included such activities as shoe making, tailoring, weaving, tool making, and barrel making. The Auburn labor system won out over the isolated industries of the Pennsylvania school because of the cost benefits to prison administrators.

During the 1800s work programs in prison took a variety of forms. Initially, the contract system was popular. Under that arrangement, businesses contracted for the services of convicts. Within the confines of the correctional institutions or on the prison-run farms, inmates performed work on the machinery or raw materials provided by the outside contractor. With the rise of the Industrial Revolution, correctional administrators turned to leasing out inmates to businesses. This method allowed for inmate labor outside of prison walls. The leasing of inmates became popular in the agricultural and mining regions of the country. Some scholars have equated this leasing procedure to a form of slavery. A third alternative approach was the state-account system. That plan involved the direct participation of prison authorities in overseeing the manufacturing of goods by inmates. Once the goods were sold on the open market, the prisoners would receive a small amount of the profits. A variation of the state-account system was the state-use form of prison industry. The intent of this program was to use inmates to produce goods that were needed in other state agencies (as an example, manufacturing license plates), or to use inmates on construction projects.

The criticism of prison work programs was inevitable. Beginning in the late 1800s, labor unions and private entrepreneurs criticized inmate labor on two grounds. First, these work programs created a competitive advantage for correctional institutions by allowing them to produce goods through the use of cheap inmate labor. And why should law-abiding citizens give up or lose jobs to criminals?

Prison industries and work programs in prison were dealt significant legislative blows with the passage of the Hawes-Cooper Act of 1929 and the Ashurst-Sumners Act of 1935. These laws were successful in restricting the interstate sale of prison-made goods. As a consequence, many state correctional institutions abandoned the use of the private sector in prison industries. This movement, however, led to the administrative problem of inmate idleness.

In 1934, Congress passed legislation creating Federal Prison Industries (FPI). After the passage of that act, the Federal Bureau of Prisons adopted FPI, or the commonly referred to

UNICOR, into federal prisons. The intent of UNICOR was to employ as many eligible inmates as possible and to limit the sale of prison-made goods to governmental agencies. UNICOR has experienced tremendous success and growth since its inception. Inmate industries now include data graphics, electronics, metal and wood, and textile and leather operations. Through their participation in these industries, federal prisoners have been trained in skills that might lead to future employment.

As the 1970s arrived, however, prisons were becoming crowded and costly to administer. Prison work programs were once again heralded by policy makers as a constructive approach to handling incarcerated criminals. The credit for resurrecting prison industries can be given to the Law Enforcement Assistance Administration's Free Venture Model, and the Congressional Percy Amendment of 1979 (later known as the Prison Industry Enhancement Act). These reform efforts were successful in removing restrictions on the interstate sale of prison-made goods and in involving private businesses in prison industries. During the 1980s and 1990s, many state laws were enacted that dealt with organization, operation, inmate compensation, purchasing, and marketing standards for prison industries and work programs. According to a 1991 national survey conducted by the American Correctional Association, there were 63,919 prisoners employed in state and federal correctional industries throughout the United States. The highest level of inmate employment was found in UNICOR (23 percent), and the lowest percent in Hawaii's Correctional Industries (0.04 percent).

Support and Maintenance, State Industry, and Private Industry

During their stay in prison, inmates may be assigned to a variety of jobs. For example, correctional administrators use prisoners for support and maintenance work (such as kitchen hands, inmate clerks, commissary clerks, library clerks, and janitors). Within the inmate social order, a hierarchy exists with respect to these work assignments. The significance of these work programs is that some prisoners attempt to improve their status by being assigned to jobs that allow them access to administrative information or to contraband material. For example, a clerical position within the records office is very high on the prestige ladder because inmates have access to information contained in files. Similarly,

kitchen duty can very easily mean access to contraband. On the other end of the spectrum, janitorial placements are the least prestigious of the support and maintenance jobs.

In addition to support and maintenance jobs, inmates may be appointed to private or state industry activities. If the private sector is involved in prison industries, the business is generally either the operator or the customer of the program. As the operator of the enterprise at or near the prison, the private firm controls the hiring, firing, supervising, and training of the inmates. On the other hand, companies can be viewed as customers if they agree to purchase a set amount of items produced by the prison industry.

Benefits and Drawbacks

Prison work programs benefit correctional institutions, offenders, and society. First, these programs have enabled institutions to reduce two precipitating forces in inmate violence: boredom and idleness. Second, prisoners who participate in work programs are provided an opportunity to develop and reinforce work habits, build self-esteem, enhance vocational skills, and prepare for reintegration back into society as productive citizens. Third, taxpayers benefit from inmate work programs because funds generated through wage deductions offset the costs of incarceration, compensate crime victims, help support inmates' families, and contribute to revenues through state and federal taxes.

The good qualities of prison work programs are counterbalanced by drawbacks. For example, worker's compensation laws have been a popular legal avenue of pursuit for inmates who have suffered injuries while working on prison projects. Generally speaking, courts have been reluctant to extend coverage to prisoners, unless a legislative statute has been passed that allows limited coverage for inmates. In a similar vein, inmate unions have been a lobbying force for improving prison work programs. They have argued for increasing wages for inmate work, ending contract labor, recognizing that inmate workers are public employees who should have statutory rights under state labor laws, and enhancing the safety of their working conditions. Finally, additional areas of concern have centered on the inmate turnover rate, the possibility of exploitation of inmates, the pool of unskilled inmates, and the lack of adequate equipment.

Gregory A. Clark

See also VOCATIONAL PROGRAMS

Bibliography

Auerbach, B., G. Sexton, F. Farrow, and R. Lawson (1988). *Work in American Prisons: The Private Sector Gets Involved.* Washington, D.C.: National Institute of Justice.

Burger, W. E. (1982). More warehouses or factories with fences? *New England Journal of Prison Law* 8(1) (Winter): 111–20.

Dwyer, D. C., and R. B. McNally (1993). Public policy, prison industries, and business: An equitable balance for the 1990s. *Federal Probation* 57(2) (June): 30–36.

Flanagan, T., and K. Maguire (1993). A full employment policy for prisons in the United States: Some arguments, estimates, and implications. *Journal of Criminal Justice* 21: 117–30.

Greiser, R. C. (1989). Do correctional industries adversely impact the private sector? *Federal Probation* 53(1): 18–24.

Hawkins, G. (1983). Prison labor and prison industries. In M. Tonry and N. Morris, eds. *Crime and Justice: An Annual Review of Research*, Vol. 5. Chicago: University of Chicago Press.

Schaller, J. (1982). Work and imprisonment: An overview of the changing role of prison labor in American prisons. *Prison Journal* 62(2): 3–12.

Work-Release Programs

In 1986 almost seventeen thousand inmates were participating in work-release programs (Champion 1990). By the beginning of 1993, the number had swelled to over 62,256. While in an absolute sense 62,256 may seem like a rather high number of participants, one must remember that there are more than one million inmates in prisons and jails and the number keeps growing. Correspondingly, work-release is only one of many approaches to managing inmates.

Traditionally, work-release programs have been defined as "Any program where inmates of jails or prisons are permitted to work in the community with minimal restriction, are compensated at the prevailing minimum wage, and must serve their nonworking hours housed in a secure facility" (McCarthy and McCarthy 1984, 159–60). Defining what constitutes a work-release program has recently become more difficult. The correctional system is now so diverse that today we have dedicated work-release centers, prerelease centers, and community-based programs that include features of work release.

Moreover, work-release programs reflect an assorted mixture of goals and decisions specific to local jurisdictions. For example, some jurisdictions have a work-release program established within the city or county jail. Eligible offenders are released from jail in the morning, report to their respective places of employment or to school (known as study-release), and report back to the institution when the work day is complete. Other jurisdictions, typically in larger metropolitan areas, have constructed dedicated work-release centers. These centers serve those about to be paroled into the community, as well as individuals sentenced directly to the center. The prime responsibility of these work-release centers is to provide parolees a transition from the structured environment of the institution to the unstructured surroundings of their communities. Much of the research on postrelease recidivism suggests that a structured transition from the institution to general society reduces the likelihood of repeat offending.

Community based sanctions have also incorporated work-release principles into many programs. For instance, Florida operates a home-confinement program that maintains a population of over ten thousand inmates. The offenders are restricted to their residence and their whereabouts are monitored by program employees. Offenders are allowed to keep their jobs—in fact, for many it is a requirement for acceptance into the program. Aside from not making use of a secure facility, the program looks much like a traditional work-release program.

Allowing an inmate to keep a job or pursue job or educational training during the day serves two important functions. First, many institutions are unconstitutionally overcrowded. Allowing inmates out during the day temporarily alleviates the crowding. In addition, a reduction in both the daytime population and the time spent in actual confinement reduces the financial costs incurred by the state. Second, inmates on work release provide for their families, participate in educational programs, and provide restitution to their victims. These tangible benefits cannot be realized if the prisoner is incarcerated around the clock. Also, it has long been recognized that, for the goal of rehabilitation to be realized (that is, making the offender a responsible member of society), the individual must develop bonds to the community and maintain a stake in conformity.

Overall, work-release programs serve a dual purpose. They meet society's expectations for punishment and provide simultaneously for the goal of rehabilitation and reintegration. Although offenders face restrictions placed on their liberties and are under the control of the state, they do spend time "free" in society. Their "free" time, however, is governed by the state and spent in responsible ventures.

The Development of Work Release

Work release was first used in 1906. Local sheriffs in Vermont would issue a "day pass" to an inmate. This pass allowed an individual the freedom to work away from the jail during the day, without any correctional oversight, on the promise that the offender would report back to the jail that night (Busher 1973). Failure to report to the jail at the assigned curfew time would result in escape charges being filed and guaranteed incarceration when apprehended.

The use of the day pass was controversial, however, and not widespread. It was not until 1913 that a state (Wisconsin) authorized through legislation the use of work release as an alternative to incarceration. The progressive era challenged many of society's notions of what constituted just punishment and subsequently produced sweeping changes in the management of prisoners (Rothman 1980). Work-release programs were first developed when the social context allowed for correctional experimentation and change. The inception of work release as a state-sanctioned correctional alternative was part of a larger transformation of the correctional system that was occurring at the time. Community and political acceptance of work-release programs was slow to come. Indeed, at the time it was a novel idea to allow convicts to mingle with the rest of society.

Over the years, work release has gained credibility and legitimacy both with the public and correctional systems. By 1975, every state, and the federal system had some form of work-release program (Champion 1990). Today, New York maintains almost fifteen thousand inmates in work-release programs, North Carolina six thousand, California over five thousand, and Illinois over four thousand. This dramatic expansion, however, has been due largely to the impressive growth of the prisoner population on whole. By 1995, the United States incarcerated well over one million people, a rate surpassing that of any other industrialized country.

The Effectiveness of Work Release

McCarthy and McCarthy (1991) have listed four objectives common to most work-release programs: offender reintegration, management, humanitarianism, and evaluation.

Reintegration

The purpose underlying most work-release programs is to reduce the likelihood that the individual will return to crime. Work-release programs attempt to do this by gradually preparing the inmate for release into the community and by maintaining or reestablishing social bonds, such as family relations. Typically, the recidivism rates for individuals in work-release centers are below the national average of 35.3 percent. Criminologists are not certain whether these low rates represent the effectiveness of work release or if they are more indicative of the low-risk nature of most individuals placed on work release.

Management

From the perspective of the inmate, work release means time away from the institution—time not spent incarcerated. The potential for work release is a powerful motivator for the inmate to behave well. Correctional administrators recognize the value placed on any temporary release program and are thus capable of using the program as a bargaining chip: If the inmate behaves well and displays a good attitude, partial freedom may be the reward. If the inmate is recalcitrant or uncooperative, work release may be revoked or denied. Regardless, work release provides correctional administrators with leverage in their dealings with inmates.

Humanitarianism

Few in society would elect to occupy a prison cell. The loss of friends, family, respect, individuality, and even feelings of self-worth may make the experience unbearable. Work release attempts to soften the harsh affects of being imprisoned by allowing the inmate to provide for family members, pay restitution, pursue an education, and remain attached to the larger society. For example, in the state of Virginia 314 offenders, 30 percent of the eligible inmate population, earned a total of $1,123,611 while on work release. Of that amount, over $65,000 went to families of inmates and $307,995 went to the state to defray the costs of incarceration (Jones 1982).

Evaluation

Placement in work-release status is dependent upon compliance with strict rules and regulations. Failure to comply with those rules can result in the individual's being revoked from work release. If that happens, the prisoner must spend the rest of the sentence behind bars. In essence then, work release provides the inmate a test that, if passed, will result in freedom—if failed, in continued incarceration.

Work release also provides administrators a tool with which to evaluate individual performance within the community. If the offender complies with the rules, administrators—particularly parole boards—may be more inclined to grant an early release. Correspondingly, if the inmate fails on work release, administrators are made aware that the offender has yet to internalize the self-control necessary for successful release. Parole boards will also most likely refuse to grant release to someone who is unable to conform to work-release requirements.

The Future of Work Release

Administrators will remain pressed with the need to manage a large number of inmates. As the inmate population continues its unprecedented growth, work release will remain a popular strategy for dealing with selected inmates. The rapid expansion of work-release programs between 1986 and 1993 highlights this point. Correspondingly, states with the largest inmate populations, such as New York, California, and Illinois, can be expected to continue to use work release in an effort to deal with crowding.

An alternative is also possible. With the continued growth of community-based sanctions, such as Intensive Supervision and House Arrest, work release, as presently defined, may disappear—or at least become part of a larger amalgamation of community sanctions. For instance, instead of having dedicated work-release centers, jurisdictions may elect to sentence eligible offenders to an Intensive Supervision program that demands from the offender both steady employment and compliance with strict curfews. In that sense, work release as an individual program ceases to exist and instead becomes part of a larger and more comprehensive approach.

Regardless of whether work release remains an individual program or becomes part of a larger design, the desire to have offenders work, and work to achieve reintegration within our communities, is unlikely to lose legitimacy in corrections, or in the eyes of the public, for some time to come.

John P. Wright
Lawrence F. Travis III

See also VOCATIONAL PROGRAMS, WORK PROGRAMS

Bibliography

Busher, W. (1973). *Ordering Time to Serve.* Washington, D.C.: U.S. Government Printing Office.

Champion, D. (1990). *Probation and Parole in the United States.* New York: Macmillan.

Jones, M. (1982). *A Report on the Virginia Work Release Program.* Richmond, Va.: Research and Reporting Unit, Division and Evaluation, Virginia Department of Corrections.

McCarthy, B., and B. McCarthy (1984). *Community Based Corrections.* Monterey, Calif.: Brooks/Cole.

McCarthy, B., and B. McCarthy (1991). *Community Based Corrections.* 2nd. ed. Monterey, Calif.: Brooks/Cole.

Rothman, D. (1980). *Conscience and Convenience: The Asylum and Its Alternatives in Progressive America.* Glenview Ill.: Scott, Foresman.

Y

Youth in Prison

As far as one can discern, application of the law in early times occurred without regard to age. Thus children were treated the same as adults by the law. Children were housed in detention facilities, prosecuted and sentenced, and then punished the same as any other offender. Prior to the 1600s, children were not viewed as a distinct social group. Among the first laws to distinguish children from adults were the Poor Laws. These laws, enacted in England in 1535, allowed for the appointment of an overseer to bind out destitute or neglected peasant children as servants. Later, the Elizabethan Poor Laws of 1601 became the model for dealing with children of the poor for two hundred years. As a result, jurists and lawmakers began to regard children differently than adults, and the children's court movement began.

In the 1827 English case *Wellesley v. Wellesley,* the concept of parens patriae was introduced as a legal doctrine. Through it the English chancery courts (whose primary interest was protecting property rights), were allowed to intervene in family life to protect the welfare of the child. By the beginning of the nineteenth century, children began to emerge as a readily distinguishable group with independent needs and interests. The concept of parens patriae grew to refer to the responsibility of the state, through the courts, to act in the best interests of children.

By 1925, juvenile justice systems had been established throughout the United States. The mandate of juvenile justice systems is the protection of the young, the incompetent, the neglected, and the delinquent. The authority of juvenile justice systems is defined by individual state juvenile codes. The major functions of the juvenile justice system are to prevent juvenile crime and to rehabilitate juvenile offenders. With the establishment of juvenile justice systems in the United States, legal jurisdiction of children has been removed from criminal courts and defined as the responsibility of juvenile or family courts. As a result, children are no longer incarcerated in prison. Instead, they are housed in facilities for juveniles where treatment and rehabilitation are emphasized.

Changing a Child into an Adult—The Legal Way

The criminal justice system regards a child as an adult when jurisdiction over the child's case is transferred, waived, certified, bound over, or remanded from the juvenile justice system to the criminal justice system. According to Champion and Mays (1991, 61), waivers or transfers of children to criminal courts are deemed appropriate when the juvenile has committed a "particularly violent, personal offense" or the juvenile has an "extensive offense history, particularly for property offenses." Juvenile cases are transferred to the criminal justice system through judicial waiver, legislative waiver, or prosecutorial waiver.

In judicial waivers, the judge has complete discretion for the transfer decision as long as the decision is based on guidelines set out in *Kent*. When judicial waiver occurs, the judge must consider the following:

1. The seriousness of the alleged offense to the community and whether the protection of the community requires waiver;
2. Whether the alleged offense was committed in an aggressive, violent, premeditated or willful manner;

3. Whether the alleged offense was against persons or against property, greater weight being given to offenses against persons especially if personal injury resulted;

4. The desirability of trial and disposition of the entire offense in one court when the juvenile's codefendants in the alleged offense are adults;

5. The sophistication and maturity of the juvenile by consideration of his home, environmental situation, emotional attitude, and pattern of living;

6. The record and previous history of the juvenile, including previous contacts with police agencies, juvenile courts, and other jurisdictions, prior periods of probation, or prior commitments to juvenile institutions;

7. The prospects for adequate protection of the public and the likelihood of reasonable rehabilitation of the juvenile (if found guilty) by the use of procedures, services, and facilities currently available to the juvenile court (Champion and Mays 1991, 62).

These factors can be grouped into two categories of concern: the dangerousness of the juvenile, and the likelihood that the juvenile can be treated.

Legislative waivers occur when the legislature decides that certain cases are not within the jurisdiction of the juvenile court. As a result, legislatures enact laws that impose jurisdictional constraints on juvenile courts. Examples of legislative waiver are laws that prohibit juvenile courts from hearing traffic offenses even though the defendant is a juvenile.

Prosecutorial waiver occurs when the prosecutor decides if the case will be prosecuted in juvenile court or criminal court. In Florida and Utah the juvenile court and criminal court share jurisdiction of juvenile cases, therefore the prosecutor must decide in which court to file the case. In a case study of prosecutorial waivers in Florida, it was determined that few of the juveniles transferred by prosecutorial waiver were the dangerous, repeat offenders for whom waiver might be justified. The prosecutorial waiver process was characterized by an absence of statutory guidelines to govern the selection of cases, the ease with which waiver is accomplished, and a lack of support among prosecutors for traditional principles of juvenile justice.

This resulted in the conclusion that prosecutorial waiver is the most controversial type of juvenile waiver.

Criminalization of the Juvenile Justice System

The use of transfers, waivers, certifications, bind-overs, or remands by juvenile courts has been growing. Since 1978, as many as forty-one states have passed legislation expanding their use. This trend has contributed to the criminalization of the juvenile justice system.

In an analysis of laws and approaches used by five states to deal with chronic juvenile offenders, it was determined that criminalization of children resulted in: (1) the automatic transfer of juveniles charged with specified serious crimes, (2) the exclusion of certain serious offenses from juvenile court jurisdiction (for example, murder, rape, and arson), (3) lowering of the age of persons under juvenile court jurisdiction, and (4) imposing mandatory incarceration periods for juveniles convicted of specified offenses. It has been suggested that although discretionary waiver of juveniles by judges and prosecutors is in need of reform, these types of waiver are preferable to legislative waivers.

It has been argued that increased use of waiver hearings were justified as necessary to address the serious crimes committed by children, although overall delinquency rates did not increase from 1980 to 1989. In an analysis of cases from four urban courts, it was determined that violent youths accounted for fewer than one-third of all children whose cases were transferred. The age of the child at the time the crime is committed and the characteristics of the offense have been found to be the more important determinants, when compared with race and prior offense record, in the decision to transfer the case to criminal court. The best predictor of certification is the level of the child's participation in the offense. Seriousness of the offense and number and nature of prior offenses are also factors in the decision to certify.

Some view waiver of juvenile cases to the criminal courts as both an indicator and cause of the criminalization of the juvenile court. For example, some say that increased use of waivers seems closely related to the public's rejection of rehabilitation and treatment and growing support for the just deserts philosophy of punishment. This results in the waiver of children to the criminal justice system based on their offense rather than their amenability to treatment or dangerousness.

Others have focused on the political nature of remanding juveniles to criminal court, suggesting that politics play an important role in influencing decisions to transfer cases. Cases are transferred, in response to the public's concern about crime in society, in an attempt to placate the public by convincing them that the justice system is taking a hard-line approach to crimes committed by children. It is also important to remember that all three types of waiver (judicial, legislative, and prosecutorial) are a result of decisions made by elected officials or political appointments.

Who Are the Children in Prison?

A widely held belief is that children in prison are the violent youth of America. Some data support this belief. For example, in 1989, violent offenses constituted 7 percent of the juvenile court caseload in ten states. Of these, 3 percent were transferred to criminal court (Butts and Connors-Beatty 1993). From an analysis of 2,335 cases that were waived to criminal court, it was determined that more than one-third of the cases involved violent index-crime offenses. In rank order from highest to lowest, robbery accounted for the largest number of the violent index-crimes, followed by aggravated assault which was ranked number three. Murder was next, and forcible rape accounted for the fewest. The evidence supports the conclusion that juvenile offenders who engage in violent crime are the most often incarcerated. The persistent property-offender receives the most frequent waivers but is the least likely to be incarcerated.

To provide the reader with a snapshot view of children incarcerated in Texas prisons, data for children certified in the second largest prison system in the United States is presented. It was determined from agency records that seventy-three children, seventeen years old or younger were incarcerated in Texas prisons at the end of October of 1993. The seventy-two boys and one girl had been transferred to the criminal courts, where they were convicted and sentenced. Over 90 percent of the children were aged sixteen or seventeen on the day they were admitted to the Texas Department of Criminal Justice—Institutional Division. Eight percent ranged in age from thirteen to fifteen. Although the majority of children were sixteen or seventeen on the day they were admitted to prison, when one considers the backlog in the courts and the amount of time spent waiting for a prison bed, it is probable that they were closer to fifteen at the time of the offense.

The majority of children (63 percent) were convicted of violent crimes, while 31.5 percent were convicted of nonviolent crimes. An overview of the violent crimes in rank order is as follows: murder, attempted murder, robbery, aggravated assault, and aggravated sexual assault. More than half of the violent crimes were committed with a deadly weapon and almost half of the murders were capital murders.

Convictions for non violent crimes, in rank order, were as follows: burglary, arson, drug charges, unauthorized use of a motor vehicle, and tampering with automobile identification numbers. The burglary convictions were characterized as follows: burglary of a building, burglary of a habitation, and burglary of a vehicle. All drug convictions involved distribution of cocaine or heroin.

There is considerable diversity in the sentences that children incarcerated in Texas prisons are serving. The sentences ranged from two years for aggravated assault to ninety-nine years for murder with a deadly weapon. The average sentence for drug offenses and all types of burglary was ten years. The average sentence for murder was about forty-five years, while the average sentence for robbery was about twenty-two years. Auto-related offenses were characterized by an average sentence of eight years.

The majority of the children (60 percent) who are incarcerated in Texas prisons were certified, then convicted in criminal courts in five metropolitan counties, Dallas, Harris, Tarrant, Bexar, and El Paso. Dallas County accounted for the largest number of incarcerated children, followed by Harris County (Houston). A quarter of the certifications were from rural counties.

The Effect of Prison on Children

Imprisonment of juveniles in adult institutions has a long-term negative impact on them. Juvenile offenders in training schools gave more positive evaluations of treatment and training programs, general services, and institutional personnel when compared with juveniles sentenced to adult correctional institutions. Children in prison report being abused by inmates and staff more often than youths in juvenile facilities. Researchers concluded that the prison socialization into crime and violence for children in adult prisons may increase the risk that these children will commit criminal acts after their release.

The incarceration of children in adult prisons poses management problems for correctional administrators. According to McShane and Williams, juvenile inmates as a group "tend to be assaultive, place inordinate demands on expensive segregation facilities, and require extra security measures"; because these youths are characterized by institutional disciplinary histories "they as a group, remain problem inmates for a longer period of time" (1989, 266).

Trends

Selective certification and waiver of older juveniles has been and continues to be the trend in many jurisdictions. Selective certification, a process analogous to selective incapacitation for adults, is based on the premises that there are special cases that deserve to be treated as adults and that our diagnostic techniques are such that we can accurately predict behavior. As one might expect, these assumptions are as problematic in selectively certifying children as they were when attempting to selectively incapacitate adults. Waiver of older children continues to be fairly routine. This is especially true for the older child, whose offense is characterized as more serious. Juvenile courts have a history of transferring cases such as this to criminal court. This emphasis on punishment, coupled with budget constraints, will probably result in increases in the number of cases handled in this fashion. Other strategies might include lowering the juvenile age. This would allow for individuals to be tried as adults at an earlier age without the need for waiver.

Eight alternatives have been proposed that would allow juvenile courts to maintain jurisdiction over children as opposed to transferring them to criminal court (Rubin 1989, 135–36):

1. Intensive probation supervision
2. Expanded work programs
3. Special schooling programs
4. Full-day school and work programs
5. School combined with adventure programs
6. Short-term secure residential placements
7. Long-term residential programs
8. Specialized foster homes combined with alternative school

Laura J. Moriarty
Elizabeth H. McConnell

Bibliography

Barnes, C. W., and R. Franz (1989). Questionably adult: Determinants and effects of the juvenile waiver decision. *Justice Quarterly* 6: 117–35.

Bishop, D. M, C. E. Fraizer, and J. C. Henretta (1989). Prosecutorial waiver: Case study of questionable reform. *Crime and Delinquency* 35: 179–210.

Butts, J., and D. J. Connors-Beatty (1993). *The Juvenile Court's Response to Violent Offenders: 1985–1989.* Washington, D.C.: U.S. Department of Justice.

Champion, D. J., and G. L. Mays (1991). *Transferring Juveniles to Criminal Courts: Trends and Implications for Criminal Justice.* New York: Praeger.

Forst, M., J. Fagan, and T. S. Vivona (1987). Youths in prison and training schools: Perceptions and consequences of the treatment–custody dichotomy. *Juvenile and Family Court Journal* 40: 1–14.

Houghtalin, M., and G. L. Mays (1991). Criminal disposition of New Mexico juveniles transferred to adult courts. *Crime and Delinquency* 37: 393–407.

McShane, M. D., and Williams, F. P. (1989). The prison adjustment of juvenile offenders. *Crime and Delinquency* 35: 254–69.

Rubin, H. T. (1989). The juvenile court landscape. In A. R. Roberts, ed. *Juvenile Justice: Policies, Programs, and Services.* Chicago: Dorsey.

Index

Irving, J. R. 30, 32
Irwin, J. 213, 217–218, 351, 353, 360, 362, 380–
381, 496
Irwin, M. 399

Jackson, B. 143
Jackson, G. 379, 416
Jackson, P. G. 259, 262–263
Jackson, R. W. 347
Jackson v. Bishop 117
Jackson v. Cain 90, 96, 305
Jackson v. Gates 302, 305
Jackson v. Virginia 285, 305
Jacobs, J. B. 105, 221, 223, 267–270, 272, 274,
334, 360, 362, 377–381, 453, 497–498
Jacobsen. V. J. 259
jailhouse lawyer 267–268, 283
James, S. V. 414
Jarrett v. Faulkner 19–20
Jaycees 33, 260, 404
Jeffords, C. 61
Jerin, B. 351
Johnson, B. R. 262–263, 403
Johnson, E. H. 20, 48, 73, 75, 162, 165, 328, 449–
451
Johnson, F. 271–272
Johnston, J 21–22
Johnson, R. 127–128, 131, 143, 200, 326, 364,
373, 381, 475
Johnson v. Avery 267, 268, 283, 292, 305
Johnson v. Glick 210–211, 288, 305
Johnson, W. 314
Johnston, N. B. 39, 99–100, 228–230, 496
Jones, A. 328
Jones, C. 284
Jones, C. H., Jr. 164–165
Jones, M. 512
Jones, R. S. 41, 443
*Jones v. North Carolina Prisoner's Labor Union,
Inc.* 469
Jordan v. Gardner 301, 305
Josi, D. A. 120, 122, 448
Judd v. Packard 19–20
judicial intervention 29, 33, 42, 136, 151, 164,
189, 232, 239–241, 244, 261, 268–274,
282–283, 329, 365, 450, 497
special master 271, 272, 323, 329
judicial waiver of juveniles 513–515
Jurik, N. C. 129–131, 380–381
Justice, W. W. 68, 272, 386

Kalinich, D. B. 114–115, 138, 263, 381, 406, 418,
450–451
Kane, J. S. 121–122
Kane, T. 15, 20, 96
Kasinsky, R. G. 261
Kassebaum, G. 163, 165
Kauffman, K. 127–128
Kay, S. 234, 322, 326
Keir, N. 436

Keller, M. 27
Kentucky v. Thompson 297, 305
Kessler, R. G. 450
Keve, P. W. 27–28, 31–32, 58, 116–117
key control 422–424, 427
Khan, A. 391
Killinger, G. 264–265
Kimball, P. 44–45
King, P. 157
King, R. D. 11
Kirchwey, G. W. 338, 445
Kirklin, J. E. 284
Kirn, H. 180
Knuckles v. Prasse 11–12
Koehler, R. J. 375–376
Koren, E. J. 234
Krajick, K. 318, 320
Kramer, N. 4
Kratcoski, P. C. 125–126, 408, 412
Krause, J. D. 105, 449
Krause, W. 174, 265
Krout, E. K. 439
Kruttschitt, C. 381
Kuhrt, J. 2, 4

L. W. v. Grubbs 305
Laaman v. Helgemoe 90, 96
LaBelle, R. 347
Laboratory of Social Hygiene 53, 141
Lachance-McCullough, M. 19
LaFave, W. R. 300
Lamott, K. 416
Langworthy, R. 194
Lanier, C. S. 79, 82–83
Lanier v. Fair 90, 96
Latessa, E. J. 459–460, 498
laundry 22, 37, 102, 112
Lavernia v. Lynaugh 286, 305
Law Enforcement Assistance Administration 375
Lawes, L. E. 225, 446
Lawrence, R. 122, 412
Lawson, R. 510
Lawson, W. T. 18, 20
Lay, D. 84, 86
lease system 32–33, 71, 116, 231, 253–254, 277–
281, 366, 377
LeClair, D. P. 356
Lee v. Washington 297, 305
legal issues, inmate
due process 11, 18, 90, 103, 139, 164–165,
174–176, 189, 221, 241, 272–273, 285–
287, 289, 293, 295–297, 303, 325, 346,
450
civil rights 16, 83–86, 89, 129, 157, 187, 210,
232, 243, 260, 269–270, 281, 283, 187–
289, 297, 301, 303, 323, 390, 417, 427,
442
equal protection 268, 283, 287, 295, 297,
390, 469, 477